Microsoft® Office
2013 IN PRACTICE

Randy Nordell
AMERICAN RIVER COLLEGE

Kari Wood
BEMIDJI STATE UNIVERSITY

Annette Easton
SAN DIEGO STATE UNIVERSITY

Pat Graves
EASTERN ILLINOIS UNIVERSITY

Connect
Learn
Succeed™

Microsoft® Office

2013

IN PRACTICE

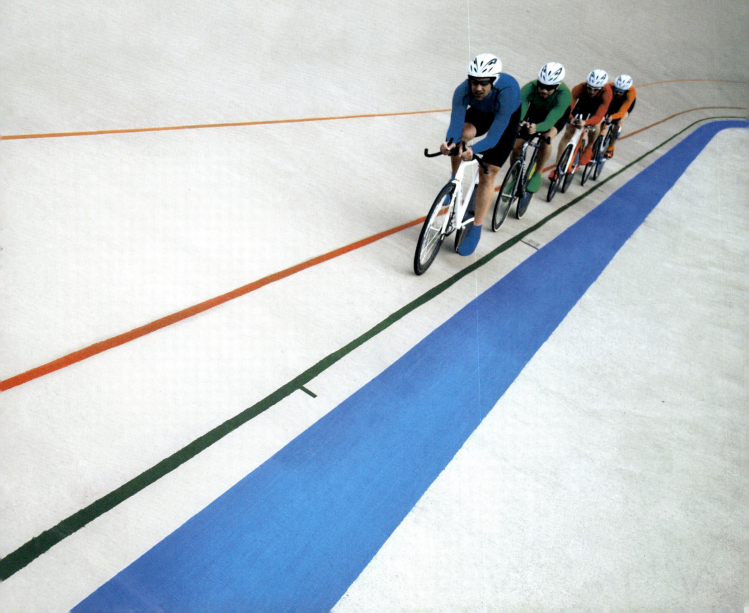

MICROSOFT OFFICE 2013: IN PRACTICE

Published by McGraw-Hill/Irwin, a business unit of The McGraw-Hill Companies, Inc., 1221 Avenue of the
Americas, New York, NY, 10020. Copyright © 2014 by The McGraw-Hill Companies, Inc. All rights reserved.
Printed in the United States of America. No part of this publication may be reproduced or distributed in any
form or by any means, or stored in a database or retrieval system, without the prior written consent of The
McGraw-Hill Companies, Inc., including, but not limited to, in any network or other electronic storage or
transmission, or broadcast for distance learning.

Some ancillaries, including electronic and print components, may not be available to customers outside the
United States.

This book is printed on acid-free paper.

6 7 8 9 0 QVS/QVS 1 0 9 8 7 6 5 4

ISBN   978-0-07-351938-8
MHID   0-07-351938-3

Senior Vice President, Products & Markets: *Kurt L. Strand*
Vice President, Content Production & Technology Services: *Kimberly Meriwether David*
Director: *Scott Davidson*
Senior Brand Manager: *Wyatt Morris*
Executive Director of Development: *Ann Torbert*
Development Editor II: *Alan Palmer*
Digital Development Editor II: *Kevin White*
Senior Marketing Manager: *Tiffany Russell*
Lead Project Manager: *Rick Hecker*
Buyer II: *Debra R. Sylvester*
Designer: *Jana Singer*
Interior Designer: *Jesi Lazar*
Cover Image: *Corbis Images*
Content Licensing Specialist: *Joanne Mennemeier*
Manager, Digital Production: *Janean A. Utley*
Media Project Manager: *Cathy L. Tepper*
Typeface: *11/13.2 Adobe Caslon Pro*
Compositor: *Laserwords Private Limited*
Printer: *Quad/Graphics*

Library of Congress Cataloging-in-Publication Data

Nordell, Randy.
    Microsoft Office 2013: in practice / Randy Nordell, American River College, Kari Wood, Bemidji
State University, Annette Easton, San Diego State University, Pat Graves, Eastern Illinois University.
        pages cm
    Includes index.
    ISBN-13: 978-0-07-351938-8 (alk. paper)
    ISBN-10: 0-07-351938-3 (alk. paper)
    1. Microsoft Office. 2. Business—Computer programs. 3. Office management—Computer programs.
I. Title.
    HF5548.4.M525N66 2014
    005.5—dc23
                                                                              2013002531

The Internet addresses listed in the text were accurate at the time of publication. The inclusion of a website
does not indicate an endorsement by the authors or McGraw-Hill, and McGraw-Hill does not guarantee the
accuracy of the information presented at these sites.

dedication

To Kelly. Thank you for your love, support, and encouragement during the seemingly endless hours of writing and editing throughout this project. Your feedback on the content and proofreading were immensely valuable. I could not have done this without you! I'm looking forward to a summer with you without deadlines.

—Randy Nordell

To my amazing husband, Woody, and to my precious children, Sammie and JD, for their love, inspiration, and patience. Thank you for your encouragement and support through the countless hours I spent on this project.

—Kari Wood

To George, Timothy, and Amanda. Your love sustains me. Your patience and willingness to put up with a boring wife and mother while I worked on this project made this book possible. George, thank you and I love you for always being my biggest fan and supporter.

—Annette Easton

To Brent. Thank you for the many ways you have helped me while I have been working on this book. Your love and support mean so much to me. I also appreciate my friends who shared their expertise and provided content for projects.

—Pat Graves

brief contents

contents

CHAPTER 2: FORMATTING AND CUSTOMIZING DOCUMENTS — W2-62

EXCEL

CHAPTER 1: CREATING AND EDITING WORKBOOKS

ACCESS

Integrating Word, Excel, and Access Skills
See www.mhhe.com/office2013inpractice

about the authors

RANDY NORDELL, Ed.D.

Randy Nordell is a Professor of Business Technology at American River College in Sacramento, California. He has been an educator for over 20 years and has taught at the high school, community college, and university levels. He holds a bachelor's degree in Business Administration from California State University, Stanislaus, a single subject teaching credential from Fresno State University, a master's degree in Education from Fresno Pacific University, and a doctorate in Education from Argosy University. Randy is the author of *Microsoft Outlook 2010*, and he speaks regularly at conferences on the integration of technology into the curriculum. When he is not teaching, he enjoys spending time with his family, cycling, skiing, swimming, and enjoying the California weather and terrain.

KARI WOOD, Ph.D.

Kari Wood is a Professor of Business at Bemidji State University in Bemidji, Minnesota. She has been an educator for over 12 years at the university level and conducted industry software training prior to her professorship. She holds a bachelor's degree in Business Management from Bemidji State University, a master's degree in Business Administration from Minnesota State University, Moorhead, and a doctorate in Organizational Management, with an emphasis in Information Technology from Capella University, in Minneapolis, Minnesota. Kari is a Microsoft Certified Trainer (MCT). She holds Quality Matters (QM) certification as a peer reviewer for online course design and is also a Certified Computer Examiner (CCE). When she is not teaching, Kari enjoys spending time with her family, playing tennis, lifting, running, reading, and watching movies.

ANNETTE EASTON, Ph.D.

Annette Easton is an Associate Professor of Management Information Systems at San Diego State University. She has been an educator for over 20 years at the university level and has served as a school board trustee for eight years. She holds a bachelor's degree in Business Administration from California State University, Fresno, and a doctorate in Management Information Systems from the University of Arizona. Annette has published articles on information technology education, electronic meeting systems, and integrating new technologies into the information systems curriculum. She co-authored *Cases for Modern Systems Development* and she presents regularly at conferences. When not teaching, she enjoys spending time with her family, travelling, and cooking.

PAT GRAVES, Ed.D.

Pat Graves is a Professor Emeritus at Eastern Illinois University in Charleston, Illinois. She began her career as a high school teacher. After receiving her doctorate in Education from Memphis State University (now the University of Memphis), she taught in the Eastern Illinois University School of Business for 20 years. Pat has been an author of PowerPoint textbooks for McGraw-Hill Higher Education since 2002 and has authored textbooks about Microsoft Office 2003, 2007, and 2010. When not writing, she travels, spends time with family and friends, enjoys the music city of Nashville, and appreciates the peacefulness of the Tennessee mountains.

preface

What We're About

We wrote *Microsoft Office 2013: In Practice* to meet the diverse needs of both students and instructors. Our approach focuses on presenting Office topics in a logical and structured manner, teaching concepts in a way that reinforces learning with practice projects that are transferrable, relevant, and engaging. Our pedagogy and content are based on the following beliefs.

Students Need to Learn and Practice Transferable Skills

Students must be able to transfer the concepts and skills learned in the text to a variety of projects, not simply follow steps in a textbook. Our material goes beyond the instruction of many texts. In our content, students practice the concepts in a variety of current and relevant projects *and* are able to transfer skills and concepts learned to different projects in the real world. To further increase the transferability of skills learned, this text is integrated with SIMnet so students also practice skills and complete projects in an online environment.

Your Curriculum Drives the Content

The curriculum in the classroom should drive the content of the text, not the other way around. This book is designed to allow instructors and students to cover all the material they need to in order to meet the curriculum requirements of their courses no matter how the courses are structured. *Microsoft Office 2013: In Practice* teaches the marketable skills that are key to student success. McGraw-Hill's Custom Publishing site, **Create**, can further tailor the content material to meet the unique educational needs of any school.

Integrated with Technology

Our text provides a fresh and new approach to an Office applications course. Topics integrate seamlessly with SIMnet with 1:1 content to help students practice and master concepts and skills using SIMnet's interactive learning philosophy. Projects in SIMnet allow students to practice their skills and receive immediate feedback. This integration with SIMnet meets the diverse needs of students and accommodates individual learning styles. Additional textbook resources found on the text's Online Learning Center (**www.mhhe.com/office2013inpractice**) integrate with the learning management systems that are widely used in many online and onsite courses.

Reference Text

In addition to providing students with an abundance of real-life examples and practice projects, we designed this text to be used as a Microsoft Office 2013 reference source. The core material, uncluttered with exercises, focuses on real-world use and application. Our text provides clear step-by-step instructions on how readers can apply the various features available in Microsoft Office in a variety of contexts. At the same time, users have access to a variety of both online (SIMnet) and textbook practice projects to reinforce skills and concepts.

Textbook Learning Approach

Microsoft Office 2013: In Practice uses the *T.I.P. approach:*

- **T**opic
- **I**nstruction
- **P**ractice

Topics

- Each Office application section begins with foundational skills and builds to more complex topics as the text progresses.
- Topics are logically sequenced and grouped by topics.
- Student Learning Outcomes (SLOs) are thoroughly integrated with and mapped to chapter content, projects, end-of-chapter review, and test banks.
- Reports are available within SIMnet for displaying how students have met these Student Learning Outcomes.

Instruction (How To)

- How To guided instructions about chapter topics provide transferable and adaptable instructions.
- Because How To instructions are not locked into single projects, this textbook functions as a reference text, not just a point-and-click textbook.
- Chapter content is aligned 1:1 with SIMnet.

Practice (Pause & Practice and End-of-Chapter Projects)

- Within each chapter, integrated Pause & Practice projects (three to five per chapter) reinforce learning and provide hands-on guided practice.
- In addition to Pause & Practice projects, each chapter has 10 comprehensive and practical practice projects: Guided Projects (three per chapter), Independent Projects (three per chapter), Improve It Project (one per chapter), and Challenge Projects (three per chapter). Additional projects can also be found on **www.mhhe.com/office2013inpractice**.
- Pause & Practice and end-of-chapter projects are complete content-rich projects, not small examples lacking context.
- Select auto-graded projects are available in SIMnet.

Chapter Features

All chapters follow a consistent theme and instructional methodology. Below is an example of chapter structure.

Main headings are organized according to the *Student Learning Outcomes (SLOs)*.

SLO 1.1 **Creating, Saving, and Opening Documents**

Microsoft Word allows you to create a variety of document types. Your cr[...]
edge of Word allow you to create, edit, and customize high-quality and pr[...]
documents.

You can create Word documents from a new blank document, from e[...]
plates, or from existing documents. Word allows you to save documents in a[...]

CHAPTER 1

Creating and Editing Documents

CHAPTER OVERVIEW

Microsoft Word (Word) has been and continues to be the leading word processing [...]
both the personal and business markets. Word improves with each new version and [...]
creating and editing personal, business, and educational documents. Word allows [...]
ate letters, memos, reports, flyers, brochures, and mailings without a vast amount o[...]
knowledge. This chapter covers the basics of creating and editing a Word documen[...]

STUDENT LEARNING OUTCOMES (SLOs)

After completing this chapter, you will be able to:

SLO 1.1 Create, save, and open a Word document (p. W1-3).

SLO 1.2 Customize a document by entering and selecting text, using word wra[...]
and using *AutoComplete*, *AutoCorrect*, and *AutoFormat* features (p. W[...]

SLO 1.3 Enhance a document using paragraph breaks, line breaks, spaces, a[...]
non-breaking spaces (p. W1-10).

SLO 1.4 Edit a document using cut, copy, paste, the *Clipboard*, and the undo, [...]
and repeat features. (p. W1-14).

SLO 1.5 Customize a document using different fonts, font sizes, and attributes [...]
(p. W1-17).

SLO 1.6 Enhance a document using text alignment and line and paragraph spa[...]
(p. W1-27).

SLO 1.7 Finalize a document using Word's proofing tools (p. W1-31).

SLO 1.8 Apply custom document properties to a document (p. W1-35).

A list of Student Learning Outcomes begins each chapter. All chapter content, examples, and practice projects are organized according to the chapter SLOs.

CASE STUDY

*Throughout this book you have the opportunity to put into practice the application features that you are learning. Each chapter begins with a case study that introduces you to the **Pause & Practice** projects in the chapter. These Pause & Practice projects give you a chance to apply and practice key skills. Each chapter contains three to five Pause & Practice projects.*

Placer Hills Real Estate *(PHRE) is a real estate company with regional offices*

throughout central California. In the Pause & Practice projects in this chapter, you create a business document related to the real estate business. PHRE encourages agents to use standard formats for their business documents. This ensures consistency in document appearance while also allowing agents to personalize their correspondence to customers and colleagues.

The *Case Study* for each chapter is a scenario that establishes the theme for the entire chapter. Chapter content, examples, figures, Pause & Practice projects, SIMnet skills, and projects throughout the chapter closely related to this case study content. The three to five Pause & Practice projects in each chapter build upon each other and address key case study themes.

How To instructions enhance transferability of skills with concise steps and screen shots.

HOW TO: Open a Document

1. Click the **File** tab to open the *Backstage* view.
2. Click the **Open** button to display the *Open* area on the *Backstage* view.
3. In the *Places* area, select the location where the document is stored.
   - You can click **Recent Documents** and select a document at the right to open it.
   - You can also open a document from *SkyDrive* or *Computer*.
4. Select a folder or click **Browse** to open the *Open* dialog box (Figure 1-5).
5. Select the file and click the **Open** button.

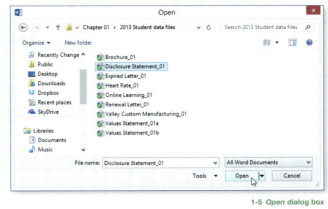

1-5 *Open* dialog box

How To instructions are easy-to-follow concise steps. Screen shots and other figures fully illustrate How To topics.

Students can complete hands-on exercises in either the Office application or in SIMnet.

Pause & Practice 1-1: Create a business letter in block format with mixed punctuation.

Pause & Practice 1-2: Edit the business letter using copy, paste, and *Format Painter.* Modify the font size, color, style, and effects of selected text.

Pause & Practice 1-3: Finalize the business letter by modifying line spacing and paragraph spacing, changing paragraph alignment, translating text, using proofing tools, and adding document properties.

Pause & Practice projects, which each cover two to three of the student learning outcomes in the chapter, provide students with the opportunity to review and practice skills and concepts. Every chapter contains three to five Pause & Practice projects.

MORE INFO

Avoid saving too many different versions of the same document. Rename only when you have a good reason to have multiple versions of a document.

More Info provides readers with additional information about chapter content.

Another Way notations teach alternative methods of accomplishing the same task or feature such as keyboard shortcuts.

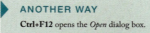
Marginal Notations present additional information and alternative methods.

End-of-Chapter Projects

Ten learning projects at the end of each chapter provide additional reinforcement and practice for students. Many of these projects are available in SIMnet for completion and automatic grading.

- *Guided Projects (three per chapter):* Guided Projects provide guided step-by-step instructions to apply Office features, skills, and concepts from the chapter. Screen shots guide students through the more challenging tasks. End-of-project screen shots provide a visual of the completed project.
- *Independent Projects (three per chapter):* Independent Projects provide students further opportunities to practice and apply skills, instructing students what to do, but not how to do it. These projects allow students to apply previously learned content in a different context.
- *Improve It Project (one per chapter):* In these projects, students apply their knowledge and skills to enhance and improve an existing document. Improve It projects are open-ended and allow students to use their critical thinking and creativity to produce attractive professional documents.
- *Challenge Projects (three per chapter):* Challenge Projects encourage creativity and critical thinking by integrating Office concepts and features into relevant and engaging projects.

Appendix

- *Office 2013 Shortcuts:* Appendix A covers the shortcuts available in Microsoft Office and within each of the specific Office applications. Information is in table format for easy access and reference.

Online Learning Center: www.mhhe.com/office2013inpractice

Students and instructors can find the following resources at the Online Learning Center, **www.mhhe.com/office2013inpractice**:

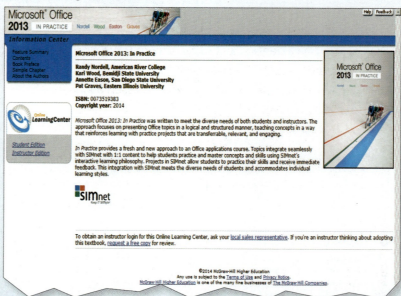

Student Resources

- **Data Files:** Files contain start files for all Pause & Practice, Integration, and end-of-chapter projects.
- **SIMnet Resources:** Resources provide getting started and informational handouts for instructors and students.
- **Check for Understanding:** A combination of multiple choice, fill-in, matching, and short answer questions are available online to assist students in their review of the skills and concepts covered in the chapter.

Integration Projects

- **Integrating Applications:** Projects provide students with the opportunity to learn, practice, and transfer skills using multiple Office applications.
- **Integrating Skills:** Projects provide students with a comprehensive and integrated review of all of the topics covered in each application (Word, Excel, Access, and PowerPoint). Available in individual application texts.

Appendices

- **SIMnet User Guide:** Appendix B introduces students to the SIMnet user interface; content demonstrates how to use SIMnet to complete lessons and projects, take quizzes, and search for specific topics as well as how to create practice exercises.
- **Office 2013 for Mac Users:** Appendix C presents instructions for Mac users on how to partition their computer drive to use the PC version of Microsoft Office 2013.
- **Business Document Formats:** Appendix D is a guide to regularly used business document formatting and includes numerous examples and detailed instructions.

Instructor Resources

- **Instructor's Manual:** An Instructor's Manual provides teaching tips and lecture notes aligned with the PowerPoint presentations for each chapter. The Manual also includes the solutions for online **Check for Understanding** questions.
- **Test Bank:** The extensive test bank integrates with learning management systems (LMSs) such as Blackboard, WebCT, Desire2Learn, and Moodle.
- **PowerPoint Presentations:** PowerPoint presentations for each chapter can be used in onsite course formats for lectures or can be uploaded to LMSs.
- **SIMnet Resources:** These resources provide getting started and informational handouts for instructors.
- **Solution Files:** Files contain solutions for all Pause & Practice, Integration, Check for Understanding, and End-of-Chapter projects.

acknowledgments

REVIEWERS

We would like to thank the following instructors, whose invaluable insights shaped the development of this series.

Frank Abnet
Baker College

Sven Aelterman
Troy University

Nisheeth Agrawal
Calhoun Community College

Jack Alanen
California State University

Doug Albert
Finger Lakes Community College

Lancie Anthony Alfonso
College of Charleston

Farha Ali
Lander University

Beverly Amer
Northern Arizona University

Penny Amici
Harrisburg Area Community College

Leon Amstutz
Taylor University

Chris Anderson
North Central Michigan College

Wilma Andrews
Virginia Commonwealth University

Mazhar Anik
Owens Community College

M. Hashem Anwari
Nova Community College

Ralph Argiento
Guilford Technical Community College

Karen M. Arlien
Bismarck State College

Gary Armstrong
Shippensburg University

Tom Ashby
Oklahoma City Community College

Laura Atkins
James Madison University

William Ayen
University of Colorado

Abida Awan
Savannah State University

Ijaz Awan
Savannah State University

Tahir Aziz
J. Sargeant Reynolds Community College

Mark Bagley
Northwestern Oklahoma State University

Greg Ballinger
Miami Dade College

David Barnes
Penn State Altoona

Emily Battaglia
United Education Institute

Terry Beachy
Garrett College

Michael Beard
Lamar University—Beaumont

Anita Beecroft
Kwantlen Polytechnic University

Julia Bell
Walters State Community College

Paula Bell
Lock Haven University of Pennsylvania

David Benjamin
Pace University

Shantanu Bhagoji
Monroe College

Sai Bhatia
Riverside City College

Cindy Hauki Blair
West Hills College

Scott Blanchard
Rockford Career College

Ann Blackman
Parkland College

Jessica Blackwelder
Wilmington University

James Boardman
Alfred State College

John Bodden
Trident Technical College

Gary Bond
New Mexico State University

Abigail Bornstein
City College of San Francisco

Gina Bowers
Harrisburg Area Community College

Craig Bradley
Shawnee Community College

Gerlinde Brady
Cabrillo College

Gerald Braun
Xavier University

Janet Bringhurst
Utah State University

Brenda Britt
Fayetteville Technical Community College

Annie Brown
Hawaii Community College

Judith Brown
University of Memphis

Menka Brown
Piedmont Technical College

Shawn Brown
Kentucky Community & Technical College

Sylvia Brown
Midland College

Cliff Brozo
Monroe College

Barbara Buckner
Lee University

Sheryl Starkey Bulloch
Columbia Southern University

Rebecca Bullough
College of Sequoias

Kate Burkes
Northwest Arkansas Community College

Sharon Buss
Hawkeye Community College

Angela Butler
Mississippi Gulf Coast Community College

Lynn Byrd
Delta State University

Carolyn Calicutt
Saint Louis Community College

Anthony Cameron
Fayetteville Technical Community College

Eric Cameron
Passaic County Community College

Michael Carrington
Nova Community College

Debby Carter
Los Angeles Pierce College

Cesar Augustus Casas
St. Thomas Aquinas College

Sharon Casseday
Weatherford College

Mary Ann Cassidy
Westchester Community College

Terri Castillo
New Mexico Military Institute

Diane Caudill
Kentucky Community & Technical College

Emre Celebi
Louisiana State University

Jim Chaffee
The University of Iowa Tippie College of Business

Jayalaxmi Chakravarthy
Monroe Community College

Bob Chambers
Endicott College

Debra Chapman
University of South Alabama

Marg Chauvin
Palm Beach Community College

Stephen Cheskiewicz
Keystone College

Mark Choman
Luzerne County Community College

Kungwen Chu
Purdue University

Carin Chuang
Purdue University—North Central

Tina Cipriano
Gateway Technical College

Angela Clark
University of South Alabama

James Clark
University of Tennessee

Steve Clements
Eastern Oregon University

Sandra Cobb
Kaplan University

Paulette Comet
Community College of Baltimore County

Marc Condos
American River College

Ronald Conway
Bowling Green State University

Margaret Cooksey
Tallahassee Community College

Lennie Cooper
Miami Dade College—North

Michael Copper
Palm Beach State College—Lake Worth

Terri Cossey
University of Arkansas

Shannon Cotnam
Pitt Community College

Missie Cotton
North Central Missouri College

Charles Cowell
Tyler Junior College

Elaine Crable
Xavier University

Grace Credico
Lethbridge Community College

Doug Cross
Clackamas Community College

Kelli Cross
Harrisburg Area Community College

Geoffrey Crosslin
Kalamazoo Valley Community College

Christy Culver
Marion Technical College

Urska Cvek
Louisiana State University

Penny Cypert
Tarrant County College

Janet Czarnecki
Brown Mackie College

Don Danner
San Francisco State University

Michael Danos
Central Virginia Community College

Louise Darcy
Texas A&M University

Tamara Dawson
Southern Nazarene University

JD Davis
Southwestern College

Elaine Day
Johnson & Wales University

Jennifer Day
Sinclair Community College

Ralph De Arazoza
Miami Dade College

Lucy Decaro
College of Sequoias

Chuck Decker
College of the Desert

Corey DeLaplain
Keiser University East Campus

Edward Delean
Nova Community College Alexandria

Darren Denenberg
University of Nevada—Las Vegas

Joy DePover
Minneapolis Community & Technical College

Charles DeSassure
Tarrant County Community College

John Detmer
Del Mar College

Michael Discello
Pittsburgh Technical College

Sallie Dodson
Radford University

Veronica Dooly
Asheville-Buncombe Technical Community College

Gretchen Douglas
State University of New York College—Cortland

Debra Duke
Cleveland State University

Michael Dumdei
Texarkana College

Michael Dunklebarger
Alamance Community College

Maureen Dunn
Penn State University

Robert Dusek
Nova Community College

Barbara Edington
St. Francis College

Margaret Edmunds
Mount Allison University

Annette Edwards
Tennessee Technology Center

Sue Ehrfurth
Aims Community College

Donna Ehrhart
Genesee Community College

Roland Eichelberger
Baylor University

Issam El-Achkar
Hudson County Community College

Glenda Elser
New Mexico State University

Emanuel Emanouilidis
Kean University

Bernice Eng
Brookdale Community College

Joanne Eskola
Brookdale Community College

Mohammed Eyadat
California State University—Dominguez Hills

Nancy Jo Evans
Indiana University-Purdue University Indianapolis

Phil Feinberg
Palomar College

Deb Fells
Mesa Community College

Patrick Fenton
West Valley College

Jean Finley
Asheville-Buncombe Technical Community College

George Fiori
Tri-County Technical College Pendleton

Richard Flores
Citrus College

Kent Foster
Winthrop University

Penny Foster
Anne Arundel Community College

Brian Fox
Santa Fe College

Deborah Franklin
Bryant & Stratton College

Judith Fredrickson
Truckee Meadows Community College

Dan Frise
East Los Angeles College

Michael Fujita
Leeward Community College

Susan Fuschetto
Cerritos College

Janos Fustos
Metropolitan State College—Denver

Samuel Gabay
Zarem Golde Ort Technical Institute

Brian Gall
Berks Technical Institute

Lois Galloway
Danville Community College

Saiid Ganjalizadeh
The Catholic University of America

Lynnette Garetz
Heald College Corporate Office

Kurt Garner
Pitt Community College

Randolph Garvin
Tyler Junior College

Deborah Gaspard
Southeast Community College

Marilyn Gastineau
University of Louisiana

Bob Gehling
Auburn University—Montgomery

Amy Giddens
Central Alabama Community College

Tim Gill
Tyler Junior College

Sheila Gionfriddo
Luzerne County Community College

Mostafa Golbaba
Langston University Tulsa

Kemit Grafton
Oklahoma State University—Oklahoma City

Deb Gross
Ohio State University

Judy Grotefendt
Kilgore College

Debra Giblin
Mitchell Technical Institute

Robin Greene
Walla Walla Community College

Nancy Gromen
Eastern Oregon University

Lewis Hall
Riverside City College

Linnea Hall
Northwest Mississippi Community College

Kevin Halvorson
Ridgewater College

Peggy Hammer
Chemeketa Community College

Patti Hammerle
Indiana University-Purdue University Indianapolis

Dr. Bill Hammerschlag
Brookhaven College

Danielle Hammoud
West Coast University Corporate Office

John Haney
Snead State Community College

Ashley Harrier
Hillsborough Community College

Ranida Harris
Indiana University Southeast

Dorothy Harman
Tarrant County College

Marie Hartlein
Montgomery County Community College

Shohreh Hashemi
University of Houston Downtown

Michael Haugrud
Minnesota State University

Rebecca Hayes
American River College

Terri Helfand
Chaffey College

Julie Heithecker
College of Southern Idaho

Gerry Hensel
University of Central Florida—Orlando

Cindy Herbert
Metropolitan Community College

Jenny Herron
Paris Junior College

Marilyn Hibbert
Salt Lake Community College

Will Hilliker
Monroe County Community College

Ray Hinds
Florida College

Rachel Hinton
Broome Community College

Emily Holliday
Campbell University

Mary-Carole Hollingsworth
Georgia Perimeter College

Terri Holly
Indian River State College

Timothy Holston
Mississippi Valley State University

David Hood
East Central College

Kim Hopkins
Weatherford College

Wayne Horn
Pensacola Junior College

Christine Hovey
Lincoln Land Community College

Derrick Huang
Florida Atlantic University

Susan Hudgins
East Central University

Jeff Huff
Missouri State University – West Plains

Debbie Huffman
North Central Texas College

Michelle Hulett
Missouri State University

Laura Hunt
Tulsa Community College

Bobbie Hyndman
Amarillo College

Jennifer Ivey
Central Carolina Community College

Bill Jaber
Lee University

Sherry Jacob
Jefferson Community College

Yelena Jaffe
Suffolk University

Rhoda James
Citrus Community College

Ted Janicki
Mount Olive College

Jon Jasperson
Texas A&M University

Denise Jefferson
Pitt Community College

John Jemison
Dallas Baptist University

Joe Jernigan
Tarrant County College—NE

Mary Johnson
Mt. San Antonio College

Mary Johnson
Lone Star College

Linda Johnsonius
Murray State University

Robert Johnston
Heald College

Irene Joos
La Roche College

Yih-Yaw Jou
University of Houston—Downtown

Jan Kamholtz
Bryant & Stratton College

Valerie Kasay
Georgia Southern University

James Kasum
University of Wisconsin

Nancy Keane
NHTI Concord Community College

Michael Keele
Three Rivers Community College

Debby Keen
University of Kentucky

Judith Keenan
Salve Regina University

Jan Kehm
Spartanburg Community College

Rick Kendrick
Antonelli College

Annette Kerwin
College of DuPage

Manzurul Khan
College of the Mainland

Julia Khan-Nomee
Pace University

Karen Kidder
Tri-State Business Institute

Hak Joon Kim
Southern Connecticut State University

James Kirby
Community College of Rhode Island

Chuck Kise
Brevard Community College

Paul Koester
Tarrant County College

Kurt Kominek
Northeast State Tech Community College

Diane Kosharek
Madison Area Technical College

Carolyn Kuehne
Utah Valley University

Ruth Kurlandsky
Cazenovia College

John Kurnik
Saint Petersburg College

Lana LaBruyere
Mineral Area College

Anita Laird
Schoolcraft College

Charles Lake
Faulkner State Community College

Marjean Lake
LDS Business College

Kin Lam
Medgar Evers College

Jeanette Landin
Empire College

Richard Lanigan
Centura College Online

Nanette Lareau
University of Arkansas Community College Morrilton

David Lee Largent
Ball State University

Linda Lannuzzo
LaGuardia Community College

Robert La Rocca
Keiser University

Dawn D. Laux
Purdue University

Deborah Layton
Eastern Oklahoma State College

Art Lee
Lord Fairfax Community College

Ingyu Lee
Troy University Troy

Kevin Lee
Guilford Technical Community College

Leesa Lee
Western Wyoming College

Thomas Lee
University of Pennsylvania

Jamie Lemley
City College of San Francisco

Linda Lemley
Pensacola State College

Diane Lending
James Madison University

Sherry Lenhart
Terra Community College

Julie Lewis
Baker College—Flint

Sue Lewis
Tarleton State University

Jane Liefert
Middlesex Community College

Renee Lightner
Florida State College

Nancy Lilly
Central Alabama Community College

Mary Locke
Greenville Technical College

Maurie Lockley
University of North Carolina

Haibing Lu
San Diego Mesa College

Frank Lucente
Westmoreland County Community College

Clem Lundie
San Jose City College

Alicia Lundstrom
Drake College of Business

Linda Lynam
Central Missouri State University

Lynne Lyon
Durham Technical Community College

Matthew Macarty
University of New Hampshire

Sherri Mack
Butler County Community College

Heather Madden
Delaware Technical Community College

Susan Mahon
Collin College Plano

Nicki Maines
Mesa Community College

Lynn Mancini
Delaware Technical Community College

Amelia Maretka
Wharton County Junior College

Suzanne Marks
Bellevue Community College

Juan Marquez
Mesa Community College

Carlos Martinez
California State University—Dominguez Hills

Santiago Martinez
Fast Train College

Lindalee Massoud
Mott Community College

Joan Mast
John Wood Community College

Deborah Mathews
J. Sargeant Reynolds Community College

Becky McAfee
Hillsborough Community College

Roberta Mcclure
Lee College

Martha McCreery
Rend Lake College

Sue McCrory
Missouri State University

Brian Mcdaniel
Palo Alto College

Rosie Mcghee
Baton Rouge Community College

Jacob McGinnis
Park University

Mike Mcguire
Triton College

Bruce McLaren
Indiana State University

Bill McMillan
Madonna University

David Mcnair
Mount Wachusett Community College

Gloria Mcteer
Ozarks Technical Community College

Dawn Medlin
Appalachian State University

Peter Meggison
Massasoit Community College

Barbara Meguro
University of Hawaii

Linda Mehlinger
Morgan State University

Gabriele Meiselwitz
Towson University

Joni Meisner
Portland Community College

Dixie Mercer
Kirkwood Community College

Donna Meyer
Antelope Valley College

Mike Michaelson
Palomar College

Michael Mick
Purdue University

Debby Midkiff
Huntington Jr. College of Business

Jenna Miley
Bainbridge College

Dave Miller
Monroe County Community College

Pam Milstead
Bossier Parish Community College

Shayan Mirabi
American Intercontinental University

Johnette Moody
Arkansas Tech University

Christine Moore
College of Charleston

Carmen Morrison
North Central State College

Gary Mosley
Southern Wesleyan University

Tamar Mosley
Meridian Community College

Ed Mulhern
Southwestern College

Carol Mull
Greenville Technical College

Melissa Munoz
Dorsey Business School

Marianne Murphy
North Carolina Central University

Karen Musick
Indiana University-Purdue University Indianapolis

Warner Myntti
Ferris State University

Brent Nabors
Reedley College

Shirley Nagg
Everest Institute

Anozie Nebolisa
Shaw University

Barbara Neequaye
Central Piedmont Community College

Patrick Nedry
Monroe County Community College

Melissa Nemeth
Indiana University-Purdue University Indianapolis

Eloise Newsome
Northern Virginia Community College

Yu-Pa Ng
San Antonio College

Fidelis Ngang
Houston Community College

Doreen Nicholls
Mohawk Valley Community College

Brenda Nickel
Moraine Park Technical College

Brenda Nielsen
Mesa Community College

Phil Nielson
Salt Lake Community College

Suzanne Nordhaus
Lee College

Ronald Norman
Grossmont College

Karen Nunam
Northeast State Technical Community College

Mitchell Ober
Tulsa Community College

Teri Odegard
Edmonds Community College

Michael Brian Ogawa
University of Hawaii

Lois Ann O'Neal
Rogers State University

Stephanie Oprandi
Stark State College of Technology

Marianne Ostrowksky
Luzerne County Community College

Shelley Ota
Leeward Community College

Youcef Oubraham
Hudson County Community College

Paul Overstreet
University South Alabama

John Panzica
Community College of Rhode Island

Donald Paquet
Community College of Rhode Island

Lucy Parker
California State University—Northridge

Patricia Partyka
Schoolcraft College

James Gordon Patterson
Paradise Valley Community College

Laurie Patterson
University of North Carolina

Joanne Patti
Community College of Philadelphia

Kevin Pauli
University of Nebraska

Kendall Payne
Coffeyville Community College

Deb Peairs
Clark State Community College

Charlene Perez
South Plains College

Lisa Perez
San Joaquin Delta College

Diane Perreault
Tusculum College

Michael Picerno
Baker College

Janet Pickard
Chattanooga State Technical Community College

Walter Pistone
Palomar College

Jeremy Pittman
Coahoma Community College

Morris Pondfield
Towson University

James Powers
University of Southern Indiana

Kathleen Proietti
Northern Essex Community College

Ram Raghuraman
Joliet Jr. College

Patricia Rahmlow
Montgomery County Community College

Robert Renda
Fulton Montgomery Community College
Margaret Reynolds
Mississippi Valley State University
David Richwine
Indian River State College—Central
Terry Rigsby
Hill College
Laura Ringer
Piedmont Technical College
Gwen Rodgers
Southern Nazarene University
Stefan Robila
Montclair State University
Terry Rooker
Germanna Community College
Seyed Roosta
Albany State University
Sandra Roy
Miss Gulf Coast Community College—Gautier
Antoon Rufi
Ecpi College of Technology
Wendy Rader
Greenville Technical College
Harold Ramcharan
Shaw University
James Reneau
Shawnee State University
Robert Robertson
Southern Utah University
Cathy Rogers
Laramie County Community College
Harry Reif
James Madison University
Shaunda Roach
Oakwood University
Ruth Robbins
University of Houston—Downtown
Randy Rose
Pensacola State College
Kathy Ruggieri
Lansdale School of Business
Cynthia Rumney
Middle Georgia Technical College
Paige Rutner
Georgia Southern University
Candice Ryder
Colorado State University
Russell Sabadosa
Manchester Community College
Gloria Sabatelli
Butler County Community College
Glenn Sagers
Illinois State University
Phyllis Salsedo
Scottsdale Community College
Dolly Samson
Hawaii Pacific University
Yashu Sanghvi
Cape Fear Community College
Ramona Santamaria
Buffalo State College
Diane Santurri
Johnson & Wales University
Kellie Sartor
Lee College
Allyson Saunders
Weber State University
Theresa Savarese
San Diego City College
Cem Saydam
University of North Carolina
Jill Schaumloeffel
Garrett College
William Schlick
Schoolcraft College
Rory Schlueter
Glendale College
Art Schneider
Portland Community College
Helen Schneider
University of Findlay
Cheryl Schroeder-Thomas
Towson University

Paul Schwager
East Carolina University
Kay Scow
North Hennepin Community College
Karen Sarratt Scott
University of Texas—Arlington
Michael Scroggins
Missouri State University
Janet Sebesy
Cuyahoga Community College Western
Vicky Seehusen
Metropolitan State College Denver
Paul Seibert
North Greenville University
Pat Serrano
Scottsdale Community College
Patricia Sessions
Chemeketa Community College
Judy Settle
Central Georgia Technical College
Vivek Shah
Texas State University
Abul Sheikh
Abraham Baldwin Agricultural College
Lal Shimpi
Saint Augustine's College
Lana Shryock
Monroe County Community College
Joanne Shurbert
NHTI Concord Community College
Sheila Sicilia
Onondaga Community College
Pam Silvers
Asheville-Buncombe Technical Community College
Eithel Simpson
Southwestern Oklahoma State University
Beth Sindt
Hawkeye Community College
Mary Jo Slater
College of Beaver County
Diane Smith
Henry Ford College
Kristi Smith
Allegany College of Maryland
Nadine Smith
Keiser University
Thomas Michael Smith
Austin Community College
Anita Soliz
Palo Alto College
Don Southwell
Delta College
Mimi Spain
Southern Maine Community College
Sri' V. Sridharan
Clemson University
Diane Stark
Phoenix College
Jason Steagall
Bryant & Stratton College
Linda Stoudemayer
Lamar Institute of Technology
Nate Stout
University of Oklahoma
Lynne Stuhr
Trident Technical College
Song Su
East Los Angeles College
Bala Subramanian
Kean University
Liang Sui
Daytona State College
Denise Sullivan
Westchester Community College
Frank Sun
Lamar University
Beverly Swisshelm
Cumberland University
Cheryl Sypniewski
Macomb Community College
Martin Schedlbauer
Suffolk University
Lo-An Tabar-Gaul
Mesa Community College

Kathleen Tamerlano
Cuyahoga Community College
Margaret Taylor
College of Southern Nevada
Sandra Thomas
Troy University
Joyce Thompson
Lehigh Carbon Community College
Jay Tidwell
Blue Ridge Community and Technical College
Astrid Todd
Guilford Technical Community College
Byron Todd
Tallahassee Community College
Kim Tollett
Eastern Oklahoma State College
Joe Torok
Bryant & Stratton College
Tom Trevethan
Ecpi College of Technology
David Trimble
Park University
Charulata Trivedi
Quinsigamond Community College
Alicia Tyson-Sherwood
Post University
Angela Unruh
Central Washington University
Patricia Vacca
El Camino College
Sue van Boven
Paradise Valley Community College
Scott Van Selow
Edison College—Fort Myers
Linda Kavanaugh Varga
Robert Morris University
Kathleen Villarreal
Apollo University of Phoenix
Asteria Villegas
Monroe Community College
Michelle Vlaich-Lee
Greenville Technical College
Carol Walden
Mississippi Delta Community College
Dennis Walpole
University of South Florida
Merrill Warkentin
Mississippi State University
Jerry Waxman
The City University of New York Queens College
Sharon Wavle
Tompkins Cortland Community College
Rebecca Webb
Northwest Arkansas Community College
Sandy Weber
Gateway Technical College
Robin Weitz
Ocean County College
Karen Welch
Tennessee Technology Center
Marcia Welch
Highline Community College
Lynne Weldon
Aiken Tech College
Jerry Wendling
Iowa Western Community College
Bradley West
Sinclair Community College
Stu Westin
University of Rhode Island
Billie Jo Whary
McCann School of Business & Technology
Charles Whealton
Delaware Technical Community College
Melinda White
Seminole State College
Reginald White
Black Hawk College
Lissa Whyte-Morazan
Brookline College
Sophia Wilberscheid
Indian River State College

Casey Wilhelm
North Idaho College
Amy Williams
Abraham Baldwin Agricultural College
Jackie Williams
University of North Alabama
Melanie Williamson
Bluegrass Community & Technical College
Jan Wilms
Union University
Rhonda Wilson
Connors State College
Diana Wolfe
Oklahoma State University—Oklahoma City
Veryl Wolfe
Clarion University of Pennsylvania
Paula Worthington
Northern Virginia Community College
Dezhi Wu
Southern Utah University
Judy Wynekoop
Florida Gulf Coast University
Kevin Wyzkiewicz
Delta College
Catherine Yager
Pima Community College
Paul Yaroslaski
Dodge City Community College
Annette Yauney
Herkimer County Community College
Yuqiu You
Morehead State University
Bahram Zartoshty
California State University—Northridge
Suzann Zeger
William Rainey Harper College
Steven Zeltmann
University of Central Arkansas
Cherie Zieleniewski
University of Cincinnati—Batavia
Mary Ann Zlotow
College of DuPage
Laurie Zouharis
Suffolk College
Matthew Zullo
Wake Technical Community College

TECHNICAL EDITORS

Chris Anderson
North Central Michigan College
Julia Bell
Walters State Community College
Gena Casas
Florida State College
Susan Fuschetto
Cerritos College
Mary Carole Hollingsworth
Georgia Perimeter College
Rhoda James
Citrus College
Sandy Keeter
Seminole State College of Florida
Amie Mayhall
Olney Central College
Vicky Seehusen
Metropolitan State College Denver
Beverly Swisshelm
Cumberland University
Sharon Wavle
Tomkins Cortland Community College
Melinda White
Seminole State College of Florida

Thank you to the wonderful team at McGraw-Hill for your confidence in us and support on this first edition. Paul, Alan, Erin, Wyatt, Tiffany, Rick, and Julianna, we thoroughly enjoy working with you all! Thank you also to Debbie Hinkle, Kathleen Stewart, Michael-Brian Ogawa, Laurie Zouharis, Amie Mayhall, Sarah Clifford, Jeanne Reed, Lyn Belisle, and all of the reviewers and technical editors for your expertise and invaluable insight, which helped shape this book.
—Randy, Kari, Annette, and Pat

CHAPTER 1

Windows 8 and Office 2013 Overview

CHAPTER OVERVIEW

Microsoft Office 2013 and Windows 8 introduce many new features including cloud storage for your files, Office file sharing, and enhanced online content. The integration of Office 2013 and Windows 8 means that files are more portable and accessible than ever when you use *SkyDrive*, Microsoft's free online cloud storage. The new user interface on Office 2013 and Windows 8 allows you to work on tablet computers and smart phones in a working environment that resembles that of your desktop or laptop computer.

STUDENT LEARNING OUTCOMES (SLOs)

After completing this chapter, you will be able to:

SLO 1.1 Use the basic features of Windows 8 and Microsoft Office 2013 products (p. O1-2).

SLO 1.2 Create, save, close, and open Office files (p. O1-12).

SLO 1.3 Print, share, and customize Office files (p. O1-20).

SLO 1.4 Use the *Ribbon*, tabs, groups, dialog boxes, task panes, galleries, and the *Quick Access* toolbar (p. O1-23).

SLO 1.5 Use context menus, mini toolbars, and keyboard shortcuts in Office applications (p. O1-27).

SLO 1.6 Customize the view and display size in Office applications and work with multiple Office files (p. O1-31).

SLO 1.7 Organize and customize Office files and Windows folders (p. O1-34).

CASE STUDY

American River Cycling Club (ARCC) is a community cycling club that promotes fitness. ARCC members include recreational cyclists who enjoy the exercise and camaraderie and competitive cyclists who compete in road, mountain, and cyclocross races throughout the cycling season.

In the Pause & Practice projects, you incorporate many of the topics covered in the chapter to create, save, customize, and share Office 2013 files.

Pause & Practice 1-1: Log into Windows using your Microsoft account, customize the Windows *Start* page, open Office files, create a new file, open and rename an existing file, and share a file.

Pause & Practice 1-2: Modify an existing document, add document properties, customize the *Quick Access* toolbar, export a file as a PDF file, and share a document by sending a link.

Pause & Practice 1-3: Modify the working environment in Office and organize files and folders.

OFFICE 2013

Using Windows 8 and Office 2013

Windows 8 is the **operating system** that makes your computer function and controls the working environment. The Office 2013 software provides you with common application programs such as Word, Excel, Access, and PowerPoint. These applications give you the ability to work with word processing documents, spreadsheets, presentations, and databases in your personal and business projects. Although the Windows 8 operating system and the Office software products work together, they have different functions on your computer.

Windows 8

The operating system on your computer makes all of the other software programs, including Office 2013, function. **Windows 8** has a new user interface—the new **Start page**—where you can select and open a program. Alternatively you can go to the **Windows desktop**, which has the familiar look of previous versions of Windows. You also have the option with Windows 8 to log in to your computer using a Windows account that synchronizes your Windows, Office, and **SkyDrive** cloud storage between computers.

Microsoft Account

In Windows 8 and Office 2013, your files and account settings are portable. In other words, your Office settings and files can travel with you and be accessed from different computers. You are not restricted to a single computer. When you create a free **Microsoft account** (Live, Hotmail, MSN, Messenger, or other Microsoft service account), you are given a free email account, a *SkyDrive* account, and access to Office Web Apps. If you do not yet have a Microsoft account, you can create one at www.live.com (Figure 1-1).

1-1 Create a Microsoft account

> **MORE INFO**
>
> You will use your Microsoft account for projects in this text.

When you sign in to your computer using Windows 8, you can log in with your Microsoft username and password. Windows uses this information to transfer your Office 2013 settings to the computer you are using and connects you to your **SkyDrive** folder.

Start Page

After logging in to Windows 8 using your Microsoft account (see *Pause & Practice: Office 1-1*, Step 1 on page O1–17), you are taken to the **Start page** (Figure 1-2), which is new to Windows 8. The *Start* page displays different **apps** (applications) as tiles (large and small buttons). Click an app tile to launch a program or task.

Windows 8 uses the term *apps* generically to refer to applications and programs. Apps include the Windows 8 Weather app, Microsoft Excel program, Control Panel, Google Chrome, or File Explorer.

When you start using Windows 8, you can customize your *Start* page. Include the apps you most regularly use, remove the apps you don't want displayed on the *Start* page, and rearrange apps tiles to your preference.

1-2 Windows *Start* page

HOW TO: Customize the Start Page

1. To move an app tile, click and drag the app tile to a new location on the *Start* page. The other app tiles shuffle to accommodate the placement of the app tile.

2. To remove an app tile from the *Start* page, right-click the app tile you want to remove to select it and display your options, and then select **Unpin from Start** (Figure 1-3).

   - When an app tile is selected, a check mark appears in the upper right corner.
   - The app tile is removed from the *Start* page, but the program or task is not removed from your computer.
   - Your options differ depending on the app tile you select.
   - You can right-click multiple app tiles, one after the other, to select and apply an option to all of them.

3. To add an app tile to the *Start* page, right-click a blank area of the *Start* page and click **All Apps** at the bottom right (Figure 1-4).

4. Right-click the app you want to add to select it and click **Pin to Start** (Figure 1-5).

5. To resize an app tile, right-click the app tile to select it and click **Larger** or **Smaller**.

   - All options do not apply to all apps.

6. To uninstall an app, right-click the app you want to uninstall to select it and click **Uninstall**.

   - Unlike the unpin option, this option uninstalls the program from your computer, not just your *Start* page.

1-3 App options

1-4 Display all apps

1-5 Pin selected app to *Start* page

Windows 8 Navigation Options

You can access the Windows 8 options and navigate quickly to other areas from the *Start* page, the Windows desktop, or anywhere on your computer. The ***Windows 8 navigation area*** and options appear on the right side of your computer monitor when you place your pointer on the small horizontal line at the bottom right corner (Figure 1-6). The following list describes the different options available from the navigation area:

- **Search:** Displays all of the apps available on your computer and opens a search area at the right of your screen.
- **Share:** Displays options for sharing selected apps with other users.
- **Start:** Displays the *Start* page.
- **Devices:** Displays the devices available on your computer.
- **Settings:** Displays options for customizing computer settings; displays power options (Figure 1-7).

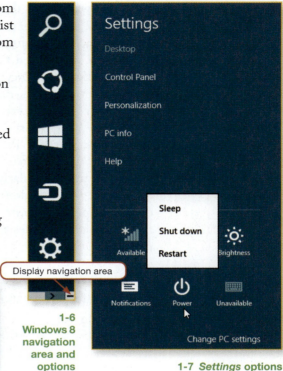

1-6
Windows 8 navigation area and options

1-7 *Settings* options

> **ANOTHER WAY**
>
> Click the bottom left corner of your computer screen to toggle between the *Start* page and the desktop.

Desktop and Taskbar

The **Windows desktop** is the working area of Windows and is similar to previous versions of Windows. Click the **Desktop** app tile on the *Start* page to go to the desktop (Figure 1-8). When you install a program on your computer, typically a shortcut to the program is added to the desktop. When you open a program from the *Start* page, such as Microsoft Word, the desktop displays and the program opens.

The *Taskbar* displays at the bottom of the desktop. You can open programs and folders from the *Taskbar* by clicking on an icon on the *Taskbar* (Figure 1-9). You can pin programs and other Windows items, such as the Control Panel or File Explorer, to the *Taskbar*.

1-8 Windows *Desktop* tile on the *Start* page

1-9 *Taskbar* at the bottom of the desktop

HOW TO: Pin a Program to the Taskbar

1. Go to the *Start* page if it is not already displayed.
   - Put your pointer in the bottom right corner of your computer monitor and select **Start** in the navigation area.
   - If you are on the desktop, you can also click the **Start page** icon that appears when you place your pointer in the bottom left corner of your monitor.

2. Right-click a program or Windows item to select it (Figure 1-10).

  • A check appears in the upper right of a selected item.
  • Options display at the bottom of the *Start* page.

3. Click **Pin to taskbar**.

1-10 Pin selected item to the *Taskbar*

File Explorer

The **File Explorer** is a window that opens on your desktop where you can browse for files stored on your computer (Figure 1-11). This window displays the libraries and folders on your computer on the left. When you select a library or folder on the left, the contents of the selection are displayed on the right. Double-click a file or folder on the right to open it.

SkyDrive

SkyDrive is a cloud storage area where you can store files in a private and secure online location that you can access from any computer. With cloud storage you don't have to be tied to one computer, and you don't have to carry your files with you on a portable storage device. When you store your files on *SkyDrive,* the files are actually saved on both your computer and on the cloud. *SkyDrive* synchronizes your files so when you change a file it is automatically updated on the *SkyDrive* cloud.

  With Windows 8, the ***Sky-Drive folder*** is one of your storage location folder options, similar to your *Documents* or *Pictures* folders (Figure 1-12). You can

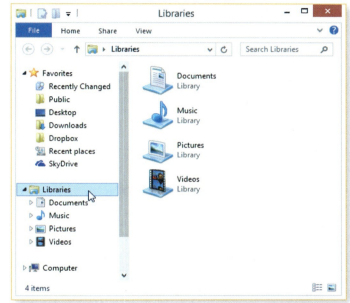

1-11 *File Explorer* window

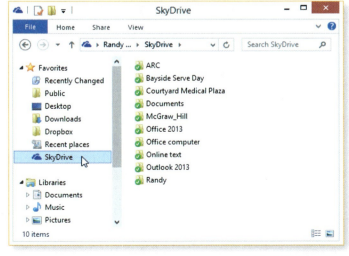

1-12 *SkyDrive* folder

save, open, and edit your *SkyDrive* files from a Windows folder. Your *SkyDrive* folder looks and functions similar to other Windows folders.

In addition to the *SkyDrive* folder on your computer, you can also access your *SkyDrive* files online using an Internet browser such as Internet Explorer, Google Chrome, or Mozilla Firefox. When you access *SkyDrive* online using a web browser, you can upload files, create folders, move and copy files and folders, and create Office files using Office Web Apps (see *Office Web Apps* later in this section).

HOW TO: Use SkyDrive Online

1. Open an Internet browser Window and navigate to the *SkyDrive* website (www.skydrive.com), which takes you to the *SkyDrive* sign in page (Figure 1-13).
   - You can use any Internet browser to access *SkyDrive* (e.g., Internet Explorer, Google Chrome, Mozilla Firefox).
2. Type in your Microsoft account email address and password.
   - If you are on your own computer, check the **Keep me signed in** box to stay signed in to *SkyDrive* when you return to the page.
3. Click the **Sign In** button to go to your *SkyDrive* web page.
   - The different areas of *SkyDrive* are listed under the *SkyDrive* heading on the left (Figure 1-14).
   - Click **Files** to display your folders and files in the folder area.
   - At the top of the page, there are buttons and drop-down menus that list the different actions you can perform on selected files and folders.

1-13 Log in to *SkyDrive* online

1-14 *SkyDrive* online

Office 2013

Microsoft Office 2013 is a suite of personal and business software applications. Microsoft Office comes in different packages and the applications included in each package vary. The common applications included in Microsoft Office and the primary purpose of each are described in the following list:

- *Microsoft Word:* Word processing software used to create, format, and edit documents such as reports, letters, brochures, and resumes.
- *Microsoft Excel:* Spreadsheet software used to perform calculations on numerical data such as financial statements, budgets, and expense reports.
- *Microsoft Access:* Database software used to store, organize, compile, and report information such as product information, sales data, client information, and employee records.
- *Microsoft PowerPoint:* Presentation software used to graphically present information in slides such as a presentation on a new product or sales trends.

- **Microsoft Outlook:** Email and personal management software used to create and send email and create and store calendar items, contacts, and tasks.
- **Microsoft OneNote:** Note-taking software used to take and organize notes, which can be shared with other Office applications.
- **Microsoft Publisher:** Desktop publishing software used to create professional-looking documents containing text, pictures, and graphics such as catalogs, brochures, and flyers.

Office Web Apps

Office Web Apps is free online software from Microsoft that works in conjunction with your online *SkyDrive* account (Figure 1-15). With Office Web Apps, you can work with Office files online, even on computers that do not have Office 2013 installed. This is a useful option when you use a computer at a computer lab or use a friend's computer that does not have Office 2013 installed.

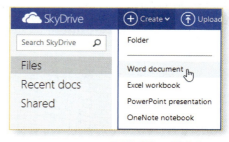

1-15 Office Web Apps

You can access Office Web Apps from your *SkyDrive* web page and create and edit Word documents, Excel workbooks, PowerPoint presentations, and OneNote notebooks. Office Web Apps is a scaled-down version of Office 2013 and not as robust in terms of features, but you can use it to create, edit, print, share, and insert comments on files. If you need more advanced features, you can open Office Web Apps files in Office 2013.

In *SkyDrive*, you can share files with others. When you share files or folders with others, you establish the access they have to the items you share. You can choose whether other users can only view files or view and edit files. To share a file or folder in your *SkyDrive*, send an email with a link to the shared items or generate a hyperlink that gives access to the shared files to others.

HOW TO: Share an Office Web Apps File

1. Log in to your *SkyDrive* account.
2. Click an Office file to open the file in Office Web Apps.
3. In read-only mode, click the **Share** button above the file. A sharing window opens with different options (Figure 1-16).
   - You can also click the **File** tab and select **Share** on the left.

1-16 Share an Office Web Apps file

4. To send an email, click **Send email**, type the recipient's email address, and type a brief message.
   - Enter a space after typing an email address to add another recipient.
   - Alternatively, you can click **Get a link** to generate a link to send to recipients.
5. Check the **Recipients can edit** box if you want the recipient to be able to edit the file.
   - Deselect this check box if you want recipients to only view the file.
   - You can also require recipients to sign in to *SkyDrive* in order to view or edit the file by checking the **Require everyone who accesses this to sign in** box.
6. Click the **Send** button.
   - Recipients receive an email containing a link to the shared file or folder.
   - A window may open, prompting you to enter a displayed code to prevent unauthorized sharing. Enter the displayed code to return to the sharing window and click **Send**.
7. Click the **X** in the upper right corner or the browser window to exit *SkyDrive*.

Office Web Apps let you synchronously (i.e., at the same time) or asynchronously (i.e., not at the same time) collaborate on an Office file with others who have access to the shared file. If two or more users are working on the same file in Office Web Apps, collaboration information is displayed at the bottom of the Office Web Apps window (Figure 1-17). You are alerted to available updates and told how many people are editing the file.

1-17 Collaboration information displayed in the *Status* bar

Click **Updates Available** in the *Status* bar to apply updates to your file. Click **People Editing** to view the names of users who are currently editing the file.

> **MORE INFO**
>
> The *Status* bar is displayed at the bottom of the application window and is available on all Office applications.

Open an Office Application

When using Windows 8, you click an app tile to open an Office application. If your *Start* page has the Office applications displayed, you can click the **Word 2013**, **Excel 2013**, **Access 2013**, or **PowerPoint 2013** tile to launch the application (Figure 1-18).

If the Office application apps are not on the *Start* page, you can search for the app.

1-18 Launch an Office 2013 application

HOW TO: Search for an App

1. Put your pointer at the bottom right corner of your computer screen to display the Windows 8 navigation options.

2. Click **Search** to display all apps and the *Search* pane on the right (Figure 1-19).

3. Type the name of the application to open (e.g., Access). Windows displays the apps matching the search text.

4. Click the app to launch it.
   - Alternatively, you can click a blank area away from the *Search* pane to close the *Search* pane, scroll through the available apps on your computer, and click an app to launch it.

1-19 Search for an app

> **MORE INFO**
>
> Add commonly used apps to your Windows *Start* page to save you time.

Office Start Page

In addition to the new *Start* page in Windows 8, most of the Office applications (except Outlook and OneNote) have a new ***Start page*** that displays when you launch the application (Figure 1-20). From this *Start* page, you can create a new blank file (e.g., a Word document, an Excel workbook, an Access database, or a PowerPoint presentation), create a file from an online template, search for an online template, open a recently used file, or open another file. These options vary depending on the Office application.

1-20 Access *Start* page

Press the **Esc** key to exit the *Start* page and enter the program. In Access, you have to open an existing database or create a new one to enter the program.

Backstage View

Office 2013 incorporates the ***Backstage view*** into all Office applications. Click the **File** tab on the *Ribbon* to open the *Backstage* view (Figure 1-21). *Backstage* options vary depending on the Office application. The following list describes some of the common tasks you can perform from the *Backstage* view:

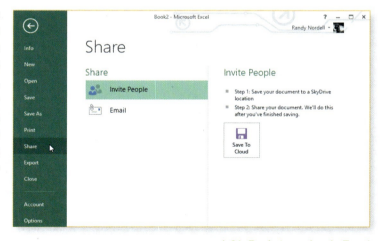

1-21 *Backstage* view in Excel

- ***Info:*** Displays document properties and other protection, inspection, and version options.
- ***New:*** Creates a new blank file or a new file from a template or theme.
- ***Open:*** Opens an existing file from a designated location or a recently opened file.
- ***Save:*** Saves a file. If the file has not been named, the *Save As* dialog box opens when you select this option.
- ***Save As:*** Opens the *Save As* dialog box.
- ***Print:*** Prints a file, displays a preview of the file, or displays print options.
- ***Share:*** Invites people to share a file or email a file.

- **Export:** Creates a PDF file from a file or saves as a different file type.
- **Close:** Closes an open file.
- **Account:** Displays your Microsoft account information.
- **Options:** Opens the *[Application] Options* dialog box (e.g., Excel Options).

Office 2013 Help

In each of the Office applications, a help feature is available where you can search for a topic and view help information related to that topic. Using the *[Application] Help* dialog box (e.g., *Access Help*), type in key words for your search. Links to online help resources display in the dialog box.

HOW TO: Use Office Help

1. Click the **Help** button (question mark) in the upper right corner of the Office application window (Figure 1-22). The *[Application] Help* dialog box opens (Figure 1-23).

1-22 *Help* button

2. In the *Search* text box, type in key words for your search and press **Enter** or click the **Search** button. A list of related articles appears in the dialog box (Figure 1-24).

- You can also click one of the links in the *Popular searches* and *Basics and beyond* areas to view related help articles.

1-23 *Access Help* dialog box

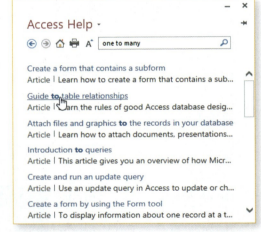

1-24 Related articles displayed in the dialog box

3. Click a link to display the article in the dialog box.

- You can use the *Back*, *Forward*, or *Home* buttons to navigate in the *Help* dialog box.
- Scroll down to the bottom of the list of articles to use the *Next* and *Previous* buttons to view more articles.

4. Click the **X** in the upper right corner to close the *Help* dialog box.

> **ANOTHER WAY**
>
> **F1** opens the *Help* dialog box.

Mouse and Pointers

If you are using Office on a desktop or laptop computer, use your mouse (or touch pad) to navigate around files, click tabs and buttons, select text and objects, move text and objects, and resize objects. The following table lists mouse and pointer terminology used in Office.

Mouse and Pointer Terminology

Term	Description
Pointer	When you move your mouse, the pointer moves on your screen. There are a variety of pointers that are used in different contexts in Office applications. The following pointers are available in most of the Office applications (the appearance of these pointers varies depending on the application and the context used): • ***Selection pointer:*** Select text or an object. • ***Move pointer:*** Move text or an object. • ***Copy pointer:*** Copy text or an object. • ***Resize pointer:*** Resize objects or table column or row. • ***Crosshair:*** Draw a shape.
Insertion point	The vertical flashing line where text is inserted in a file or text box. Click the left mouse button to position the insertion point.
Click	Click the left mouse button. Used to select an object or button or to place the insertion point in the selected location.
Double-click	Click the left mouse button twice. Used to select text.
Right-click	Click the right mouse button. Used to display the context menu and the mini toolbar.
Scroll	Use the scroll wheel on the mouse to scroll up and down through your file. You can also use the horizontal or vertical scroll bars at the bottom and right of an Office file window to move around in a file.

Office 2013 on a Tablet

The new user interface in Windows 8 and Office 2013 is designed to facilitate use of Windows and the Office applications on a tablet computer or smart phone. With tablets and smart phones, you use a touch screen rather than using a mouse, so the process of selecting text and objects and navigating around a file is different from when you select and navigate on a desktop or laptop computer. The following table lists some of the gestures used when working on a tablet or smart phone (some of these gestures vary depending on the application used and the context).

Tablet Gestures

Gesture	Used To	How To
Tap	Make a selection or place the insertion point. Double tap to edit text in an object or cell.	
Pinch	Zoom in or resize an object.	
Stretch	Zoom out or resize an object.	
Slide	Move an object or selected text.	
Swipe	Select text or multiple objects.	

Creating, Saving, Closing, and Opening Files

Creating, saving, and opening files is primarily done from the *Start* page or *Backstage* view. These areas provide you with many options and a central location to perform these tasks. You can also use shortcut commands to create, save, and open files.

Create a New File

When you create a new file in an Office application, you can create a new blank file or a new file based on a template (in PowerPoint, you can also create a presentation based on a theme). On the *Start* page, click **Blank [file type]** to create a new blank file in the application you are using (in Word, you begin with a blank document; in Excel, a blank workbook; in Access, a blank desktop database; and in PowerPoint, a blank presentation). From the *Backstage* view, the new file options are available in the *New* area.

HOW TO: Create a New File from the Start Page

1. Open the Office application you want to use. The *Start* page displays when the application opens.
2. From the *Start* page, click **Blank [file type]** or select a template or theme to use for your new blank file. A new file opens in the application you are using.
   - The new file is given a generic file name (e.g., *Document1*, *Book1*, or *Presentation1*). You can name and save this file later.
   - When creating a new Access database, you are prompted to name the new file when you create it.
   - Some templates and themes (in PowerPoint only) are displayed on the *Start* page, but you can search for other online templates and themes using the *Search* text box at the top of the *Start* page.

> **MORE INFO**
>
> **Esc** closes the *Start* page and takes you into the Office application (except in Access).

If you have been using an application already and want to create a new file, you create it from the *Backstage* view.

HOW TO: Create a New File from the Backstage View

1. Click the **File** tab to display the *Backstage* view.
2. Select **New** on the left to display the *New* area (Figure 1-25).
3. Click **Blank [file type]** or select a template or theme to use in your new blank file. A new file opens in the application.
   - The new file is given a generic file name (e.g., *Document1*, *Book1*, or *Presentation1*). You can name and save this file later.
   - When you are creating a new Access database, you are prompted to name the new file when you create it.
   - Some templates and themes (in PowerPoint only) are displayed on the *Start* page, but you can search for other online templates and themes using the *Search* text box at the top of the *Start* page.

1-25 *New* area in Word

Save a File

In Access, you name a file as you create it, but in Word, Excel, and PowerPoint, you name a file after you have created it. When you save a file, you type a name for the file and select the location where the file is saved.

HOW TO: Save a File

1. Click the **File** tab to display the *Backstage* view.
2. Select **Save** or **Save As** on the left to display the *Save As* area (Figure 1-26).
   - If the file has not already been saved, clicking *Save* or *Save As* takes you to the *Save As* area on the *Backstage* view.
3. Select a place to save your file in the *Places* area.
4. On the right, click a folder in the *Recent Folders* area or click the **Browse** button to open the *Save As* dialog box (Figure 1-27).
5. In the *Folder* list on the left, select a location to save the file.
6. In the *File name* area, type a name for the file.
7. In the *Save as type*, select the file type to save.
   - By default, Office selects the file type, but you can change the file type in this area.
8. Click **Save** to close the dialog box and save the file.

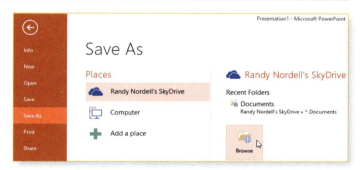

1-26 *Save As* area in PowerPoint

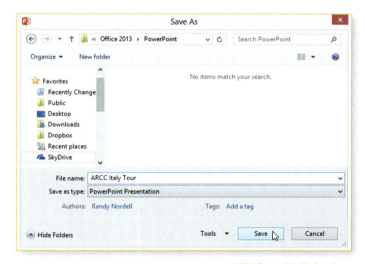

1-27 *Save As* dialog box

Create a Folder

When saving files, it is a good idea to create folders to organize your files. Organizing your files in folders makes it easier to find your files and saves you time when you are searching for a specific file (see *SLO 1.7: Organizing and Customizing Folders and Files* for more information on this topic). When you save an Office file, you can also create a folder in which to store that file.

HOW TO: Create a Folder

1. Click the **File** tab to display the *Backstage* view.
2. Select **Save As** on the left to display the *Save As* area.
3. Select a place to save your file in the *Places* area.
4. On the right, click a folder in the *Recent Folders* area or the **Browse** button to open the *Save As* dialog box.
5. In the *Folder* list at the left, select a location to save the file.
6. Click the **New Folder** button to create a new folder (Figure 1-28).
7. Type a name for the new folder and press **Enter**.

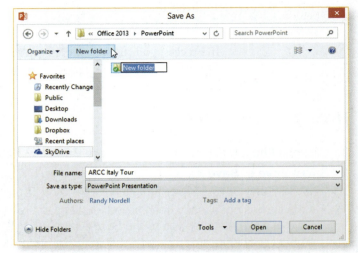

1-28 Create a new folder

> **ANOTHER WAY**
>
> **F12** opens the *Save As* dialog box (except in Access).

Save As a Different File Name

After you have saved a file, you can save it again with a different file name. If you do this, you have preserved the original file and you can continue to revise the second file for a different purpose. For example, you might want to save a different version of a file with a different file name.

HOW TO: Save As a Different File Name

1. Click the **File** tab to display the *Backstage* view.
2. Select **Save As** on the left to display the *Save As* area.
3. Select the location where you want to save your file in the *Places* area.
4. On the right, click a folder in the *Recent Folders* area or the **Browse** button to open the *Save As* dialog box.
5. In the *Folder* list on the left, select a location to save the file.
6. In the *File name* area, type a name for the file.
7. Click **Save** to close the dialog box and save the file.

Office 2013 File Types

When you save an Office file, by default Office saves the file in the most recent file format for that application. You also have the option of saving files in older versions of the Office application you are using. For example, you can save a Word document as an older version to share with or send to someone who uses an older version of Word. Each file has an extension at the end of the file name that determines the file type. The *file name extension* is automatically added to a file when you save it.

The following table lists some of the common file types used in the different Office applications.

Office File Types

File Type	Extension
Word Document	.docx
Word Template	.dotx
Word 97-2003 Document	.doc
Rich Text Format	.rtf
Excel Workbook	.xlsx
Excel Template	.xltx
Excel 97-2003 Workbook	.xls
Comma Separated Values (CSV)	.csv
Access Database	.accdb
Access Template	.accdt
Access Database (2000-2003 format)	.mdb
PowerPoint Presentation	.pptx
PowerPoint Template	.potx
PowerPoint 97-2003 Presentation	.ppt
Portable Document Format (PDF)	.pdf

Close a File

There are a few different methods you can use to close a file.

- Click the **File** tab and select **Close** on the left.
- Press **Ctrl+W**.
- Click the **X** in the upper right corner of the file window. This method closes the file and the program.

When you close a file, you are prompted to save the file if it has not been named or if changes were made after the file was last saved (Figure 1-29). Click **Save** to save and close the file or click **Don't Save** to close the file without saving. Click **Cancel** to return to the file.

1-29 Prompt to save a document before closing

Open an Existing File

You can open an existing file from the *Start* page when you open an Office application or you can open an existing file while you are working on another Office file.

HOW TO: Open a File from the Start Page

1. Open an Office application to display the *Start* page (Figure 1-30).
2. Select a file to open in the *Recent* area on the left.
   - If you select a file in the *Recent* area, the file must be located on the computer or an attached storage device in order to open. If the file has been renamed, moved, or on a storage device not connected to the computer, you received an error message.
3. Alternatively, click the **Open Other [file type]** (e.g., Documents, Workbooks, Files, or Presentations) link to open the *Open* area of the *Backstage* view (Figure 1-31).
4. Select a location in the *Places* area.
5. Select a folder in the *Recent Folders* area or click the **Browse** button to open the *Open* dialog box (Figure 1-32).
6. Select a location from the *Folder* list on the left.
7. Select the file to open and click the **Open** button.

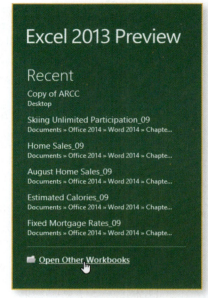

1-30 Open a file from the *Start* page

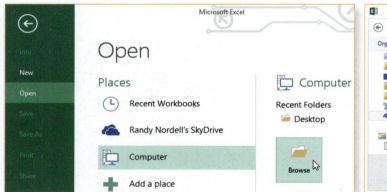

1-31 *Open* area in the *Backstage* view

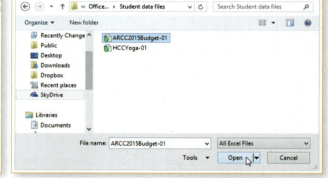

1-32 *Open* dialog box

To open a file from within an Office application, click the **File** tab to open the *Backstage* view and select **Open** on the left to display the *Open* area. Follow steps 4–7 above to open a file.

You can also open a file from a Windows folder. When you double-click a file in a Windows folder, the file opens in the appropriate Office application. Windows recognizes the file name extension and launches the correct program.

> ▶ **ANOTHER WAY**
>
> **Ctrl+F12** opens the *Open* dialog box when you are in the working area of an Office application (except in Access).

O1-16

For this project, you log in to Windows using your Microsoft account, customize the Windows *Start* page, create and save a PowerPoint presentation, create a folder, open and rename an Excel workbook, use *Help*, and share a file in *SkyDrive*.

Note to Students and Instructor:

Students: *For this project, you share an Office Web App file with your instructor. You also create a Microsoft account if you don't already have one.*

Instructor: *In order to complete this project, your students need your Microsoft email address. You can create a new Live or Hotmail account for projects in this chapter.*

File Needed: **ARCC2015Budget-01.xlsx**
Completed Project File Names: **[your initials] PP O1-1a.pptx** and **[your initials] PP O1-1b.xlsx**

1. Log in to Windows using your Microsoft account if you are not already logged in.
   a. If you are not logged in to Windows using your Microsoft account, you might need to log out or restart to display the log in page. When Windows opens, type in your Windows account username and password.
   b. If you have not yet created a Microsoft account, open a browser Window and go to www.live.com and click the **Sign up now** link. Enter the required information to create your free Windows account.

2. After logging in to Windows, customize the *Start* page to include Office 2013 apps. If these apps tiles are already on the *Start* page, skip steps 2a–e.
   a. Right-click a blank area of the *Start* page.
   b. Click **All apps** on the bottom right to display the *Apps* area of Windows.
   c. Locate and right-click **Word 2013** to select it (Figure 1-33).
   d. Click **Pin to Start** on the bottom left to add this app to the *Start* page.
   e. Repeat steps 2a–d to pin *Excel 2013*, *Access 2013*, and *PowerPoint 2013* to the *Start* page.

1-33 Word 2013 selected

3. Return to the *Start* page and arrange apps.
   a. Place your pointer on the bottom right of your screen and select **Start** from the Windows navigation options.

> **ANOTHER WAY**
>
> Click the bottom left corner of your screen to return to the *Start* page.

   b. Drag the app tiles you added to the *Start* page to your preferred locations.

4. Create a PowerPoint presentation and save in a new folder.
   a. Click the **PowerPoint 2013** app tile on your *Start* page to open the application.
   b. On the PowerPoint *Start* page, click **Blank presentation** to create a new blank presentation (Figure 1-34). A new blank presentation opens.

1-34 Create a new blank PowerPoint presentation

c. Click in the **Click to add title** area and type American River Cycling Club.

d. Click the **File** tab to open the *Backstage* view and click **Save As** on the left to display the *Save As* area.

e. Click *[your name's]* **SkyDrive** in the *Places* area and click **Browse** to open the *Save As* dialog box (Figure 1-35).

f. Click the **New Folder** button to create a new folder in your *SkyDrive* folder.

g. Type American River Cycling Club and press **Enter**.

h. Double-click the folder you created to open it.

i. In the *File name* area, type [your initials] PP O1-1a (Figure 1-36).

j. Click **Save** to close the dialog box and save the presentation.

k. Click the **X** in the upper right corner of the window to close the file and PowerPoint.

1-35 Save the file in *SkyDrive*

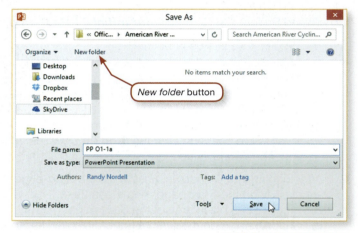

New folder button

1-36 *Save As* dialog box

5. Open an Excel file and save as a different file name.

a. Return to the Windows *Start* page.

b. Click the **Excel 2013** app tile to open it.

c. From the Excel *Start* page, click the **Open Other Workbooks** link on the bottom left to display the *Open* area of the *Backstage* view.

d. Click **Computer** in the *Places* area and click **Browse** to open the *Open* dialog box (Figure 1-37).

e. Browse to your student data files and select the ***ARCC2015Budget-01*** file.

f. Click **Open** to open the workbook.

g. Press **F12** to open the *Save As* dialog box.

h. Click **SkyDrive** in the *Folder* list on the left.

i. Double-click the **American River Cycling Club** folder to open it.

j. In the *File name* area type [your initials] PP O1-1b.

k. Click **Save** to close the dialog box and save the workbook.

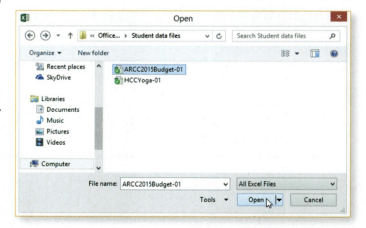

1-37 *Open* dialog box

6. Use *Excel Help* to find articles about selected topics.

a. Click the **Help** button in the upper right corner of the Excel window. The *Excel Help* dialog box opens.

b. Type pivot table in the *Search* text box and press **Enter**.

c. Click one of the displayed articles and quickly read about pivot tables.

d. Click the **Home** button to return to the home page of Excel help.

e. Type sum function in the *Search* text box and press **Enter**.

f. Click one of the displayed articles and quickly read about sum functions.

g. Click the **X** in the upper right corner to close the *Excel Help* dialog box.

h. Press **Ctrl+W** to close the Excel workbook.

i. Click the **X** in the upper right corner of the Excel window to close Excel.

7. Share an Office Web Apps file on *SkyDrive* with your instructor.

a. Return to the Windows *Start* page.

b. Open an Internet browser window and go to the *SkyDrive* (www.skydrive.com) sign-in page (Figure 1-38).

c. Type in your Microsoft account email address and password and click the **Sign In** button to go to your *SkyDrive* web page.

d. Click the navigation button on the upper left and select **SkyDrive** (if your *SkyDrive* is not already displayed) (Figure 1-39).

e. Click the **American River Cycling Club** folder to open it.

f. Click the **PP O1-1b** Excel workbook to open it in Office Web Apps (Figure 1-40).

g. Click the **File** tab to open the *Backstage* view.

h. Click **Share** on the left and select **Share with People**. A sharing window opens with different options (Figure 1-41). Sharing requires the recipient to have a Microsoft account. Also, you might be directed to complete an online form for security purposes the first time you share a file.

i. Click **Send email**, type your instructor's email address, and type a brief message.

j. Check the **Recipients can edit** check box.

k. Click the **Share** button.

8. Select **[your name]** on the upper right of the *SkyDrive* window and select the **Sign out** from the *Account* drop-down list.

1-38 Log in to *SkyDrive* online

1-39 Go to your *SkyDrive*

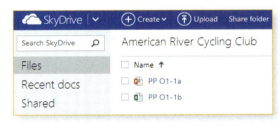

1-40 Open a file in Office Web Apps

1-41 Share an Office Web App file

Printing, Sharing, and Customizing Files

On the *Backstage* view of any of the Office applications, you can print a file and customize how a file is printed. You can also export an Office file as a PDF file in most of the Office applications. In addition, you can add and customize document properties for an Office file and share a file in a variety of formats.

Print a File

You can print an Office file if you need a paper copy of it. The *Print* area on the *Backstage* view displays a preview of the open file and many print options. For example, you can choose which page or pages to print and change the margins of the file in the *Print* area. Some of the print settings vary depending on the Office application you are using and what you are printing.

HOW TO: Print a File

1. Open the file you want to print from a Windows folder or within an Office program.
2. Click the **File** tab to open the *Backstage* view.
3. Click **Print** on the left to display the *Print* area (Figure 1-42).

   - A preview of the file displays on the right. Click the **Show Margins** button to adjust margins or **Zoom to Page** button to change the view in the *Preview* area. The *Show Margins* button is only available in Word and Excel.
   - On the left a variety of options are listed in the *Settings* area.
   - The *Settings* options vary depending on the Office application you are using and what you are printing.

4. In the *Copies* area, you can change the number of copies to print.

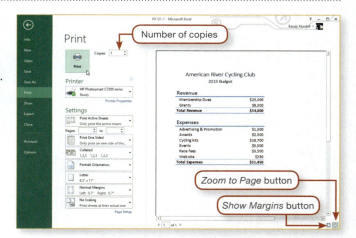

1-42 *Print* **area on the** *Backstage* **view**

5. The default printer for your computer is displayed in the *Printer* drop-down list.

   - Click the **Printer** drop-down list to select a different printer.

6. In the *Settings* area, you can customize what is printed and how it is printed.

   - In the *Pages* area (*Slides* area in PowerPoint), you can select a page or range of pages (slides) to print.
   - By default all pages (slides) are printed when you print a file.

7. Click the **Print** button to print your file.

> ▶ **ANOTHER WAY**
>
> **Ctrl+P** opens the *Print* area on the *Backstage* view.

Export as a PDF File

Portable document format, or **PDF**, is a specific file format that is often used to share files that are not to be changed or to post files on a web site. When you create a PDF file from an Office application file, you are actually exporting a static image of the original file, similar to taking a picture of the file.

The advantage of working with a PDF file is that the format of the file is retained no matter who opens the file. PDF files open in Adobe Reader, which is free software that is installed on most computers, or Adobe Acrobat, which is software users have to buy. Because a PDF file is a static image of a file, it is not easy for other people to edit your files. When you want people to be able to view a file but not make changes, PDF files are a good choice.

> **MORE INFO**
>
> Word 2013 allows you to open PDF files and edit the file as a Word document.

When you export an Office application file as a PDF file, Office creates a static image of your file and prompts you to save the file. The file is saved as a PDF file.

HOW TO: Export a File as a PDF File

1. Open the file you want to export to a PDF file.
2. Click the **File** tab and click **Export** to display the *Export* area on the Backstage view (Figure 1-43).
3. Select **Create PDF/XPS Document** and click the **Create PDF/XPS**. The *Publish as PDF or XPS* dialog box opens.
4. Select a location to save the file.
5. In the *File name* area, type a name for the file.
6. Click **Publish** to close the dialog box and save the PDF file.
   - A PDF version of your file may open. You can view the file and then close it.

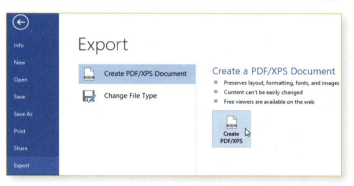

1-43 Export a file as a PDF file

Document Properties

Document properties are hidden codes in a file that contain identifying information about that file. Each piece of document property information is called a *field*. You can view and modify document properties in the *Info* area of the *Backstage* view.

Some document properties fields are automatically generated when you work on a file, such as *Size, Total Editing Time, Created,* and *Last Modified*. But you can modify other document properties fields, such as *Title, Comments, Subject, Company,* and *Author*. You can use document property fields in different ways such as inserting the *Company* field in a document footer.

HOW TO: View and Modify Document Properties

1. Click the **File** tab and click **Info**. The document properties display on the right (Figure 1-44).
2. Click in the text box area of a field that can be edited (e.g., *Add a title* or *Add a tag*) and type your custom document property information.
3. Click the **Show All Properties** link at the bottom to display additional document properties.
   - When all properties are displayed, click **Show Fewer Properties** to display fewer properties.
   - This link toggles between *Show All Properties* and *Show Fewer Properties*.
4. Click the **File** tab to return to the file.

1-44 Document properties

Share a File

Windows 8 and Office 2013 have been developed to help you share and collaborate effectively. The *Share* area on the *Backstage* view provides different options for sharing files from within an Office application. When you save a file to your *SkyDrive*, Office gives you a variety of options to share your file (Figure 1-45). Your sharing options vary depending on the Office application you are using. The following list describes some common ways you can share files with others:

1-45 Share an Office file

- *Invite People* to view or edit your file.
- *Get a Link* to the online file that you can send to others or post online.
- *Post to Social Networks* such as LinkedIn or Facebook.
- *Email* the file as an attachment, link, or PDF file.

> **MORE INFO**
>
> There is not a *Sharing* area on the *Backstage* view in Access.

HOW TO: Share a File

1. Click the **File** tab and select **Share**.
   - If your file is not saved on *SkyDrive*, select **Invite People** and click **Save to Cloud** (Figure 1-46).
   - Save your file to your *SkyDrive* folder.
   - If your file is not saved to *SkyDrive*, you will not have all of the sharing options.
2. Select one of the *Share* options on the left. Additional information is displayed on the right (Figure 1-47).
   - In most of the *Share* options, you can set the permission level to **Can view** or **Can edit**, which controls what others can do with your file.
   - In order to post a file to a social network site, you must connect your social network site to your Microsoft account. Go to the *Account* area of the *Backstage* view to connect to social network sites.

1-46 Save a file to the cloud before sharing

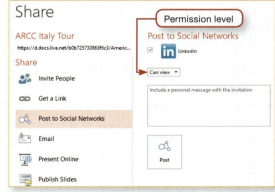

1-47 Share a file on a social network site

Program Options

Using the program options, you can make changes that apply globally to the Office program. For example, you can change the default save location to your *Sky-Drive* folder or you can turn off the *Start* page that opens when you open an Office application.

Click the **File** tab and select **Options** on the left to open the **[Program] Options** dialog box (e.g., Word Options, Excel Options, etc.) (Figure 1-48). Click one of the categories on the left to display the category options on the right. The categories and options vary depending on the Office application you are using.

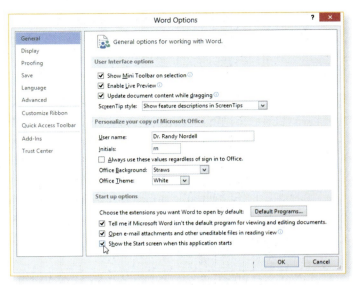

1-48 *Word Options* dialog box

SLO 1.4

Using the Ribbon, Tabs, and Quick Access Toolbar

You can use the *Ribbon*, tabs, groups, buttons, drop-down lists, dialog boxes, task panes, galleries, and the *Quick Access* toolbar to modify your Office files. This section describes the different tools you can use to customize your files.

The Ribbon, Tabs, and Groups

The **Ribbon**, which appears at the top of an Office file window, displays the many features available to use on your files. The *Ribbon* is a collection of **tabs**. On each tab are **groups** of features. The tabs and groups that are available on each Office application vary. Click a tab to display the groups and features available on that tab.

Some tabs are always displayed on the *Ribbon* (e.g., *File* tab and *Home* tab). Other tabs are **context-sensitive**, which means that they only appear on the *Ribbon* when a specific object is selected in your file. Figure 1-49 displays the context-sensitive *Table Tools Table* tab that displays in Access when you open a table.

1-49 Context-sensitive *Table Tools Table* tab displayed

Ribbon Display Options

The *Ribbon* is by default displayed when an Office application is open, but you can customize how the *Ribbon* displays. The **Ribbon Display Options** button is in the upper right corner of an Office application window (Figure 1-50). Click the **Ribbon Display Options** button to select one of the three options.

1-50 *Ribbon Display Options*

- *Auto-Hide Ribbon:* Hides the *Ribbon*. Click at the top of the application to display the *Ribbon*.
- *Show Tabs:* *Ribbon* tabs display. Click a tab to open the *Ribbon* and display the tab.
- *Show Tabs and Commands:* Displays the *Ribbon* and tabs, which is the default setting in Office applications.

> **▶ MORE INFO**
>
> **Ctrl+F1** collapses or expands the *Ribbon* to display only tabs.

Buttons, Drop-Down Lists, and Galleries

Groups on each of the tabs contain a variety of *buttons*, *drop-down lists*, and *galleries*. The following list describes each of these features and how they are used:

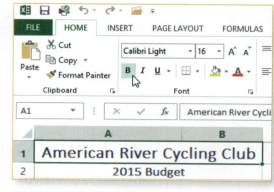

1-51 *Bold* button in the *Font* group on the *Home* tab

- *Button:* Applies a feature to selected text or object. Click a button to apply the feature (Figure 1-51).
- *Drop-Down List:* Displays the various options available for a feature. Some buttons are drop-down lists only, which means when you click one of these buttons the drop-down list of options appears (Figure 1-52). Other buttons are *split buttons*, which have both a button you click to apply a feature and an arrow you click to display a drop-down list of options (Figure 1-53).

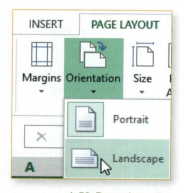

1-52 Drop-down list

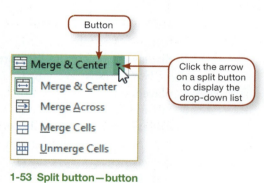

1-53 Split button—button and drop-down list

- *Gallery:* Displays a collection of option buttons. Click an option in a gallery to apply the feature. Figure 1-54 is the *Styles* gallery. You can click the **More** button to display the entire gallery of options or click the **Up** or **Down** arrow to display a different row of options.

1-54 *Styles* gallery in Word

Dialog Boxes, Task Panes, and Launchers

Not all of the features that are available in an Office application are displayed in the groups on the tabs. Additional options for some groups are displayed in a *dialog box* or *task pane*. A *launcher*, which is a small square in the bottom right of some groups, opens a dialog box or displays a task pane when you click it (see Figure 1-56).

- *Dialog box:* A new window that opens to display additional features. You can move a dialog box by clicking and dragging on the title bar, which is the top of the dialog box where the title is displayed. Figure 1-55 is the *Datasheet Formatting* dialog box that opens when you click the *Text Formatting* launcher in Access.
- *Task pane:* Opens on the left or right of the Office application window. Figure 1-56 is the *Clipboard* pane, which is available in all Office applications. Task panes are named according to their feature (e.g., *Clipboard* pane or *Navigation* pane). You can resize a task pane by clicking and dragging on its left or right border. Click the **X** in the upper right corner to close a task pane.

1-55 *Datasheet Formatting* dialog box

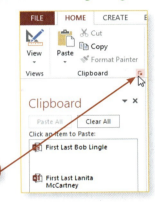

1-56 *Clipboard* pane

ScreenTips

ScreenTips display descriptive information about a button, drop-down list, launcher, or gallery selection in the groups on the *Ribbon*. When you put your pointer on an item on the *Ribbon*, a ScreenTip displays information about the selection (Figure 1-57). The ScreenTip appears temporarily and displays the command name, keyboard shortcut (if available), and a description of the command.

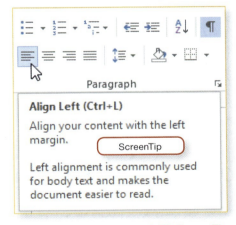

1-57 ScreenTip

Radio Buttons, Check Boxes, and Text Boxes

Within dialog boxes and task panes there are a variety of features you can apply using radio buttons, check boxes, text boxes, drop-down lists, and other buttons. A *radio button* is a round button that you click to select one option from a list of options. A selected radio button has a solid dot inside the round button. When you see a *check box*, you can use it to select one or more options. A check appears in a check box you have selected. A *text box* is an area where you can type text.

A task pane or dialog box may also include drop-down lists or other buttons that open additional dialog boxes. Figure 1-58 shows the *Page Setup* dialog box in Excel, which includes a variety of radio buttons, check boxes, text boxes, drop-down lists, and other buttons that open additional dialog boxes.

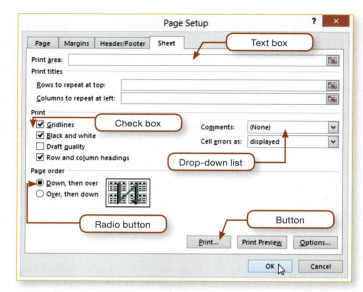

1-58 *Page Setup* dialog box in Excel

Quick Access Toolbar

The **Quick Access toolbar** is located above the *Ribbon* on the upper left of each Office application window. It contains buttons you can use to apply commonly used features such as *Save, Undo, Redo,* and *Open* (Figure 1-59). The *Undo* button is a split button. You can click the button to undo the last action performed or you can click the drop-down arrow to display and undo multiple previous actions.

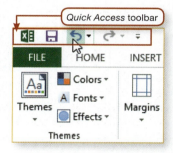

1-59 *Quick Access* toolbar

Customize the Quick Access Toolbar

You can customize the *Quick Access* toolbar to include features you regularly use, such as *Quick Print, New,* and *Spelling & Grammar.* The following steps show how to customize the *Quick Access* toolbar in Word. The customization process is similar for the *Quick Access* toolbar in the other Office applications.

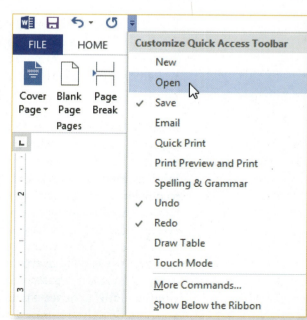

HOW TO: Customize the Quick Access Toolbar

1. Click the **Customize Quick Access Toolbar** drop-down list on the right edge of the *Quick Access* toolbar (Figure 1-60).

2. Select a command to add to the *Quick Access* toolbar. The command appears on the *Quick Access* toolbar.

   • Items on the *Customize Quick Access Toolbar* drop-down list with a check mark are displayed on the *Quick Access* toolbar.
   • Deselect a checked item to remove it from the *Quick Access* toolbar.

3. To add a command that is not listed on the *Customize Quick Access Toolbar,* click the **Customize Quick Access Toolbar** drop-down list and select **More Commands**.

1-60 Customize the *Quick Access* toolbar

The *Word Options* dialog box opens with the *Quick Access Toolbar* area displayed (Figure 1-61).

4. Click the **Customize Quick Access Toolbar** drop-down list on the right and select **For all documents** or the current document.

- If you select *For all documents*, the change is made to the *Quick Access* toolbar for all documents you open in Word.
- If you select the current document, the change is made to the *Quick Access* toolbar in that document only.

5. On the left, select the command you want to add.

- If you can't find the command you're looking for, click the **Choose commands from** drop-down list and select **All Commands**.

6. Click the **Add** button and the command name appears in the list on the right.

7. Add other commands as desired.

8. To rearrange commands on the *Quick Access* toolbar, select the command to move and click the **Move Up** or **Move Down** button.

9. Click **OK** to close the *Word Options* dialog box.

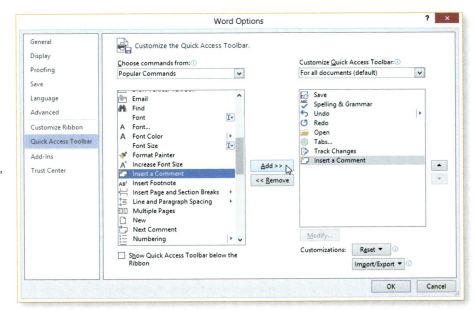

1-61 Customize the *Quick Access* toolbar in the *Word Options* dialog box

---

> **MORE INFO**
>
> To remove an item from the *Quick Access* toolbar, right-click an item and select **Remove from Quick Access Toolbar**.

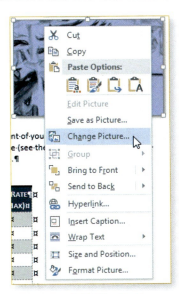

1-62 Context menu

SLO 1.5

Using a Context Menu, Mini Toolbar, and Keyboard Shortcuts

Most of the formatting and other features you will want to apply to text are available in groups on the different tabs. But many of these features are also available using content menus, mini toolbars, and keyboard shortcuts. You can use these tools to quickly apply formatting or other options to text or objects.

Context Menu

A **context menu** is displayed when you right-click text, a cell, or an object such as a picture, drawing object, chart, or *SmartArt* (Figure 1-62). The context menu is a vertical rectangle menu that lists a variety of options. These options are context-sensitive, which means they vary depending on what you right-click.

Some options on the context menu are buttons that perform an action (e.g., *Cut* or *Copy*), some are buttons that open a dialog box or task pane (e.g., *Save as Picture* or *Size and Position*), and some are selections that display a drop-down list of selections (e.g., *Bring to Front* or *Wrap Text*).

Mini Toolbar

The ***mini toolbar*** is another context menu that displays when you right-click text, a cell, or an object in your file (Figure 1-63). The mini toolbar is a horizontal rectangle menu that lists a variety of formatting options. These options vary depending on what you right-click. The mini toolbar contains a variety of buttons and drop-down lists. Some mini toolbars automatically display when you select text or an object, such as when you select a row of a table in Word or PowerPoint.

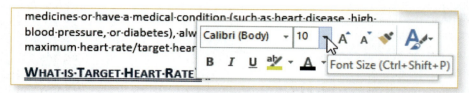

1-63 Mini toolbar

Keyboard Shortcuts

You can also use a ***keyboard shortcut*** to quickly apply formatting or perform actions. A keyboard shortcut is a keyboard key or combination of keyboard keys that you press at the same time. These can include the *Ctrl, Shift, Alt,* letter, number, and function keys (e.g., *F1* or *F7*). The following table lists some common Office keyboard shortcuts.

> **MORE INFO**
>
> See Appendix A for more Office 2013 keyboard shortcuts.

Common Office Keyboard Shortcuts

Keyboard Shortcut	Action or Displays	Keyboard Shortcut	Action or Displays
Ctrl+S	Save	**Ctrl+Z**	Undo
F12	*Save As* dialog box	**Ctrl+Y**	Redo or Repeat
Ctrl+O	*Open* area on the *Backstage* view	**Ctrl+1**	Single space
Shift+F12	*Open* dialog box	**Ctrl+2**	Double space
Ctrl+N	New blank file	**Ctrl+L**	Align left
Ctrl+P	*Print* area on the *Backstage* view	**Ctrl+E**	Align center
Ctrl+C	Copy	**Ctrl+R**	Align right
Ctrl+X	Cut	**F1**	*Help* dialog box
Ctrl+V	Paste	**F7**	*Spelling* pane
Ctrl+B	Bold	**Ctrl+A**	Select All
Ctrl+I	Italic	**Ctrl+Home**	Move to the beginning
Ctrl+U	Underline	**Ctrl+End**	Move to the end

For this project, you work with a document for the American River Cycling Club. You modify the existing document, add document properties, customize the *Quick Access* toolbar, export the document as a PDF file, and share a link to the document.

Note to Instructor:
Students: *For this project, you share an Office Web App file with your instructor.*
Instructor: *In order to complete this project, your students need your Microsoft email address. You can create a new Live or Hotmail account for projects in this chapter.*

File Needed: **ARCCTraining-01.docx**
Completed Project File Names: **[your initials] PP O1-2.docx** and **[your initials] PP O1-2.pdf**

1. Open Word 2013 and open the **ARCCTraining-01** file from your student data files.

2. Save this document as **[your initials] PP O1-2** in the *American River Cycling Club* folder in your *SkyDrive* folder.

3. Use a button, drop-down list, and dialog box to modify the document.
   a. Select the first heading, "**What is Maximum Heart Rate?**"
   b. Click the **Bold** button [*Home* tab, *Font* group].
   c. Click the **Underline** drop-down arrow and select **Double underline** (Figure 1-64).
   d. Click the **launcher** in the *Font* group [*Home* tab] to open the *Font* dialog box (Figure 1-65).
   e. In the *Size* area, select **12** from the list or type 12 in the text box.
   f. In the *Effects* area, click the **Small caps** check box to select it.
   g. Click **OK** to close the dialog box and apply the formatting changes.
   h. Select the next heading, "**What is Target Heart Rate?**"
   i. Repeat steps 3b–g to apply formatting to selected text.

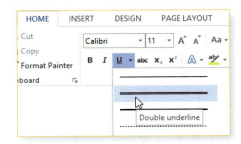

1-64 Apply *Double underline* to selected text

4. Add document properties.
   a. Click the **File** tab to display the *Backstage* view.
   b. Select **Info** on the left. The document properties are displayed on the right.
   c. Click in the **Add a title** text box and type ARCC Training.
   d. Click the **Show All Properties** link near the bottom to display more document properties.
   e. Click in the **Specify the subject** text box and type Heart rate training.
   f. Click in the **Specify the company** text box and type American River Cycling Club.
   g. Click the **Show Fewer Properties** link to display fewer document properties.
   h. Click the **Back** arrow on the upper left to close the *Backstage* view and return to the document.

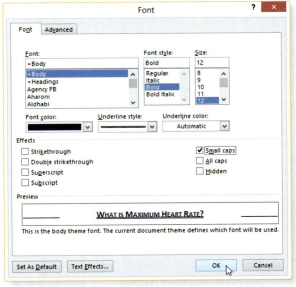

1-65 *Font* dialog box

5. Customize the *Quick Access* toolbar.
   a. Click the **Customize Quick Access Toolbar** drop-down arrow and select **Open** (Figure 1-66).
   b. Click the **Customize Quick Access Toolbar** drop-down arrow again and select **Spelling & Grammar**.
   c. Click the **Customize Quick Access Toolbar** drop-down arrow and select **More Commands**. The *Word Options* dialog box opens (Figure 1-67).
   d. Click the **Customize Quick Access Toolbar** drop-down list on the right and select **For all documents**.

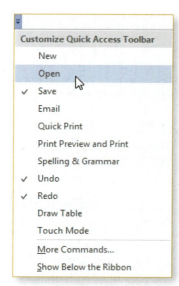

1-66 *Customize Quick Access Toolbar* drop-down list

1-67 Customize the *Quick Access* toolbar in the *Word Options* dialog box

   e. In the list of commands at the left, click **Insert a Comment**.
   f. Click the **Add** button to add it to your *Quick Access* toolbar list on the right.
   g. Click **OK** to close the *Word Options* dialog box.
   h. Click the **Save** button on the *Quick Access* toolbar to save the document.

6. Export the file as a PDF file.
   a. Click the **File** tab to go to the *Backstage* view.
   b. Select **Export** on the left.
   c. Select **Create PDF/XPS Document** and click the **Create PDF/XPS** button. The *Publish as PDF or XPS* dialog box opens (Figure 1-68).
   d. Select the **American River Cycling Club** folder in your *SkyDrive* folder as the location to save the file.
   e. In the *File name* area, type [your initials] PP O1-2 if it is not already there.
   f. Deselect the **Open file after publishing** check box if it is checked.

1-68 *Publish as PDF or XPS* dialog box

O1-30

g. Select the **Standard** (publishing online and printing) radio button.

h. Click **Publish** to close the dialog box and create a PDF version of your file.

7. Get a link to share a document with your instructor.

a. Click the **File** tab to open the *Backstage* view.

b. Select **Share** at the left. Your file is already saved to *SkyDrive* so all of the *Share* options are available.

c. Select **Get a Sharing Link** on the left (Figure 1-69).

d. In the *View Link* area, click the **Create Link** button. A link for the document is created and displayed on the right of the button.

e. Select this link and press **Ctrl+C** to copy the link.

f. Click the **Back** arrow to close the *Backstage* view and return to your document.

8. Save and close the document (Figure 1-70).

9. Email the sharing link to your instructor.

a. Using your email account, create a new email to send to your instructor.

b. Include an appropriate subject line and a brief message in the body.

c. Press **Ctrl+V** to paste the link to your document in the body of the email.

d. Send the email message.

1-69 *Get a Link* to share a file

1-70 PP O1-2 completed

Working with Files

When you work with Office files, there are a variety of views to display your file. You can change how a file is displayed, adjust the display size, work with multiple files, and arrange the windows to view multiple files. Because most people work with multiple files at the same time, Office makes it intuitive to move from one file to another or display multiple document windows at the same time.

File Views

Each of the different Office applications provides you with a variety of ways to view your document. In Word, Excel, and PowerPoint, the different views are available on the *View* tab

(Figure 1-71). You can also change views using the buttons on the right side of the *Status* bar at the bottom of the file window (Figure 1-72). In Access, the different views for each object are available in the *Views* group on the *Home* tab.

The following table lists the views that are available in each of the different Office applications.

1-71 *Workbook Views* group on the *View* tab in Excel

1-72 PowerPoint views on the *Status* bar

File Views

Office Application	Views	Office Application	Views
Word	Read Mode Print Layout Web Layout Outline Draft	Access *(Access views vary depending on active object)*	Layout View Design View Datasheet View Form View SQL View Report View Print Preview
Excel	Normal Page Break View Page Layout View Custom Views	PowerPoint	Normal Outline View Slide Sorter Notes Page Reading View Presenter View

Change Display Size

You can use the ***Zoom feature*** to increase or decrease the display size of your file. Using *Zoom* to change the display size does not change the actual size of text or objects in your file; it only changes the size of your display. For example, if you change the *Zoom* level to 120%, you increase the display of your file to 120% of its normal size (100%), but changing the display size does not affect the actual size of text and objects in your file. You could also decrease the *Zoom* level to 80% to display more of your file on the screen.

There are a few different ways you can increase or decrease the *Zoom* level on your file. Your *Zoom* options vary depending on the Office application you are using.

- ***Zoom level on the* Status *bar*** (Figure 1-73): Click the + or − buttons to increase or decrease *Zoom* level.

1-73 *Zoom* level area on the *Status* bar in PowerPoint

- ***Zoom group on the View tab*** (Figure 1-74): There are a variety of *Zoom* options in the *Zoom* group. These vary depending on application.

1-74 *Zoom* group in Excel

- **Zoom dialog box** (Figure 1-75): Click the **Zoom** button in the *Zoom* group on *View* tab or click **Zoom level** on the *Status* bar to open the *Zoom* dialog box.

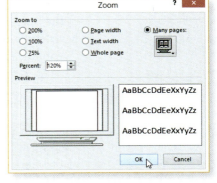

 MORE INFO

The *Zoom* feature is only available in Access in *Print Preview* view when you are working with reports.

1-75 *Zoom* dialog box in Word

Manage Multiple Open Files and Windows

When you are working on multiple files in an Office application, each file is opened in a new window. You can **minimize** an open window to place the file on the Windows *Taskbar* (the bar at the bottom of the Windows desktop), **restore down** an open window so it does not fill the entire computer screen, or **maximize** a window so it fills the entire computer screen. The *Minimize, Restore Down/Maximize,* and *Close* buttons are in the upper right of a file window (Figure 1-76).

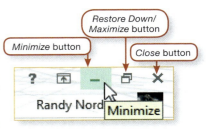

1-76 Window options buttons

 MORE INFO

You can open only one Access file at a time. If you open another Access file, the first one closes.

- **Minimize:** Click the **Minimize** button to hide this window. When a document is minimized, it is not closed. It is collapsed so the window is not displayed on your screen. Click the application icon on the Windows *Taskbar* at the bottom to display thumbnails of open files. You can click an open file thumbnail to display the file (Figure 1-77).
- **Restore Down/Maximize:** Click the **Restore Down/Maximize** button to decrease the size of an open window or maximize the window to fill the entire screen. This button toggles between *Restore Down* and *Maximize.* When

1-77 Display open files on the Windows *Taskbar*

a window is restored down, you can change the size of a window by clicking and dragging on a border of the window. You can also move the window by clicking and dragging on the title bar at the top of the window.
- **Close:** Click the **Close** button to close the window. If there is only one open file, the Office application also closes when you click the *Close* button on the file.

You can switch between open files or arrange the open files to display more than one window at the same time. There are a few ways to do this.

- **Switch Windows button:** Click the **Switch Windows** button [*View* tab, *Window* group] (not available in Access) to display a drop-down list of open files. Click a file from the drop-down list to display the file.

- *Windows Taskbar:* Click an Office application icon on the Windows *Taskbar* to display the open files in that application. Click an open file to display it (see Figure 1-77).
- *Arrange All button:* Click the **Arrange All** button [*View* tab, *Window* group] to display all windows in an application. You can resize or move the open file windows.

SLO 1.7

Organizing and Customizing Folders and Files

The more you use your computer and create and use files, the more important it is to stay organized. You can do this by using folders to store related files, which makes it easier for you to find, edit, and share your files. For example, you can create a folder for the college you attend. Inside the college folder, you can create a folder for each of your courses. Inside each of the course folders you might create a folder for student data files, solution files, and group projects. Folders can store any type of files, and you are not limited to Office files.

Create a Folder

You can create folders inside of other folders. In *SLO 1.2: Creating, Saving, Closing, and Opening Files,* you learned how to create a new folder when saving an Office file in the *Save As* dialog box. You can also create a folder using a Windows folder.

HOW TO: Create a Windows Folder

1. Open a Windows folder.
   - From the Windows *Start* page, click **File Explorer**, **Computer**, or **Documents** to open a Windows window.
   - Your folders and computer locations are listed on the left.
2. Select the location where you want to create a new folder.
3. Click the **New folder** button on the top left of the window. A new folder is created in the folders area (Figure 1-78).
   - You can also click the **Home** tab and click the **New folder** button [*New* group].
4. Type the name of the new folder and press **Enter**.

1-78 Create a new Windows folder

> **ANOTHER WAY**
>
> **Ctrl+Shift+N** creates a new folder in a Windows folder.

Move and Copy Files and Folders

You can move or copy files and folders using the *Move to* or *Copy to* buttons on the *Home* tab of a Windows folder. You can also use the move or copy keyboard shortcuts (**Ctrl+X, Ctrl+C, Ctrl+V**) or the drag and drop method. When you move a file or folder, you cut it from one location and paste it in another location. When you copy a file or folder, you create a copy of it and paste it in another location so the file or folder is in two or more locations. If there are files in a folder you move or copy, the files in the folder are moved or copied with the folder.

To move or copy multiple folders or files at the same time, press the **Ctrl** key and select multiple items to move or copy. Use the *Ctrl* key to select or deselect multiple non-adjacent files or folders. You can also use the *Shift* key to select a range of files or folders. Click the first file or folder in a range, press the **Shift** key, and select the last file or folder in the range to select all of the items in the range.

HOW TO: Move or Copy a File or Folder

1. In a Windows folder, select a file or folder to move or copy.
2. Click the **Home** tab to display the tab in the open window.
3. Click the **Move to** or **Copy to** button [*Organize* group] and select the location where you want to move or copy the file or folder (Figure 1-79).

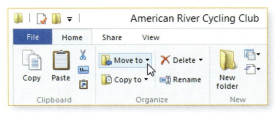

1-79 Move or copy a selected file or folder

- If the folder you want is not available, select **Choose location** to open the *Move Items* or *Copy Items* dialog box.
- To use the keyboard shortcuts, press **Ctrl+X** to cut the file or folder or **Ctrl+C** to copy the file or folder from its original location, go to the desired new location, and press **Ctrl+V** to paste it.
- To use the drag and drop method to move a file or folder, select the file or folder and drag and drop on the new location.
- To use the drag and drop method to copy a file or folder, press the **Ctrl** key, select the file or folder, and drag and drop on the new location.

> **ANOTHER WAY**
> Right-click a file or folder to display the context menu where you can select **Cut**, **Copy**, or **Paste**.

Rename Files and Folders

When you need to change the name of a file or folder, you can rename these in a Windows folder.

HOW TO: Rename a File or Folder

1. In a Windows folder, select the file or folder you want to rename.
2. Click the **Rename** button [*Home* tab, *Organize* group].
3. Type the new name of the file or folder and press **Enter**.

> **ANOTHER WAY**
> Select a file or folder to rename, press **F2**, type the new name, and press **Enter**. You can also right-click a file or folder and select **Rename** from the context menu.

Delete Files and Folders

You can also easily delete files and folders. When you delete a file or folder, it is moved from its current location to the **Recycle Bin** on your computer, which is the location where deleted items are stored. If a file or folder is in the *Recycle Bin*, you can restore this item to its original location or move it to a different location. You also have the option to permanently delete a file or folder; the item is deleted and not moved to the *Recycle Bin*. If an item is permanently deleted, you do not have the restore option.

There are several ways to delete a file or folder. To ensure that you don't delete anything by mistake, when you delete a file or folder, a confirmation dialog box opens, prompting you to confirm whether or not you want to delete the selected file or folder.

HOW TO: Delete Files and Folders

1. Select the file or folder you want to delete.
   - You can select multiple files and folders to delete at the same time.
2. Click the **Delete** drop-down arrow [*Home* tab, *Organize* group] to display the list of delete options (Figure 1-80).
3. Click **Recycle** or **Permanently delete**. A confirmation dialog box opens.
   - *Recycle* deletes the selected item(s) and moves them to the *Recycle Bin.*
   - *Permanently delete* deletes the item(s) from your computer.
   - The default action when you click the *Delete* button (not the drop-down arrow) is *Recycle.*
4. Click **Yes** to delete.

1-80 Delete selected files and folders

> ### ANOTHER WAY
> Press **Ctrl+D** or the **Delete** key on your keyboard to recycle selected item(s).
> Press **Shift+Delete** to permanently delete selected item(s).

Compressed and Zipped Folders

If you want to share multiple files or a folder of files with classmates, coworkers, friends, or family, you can *zip* the files into a *zipped folder* (also called a *compressed folder*). For example, you can't attach an entire folder to an email message, but you can attach a zipped folder to an email message. Compressing files and folders decreases their size. You can zip a group of selected files, a folder, or a combination of files and folders, and then share the zipped folder with others through email or in a cloud storage location such as *SkyDrive.*

HOW TO: Create a Zipped Folder

1. Select the file(s) and/or folder(s) you want to compress and send.
2. Click the **Zip** button [*Share* tab, *Send* group] (Figure 1-81). A zipped folder is created.
   - The name of the zipped folder is the name of the first item you selected to zip. You can rename this folder.
   - The icon for a zipped folder looks similar to the icon for a folder except it has a vertical zipper down the middle of the folder.

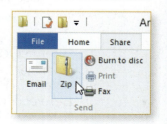

1-81 Create a zipped folder

If you receive a zipped folder from someone via email, save the zipped folder and then you can *extract* its contents. Extracting a zipped folder creates a regular Window folder from the zipped folder.

HOW TO: Extract a Zipped Folder

1. After saving the zipped folder to a location on your computer, select the folder (Figure 1-82).
2. Click the **Extract all** button [*Compress Folder Tools Extract* tab]. The *Extract Compressed (Zipped) Folders* dialog box opens (Figure 1-83).
3. Click **Extract** to extract the folder.
   - Both the extracted folder and the zipped folder display in the folder where they are located.
   - If you check the **Show extracted files when complete** check box, the extracted folder will open after extracting.

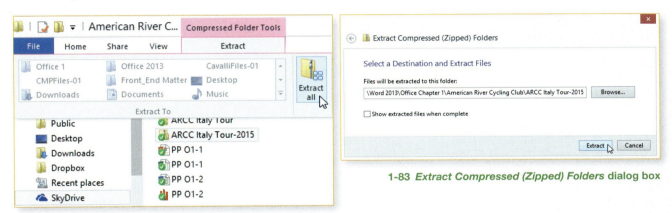

1-82 **Extract files from a zipped folder**

1-83 *Extract Compressed (Zipped) Folders* dialog box

PAUSE & PRACTICE: OFFICE 1-3

For this project, you copy and rename files in your *SkyDrive* folder on your computer, create a folder, move and copy files, create a zipped folder, and rename a zipped folder.

Files Needed: ***[your initials] PP O1-1a.pptx***, ***[your initials] PP O1-1b.xlsx***, and ***[your initials] PP O1-2.docx***
Completed Project File Names: ***[your initials] PP O1-3a.pptx***, ***[your initials] PP O1-3b.xlsx***, ***[your initials] PP O1-3c.docx***, and ***ARCC Italy Tour-[current year]*** (zipped folder)

1. Open your *SkyDrive* folder.
   a. From the Windows *Start* page, click the **File Explorer** or **Computer** tile to open a Windows folder. If these options are not available on the *Start* page, use *Search* to find and open the *File Explorer* or *Computer* window.

b. Click the **SkyDrive** folder on the left to display the folders in your *SkyDrive* folder.
c. Double click the **American River Cycling Club** folder to open it.

2. Copy and rename files.
   a. Select the *[your initials] PP O1-1a* file (this is a PowerPoint file).
   b. Click the **Copy to** button [*Home* tab, *Organize* group] and select **Choose Location** to open the *Copy Items* dialog box (Figure 1-84).
   c. Select the **American River Cycling Club** folder in your *SkyDrive* folder and click **Copy**.
   d. Select the copy of the file (*[your initials] PP O1-1a – Copy*) and click the **Rename** button [*Home* tab, *Organize* group].
   e. Type [your initials] PP O1-3a and press **Enter**.
   f. Select the *[your initials] PP O1-1b* file (this is an Excel file).
   g. Press **Ctrl+C** to copy the file and then press **Ctrl+V** to paste a copy of the file.
   h. Rename this file [your initials] PP O1-3b.
   i. Right-click the *[your initials] PP O1-2* file (this is a Word file and the third one in the list) and select **Copy** from the context menu.
   j. Right-click a blank area of the open window and select **Paste** from the context menu.
   k. Rename this file [your initials] PP O1-3c.

3. Create a new folder and move files.
   a. With the *American River Cycling Club* folder still open, click the **New folder** button on the upper left.
   b. Type ARCC Italy Tour and press **Enter**.
   c. Select the *[your initials] PP O1-3a* file.
   d. Hold down the **Ctrl** key, select the *[your initials] PP O1-3b* and *[your initials] PP O1-3c* files.
   e. Click the selected files and drag and drop on the *ARCC Italy Tour* folder (don't hold down the *Ctrl* key while dragging). The files are moved to the *ARCC Italy Tour* folder.
   f. Double-click the **ARCC Italy Tour** folder to open it and confirm the files are moved.
   g. Click the **Up** or **Back** arrow to return to the *American River Cycling Club* folder.

4. Create a zipped folder.
   a. Select the **ARCC Italy Tour** folder.
   b. Click the **Zip** button [*Share* tab, *Send* group]. A zipped (compressed) folder is created.
   c. Right-click the zipped folder and select **Rename** from the context menu.
   d. At the end of the folder name, type - (a hyphen), type the current year, and press **Enter** (Figure 1-85).

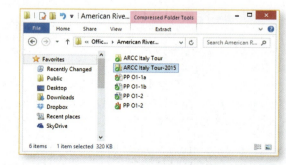

1-84 Copy selected file

1-85 PP O1-3 completed

5. Email the zipped folder to your instructor.
   a. Using your email account, create a new email to send to your instructor.
   b. Include an appropriate subject line and a brief message in the body.
   c. Attach the *ARCC Italy Tour-[current year]* zipped folder to the email message.
   d. Send the email message.

Chapter Summary

1.1 Use the basic features of Windows 8 and Microsoft Office 2013 products (p. O1-2).

- **Windows 8** is the operating system on your computer.
- A **Microsoft account** is a free account you create. When you create a Microsoft account, you are given an email address, a **SkyDrive** account, and access to **Office Web Apps**.
- **SkyDrive** is the **cloud storage** area where you can store files in a private and secure online location.
- In Windows 8, the **SkyDrive folder** is one of your file storage location options.
- The **Start page** in Windows 8 is where you select what you want to do on your computer.
- The **Windows desktop** is the working area of Windows and the **Taskbar** is at the bottom of the desktop. You can pin applications to the *Taskbar*.
- The **File Explorer** is a window that displays libraries, files, and folders on your computer.
- You can access your *SkyDrive* folders and files using an Internet browser window.
- **Apps** are the applications or programs on your computer. App buttons are arranged in tiles on the Windows 8 *Start* page.
- You can customize the *Start* page to add, remove, or arrange apps.
- **Navigation options** display on the right side of your computer monitor when you put your pointer in the bottom right corner.
- **Office 2013** is application software that contains **Word**, **Excel**, **Access**, **PowerPoint**, **Outlook**, **OneNote**, and **Publisher**.
- **Office Web Apps** is free online software that works in conjunction with your online *SkyDrive* account.
- In *SkyDrive*, you can share Office files with others.
- When you open each of the Office applications, a **Start page** is displayed where you can open an existing file or create a new file.
- In the **Backstage view** in each of the Office applications, you can perform many common tasks such as saving, opening an existing file, creating a new file, printing, and sharing.
- **Office Help** contains searchable articles related to specific topics.

- Use the mouse (or touch pad) on your computer to navigate the pointer on your computer screen. Use the pointer or click buttons to select text or objects.
- When using Office 2013 on a tablet, use the touch screen to perform actions.

1.2 Create, save, close, and open Office files (p. O1-12).

- You can create a new Office file from the *Start* page or *Backstage* view of the Office application you are using.
- When you **save a file** for the first time, you give it a **file name**.
- You can create **folders** to organize saved files, and you can save a file as a different file name.
- A variety of different **file types** are used in each of the Office applications.
- You can close an Office file when you are finished working on it. If the file has not been saved or changes have been made to the file, you are prompted to save the file before closing.
- In each of the Office applications, you can open an existing file from the *Start* page or from the *Backstage* view.

1.3 Print, share, and customize Office files (p. O1-20).

- You can print a file in a variety of formats. The *Print* area on the *Backstage* view lists your print options and displays a preview of your file.
- You can export a file as a **PDF file** and save the PDF file to post to a web site or share with others.
- **Document properties** contain information about a file.
- You can **share** Office files in a variety of ways and allow others to view or edit shared files.
- **Program options** are available on the *Backstage* view. You can use the program options to make global changes to an Office application.

1.4 Use the Ribbon, tabs, groups, dialog boxes, task panes, galleries, and the Quick Access toolbar (p. O1-23).

- The **Ribbon** appears at the top of an Office window. It contains **tabs** and **groups** that allow you to access features you regularly use.

O1-39

- The **Ribbon Display Options** provides different ways the *Ribbon* can be displayed in Office applications.
- Within groups on each tab are a variety of **buttons**, **drop-down lists**, and **galleries**.
- **Dialog boxes** contain additional features not always displayed on the *Ribbon*.
- Click the **launcher** in the bottom right corner of some groups to open a dialog box for that group.
- A **ScreenTip** displays information about commands on the *Ribbon*.
- Dialog boxes contain **radio buttons**, **check boxes**, **drop-down lists**, and **text boxes** you can use to apply features.
- The **Quick Access toolbar**, which contains buttons that allow you to perform commands, is displayed in all Office applications on the upper left.
- You can add or remove commands on the *Quick Access* toolbar.

1.5 Use context menus, mini toolbars, and keyboard shortcuts in Office applications (p. O1-27).

- A **context menu** displays when you right-click text or an object. The context menu contains different features depending on what you right-click.
- The **mini toolbar** is another context menu that displays formatting options.
- You can use **keyboard shortcuts** to apply features or commands.

1.6 Customize the view and display size in Office applications and work with multiple Office files (p. O1-31).

- In each of the Office applications, there are a variety of **views**.
- The **Zoom feature** changes the display size of your file.
- You can work with multiple Office files at the same time and switch between open files.

1.7 Organize and customize Office files and Windows folders (p. O1-34).

- **Folders** store and organize your files.
- You can create, move, or copy files and folders. Files stored in a folder are moved or copied with that folder.
- You can rename a file to change the file name.
- When you delete a file or folder, it is moved to the **Recycle Bin** on your computer by default. Alternatively, you can permanently delete files and folders.
- A **zipped (compressed) folder** makes it easier and faster to email or share multiple files. You can zip files and/or folders into a zipped folder.
- When you receive a zipped folder, you can **extract** the zipped folder to create a regular Windows folder and access its contents.

Check for Understanding

In the **Online Learning Center** for this text (www.mhhe.com/office2013inpractice), there are a variety of resources that can be used to review the concepts covered in this chapter.

The following Online Learning Resources are available in the Online Learning Center:

- Multiple choice questions
- Short answer questions
- Matching exercises

In these projects, you use your *SkyDrive* to store files. If you don't have a Microsoft account, see *SLO 1.1: Using Windows 8 and Office 2013* for information about obtaining a free personal Microsoft account.

Guided Project 1-1

For this project, you organize and edit files for Emma Cavalli at Placer Hills Real Estate. You extract a zipped folder, rename files, manage multiple documents, and apply formatting.
[Student Learning Outcomes 1.1, 1.2, 1.4, 1.5, 1.6, 1.7]

Files Needed: ***CavalliFiles-01*** (zipped folder)
Completed Project File Names: ***[your initials] Office 1-1a.docx***, ***[your initials] Office 1-1b.docx***, ***[your initials] Office 1-1c.xlsx***, and ***[your initials] Office 1-1d.pptx***

Skills Covered in This Project

- Copy and paste a zipped folder.
- Create a new folder in your *SkyDrive* folder.
- Extract a zipped folder.
- Move a file.
- Rename a file.
- Open a Word document.
- Switch between two open Word documents.

- Save a Word document with a different file name.
- Change display size.
- Use a mini toolbar, keyboard shortcut, context menu, and dialog box to apply formatting to selected text.
- Close a Word document.

1. Copy a zipped folder and create a new *SkyDrive* folder.
   a. From the Windows *Start* page, click **File Explorer** or **Computer** to open a Windows folder. If these options are not available on the *Start* page, use *Search* to find and open a Windows folder.
   b. Browse to the location on your computer where you store your student data files.
   c. Select the ***CavalliFiles-01*** zipped folder and press **Ctrl+C** to copy the folder.
   d. Select your **SkyDrive** folder at the left and click the **New folder** button to create a new folder.
   e. Type PHRE and press **Enter**.
   f. Press **Enter** again to open the *PHRE* folder.
   g. Press **Ctrl+V** to paste the copied ***CavalliFiles-01*** zipped folder in the *PHRE* folder.

2. Extract a zipped folder.
   a. Select the ***CavalliFiles-01*** zipped folder.
   b. Click the **Compressed Folder Tools Extract** tab and click the **Extract all** button. The *Extract Compressed (Zipped) Folders* dialog box opens.
   c. Deselect the **Show extracted files when complete** check box.
   d. Click the **Extract** button. The zipped folder is extracted and there are now two *CavalliFiles-01* folders. One folder is zipped and the other is a regular folder.
   e. Select the zipped ***CavalliFiles-01*** folder and press **Delete** to delete the zipped folder.

3. Move and rename files.
   a. With the *PHRE* folder still open, double-click the **CavalliFiles-01** folder to open it.
   b. Click the first file, press and hold the **Shift** key, and click the last file to select all four files.
   c. Press **Ctr+X** to cut the files from the current location.

d. Click the **Up** button to move up to the *PHRE* folder (Figure 1-86).

e. Press **Ctrl+V** to paste and move the files.

f. Select the ***Cavalli files-01*** folder and press **Delete** to delete the folder.

g. Select the ***CavalliPHRE-01*** file, click the **File** tab, and click the **Rename** button [*Organize* group].

h. Type [your initials] Office 1-1a and press **Enter**.

i. Right-click the ***FixedMortgageRates-01*** file and select the **Rename** from the context menu.

j. Type [your initials] Office 1-1b and press **Enter**.

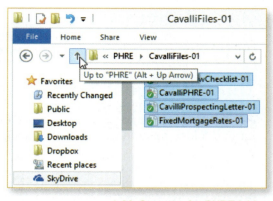

1-86 Go up to the *PHRE* folder

4. Open two Word documents and rename a Word document.

a. Press the **Ctrl** key and click the ***BuyerEscrowChecklist-01*** and ***CavalliProspectingLetter-01*** files to select both files.

b. Press the **Enter** key to open both files in Word.

c. If the *BuyerEscrowChecklist-01* document is not displayed, click the **Switch Documents** button [*View* tab, *Window* group] and select ***BuyerEscrowChecklist-01***. You can also switch documents by selecting the document on the *Taskbar*.

d. Click the **File** tab and select **Save As** at the left.

e. Select **[your name's] SkyDrive** in the *Places* area and select the **PHRE** folder or click **Browse** and select the **PHRE** folder. The *Save As* dialog box opens.

f. Type [your initials] Office 1-1c in the *File name* text box and click **Save**.

g. Press **Ctrl+W** to close the document. The *Cavalli Prospecting Letter_01* remains open.

5. Change display size and edit and rename a Word document.

a. Click the **Zoom In** or **Zoom Out** button at the bottom right of the document window to change the display size to 120% (Figure 1-87). This will vary depending on the current display size.

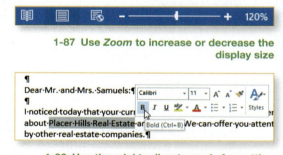

1-87 Use *Zoom* to increase or decrease the display size

b. Select "**Placer Hills Real Estate**" in the first body paragraph of the letter and the mini toolbar is displayed (Figure 1-88).

c. Click the **Bold** button on the mini toolbar to apply bold formatting to the selected text.

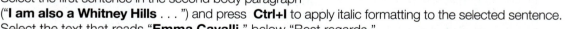

1-88 Use the mini toolbar to apply formatting

d. Select the first sentence in the second body paragraph ("**I am also a Whitney Hills** . . . ") and press **Ctrl+I** to apply italic formatting to the selected sentence.

e. Select the text that reads "**Emma Cavalli,**" below "Best regards."

f. Right-click the selected text and select **Font** from the context menu to open the *Font* dialog box.

g. Check the **Small Caps** check box in the *Effects* area and click **OK** to close the *Font* dialog box.

h. With "**Emma Cavalli**" still selected, click the **Bold** button [*Home* tab, *Font* group].

i. Press **F12** to open the *Save As* dialog box.

j. Type [your initials] Office 1-1d in the *File name* text box and click **Save**.

k. Click the **X** in the upper right corner of the document window to close the document and close Word.

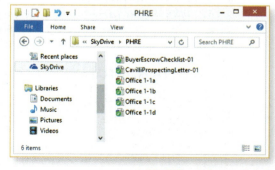

6. Your *PHRE* folder should contain the files shown in Figure 1-89.

1-89 Office 1-1 completed

Guided Project 1-2

For this project, you modify an Excel file for Hamilton Civic Center. You rename a file, add document properties, use *Help* to search a topic, share the file, and export a file as a PDF file.
[Student Learning Outcomes 1.1, 1.2, 1.3, 1.4]

Note to Students and Instructor:

Students: *For this project, you share an Office file with your instructor.*
Instructor: *In order to complete this project, your students need your Microsoft email address. You can create a new Live or Hotmail account for projects in this chapter.*

File Needed: ***HCCYoga-01.xlsx***
Completed Project File Names: ***[your initials] Office 1-2.xlsx*** and ***[your initials] Office 1-2.pdf***

Skills Covered in This Project

- Open Excel and an Excel workbook.
- Create a new *SkyDrive* folder.
- Save an Excel workbook with a different file name.
- Add document properties to a file.

- Use *Microsoft Excel Help* to search for a topic.
- Open a Word document.
- Share a file.
- Export a file as a PDF file.

1. Open Excel 2013 and open an Excel workbook.
   a. From the Windows *Start* page, click **Excel 2013** to open this application. If Excel 2013 is not available on the *Start* page, use *Search* to find and open it.
   b. From the Excel *Start* page, click **Open Other Workbooks** to display the *Open* area of the *Backstage* view.
   c. In the *Places* area, select where your student data files are stored and click the **Browse** button to open the *Open* dialog box.
   d. Browse to the location where your student data files are stored, select the ***HCCYoga-01*** file, and click **Open** to open the Excel workbook.

2. Save a file as a different file name in your *SkyDrive* folder.
   a. Click the **File** tab to open the *Backstage* view and select **Save As** at the left.
   b. In the *Places* area, select **[your name's] SkyDrive**.
   c. Click the **Browse** button to open the *Save As* dialog box.
   d. Select the **SkyDrive** folder on the left and click the **New folder** button to create a new folder.
   e. Type HCC and press **Enter**.
   f. Double-click the **HCC** folder to open it.
   g. In the *File name* area, type [your initials] Office 1-2 and click **Save** to close the dialog box and save the file.

3. Add document properties to the Excel workbook.
   a. Click the **File** button to open the *Backstage* view and select **Info** on the left. The document properties are displayed on the right.
   b. Put your insertion point in the *Title* text box ("Add a title") and type Yoga Classes.
   c. Click the **Show All Properties** link to display more properties.

d. Put your insertion point in the *Company* text box and type Hamilton Civic Center.
   e. Click the **back arrow** in the upper left of the *Backstage* window to return to the Excel workbook.

4. Use *Help* to learn about a topic.
   a. Click **Microsoft Excel Help** button (question mark) in the upper right corner of the Excel window or press **F1** to open the *Excel Help* dialog box.
   b. Put your insertion point in the *Search help* text box, type AutoSum, and press **Enter**.
   c. Click the first link and read about *AutoSum*.
   d. Click the **Back** button to return to the search list of articles and click the second link.
   e. Read about *AutoSum* and then click the **X** in the upper right corner to close the *Excel Help* dialog box.

5. Share an Excel workbook with your instructor.
   a. Click the **File** tab and select **Share** at the left.
   b. In the *Share* area, select **Invite People** (Figure 1-90).
   c. Type your instructor's email address in the *Type names or email addresses* area.
   d. In the drop-down list to the right of the email address, select **Can edit**.
   e. In the body, type a brief message.
   f. Click the **Share** button.
   g. Click the **Save** button to save and return to the workbook.

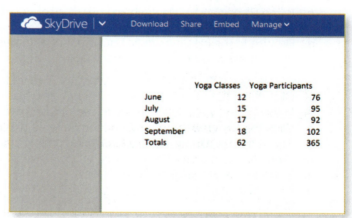

1-90 Invite people to share a file

6. Export the Excel workbook as a PDF file.
   a. Click the **File** button and select **Export** at the left.
   b. In the *Export* area, select **Create PDF/XPS Document** and click the **Create PDF/XPS** button. The *Publish as PDF or XPS* dialog box opens.
   c. Check the **Open file after publishing** check box. The publish location and file name are the same as the Excel file; don't change these.
   d. Click **Publish** to create and open the PDF file (Figure 1-91). The PDF file opens in an Internet browser window in *SkyDrive*.
   e. Close the Internet browser window.

7. Save and close the Excel file.
   a. Click the **Excel** icon on the Windows *Taskbar* to display the Excel file.
   b. Press **Ctrl+S** to save the file.
   c. Click the **X** in the upper right corner of the Excel window to close the file and Excel.

1-91 PDF file displayed in *SkyDrive*

Independent Project 1-3

For this project, you organize and edit files for Courtyard Medical Plaza. You extract a zipped folder, rename files, export a file as a PDF file, and share a file in *SkyDrive*.
[Student Learning Outcomes 1.1, 1.3, 1.6, 1.7]

Note to Students and Instructor:
Students: *For this project, you share an* Office Web App *file with your instructor.*
Instructor: *In order to complete this project, your students need your Microsoft email address. You can create a new Live or Hotmail account for projects in this chapter.*

Files Needed: **CMPFiles-01** (zipped folder)
Completed Project File Names: **[your initials] Office 1-3a.pptx**, **[your initials] Office 1-3a-pdf.pdf**, **[your initials] Office 1-3b.accdb**, **[your initials] Office 1-3c.xlsx**, and **[your initials] Office 1-3d.docx**

Skills Covered in This Project

- Copy and paste a zipped folder.
- Create a new folder in your *SkyDrive* folder.
- Extract a zipped folder.
- Move a file.
- Rename a file.
- Open a PowerPoint presentation.
- Export a file as a PDF file.
- Use *SkyDrive* to share a file.

1. Copy a zipped folder and create a new *SkyDrive* folder.
   a. Using a Windows folder, browse to locate the **CMPFiles-01** zipped folder in your student data files and copy the zipped folder.
   b. Go to your *SkyDrive* folder and create a new folder named Courtyard Medical Plaza within the *SkyDrive* folder.

2. Copy and extract the zipped folder and move files.
   a. Paste the zipped folder in the *Courtyard Medical Plaza* folder.
   b. Extract the zipped folder and then delete the zipped folder.
   c. Open the **CMPFiles-01** folder and move all of the files to the *Courtyard Medical Plaza* folder.
   d. Delete the **CMPFiles-01** folder.

3. Rename files in the *Courtyard Medical Plaza* folder.
   a. Rename the **CMPStayingActive-01** PowerPoint file to [your initials] Office 1-3a.
   b. Rename the **CourtyardMedicalPlaza-01** Access file to [your initials] Office 1-3b.
   c. Rename the **EstimatedCalories-01** Excel file to [your initials] Office 1-3c.
   d. Rename the **StayingActive-01** Word file to [your initials] Office 1-3d.

4. Export a PowerPoint file as a PDF file.
   a. From the *Courtyard Medical Plaza* folder, open the **[your initials] Office 1-3a** file. The file opens in PowerPoint.
   b. Export this file as a PDF file. Don't have the PDF file open after publishing.
   c. Save the file as [your initials] Office 1-3a-pdf and save in the *Courtyard Medical Plaza* folder.
   d. Close the PowerPoint file and exit PowerPoint.

5. Use *SkyDrive* to share a file with your instructor.
   a. Open an Internet browser window and log in to your *SkyDrive* (www.skydrive.com) using your Microsoft account.
   b. Go to your *SkyDrive* files and open the **Courtyard Medical Plaza** folder.
   c. Open the *[your initials] Office 1-3a* file in PowerPoint Web App.
   d. Share this file with your instructor.
   e. Send an email to share the file and include your instructor's email address and a brief message. Allow your instructor to edit the file.
   f. Sign out of *SkyDrive*.

6. Close the Windows folder containing the files for this project (Figure 1-92).

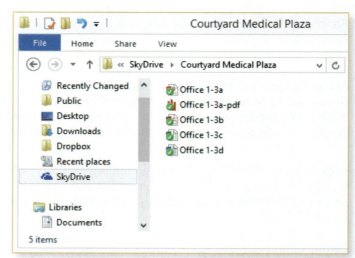

1-92 Office 1-3 completed

Independent Project 1-4

For this project, you modify a Word file for Life's Animal Shelter. You rename the document, add document properties, modify the document, share a link to the document, export a document as a PDF file, and create a zipped folder.
[Student Learning Outcomes 1.1, 1.2, 1.3, 1.4, 1.5, 1.6, 1.7]

Note to Students and Instructor:
Students: For this project, you share an Office file with your instructor.
Instructor: In order to complete this project, your students need your Microsoft email address. You can create a new Live or Hotmail account for projects in this chapter.

File Needed: **LASSupportLetter-01.docx**
Completed Project File Names: *[your initials] Office 1-4.docx*, *[your initials] Office 1-4.pdf*, and **LAS files** (zipped folder)

Skills Covered in This Project

- Open Excel and an Excel file.
- Create a new *SkyDrive* folder.
- Save a file with a different file name.
- Apply formatting to selected text.
- Add document properties to the file.

- Use *Microsoft Excel Help* to search for a topic.
- Open a Word document.
- Share a file.
- Export a file as a PDF file.

1. Open Word 2013 and open a Word document.
   a. From the Windows *Start* page, open Word 2013.
   b. From the Word *Start* page, open the ***LASSupportLetter-01*** document from your student data files.

2. Create a new folder and save the document with a different file name.
   a. Open the **Save As** dialog box and create a new folder named LAS in your *SkyDrive* folder.
   b. Save this document as [your initials] Office 1-4.

3. Apply formatting changes to the document using a dialog box, keyboard shortcut, and mini toolbar.
   a. Select "**To**" and use the **launcher** to open the *Font* dialog box.
   b. Apply **Bold** and **All caps** to the selected text.
   c. Repeat the formatting on the other three memo guide words: "**From**," "**Date**," and "**Subject**."
   d. Select "**Life's Animal Shelter**" in the first sentence of the first body paragraph and use the keyboard shortcut to apply **bold** formatting.
   e. Select the first sentence in the second body paragraph ("**Would you again consider** . . . ") and use the mini toolbar to apply **italic** formatting.

4. Add the following document properties to the document:
   Title: Support Letter
   Company: Life's Animal Shelter

5. Get a link to share this document with your instructor.
   a. Create and copy an **Edit Link** you can email to your instructor.
   b. Create a new email to send to your professor using the email you use for this course.
   c. Include an appropriate subject line and a brief message in the body.
   d. Paste the link in the body of the email message and send the message.

6. Use the keyboard shortcut to **save** the file before continuing.

7. Export this document as a PDF file.
   a. Save the file in the same location and use the same file name.
   b. Close the PDF file if it opens after publishing.

8. Save and close the Word file and exit Word (Figure 1-93).

9. Create a zipped folder.
   a. Using a Windows folder, open the **LAS** folder in your *SkyDrive* folder.
   b. Select the two files and create a zipped folder.
   c. Rename the zipped folder LAS files (Figure 1-94).

10. Close the open Windows folder.

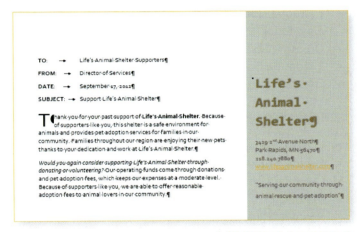

1-93 Office 1-4 completed

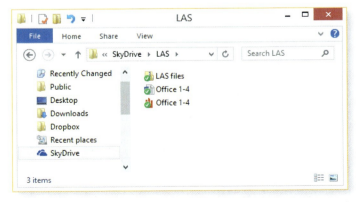

1-94 Office 1-4 completed

Projects www.mhhe.com/office2013inpractice

Challenge Project 1-5

For this project, you create folders to organize your files for this class and use *SkyDrive* to share a link with your professor.
[Student Learning Outcomes 1.1, 1.7]

Note to Students and Instructor:
Students: *For this project, you share an Office file with your instructor.*
Instructor: *In order to complete this project, your students need your Microsoft email address. You can create a new Live or Hotmail account for projects in this chapter.*

File Needed: None
Completed Project File Name: Email link to shared folder to your instructor

Using a Windows folder, create *SkyDrive* folders to contain all of the files for this class. Organize your files and folders according to the following guidelines:

- Create a *SkyDrive* folder for this class.
- Create a *Student data files* folder inside the class folder.
- Extract student data files if you have not already done so. Make sure they are in the *Student data files* folder.
- Create a *Solution files* folder inside the class folder.
- Inside the *Solution files* folder, create a folder for each chapter.
- Create a folder to store miscellaneous class files such as the syllabus and other course handouts.

Using an Internet browser, log in to your *SkyDrive* and share your class folder with your instructor.

- In *SkyDrive*, select the check box to the right of your class folder and click the **Share** button.
- Create a link to *View only* the folder.
- Create an email to your professor and include an appropriate subject line and a brief message in the body.
- Paste the link to your *SkyDrive* class folder in the body of the email message and send the email.

Challenge Project 1-6

For this project, you save a file as a different file name, customize the *Quick Access* toolbar, share a file with your professor, and export a file as a PDF file.
[Student Learning Outcomes 1.1, 1.2, 1.3, 1.4]

Note to Students and Instructor:

Students: *For this project, you share an Office file with your instructor.*
Instructor: *In order to complete this project, your students need your Microsoft email address. You can create a new Live or Hotmail account for projects in this chapter.*

File Needed: Use an existing Office file
Completed Project File Name: *[your initials] Office 1-6*

Open an existing Word, Excel, or PowerPoint file. Save this file in a *SkyDrive* folder and name it *[your initials] Office 1-6*. If you don't have any of these files, use one from your Pause & Practice projects or select a file from your student data files.

With your file open, perform the following actions:

- Customize the *Quick Access* toolbar to add command buttons. Add commands such as *New, Open, Quick Print*, and *Spelling* that you use regularly in the Office application.
- Share your file with your instructor. Use *Invite People* and include your instructor's email, an appropriate subject line, and a brief message in the body. Allow your instructor to edit the file.
- Export the document as a PDF file. Use the same file name and save it in the same *SkyDrive* folder as your open file.

Microsoft® Office
IN PRACTICE

word

Creating and Editing Documents

CHAPTER OVERVIEW

Microsoft Word (Word) has been and continues to be the leading word processing software in both the personal and business markets. Word improves with each new version and is used for creating and editing personal, business, and educational documents. Word allows you to create letters, memos, reports, flyers, brochures, and mailings without a vast amount of computer knowledge. This chapter covers the basics of creating and editing a Word document.

STUDENT LEARNING OUTCOMES (SLOs)

After completing this chapter, you will be able to:

SLO 1.1 Create, save, and open a Word document (p. W1-3).

SLO 1.2 Customize a document by entering and selecting text, using word wrap, and using *AutoComplete*, *AutoCorrect*, and *AutoFormat* features (p. W1-6).

SLO 1.3 Enhance a document using paragraph breaks, line breaks, spaces, and non-breaking spaces (p. W1-10).

SLO 1.4 Edit a document using cut, copy, paste, the *Clipboard*, and the undo, redo, and repeat features. (p. W1-14).

SLO 1.5 Customize a document using different fonts, font sizes, and attributes (p. W1-17).

SLO 1.6 Enhance a document using text alignment and line and paragraph spacing (p. W1-27).

SLO 1.7 Finalize a document using Word's proofing tools (p. W1-31).

SLO 1.8 Apply custom document properties to a document (p. W1-35).

CASE STUDY

*Throughout this book you have the opportunity to put into practice the application features that you are learning. Each chapter begins with a case study that introduces you to the **Pause & Practice** projects in the chapter. These Pause & Practice projects give you a chance to apply and practice key skills. Each chapter contains three to five Pause & Practice projects.*

Placer Hills Real Estate (PHRE) is a real estate company with regional offices throughout central California. In the Pause & Practice projects in this chapter, you create a business document related to the real estate business. PHRE encourages agents to use standard formats for their business documents. This ensures consistency in document appearance while also allowing agents to personalize their correspondence to customers and colleagues.

Pause & Practice 1-1: Create a business letter in block format with mixed punctuation.

Pause & Practice 1-2: Edit the business letter using copy, paste, and *Format Painter.* Modify the font size, color, style, and effects of selected text.

Pause & Practice 1-3: Finalize the business letter by modifying line spacing and paragraph spacing, changing paragraph alignment, translating text, using proofing tools, and adding document properties.

> **MORE INFO**
>
> *Appendix D* (online resource) contains examples of business documents.

SLO 1.1 # Creating, Saving, and Opening Documents

Microsoft Word allows you to create a variety of document types. Your creativity and knowledge of Word allow you to create, edit, and customize high-quality and professional-looking documents.

You can create Word documents from a new blank document, from existing Word templates, or from existing documents. Word allows you to save documents in a variety of formats.

Create a New Document

All new documents are based on the ***Normal template*** (*Normal.dotx*). When you open Word, a blank document is displayed in the Word window. This document has default fonts, font sizes, line and paragraph spacing, and margins, all of which are controlled by the *Normal* template.

HOW TO: Create a New Document

1. Click the **File** tab to open the *Backstage* view (Figure 1-1).
2. Click the **New** button.
3. Select **Blank document**. A new blank document opens in Word.

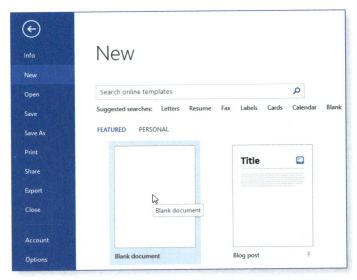

1-1 Open a blank document

> **ANOTHER WAY**
>
> **Ctrl+N** opens a new blank document.

Save a Document

When you create a blank document, Word automatically assigns a generic file name to this document, such as *Document1*. Save all your new documents using the ***Save As dialog box.***

You can save a Word document in a variety of formats. By default, a Word document is saved as a *.docx* file. If you are sharing a document with someone who is using an older version of Word, you might want to save your file as an older version of Word. To change the type of document format, select the format of your choice from the *Save as type* area of the *Save As* dialog box. The following table lists some of the more commonly used available formats.

Save Formats

Type of Document	File Extension	Uses
Word Document	.docx	Standard Word 2013 document
Word Macro-Enabled Document	.docm	Word document with embedded macros
Word 97-2003 Document	.doc	Word document that is compatible with previous versions of Microsoft Word
Word Template	.dotx	Creates a new document based upon a template
Word Macro-Enabled Template	.dotm	Creates a new document based upon a template with embedded macros
Portable Document Format (PDF)	.pdf	PDF files, which are more like pictures of a document, are used to preserve the formatting of a document
Rich Text Format (RTF)	.rtf	RTF files are in a more generic file format and can be read by many different types of word processors while retaining the basic format of the document
Plain Text	.txt	Plain text files contain only text with no special formatting and can be opened with most word processing programs
Open Document Text	.odt	This format is used in the Open Office word processing program

HOW TO: Save a New Document

1. Click the **File** tab to open the *Backstage* view.
2. Click **Save** or **Save As** to display the *Save As* area on the *Backstage* view (Figure 1-2).
3. Select the location where you want to store your document.
   - You can save to your *SkyDrive*, computer, or storage device.

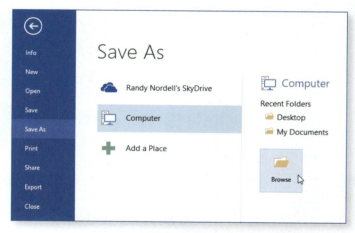

1-2 *Save As* area of the *Backstage* view

4. Select a folder in the *Recent Folders* area or click the **Browse** button to open the *Save As* dialog box (Figure 1-3).

5. Browse to the location on your *SkyDrive*, computer, or USB drive to save the file.

6. Type the file name in the *File name* area.

7. Click the **Save** button.

1-3 *Save As* dialog box

ANOTHER WAY

F12 opens the *Save As* dialog box.

After you have saved a document once, you can save the document again by pressing **Ctrl+S** or clicking the **Save** button on the *Quick Access* toolbar. Word saves changes to an existing document without opening the *Save As* dialog box.

Save As a Different File Name

You can save a document as a different name by opening the *Save As* dialog box and giving the document a different file name. When you save as a different file name, the original document is not changed and is still available. Saving as a different file name creates a new version of the original document, but the new document has a different file name.

HOW TO: Save As a Different File Name

1. Click the **File** tab to open the *Backstage* view.

2. Click the **Save As** button to display the *Save As* area.

3. Select a recent folder or click the **Browse** button. The *Save As* dialog box opens (see Figure 1-3).
   • From within Word (not the Backstage view), you can also press **F12** to open the *Save As* dialog box.

4. Browse to the location on your computer or USB drive to save the file.

5. Type the file name in the *File name* area.

6. Click the **Save** button.

> **MORE INFO**
>
> Avoid saving too many different versions of the same document. Rename only when you have a good reason to have multiple versions of a document.

Share and Export Options

Word 2013 provides you with other sharing and export options. From the **Share** and **Export** area of the *Backstage* view, you have the options of saving a document to the cloud (*SkyDrive*), emailing a document, or saving it as a PDF document. Here are the *Share* and *Export* options, also seen in Figure 1-4.

• Invite People [*Share* area]
• Email [*Share* area]

- Present Online [*Share* area]
- Publish as Blog Post [*Share* area]
- Create PDF/XPS Document [*Export* area]
- Change File Type [*Export* area]

Open a Document

You can open an existing document from your computer, USB drive, SkyDrive drive, or an attachment from an email. One advantage of using Microsoft Word is the program's ability to open different types of file formats and to save documents as different types of files.

1-4 *Share* area of the *Backstage* view

HOW TO: Open a Document

1. Click the **File** tab to open the *Backstage* view.

2. Click the **Open** button to display the *Open* area on the *Backstage* view.

3. In the *Places* area, select the location where the document is stored.

   - You can click **Recent Documents** and select a document at the right to open it.
   - You can also open a document from *SkyDrive* or *Computer*.

4. Select a folder or click **Browse** to open the *Open* dialog box (Figure 1-5).

5. Select the file and click the **Open** button.

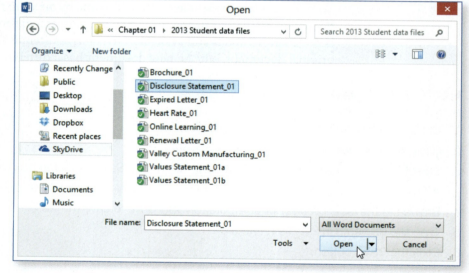

1-5 *Open* dialog box

> **ANOTHER WAY**
> **Ctrl+F12** opens the *Open* dialog box.

SLO 1.2

Entering and Selecting Text

When creating or editing a document, you can type new text, insert text from another document, or copy text from a web page or another document. It is important to understand how to enter text, use word wrap, and select text to create clean and professional-looking documents. Word provides you with options to automatically insert and correct text as well as the ability to control which words are automatically corrected by Word.

Type Text and Word Wrap

Word inserts text at the point in the document where the insertion point is flashing. By default, text is aligned at the left margin and the text wraps to the next line when it reaches the right margin, which is called *word wrap*.

Show/Hide Formatting Symbols

You can turn on or off the display of formatting symbols. When the *Show/Hide* feature is turned on, the formatting symbols are visible in the document. You are able to see paragraph breaks, line breaks, spaces, tabs, and other formatting symbols that help you create clean documents and edit existing documents (Figure 1-6).

Click the **Show/Hide** button in the *Paragraph* group on the *Home* tab to toggle on and off *Show/Hide*. These symbols do not print, but they allow you to see the formatting that is in the document when you view it on your screen.

> **ANOTHER WAY**
> **Ctrl+Shift+8** turns on/off *Show/Hide*.

> **MORE INFO**
> When editing a document that has inconsistent formatting, begin by turning on **Show/Hide**.

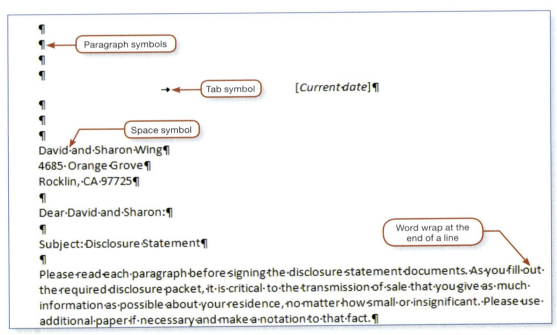

1-6 Document with *Show/Hide* turned on

Select Text

Word allows you select words, lines, sentences, paragraphs, or the entire document. You do this by clicking and dragging the pointer over the desired text, but there are a variety of additional quick methods to select text. The following table lists ways to select text.

> **ANOTHER WAY**
> **F8** is the selection function key.
>
> Press once—use the arrow keys to select text.
> Press twice—select word.
> Press three times—select sentence.
> Press four times—select paragraph.
> Press five times—select entire document.
>
> Press **Esc** to turn off **F8** selection.

Selecting Text

Select	Method
Word	Double-click the word.
Line	Click in the *Selection* area, which is to the left of the left margin. Your pointer becomes a right-pointing arrow.
Multiple lines of text	Click in the *Selection* area and drag up or down.
Sentence	Press **Ctrl+Click**. Hold down the **Ctrl** key and click the sentence.
Paragraph	Double-click in the *Selection* area to the left of the paragraph.
Multiple paragraphs	Click in the *Selection* area to the left of the first line of the paragraph and drag down.
Entire document	Press **Ctrl+A** or **Ctrl+Click** in the *Selection* area. You can also click the **Select** button [*Home* tab, *Editing* group] and choose **Select All**.
Non-adjacent text	Select text, press and hold the **Ctrl** key, and select non-adjacent text.

AutoComplete

When you type a day, month, or date, Word uses the *AutoComplete* feature to automatically complete typing the day, month, or date for you, which saves you a few key strokes and allows you to be more efficient and accurate when entering dates. As you begin to type the date, Word displays the information in an *AutoComplete* tag (Figure 1-7). Press **Enter** to accept the *AutoComplete* entry. If you do not want this *AutoComplete* entry, keep typing and the *AutoComplete* entry disappears.

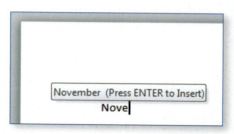

1-7 *AutoComplete*

AutoCorrect and AutoFormat

When you're typing, do you ever misspell a word by transposing letters or omitting a letter or adding a letter? Because we all regularly make typing mistakes, the *AutoCorrect* feature recognizes and corrects commonly misspelled words.

Word automatically makes the following corrections:

- Eliminates two initial capitals in a word
- Capitalizes the first letter of a sentence
- Capitalizes the first letter of table cells
- Capitalizes the names of days
- Resolves accidental usage of the Caps Lock key

Word's *AutoFormat* controls the formatting of items such as numbered and bulleted lists, fractions, ordinal numbers, hyphens and dashes, quotes, indents, and hyperlinks. For example, when you type ¾ followed by a space, *AutoFormat* automatically changes the format of the fraction to ¾.

AutoCorrect Options

When Word automatically makes a correction or formatting change, you have the option to accept the change, undo the change, stop Word from making the change, or open the *AutoCorrect Options* dialog box. If you keep typing, the change is accepted. Often when Word automatically corrects a word, you don't even recognize a change has been made.

AutoCorrect Smart Tag

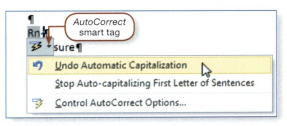

1-8 *AutoCorrect Options*

If you do not want to accept a change, you can click the ***AutoCorrect Options smart tag*** on the changed word to open the *AutoCorrect Options* menu (Figure 1-8). For example, when you type reference initials at the end of a business letter, Word automatically capitalizes the first letter. You can undo this automatic capitalization by clicking on the *AutoCorrect Options* smart tag and selecting **Undo Automatic Capitalization**.

> **ANOTHER WAY**
> **Ctrl+Z** is *undo*. Press **Ctrl+Z** to reverse an automatic correction made by Word.

Add Custom AutoCorrect Entry

The *AutoCorrect* dialog box allows you to customize how Word automatically corrects and formats items in a document. In this dialog box, you can also add custom items to the *Auto-Correct* menu. For example, you can add a custom entry to the *AutoCorrect* menu to type your name every time you type your initials.

HOW TO: Add a Custom AutoCorrect Entry

1. Click the **File** tab to open the *Backstage* view.
2. Choose the **Options** button to open the *Word Options* dialog box.
3. Click the **Proofing** button on the left.
4. Select the **AutoCorrect Options** button. The *AutoCorrect* dialog box opens (Figure 1-9).
5. Type in the text you want to replace in the *Replace* box.
6. Type in the word(s) to replace the original text in the *With* box.
7. Choose **Add** to add this custom *AutoCorrect* entry.
8. Click **OK** to close the *AutoCorrect* dialog box.
9. Click **OK** to close the *Word Options* dialog box.

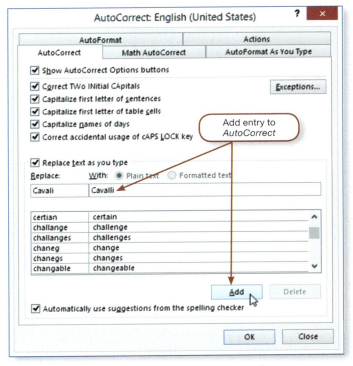

1-9 *AutoCorrect* dialog box

You can delete *AutoCorrect* entries in the *AutoCorrect* dialog box by selecting the entry and pressing **Delete**. You can also add exceptions to *AutoCorrect* by clicking the **Exceptions** button.

Using Paragraph Breaks, Line Breaks, and Non-Breaking Spaces

It is important to create attractive and readable documents. Using paragraph and line breaks allows you to break up a document into more readable chunks of information. The different types of breaks can be used for different purposes when you are formatting documents.

Paragraph Breaks

The **Enter** key inserts a *paragraph break* and is marked by a *paragraph symbol* that displays at the end of each paragraph when *Show/Hide* is turned on (Figure 1-10). Use paragraph breaks to control the amount of white space between paragraphs of text within a document.

Many formatting features, such as indents, numbering, bullets, text alignment, line spacing, and paragraph spacing, are applied to an entire paragraph. For example, if your insertion point is within a paragraph and you change the line spacing to double space,

¶
David·and·Sharon·Wing¶ — Paragraph symbols
4685·Orange·Grove¶
Rocklin,·CA·97725¶
¶
Dear·David·and·Sharon:¶
¶
Subject:·Disclosure·Statement¶
¶
Please·read·each·paragraph·before·

1-10 Paragraph breaks after and between lines

double spacing is applied to that paragraph only. It is not applied to the entire document or just the line where the insertion point is located.

Line Breaks

You can use **line breaks** to control breaks between lines or sentences of text. They function similar to the way a paragraph break functions. The distinction between a paragraph break and a line break is that when line breaks are used, the text separated by line breaks is treated as one paragraph.

You can use line breaks within a numbered or bulleted list to allow for multiple lines of text on separate lines and blank lines between the text without creating a new number or bullet (Figure 1-11). You can also use line breaks to control the amount of space between paragraphs when you are using before and after spacing for paragraphs. For more on before and after paragraph spacing, see *SLO 1.6: Changing Text Alignment, Line Spacing, and Paragraph Spacing*.

Press **Shift+Enter** to insert a line break.

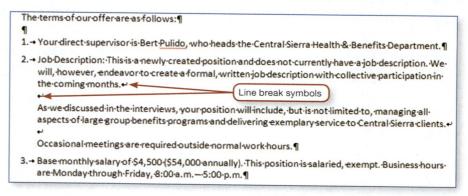

1-11 Line breaks used in a numbered list

Spaces and Non-Breaking Spaces

Spaces are included between words. Use the **spacebar** to insert a space. Add just one space after most punctuation marks, including periods, commas, semicolons, and ending quotation marks. Do not use spaces after a beginning quotation mark, before or after a hyphen in a hyphenated word, or when using a dash.

There might be times when you are typing a document and word wrap breaks up words that you want to keep together. For example, you might want to keep a person's first and last name or a date together on the same line, but you don't want to add a line break or paragraph break at that point in your document. In this case, you can use a ***non-breaking space*** to keep these words together. In Figure 1-12, there is a non-breaking space between 8:00 and a.m., which keeps this information together.

3.→ Base·monthly·salary·of·$4,500·($54,000·annually).·Business·hours·are·Monday·through·Friday,·
8:00°a.m.—5:00·p.m.¶

non-breaking space

1-12 Non-breaking space used to keep text together

Press **Ctrl+Shift+Spacebar** to insert a non-breaking space between words. Don't insert an additional regular space between words when using a non-breaking space.

PAUSE & PRACTICE: WORD 1-1

In this project, you create a block format business letter for Emma Cavalli, a realtor consultant for Placer Hills Real Estate. In a block format business letter, all lines begin at the left margin. This document uses mixed punctuation, which means there is a colon after the salutation and a comma after the complimentary close (e.g., Best regards,). For more examples of business documents, see *Appendix D* (online resource).

File Needed: None
Completed Project File Name: ***[your initials] PP W1-1.docx***

1. Open a new document.
   a. Press **Ctrl+N** or click the **File** tab, click **New**, and click **Blank Document**.
2. Save the document.
   a. Press **F12** to open the *Save As* dialog box (Figure 1-13). You can also use **Save** or **Save As** in the *Backstage* view.
   b. Browse to the location on your computer or storage device to save the document.
   c. Type [your initials] PP W1-1 in the *File name* area.
   d. Click **Save** to close the dialog box and save the document.

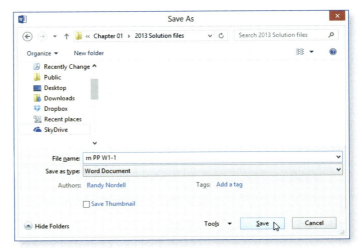

m PP W1-1 docx

1-13 *Save As* dialog box

3. Create an *AutoCorrect* entry.
   a. Click the **File** tab to open the *Backstage* view and select **Options** to open the *Word Options* dialog box.
   b. Click the **Proofing** button on the left and select **AutoCorrect Options** to open the *AutoCorrect* dialog box (Figure 1-14).
   c. Click the **AutoCorrect** tab.
   d. Type Cavali in the *Replace* area and Cavalli in the *With* area.
   e. Click the **Add** button to add the *AutoCorrect* entry.
   f. Click **OK** to close the *AutoCorrect* dialog box.
   g. Click **OK** to close the *Word Options* dialog box.

4. Click the **Show/Hide** button [*Home* tab, *Paragraph* group] to turn on the *Show/Hide* feature.

5. Type the current date on the first line of the document. Type the date in month, day, year format (e.g., September 1, 2015).
   a. If the *AutoComplete* tag appears, press **Enter**, and the month is automatically inserted (Figure 1-15).
   b. Continue typing the rest of the date; press **Enter** if the *AutoCorrect* tag displays the current date.

6. Press **Enter** two times after typing the date.

7. Type the following information as the inside address of the letter (the recipient of the letter).
   a. Press **Shift+Enter** to insert a line break after the first and second lines to keep the lines together.

   David and Sharon Wing
   4685 Orange Grove Road
   Rocklin, CA 97725

   b. Press **Enter** after the last line of the inside address.

8. Type the following salutation and subject line. Press **Enter** after typing each line.

   Dear Mr. and Mrs. Wing:
   Subject: Disclosure Statement

1-14 Add an *AutoCorrect* entry

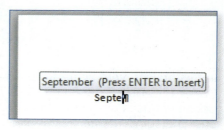

1-15 *AutoComplete* tag

> **MORE INFO**
>
> In a business letter, use "Dear" followed by a courtesy title (such as Mr., Mrs., Ms., Miss, or Dr.) and the person's last name.

9. Type the body paragraphs below.
   a. Use word wrap for line endings. Do not press Enter at the end of each line.
   b. Press **Enter** at the end of each paragraph.

c. Press **Ctrl+Shift+Spacebar** to insert a non-breaking space between the words "Real" and "Estate" in the second paragraph. Use only a single non-breaking space; do not include a regular space.

Please read each paragraph before signing the disclosure statement documents. As you fill out the required disclosure packet, it is critical to the transmission of sale that you give as much information as possible about your residence, no matter how small or insignificant. Please use additional paper if necessary and make a notation to that fact.

If there is information about the neighborhood or neighbors that you as a buyer would want to know about, be sure to reveal that information. Be sure to address those types of questions on the Real Estate Transfer Disclosure Statement, item #11 on page 2.

10. Type Best regards, as the complimentary close and press **Enter** two times after. Be sure to include the comma after the complimentary close.

11. Type the letter writer's name, title, and company name.
    a. Insert a line break (**Shift+Enter**) at the end of the first two lines.

    Emma Cavalli
    Realtor Consultant
    Placer Hills Real Estate

    b. Press **Enter** after the company name.

12. Type your initials in lower case letters and press **Shift+Enter** to insert a line break.
    a. Word automatically capitalizes the first letter because it is the first word in a new paragraph.
    b. Click the **AutoCorrect** smart tag and select **Undo Automatic Capitalization** (Figure 1-16) or press **Ctrl+Z** to undo automatic capitalization.

1-16 *AutoCorrect* smart tag

13. On the next line below the reference initials, type Enclosure. An enclosure notation indicates to the reader that something is enclosed with the letter.

14. Press **Ctrl+S** to save the document (Figure 1-17). You can also save the document by clicking on the **Save** button on the *Quick Access* toolbar or in the *Backstage* view.

15. Click the **File** tab and select **Close** (or press **Ctrl+W**) to close the document.

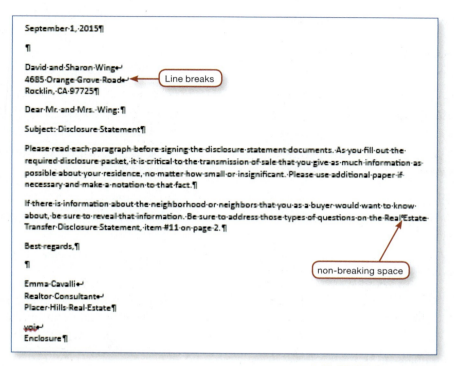

September·1,·2015¶

¶

David·and·Sharon·Wing↵
4685·Orange·Grove·Road↵   Line breaks
Rocklin,·CA·97725¶

Dear·Mr.·and·Mrs.·Wing:¶

Subject:·Disclosure·Statement¶

Please·read·each·paragraph·before·signing·the·disclosure·statement·documents.·As·you·fill·out·the·required·disclosure·packet,·it·is·critical·to·the·transmission·of·sale·that·you·give·as·much·information·as·possible·about·your·residence,·no·matter·how·small·or·insignificant.·Please·use·additional·paper·if·necessary·and·make·a·notation·to·that·fact.¶

If·there·is·information·about·the·neighborhood·or·neighbors·that·you·as·a·buyer·would·want·to·know·about,·be·sure·to·reveal·that·information.·Be·sure·to·address·those·types·of·questions·on·the·Real°Estate·Transfer·Disclosure·Statement,·item·#11·on·page·2.¶   non-breaking space

Best·regards,¶

¶

Emma·Cavalli↵
Realtor·Consultant↵
Placer·Hills·Real·Estate¶

yois↵
Enclosure¶

1-17 PP W1-1 completed

SLO 1.4

Moving and Copying Text

Editing is an important phase in document creation. Editing involves not only proofreading and correcting grammar and spelling mistakes but also arranging text within a document, which can include cutting, copying, and pasting. Word makes it easy to move and copy information within a document or between multiple documents.

> **ANOTHER WAY**
>
> **Ctrl+C** to copy
> **Ctrl+X** to cut
> **Ctrl+V** to paste

Move Text

Moving is actually removing text from one location (cutting) and placing it in another location (pasting). There are two methods you can use to move text: ***drag and drop*** or **cut** and ***paste.***

HOW TO: Move Text Using Drag and Drop

1. Select the text you want to move.
2. Click and hold the selected text with your pointer.
3. Drag the text to the desired new location and release the pointer (Figure 1-18).

Drag pointer

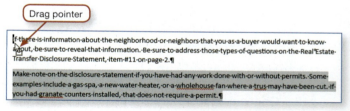

1-18 Move using drag and drop

There are a variety of ways to move text using cut and paste.

- ***Cut and Paste buttons:*** These buttons are in the *Clipboard* group on the *Home* tab.
- ***Shortcut commands:*** Press **Ctrl+X** to cut and **Ctrl+V** to paste.
- ***Context menu:*** Right-click the selected text to display this menu.

HOW TO: Move Text Using Cut and Paste

1. Select the text you want to move.
2. Click the **Cut** button [*Home* tab, *Clipboard* group].
   - You can also press **Ctrl+X** or right-click the selected text and choose **Cut** from the context menu.
3. Place your insertion point in the desired location.
4. Click the **Paste** button [*Home* tab, *Clipboard* group].
   - You can also press **Ctrl+V** or right-click the selected text and click the first **Paste** icon. *Note: See the **Paste Text and Paste Options** section below for the different paste options available.*

Copy Text

An efficient method of inserting text into a document is to copy it from another location, such as a web page or a different document, and paste it into your document. Copying text leaves the text in its original location and places a copy of the text in a new location.

You can **copy** text by using the **drag and drop** method or the **Copy and Paste** buttons. Use the drag and drop method when copying text within the same document. The drag and drop method for copying is similar to the method for moving, except that you hold the **Ctrl** key when dragging the text to be copied to an additional location. A + (plus sign) appears next to your pointer, indicating this text is being copied.

HOW TO: Copy Text Using Drag and Drop

1. Select the text you want to copy.
2. Hold the **Ctrl** key and click and hold the selected text with your pointer.
3. Drag to the desired new location and release the pointer (Figure 1-19).

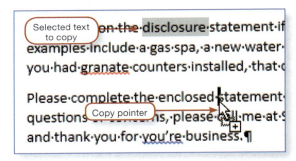

1-19 **Copy using drag and drop**

Copying text using the following copy and paste method is similar to moving text using the cut and paste method.

- **Copy and Paste buttons:** These buttons are in the *Clipboard* group on the *Home* tab.
- **Shortcut commands:** Press **Ctrl+C** to copy and **Ctrl+V** to paste.
- **Context menu:** Right-click the selected text to display this menu.

Paste Text and Paste Options

You might want to paste text into a document and only want the plain text, or you might want to merge the format from the source document into the new document. Word provides multiple paste options.

You have three primary paste options when you use the *Paste* button in the *Clipboard* group (Figure 1-20) or from the context menu.

1-20 *Paste* options

- ***Keep Source Formatting***—*retains formatting from source document (the document where the text was copied)*
- ***Merge Formatting***—*merges formatting from source document and current document*
- ***Keep Text Only***—*pastes only unformatted text*

The default paste option is *Keep Source Formatting*. In addition to these paste options, there are other context-specific paste options that are available when you paste information from lists or paste text with a style applied.

> **MORE INFO**
>
> If you're having trouble with the format of pasted text, try pasting the text as plain text and formatting the text *after* you have pasted it into the document.

The Clipboard

When you copy or cut an item from a document, Word stores this information in the ***Clipboard.*** From the *Clipboard*, you can select a previously copied item and paste it into a document. When Word is open, the *Clipboard* stores multiple items copied from Word documents and also items from web pages or other documents. The *Clipboard* stores text, pictures, tables, lists, and graphics.

Open the Clipboard Task Pane

The ***Clipboard task pane*** displays all of the items stored in *Clipboard*. To display the *Clipboard* task pane, click the **launcher** in the bottom right corner of the *Clipboard* group on the *Home* tab (Figure 1-21). The *Clipboard* task pane is displayed on the left side of the Word window.

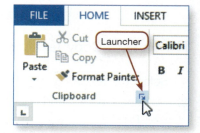

1-21 *Clipboard* launcher

> **MORE INFO**
>
> The ***launcher*** (also referred to as the ***dialog box launcher***) is referred to throughout this text. Click the **launcher** in the bottom right corner of a group to open a dialog box or pane to give you additional options.

Paste from the Clipboard

To paste an item from the *Clipboard* into a document at the insertion point in the document, select the item or click the drop-down arrow to the right of the item and choose **Paste** (Figure 1-22).

Other Clipboard Options

Paste All pastes all of the items in the *Clipboard* at the insertion point in the document. Selecting **Clear All** empties the content of the *Clipboard*. When you exit Word, the contents of the *Clipboard* are removed.

1-22 *Clipboard* task pane

At the bottom of the *Clipboard* task pane, there are a variety of display options. Choose from these by clicking on the **Options** button (Figure 1-23). Click the **X** in the upper right corner of the pane to close it.

1-23 *Clipboard* options

Undo, Redo, and Repeat Changes

You can undo, redo, or repeat previous actions. All of these buttons are available on the *Quick Access toolbar*.

Undo

When you click the **Undo** button, the last action you performed is undone. You can undo multiple actions by clicking on the **Undo** drop-down arrow to the right of the button and selecting the items to undo (Figure 1-24).

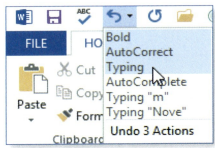

1-24 *Undo* button on the *Quick Access* toolbar

Redo and Repeat

The **Redo** and **Repeat** features are similar to the undo feature. The same button is used for both of these features, and it is context sensitive. Depending on the previous action performed, the button is either *Redo* or *Repeat*.

When you use the *Undo* button, the *Redo* button is activated so you can redo the previous change (Figure 1-25).

When you perform an action or apply formatting in a document, the *Repeat* button is activated so you can repeat the previous action or formatting (Figure 1-26). For example, if you need to copy the date or a name into a document in multiple places, you can use the *Repeat* feature to accomplish this task quickly and accurately.

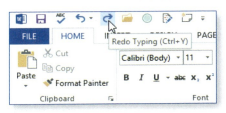

1-25 *Redo* button on the *Quick Access* toolbar

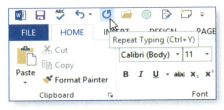

1-26 *Repeat* button on the *Quick Access* toolbar

> ## ANOTHER WAY
> **Ctrl+Z** is undo.
> **Ctrl+Y** is redo and repeat.

SLO 1.5

Changing Fonts, Font Sizes, and Attributes

Word has many features that you can use to customize the appearance of the text within a document. You can change the font and size of font; add styles such as bold, italics, and underlining; change the case of the text; add font and text effects; adjust the scale, spacing, and position of text; and change the default font settings. You can use buttons in the *Font* group on the *Home* tab, the *Font* dialog box, and the mini toolbar to apply formatting to text.

Font and Font Size

There are two main categories of fonts: serif and sans serif. **Serif fonts** have structural details (flair) at the top and bottom of most of the letters. Some commonly used serif fonts are Cambria, Times New Roman, and Courier New. **Sans serif fonts** have no structural details on the letters. Commonly used sans serif fonts are Calibri, Arial, and Century Gothic.

Font size is measured in **points** (pt.); the larger the point, the larger the font. Most documents use between 10 and 12 pt. font sizes. Titles and headings generally are larger font sizes.

MORE INFO

The default font and font size in Microsoft Word are *Calibri* and *11 pt.*, respectively.

Font size of 72 pt. is approximately 1" in height.

1-27 *Font drop-down list*

HOW TO: Change Font and Font Size

1. Select the text you want to change.
2. Click the **Font** drop-down list to display the list of available fonts (Figure 1-27).
   - The *Font* drop-down list has three sections: *Theme Fonts, Recently Used Fonts,* and *All Fonts.*
3. Select the font you want to apply to the selected text.
4. Click the **Font Size** drop-down list to display the list of available font sizes (Figure 1-28).
5. Select a font size to apply to selected text.
   - You can also click in the **Font Size** area and type a size.
   - Use the **Increase Font Size** and **Decrease Font Size** buttons to increase or decrease the size of the font in small increments.

ANOTHER WAY

Ctrl+> (**Ctrl+Shift+.**) is *Increase Font Size.*
Ctrl+< (**Ctrl+Shift+,**) is *Decrease Font Size.*

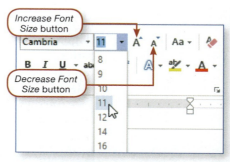

1-28 *Font Size drop-down list*

When creating a new document, you can choose a font and it applies to the entire document. If you want to change the font of an existing document, you must first select the text before applying the change.

Font Styles

You can add styles such as **Bold, Italic,** and **Underline** to fonts to improve their appearance or call attention to specific text. The font style buttons for *Bold, Italic,* and *Underline* are available in the *Font* group on the *Home* tab.

Bold, Italic, and Underline

To apply a font style, select the desired text and click the **Bold**, **Italic**, or **Underline** button in the *Font* group on the *Home* tab (Figure 1-29). You can also click one or more of the font style buttons to turn on a style. Type the text and click the font style button(s) again to turn off the style.

The *mini toolbar* displays when you select or right-click text (Figure 1-30). You can use the mini toolbar to apply text formatting. Like the content menu, the mini toolbar is context-sensitive and displays different options depending on the selection you right-click.

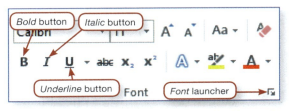

1-29 *Font* group on the *Home* tab

> ▶ **ANOTHER WAY**
>
> **Ctrl+B** is *Bold.*
> **Ctrl+I** is *Italic.*
> **Ctrl+U** is *Underline.*

1-30 Select or right-click text to display the mini toolbar

Other Font Style Buttons

There are other styles and effects in the *Font* group on the *Home* tab and on the mini toolbar.

- *Strikethrough*
- *Subscript*
- *Superscript*
- *Text Effects and Typography*, which includes *Outline, Shadow, Reflection, Glow, Number Styles, Ligatures, and Style Sets*
- *Text Highlight Color*
- *Font Color*

Change Case

The **Change Case** feature is a quick and easy way to change the case of a single word or group of words. The *Change Case* button is in the *Font* group on the *Home* tab (Figure 1-31).

Your different case options are:

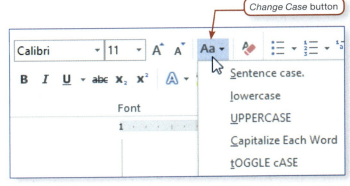

1-31 *Change Case* options

- *Sentence* case (capitalizes the first letter of the sentence)
- *lowercase*
- *UPPERCASE*
- *Capitalize Each Word*
- *tOGGLE cASE* (changes letters that are uppercase to lowercase and lowercase letters to uppercase)

Font Dialog Box

The **Font dialog box** combines many of the font style and **effect options** in one location for easy access. You can open the *Font* dialog by clicking the **Font** launcher in the bottom right corner of the *Font* group (Figure 1-32).

In addition to the *Font, Font Style,* and *Size* areas on the *Font* tab in this dialog box, there are also areas to change *Font Color, Underline Style, Underline Color,* and *Effects.* The *Preview* area gives you a preview of applied changes, styles, and effects.

The *Advanced* tab lists *Character Spacing* options such as *Scale, Spacing, Position,* and *Kerning.* From this tab, you can also open the *Format Text Effects* dialog box.

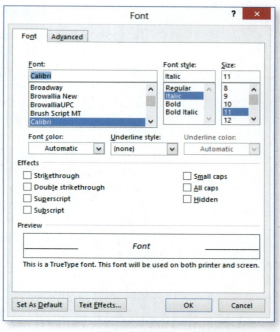

1-32 *Font* dialog box

> ▶ **ANOTHER WAY**
>
> **Ctrl+D** opens the *Font* dialog box.

Font Color

By default, the font color in a Word document is black. You can change the font color of selected text to add emphasis. The **Font Color** drop-down list in the *Font* dialog box displays a list of available font colors.

HOW TO: Change Font Color

1. Select the text you want to be a different color.
2. Click the **Font** launcher [*Home* tab, *Font* group]. The *Font* dialog box opens (Figure 1-33).
3. Click the **Font Color** drop-down arrow to display the list of font colors.
   - The drop-down list of font color options includes *Theme Colors, Standard Colors,* and *More Colors.* Theme colors are those colors associated with the theme of the document. For more on themes, see *Section 2.7: Using Styles and Themes.*
4. Choose **OK** to close the *Font* dialog box.

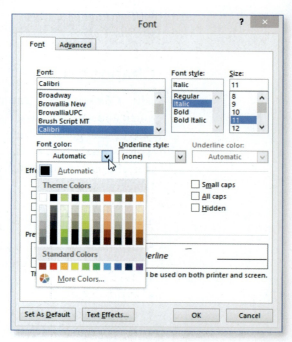

1-33 **Change font color in the *Font* dialog box**

> **ANOTHER WAY**
>
> Change the font color by clicking on the **Font Color** button [*Home* tab, *Font* group].

Underline Style and Color

When you underline selected text, the default underline style is a solid black underline. Word provides a variety of additional underline styles. You can also change the color of the underline.

The ***Underline Style*** and ***Underline Color*** drop-down lists are available in the *Font* dialog box (Figure 1-34). A preview of how the formatted text will appear in your document is displayed in the *Preview* area of the *Font* dialog box.

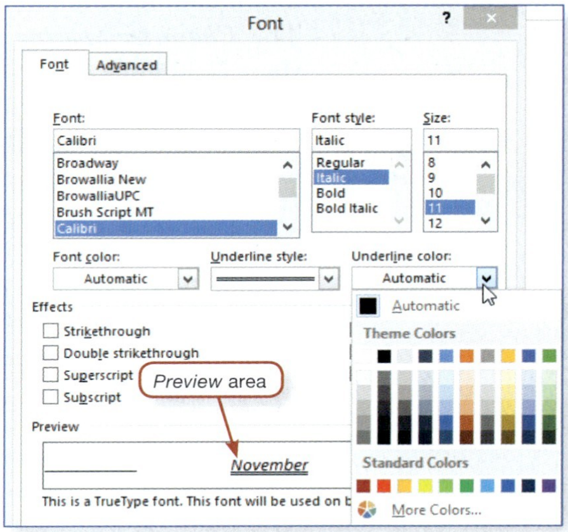

1-34 Change *Underline* style and color

Font Effects

In the *Font* dialog box you can choose a variety of font effects from the ***Effects*** section. Some of these font effects are available in the *Font* group on the *Home* tab. The following table lists the different font styles and effects.

Font Styles and Effects

Style/Effect	Example
Bold	This **word** is in bold.
Italic	This *word* is in italic.
Bold and Italic	This ***word*** is in bold and italic.
Underline	This sentence is underlined.
Double Underline	This word is double underlined.
Underline Words Only	This sentence is words only underlined.
Thick Underline with Color	This word has a thick, colored underline.
Strikethrough	This ~~word~~ has a strikethrough.
Double Strikethrough	~~This sentence has a double strikethrough.~~
Subscript	H_2O uses a subscript number.
Superscript	Footnotes and endnotes use superscript numbers or letters.[1]
Small Caps	MICROSOFT WORD 2013 is in small caps.
All Caps	THIS SENTENCE IS IN ALL CAPS.
Hidden	
Text Highlight Color	This word has a highlight color.
Font Color	This sentence has a font color applied.

Character Spacing

The ***Character Spacing*** options allow you to add more or less space between letters and words. You can also raise and lower letters and words (Figure 1-35).

The ***Scale*** option allows you to change the spacing of a word or group of words by a percentage. You can choose from preset percentages, or you can type in a custom percentage for scaling.

Spacing has three options: *Normal*, *Expanded*, and *Condensed*. For *Expanded* and *Condensed*, you can choose the amount of points by which to expand the selected text.

The ***Position*** option raises or lowers text by a selected number of points.

Kerning adjusts the space between letters in a proportional font.

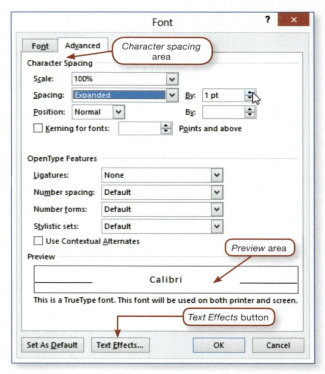

1-35 *Font* dialog box *Advanced* tab

Text Effects

With ***Text Effects,*** you can add special formatting features to selected text, such as *Outline*, *Shadow*, *Reflection*, and *Glow* (Figure 1-36).

The *Text Effects* button is located in the *Font* group on the *Home* tab. There are many preset options for each of the different text effects, and there are more custom text effect options available in the *Format Text Effects* dialog box.

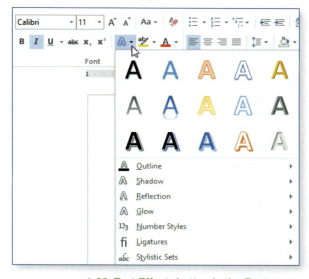

1-36 *Text Effects* button in the *Font* group

HOW TO: Use the Format Text Effects Dialog Box

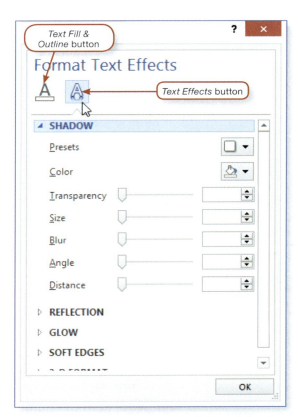

1. Select the text you want to format.

2. Click the **Font** launcher [*Home* tab, *Font* group]. The *Font* dialog box opens.

3. Click the **Text Effects** button at the bottom. The *Format Text Effects* dialog box opens (Figure 1-37).

4. Click the **Text Fill & Outline** button to display fill and outline options.
   - Select **Text Fill** or **Text Outline** to expand and display options.

5. Click the **Text Effects** button to display text effect options.
   - Select **Shadow**, **Reflection**, **Glow**, **Soft Edges**, or **3-D Format** to expand and display options.
   - Each of these categories has *Presets* you can choose or you can customize the effect.

6. Select the text effect of your choice on the left.

7. To the right of each option you can choose a preset option from the drop-down list or customize the text effect as desired.

8. Click **OK** to close the *Format Text Effects* dialog box and click **OK** to close the *Font* dialog box.

1-37 *Format Text Effects* dialog box

Format Painter

The **Format Painter** copies font, font size, line spacing, indents, bullets, numbering, styles, and many other features in Word and applies the formatting to a word, phrase, or entire paragraph. This feature saves time in applying formats and keeps your document consistent in format.

HOW TO: Use the Format Painter

1. Select the text that has the formatting you want to copy.

2. Click the **Format Painter** button [*Home* tab, *Clipboard* group (Figure 1-38). The *Format Painter* icon appears as your pointer (Figure 1-39).

3. Click the word or select the paragraph you want to format and Word applies the formatting to the selected text.
   - Double-click the **Format Painter** button to apply formatting to multiple non-adjacent selections.
   - Click the **Format Painter** button again to turn off the *Format Painter*.

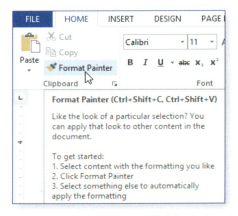

1-38 *Format Painter* button

1-39 *Format Painter* icon

Clear Formatting

If you have applied multiple formatting features to text and you decide to remove the formatting, you don't have to individually deselect all of the formatting options previously selected. The ***Clear Formatting*** feature allows you to remove all formatting for the selected text and change it back to plain text (Figure 1-40).

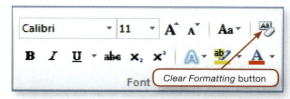

1-40 *Clear Formatting* button in the *Font* group

> **MORE INFO**
>
> Be careful when using the *Clear Formatting* feature. It not only clears all text formatting but also clears line and paragraph spacing, numbering, bullets, and style formatting.

Change Default Font and Font Size

Recall that the default font in Microsoft Word is *Calibri,* and the default font size is *11 pt.* This ***default*** setting is used on each new blank document you create. Each new document is based on the *Normal.dotx* template. This template stores the default settings for documents and controls document elements such as font, font size, line spacing, paragraph spacing, alignment, and styles.

You can change the default settings on the current document only or change the default settings in the *Normal* template. If you change the default settings for the *Normal* template, each new blank document you create uses this new default font and font size.

HOW TO: Change the Default Font and Font Size

1. Select the text you want to format.
2. Click the **Font** launcher [*Home* tab, *Font* group]. The *Font* dialog box opens (Figure 1-41).
3. Click the **Font** tab if it is not already selected.
4. Select the font and font size to set as the default.
5. Click the **Set As Default** button at the bottom left. A confirmation dialog box opens giving you two options: *This document only?* or *All documents based on the Normal template?* (Figure 1-42).
6. Select an option.
7. Click **OK** to close the dialog box.

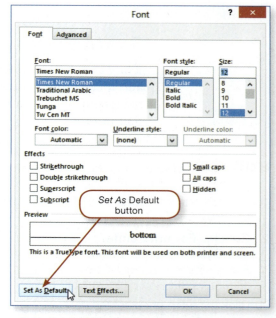

1-41 *Set As Default* button in the *Font* dialog box

> **MORE INFO**
>
> Be careful about changing the default settings in the *Normal* template. Do this only when you are sure you want to make this global default settings change.

Microsoft Word

Do you want to set the default font to Times New Roman, 12 pt for:

○ This document only?

○ All documents based on the Normal template?

OK   Cancel

1-42 **Change default setting confirmation options**

In this Pause & Practice project, you customize the content of your block format letter using cut, copy, paste, and the *Clipboard.* You also enhance your document by changing the font and applying font attributes.

Files Needed: *[your initials] PP W1-1.docx*, *DisclosureStatement-01.docx*
Completed Project File Name: *[your initials] PP W1-2.docx*

1. Open the *[your initials] PP W1-1* document.

2. Save this document as *[your initials] PP W1-2*.
   a. Press **F12** to open the *Save As* dialog box.
   b. Change the file name to [your initials] PP W1-2.
   c. Click **Save** to rename the document and close the *Save As* dialog box.

3. Open the *DisclosureStatement-01* document. Ignore any spelling and grammar errors in this document; you will fix these in Pause & Practice 1-3.

4. In the *DisclosureStatement-01* document, copy both paragraphs of text to the *Clipboard.*
   a. Press **Ctrl+A** to select the text.
   b. Press **Ctrl+C** or click the **Copy** button [*Home* tab, *Clipboard* group].
   c. Close the document without saving.

5. Paste the contents of the *Clipboard* into the document.
   a. In the *[your initials] PP W1-2* document, place your insertion point to the left of "Best regards,".
   b. Click the **Clipboard** launcher [*Home* tab, *Clipboard* group] to display the *Clipboard* pane.
   c. Click the **drop-down arrow** to the right of the copied text in the *Clipboard* (Figure 1-43).
   d. Select **Paste**. The paragraphs of text are pasted in the document at the insertion point.
   e. Close the *Clipboard* by clicking on the **X** in the upper right corner.

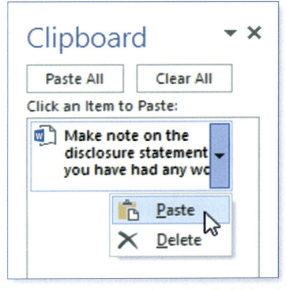

1-43 Paste text from the *Clipboard*

6. Copy the formatting of the first paragraph to the two new paragraphs.
   a. Place your insertion point in the first body paragraph of the letter.
   b. Click the **Format Painter** button [*Home* tab, *Clipboard* group].
   c. Select the last two paragraphs in the body of the letter. Be sure to include the paragraph mark at the end of the last body paragraph (Figure 1-44).

> Make note on the disclosure statement if you have had any work done with or without permits. Some examples include a gas spa, a new water heater, or a wholehouse fan where a trus may have been cut. If you had granate counters installed, that does not require a permit.¶
> Please complete the enclosed statement by [date] and return it to me. As always, if you have any questions or concerns, please call me at 916-450-3334 or email me at ecavalli@phre.com. Best wishes and thank you for you're business.¶ 🖌
> Best regards,¶

1-44 Apply the *Format Painter* to selected text

7. Copy text using the drag and drop method.
   a. Select the word "**disclosure**" in the first sentence of the third body paragraph.
   b. Hold down the **Ctrl** key and drag and drop the text between the words "enclosed" and "statement" (Figure 1-45).

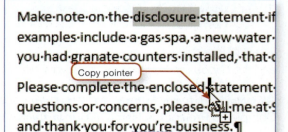

1-45 Copy text using drag and drop

8. Move the third body paragraph ("Make note . . .") so it becomes the second body paragraph.
   a. Select the third paragraph in the body of the letter, including the paragraph mark at the end of the paragraph.
   b. Click the **Cut** button [*Home* tab, *Clipboard* group] or press **Ctrl+X**. The selected paragraph is cut from the document and stored in the *Clipboard.*
   c. Place your insertion point at the beginning of the second body paragraph.
   d. Click the **Paste** button [*Home* tab, *Clipboard* group] or press **Ctrl+V**.

9. Insert and format a date.
   a. Replace the placeholder "[date]" in the last paragraph with the date one week from today.
   b. Use month, day, year format (e.g., September 8, 2015).
   c. Select the date.
   d. On the **Text Highlight Color** drop-down list button [*Home* tab, *Font* group], choose **yellow** text highlight color (Figure 1-46).

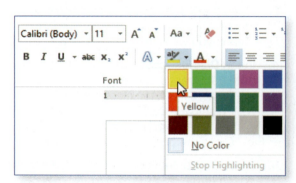

1-46 Apply text highlight color

10. Change the font and font size of the entire document.
    a. Press **Ctrl+A** to select all of the text in the document.
    b. Click the **Font** drop-down list button [*Home* tab, *Font* group] and select **Cambria**.
    c. Click the **Font Size** drop-down list button [*Home* tab, *Font* group] and select **12**.

11. Change the case and spacing of selected text.
    a. Select the word "**Subject**" in the subject line of the document.
    b. Click the **Change Case** button [*Home* tab, *Font* group] and select **UPPERCASE**.
    c. Select the entire subject line.
    d. Click the **Font** launcher [*Home* tab, *Font* group] to open the *Font* dialog box. **Ctrl+D** also opens the *Font* dialog box (Figure 1-47).
    e. Click the **Advanced** tab.
    f. In the *Character Spacing* area, click the **Spacing** drop-down list and select **Expanded**.
    g. In the *By* area to the right of *Spacing*, click the up arrow to change the character spacing to be expanded by **1.5 pt**.
    h. Click **OK** to close the *Font* dialog box.

1-47 Change character spacing

12. Apply font styles to selected text.
    a. Select the email address "**ecavalli@phre.com**" in the last body paragraph.
    b. Click the **Font Color** drop-down list button [*Home* tab, *Font* group] and select **Dark Blue** in the *Standard Colors* area.
    c. Click the **Underline** button or press **Ctrl+U** to apply an underline to the selected email address.
    d. Select the writer's name "**Emma Cavalli**" (below "Best regards,") and open the *Font* dialog box.
    e. In the *Effects* area on the *Font* tab, check the **Small caps** box.
    f. Click **OK** to close the *Font* dialog box.
    g. Select the writer's title "**Realtor Consultant**" and click the **Italic** button or press **Ctrl+I**.
    h. Select the company name "**Placer Hills Real Estate**" and click the **Bold** button or press **Ctrl+B**.

13. Save and close the document (Figure 1-48).

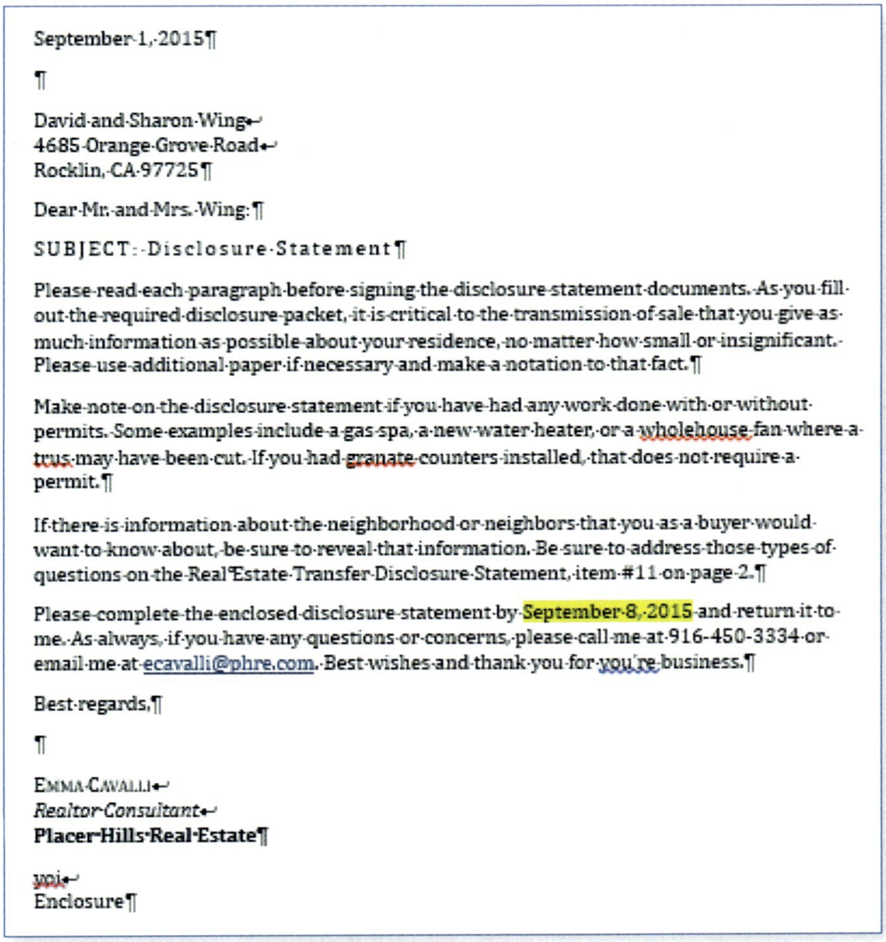

September·1,·2015¶

¶

David·and·Sharon·Wing↵
4685·Orange·Grove·Road↵
Rocklin,·CA·97725¶

Dear·Mr.·and·Mrs.·Wing:¶

S U B J E C T :··Disclosure·Statement¶

Please·read·each·paragraph·before·signing·the·disclosure·statement·documents.·As·you·fill·out·the·required·disclosure·packet,·it·is·critical·to·the·transmission·of·sale·that·you·give·as·much·information·as·possible·about·your·residence,·no·matter·how·small·or·insignificant.·Please·use·additional·paper·if·necessary·and·make·a·notation·to·that·fact.¶

Make·note·on·the·disclosure·statement·if·you·have·had·any·work·done·with·or·without·permits.·Some·examples·include·a·gas·spa,·a·new·water·heater,·or·a·wholehouse·fan·where·a·trus·may·have·been·cut.·If·you·had·granate·counters·installed,·that·does·not·require·a·permit.¶

If·there·is·information·about·the·neighborhood·or·neighbors·that·you·as·a·buyer·would·want·to·know·about,·be·sure·to·reveal·that·information.·Be·sure·to·address·those·types·of·questions·on·the·Real·Estate·Transfer·Disclosure·Statement,·item·#11·on·page·2.¶

Please·complete·the·enclosed·disclosure·statement·by·September·8,·2015·and·return·it·to·me.·As·always,·if·you·have·any·questions·or·concerns,·please·call·me·at·916-450-3334·or·email·me·at·ecavalli@phre.com.·Best·wishes·and·thank·you·for·you're·business.¶

Best·regards,¶

¶

EMMA·CAVALLI↵
Realtor·Consultant↵
Placer·Hills·Real·Estate¶

you↵
Enclosure¶

1-48 PP W1-2 completed

Changing Text Alignment, Line Spacing, and Paragraph Spacing

In addition to word wrap, line breaks, and paragraphs breaks, you can use text alignment, line spacing, and paragraph spacing to control the layout and the white space between parts of your document.

Understand Default Settings

Just as there are default settings for font and font size, there are default settings for paragraph alignment, line spacing, and paragraph spacing. These default settings are stored in the *Normal* template on which all new blank documents are based. The following table summarizes these default settings:

Normal Template Default Settings

Setting	Default Setting
Font	Calibri
Font Size	11 pt.
Horizontal Paragraph Alignment	Left
Line Spacing	1.08 lines
Paragraph Spacing—Before	0 pt.
Paragraph Spacing—After	8 pt.

Paragraph Alignment

Paragraph alignment controls how a paragraph is aligned horizontally on the page. A paragraph can be a single word, a group of words, a sentence, or multiple sentences. Paragraphs are separated by paragraph breaks. A group of words using word wrap and line breaks is considered one paragraph.

The four different paragraph alignment options are:

- *Left* (default): The paragraph is aligned at the left margin.
- *Center:* The paragraph is centered between the left and right margins.
- *Right:* The paragraph begins and is aligned at the right margin.
- *Justify:* The paragraph is aligned flush with both the left and right margins.

Change the alignment of a paragraph by clicking a paragraph alignment button in the *Paragraph* group on the *Home* tab (Figure 1-49). When changing the alignment of a paragraph, the entire paragraph need not be selected; the insertion point only needs to be within the paragraph for the alignment to be applied. Text alignment can also be changed in the *Paragraph* dialog box, which we discuss later.

1-49 Paragraph alignment options in the *Paragraph* group

Line Spacing

Line spacing refers to the amount of blank space between lines of text within a paragraph. The default setting in Word is 1.08 lines, which is slightly more than single spaced. Most documents you type are single spaced or 1.08 line spacing, but there are times you may want to use double spacing (2 lines), such as when typing an academic report.

As with paragraph alignment, you can apply line spacing to an individual paragraph, multiple paragraphs, or an entire document.

You can change the line spacing using the **Line and Paragraph Spacing** button in the *Paragraph* group on the *Home* tab (Figure 1-50). You can choose from the preset line spacing options, or you can select **Line Spacing Options** and set custom line spacing in the *Paragraph* dialog box.

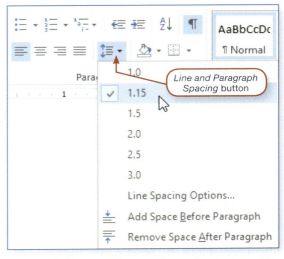

1-50 *Line and Paragraph Spacing* button in the *Paragraph* group

> ▶ **ANOTHER WAY**
>
> **Ctrl+1** is single space (1 line).
> **Ctrl+5** is 1.5 line spacing.
> **Ctrl+2** is double space (2 lines).

When you select **Line Spacing Options**, the *Paragraph* dialog box opens. In the box, you see different line spacing options (Figure 1-51).

The *At Least* and *Exactly* options allow you to specify points of spacing, rather than lines of spacing, between lines of text. The *Multiple* option allows you to set a line spacing option that is not a whole number, such as 1.3 or 2.25 line spacing.

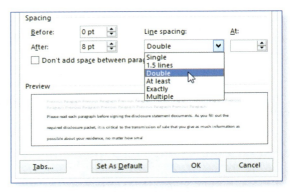

1-51 Line spacing options in the *Paragraph* dialog box

> ▶ **MORE INFO**
>
> If a document has inconsistent line spacing, it looks messy and unprofessional. Select the entire document and set the line spacing to enhance consistency. Consistent line spacing also improves readability.

Paragraph Spacing

While line spacing controls the amount of space between lines of text in a paragraph, *paragraph spacing* controls the amount of spacing before and after paragraphs (before and after a paragraph break). For example, you might want the text of a document to be single spaced, but you prefer to have more blank space between paragraphs. You can use paragraph spacing to accomplish this task. You can also do this by inserting multiple paragraph breaks—pressing *Enter* more than once.

Before and *After* paragraph spacing is set in points. The default after paragraph spacing in Word is 8 pt., which is a little less than one blank line.

Change before and after paragraph spacing from the *Paragraph* group on the *Page Layout* tab (Figure 1-52). You can also change before and after paragraph spacing in the *Paragraph* dialog box and from the *Line and Paragraph Spacing* button in the *Paragraph* group on the *Home* tab.

From the *Line and Paragraph Spacing* button in the *Paragraph* group on the *Home* tab, you can **Add/Remove Space Before Paragraph** or **Add/Remove Space After Paragraph** (Figure 1-53). These options are context sensitive, depending on whether there is already *Before* or *After* paragraph spacing.

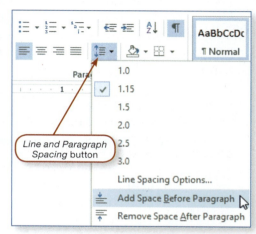

1-52 *Paragraph* group on the *Page Layout* tab

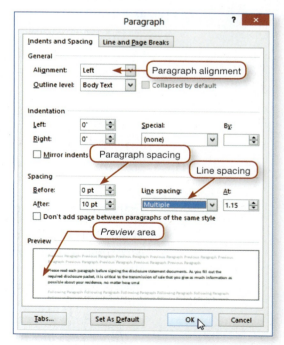

1-53 Add/Remove paragraph spacing options

> ### MORE INFO
>
> Use line breaks to keep lines of text together. *Before* and *After* paragraph spacing is not applied to lines of text where line breaks are used.

Paragraph Dialog Box

The ***Paragraph dialog box*** combines many of the alignment and spacing options included in the *Paragraph* groups on the *Home* and *Page Layout* tabs.

HOW TO: Change Alignment and Spacing in the Paragraph Dialog Box

1. Select the text you want to format.
2. Click the **Paragraph** launcher [*Home* or *Page Layout* tab, *Paragraph* group] to open the *Paragraph* dialog box (Figure 1-54).
3. Click the **Alignment** drop-down list in the *General* area and select **Left**, **Centered**, **Right**, or **Justified**.
4. The *Indentation* section of this dialog box lets you control indents. (For more on indents, see Chapter 2.)
5. In the *Spacing* section, you can change paragraph spacing and line spacing.
   - Type the number of points for spacing or use the up and down arrows.
   - The *Don't add space between paragraphs of the same style* check box controls paragraph spacing between paragraphs of the same style, which is primarily used with numbered and bulleted lists and outlines.
6. Click the **Line spacing** drop-down list to select line spacing.
   - You can select **Multiple** and type in a specific line spacing in the *At* area.
7. The *Preview* area displays how your document will look with changes.
8. Click **OK** to close the *Paragraph* dialog box.

1-54 *Paragraph* dialog box

Change Default Line and Paragraph Spacing

You can set default paragraph alignment and spacing settings in the *Paragraph* dialog box. This process is similar to changing the font and font size default settings.

HOW TO: Change the Default Paragraph Alignment and Spacing

1. Click the **Paragraph** launcher [*Home* or *Page Layout* tab, *Paragraph* group] to open the *Paragraph* dialog box.
2. Click the **Indents and Spacing** tab if it is not already selected.
3. Make the desired changes to paragraph and line spacing.
4. Click the **Set As Default** button on the bottom left. Select one of the two options in the confirmation dialog box that opens: *This document only* or *All documents based on the Normal template* (Figure 1-55).
5. Click **OK**.

Microsoft Word

Do you want to set the default alignment, indentation, and spacing of the paragraphs for:
- ⦿ This document only?
- ◯ All documents based on the Normal template?

OK   Cancel

1-55 Change default setting confirmation options

SLO 1.7 # Checking Spelling and Grammar and Using the Thesaurus

The words and grammar you use in a document reflect your professionalism and the reputation of your organization. Word provides you with many proofing and editing tools to improve the quality of the documents you produce. The spelling, grammar, thesaurus, and research features help you to produce high-quality and professional-looking documents.

Automatic Spelling and Grammar Notifications

Recall that Word uses *AutoCorrect* to automatically correct many commonly misspelled words. But there are many ***spelling errors*** that Word does not automatically correct. When you are typing a document, Word is constantly checking the words you type against the words in its dictionary. When Word doesn't recognize a word, it marks it with a ***red wavy underline.***

Word also checks the grammar of what you are typing and marks potential word choice or ***grammatical errors*** with a ***blue wavy underline.***

> **MORE INFO**
>
> Just because Word marks a word as a possible spelling or grammatical error, it does not necessarily mean that the word is misspelled. Many proper nouns are not included in the dictionary.

HOW TO: Correct Spelling and Grammatical Errors

1. Right-click a word that has a red or blue wavy underline. A context menu opens (Figure 1-56).
2. This menu provides different editing options.
   - Select the correct word from the list to replace the misspelled word.

HOW TO: Find Synonyms Using the Context Menu

1. **Select** the word you want to replace with an appropriate synonym.
2. Right-click the selected word to display the context menu (Figure 1-60).
3. Put your pointer on **Synonyms**. Another context menu appears with a list of synonym choices.
4. Select the synonym you prefer. The selected synonym replaces the selected word in the text and the menus close.

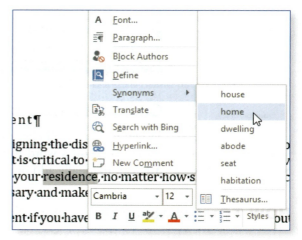

1-60 Use *Thesaurus* to find synonyms

You can also use the *Thesaurus* feature in the *Thesaurus* pane. This method allows you to search for synonyms of any word, not just a selected word in your document.

HOW TO: Use the Thesaurus

1. Click the **Thesaurus** button [*Review* tab, *Proofing* group]. The *Thesaurus* pane opens on the right side of the Word window (Figure 1-61).
2. Type a word in the *Search* text box and press **Enter** or click the **Search** button (magnifying glass icon). A list of synonyms appears in the *Thesaurus* area.
3. Choose from the synonyms listed.
   - Click the **arrow** to the right of the word to display the drop-down list. You have options to *Insert* or *Copy* the synonym.
   - You can also click a synonym in the list to look up synonyms for that word. Click the **Back** button to return to the previous synonym list.
4. Click the **X** in the upper right corner of the *Thesaurus* pane to close this pane.

1-61 *Thesaurus* pane

> **ANOTHER WAY**
> **Shift+F7** opens the *Thesaurus* pane.

Word Count

Word also provides you with a *word count* option. Click the **Word Count** button in the *Proofing* group on the *Review* tab (Figure 1-62) to get the following information: number of pages, words, characters (no spaces), characters (with spaces), paragraphs, and lines (Figure 1-63). You can also choose to have Word count words in text boxes, footnotes, and endnotes, which are not by default included in the word count.

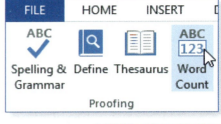

1-62 *Word Count* button

> **ANOTHER WAY**
>
> Click **WORDS** at the bottom left of the *Status* bar to open the *Word Count* dialog box.

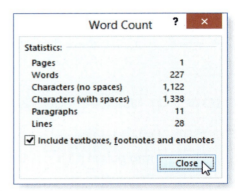

1-63 *Word Count* dialog box

SLO 1.8

Customizing Document Properties

Word allows you to include details about a document, which are called *document properties.* These details are not visible in the text of the document but are included as hidden information within the document. These include fields such as *Title, Author, Comments, Subject, Company, Created,* and *Last Modified.* Some of the document properties are automatically generated, such as *Words, Total Editing Time,* and *Last Modified,* whereas other document property details can be edited individually.

Document Properties

The document properties can be viewed and edited in the *Info* area on the *Backstage* view. Document properties are saved within the document and can be viewed by others who view or use the document.

HOW TO: Add Document Properties

1. Click the **File** tab to display the *Backstage* view.
2. Click the **Info** button if it is not already selected.
3. The document properties are displayed on the right side of the window (Figure 1-64).
4. Document property field names are listed on the left, and the information in these fields is listed on the right.
5. Click in a field and type information to edit the document property.
   - Some properties cannot be changed. These properties are automatically generated by Word.

1-64 Document properties on the *Backstage* view

6. Click the **Show All/Fewer Properties** link at the bottom to display more or fewer document property fields.

7. After entering document properties, click the **Back** arrow in the upper left corner of the Backstage view to return to the document.

Document Panel

In addition to viewing and editing the document properties on the *Backstage* view, you can also display the properties in the ***Document panel,*** which appears in the regular Word window above the document and below the tab.

HOW TO: Use the Properties Panel

1. Click the **File** tab to display the *Backstage* view.
2. Click the **Info** button if it is not already selected.
3. Click the **Properties** drop-down list at the top of the *Properties* area (Figure 1-65).
4. Select **Show Document Panel**. The *Backstage* view closes and the *Document* panel is displayed above the document in the Word window (Figure 1-66).
5. Edit or add text in the *Document Properties* fields as desired.
6. Click the **X** in the upper right corner of the *Document* panel (not the Word window) to close the panel.

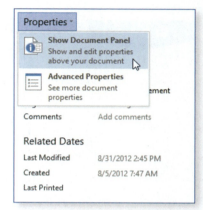

1-65 *Show Document Panel*

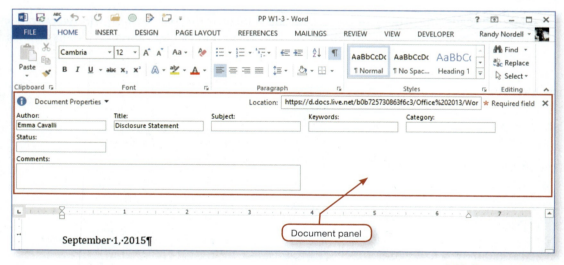

1-66 *Document* panel

In the final Pause & Practice project in this chapter, you put the finishing touches on a document. You customize paragraph and line spacing, change paragraph alignment, and use spelling and grammar checkers to produce an error-free document. You also modify the document properties.

File Needed: *[your initials] PP W1-2.docx*
Completed Project File Name: *[your initials] PP W1-3.docx*

1. Open the *[your initials] PP W1-2* document.

2. Save this document as *[your initials] PP W1-3*.
   a. Press **F12** to open the *Save As* dialog box.
   b. Change the file name to [your initials] PP W1-3.
   c. Click **Save** to rename the document and close the *Save As* dialog box.

3. Change the line and paragraph spacing on the entire document and set as the default for this document only.
   a. Press **Ctrl+A** to select the entire document.
   b. Click the **Paragraph** launcher [*Home* or *Page Layout* tab, *Paragraph* group] to open the *Paragraph* dialog box (Figure 1-67).
   c. Change the *Line spacing* to **Single**.
   d. Change the *After* spacing to **12 pt**., using the up arrow or typing in the amount of spacing.
   e. Click the **Set As Default** button. A dialog box opens.
   f. Click the **This document only?** radio button and click **OK** to close the dialog box.

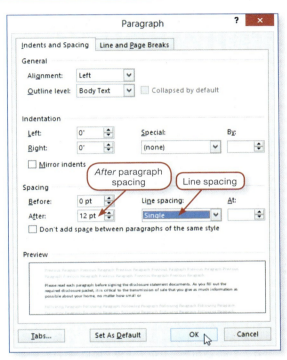

1-67 Change line and paragraph spacing in the *Paragraph* dialog box

> ▶ **ANOTHER WAY**
>
> Change line spacing in the *Paragraph* group on the *Home* tab. Change *Before* and *After* paragraph spacing in the *Paragraph* group on the *Page Layout* tab.

4. Add paragraph spacing before the date line of the business letter.
   a. Select or place your insertion point in the first line (date line) of the business letter.
   b. Click the **Page Layout** tab.
   c. Change the *Before* spacing to **72 pt**. Note: 72 pt. is approximately 1", which is commonly used as the spacing before the date line on business letters (Figure 1-68).

1-68 Change paragraph spacing in the *Paragraph* group

5. Change the paragraph alignment of selected text.
   a. Select or place your insertion point in the subject line of the business letter.
   b. Click the **Center** button [*Home* tab, *Paragraph* group] or press **Ctrl+E**.

6. Use the *Thesaurus* to find synonyms for selected words.
   a. Select the word "**reveal**" in the third body paragraph.
   b. Click the **Thesaurus** button [*Review* tab, *Proofing* group]. The *Thesaurus* pane opens on the right side of the Word window with a list of synonyms for the selected word (Figure 1-69).
   c. Click the **drop-down arrow** to the right of the word "divulge" and choose **Insert**. The word "reveal" is replaced with "divulge."
   d. Click the **X** in the upper right corner of the *Thesaurus* pane to close the pane.
   e. Right-click the word "**residence**" in the first body paragraph. A context menu opens.
   f. Put your pointer on **Synonyms** and a list of synonyms appears.
   g. Select "**home**" from the list of synonyms. The word "residence" is replaced with "home."

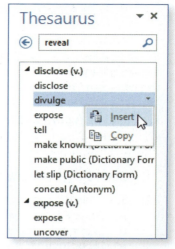

1-69 Insert a synonym from the *Thesaurus* pane

7. Add a word to the custom dictionary.
   a. Click the **File** tab to open the *Backstage* view.
   b. Click the **Options** button to open the *Word Options* dialog box.
   c. Click the **Proofing** button.
   d. Click the **Custom Dictionaries** button in the *When correcting spelling in Microsoft Office programs* area. The *Custom Dictionaries* dialog box opens.
   e. Select **RoamingCustom.dic** in the *Dictionary List*.
   f. Click the **Edit Word List** button. The *RoamingCustom.dic* dialog box opens (Figure 1-70).
   g. Type your last name in the *Word(s)* area and click the **Add** button.
   h. Click **OK** to close the *RoamingCustom.dic* dialog box.
   i. Click **OK** to close the *Custom Dictionaries* dialog box.
   j. Click **OK** to close the *Word Options* dialog box.

1-70 Add a word to the custom dictionary

8. Spell and grammar check the document.
   a. Right-click the word "**whole house**" in the second paragraph. A context list of words appears (Figure 1-71).
   b. Select "**whole house**." The correctly spelled word replaces the incorrectly spelled word.
   c. Click the **Spelling & Grammar** button [*Review* tab, *Proofing* group] or press **F7** to open the *Spelling* pane on the right (Figure 1-72).
   d. Select "**truss**" and click **Change**.
   e. Continue spell checking the remainder of the document. Change "granate" to "granite" and "you're" to "your."
   f. Click **Add** for "Cavalli."

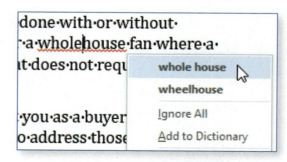

1-71 Correct spelling using the context menu

g. Click **Ignore** for your reference initials (if it is marked as incorrect).

h. Click **Ignore** for the capitalization grammar error (lower case reference initials).

i. Click **OK** to close the dialog box that opens and informs you that the spelling and grammar check is complete. The *Spelling and Grammar* pane closes.

9. Add document properties to your letter.

a. Click the **File** tab to open the *Backstage* view.

b. Click the **Info** button on the left if it is not already selected. The document properties are displayed on the right side of the *Backstage* view (Figure 1-73).

c. Click in the *Title* field and type Disclosure Statement.

d. In the *Author* area, right-click the existing author and select **Remove Person**.

e. In the *Author* area, click **Add an author**, type Emma Cavalli, and press **Tab**.

f. Click the **Show All Properties** link at the bottom. More document properties are displayed.

g. Click in the *Company* area and type Placer Hills Real Estate.

h. Click the **Properties** drop-down list at the top of the *Properties* area and choose **Show Document Panel**. The document properties are displayed in the *Document* panel.

i. Click the **X** in the upper right corner of the *Document* panel to close it.

10. Save and close the document (Figure 1-74).

1-72 *Spelling and Grammar* pane

September 1, 2015¶

¶

David and Sharon Wing↵
4685 Orange Grove Road↵
Rocklin, CA 97725¶

Dear Mr. and Mrs. Wing: ¶

SUBJECT: Disclosure Statement¶

Please read each paragraph before signing the disclosure statement documents. As you fill out the required disclosure packet, it is critical to the transmission of sale that you give as much information as possible about your home, no matter how small or insignificant. Please use additional paper if necessary and make a notation to that fact. ¶

Make note on the disclosure statement if you have had any work done with or without permits. Some examples include a gas spa, a new water heater, or a whole house fan where a truss may have been cut. If you had granite counters installed, that does not require a permit.¶

If there is information about the neighborhood or neighbors that you as a buyer would want to know about, be sure to divulge that information. Be sure to address those types of questions on the Real Estate Transfer Disclosure Statement, item #11 on page 2.¶

Please complete the enclosed disclosure statement by September 8, 2015 and return it to me. As always, if you have any questions or concerns, please call me at 916-450-3334 or email me at ecavalli@phre.com. Best wishes and thank you for your business.¶

Best regards,¶

¶

EMMA CAVALLI↵
Realtor Consultant↵
Placer Hills Real Estate¶

yoi↵
Enclosure¶

1-74 PP W1-3 completed

1-73 Document properties on the *Backstage* view

Chapter Summary

1.1 Create, save, and open a Word document (p. W1-3).

- New Word documents are based on the **Normal template** (*Normal.dotx*).
- You can save documents with the existing file name or with a different file name.
- A **Word document** (*.docx*) is the standard file format. There are a variety of Word file formats in which to save a document.
- You can open, edit, and save existing Word documents.

1.2 Customize a document by entering and selecting text, using word wrap, and using AutoComplete, AutoCorrect, and AutoFormat features (p. W1-6).

- **Word wrap** automatically wraps text to the next line as you reach the right margin of the document.
- The **Show/Hide** button displays formatting symbols in the document to properly and consistently format documents.
- You can select text in a variety of ways, and you can select individual words, an entire line, multiple lines of text, a sentence, a paragraph, multiple paragraphs, or the entire document.
- **AutoComplete** automatically completes a day, month, or date for you.
- **AutoCorrect** automatically corrects commonly misspelled words and capitalization errors.
- **AutoFormat** automatically controls the formatting of items such as numbered and bulleted lists.
- You can add, delete, and edit *AutoCorrect* entries and customize *AutoCorrect* options in Word.

1.3 Enhance a business document using paragraph breaks, line breaks, spaces, and non-breaking spaces (p. W1-10).

- The **Enter** key on the keyboard inserts a **paragraph break**. The **paragraph symbol** is visible when Show/*Hide* is turned on.
- **Line breaks** control breaks between lines or sentences to retain paragraph formatting between lines.
- **Non-breaking spaces** keep related words together.

1.4 Edit a business document using cut, copy, paste, the Clipboard, and the undo, redo, and repeat features (p. W1-14).

- You can move or copy selected text within a document. There are a variety of methods to **cut**, **copy**, and **paste** text in a document.
- The **Clipboard** stores text that you have cut or copied. You can use the *Clipboard* to paste text into your document.
- You can **Undo**, **Redo**, and **Repeat** previous actions when working on a document. These features are available on the **Quick Access** toolbar.

1.5 Customize a business document using different fonts, font sizes, and attributes (p. W1-17).

- **Serif** and **sans serif** are the two main categories of **fonts**.
- Fonts are measured in **points** (pt.). Most documents use between 10 and 12 pt. font size.
- You can change fonts and font size for specific text or the entire document.
- **Bold**, **italic**, and **underline** are font styles that you can apply quickly to text.
- Other font effects include **strikethrough**, **subscript**, **superscript**, **small caps**, and **all caps**.
- You can change the case of text in Word.
- The **Font dialog box** provides many font, size, style, and **effect** options.
- You can modify the **scale**, **spacing**, **position**, and **kerning** of selected text.
- The **Format Painter** applies formatting from selected text to other text.
- The **Clear Formatting** feature removes all formatting applied to selected text.
- You can change the **default** font and font size in Word.

1.6 Enhance a document using text alignment and line and paragraph spacing. (p. W1-27).

- **Paragraph alignment** describes how text is aligned horizontally between the margins of a document: **left**, **center**, **right**, or **justified**.
- **Line spacing** refers to the amount of blank space between lines of text in a paragraph.
- **Paragraph spacing** is the amount of space between paragraphs. Paragraph spacing is measured in points.

- You can modify alignment, line spacing, and paragraph spacing on the *Home* or *Page Layout* tab or in the **Paragraph dialog box**.

- You can change the default line and paragraph spacing in Word.

1.7 Finalize a document using Word's proofing tools (p. W1-31).

- By default, Word automatically checks documents for **spelling** and **grammatical errors**.

- Word marks potential spelling, incorrect word, or grammatical errors with a colored wavy line under the words. You can correct errors by selecting from options in the context menu.

- You can manually spell and grammar check a document using the *Spelling and Grammar* pane.

- You can customize the **Word dictionary** by adding, deleting, or modifying words in the word list.

- The **Thesaurus** finds synonyms for words in your document.

- Word also provides you with **Word Count**.

1.8 Apply custom document properties to a document (p. W1-35).

- *You can add **document properties**, such as Title, Author, Company, Subject, Created, and Last Modified, into a document.*

- You can add document properties on the *Backstage* view or in the **Document panel**.

Check for Understanding

In the **Online Learning Center** for this text (**www.mhhe.com/office2013inpractice**), there are a variety of resources that can be used to review the concepts covered in this chapter.

The following Online Learning Resources are available in the Online Learning Center.

- Multiple choice questions
- Short answer questions
- Matching exercises

Guided Project 1-1

In this project, Jennie Owings at Central Sierra Insurance is writing a business letter to Hartford Specialty regarding the renewal of the insurance policy for Valley Custom Manufacturing. This business letter is typed in block format and uses open punctuation. See *Appendix D* (online reference) for an example of a block format business letter and open and mixed punctuation.
[Student Learning Outcomes 1.1, 1.2, 1.3, 1.4, 1.5, 1.6, 1.7]

File Needed: ***ValleyCustomManufacturing-1.docx***
Completed Project File Name: ***[your initials] Word 1-1.docx***

Skills Covered in This Project

- Use business letter format.
- Change line spacing.
- Change paragraph spacing.
- Use *AutoComplete*.
- Use paragraph breaks for proper spacing between the parts of a business letter.
- Copy and paste using the *Clipboard*.

- Use *Show/Hide*.
- Undo automatic capitalization.
- Change font size.
- Apply font styles.
- Use spelling and grammar checker.
- Add words to dictionary.

1. Open a new Word document and save it as ***[your initials] Word 1-1***.

2. Change the line and paragraph spacing of the document.
   a. Click the **Paragraph** launcher [*Home* or *Page Layout* tab, *Paragraph* group]. (Figure 1-75).
   b. Change the *Line spacing* to **Single**.
   c. Change the *After* paragraph spacing to **0 pt**.
   d. Choose **OK** and close the *Paragraph* dialog box.

3. Type the current date on the first line of the document.
   a. Use month, day, year format (e.g., September 1, 2015).
   b. As you begin typing the date, press **Enter** as *AutoComplete* completes the month and current date.
   c. Press **Enter** four times (quadruple space, QS) after the date.

4. Type the inside address.
   a. Press **Enter** once (single space, SS) at the end of each of the first three lines.

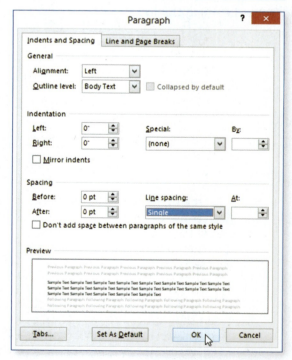

1-75 *Paragraph* dialog box

b. Press **Enter** twice (double space, DS) after the last line of the inside address.

Mrs. Cammie Speckler
Hartford Specialty
4788 Market Street, Suite A205
San Francisco, CA 95644

5. Type Dear Mrs. Speckler as the salutation. No colon is used after the salutation when using open punctuation.

6. Press **Enter** two times.

7. Type RE: Valley Custom Manufacturing as the subject line.

8. Press **Enter** two times.

9. Copy text from another document and paste it into the current document.
   a. Open the **ValleyCustomManufacturing-01** document from your student data files.
   b. Press **Ctrl+A** to select the entire document.
   c. Click the **Copy** button [*Home* tab, *Clipboard* group] or press **Ctrl+C**.
   d. Close **ValleyCustomManufacturing-01** without saving the document.
   e. In the **[your initials] Word 1-1** document, place your insertion point at the end of the document (a DS below the subject line).
   f. Click the **Clipboard** launcher [*Home* tab, *Clipboard* group] to open the *Clipboard* pane (Figure 1-76).
   g. Select the **drop-down arrow** to the right of the copied text in the *Clipboard* and click **Paste**. The paragraphs of text are pasted in the body of the document.
   h. Click the **X** in the upper left corner of the *Clipboard* pane to close it.

1-76 Paste from the *Clipboard*

10. Use the *Format Painter* to format the inserted paragraphs.
    a. Place your insertion point in the first line of the document.
    b. Click the **Format Painter** button [*Home* tab, *Clipboard* group].
    c. Select the body paragraphs of the letter to apply the formatting (Figure 1-77).

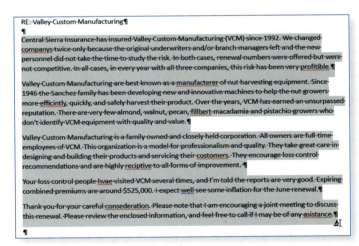

1-77 Use the *Format Painter* to copy formatting

11. Insert a blank line between each of the body paragraphs so there is a double space after each body paragraph (one blank line between paragraphs).
    a. Turn on **Show/Hide** [*Home* tab, *Paragraph* group] if it is not already turned on.
    b. Place your insertion point at the end of the first body paragraph and press **Enter**.
    c. Repeat for each of the body paragraphs.

12. Enter the closing lines of the document.
   a. Place your insertion point on the blank line below the body of the letter, press **Enter**, and type Sincerely. No comma is used after the salutation when using open punctuation.
   b. Press **Enter** four times and type the writer's name, title, and company.

   Jennie Owings, Vice President
   Central Sierra Insurance

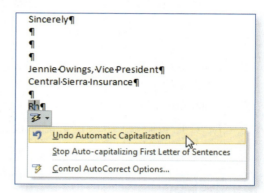

1-78 *AutoCorrect* **smart tag**

   c. Press **Enter** two times and type your reference initials (your first and last initials in lower case letters).
   d. Press **Enter**. *AutoCorrect* automatically capitalizes the first letter of your reference initials.
   e. Click the **AutoCorrect Options** smart tag (Figure 1-78). The *AutoCorrect Options* smart tag appears when you place your pointer below your reference initials.
   f. Click **Undo Automatic Capitalization** to undo the automatic capitalization of your reference initials.
   g. Place your insertion point on the blank line below your reference initials and type Enclosure.

13. Select the entire document (**Ctrl+A**) and change the font size to **10 pt**.

14. Add paragraph spacing before the date line.
   a. Select or place your insertion point in the date line.
   b. Click the **Page Layout** tab.
   c. Change the *Before* spacing to **72 pt**. [*Paragraph* group] (Figure 1-79).

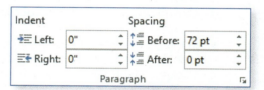

1-79 **Change** *Before* **paragraph spacing on the date line**

15. Apply font styles to selected text.
   a. Select the words "**Central Sierra Insurance**" in the first paragraph.
   b. Click the **Underline** button [*Home* tab, *Font* group] or press **Ctrl+U**.
   c. Select the words "**Valley Custom Manufacturing (VCM)**" in the first paragraph.
   d. Click the **Bold** button [*Home* tab, *Font* group] or press **Ctrl+B**.

16. Spell and grammar check the entire document.
   a. Press **Ctrl+Home** to move to the top of the document.
   b. Click the **Review** tab.
   c. Click the **Spelling & Grammar** button [*Proofing* group]. The *Spelling* pane opens (Figure 1-80).
   d. Click **Add** to add "Cammie" and "Speckler" to the dictionary.

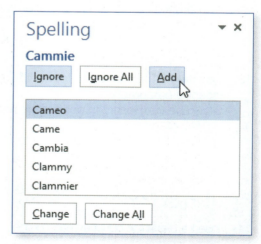

1-80 **Add word to the dictionary**

e. Change other words as necessary to correct spelling, incorrect word usage, and grammatical errors. If prompted to continue checking the document from the beginning, choose **Yes**.

f. Click **Ignore Once** if your reference initials are marked as a potential spelling or grammatical error.

17. Save and close the document (Figure 1-81).

September 1, 2015¶
¶
¶
¶
Mrs. Cammie Speckler¶
Hartford Specialty¶
4788 Market Street, Suite A205¶
San Francisco, CA 95644¶
¶
Dear Mrs. Speckler¶
¶
RE: Valley Custom Manufacturing¶
¶
Central Sierra Insurance has insured Valley Custom Manufacturing (VCM) since 1992. We changed companies twice only because the original underwriters and/or branch managers left and the new personnel did not take the time to study the risk. In both cases, renewal numbers were offered but were not competitive. In all cases, in every year with all three companies, this risk has been very profitable.¶
¶
Valley Custom Manufacturing are best known as a manufacturer of nut harvesting equipment. Since 1946 the Sanchez family has been developing new and innovative machines to help the nut growers more efficiently, quickly, and safely harvest their product. Over the years, VCM has earned an unsurpassed reputation. There are very few almond, walnut, pecan, filbert-macadamia and pistachio growers who don't identify VCM equipment with quality and value.¶
¶
Valley Custom Manufacturing is a family owned and closely held corporation. All owners are full-time employees of VCM. This organization is a model for professionalism and quality. They take great care in designing and building their products and servicing their customers. They encourage loss control recommendations and are highly receptive to all forms of improvement.¶
¶
Your loss control people have visited VCM several times, and I'm told the reports are very good. Expiring combined premiums are around $525,000. I expect we'll see some inflation for the June renewal.¶
¶
Thank you for your careful consideration. Please note that I am encouraging a joint meeting to discuss this renewal. Please review the enclosed information, and feel free to call if I may be of any assistance.¶
¶
Sincerely¶
¶
¶
¶
Jennie Owings, Vice-President¶
Central Sierra Insurance¶
¶
yoi¶
Enclosure¶

1-81 Word 1-1 completed

Guided Project 1-2

Sierra Pacific Community College District is a multi-campus community college district. In this project, you format an informational handout regarding online learning.
[Student Learning Outcomes 1.1, 1.3, 1.4, 1.5, 1.6, 1.7, 1.8]

File Needed: ***OnlineLearning-01.docx***
Completed Project File Name: *[your initials] Word 1-2.docx*

Skills Covered in This Project

- Open and edit an existing document.
- Change line spacing.
- Change paragraph spacing.
- Change default paragraph settings in your current document.
- Use *Show/Hide*.
- Change font size and apply color, styles, and effects.

- Cut and paste to move a paragraph.
- Use drag and drop to move a paragraph.
- Apply a shadow text effect.
- Use the *Format Painter*.
- Use spelling and grammar checker.
- Add document properties.

---

1. Open the **OnlineLearning-01** document from your student data files.

2. Save this document as **[your initials] Word 1-2**.

3. Change the line and paragraph spacing of the entire document, and use these settings as the default for this document.
   a. Press **Ctrl+A** to select the entire document.
   b. Click the **Paragraph** launcher [*Home* or *Page Layout* tab, *Paragraph* group] to open the *Paragraph* dialog box (Figure 1-82).
   c. In the *Line spacing* area, select **Multiple** from the drop-down list.
   d. In the *At* area, type 1.2.
   e. Change the paragraph spacing *After* to **12 pt**.
   f. Click **Set As Default**. A dialog box opens (Figure 1-83).
   g. Select the **This Document Only?** radio button.
   h. Click **OK** to close the *Paragraph* dialog box.

4. Turn on **Show/Hide** [*Home* tab, *Paragraph* group] and **delete** the one extra blank line between each paragraph including the title.

5. Change the font and font size of the entire document.
   a. Select the entire document (**Ctrl+A**).
   b. Change the font to **Cambria** and the size to **11 pt**. [*Home* tab, *Font* group].

6. Change the paragraph spacing, alignment, font size, styles, effects, and color of the title.
   a. Select the title of the document (**Online Learning Information**).
   b. Click the **Page Layout** tab.
   c. Change the *Before* spacing to **36 pt**. and the *After* spacing to **18 pt**. [*Paragraph* group].
   d. Click the **Center** button [*Home* tab, *Paragraph* group].
   e. Click the **launcher** [*Font* group]. The *Font* dialog box opens (Figure 1-84).
   f. Change the *Font* style to **Bold**.

1-82 Change line and *After* paragraph spacing

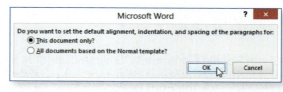

1-83 Set as default for this document only

g. Change the *Size* to **24**.

h. In the *Effects* area, click the **Small caps** check box.

i. On the **Font color** drop-down list [*Font* group], choose **Blue-Gray**, **Text 2** from the *Theme Colors*.

j. Click the **Advanced** tab.

k. Click the **Spacing** drop-down list and select **Expanded**. Change the *By* to **1.2**.

l. Click **OK** to close the *Font* dialog box.

7. Move paragraphs in the document and insert a heading.

a. Select the last paragraph in the document, including the paragraph mark at the end of the document.

b. Click the **Cut** button [*Home* tab, *Clipboard* group] or press **Ctrl+X**.

c. Place your insertion point before the second line of the document ("Definition of Online Learning Modalities").

d. Click the **Paste** button [*Home* tab, *Clipboard* group] or press **Ctrl+V**.

e. Click at the beginning of the pasted paragraph and type Where are we now with Online Learning?

f. Press **Enter**.

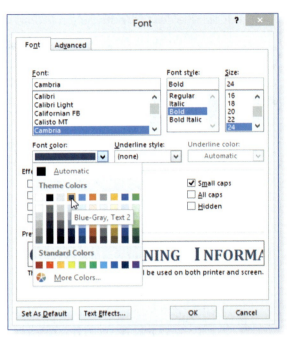

1-84 Change font style, size, effects, and color

g. Select the paragraph that begins "Hybrid Course:", including the paragraph mark at the end of the paragraph.

h. Move this paragraph using the drag and drop method so it appears before the paragraph that begins with "Television or Tele-Web Course:" (Figure 1-85).

> Television or Tele-Web Course: This type of course uses cable TV to deliver some or all of the course content. A tele-web course merges online and TV delivery. Typically, only a limited number of face-to-face meetings are held and the remainder of the course is conducted using television delivery of content and web-based activities, communication and discussion.¶
>
> Hybrid Course: A hybrid course is a course that is taught online using similar web-based tools and activities as an online class. Some potion of the course meeting time is conducted online, and the remaining percentage of the class is conducted in a traditional classroom manner.¶

1-85 Move paragraph using drag and drop

8. Format section headings in the document.

a. Select the first section heading ("**Where are we now with online learning?**").

b. Click the **Font** launcher [*Home* tab, *Font* group] to open the *Font* dialog box (Figure 1-86).

c. Change the font *Size* to **12 pt**.

d. Change the *Font color* to **Blue-Gray**, **Text 2**.

e. Change the *Underline style* to **Double Underline**.

f. Change the *Underline color* to **Blue-Gray**, **Text 2**.

g. In the *Effects* area, click the **All caps** check box.

h. Click **OK** to close the *Font* dialog box.

   i. Click the **Text Effects** button [*Home* tab, *Font* group].

   j. Put your pointer on **Shadow;** a list of shadow options is displayed (Figure 1-87).

   k. Select **Offset Diagonal Bottom Right**.

   l. With the formatted heading still selected, click the **Format Painter** button [*Home* tab, *Clipboard* group].

   m. Select the next heading (**"Definition of Online Learning Modalities"**) to apply formatting.

9. Format paragraph headings in the document.
   a. Select the first paragraph heading ("**Online Course:**"), including the colon.
   b. Click the **Font** launcher [*Home* tab, *Font* group] to open the *Font* dialog box.
   c. Change the *Font color* to **Blue-Gray**, **Text 2**.
   d. In the *Effects* area, click the **Small caps** check box.
   e. Click **OK** to close the *Font* dialog box.
   f. Use the **Format Painter** to copy this format to the other paragraph headings ("Hybrid Course:", "Television or Tele-Web Course:", "Web-Enhanced Course:"). Double-click the **Format Painter** button to apply this formatting to multiple selections. Click the **Format Painter** button again to turn off the *Format Painter*.

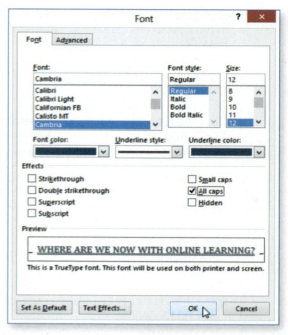

1-86 Format heading using *Font* dialog box

1-87 Apply *Shadow* text effect

10. Correct spelling and grammar in the document using the context menu.
    a. Right-click the first misspelled word ("**management**") and choose the correct spelling from the list of options.
    b. Repeat this process for "**potion**".
    c. Click **Ignore All** or **Ignore Once** on the other words that are marked as potentially incorrect.

11. Select the sentence in parentheses at the end of the document, including the parentheses, and click the **Italic** button [*Home* tab, *Font* group] or press **Ctrl+I**.

12. Add document properties using the *Document* panel.
    a. Click the **File** tab to open the *Backstage* view.
    b. Click the **Info** button if it is not already selected.
    c. Click the **Properties** button on the right and choose **Show Document Panel**. The *Document* panel is displayed above the document.
    d. In the *Author* area, delete the existing author name and type Tanesha Morris.
    e. In the *Title* area, type Online Learning Information.
    f. In the *Subject* area, type Online Learning.
    g. In the *Status* area, type Draft.
    h. Click the **X** in the upper right of the *Document* panel to close it.

13. Save and close the document (Figure 1-88).

ONLINE·LEARNING·INFORMATION¶

WHERE·ARE·WE·NOW·WITH·ONLINE·LEARNING?¶

SPCCD·was·a·pioneer·in·online·education·and·was·one·of·the·first·community·colleges·in·California·
to·offer·fully·online·courses·in·1998.·However·over·the·next·few·years·there·was·limited·growth·in·
online·offerings·and·only·15·course·sections·were·taught·online·during·Fall·2000.·The·adoption·of·a·
learning·management·system·in·Spring·2001,·and·the·availability·of·training·to·teach·online,·and·
recruitment·of·new·faculty·interested·in·teaching·online·resulted·in·a·rapid·increase·in·online·
offerings.¶

DEFINITION·OF·ONLINE·LEARNING·MODALITIES¶

All·online·learning·modes·offered·at·SPCCD·will·be·considered·in·the·plan.·Currently,·these·include·
the·following:·online,·hybrid,·television,·and·tele-web.¶

ONLINE·COURSE:·An·online·course·is·a·course·that·is·offered·over·the·Internet.·Typically,·content·is·
presented·through·web·pages·and·class·discussions·using·a·combination·of·email,·mailing·lists,·
bulletin·boards,·chat·rooms,·or·newsgroups.·All·class·meetings,·assignments,·lectures,·and·
assessments·are·online·(with·the·exception·of·orientation·meetings·or·other·face-to-face·
examinations·as·determined·by·the·professor).¶

HYBRID·COURSE:·A·hybrid·course·is·a·course·that·is·taught·online·using·similar·web-based·tools·and·
activities·as·an·online·class.·Some·portion·of·the·course·meeting·time·is·conducted·online,·and·the·
remaining·percentage·of·the·class·is·conducted·in·a·traditional·classroom·manner.¶

TELEVISION·OR·TELE-WEB·COURSE:·This·type·of·course·uses·cable·TV·to·deliver·some·or·all·of·the·
course·content.·A·tele-web·course·merges·online·and·TV·delivery.·Typically,·only·a·limited·number·
of·face-to-face·meetings·are·held·and·the·remainder·of·the·course·is·conducted·using·television·
delivery·of·content·and·web-based·activities,·communication,·and·discussion.¶

WEB-ENHANCED·COURSE:·This·type·of·course·is·taught·face-to-face·for·100%·of·the·course·meeting·
time,·but·classroom·assignments·and·materials·are·supplemented·with·web-based·activities.·
Examples·are:·online·projects,·hand-outs·and·materials,·online·discussion,·or·online·testing·(Note:·
this·is·a·definition·of·a·non-online·learning·course·which·uses·online·learning·tools).¶

1-88 Word 1-2 completed

Guided Project 1-3

In this project, you create a memo about using heart rate to increase the effectiveness of training to send out to American River Cycling Club members.
[Student Learning Outcomes 1.1, 1.2, 1.3, 1.5, 1.6, 1.7, 1.8]

File Needed: *HeartRate-01.docx*
Completed Project File Name: *[your initials] Word 1-3.docx*

Skills Covered in This Project

- Open and edit an existing document.
- Change line spacing.
- Change paragraph spacing.
- Use *Show/Hide*.
- Add a memo heading to a document.
- Change paragraph alignment.
- Change font size and apply styles and effects.

- Use the *Format Painter*.
- Add text highlight color.
- Use non-breaking space.
- Use *Thesaurus*.
- Add words to the dictionary.
- Add document properties.

1. Open the **HeartRate-01** document from your student data files.

2. Save the document as **[your initials] Word 1-3**.

3. Change line and paragraph spacing of the entire document and insert a paragraph break between each paragraph.
   a. Press **Ctrl+A** to select the entire document.
   b. Click the **Paragraph** launcher [*Home* or *Page Layout* tab, *Paragraph* group].
   c. In the *Line spacing* area, select **Single** from the drop-down list.
   d. Change the *After* paragraph spacing to **0 pt**.
   e. Click **OK** to close the *Paragraph* dialog box.
   f. Turn on **Show/Hide** [*Home* tab, *Paragraph* group].
   g. Click at the end of each paragraph and press **Enter** once to add a blank line between each of the paragraphs.

4. Add a memo heading to the document.
   a. Place your insertion point at the beginning of the first paragraph and press **Enter**.
   b. Press the **up arrow** key on keyboard to move to the blank line above the first paragraph.
   c. Type TO: and press **Tab** two times.
   d. Type All ARCC Club Members and press **Enter** two times.
   e. Type FROM: and press **Tab** two times.
   f. Type Taylor Mathos, ARCC Coach and press **Enter** two times.
   g. Type DATE: and press **Tab** two times.
   h. Type the current date in month, day, year format (e.g., September 1, 2015) and press **Enter** two times.
   i. Type SUBJECT: and press **Tab** once.
   j. Type Heart Rate Training and press **Enter** two times.

5. Change paragraph alignment and font styles of selected text.
   a. Select the second and third paragraphs in the body of the memo (beginning with "**220 – Your Age. . .**" and ending with "**. . .heart rate is 180.)**"), including the paragraph mark at the end of the third paragraph.
   b. Click the **Center** button [*Home* tab, *Paragraph* group] or press **Ctrl+E**.
   c. Select the paragraph beginning "220 – Your Age . . . " and click the **Bold** button [*Home* tab, *Font* group] or press **Ctrl+B**.
   d. Select the next paragraph and click the **Italic** button [*Home* tab, *Font* group] or press **Ctrl+I**.
   e. Delete the blank line between the second and third paragraphs (Figure 1-89).

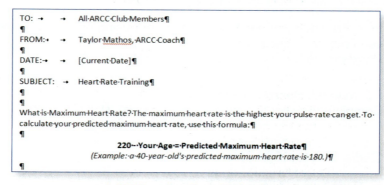

1-89 Memo heading added and paragraphs formatted

6. Change the font and style of selected text.
   a. Press **Ctrl+A** to select the entire document.
   b. Click the **Increase Font Size** button [*Home* tab, *Font* group] to increase the font size to 12 pt. (Figure 1-90).
   c. In the first sentence of the first body paragraph, select the words "**Maximum Heart Rate**".

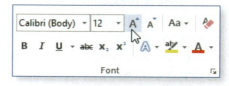

1-90 *Increase Font Size* button

d. Click the **Font** launcher [*Home* tab, *Font* group] to open the *Font* dialog box (Figure 1-91).

e. Change the *Font style* to **Bold**.

f. Change the *Underline style* to **Words only**.

g. Change the *Underline color* to **Green, Accent 6**.

h. In the *Effects* area, select the **Small caps** check box.

i. Click **OK** to close the *Font* dialog box.

j. With the words still selected, click the **Format Painter** button [*Home* tab, *Clipboard* group].

k. Select the words "**Target Heart Rate Zone**" in the first sentence of the fifth paragraph in the body ("You gain the most benefits . . ."). The *Format Painter* applies the formatting to the selected words.

l. Select the last two sentences of the fifth paragraph ("Do not exercise above 85 percent . . .").

m. Click the **Text Highlight Color** drop-down arrow [*Home* tab, *Font* group] (Figure 1-92).

n. Select **Gray-25%** text highlighting.

7. Use a non-breaking space to keep words together.

a. In the first sentence of the fifth paragraph in the body ("You gain the most benefits . . ."), delete the space between the words "Target" and "Heart."

b. Place your insertion point between these two words and press **Ctrl+Shift+Spacebar** to insert a non-breaking space. "Target" is wrapped to the next line so the words do not break between lines.

8. Add paragraph spacing before the first line of the document.

a. Select the first line of the document.

b. Change the *Before* spacing to **72 pt**. [*Page Layout* tab, *Paragraph* group].

9. Use the thesaurus to find synonyms for selected words.

a. Right-click the word "**medicines**" in the third sentence of the first body paragraph.

b. Put your pointer on **Synonyms** to display a list of synonyms (Figure 1-93).

c. Select "**medications**" as the synonym.

d. In the last sentence of the fifth paragraph ("You gain the most benefits . . ."), right-click the word "**added**."

e. Put your pointer on **Synonyms** and select "**additional**."

10. Add reference initials to the document.

a. Click at the end of the last paragraph and press **Enter** two times.

b. Type your reference initials in lower case letters.

1-91 Change font style and effects

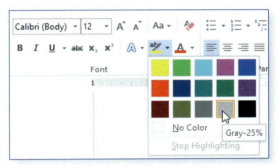

1-92 *Text Highlight Color* button and drop-down list

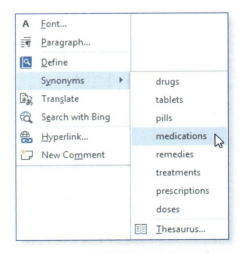

1-93 Select synonym from context menu

11. Add document properties.
    a. Click the **File** tab to open the *Backstage* view.
    b. Click the **Info** button if it is not already selected to display the document properties at the right.
    c. In the *Title* area, type Heart Rate Training.
    d. In the *Author* area, right-click the existing author and select **Remove Person**.
    e. In the *Author* area, type Taylor Mathos.
    f. Click the **Show All Properties** link at the bottom of the document properties.
    g. In the *Company* area, type ARCC.
    h. Click the **Back** arrow in the upper left of the *Backstage* view to the document.

12. Add words to the dictionary.
    a. Right-click the word "**Mathos**" in the second line of the memo heading.
    b. Choose **Add to Dictionary** from the context menu.
    c. If your reference initials are marked as incorrectly spelled (red wavy underline), right-click them and choose **Add to Dictionary**.

13. Save and close the document (Figure 1-94).

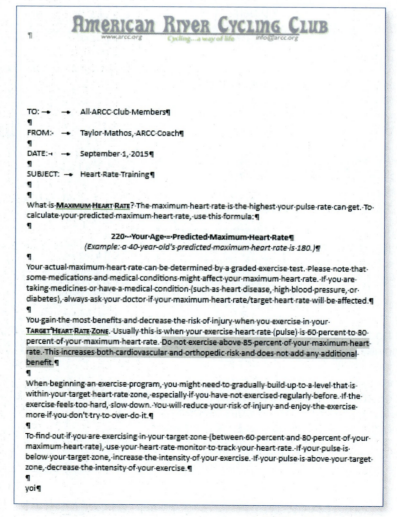

1-94 Word 1-3 completed

Independent Project 1-4

In this project, you format a business letter for Emma Cavalli to send to clients whose current home listings are expiring.
[Student Learning Outcomes 1.1, 1.2, 1.3, 1.4, 1.5, 1.6, 1.7, 1.8]

File Needed: *ExpiredLetter-01.docx*
Completed Project File Name: *[your initials] Word 1-4.docx*

Skills Covered in This Project

- Open and edit an existing document.
- Change line spacing.
- Change paragraph alignment and spacing.
- Change font and font size.
- Use *Show/Hide*.
- Format document as a block format business letter with mixed punctuation.

- Use *AutoCorrect*.
- Move text.
- Change font styles and effects.
- Use spelling and grammar checker.
- Add document properties.

1. Open the *ExpiredLetter-01* document from your student data files.
2. Save this document as *[your initials] Word 1-4*.
3. Select the entire document and make the following formatting changes:
   a. Change the before and after paragraph spacing to **0 pt**.
   b. Change the line spacing to **Single**.
   c. Change the paragraph alignment to **Left**.
   d. Change the font and font size to **Calibri** and **11 pt**.
4. Turn on **Show/Hide** and press **Enter** to add an extra space between each paragraph.
5. Add the following information to the top of the business letter:
   a. Press **Ctrl+Home** to move your insertion point to the top of the document.
   b. Type the current date and press **Enter** four times.
   c. Type the following inside address and press **Enter** two times after the last line.

   Mr. Rick Hermann
   9035 Masi Drive
   Fair Oaks, CA 95528

   d. Supply an appropriate salutation and use mixed punctuation.
   e. Press **Enter** two times after the salutation; there should be one blank line between the salutation and the body of the letter.
   f. Add **72 pt**. *Before* paragraph spacing on the date line.
6. Press **Enter** two times after the last paragraph and type in the closing lines.
   a. Type Best regards, and press **Enter** four times.
   b. Type the following closing lines.

   Emma Cavalli
   Realtor Consultant
   Placer Hills Real Estate

   c. Press **Enter** two times after the company name and type your reference initials in lower case letters.

7. Move the third body paragraph so it appears before the second body paragraph. Make sure there is one blank line between each of the body paragraphs.

8. In the second body paragraph ("There was a lot of detail . . ."), move the last two sentences to the beginning of the paragraph. Make sure there is proper spacing between sentences.

9. Select "**Placer Hills Real Estate**" in the first body paragraph and make the company name **Bold**, **Underline**, and **Small caps**.

10. Select the first sentence in the third paragraph ("The service and experience . . .") and make it **Italic**.

11. Apply formatting to the closing lines of the business letter.
    a. Select the writer's name at the bottom and make it **Small caps**.
    b. Select the writer's title and make it **Italic**.
    c. Select the company name below the writer's title and make it **Bold**.

12. Add the following document properties:
    a. *Title*: Expired Letter
    b. *Company*: Placer Hills Real Estate
    c. *Manager*: Kelsey Kroll
    d. *Author*: Emma Cavalli

13. Spell and grammar check the entire document, ignoring proper nouns.

14. Save and close the document (Figure 1-95).

1-95 Word 1-4 completed

Independent Project 1-5

In this project, you combine information from different documents to create a memo for Sierra Pacific Community College District. This memo is a draft of the values statement for the district.
[Student Learning Outcomes 1.1, 1.3, 1.4, 1.5, 1.6, 1.8]

File Needed: *ValuesStatement-01a.docx*, *ValuesStatement-01b.docx*
Completed Project File Name: *[your initials] Word 1-5.docx*

Skills Covered in This Project

- Open and edit an existing document.
- Change line spacing.
- Change paragraph spacing.
- Change font and font size.
- Format document as a memo.
- Use spelling and grammar checker.
- Add words to the dictionary.
- Change font styles and effects.
- Use the *Format Painter*.
- Move text.
- Add document properties.

1. Open the ***ValuesStatement-01a*** document from your student data files.

2. Save this document as ***[your initials] Word 1-5***.

3. Open the ***ValuesStatement-01b*** document from your student data files.

4. Select all of the text in this document and copy to the *Clipboard.*

5. Close the ***ValuesStatement-01b*** document without saving.

6. In the ***[your initials] Word 1-5*** document, press **Enter** at the end of the document and paste the copied text from the *Clipboard.*

7. **Delete** the extra paragraph breaks between the first four paragraphs and at the end of the document.

8. Select the entire document and make the following formatting changes:
   a. Change after paragraph spacing to **12 pt**.
   b. Change the line spacing to **1.15**.
   c. Change the font and font size to **Calibri** and **10 pt**.

9. Press **Enter** at the top of the document and add the memo information above the existing text.
   a. Press **Tab** (once or twice) after the guidewords to line up information at 1".
   b. Press **Enter** once at the end of the first three lines of the memo heading.

   TO: All SPCCD faculty, staff, and managers
   FROM: Lanita Morrow, Chancellor
   DATE: [Current Date]
   SUBJECT: Draft of SPCCD Values Statement

10. Select the first line of the memo heading and change the before paragraph spacing to **24 pt**.

11. Select the last line of the memo heading and change the after paragraph spacing to **18 pt**.

12. Spell and grammar check the entire document.

13. Add the chancellor's first and last names to the dictionary if they are marked as potential spelling errors.

14. Select the first paragraph heading (**"Access"**) in the body of the memo and apply the following style changes:
    a. *Font style*: **Bold**
    b. *Font color*: **Blue-Gray, Text 2**
    c. *Underline*: **Double Underline**
    d. *Underline color*: **Blue-Gray, Text 2**
    e. *Effects*: **Small caps**

15. Use the *Format Painter* to apply these styles to each of the other paragraph headings in the body of the memo.

16. Use cut and paste or drag and drop to move the body paragraphs so they are ordered alphabetically by paragraph heading. Exclude the first body paragraph. Be sure to include the paragraph symbol at the end of each paragraph when cutting or dragging.

17. Delete any extra blank lines at the end of the document so this document fits on one page.

18. Add the following document properties:
    a. *Title*: SPCCD Values Statement
    b. *Company*: Sierra Pacific Community College District
    c. *Author*: Yoon Soo Park

19. Save and close the document (Figure 1-96).

1-96 Word 1-5 completed

Independent Project 1-6

In this project, you use formatting features in Word to create a professional and appealing brochure for Emma Cavalli at Placer Hills Real Estate.
[Student Learning Outcomes 1.1, 1.2, 1.3, 1.4, 1.5, 1.6, 1.7, 1.8]

File Needed: ***Brochure-01.docx***
Completed Project File Name: *[your initials] Word 1-6.docx*

Skills Covered in This Project

- Open and edit an existing document.
- Change font and font size.
- Change paragraph spacing.
- Change line spacing.
- Use line breaks.
- Change paragraph alignment.

- Change font styles and effects.
- Use the *Format Painter*.
- Move text.
- Use the thesaurus to find synonyms.
- Add document properties.

1. Open the **Brochure-01** document from your student data files.

2. Save this document as **[your initials] Word 1-6**.

3. Select the entire document and make the following formatting changes:
   a. Change the font and font size to **Candara** and **10 pt**.
   b. Change the after-paragraph spacing to **6 pt**.
   c. Change the line spacing to **Single**.

4. On the first five lines of the document ("Emma Cavalli to E-mail . . ."), delete the paragraph symbols at the end of each line and insert a line break (**Shift+Enter**).

5. **Center** the first six lines of the document ("Emma Cavalli to Web . . .").

6. Select the first line of the document and make the following changes:
   a. *Font style*: **Bold**
   b. *Size*: **12 pt**.
   c. *Font color*: **Green**, **Accent 6**, **Darker 50%**
   d. *Underline style*: **Thick Underline**
   e. *Underline color*: **Green**, **Accent 6**, **Darker 50%**

7. Select the second line of the document and make it **Bold**.

8. Select the third line of the document and make it **Italic**.

9. Select the first section heading, "**Personal Statement**," and apply **Bold**, **Underline**, and **Small Caps** formatting. Change the before paragraph spacing to **12 pt**. and the after paragraph spacing to **3 pt**.

10. Use the *Format Painter* to copy this formatting to the other section headings ("Real Estate Experience," "Why I am a Real Estate Agent," "What Clients are Saying," "Professional Credentials," and "Education & Training").

11. In the "Why I am a Real Estate Agent" section, combine the four sentences into one paragraph, deleting paragraph marks and inserting spaces as needed.

12. In the "What Clients are Saying" section, make the following changes:
    a. Select the first quote (don't include the names of the individuals who said the quote), make it **Italic**, and change the after spacing to **0 pt**.
    b. Select the source of the quote ("**-Rod & Luisa Ellisor**, **Rocklin**, **CA**") and right-align this text.
    c. Repeat the above two steps for the second quote in this section.

13. Move the third section heading and the paragraph below it ("Why I am a Real Estate Agent") so it appears before the second section ("Real Estate Experience").

14. Select the lines of text in the "Professional Credentials" section (don't include the heading) and change the after-paragraph spacing to **3 pt**.

15. Use the *Format Painter* to repeat the above formatting to the lines of text (excluding the heading) in the "Education & Training" section.

16. Use the thesaurus to find an appropriate synonym for the following words:
    a. Replace "surpass" (in the "Personal Statement" section) with "**exceed**."
    b. Replace "emotions" (in the "Why I am a Real Estate Agent" section) with "**sentiments**."

17. Add the following document properties:
    a. *Title*: Brochure
    b. *Company*: Placer Hills Real Estate
    c. *Author*: Emma Cavalli

18. Save and close the document (Figure 1-97).

1-97 Word 1-6 completed

Improve It Project 1-7

In this project, you create a block format business letter for Margaret Jepson, an insurance agent at Central Sierra Insurance. You fix the formatting and text in this document and add opening and closing lines to create a properly formatted business letter. For more information on creating a correctly formatted block format business letter, see *Appendix D* (online reference).
[Student Learning Outcomes 1.1, 1.2, 1.3, 1.5, 1.6, 1.8]

File Needed: *RenewalLetter-01.docx*
Completed Project File Name: *[your initials] Word 1-7.docx*

Skills Covered in This Project

- Open and edit an existing document.
- Change font and font size.
- Change paragraph spacing.
- Change line spacing.
- Use spelling and grammar checker.

- Format a business letter.
- Change paragraph alignment.
- Change font styles and effects.
- Use the *Format Painter*.
- Add document properties.

1. Open the **RenewalLetter-01** document from your student data files.

2. Save this document as *[your initials] Word 1-7*.

3. Use **Single** line spacing and **0 pt**. before- and after-paragraph spacing on the entire document.

4. Use **Calibri** font and **11 pt**. font size.

5. Correct spelling and grammar as needed.

6. Type the current date at the top of the document.

7. Type the inside address.

   Mr. Rick DePonte
   8364 Marshall Street
   Granite Bay, CA 95863

8. Include an appropriate salutation. Use mixed punctuation.

9. Include the insurance policy information in the subject line.

   Policy HO-2887-5546-B

10. At the end of the document, supply an appropriate complimentary close. Use mixed punctuation.

11. Type the information below as the writer's name, title, and company.

    Margaret Jepson, ARM, CIC, CRM
    Insurance Agent
    Central Sierra Insurance

12. Include your reference initials and an enclosure notation at the end of the business letter.

13. **Center** the four lines of renewal premium information in the body of the letter.

14. Apply **Bold** and **Small caps** formatting to the headings for each of these four lines of renewal premium information.

15. Format the "Total Premium" amount as **Bold**, *Italic*, and **Double Underline**.

16. Replace *[Company Name]* with Hartford Specialty.

17. Replace *[First Name]* with the appropriate information.

18. Use **72 pt**. before paragraph spacing on the date line.

19. Add *Title* (Renewal Letter), *Company*, and *Author* document properties to the letter.

20. Proofread and edit the document carefully. Make sure there is proper spacing between each of the parts of the block format business letter. This document fits on one page.

21. Save and close the letter (Figure 1-98).

1-98 Word 1-7 completed

Challenge Project 1-8

Create a cover letter for a job application. A cover letter typically accompanies a resume to introduce an applicant to a prospective employer. You can use and modify an existing cover letter, or you can create a new one. It is important to customize each cover letter for each job for which you are applying.

There are many online resources available to help you with both content and format. One of the best online resources for writing is the Online Writing Lab (OWL) from Purdue University (http://owl.english .purdue.edu/owl/). You can search this site for helpful information about cover letters.
[Student Learning Outcomes 1.1, 1.2, 1.3, 1.4, 1.5, 1.6, 1.7, 1.8]

File Needed: None
Completed Project File Name: *[your initials] Word 1-8.docx*

Open a new document and save this document as *[your initials] Word 1-8*.

Type this document as a personal business letter in block format. For more information on formatting a personal business letter see *Appendix D* (online reference). Modify your document according to the following guidelines:

- Move sentences and paragraphs as needed to produce a well-organized cover letter.
- Add words to the dictionary as needed.
- Use the thesaurus to find synonyms as needed.
- Include document properties and spell and grammar check the document.

Challenge Project 1-9

Create a list of five places you would like to visit in the next five years. For each of the places you list, compose a short paragraph about that place and why it is interesting to you. Research each of the places you choose on the Internet. Use your own words when composing the paragraphs about each place.
[Student Learning Outcomes 1.1, 1.2, 1.3, 1.4, 1.5, 1.6, 1.7, 1.8]

File Needed: None
Completed Project File Name: *[your initials] Word 1-9.docx*

Open a new document and save it as *[your initials] Word 1-9*. Modify your document according to the following guidelines:

- Create and format a title for the document.
- Format each of the headings by modifying the font, style, and attributes.
- Change line and paragraph spacing as needed to create an attractive and readable document.
- Use consistent line and paragraph spacing throughout the document.
- Use the *Format Painter* to keep formatting consistent throughout the document.
- Move the paragraphs so the places are listed in order of your preference.
- Include document properties and spell and grammar check the document.

Challenge Project 1-10

Create a flyer for an upcoming event for an organization to which you belong. Be sure to include all the relevant information for this event and arrange it attractively and professionally on the page. [Student Learning Outcomes 1.1, 1.2, 1.3, 1.5, 1.6, 1.7, 1.8]

File Needed: None
Completed Project File Name: *[your initials] Word 1-10.docx*

Open a new document and save it as *[your initials] Word 1-10*. Modify your document according to the following guidelines:

- Create and format a title for the document.
- Format the information by modifying the fonts, styles, and attributes.
- Change line and paragraph spacing as needed to create an attractive and readable document.
- Change the text alignment as desired.
- Use the *Format Painter* to keep formatting consistent throughout the document.
- Include document properties and spell and grammar check the document.

Formatting and Customizing Documents

CHAPTER OVERVIEW

In addition to giving you the ability to create basic business documents, Microsoft Word 2013 provides formatting and editing tools you can use to customize a variety of documents. Formatting features such as custom margins, tab stops, indents, page numbering, headers, footers, breaks, lists, styles, themes, borders, and shading help you to produce readable and attractive professional and personal documents.

STUDENT LEARNING OUTCOMES (SLOs)

After completing this chapter, you will be able to:

SLO 2.1   Format a document by customizing margins, page orientation, paper size, and vertical alignment (p. W2-63).

SLO 2.2   Improve alignment and white-space usage by setting, using, and editing tab stops in a document (p. W2-66).

SLO 2.3   Understand and apply indents to control text alignment (p. W2-71).

SLO 2.4   Enhance document layout by effectively using page numbers, headers, and footers (p. W2-76).

SLO 2.5   Control pagination with page and section breaks (p. W2-83).

SLO 2.6   Present information using customized bulleted and numbered lists (p. W2-85).

SLO 2.7   Increase document consistency and format with styles and themes (p. W2-89).

SLO 2.8   Effectively edit a document using find and replace (p. W2-93).

SLO 2.9   Improve overall document design and format with borders, shading, horizontal lines, and hyperlinks (p. W2-96).

CASE STUDY

Courtyard Medical Plaza has a preschool for its employees' children. The preschool is currently looking for qualified applicants to fill a vacant teacher position.

In the Pause & Practice projects, you are modifying a resume for Richelle Wilkinson. You use features covered in this chapter to create an attractive and informative resume.

Pause & Practice 2-1: Edit the resume to change margins and include tab stops and indents.

Pause & Practice 2-2: Modify the resume to include a header with text and a page number.

Pause & Practice 2-3: Enhance the resume by using bulleted lists, a page break, and a theme.

Pause & Practice 2-4: Finalize the resume by using find and replace, borders, shading, and hyperlinks.

WORD

Customizing Margins and Page Layout

You can use margins to create *white space* around the edges of a document. White space improves the readability of a document and prevents the document from appearing cluttered. The document type and content influence the margins you choose for the document. You can also customize a document by changing the orientation, page size, or vertical alignment.

Page Layout Settings

When you open a new Word document, the default settings control margins, page orientation, paper size, and vertical alignment. The default settings for a new document are as follows:

Default Page Layout Settings

Page Layout Option	Default Setting
Margins	1" top, bottom, left, and right
Page Orientation	Portrait
Paper Size	8.5"×11" (Letter)
Vertical Alignment	Top

These settings are applied to the entire Word document, and you can easily change all of these settings in Word.

Margin Settings

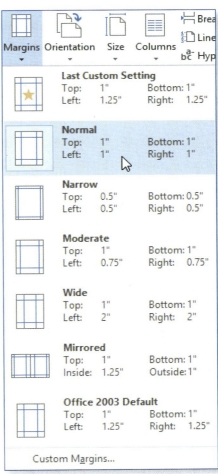

Margin settings are measured in inches; the default margin settings for a new Word document are 1". Word provides you with a variety of *preset margins settings.* You can choose and change margins on the *Page Layout* tab.

HOW TO: Change Margin Settings

1. Click the **Page Layout** tab.
2. Click the **Margins** button [*Page Setup* group]. Preset margin options appear in the *Margins* drop-down list (Figure 2-1).
3. Select the desired margin settings from the drop-down list of options.

The *Margins* drop-down list provides preset margin options. You are not limited to these preset options; you can also create your own custom margin settings.

> **MORE INFO**
>
> At the top of this *Margins* list, the **Last Custom Setting** option displays the most recent custom margin settings you have used.

2-1 Preset margin settings drop-down list

Page Setup Dialog Box

If you want margin settings that are not listed in the preset margin settings in the *Margins* drop-down list, use the ***Page Setup dialog box*** (Figure 2-2) to change one or more of the margin settings and create custom margins.

HOW TO: Set Custom Margins

1. Click the **Page Layout** tab.
2. Click the **Margins** button [*Page Setup* group]. The *Margins* drop-down list opens.
3. Click **Custom Margins**. The *Page Setup* dialog box opens (Figure 2-2).
4. Click the **Margins** tab if it is not already selected.
5. Change the *Top, Bottom, Left,* and *Right* margin settings as desired. You can do this in two different ways.
   - Click in the **Top**, **Bottom**, **Left**, or **Right** margin box, and type in your desired margin setting.
   - Click the **up** or **down arrow** to increase or decrease the margin size. Each click of the *up* or *down arrow* increases or decreases the margins by 0.1".
6. The *Preview* area displays how the margin settings appear when applied to the document.
7. Click **OK** to apply the margin settings.

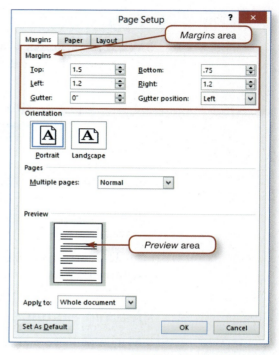

2-2 *Page Setup* dialog box

> **MORE INFO**
>
> Margin settings are applied to the entire document by default. However, you can apply different margin settings to different sections of a document. Sections and section breaks are covered later in this chapter.

Page Orientation

Page orientation refers to the direction of the page. The two different orientation options in Word are ***Portrait*** and ***Landscape.*** Portrait is the tall orientation (8.5"×11") which is the default setting in Word. Landscape is the wide orientation (11"×8.5").

You can change page orientation by clicking the **Orientation** button in the *Page Setup* group on the *Page Layout* tab (Figure 2-3). By default, orientation is applied to the entire document. You can also change page orientation in the *Page Setup* dialog box.

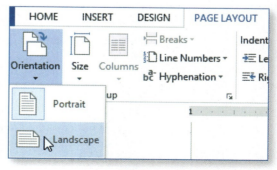

2-3 Page orientation settings

Paper Size

Paper size refers to the actual size of the paper of your final printed document. A new document in Word is letter size, which is 8.5"×11" by default. Word also provides other preset paper size settings, some of which are displayed in Figure 2-4.

You can change paper size by clicking the **Size** button in the *Page Setup* group on the *Page Layout* tab. You can also set a custom paper size in the *Page Setup* dialog box. When a different paper size is set, the margins of the document remain the same. You can change the margins if necessary.

Vertical Alignment

If you are creating a flyer or a title page for a report, you might want to balance or center the information vertically on the page. Changing the ***vertical alignment*** of a page, section, or document is a much more effective method than using paragraph breaks (pressing *Enter* multiple times) to align information vertically.

Word gives you four different vertical alignment options.

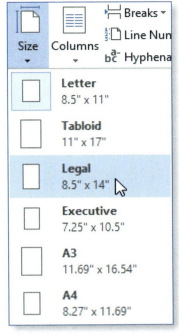

2-4 Paper size preset setting options

- ***Top***—The text begins at the top of the document.
- ***Center***—Information is centered vertically between the margins.
- ***Justified***—Space is automatically added between lines to fill up the entire vertical space between the top and bottom margins.
- ***Bottom***—The text begins at the bottom of the document.

HOW TO: Change Vertical Alignment

1. Click the **Page Layout** tab.
2. Click the **Page Setup** launcher [*Page Setup* group]. The *Page Setup* dialog box opens.
3. Click the **Layout** tab.
4. In the *Page* area, click the **Vertical alignment** drop-down list (Figure 2-5).
5. Select the vertical alignment option of your choice.

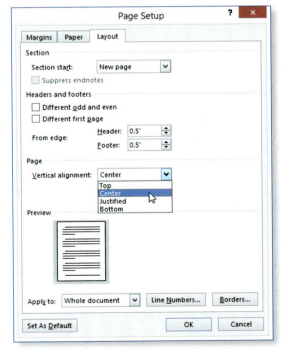

2-5 Change vertical alignment

Use the Ruler

Microsoft Word provides horizontal and vertical rulers that displays both the typing line length and the vertical typing space available in a document. The rulers are broken into 1/8" increments. Half-inch markers are longer vertical lines and inch markers are numerical. The typing area on the rulers is displayed in white, while the margin area is shaded (Figure 2-6).

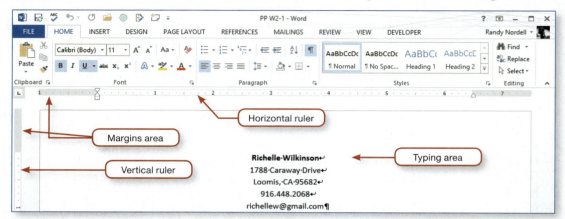

2-6 Horizontal and vertical rulers displayed

To display the rulers, select the **Ruler** check box on the *View* tab in the *Show* group. This check box toggles on and off the display of the rulers.

> **MORE INFO**
>
> The rulers are increasingly important and useful as you begin using tab stops, indents, columns, tables, and section breaks.

SLO 2.2

Setting, Using, and Editing Tab Stops

Tabs are useful tools that you can employ to control the alignment of text. A tab is often used to indent the first line of a paragraph. A ***tab stop*** is where your insertion point stops when you press the *Tab* key. Tabs can also be used, for example, to align text in columns, or to begin the date at the horizontal midpoint on a modified block business letter.

The five different types of tabs stops that you can set and use in your documents are described in the following table.

Types of Tab Stops

Type of Tab Stop	Description	Tab Stop Indicator	Tab Stop in Use
Left	Text is left aligned at the tab stop	⌞	Left tab
Center	Text is centered on the tab stop	⊥	Center tab
Right	Text is right aligned at the tab stop	⌟	Right tab
Decimal	Decimal point is aligned at the tab stop	⊥·	Decimal tab 620.50 8.375
Bar	A vertical bar (line) is inserted at the tab stop	I	There is a bar | tab between these words

Set Tabs Stops

Tabs are different from margins because tab stops apply to a paragraph or selected paragraphs rather than an entire document or sections of a document. This is important to keep in mind when setting, using, and editing tab stops.

You can set tab stops before text is typed, or you can set tab stops on existing text. If you open a *new* document and set a left tab stop at 3.25", that tab stop is set on the first line of the document and is set on each subsequent line and paragraph in the document.

On the other hand, if you open an *existing* document and set a tab stop on the first line, the tab stop is only set for that paragraph. When setting a tab stop on existing documents or text, remember to select all the text or paragraphs where you want the tab settings to apply.

There are two ways to set a tab stop in Word.

- *Tabs* dialog box
- Ruler

Use the Tabs Dialog Box to Set Tab Stops

The ***Tabs dialog box*** is an effective and easy method to set single or multiple tab stops. The *Tabs* dialog box is available from the *Paragraph* dialog box, which you can open from the *Paragraph* group on either the *Home* or *Page Layout* tabs.

EXPERIENCE¶

HEAD·TEACHER, ·LOOMIS·LEARNING·CENTER¶

Loomis, ·CA → October·2010-Present¶

Develop·and·implement·a·developmentally·appropriate·preschool the·ages·of·two·and·four·years.¶

2-7 Select text before setting tab stops

HOW TO: Set Tab Stops Using the Tabs Dialog Box

1. Select the text where you want to set a tab stop (Figure 2-7).
2. Click the **Home** tab.
3. Click the **Paragraph** launcher to open the *Paragraph* dialog box.
4. Click the **Tabs** button (Figure 2-8). The *Tabs* dialog box opens.
5. Click in the **Tab stop position** area and type the desired tab stop position.
6. In the *Alignment* area, select the type of tab stop radio button you want.
7. Click the **Set** button. The tab stop appears in the list of tab stops below the *Tab stop position* area (Figure 2-9).
8. Click **OK** to close the *Tabs* dialog box.
   - The tab stop is applied to the selected text.
   - The tab stop is visible on the ruler.

2-8 Tabs button in the Paragraph dialog box

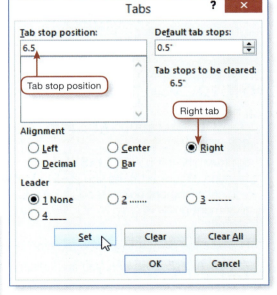

2-9 Set 6.5" right tab stop in the Tabs dialog box

> **MORE INFO**
>
> Set and use tab stops to line up and balance columns of text rather than pressing *Tab* multiple times between columns.

Use the Ruler to Set Tab Stops

Using the ruler to set tab stops is a quick way to add them to a document. You can also easily move or remove tab stops using the ruler. Use the *tab selector* to select the type of tab stop you want. The tab selector is located at the top of the vertical ruler on the left side of the Word window. When setting tab stops on an existing document, it is very important to select the text or paragraphs where you want the tab stop to apply before setting the tab stop.

HOW TO: Set Tab Stops Using the Ruler

1. Select the text where you want the new tab stop(s) to appear.
2. Click the **tab selector** to select the type of tab stop to apply (Figure 2-10).
3. Click the ruler to set a tab stop.
   - When setting tab stops using the ruler, click the bottom edge of the ruler to set a tab stop (Figure 2-11).

2-10 *Tab Selector* button

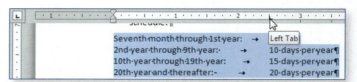

2-11 Set left tab stop at 2.5" on the ruler

> **MORE INFO**
>
> Use the *Format Painter* to copy tab stops from one area of your document to other areas.

Edit Tab Stops

Aligning text using tab stops can sometimes be tedious. It can be challenging to get text aligned correctly and balanced between columns. But as you set and use tab stop more regularly, you become more comfortable selecting the correct type of tab stop to use, adjusting the settings of existing tab stops, and removing tab stops. When using multiple columns, adjust tab stops so you have about the same amount of white space between columns.

Move Tab Stops

The easiest way to move tab stops is by using the ruler. When using the ruler to adjust a tab stop, be sure to select the appropriate text before moving a tab stop.

HOW TO: Move Tab Stops

1. Select the text or paragraphs where the tab stops you want to edit are set.
2. On the ruler, left click the **tab stop** and drag it to the new location (Figure 2-12). As you click the tab stop to be moved, a vertical alignment guide appears on your document. This alignment guide is used to help you see where your text is aligned.
3. Release the pointer to set the tab stop in the new location.
4. Repeat this process until you are satisfied with the placement of your tab stops.

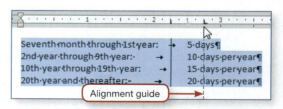

2-12 Move a tab stop using the ruler

> **ANOTHER WAY**
>
> Adjust tab stops in the *Tabs* dialog box by clearing an existing tab stop and setting a new tab stop.

If you hold down the **Alt** key when you are moving a tab stop, a different ruler appears that allows you to place the tab stop at a specific measurement (Figure 2-13).

2-13 Use the *Alt* key to adjust a tab stop

Remove Tab Stops

Occasionally, when setting tab stops using the ruler, you unintentionally add unwanted tab stops. Or sometimes you might just want to remove unwanted tab stops to clean up an existing document. It is very important to select the text or paragraphs where the tab stops you want to remove are before performing these actions. Following are three different ways to remove tab stops.

- Drag a tab stop off the ruler.
- Clear a single tab stop in the *Tabs* dialog box.
- Clear all tab stops in the *Tabs* dialog box.

To clear a single tab stop using the ruler, select the text or paragraphs, select the tab stop you want to remove, drag down below the ruler, and release the pointer.

When using the *Tabs* dialog box to remove tab stops, you can clear a single tab stop or clear all existing tab stops on the selected text or paragraphs.

HOW TO: Clear Tab Stops Using the Tabs Dialog Box

1. Select the text or paragraphs that contain the tab stops you want to remove.
2. Click the **Paragraph** launcher [*Home* or *Page Layout* tab] to open the *Paragraph* dialog box.
3. Click the **Tabs** button to open the *Tabs* dialog box.
4. To clear a single tab stop, select the tab stop to be cleared in the list of existing tab stops and click the **Clear** button (Figure 2-14). Repeat on any other tab stops you want to remove.
   - To clear all tab stops, click the **Clear All** button.
5. Click **OK** to close the *Tabs* dialog box.

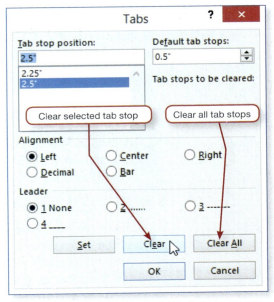

2-14 Clear tab stops in the *Tabs* dialog box

Tab Leaders

You can use **leaders** to insert dots or a line between information when using tab stops. The most common type of leader is the dot leader, which is regularly used in a table of contents. In a table of contents, a dot leader is inserted between the text and the right aligned page number. Leaders make it easier for readers to read across a line where there is a gap on the same line. Leaders can also be used to insert a dashed line in the blank space between columns or to create a solid underline when creating a printed form.

Word has three different types of leaders. Examples of each of these are in the following table.

Types of Leaders

Leader	Example of Use
Dot	Chapter 1 4
Dash	Vacation Days ------- 10 days per year
Solid Underline	Name _____

You can add leaders to existing or new tab stops, but they can only be added in the *Tabs* dialog box.

HOW TO: Add a Tab Leader

1. Select the text or paragraphs where you want to add a tab leader.
2. Click the **Paragraph** launcher [*Home* or *Page Layout* tab] to open the *Paragraph* dialog box.
3. Click the **Tabs** button to open the *Tabs* dialog box.
4. Select an existing tab stop or type in the *Tab stop position* text box for a new tab stop.
5. In the *Leader* area, select the type of leader to be applied.
6. Click **Set**. Figure 2-15 is an example of a dash leader.
7. Click **OK** to close the *Tabs* dialog box.

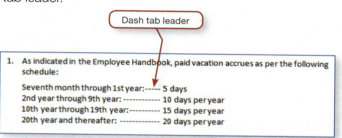

2-15 Tab stop with a dash leader

Change Default Tab Stops

By default, Word has a left tab stop every 0.5". When you set a tab stop in Word, this custom tab stop overrides all preceding default tab stops. The default tab stops after your custom tab stop still remain. For example, if you set a left tab stop at the horizontal midpoint (typically 3.25") and press *Tab* to move to the horizontal midpoint, your insertion point will move to the midpoint, not 0.5". But if you press *Tab* again, your insertion point will stop at the next default tab stop, which would be 3.5".

You can customize the default tab stops. If you change the default tab stop setting, this change affects only the document on which you are working, not all new documents.

HOW TO: Change Default Tab Stops

1. Click the **Paragraph** launcher [*Home* or *Page Layout* tab] to open the *Paragraph* dialog box.
2. Click the **Tabs** button to open the *Tabs* dialog box.
3. In the *Default tab stops* area, use the up or down arrow to change the default tab stops (Figure 2-16).
4. Click **OK** to close the *Tabs* dialog box.

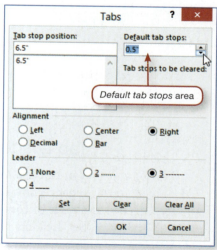

2-16 Change default tab stops

Using Indents

Indents are another powerful tool to help you control how text is arranged between the left and right margins. Indents can be thought of as temporary margins. You can use indents to indent the first line of each paragraph, set off a long quote in a report, or indent the carry-over lines when creating bulleted or numbered lists.

The four different types of indents that you can set and use in your document are described in the following table.

Types of Indents

Indent	Example of Use	Ruler Indent Marker
Left Indent	This line has a **left indent**.	Left Indent
Right Indent	This line has a **right indent**.	Right Indent
First Line Indent	This line has a **first line indent**.	First Line Indent
Hanging Indent	This line has a **hanging indent**.	Hanging Indent

Similar to setting tab stops, it is important to select the text where you want to apply the indent settings before applying the new settings. You can set indents using the ruler, the *Paragraph* group on the *Page Layout* tab, or the *Paragraph* dialog box.

Left and Right Indents

Indents are applied to paragraphs, not just lines of text within a paragraph. When setting an indent, select the text or paragraphs on which to apply the indent. If your insertion point is in a paragraph, the indent you set is applied to that paragraph only.

HOW TO: Set a Left and Right Indent

1. Select the text or paragraph where you want to apply the indent. If it is just one paragraph, place your insertion point in that paragraph.
2. Click the **Page Layout** tab.
3. Change the *Left* and *Right* indent settings [*Paragraph* group]. This change is applied to the selected text (Figure 2-17).

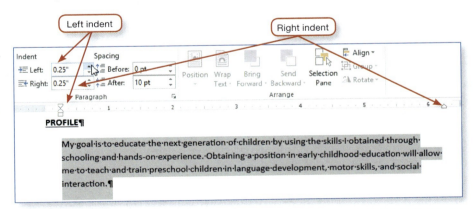

2-17 Change left and right indents

When an indent is set on a paragraph and you press *Enter* at the end of the paragraph, the indent carries over to the next paragraph.

Indents can also be set using the ruler by dragging the indent marker to the desired location after you select the text you want to indent. As you drag the indent marker, an alignment guide appears to display where your text aligns.

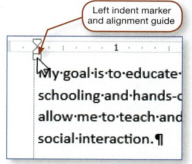

2-18 **Change left indent using the ruler**

HOW TO: Use the Ruler to Set Indents

1. Select the text or paragraph you want to indent. If it is just one paragraph, place your insertion point in that paragraph.
2. Left click the **left indent marker**, drag to the desired location, and release the pointer. The left indent is applied to the text (Figure 2-18).
3. Left click the **right indent marker**, drag to the desired location, and release the pointer. The right indent is applied to the text (Figure 2-19).

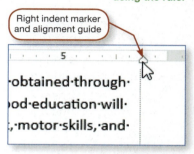

2-19 **Change right indent using the ruler**

ANOTHER WAY

Set left and right indents using the *Paragraph* dialog box. Click the **Paragraph** launcher to open the *Paragraph* dialog box.

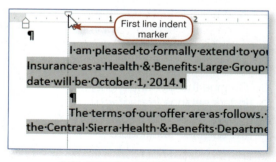

2-20 *Decrease Indent* and *Increase Indent* **buttons**

The **Decrease Indent** and **Increase Indent** buttons in the *Paragraph* group on the *Home* tab increase or decrease the left indent in increments of 0.5" (Figure 2-20). Remove a left indent by clicking at the beginning of the paragraph and pressing **Backspace**.

First Line and Hanging Indents

You can use *first line indents* to indent the first line of a paragraph instead of using a tab. *Hanging indents* are typically used with bulleted and numbered lists but can be used effectively to indent text that wraps to a second or more lines.

When using the ruler to set a first line indent, select the text or paragraph you want to indent and drag the first line indent marker to the desired location (Figure 2-21). The alignment guide displays where the first line of each paragraph will align.

2-21 **Set a first line indent using the ruler**

To set a hanging indent, select the text or paragraph on which to apply the indent and drag the hanging indent marker to the desired location (Figure 2-22). The alignment guide displays where the carryover lines of the paragraph will align.

You can use the *Paragraph* dialog box to set either a first line or a hanging indent.

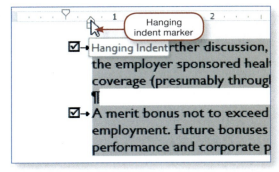

2-22 Set a hanging indent using the ruler

HOW TO: Set a First Line or a Hanging Indent Using the Paragraph Dialog Box

1. Select the text or paragraph you want to indent.
2. Click the **Paragraph** launcher [*Home* or *Page Layout* tab] to open the *Paragraph* dialog box.
3. Click the **Special** drop-down list in the *Indentation* area and choose the type of indent (Figure 2-23).
4. In the *By* area, either type the indent amount or use the up or down buttons to increase or decrease the amount of the indent.
   - The *Preview* area displays how the text will look with the indent applied.
5. Click **OK** to close the *Paragraph* dialog box.

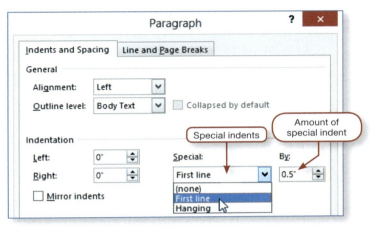

2-23 Set first line or hanging indent using the *Paragraph* dialog box

An ***outdent*** can be used to line up information outside the left or right margins. Outdents are sometimes used to set off section headings so they are slightly to the left of the left margin. You can do this by setting a ***negative value*** (–0.25") in the indents area in the *Paragraph* dialog box or *Paragraph* group on the *Page Layout* tab or by dragging the indent marker outside of the left or right margins.

Remove Indents

Removing indents moves the indent markers back to either the left or right margin, so the margins control the alignment of text rather than the indents. Remember to select the paragraph or paragraphs before removing the indents. You can remove indents using the *Paragraph* dialog box or the *Paragraph* group on the *Page Layout* tab. When using either of these methods, set the indents value to 0" (Figure 2-24).

The ruler can also be used to remove indents. When using this method, select the text or paragraphs on which to remove the indents, and drag the indent marker(s) to the margin.

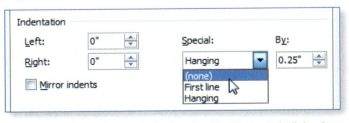

2-24 Remove indents using the *Paragraph* dialog box

In this Pause & Practice project, you format a resume for Richelle Wilkinson. This resume is a two-page document, and you change the margins, set tab stops and leaders, and use indents.

File Needed: **Resume-02.docx**
Completed Project File Name: **[your initials] PP W2-1.docx**

1. Open the **Resume-02** document in your student data files.

2. Save this document as **[your initials] PP W2-1.**

3. Change the margins of the resume.
   a. Click the **Page Layout** tab.
   b. Click the **Margins** button [*Page Setup* group]. A drop-down list appears.
   c. Select **Custom Margins** at the bottom of the list. The **Page Setup** dialog box opens.
   d. In the *Margins* area (Figure 2-25), click in the *Top* box, delete the existing margin, and type .75.
   e. Click in the *Bottom* box, delete the existing margin, and type .75.
   f. Click the **down arrow** to the right of the *Left* box to change the left margin to **1"**.
   g. Click the **down arrow** to the right of the *Right* box to change the right margin to **1"**.
   h. Click the **Apply to** drop-down list at the bottom of the dialog box and select **Whole document**.
   i. Click **OK** to apply the new margin settings and close the dialog box.

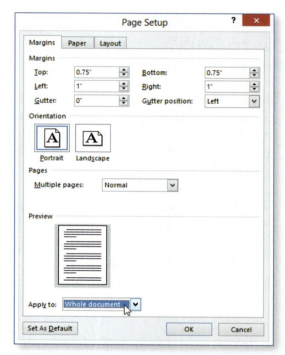

2-25 Change margins in the *Page Setup* dialog box

4. Set a right tab stop with a dash leader.
   a. Select **"Loomis, CA October 2011Present"** below *"Head Teacher, Loomis Learning Center."*
   b. Click the **Paragraph** launcher [*Page Layout or Home* tab]. The *Paragraph* dialog box opens.
   c. Click the **Tabs** button in the bottom left of the *Paragraph* dialog box. The *Tabs* dialog box opens (Figure 2-26).
   d. In the *Tab stop position* area, type 6.5.
   e. In the *Alignment* area, click the **Right** radio button.
   f. In the *Leader* area, click the **3** (dash leader) radio button.
   g. Click the **Set** button to set this tab stop and leader.
   h. Click the **OK** button to close the dialog box.

5. Use the *Format Painter* to apply the tab setting to multiple areas of the resume.
   a. Place the insertion point somewhere in the line you just formatted.
   b. Double-click the **Format Painter** button [*Home* tab, *Clipboard* group].

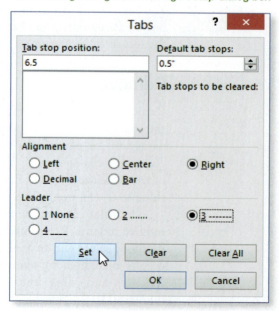

2-26 Set a right tab stop with a dash leader

c. Click each of the city/date lines in the "Experience" and "Education" sections to apply the tab settings to these lines as shown in Figure 2-27.

d. Click the **Format Painter** button to turn it off.

6. Remove an existing tab stop and set a left tab stop.
   a. On the second page, select the lines of text below the "References" heading.
   b. Click the **Paragraph** launcher [*Page Layout* or *Home* tab] to open the *Paragraph* dialog box.
   c. Click the **Tabs** button in the bottom left of the *Paragraph* dialog box. The *Tabs* dialog box opens (Figure 2-28).
   d. In the *Tab stop position* area, select the existing tab stop and click the **Clear** button to remove the existing tab.
   e. In the *Tab stop position* area, type 3.75.
   f. In the *Alignment* area, click the **Left** radio button.
   g. In the *Leader* area, click the **1 None** radio button.
   h. Click the **Set** button to set this left tab stop.
   i. Click the **OK** button to close the dialog box.

2-27 Use the *Format Painter* to apply tab settings

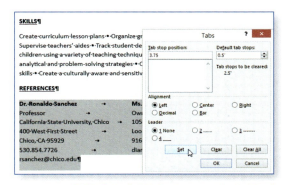

2-28 Set a left tab stop on selected text

7. Apply a left and right indent to selected text.
   a. Place the insertion point in the paragraph below the "Profile" heading on the first page.
   b. Click the **Page Layout** tab.
   c. Click in the **Left** indent area [*Paragraph* group], type .25, and press **Enter**.
   d. Click in the **Right** indent area, type .25, and press **Enter**.

8. Save and close this document (Figure 2-29).

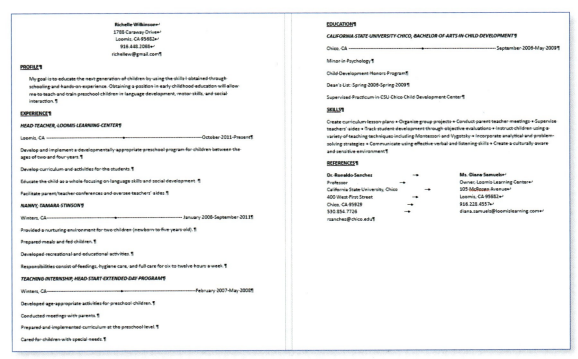

2-29 PP W2-1 completed

Inserting Page Numbers, Headers, and Footers

Page numbering, **headers,** and **footers** are regularly used in multiple-page documents. You can set the header and footer information to appear on each page of the document, which means you only have to type the information once, and Word repeats that information on each of the subsequent pages. The header area of a document is above the top margin, and the footer is below the bottom margin.

Page Numbering

When you use Word to insert page numbers, a ***page number field*** is inserted in the header or footer of the document. This page number field automatically displays the current page number. You can control where the page number is placed and the page number format.

Insert Page Number

Word gives you a variety of page number locations, horizontal alignment options, and number format options. The following is a list of the basic page number placement options.

- Top of Page
- Bottom of Page
- Page Margins
- Current Position

Page numbers at the top or bottom of the document can be aligned at the left, center, or right.

HOW TO: Insert a Page Number

1. Click the **Insert** tab.
2. Click the **Page Number** button [*Header & Footer* group]. A drop-down list of options appears (Figure 2-30).
3. Click either **Top of Page** or **Bottom of Page**. Another drop-down list of page number options appears.
   - The top three options in this list are simple page numbers aligned at the left, center, or right.
   - Further down this list there are custom page number options.
4. Click one of the page number options to insert the current page number. The header and footer open with the page number inserted, and the *Headers & Footer Tools Design* tab opens (Figure 2-31).
5. Click the **Close Header and Footer** button [*Close* group].

2-30 Insert page number

> ▸ **ANOTHER WAY**
>
> Close the header and footer by **double-clicking** in the body of the document.

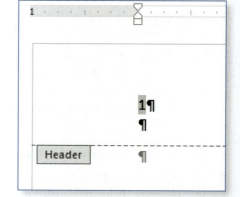

2-31 Page number inserted in the header on the left

When you close the header and footer, the page number appears in gray rather than black like the text of the document. The header and footer are outside the boundaries of the margins. If you want to edit the page number or contents of the header and footer, you have to open the header and footer. There are three ways to do this.

- Double-click in the header or footer area of the document.
- Click the **Insert** tab, click the **Header** or **Footer** button in the *Header & Footer* group, and choose **Edit Header** or **Edit Footer**.
- Right-click the header or footer and select **Edit Header** or **Edit Footer**.

Different First Page

There are times when you might not want the page number and header or footer to print on the first page, but you want it to appear on the second and continuing pages. For example on both multiple-page business letters and reports, the page number is typically not on the first page but is on the second and subsequent pages. Word gives you the option to set a *different first page*.

HOW TO: Set a Different First Page Header and Footer

1. After inserting a page number in the header or footer, open the header and footer if it is not already open.
2. Click the **Different First Page** check box [*Options* group] (Figure 2-32).
3. Click the **Close Header and Footer** button [*Close* group]. The page number, header, and footer no longer appear on the first page but do appear on the second and continuing pages.

2-32 ***Different First Page* option check box**

> ### MORE INFO
>
> When inserting a page number, header, or footer, it is best to insert it on the first page of the document. This becomes increasingly important as you add section breaks to a document.

Page Number Format

When using page numbering, you might want a different type of page number format, numbering to begin with a different page number, or a chapter number before the page number. The *Page Number Format* dialog box provides you with page numbering options (Figure 2-33).

HOW TO: Format Page Numbers

1. After inserting a page number, click the **Page Number** button [*Insert* tab, *Header & Footer* group].
2. From the drop-down list, select **Format Page Numbers**. The *Page Number Format* dialog box opens (Figure 2-33).
3. In the *Number format* area, click the **drop-down list** and select a page number format. There are six preset page numbering options from which to choose.
4. In the *Page numbering* section, you have the option to *Continue from previous section* (default setting) or *Start at* a different page number.
5. Click the **Start at** radio button to set a different starting page number.
6. Type in the starting page number or use the up or down arrow to set the starting page number.
7. Click **OK** to close the *Page Number Format* dialog box.

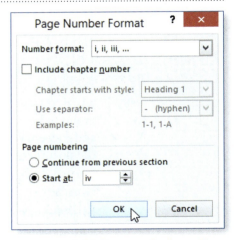

2-33 **Page numbering options**

Remove Page Number

If you want to remove the page numbering from a document, there are two different ways to do this.

- Open the header and footer and manually delete the page number.
- Select **Remove Page Numbers** from the *Page Numbers* drop-down list (Figure 2-34).

Insert Header and Footer Content

In addition to inserting page numbers into the header or footer of a document, you might want to include the number of pages in the document, date or time, title of the document, or company name. You can enter information manually into the header or footer, or you can have Word insert document property fields.

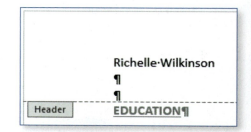

2-34 Remove page numbers

HOW TO: Manually Enter Information in the Header or Footer

1. Click the **Insert** tab.
2. Click the **Header** button and choose **Edit Header** in the drop-down list, or double-click in the *Header* area of the document (above the top margin). The header of the document opens and the *Header & Footer Tools Design* tab is displayed.
3. In the *Header* area, type in your information (Figure 2-35).
   - You can change the formatting and alignment as desired.
   - You can insert a page number with the header or footer open.
4. Close the header.

Richelle·Wilkinson
¶
¶
Header   **EDUCATION**¶

2-35 Manually enter information in the header

> **MORE INFO**
>
> In the header and footer, there is a center tab stop at the horizontal midpoint and a right tab stop at the right margin. You can move these tab stops, remove them, or add additional tab stops.

When you edit a header or footer, both the header and footer open and the *Header & Footer Tools Design* tab is displayed. On this tab, there is a *Navigation* group to help you move between the header and footer and move through the different headers and footers in the document (Figure 2-36).

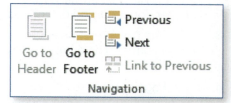

2-36 *Navigation* group in the *Header & Footer Tools Design* tab

Number of Pages Field

In addition to inserting the current page number in a document, you can add a field code to automatically insert the total number of pages in a document (*NumPages* field).

HOW TO: Insert the Number of Pages Field

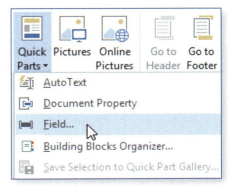

1. Open the header or footer. The page number should already be inserted in the document.

2. Click before the page number, type Page, and press **spacebar**.

3. Click after the page number and press **spacebar**, type of, and press **spacebar**.

4. Click the **Quick Parts** button [*Header & Footer Tools Design* tab, *Insert* group] (Figure 2-37).

5. Select **Field** from the drop-down list. The *Field* dialog box opens (Figure 2-38).

2-37 Insert field code

6. In the *Field names* area, scroll down and select **NumPages**. The description of the field is displayed in the *Description* area.

7. In the *Format* area, click **1**, **2**, **3**. This is the format of the page number.

8. Click **OK** to close the *Field* dialog box. The number of pages in the document is inserted (Figure 2-39).

9. Close the header or footer.

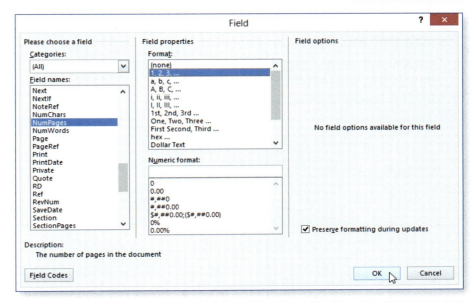

2-38 Insert *NumPages* field from the *Field* dialog box

> **MORE INFO**
>
> When inserting text before or after a page number, be sure to include a space between the word and the page number. Word does not automatically do this for you.

2-39 Page number and number of pages fields inserted into the header

Date and Time

You can type a date or the time in the header or footer of a document, or you can have Word insert this information. The advantages of inserting the date and time are that you have a variety of date and time formats from which to choose, and you can choose to have the date and time update automatically.

HOW TO: Insert the Date and Time

1. Open the header or footer and position the insertion point at the position where you want the date inserted.

2. Click the **Date & Time** button [*Header & Footer Tools Design* tab, *Insert* group]. The *Date and Time* dialog box opens (Figure 2-40).

3. In the *Available formats* area, select the date or time format to use

4. If you want the date to update automatically, check the **Update automatically** check box.

   • Don't use the *Update automatically* on time-sensitive documents where the date should remain constant.

5. Click **OK** to close the *Date and Time* dialog box. The date is inserted into the header.

6. Close the header or footer.

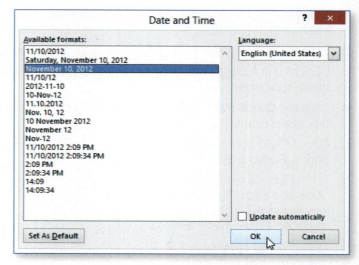

2-40 *Date and Time* **dialog box**

> ### MORE INFO
>
> Inserting a date or time is not limited to headers and footers. You can insert the date or time in the body of a document by clicking **Date & Time** [*Insert* tab, *Text* group].

Document Properties

When you have entered document properties in a Word document, you can automatically insert this information in the header or footer. For example, you might want to include the title of the document, name of the author, or date last modified. One of the advantages of inserting document properties rather than typing this information is that when you update the document properties, these fields are automatically updated in the header or footer and throughout the document.

HOW TO: Insert Document Properties

1. Open the header or footer and place the insertion point at the location where you want the document property inserted.

2. Click the **Document Info** button [*Header & Footer Tools Design* tab, *Insert* group] (Figure 2-41).

3. Select the document property field or click **Document Property** and select the document property field of your choice from the drop-down list. The document property field is inserted in the document.

   • You can also click the **Quick Parts** button [*Header & Footer Tools Design* tab, *Insert* group] and select **Document Property**.

4. Close the header or footer.

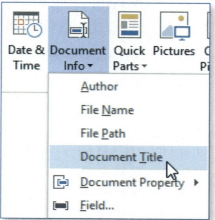

2-41 **Insert document property field**

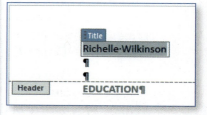

2-42 *Title* **document property field inserted in the header**

Built-In Headers, Footers, and Page Numbers

In addition to inserting basic page numbers, manually adding header or footer content, and inserting date and time, Word provides you with a variety of built-in custom header, footer, and page number format options. Many of the header and footer options include document properties that are automatically inserted and updated.

HOW TO: Insert a Built-In Header

1. Click the **Insert** tab.
2. Click the **Header** button [*Header & Footer* group] and select a built-in header from the choices in the drop-down list. (Figure 2-43) The selected header is inserted into the document.
   - Document property fields are automatically updated with the document information.
   - Some fields, such as *Pick the date,* require you to input or select information.
3. Close the header.

2-43 List of built-in headers

Keep in mind when you are using built-in headers, footers, and page numbers that many of these use tables, graphics, and advanced formatting, which makes editing more challenging without a thorough understanding of this type of content.

PAUSE & PRACTICE: WORD 2-2

In this Pause & Practice project, you modify the resume from *Pause & Practice 2-1*. You add a header that appears only on the second page of this document and insert a document property field, page number, and Word field into the header.

File Needed: ***[your initials] PP W2-1.docx***
Completed Project File Name: ***[your initials] PP W2-2.docx***

1. Open the ***[your initials] PP W2-1*** document created in *Pause & Practice 2-1*.
2. Save this document as ***[your initials] PP W2-2***.

3. Edit the document properties.
   a. Click the **File** tab to open the *Backstage* view.
   b. In the *Info* area, click in the *Title* document property text box and type Richelle Wilkinson.
   c. Click the **Back** arrow to return to the resume.

4. Insert a document property field in the header of the resume.
   a. Place the insertion point at the beginning of the first page.
   b. Click the **Insert** tab.
   c. Click the **Header** button [*Header & Footer* group], and select **Edit Header** from the drop-down list. The header on the first page opens.
   d. Click the **Quick Parts** button [*Header & Footer Tools Design* tab, *Insert* group], select **Document Property**, and select **Title** from the drop-down list.
   e. Press the **right arrow** key once to deselect the document property field you just inserted.
   f. Press **Tab** two times to move to the right margin.
   g. Type Page and **space** once. Leave the header open.

5. Insert a page number and number of pages field to the header and make it display only on the second page.
   a. With the header still open, click the **Page Number** button [*Header & Footer* group].
   b. From the drop-down list, select **Current Position**, and then select **Plain Number**. The page number is inserted.
   c. **Space** once, type of, and **space** once.
   d. Click the **Quick Parts** button [*Header & Footer Tools Design* tab, *Insert* group] and select **Field** from the drop-down list. The *Field* dialog box opens (Figure 2-44).
   e. In the *Field names* area, scroll down and select **NumPages**. This is a field code to insert the total number of pages in the document.
   f. In the *Format* area, select **1, 2, 3**.
   g. Click **OK** to insert the number of pages in the header.
   h. Press **Enter** two times to insert two blank lines after the header.
   i. Check to ensure that there are spaces between each of the words and page numbers.
   j. Check the **Different First Page** check box [*Options* group]. This removes the page number from the first page; the page number is still displayed on the second and subsequent pages (Figure 2-45).

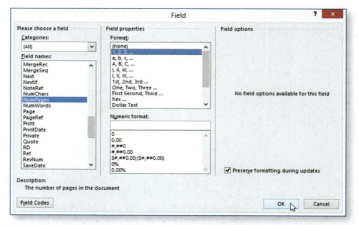

2-44 Insert *NumPages* field

2-45 Header with custom text, page number, and number of pages

   k. Click the **Close Header and Footer** button [*Close* group] to close the header and return to the document.

6. Save and close the document (Figure 2-46).

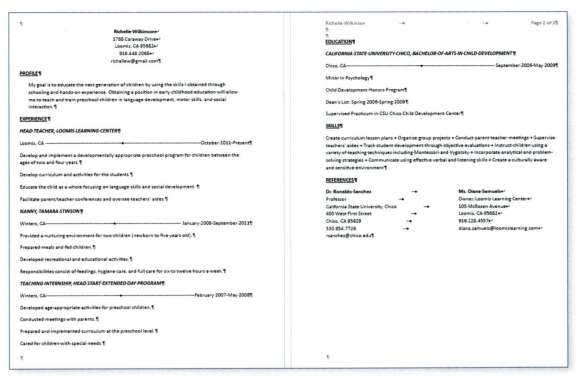

2-46 PP W2-2 completed

Using Page and Section Breaks

As you're typing a document and you get to the bottom of the page, Word automatically moves to the top of the next page so you can continue typing; this is referred to as a *soft page break.* The document's content and margins determine how much information fits on a page and what information flows to a new page.

There may be times when you want to start a new page before you get to the bottom margin or you might want different margins or page orientation in a different section of your document. When this happens, Word provides options for page and section breaks (Figure 2-47).

> **MORE INFO**
>
> Turn **Show/Hide** [*Home* tab, *Paragraph* group] on when working with page and section breaks, so you can view the placement of these breaks.

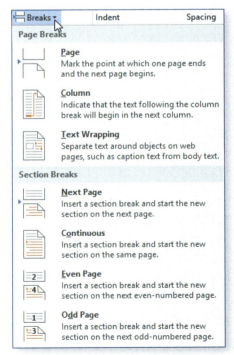

2-47 Page and section breaks

Page Breaks

Page breaks end one page and begin a new page. When you insert page breaks, you, rather than the margins, control where one page ends and a new page begins. There are three different types of page breaks: *Page*, *Column*, and *Text Wrapping*.

HOW TO: Insert a Page Break

1. Position the insertion point at the point in your document where you want to end one page and begin a new page.
2. Click the **Page Layout** tab.
3. Click the **Breaks** button [*Page Setup* group]. A drop-down list appears (Figure 2-48).
4. Select **Page** from the drop-down list. A page break is inserted in the document.
   - Make sure *Show/Hide* [*Home* tab, *Paragraph* group] is turned on.
   - The *Page Break* indicator is visible and displays where the page breaks (Figure 2-49).

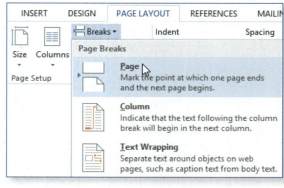

2-48 Insert page break

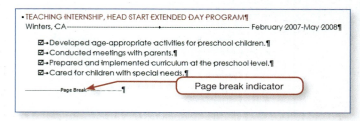

2-49 Page break inserted in a document

> **ANOTHER WAY**
>
> Press **Ctrl+Enter** to insert a page break at the insertion point.

Section Breaks

Section breaks allow you even more formatting control over your document than page breaks. Section breaks can be used to format different headers, footers, and page numbering in different sections of your document. For example, if you want one page in your document to be landscape orientation, you can use a section break to control this. There are four different types of section breaks: *Next Page*, *Continuous*, *Even Page*, and *Odd Page*.

HOW TO: Insert a Next Page Section Break

1. Position the insertion point at the point in your document where you want to end one page and begin a new page.
2. Click the **Page Layout** tab.
3. Click the **Breaks** button [*Page Setup* group]. A drop-down list appears.
4. Select **Next Page** from the drop-down list. A next page section break is inserted in the document.
   - Make sure *Show/Hide* [*Home* tab, *Paragraph* group] is turned on.
   - The *Section Break (Next Page)* indicator is visible and displays where the next page section break occurs (Figure 2-50).

2-50 *Next Page* section break inserted in a document

Edit Page and Section Breaks

When finalizing a document, you might need to change the placement of a page or section break or remove one or more of these from the document. You can move and delete breaks in the same way you move or delete text from a document.

There are two different ways to move a section or page break to a new location. First select the **Page Break** or **Section Break**, and then use one of the move options below.

- Cut and paste
- Drag and drop (Figure 2-51)

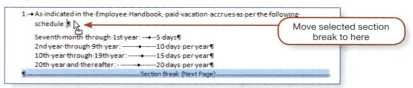

1.→ As·indicated·in·the·Employee·Handbook,·paid·vacation·accrues·as·per·the·following·
schedule:¶

Seventh·month·through·1st·year: →·····→·5·days¶
2nd·year·through·9th·year: ·······→·······10·days·per·year¶
10th·year·through·19th·year: ·····→·······15·days·per·year¶
20th·year·and·thereafter: ·········→·······20·days·per·year¶
¶ ···Section·Break·(Next·Page)································

Move selected section break to here

2.51 Move section break using drag and drop

To delete a page or section break, select the break and press **Delete**.

SLO 2.6

Using Bulleted and Numbered Lists

Bulleted and *numbered lists* highlight important information. Generally, bulleted lists are used when the order of information is not important, while numbered lists are used for sequential information. Word provides you with automatic bulleted and numbered lists, but you can also customize how your list information is displayed and aligned.

> ### MORE INFO
>
> When using bulleted and numbered lists, do not use a period at the end of lists containing only words or short phrases. If you are using complete sentences in your list, use a period at the end of each sentence.

Create Bulleted Lists

You can create a bulleted list from existing text or you can create a new bulleted list. When you turn on bullets, you choose the type of bullet to use from a library of bullet options.

HOW TO: Create a Bulleted List

1. Select the text to be converted to a bulleted list, or, if you are beginning a new bulleted list, place the insertion point at the location where you want to begin the list.

2. Click the **Home** tab.

3. Click the **Bullets** drop-down arrow [*Paragraph* group] to open the library of bullet options (Figure 2-52).
   - If you click the *Bullets* button, the most recently used bullet will be applied.

4. Select the bullet to be used from the list of options.

5. Type your information after the bullet.

6. Press **Enter** to add another bullet.

7. Click the **Bullet** button to turn off bullets or press **Enter** two times after the last bullet.

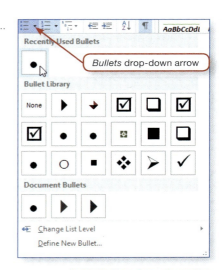

Bullets drop-down arrow

2-52 Bullets drop-down list

By default, bulleted lists are formatted using a hanging indent. The first line is indented 0.25" and the hanging indent is set at 0.5". You can adjust the indent using the *Decrease Indent* or *Increase Indent* buttons, ruler, or *Paragraph* dialog box.

You can add new bulleted items in the middle or at the end of the list by pressing **Enter** in front of or at the end of an existing bulleted item. To add a bulleted item before the first item in the list, click at the beginning of the first item and press **Enter**.

> ▶ **MORE INFO**
>
> You can use a line break (**Shift+Enter**) at the end of a bulleted sentence to add a blank line between bulleted items.

Customize Bullets

In addition to using the bullets listed in the bullets library, you can select and use a custom bullet. You have the option of using a symbol from one of the font groups or you can use a picture. If you are using a picture, you can select one from the picture library or import a graphic of your own to use as a bullet.

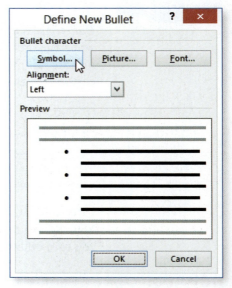

2-53 *Define New Bullet dialog box*

HOW TO: Use Custom Bullets

1. Click the **Bullets** drop-down arrow [*Home* tab, *Paragraph* group] and select **Define New Bullet**. The *Define New Bullet* dialog box opens (Figure 2-53).

2. Click the **Symbol** or **Picture** button to open the *Symbol* or *Picture Bullet* dialog box.
   - If you click the **Symbol** button, the *Symbol* dialog box opens (Figure 2-54). You can select a symbol from any of the font sets (the most common are *Symbol, Wingdings,* and *Webdings*) or from *Recently used symbols*.
   - If you click the **Picture** button, the *Insert Pictures* dialog box opens. You can import your own picture bullet from a file or search Office.com or Bing for a picture to use as a bullet.

3. Select the bullet to use and click **OK** (or **Insert** or **Open** depending on the open dialog box) to close the dialog box.

4. Click **OK** to close the *Define New Bullet* dialog box.

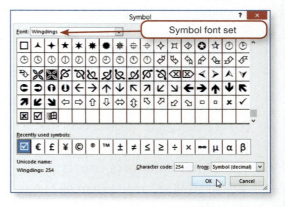

2-54 *Symbol dialog box*

You also have the option of having multiple levels of bullets with a different bullet for each level. Each subsequent level of bullet is indented to distinguish it from the previous level. There are a few ways to increase or decrease the bullet level.

- Click the **Bullets** drop-down arrow [*Home* tab, *Paragraph* group], and select a bullet list level from the **Change List Level** drop-down list (Figure 2-55).
- Select or click at the beginning of a bulleted item, and press **Tab** to increase bullet level.
- Select or click at the beginning of a bulleted item and click the **Increase Indent** button [*Home* tab, *Paragraph* group] to increase bullet level.

2-55 Change bulleted list level

> ▶ **MORE INFO**
>
> **Shift+Tab** or **Decrease Indent** decreases the bullet level.

Create Numbered Lists

Creating a numbered list is similar to creating a bulleted list. There is a ***Numbering Library*** that contains number format options.

HOW TO: Create a Numbered List

1. Select the text you want to convert to a numbered list, or, if you are beginning a new numbered list, place the insertion point at the location where you want to begin the list.
2. Click the **Home** tab.
3. Click the **Numbering** drop-down arrow [*Paragraph* group] to open the *Numbering Library* of number format options (Figure 2-56).
   - If you click the *Numbering* button, the most recently used number format is applied.
4. Select the number format to be used from the list of options. The number format is applied to selected text.

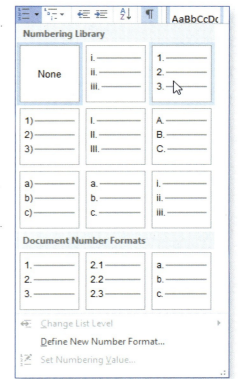

2-56 Number format options

> ▶ **ANOTHER WAY**
>
> Both the *Numbering* and *Bullets* drop-down lists are available from the context menu.

Customize Numbering

In addition to being able to select a format from the *Numbering Library*, you also have the options to *Change List Level*, *Define New Number Format*, and *Set Numbering Value*.

The *Change List Level* option in the *Numbering* drop-down list allows you to select the level of the list. The numbering of each subsequent level of the list is dependent upon the number format you select.

You are not limited to the numbering formats available in the *Numbering* drop-down list. The *Define New Number Format* option allows you to customize how the numbered list is displayed.

HOW TO: Define New Number Format

1. Select the text where you want to change the number format, or, if you are beginning a new numbered list, place the insertion point at the location where you want to begin the list.

2. Click the **Numbering** drop-down arrow [*Home* tab, *Paragraph* group], and select **Define New Number Format**. The *Define New Number Format* dialog box opens (Figure 2-57).

3. In the *Number style* area, you can select from a list of number format options. You can also change the font of the numbering.

4. In the *Number format* area, you can customize how the numbers are displayed. Typically, a period follows the numbers, but you can change this to an ending parenthesis, hyphen, other character, or nothing.

5. Numbers are aligned at the left by default, but you can change the number alignment to center or right in the *Alignment* area.

6. The *Preview* area displays how your number format will appear in your document.

7. Click **OK** to apply the number format and close the dialog box.

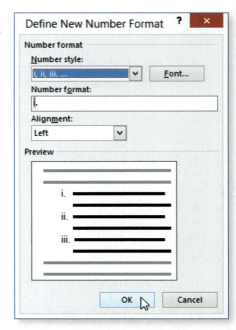

2-57 *Define New Number Format* **dialog box**

The *Set Numbering Value* option allows you to *Start new list* or *Continue from previous list*. You can also set the number value to begin a new list. The *Set Numbering Value* dialog box can be opened from the *Numbering* drop-down list or from the context menu (Figure 2-58).

When using numbering, the context menu gives you the options to *Adjust List Indents*, *Restart at 1*, *Continue Numbering*, and *Set Numbering Value* (Figure 2-59).

2-58 *Set Numbering Value* **dialog box**

> **MORE INFO**
>
> Use the *Format Painter* to copy numbered or bulleted list formatting to other areas in a document.

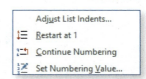

2-59 **Context menu numbering options**

Multilevel Lists

Multilevel lists allow you to customize a list using a combination of numbers, letters, or bullets. Word provides you with a *List Library* from which to select a multilevel list. You can customize an existing multilevel list or you can define your own.

As you define a new multilevel list, you have the option to make the following customizations on each level of the list.

- Number format including font and starting number
- Number style, which can be a number, letter, Roman numeral, or bullet
- Position of the number and the text that follows

HOW TO: Define a New Multilevel List

1. Select the text or the beginning point on which to apply a multilevel list.

2. Click the **Multilevel List** button [*Home* tab, *Paragraph* group].

3. From the drop-down list, select **Define new Multilevel list**. The *Define new Multilevel list* dialog box opens (Figure 2-60).

4. Click the **More** button at the bottom left of the dialog box to display all formatting options.

5. In the *Click level to modify* area, select the level you want to modify.

6. In the *Number format* area, select the number format, starting number, and number style for the selected level.

7. In the *Position* area, set the number alignment, the position at which the number is aligned, and the position of the text indent (which is a hanging indent).

8. The **Set for All Levels** button opens a dialog box that allows you to set the indents for all levels.

9. Click **OK** to apply the multilevel list settings.

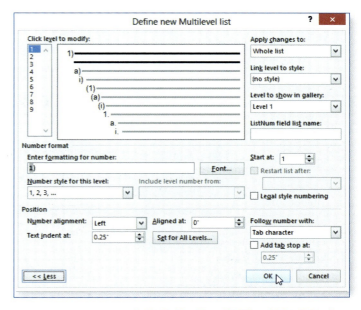

2-60 *Define New Multilevel List* dialog box

SLO 2.7 — Using Styles and Themes

Styles are a collection of preset formatting that you can apply to selected text. You can use styles to apply preset formatting to titles, section headings, paragraph headings, text, lists, and tables. *Themes* are a collection of fonts, colors, and effects that you can apply to an entire document. Both styles and themes keep the formatting consistent throughout a single document or multiple documents.

Style Gallery

The *Style gallery* in the *Styles* group on the *Home* tab provides you with numerous built-in styles to apply to selected text in a document (Figure 2-61). The *Style* gallery does not display all of the available styles but rather a list of the more commonly used styles.

2-61 *Style* gallery

Apply Built-In Styles

You can quickly preview or apply styles to selected text or paragraphs. To preview a style, put the pointer on a style in the *Style* gallery. A live preview of the style is displayed on the selected text or paragraph. You can apply a style to the text by clicking a style.

HOW TO: Use the Style Gallery

1. Select the text or paragraph where you want to apply the style.

2. From the *Style* gallery [*Home* tab, *Styles* group], select a style to apply to the text.
   - To see the second row of styles available in the *Style* gallery, click the **down arrow** at the right side of the gallery (Figure 2-62).
   - To see all of the styles in the *Style* gallery, click the **More** button.

More button

Click to display next row

2-62 Display more styles

Edit Styles

A style is a collection of fonts, font sizes, styles, color, effects, indents, line spacing, paragraph spacing, and borders. Once a style has been applied to the text, you can change the formatting of this text. One way to do this is to make changes to font, font size, color, style, effects, etc. to the selected text without actually changing the style. The other option you have is to modify the style. The advantage of modifying a style when you make a change is that the style will be consistent when applied to text in a document. When a style is modified, existing text with that style applied is automatically updated to match the modified style.

There are two ways to modify a style.

- Update style to match selection
- Modify style

HOW TO: Update Style to Match Selection

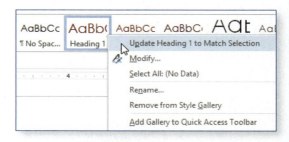

1. Apply a style to selected text.
2. Make the desired changes to the text where the style was applied.
3. Select the text that you changed.
4. Right-click the style in the *Style* gallery and choose **Update [name of style] to Match Selection** (Figure 2-63).

2-63 Update style from the *Style* gallery

You can also modify a style using the *Modify Style* dialog box.

HOW TO: Modify an Existing Style

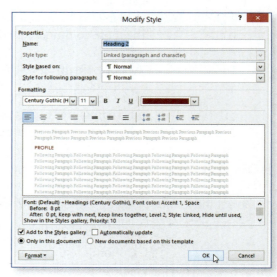

1. Right-click the style to modify in the *Style* gallery and select **Modify**. The *Modify Style* dialog box opens (Figure 2-64).
2. Make desired changes to the style. You can make basic formatting changes from this dialog box.
   - Click the **Format** button to open other dialog boxes, such as *Font, Paragraph, Tabs, Borders,* etc.
   - Click **OK** to apply changes from another dialog box.
   - The formatting changes are shown and described in the *Preview* area.
3. Click **OK** to apply the style change and close the *Modify Style* dialog box.

2-64 *Modify Style* dialog box

Apply Themes

A theme is a collection of fonts, colors, and effects. Themes are similar to styles, but instead of applying to just selected text, themes apply to an entire document. All documents have a theme; the default theme for a new document is *Office*. You can change the theme of a document or you can individually change the colors, fonts, or effects set in a document.

HOW TO: Change the Document Theme

1. Click the **Design** tab.
2. Click the **Themes** button [*Document Formatting* group].
3. From the *Themes* gallery, select the theme to be applied (Figure 2-65).
4. You can also click the **Colors**, **Fonts**, or **Effects** buttons to change each of these individually within the existing theme.

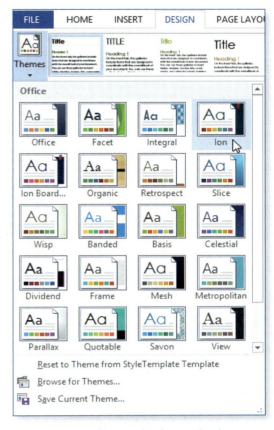

2-65 Change the theme of a document

PAUSE & PRACTICE: WORD 2-3

In this Pause & Practice project, you modify the resume you edited in *Pause & Practice 2-2*. You add a bulleted list, customize the bulleted list, insert a page break, apply and modify styles, and apply a document theme.

File Needed: *[your initials] PP W2-2.docx*
Completed Project File Name: *[your initials] PP W2-3.docx*

---

1. Open the *[your initials] PP W2-2* document created in *Pause & Practice 2-2*.
2. Save this document as *[your initials] PP W2-3*.
3. Convert text to bulleted list and customize the bullet.
   a. Select the four paragraphs of text below the "Experience" heading and the city, state, and date line.
   b. Click the **Bullets** button [*Home* tab, *Paragraph* group]. The selected text is converted to a bulleted list (Figure 2-66).

c. With the bulleted paragraphs still selected, click the **Bullets** drop-down arrow, and select **Define New Bullet**. The *Define New Bullet* dialog box opens.

d. Click the **Symbol** button. The *Symbol* dialog box opens (Figure 2-67).

e. Click the **Font** drop-down list and scroll down to select **Wingdings**.

f. In the list of symbols, scroll down and select the **check box** symbol (*Character code 254*).

g. Click **OK** to close the *Symbol* dialog box.

h. Click **OK** to close the *Define New Bullet* dialog box.

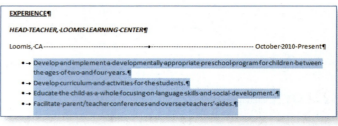

2-66 **Apply bullets to selected text**

4. Use the *Format Painter* to apply this bullet format to lines of text in the other "Experience" sections and the "Education" section. Don't apply bullet formatting to the city, state, and date lines with the tab stop and leader applied.

5. Insert a page break in the document.
   a. Turn on the **Show/Hide** feature [*Home* tab, *Paragraph* group].
   b. Place the insertion point in front of the "Education" heading.
   c. Click the **Page Layout** tab.
   d. Click the **Breaks** button [*Page Setup* group].
   e. From the drop-down list select **Page** in the *Page Breaks* section. A page break is inserted at the bottom of the first page and the "Education" section is pushed to the next page.

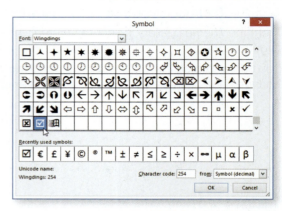

2-67 *Symbol* **dialog box**

> **ANOTHER WAY**
>
> **Ctrl+Enter** inserts a page break.

6. Change the theme of the document.
   a. Click the **Design** tab.
   b. Click the **Themes** button [*Document Formatting* group].
   c. Scroll down the list of themes and select **Ion**.

7. Apply styles from the *Style* gallery to text.
   a. On the first page of the letter, select **"Richelle Wilkinson"** and click the **Title** style from the *Style* gallery [*Home* tab].
   b. With this text still selected, change the font size to **20 pt**.
   c. Apply the **Heading 1** style to each of the main headings ("Profile," "Experience," "Education," "Skills," and "References").
   d. Apply the **Heading 2** style to each of the bold and italicized subheadings in the "Experience" and "Education" sections.

8. Modify a style.
   a. Select the **"Profile"** heading.
   b. Change the *Before* paragraph spacing to **16 pt**.

c. Right-click the **Heading 1** style in the *Style* gallery and select **Update Heading 1 to Match Selection** (Figure 2-68). This style change is applied to all text with *Heading 1* style.

d. On the second page, select **"CALIFORNIA STATE UNIVERSITY CHICO, BACHELOR OF ARTS IN CHILD DEVELOPMENT"** and change the font size to **11 pt**.

e. Right-click the **Heading 2** style in the *Style* gallery and select **Update Heading 2 to Match Selection**.

9. Save and close the document (Figure 2-69).

2-68 Update style to match selection

2-69 PP W2-3 completed

Using Find and Replace

Find and ***Replace*** are two extremely useful and powerful tools in Word. The *Find* feature allows you to search for and locate words and phrases in a document. The *Replace* feature allows you to search for a word or phrase and replace it with other text. You can also use *Find* and *Replace* to search for a specific type of formatting in a document and replace it with different formatting. These features are particularly useful in longer documents.

Find

You can use the *Navigation* pane in Word to search for text and display all instances of the matching text. Word highlights in yellow each instance of the matching text in the document. You are able to navigate through the document, see each instance, and make edits as desired.

1. Click the **Find** button [*Home* tab, *Editing* group]. The *Navigation* pane is displayed at the left side of the Word window.

2. Click in the **Search Document** text box at the top of the *Navigation* pane and type in the text you want to search. The matching results are displayed below the text box and the matching text in the document is highlighted.

3. Click the **Next** or **Previous** search result buttons to move through each matching instance in the document (Figure 2-70). You can also click the matching instances below the *Search Document* text box to go to a specific occurrence of the matching text.

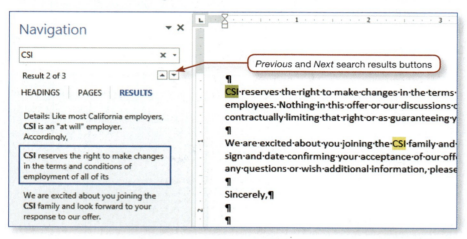

2-70 Use *Find* in the *Navigation* pane

4. Edit the highlighted text in the document if you want to make changes.

5. Click the **X** to the right of the *Search Document* text box to clear the current search.

6. Click the **X** in the upper right of the *Navigation* pane to close the pane.

> **ANOTHER WAY**
>
> **Ctrl+F** opens the *Find* feature in the *Navigation* pane.

Find and Replace

The ***Find and Replace*** dialog box gives you three different advanced options for searching your document.

- Find
- Replace
- Go To

The *Find* tab of the *Find and Replace* dialog box not only searches for text in your document but also searches for specific formatting (such as font styles, line spacing, or paragraph spacing). For example, you can search for all text that is bold or italic, or that has 6 pt. after paragraph spacing.

Using the *Replace* feature you can search for text, formatting, or a combination of text and formatting and replace the matching text with other text, formatting, or formatted text. This feature is a quick and efficient way to find and replace information in a document.

HOW TO: Use Replace

1. Click the **Replace** button [*Home* tab, *Editing* group] or press **Ctrl+H**. The *Find and Replace* dialog box opens with the *Replace* tab displayed (Figure 2-71).

2. Click in the **Find what** text box and type the text for which you are searching.

3. Click in the **Replace with** text box and type the text you want to replace the found text.

4. Click the **More** button to display advanced find options. The *Less* button hides the advanced find options.

5. Click the **Format** or **Special** button to add formatting options or special characters to either the text for which you are searching or the replacement text.

6. When the first occurrence is found you have the options to *Replace* (this occurrence), *Replace All* (all occurrences), or *Find Next* (skip this occurrence without replacing and move on to the next).

7. Click the **Find Next** button to move to the next occurrence of the matching text and formatting.

8. When you finish finding and replacing text in the document, a dialog box opens informing you that Word has finished searching the document. Click **OK** to close this dialog box.

9. Click the **X** in the upper right corner to close the *Find and Replace* dialog box.

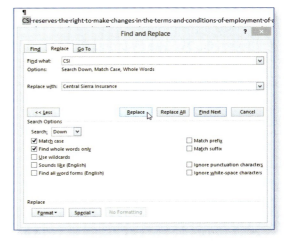

2-71 Replace text

When using *Find* or *Replace*, wildcards can be used to help find information. You can use wildcards before, after, or between words.

- Use the question mark (?) as a wildcard for a single character. For example, ***w*???** finds any words that begins with "w" and contains four letters (e.g., when, with, or wish).
- Use an asterisk (*) as a wildcard for a string of characters. For example, **search*** finds any form of the word "search" (e.g., searches, searching, or searched).

> **ANOTHER WAY**
>
> **Ctrl+H** opens the *Find and Replace* dialog box.

> **MORE INFO**
>
> It is a good idea to use **Match Case** when replacing acronyms (capital letters) with words so the replaced words will not be all upper case. Also, use **Find whole words only** to refine your search.

Go To

The *Go To* feature allows you to go quickly to specific items in your document. This feature is available in the *Find and Replace* dialog box. This feature is different from *Find* in that *Go To* moves you to specific objects in your document such as a page, section, or bookmark.

HOW TO: Use the Go To Feature

1. Click the **Find** drop-down arrow [*Home* tab, *Editing* group].

2. Select **Go To**. The *Find and Replace* dialog box opens with the *Go To* tab displayed (Figure 2-72).

3. In the *Go to what* area, select the item to go to from the list of options. The text box to the right is context sensitive and changes depending on the item chosen.

4. In the text box to the right, type in a page number, section, line, etc.

5. Click the **Go To** button.

6. Click **Close** to close this dialog box.

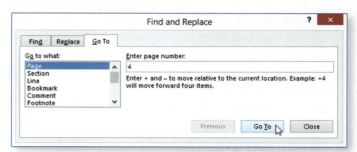

2-72 *Go To* in the *Find and Replace* dialog box

> **ANOTHER WAY**
>
> **Ctrl+G** or **F5** opens the *Find and Replace* dialog box with the *Go To* tab selected.

SLO 2.9

Using Borders, Shading, and Hyperlinks

Borders and *shading* are excellent ways to set off or emphasize important information in a document. In Word, there are many different border and shading options including many preset border options. You also have the option of applying custom borders and shading to selected text or areas of your document.

A *hyperlink* functions like a button and can be used to take a reader to a web page, open an existing or new document, open an email message, or take a reader to another location in the current document. You can add a hyperlink to text or a graphic in a document.

Apply Built-In Borders

You can use the built-in border options to quickly apply borders to selected text. Borders are typically applied to paragraphs, but they can also be applied to other selected text. Borders are, by default, applied to the paragraph where your insertion point is unless specific text is selected.

The built-in borders are available from the *Borders* button in the *Paragraph* group on the *Home* tab. Figure 2-73 shows the different types of built-in borders.

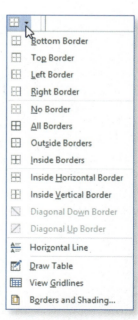

HOW TO: Apply Built-In Borders

1. Select the paragraph or place the insertion point in the paragraph where you want to apply the border.

2. Click the **Home** tab.

3. Click the **Borders** drop-down arrow [*Paragraph* group] (Figure 2-73).

4. Click the border option to apply to the paragraph.

2-73 *Borders* drop-down list

W2-96

Customize Borders

The **Borders and Shading** dialog box gives you many more options to customize the type of border you use. Not only can you customize the style, width, and color of border line, but also you can customize where the border is placed in relation to the selected text. The *Borders and Shading* dialog box is available from the *Borders* drop-down list in the *Paragraph* group on the *Home* tab.

HOW TO: Apply Custom Borders

1. Select the paragraph(s) you want to border.

2. Click the **Borders** drop-down arrow [*Home* tab, *Paragraph* group] and choose the **Borders and Shading** option at the bottom of the list. The *Borders and Shading* dialog box opens (Figure 2-74).

3. In the *Setting* area, select the type of border to use. Your options are *None, Box, Shadow, 3-D,* and *Custom.*

4. In the *Style* area, select a style of the line from the list of options.

5. In the *Color* area, select line color.

6. In the *Width* area, select the width of the border line. The width of the line is measured in points.

7. The *Preview* area shows you how the border will appear in your document.
   - You can turn on or off a specific border by either clicking any of the border buttons in the *Preview* area or clicking the border itself.

8. Click the **Options** button to open the *Borders and Shading Options* dialog box (Figure 2-75). This dialog box gives you the option to add in additional space (padding) between the border and the text at the *Top, Bottom, Left,* and *Right.* The spacing is measured in points.

9. Click **OK** to close the *Borders and Shading Options* dialog box.

10. Click **OK** to close the *Borders and Shading* dialog box.

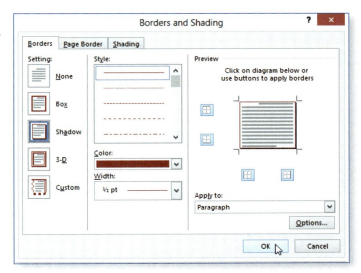

*2-74 **Borders and Shading** dialog box*

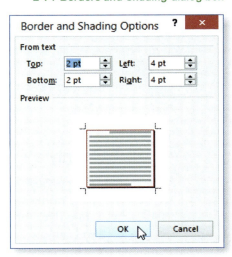

*2-75 **Border and Shading Options** dialog box*

Apply Shading

Applying shading to a paragraph or text is very similar to applying borders. The *Shading* option is available from the *Shading* button in the *Paragraph* group on the *Home* tab or in the *Borders and Shading* dialog box on the *Shading* tab.

The shading colors available are dependent upon the theme of the document. In the *Shading* drop-down list, you can select from *Theme Colors* or *Standard Colors* (Figure 2-76). If you want a color that is not available in the menu, you can click *More Colors* to select from a color palette.

2-76 Shading color options from the *Shading* drop-down list

HOW TO: Apply Shading from the Borders and Shading Dialog Box

1. Select the paragraph(s) you want to shade.
2. Click the **Borders** drop-down arrow [*Home* tab, *Paragraph* group] and choose the **Borders and Shading** option at the bottom of the list. The *Borders and Shading* dialog box opens (Figure 2-77).
3. Click the **Shading** tab.
4. In the *Fill* area, select a shading color.
5. In the *Patterns* area, you can select a shading *Style* and *Color*.
   - From the *Style* drop-down list, you can select a gradient percent or a fill pattern as the shading style.
   - From the *Color* drop-down list, you can select a fill color for the gradient or pattern you selected.
   - You do not have to use a pattern style or color for shading. Usually just a fill color is sufficient.
6. Click **OK** to close the *Borders and Shading* dialog box.

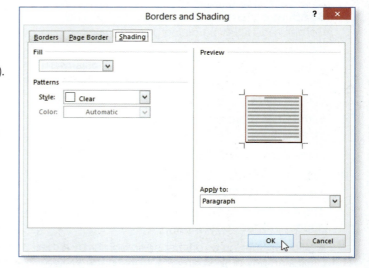

2-77 Shading options in the *Borders and Shading* dialog box

Apply a Page Border

Page borders are different from paragraph or text borders; a page border is around the entire page rather than selected paragraphs or text. Page borders are useful and attractive when creating flyers or handouts. A page border can be a line with varying styles, widths, and colors, or you can use art graphics as a page border.

HOW TO: Apply a Page Border

1. Click the **Design** tab.
2. Click the **Page Borders** button [*Page Background* group]. The *Borders and Shading* dialog box opens with the *Page Border* tab displayed (Figure 2-78).
3. In the *Setting* area, select the type of page border you want to apply.

4. You can select either a page border *Style* or *Art* from the drop-down lists.

5. You can change the *Color* and *Width* as desired.

6. In the *Preview* area, you can customize how the page border appears by turning on or off top, bottom, left, or right borders.

7. In the *Apply to* area, you can select the page(s) where you want to apply the page border. Your options are:

   - *Whole document*
   - *This section*
   - *This section – First page only*
   - *This section – All except first page*

8. Click **OK** to close the *Borders and Shading* dialog box.

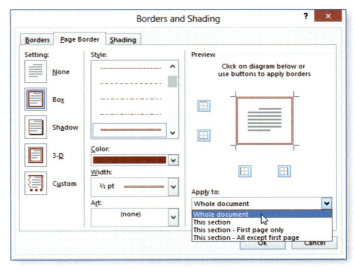

2-78 Apply a page border

> ## MORE INFO
>
> When you apply a page border, the text in the document is not affected because the page border is placed outside the margin boundaries.

Insert a Horizontal Line

In addition to being able to insert top and bottom borders on selected text, you can also insert a ***horizontal line*** to use as a border to separate information on a page. A horizontal line is actually a graphic that is inserted into the document. When you insert a horizontal line, the line is the width of the page. More information about using and customizing graphics is covered in *SLO 4.5: Working with Graphics*.

HOW TO: Insert a Horizontal Line

1. Place your insertion point in the document where you want a horizontal line.

2. Click the **Borders** drop-down arrow *[Home tab, Paragraph group]*.

3. Select **Horizontal Line** from the drop-down list (Figure 2-79).

   - The horizontal line is treated as a separate paragraph and has a paragraph mark to the right.

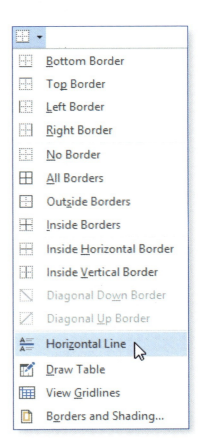

2-79 Insert a horizontal line

Create a Hyperlink

A hyperlink is an excellent way to direct users to information on a web site, another document, or a location in the same document. You can also create a hyperlink for an email address, which automatically opens a new Outlook email message addressed to the recipient. You can create a hyperlink by selecting the text or figure you want to turn into a hyperlink and then providing the information about the online location where the user will be directed. You can also customize the ScreenTip and the target frame.

> ### MORE INFO
>
> Typically, hyperlinks are underlined and a different color to distinguish them from regular text in a document. In a Word document, **Ctrl+Click** opens a hyperlink.

The *ScreenTip* is the text that is displayed when you place your pointer over the hyperlink in the document. The *target frame* is the window where the hyperlink document or web site opens. There are many different target frame options from which to choose. Usually it is best to choose **New window** if the link is to a different document or a web page. An email message always opens in a new window.

HOW TO: Create a Hyperlink

1. Select the text or graphic where you want to create a hyperlink.
2. Click the **Insert** tab.
3. Click the **Hyperlink** button [*Links* group]. The *Insert Hyperlink* dialog box opens (*Figure 2-80*).
4. In the *Link to* area, select the type of hyperlink you want to create. Your options are:
   - *Existing File or Web Page*
   - *Place in This Document*
   - *Create New Document*
   - *E-mail Address*

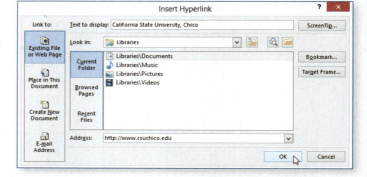

2-80 *Insert Hyperlink* dialog box

5. The text you selected in the document as the hyperlink is displayed in the *Text to display* area. If you type other text in this text box, it will replace the text you selected in the document.
6. Select the file to link to in the *Look in* area, or type a web address in the *Address* area.
   - If you are linking to a file, you can browse your computer in the *Look in* area to locate and select the file.
   - If you are linking to a place in the document, you are given a list of headings and bookmarks from which to choose.
   - If you are inserting a link to create a new document, you are given options for the new document.
   - If you are linking to an email address, you type in the email address and are given the option to create a subject line for the email.
7. Click the **ScreenTip** button to insert text that will be displayed when the pointer is placed over the hyperlink (Figure 2-81).
8. Type the ScreenTip text.
9. Click **OK** to close the *Set Hyperlink ScreenTip* dialog box.

2-81 *Set Hyperlink ScreenTip* dialog box

10. Click the **Target Frame** button to open the *Set Target Frame* dialog box (Figure 2-82)

- From the drop-down list of options, select where the hyperlink destination will be opened .
- The *Set as default for all hyperlinks* check box allows you to make your target frame selection the default for all hyperlinks in your document.

11. Click **OK** to close the *Set Target Frame* dialog box.
12. Click **OK** to insert the hyperlink and close the *Insert Hyperlink* dialog box.

2-82 *Set Target Frame* dialog box

▶ ANOTHER WAY

Ctrl+K opens the *Insert Hyperlink* dialog box.

Edit or Remove a Hyperlink

There might be times when you have incorporated text from a web site or another document that includes hyperlinks to a document, or you might want to edit a hyperlink in an existing document. Word allows you to quickly edit hyperlinks to change hyperlink information, add a ScreenTip, or change the target frame.

HOW TO: Edit a Hyperlink

1. Select or click the hyperlink to be edited.
2. Click the **Hyperlink** button [*Insert* tab, *Links* group]. You can also press **Ctrl+K** or right-click the selected hyperlink and select **Edit Hyperlink**. The *Edit Hyperlink* dialog box opens.
3. Make the desired changes to the hyperlink information or options.
4. Click **OK** to close the *Edit Hyperlink* dialog box.

You can quickly remove a hyperlink from a document without deleting the text in the document. When you remove a hyperlink from existing text, the text is not deleted. Only the hyperlink attached to the text is deleted.

HOW TO: Remove a Hyperlink

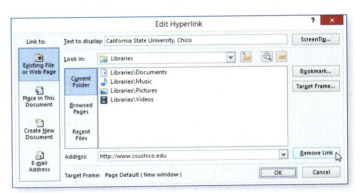

1. Select or click the hyperlink to be removed.
2. Click the **Hyperlink** button [*Insert* tab, *Links* group] or press **Ctrl+K** to open the *Edit Hyperlink* dialog box (Figure 2-83).
3. Click the **Remove Link** button.
4. Click **OK** to close the *Edit Hyperlink* button.

2-83 Remove hyperlink

▶ ANOTHER WAY

Right-click a hyperlink and select **Remove Hyperlink**.

In this Pause & Practice project, you finalize the resume you worked on in *Pause & Practice 2-3*. You use *Find and Replace,* apply borders and shading to selected text, and add hyperlinks to the document.

File Needed: ***[your initials] PP W2-3.docx***
Completed Project File Name: ***[your initials] PP W2-4.docx***

1. Open the ***[your initials] PP W2-3*** document created in *Pause & Practice 2-3*.

2. Save this document as ***[your initials] PP W2-4.***

3. Use *Find and Replace* to replace the hyphen between dates with an en dash.
    a. Press **Ctrl+Home** to move to the top of the document.
    b. Click the **Replace** button [*Home* tab, *Editing* group] or press **Ctrl+H** to open the *Find and Replace* dialog box (Figure 2-84).
    c. Type **-** (hyphen) in the *Find what* text box.
    d. Place the insertion point in the *Replace with* text box.
    e. Click the **More** button if the *Search Options* are not already displayed.
    f. Click the **Special** button and select **En Dash**.
    g. Click the **Less** button to make the **Find and Replace** dialog box smaller.
    h. Click the **Find Next** button to locate the first instance of the text for which you are searching.

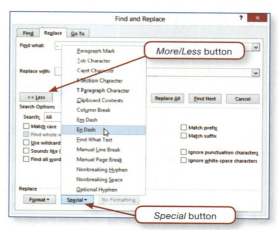

2-84 Use Find and Replace

> ## MORE INFO
>
> Word highlights each found occurrence. If you need to, you can move the *Find and Replace* dialog box to view highlighted text.

    i. Choose **Find Next** to skip the hyphenated word in the first paragraph.
    j. Click the **Replace** button to replace the hyphen between the dates with an en dash.
    k. Choose **Replace** to replace each occurrence of a hyphen between dates; choose **Find Next** to skip and not replace each occurrence of a hyphenated word.
    l. Click **OK** when Word has finished searching the document.
    m. Click **Close** to close the *Find and Replace* dialog box.

4. Add borders and shading to a paragraph.
    a. Select the paragraph after the "Profile" heading on the first page. Be sure to include the paragraph mark at the end of the paragraph.
    b. Click the **Borders** drop-down arrow [*Home* tab, *Paragraph* group] and select **Borders and Shading** to open the *Borders and Shading* dialog box (Figure 2-85).

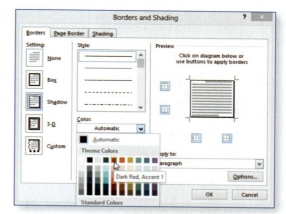

2-85 Select border color in the *Borders and Shading* dialog box

c. Select **Shadow** in the *Setting* area.
d. Select the **solid line** in the *Style* area.
e. Click the **Color** drop-down list and select **Dark Red**, **Accent 1**.
f. Select **½ pt** in the *Width* area.
g. Select **Paragraph** in the *Apply to* area.
h. Click the **Options** button to open the *Borders and Shading Options* dialog box.
i. Change *Top* and *Bottom* to **2 pt**.
j. Click **OK** to close the *Borders and Shading Options* dialog box.
k. Click the **Shading** tab (Figure 2-86).
l. Click the **Fill** drop-down list and choose **White**, **Background 1**, **Darker 5%**.
m. Click **OK** to close the *Borders and Shading* dialog box.

2-86 Apply shading to selected text

5. Add bottom border to the header.
   a. Double-click the header on the second page of the resume to open the second-page header.
   b. Place the insertion point in the first line of the header.
   c. Click the **Borders** drop-down arrow [*Home* tab, *Paragraph* group].
   d. Select **Bottom Border**. A bottom border is applied below the header text.
   e. Click the **Close Header and Footer** button [*Header & Footer Tools Design* tab, *Close* group].

6. Insert a hyperlink to an email address.
   a. Select the email address in the heading information on the first page.
   b. Click the **Hyperlink** button [*Insert* tab, *Links* group] or press **Ctrl+K** to open the *Insert Hyperlink* dialog box (Figure 2-87).
   c. Click the **E-mail Address** button in the *Link to* area.
   d. Type richellew@gmail.com in the *Text to display* area.
   e. Type richellew@gmail.com in the *E-mail address* area. Word automatically inserts "mailto:" before the email address.
   f. Click **OK** to close the *Insert Hyperlink* dialog box.

2-87 Insert hyperlink to an email address

7. Insert a hyperlink to a web site.
   a. Select **"California State University, Chico"** in the "References" section on the second page.
   b. Click the **Hyperlink** button or press **Ctrl+K** to open the *Insert Hyperlink* dialog box (Figure 2-88).
   c. Select **Existing File or Web Page** in the *Link to* area. The *Text to display* area has *California State University, Chico* already filled in.
   d. In the *Address* area, type www.csuchico.edu. Word automatically inserts "*http://*" before the web address.
   e. Click the **ScreenTip** button. The *Set Hyperlink ScreenTip* dialog box opens (Figure 2-89).
   f. Type CSU Chico web site in the *ScreenTip text* area.

2-88 Insert hyperlink to a web page

2-89 *Set Hyperlink ScreenTip* dialog box

g. Click **OK** to close the *Set Hyperlink ScreenTip* dialog box.

h. Click the **Target Frame** button in the *Insert Hyperlink* dialog box to open the *Set Target Frame* dialog box (Figure 2-90).

i. Select **New window** from the drop-down list.

j. Check the **Set as default for all hyperlinks** check box.

k. Click **OK** to close the *Set Target Frame* dialog box.

l. Click **OK** to close the *Insert Hyperlink* dialog box.

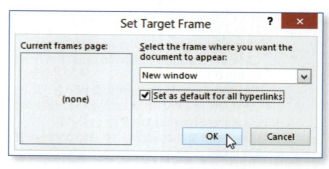

2-90 *Set Target Frame* dialog box

8. Automatically add hyperlinks to email addresses.

a. Place the insertion point after "rsanchez@chico.edu" in the "References" section on the second page.

b. Press the **spacebar** once to automatically add a hyperlink to the email address.

c. Repeat the above steps to automatically add a hyperlink to the "diana.samuels@loomislearning.com" email address.

9. Save and close the document (Figure 2-91).

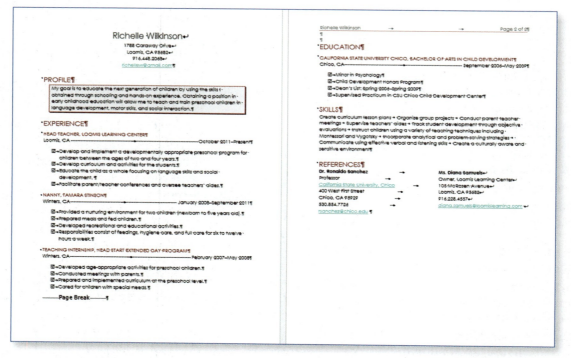

2-91 **PP W 2-4 completed**

Chapter Summary

2.1 Format a document by customizing margins, page orientation, paper size, and vertical alignment (p. W2-63).

- Adjust the **margins** of a document to increase or decrease the **white space** surrounding the text. You can adjust the top, bottom, left, and right margins of a document.
- **Landscape** and **portrait** are the two **page orientation** options.
- A standard sheet of paper is 8½"×11". Select other paper sizes or create a custom paper size.
- By default, text is aligned vertically at the top of the document. You can also **vertically align** text center, justified, or bottom.
- Use horizontal and vertical **rulers** to display the typing area on a document.
- You can change default page settings in the *Page Setup* dialog box.

2.2 Improve alignment and white-space usage by setting, using, and editing tab stops in a document (p. W2-66).

- There are five different types of tab stops: **left**, **center**, **right**, **decimal**, and **bar**.
- Set, modify, or remove tab stops using the ruler or the *Tabs* dialog box.
- Leaders can be used with tab stops. There are three different types of leaders: **dot**, **dash**, and **solid underline**.
- In a Word document, default tab stops are set every 0.5". You can change the default tab stops.

2.3 Understand and apply indents to control text alignment (p. W2-71).

- **Indents** can function as temporary margins and allow you to arrange paragraphs horizontally between the margins.
- There are four different types of indents: **left**, **right**, **first line**, and **hanging**.
- You can apply, modify, and remove indents with the ruler, *Page Layout* tab, or *Paragraph* dialog box.

2.4 Enhance document layout by effectively using page numbers, headers, and footers (p. W2-76).

- You can insert a **page number** into the header or footer in various locations.

- The **Different First Page** option allows you to remove a page number from the first page or have a header and footer.
- **Headers** and **footers** are areas above and below a document's top and bottom margins.
- You type header and footer content once and it appears on subsequent pages.
- You can customize headers and footers with text, page numbers, the date, and other document property fields.
- You have a variety of built-in header, footer, and page numbering options.

2.5 Control pagination with page and section breaks (p. W2-83).

- Use **page breaks** to control the ending and beginning of pages in a document.
- Use **section breaks** to allow for different page setup formatting on different sections of a document.
- There are four different types of section breaks: **next page**, **continuous**, **even page**, and **odd page**.
- Section breaks are visible in a document when the *Show/Hide* feature is turned on.

2.6 Present information using customized bulleted and numbered lists (p. W2-85).

- Use **bulleted** and **numbered lists** to emphasize important information.
- You can customize lists by using different symbols or pictures as bullets.
- Use numbering to display an ordered list.
- You can customize number format and levels.
- **Multilevel lists** allow you to customize a list using a combination of numbers, letters, or bullets.

2.7 Increase document consistency and format with styles and themes (p. W2-89).

- A **style** is a collection of preset formatting that you can apply to selected text.
- The **Style gallery** is a collection of built-in styles available in a document.
- You can modify existing styles.
- A **theme** is a collection of fonts, colors, and effects that you can apply to a document.

2.8 Effectively edit a document using find and replace (p. W2-93).

- The *Find* feature in Word allows you to search for specific information in a document.
- The *Navigation pane* displays all occurrences of the text for which you are searching.
- The *Replace* feature allows you to search for specific information in a document and replace it with other information.
- Both *Find* and *Replace* allow you to search for and replace formatting in a document.
- Use the *Go To* feature to go directly to a page, section, line, or other area in your document.

2.9 Improve overall document design and format by using borders, shading, horizontal lines, and hyperlinks (p. W2-96).

- *You can apply **borders** and **shading** to text and paragraphs in a document.*
- Word provides a variety of built-in border and shading options that you can apply to text, or you can customize borders and shading using the *Borders and Shading* dialog box.
- You can apply *page borders* to an individual page or all pages in a document.
- A *horizontal line* is a graphic that you can insert into a document.
- A *hyperlink* takes readers to a web page, a different document, or a different location in a document.

Check for Understanding

On the *Online Learning Center* for this text (www.mhhe.com/office2013inpractice), there are a variety of resources that can be used to review the concepts covered in this chapter.

The following Online Learning Resources are available on the Online Learning Center.

- Multiple choice questions
- Short answer questions
- Matching exercises

Guided Project 2-1

In this project, you create a form for contractors seeking insurance coverage at Central Sierra Insurance. You use a theme, styles, a multilevel list, tab stops, leaders, indents, borders and shading, a page break, and page numbering.
[Student Learning Outcomes 2.1, 2.2, 2.3, 2.4, 2.5, 2.6, 2.7, 2.9]

File Needed: ***InsuranceQuestionnaire-02.docx***
Completed Project File Name: ***[your initials] Word 2-1.docx***

Skills Covered in This Project

- Modify an existing document.
- Change margins.
- Apply a document theme.
- Change font size, line spacing, and paragraph spacing.
- Apply a style to selected text.
- Modify an existing style.

- Apply borders and shading to selected text.
- Set and use a tab stop with an underline leader.
- Apply and modify a multilevel list.
- Insert a page break.
- Insert a page number in the footer.

1. Open the ***InsuranceQuestionnaire-02*** document from your student data files.

2. Save this document as ***[your initials] Word 2-1***.

3. Change the margins of the document.
   a. Click the **Margins** button [*Page Layout* tab, *Page Setup* group] and select **Custom Margins**. The *Page Setup* dialog box opens.
   b. Change the *Left* and *Right* margins to **0.75"**.
   c. Click **OK** to close the *Page Setup* dialog box.

4. Change the theme and color set of the document.
   a. Click the **Themes** button [*Design* tab, *Document Formatting* group].
   b. Select **Integral** from the drop-down list.
   c. Click the **Colors** button [*Document Formatting* group] (Figure 2-92).
   d. Select **Aspect** from the drop-down list.

5. Change the font size, paragraph spacing, and line spacing on the entire document.
   a. Press **Ctrl+A** to select the entire document.
   b. Change the font size to **11 pt**.
   c. Change the line spacing to **Single** (1.0).
   d. Change the *After* paragraph spacing to **6 pt**.

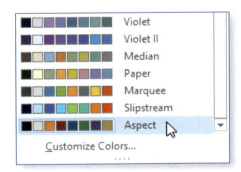

2-92 Select color set

6. Apply styles to selected text.
   a. Place the insertion point in the first line of text ("Contractor's Insurance Questionnaire").
   b. Click the **Title** style [*Home* tab, *Styles* group] in the *Style* gallery.
   c. Select the second line of the document (**"Please carefully . . . "**).
   d. Right-click the selected text and click **Styles** on the mini toolbar. The *Style* gallery list appears.
   e. Select **Book Title** from the *Style* gallery.
   f. With this text still selected, click the **Change Case** button in the *Font* group, and select **UPPERCASE**.
   g. Select **"Applicant's Instructions"** and apply the **Intense Quote** style from the *Style* gallery.
   h. In the next paragraph ("Please answer ALL questions . . ."), apply the **Strong** style to the three words in all caps ("ALL," "NONE," and "NONE").
   i. On the second page of the document, select **"Insurance Application Disclaimer"** and apply the **Intense Quote** style.

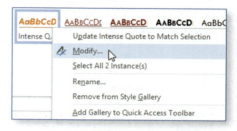

2-93 **Modify an existing style**

7. Modify an existing style.
   a. Click the **More** button [*Home* tab, *Styles* group] to display the *Style* gallery.
   b. Right-click the **Intense Quote** style in the *Style* gallery and select **Modify** (Figure 2-93). The *Modify Style* dialog box opens.
   c. In the *Formatting* area, change the font size to **12 pt**.
   d. Click the **Format** button on the bottom left and select **Paragraph**. The *Paragraph* dialog box opens.
   e. Change the *Left* and *Right* indent to **0**.
   f. Click **OK** to close the *Paragraph* dialog box.
   g. Click the **Only in this document** radio button to apply the style changes to only this document.
   h. Click **OK** to close the *Modify Style* dialog box. The change should be applied to all text formatted with the *Intense Reference* style on both the first and second pages.

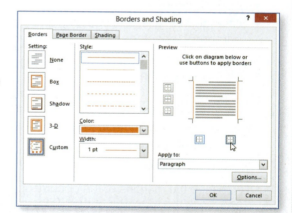

2-94 **Border option settings**

8. Add borders and shading to selected text.
   a. On the second page, select the three paragraphs below "Insurance Application Disclaimer."
   b. Click the **Borders** drop-down arrow [*Home* tab, *Paragraph* group] and select **Borders and Shading**. The *Borders and Shading* dialog box opens (Figure 2-94).
   c. In the *Setting* area, select **Custom**.
   d. In the *Style* area, select the solid line border.
   e. In the *Color* area, select **Orange, Accent 1**.
   f. In the *Width* area, select **1 pt**.
   g. In the *Preview* area, click the **Left** and **Right** border buttons.
   h. In the *Apply to* area, select **Paragraph**.
   i. Click the **Options** button. The *Border and Shading Options* dialog box opens.
   j. Change the *Left* and *Right* settings to **5 pt**. and click **OK** to close the *Border and Shading Options* dialog box.
   k. Click the **Shading** tab (Figure 2-95).
   l. From the *Fill* drop-down list, select **Orange, Accent 1, Lighter 80%**.
   m. Click **OK** to close the *Borders and Shading* dialog box.

9. Change the paragraph spacing and add a tab stop with an underline leader to selected text.
   a. Select the last three lines of text on the second page.
   b. Click the **Paragraph** launcher [*Home* or *Page Layout* tab].

2-95 **Select shading fill color**

c. Change the *Before* paragraph spacing to **12 pt**.

d. Click the **Tabs** button to open the *Tabs* dialog box (Figure 2-96).

e. In the *Tab stop position* area, type 7.

f. Click the **Right** radio button in the *Alignment* area.

g. Click the **4** (solid underline) radio button in the *Leader* area.

h. Click the **Set** button to set this tab stop.

i. Click **OK** to close the *Tabs* dialog box.

j. Click at the end of the "Name and Title of the Insured" line and press **Tab**. A solid underline is inserted across the page to the right margin.

k. Repeat the above step (j.) on the next two lines.

10. Add a multilevel list to selected text and modify lists settings.

a. Select the lines of text beginning with "Applicant" on the first page and ending with the last "If yes, please explain:" on the second page.

b. Click the **Multilevel List** button [*Home* tab, *Paragraph* group] and select the **1), a), i)** option.

c. With the text still selected, click the **Multilevel List** button and select **Define new Multilevel list**. The *Define new Multilevel list* dialog box opens (Figure 2-97).

d. Click the **Set for All Levels** button. The *Set for All Levels* dialog box opens.

e. Set the *Bullet/Number position for first level* to **0"**.

f. Set the *Text position for first level* to **0.3"**.

g. Set the *Additional indent for each level* to **0.3"**.

h. Click **OK** to close the *Set for All Levels* dialog box.

i. Click **OK** to close the *Define new Multilevel list* dialog box.

11. Increase indent on selected lines.

a. Click anywhere on the list to deselect it.

b. Place your insertion point in 13 in the numbered list ("If yes, . . .") and click **Increase Indent** [*Home* tab, *Paragraph* group]. This line is now letter *a)*.

c. Repeat the above step (b.) on each of the lines in the list that begin with "If yes, . . .". There should be 28 numbered items in the list when you finish this process.

12. Change paragraph spacing to the multilevel list and add a right tab stop with an underline leader.

a. Select the entire multilevel list.

b. Click the **Paragraph** launcher [*Home* or *Page Layout* tab].

c. Deselect the **Don't add space between paragraphs of the same style** check box (Figure 2-98).

d. Click the **Tabs** button to open the *Tabs* dialog box.

e. In the *Tab stop position* area, type 7.

f. Click the **Right** radio button in the *Alignment* area.

g. Click the **4** (solid underline) radio button in the *Leader* area.

h. Click the **Set** button to set this tab stop.

2-96 Set a right tab stop with an underline leader

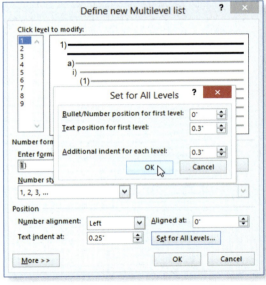

2-97 Change settings for a multilevel list

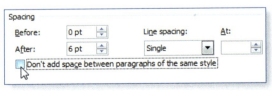

2-98 Add spacing between lines of text with the same style

i. Click **OK** to close the *Tabs* dialog box.

j. Click at the end of the first numbered item ("Applicant:") and press **Tab**. A solid underline will be inserted across the page to the right margin.

k. Repeat the above step (j.) on each of the numbered and lettered paragraphs.

13. Insert a page break in the document.

a. Place the insertion point before the text in number 22 in the multilevel list.

b. Click the **Breaks** button [*Page Layout* tab, *Page Setup* group] and select **Page Break**, or press **Ctrl+Enter** to insert a page break.

14. Add a page number in the footer of the document.

a. Press **Ctrl+Home** to move to the top of the document.

b. Click the **Page Number** button [*Insert* tab, *Header & Footer* group].

c. Put your pointer on **Bottom of Page** to display the drop-down list.

d. Scroll down and choose **Bold Numbers 3** in the *Page X of Y* section. The page number is inserted at the right of the footer.

e. Click the blank line below the page number in the footer and press **Backspace** to delete the blank line.

f. Click the **Close Header and Footer** button [*Header & Footer Tools Design* tab, *Close* group].

15. Save and close the document (Figure 2-99).

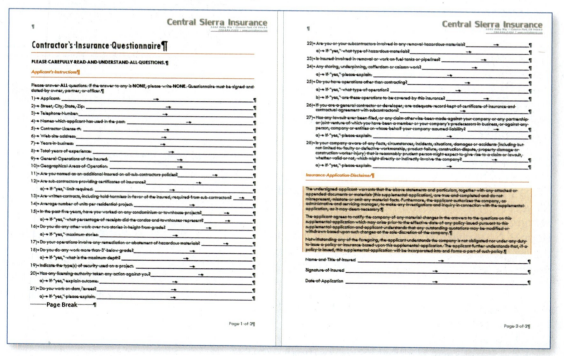

2-99 Word 2-1 completed

Guided Project 2-2

In this project, you create a checklist for employees at Placer Hills Real Estate to track the tasks they need to complete when a house enters escrow. You create a bulleted list, modify a bullet in a list, set and modify tab stops, apply and modify styles, and insert document properties in the footer. [Student Learning Outcomes 2.1, 2.2, 2.3, 2.4, 2.6, 2.7, 2.9]

File Needed: ***SellerEscrowChecklist-02.docx***
Completed Project File Name: ***[your initials] Word 2-2.docx***

Skills Covered in This Project

- Modify an existing document.
- Change margins, line spacing, font, and font size.
- Set a tab stop using the ruler.
- Set a tab stop with leader.
- Apply a style to selected text.

- Modify an existing style.
- Apply and customize a bulleted list.
- Use the *Format Painter*.
- Insert a document property field and date in the footer.
- Apply a border in the footer.

1. Open the ***SellerEscrowChecklist-02*** document from your student data files.
2. Save this document as ***[your initials] Word 2-2***.
3. Change margins, vertical alignment, line spacing, and font and font size, and delete blank lines.
   a. Click the **Margins** button [*Page Layout* tab, *Page Setup* group].
   b. Select **Normal** from the drop-down list.
   c. Click the **Page Setup** launcher to open the *Page Setup* dialog box.
   d. Click the **Layout** tab.
   e. In the *Page* area, change *Vertical alignment* to **Center**.
   f. Click **OK** to close the *Page Setup* dialog box.
   g. Press **Ctrl+A** to select the entire document.
   h. Change the font to **Calibri**.
   i. Change the font size to **12 pt**.
   j. Change the line spacing to **2.0** (Double).
   k. Turn on **Show/Hide** and delete all of the blank lines between the lines of text.
4. Add text to the document.
   a. Click after "Seller" in the second line of the document and press **Tab** once.
   b. Type Property Address.
   c. Click after "Escrow Company" and press **Tab** once.
   d. Type Escrow #.
   e. Click after "Tasks to be Completed" and press **Tab** once.
   f. Type Date Completed.
5. Set tab stops using the ruler to line up information.
   a. Select the second and third lines of text (beginning with "Seller").
   b. Ensure that the **Left Tab** is selected in the tab selector area to the left of the horizontal ruler.
   c. Click the ruler at **3.5"**. If you click the wrong location on the ruler, drag the tab stop to the correct location (Figure 2-100).
   d. Select the fourth line of text (beginning with "Tasks").
   e. Click to the **tab selector** to change to a center tab stop (Figure 2-101).
   f. Click the ruler at **5.5"**.

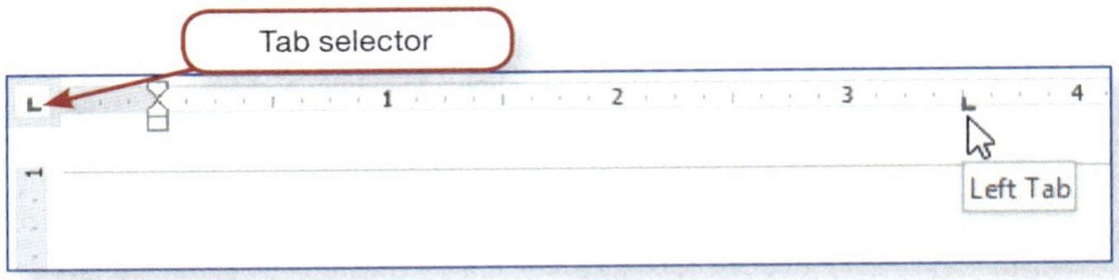

2-100 Set left tab stop using the ruler

2-101 Center tab stop

6. Set tab stops and add leaders to create lines for users to fill in information.
   a. Select the second and third lines of text (beginning with "Seller").
   b. Click the **Paragraph** launcher. The *Paragraph* dialog box opens.
   c. Click the **Tabs** button. The *Tabs* dialog box opens.
   d. In the *Tab stop position* area, type 3.
   e. Click the **Right** radio button in the *Alignment* area.
   f. Click the **4** (solid underline) radio button in the *Leader* area.
   g. Click the **Set** button to set this tab stop.
   h. In the *Tab stop position* area, type 6.5.
   i. Click the **Right** radio button in the *Alignment* area.
   j. Click the **4** (solid underline) radio button in the *Leader* area.
   k. Click the **Set** button to set this tab stop.
   l. Click **OK** to close the *Tabs* dialog box.

7. Use tab stops to align text.
   a. Place the insertion point before "Property Address" and press **Tab** once.
   b. Click after "Property Address" and press **Tab** once.
   c. Place the insertion point before "Escrow #" and press **Tab** once.
   d. Click after "Escrow #" and press **Tab** once.

8. Apply styles to selected text and modify a style.
   a. Place the insertion point in the first line of text ("Seller Escrow Checklist").
   b. Select **Title** style in the *Style* gallery [*Home* tab, *Styles* group].
   c. Change the *After* paragraph spacing to **24 pt**. [*Page Layout* tab, *Paragraph* group].
   d. Click the **Center** alignment button to center the title.
   e. Select **"Tasks to be Completed"**.
   f. Apply the **Book Title** style from the *Style* gallery.
   g. Change the font size of the selected text to **14 pt**. and apply a **Double underline**.
   h. Right-click the **Book Title** style in the *Style* gallery and select **Update Book Title to Match Selection**. The *Book Title* style is updated.
   i. Select **"Date Completed"** and apply the **Book Title** style.

9. Create a bulleted list to selected text and apply a custom bullet.
   a. Select the remaining lines of text beginning with "Open Escrow . . .".
   b. Click the **Bullets** drop-down arrow [*Home* tab, *Paragraph* group] and select **Define New Bullet**. The *Define New Bullet* dialog box opens.
   c. Click the **Symbol** button. The *Symbol* dialog box opens (Figure 2-102).
   d. Click the **Font** drop-down arrow and select **Wingdings**.
   e. Scroll down the list and select the **open square** bullet (Character code 113).
   f. Click **OK** to close the *Symbol* dialog box.
   g. Click the **Font** button in the *Define New Bullet* dialog box. The *Font* dialog box opens.
   h. Change the *Size* to **14 pt**.
   i. Click **OK** to close the *Font* dialog box.
   j. Click **OK** to close the *Define New Bullet* dialog box.
   k. With the bulleted list still selected, click the **Decrease Indent** button to align the bullet at the left margin.

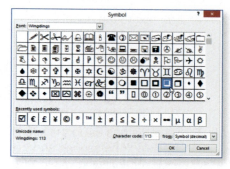

2-102 **Select a symbol for a custom bullet**

10. Change the hanging indent and add tab stops.
    a. Select the bulleted list.
    b. Click the **Paragraph** launcher to open the *Paragraph* dialog box.
    c. Change the hanging indent to **0.3"**.

d. Click the **Tabs** button. The *Tabs* dialog box opens (Figure 2-103).

e. In the *Tab stop position* area, type 4.5.

f. Click the **Left** radio button in the *Alignment* area.

g. Click the **1 None** radio button in the *Leader* area.

h. Click the **Set** button to set this tab stop.

i. In the *Tab stop position* area, type 6.5.

j. Click the **Right** radio button in the *Alignment* area.

k. Click the **4** (solid underline) radio button in the *Leader* area.

l. Click the **Set** button to set this tab stop.

m. Click **OK** to close the *Tabs* dialog box.

n. Place the insertion point after "Open Escrow with Escrow Company" and press **Tab** two times. A solid underline is inserted between 4.5" and 6.5".

o. Repeat the step above (n.) on the remaining lines in the bulleted list.

2-103 *Tabs* dialog box

11. Add text to the document.

a. Press **Enter** after the last line of text in the document.

b. Click the **Bullets** button [*Home* tab, *Paragraph* group] to turn off the bullet on this line.

c. Type Fax/Email Clear Pest Report and press **Enter**.

d. Type Title and press **Enter**.

e. Type Lender and press **Enter**.

f. Type Buyer's Agent.

12. Apply a style to selected text and use the *Format Painter*.

a. Select **"Fax/Email Clear Pest Report"** and apply the **Subtle Reference** style.

b. Click one of the bulleted items.

c. Click the **Format Painter** button [*Home* tab, *Clipboard* group] to copy the formatting of this bulleted item.

d. Select the last three lines of text (beginning with "Title . . ."). The *Format Painter* copies the bullet formatting and tab settings to these lines of text.

e. Press **Tab** two times after each of these last three lines to insert the tab stops and leaders.

13. Insert a document property field, the date, and a border in the footer of the document.

a. Click the **Footer** button [*Insert* tab, *Header & Footer* group].

b. Select **Edit Footer** from the drop-down list. The footer opens.

c. Click the **Quick Parts** button [*Header & Footer Tools Design* tab, *Insert* group].

d. Click **Document Property** and select **Company**. The *Company* document property field is inserted.

e. Press the **right arrow** key once to deselect the *Company* field.

f. Press **Tab** two times, type Last Updated:, and **space** once. The text aligns at the right side of the footer.

g. Click the **Date & Time** button [*Header & Footer Tools Design* tab, *Insert* group]. The *Date and Time* dialog box opens.

h. Select the third option (month, day, year) and click the **Update automatically** check box.

i. Click **OK** to close the dialog box.

j. Select all of the text in the footer and change the font to **Calibri** and the font size to **10 pt**.

k. Click the **Borders** drop-down arrow [*Home* tab, *Paragraph* group] and select **Top Border**.

l. Click the **Close Header and Footer** button [*Header & Footer Tools Design* tab, *Close* group].

14. Save and close the document (Figure 2-104).

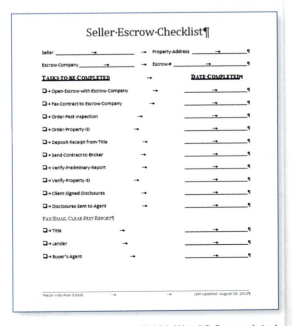

2-104 Word 2-2 completed

Guided Project 2-3

In this project, you edit and format the personal training guide for the American River Cycling Club to improve readability and effectiveness. You use find and replace, apply a document theme, modify styles, customize numbered and bulleted lists, apply borders and shading, and insert headers, footers, and document properties.
[Student Learning Outcomes 2.3, 2.4, 2.6, 2.7, 2.8, 2.9]

File Needed: ***PersonalTrainingProgram-02.docx***
Completed Project File Name: ***[your initials] Word 2-3.docx***

Skills Covered in This Project

- Modify an existing document.
- Apply a document theme.
- Change line spacing and paragraph spacing.
- Apply a style to selected text.
- Modify an existing style.
- Apply borders and shading to selected text.

- Customize a multilevel bulleted list.
- Use *Find* and *Replace*.
- Insert a hyperlink.
- Insert header, footer, page number, and document properties.

1. Open the ***PersonalTrainingProgram-02*** document from your student data files.

2. Save this document as ***[your initials] Word 2-3***.

3. Apply a document theme and change the line and paragraph spacing.
   a. Click the **Themes** button [*Design* tab, *Document Formatting* group].
   b. Select **Slice** from the drop-down list of theme options.
   c. Select the entire document.
   d. Change the line spacing to **1.15**.
   e. Change the after paragraph spacing to **10 pt**.
   f. Turn on **Show/Hide** and delete any blank lines in the document.

4. Apply styles to the title, subtitle, and section headings.
   a. Select the title (first line) of the document.
   b. Apply the **Title** style from the *Style* gallery [*Home* tab, *Styles* group].
   c. Change the font size to **20 pt.**, make it **bold**, and **center** it horizontally.
   d. Select the subtitle (second line) of the document.
   e. Apply the **Subtitle** style from the *Style* gallery.
   f. Change the font size to **16 pt**. and **center** horizontally.
   g. Select the first section heading **("General Guidelines")**.
   h. Apply the **Heading 1** style from the *Style* gallery.
   i. Apply the **Heading 1** style to the remaining section headings in the document *("Personal Training Program Guidelines," "More About Long Rides," "Training Intensity and Heart Rate," "Tracking Training Miles versus Hours,"* and *"Using a Training Log"*).

5. Modify styles in the document.
   a. Select the first section heading **("General Guidelines")** including the paragraph mark at the end of the line.
   b. Change the *Before* paragraph spacing to **12 pt**. and the *After* paragraph spacing to **6 pt**.
   c. Click the **Borders** drop-down arrow [*Home* tab, *Paragraph* group] and select **Borders and Shading**. The *Borders and Shading* dialog box opens.

d. In the *Setting* area, select **Shadow**.

e. In the *Style* area, select the solid line.

f. In the *Color* area, select **Dark Blue**, **Accent 1**, **Darker 50%** (Figure 2-105).

g. In the *Width* area, select **1 pt**.

h. In the *Apply to* area, make sure that **Paragraph** is selected.

i. Click the **Shading** tab and in the *Fill* area, select **Dark Blue**, **Accent 1**, **Lighter 80%**.

j. In the *Apply to* area, make sure that **Paragraph** is selected and click **OK** to close the *Borders and Shading* dialog box.

k. With the heading still selected, right-click the **Heading 1** style in the *Style gallery*.

l. Select **Update Heading 1 to Match Selection**. All of the headings with the *Heading 1* style applied are automatically updated in the document.

2-105 Select border line color

6. Customize the bullets and indents for the bulleted list.

a. Right-click the first bulleted item on the first page and select **Adjust List Indents**. The *Define new Multilevel list* dialog box opens.

b. Click **1** in the *Click level to modify* area.

c. In the *Number style for this level* area, select **New Bullet** from the drop-down list (Figure 2-106). The *Symbol* dialog box opens.

d. In the *Font* area, select **Webdings** from the drop-down list (Figure 2-107).

e. Click the **right pointing triangle** (Character code 52) and click **OK** to close the *Symbol* dialog box.

f. Click **2** in the *Click level to modify* area in the *Define new Multilevel list* dialog box.

g. In the *Number style for this level* area, select **New Bullet** from the drop-down list. The *Symbol* dialog box opens.

h. In the *Font* area, select **Webdings** from the drop-down list.

i. Click the **double right pointing triangle** (Character code 56) and click **OK** to close the *Symbol* dialog box.

j. Click the **Set for All Levels** button in the *Define new Multilevel list* dialog box. The *Set for All Levels* dialog box opens (Figure 2-108).

k. Change the *Bullet/Number position for first level* to **0.25"**.

l. Change the *Text position for first level* to **0.5"**.

m. Change *Additional indent for each level* to **0.25"**.

n. Click **OK** to close the *Set for All Levels* dialog box.

o. Click **OK** to close the *Define new Multilevel list* dialog box. All of the first and second level bullets and indents in the entire document are changed.

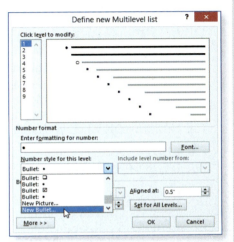

2-106 Customize bulleted list

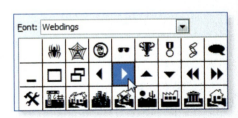

2-107 Select bullet from Webdings font set

7. Use the *Find* feature to find text in the document.

a. Press **Ctrl+Home** to go to the beginning of the document.

b. Press **Ctrl+F** to open *Find* in the *Navigation* pane.

c. Type personal training program in the *Search Document* area. All instances of this text appear below in the *Navigation* pane.

d. Click after "personal training program" in the first body paragraph on the first page and type (PTP). Make sure there is one space before and after the parentheses.

e. Select **"PTP"** and make **italic**.

f. Click the **X** in the upper right of the *Navigation* pane to close this pane.

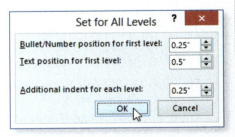

2-108 Set indents for all levels

8. Use the replace feature to find and replace text in the document.
   a. Press **Ctrl+Home** to go to the beginning of the document.
   b. Click the **Replace** button [*Home* tab, *Editing* group]. The *Find and Replace* dialog box opens with the *Replace* tab selected (Figure 2-109).
   c. In the *Find what* area, type personal training program.
   d. In the *Replace with* area, type PTP.
   e. Click the **More** button to display more search options.
   f. Click the **Format** button and select **Font**. The *Replace Font* dialog box opens.
   g. Click **Italic** in the *Font style* area and click **OK** to close the *Replace Font* dialog box.
   h. Click the **Less** button to make the *Find and Replace* dialog box smaller.
   i. Click the **Find Next** button to find the first occurrence of "personal training program" in the document.
   j. Do not replace this text in the title, first body paragraph, or section heading. Replace all other occurrences of "personal training program" with "*PTP.*" Click the **Replace** button to replace the highlighted occurrence or click the **Find Next** button to skip and not replace an occurrence.
   k. Click **OK** when you are finished searching the document.

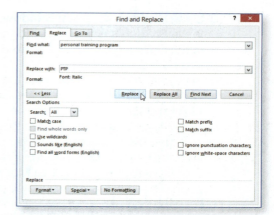

2-109 Replace text with text and formatting

9. Use the replace feature to replace some hyphens with an em dash.
   a. With the *Find and Replace* dialog box still open, delete the text in the *Find what* area and type - (hyphen).
   b. Click the **More** button.
   c. Delete the text in the *Replace with* area.
   d. Click the **No Formatting** button at the bottom of the dialog box to clear the *Replace with* formatting.
   e. Click the **Special** button and select **Em Dash**.
   f. Click the **Less** button.
   g. Click the **Find Next** button to find the first occurrence of the hyphen. Replace the hyphen with an em dash when a hyphen is used to set off part of a sentence; skip (click **Find Next**) when the hyphen is used in a hyphenated word.
   h. Click **OK** when you are finished searching the document (click **No** if a dialog box opens asking if you want to search from the beginning of the document).
   i. Click **Close** to close the *Find and Replace* dialog box.

10. Add a hyperlink to the document.
    a. Select the subtitle of the document (**"American River Cycling Club"**).
    b. Click the **Hyperlink** button [*Insert* tab, *Links* group] or press **Ctrl+K**. The *Insert Hyperlink* dialog box opens.
    c. Click the **Existing File or Web Page** button in the *Link to* area.
    d. Type www.arcc.org in the *Address* area.
    e. Click the **Target Frame** button. The *Set Target Frame* dialog box opens.
    f. Select **New window** from the drop-down list.
    g. Click **OK** to close the *Set Target Frame* dialog box.
    h. Click **OK** to close the *Insert Hyperlink* dialog box.

11. Insert header and footer on the second and continuing pages.
    a. Press **Ctrl+Home** to move to the beginning of the document.
    b. Click the **Page Number** button [*Insert* tab, *Header & Footer* group].
    c. Click **Top of Page** and select **Accent Bar 2** from the drop-down list. The header is inserted and remains open with the *Header & Footer Tools Design* tab displayed.
    d. Check the **Different First Page** check box [*Options* group] to remove the header from the first page so it only displays on the second and continuing pages.

12. Insert document property fields in the footer.
    a. With the header still open, click the **Go to Footer** button [*Navigation* group].
    b. Click the **Next** button [*Navigation* group] to move to the footer on the second page.
    c. Click the **Quick Parts** button [*Insert* group] and select **Document Property**.
    d. Select **Company** to insert the company document property field.
    e. Press the **right arrow** key once to deselect the property field.
    f. Press **Tab** two times to move the insertion point to the right margin in the footer.
    g. Click the **Quick Parts** button [*Insert* group] and select **Document Property**.
    h. Select **Title** to insert the title document property field.
    i. Press **Ctrl+A** to select all of the text in the footer.
    j. Make this text **bold** and *italic*.
    k. Click the **Close Header and Footer** button [*Header & Footer Tools Design* tab, *Close* group]. The header and footer information should appear on the second and continuing pages in the document.

13. Save and close the document (Figure 2-110).

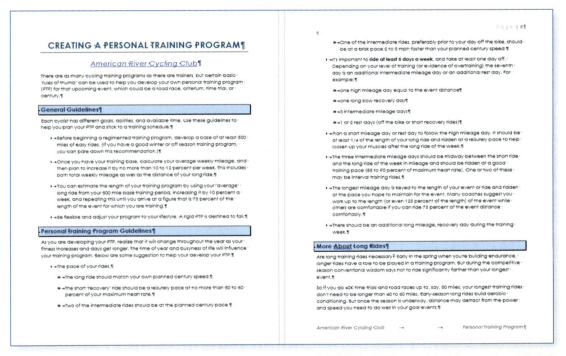

2-110 Word 2-3 completed (pages 1 and 2 of 5)

Independent Project 2-4

In this project, you use styles, indents, lists, tab stops, the replace feature, footers, and document properties to customize the Emergency Procedures document for Sierra Pacific Community College District.
[Student Learning Outcomes 2.1, 2.2, 2.3, 2.4, 2.6, 2.7, 2.9]

File Needed: ***EmergencyProcedures-02.docx***
Completed Project File Name: ***[your initials] Word 2-4.docx***

Skills Covered in This Project

- Modify an existing document.
- Apply a document theme.
- Change margins and font size.
- Apply and modify a style.
- Apply borders to selected text.
- Apply and customize a numbered and bulleted list.
- Use the *Format Painter*.
- Set and modify tab stops.
- Use *Replace*.
- Insert a footer with document properties and current date.
- Insert a page border.
- Center text vertically.

---

1. Open the **EmergencyProcedures-02** document from your student data files.

2. Save this document as **[your initials] Word 2-4**.

3. Format the entire document.
   a. Change the document theme to **Integral** and the color set to **Red**.
   b. Change the top, bottom, left, and right margins to **0.75"**.
   c. Select the entire document and change the font size to **12 pt**.

4. Format the title of the document.
   a. Select the title of the document and apply **Heading 1** style.
   b. Format this text in **all caps**.
   c. Change the font size to **16 pt**.
   d. Change the before paragraph spacing to **0 pt**.
   e. Add a **bottom border** to the title.

5. Select each of the section headings and apply the **Heading 2** style.

6. Modify the **Heading 2** style. Select the first section heading **("Emergency Telephones [Blue Phones]")** and make the following changes.
   a. Change before paragraph spacing to **12 pt**. and after paragraph spacing to **3 pt**.
   b. Apply **small caps** effect and **underline**.
   c. Update **Heading 2** style to match this heading. All of the section headings are updated.

7. Delete all of the blank lines in the document.

8. Select the bulleted list in the first section and change to a numbered list.

9. Apply numbering format, make formatting changes, and use the *Format Painter*.
   a. Apply numbering format to the text in the following sections: *"Assaults, Fights, or Emotional Disturbances"; "Power Failure"; "Fire"; "Earthquake"; and "Bomb Threat."*
   b. With the numbered list in the "Bomb Threat" section selected, use the *Paragraph* dialog box to set before and after paragraph spacing to **2 pt**., and deselect the **Don't add space between paragraphs of the same style** check box.
   c. Use the **Format Painter** to copy this numbering format to each of the other numbered lists.
   d. Reset each numbered list so it begins with **1**.

10. Select the text in the "Accident or Medical Emergency" section and apply and customize a bulleted list.
    a. Use a **solid square bullet** (Wingdings, Character code 110).
    b. Set left indent at **0.25"** and hanging indent at **0.25"**.
    c. Set before and after paragraph spacing to **2 pt**.
    d. Deselect the **Don't add space between paragraphs of the same style** check box.

11. Use the *Format Painter* to apply this bulleted list format to the following text in the following sections: *"Tips to Professors and Staff"* and *"Response to Students."*

12. Select the text in the "Emergency Telephone Locations" section and change indent, paragraph spacing, and style.

a. Set a **0.25"** left indent.
b. Set before and after paragraph spacing to **2 pt**.
c. Deselect the **Don't add space between paragraphs of the same style** check box.
d. Apply **Book Title** style to each of the telephone locations. Select only the location, not the text in parentheses or following text.

13. Select the text in the "Emergency Phone Numbers" section, change left indent and paragraph spacing, and set a tab stop with a dot leader.
    a. Set a **0.25"** left indent for this text.
    b. Set before and after paragraph spacing to **2 pt**.
    c. Deselect the **Don't add space between paragraphs of the same style** check box.
    d. Set a **right tab stop** at the right margin and use a **dot leader (2)**.
    e. Press **Tab** before the phone number on each of these lines. The phone numbers align at the right margin with a dot leader between the text and phone number.

14. Apply the **Intense Reference** style to the paragraph headings in the "Accident or Medical Emergency" section ("*Life-Threating Emergencies*" and "*Minor Emergencies*").

15. Use the *Replace* feature to replace all instances of "Phone 911" with "PHONE 911" with **bold** font style.

16. Insert a footer with document property fields and the current date that appears on every page.
    a. Edit the footer and use the ruler to move the center tab stop to **3.5"** and the right tab stop to **7"**.
    b. Insert the **Title** document property field at the left.
    c. Insert the **Company** document property field at center. Use the center tab stop for alignment.
    d. Insert the **current date** (third date format) that is updated automatically at the right. Use the right tab stop for alignment.
    e. Change the font size of all the text in the footer to **10 pt**.
    f. Add a **top border** to the text in the footer.

17. Insert a page border on the entire document. Use **Shadow** setting, **solid line** style, **Dark Red**, **Accent 1** color, and **1 pt**. line width.

18. Center the entire document vertically.

19. Save and close the document (Figure 2-111).

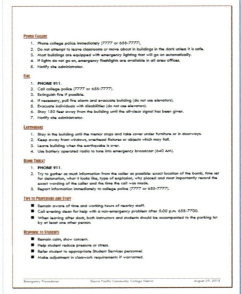

2-111 Word 2-4 completed

Independent Project 2-5

In this project, you format a bank authorization letter for Placer Hills Real Estate. You modify the formatting of an existing document, apply a theme, apply and modify styles, set tab stops, apply borders, and insert and edit hyperlinks.
[Student Learning Outcomes 2.1, 2.2, 2.7, 2.9]

File Needed: **BankAuthorization-02.docx**
Completed Project File Name: **[your initials] Word 2-5.docx**

Skills Covered in This Project

- Modify an existing document.
- Apply a document theme.
- Change margins.
- Insert automatically updated date.
- Apply and modify a style.
- Expand font spacing.

- Change paragraph spacing.
- Use the *Format Painter*.
- Set and use tab stops.
- Apply borders and shading to selected text.
- Insert a hyperlink.
- Edit a hyperlink.

---

1. Open the **BankAuthorization-02** document from your student data files.

2. Save this document as **[your initials] Word 2-5**.

3. Format the document.
   a. Change the document theme to **Whisp**.
   b. Change the margins to **Normal**.
   c. Select the entire document and change the after paragraph spacing to **18 pt**.

4. Insert a blank line after the first line of the document and insert the **current date** (third date format) that is updated automatically.

5. Click at the end of the document, press **Enter**, and type the following information. Use line breaks after the first three lines. (Note: the email address is automatically converted to a hyperlink; you will edit this later).

   Emma Cavalli
   Placer Hills Real Estate
   ecavalli@phre.com
   916-450-3334

6. Select the date line and change the after paragraph spacing to **30 pt**. Use the *Format Painter* to copy this formatting to the "Sincerely," line.

7. Apply the **Title** style to the first line of the document and change the before paragraph spacing to **36 pt**.

8. Select **"Authorization Letter to Lender,"** apply the **Intense Reference** style, and expand the font spacing to **1 pt**. on this text.

9. Select the five lines of text beginning "Bank/Financial Institution" and apply the **Book Title** style. Use the *Format Painter* to copy the style to "Seller/Borrower Signature(s)".

10. Select the five lines of text beginning "Bank/Financial Institution" and set a **right tab stop** at the right margin with a **solid underline leader**. Press **Tab** after each of these lines to insert the solid underline leader to the right margin.

11. Select the paragraph beginning "Please consider . . ." and apply a border and shading to the paragraph.
    a. Use **Shadow** setting, **solid line** style, **Black, Text 1, Lighter 50%** color, and **1½ pt.** line width.
    b. Change the options so there is **4 pt.** padding from text on the top, bottom, left, and right.
    c. Set the shading fill color to **White, Background 1, Darker 5%**.

12. Select the **"Seller/Borrower Signature(s)"** line and apply a top border that is **solid line**, **black**, and **2¼ pt.** width.

13. Select **"Placer Hills Real Estate"** in the closing lines and insert a hyperlink.
    a. Type www.phre.com as the web page address.
    b. Set the target frame to **New window** and make this the default for all hyperlinks.

14. Edit the "ecavalli@phre.com" email hyperlink and type Email Emma Cavalli as the ScreenTip.

15. Save and close the document (Figure 2-112).

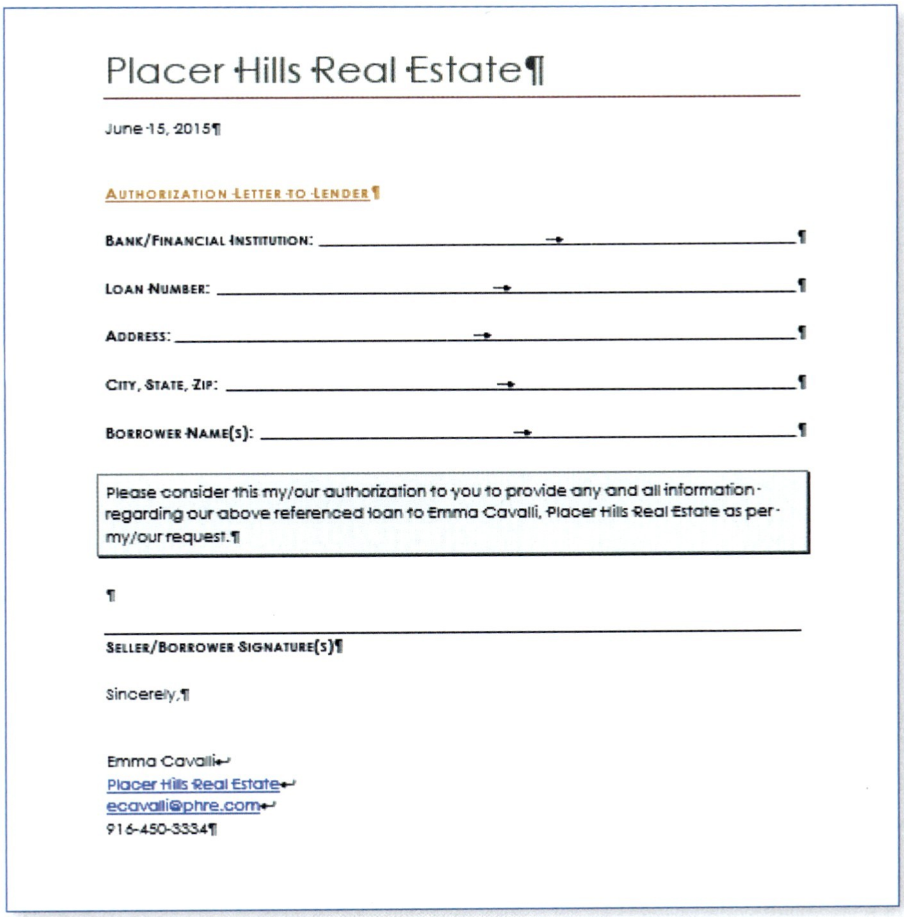

2-112 Word 2-5 completed

Independent Project 2-6

In this project, you edit, format, and customize the conference registration form for Central Sierra Insurance's Agriculture Insurance Conference. You use a continuous section break, *Find and Replace*, tab stops and leaders, styles, bullets, indents, borders, shading, and hyperlinks.
[Student Learning Outcomes 2.1, 2.2, 2.3, 2.4, 2.5, 2.6, 2.7, 2.9]

File Needed: ***ConferenceRegistrationForm-02.docx***
Completed Project File Name: ***[your initials] Word 2-6.docx***

Skills Covered in This Project

- Modify an existing document.
- Change margins, font, font size, line spacing, and paragraph spacing.
- Insert a header.
- Apply a style.
- Use *Find and Replace*.
- Insert a continuous section break.

- Insert a horizontal line.
- Set different margins for different sections.
- Customize a bulleted list and indents.
- Set and use tab stops and leaders.
- Apply borders and shading to selected text.
- Insert hyperlinks.

1. Open the **ConferenceRegistrationForm-02** document from your student data files.

2. Save this document as **[your initials] Word 2-6**.

3. Format the document.
   a. Change the top and bottom margins to **0.5"**.
   b. Select all of the text in the document and change the font size to **10 pt.**, line spacing to **1** (SS), and after paragraph spacing to **6 pt**.

4. Apply styles to title and subtitle.
   a. Cut the first line of the document and paste it in the header. Apply **Title** style, align **center**, and change the after paragraph spacing to **6 pt**.
   b. Delete the blank line below the text in the header.
   c. In the body of the document, select the first two lines beginning with "Central Sierra Insurance," apply **Subtitle** style, align **center**, and change the after paragraph spacing to **6 pt**.

5. Use *Find* and *Replace*.
   a. Use *Find* to find all occurrences of "Agriculture Insurance Conference."
   b. Apply **italic** formatting to each occurrence except in the header.
   c. Use *Replace* to find all occurrences of "Oct." and replace with **"May"**.
   d. Use *Replace* to find all occurrences of "Westfield Hotel & Spa" and replace with **"Northgate Resort"** with **bold** and **italic** font style.

6. Click at the end of the second body paragraph ("Please help us to determine . . .") and insert a **continuous** section break.

7. On the blank line below the section break, insert a **horizontal line**.

8. Click in the document below the section break and change the left and right margins to **1.25"** and apply to **This section**.

9. Select the two lines of text below the horizontal line and set a **right tab stop** with a **solid underline leader** at the right margin. Press **Tab** after each of these lines to insert the **solid underline leader** to the right margin.

10. Customize bullets and indents for the different levels.
    a. Use the *Define new Multilevel list* dialog box (in the *Multilevel List* drop-down list).
    b. On the first, second, and third levels, change the bullet to an open square bullet and change the font size of the bullet to **12 pt**.
    c. Set the indents for all levels so that the first level begins at **0"**, the text for the first level begins at **0.25"**, and additional indent for each level is **0.25"**.
    d. Apply this formatting to all of the bulleted lists.

11. Set tab stops with a leader.
    a. Select the **"Flying—Arrival time:"** line and set a **right tab stop** at **3"** with a solid underline leader.
    b. Press **Tab** after this line to insert the leader.
    c. Select the **"I need directions to *Northgate Resort* from:"** line and set a **right tab stop** at **5"** with a **solid underline leader**.
    d. Press **Tab** after this line to insert the leader.

12. Change indents and apply custom borders and shading to selected text.
    a. Select the last two lines of the document, align **center**, and change the left and right indents to **1"**.
    b. With these two lines selected, apply a double border, **¾ pt.**, and **Dark Blue**, **Text 2** to the top and bottom border of the selected text.
    c. Apply **Dark Blue**, **Text 2**, **Lighter 80%** shading to the selected text.

13. Insert a hyperlink to an email address at each of the two occurrences of "apelandale@centralsierra.com."
    a. Make sure the *Text to display* area just displays the email address and not "mailto: . . ."
    b. Type Email Asia Pelandale as the ScreenTip for each of these hyperlinks.

14. Save and close the document (Figure 2-113).

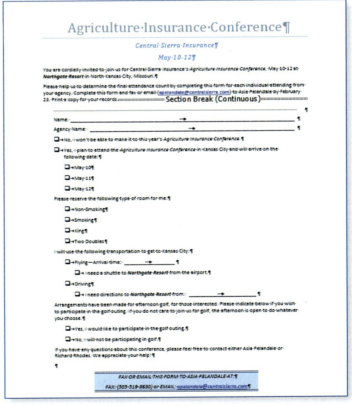

2-113 Word 2-6 completed

Improve It Project 2-7

In this project, you clean up a document that contains shortcuts for Microsoft Outlook. Courtyard Medical Plaza wants to make this document available to all of its employees. You use tab stops, styles, and many other page layout features that you have learned in this chapter to create a professional and attractive reference document.
[Student Learning Outcomes 2.1, 2.2, 2.4, 2.5, 2.7, 2.9]

File Needed: *OutlookShortcuts-02.docx*
Completed Project File Name: *[your initials] Word 2-7.docx*

Skills Covered in This Project

- Modify an existing document.
- Change margins, line spacing, and paragraph spacing.
- Apply and modify a style.
- Apply borders and shading to selected text.
- Set and modify tab stops and leaders.
- Use the *Format Painter*.
- Insert a page break.
- Edit footer content and tab stops.

1. Open the **OutlookShortcuts-02** document from your student data files.

2. Save this document as *[your initials] Word 2-7*.

3. Format the document.
   a. Change the page orientation to **Landscape**.
   b. Change the top margin to **0.5"** and the bottom, left, and right margins to **0.75"**.
   c. Select the entire document and change the line spacing to **1** and the after paragraph spacing to **4 pt**.

4. Modify and apply styles.
   a. Remove the bottom border from the title and change the after paragraph spacing to **0 pt**.
   b. Select **"Global Outlook Commands,"** add a **1 pt.**, **Dark Blue**, **Text 2** top and bottom border, and apply **White**, **Background 1**, **Darker 5%** shading.
   c. Change the before paragraph spacing to **12 pt.** and the after spacing to **0 pt**.
   d. Update **Heading 1** to match selected text.
   e. Apply the **Heading 1** style to each of the remaining headings ("*Mail*," "*Calendar*," "*Contacts*," "*Tasks*," "*Notes*," "*Journal*," and "*Formatting*").
   f. Select the third line of text on the first page ("Activity Shortcut . . .") and change the before paragraph spacing to **6 pt.** and the after spacing to **3 pt**.
   g. Set **left tab stops** on the selected text at **3"**, **5"**, and **8.25"**.
   h. Update **Heading 2** to match selected text.
   i. Apply the **Heading 2** style to the first line of text ("Activity Shortcut . . .") after each section heading.

5. Select the tabbed text below the column headings ("Activity Shortcut . . .") in the first section and set tab stops to match the column headings. Include a dot leader between the text in the first and second columns and between the third and fourth columns.

6. Use the *Format Painter* to apply the tab settings to the text in the other sections.

7. Delete any blank lines and extra tabs.

8. Remove the existing footer and insert a footer with **Courtyard Medical Plaza** at the left, **Outlook Shortcuts** aligned at the center tab stop, and **Page X of Y** aligned at the right tab stop.
   a. You need to adjust the tab stops on the ruler in the footer.
   b. For the page number, use *Page X of Y* format where *X* is the page number and *Y* is the number of pages in the document (Hint: for *Y*, insert *NumPages* field).
   c. Apply a **1 pt.**, **Dark Blue**, **Text 2** top border in the footer.
   d. Set the footer so it does not appear on the first page.

9. Insert page breaks where necessary to keep groupings together. This document fits on four pages.

10. Check the document for consistent formatting. Make any necessary changes.

11. Save and close the document (Figure 2-114).

2-114 Word 2-7 completed (pages 1 and 2 of 4)

Challenge Project 2-8

Create an agenda for an upcoming meeting for an organization you are a member of, such as a club, church, volunteer organization, student group, or neighborhood association. Do some online research to find out some of the common components of agendas. Robert's Rules of Order is a good source of information about meetings and guidelines for meeting protocol.
[Student Learning Outcomes 2.1, 2.2, 2.3, 2.6, 2.7, 2.9]

File Needed: None
Completed Project File Name: *[your initials] Word 2-8.docx*

Create a new document and save it as *[your initials] Word 2-8*. An agenda can include, but is not limited to, the following items:

- Organization name as the title
- Meeting date, start time, and end time

- Meeting location
- Meeting attendees
- Topic headings
- Topic subheadings—include details for each topic heading
- The time each topic is expected to last

Modify your document according to the following guidelines:

- Apply styles.
- Use a multilevel list for the agenda items and subheadings.
- Customize number or bullet format and indents as needed.
- Use a right tab stop with a leader to line up the amount of time to be spent on each main topic heading.
- Apply borders, shading, and/or a horizontal line to create an attractive agenda.
- Adjust margins as needed.
- Include an appropriate header and/or footer.

Challenge Project 2-9

Update your resume using some of the document formatting features learned in this chapter. Edit your resume so it is consistently formatted, easy to read, and professional looking. Do some online research on resumes to get ideas about formatting and content.
[Student Learning Outcomes 2.1, 2.2, 2.3, 2.4, 2.5, 2.6, 2.7, 2.8, 2.9]

File Needed: None
Completed Project File Name: *[your initials] Word 2-9.docx*

Open your existing resume or create a new document and save it as *[your initials] Word 2-9*. Modify your document according to the following guidelines:

- Apply a document theme.
- Apply styles to headings and subheadings to improve consistency in format.
- Adjust margins as needed.
- Use bulleted lists with customized bullets and indents to attractively arrange information.
- Set and use tab stops and indents as necessary to line up information.
- Apply borders, shading, and/or a horizontal line to set off information in your resume.
- Use page or section breaks as needed.
- Use *Find and Replace* as needed.
- Insert hyperlinks for appropriate information (e.g., email address and company names).
- If your resume is more than one page, include a header and/or footer on the second and continuing pages.

Challenge Project 2-10

Format your favorite recipe using some of the formatting features learned in this chapter. You can look up recipes online on the Food Network, Epicurious, Simply Recipes, or other food web sites. [Student Learning Outcomes 2.1, 2.2, 2.3, 2.6, 2.7, 2.9]

File Needed: None
Completed Project File Name: *[your initials] Word 2-10.docx*

Create a new document and save it as *[your initials] Word 2-10*. Your recipe should include, but is not limited to, the following:

- Recipe title
- Descriptive paragraph about the recipe
- Tab stops to arrange quantity and ingredients (and special instructions if needed)
- Numbered, step-by-step instructions
- Recipe source and/or additional information

Modify your document according to the following guidelines:

- Apply a document theme.
- Apply styles.
- Adjust margins as needed.
- Set and use a combination of tab stops (e.g., left, right, center, decimal, bar, and leaders) as necessary to attractively line up information.
- Use a numbered list for instructions.
- Use left, right, first line, and/or hanging indents as necessary.
- Apply borders, shading, page border, and/or a horizontal line to set off information in your recipe.
- Insert hyperlinks to appropriate information (e.g., link to online recipe).

Working with Reports and Multipage Documents

CHAPTER OVERVIEW

Creating a long report with a table of contents, citations, footnotes or endnotes, a reference page, and headers and footers can be a challenging task. Word 2013 has numerous tools that automatically create these components in report or multipage document. Using these tools not only saves you time when you are working on this type of document, but also improves consistency within your documents.

STUDENT LEARNING OUTCOMES (SLOs)

After completing this chapter, you will be able to:

SLO 3.1 Insert and edit footnotes and endnotes in a document (p. W3-129).

SLO 3.2 Create a bibliography with properly formatted sources and insert citations into a document (p. W3-134).

SLO 3.3 Create and edit a table of contents based on headings (p. W3-144).

SLO 3.4 Insert a cover page and modify content and content control fields (p. W3-148).

SLO 3.5 Integrate bookmarks into a multipage document (p. W3-153).

SLO 3.6 Apply and customize headers and footers in a multipage document (p. W3-156).

Case Study

American River Cycling Club (ARCC) is a community cycling club that promotes fitness for the entire region. ARCC members include recreational cyclists who enjoy the exercise and camaraderie and competitive cyclists who compete in road, mountain, and cyclo-cross races throughout the cycling season.

For the Pause & Practice projects, you create a report for club members about how to develop a personal training program. In this report, you incorporate many of the report features covered in the chapter to produce a professional-looking and useful report.

Pause & Practice 3-1: Insert endnotes into the report, convert endnotes to footnotes, add reference sources, insert citations, and create a bibliography page.

Pause & Practice 3-2: Apply styles to headings in the report, create a table of contents based on the headings in the document, modify the table of contents, and insert a cover page.

Pause & Practice 3-3: Insert and view bookmarks, create hyperlinks and cross-references to bookmarks, and customize headers and footers in the report.

Using Footnotes and Endnotes

Footnotes and *endnotes* cite reference sources used in a document. You can also use them to include additional notational information that does not cleanly fit within the text of the document. Footnotes appear at the bottom of each page, while endnotes are listed at the end of the document.

As you insert footnotes and endnotes into your document, Word numbers them consecutively. If another footnote or endnote is inserted before or between existing notes, Word automatically reorders notes. You can also customize number format and convert footnotes to endnotes or endnotes to footnotes.

Insert Footnotes

When a footnote is inserted into a document, a ***reference marker,*** which is a number or letter in superscript format (in a smaller font and slightly raised above the typed line), is inserted directly after the word. Word then places the insertion point at the bottom of the page to insert the text of the footnote. A thin top border above the note distinguishes it from the text in the body of the document.

Footnotes are placed in the body of the document at the bottom of the page, not in the footer, and the text on a page with a footnote is adjusted to allow space for the footnote.

HOW TO: Insert a Footnote

1. Position the insertion point directly after the word where the footnote is to be inserted.
2. Click the **References** tab.
3. Click the **Insert Footnote** button [*Footnotes* group] (Figure 3-1). A reference marker is inserted in the body of the document (Figure 3-2), and the insertion point is positioned after the corresponding reference marker in the footnote area of the page.

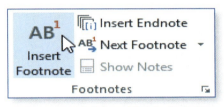

3-1 *Insert Footnote* button

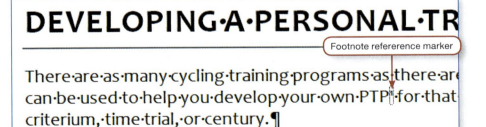

3-2 Footnote reference marker in the body of the document

4. Type the footnote text in the footnote area of the page (Figure 3-3).

3-3 Footnote text at the bottom of the page

Insert Endnotes

Inserting endnotes is similar to inserting footnotes. The main difference is the text for the endnote is placed after the text at the end of the document rather than at the bottom of the page where the note appears.

HOW TO: Insert an Endnote

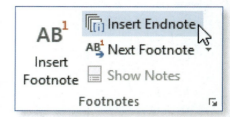

3-4 *Insert Endnote* button

1. Position the insertion point directly after the word where the endnote is to be inserted.
2. Click the **References** tab.
3. Click the **Insert Endnote** button [*Footnotes* group] (Figure 3-4). The reference marker is inserted in the body of the document and the insertion point is positioned after the corresponding reference marker at the end of the document.
4. Type the endnote text.

> **ANOTHER WAY**
>
> **Alt+Ctrl+F** inserts a footnote.
> **Alt+Ctrl+D** inserts an endnote.

View Footnotes and Endnotes

Once you have footnotes or endnotes in your document, it is easy to see the footnote or endnote text at the bottom of a page or at the end of the document, but you might have a difficult time locating the reference markers in the body of the document. Word provides you with a tool to easily locate footnote reference markers in your document.

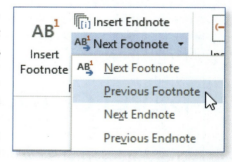

3-5 *Next Footnote* drop-down list

Click the **Next Footnote** button in the *Footnotes* group on the *References* tab to move to the next footnote (Figure 3-5). Click the **Next Footnote** drop-down arrow to display a list of options to move to next or previous footnotes or endnotes. Click the **Show Notes** button in the *Footnotes* group to toggle between the note reference markers and the note text.

3-6 Footnote text displayed

Word also displays the text of the footnote or endnote when you place your pointer over a reference marker (Figure 3-6).

Customize Footnotes and Endnotes

By default, footnotes are numbered consecutively with numbers (e.g., 1, 2, 3) and endnotes are numbered with lowercase Roman numerals (e.g., i, ii, iii). You might decide to use letters or symbols such as an asterisk (*), section mark (§), or number or pound symbol (#) as reference markers. You can customize how notes are numbered and where they are displayed in a document.

HOW TO: Customize Footnotes and Endnotes

1. Select the **References** tab.
2. Click the **Footnotes** launcher [*Footnotes* group] to open the *Footnote and Endnote* dialog box (Figure 3-7).
3. In the *Location* area, select either **Footnotes** or **Endnotes**.
   - In the drop-down list for *Footnotes,* you have the option to position the footnote text at the *Bottom of page* (default) or *Below text*.
   - In the drop-down list for *Endnotes,* you have the option to position the endnote text at the *End of document* (default) or *End of section*.
4. In the *Format* area, you can change any of the following: *Number format, Custom mark, Start at,* or *Numbering.*
5. In the *Apply changes* area, you can apply changes to the *Whole document* or *This section* (if there are sections in your document).
6. Click **Apply** to close the dialog box and apply the changes. Do not press *Insert,* which inserts a footnote or endnote in the document.

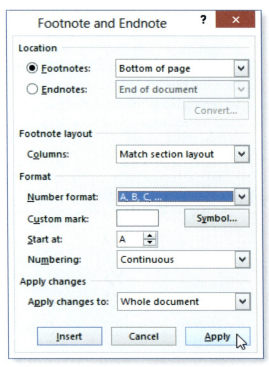

3-7 *Footnote and Endnote* dialog box

> **MORE INFO**
>
> You can also use the *Footnote and Endnote* dialog box to insert a footnote or endnote.

Modify Footnote and Endnote Format

In addition to customizing placement and note format, you can also change how the text of the footnotes and endnotes appears. You do this the same way you format regular text in the document.

Select the footnote or endnote text and apply any formatting changes such as font, font size, style, line or paragraph spacing, or text effects (Figure 3-8). You can apply changes using the buttons on the *Home* or *Page Layout* tab, the context menu (right-click selected text), the mini toolbar, or keyboard shortcuts.

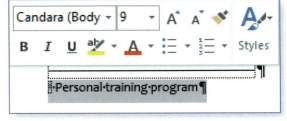

3-8 **Apply formatting to footnote text**

Modify Footnote and Endnote Styles

The appearance of the footnotes and endnotes in your document is determined by styles. Styles control the font, font size, text styles and effects, and paragraph formatting. When you insert a footnote in your document, Word applies the *Footnote Text* style; this style controls the formatting of all of the footnote text in your document.

You can modify the footnote or endnote style, which automatically updates all of your footnote or endnote text to reflect the changes you made to the style.

HOW TO: Modify the Footnote or Endnote Style

1. Right-click the footnote or endnote text and select **Style** from the context menu. The *Style* dialog box opens and the name of the style is displayed in the *Styles* area (Figure 3-9).
2. Click the **Modify** button to open the *Modify Style* dialog box.
3. You can change the basic font formatting in the *Formatting* area.
4. Click the **Format** button to display a list of other formatting options (Figure 3-10).
   - When you select an option, another dialog box opens.
   - Make any desired formatting changes and click **OK** to close the dialog box.
5. Click **OK** to close the *Modify Style* dialog box.

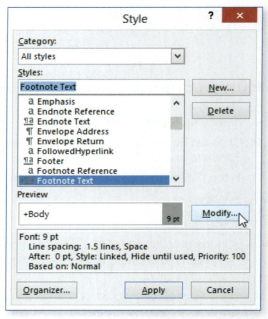

3-9 *Style* dialog box

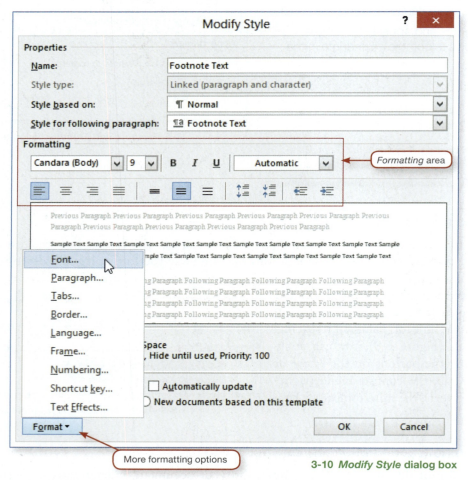

3-10 *Modify Style* dialog box

6. Click **Apply** to apply any changes to the style and close the *Style* dialog box.

Convert Footnotes and Endnotes

There might be times when you want to convert footnotes to endnotes or endnotes to footnotes. Rather than deleting and re-creating them, you can convert notes. When you convert notes, Word automatically renumbers the reference markers and moves the note text to the correct location in the document.

HOW TO: Convert All Notes

1. Click the **Footnotes** launcher [*References* tab, *Footnotes* group] to open the *Footnote and Endnote* dialog box.
2. In the *Location* area, click the **Convert** button. The *Convert Notes* dialog box opens (Figure 3-11).
3. Select from one of the three convert options.
4. Click **OK** to close the *Convert Notes* dialog box.
5. Click **Close** to close the *Footnote and Endnote* dialog box. Do not click *Insert* or Word will insert a footnote or endnote.

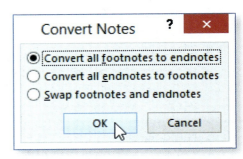

3-11 *Convert Notes* dialog box

> **MORE INFO**
>
> All three of the convert options are active *only* if you have both footnotes and endnotes in your document. Otherwise, only one option is active.

You can convert individual notes using the context menu. Right-click a footnote or endnote (*not* the reference marker in the text of the document) and select **Convert to Endnote** or **Convert to Footnote** (Figure 3-12).

Move Footnotes and Endnotes

You can move footnotes and endnotes in the same way you move text in a document. To move a note, select the **reference marker** in the body of the document (Figure 3-13) and use one of the following methods:

- Drag and drop
- **Ctrl+X** to cut and **Ctrl+V** to paste
- **Cut** and **Paste** buttons [*Home* tab, *Clipboard* group]
- **Cut** and **Paste** options in the context menu

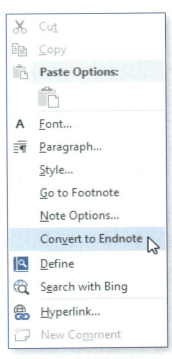

3-12 Convert individual notes

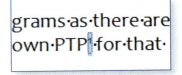

3-13 Select note to move

> **MORE INFO**
>
> When moving a note, select the note carefully to ensure that you are only moving the note and not any spaces or text.

Delete Footnotes and Endnotes

When you delete a note, Word removes the reference marker and the text of the note. Your remaining notes are renumbered and remain in consecutive order.

HOW TO: Delete a Note

1. Select the **reference marker** in the body of the document (*not* the text of the footnote or endnote at the bottom of the page or end of the document).
2. Press **Delete** on the keyboard.
   - Deleting footnote or endnote text in footnote or endnote area will not delete note reference.
3. Check to ensure proper spacing around text where the note was deleted.

SLO 3.2

Creating a Bibliography and Inserting Citations

Typically, the most tedious and time-consuming aspect of writing a research paper is compiling sources, creating a bibliography page, and citing sources in the body of the report. A *source* is the complete bibliographic reference for a book, journal article, or web page. A *citation* is the abbreviated source information that you place in the body of the report to give credit to the source of the information you use. A *bibliography* or *works cited* page lists the sources used in the report. Word has tools to create sources, insert citations, and create a bibliography or works cited page at the end of your report.

Report Styles

There are a variety of report styles, and each differs not only in the overall format of the report but also in the format for sources and citations. The most common report styles are the following:

- APA (American Psychological Association)
- Chicago *(The Chicago Manual of Style)*
- MLA (Modern Language Association)
- Turabian

MLA and APA are the two most common report formats. The following table lists some of the general characteristics of each of these two report styles. Within each of these report formats, there can be much variance depending on the preference of your instructor. Always follow the formatting instructions your instructor provides.

Common Report Styles

Report Features	APA	MLA
Font	11 or 12 pt.	11 or 12 pt.
Line Spacing	Academic APA is double spaced and business APA is single spaced.	Double space.
Margins	For an unbound report use 1" for all margins. For a left bound report use 1.5" left margin and 1" top, bottom, and right margins.	Use 1" margins.

Heading Information	Heading information is typically typed on a title page.	Left align at the top of the first page and include author's name, instructor's name, class, and date on separate lines.
Title	The title is either on the title page or centered on the first page of the report.	Centered on the first page of the report.
Header	Include report title and page number on the right.	Include author's last name and page number on the right.
Uses	Typically use in social and behavioral sciences, business, and nursing.	Typically use in humanities.

Bibliography Styles

As you begin compiling your sources for your report, the first thing you need to do is select the ***bibliography style*** of the report. Most likely your instructor will tell you what style to use. You can then select this bibliography style in Word so Word correctly formats sources and citations.

HOW TO: Set the Bibliography Style of the Report

1. Click the **Reference** tab.
2. Click the **Style** drop-down arrow [*Citations & Bibliography* group].
3. Select the style of the report from the drop-down list of report styles (Figure 3-14).

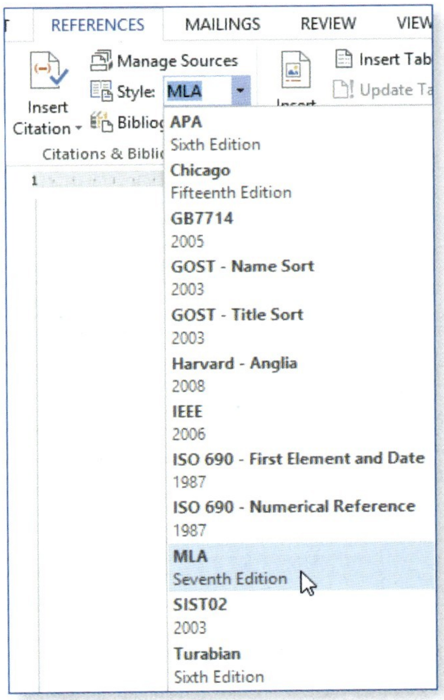

> **MORE INFO**
>
> The report style you select controls the formatting of sources and citations; it does not control the overall formatting of your report. To do that, you must apply the correct formatting to the body of your report.

REFERENCES	MAILINGS	REVIEW	VIEW

Manage Sources   Insert Tab
Style: MLA ▾   Update Ta
Insert Citation ▾ Biblio
Citations & Biblio

APA
Sixth Edition
Chicago
Fifteenth Edition
GB7714
2005
GOST - Name Sort
2003
GOST - Title Sort
2003
Harvard - Anglia
2008
IEEE
2006
ISO 690 - First Element and Date
1987
ISO 690 - Numerical Reference
1987
MLA
Seventh Edition
SIST02
2003
Turabian
Sixth Edition

3-14 **Select bibliography style**

Add a New Source

As you are writing a report, you should be gathering bibliographic information about sources used in your report (e.g., author; title of book, journal, or article; publication date and edition; publisher or online location). You need to add this information to your report in Word. Word inserts a citation in your report at the insertion point and stores this source information. You then can access these stored sources to insert additional citations and create a bibliography page.

HOW TO: Add a New Source

1. Position the insertion point in your document at the point where you want to insert a citation.
2. Click the **Insert Citation** button [*References* tab, *Citations & Bibliography* group].

3. Select **Add New Source**. The *Create Source* dialog box opens (see Figure 3-16).

4. Select the type of source in the *Type of Source* area.

   - The fields for the source change depending on the type of source you choose.

5. Click the **Edit** button to the right of the *Author* area. The *Edit Name* dialog box opens (Figure 3-15).

   - Type the author name in this box so you can specify first, middle, and last names.
   - Add additional authors if your source has more than one author.
   - If the source is an organization or company (e.g., USA Cycling or Velo News), click the **Corporate Author** check box instead of the *Edit* button in the *Create Source* dialog box (see Figure 3-16).

6. Type in the author information and click **OK** when finished (see Figure 3-15).

   - Click the **Add** button to add additional authors.
   - You can also reorder multiple authors by selecting an author in the *Names* area and clicking the **Up** or **Down** button.

7. Type in other source information as needed (Figure 3-16).

   - As you type in other source information, Word automatically creates a *Tag name* for your source.
   - You can edit the *Tag name* if desired.

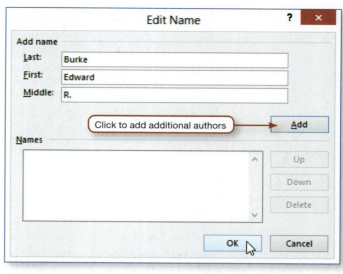

3-15 *Edit Name* dialog box

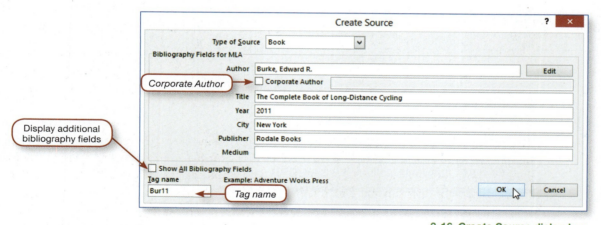

3-16 *Create Source* dialog box

8. Click the **Show All Bibliography Fields** check box to display more fields. For example, you might need to type in the edition of the book.

9. Click **OK** to close the *Create Source* dialog box.

10. The citation is inserted in the document in the report style you selected (Figure 3-17).

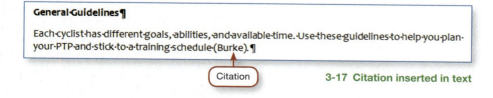

3-17 Citation inserted in text

Insert Citations

Many times you will cite a source more than once in a report. Once you have added a source to your document, you can insert this same citation again in your document without entering source information again. When inserting a citation, you can choose from citations you have previously created.

HOW TO: Insert a Citation

1. Position the insertion point in your document at the point where you want a citation inserted.
2. Click the **Insert Citation** button [*References* tab, *Citations & Bibliography* group].
   - A list of previously used or created sources is displayed in the drop-down list (Figure 3-18).
3. Select from your list of sources.
4. The citation is inserted in the document.
   - When a citation is inserted, Word automatically inserts a space between the citation and the preceding word.

> **MORE INFO**
>
> When inserting citations, the citation typically is placed one space after the preceding word and directly before the punctuation mark. Always check your document to ensure proper spacing.

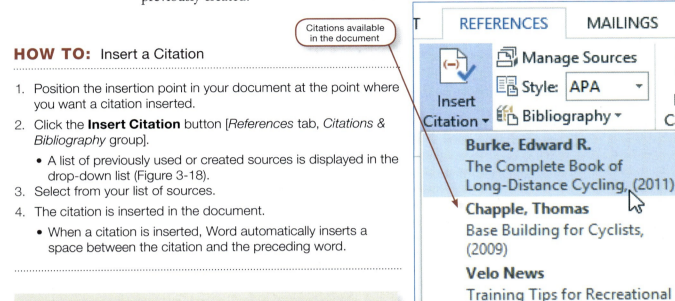

Citations available in the document

3-18 Insert citation from a previously created source

Insert a Placeholder

There might be times when you need to insert a citation but do not have all of the bibliographic information to create the source. You can insert a *placeholder* in the report to temporarily mark a spot where a citation needs to be completed. Later, you can go back in and add bibliographic source information for any placeholders inserted in the document.

HOW TO: Insert a Placeholder

1. Position the insertion point in your document at the point where you want a placeholder inserted.
2. Click the **Insert Citation** button [*References* tab, *Citations & Bibliography* group].
3. Select **Add New Placeholder**. The *Placeholder Name* dialog box opens (Figure 3-19).

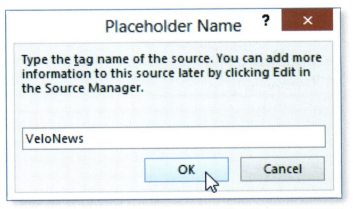

3-19 Insert a placeholder

4. Type in the name of the placeholder.
   - You can't use spaces between words in the placeholder text.
   - Use an underscore or merge words together when naming a placeholder.
5. Click **OK**. The placeholder is inserted into the document and looks similar to a citation (Figure 3-20).

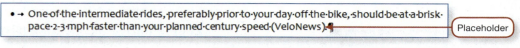

One·of·the·intermediate·rides,·preferably·prior·to·your·day·off·the·bike,·should·be·at·a·brisk·pace·2-3·mph·faster·than·your·planned·century·speed·(VeloNews). — Placeholder

3-20 Placeholder in the body of the document

Manage Sources

The ***Source Manager*** dialog box allows you to create sources, copy sources created and used in other documents, modify sources, and add bibliographic information to placeholders. This dialog box displays which sources are used in your report and the placeholders that need bibliographic information.

HOW TO: Manage Sources

1. Click the **Manage Sources** button [*References* tab, *Citations & Bibliography* group]. The *Source Manager* dialog box opens (Figure 3-21).
   - The *Master List* of sources on the left displays *all* available sources. Some of these may have been created in other Word documents.
   - The *Current List* displays the sources available in your current document.
   - The *Preview* area displays the contents of your source.
   - The sources in the *Current List* that are cited in the document have a check mark next to them.
   - The sources in the *Current List* that are placeholders have a question mark next to them. These placeholders need additional information.

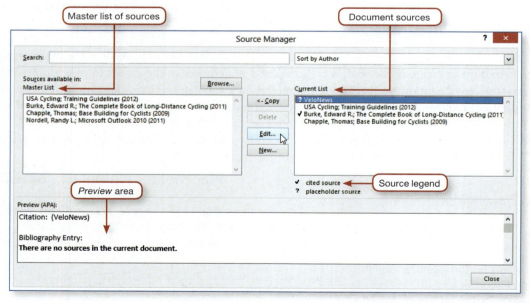

3-21 *Source Manager* dialog box

2. To copy a source from the *Master List* to the *Current List,* select the source and press the **Copy** button. The copied source remains on the *Master List.*

3. To edit a source from either list, select the source and click the **Edit** button. The *Edit Source* dialog box opens.

- Make changes to the source and press **OK**.
- Word automatically updates any citations in your document if you make changes to the source.

4. To add bibliographic information to a placeholder, select the placeholder and click the **Edit** button. The *Edit Source* dialog box opens.

- Add bibliographic information to the placeholder and press **OK**.
- When bibliographic information is added to a placeholder, it becomes a complete source and the question mark next to it changes to a check.
- Word automatically replaces the placeholder with a citation in your document when you add bibliographic information to a placeholder.

5. Click the **New** button to create a new source. The *Create Source* dialog box opens.

- Type in the bibliographic information and press **OK**.
- This source is now available as a citation to insert in your document.
- This source is also added to the *Master List*.

6. To delete a source from either list, select the source and click the **Delete** button.

- You cannot delete a source from the *Current List* if it is cited in the document.
- If a source is in both lists and you delete it from one list, it is not deleted from the other list.

7. Click **Close** to close the *Source Manager* dialog box and apply any changes made.

Edit Citations and Sources

After citations are inserted into the document, you can edit the citation or source without using the *Source Manager* dialog box. When you click a citation in your document, you see a drop-down list of editing options (Figure 3-22).

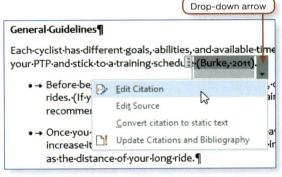
3-22 Edit citation options

- **Edit Citation:** Options in the *Edit Citation* dialog box allow you to add a page number to the citation or suppress any currently displayed information.
- **Edit Source:** Options in the *Edit Source* dialog box allow you to update source bibliographic information.
- **Convert citation to static text:** This option changes the citation from a Word field that is automatically generated and updated to static text that is not updated.
- **Update Citations and Bibliography:** This option updates your bibliography page to reflect any changes you have made to citations or sources.

> **MORE INFO**
>
> You can edit placeholders using either the drop-down list or context menu.

You can move or delete a citation or placeholder in the body of the text by clicking the citation or placeholder handle on the left and dragging to a new location (to move) or by pressing **Delete** (to delete) on your keyboard (Figure 3-23).

3-23 **Select a citation to move or delete**

Insert a Bibliography

Once you have created your sources and inserted citations in the body of the report, you are now ready to create a bibliography page. The bibliography page is automatically generated from the sources in your document and is formatted according to the style of report you selected. Word provides you with a few bibliography options.

The *Bibliography, References*, and *Works Cited* built-in options insert a title before the sources. The *Insert Bibliography* option just inserts the sources; you can add a title of your choice. If you are planning on using a table of contents in your report, it is best to use one of the built-in options because Word applies a style for the bibliography title, which allows the bibliography page to automatically be included in the table contents.

HOW TO: Insert a Bibliography

1. Position the insertion point in your document at the point where you want the bibliography to begin.
    - It is usually good to insert a page break (**Ctrl+Enter**) at the end of the document and begin the bibliography on a new page.
2. Click the **Bibliography** button [*References* tab, *Citations & Bibliography* group] to display the list of options (Figure 3-24).
3. Select your bibliography option. The bibliography is inserted in the document.

If changes are made to sources after the bibliography page has been inserted, you have to update the bibliography. Click one of the references on the bibliography page to select the entire bibliography and click the **Update Citations and Bibliography** (Figure 3-25).

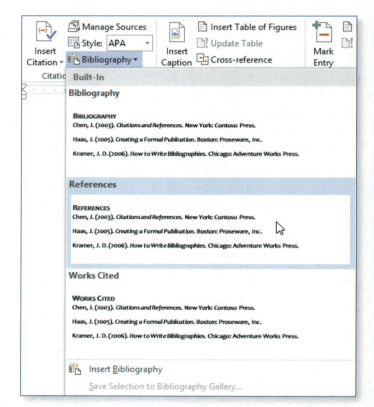

3-24 Insert bibliography

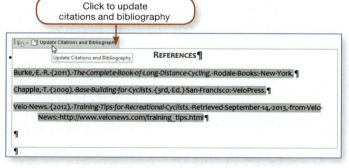

3-25 Bibliography inserted into the document

> **ANOTHER WAY**
>
> Right-click your bibliography and choose **Update Field** or press **F9** to update your bibliography.

For this Pause & Practice project, you modify the *Developing a Personal Training Program* report for American River Cycling Club. You select the report style, add and modify notes, add sources and citations, and insert a bibliography page.

File Needed: ***PersonalTrainingProgram-03.docx***
Completed Project File Name: ***[your initials] PP W3-1.docx***

1. Open the ***PersonalTrainingProgram-03*** document from your student data files.

2. Save this document as ***[your initials] PP W3-1***.

3. Insert endnotes into the report.
   a. Position the insertion point after "PTP" (first page, first paragraph).
   b. Click **Insert Endnote** [*References* tab, *Footnotes* group]. Word moves the insertion point to the endnote area on the last page.
   c. Type Personal training program.
   d. Position the insertion point after the first instance of "Max VO2" (third page, "Training Intensity and Heart Rate" section).

> **MORE INFO**
>
> Use the *Find* feature in the *Navigation* pane to locate specific words.

   e. Click **Insert Endnote** [*References* tab, *Footnotes* group].
   f. Type The highest rate of oxygen consumption attainable during maximal or exhaustive exercise.
   g. Position the insertion point after "RPM" (third page, "Training Intensity and Heart Rate" section).
   h. Click **Insert Endnote** [*References* tab, *Footnotes* group].
   i. Type Revolutions per minute.
   j. Apply **bold** and *italic* formatting to the words "maximal" and "exhaustive" in the second endnote (Figure 3-26).

Personal·training·program¶
The·highest·rate·of·oxygen·consumption·attainable·during·*maximal*·or·*exhaustive*·exercise¶
Revolutions·per·minute¶

3-26 Endnotes added to report

4. Convert endnotes to footnotes and change numbering.
   a. Click the **Footnotes** launcher [*References* tab, *Footnotes* group]. The *Footnote and Endnote* dialog box opens.
   b. Click the **Convert** button to open the *Convert Notes* dialog box (Figure 3-27).
   c. Select **Convert all endnotes to footnotes** and click **OK**.

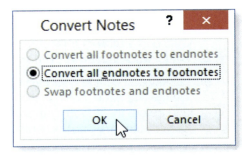

3-27 Convert endnotes to footnotes

d. Click **Close** to the close the *Footnote and Endnote* dialog box.

e. Click the **Footnotes** launcher again to open the *Footnote and Endnote* dialog box.

f. Click the **Footnotes** radio button.

g. Click the **Number format** drop-down arrow and select **a, b, c . . .** option (Figure 3-28). Don't change any of the other *Format* settings.

h. Choose **Apply** to close the *Footnote and Endnote* dialog box and apply the changes.

i. Check your document to confirm that endnotes have been converted to footnotes and that the number format has been changed.

5. Change the style of the footnotes.

a. Right-click the footnote text at the bottom of the first page.

b. Select **Style** from the context menu. The *Style* dialog box opens.

c. Click the **Modify** button to open the *Modify Style* dialog box (Figure 3-29).

d. Change the font size to **9 pt**.

e. Change line spacing to **1.5**.

f. Click **OK** to close the *Modify Style* dialog box.

g. Choose **Apply** to close the *Style* dialog box.

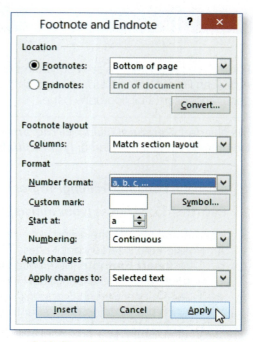

3-28 **Change number format of footnotes**

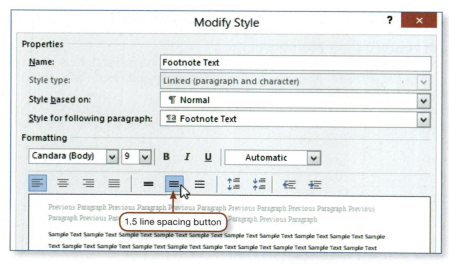

3-29 **Modify *Footnote Text* style**

6. Select the report style for sources and citations.

a. Click the **Style** drop-down list [*References* tab, *Citations & Bibliography* group].

b. Select **MLA Seventh Edition**.

7. Add a new source and insert a citation.

a. On the first page, position the insertion point after the word "schedule" and before the period (first paragraph, "General Guidelines" section).

b. Click the **Insert Citation** button [*References* tab, *Citations & Bibliography* group].

c. Select **Add New Source**. The *Create Source* dialog box opens.

d. Select **Book** as the type of source.

    e. Click the **Edit** button to open the *Edit Name* dialog box.

    f. In the *Author* area, type Burke for *Last,* Edward for *First,* and R. for *Middle*.

    g. Click **OK** to close the dialog box.

    h. Type the following in the *Create Source* dialog box:

> *Title:* The Complete Book of Long-Distance Cycling
> *Year:* 2011
> *City:* New York
> *Publisher:* Rodale Books
> *Tag name:* Burke

    i. Click **OK** to add the source, insert the citation, and close the dialog box.

8. Add a placeholder to the report.

    a. On the first page, position the insertion point after the word "speed" and before the period (last bulleted item, "Pace of Rides" section).

    b. Click the **Insert Citation** button [*References* tab, *Citations & Bibliography* group].

    c. Select **Add New Placeholder**. The *Placeholder Name* dialog box opens.

    d. Type VeloNews (no space between words) as the placeholder text.

    e. Press **OK** to insert the placeholder and close the dialog box.

9. Manage sources to add a new source and complete bibliographic information for the placeholder.

    a. Click the **Manage Sources** button [*References* tab, *Citations & Bibliography* group]. The *Source Manager* dialog box opens.

    b. Select **VeloNews** in the *Current List* area and click the **Edit** button.

    c. Type the following:

> *Type of Source:* **Document from Web Site**
> *Corporate Author* (check **Corporate Author** check box): Velo News
> *Name of Web Page:* Training Tips for Recreational Cyclists
> *Name of Web Site:* Velo News
> *Year:* 2012
> *Year Accessed:* 2013 (check **Show All Bibliography Fields** box)
> *Month Accessed:* September
> *Day Accessed:* 14
> *URL:* http://www.velonews.com/training_tips.html

    d. Click **OK** to close the *Edit Source* dialog box. The placeholder is updated as a complete source.

    e. Click the **New** button to create a new source.

    f. Type the following:

> *Type of Source:* **Book**
> *Author:* Thomas Chapple
> *Title:* Base Building for Cyclists
> *Year:* 2009
> *City:* San Francisco
> *Publisher:* VeloPress
> *Edition* (check **Show All Bibliography Fields** check box): 3rd
> *Tag name:* Chapple

    g. Click **OK** to close the *Create Source* dialog box.

    h. Click **Close** to close the *Source Manager* dialog box.

10. Insert citations into the report.

    a. On the second page, position the insertion point after "rest day" and before the period (first paragraph, "Number of Rides per Week" section).

b. Click the **Insert Citation** button [*References* tab, *Citations & Bibliography* group] (Figure 3-30).

c. Select the **Chapple**, **Thomas** source. The citation is inserted into the report.

d. Using the **Insert Citation** button, insert the following citations:

Burke, **Edward**, **R.**: after "training week" and before the period (page 2, last bulleted item in the "Duration of Rides" section).

Chapple, **Thomas**: after "maximum heart rate" and before the period (page 3, first paragraph in "Training Intensity and Heart Rate" section).

Velo News: after "overtraining" and before the period (page 3, at the end of "Other Heart Rate Factors" section).

11. Insert a bibliography and change report style.

a. Position the insertion point on the blank line at the end of the document and press **Ctrl+Enter** to insert a page break.

b. Click the **Bibliography** button [*References* tab, *Citations & Bibliography* group] and select **References** from the drop-down list. The *Reference* page is inserted on the blank page at the end of the document.

c. **Center** the *References* title and apply **10 pt**. after paragraph spacing.

d. Click the **Style** drop-down list [*References* tab, *Citations & Bibliography* group].

e. Select **APA Sixth Edition**.

12. Save and close the document (Figure 3-31).

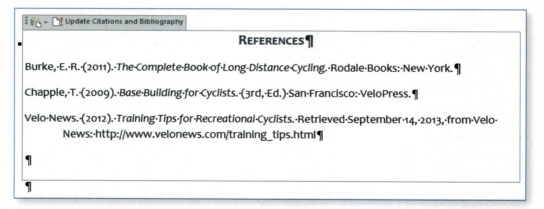

3-30 Insert a citation

3-31 PP W3-1 References page

SLO 3.3 # Inserting a Table of Contents

Most long reports have a ***table of contents*** to provide readers with an overview of the material covered in the report. The table of contents reflects the headings in the report; some tables of contents list only the main headings while others might list second- and third-level headings. Typically, a table of contents lists headings on the left and page numbers on the right with a dot leader separating them.

You can create a table of contents manually by typing in the headings, using a tab with a dot leader, and then typing the page number. But with Word you can automatically generate a table of contents based upon the headings in your report. This saves you time, and, if you generate your table of contents this way, it automatically updates if topics are moved or page numbering changes in the report.

Use Heading Styles for a Table of Contents

Word can automatically generate a table of contents listing the headings in your report if **heading styles** are applied to each heading. Styles control the appearance of text by applying a specific font, font size, color, font styles and effects, and spacing to the text on which a style is applied. The document **theme** determines the appearance of the styles. Many of the commonly used styles are displayed in the *Styles* gallery.

> ▶ **MORE INFO**
>
> Styles and themes were introduced in Chapter 2.

The first step in automatically generating a table of contents in a report is to apply a heading style to each heading in the document. Word provides you with multiple levels of heading styles (e.g., Heading 1, Heading 2, etc.).

HOW TO: Apply Heading Styles

1. Select the heading where you want to apply a style.
2. Click the heading style to apply [*Home* tab, *Styles* group] (Figure 3-32). The style is applied to the heading.
   - Apply *Heading 1* to main headings, *Heading 2* to second level headings, and other heading styles as needed.
   - When you place the insertion point on a style, Word displays a live preview of the style and temporarily applies the style to the selected text.
   - Click the **More** button to expand the *Style* gallery to display more styles.

3-32 Document styles displayed in the *Style* gallery

3. Continue to select headings and apply styles. Every heading that you want to have in your table of contents must have a style.
   - When a heading style has been applied to text, there is an *Expand/Collapse* button to the left of the heading (Figure 3-33). Click the **Expand/Collapse** button to expand or collapse the text below the heading.

3-33 Expand or collapse text below heading

Insert a Built-In Table of Contents

You can insert a built-in table of contents that includes the headings in your document. Word inserts the table of contents at the point in your report where the insertion point is located. It is a good idea to insert a blank page before the first page of your report for your table of contents.

HOW TO: Insert a Built-In Table of Contents

1. Place the insertion point before the first line of the report and press **Ctrl+Enter** to insert a page break.
2. Position the insertion point at the top of the new first page.
3. Click the **References** tab.
4. Click the **Table of Contents** button [*Table of Contents* group] (Figure 3-34).
5. Select a built-in table of contents to insert. The table of contents is inserted into your report (Figure 3-35).

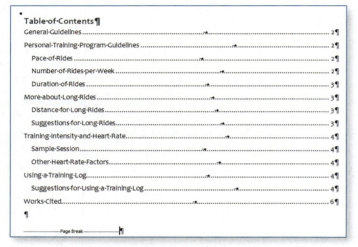

3-35 Table of contents inserted into the report

3-34 Insert built-in table of contents

Insert a Custom Table of Contents

You can also insert a table of contents and customize the format and appearance of the table. When you insert a custom table of contents, the "Table of Contents" title is not automatically inserted as it is when you insert a built-in table of contents. If you want a title on your custom table of contents page, you should type it before inserting your table of contents.

> **MORE INFO**
>
> It is usually best to just apply font formatting (not a heading style) to the table of contents title. If a heading style is applied to the table of contents title, the table of contents title is included as an item in the table of contents when it is updated.

HOW TO: Insert a Custom Table of Contents

1. Place the insertion point before the first line of your report and press **Ctrl+Enter** to insert a page break.
2. Position the insertion point at the top of the new first page.
   - If desired, type a title for the table of contents and press **Enter**. Do not apply a heading style to the title.
3. Click the **Table of Contents** button [*References* tab, *Table of Contents* group].

4. Select **Custom Table of Contents**. The *Table of Contents* dialog box opens (Figure 3-36).

- A preview of the table of contents appears in the *Print Preview* area.
- Below the *Print Preview* area, you can choose to not display page numbers or not have them aligned on the right and select the type of leader to use with right-aligned page numbers.

5. In the *General* area, select a table of contents format from the **Formats** drop-down list.

6. Select the number of heading levels to display in the *Show levels* area.

7. Click **OK** to insert the table of contents.

3-36 *Table of Contents* dialog box

Modify a Table of Contents

After inserting a table of contents, you might decide that you want a different format or to change the levels of headings that are displayed. When you update a table of contents, you are actually replacing the old table of contents with a new one.

HOW TO: Modify a Table of Contents

1. Click anywhere in the table of contents.
2. Click the **Table of Contents** button [*References* tab, *Table of Contents* group].
3. Select **Custom Table of Contents**. The *Table of Contents* dialog box opens.
4. Make changes to the table of contents.
5. Click **OK**. A dialog box opens, confirming you want to replace the existing table of contents (Figure 3-37).
6. Click **YES** to insert the new table of contents.

3-37 **Replace existing table of contents**

Update a Table of Contents

When you make changes to your report such as adding or modifying headings, content, or page breaks, the content and page numbers in the table of contents may no longer be accurate. You need to update the table of contents to reflect these changes. You have the option of updating only page numbers or updating the entire table of contents, which includes both content and page numbers.

HOW TO: Update a Table of Contents

1. Click anywhere in the table of contents.
2. Click the **Update Table** button [*References* tab, *Table of Contents* group]. The *Update Table of Contents* dialog box opens (Figure 3-38).
3. Select either **Update page numbers only** or **Update entire table**.
4. Click **OK** to update the table of contents.

3-38 **Update table of contents**

▶ **ANOTHER WAY**

Press **F9** or right-click the table of contents and select **Update Field** to update the table of contents.

Remove a Table of Contents

If you no longer want a table of contents in your report, you can easily remove it. Click the **Table of Contents** button in the *Table of Contents* group on the *References* tab and select **Remove Table of Contents.** The table of contents is removed from your document (Figure 3-39).

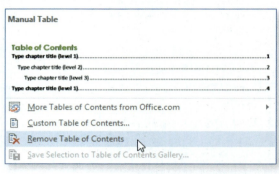

3-39 Remove table of contents

SLO 3.4

Inserting a Cover Page

Some reports have a title page as the cover or introduction. If you're writing a formal report in APA style, there is a specific way you must organize the title page. But if you're present-ing a market analysis or product feasibility report at work, you might want a *cover page* to introduce the report with professional appeal. Word provides you with a variety of cover page options.

Insert a Built-In Cover Page

When you insert a cover page into a document, Word automatically inserts it at the beginning of the document and inserts a page break to push the existing first page content to the sec-ond page.

To insert a cover page, click the **Cover Page** button in the *Pages* group on the *Insert* tab and select one of the built-in cover pages from the drop-down list (Figure 3-40). More custom cover pages are available on Office.com. Select **More Cover Pages from Office.com** to display a list of additional cover pages.

3-40 Insert built-in cover page

Customize Cover Page Content

The built-in cover pages in Word are arrange-ments of graphics, text boxes, and Word fields. Some of the fields are document property fields and some are *content control fields,* fields where you can type custom information. You can customize the content of the fields, delete unwanted Word fields, and modify the graphics and text boxes on the cover page. Cover pages are controlled by the theme of your document, which means the colors and fonts change depending on the theme selected for the document.

Customize Document Property Content

If you have added information to the document properties of your document, Word automatically populates the document properties fields in the cover page. When you type information into a document property field on the cover page, Word adds this information to your document properties.

HOW TO: Customize Document Properties

1. Click the **File** tab to open the *Backstage* view and select **Info** to display document properties (Figure 3-41).
2. Click the **Show All Properties** link at the bottom.
   - This link toggles between *Show All Properties* and *Show Fewer Properties*.
3. Add or modify document property content.
   - Some fields, such as *Last Modified* and *Created,* cannot be modified.
   - To remove the *Author,* right-click the author and select **Remove Person**.
4. Click the **Back** arrow to return to the document. Word updates the document property fields on the cover page.

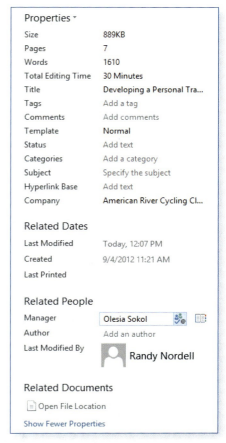

Properties ▾	
Size	889KB
Pages	7
Words	1610
Total Editing Time	30 Minutes
Title	Developing a Personal Tra...
Tags	Add a tag
Comments	Add comments
Template	Normal
Status	Add text
Categories	Add a category
Subject	Specify the subject
Hyperlink Base	Add text
Company	American River Cycling Cl...

Related Dates

Last Modified	Today, 12:07 PM
Created	9/4/2012 11:21 AM
Last Printed	

Related People

Manager	Olesia Sokol
Author	Add an author
Last Modified By	Randy Nordell

Related Documents

Open File Location

Show Fewer Properties

3-41 Document properties on the *Backstage* view

Add or Remove Document Property Fields

You can also add document property fields to the cover page or remove them. When you add a document property field to a cover page, the content of this field is automatically populated with the information from your document properties.

HOW TO: Add Document Property Fields

1. Position the insertion point at the place where you want to insert the document property field.
2. Click the **Insert** tab.
3. Click the **Quick Parts** button [*Text* group] (Figure 3-42).
4. Choose **Document Property**.
5. Select a document property field from the drop-down list. The document property field is inserted into the document.

> ▶ **MORE INFO**
>
> You can insert document property fields anywhere in a document.

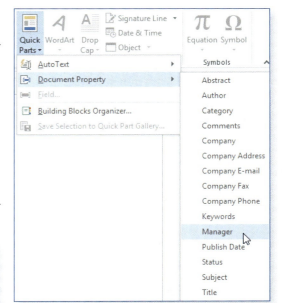

3-42 Insert document property field

To remove a document property field, click the **field handle** and press **Delete** (Figure 3-43). Make sure to check for proper spacing and paragraph breaks when you delete a document property field.

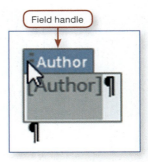

3-43 Delete document property field

Print Document Properties

After customizing document properties, you can print the document properties included in a document. When you print document properties, only a page listing the document properties prints, not the document itself.

HOW TO: Print Document Properties

1. Click the **File** tab to open the *Backstage* view.
2. Click **Print** on the left.
3. Click **Print All Pages** and select **Document Info** from the drop-down list (Figure 3-44).
4. Click the **Print** button to print the document properties.

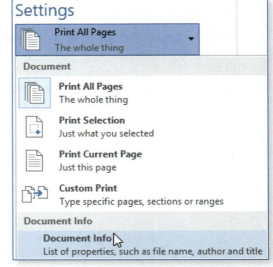

3-44 Print document properties

Customize Content Control Fields

When you insert a cover page into a document, many of the fields are content control fields, which are fields where you type or select custom content (Figure 3-45). You may want to add content to some of these fields and remove others. You can remove Word content control fields the same way you remove a document property field (see Figure 3-43).

To insert custom content into a content control field, click in the field and type the information. You can type whatever information you want into a content control field. For example, you can type a web address into the *Address* field (Figure 3-45).

3-45 Insert text into a content control field

Remove a Cover Page

You might decide that you no longer want a cover page or that you want to insert a different one. Removing a cover page is similar to removing a table of contents. Click the **Cover Page** button and select **Remove Current Cover Page** (Figure 3-46). When you remove a cover page, Word deletes the entire contents of the cover page and removes the page break.

3-46 Remove cover page

For the Pause & Practice project, you continue to modify the *Personal Training Program* report for American River Cycling Club. You apply styles to headings in the report, insert and modify a table of contents, and insert and modify a cover page.

File Needed: ***[your initials] PP W3-1.docx***
Completed Project File Name: ***[your initials] PP W3-2.docx***

---

1. Open the ***[your initials] PP W3-1*** document created in *Pause & Practice 3-1*.

2. Save this document as ***[your initials] PP W3-2***.

3. Apply styles to the headings in the report.
   a. Select the "**General Guidelines**" heading on the first page.
   b. Click the **Heading 1** style [*Home* tab, *Styles* group] to apply this style to the selected heading (Figure 3-47). If the *Heading 1* style is not visible, click the **More** button to display the entire *Styles* gallery.

   3-47 Apply *Heading 1* style

   c. Apply the **Heading 1** style to the following headings (bolded headings in the document):

   Personal Training Program Guidelines
   More about Long Rides
   Training Intensity and Heart Rate
   Using a Training Log

   d. Apply the **Heading 2** style to the following headings (underlined headings in the document):

   Pace of Rides
   Number of Rides per Week
   Duration of Rides
   Distance for Long Rides
   Suggestions for Long Rides
   Sample Session
   Other Heart Rate Factors
   Suggestions for Using a Training Log

4. Insert a page break and add a table of contents.
   a. Turn on **Show/Hide** [*Home* tab, *Paragraph* group].
   b. Position the insertion point at the beginning of the document before the title ("Developing a Personal Training Program") and press **Ctrl+Enter** to insert a page break.
   c. Position the insertion point before the page break on the new first page.
   d. Click the **Table of Contents** button [*References* tab, *Table of Contents* group] (Figure 3-48).
   e. Select **Automatic Table 2** from the drop-down list. The table of contents is inserted on the first page of the report.

   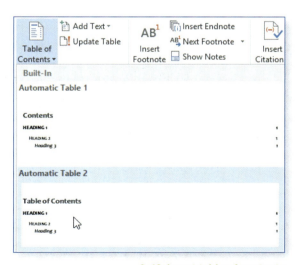

   3-48 Insert table of contents

5. Customize the table of contents.
   a. Position the insertion point anywhere in the body of the table of contents.
   b. Click the **Table of Contents** button [*References* tab, *Table of Contents* group].
   c. Select **Custom Table of Contents** to open the *Table of Contents* dialog box (Figure 3-49).
   d. Click the **Formats** drop-down list and select **Formal**.
   e. In the *Show levels* area, set the number of levels at **2**.
   f. Check the **Right align page numbers** check box if it is not already checked.
   g. Select the dot leader option from the *Tab leader* drop-down list if it is not already selected.
   h. Click **OK** to close the dialog box. A dialog box opens, confirming you want to replace the existing table of contents (Figure 3-50).
   i. Click **YES** to replace the existing table of contents.

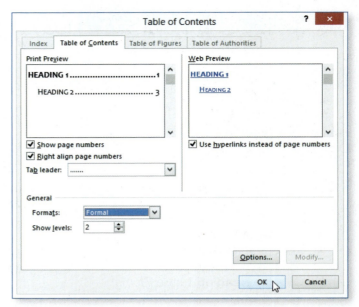

3-49 Customize table of contents

6. Insert page breaks and update table of contents.
   a. On the second page, position the insertion point in front of the "Number of Rides per Week" heading and press **Ctrl+Enter** to insert a page break and push this heading to the next page.
   b. Repeat this process on the following headings:

      Suggestions for Long Rides
      Using a Training Log

   c. Press **Ctrl+Home** to move to the beginning of the document.
   d. Click the **Update Table** button [*References* tab, *Table of Contents* group]. The *Update Table of Contents* dialog box opens (Figure 3-51).
   e. Select the **Update entire table** radio button and click **OK**.
   f. If there is a blank line above the table of contents, select it and press **Delete**.

3-50 Replace existing table of contents

3-51 Update entire table of contents

7. Customize document properties.
   a. Click the **File** tab to open the *Backstage* view and select **Info** to display document properties.
   b. Click the **Show All Properties** link in the document properties area.
   c. Add the following document properties:
      Title: Developing a Personal Training Program
      Company: American River Cycling Club
      Manager: Olesia Sokol
   d. In the *Author* area, right-click the author's name and select **Remove Person**.
   e. Click the **Back** arrow to return to the report.

8. Add a cover page and customize fields.
   a. Click the **Cover Page** button [*Insert* tab, *Pages* group] and select **Semaphore**. The cover page is inserted on a page before the table of contents.
   b. Click the **Date** field drop-down arrow to display the calendar and select the current date.
   c. Click the **Author** document property field, select the field handle, and press **Delete** to delete the field (Figure 3-52). The insertion point is positioned on the blank line where the *Author* field was removed.

3-52 Delete document property field

   d. Click the **Quick Parts** button [*Insert* tab, *Text* group].
   e. Choose **Document Property** and select **Manager** from the drop-down list. The *Manager* document property field is inserted into the cover page.
   f. Click in the **Company Address** field and type: www.arcc.org.
   g. Select and delete the **Subject** field ("[Document Subtitle]").
   h. Click in the **Title** field and apply **bold** format. The bold formatting is applied to the entire title.

9. Save and close the document (Figure 3-53).

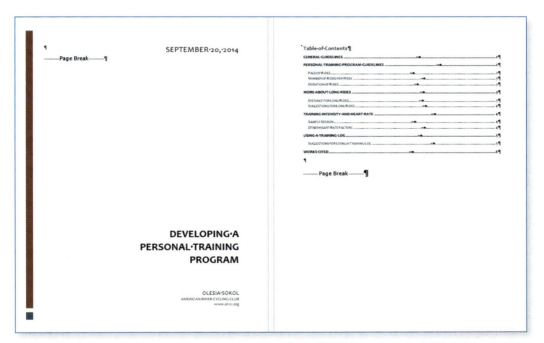

3-53 PP W3-2 cover page and table of contents

SLO 3.5

Using Bookmarks

When working with long documents, you can add a ***bookmark*** for a location or selected text in the document. Once you have inserted a bookmark, you can create a hyperlink to this location, create a cross-reference to this location, or index the bookmark to be included on an index page.

Add a Bookmark

Use bookmarks to mark a specific location, a word, or selected text, including a table.

HOW TO: Add a Bookmark

1. Position the insertion point or select the text you want to bookmark.
2. Click the **Insert** tab.
3. Click the **Bookmark** button [*Links* group] to open the *Bookmark* dialog box (Figure 3-54).
4. Type the name of the bookmark.
   - Bookmark names must be one word.
5. Click **Add** to add the bookmark and close the dialog box.

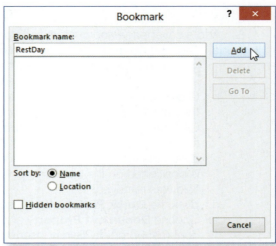

3-54 *Bookmark* dialog box

View Bookmarks in a Document

When a bookmark is added, by default it is not visible in your document. But you can make bookmarks visible in Word by changing a setting in the *Word Options* dialog box.

HOW TO: Make Bookmarks Visible in Your Document

1. Click the **File** tab to open the *Backstage* view.
2. Click the **Options** button to open the *Word Options* dialog box.
3. Select **Advanced** on the left of the *Word Options* dialog box (Figure 3-55).
4. Check the **Show bookmarks** check box in the *Show document content* area.
5. Click **OK** to close the dialog box.

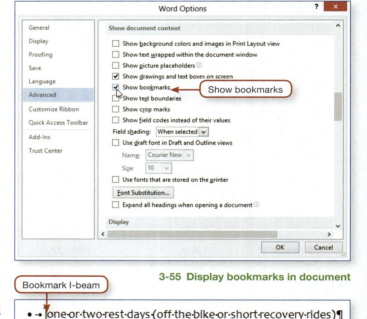

3-55 Display bookmarks in document

When bookmarks are made visible, a bookmark at a specific location is marked with a gray I-beam (Figure 3-56), and a bookmark on selected text is marked with gray brackets (Figure 3-57).

Bookmark I-beam

• → one·or·two·rest·days·(off·the·bike·or·short·recovery·rides)¶

3-56 Bookmark at specific location in the document

Go To a Bookmark

There are a couple of ways to quickly move to a bookmark in your document.

- **Insert Bookmark** button [*Insert* tab, *Links* group]: In the *Bookmark* dialog box, select the bookmark and click **Go To.**
- **Find and Replace** dialog box: Click the **Find** drop-down arrow [*Home* tab, *Editing* group] and select **Go To** (Figure 3-58). Select **Bookmark** in the *Go to what* area, select the bookmark, and click **OK.**

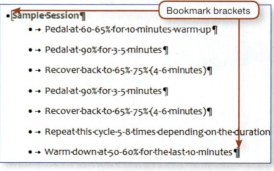

3-57 Bookmark on selected text

3-58 Go to selected bookmark

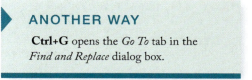

▶ **ANOTHER WAY**

Ctrl+G opens the *Go To* tab in the *Find and Replace* dialog box.

Hyperlink to a Bookmark

You can create a *hyperlink* in your document that takes the reader to the bookmarked area.

HOW TO: Create a Hyperlink to a Bookmark

1. Select the text on which to create a hyperlink.
2. Click the **Hyperlink** button [*Insert* tab, *Links* group] or press **Ctrl+K**. The *Insert Hyperlink* dialog box opens (Figure 3-59).
3. Choose **Place in This Document** in the *Link to* area.

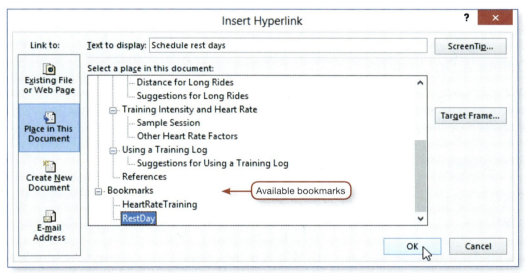

3-59 Insert hyperlink to a bookmark

4. Select from the available bookmarks.
5. Click **OK** to insert the hyperlink and close the dialog box.
   - The selected text is blue and underlined.
   - Press **Ctrl** and click the hyperlink to move to the bookmark.

Cross-Reference a Bookmark

You can also *cross-reference* a bookmark. For example, you can insert a page number that references a bookmark at another location in the document (e.g., "Schedule rest days (*see page 3*)"). When a cross-reference page number is linked to a bookmark, the page number is automatically updated if the bookmarked text moves to a different page.

HOW TO: Create a Cross-Reference to a Bookmark

1. Type any preceding text and position the insertion point where you want the cross-reference inserted.

2. Click the **Cross-reference** button [*Insert* tab, *Links* group]. The *Cross-reference* dialog box opens (Figure 3-60).

3. Select **Bookmark** in the *Reference type* area.
   - Check the **Insert as hyperlink** check box if you want the cross-reference to be a hyperlink to the bookmark.

4. In the *Insert reference to* area, select the type of reference from the drop-down list.
   - You can reference a page number, the bookmarked text, or the words "above" or "below."
   - If you choose *Page number,* you can also include the words "above" or "below" after the page number (e.g., "see page 3 above").

5. Select the bookmark in the *For which bookmark* area.

6. Click **Insert** to insert the cross-reference.

7. Click **Close** to close the dialog box.

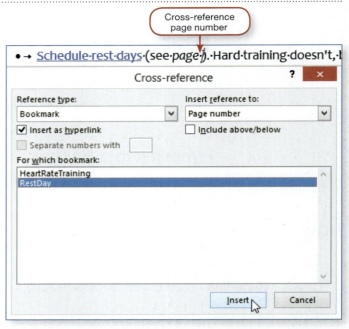

3-60 Insert cross-reference to a bookmark

Delete a Bookmark

When you delete a bookmark from a document, Word does not remove hyperlinks or cross-references associated with this bookmark. You must manually remove a hyperlink or cross-reference to a bookmark.

HOW TO: Delete a Bookmark

1. Click the **Bookmark** button [*Insert* tab, *Links* group]. The *Bookmark* dialog box opens.

2. Select the bookmark to delete.

3. Click **Delete**.

4. Click **Close** to close the *Bookmark* dialog box.

Using Advanced Headers and Footers

You can use headers and footers to include page numbers and document information at the top or bottom of each page in a report or multipage document. Headers appear at the top of the page and footers appear at the bottom. You type headers and footers just once and then they are automatically displayed on subsequent pages. Page numbers can automatically be inserted in the header or footer. You can also add custom content such as text, document property fields, the date, or borders.

Page and Section Breaks

For multipage documents, it is a good idea to insert page or section breaks to control page endings or special formatting in different sections. A *Page* break controls where one page ends and another begins. Use a *Next Page* section break when special document layout formatting is applied to a whole page or multiple pages of a document, such as landscape orientation to one page of the document. Use a *Continuous* section break when special formatting is applied to a section of the document, such as two-column format to specific text on one page.

> **MORE INFO**
>
> Don't use a section break to control page endings where a page break will suffice.

HOW TO: Insert a Page or Section Break

1. Place the insertion point in the document at the point where you want the page or section break.
   - If you are inserting a continuous section break, it is best to select the text on which to apply the section break.
   - When you insert a continuous break on selected text, Word inserts a continuous section break before and after the selected text.
2. Click the **Breaks** button [*Page Layout* tab, *Page Setup* group] (Figure 3-61).
3. Select the type of break from the drop-down list.

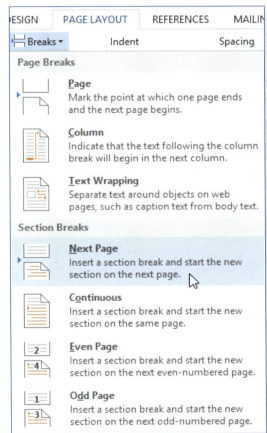

3-61 Insert page or section break

> **ANOTHER WAY**
>
> **Ctrl+Enter** inserts a page break.

When working with page and section breaks, it is best to have the *Show/Hide* feature turned on so you can see where these breaks are located in a document. To delete a page or section break, select the break and press **Delete.**

Built-In Headers, Footers, and Page Numbers

Word provides you with a variety of built-in headers, footers, and page numbering options that you can insert into a document. You can also customize this built-in content. You can insert this content with the header or footer open or while you are in the main document.

HOW TO: Insert a Built-In Header or Footer

1. Click the **Insert** tab.
2. Click the **Header**, **Footer**, or **Page Number** button [*Header & Footer* group].

3. Select the built-in header, footer, or page number from the drop-down list (Figure 3-62). The content is inserted and the header or footer opens.

- If you're inserting a page number, select the position (*Top of Page, Bottom of Page, Page Margins,* or *Current Position*) to insert the page number.
- The colors and fonts of the built-in headers, footers, and page numbers are determined by the theme of your document.
- More built-in headers, footers, and page numbers are displayed when you place your pointer on *More Headers (Footer* or *Page Numbers) from* Office.com.
- You can insert odd and even headers, footers, and page numbering into a document. We discuss odd and even headers and footers in the next section.

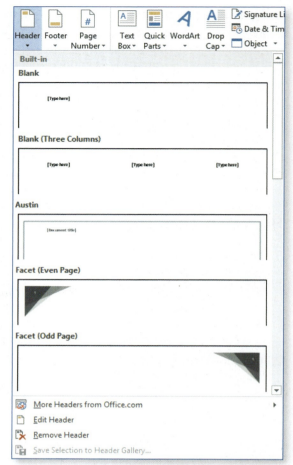

3-62 Insert built-in header

Many of the built-in headers and footers in Word contain document property fields or content control fields. You can enter information in the document property area and these fields are automatically populated. For content control fields such as *Date* or *Year,* you can select or type the content to be displayed in these fields (see Figure 3-62).

Customize Header and Footer Content

You are not limited to built-in content in the header and footer of your document. You can type text or insert content control fields. You can format header and footer text as you would other text in your document; you can apply font formatting and borders, insert graphics, and modify or set tabs for alignment.

You can open a header or footer in the following ways:

- Double-click on the header or footer area of the document.
- Right-click the header or footer area and select **Edit Header** or **Edit Footer.**
- Click the **Header** or **Footer** button [*Insert* tab, *Header & Footer* group] and select **Edit Header** or **Edit Footer.**

HOW TO: Insert Custom Content in the Header or Footer

1. Open the header or footer. See above for different ways to open the header or footer. The *Header & Footer Tools Design* tab open (Figure 3-63).
2. Insert content from the *Header & Footer Tools Design* tab.

3-63 *Header & Footer Tools Design* tab

W3-158

3. Type content to display in the header or footer.

4. Align information in the header or footer (Figure 3-64).

   - By default a center tab is set at the midpoint between the left and right margins and a right is set at the right margin.
   - You can insert a tab by clicking the **Insert Alignment Tab** button [*Position* group].
   - You can modify, add, or remove tabs on the ruler or in the *Tabs* dialog box [*Paragraph* dialog box, *Tabs* button].

3-64 Built-in and custom content inserted in the footer

5. You can change the position of the header and footer in the *Position* group.

   - By default, the header and footer are positioned 0.5" from the top and bottom of the page.
   - The settings can also be changed in the *Page Setup* dialog box on the *Layout* tab.

6. Click **Close Header and Footer** to return to the main document.

Different Headers and Footers

It's common on long documents to have different header and footer content on different pages. Word options allow you to have a different first page header and footer as well as different headers and footers on odd and even pages.

Different First Page

On many reports, you don't include a page number or header and footer content on the first page, but this information is included on subsequent pages. When you select the ***Different First Page*** option, Word removes existing content from the header and footer on the first page. You can choose to leave the first page header and footer blank, or you can insert content that is different from the second and subsequent pages headers and footers.

HOW TO: Insert a Different First Page Header and Footer

1. Open the header or footer on the first page of the document.

2. Check the **Different First Page** check box [*Header & Footer Tools Design* tab, *Options* group] (Figure 3-65).

   - When the *Different First Page* check box is checked, the header (or footer) tab displays *First Page Header* (or *First Page Footer*) to distinguish it from other headers and footers in the document, which are labeled *Header* (or *Footer*) (Figure 3-66).
   - The header (or footer) tab label changes when you apply other header and footer formatting such as odd and even pages or have different headers for different sections of your document.

3. Click **Close Header and Footer**.

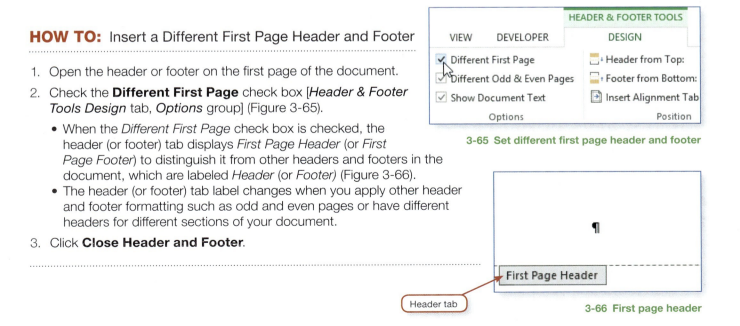

3-65 Set different first page header and footer

3-66 First page header

Different Odd and Even Pages

Just as you can have different header and footer content on the first page, Word provides you with the option of having *different odd and even* header and footer content on a multipage document. For example, you might want the title of the report to appear on all even pages in the footer and the page number and a company name to appear on odd pages.

> **MORE INFO**
> It's best to insert header and footer content on the first page of your document and then make any desired header and footer option changes.

HOW TO: Insert Different Odd and Even Headers and Footers

1. Open the header or footer on the first page of the document.
2. Check the **Different Odd & Even Pages** check box [*Header & Footer Tools Design* tab, *Options* group].
   - When the *Different Odd & Even Pages* check box is checked, the header (or footer) tab displays *Odd* (or *Even*) *Page Header* (or *Footer*) to distinguish it from other headers and footers in the document (Figure 3-67).
3. Click **Close Header and Footer**.

3-67 Odd page footer

Link to Previous

When you have different sections in your document, the headers and footers are by default linked to previous headers and footers. For example, a page number that appears in the footer of the first section of a document will also appear in the same position in the next section footer because it is linked to the previous footer. You can break this link to format header and footer content in one section independently of the header or footer in another section.

HOW TO: Link or Unlink Headers or Footers

1. Open the header or footer to be unlinked from the previous section (Figure 3-68).
   - By default the *Link to Previous* button is on (highlighted).
   - The *Same as Previous* label is displayed on the right of the header or footer.

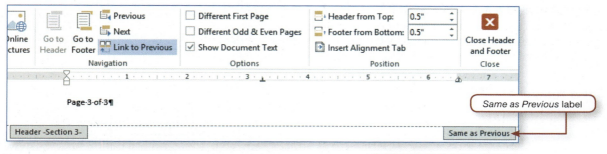

3-68 *Link to Previous* button

2. Click the **Link to Previous** button [*Header & Footer Tools Design* tab, *Navigation* group] to unlink it from the previous section.

- The *Same as Previous* label is no longer displayed.
- The header or footer content is still displayed, but you can now change it without it changing the header or footer content in the previous section.
- The *Link to Previous* button is no longer highlighted.

3. If you want to link header or footer content to a previous section after it has been unlinked, click the **Link to Previous** button. A dialog box opens asking if you want to link the header or footer to the previous section (Figure 3-69).

4. Click **Yes**.

5. Click **Close Header and Footer**.

3-69 Link header or footer to previous section

Format Page Numbers

When you number the pages in your document, you can change the page number format and starting page number. For example, on a report you might want to number the front matter pages (title page, table of contents, executive summary) with Roman numerals and number the body pages with regular numbers. If you are using different numbering for different sections of a document, you need to insert a next page section break between sections. This allows you to format the page numbering of each section differently.

HOW TO: Format Page Numbers

1. Select the page number to format in the header or footer.

2. Click the **Page Number** button [*Header & Footer Tools Design* tab, *Header & Footer* group].

3. Select **Format Page Numbers** from the drop-down list. The *Page Number Format* dialog box opens (Figure 3-70).

4. In the *Number format* area, select the number format from the drop-down list.

5. In the *Page numbering* area, select either the **Continue from previous section** or **Start at** radio button.

- If you select *Continue from previous section,* the numbering continues consecutively from the previous section.
- If you select *Start at,* you select the starting page number for the section.

6. Click **OK** to close the *Page Number Format* dialog box.

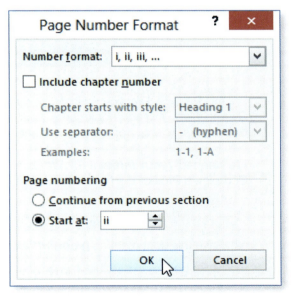

3-70 *Page Number Format* dialog box

When you include a Word cover page in a multipage document, the cover page is *not* considered the first page. Word considers the cover page as "page 0" when inserting page numbers in the header or footer, table of contents, or cross-reference links. For this reason, the page numbering in your document might be different from the page number displayed in the *Status* bar (bottom left of the Word window) of the document.

Navigate between Headers and Footers

When you are in a header or footer of a document, there are a variety of buttons you can use to move from the header to the footer or to the next or previous header or footer. These navigation buttons are in the *Navigation* group on the *Header & Footer Tools Design* tab (Figure 3-71).

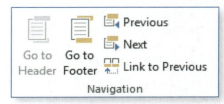

3-71 Header and footer navigation buttons

Remove Headers and Footers

To remove a header or footer from a document, you can open the header or footer and manually delete the content. All linked header or footer content is also removed when you do this. Word can also automatically remove the header or footer from a document.

HOW TO: Remove a Header or Footer

1. Click the **Insert** button.
2. Click the **Header or Footer** button [*Header & Footer* group].
3. Select **Remove Header** or **Remove Footer** from the drop-down list (Figure 3-72). The header or footer content is removed.

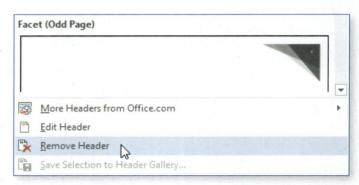

3-72 Remove header

PAUSE & PRACTICE: WORD 3-3

For this Pause & Practice project, you finalize the *Personal Training Program* report for American River Cycling Club. You add bookmarks, create hyperlinks to bookmarks, create cross-reference links to bookmarks, and customize headers and footers.

File Needed: *[your initials] PP W3-2.docx*
Completed Project File Name: *[your initials] PP W3-3.docx*

1. Open the *[your initials] PP W3-2* document created in *Pause & Practice 3-2*.

2. Save this document as *[your initials] PP W3-3*.

3. Make bookmarks visible in your document.
   a. Click the **File** tab to open the *Backstage* view.
   b. Select **Options** to open the *Word Options* dialog box (Figure 3-73).
   c. Select **Advanced** on the left.
   d. Check the **Show bookmarks** check box in the *Show document content* area.
   e. Click **OK** to close the dialog box.

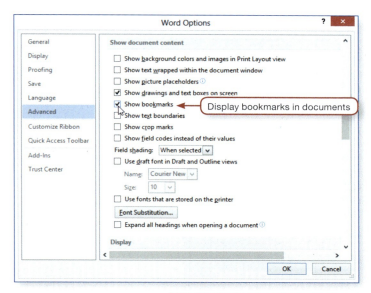

3-73 Display bookmarks in document

4. Insert bookmarks.
   a. Place the insertion point before "one or two rest days" (fourth page, fourth bullet).
   b. Click the **Bookmark** button [*Insert* tab, *Links* group]. The *Bookmark* dialog box opens (Figure 3-74).
   c. Type RestDay and click **Add** to add the bookmark and close the dialog box. An I-beam bookmark is displayed before the text.
   d. On the fifth page, select the text beginning with "**Sample Session**" and ending with the last bulleted item in that section.
   e. Click the **Bookmark** button.
   f. Type HeartRateTraining and click **Add** to add the bookmark and close the dialog box. Bookmark brackets are displayed around the selected text.

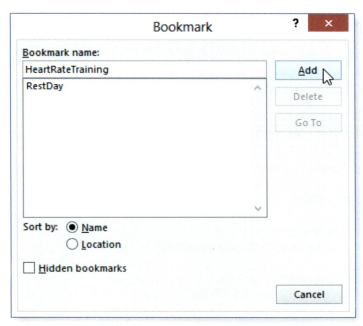

3-74 Insert bookmarks

5. Insert a cross-reference to a bookmark.
   a. On the sixth page, place your insertion point after "Record heart rate levels" (second bulleted item) and before the period.
   b. **Space** once and type (see Sample Session and **space** once.
   c. Click the **Cross-reference** button [*Insert* tab, *Links* group] to open *the Cross-reference* dialog box (Figure 3-75).

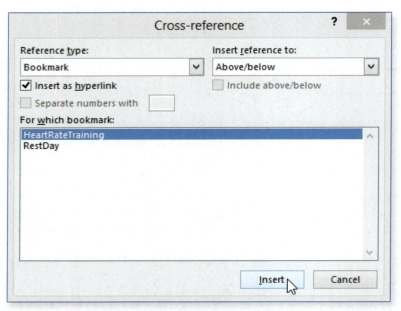

3-75 Insert cross-reference to a bookmark

   d. Select **Bookmark** from the *Reference type* drop-down list.
   e. Select **Above/below** from the *Insert reference to* drop-down list.
   f. Select **HeartRateTraining** in the *For which bookmark* area.
   g. Click **Insert** to insert the cross-reference and then click **Close**. The word "above" is inserted after the text.
   h. Type) after the inserted cross-reference and before the period.
   i. Select the words "**Sample Session**" and apply **italic** formatting.

6. Insert a page number cross-reference to a bookmark.
   a. On the sixth page, place your insertion point after "Schedule rest days" (fifth bulleted item) and before the period.
   b. **Space** once and type (see page and **space** once.
   c. Click the **Cross-reference** button.
   d. Select **Bookmark** from the *Reference type* drop-down list.
   e. Select **Page number** from the *Insert reference to* drop-down list. Do not check the *Include above/below* check box.
   f. Select **RestDay** in the *For which bookmark* area.
   g. Click **Insert** to insert the cross-reference and then click **Close**. The page number "3" is inserted after the text.
   h. Type) after the inserted cross-reference and before the period.
   i. Select the words "**page 3**" and apply **italic** formatting.

7. Insert hyperlinks to bookmarks.
   a. On the sixth page, select "**Record heart rate levels**" (second bulleted item).
   b. Click the **Hyperlink** button [*Insert* tab, *Links* group] to open *the Insert Hyperlink* dialog box (Figure 3-76).

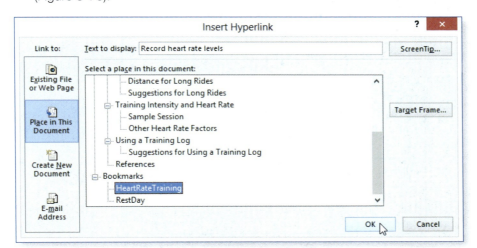

3-76 Insert hyperlink to a bookmark

   c. Select **Place in This Document** in the *Link to* area.
   d. Select **HeartRateTraining** in the *Bookmarks* list.
   e. Click **OK** to insert the hyperlink to the bookmark.
   f. On the sixth page, select "**Schedule rest days**" (fifth bulleted item).
   g. Click the **Hyperlink** button [*Insert* tab, *Links* group] to open *the Insert Hyperlink* dialog box.
   h. Select **Place in This Document** in the *Link to* area.
   i. Select **RestDay** in the *Bookmarks* list.
   j. Click **OK** to insert the hyperlink to the bookmark (Figure 3-77).

8. Insert odd page and even page footers.
   a. Press **Ctrl+Home** to move to the top of the document.
   b. Click the **Footer** button [*Insert* tab, *Header & Footer* group] and select **Edit Footer** to open the footer.
   c. Check the **Different First Page** (if it is not already checked) and the **Different Odd & Even Pages** check boxes [*Header & Footer Tools Design* tab, *Options* group].
   d. Click the **Next** button [*Navigation* group] to move to the footer on the second page (Figure 3-78).

- → <u>Record·heart·rate·levels</u>·(see·*Sample·Session*·above). amount·of·time·spent·in·each·zone.·Lump-sum·hours near·or·above·lactate·threshold.·In·other·words,·qua

- → Keep·record·of·your·body·statistics.·Regularly·check· mass,·and·muscle·mass,·and·body·water.·A·good·scal measurements.¶

- → Record·how·do·you·feel.··More·important·than·intens overall·well-being.·Mental·state·is·one·of·the·best·ind doing·too·much.·Do·you·feel·vigorous·or·flat?·Am·I·ea the·motions?·Do·rides·feel·so·good·that·I·extend·ther through·a·lackluster·hour·and·head·home?¶

- → <u>Schedule·rest·days</u>·(see·*page·3*).·Hard·training·doesn' and·recovery·are·the·essential·catalysts.·If·you·don't· Record·this·information·in·your·electronic·diary·(inclu

3-77 Cross-references and hyperlinks to bookmarks

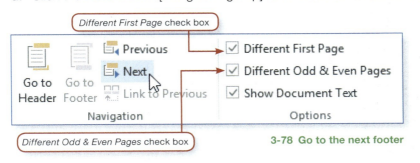

3-78 Go to the next footer

e. Click the **Page Number** button [*Header & Footer* group].

f. Select **Bottom of Page** and select **Two Bars 1** from the drop-down list of built-in page numbers (Figure 3-79). The page number "1" is inserted on the second page.

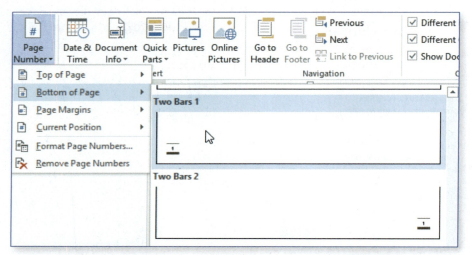

3-79 Select built-in page number

> **MORE INFO**
>
> Word considers the cover page as page 0. The table of contents page is page 1.

g. Click the **Next** button [*Navigation* group] to move to the footer on the next page.

h. Click the **Page Number** button [*Header & Footer* group].

i. Select **Bottom of Page** and select **Two Bars 2** from the drop-down list of built-in page numbers. The page number "2" is inserted on the right. Leave the footer open to add custom content in the next step.

9. Add custom content to the odd and even footers.

a. The insertion point should be in the even page footer.

b. Press **Ctrl+R** to align the insertion point on the right.

c. Click the **Document Info** button [*Header & Footer Tools Design* tab, *Insert* group] (Figure 3-80).

d. Select **Document Property** and choose **Company** from the drop-down list. The *Company* document property field is inserted with the company name displayed in this field.

e. Select the **Company** document property field, change the font size to **10 pt.**, and apply **bold** formatting.

f. Click the **Previous** button [*Header & Footer Tools Design* tab, *Navigation* group] to move to the odd page footer on the previous page. The insertion point should be on the left after the page number "1."

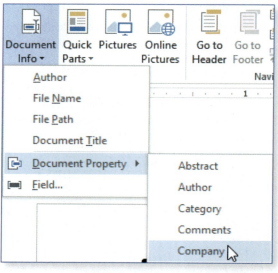

3-80 Insert document property field

g. Click the **Quick Parts** button [*Header & Footer Tools Design* tab, *Insert* group].

h. Select **Document Property** and choose **Title** from the drop-down list. The *Title* document property field is inserted with the document title displayed in this field.

i. Select the **Title** document property field, change the font size to **10 pt.**, and apply **bold** formatting.

j. Click the **Close Header and Footer** button [*Header & Footer Tools Design* tab, *Close* group].

10. Review the document to ensure correct page numbering.

   a. There should be no header or footer on the cover page of the document.

   b. The table of contents page should be numbered "1" in the footer on the left with the title of the report following the page number.

   c. The first body page of the report should be numbered "2" in the footer on the right with the company name preceding the page number.

   d. Each subsequent page should be numbered consecutively with odd and even footers.

11. Save and close the document (Figure 3-81).

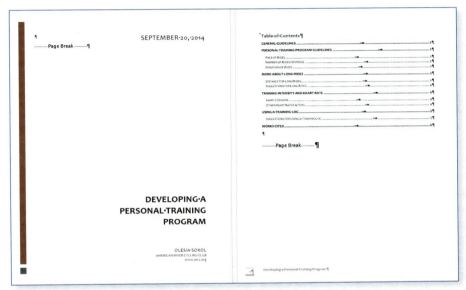

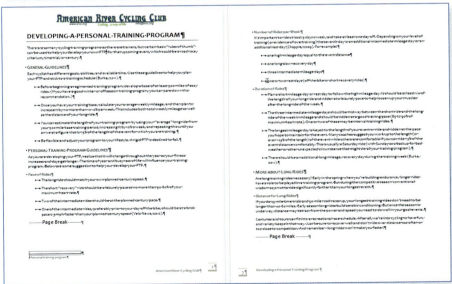

3-81 PP W3-3 completed (first four of seven pages)

Chapter Summary

3.1 Insert and edit footnotes and endnotes in a document (p. W3-129).

- *Use **Footnotes** and **endnotes*** to include additional information or reference sources.
- Footnotes appear at the bottom of the page and endnotes appear at the end of the document.
- A ***reference marker*** is a number, letter, or symbol that marks a footnote or endnote in the body of the document.
- Change the location, number format, and starting number for footnotes and endnotes in the ***Footnote and Endnote*** dialog box.
- Word styles control the format of footnotes and endnotes. Change these styles to modify how your footnote and endnote text appears in the document.
- Convert footnotes to endnotes or endnotes to footnotes using the ***Convert Notes*** dialog box.
- Move footnotes and endnotes using the drag and drop method or using cut and paste.
- When you delete a footnote or endnote reference marker, the associated footnote and endnote text is also deleted. Footnotes and endnotes are automatically renumbered if one is deleted or inserted.

3.2 Create a bibliography using proper source format and insert citations in a document (p. W3-134).

- A ***source*** is the complete bibliographic information for a reference (e.g., book, web page, journal article) used in a report.
- A ***citation*** is the abbreviated source information used in the body of a report.
- The ***bibliography style*** controls the format of the sources on the bibliography page and citations in the body of the document.
- Add a ***placeholder*** to temporarily mark a citation in the body of a report.
- Use the ***Source Manager*** dialog box to create and edit sources, edit placeholders, and view available sources.
- Insert a ***bibliography*** or ***works cited*** page to list the sources in your document.

3.3 Create and edit a table of contents based on headings in a document (p. W3-144).

- Word can automatically generate a ***table of contents*** for a document.

- ***Heading styles*** (e.g., Heading 1, Heading 2) determine the content for a table of contents.
- You can use built-in table of contents formats or customize the format of the table of contents.
- Use the ***Table of Contents*** dialog box to customize the format and levels displayed in the table of contents.
- When document heading or pagination is changed, the table of contents can be updated to reflect these changes.

3.4 Insert a cover page and modify content and document fields (p. W3-148).

- There are a variety of built-in ***cover pages*** available to use on your documents.
- A cover page has graphics, colors, text boxes, and Word fields that you can customize. The document theme controls the colors and fonts on the cover page.
- Use ***document property*** and ***content control fields*** to display information on the cover page. This content can be customized or deleted.

3.5 Integrate bookmarks into a multipage document (p. W3-153).

- Use a ***bookmark*** to mark a specific location or selected text in a document.
- In ***Word Options***, you can set bookmarks in your documents.
- You can add a ***hyperlink*** to a bookmark; this takes the user to the bookmark when the hyperlink is clicked.
- You can add a ***cross-reference*** to a bookmark; this provides the page number for the bookmark or a general location in the document.

3.6 Apply custom headers and footers in multipage documents (p. W3-156).

- ***Headers*** and ***footers*** provide information and page numbers in a document. Headers are located at the top and footers are located at the bottom of a document.
- ***Page*** and ***section breaks*** control pagination and page numbering in a document.
- You can insert a variety of built-in headers, footers, and page numbers into a document.
- You can customize content and page numbering in headers and footers.

- **Different first page** headers and footers allow you to include different information on the first page of a document.
- Use **odd and even page** headers and footers to display different information on odd and even pages in a document.

- Change the page number format and starting page number in the **Page Number Format** dialog box.

Check for Understanding

In the **Online Learning Center** for this text (www.mhhe.com/office2013inpractice), there are a variety of resources that can be used to review the concepts covered in this chapter.

The following Online Learning Resources are available in the Online Learning Center:

- Multiple-choice questions
- Short answer questions
- Matching exercises

Guided Project 3-1

For this project, you customize the *Online Learning Plan* for Sierra Pacific Community College District. You add a customized cover page, apply styles, create a table of contents, insert and modify footnotes, and insert headers and footers.
[Student Learning Outcomes 3.1, 3.3, 3.4, 3.6]

File Needed: **OnlineLearningPlan-03.docx**
Completed Project File Name: **[your initials] Word 3-1.docx**

Skills Covered in This Project

- Customize document properties.
- Insert a cover page and add content.
- Delete and add document property fields.
- Apply font formatting to text.
- Apply styles to selected text.
- Insert page breaks.
- Create a table of contents based on heading styles.

- Insert footnotes.
- Modify footnote number format.
- Insert built-in page numbers in the header.
- Insert document property fields and the date in the footer.
- Modify header and footer text formatting.
- Update a table of contents.

1. Open the **OnlineLearningPlan-03** document from your student data files.

2. Save this document as **[your initials] Word 3-1**.

3. Add document properties.
   a. Click the **File** tab to open the *Backstage* view.
   b. Click **Show All Properties** in the *Properties* area.
   c. Add the following document properties:

      Title: Online Learning Plan
      Company: Sierra Pacific Community College District
      Manager: Hasmik Kumar

   d. Click the **Back** arrow to return to the document.

4. Insert a cover page and modify content control fields.
   a. Press **Ctrl+Home** to move to the top of the document.
   b. Click the **Cover Page** button [*Insert* tab, *Pages* group].
   c. Select the **Austin** built-in cover page from the drop-down list. The cover page is inserted before the first page of the document.
   d. Click the **Subtitle** content control field handle and press **Delete** (Figure 3-82).

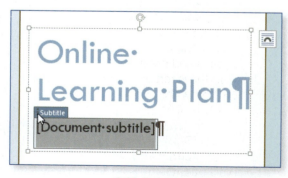

3-82 Delete content control field

e. Delete the blank line after the *Title* field.

f. Select the **Title** field and change the font size to **48 pt**.

g. Click the **Abstract** content control field and type This report was developed by the Online Learning Task Force at Sierra Pacific Community College District to review and update the district's strategic plan for online learning.

h. Select the **Abstract** field, change the text alignment to **left**, and apply **italic** formatting.

i. Click the **Author** content control field handle and press **Delete**.

j. With the insertion point on the blank line where the *Author* field was deleted, click the **Quick Parts** button [*Insert* tab, *Text* group] (Figure 3-83).

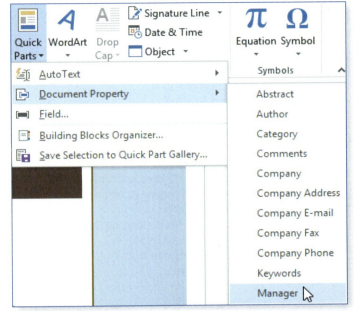

3-83 Insert document property field

k. Select **Document Property** and select **Manager** from the drop-down list.

l. Apply **bold** formatting to the *Manager* document property field.

5. Apply styles to the document.
   a. Apply the **Heading 1** style to all of the main headings (those in all caps and bold) in the document. Do not include information on the cover page.
   b. Apply the **Heading 2** style to all subheadings (those underlined) in the document.
   c. On the second page of the document, select the title ("**Online Learning Plan**") and apply the **Title** style.
   d. On the second page of the document, select the subtitle ("**Sierra Pacific Community College District**") and apply the **Subtitle** style.

6. Insert a table of contents into the report.
   a. Click in front of the first main heading in the document ("Purpose of this Plan") and insert a page break.
   b. On the second page of the document, click directly after the subtitle and press **Enter**.
   c. With the insertion point on the blank line below the subtitle, click the **Table of Contents** button [*References* tab, *Table of Contents* group] (Figure 3-84).
   d. Select **Automatic Table 2**. The table of contents is inserted below the subtitle.

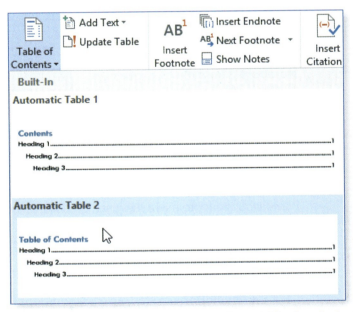

3-84 Insert table of contents

e. Select the words "**Table of Contents**" in the table of contents and apply **Black, Text 1** font color.

f. If there is a blank line between the subtitle and "Table of Contents," delete it.

7. Insert footnotes into the document.

a. On the third page of the document, position the insertion point after "Web-Enhanced course."

b. Click the **Insert Footnote** button [*References* tab, *Footnotes* group]. A footnote reference marker is inserted after the text and the insertion point is positioned at the bottom of the page in the *Footnotes* area.

c. In the *Footnotes* area, type Just for clarification, this is a non-OL course that uses OL tools.

d. On the third page of the document, position the insertion point after "online learning" (first body paragraph, second sentence).

e. Click the **Insert Footnote** button and in the footnote area type Online learning will be referred to as OL throughout this document. This footnote becomes footnote 1 and the other footnote automatically becomes number 2.

8. Modify footnote number format.

a. Click the **Footnotes** launcher to open the *Footnote and Endnote* dialog box (Figure 3-85).

b. Select **i, ii, iii, . . .** from the *Number format* drop-down list.

c. Click **Apply** to close the dialog box and apply the number format change.

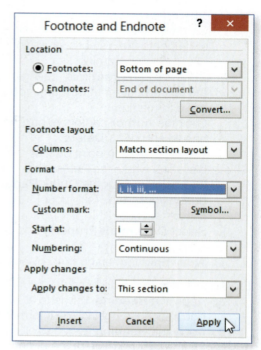

3-85 Modify footnote number format

9. Insert and modify content in the header.

a. Position the insertion point at the top of the table of contents page.

b. Click the **Page Number** button [*Insert* tab, *Header & Footer* group].

c. Select **Top of Page** and select **Bold Numbers 3** from the drop-down list (Figure 3-86).

d. Delete the blank line below the page number.

e. Select the text in the header and change the font size to **10 pt**.

3-86 Insert page number

10. Insert and modify content in the footer.

a. With the header still open, click the **Go to Footer** button [*Header & Footer Tools Design* tab, *Navigation* group] to move the insertion point to the footer.

b. Click the **Quick Parts** button [*Header & Footer Tools Design* tab, *Insert* group], select **Document Property**, and select **Title** from the drop-down list to insert the *Title* document property field into the footer.

c. Press the **right arrow** once to deselect the document property field and press **Tab** to move to the center preset tab.

d. Click the **Quick Parts** button, select **Document Property**, and select **Company** from the drop-down list.

e. Press the **right arrow** once to deselect the document property field and press **Tab** to move to the right preset tab.

f. Type Last modified: and **space** once.

g. Click the **Date & Time** button [*Header & Footer Tools Design* tab, *Insert* group] to open the *Date and Time* dialog box.

h. Select the first date format (e.g., 1/31/2015) and deselect the **Update automatically** check box.

i. Click **OK** to close the dialog box and insert the date.

j. Select the text in the footer and change the font size to **10 pt**.

k. Click the **Close Header and Footer** button [*Header & Footer Tools Design* tab, *Close* group].

11. Insert a page break.

a. Position the insertion point before the last subheading ("How are Courses and Programs Selected for Online Learning Delivery?") on the first body page of the report (the page after the table of contents).

b. Press **Ctrl+Enter** to insert a page break.

12. Update the table of contents.

a. Click in the table of contents.

b. Click the **Update Table** button [*References* tab, *Table of Contents* group]. The *Update Table of Contents* dialog box opens (Figure 3-87).

c. Select the **Update entire table** radio button.

d. Click **OK** to close the dialog box and update the table.

13. Save and close the document (Figure 3-88).

3-87 *Update Table of Contents* dialog box

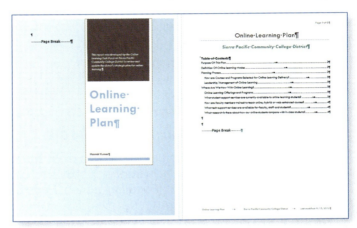

3-88 Word 3-1 completed (first four of six pages)

Guided Project 3-2

For this project, you create a multipage insurance renewal letter that Central Sierra Insurance will send on behalf of Valley Custom Manufacturing. You format this document as a business letter, insert and customize header content, use footnotes and endnotes, and insert a bookmark.
[Student Learning Outcomes 3.1, 3.5, 3.6]

File Needed: ***ValleyCustomManufacturing-03.docx***
Completed Project File Name: ***[your initials] Word 3-2.docx***

Skills Covered in This Project

- Format an existing document as a block format business letter.
- Insert a next page section break.
- Change margins and header location on a section of a document.
- Use a different first page header.
- Insert header content and page number.
- Format the page number in the header.

- Apply bottom border.
- Insert footnotes.
- Convert footnotes to endnotes and change number format.
- Insert a bookmark for selected text.
- Insert a cross-reference to a bookmark.
- Create a hyperlink to a bookmark.
- Insert a page break to control pagination.

---

1. Open the ***ValleyCustomManufacturing-03*** document from your student data files.

2. Save this document as ***[your initials] Word 3-2***.

3. Format the first page of the document as a block format business letter.
   a. Place your insertion point in front of "LIABILITY" on the first page.
   b. Click the **Breaks** button [*Page Layout* tab, *Page Setup* group] and select **Next Page** section break from the drop-down list.
   c. On the last blank line on the first page, type Sincerely, and press **Enter** four times.
   d. Type Jennie Owings, Vice President and press **Enter** once.
   e. Type Central Sierra Insurance and press **Enter** two times.
   f. Type your initials in lower case letters with no spaces or punctuation and press **Enter**. Word automatically capitalizes the first letter of your initials. Use the **smart tag** to undo automatic capitalization or press **Ctrl+Z** to undo the last action (Figure 3-89).

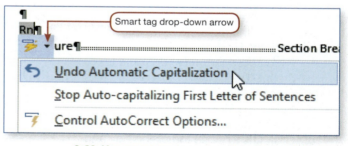

3-89 Use smart tag to undo automatic capitalization

   g. Type Enclosure on the line after your reference initials.
   h. Press **Ctrl+Home** to go to the top of the document and press **Enter** four times.
   i. Place the insertion point on the first blank line at the top and click the **Date & Time** button [*Insert* tab, *Text* group]. The *Date and Time* dialog box opens.
   j. Select the date in proper business letter format (e.g., April 12, 2014) and check the **Update automatically** check box.
   k. Click **OK** to close the dialog box and insert the date.
   l. On the dateline, apply **24 pt**. before paragraph spacing.

4. Modify the margins and header position in the second section of the document.
   a. Place your insertion point in the second section of the document (page 2 or 3).
   b. Click the **Margins** button [*Page Layout* tab, *Page Setup* group] and select **Custom Margins** from the drop-down list. The *Page Setup* dialog box opens.
   c. Change the *Top* margin to **1.5"** and the *Left* and *Right* margins to **1.25"**.

d. Click the **Layout** tab (Figure 3-90).

e. In the *Headers and footers* area, change the *From edge Header* setting to **1"**.

f. In the *Apply to* area, select **This section** from the drop-down list.

g. Click **OK** to close the dialog box and apply the settings.

5. Insert header content on the second and continuing pages.

a. Press **Ctrl+Home** to move to the top of the document.

b. Click the **Header** button [*Insert* tab, *Header & Footer* group].

c. Select **Edit Header** from the drop-down list.

d. Check the **Different First Page** check box [*Header & Footer Tools Design* tab, *Options* group].

e. Click the **Next** button [*Header & Footer Tools Design* tab, *Navigation* group] to move to the header in section 2.

f. Type Valley Custom Manufacturing and press **Enter**.

g. Click the **Date & Time** button [*Header & Footer Tools Design* tab, *Insert* group]. The *Date and Time* dialog box opens.

h. Select the date in proper business letter format (e.g., April 12, 2014) and check the **Update automatically** check box.

i. Click **OK** to close the dialog box and insert the date.

6. Insert page number in the header and format page number.

a. With the header still open, press **Enter** after the date.

b. Type Page and **space** once.

c. Click the **Page Number** button [*Header & Footer Tools Design* tab, *Header & Footer* group].

d. Select **Current Position** and **Plain Number** from the drop-down list of page number options.

e. Click the **Page Number** button and select **Format Page Numbers** to open the *Page Number Format* dialog box (Figure 3-91).

f. In the *Page numbering* area, click the **Start at** radio button and change the page number to **2**.

g. Click **OK** to close the dialog box.

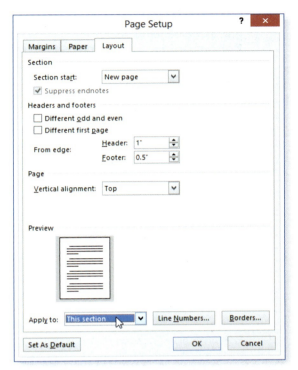

3-90 Change header position in this section of the document

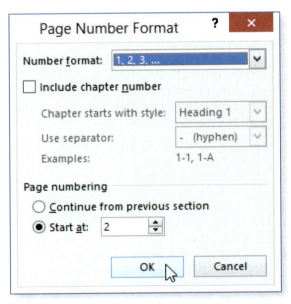

3-91 Format page number

h. Place the insertion point after the page number and press **Enter** two times.

i. Select the page number line, click the **Borders** button [*Home* tab, *Paragraph* group], and select **Bottom Border** from the drop-down list.

j. Click the **Close Header and Footer** button [*Header & Footer Tools Design* tab, *Close* group].

7. Insert footnotes.

a. Place the insertion point after the period at the end of the last line of text on page 4.

b. Click the **Insert Footnote** button [*References* tab, *Footnotes* group].

c. In the footnotes area, type A list of drivers was faxed as a separate attachment.

d. On the first page, place the insertion point at the end of the fourth body paragraph (after "2013 renewal.").

e. Click the **Insert Footnote** button.

f. In the footnotes area, type Inflation is anticipated to be 2 percent.

3-92 Convert footnotes to endnotes

8. Convert footnotes to endnotes and change number format.

a. Click the **Footnotes** launcher to open the *Footnote and Endnote* dialog box.

b. Click the **Convert** button. The *Convert Notes* dialog box opens (Figure 3-92).

c. Select the **Convert all footnotes to endnotes** radio button and click **OK** to close the *Convert Notes* dialog box.

d. Click **Close** to close the *Footnote and Endnote* dialog box.

e. Click the **Footnotes** launcher to open the *Footnote and Endnote* dialog box (Figure 3-93).

f. Select the **Endnotes** radio button if it is not selected.

g. In the *Number format* area, select **a, b, c, . . .** from the drop-down list.

h. In the *Apply changes to* area, select **Whole document** from the drop-down list.

i. Click **Apply** to close the dialog box and apply the changes.

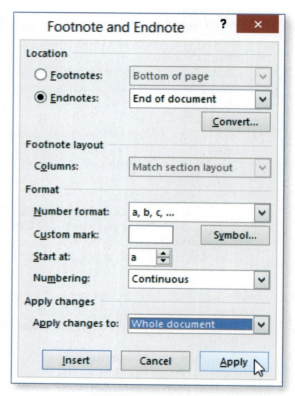

3-93 Change endnote number format

9. Insert a bookmark for selected text.

a. On page 3, select the "Parts and Inventory Building" paragraph. Include the line break at the end of the paragraph, but do *not* include the paragraph break on the blank line below.

b. Click the **Bookmark** button [*Insert* tab, *Links* group]. The *Bookmark* dialog box opens (Figure 3-94).

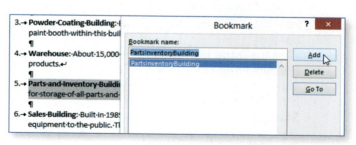

3-94 Insert bookmark on selected text

c. In the *Bookmark name* area, type PartsInventoryBuilding.

d. Click **Add** to close the dialog box and add the bookmark for selected text.

10. Insert a cross-reference link to a bookmark.

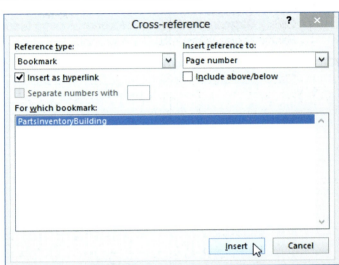

a. On page 2 in the "Farm Equipment Dealers" section, place the insertion point after "2001" and before the period.

b. **Space** once and type (see #5 on page and **space** once.

c. Click the **Cross-reference** button [*Insert* tab, *Links* group] to open the *Cross-reference* dialog box (Figure 3-95).

d. In the *Reference type* area, select **Bookmark**.

e. In the *Insert reference to* area, select **Page number**.

f. In the *For which bookmark* area, select **PartsInventoryBuilding**.

3-95 Insert cross-reference to a bookmark

g. Click **Insert** and then click **Close**.

h. Type) after the inserted cross-reference page number.

11. Create a hyperlink to a bookmark.

a. On page 2 in the "Farm Equipment Dealers" section, select "**new building completed in 2001**."

b. Click the **Hyperlink** button [*Insert* tab, *Links* group] to open the *Insert Hyperlink* dialog box (Figure 3-96).

c. In the *Link to* area, select **Place in This Document**.

d. In the *Select a place in this document* area, select the **PartsInventoryBuilding** bookmark.

e. Click **OK** to close the dialog box and insert the hyperlink.

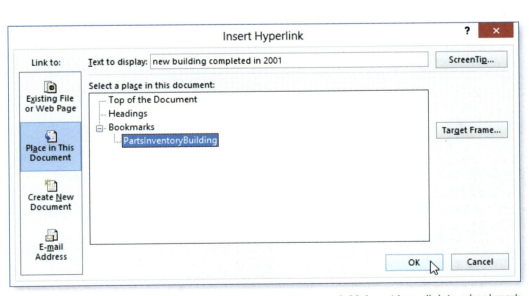

3-96 Insert hyperlink to a bookmark

12. Insert a page break to control pagination.
    a. On page 2, place the insertion point in front of the "PROPERTY" heading.
    b. Click the **Breaks** button [*Page Layout* tab, *Page Setup* group].
    c. Select **Page** in the *Page Breaks* area. A page break is inserted and the "PROPERTY" heading and following text are moved to page 3.

13. Save and close the document (Figure 3-97).

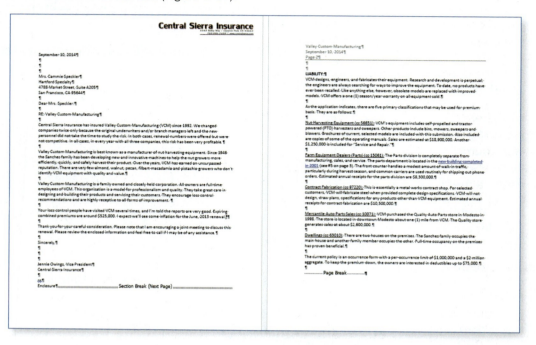

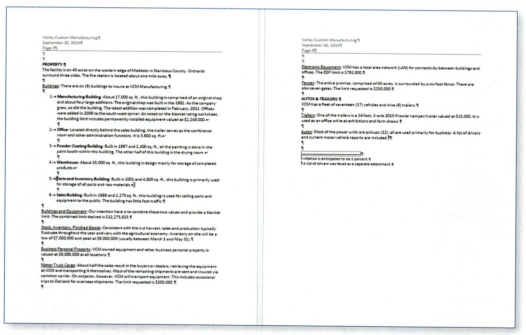

3-97 **Word 3-2 completed**

Guided Project 3-3

For this project, you customize the *Teen Substance Abuse* report for Courtyard Medical Plaza. You insert citations and a placeholder, manage sources, create a bibliography, and use odd and even page headers and footers.
[Student Learning Outcomes 3.2, 3.3, 3.6]

File Needed: ***TeenSubstanceAbuse-03.docx***
Completed Project File Name: ***[your initials] Word 3-3.docx***

Skills Covered in This Project

- Set bibliography style.
- Insert a placeholder for a citation.
- Create a source and insert a citation.
- Use the *Source Manager* to edit a placeholder and create a new source.
- Insert a bibliography page.
- Use styles to format title and headings.

- Create a table of contents.
- Insert built-in odd and even headers and footers.
- Insert a document property field into a header.
- Update a table of contents.

1. Open the **TeenSubstanceAbuse-03** document from your student data files.

2. Save this document as ***[your initials] Word 3-3***.

3. Select the report style and insert placeholders for a citation.
   a. Click the **Style** drop-down list [*References* tab, *Citations & Bibliography* group].
   b. Select **Chicago Fifteenth Edition**.
   c. On the first page in the "What Problems Can Teen Substance Abuse Cause?" section, place the insertion point at the end of the last sentence in the second paragraph and before the period.
   d. Click the **Insert Citation** button [*References* tab, *Citations & Bibliography* group].
   e. Select **Add New Placeholder**. The *Placeholder Name* dialog box opens.
   f. Type Foundation and click **OK**. The placeholder for the citation is inserted into the report.
   g. On the second page in the "Can Teen Substance Use And Abuse Be Prevented?" section, place the insertion point at the end of the last sentence in the first paragraph and before the period.
   h. Click the **Insert Citation** button and select the **Foundation** placeholder from the drop-down list (Figure 3-98).

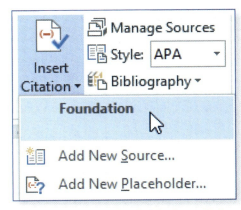

3-98 Insert placeholder for a citation

4. Insert a citation into the report.
   a. On the first page in the "What Is Teen Substance Abuse?" section, place the insertion point at the end of the last sentence in the second paragraph and before the period.

b. Click the **Insert Citation** button and select **Add New Source**. The *Create Source* dialog box opens (Figure 3-99).

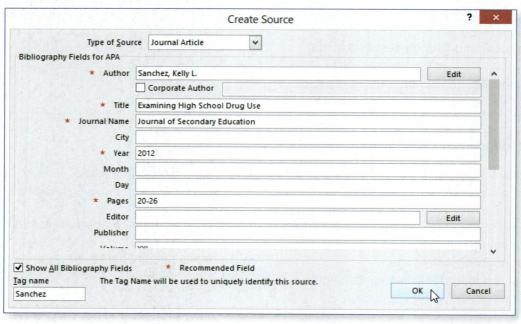

3-99 *Create Source* dialog box

c. Create a new source with the following information:

Type of Source: **Journal Article**
Author: Kelly L. Sanchez
Title: Examining High School Drug Use
Journal Name: Journal of Secondary Education
Year: 2012
Pages: 22-26
Volume: XXI (check the **Show All Bibliography Fields** check box to display these last two fields)
Issue: 2
Tag Name: Sanchez

d. Click **OK** to close the dialog box and insert the citation. The citation is inserted into the report.

5. Use the *Source Manager* to create a new source and provide source information for a placeholder.
   a. Click the **Manage Sources** button [*References* tab, *Citations & Bibliography* group] to open the *Source Manager* dialog box.
   b. In the *Current List* area, select the **Foundation** placeholder and click **Edit**. The *Edit Source* dialog box opens.
   c. Use the following information to edit the placeholder source:

Type of Source: **Web site**
Corporate Author: Foundation for Teen Health
Name of Web Page: Making Good Choices
Year: 2013
Year Accessed: 2013
Month Accessed: June
Day Accessed: 25
URL: http://foundationforteenhealth.org/choices.htm
Tag Name: Foundation

d. Click **OK** to close the dialog box and update the placeholders. The placeholders in the report are updated with the proper citation from the source information.

e. With the *Source Manager* dialog box still open, click the **New** button. The *Create Source* dialog box opens.

f. Create a new source with the following information:

Type of Source: **Document From Web site**
Corporate Author: Courtyard Medical Plaza
Name of Web Page: Teen Mental Health
Name of Web Site: Courtyard Medical Plaza
Year: 2013
Month: March
Day: 6
URL: http://cmp.com/Teen_Mental_Health.pdf
Tag Name: CMP

g. Click **OK** to close the dialog box and click **Close** to close the *Source Manager* dialog box.

6. Insert citations into the report.
   a. On the first page in the "Why Do Teens Abuse Drugs and Alcohol?" section, place the insertion point at the end of the last sentence in the second paragraph and before the period.
   b. Click the **Insert Citation** button and select the **Courtyard Medical Plaza** citation from the drop-down list.
   c. On the second page in the "What You Should Do If You Find Out That Your Teen Is Using?" section, place the insertion point at the end of the last sentence in the second paragraph and before the period.
   d. Click the **Insert Citation** button and select the **Sanchez, Kelly L**. citation from the drop-down list.

7. Insert a bibliography page at the end of the document.
   a. Press **Ctrl+End** to move to the end of the document.
   b. Insert a **page break**.
   c. With the insertion point on the blank last page, click the **Bibliography** button [*References* tab, *Citations & Bibliography* group].
   d. Select **Bibliography** to insert a bibliography into the document.

8. Apply styles to the title and section headings and insert a table of contents.
   a. Apply the **Title** style to the title of the report on the first page.
   b. Apply the **Heading 1** style to each of the bold section headings in the report.
   c. Press **Ctrl+Home** to move the insertion point to the beginning of the report.
   d. Click the **Blank Page** button [*Insert* tab, *Pages* group] to insert a blank page before the first page of the report.
   e. Place your insertion point at the top of the new first page, type Teen Substance Abuse, and press **Enter**. The text should be formatted as *Title* style. If it's not, apply the **Title** style.
   f. Click the **Table of Contents** button [*References* tab, *Table of Contents* group] and select **Automatic Table 1** from the drop-down list. The table of contents is inserted below the title.

9. Insert odd and even page headers and customize content.
   a. With the insertion point still on the first page, click the **Header** button [*Insert* tab, *Header & Footer* group] and click **More Headers from Office.com**.
   b. Select **Origin (Odd Page)** from the drop-down list of built-in headers.
   c. In the header, click the **Title** document property handle and press **Delete**.
   d. Click the **Document Info** button, click **Document Property**, and select **Company** from the drop-down list.

e. Select the **Company** document property field and change the after paragraph spacing to **0 pt**. and line spacing to **1** (single).
f. Check the **Different Odd & Even Pages** check box [*Header & Footer Tools Design* tab, *Options* group and click the **Next** button to move to the *Even Page Header*.
g. Click the **Header** button [*Header & Footer Tools Design* tab, *Header & Footer* group].
h. Click **More Headers from Office.com** and select **Origin (Even Page)** from the drop-down list.
i. Delete the **Title** document property field and insert the **Company** document property field.
j. Select the **Company** document property field and change the after paragraph spacing to **0 pt**. and line spacing to **1**.

10. Insert odd and even page footers.
a. With the header still open, click the **Go to Footer** button [*Header & Footer Tools Design* tab, *Navigation* group] to move to the *Even Page Footer*.
b. Click the **Page Number** button [*Header & Footer* group], click **Bottom of Page**, and select **Brackets 2**.
c. Click the **Previous** button [Navigation group] to move to the *Odd Page Footer*.
d. Click the **Page Number** button [*Header & Footer* group], click **Bottom of Page**, and select **Brackets 2**.
e. Click the **Close Header and Footer** button [*Close* group].

11. Insert page breaks to control pagination.
a. On page 2, click before the last section heading and insert a **page break**.
b. On page 3, click before the last section heading and insert a **page break**.

12. Update the table of contents.
a. Click the table of contents on the first page.
b. Click the **Update Table** button at the top of the content control field. The *Update Table of Contents* dialog box opens (Figure 3-100).

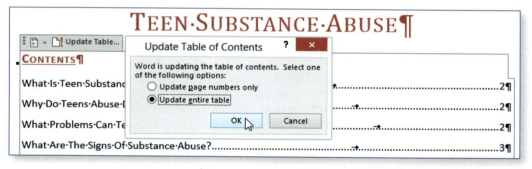

3-100 Update table of contents

c. Select the **Update entire table** radio button and click **OK**.

13. Save and close the document (Figure 3-101).

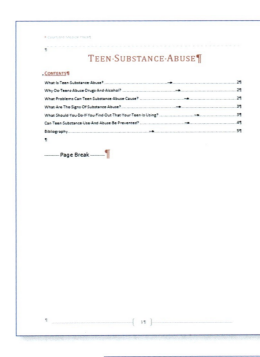

TEEN·SUBSTANCE·ABUSE¶

·CONTENTS¶

¶

----------Page Break----------¶

¶ —[1¶]—

TEEN·SUBSTANCE·ABUSE¶

·WHAT IS TEEN SUBSTANCE ABUSE?¶

Many teens try alcohol, tobacco, or drugs, but using these substances is not safe or legal. Some teens try these substances only a few times and stop. Others can't control their urges or cravings for them. This is substance abuse.¶

Teens may try a number of substances, including cigarettes, alcohol, household chemicals (inhalants), prescription and over-the-counter medicines, and illegal drugs. Marijuana is the illegal drug that teens use most often (Sanchez 2012).¶

·WHY DO TEENS ABUSE DRUGS AND ALCOHOL?¶

Teens use alcohol and other drugs for many reasons. They may do it because they want to fit in with friends or certain groups. They may also take a drug or drink alcohol because they like the way it makes them feel. Or they may believe that it makes them more grown up. Teens tend to try new things and take risks, and they may take drugs or drink alcohol because it seems exciting.¶

Teens with family members who have problems with alcohol or other drugs are more likely to have serious substance abuse problems. Also, teens who feel that they are not connected to or valued by their parents are at greater risk. Teens with poor self-esteem or emotional or mental health problems, such as depression, also are at increased risk (Courtyard Medical Plaza 2013).¶

·WHAT PROBLEMS CAN TEEN SUBSTANCE ABUSE CAUSE?¶

Substance abuse can lead to serious problems such as poor schoolwork, loss of friends, problems at home, and lasting legal problems. Alcohol and drug abuse is a leading cause of teen death or injury related to car accidents, suicides, violence, and drowning. Substance abuse can increase the risk of pregnancy and sexually transmitted diseases (STDs), including HIV, because of unprotected sex.¶

Even casual use of certain drugs can cause severe medical problems, such as an overdose or brain damage. Many illegal drugs today are made in home labs, so they can vary greatly in strength. These drugs also may contain bacteria, dangerous chemicals, and other unsafe substances (Foundation for Teen Health 2013).¶

----------Page Break----------¶

¶ —[2¶]—

¶

·BIBLIOGRAPHY¶

Courtyard Medical Plaza. "Teen Mental Health." *Courtyard Medical Plaza.* March 6, 2013. http://cmp.com/Teen_Mental_Health.pdf.¶

Foundation for Teen Health. *Making Good Choices.* 2013. http://foundationforteenhealth.org/choices.htm (accessed June 25, 2013).¶

Sanchez, Kelly L. "Examining High School Drug Use." *Journal of Secondary Education* XXI, no. 2 (2012): 22-26.¶
¶
¶

¶ —[5¶]—

3-101 Word 3-3 completed (pages 1, 2, and 5 displayed)

Independent Project 3-4

For this project, you modify the *Tips for Better Heart Rate Monitor Training* document from the American River Cycling Club. You insert and modify endnotes, insert placeholders, create sources, insert a bibliography page, bookmark selected text, and use custom headers and footers.
[Student Learning Outcomes 3.1, 3.2, 3.4, 3.5, 3.6]

File Needed: ***HeartRateMonitorTraining-03.docx***
Completed Project File Name: ***[your initials] Word 3-4.docx***

Skills Covered in This Project

- Insert endnotes.
- Insert a placeholder for a citation.
- Use the *Source Manager* to edit placeholders and create a new source.
- Change the bibliography style.
- Insert a bibliography page.
- Create a bookmark for selected text.
- Create a hyperlink to a bookmark.
- Add document properties.
- Insert and modify a cover page.
- Insert custom headers and footers.
- Insert page breaks.

1. Open the ***HeartRateMonitorTraining-03*** document from your student data files.

2. Save this document as ***[your initials] Word 3-4***.

3. Insert endnotes.
   a. Insert an endnote at the end of the first paragraph on the first page.
   b. In the endnote area, type See the bibliography for related books and articles.
   c. Insert an endnote at the end of the first sentence in the "Analyze Your Heart Rate Data" section.
   d. In the endnote area, type See the ARCC web site (www.arcc.org) for information about specific heart rate monitors.
   e. Insert an endnote at the end of the second sentence of the second paragraph in the "Comparing Heart Rate Values with Others" section.
   f. In the endnote area, type 220-age is a rough estimate of maximum heart rate.

4. Insert placeholders for citations.
   a. Place the insertion point at the end of the last sentence and before the period in the "Know Your Resting Heart Rate" section.
   b. Insert a placeholder named **VeloNews**.
   c. Place the insertion point at the end of the last sentence and before the period in the "Perform a Threshold Test" section.
   d. Insert a placeholder named **Burke**.
   e. Place the insertion point at the end of the last sentence and before the period in the "Analyze Your Heart Rate Data" section.
   f. Insert a placeholder named **Chapple**.
   g. Place the insertion point at the end of the last sentence and before the period in the "A Heart Rate Monitor Is Not Effective for Anaerobic Intervals" section.
   h. Insert the **Chapple** placeholder.

5. Use the *Source Manager* dialog box to provide source information for the three placeholders.
   a. Edit the *VeloNews* placeholder to include the following information:

Type of Source: **Web site**
Corporate Author: Velo News
Name of Web Page: Training Tips for Recreational Cyclists
Year: 2012
Year Accessed: 2013
Month Accessed: May
Day Accessed: 2
URL: http://velonews.com/training_tips.html

   b. Edit the *Burke* placeholder to include the following information. When you save the edit, click **No** if a dialog box opens and asks if you want to update the source.

Type of Source: **Book**
Author: Edward R. Burke
Title: The Complete Book of Long-Distance Cycling
Year: 2011
City: New York
Publisher: Rodale Books

   c. Edit the *Chapple* placeholder to include the following information. When you save the edit, click **No** if a dialog box opens and asks if you want to update the source.

Type of Source: **Book**
Author: Thomas Chapple
Title: Base Building for Cyclists
Year: 2009
City: San Francisco
Publisher: VeloPress

6. Change the style of the report to **APA Sixth Edition**.

7. Convert all endnotes to footnotes and change the footnote number format to **A**, **B**, **C**.

8. Insert a bibliography at the end of the document.
   a. Insert a page break at the end of the document.
   b. Insert the built-in **References** page on the last page.
   c. **Center** the *References* heading.

9. Insert a bookmark for selected text.
   a. Select the "**Perform a Threshold Test**" heading on the first page and insert a bookmark.
   b. Name the bookmark **LactateThreshold**.

10. Create a hyperlink to a bookmark.
    a. On the first page, select "**maximum heart rate**" in the first paragraph (third sentence).
    b. Insert a hyperlink to the **LactateThreshold** bookmark.

11. Add the following text to the document properties.

Title: Tips for Better Heart Rate Training
Company: American River Cycling Club
Manager: Olesia Sokol

12. Insert a cover page.
    a. Insert the **Ion (Dark)** built-in cover page.
    b. In the *Year* field, select the current date.
    c. Delete the **Subtitle** and **Author** fields.
    d. In the *Company Address* field, type www.arcc.org.
    e. Select the **Title** field, change the font size to **40 pt**., apply **bold** formatting, and align **center**.

13. Insert a header and footer.
   a. In the header of the second page, type Page, **space** once, and insert a plain page number in the current position.
   b. **Right align** the header information.
   c. In the footer, type American River Cycling Club on the left and www.arcc.org on the right (use tabs to align the text on the right).
   d. Change the font size of the information in the header and footer to **10 pt**.
   e. Apply a **½ pt**. **top** and **bottom black border** to the information in the footer.
   f. No header or footer should appear on the cover page.

14. Insert **page breaks** where necessary to keep headings on the same page with the text that follows.

15. Save and close the document (Figure 3-102).

3-102 Word 3-4 completed (cover page and page 1 displayed)

Independent Project 3-5

Sierra Pacific Community College District gives incoming college students a *Student Success Tips* document. For this project, you modify the document to include heading styles, a table of contents, footnotes, and bookmarks.
[Student Learning Outcomes 3.1, 3.3, 3.5, 3.6]

File Needed: **StudentSuccess-03.docx**
Completed Project File Name: **[your initials] Word 3-5.docx**

Skills Covered in This Project

- Change margins.
- Apply title and heading styles.
- Insert a bookmark for selected text.
- Create a cross-reference and a hyperlink to a bookmark.
- Insert and modify footnotes.
- Insert a table of contents.

- Use a different first page footer.
- Insert page numbers and a document property field into the footer.
- Modify text format and right indent.
- Insert page breaks.
- Update a table of contents.

---

1. Open the **StudentSuccess-03** document from your student data files.

2. Save this document as **[your initials] Word 3-5**.

3. Change the margins to **1"** top, bottom, left, and right on the entire document.

4. Apply styles to the title and headings.
   a. Apply the **Title** style to the title on the first page.
   b. Apply the **Heading 1** style to all the bold headings
   c. Apply the **Heading 2** style to all the underlined headings.

5. Insert a bookmark for selected text.
   a. Select the "**Procrastination**" heading and all of the text in that section.
   b. Insert a bookmark named **Procrastination** on the selected text.
   c. If bookmarks are not visible in your document, change the *Word Options* settings to make them visible.

6. Create a cross-reference to a bookmark.
   a. Find the word "Procrastination" in the "How to Reduce Test Anxiety" section.
   b. After "Procrastination," create a cross-reference to insert the page number of the *Procrastination* bookmark.
   c. Insert text so the cross-reference reads "(see page x)" where "x" is the inserted page number of the bookmark.

7. Create a hyperlink to a bookmark.
   a. Select the word "**Procrastination**" in the "How to Reduce Test Anxiety" section.
   b. Insert a hyperlink to the **Procrastination** bookmark on the selected text.
   c. Test the hyperlink to make sure it takes the reader to the *Procrastination* bookmark.

8. Insert footnotes and apply text formatting.
   a. Insert a footnote after "Weekly Schedules" in the "Schedule Your Time" section on the first page.
   b. For the footnote text, type Weekly Schedules are available from your counselor or in the college bookstore.
   c. In the "Schedule Your Time" section, insert a footnote at the end of "Be sure to schedule your time for all these in your 119 hours."
   d. For the footnote text, type Be sure to schedule recreational and down time in your 119 hours.
   e. Apply **italic** formatting to the text of the footnotes.

9. Move a footnote and modify footnote number format.
   a. Move the first footnote so it appears after "Weekly Schedule" in the "Track Your Time" section.
   b. Change the footnote number format to **a, b, c**.

10. Insert a table of contents.
    a. Insert a page break before the first page.
    b. Type Student Success Tips on the first line on the new first page and press **Enter**.

c. Apply the **Title** style to the title on the new first page.

d. On the blank line below the title, insert the **Automatic Table 1** table of contents.

11. Insert a footer on the second and continuing pages.

    a. Edit the footer on the first page of the document (table of contents).

    b. Set the first page footer to be different from the remaining footers.

    c. Go to the footer on the second page.

    d. Insert the **Vertical**, **Right** built-in page number format from the *Page Margins* page numbering options.

    e. In the footer, change the alignment to **right** and insert the **Company** document property field (Figure 3-103).

    f. Change the font size to **10 pt**. and apply **bold** formatting to the document property field.

    g. Change the right indent in the footer to **–.5"**.

    h. Close the footer.

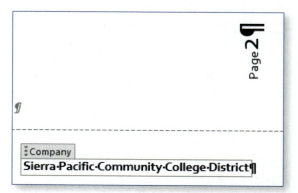

3-103 Footer on second and continuing pages

12. Insert page breaks to keep headings and text together.

13. Update the table of contents.

14. Save and close the document (Figure 3-104).

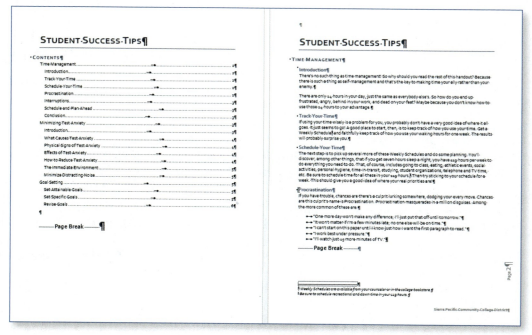

3-104 Word 3-5 completed (first two pages of six)

Independent Project 3-6

Courtyard Medical Plaza works closely with the Skiing Unlimited winter ski program. In this project, you modify the *Skiing Unlimited Training Guide* to include a table of contents, cover page, and odd and even headers.
[Student Learning Outcomes 3.3, 3.5, 3.6]

File Needed: ***SkiingUnlimitedTrainingGuide-03.docx***
Completed Project File Name: ***[your initials] Word 3-6.docx***

Skills Covered in This Project

- Change margins.
- Edit document properties.
- Apply title and heading styles.
- Insert a custom table of contents.
- Insert and customize odd and even headers.
- Insert a document property field into headers.

- Insert a cover page.
- Customize content and insert document property fields.
- Insert page breaks.
- Update a table of contents.

1. Open the ***SkiingUnlimitedTrainingGuide-03*** document from your student data files.

2. Save this document as ***[your initials] Word 3-6***.

3. Change the left and right margins to **1"**.

4. Edit the following document properties.
    Title: Skiing Unlimited Training Guide
    Company: Courtyard Medical Plaza
    Manager: Kallyn Nickols

5. Apply styles to the title and headings.
    a. Apply the **Title** style to the title on the first page.
    b. Apply the **Heading 1** style to all the bold headings.
    c. Apply the **Heading 2** style to all the underlined headings.
    d. Apply the **Heading 3** style to all the italicized headings.

6. Insert a custom table of contents.
    a. Insert a page break before the first page.
    b. Type Table of Contents on the first line on the new first page and press **Enter**.
    c. Apply the **Title** style to the title on the new first page.
    d. On the blank line below the title and before the page break, click the **Table of Contents** button and select **Custom Table of Contents** to insert a custom table of contents.
    e. Select **Fancy** format and show **2** levels of headings.

7. Insert header and footer.
    a. On the first page, insert the **Bold Numbers 3** built-in page number at the top of the page.
    b. Delete the extra **Enter** in the header.
    c. In the footer, insert the **Title** document property field on the left and the **Company** field on the right. Use tabs to align the field on the right.
    d. **Bold** the text in the footer.

8. Insert and modify a cover page.
   a. Insert the **Grid** cover page.
   b. Delete the **Subtitle** field and insert the **Company** document property field.
   c. Change the font size of the *Company* document property field to **20 pt**.
   d. In the *Abstract* field, type On behalf of the Skiing Unlimited winter ski program, Courtyard Medical Plaza has developed this training guide for Skiing Unlimited volunteers.
   e. On the Abstract field, apply **italic** formatting and change the text color to **Black, Text 1**.

9. Insert page breaks where necessary to keep headings with the text below.
   a. Insert a page break before the "Visual Impaired (VI)" heading.
   b. Insert other page breaks as necessary to keep headings with the text below.

10. Update the table of contents.

11. Save and close the document (Figure 3-105).

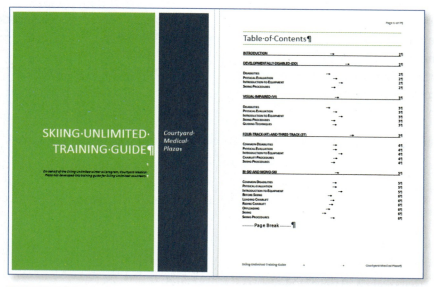

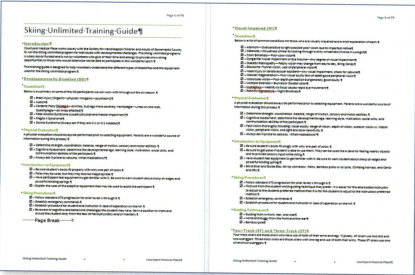

3-105 Word 3-6 completed (first four pages of eight)

Improve It Project 3-7

American River Cycling Club is working with a cycling tour company to set up a trip to cycle through the Tuscany region of Italy. The original document from the cycling tour company needs to be improved. Modify this document to remove some of the existing content and add a cover page, footnotes, bookmarks, and a footer.
[Student Learning Outcomes 3.1, 3.4, 3.5, 3.6]

File Needed: *ItalyTourItinerary-03.docx*
Completed Project File Name: *[your initials] Word 3-7.docx*

Skills Covered in This Project

- Change margins.
- Edit document properties.
- Apply a title and heading styles.
- Insert a custom table of contents.
- Insert and customize odd and even headers.
- Insert a document property field into headers.

- Insert a cover page.
- Customize content and insert document property fields.
- Insert and align pictures.
- Insert page breaks.
- Update a table of contents.

1. Open the *ItalyTourItinerary-03* document from your student data files.

2. Save this document as *[your initials] Word 3-7*.

3. Remove existing content.
   a. Remove the existing cover page.
   b. Remove the existing table of contents.
   c. Remove the existing headers and footers on all pages of the itinerary.
   d. Delete the existing bookmark in the document.

4. Change the page orientation to **Landscape**.

5. Apply the **Day** style to each of the day headings in the itinerary.

6. Insert page breaks.
   a. Click in front of "Day 3" and insert a page break.
   b. Repeat this on each of the odd numbered days so only two days appear on each page.

7. Add text and apply style.
   a. Place your insertion point on the blank line after the text in the "Day 2" section.
   b. Press **Enter** and type Notes and Questions at the insertion point.
   c. Apply **Day** style to the text you just typed.
   d. Repeat steps b and c to insert this information at the end of the "Day 4," "Day 6," and "Day 8" sections.

8. Insert a bookmark for selected text.
   a. On the last page, select the text beginning with "**Kilometers to Miles Conversion**" to "**49.6 miles.**"
   b. Insert a bookmark named **kmConversion** for the selected text.

9. Insert hyperlinks to a bookmark.
   a. On the first page in the "Day 2" section, select "**Distance: 83 km**" (don't select the paragraph mark) and insert a hyperlink to the **kmConversion** bookmark.
   b. Repeat this on each of the other riding days of the tour. Don't select the footnote after the "Day 3" distance.
   c. Test the hyperlink on page 1. It should take you to the bookmarked text on page 4.

10. Move and delete footnotes.
    a. Move the first footnote (after the distance on "Day 3") to appear after the distance on "Day 2."
    b. Change the footnote text to Day 2 is the longest day of the tour.
    c. Delete the second footnote reference marker after "Day 4." The footnote text is removed when you delete the footnote reference marker.

11. Insert footnotes.
    a. After the "Day 4" distance, insert a footnote and type Day 4 is an optional riding day.
    b. After the "Day 5" distance, insert a footnote and type Day 5 has two routes from which to choose.
    c. After the "Day 6" distance, insert a footnote and type Day 6 has three routes from which to choose. The 68 km route has a couple of substantial climbs.

12. Edit the following document properties.
    Title: Cycling Classic Tuscany: Tour Itinerary
    Company: American River Cycling Club

13. Insert and modify a cover page.
    a. Insert the **Semaphore** cover page.
    b. Select next **June 15** as the date.
    c. Change the font size of the *Title* field to **32 pt.**
    d. Delete the **Subject** (*Document Subtitle*) and **Author** fields.
    e. Change the font size of the *Company* field to **14 pt**.
    f. In the *Address* field, type www.arcc.org.

14. Insert footers on the second and continuing pages.
    a. On the second page of the document, edit the footer.
    b. Change the alignment to **right**, insert the **Company** document property field, deselect the field, and **space** once.
    c. Type | (horizontal line; **Shift+**) and **space** once.
    d. Type Page followed by a **space**.
    e. Insert a plain page number in the current position.
    f. **Bold** all of the text in the footer.

15. Save and close the document (Figure 3-106).

3-106 Word 3-5 completed (first two pages of five)

Challenge Project 3-8

Modify a report you have written for another class to include citations, a bibliography or works cited page, and headers and footers.
[Student Learning Outcomes 3.2, 3.6]

File Needed: None
Completed Project File Name: **[your initials] Word 3-8.docx**

Open an existing report you have and save it as **[your initials] Word 3-8**.

Modify your document according to the following guidelines:

- Select the citation style to use for your report (e.g., APA, MLA, Chicago).
- Add citations to the body of your report and create sources.
- Add placeholders for citations in the body of your report.
- Insert a bibliography or works cited page at the end of your report.
- Use the *Source Manager* dialog box to edit placeholders and sources and add new sources, if necessary.
- Insert other citations in the body as necessary.
- Update the bibliography page.
- Insert a header, footer, and page number from the built-in list of options.
- Use different first page headers and footers.
- Insert page breaks to control pagination as necessary.

Challenge Project 3-9

Add footnotes and endnotes, bookmarks, and headers and footers to a multipage document that you have written.
[Student Learning Outcomes 3.1, 3.5, 3.6]

File Needed: None
Completed Project File Name: *[your initials] Word 3-9.docx*

Open an existing report you have written for another class and save it as *[your initials] Word 3-9*.

Modify your document according to the following guidelines:

- Add endnotes to the document.
- Convert endnotes to footnotes.
- Change the number format for footnotes.
- Move a footnote to a new location.
- Delete a footnote.
- Add two bookmarks. Insert one at a specific location in your document and another one for selected text.
- Create a hyperlink to a bookmark.
- Create a cross-reference to a bookmark.
- Insert a custom header or footer in your document.
- Add a page number in the header or footer of the document.
- Insert page breaks to control pagination as necessary.

Challenge Project 3-10

Modify a report or multipage document you have written for another class to include a table of contents, a cover page, and headers and footers.
[Student Learning Outcomes 3.3, 3.4, 3.6]

File Needed: None
Completed Project File Name: **[your initials] Word 3-10.docx**

Open an existing report or multipage document and save it as **[your initials] Word 3-10**.

Modify your document according to the following guidelines:

- Apply *Heading 1* and *Heading 2* styles to the headings of your document. If the document does not have headings, add two levels of headings to the document.
- Insert a built-in or custom table of contents as the first page of your document.
- Include two levels of headings in the table of contents.
- Customize the title, company, and author document property fields.
- Insert a cover page of your choice.
- Customize the cover page by adding or removing a document property or content control fields.
- Add custom content to content control fields.
- Insert a header, footer, and page number from the built-in list of options.
- Use different first page headers and footers.
- Insert page breaks to control pagination as necessary.
- Update the table of contents.

CHAPTER
4

Using Tables, Columns, and Graphics

CHAPTER OVERVIEW

Tables, columns, and graphics enhance the appearance and readability of your Word documents. For example, you can use tables to attractively arrange and align information in column and row format. Columns improve readability and provide additional white space in a document. You can also insert and manipulate graphics to add attention-grabbing visual elements to your documents. This chapter introduces you to the Word tools that allow you to add and customize tables, columns, and graphics.

STUDENT LEARNING OUTCOMES (SLOs)

After completing this chapter, you will be able to:

SLO 4.1 Improve the design and readability of a document by using tables to present and arrange information (p. W4-197).

SLO 4.2 Modify a table by changing column and row size, aligning text, using the *Table Properties* dialog box, sorting data, and using *AutoFit* (p. W4-201).

SLO 4.3 Enhance the appearance and function of a table by using the *Table Tools* tabs, applying borders and shading, using table styles, inserting formulas, and converting text into a table (p. W4-207).

SLO 4.4 Modify the layout and design of a document using columns to present information (p. W4-214).

SLO 4.5 Enrich a document by adding and modifying visual elements such as pictures, shapes, *SmartArt,* and *WordArt* (p. W4-218).

Case Study

Placer Hills Real Estate (PHRE) is a real estate company with regional offices throughout central California. In the Pause & Practice projects in this chapter, you modify a brochure for Emma Cavalli, a realtor consultant with PHRE. In the past, Emma distributed brochures that were poorly laid out and designed and that negatively impacted the effectiveness of her message. You modify one of Emma's brochures to include tables, columns, and graphics. Your modifications will improve the overall layout and effectiveness of the document.

Pause & Practice 4-1: Modify an existing brochure to include a table that presents information attractively.

Pause & Practice 4-2: Enhance the table in the brochure by using borders, shading, and table styles.

Pause & Practice 4-3: Improve the readability of the brochure by arranging text in columns.

Pause & Practice 4-4: Add visual elements to the brochure to improve the overall design of the document.

Creating and Editing Tables

In Chapter 2 you learned about aligning information into column and row format using tab stops. *Tables* are another tool that you can use to organize information into column and row format. In addition to lining up information, tables allow you more formatting options than tabs do for alignment.

> **MORE INFO**
>
> On web pages, most of the information is organized into table and row format even though you might not see table borders or structure.

Tables

You can insert tables almost anywhere in a Word document. A table is made up of individual *cells*. You enter information in the cells of a table. Cells are grouped into *columns* and *rows*. When using tables, it is important to distinguish between cells, columns, and rows (Figure 4-1).

- *Cell:* The area where a column and row intersect
- *Column:* A vertical grouping of cells (think of vertical columns that support a building)
- *Row:* A horizontal grouping of cells (think of horizontal rows of seating in a stadium or auditorium)

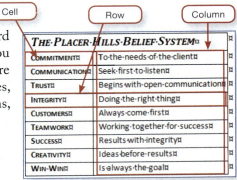

| Cell | Row | Column |

THE·PLACER·HILLS·BELIEF·SYSTEM¤		¤
COMMITMENT¤	To·the·needs·of·the·client¤	¤
COMMUNICATION¤	Seek·first·to·listen¤	¤
TRUST¤	Begins·with·open·communication¤	¤
INTEGRITY¤	Doing·the·right·thing¤	¤
CUSTOMERS¤	Always·come·first¤	¤
TEAMWORK¤	Working·together·for·success¤	¤
SUCCESS¤	Results·with·integrity¤	¤
CREATIVITY¤	Ideas·before·results¤	¤
WIN-WIN¤	Is·always·the·goal¤	¤

4-1 Table

HOW TO: Insert a Table

1. Place your insertion point in your document where you want to insert a table.
2. Click the **Insert** tab.
3. Click the **Table** button [*Tables* group] to open the drop-down list.
4. Click and drag across the *Insert Table* grid to select the number of columns and rows you want to have in the table (Figure 4-2).
   - As you drag across the grid, the *Insert Table* label changes to display the size of the table (e.g., *3x2 Table*).
5. Select the desired table size to insert into the document. The table is inserted into your document.

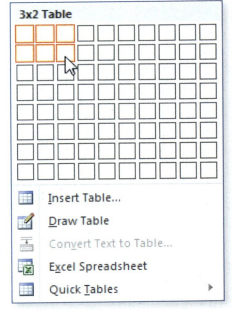

4-2 *Insert Table* drop-down list

> **MORE INFO**
>
> Word lists table dimensions in column and row format. For example, a three column and two row table is a 3x2 table.

When you insert a table using the *Insert Table* grid, the table size is limited depending on the size and resolution of your computer screen. You can also insert a table using the ***Insert Table*** dialog box.

HOW TO: Insert a Table Using the Insert Table Dialog Box

1. Click the **Insert** tab.
2. Click the **Table** button [*Tables* group] to open the drop-down list.
3. Select **Insert Table.** The *Insert Table* dialog box opens (Figure 4-3).
4. In the *Table size* area, select the desired number of columns and rows.
5. Choose **OK** to insert the table.

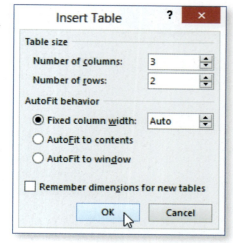

4-3 *Insert Table* dialog box

Navigate within a Table

To move the insertion point within a table, press **Tab** to move forward one cell in the current row. When you get to the end of a row and press *Tab,* the insertion point moves to the first cell in the next row. **Shift+Tab** moves you back one cell at a time. You can also use your pointer and click in a cell to insert the insertion point.

Table Tools Layout Tab

When a table is inserted into a document, the ***Table Tools tabs*** are displayed. There are two *Table Tools* tabs: ***Design*** and ***Layout***. These context-sensitive toolbars are activated whenever the insertion point is in the table or when a region of the table is selected. The *Table Tools Layout* tab lists a variety of formatting options (Figure 4-4). For more on the *Table Tools Design* tab, see *SLO 4.3: Formatting and Editing Tables*.

4-4 *Table Tools Layout* tab

Select Table and Text

When you are working with tables, at times you will want to select the entire table, a cell, column, or row, or multiple cells, columns, or rows. Word provides a variety of table selection tools.

- ***Table selector handle:*** This handle appears at the upper left of the table when the pointer is on the table (Figure 4-5). Click the **table selector** to select the entire table.
- ***Row selector:*** The row selector is the right-pointing arrow when your pointer is just to the left of the table row (Figure 4-6). When the pointer becomes the row selector, click to select a single row. To select multiple rows, click and drag up or down.

4-5 Table selector handle

4-6 Row selector

- **Column selector:** The column selector is the thick, black down arrow when your pointer is on the top of a column (Figure 4-7). When the pointer becomes the column selector, click to select a single column. To select multiple colums, click and drag left or right.

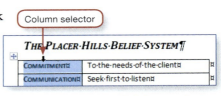

4-7 **Column selector**

- **Cell selector:** The cell selector is the thick, black right-pointing arrow when your pointer is just inside the left border of a cell (Figure 4-8). When the pointer becomes the cell selector, click to select a single cell. To select multiple cells, click and drag left, right, up, or down. When the cell selector is displayed, double-click to select the entire row.

4-8 **Cell selector**

- **Select button:** The select button is on the *Table Tools Layout* tab in the *Table* group. Click the **Select** button to access a drop-down list of table selection options (Figure 4-9).

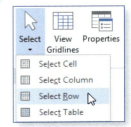

4-9 *Select* **drop-down list**

Add Rows and Columns

When you insert a table into a document, you are not locked into your original table dimensions; you can always add columns and rows to the table in a variety of ways.

- **Insert Control:** Place your pointer on the left outside edge of a row or top outside edge of a column to display the insert row or column control (plus sign). Click the **insert control** to add a row or column (Figure 4-10). Select multiple rows or columns and click the insert control to add the number or rows or columns selected.

4-10 **Insert row control**

- **Table Tools Layout tab**—In the *Rows & Columns* group, you can insert a row above or below the current row or a column to the left or right of the current column (see Figure 4-4).
- **Mini toolbar:** Select a cell, row, column, or table to display the mini toolbar. You can also right-click the table to display the mini toolbar. Click the **Insert** button to display a list of insert options (Figure 4-11).

4-11 **Use the mini toolbar to insert a row**

- **Insert Cells dialog box:** Open this dialog box by clicking the **Rows & Columns** launcher on the *Table Tools Layout* tab (Figure 4-12).
- **Tab:** When your insertion point is in the last cell in the last row, you can press **Tab** to insert a new row below the last row.

> **MORE INFO**
>
> Be careful about *using Shift cells right* from the *Insert Cells* dialog box. This pushes cells to the right creating a new column in that one row, not the entire table.

4-12 *Insert Cells* **dialog box**

Merge and Split Cells

Many times when you use tables you want to span information across multiple columns, such as when you are inserting a title or subtitle in a table. You can do this by merging columns, rows, and cells.

HOW TO: Merge Cells

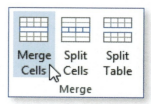

1. Select the cells to be merged.
2. Click the **Table Tools Layout** tab.
3. Click the **Merge Cells** button [*Merge* group] (Figure 4-13). The cells are merged into one cell.

4-13 *Merge Cells* button

Word also allows you to split a cell into multiple cells. You can split cells that have previously been merged or split a single cell into multiple columns and rows. When you are splitting cells, the *Split Cells* dialog box prompts you to specify the number of columns and rows.

HOW TO: Split Cells

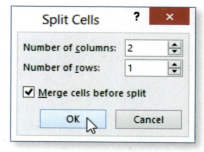

1. Select the cell(s) to be split.
2. Click the **Table Tools Layout** tab.
3. Click the **Split Cells** button [*Merge* group]. The *Split Cells* dialog box opens (Figure 4-14).
4. Select the number of columns and rows that you want in the split cell.
   - By default, the *Merge cells before split* check box is selected. When this check box is selected, Word merges the selected cells before splitting them into the desired number of columns and rows.
5. Click **OK** to split the cells.

4-14 *Split Cells* dialog box

> **ANOTHER WAY**
> Both *Merge Cells* and *Split Cells* are available from the context menu.

Copy or Move Columns and Rows

You can copy or move columns and rows in a table similar to how you copy or move text in a document. Select the column or row to copy or move, and use one of the following methods:

- *Drag and drop:* Drag and drop the column or row in the new location to move it. Hold the **Ctrl** key while dragging and dropping to copy a column or row.
- *Keyboard Shortcuts:* **Ctrl+C** (copy), **Ctrl+X** (cut), and **Ctrl+V** (paste).
- *Context menu:* Right-click on the selected column or row and select **Cut, Copy,** or **Paste**.
- *Clipboard group on the Home tab:* Use the **Cut, Copy,** and **Paste** buttons in this group.

Remove Columns and Rows

At some point, you will need to remove columns or rows from your table. Removing columns and rows is very similar to inserting columns and rows. Use the *Delete* button in the *Rows & Columns* group on the *Table Tools Layout* tab or the mini toolbar to remove cells, columns, rows, or an entire table. You have the following options (Figure 4-15):

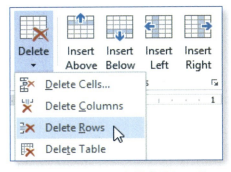

4-15 *Delete* options

- *Delete Cells . . .*: This will open the *Delete Cells* dialog box.
- *Delete Columns*
- *Delete Rows*
- *Delete Table*

Delete a Table

If you select an entire table and press *Delete* on your keyboard, only the information in the table is deleted; the blank table remains in your document. To delete a table, you select the **Delete Table** option from the *Delete* button on the *Table Tool Layout* tab or mini toolbar (see Figure 4-15).

SLO 4.2

Arranging Text in Tables

You can adjust the width of columns and the height of rows and control how text is aligned within the cells of a table. Word provides you with a variety of table resizing and text alignment options. You also can sort information automatically within a table.

Resize Columns and Rows

Many times you need to adjust columns and rows to better fit the information in the table. When you insert a table into a document, the default size for the table is the width of the document. You can manually adjust the width of columns and height of rows in a couple of ways.

You can manually drag the column or row borders to increase or decrease the size of a column or row. When you put your pointer on the vertical border of a column, the pointer changes to a *resizing pointer* (Figure 4-16). You can drag the column border to the left or right to adjust the size of the column. You can use the same method to adjust the height of a row by dragging the top or bottom border of a row up or down.

Resizing pointer

4-16 Manually adjust column width

> ### MORE INFO
> When you manually adjust the height of a row, it adjusts the height of the selected row only. Normally, you want to keep the height of rows consistent.

Word also allows you to type in a specific size for columns and rows. It is difficult to adjust column and row sizes of a table with merged cells. It is best to adjust the size of columns and rows before merging cells. If you're adjusting the size of columns or rows after merging cells, be very specific about the cells you select.

HOW TO: Resize Columns and Rows

1. Select the cells, columns, or rows you want to resize.
2. Click the **Table Tools Layout** tab.
3. Change the height or width to the desired size [*Cell Size* group] (Figure 4-17).
   - Manually type in the specific size or use the up or down arrows (spinner box) to resize.

4-17 Set cell *Height* and *Width*

AutoFit Tables

When you insert a table into a document, the table is automatically set to the width of the document (inside the left and right margins). Word has three different **AutoFit** options to adjust the column width of the table. The *AutoFit* options are in the *Cell Size* group on the *Table Tools Layout* tab (Figure 4-18).

- **AutoFit Contents:** Adjusts column widths to fit the contents of the table.
- **AutoFit Window:** Distributes the column widths so the table fits across the width of the page (this is the default setting when you insert a table into a document).
- **Fixed Column Width:** Adjusts columns to a fixed column width.

4-18 *AutoFit* options

> **MORE INFO**
>
> When you insert a table, the table has the same formatting as the text in the document. If your rows seem too high, it might be because your document contains before or after paragraph spacing that is controlling the height of the rows in your table.

Distribute Rows and Columns

There might be times when you adjust the sizes of columns and rows in a table and the table seems cluttered or uneven afterwards, or you might just want your columns and rows to be the same size as a starting point. Word provides you with features to evenly distribute rows and columns. **Distribute Rows** and **Distribute Columns** are on the *Table Tools Layout* tab in the *Cell Size* group (Figure 4-19).

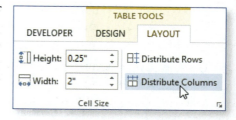

4-19 Distribute rows and columns

- **Distribute Rows:** This feature evenly distributes the rows based on the height of the existing table, making all rows a consistent height.
- **Distribute Columns:** This feature evenly distributes the columns based on the width of the existing table, making all columns the same width.

> **ANOTHER WAY**
>
> *AutoFit* and *Distribute* options are available from the context menu when a table is selected.

Text Alignment

In Chapter 1, you learned about paragraph alignment and how to left align, right align, center, or justify text. You learned how to change the vertical alignment of a page or section in Chapter 2. Similarly, when using tables, you have both horizontal and vertical alignment options. Text can be aligned vertically and horizontally within a cell and can be aligned independently of other cells. There are nine alignment options within the cell of a table. The following alignment options are in the *Alignment* group on the *Table Tools Layout* tab (Figure 4-20):

- *Align Top Left*
- *Align Top Center*
- *Align Top Right*
- *Align Center Left*
- *Align Center*
- *Align Center Right*
- *Align Bottom Left*
- *Align Bottom Center*
- *Align Bottom Right*

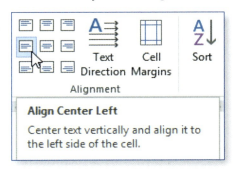

4-20 **Text alignment options in a table**

> **MORE INFO**
>
> For horizontal alignment, text in the table is usually aligned on the left and numbers are aligned on the right. If you increase row height, it's generally best to vertically center text within a cell.

Cell Margins

In addition to being able to change alignment in cells, you can also adjust **cell margins**. Just like the margins on a Word document, the cells of a table have top, bottom, left, and right margins. The default cell margins are 0" top and bottom, and 0.08" left and right.

HOW TO: Change Cell Margins

1. To change the cell margins on the entire table, select the entire table. Cell margins can also be changed on individual cells.
2. Click the **Table Tools Layout** tab.
3. Click the **Cell Margins** button [*Alignment* group]. The *Table Options* dialog box opens (Figure 4-21).
4. Make the desired changes to the *Top, Bottom, Left,* and *Right* cell margins.
   - You can also add spacing between cells in the *Default cell spacing* area. This puts padding (space) around the outside of the cells.
   - If you don't want the size of your table to be automatically adjusted, deselect the **Automatically resize to fit contents** check box.
5. Click **OK** to apply the cell margin settings.

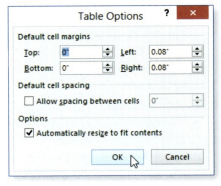

4-21 *Table Options* **dialog box**

Table Properties Dialog Box

The *Table Properties* dialog box consolidates some of table sizing and alignment options in one location. In the dialog box, there are separate tabs for *Table, Row, Column, Cell,* and *Alt Text*. To open the *Table Properties* dialog box, click the **Properties** button in the *Table* group on the *Table Tools Layout* tab (Figure 4-22). You can also open the *Table Properties* dialog box from the context menu.

- *Table* tab: Adjusts the size of the table, alignment, text wrapping, positioning, borders and shading, and cell margins.
- *Row* tab: Adjusts the height of rows and controls how rows break between pages.
- *Column* tab: Adjusts the width of columns.
- *Cell* tab: Adjusts the width of cells, vertical alignment of information in cells, and cell margins.
- *Alt Text* tab: Alternative text (Alt text) is an information tag that is displayed when the pointer is placed on the table. Alt text is also used with screen readers to accommodate those with visual impairments. Alt text is very common with web pages.

4-22 *Table Properties* dialog box

Sort Data in Tables

A very useful feature in Word is the ability to sort information within a table. You might want to arrange the text in the first column of a table alphabetically or sort numbers in descending order. When you use the *Sort* feature on a table, rows of information are rearranged according to how you specify the sort.

HOW TO: Sort Information in a Table

1. Place your insertion point somewhere in the table.
2. Select the **Table Tools Layout** tab.
3. Click the **Sort** button [*Data* group]. The entire table is selected and the *Sort* dialog box opens (Figure 4-23).
4. Click the **Sort by** drop-down list and select the column to use to sort the table. You can sort by any of the columns in the table.
5. Click the **Type** drop-down list and select the type of sort to be performed. You can sort by *Text, Number,* or *Date.*
6. Click the **Using** drop-down list and select the cell information to be used in the sort. *Paragraphs* is the default option and usually this is the only option available.
7. Select **Ascending** (A to Z or 1 to 10) or **Descending** (Z to A or 10 to 1) for the sort order.
8. If desired, you can add a second or third sort on different columns. Use the *Then by* options to add additional sorts.
9. If your table has a header row (title or column headings), click the **Header row** radio button to omit this row from the sort.
10. Click **OK** to perform the sort. Your table is sorted according to your settings.

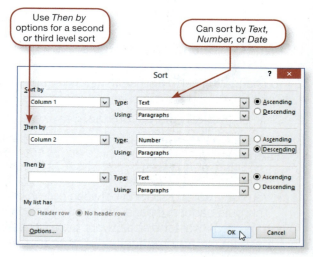

4-23 *Sort* dialog box

PAUSE & PRACTICE: WORD 4-1

For this Pause & Practice project, you begin modifying Emma Cavalli's brochure. You add a table to the end of this document and then modify the table.

File Needed: ***Brochure-04.docx***
Completed Project File Name: ***[your initials] PP W4-1.docx***

1. Open the ***Brochure-04*** document from your student data files.

2. Save this document as ***[your initials] PP W4-1***.

3. Move to the end of the document and insert a 3x7 table.
   a. Press **Ctrl+End** to move to the end of the document.
   b. Click the **Insert** tab.
   c. Click the **Table** button [*Tables* group] and select a 3x7 table using the table grid. The table is inserted into the document.

4. Type the information in the following table. Press **Tab** to move from one cell to the next cell in the row. Leave the third column blank.

Commitment	To the needs of the client	
Communication	Seek first to listen	
Integrity	Doing the right thing	
Customers	Always come first	
Teamwork	Work together for success	
Success	Results with integrity	
Creativity	Ideas before results	

5. Delete a column and insert rows.
   a. Place the insertion point in any cell in the last column and click the **Delete** button [*Table Tools Layout* tab, *Rows & Columns* group].
   b. Select **Delete Columns**.
   c. Place the insertion point in the second row and click the **Insert Below** button [*Table Tools Layout* tab, *Rows & Columns* group]. A blank row is inserted below the second row.

d. Type the following information in the third row:

Trust	Begins with communication

e. Click in the last cell of the table (bottom right cell) and press **Tab.** A new row is inserted at the bottom of the table.

f. Type the following information in the third row:

Win-Win	Is always the goal

6. *AutoFit* table and adjust column and row size.
   a. Place your insertion point somewhere in the table.
   b. Click the **AutoFit** button [*Table Tools Layout* tab, *Cell Size* group] and select **AutoFit Contents.** The column widths are adjusted to fit the contents of the table.
   c. Place the insertion point in the first column.
   d. Change the *Width* to **1.2"** [*Table Tool Layout* tab, *Cell Size* group]
   e. Place the insertion point in the second column.
   f. Change the *Width* to **2".**
   g. Use the table selector handle to select the entire table.
   h. Click the **Properties** button [*Table Tool Layout* tab, *Table* group] to open the *Table Properties* dialog box (Figure 4-24).
   i. Click the **Row** tab and check the **Specify height** check box.
   j. Type .25 in the *Specify height* field and select **Exactly** in the *Row height is* drop-down list.

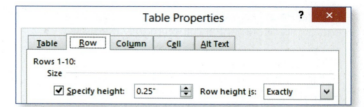

4-24 Change row height on the selected table

   k. Click **OK** to close the *Tables Properties* dialog box and apply these settings.

7. Insert a row and merge cells.
   a. Click anywhere in the table so the entire table is no longer selected.
   b. Select the first row of the table, select **Insert** on the mini toolbar, and click **Insert Above.** A new row is inserted at the top of the table.
   c. With the first row selected, click the **Merge Cells** button [*Table Tools Layout* tab, *Merge* group]. The cells in the first row are merged into one cell.
   d. Type The Placer Hills Belief System in the merged first row.

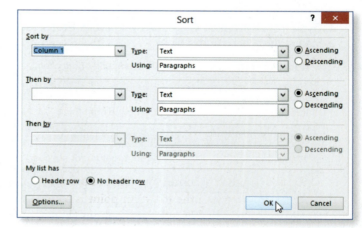

4-25 Sort the table by the first column in ascending order

8. Sort the table by text in the first column.
   a. Select the **second through tenth (last) rows** of the table.
   b. Click the **Sort** button [*Table Tools Layout* tab, *Data* group]. The *Sort* dialog box opens (Figure 4-25).
   c. Sort by **Column 1** in **Ascending** order. Leave *Type* as **Text** and *Using* as **Paragraphs.**
   d. Click **OK** to perform the sort. The rows below the title are sorted in ascending order.

W4-206

9. Change cell margins and text alignment.
   a. Select the entire table.
   b. Click the **Cell Margins** button [*Table Tools Layout* tab, *Alignment* group]. The *Table Options* dialog box opens (Figure 4-26).
   c. In the *Left* and *Right* cell margins, type .05.
   d. Select the **Automatically resize to fit contents** check box and press **OK**.
   e. With the table still selected, click the **Align Center Left** button (first button in the second row) [*Table Tools Layout* tab, *Alignment* group].
   f. Click in the first row of the table to deselect the table.
   g. Right-click the first row of the table.
   h. Click the **Center** button on the mini toolbar. The title is centered horizontally.

10. Save and close this document (Figure 4-27).

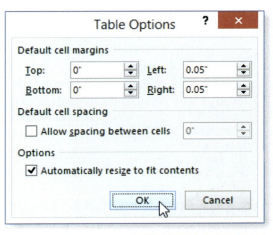

4-26 Change cell margins

The·Placer·Hills·Belief·System¤		¤
Commitment¤	To·the·needs·of·the·client¤	¤
Communication¤	Seek·first·to·listen¤	¤
Creativity¤	Ideas·before·results¤	¤
Customers¤	Always·come·first¤	¤
Integrity¤	Doing·the·right·thing¤	¤
Success¤	Results·with·integrity¤	¤
Teamwork¤	Work·together·for·success¤	¤
Trust¤	Begins·with·communication¤	¤
Win-Win¤	Is·always·the·goal¤	¤

4-27 PP W4-1 completed (table only displayed)

SLO 4.3

Formatting and Editing Tables

In addition to the ability to adjust the structure of tables, Word provides you with many tools to enhance the overall appearance of tables. For example, you can add custom borders and shading and table styles to tables. You can also add formulas to tables and convert text into tables.

Table Tools Design Tab

Word provides you with two *Table Tools* tabs when you work with tables: *Design* and *Layout*. Both tabs are context-sensitive and are only displayed when the table or portion of the table is selected or when the insertion point is somewhere in the table. The ***Table Tools Design tab*** allows you to apply table styles and options (Figure 4-28). You can also draw tables using the tools on this tab.

4-28 *Table Tools Design* tab

Table Borders

The *Borders* button is on the *Table Tools Design* tab in the *Borders* group or on the mini toolbar. On the *Borders* drop-down list, there are a variety of border options (Figure 4-29). You can also apply borders using the *Borders and Shading* dialog box.

You can apply borders to an individual cell, a group of cells, or an entire table. When applying borders, it is important to be very specific when selecting the area of the table on which to apply the borders.

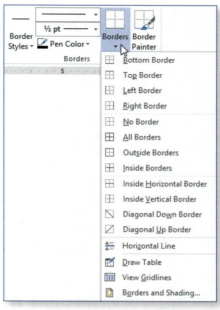

4-29 *Borders* drop-down list

HOW TO: Apply Borders to a Table Using the Borders and Shading Dialog Box

1. Select the entire table or the desired area of the table where you want borders.

2. Click the **Borders** button [*Table Tools Design* tab, *Borders* group].

3. Select **Borders and Shading** to open the *Borders and Shading* dialog box (Figure 4-30).

4. In the *Apply to* area, select the portion of the table where you want to apply the border settings.

5. In the *Setting* area, select the border from the list of options.
   - You can remove all borders by selecting **None**.

6. Select the *Style* of the border from the list of options.

7. Choose the color of the border from the *Color* drop-down list.

8. Change the width of the border with the *Width* drop-down list.

9. In the *Preview* area, you can see how your borders will be applied to your table.
   - In the *Preview* area, you can also apply or deselect borders on specific areas of your table.
   - You can click the buttons in the *Preview* area or click the displayed borders to turn borders on or off.

10. Click **OK** to apply the border settings and close the *Borders and Shading* dialog box.

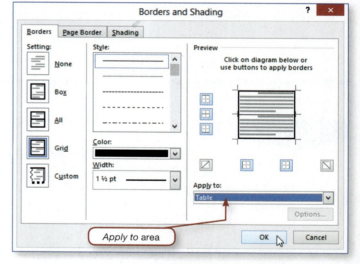

4-30 *Borders and Shading* dialog box

> **MORE INFO**
>
> Without borders, it is difficult to see the structure of your table. If you don't have borders, click **View Gridlines** [*Table Tools Layout* tab, *Table* group]. Gridlines are displayed in the document only; they do not print.

Table Shading

Like table borders, you can apply shading to specific cells or to an entire table. In the *Shading* drop-down list in the *Table Styles* group on the *Table Tools Design* tab, you can choose from *Theme Colors* or *Standard Colors* (Figure 4-31). Theme colors change depending on the theme of your document. You can choose a custom color by selecting **More Colors**, which opens the *Colors* dialog box. You can also remove shading by selecting **No Color**.

You can also apply, change, or remove shading with the *Shading* tab in the *Borders and Shading* dialog box.

4-31 Table *Shading* options

ANOTHER WAY

Apply borders and shading from the mini toolbar by right-clicking the table or a portion of the table.

Table Styles

Table Styles are built-in styles that you can apply to your tables. These table styles include a variety of borders, shading, alignment, and formatting options. Word provides a wide variety of built-in table styles in the *Table Styles* group on the *Table Tools Design* tab. Click the **More** button on the bottom right to display the *Table Styles* gallery (Figure 4-32).

After you have applied a table style to a table, you can still customize all aspects of the table. You can also remove all formatting of a table by selecting the **Clear** option at the bottom of the *Table Styles* gallery.

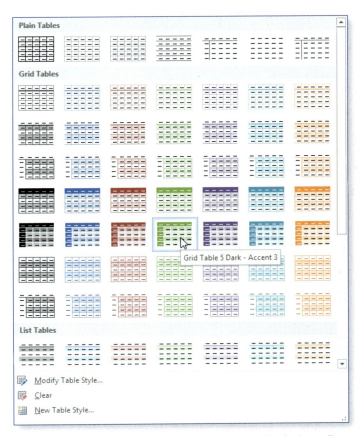

4-32 *Table Styles* gallery

Table Style Options

Word offers a variety of ***Table Style Options*** to customize tables (Figure 4-33). For example, many tables have a header row or column, or a total or last row, where you might want to apply special formatting for emphasis. When any of these options is selected, Word includes special formatting when a table style is applied. Select your table style options before applying a table style.

☑ Header Row	☑ First Column
☐ Total Row	☐ Last Column
☑ Banded Rows	☐ Banded Columns
Table Style Options	

4-33 *Table Style Options* group

HOW TO: Apply a Table Style and Options

1. Select the table on which to apply a table style.
2. Click the **Table Tools Design** tab.
3. Select the options you want to apply to the table [*Table Style Options* group].
   - Consider the content of your table when deciding which table style options to choose.
   - When you select or deselect table style options, the thumbnails of the table styles in the *Table Styles* gallery change to reflect the options you have chosen.
4. Click the **More** button to display the *Table Styles* gallery.
   - You can scroll down in the *Table Styles* gallery to view more table styles.
5. Choose a table style. Word applies the style and options to your table.

Add Formulas to Tables

In addition to making your tables more attractive and easier to read with formatting and style options, you can add *formulas* to tables to automatically calculate amounts. For example, you can add a formula in a total row of the table to total the numbers in the rows above (Figure 4-34).

Formula that adds the numbers above

Placer·Hills·Real·Estate↵	¤
Monthly·Home·Sales¤	
Week·1¤	15¤
Week·2¤	24¤
Week·3¤	19¤
Week·4¤	28¤
Total¤	86¤

4-34 Formula in a table

Insert a Formula

Most formulas used in tables in Word are simple formulas that calculate numbers in a column or row. When you insert a formula, Word, by default, inserts the **SUM** formula and adds the range of numbers in the column or row. Word also allows you to insert more complex formulas.

HOW TO: Insert a Formula in a Table

1. Place the insertion point in the cell where you want to insert the formula.
2. Click the **Table Tools Layout** tab.
3. Click the **Formula** button [*Data* group]. The *Formula* dialog box opens (Figure 4-35).
4. The formula appears in the *Formula* box.
   - You can select different formula functions from the *Paste function* drop-down list.
5. In the *Number format* area, select number format from the drop-down list.
6. Click **OK** to insert the formula.

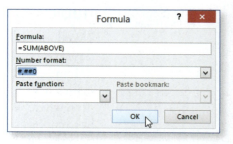

4-35 *Formula* dialog box

Update a Formula

A formula automatically adds values in a table, and you can automatically update it if any of the values change. There are two ways to update a formula:

- Right-click the formula and select **Update Field**.
- Select the formula and press the **F9** function key.

Convert Text into a Table

You will not always be creating a table from scratch. Many times you want to create a table from existing text. For example, you might want to convert information that is arranged into a table using tabs, or you might want to convert a table into text. Word provides you with options to *convert text to a table* or *convert a table to text*.

When converting text into a table, the selected text must be separated by tabs, commas, paragraph breaks, or other characters. Word uses these characters to separate text into individual cells in the table.

HOW TO: Convert Text to a Table

1. Select the text to be converted to a table.
2. Click the **Insert** tab.
3. Click **Tables** [*Tables* group] and select **Convert Text to Table**. The *Convert Text to Table* dialog box opens (Figure 4-36).
4. In the *Table size* area, make desired changes to the number of columns or rows.
   - Word automatically detects the size of the table you need.
   - You might not be able to change one or both of the values, depending on the text you selected.
5. In the *AutoFit behavior* area, select an *AutoFit* option. The default setting is *Fixed column width*.
6. In the *Separate text at* area, select how you want Word to separate columns and rows.
   - Word automatically picks an option based on the text you have selected.
7. Click **OK** to convert the text to a table.

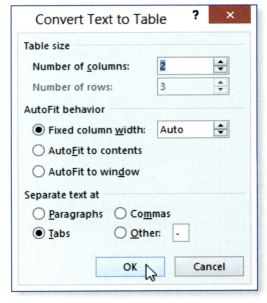

4-36 *Convert Text to Table* dialog box

> **MORE INFO**
>
> To convert a table to text, click the **Convert to Text** button [*Table Tool Layout* tab, *Data* group] to open the *Convert Table to Text* dialog box.

For this Pause & Practice project, you continue to modify Emma's brochure. You apply a table style and table style options to the table you created in the previous Pause & Practice project. You also convert text to a table and apply borders and shading.

File Needed: ***[your initials] PP W4-1.docx***
Completed Project File Name: ***[your initials] PP W4-2.docx***

---

1. Open the ***[your initials] PP W4-1*** file you created in *Pause & Practice 4-1.*

2. Save this document as ***[your initials] PP W4-2***.

3. Apply table style options and a table style.
   a. Select the table at the end of the document.
   b. Click the **Table Tools Design** tab.
   c. Select **Header Row**, **Banded Rows**, and **First Column** [*Table Style Options* group] if they are not already selected. The other check boxes should not be selected.
   d. Click the **More** button in the *Table Styles* group to open the *Table Styles* gallery.
   e. Select the **Grid Table 5 Dark – Accent 3** style (Figure 4-37). The style is applied to the table.

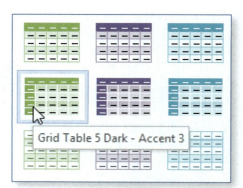

4-37 Select table style

4. Apply a custom top and bottom border to the table.
   a. Select the **first row** (title) of the table.
   b. Click the **Borders** button [*Table Tools Design* tab, *Borders* group or on the mini toolbar] and select **Borders and Shading.** The *Borders and Shading* dialog box opens (Figure 4-38).
   c. In the *Setting* area, select **Custom.**
   d. Select **Black**, **Text 1** from the *Color* drop-down list.
   e. Select **1½ pt.** from the *Width* drop-down list.
   f. Select the **solid line** (first line style in the list) in the *Style* area if it is not already selected.
   g. In the *Preview* area, click the **top boundary** of the cell to add a top border.

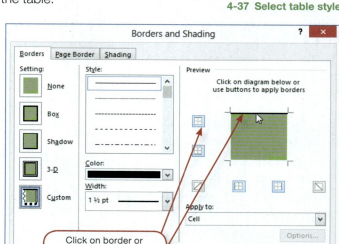

4-38 Apply custom borders

   h. Click **OK** to close the dialog box and add the border.
   i. Select the **bottom row** of the table.
   j. Open the *Borders and Shading* dialog box and apply the same custom border to the bottom of the selected row (**Black, 1½ pt., solid line**).
   k. Click **OK** to add the border and close the dialog box.

5. Vertically align text in cells.
   a. Select the entire table and click the **Properties** button [*Table Tools Layout* tab, *Table* group] to open the *Table Properties* dialog box.

b. Click the **Cell** tab and select **Center** in the *Vertical alignment* area.

c. Click **OK** to close the dialog box.

6. Make formatting changes to the text in the table.
   a. Select the first row.
   b. Open the *Font* dialog box, change *Size* to **12** and *Font color* to **Black**, **Text 1**, and check **All caps** in the *Effects* area.
   c. Click **OK** to close the *Font* dialog box.
   d. Select the first column, not including the title.
   e. Open the *Font* dialog box and check **Small caps** in the *Effects* area.
   f. Click **OK** to close the *Font* dialog box.

7. Convert text to a table.
   a. On the first page, select the three lines of text after "Realtor Consultant" ("Phone" through "www.phre.com/ecavalli"). Be sure to include the paragraph mark at the end of the third line.
   b. Click the **Insert** tab.
   c. Click the **Table** button [*Tables* group] and select **Convert Text to Table**. The *Convert Text to Table* dialog box opens (Figure 4-39).
   d. Change the *AutoFit behavior* to **AutoFit to contents.**
   e. Click **OK** to convert selected text to a table.

8. Remove all borders and add custom borders and shading.
   a. With the table selected, click the **Borders** drop-down arrow [*Table Tools Design* tab, *Borders* group].
   b. Select **No Border** to remove all borders.
   c. With the table still selected, click the **Borders** drop-down arrow and select **Top Border.**
   d. With the table still selected, click the **Borders** drop-down arrow and select **Bottom Border**.
   e. With the table still selected, click the **Shading** drop-down arrow [*Table Tools Design* tab, *Table Styles* group] and select **Olive Green, Accent 3, Lighter 80%** (Figure 4-40).

9. Save and close the document (Figure 4-41).

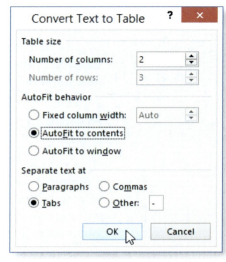

4-39 *Convert Text to Table* dialog box

4-40 Select *Shading* color

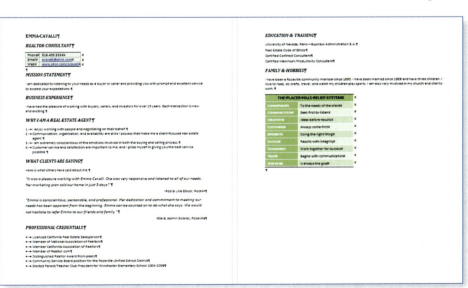

4-41 PP W4-2 completed

Using Columns

You can use columns to arrange text and tables into narrower widths and improve the readability, layout, and design of a document. In a normal Word document, text is arranged in a single column. You can apply columns to an entire document or to selected sections of a document. Word has preset column setting options or you can customize column settings to meet your needs. You can use column and section breaks to control column endings and balance columns.

Preset Column Settings

You can apply column settings to a new document or to a document with existing text. To apply preset column settings, click the **Columns** button on the *Page Layout* tab in the *Page Setup* group (Figure 4-42). The *Two* and *Three* column options set columns with equal width, while the *Left* and *Right* column options arrange your document in two columns of unequal width.

When you apply columns to a document, the column settings are applied only to that section of the document. If there are no section breaks, columns are applied to the entire document.

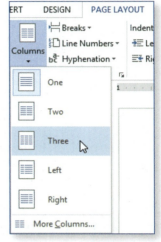

4-42 Preset column options

Customize Columns

Use the **Columns dialog box** to apply column settings or customize current column settings. In the *Columns* dialog box you can select the number of columns, adjust the column width and space between columns, insert a line between columns, and select the portion of the document where the column settings will be applied.

HOW TO: Customize Columns Using the Columns Dialog Box

1. Click the **Page Layout** tab.
2. Click the **Columns** button [*Page Setup* group].
3. Select **More Columns**. The *Columns* dialog box opens (Figure 4-43).
4. Select column settings from the *Presets* options or *Number of columns* box.
   - Based on the number of columns you choose, Word automatically sets the column width and spacing.
   - The default spacing between columns is 0.5".
5. In the *Width and spacing* area, adjust the column widths and spacing as desired.
6. To apply unequal column widths, deselect the **Equal column widths** check box.
   - When *Equal column width* is deselected, you can adjust the width and spacing of each column individually.
   - When *Equal column width* is selected, you can adjust the width and spacing to apply to all columns.
7. In the *Apply to* area, select the portion of the document where you want to apply column settings.
   - You can apply column settings to the *Whole document* or from *This point forward*.

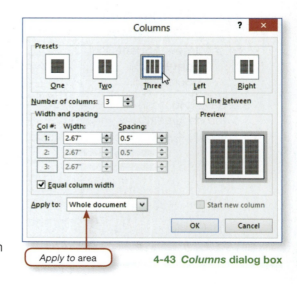

4-43 Columns dialog box

- When *This point forward* is selected, Word inserts a continuous section break at the insertion point in the document and applies column settings to the text after the continuous section break.
- If you select text, you will be given the option to apply column settings to *Selected text* in the *Apply to* area.

8. Check the **Line between** check box to insert a vertical line between columns.
9. The *Preview* area displays a thumbnail of how your columns will appear.
10. Click **OK** to apply column settings.

Convert Text to Columns

You can apply column settings to the *whole document,* from *this point forward,* or to *selected text.* Depending on the portion of the document where you are applying column settings, Word applies the column settings and inserts any needed section breaks. These options are in the *Columns* dialog box in the *Apply to* area. The following table describes how Word handles each of the options.

Apply to Column Options

Columns Applied to	Actions
Whole Document	Word applies column settings to the entire document. No section breaks are added.
This point forward	Word inserts a continuous section break before the insertion point in the document and applies the column setting beginning at the insertion point, which becomes a new section of the document.
Selected text	When text is selected and column settings are applied, Word inserts a continuous section break before and after the selected text. The column settings apply only to that section.

Use Column Breaks

Column widths control the horizontal text wrapping, while the top and bottom margins or section breaks control where a column ends and wraps to the next column. You can insert **column breaks** to end a column and push subsequent text to the next column.

HOW TO: Insert a Column Break

1. Place the insertion point where you want the column to end or the next column to begin.
2. Click the **Page Layout** tab.
3. Click the **Breaks** button [*Page Layout* group].
4. Select **Column** in the *Page Breaks* options (Figure 4-44).
   - You see a column break indicator when *Show/Hide* is turned on (Figure 4-45).

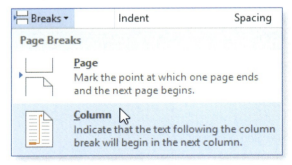

4-44 Insert column break

WHY·I·AM·A·REAL·ESTATE·AGENT¶

1.→ I·enjoy·working·with·people·and· negotiating· on·their·behalf.¶
2.→ Communication,· organization,· and· availability· are·skills·I·possess·that· make· me·a·client-focused·real·estate·agent.¶
3.→ I·am·extremely·conscientious·of·the· emotions·involved·in·both·the·buying·and· selling·process.¶
4.→ Customer·service·and·satisfaction· are· important· to·me,·and·I·pride·myself·in· giving·you·the·best·service·possible.¶

·················· Column Break ··················

4-45 Column break inserted

> ## MORE INFO
>
> Always turn on *Show/Hide* (**Ctrl+Shift+8**) when using page, section, or column breaks to help you see these elements in your document.

Balance Columns

Column breaks are one way to balance columns on a page. Another way is to use a ***continuous section break***. To make columns approximately equal in length on a page, insert a continuous section break at the end of the last column on the page. Word automatically adjusts your columns so they are about the same length.

HOW TO: Balance Columns Using a Continuous Section Break

1. Place the insertion point at the end of the last column in your document.
2. Click the **Page Layout** tab.
3. Click the **Breaks** button [*Page Layout* group].
4. Select **Continuous** in the *Section Breaks* options.
   - You see a continuous section break indicator when *Show/Hide* is turned on.

> ## MORE INFO
>
> Balancing columns using a continuous section break works only if there are no other column breaks controlling column endings on that page.

PAUSE & PRACTICE: WORD 4-3

For this Pause & Practice project, you apply columns to Emma's brochure. With the use of columns and column breaks, you attractively arrange the columns and make the document fit on one page.

File Needed: ***[your initials] PP W4-2.docx***
Completed Project File Name: ***[your initials] PP W4-3.docx***

1. Open the ***[your initials] PP W4-2*** file you saved in *Pause & Practice 4-2*.
2. Save this document as ***[your initials] PP W4-3***.
3. Change the page orientation and margins.
   a. Click the **Orientation** button [*Page Layout* tab, *Page Setup* group].
   b. Select **Landscape**.

c. Click the **Margins** button and choose *Custom Margins.*

d. Change the *Top* margin to **1.2"**, and the *Bottom, Left,* and *Right* margins to **0.5"**.

e. Click **OK** to close the dialog box and apply the margin settings. If a dialog box opens informing you that the margins are outside the printable area, click **Ignore**.

4. Arrange the text in columns.
   a. Move to the top of the document.
   b. Click the **Columns** button [*Page Layout* tab, *Page Setup* group] and choose **Two**. The text is arranged into two columns.

5. Customize column settings using the *Columns* dialog box.
   a. Click the **Columns** button [*Page Layout* tab, *Page Setup* group] and choose **More Columns**. The *Columns* dialog box opens (Figure 4-46).
   b. In the *Presets* area, select **Three**.
   c. In the *Width and spacing* area, change the *Spacing* to **0.6"**.
   d. In the *Apply to* area, select **Whole document**.
   e. Click **OK** to apply custom column settings.

6. Use column breaks to control column endings.
   a. Place the insertion point in front of "What Clients are Saying."
   b. Click the **Breaks** button [*Page Layout* tab, *Page Setup* group].
   c. Select **Column** in the *Page Breaks* options to insert a column break.
   d. Place the insertion point in front of "Education & Training."
   e. Press **Ctrl+Shift+Enter** to insert a column break.

7. Save and close the document (Figure 4-47).

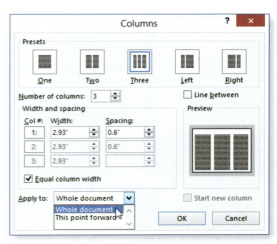

4-46 Customize column settings

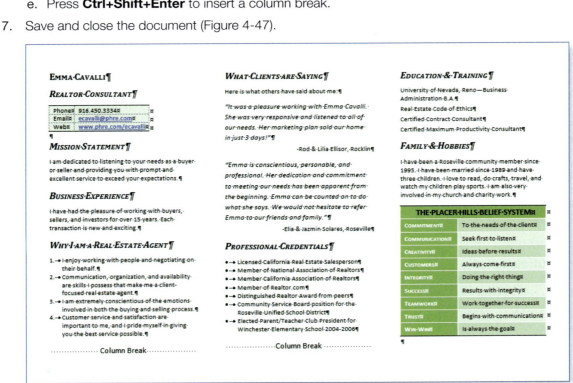

4-47 PP W4-3 completed

Working with Graphics

You can use graphics to visually present information and enhance a document. Graphics can be pictures stored on your computer, online pictures or clip art, shapes, *SmartArt*, and *WordArt*. You can insert and customize each of these to meet your specific needs and effectively present information visually.

Pictures and Online Pictures

You can use *pictures* and *clip art* to enhance your documents with a visual element. Word provides a library of media that includes illustrations, photographs, video, and audio. In addition to using Word's media library, you can also add your own pictures and graphics to Word documents. Word uses the term *picture* generically to refer to any type of visual image that is saved as a graphic file. Below is a table of common types of graphic formats.

Types of Graphics

Format	Full Name	Extension	Details
PNG	Portable Network Graphics	.png	Used with pictures and editing pictures. High-quality resolution.
JPEG	Joint Photographic Experts Group	.jpeg or .jpg	Relatively small file size. Many pictures are saved and distributed in JPEG format.
TIFF	Tagged Image File Format	.tiff	Used with high-quality digital photos and has a larger file size than JPEG or PNG.
GIF	Graphics Interchange Format	.gif	Used with graphics and clip art with fewer colors.
WMF	Windows Metafile	.wmf	Windows format used with many clip art and graphic images.
BMP	Windows Bitmap	.bmp	Proprietary Windows format used with many Microsoft clip art and graphic images.

Insert a Picture

You can use your own picture or a picture from the media library in Word. See the steps below to insert a picture into a document.

HOW TO: Insert a Picture

1. Place the insertion point in the document at the approximate area where you want the picture inserted.

2. Click the **Insert** tab.

3. Click the **Pictures** button [*Illustrations* group]. The *Insert Picture* dialog box opens (Figure 4-48).

4. Browse to the location on your computer and select a picture.

5. Click the **Insert** button to insert the picture and close the *Insert Picture* dialog box.

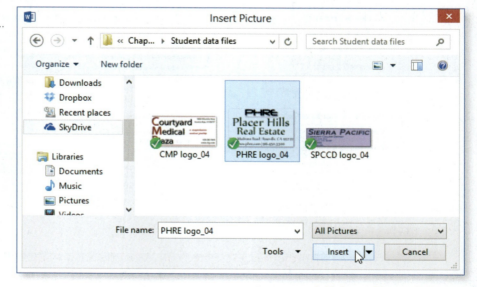

4-48 *Insert Picture* dialog box

You might find a picture on the Internet and want to use it in a document. You can either save the picture and insert it as explained above or copy the picture and paste it into your document. Press **Ctrl+C** to copy the picture and **Ctrl+V** to paste the picture.

Include pictures obtained from the web only if you have permission from the image owner to avoid copyright infringement. For academic purposes, you may include images if you reference their sources as you would any other research citation.

>
> ### ANOTHER WAY
> Use the context menu (right-click) to both copy the picture and paste it into a document.

Search for an Online Picture

Word provides a variety of clip art and picture choices in its royalty-free media library on Office.com. You can also search for images using *Bing Image Search*. When using an image from *Bing Image Search*, make sure you have the permission of the image owner to avoid copyright infringement.

HOW TO: Search for and Insert Online Pictures

1. Place the insertion point in the document where you want the picture inserted.
2. Click the **Insert** tab.
3. Click the **Online Pictures** button [*Illustrations* group] to open the *Insert Pictures* dialog box.
4. Click in the *Office.com Clip Art* or *Bing Image Search* text box, type the keywords for the graphic you want to find, and press **Enter**. Thumbnails of the pictures appear in the list below (Figure 4-49).

4-49 Insert graphic from the *Insert Pictures* dialog box

5. Select the picture to insert into your document.
   - Click the **View Larger** button in the bottom right corner of a graphic to view a larger picture.
   - Click the **X** in the upper right corner to close the larger image.
6. Click the **Insert** button to insert the picture into your document.

In the *Insert Pictures* dialog box, you are not limited to inserting clip art only. When you search for a picture, Word provides you with a list of pictures and clip art that match the keywords in your search.

Arrange Graphics within a Document

Once you have inserted an image into a document, you can adjust its size and arrange it in the document. Word provides you with a number of options to resize, align, and wrap text around graphics in your document.

Resize a Graphic

In most cases you will need to resize your graphic to fit properly in your document. You can do this a couple of different ways. You can drag the top, bottom, side, or corner handles to resize the graphic manually, or you can set a specific size for the graphic.

When you select (click) a graphic, *sizing handles* appear on each side and in each corner (Figure 4-50). To resize the graphic, click and hold one of the handles and drag in or out to decrease or increase the size of the graphic. Use the corner handles to keep the resized image proportional. If you use the side, top, or bottom handles to resize, the proportions of the image may become distorted. You can also resize the image to a specific size or to a percentage of its original size.

4-50 Resize graphic using the sizing handles

HOW TO: Resize an Image

1. Click the image to select it. The *Picture Tools Format* tab opens.

2. Click the **up** or **down** arrows in the *Height* or *Width* area [*Size* group] to increase or decrease the size (Figure 4-51). Resizing in this manner keeps the graphic proportional.

3. You can also resize the graphic in the *Layout* dialog box.

4. Click the **Size** launcher. The *Layout* dialog box opens with the *Size* tab displayed (Figure 4-52).

5. You can change the size of the graphic to a specific size in the *Height* and *Width* area. You can also scale the graphic to make it a percentage of its original size in the *Scale* area.

   - Keep the *Lock aspect ratio* box selected to prevent the graphic from becoming distorted in size.
   - In the *Original size* area, the original size of the graphic is displayed. You can reset the graphic to its original size by clicking the **Reset** button.

6. Click **OK** to resize the graphic and close the dialog box.

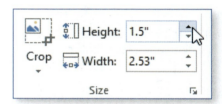

4-51 *Size* group on the *Picture Tools Format* tab

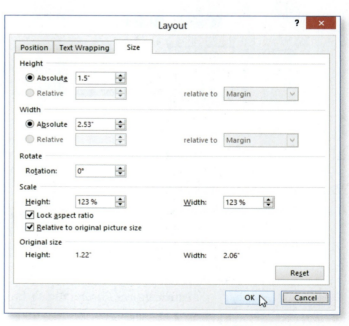

4-52 *Layout* dialog box

> **ANOTHER WAY**
>
> Open the *Layout* dialog box by right-clicking the graphic and selecting **Size and Position**.

Wrap Text around a Graphic

You can select how the text aligns or wraps around your graphic with a variety of ***text wrapping*** options. You can control how the text wraps around the graphic and choose to position the graphic in front of or behind the text.

HOW TO: Wrap Text

1. Click the graphic to select it.
2. Click the **Wrap Text** button [*Picture Tools Format* tab, *Arrange* group] (Figure 4-53).
3. Select a text wrapping option.
   - Select **More Layout Options** to open the *Layout* dialog box with the *Text Wrapping* tab displayed. Options in this dialog box allows you to customize text wrapping.
   - You can also click the **Layout Options** button to the right of a selected graphic and select a text wrapping option.

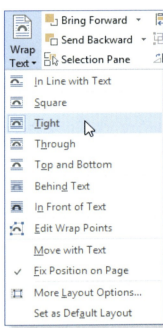

4-53 *Wrap Text* options

In the *Layout* dialog box on the *Text Wrapping* tab, there are additional options to control how text wraps around a graphic (Figure 4-54). In the ***Wrap text*** area, you can choose *Both sides, Left only, Right only,* or *Largest only.* In the ***Distance from text*** area, you can set a specific distance from the graphic to wrap text.

> **MORE INFO**
>
> *In Line with Text* is the default option when a graphic is inserted into a document.

Position a Graphic

In addition to adjusting the size of a graphic and specifying how text wraps around a graphic, you can also determine the position of the graphic in your document. You can align a graphic left, right, or center by selecting the graphic and clicking the **Align** button in the *Arrange* group on the *Picture Tools Format* tab (Figure 4-55).

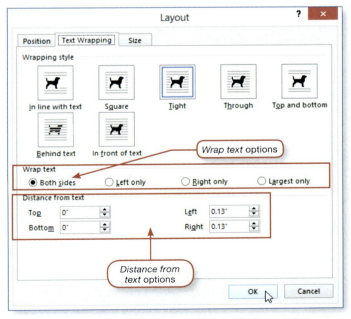

4-54 *Text Wrapping* tab in the *Layout* dialog box

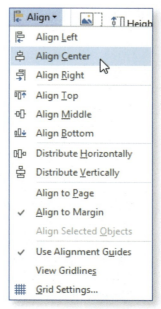

4-55 *Align* options

You can position a graphic in a document in a specific location by dragging the graphic to the desired location. You can also specify the location relative to the margins, page, or column. For example, you can position a graphic 5" from the left margin and 6" from the top margin of the document. The *Position* tab in the *Layout* dialog box offers customization options (see Figure 4-56).

HOW TO: Position a Graphic

1. Select the graphic to be positioned.
2. Click the **Picture Tools Format** tab.
3. Click the **Position** button [*Arrange* group] and select **More Layout Options**. The *Layout* dialog box opens with the *Position* tab selected (Figure 4-56).
4. In this dialog box, you can set both the horizontal and vertical alignment of the graphic.
   - In the *Horizontal* area, you have the following positioning options: *Alignment, Book layout, Absolute position,* and *Relative position.*
   - In the *Vertical* area, you have the following positioning options: *Alignment, Absolute position,* and *Relative position.*
5. Use the radio buttons in these areas to select how the graphic is aligned.
6. Click **OK** to close the dialog box.

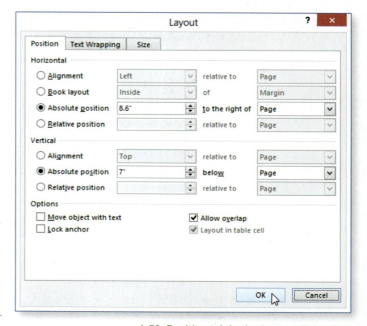

4-56 *Position* tab in the *Layout* dialog box

Insert a Caption

You might want to add a caption to a picture or chart that you insert into a document. The *Insert Caption* option creates a text box below the graphic where you can enter a caption (Figure 4-57).

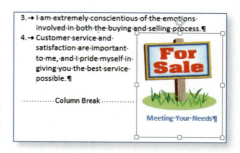

4-57 Graphic with caption below

HOW TO: Insert a Caption

1. Select the graphic that needs a caption.

2. Right-click the graphic and select **Insert Caption** from the context menu. The *Caption* dialog box opens (Figure 4-58).

   - Word automatically creates a caption for the object you have selected.
   - In the *Caption* area, you can add a description after the label, but you cannot delete the label.
   - After a caption is added to a graphic, you can delete the label and number and customize the caption text.

3. In the *Label* area, choose *Equation, Figure,* or *Table.*

   - You can add a custom label by clicking the *New Label* button and typing a custom label.
   - You can remove the label (but not the number) by checking the *Exclude label from caption* option.

4. In the *Position* area, you can choose to place the caption below or above the selected item.

5. Click **OK** to insert the caption.

6. You can edit the caption in the text box after it is added to the graphic (Figure 4-59). You can also customize the size and color of the caption text and adjust the size and positioning of the text box.

4-58 *Caption* dialog box

4-59 **Caption added to graphic**

ANOTHER WAY

Insert a caption by clicking the **Insert Caption** button [*References* tab, *Captions* group].

Group Graphics Objects

When you work with graphics, you may want to ***group*** together related graphics and objects. For example, you might want to group a picture and caption. The advantage of doing this is that the grouped graphics become one object that can be resized and positioned together.

HOW TO: Group and Ungroup Graphics

1. Hold down the **Ctrl** key and click the graphics to be grouped (Figure 4-60).

2. Click the **Group** button [*Picture Tools Format* tab, *Arrange* group].

3. Select **Group**. The selected objects become one grouped object (Figure 4-61).

4. To ungroup grouped items, click the **Group** button in the *Arrange* group on the *Picture Tools Format* tab and select **Ungroup**.

4-60 **Multiple objects selected**   4-61 **Grouped objects**

ANOTHER WAY

Group and *Ungroup* options are available in the context menu by right-clicking a graphic.

Shapes, SmartArt, and WordArt

In addition to pictures and clip art, you can insert other types of graphic items into your Word documents. For example, Word provides a variety of **shapes** that you can insert into your document. **SmartArt** and **WordArt** can also be added to enhance documents.

Insert Shapes

Word's *Shapes* gallery groups shapes into categories (Figure 4-62). When you insert a shape or line into your document, you are actually drawing the object in your document. Once the object is drawn in your document, you can edit the size, position, alignment, and text wrapping of the object.

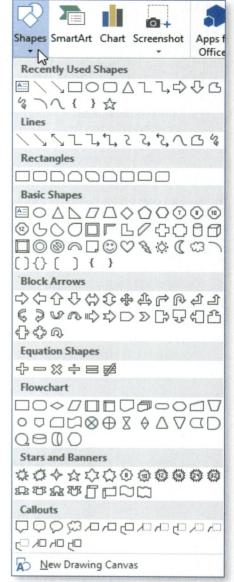

4-62 *Shapes* drop-down list

HOW TO: Insert a Shape

1. Click the **Insert** tab.
2. Click the **Shapes** button [*Illustrations* group] to display the gallery of shape options.
3. Select the shape you want to use. Your pointer becomes a drawing crosshair (large dark plus sign).
4. Click and drag to create the shape (Figure 4-63). When you release the pointer, the shape is inserted into the document.

4-63 Draw a shape

- You don't have to be perfectly accurate when you create the shape because you can easily resize the shape after it is inserted.
- You can change the text wrapping on a shape so the shape appears on top of or behind the text, or you can have text wrap around a shape.

> ### MORE INFO
>
> If you want to create a perfect square or circle or to draw a straight line, hold down the **Shift** key while drawing.

Customize Shapes

Once a shape has been inserted into a document, you can move or resize it. Also, you can change the line size, color, and fill of the shapes. See Figure 4-64 and its callouts for examples of the available selection and sizing handles. The following is a list of those options:

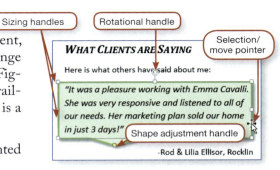

4-64 Shape selected with handles displayed

- *Selection/move pointer:* This pointer (four-pointed arrow) allows you to select and move objects. Select multiple objects by holding down the *Ctrl* key.
- *Sizing handles:* There are sizing handles in each corner and on each side of the shape. When you select one of these, the pointer becomes a sizing pointer (two-pointed arrow).
- *Rotation handle:* The rotation handle is the circle at the top of the selected shape. Rotate a shape by clicking and dragging this handle to the left or right.
- *Shape Adjustment handle:* This handle is the yellow diamond. You can use this handle to change the shape of an object (not all shapes have this handle available). You can also use this handle to change the size or location of a callout, corner roundness, and other shape elements.

You can change the **Shape Fill**, **Shape Outline**, and **Shape Effects** of a shape. Each of these areas includes many customization options to enhance shapes. When the shape is selected, the *Drawing Tools Format* tab is displayed (Figure 4-65).

4-65 *Drawing Tools Format* tab

Insert SmartArt

SmartArt allows you to graphically present information in your document in a visually attractive way. There are a variety of categories of *SmartArt* and within each category there are numerous options available (Figure 4-66).

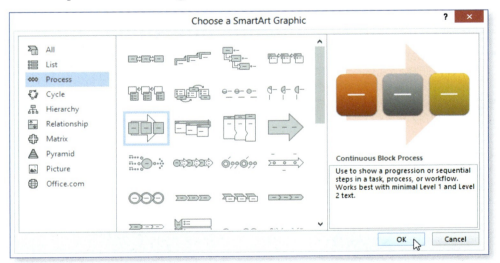

4-66 *Choose a SmartArt Graphic* dialog box

Customize SmartArt

SmartArt graphics are a combination of shapes and text boxes. Once you insert a *SmartArt* graphic into a document, you can use *SmartArt Tools Design* and *Format* tabs to customize the text content and the graphic's structure.

HOW TO: Insert and Customize SmartArt

1. Position your insertion point in your document where you want to insert the *SmartArt.*
2. Click the **Insert** tab.
3. Click the **SmartArt** button [*Illustrations* group]. The *Choose a SmartArt Graphic* dialog box opens (see Figure 4-66).
4. Select a *SmartArt* graphic. A preview and description of the *SmartArt* are displayed on the right of the dialog box.
5. Click **OK** to insert the *SmartArt* into the document.
6. Customize the graphic using the *SmartArt Tools Design* and *Format* tabs.
   - The *SmartArt Tools Design* tab controls the overall design and colors of the *SmartArt* objects.
   - The *SmartArt Tools Format* tab allows you to customize the shape of objects, colors, borders, fill, and effects.

Insert WordArt

WordArt can visually enhance a title of a document or add emphasis to certain text within a document. When you insert *WordArt,* you are actually inserting a text box in the document which can then be manipulated as a graphic. Once you insert *WordArt* in a document, you can resize and move it, and you can change the color, fill, and effects of this object.

HOW TO: Insert WordArt

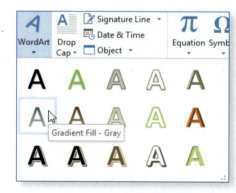

4-67 *WordArt* gallery

1. Position your insertion point in your document where you want to insert the *WordArt.*
2. Click the **Insert** tab.
3. Click the **WordArt** button [*Text* group] and select a *WordArt* style from the gallery of options (Figure 4-67). The *WordArt* text box is inserted into your document.
4. Type the text you want to format as *WordArt.*
   - The placeholder text (*Your text here*) is selected when you insert the *WordArt* (Figure 4-68). Type to replace the placeholder text. If the placeholder text is deselected, select it before typing in your text.
5. Click your document away from the text box to deselect the *WordArt* graphic.

4-68 WordArt inserted into a document

> **ANOTHER WAY**
>
> To select text in your document to be converted to *WordArt,* first select the text and then select the *WordArt* format. The selected text is converted to *WordArt* and placed in a text box.

Customize WordArt

Customizing *WordArt* is similar to customizing other graphic objects in Word. When the *WordArt* text box is selected, the *Design Tools Format* tab is displayed (Figure 4-69). From this tab, you can change the style of the *WordArt*, add a border to the text box, and change the fill, outline, and effects of the *WordArt* text.

4-69 *Drawing Tools Format* tab

Resize *WordArt* by using the sizing handles on the corners and sides. Rotate the *WordArt* text box with the rotation handle. You can change the position and text wrapping of the *WordArt* in the same way you manipulate other graphics.

Enhance Graphics with Styles

Each of the different types of graphics has a variety of styles, fills, outlines, and effects that you can apply. Context-sensitive tabs appear when you select a graphic object. On each of these context-sensitive tabs, there are a variety of ***styles galleries*** (Figure 4-70).

When applying styles to graphics, Word provides you with a ***live preview***. When you place your pointer on a style from one of the style galleries, Word temporarily applies the style to the selected graphic to preview how it will appear in the document.

4-70 *Picture Styles* gallery

Insert Symbols and Special Characters

In addition to pictures, Clip Art, *WordArt*, shapes, *SmartArt*, and other types of graphic objects, Word has a variety of symbols and other special characters that you can insert into a document (Figure 4-71). The *Symbols, Wingdings,* and *Webdings* font sets have an assortment of characters and symbols that can be inserted into a document. There are also additional special characters available, such as the em dash, en dash, and copyright and trademark symbols.

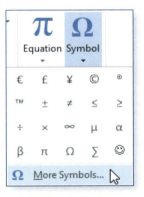

4-71 *Symbol* button on the *Insert* tab

HOW TO: Insert a Symbol

1. Click the **Insert** tab.
2. Click the **Symbol** button [*Symbols* group]. A drop-down list of recently used symbols is displayed.
3. Select **More Symbols** (see Figure 4-71). The *Symbol* dialog box opens (Figure 4-72).
4. Click the **Font** drop-down list on the *Symbols* tab to select the font set.
   - Or click the **Special Character** tab to display the list of available special characters.
5. Click a symbol or special character to insert.
6. Click **Insert** to insert the symbol in the document.
7. Click **Close** to close the dialog box.

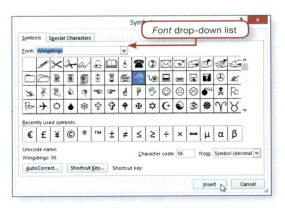

4-72 *Symbol* dialog box

For this Pause & Practice project, you finalize Emma's brochure by inserting a picture, clip art, shapes, and *WordArt.* You format and arrange these graphic objects attractively in the document.

Files Needed: ***[your initials] PP W4-3.docx*** and ***PHRElogo-04.png***
Completed Project File Name: ***[your initials] PP W4-4.docx***

1. Open the ***[your initials] PP W4-3*** file you saved in *Pause & Practice 4-3.*

2. Save this document as ***[your initials] PP W4-4.***

3. Insert the Placer Hills Real Estate logo at the bottom right corner of the document.
   a. Position the insertion point below the table in the third column.
   b. Click the **Pictures** button [*Insert* tab, *Illustrations* group]. The *Insert Picture* dialog box opens.
   c. Select the ***PHRElogo-04*** file from the student data files and click **Insert.**

4-73 Adjust the size of a graphic

4. Arrange and format the logo.
   a. With the logo selected, click the **Wrap Text** button [*Picture Tools Format* tab, *Arrange* group] and choose **In Front of Text**.
   b. In the *Height* box [*Size* group] type 1.2 and press **Enter** (Figure 4-73). The width automatically adjusts to keep the graphic proportional.
   c. Click in the middle of the graphic and drag the graphic near the bottom right corner of the document.
   d. Click the **Picture Border** button [*Picture Styles* group] and select **Olive Green**, **Accent 3** (Figure 4-74).
   e. Click the **Picture Border** again, click **Weight**, and select **1½ pt**.
   f. Click the **Position** button [*Arrange* group] and select **More Layout Options.** The *Layout* dialog box opens with the *Position* tab displayed (Figure 4-75).
   g. In the *Horizontal* area, select the **Absolute position** radio button, type 8.6, click the ***to the right of*** drop-down list, and select **Page**.
   h. In the *Vertical* area, select the **Absolute position** radio button, type 7, click the ***below*** drop-down list, and select **Page**.
   i. Click **OK** to close the dialog box.

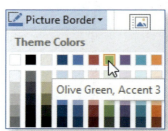

4-74 Select *Picture Border* color

4-75 *Layout* dialog box

5. Add clip art near the bottom of the first column.
   a. Click at the end of the fourth numbered item in the first column.
   b. Click the **Online Pictures** button [*Insert* tab, *Illustrations* group]. The *Insert Pictures* dialog box opens.
   c. Type for sale in the *Office.com Clip Art* text box and press **Enter**. A list of clip art options appears in the dialog box.

d. Select the clip art shown in Figure 4-76 and click **Insert.** The clip art is inserted into the document. Don't be concerned about the clip art at this point. If this clip art is not available, you can insert the **ForSale-04** picture from your student data files.

e. With the clip art selected, change the *Height* [*Picture Tools Format* tab, *Size* group] to **1.2"** and press **Enter.**

f. Right-click the clip art, choose **Wrap Text**, and select **Square**.

g. Select the graphic and position it so it is to the right of the fourth numbered item in the first column.

6. Insert a caption for the clip art.
   a. Right-click the clip art and choose **Insert Caption.** The *Caption* dialog box opens.
   b. Click **OK** to close the *Caption* dialog box and insert the caption.
   c. In the caption text box, delete the placeholder text and type Meeting Your Needs.
   d. Press **Ctrl+E** or click the **Center** button [*Home* tab, *Paragraph* group] to center the text in the caption.
   e. With the caption still selected, hold down the **Ctrl** key and click the clip art to select it also. Both the clip art and the caption should be selected.
   f. Click the **Group** button [*Picture Format Tools* tab, *Arrange* group] and choose **Group**. The two objects are grouped into one object (Figure 4-77).

7. Change the paragraph spacing on the two quotes in the second column.
   a. Click in the first quoted paragraph in the second column (beginning with "It was a pleasure . . .").
   b. Change the *After* paragraph spacing to **12 pt**.
   c. Click in the second quoted paragraph in the second column (beginning with "Emma is conscientious . . .").
   d. Change the *After* paragraph spacing to **12 pt**.

8. Add and format a shape to the quoted text.
   a. Click the **Shapes** button [*Insert* tab, *Illustration* group] and select **Rectangular Callout** (Figure 4-78). Your pointer changes to a crosshair (dark plus sign).
   b. On the first quote in the second column, drag from the upper left to the lower right to draw the shape over the quoted text (Figure 4-79).
   c. With the shape still selected, click the **Send Backward** drop-down arrow [*Drawing Tools Format* tab, *Arrange* group] and select **Send Behind Text** (Figure 4-80). The text is displayed over the shape.
   d. Click the **More** button [*Drawing Tools Format* tab, *Shape Styles* group] to display the gallery of shape styles.
   e. Select **Colored Outline – Olive Green**, **Accent 3** (Figure 4-81).
   f. Click the **Shape Fill** button [*Drawing Tools Format* tab, *Shape Styles* group] and select **Olive Green**, **Accent 3**, **Lighter 80%**.

4-76 Insert clip art

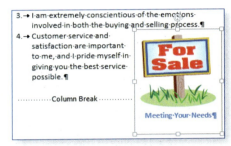

4-77 Clip art and captions grouped

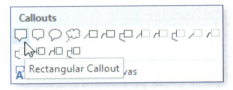

4-78 Select shape

4-79 Draw rectangular shape

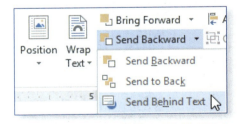

4-80 *Send Behind Text*

4-81 Apply shape style

g. Click the **Shape Effects** button [*Drawing Tools Format* tab, *Shape Styles* group], select **Shadow**, and choose **Offset Diagonal Bottom Right** (Figure 4-82).

h. With the shape still selected, change the *Shape Height* to **0.9"** and the *Shape Width* to **3"** [*Drawing Tools Format* tab, *Size* group].

i. Drag the shape so it is evenly positioned behind the text. You can also use the keyboard arrow keys to position a selected shape.

9. Replicate and align the callout shape.
   a. With the shape still selected, press **Ctrl+C** to copy it and **Ctrl+V** to paste the copy of the shape into the document.
   b. Drag the new shape over the second quote.
   c. With the second shape still selected, change the *Shape Height* to **1.4"** [*Drawing Tools Format* tab, *Size* group].
   d. Drag the shape so it is evenly positioned behind the text (Figure 4-83).
   e. With the second shape selected, hold down the **Shift** key and click the right edge of the first shape to select both shapes.
   f. Click the **Align** button [*Drawing Tools Format* tab, *Arrange* group] and select **Align Center**.
   g. Make any necessary minor vertical position adjustments by selecting the shape and using the up or down arrow keys.

10. Add *WordArt* to the brochure and customize it.
   a. At the top of the first column, select the text **"Emma Cavalli"** (including the paragraph mark).
   b. Click the **WordArt** button [*Insert* tab, *Text* group].
   c. In the *WordArt* gallery, select **Gradient Fill – Gray** (Figure 4-84). The selected text is converted to *WordArt*.
   d. With the *WordArt* selected, change the *Shape Height* to **0.8"** and the *Shape Width* to **3.6"** [*Drawing Tools Format* tab, *Size* group].
   e. Click the **Text Effects** button [*Drawing Tools Format* tab, *WordArt Styles* group], click **Reflection**, and select **Tight Reflection, touching** (Figure 4-85).

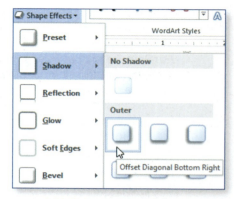

4-82 Select a shape *Shadow* option

4-83 Shapes positioned behind text

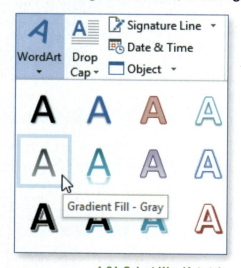

4-84 Select *WordArt* style

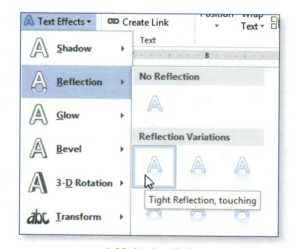

4-85 Apply a *Reflection* text effect

f. Click the **Position** button [*Drawing Tools Format* tab, *Arrange* group] and select **More Layout Options.** The *Layout* dialog box opens.

g. In the *Horizontal* area, change the *Absolute position* to **0.2"** *to the right of* **Page**.

h. In the *Vertical* area, change the *Absolute position* to **0.2"** *below* **Page**.

i. Click **OK** to close the *Layout* dialog box.

11. Save and close the document (Figure 4-86).

Emma Cavalli

REALTOR CONSULTANT

Phone	916.450.3334
Email	ecavalli@phre.com
Web	www.phre.com/ecavalli

MISSION STATEMENT

I am dedicated to listening to your needs as a buyer or seller and providing you with prompt and excellent service to exceed your expectations.

BUSINESS EXPERIENCE

I have had the pleasure of working with buyers, sellers, and investors for over 15 years. Each transaction is new and exciting.

WHY I AM A REAL ESTATE AGENT

1. I enjoy working with people and negotiating on their behalf.
2. Communication, organization, and availability are skills I possess that make me a client-focused real estate agent.
3. I am extremely conscientious of the emotions involved in both the buying and selling process.
4. Customer service and satisfaction are important to me, and I pride myself in giving you the best service possible.

Meeting Your Needs

WHAT CLIENTS ARE SAYING

Here is what others have said about me:

"It was a pleasure working with Emma Cavalli. She was very responsive and listened to all of our needs. Her marketing plan sold our home in just 3 days!"

-Rod & Lilia Ellisor, Rocklin

"Emma is conscientious, personable, and professional. Her dedication and commitment to meeting our needs has been apparent from the beginning. Emma can be counted on to do what she says. We would not hesitate to refer Emma to our friends and family."

-Elia & Jazmin Solares, Roseville

PROFESSIONAL CREDENTIALS

- Licensed California Real Estate Salesperson
- Member of National Association of Realtors
- Member California Association of Realtors
- Member of Realtor.com
- Distinguished Realtor Award from peers
- Community Service Board position for the Roseville Unified School District
- Elected Parent/Teacher Club President for Winchester Elementary School 2004-2006

EDUCATION & TRAINING

University of Nevada, Reno—Business Administration B.A.

Real Estate Code of Ethics

Certified Contract Consultant

Certified Maximum Productivity Consultant

FAMILY & HOBBIES

I have been a Roseville community member since 1995. I have been married since 1989 and have three children. I love to read, do crafts, travel, and watch my children play sports. I am also very involved in my church and charity work.

THE PLACER HILLS BELIEF SYSTEM	
COMMITMENT	To the needs of the client
COMMUNICATION	Seek first to listen
CREATIVITY	Ideas before results
CUSTOMERS	Always come first
INTEGRITY	Doing the right thing
SUCCESS	Results with integrity
TEAMWORK	Work together for success
TRUST	Begins with communication
WIN-WIN	Is always the goal

PHRE
Placer Hills
Real Estate
7100 Madrone Road | Roseville, CA 95722
www.phre.com | 916.450.3300

4-86 PP W4-4 completed

Chapter Summary

4.1 Improve the design and readability of a document by using tables to present and arrange information (p. W4-197).

- **Tables** organize information in column and row format. A **column** is a vertical grouping of cells, and a **row** is a horizontal grouping of cells.
- A **cell** is where a column and row intersect.
- Use **Tab** to move forward to the next cell and **Shift+Tab** to move to the previous cell.
- **Table Tools Layout** and **Table Tools Design** tabs provide you with many table formatting features.
- You can copy or move columns or rows in a table.
- You can add or delete columns and rows from existing tables.
- When working with tables, you can select individual cells, a range of cells, rows, columns, or an entire table.
- A group of cells can be **merged** to create one cell. Cells can also be **split** into multiple cells.

4.2 Modify a table by changing the column and row size, aligning text, using the *Table Properties* dialog box, sorting data in tables, and using *AutoFit* (p. W4-201).

- You can resize columns and rows in a table.
- The **AutoFit** feature allows you to automatically resize the table to fit the contents or window or change to a fixed width.
- Text in a cell can be **aligned** both horizontally and vertically.
- **Cell margins** control the amount of spacing around the text within a cell.
- The **Table Properties** dialog box provides size and alignment options for cells, rows, columns, or an entire table.
- You can sort table information in ascending or descending order.

4.3 Enhance the appearance and function of a table by using the *Table Tools* tabs, applying borders and shading, using table styles, inserting formulas, and converting text into a table (p. W4-207).

- You can apply **borders** and **shading** to parts of a table or to the entire table.
- **Table Styles** are collections of borders, shading, and formatting that you can apply to a table. Word provides a gallery of table styles.
- You can apply **Table Style Options** to a header row, total row, banded rows, first column, or last column.
- **Formulas** in a table perform mathematical calculations.
- You can convert existing text into a table in Word.

4.4 Modify the layout and design of a document by using columns to present information (p. W4-214).

- You can arrange text in a document in **columns**.
- You can choose from preset column settings or you can customize column settings and space between columns using the **Columns dialog box.**
- **Column breaks** control column endings.
- Balance columns with column breaks or a **continuous section break**.

4.5 Enrich a document by adding and modifying visual elements such as pictures, shapes, *SmartArt,* and *WordArt* (p. W4-218).

- **Pictures** and **clip art** add visual appeal to a document. Word can insert a variety of graphic file types.
- You can **resize** and **position** graphics at specific locations in a document.
- **Text wrapping** controls how text wraps around graphics.
- The **Layout dialog box** has options to change the position, text wrapping, and size of graphic objects.
- You can insert customized **captions** for graphics.
- Graphic objects can be **grouped** together to create one graphic object, which makes resizing and positioning easier.
- **Shapes** can be inserted into a document and resized and customized. You can change fill color, outline color and width, and shape effects.
- **SmartArt** graphically presents information in a document.
- **WordArt** is special text formatting that you can insert into a document.
- Word provides a variety of formatting options and styles for *SmartArt, WordArt,* and other graphic objects.
- You can insert a variety of **symbols** and **special characters** into documents. Use the **Symbols dialog box** to select different symbols and characters.

Check for Understanding

In the **Online Learning Center** for this text (www.mhhe.com/office2013inpractice), there are a variety of resources that can be used to review the concepts covered in this chapter.

The following Online Learning Resources are available in the Online Learning Center:

- Multiple choice questions
- Short answer questions
- Matching exercises

Guided Project 4-1

For this project, you modify the values statement document for Sierra Pacific Community College District to arrange text in columns, insert the company logo, and use shapes.
[Student Learning Outcomes 4.4, 4.5]

Files Needed: *ValuesStatement-04.docx* and *SPCCDlogo-04.png*
Completed Project File Name: *[your initials] Word 4-1.docx*

Skills Covered in This Project

- Modify an existing document.
- Change page orientation.
- Change margins.
- Apply columns to text.
- Modify column settings.
- Insert a column break.

- Insert a picture.
- Change picture color.
- Modify picture size and position.
- Insert a shape.
- Modify shape size and position.
- Modify shape fill and outline.

1. Open the **ValuesStatement-04** document from your student data files.

2. Save this document as **[your initials] Word 4-1.**

3. Change the orientation and change the margins of the document.
   a. Change the orientation of the document to **Landscape**.
   b. Change the top and bottom margins to **0.5"**.
   c. Change the left and right margins to **0.75"**.

4. Apply column formatting to the text in the body of the document.
   a. Place the insertion point in front of the first paragraph heading ("Access").
   b. Click the **Columns** button [*Page Layout* tab, *Page Setup* group] and select **More Columns**. The *Columns* dialog box opens (Figure 4-87).
   c. Select **Three** in the *Presets* area.
   d. In the *Width and spacing* area, change the *Spacing* to **0.4"**.
   e. In the *Apply to* area, select **This point forward** from the drop-down list.
   f. Click **OK** to close the *Columns* dialog box.

5. Insert a column break to balance the columns on the page.
   a. Place the insertion point in front of the "Student Learning Outcomes" paragraph heading.
   b. Click the **Breaks** button [*Page Layout* tab, *Page Setup* group] and select **Column**.

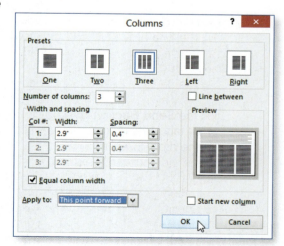

4-87 *Columns* dialog box

6. Insert the company logo on the bottom left of the document and resize and position it.
   a. Click at the end of the first column.
   b. Click the **Pictures** button [*Insert* tab, *Illustrations* group].
   c. Select the ***SPCCDlogo-04*** file from the student data files and click **Insert**.
   d. Click the **Wrap Text** button [*Picture Tools Format* tab, *Arrange* group] and select **Behind Text**.
   e. Right-click the logo and choose **Size and Position**. The *Layout* dialog box opens (Figure 4-88).
   f. In the *Scale* area, change the *Height* to **120%** and press **Tab**. The width automatically adjusts to keep the logo proportional.
   g. Click the **Position** tab.
   h. In the *Horizontal* area, change the *Absolute position* to **0.3"** *to the right of* **Page**.
   i. In the *Vertical* area, change the *Absolute position* to **7.2"** *below* **Page**.
   j. Click **OK** to close the *Layout* dialog box.

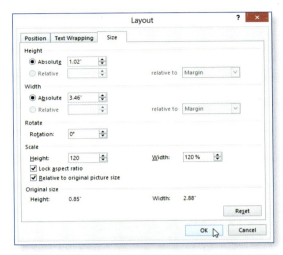

4-88 Resize logo as a percentage of its original size

7. Change the color of the logo.
   a. With the logo selected, click the **Color** button [*Picture Tools Format* tab, *Adjust* group].
   b. Select **Saturation: 0%** in the *Color Saturation* area (Figure 4-89).

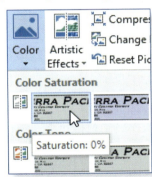

4-89 Change *Color Saturation*

8. Add a shape around the title, and then resize the shape and modify the outline and fill.
   a. Click the **Shapes** button [*Insert* tab, *Illustrations* group].
   b. Select **Snip Single Corner Rectangle** from the *Shapes* gallery. Your pointer becomes a crosshair (dark plus sign) (Figure 4-90).
   c. Click and drag the crosshair over the title and then release the pointer (Figure 4-91).
   d. Click the **Shape Fill** button [*Drawing Tools Format* tab, *Shape Styles* group] and select **White, Background 1, Darker 15%**.
   e. Click the **Shape Outline** button [*Drawing Tools Format* tab, *Shape Styles* group] and select **White, Background 1, Darker 50%**.
   f. Click the **Shape Outline** button again, select **Weight**, and select **1½ pt**.
   g. Click the **Send Backward** drop-down arrow [*Drawing Tools Format* tab, *Arrange* group] and select **Send Behind Text** from the drop-down list.
   h. Change the *Shape Height* [*Drawing Tools Format* tab, *Size* group] to **0.4"** and the *Shape Width* to **6.3"**.
   i. Click the **Align** button [*Drawing Tools Format* tab, *Arrange* group] and select **Align Center**.
   j. Use the up and down arrow keys on the keyboard to vertically center the shape behind the title.

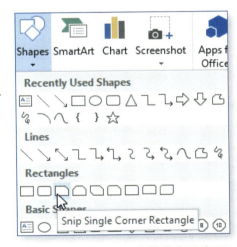

4-90 Select shape

SIERRA·PACIFIC·COMMUNITY·COLLEGE·DISTRICT·VALUES¶

4-91 Draw shape around the title

9. Save and close the document (Figure 4-92).

SIERRA·PACIFIC·COMMUNITY·COLLEGE·DISTRICT·VALUES¶

ACCESS¶

Students·are·the·reason·we·exist·and·their·education·is·our·primary·purpose.·We·recognize·that·residents·of·the·region·are·entitled·to·an·opportunity·to·attend·and·to·be·successful·in·college.¶

BENEFITS·OF·EDUCATION¶

Individuals·and·society·benefit·from·citizens·who·achieve·the·full·extent·of·their·personal,·intellectual,·and·physical·ability;·engage·in·critical·and·creative·thinking;·exhibit·responsible·citizenship;·succeed·in·a·competitive·global·work·environment;·and·participate·in·lifelong·learning.¶

EXCELLENCE¶

Excellence·in·instruction·and·student·services·is·essential·to·develop·the·full·potential·of·each·student.¶

LEADERSHIP¶

Responsible·leadership·and·service·among·all·Sierra·Pacific·Community·College·District·faculty,·staff,·and·students·are·nurtured·and·encouraged·so·the·college·will·be·a·leader·for·positive·change,·growth,·and·transformation·in·student-oriented·educational·practices.¶

·················· Column Break ··················

SIERRA PACIFIC
COMMUNITY COLLEGE DISTRICT
7300 COLLEGE AVE
SACRAMENTO, CA 92387
209.658.4466
WWW.SPCCD.EDU

STUDENT·LEARNING·OUTCOMES¶

Identification·and·assessment·of·student·learning·outcomes·promotes·and·improves·student·success·and·the·effective·use·of·SPCCD·resources·to·create·innovative·and·flexible·learning·opportunities.¶

DIVERSITY¶

We·are·a·community·enriched·by·the·experience·of·students,·faculty,·staff,·and·administrators·from·a·variety·of·cultures,·ethnic·and·economic·backgrounds,·age·is·and·abilities.·We·are·committed·to·providing·and·nurturing·a·safe·environment·for·the·free·exchanges·of·ideas.¶

COMMUNITY·DEVELOPMENT¶

The·curricular·and·co-curricular·programs·and·services·of·the·college·benefit·the·region·served·through·enhanced·intellectual·and·physical·growth,·economic·development,·and·exposure·to·the·arts,·sciences,·and·humanities.¶

HUMAN·RESOURCES¶

Faculty·and·staff·members·are·our·most·important·resources·and·are·entitled·to·a·supportive,·collegial·work·environment·that·recognizes·excellence,·provides·opportunities·for·professional·development,·service·and·leadership,·and·encourages·meaningful·involvement·in·an·interest-based·decision-making·process.¶

COMMUNICATION¶

Achievement·of·the·Sierra·Pacific·Community·College·District·mission·and·vision·requires·an·effective·system·of·communication·with·internal·and·external·constituencies·that·is·based·on·honesty,·trust,·civility,·and·mutual·respect.¶

INNOVATION·AND·RISK·TAKING¶

Addressing·challenges·and·change·requires·creativity,·assessment,·flexibility,·and·responsible·risk-taking·to·achieve·our·vision,·mission·and·goals.¶

FISCAL·RESPONSIBILITY¶

It·is·necessary·to·maintain·a·fiscally-sound,·efficient,·and·effective·operation·that·achieves·our·mission·within·the·resources·available.¶

EVALUATION¶

Efficient·and·effective·accomplishment·of·the·ARC·mission,·vision,·and·student·learning·outcomes·requires·regular·and·ongoing·data-based·evaluation.¶

4-92 Word 4-1 completed

Guided Project 4-2

For this project, you modify a document about maximum and target heart rate for the American River Cycling Club. You arrange text in a table and insert and modify *SmartArt* and clip art.
[Student Learning Outcomes 4.1, 4.2, 4.3, 4.5]

File Needed: ***MaximumHeartRate-04.docx***
Completed Project File Name: ***[your initials] Word 4-2.docx***

Skills Covered in This Project

- Modify an existing document.
- Insert and resize *WordArt*.
- Position and modify *WordArt*.
- Convert text to a table.
- Apply a table style.
- Modify table and text alignment.

- Change cell margins in a table.
- Insert and add text to a *SmartArt* graphic.
- Resize, position, and format *SmartArt*.
- Insert, resize, and position a graphic.
- Insert a caption
- Align and group graphic objects.

---

1. Open the **MaximumHeartRate-04** document from your student data files.

2. Save this document as *[your initials] Word 4-2.*

3. Insert *WordArt* as the title of the document and modify the *WordArt*.

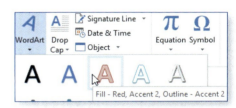

4-93 Insert WordArt

   a. Select the title of the document, **"American River Cycling Club."**
   b. Click the **WordArt** button [*Insert* tab, *Text* group].
   c. Select **Fill – Red**, **Accent 2**, **Outline – Accent 2** from the *WordArt* gallery (Figure 4-93).
   d. Change the *Shape Width* [*Drawing Tools Format* tab, *Size* group] to **6.5"**.
   e. Click the **Position** button [*Drawing Tools Format* tab, *Arrange* group] and select **More Layout Options**. The *Layout* dialog box opens (Figure 4-94).
   f. In the *Horizontal* area select **Alignment** and **Centered** *relative to* **Margin**.
   g. In the *Vertical* area select **Absolute position** and enter **0.2"** *below* **Page**.
   h. Click **OK** to close the *Layout* dialog box.
   i. Click the **Text Effects** button [*Drawing Tools Format* tab, *WordArt Styles* group] and select **Reflection**.
   j. Select **Tight Reflection, touching** (Figure 4-95).

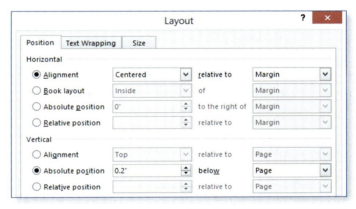

4-94 Adjust position of WordArt

4. Convert text into a table and format the table.
   a. Select all of the tabbed text at the bottom of the document.
   b. Click the **Table** button [*Insert* tab, *Tables* group] and select **Convert Text to Table**. The *Convert Text to Table* dialog box opens.
   c. In the *AutoFit behavior* area, click the **AutoFit to contents** radio button.
   d. Click **OK** to close the dialog box.
   e. Click the **Table Tools Design** tab.
   f. Select the **Header Row** and **Banded Rows** check boxes [*Table Style Options* group] and deselect the other check boxes.
   g. In the *Table Styles* group, click the **More** button to display the *Table Styles* gallery.

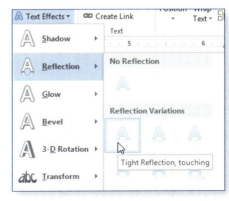

4-95 Reflection options

h. Select **Grid Table 4 – Accent 2** (Figure 4-96).

i. In the second column of the first row, place the insertion point before "Zone" and press **Enter**.

j. In the third column of the first row, place the insertion point before "Heart" and press **Enter**.

5. Adjust the size and alignment of the table.

a. Use the table selector handle to select the entire table.

b. Click the **Align Center** button [*Table Tool Layout* tab, *Alignment* group] (Figure 4-97).

c. With the table still selected, click the **Properties** button [*Table Tools Layout* tab, *Table* group].

d. Click the **Table** tab, select **Center** in the *Alignment* area, and click **OK** to close the dialog box.

e. Click the **Cell Margins** button [*Table Tools Layout* tab, *Alignment* group]. The *Table Options* dialog box opens.

f. Change the *Top* and *Bottom* cell margins to **0.03"** and the *Left* and *Right* cell margins to **0.1"**.

g. Click **OK** to close the *Table Options* dialog box.

4-96 *Table Styles* gallery

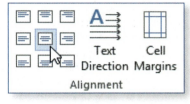

4-97 *Text alignment options*

6. Insert and modify a *SmartArt* graphic.

a. Place the insertion point at the end of the "(Example: . . ." line near the top of the document.

b. Click the **SmartArt** button [*Insert* tab, *Illustrations* group]. The *Choose a SmartArt Graphic* dialog box opens (Figure 4-98).

c. Click **Process** in the list of *SmartArt* types.

d. Select **Continuous Block Process** and press **OK** to insert the *SmartArt*.

e. Click the first placeholder text (*[Text]*) and type 220, **space** once, and type – (hyphen or minus).

f. Click the next placeholder text and type Your Age, **space** once, and type =.

g. Click the last placeholder text and type Predicted Maximum Heart Rate.

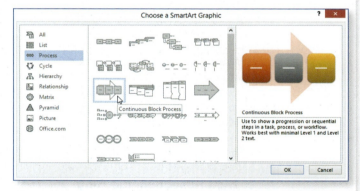

4-98 *Choose a SmartArt Graphic* dialog box

7. Format, resize, and position the *SmartArt*.

a. Click the outside frame of the *SmartArt* graphic. *Note: make sure the entire SmartArt is selected and not an object within the graphic.*

b. In the *Size* group [*SmartArt Tools Format* tab], change the *Shape Height* to **1.5"** and the *Shape Width* to **2.6"**.

c. Click the **Wrap Text** button [*SmartArt Tools Format* tab, *Arrange* group] and select **Square**.

d. Click the **Position** button [*SmartArt Tools Format* tab, *Arrange* group] and select **More Layout Options**. The *Layout* dialog box opens (Figure 4-99).

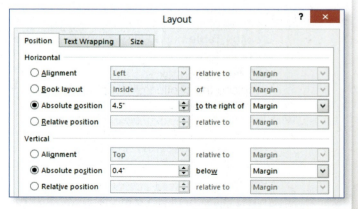

4-99 Adjust *SmartArt* position

e. In the *Horizontal* area select **Absolute position** and enter **4.5"** *to the right of* **Margin**.

f. In the *Vertical* area select **Absolute position** and enter **0.4"** *below* **Margin**.

g. Click **OK** to close the *Layout* dialog box.

h. With the *SmartArt* still selected, select **Intense Effect** as the *SmartArt* style [*SmartArt Tools Design* tab, *SmartArt Styles* group] (Figure 4-100).

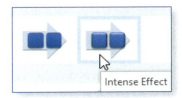

4-100 Apply *SmartArt* style

i. Click the edge of the first text box to select it, and press **Ctrl+B** to make the text bold. Repeat this on the other two text boxes.

j. Select the last text box and click the **SmartArt Tools Format** tab.

k. Click the **Shape Fill** button and select **Red**, **Accent 2** as the fill color (Figure 4-101).

8. Insert clip art and resize and position the graphic.

a. Place the insertion point at the end of the second paragraph heading ("Target Heart Rate").

b. Click the **Online Pictures** button [*Insert* tab, *Illustrations* group] to open the *Insert Pictures* dialog box.

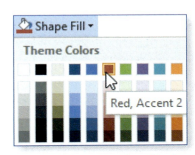

4-101 Change text box fill color

c. Type heart rate in the *Office.com Clip Art* text box and press **Enter**.

d. Select the **Heart cardiogram illustration** clip art and click **Insert** to insert it into the document (Figure 4-102). If this clip art is not available, insert the ***HeartRate-04*** picture from your student data files.

e. Change the *Height* [*Picture Tools Format* tab, *Size* group] to **1"** and press **Enter**. The width automatically adjusts.

f. Click the **Wrap Text** button [*Picture Tools Format* tab, *Arrange* group] and select **Tight**.

g. Drag the clip art to the right of the heading and first paragraph in the "Target Heart Rate" section and place it approximately 0.5" from the right edge of the document.

4-102 Insert clip art

9. Format the clip art and insert a caption.

a. With the clip art selected, click the **More** button in the *Pictures Styles* group [*Picture Tools Format* tab] to display the gallery of styles.

b. Select the **Bevel Rectangle** picture style (Figure 4-103).

c. Right-click the clip art and select **Insert Caption** from the context menu. The *Insert Caption* dialog box opens.

d. Press **Enter** to insert the caption.

e. Select the caption text, click the **Text Fill** button [*Drawing Tools Format* tab, *WordArt Styles* group], and select **Red**, **Accent 2** as the text color.

4-103 Apply *Picture Style* to clip art

f. With the caption text still selected, type Know your target heart rate to replace the caption placeholder text.

g. In the *Size* group [*Drawing Tools Format* tab], change the *Height* to **0.2"** and the *Width* to **1.5"**.

h. Press the **Ctrl** key and click the clip art. Both the caption and text box should be selected.

i. Click the **Align** button [*Drawing Tools Format* tab, *Arrange* group] and select **Align Center**.

j. Click the **Group** button [*Arrange* group] and select **Group**. The clip art and caption are grouped into one object.

k. Drag the grouped clip art and caption so it is approximately 0.5" from the right edge of the document.

10. Save and close the document (Figure 4-104).

American River Cycling Club

WHAT IS MAXIMUM HEART RATE?

The maximum heart rate is the highest your pulse rate can get. To calculate your **predicted maximum heart rate**, use this formula:

(Example: a 40-year-old's predicted maximum heart rate is 180.)

Your actual maximum heart rate can be determined by a graded exercise test. Please note that some medicines and medical conditions might affect your maximum heart rate. If you are taking medicines or have a medical condition (such as heart disease, high blood pressure, or diabetes), always ask your doctor if your maximum heart rate/target heart rate will be affected.

TARGET HEART RATE

You gain the most benefits and decrease the risk of injury when you exercise in your target heart rate zone. Usually this is when your exercise heart rate (pulse) is 60 percent to 80 percent of your maximum heart rate. Do not exercise above 85 percent of your maximum heart rate. This increases both cardiovascular and orthopedic risk and does not add any extra benefit.

Know your target heart rate

When beginning an exercise program, you might need to gradually build up to a level that is within your target heart rate zone, especially if you have not exercised regularly before. If the exercise feels too hard, slow down. You will reduce your risk of injury and enjoy the exercise more if you don't try to over-do it.

To find out if you are exercising in your target zone (between 60 percent and 80 percent of your maximum heart rate), use your heart rate monitor to track your heart rate. If your pulse is below your target zone (see the chart below), increase your rate of exercise. If your pulse is above your target zone, decrease your rate of exercise.

Age	Target Heart Rate (HR) Zone (60-85%)	Predicted Maximum Heart Rate
20	120-170	200
25	117-166	195
30	114-162	190
35	111-157	185
40	108-153	180
45	105-149	175
50	102-145	170
55	99-140	165
60	96-136	160
65	93-132	155
70	90-128	150

4-104 Word 4-2 completed

Guided Project 4-3

For this project, you format a buyer escrow checklist for Placer Hills Real Estate. You convert text to a table, format the table, and insert clip art and a picture.
[Student Learning Outcomes 4.1, 4.2, 4.3, 4.5]

Files Needed: ***BuyerEscrowChecklist-04.docx*** and ***PHRElogo-04.png***
Completed Project File Name: ***[your initials] Word 4-3.docx***

Skills Covered in This Project

- Modify an existing document.
- Convert text to a table.
- Add columns to a table.
- Apply bullets and modify alignment.
- Apply table styles and borders.
- Modify row width and column height.

- Center text vertically in a table.
- Insert and position clip art.
- Insert and resize a graphic.
- Use absolute position and text wrapping.
- Insert and resize a picture.
- Apply border and effects to a picture.

---

1. Open the **BuyerEscrowChecklist-04** document from your student data files.

2. Save this document as **[your initials] Word 4-3**.

3. Convert text to a table.
   a. Select the text beginning with **"Task"** through **"Verify Preliminary Report with Lender."**
   b. Click the **Table** button [*Insert* tab, *Tables* group].
   c. Click the **Convert Text to Table** button. The *Convert Text to Table* dialog box opens.
   d. Click **OK** to accept the default settings. The text is converted to a table with 1 column and 14 rows.

4. Add columns and column headings to the table.
   a. With the table selected click the **Table Tools Layout** tab.
   b. Click the **Insert Right** button [*Rows & Columns* group]. A blank column is inserted to the right of the existing column.
   c. Click the **Insert Right** button two more times to insert two more columns. Your table should now have four columns.
   d. Type the following column headings in the first row:
      Column 2: Date Completed
      Column 3: Initials
      Column 4: Notes
   e. **Center** column headings.

5. Add bullets to selected text.
   a. Select all of the text in the first column below "Task."
   b. Apply an **open square bullet** to these items.
   c. Click the **Decrease Indent** button once so the first line indent is at 0" and the hanging indent is at 0.25".

6. Apply table style and apply formatting.
   a. Place your insertion point in the first cell in the first column.
   b. Click the **AutoFit** button [*Table Tools Layout* tab, *Cell Size* group] and select **AutoFit Contents**.
   c. Click the **Table Tools Design** tab.
   d. In the *Table Style Options* group, select **Header Row** and **Banded Rows**. The other options should be unchecked.
   e. Click the **More** button in the *Table Styles* group to open the gallery of table styles.
   f. Select **Grid Table 5 Dark** style (Figure 4-105).
   g. Select the column headings (first row of the table).
   h. **Bold** the column headings.

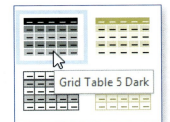

4-105 Apply table style

7. Modify cell size and alignment.
   a. Use the table selector handle to select the entire table, or use the **Select** button [*Table Tools Layout* tab, *Table* group] and click **Select Table**.

b. Change the *Height* [*Table Tools Layout* tab, *Cell Size* group] to **0.35"**. The row height changes on the entire table.

c. With the table still selected, click the **Properties** [*Table Tools Layout* tab, *Table* group] button. The *Table Properties* dialog box opens.

d. Click the **Cell** tab and select **Center** in the *Vertical alignment* area.

e. Click **OK** to close the *Table Properties* dialog box

f. Place your insertion point in the fourth column and change the *Width* [*Table Tools Layout* tab, *Cell Size* group] to **1.5"**.

8. Insert clip art and position it in the document.

a. Place your insertion point at the end of the "Buyer(s):" line after the solid underline tab leader.

b. Click the **Online Pictures** button [*Insert* tab, *Illustrations* group]. The *Insert Pictures* dialog box opens.

c. In the *Office.com Clip Art* text box, type check and press **Enter**.

d. Select the clip art shown in Figure 4-106 and click **Insert**. If this clip art is not available, insert the **Check-04** picture from your student data files.

4-106 Insert clip art

e. In the *Size* group [*Picture Tools Format* tab], change the *Height* to **1.5"** and press **Enter**. The width automatically adjusts to keep the clip art proportional.

f. Click the **Wrap Text** button [*Picture Tools Format* tab, *Arrange* group] and select **Tight**.

g. Click the **Position** button [*Picture Tools Format* tab, *Arrange* group] and select **More Layout Options** to open the *Layout* dialog box (Figure 4-107).

h. In the *Horizontal* area, change the *Absolute position* to **5.2"** *to the right of* **Margin**.

i. In the *Vertical* area, change the *Absolute position* to **0.8"** *below* **Margin**.

j. Click **OK** to close the *Layout* dialog box.

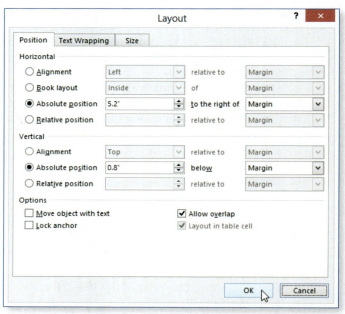

4-107 Position clip art

9. Insert a picture in the upper right of the document.

a. Place your insertion point at the end of the title.

b. Click the **Pictures** button [*Insert* tab, *Illustrations* group]. The *Insert Picture* dialog box opens.

c. Select the **PHRElogo-04** file from the student data files and click **Insert**.

d. Right-click the picture, select **Wrap Text**, and choose **In Front of Text**.

e. Drag the picture so it is near the upper right corner of the document.

f. Click the **Picture Border** button [*Picture Tools Format* tab, *Picture Styles* group] and select **Olive Green**, **Accent 2** (Figure 4-108).

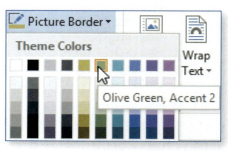

4-108 Apply *Picture Border* color

g. Click the **Picture Border** button, click **Weight**, and select **1½ pt**.
h. Click the **Picture Effects** button [*Picture Tools Format* tab, *Picture Styles* group], select **Shadow**, and select **Offset Bottom** (middle option in first row).

10. Save and close the document (Figure 4-109).

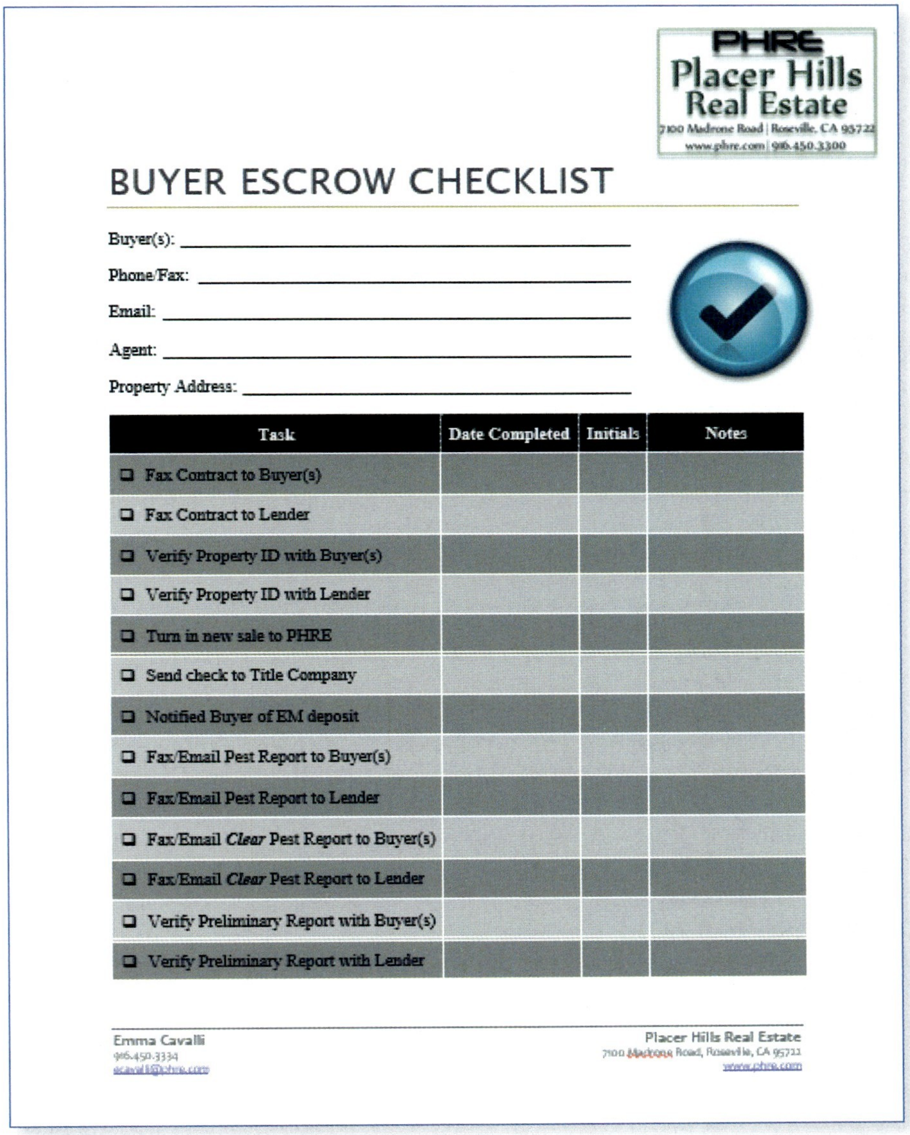

PHRE
Placer Hills Real Estate
7100 Madrone Road | Roseville, CA 95722
www.phre.com | 916.450.3300

BUYER ESCROW CHECKLIST

Buyer(s): ____________________

Phone/Fax: ____________________

Email: ____________________

Agent: ____________________

Property Address: ____________________

Task	Date Completed	Initials	Notes
❑ Fax Contract to Buyer(s)			
❑ Fax Contract to Lender			
❑ Verify Property ID with Buyer(s)			
❑ Verify Property ID with Lender			
❑ Turn in new sale to PHRE			
❑ Send check to Title Company			
❑ Notified Buyer of EM deposit			
❑ Fax/Email Pest Report to Buyer(s)			
❑ Fax/Email Pest Report to Lender			
❑ Fax/Email ***Clear*** Pest Report to Buyer(s)			
❑ Fax/Email ***Clear*** Pest Report to Lender			
❑ Verify Preliminary Report with Buyer(s)			
❑ Verify Preliminary Report with Lender			

Emma Cavalli
916.450.3334
ecavalli@phre.com

Placer Hills Real Estate
7100 Madrone Road, Roseville, CA 95722
www.phre.com

4-109 Word 4-3 completed

Independent Project 4-4

For this project, you format a vaccination schedule for Courtyard Medical Plaza by converting text to a table, formatting the table, and inserting a picture.
[Student Learning Outcomes 4.1, 4.2, 4.3, 4.5]

Files Needed: **VaccinationSchedule-04.docx, CMPLogo-04.png,** and **Vaccination-04.png**
Completed Project File Name: **[your initials] Word 4-4.docx**

Skills Covered in This Project

- Modify an existing document.
- Convert text to a table.
- Apply a table style.
- *AutoFit* table and change row height.
- Center text vertically.
- Sort text in a table.
- Insert rows and add information.
- Merge cells.
- Apply custom borders.

- Apply a style to text.
- Insert a picture.
- Adjust size and position.
- Apply picture effect.
- Insert and position clip art.
- Resize clip art.
- Add and format a caption.
- Align and group caption and clip art.

1. Open the **VaccinationSchedule-04** document from your student data files.

2. Save this document as **[your initials] Word 4-4.**

3. Convert the tabbed text in the middle of the document to a table.

4. Select the entire table and make the following changes:
   a. Select **Banded Rows** in the *Table Style Options* group [*Table Tools Design* tab] and deselect all other check boxes.
   b. Apply the **List Table 1 Light – Accent 2** table style.
   c. Change the font size to **10 pt**.
   d. Choose **AutoFit Window**.
   e. Change row height to **0.25"**.
   f. Center all text vertically within each cell (*Hint: Use the* Cell *tab in the* Table Properties *dialog box*).
   g. Sort the table in ascending order by **Name of Vaccine**. Be sure to select **Header row** in the *My list has* area of the *Sort* dialog box.

5. Make the following changes to the table:
   a. Insert a row above the first row.
   b. Merge the three cells in the new first row and type **RECOMMENDED VACCINATION SCHEDULE**.
   c. **Bold** and **center** the first row.
   d. **Bold** and **italicize** the second row.
   e. On the first row, apply a **black**, **1½ pt**. top and bottom border.
   f. On the second row, apply a **black**, **1½ pt**. bottom border.
   g. On the last row, apply a **black**, **1½ pt**. bottom border.
   h. Horizontally center the column headings and the text in the third column.

6. Insert the following information alphabetically into the table. Insert rows where needed.

Meningococcal conjugate (MCV)	At 11-12 years	1
Hepatitis B (HepB)	At birth, 1-2 months, and 6 months	3

7. Modify the title of the document ("Vaccination Schedule").
   a. Apply **Title** style to the title of the document.
   b. Change the *After* paragraph spacing to **8 pt**.
   c. **Center** the title horizontally.
   d. Apply **small caps** and **bold** formatting to the title.

8. Insert the **CMPLogo-04** picture in the upper left of the document.
   a. Change text wrapping to **Top and Bottom**.
   b. Change the height of the logo to **1"**. Make sure that the logo remains proportional.
   c. Apply the **Offset Diagonal Bottom Right** shadow picture effect.
   d. Set the horizontal and vertical absolute position at **0.2"** to the right of and below page.

9. Insert clip art and add a caption.
   a. Search for vaccination in *Office.com Clip Art.*
   b. Insert the clip art displayed in Figure 4-110. If this clip art is not available, insert the **Vaccination-04** picture from your student data files.
   c. Change the text wrapping to **Square**.
   d. Change the height of the clip art to **1.3"**. Make sure the graphic remains proportional.
   e. Position the clip art so it is to the right of the first and second paragraphs.
   f. Add Don't neglect your vaccinations! as the caption.
   g. **Center** the caption text, change the font color to **Red, Accent 2**, and turn off italics if it is applied to the text.
   h. Adjust the size of the caption text box as needed.
   i. Select the caption and the clip art and **Align Center**.
   j. **Group** the caption and the clip art.
   k. Position the grouped graphic to the right of the first and second paragraphs approximately 0.5" from the right edge of the document and adjust vertically so it does not interfere with the title alignment or the table.

10. Save and close the document (Figure 4-111).

4-110 Insert clip art

4-111 Word 4-4 completed

Independent Project 4-5

For this project, you create an emergency telephone information sheet for Sierra Pacific Community College District (SPCCD). You add and modify a *SmartArt* graphic, convert text to a table, insert a new table, format the tables, and insert the company logo.
[Student Learning Outcomes 4.1, 4.2, 4.3, 4.5]

Files Needed: ***EmergencyTelephones-04.docx*** and ***SPCCDlogo.png***
Completed Project File Name: ***[your initials] Word 4-5.docx***

Skills Covered in This Project

- Modify an existing document.
- Insert a *SmartArt* graphic.
- Add text to a *SmartArt* graphic.
- Resize, change color of, and apply style to *SmartArt.*
- Convert text to a table and *AutoFit.*
- Sort text in a table.
- Insert a row, merge cells, and add information.

- Apply a table style.
- Change cell margins and alignment.
- Apply a style to text.
- Insert a table and type text.
- Insert a picture.
- Adjust picture size and position.
- Insert a symbol and the current date.

1. Open the ***EmergencyTelephones-04*** document from your student data files.

2. Save this document as ***[your initials] Word 4-5.***

3. Insert a *SmartArt* graphic and add text.
   a. Place your insertion point in front of the second section heading ("Emergency Telephone Locations").
   b. Insert the **Vertical Chevron List** *SmartArt* graphic (Figure 4-112).
   c. Type 1 in the graphic text box in the upper left of the *SmartArt* graphic.
   d. Type 2 in the graphic text box below and type 3 in the third graphic text box in the first column of the graphic.
   e. Type the following text in the bulleted text boxes in the second column. You do not need to add bullets because bullets are already included in the *SmartArt.*

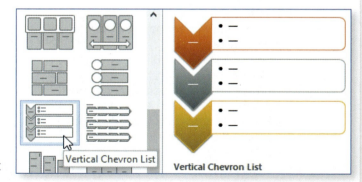

4-112 Insert *SmartArt* graphic

• Press the "Help" button • Speak when the light comes on
• Stay on the line • You will be connected with the college police
• State clearly the nature of the emergency and your location

   f. Delete the extra bullet in the last graphic in the second column.

4. Resize and format the *SmartArt* graphic.
   a. Change the size of the *SmartArt* to **70%** of its original size. Be sure to lock aspect ratio.
   b. Change the text wrapping to **Top and Bottom**.
   c. Change the color of the entire *SmartArt* graphic to **Dark 2 Fill** (Figure 4-113).
   d. Apply the **Intense Effect** *SmartArt* style.

5. Convert text to a table.
   a. Select the tabbed text below the second section heading ("Emergency Telephone Locations"). Do not select the paragraph mark below the last row.
   b. Convert this text to a table and **AutoFit to contents**.

6. Sort the table text in ascending order by the first column.

7. Add a title row and insert text.
   a. Add a row above the first row.
   b. Merge the cells in this row.
   c. Type Blue Emergency Telephones in the merged first row.

8. Format the table.
   a. In the *Table Style Options* group, select **Header Row**, **First Column**, and **Banded Rows**.
   b. Apply the **List Table 2 – Accent 4** table style.
   c. Select the entire table and change the top and bottom cell margins to **0.04"** and the left and right cell margins to **0.1"**.
   d. Vertically **center** all text in the table *(Hint: use the* Cell *tab in the* Table Properties *dialog box).*
   e. Horizontally **center** the text in the first row. This text should be centered vertically and horizontally.

9. Insert, resize, and position the SPCCD logo.
   a. Insert the ***SPCCDlogo_04*** picture at the top of the document.
   b. Change the width to **3"** and keep the size proportional.
   c. Change the text wrapping to **Top and Bottom** and drag the logo above the title.
   d. Set the horizontal and vertical absolute position at **0.3"** to the right of the page and below the page.

10. Modify the footer to include a symbol and the current date.
    a. Open the footer and **space** once at the end of the footer.
    b. Insert a **solid circle** from the *Symbol* font set (Character code 183) and **space** once after it.
    c. Type Revised: and **space** once.
    d. Insert the current date in MM/DD/YY format and set it so that it does not update automatically.

11. Save and close the document (Figure 4-114).

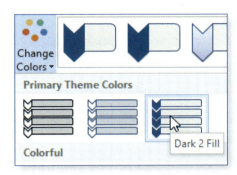

4-113 Change the *SmartArt* colors

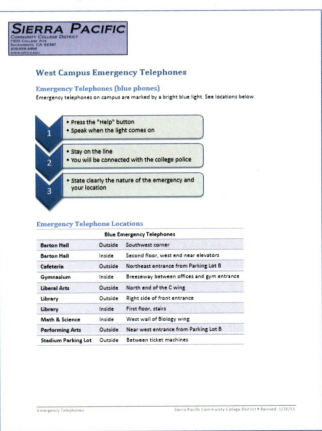

4-114 Word 4-5 completed

Independent Project 4-6

For this project, you modify a memo for Life's Animal Shelter. You edit an existing table, add rows and a column, format the table, insert formulas into the table, and insert and modify *WordArt*.
[Student Learning Outcomes 4.1, 4.2, 4.3]

File Needed: ***WeeklyExpenses-04.docx***
Completed Project File Name: ***[your initials] Word 4-6.docx***

Skills Covered in This Project

- Modify an existing document.
- Modify a table row height.
- Change cell alignment.
- Add rows and a column to a table.
- Merge table rows.
- Modify borders and shading of the table.
- Insert formulas into a table.

- Set formula number format.
- Update formulas.
- Format selected text.
- Insert *WordArt*.
- Modify and position *WordArt*.
- Change paragraph spacing.
- Insert a date.

1. Open the **WeeklyExpenses-04** document from your student data files.

2. Save this document as **[your initials] Word 4-6.**

3. Select the entire table and change the font size to **10 pt**.

4. Sort the table in ascending order by the first column excluding the header row.

5. Add rows, a column, and text to the table.
   a. Insert two rows above the first row.
   b. Insert one row below the last row.
   c. Insert one column to the right of the last column.
   d. Merge the cells in the first row.
   e. Merge the cells in the second row.
   f. In the first row, type Life's Animal Shelter.
   g. In the second row, type Weekly Expenses.
   h. If there is a paragraph symbol at the end of the title and subtitle text, delete the paragraph symbols in these two rows.
   i. In the last column in the third row, type Totals.
   j. In the first column in the last row, type Totals.

6. Modify row height and text alignment.
   a. Change the row height on the entire table to **0.3"**.
   b. **Align Center** (vertical and horizontal) the first two rows.
   c. **Align Center Left** the first column below the two merged rows.
   d. **Align Center Right** columns 2-9 below the two merged rows.

7. Modify table borders and shading.
   a. Select the table and remove all borders.
   b. Add a **1½ pt**, **black**, **double line** top border to the first row.
   c. Add a **1½ pt**, **black**, **double line** bottom border to the last row.
   d. Add a **½ pt**, **black**, **single line** top and bottom border to the third row.

e. Add a **½ pt**, **black**, **single line** top border to the last row.
f. Add a **½ pt**, **black**, **single line** right border to the first column. Don't include the first two rows (title and subtitle).
g. Add a **½ pt.**, **black**, **single line** left border to the last column. Don't include the first two rows (title and subtitle).
h. Apply **Orange**, **Accent 6**, **Lighter 60%** shading fill to the first two rows.
i. Apply **Orange**, **Accent 6**, **Lighter 60%** shading fill to the last row.
j. Apply **Orange**, **Accent 6**, **Lighter 60%** shading fill to the last column.

8. Insert formulas into the table.

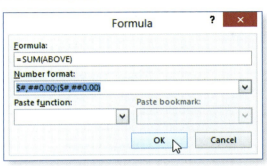

4-115 Insert a formula into the table

a. In the last row of the second column, insert a formula [*Table Tools Layout* tab, *Data* group] to add the figures above. The formula should be **=SUM(ABOVE)**. Use the **$#,##0.00;($#,##0.00)** number format (Figure 4-115).
b. Insert the same formula and number format in remaining cells in the last row.
c. In the last column of the fourth row, insert a formula to add the figures to the left. The formula should be **=SUM(LEFT)**. Use the **$#,##0.00;($#,##0.00)** number format.
d. Insert the same formula and number format in remaining rows in the last column. Make sure to insert the correct formula in each of these cells **=SUM(LEFT)**. Replace "ABOVE" with "LEFT" in the formula, if needed.

9. Change expense data and update formulas.
a. Change the wages for Wednesday to 592.75.
b. Select the total amounts in this column and row and press **F9** to update the formulas.
c. Use **F9** to update the formulas for the wages total and grand total (bottom right cell).

10. Format text in the table.
a. Apply **bold**, **small caps**, and **12 pt**. font size to the text in the first two rows.
b. **Bold** and **italicize** text in the third and last rows.
c. **Bold** and **italicize** text in the last column.
d. **Italicize** the expense categories in the first column.
e. Select the table and **AutoFit Contents**.

11. Insert *WordArt* for the company logo.

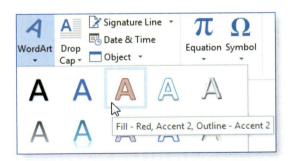

4-116 Insert *WordArt*

a. At the top of the document, insert *WordArt* and use **Fill – Red**, **Accent 2**, **Outline – Accent 2** (Figure 4-116).
b. Type Life's Animal Shelter as the text for the *WordArt*.

12. Modify and position *WordArt*.
a. Change the text to **small caps** and **40 pt**.
b. Change the text fill to **Orange**, **Accent 6**.
c. Change the **Shadow** text effect to **Offset Right**.
d. Using the *Layout* dialog box, change the horizontal **Alignment** to **Centered** relative to **Margin** and change vertical **Absolute position** to **0.2"** below **Page**.

13. Modify the heading lines of the memo.
   a. Add **36 pt**. before paragraph spacing on the first line ("TO: . . .") of the document.
   b. Insert the current date on the date line in the memo heading to replace the placeholder text and set it to update automatically.

14. Save and close the document (Figure 4-117).

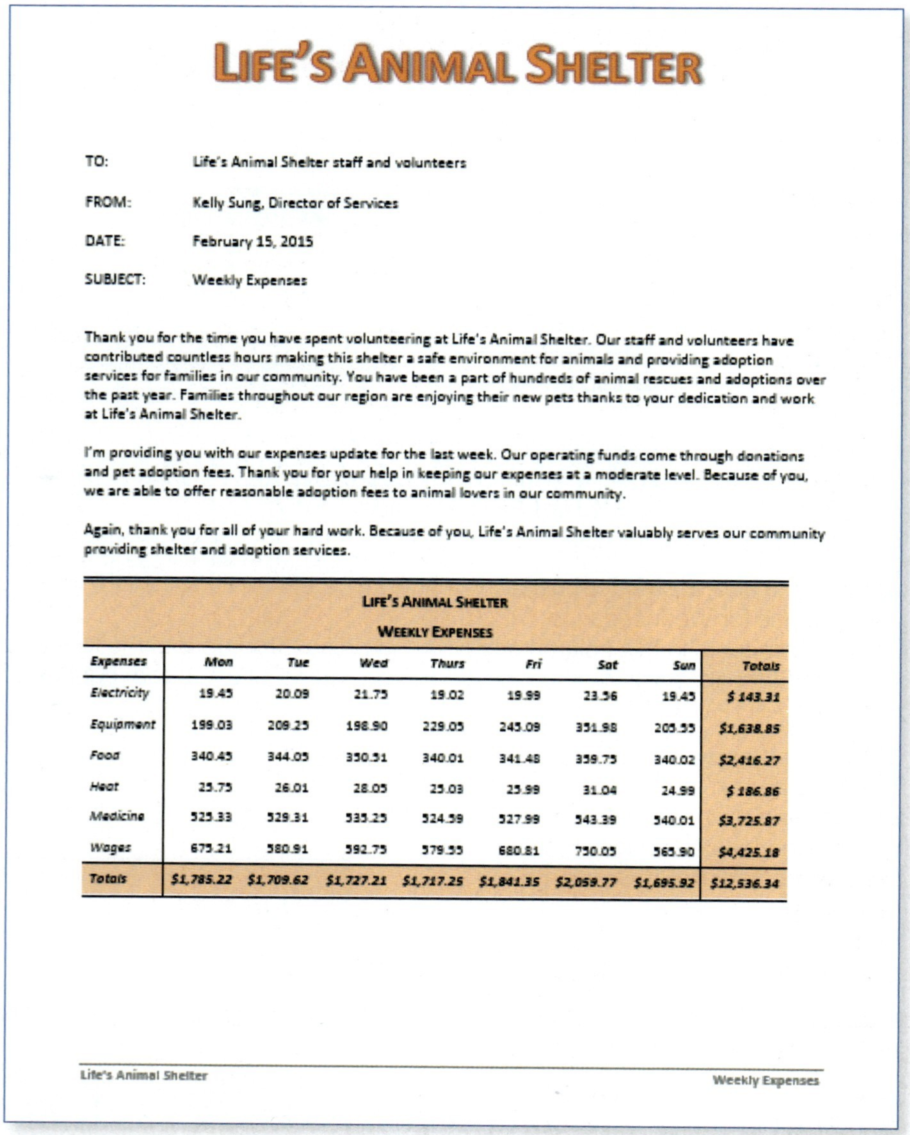

LIFE'S ANIMAL SHELTER

TO: Life's Animal Shelter staff and volunteers

FROM: Kelly Sung, Director of Services

DATE: February 15, 2015

SUBJECT: Weekly Expenses

Thank you for the time you have spent volunteering at Life's Animal Shelter. Our staff and volunteers have contributed countless hours making this shelter a safe environment for animals and providing adoption services for families in our community. You have been a part of hundreds of animal rescues and adoptions over the past year. Families throughout our region are enjoying their new pets thanks to your dedication and work at Life's Animal Shelter.

I'm providing you with our expenses update for the last week. Our operating funds come through donations and pet adoption fees. Thank you for your help in keeping our expenses at a moderate level. Because of you, we are able to offer reasonable adoption fees to animal lovers in our community.

Again, thank you for all of your hard work. Because of you, Life's Animal Shelter valuably serves our community providing shelter and adoption services.

LIFE'S ANIMAL SHELTER WEEKLY EXPENSES								
Expenses	Mon	Tue	Wed	Thurs	Fri	Sat	Sun	Totals
Electricity	19.45	20.09	21.75	19.02	19.99	23.56	19.45	$ 143.31
Equipment	199.03	209.25	198.90	229.05	245.09	351.98	205.55	$1,638.85
Food	340.45	344.05	350.51	340.01	341.48	359.75	340.02	$2,416.27
Heat	25.75	26.01	28.05	25.03	25.99	31.04	24.99	$ 186.86
Medicine	525.33	529.31	535.25	524.59	527.99	543.39	540.01	$3,725.87
Wages	675.21	580.91	592.75	579.55	680.81	750.05	565.90	$4,425.18
Totals	$1,785.22	$1,709.62	$1,727.21	$1,717.25	$1,841.35	$2,059.77	$1,695.92	$12,536.34

Life's Animal Shelter   Weekly Expenses

4-117 Word 4-6 completed

Improve It Project 4-7

For this project, you edit a document for Courtyard Medical Plaza. You arrange text in columns, position the company logo, and apply formatting to improve the overall layout of the document.
[Student Learning Outcomes 4.4, 4.5]

Files Needed: **StayingActive-04.docx** and **CMPlogo.png**
Completed Project File Name: **[your initials] Word 4-7.docx**

Skills Covered in This Project

- Modify an existing document.
- Apply style formatting to the title and headings.
- Change font size and alignment.
- Change paragraph spacing.
- Arrange text in columns.
- Change spacing between columns.
- Use a column break to balance columns.

- Insert a picture.
- Update formulas.
- Format selected text.
- Insert *WordArt*.
- Modify and position *WordArt*.
- Change paragraph spacing.
- Insert a date.

---

1. Open the **StayingActive-04** document from your student data files.

2. Save this document as **[your initials] Word 4-7**.

3. Modify the title of the document.
   a. Apply **Intense Reference** style.
   b. Change to **18 pt**. font size.
   c. Align **center**.
   d. Change paragraph spacing to **36 pt**. before and **12 pt**. after.

4. Modify section headings of the document ("Try Some of the Following Suggestions" and "To Keep Exercise Fun and Interesting").
   a. Apply **Subtle Reference** style.
   b. Change to **14 pt**. font size.
   c. Align **center**.
   d. Change paragraph spacing to **12 pt**. before and **6 pt**. after.

5. Format the last line of the document to make it part of the bulleted list that precedes it and format it consistently with the other bulleted items.

6. Apply column format to the multilevel list following the first section heading.
   a. Arrange the multilevel list in two-column format. Do not include the section heading. If the section break above the list has a number, turn off numbering on this line.
   b. Use **0.75"** space between columns.

7. Apply column format to the bulleted list following the second section heading.
   a. Arrange the bulleted list in two-column format. Do not include the section heading. If the section break above the list has a bullet, turn off bullets on this line.
   b. Use **0.75"** space between columns.
   c. Insert a **column break** before the third bulleted item to balance the columns.

8. Insert the *CMPlogo-04* picture at the top of the document.

9. Resize and position the logo.
   a. Change the width to **2.5"** and keep the size proportional.
   b. Change the text wrapping to **In Front of Text**.
   c. Set the horizontal and vertical absolute position at **0.2"** to the right of and below page.

10. Save and close the document (Figure 4-118).

Courtyard
9660 Alhandra Way
Granite Bay, CA 95517

Medical *a comprehensive medical facility*

Plaza
559.288.9660
www.cmp.com

TIPS FOR STAYING ACTIVE

Almost any activity that gets you moving and strengthens your muscles is good for your health and can help you meet your fitness and weight goal. If you haven't been exercising regularly, start out slowly and gradually increase duration, frequency, and intensity. If you have been exercising regularly, keep it up!

TRY SOME OF THE FOLLOWING SUGGESTIONS:

1) AIM FOR AT LEAST 30 TO 60 MINUTES OF MODERATE INTENSITY ACTIVITY ON MOST DAYS.
   a) You can get your exercise all at once, or spread it out during the day.
      i) For example, exercising for three 10-minute periods is just as effective as exercising for 30 minutes at a time.
   b) The more physical activity you do, the more calories you burn and the greater the health benefit.

2) IF YOU DON'T LIKE COUNTING CALORIES, TRY COUNTING YOUR STEPS! WALKING 10,000 STEPS A DAY CAN HELP YOU MANAGE YOUR WEIGHT.
   a) Use a pedometer (an easy-to-wear device that senses your body's motion) to count your steps and motivate you to increase your activity.
   b) Use a journal to track your walking.

3) USE BOTH AEROBIC AND STRENGTHENING ACTIVITIES ARE IMPORTANT TO LOSING WEIGHT AND KEEPING IT OFF.
   a) As you grow older, your body slows down and your metabolism—the rate at which your body burns calories—naturally decreases.
   b) Taking a brisk walk will boost your metabolism and keep you burning calories for hours afterward.

4) REMEMBER THAT ANY FORM OF EXERCISE IS GOOD FOR YOU.
   a) Household chores
      i) Cleaning windows
      ii) Vacuuming
      iii) Folding clothes
   b) Yard work and gardening
   c) Using stairs rather than an elevator
   d) Getting up and moving regularly at work

TO KEEP EXERCISE FUN AND INTERESTING:

✓ PICK ONE OR MORE ACTIVITIES YOU ENJOY. Regular exercise is more likely to become a healthy habit when it's fun as well as rewarding. Varying your activities can help prevent boredom.

✓ EXERCISE WITH A FRIEND. The support and companionship will help keep you going.

✓ THINK ABOUT THE PAYOFFS. Exercise not only helps control weight, it is beneficial to the body and mind in a number of ways. It improves health, boosts your immune system, helps control appetite, helps you feel more energetic and relaxed, and raises your self-confidence!

✓ SET REALISTIC EXERCISE GOALS. Reward yourself in healthy ways when you achieve them.

4-118 Word 4-7 completed

Challenge Project 4-8

It is always good to live within your means. A budget can help you track actual or anticipated spending and compare the amount you spend with your earnings. Using some of the skills you learned in this chapter, for this project you create a weekly or monthly budget.
[Student Learning Outcomes 4.1, 4.2, 4.3, 4.5]

File Needed: None
Completed Project File Name: *[your initials] Word 4-8.docx*

Create a new document and save it as *[your initials] Word 4-8.*

A budget can include, but is not limited to, the following elements:

- Document title
- Time frame of the budget
- Expenditure categories
- Days in the week or weeks in the month
- Row and column totals

Modify your document according to the following guidelines:

- Set up your budget in table format.
- Use column headings for days or weeks.
- Use row headings for expense categories.
- Use formulas to total rows and columns.
- Sort table by expenditure amounts.
- Apply table style formatting.
- Adjust shading and borders as needed.
- Adjust column width and row height.
- Modify cell margins.
- Format row and column totals.
- Insert a picture or clip art.
- Format, resize, and position clip art.
- Adjust document margins as needed.
- Include an appropriate header and/or footer.

Challenge Project 4-9

Most newspapers and magazines arrange text in column format to improve readability and overall attractiveness of the document. For this project, you arrange an existing document you have written (such as an essay, blog entry, article for a newspaper, or posting for Craigslist) in column format. [Student Learning Outcomes 4.4, 4.5]

File Needed: None
Completed Project File Name: *[your initials] Word 4-9.docx*

Create a new document and save it as *[your initials] Word 4-9.*

A document in column format can include, but is not limited to, the following elements:

- Document title
- Byline
- Section headings
- Graphics

Modify your document according to the following guidelines:

- Set up your article in column format. Don't include the title as part of the columns.
- Change space and/or add a line between columns.
- Use a column or continuous section break to balance the columns.
- Insert a graphic.
- Adjust size, wrapping, and position of the graphic.
- Add a caption to the graphic.
- Adjust margins as needed.
- Include an appropriate header and/or footer.

Challenge Project 4-10

A weekly schedule can help you get organized and manage work, school, family, and personal time more effectively. In this project, you use a table to create a weekly schedule and figure out the time you spend on each activity you engage in each day.
[Student Learning Outcomes 4.1, 4.2, 4.3, 4.5]

File Needed: None
Completed Project File Name: *[your initials] Word 4-10.docx*

Create a new document and save it as *[your initials] Word 4-10.*

A weekly schedule can include, but is not limited to, the following elements:

- Document title
- Days of the week
- Time commitment categories
- Row and column totals

Modify your document according to the following guidelines:

- Set up your weekly schedule in table format.
- Use column headings for days of the week.
- Use row headings for time commitment categories.
- Use formulas to total rows and columns.
- Apply table style formatting.
- Adjust shading and borders as needed.
- Adjust column width and row height.
- Adjust cell margins as needed.
- Format row and column totals.
- Insert a picture or clip art.
- Format, resize, and position clip art.
- Adjust document margins as needed.
- Include an appropriate header and/or footer.

Microsoft® Office

IN PRACTICE

excel

Creating and Editing Workbooks

CHAPTER OVERVIEW

Microsoft Excel (Excel) is a spreadsheet program you can use to create electronic workbooks to organize numerical data, perform calculations, and create charts. Using Excel, both new and advanced users can create useful and powerful business spreadsheets. This chapter covers the basics of creating and editing an Excel workbook.

STUDENT LEARNING OUTCOMES (SLOs)

After completing this chapter, you will be able to:

SLO 1.1 Create, save, and open an Excel workbook (p. E1-3).

SLO 1.2 Edit a workbook by entering and deleting text and numbers, using the *Fill Handle* to complete a series, and using the cut, copy, and paste features (p. E1-6).

SLO 1.3 Create a basic formula using *AutoSum* (p. E1-16).

SLO 1.4 Format a worksheet using different font attributes, borders, shading, cell styles, themes, and the *Format Painter* (p. E1-19).

SLO 1.5 Resize, insert, delete, and hide and unhide columns and rows in a worksheet (p. E1-26).

SLO 1.6 Insert, delete, edit, format, and rearrange worksheets (p. E1-31).

SLO 1.7 Customize the Excel window by changing views, adjusting zoom level, freezing panes, and splitting a worksheet (p. E1-36).

SLO 1.8 Finalize a workbook by spell checking, adding document properties, applying page setup options, and printing (p. E1-41).

CASE STUDY

Paradise Lakes Resort (PLR) is a vacation company with four resort chains located throughout northern Minnesota. PLR asks employees to use standard formats for spreadsheets to ensure consistency in spreadsheet appearance. In the Pause & Practice projects for Chapter 1, you create business workbooks for the Paradise Lakes Resort.

Pause & Practice 1-1: Create a business workbook.

Pause & Practice 1-2: Create basic formulas using *AutoSum* and format a workbook.

Pause & Practice 1-3: Customize cell contents and edit spreadsheet structure.

Pause & Practice 1-4: Customize the window and finalize the workbook.

EXCEL

Creating, Saving, and Opening Workbooks

In Microsoft Excel, the file you create and edit is called a **_workbook_**. You can create an Excel workbook from a blank workbook or from an existing, customizable Excel template. Each workbook file contains many **_worksheets_**, which are comparable to individual pages in a Word document. A worksheet is also referred to as a **_spreadsheet_** or a **_sheet_**, and you can use these terms interchangeably. This book also uses the terms "workbook" and "file" interchangeably. To create a new workbook, first open Excel on your computer.

Create a New Workbook

By default, a workbook includes one worksheet, but a workbook can include multiple worksheets. The worksheet tab is located near the bottom left of the workbook window and is labeled _Sheet1_.

When you first open Excel, the **_Excel Start page_** displays. From the _Start_ page, you can create a new blank workbook, open a previously saved workbook, or create a new workbook from an Excel template. Click **Blank workbook** to open a new blank workbook. Alternatively, you can create a new blank workbook from the _New_ area on the **_Backstage view_**.

> **ANOTHER WAY**
>
> Press **Esc** to leave the Excel _Start_ page and open a blank workbook.

HOW TO: Create a New Workbook

1. Click the **File** tab to display the _Backstage_ view.
2. Select **New** on the left to display the _New_ area on the _Backstage_ view (Figure 1-1).
3. Click **Blank workbook** to create a new blank workbook.

> **ANOTHER WAY**
>
> **Ctrl+N** opens a new blank workbook.

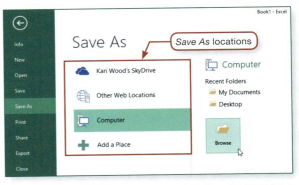

1-1 _Backstage_ view for creating new workbooks

Save a Workbook

When you open a blank workbook, Excel automatically assigns a file name to the file, such as _Book1_. The first time you save a new workbook you must type a file name for the workbook into the _Save As_ dialog box (see Figure 1-3).

1-2 _Save As_ locations

HOW TO: Save a New Workbook

1. Click the **File** tab to display *Backstage* view.
2. Select **Save As** on the left to display the *Save As* area (see Figure 1-2).
   - You can also press **Ctrl+S** to open the *Save As* area on *Backstage* view when saving a workbook that has not yet been saved.
3. Select the location where you want to save your document.
   - You can save the document on your computer, in a *SkyDrive* folder, or on an external storage device.
   - If you click one of the *Recent Folders* options, the *Save As* dialog box opens.
4. Click the **Browse** button to open the *Save As* dialog box (Figure 1-3).
5. Select the location where you want to save the workbook in the left area of the *Save As* dialog box.
6. Type the name of the file in the *File name* area.
7. Click **Save** to close the *Save As* dialog box and save the file.

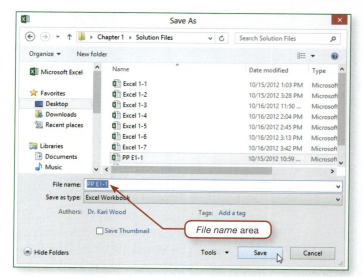

1-3 *Save As* dialog box

> **▶ ANOTHER WAY**
>
> Press **F12** to open the *Save As* dialog box.

Once a workbook has been saved, you can re-save it by pressing **Ctrl+S** or clicking the **Save** button on the *Quick Access* toolbar.

Save a Workbook with a Different File Name

You can save a workbook as a different name by opening the *Save As* dialog box and giving the workbook a different file name. This action does not remove the existing workbook but instead creates a copy of the file with a new name. For example, you might want to rename an existing expense report before updating it with current data. Saving a workbook with a different file name is similar to saving a new workbook.

HOW TO: Save As a Different File Name

1. Click the **File** tab to open *Backstage* view.
   - You can also press **F12** from the working area of Excel to open the *Save As* dialog box.
2. Click **Save As** to display the *Save As* area.
3. Select the location to save your document.
4. Click the **Browse** button to open the *Save As* dialog box (see Figure 1-3).
5. Select the location where you want to save the workbook in the left pane of the *Save As* dialog box.
6. Type the name of the file in the *File name* area.
7. Click **Save** to close the *Save As* dialog box and save the file.

Workbook File Formats

You can save an Excel workbook in a variety of formats. For example, you might want to save a workbook in an older Excel format to share with someone who uses an earlier version of Excel, or you may want to save a workbook in portable document format (.pdf) to create a static image of the file.

By default, Excel workbooks are saved as *.xlsx* files. To change the type of file format, select the format of your choice from the *Save as type* area of the *Save As* dialog box (Figure 1-4). The following table lists several common formats for saving an Excel workbook.

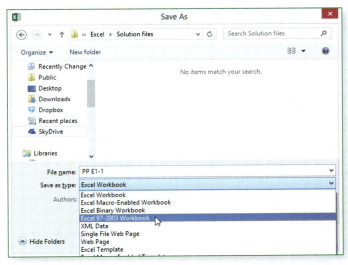

1-4 Workbook file formats

Save Formats

Type of Document	File Extension	Uses of This Format
Excel Macro-Enabled Workbook	.xlsm	Excel workbook with embedded macros
Excel 97-2003 Workbook	.xls	Excel workbook compatible with older versions of Microsoft Excel
Excel Template	.xltx	A new workbook based on a template
Excel Macro-Enabled Template	.xltm	A new workbook based on a template with embedded macros
Portable Document Format (PDF)	.pdf	A static image, similar to a picture, of a workbook; used to preserve the formatting of a file
Plain Text	.txt	Workbook can be opened with most spreadsheet applications and contains text only, with no special formatting.
Comma Separated Values (CSV)	.csv	A common file format that can be opened by most spreadsheet programs and is used to import and export data
Open Document Text	.ods	The spreadsheet software in the Open Office suite
Web Page	.htm, .html	A workbook that is formatted for web sites

Open a Workbook

You can open workbooks from your computer, USB drive, or *SkyDrive*. You can open a previously saved workbook from the *Start* page, *Open* area on the *Backstage* view, or *Open* dialog box.

HOW TO: Open a Workbook

1. Click the **File** tab to open *Backstage* view.
2. Click **Open** to display the *Open* area.
   - Select a workbook to open in the *Recent Workbooks* area or click one of the options in the *Open* area.
3. Select the location where the workbook is stored.
4. Click **Browse** or click a folder to display the *Open* dialog box.
5. Select the workbook and click **Open** (Figure 1-5).

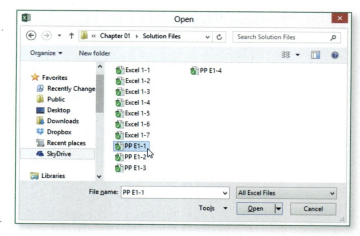

1-5 *Open* dialog box

SLO 1.2

Working with Text and Numbers

When you create or edit a workbook, you can type data, import data from another file, or copy data from a web page or another source. It is important to enter text and numbers correctly to create professional-looking workbooks. A *label* is text in a worksheet that identifies a title and subtitle, row and column headings, and other descriptive information. Labels are not included in calculations. A *value* is a number that you type in a cell. Use values for numbers, currency, dates, and percentages. Values are included in calculations. Occasionally you may need to enter a number as a label. To type a number as a label, click the cell, type an apostrophe ('), and type the number value.

A worksheet is arranged in *columns* (vertical) and *rows* (horizontal). Columns are labeled with letters and rows are labeled with numbers. You type text and numbers in a *cell*, which is the intersection of a column and a row. Each cell is identified with a *cell reference* (or *cell address*), which is the column letter and row number that represent the location of the cell. Cell A1 is the intersection of column A and row 1.

Before entering data in a worksheet, verify the workbook view settings. Click the **View** tab, and select the **Gridlines**, **Formula Bar**, and **Headings** options in the *Show* group. *Gridlines* display the cell boundaries, and the *Headings* option displays row and column headings. Use the *Formula bar* to insert formulas and to edit data.

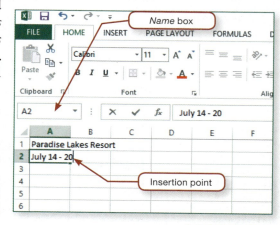

Enter Text and Numbers

To enter data into a spreadsheet, click the cell with your pointer to activate the cell. The *active cell* displays a solid border around the cell, and the reference for the active cell appears in the *Name box* (Figure 1-6).

1-6 Entering text

HOW TO: Enter Data into a Workbook

1. Select the cell and type the information.
   - The text appears inside the active cell with a blinking insertion point (see Figure 1-6).
2. Press **Enter** to accept the information you typed in the cell and to activate the cell below.
   - Press **Tab** to activate the cell to the right.
   - You can also use the arrow keys on your keyboard to activate a cell.

> ### MORE INFO
> When text is longer than the width of the cell, the text displays only if adjacent cells are empty. If the adjacent cells are not empty, the text appears cut off in the cell, but the *Formula bar* displays the entire entry. To display the entire entry, adjust the column width.

Edit Cell Contents

You can edit the content of the cell as you type or after the entry is complete. To edit text as you type (before you press *Enter*), use the **Backspace** key to delete characters to the left of the insertion point. Use arrow keys to move the insertion point, and use the **Delete** key to delete characters to the right of the insertion point. To edit a completed entry (after you press *Enter*), you must activate *edit mode* in the cell. To activate edit mode, double-click the cell or press **F2**. Either method displays an insertion point, and "EDIT" displays on the *Status bar*.

> ### ANOTHER WAY
> Click the **Enter** button on the *Formula bar* to complete an entry.

HOW TO: Edit Cell Contents (Completed Entry)

1. Activate edit mode by double-clicking the cell (Figure 1-7).
   - Another way to activate edit mode is to press **F2**.
2. Position the insertion point and edit the contents of the cell.
3. Press **Enter**.

Replace or Clear Cell Contents

To replace the contents of an existing cell, click to activate the cell, and type the new text. Press **Enter** or click the **Enter** button on the *Formula bar*. To remove the contents of the cell, select the cell and press **Delete** or click the **Clear** button [*Home* tab, *Editing* group]. When you click the *Clear* button, you can choose to *Clear All, Clear Formats,* or *Clear Contents*.

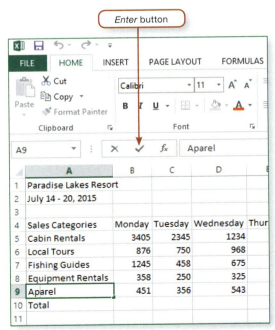

1-7 Activated cell for editing

HOW TO: Clear Cell Contents

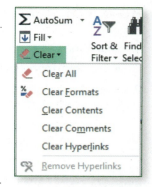

1. Select the cell or cells.
2. Click the **Clear** button [*Home* tab, *Editing* group].
   - Another way to remove cell contents is to press **Delete**.
3. Choose an option from the drop-down list (Figure 1-8).
   - *Clear All* removes formatting and content.
   - *Clear Formats* only clears formatting.
   - *Clear Contents* deletes content.

1-8 *Clear* options

Align and Indent Cell Contents

Excel recognizes any combination of letters, numbers, spaces, and other characters as text and aligns each entry in the bottom left corner of the cell. When you type only numbers into a cell, Excel recognizes your entry as numeric data (values). Excel aligns numeric entries in the bottom right corner of the cell.

You can change both the vertical and horizontal *alignment* of information in a cell. A number of horizontal and vertical alignment and indent options are available in the *Alignment* group on the *Home* tab (Figure 1-9). The vertical alignment options are *Top Align*, *Middle Align*, and *Bottom Align*. Horizontal alignment options are *Align Left*, *Center*, and *Align Right*.

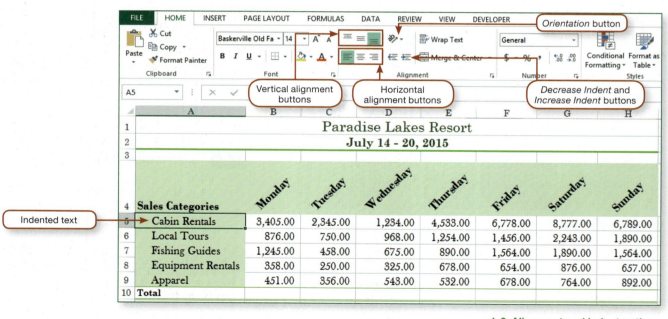

1-9 Alignment and indent options

You can also indent information in a cell. An **indent** increases the distance between the cell contents and the left boundary of the cell. It is common practice to indent row headings in a worksheet (see Figure 1-9). Use **Increase Indent** [*Home* tab, *Alignment* group] to indent cell contents to the right. Use **Decrease Indent** [*Home* tab, *Alignment* group] to remove a previously added indent and move cell contents to the left.

HOW TO: Align and Indent Text

1. Select the cell.
2. Select a horizontal alignment option [*Home* tab, *Alignment* group].
   - *Align Left* aligns text on the left side of the cell.
   - *Center* centers text between the left and right sides of the cell.
   - *Right Align* aligns text on the right side of the cell.
3. Select a vertical alignment option [*Home* tab, *Alignment* group].
   - *Top Align* aligns text at the top of the cell.
   - *Middle Align* aligns text between the top and bottom of the cell.
   - *Bottom Align* aligns text at the bottom of the cell.
4. Select an indent option [*Home* tab, *Alignment* group].
   - *Increase Indent* moves text to the right of the left cell boundary.
   - *Decrease Indent* moves text toward the left cell boundary.

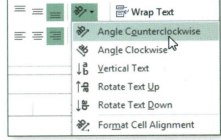

1-10 Text orientation options

By default, text and values are oriented horizontally from left to right, but you can change *text orientation* to display text vertically or at an angle. Click the **Orientation** button [*Home* tab, *Alignment* group] to select a text orientation from the drop-down list (Figure 1-10). Select the **Format Cell Alignment** option from the *Orientation* drop-down list to open the *Format Cells* dialog box and adjust the orientation to a specific degree.

> **MORE INFO**
>
> Click the **Alignment** launcher [*Home* tab, *Alignment* group] or press **Ctrl+1** to open the *Format Cells* dialog box, where you can further customize cell contents.

Select Cells

When you format or edit worksheets, the first step is to select a cell, ranges, columns, or rows. A group of cells is a *range* (or cell range). In a range of cells, a colon is used to represent "through" while a comma is used to represent "and." For example, (A1:A3) includes the cell A2 while (A1, A3) does not.

Excel uses multiple *pointers* to indicate various selecting, copying, and moving options within a worksheet. The following table describes the pointers in Excel.

Pointers

Pointer Icon	Pointer Use
	Selection pointer (block plus sign) selects a cell or *cell range* (group of cells); the selection pointer appears when you move your pointer over the center of a cell.
	Fill pointer (crosshair or thin black plus sign) copies cell contents, completes lists, and fills patterns of selected data; it appears when you place your pointer on the *Fill Handle* or black square in the bottom right corner of an active cell or cells.
	Move pointer (white pointer and four-pointed arrow) moves data; it appears when you place your pointer on the border of an active cell or cells.
	Resize pointer (two-pointed arrow) adjusts cell ranges in a formula and adjusts object sizes; it appears when you place your pointer on the selection handle in a range in a formula or on a sizing handle when an object is selected.

There are many different ways to select data in a worksheet (Figure 1-11). The following table lists the various selection methods.

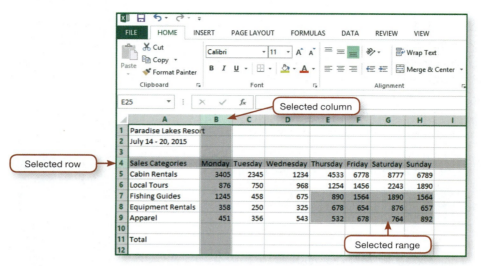

1-11 Selected text

Selection Methods

Name	Instructions
Select an Entire Column or Row	To select an entire column, point to and click a column heading. To select an entire row, point to and click a row heading.
Select the Worksheet	Press **Ctr+A** or click the **Select All** button (above the row 1 heading and to the left of the column A heading) to select the entire sheet.
Select Adjacent Cells	To select groups of cells that are *adjacent* (next to each other), click and drag the selection pointer over the range of cells. Alternatively, you can select the first cell in the range, press **Shift**, and select the last cell in the range. You can also use the **arrow keys+Shift** to select adjacent cells.
Select Non-Adjacent Cells	To select groups of cells that are *non-adjacent* (not next to each other), use the selection pointer to select the first cell(s), hold down **Ctrl**, and select the next cell(s).
Use the *Name Box* to Select Cells	Type a cell reference or cell range in the *Name* box and press **Enter** to select cells. Type a colon (:) between cell references to select a range of cells.

Fill Handle

When you are typing data that is in a series, such as days of the week or months of the year, you can use the ***Fill Handle*** to complete the list. You can also use this tool to repeat numeric patterns, such as in a numbered list, or to copy cell contents to another location.

HOW TO: Use the Fill Handle to Create a Series

1. Type the first item in the series.

2. Press **Enter** and reselect the cell.

3. Place your pointer on the *Fill Handle* (small black square in the lower right corner of the cell) until a fill pointer (thin black plus sign) appears (Figure 1-12).

4. Click and drag the fill pointer through the last cell in the range. Release the pointer to complete the series.

   - The items in the series appear in the cell range.
   - The *Auto Fill Options* button displays and includes options to change the fill selection (Figure 1-13).

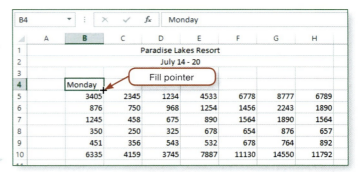

1-12 Use the *Fill Handle* to complete a series

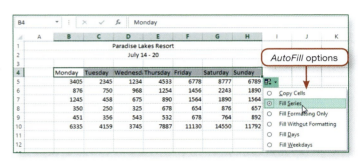

1-13 Completed series

Cut, Copy, and Paste Cell Contents

You can reorganize labels or numeric data quickly using *Cut, Copy,* and *Paste*. Use the *Cut* command to move cells or a cell range. The *Copy* command duplicates cell content from one cell or range to another location. When you cut or copy a cell or a range of cells, it is stored on the Windows *Clipboard*. When you use *Cut, Copy,* and *Paste* commands, the cell you cut or copy from is a ***source cell*** or cells and the cell you paste to is a ***destination cell*** or cells.

> **ANOTHER WAY**
>
> Use **Ctrl+C** to copy.
> Use **Ctrl+X** to cut.
> Use **Ctrl+V** to paste.

Move or Cut Cell Contents

You can move cell content using drag and drop, keyboard shortcuts, or *Cut* and *Paste* in the *Clipboard* group on the *Home* tab. When you use the drag and drop method, the selected cells are not placed on the clipboard.

HOW TO: Move Cell Contents Using Drag and Drop

1. Select the cell(s) you want to move.

2. Place your pointer on the border of the selection until the move pointer (white pointer and four-pointed arrow) appears.

3. Click and hold the move pointer on the border of the selected cell(s) (Figure 1-14).

4. Drag to the desired new location and release the pointer.

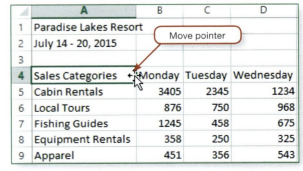

1-14 Move pointer

After you select and cut cells, the cells are placed on the *Clipboard*. To place the contents of the *Clipboard* in the spreadsheet, use the *Paste* command. There are three ways to move text using *Cut* and *Paste*.

- **Ribbon buttons: Cut** and **Paste** buttons [*Home* tab, *Clipboard* group]
- **Shortcut commands: Ctrl+X** to cut and **Ctrl+V** to paste
- **Context menu:** Right-click a cell or range of cells to display the context menu, and click **Cut**.

HOW TO: Move Cell Contents Using Cut and Paste

1. Select the cell or cell range you want to move.
2. Click **Cut** [*Home* tab, *Clipboard* group]. A moving border appears around the selected source cell or cell range (Figure 1-15).
   - If you choose not to move data, press **Esc** to remove the moving border.
3. Select the destination cell location.
   - Click the cell in the top left of the range where you want to paste.
4. Click **Paste** [*Home* tab, *Clipboard* group].
   - If the destination cell or cell range is not empty, pasted data overwrites existing data. To prevent loss of data, use **Insert Cut Cells** [*Home* tab, *Insert* group].
   - You can paste data that you cut only one time.

1-15 **Moving cell contents using *Cut* and *Paste***

> **ANOTHER WAY**
>
> Press **Ctrl+X** to cut or right-click the cell and select **Cut** from the context menu. Alternatively, you can press **Ctrl+V** to paste or right-click the destination cell and select **Paste** from the context menu.

Office Clipboard

The Office *Clipboard* stores cut or copied data from Excel or other Office applications, and the data stored on the *Clipboard* is available to Excel or to other applications such as Word and PowerPoint. The *Clipboard* can hold up to 24 items. Click the **Clipboard** launcher to open the *Clipboard* pane. Each time you cut or copy, the item appears at the top of the *Clipboard* pane. You can paste one item from the *Clipboard* or paste the entire contents of the *Clipboard*.

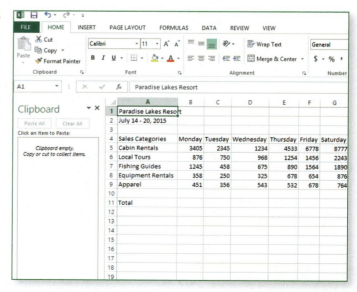

HOW TO: Use the Office Clipboard

1. Click the **Home** tab.
2. Click the **Clipboard** launcher to display the *Clipboard* pane (Figure 1-16).
3. Click **Clear All** to empty the *Clipboard*.

1-16 *Clipboard* pane

4. Cut or copy spreadsheet data to place data on the *Clipboard*. Each item you cut or copy is added to the top of the *Clipboard* pane.

5. Paste items from the *Clipboard* by clicking the item in the task pane. The data is pasted in the active cell.

6. Delete an item from the *Clipboard* by pointing to a *Clipboard* item and clicking the drop-down arrow that appears to the right of the item. Choose **Delete**.

7. Click **Close** to hide the *Clipboard*.

Copy Cell Contents

Copying a cell or a cell range places a duplicate of the selection on the *Clipboard*. The selected data remains in its original location, and a copy of the cell data is pasted in another location. You can copy text using the drag and drop method or *Copy* and *Paste* commands. Data that is copied can be pasted multiple times and in multiple locations.

HOW TO: Copy Using Drag and Drop

1. Select the cell(s) you want to copy.

2. Place your pointer over the border of the selection until the move pointer appears.

3. Press and hold **Ctrl** and click the border of the selected cell(s).

   • A small plus sign appears next to the pointer indicating the move pointer has changed to the copy pointer.

4. Drag the cell or cell range to the desired new location on the worksheet, release the pointer first, and then release **Ctrl** (Figure 1-17).

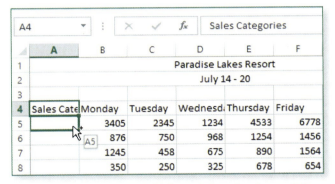

1-17 **Copy data using drag and drop**

Copying cells using the copy and paste method is similar to moving cells using the cut and paste method. The *Copy* command places the selection on the *Clipboard,* and the *Paste* command places the *Clipboard* contents in the worksheet.

• *Ribbon buttons:* **Copy** and **Paste** buttons [*Home* tab, *Clipboard* group]
• *Shortcut commands:* **Ctrl+C** to copy and **Ctrl+V** to paste
• *Context menu:* Right-click to display the menu, and click **Copy**.

Paste Cell Contents and Paste Options

When you are pasting cell data into a worksheet, you may want to paste plain text or cell formatting or formulas. Excel provides multiple paste options. After copying or cutting cells from your worksheet, click the bottom half of the **Paste** button in the *Clipboard* group on the *Home* tab to display the **Paste Options gallery** (Figure 1-18). The following groups are available in the *Paste Options* gallery:

• *Paste*
• *Paste Values*
• *Other Paste Options*

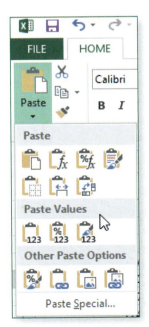

1-18 *Paste Options* gallery

Within these paste groups, there are many context-sensitive paste options. The following table describes each of these paste options.

Paste Options

Group	Paste Icon	Paste Option	Description
Paste		Paste	Copy contents and format of source cell(s); this is the default option.
		Formulas	Copy formulas from the source cell(s) but not contents or formats.
		Formulas & Number Formatting	Copy formulas and format for numbers and formulas of source area but not the contents.
		Keep Source Formatting	Copy contents, format, and styles of source cell.
		No Borders	Copy contents and format of source area but not borders.
		Keep Source Column Widths	Copy contents and format of source cell(s); change destination column widths to source column widths.
		Transpose	Copy the contents and format of the source cell(s), but transpose the rows and columns.
		Merge Conditional Formatting	Context-sensitive: Copy the contents, format, and *Conditional Formatting* rules of the source cell(s) to the destination cell(s).
Paste Values		Values	Copy contents of source cell(s) without formatting or formulas.
		Values & Number Formatting	Copy contents and formatting of source cell(s), but use the format of the destination area for labels.
		Values & Source Formatting	Copy contents and formatting of source cell(s) without formulas.
Other Paste Options		Formatting	Copy format of source cell(s) without the contents.
		Paste Link	Copy contents and format and link cells so that a change to the cells in the source area updates corresponding cells in the destination area.
		Picture	Copy an image of the source cell(s) as a picture.
		Linked Pictures	Copy an image of the source area as a picture so that a change to the cells in the source area updates the picture in the destination area.

> **MORE INFO**
> The default paste option is *Keep Source Formatting*. This option applies when you click the top half of the *Paste* button [*Home* tab, *Clipboard* group].

Businesses use spreadsheets to display data in a useful and meaningful manner. For this project, you create a business spreadsheet that displays one week's sales for Paradise Lakes Resort.

File Needed: None
Completed Project File Name: **[your initials] PP E1-1.xlsx**

1. Create a new workbook.
   a. Click the **File** tab.
   b. Click **New**.
   c. Click **Blank workbook** to open a new workbook.

2. Save the workbook.
   a. Press **F12** to open the *Save As* dialog box.
   b. Select a location to save the workbook (Figure 1-19).
   c. Name the file **[your initials] PP E1-1** in the *File name* area.
   d. Click **Save**. The *Save As* dialog box closes.

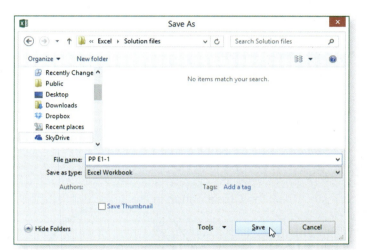

1-19 *Save As* dialog box

3. Enter data.
   a. Click to select cell **A1**, and type Paradise Lakes Resort.
   b. Press **Enter** and type July 14 – 20, 2015.
   c. Press **Enter** again.
   d. Type the remaining data in Figure 1-20. The data in the spreadsheet is displayed so that you can easily read the text for each column and row. You will learn the procedure to increase column width in SLO 1.5. To widen column A, drag the right column heading border to the right.

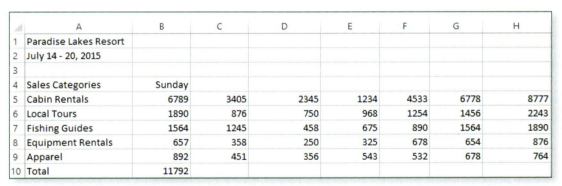

	A	B	C	D	E	F	G	H
1	Paradise Lakes Resort							
2	July 14 - 20, 2015							
3								
4	Sales Categories	Sunday						
5	Cabin Rentals	6789	3405	2345	1234	4533	6778	8777
6	Local Tours	1890	876	750	968	1254	1456	2243
7	Fishing Guides	1564	1245	458	675	890	1564	1890
8	Equipment Rentals	657	358	250	325	678	654	876
9	Apparel	892	451	356	543	532	678	764
10	Total	11792						

1-20 **PP E1-1 data**

4. Use the *Fill Handle* to create a series.
   a. Select **B4**.
   b. Place the pointer on the *Fill Handle* (small black square in the lower right corner of the cell) until a fill pointer appears.
   c. Click and drag to cell **H4**.
   d. Release the pointer.

5. Edit worksheet data.
   a. Select **B10**.
   b. Press **Delete** to remove the contents.
   c. Select **F5**.
   d. Type 4583 and press **Enter**.

6. Indent and align text.
   a. Select **A5:A9**.
   b. Click the **Increase Indent** button [*Home* tab, *Alignment* group].
   c. Select **B4:H4**.
   d. Click the **Align Right** button [*Home* tab, *Alignment* group].

7. Move text.
   a. Select **B4:B9**.
   b. Click the **Cut** button [*Home* tab, *Clipboard* group].
   c. Select **I4**.
   d. Click the **Paste** button [*Home* tab, *Clipboard* group].
   e. Select **C4:I9**.
   f. Point to the right border of the selected cell range.
   g. Drag the selected cells to **B4** and release the move pointer.

8. Save and close the workbook (Figure 1-21).
   a. Press **Ctrl+S** to save the workbook.
   b. Click the **Close** button in the upper right corner.

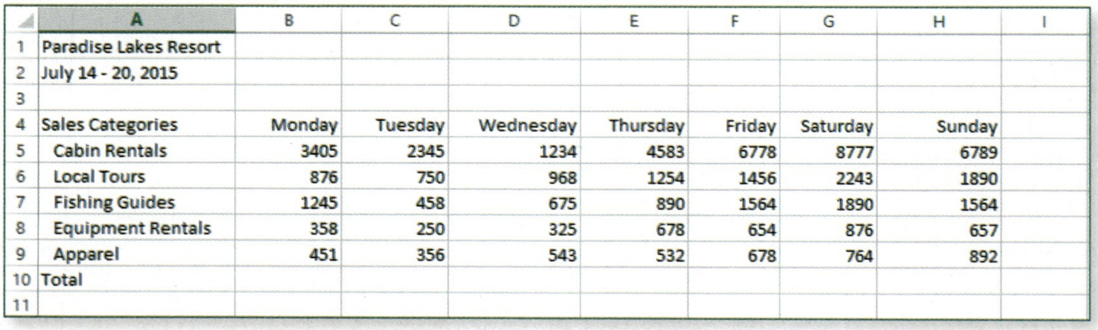

	A	B	C	D	E	F	G	H	I
1	Paradise Lakes Resort								
2	July 14 - 20, 2015								
3									
4	Sales Categories	Monday	Tuesday	Wednesday	Thursday	Friday	Saturday	Sunday	
5	Cabin Rentals	3405	2345	1234	4583	6778	8777	6789	
6	Local Tours	876	750	968	1254	1456	2243	1890	
7	Fishing Guides	1245	458	675	890	1564	1890	1564	
8	Equipment Rentals	358	250	325	678	654	876	657	
9	Apparel	451	356	543	532	678	764	892	
10	Total								
11									

1-21 PP E1-1 completed

SLO 1.3

Using the Sum Function

Sum is a built-in formula that adds the values in a selected range. To insert the *Sum* function, click the cell to make it active. When you click **AutoSum** [*Home* tab, *Editing* group], a formula (=SUM) displays in the cell followed by the suggested range of cells (for example, B5:B9). A moving border surrounds the cells in the range, and the function displays. Press **Enter** to complete the formula or adjust the cell range. The cell displays the result of the sum function, and the *Formula bar* displays the formula. Once a formula has been entered, it is automatically updated if the content of the worksheet is edited.

> **ANOTHER WAY**
>
> The *Function Library* group on the *Formulas* tab includes the *AutoSum* function.

HOW TO: Use the Sum Function

1. Click the cell where you want to display the calculation results.
2. Click the **AutoSum** button [*Home* tab, *Editing* group].
3. Press **Enter** to complete the formula (Figure 1-22).
   - You can double-click **AutoSum** to enter the formula. Click once to see the range and click a second time to complete the entry.

MORE INFO

To display formulas in the worksheet, click the **Formula** tab, and click **Show Formulas** or press **CTRL+`**.

1-22 *AutoSum* function

Copy the Sum Function

The *Fill Handle* is a useful tool to copy functions and formulas, such as *Sum,* into adjacent cells. Notice that in Figure 1-23 each day of the week contains the same number of figures to total. The formula to sum the numbers in the "Tuesday" column is the same as the formula to add the numbers in the "Monday" column except for the cell references. When you drag the *Fill Handle,* Excel automatically adjusts cell references. The formula automatically changes relative to its location on the worksheet.

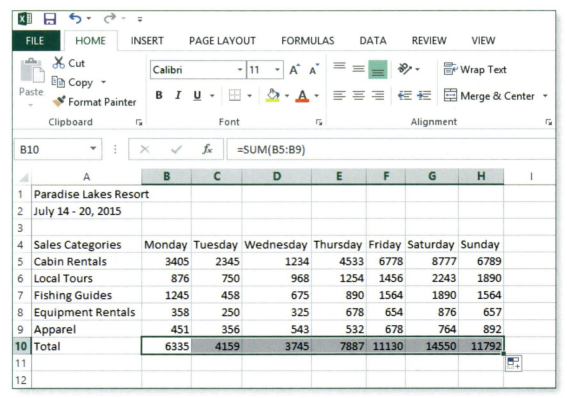

1-23 Using the *Fill Handle* to copy a formula

HOW TO: Use the Fill Handle to Copy Formulas

1. Click the cell containing the formula.
2. Point to the *Fill Handle* in the lower right corner of the cell.
3. Click and drag the fill pointer to the adjacent cells (see Figure 1-23).

Edit the Formula Cell Range

As you edit worksheet structure and contents, it may be necessary to adjust the cell range in a formula. You can edit the cell range using the *Formula bar* or by dragging the border that surrounds a range of cells. Remember that a cell displays the result of the formula and the *Formula bar* displays the formula.

You can also edit a cell reference or the cell range in a formula by dragging the border to reduce or expand the range. When dragging to include more or fewer cells, you will see a two-pointed arrow (resize pointer) when you point to a selection handle on the border.

HOW TO: Edit a Cell Reference Range Using the Formula Bar

1. Select the cell containing the formula.
2. Click the cell range displayed in the *Formula bar*. The range is highlighted, and a border displays around the cell range (Figure 1-24).
3. Edit the cell range.
4. Press **Enter**.

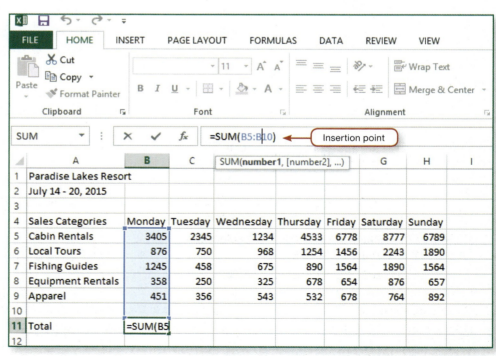

1-24 Editing the cell range in the *Formula bar*

HOW TO: Edit a Formula Cell Range by Dragging

1. Double-click the cell containing the formula.
2. Drag the border handle in the lower right corner to expand or contract the border (Figure 1-25).
3. Press **Enter** to complete the edit.
   - Click the **Enter** button on the *Formula bar* to complete an entry.

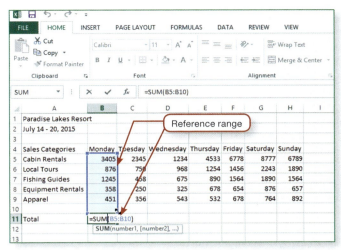

1-25 Edit a cell reference range by dragging

SLO 1.4

Formatting a Worksheet

There are a variety of ways you can change the appearance of your worksheet. You can apply font attributes and add borders, or you can apply a format using ***cell styles***. ***Themes*** provide consistency in format and help you create professional-looking workbooks.

Font Face, Size, Style, and Color

A font is a type design applied to an entire set of characters including the alphabet, numbers, punctuation marks, and other keyboard symbols. *Font size* describes the size of text and is measured in points. There are 72 points in one inch. *Font style* is the weight or angle of text, such as **bold**, underline, or *italic text*. *Font color* refers to the color of the characters. You can change the font attributes in a single cell, a group of cells, a worksheet, or an entire workbook.

The default font attributes for Excel 2013 workbooks are:

- ***Font:*** Calibri
- ***Font Size:*** 11 pt.
- ***Font Color:*** Black, Text 1

> **MORE INFO**
>
> The *Font* drop-down list has two sections: *Theme Fonts* and *All Fonts*.

HOW TO: Customize Font, Style, Font Size, and Font Color

1. Select the cell or range of cells to be formatted and choose an option from the *Font* group [*Home* tab] (Figure 1-26).
2. Click the **Font** drop-down list and select a font.
3. Click the **Font Size** drop-down list and select a font size or type a font size in the *Font Size* area.
   - You can also click the **Increase Font Size** or **Decrease Font Size** buttons to change the font size.
4. Click **Bold**, **Italic**, or **Underline** to apply one or more font styles.
5. Click the **Font Color** drop-down list [*Home* tab, *Font* group] and select a color.
   - Click the **Font Color** button (left of the drop-down arrow) to apply the last font color selected.

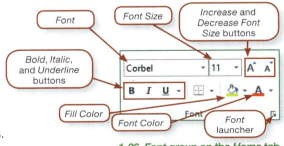

1-26 *Font* group on the *Home* tab

You can also apply font formats using one of the following methods:

1-27 Mini toolbar

- *Mini toolbar:* Right-click a cell or range of cells to display the mini toolbar (Figure 1-27).
- *Format Cells dialog box:* Click the **Font** launcher in the bottom right corner of the *Font* group on the *Home* tab or press **Ctrl+1** (Figure 1-28).
- *Context menu:* Right-click a cell or range of cells and select **Format Cells**.
- Keyboard shortcuts
  Bold: **Ctrl+B**
  Italic: **Ctrl+I**
  Underline: **Ctrl+U**

1-28 *Format Cells* dialog box

Format Painter

The ***Format Painter*** option allows you to copy formatting attributes and styles from one cell to another cell or group of cells. This method is a quick and easy way to apply a consistent look to worksheet data.

HOW TO: Use the Format Painter Button

1. Select the cell that contains the formatting you want to copy.
2. Click **Format Painter** [*Home* tab, *Clipboard* group].
3. Select the cell(s) where you want to apply the copied format (Figure 1-29).

   - The *Format Painter* automatically turns off after you apply the copied format one time.
   - To apply formatting to multiple areas, double-click **Format Painter**, apply the copied format to multiple areas, and click **Format Painter** again to turn off the option. You can also press **Esc** to cancel copying format.

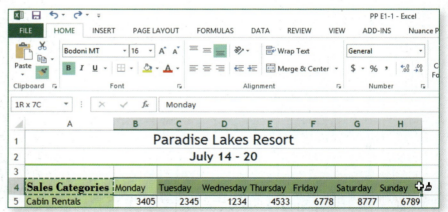

1-29 Copy formats to a range using *Format Painter*

Number Formats

In addition to text formatting, you can apply various number formats to cells so the numbers in your worksheet are clear and easy to understand. Common numeric formats used in worksheets include *Currency*, *Accounting*, and *Percentage*. You can also specify the number of decimal places a number displays by using the *Increase Decimal* or *Decrease Decimal* button. Open the *Format Cells* dialog box to customize number formatting. For example, the *Currency* format includes options to specify the number of decimal places, apply the $ symbol or no symbol, and control the appearance of negative numbers.

HOW TO: Format Numbers

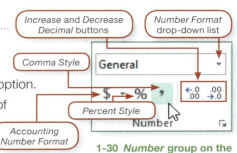

1-30 *Number* group on the *Home* tab

1. Select the cell range you want to format.
2. Click one of the numeric format buttons [*Home* tab, *Number* group] (Figure 1-30) or click the **Number Format** drop-down list and select an option.
3. Click **Increase Decimal** or **Decrease Decimal** to specify the number of decimal places after the whole number.
   - If pound signs (###) appear in any cell, it means your column is not wide enough to accommodate the entry. Adjusting column width is covered in *SLO 1.5: Editing Columns and Rows*.

> ▶ **MORE INFO**
>
> Click the **Number** launcher [*Home* tab, *Number* group] or press **Ctrl+1** to open the *Format Cells* dialog box where you can further customize a number format.

Borders and Shading

You can apply borders to a worksheet to place lines under headings, to show totals, or to group information. Use shading (or fill) to apply a background color or pattern to cells. You can use the *Ribbon* or *Format Cells* dialog box to apply a border or shading to selected cells.

HOW TO: Add Borders and Shading Using the Ribbon

1. Select the cell or range of cells to be formatted.
2. Click the arrow next to the *Borders* button [*Home* tab, *Font* group] and select a border option from the *Borders* drop-down list (Figure 1-31).
   - The *Borders* button displays the most recently used border style.
   - To remove a cell border, choose the **No Border** option from the *Borders* drop-down list.
3. Click the arrow next to the *Fill Color* button [*Home* tab, *Font* group] and select a background color (Figure 1-32).
   - Click **More Colors** to apply a custom color.
   - Click the **Fill Color** button to apply the most recently selected color.
   - To remove cell shading, click the arrow next to *Fill Color* and then select **No Fill**.

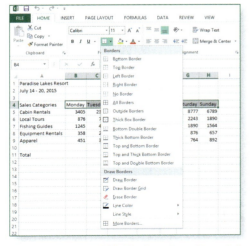

1-31 *Borders* drop-down list

1-32 *Fill Color* palette

The *Format Cells* dialog box includes a tab for defining borders and applying a fill to selected cells. Each tab provides more borders and fill color choices than the *Ribbon* does. When creating a border design, select the border color and border line style before you apply the border to a preset or custom location. When selecting a solid or pattern fill, consider the content of the cell and whether readability will be affected.

HOW TO: Add Borders and Shading Using the Format Cells Dialog Box

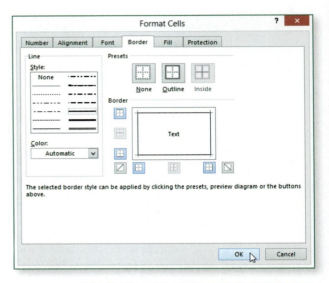

1-33 *Border* tab in the *Format Cells* dialog box

1. Select the cell or range of cells to be formatted.
2. Click the **Font** launcher [*Home* tab, *Font* group] or press **Ctrl+1** to display the *Format Cells* dialog box.
3. Click the **Border** tab (Figure 1-33).
4. Select a line style in the *Style* area.
5. Choose a color from the *Color* drop-down list.
6. Click **Outline** in the *Presets* area to apply an outside border.
   - The *Preview* area displays the change.
7. Click **None** to remove the border.
8. Set individual borders by clicking a button in the *Border* area.
9. Click the **Fill** tab (Figure 1-34).
10. Select a color under *Background Color*.
    - To create a pattern with two colors, click a color in the *Pattern Color* box.
    - To create a gradient special effect, click **Fill Effects**, and select color and shading options.
11. Click a pattern style in the *Pattern Style* box.
12. Click **OK** to close the *Format Cells* dialog box.

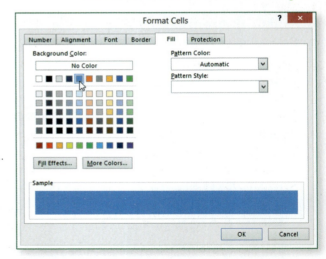

1-34 *Fill* tab in the *Format Cells* dialog box

Cell Styles

Cell Styles are a set of predefined formatting you can apply to titles, subtitles, column headings, row totals, and other areas of your worksheet. Styles apply formatting to the text, background, and border of a cell. You can also create your own cell styles to include specific character formatting, numeric formatting, borders, shading, or alignment. If you plan to use a *Cell Style*, apply the cell style before changing individual font attributes because the *Cell Style* overwrites other formats. Your screen may differ from the figures in this section. If you do not see a style gallery, click the **Cell Styles** button.

HOW TO: Apply Cell Styles to a Range of Cells

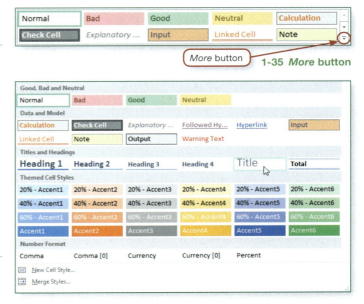

1-35 *More button*

1. Select the cell or cell range where you want to apply a *Cell Style*.
2. Click the **More** button or the **Cell Styles** button [*Home* tab, *Styles* group] to display the *Cell Styles* gallery (Figure 1-35).
3. Select a style to apply to the selected cell(s) (Figure 1-36).
   - When you position your pointer on a *Cell Style* in the *Cell Styles* gallery, Excel provides a live preview of the style by temporarily applying the style to the selected cell(s).

1-36 *Cell Syles* **gallery**

Workbook Themes

Applying a ***theme*** to a workbook formats a workbook quickly and applies a consistent design to the entire workbook. Themes include three combined elements: colors, fonts, and effects. The *Themes* gallery includes several themes to format a workbook; the default theme is called ***Office***. Themes can be customized, and you can individually change ***theme colors***, ***theme fonts***, or ***theme effects***. Additional themes are available online.

HOW TO: Apply Themes to a Workbook

1. Open the workbook.
2. Click the **Theme** button [*Page Layout* tab, *Themes* group] to display the *Themes* gallery (Figure 1-37).
   - Place your pointer on a theme to temporarily apply a live preview of the theme in your workbook.
3. Select a theme to apply to a workbook.
   - You can individually apply theme colors, theme fonts, or theme effects by clicking the **Colors**, **Fonts**, and **Effects** buttons [*Page Layout* tab, *Themes* group] and selecting from the drop-down lists.

> ### MORE INFO
> Themes change the colors that are available in a workbook. Place your pointer over each button in the *Themes* group on the *Page Layout* tab to view the current theme.

1-37 *Themes* **gallery**

For this project you continue working on the spreadsheet you created in *Pause & Practice Excel 1-1*. You add totals to the worksheet using *Sum* and copy formulas using *AutoFill*. You also format the spreadsheet. Formatting changes you apply in this exercise may cause the spreadsheet data to appear crowded or missing. You will adjust column width for the spreadsheet in Student Learning Objective 1.5.

File Needed: *[your initials] PP E1-1.xlsx*
Completed Project File Name: *[your initials] PP E1-2.xlsx*

1. Open the workbook and save it as a different name.
   a. Click the **File** tab and then click the **Open** button.
   b. Locate the folder where your files are saved.
   c. Open the workbook *[your initials] PP E1-1*.
   d. Press **F12** to open the *Save As* dialog box.
   e. Locate the folder where your files are saved.
   f. Save the workbook as *[your initials] PP E1-2*.

2. Calculate daily totals using *Sum*.
   a. Click cell **B10**.
   b. Click the **AutoSum** button [*Home* tab, *Editing* group].
   c. Press **Enter** to complete the formula.

3. Copy a formula across cells using the *Fill Handle*.
   a. Click cell **B10**.
   b. Point to the *Fill Handle* in the lower right corner of the cell.
   c. Click and drag to cell **H10** (Figure 1-38).

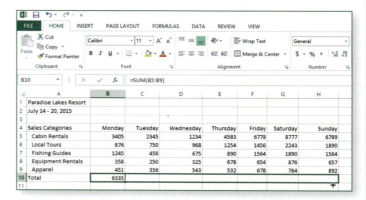

1-38 Copying a formula

4. Calculate sales category totals.
   a. Click cell **J5**.
   b. Double-click the **AutoSum** button [*Home* tab, *Editing* group].

5. Edit the cell reference range to remove the blank cell reference.
   a. Click cell **J5**.
   b. Click the cell range **B5:I5** in the *Formula bar* (Figure 1-39).

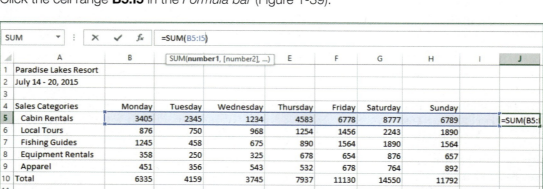

1-39 Edit cell reference in *Formula bar*

c. Change the cell range to **B5:H5**.

d. Press **Enter**.

6. Copy a formula down using the *Fill Handle*.

   a. Select **J5**.

   b. Point to the *Fill Handle* in the lower right corner of the cell.

   c. Click and drag to **J10**.

7. Apply *Cell Styles*.

   a. Select **A1** and then click the **More** button or the **Cell Styles** button [*Home* tab, *Styles* group] to display the *Styles* gallery (Figure 1-40).

1-40 *More* button

   b. Locate the *Titles and Headings* category and select **Title**.

   c. Select **A2** and click the **More** button or the **Cell Styles** button [*Home* tab, *Styles* group].

   d. Locate the *Titles and Headings* category and select **Heading 2**.

   e. Drag to select **A10:H10** and then click the **More** button [*Home* tab, *Styles* group].

   f. Select **Total** in the *Titles and Headings* category.

   g. Select **A4:A9**, hold down and press **Ctrl**, and then select **B4:H4**.

   h. Click the **More** button [*Home* tab, *Styles* group].

   i. Select **20%**, **Accent 1** in the *Themed Cell Styles* category.

8. Apply themes.

   a. Click the **Themes** button [*Page Layout* tab, *Themes* group], and choose **Facet** from the gallery.

   b. Click the **Theme Fonts** button [*Page Layout* tab, *Themes* group] and select **Candara** from the gallery.

9. Apply font attributes to cell A4.

   a. Select **A4** and click the **Home** tab.

   b. Click the **Font** drop-down list [*Font* group], and select **Bodoni MT** in the *All Fonts* section.

   c. Click the **Font Size** drop-down list and select **16 pt**.

   d. Click the **Bold** button.

   e. Click the **Font Color** button and select **Blue-Grey**, **Text 2**, **Darker 50%** (fourth column, last row). Drag column heading border to widen if needed.

10. Apply font attributes to cells A1:A2.

    a. Select **A1:A2**.

    b. Click the **Font Color** button [*Home* tab, *Font* group].

    c. Select **Green**, **Accent 1**, **Darker 50%** (fifth column, last row in the *Theme Colors* category).

11. Apply font attributes to the cell range A5:H10.

    a. Select **A5:H10**.

    b. Change the font to **Arial Narrow** [*Home* tab, *Font* group, *Font*].

    c. Click the **Font Size** drop-down arrow and choose **12 pt**.

12. Use the *Format Painter* button to apply the formatting in A4 to the cell range B4:H4.

    a. Click **A4**.

    b. Double-click **Format Painter** [*Home* tab, *Clipboard* group] to turn on the option.

    c. Select the range **B4:H4** by clicking and dragging your pointer or select each cell in the range.

    d. Click **Format Painter** [*Home* tab, *Clipboard* group] to turn off the option.

13. Apply numeric formatting and align text.

    a. Select **B5:H9**.

    b. Click **Comma Style** [*Home* tab, *Number* group].

    c. Select **B10:H10**.

    d. Click the **Accounting Number Format** button [*Home* tab, *Number* group].

    e. Select **B4:H4**.

    f. Click **Align Right** [*Home* tab, *Alignment* group].

14. Delete text.

    a. Select the cell range **J5:J10**.

    b. Press **Delete**.

15. Add a bottom border and an outside border.

    a. Select cells **A1:H10**.

    b. Press **Ctrl+1** to display the *Format Cells* dialog box.

    c. Click the **Border** tab.

    d. Click a thick solid line style (second column, fifth style).

    e. Click the **Color** drop-down list, and select **Black** (Automatic).

    f. Click **Outline** in the *Presets* area.

    g. Click **OK** to close the *Format Cells* dialog box.

    h. Select **A4:H4**.

    i. Click the **Border** button drop-down list [*Home* tab, *Font* group] (Figure 1-41).

    j. Select **Bottom Border**.

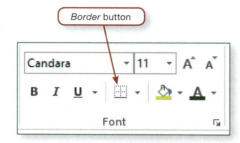

1-41 *Border* button

16. Press **Ctrl+S** to save the workbook (Figure 1-42). You can also save the workbook by clicking the **Save** button on the *Quick Access* toolbar or in *Backstage* view.

Paradise Lakes Resort							
July 14 - 20, 2015							
Sales Categories	**Monday**	**Tuesday**	**Wednesday**	**Thursday**	**Friday**	**Saturday**	**Sunday**
Cabin Rentals	3,405.00	2,345.00	1,234.00	4,583.00	6,778.00	8,777.00	6,789.00
Local Tours	876.00	750.00	968.00	1,254.00	1,456.00	2,243.00	1,890.00
Fishing Guides	1,245.00	458.00	675.00	890.00	1,564.00	1,890.00	1,564.00
Equipment Rentals	358.00	250.00	325.00	678.00	654.00	876.00	657.00
Apparel	451.00	356.00	543.00	532.00	678.00	764.00	892.00
Total	$ 6,335.00	$ 4,159.00	$ 3,745.00	$ 7,937.00	$ 11,130.00	$ 14,550.00	$ 11,792.00

1-42 PP E1-2 completed

17. Click the **File** tab and click **Close**, or press **Ctrl+W** to close the workbook.

SLO 1.5

Editing Columns and Rows

There are many ways to control the display of data within each column and row. Often the default column width and row height settings of Excel do not fit the requirements of the cell contents and require adjustment. You may also want to hide columns or rows containing sensitive data such as employee salaries. This section teaches you how to adjust column width and row height, as well as how to insert, delete, hide, and unhide columns and rows.

> **MORE INFO**
>
> Excel 2013 has 16,384 columns and 1,048,576 rows.

Adjust Column Width and Row Height

The default setting for each column is 8.43 characters. This number represents the number of characters that are viewable within the cell in the default font. You may change this width to any value between 0 and 255 characters. The default height of each row is 15 points. There are several ways to edit column width or row height, including dragging column or row heading borders, displaying the context menu, or selecting options from the *Format* drop-down list [*Home* tab, *Cells* group]. When you adjust column width or row height, the entire column or row changes.

HOW TO: Change Column Width or Row Height

1. Select a cell in the column or row you want to adjust.
    - To apply the same column width or row height to multiple columns or rows, select multiple columns or rows.
2. Click the **Format** button [*Home* tab, *Cells* group] and select **Row Height** or **Column Width** from the drop-down list to open the *Row Height* or *Column Width* dialog box (Figure 1-43).
3. Enter the desired height or width.
4. Click **OK** to close the dialog box.

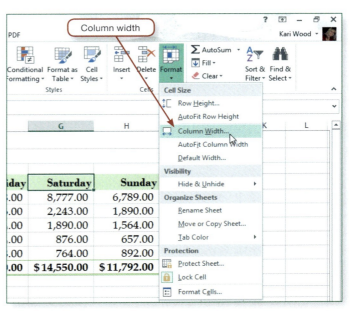

1-43 *Format* button drop-down list

> **ANOTHER WAY**
>
> To apply the same column width or row height to multiple columns or rows, select the columns or rows and right-click. Choose **Column Width** or **Row Height** from the context menu. Enter the new measurement and click **OK**.

> **MORE INFO**
>
> You can change the default sheet settings for column width by selecting the sheet tab or tabs, clicking **Format** [*Home* tab, *Cells* group], and selecting **Default Width** in the *Cell Size* category. Enter the new width for the selected sheets.

AutoFit Columns and Rows

The *AutoFit* feature resizes column width or row height to accommodate the width or height of the largest entry. You can use the *Format* button in the *Cells* group on the *Home* tab, or the context menu to *AutoFit* columns and rows. Another way to *AutoFit* a column is to double-click the right border of the column heading. When you point to the border, the pointer changes to a *sizing pointer* (Figure 1-44). To *AutoFit* a row, double-click the bottom border of the row heading.

HOW TO: Change Column Width or Row Height Using AutoFit

1. Select the columns or rows to adjust.
2. Click **Format** [*Home* tab, *Cells* group].
3. Click **AutoFit Column Width** or **AutoFit Row Height** (see Figure 1-44).

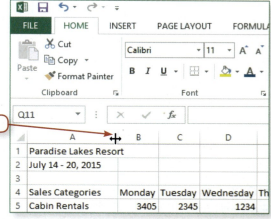

1-44 Double-click a column border to *AutoFit* column contents

Wrap Text and Merge Cells

The ***Wrap Text*** feature enables you to display the contents of a cell on multiple lines. You can format the cell to wrap text automatically, or you can enter a manual line break by pressing **Alt+Enter**. The cell contents wrap to fit the width of the column. If the text is not visible, it may be necessary to adjust the row height.

HOW TO: Wrap Text in a Cell

1. Select the cells to format.
2. Click the **Home** tab.
3. Click the **Wrap Text** button [*Alignment* group] (Figure 1-45).

1-45 *Wrap Text* button

> ▶ **ANOTHER WAY**
>
> Double-click a cell or press **F2** to activate edit mode in a cell and click to position the insertion point where you want to break the line. Press **Alt+Enter**.

The ***Merge & Center*** command combines two or more cells into one cell and centers the text. This feature is useful for centering worksheet titles over multiple columns. Before you merge cells, be sure the data appears in the upper-left cell. All data included in any other selected cell will be overwritten during the merge process.

HOW TO: Merge and Center

1. Select the cells you want to merge and center.
2. Click the **Home** tab.
3. Click the **Merge & Center** button [*Alignment* group] (Figure 1-46).

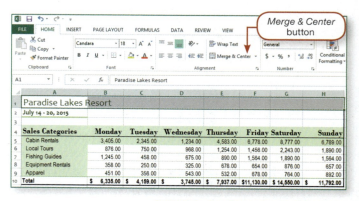

1-46 Select cells to merge and center

To merge cells without centering text, click the arrow next to *Merge & Center,* and choose **Merge Across** or **Merge Cells**. To unmerge cells, click the **Merge & Center** button or click the **Merge & Center** drop-down list and choose **Unmerge Cells**.

MORE INFO

Use the *Undo* button on the *Quick Access* toolbar or press **Ctrl+Z** to undo single or multiple actions.

Insert and Delete Columns and Rows

There are times when you need to insert or delete a row or column of information in your spreadsheet. For example, you can insert a row for an additional sales category or you might want to combine Saturday and Sunday sales figures into one column and delete the extra column. When you insert or delete columns and rows, Excel automatically shifts cells to make room for the new cells or fills the gap for deleted cells.

HOW TO: Insert Columns or Rows

1. Select a cell in the column that is to the right of where you want to insert a column, or click the row immediately below the row where you want to insert a new row.
2. Click the bottom half of the **Insert** button [*Home* tab, *Cells* group].
3. Select **Insert Sheet Rows** to add a row (Figure 1-47).
   - The new row appears directly above the originally selected row.

1-47 Insert a row

4. Select **Insert Sheet Columns** to add a column.
   - The new column appears directly to the left of the column you originally selected.
5. Select an individual cell and click the top half of the *Insert* button to insert a single cell rather than an entire row.
6. Select an entire column or row and click the top half of the *Insert* button to insert a column or row. To insert multiple columns or rows, select the number of columns or rows you want to insert.

ANOTHER WAY

To insert a column or row, select a column heading or row heading, right-click, and select **Insert** from the context menu. An alternative is to select column(s) or row(s), and press **Ctrl+plus sign (+)** on the numeric keypad.

When you delete a column or row, the contents in the cells of that column or row are deleted. Remaining columns and rows shift to the left or up after a deletion.

HOW TO: Delete Columns or Rows

1. Select a cell in the column or row you want to delete.
2. Click the bottom half of the **Delete** button [*Home* tab, *Cells* group].
3. Select **Delete Sheet Rows** to remove a row (Figure 1-48).
   - All the remaining rows below the deleted row shift up.

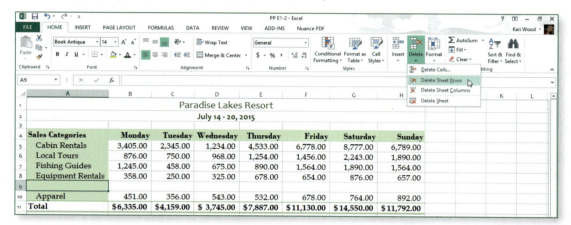

1-48 Delete a row

4. Select **Delete Sheet Columns** to remove a column.
   - All remaining columns to the right of the deleted column shift to the left.
5. Select an individual cell and click the top half of the *Delete* button to delete a cell rather than an entire row.
6. Select an entire column or row and click the top half of the *Delete* button to delete the column or row.

> **MORE INFO**
>
> Delete or insert single cells by choosing **Insert Cells** from the *Insert* drop-down list or **Delete Cells** from the *Delete* drop-down list [*Home* tab, *Cells* group].

Hide and Unhide Columns and Rows

If there is sensitive data in a worksheet, you may want to hide it before sharing the worksheet with others. Hiding a column or row does not delete the information in the worksheet nor does it affect the results of calculations. After hiding a column or row, you can unhide it so it again displays in the worksheet.

HOW TO: Hide and Unhide Columns or Rows

1. Select the column or row (or a cell in the column or row) you want to hide.
   - The hide feature applies to an entire column or row, not individual cells.
   - You can select multiple columns or rows to hide.
2. Click the **Format** button [*Home* tab, *Cells* group] and select **Hide & Unhide** in the *Visibility* category.

3. Select **Hide Columns** or **Hide Rows**.
  - When a column or row is hidden, there is a small gap between the letters in column headings or numbers in row headings indicating that the column or row is hidden.
  - Column or row headings are not lettered or numbered consecutively when a column or row is hidden.
4. To unhide a column or row, select the columns to the left and right of the hidden column or select the rows above and below the hidden row.
5. Click the **Format** button and select **Hide & Unhide** in the *Visibility* category (Figure 1-49).

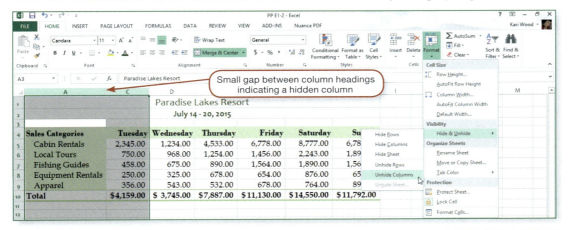

1-49 Unhide a column

6. Select **Unhide Columns** or **Unhide Rows** to display the hidden column or row.

> ▶ **ANOTHER WAY**
>
> **Ctrl+9** hides selected rows.
> **Ctrl+Shift+(** unhides hidden rows from a selection.
> **Ctrl+0** hides selected columns.

> ▶ **MORE INFO**
>
> To hide or unhide multiple columns or rows, select the columns or rows, right-click one of the selected columns or rows, and choose **Hide** or **Unhide** from the context menu.

SLO 1.6

Customizing Worksheets

An Excel workbook consists of one or more worksheets (or sheets), and each worksheet has a ***worksheet tab*** near the bottom left of the Excel window that displays the name of the worksheet.

The number of worksheets you can insert in a workbook is limited only by the amount of memory available on your computer. By default each workbook contains one sheet. Excel provides options to insert additional sheets, delete unwanted sheets, rename sheets, and change the tab color of sheets. Also, you may want to hide sheets if sensitive data should not be available to others. In this section, you learn to format, name, insert, delete, copy, rearrange, hide, and unhide worksheet tabs.

Insert and Delete Worksheets

There are times when you need to insert a worksheet to store additional information in your workbook. When there is more than one worksheet in a workbook, you select a worksheet by clicking the worksheet tab. There are multiple ways to both insert and delete worksheets. Inserted worksheets are automatically named.

> **MORE INFO**
>
> Press **Ctrl+Page Down** to move to the next worksheet. Press **Ctrl+Page Up** to move to the previous worksheet.

HOW TO: Insert and Delete Worksheets

1. Select a cell in the current worksheet.
2. To insert a worksheet, use one of the following methods:
   - Click the **New Sheet** button (plus sign) to the right of the existing worksheet tabs (Figure 1-50).
   - Click the bottom half of the **Insert** button [*Home* tab, *Cells* group] and select **Insert Sheet** (Figure 1-51).
   - Right-click a worksheet tab and select **Insert** from the context menu to open the *Insert* dialog box. Select **Worksheet** and click **OK**.
3. To delete a worksheet from a workbook, click the bottom half of the **Delete** button [*Home* tab, *Cells* group] and select **Delete Sheet** to remove the active worksheet.
   - Alternatively, you can right-click the worksheet tab and select **Delete** from the context menu.

1-50 **New Sheet** button

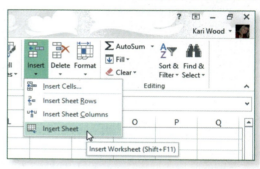

1-51 **Insert** button: Adding a new worksheet

> **ANOTHER WAY**
>
> Press **Shift+F11** to insert a new worksheet.

> **MORE INFO**
>
> To delete or insert multiple worksheets, click the worksheet tabs while pressing **Ctrl**, right-click one of the selected worksheet tabs, and choose **Delete** or **Insert** from the context menu.

Rename Worksheets and Change Tab Color

The default names for the sheets within a workbook are *Sheet1*, *Sheet2*, and so on. After adding worksheets to a workbook, you might want to **rename** each worksheet with a more meaningful name. The size of the sheet tab adjusts to fit the name. You can also apply a **tab color** to further distinguish each worksheet. There is no default color for worksheet tabs.

HOW TO: Rename a Worksheet and Apply a Tab Color

1. Right-click the worksheet tab and choose **Rename** from the context menu (Figure 1-52).

2. Type the new name on the worksheet tab and press **Enter**.
   - You can also click the **Format** button [*Home* tab, *Cells* group] and select **Rename Sheet**.

3. Right-click the worksheet tab, choose **Tab Color** from the context menu, and select a color to apply to the background of the worksheet tab.
   - When a worksheet tab is active (selected), it displays as a light version of the tab color, and when a worksheet is not active, it displays the tab color (Figure 1-53).
   - You can also apply a tab color to the active worksheet by clicking the **Format** button, selecting **Tab Color**, and then choosing a color.

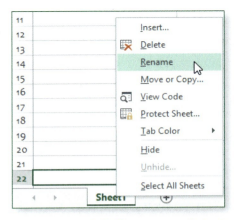

1-52 Rename a worksheet

1-53 Tab color applied to a worksheet

> **MORE INFO**
>
> To color multiple sheet tabs in a workbook the same color at the same time, select the sheet tabs you want to apply the color to, right-click one of the selected sheet tabs, and choose **Tab Color** from the context menu.

> **ANOTHER WAY**
>
> Rename a sheet tab by double-clicking the sheet tab name, typing the new name, and pressing **Enter**.

Move and Copy Worksheets

You can use the move feature to change the order of worksheets within a workbook or to move worksheets to a different workbook. The copy feature saves time by eliminating the need to reenter data. If you need to move or copy a worksheet a short distance, use the drag and drop method. Otherwise, use move, copy, and paste.

HOW TO: Move Worksheets

1. Right-click the worksheet tab you want to move.

2. Select **Move or Copy** from the context menu (Figure 1-54). The *Move or Copy* dialog box opens (Figure 1-55).
   - Alernatively, you can click the **Format** button [*Home* tab, *Cells* group] and select **Move or Copy Sheet**.
   - To move or copy the selected worksheet into a workbook other than the current one, select a different workbook from the *To book* drop-down list.
   - If you are moving a worksheet between workbooks, the destination workbook must be open prior to opening the *Move or Copy* dialog box.

3. Locate the *Before sheet* area, and select the worksheet that the active sheet will precede when it is moved.

4. Deselect the **Create a copy** check box if it is checked.

5. Click **OK** to close the dialog box.

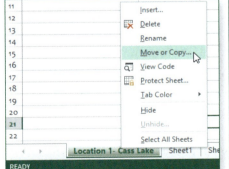

1-54 Move or copy a worksheet

1-55 *Move or Copy* dialog box

When you move or copy worksheets, you can select multiple sheets to move or copy. Selecting multiple worksheets creates a group, and the title bar displays "[Group]" after the workbook name. To select multiple sheets, select a sheet tab, press **Shift**, and click another sheet tab. Once you have moved or copied the grouped worksheets, "[Group]" disappears from the title bar. To ungroup the sheets (prior to moving or copying), right-click a grouped tab, and choose **Ungroup**.

HOW TO: Copy Worksheets

1. Right-click the worksheet tab you want to copy and select **Move or Copy** from the context menu (see Figure 1-54). The *Move or Copy* dialog box opens (see Figure 1-55).
   - You can also click the **Format** button [*Home* tab, *Cells* group] and select **Move or Copy Sheet**.
   - To copy the selected worksheet into a workbook other than the current one, select a destination workbook from the *To book* drop-down list.
   - If you are copying a worksheet between workbooks, the destination workbook must be open prior to opening the *Move or Copy* dialog box.
2. Select the worksheet that the active sheet will precede when it is copied in the *Before sheet* area.
3. Check the **Create a copy** box in the bottom left corner of the dialog box.
4. Click **OK** to close the dialog box.
   - The copied sheet has the same name as the original worksheet with a (2) after it, as shown in Figure 1-56.

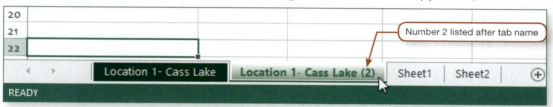

1-56 New worksheet copy

> ▶ **ANOTHER WAY**
>
> To move a worksheet, click the worksheet tab and drag to the left or right. To copy a worksheet, press and hold **Ctrl** while you drag the worksheet tab to the left or right.

PAUSE & PRACTICE: EXCEL 1-3

For this project, you open your previous Pause & Practice file (*[your initials] PP E1-2*) to adjust the column and row widths; insert a row for a new sales category; delete unwanted sheets; and copy, rename, and format a spreadsheet for another location of Paradise Lakes Resorts.

File Needed: *[your initials] PP E1-2.xlsx*
Completed Project File Name: *[your initials] PP E1-3.xlsx*

1. Open the *[your initials] PP E1-2* workbook.
2. Save the file as *[your initials] PP E1-3*.

3. Change the width of columns B through H.
   a. Click and drag column headings **B** through **H** to select the columns.
   b. Click the **Format** button [*Home* tab, *Cells* group].
   c. Select **Column Width** from the menu.
   d. Enter 20.0 characters as the new width.
   e. Click **OK**.

4. Apply new row heights to rows 4 and 10.
   a. Click row heading **4**, hold down **Ctrl**, and click row heading **10**.
   b. Right-click row heading **4**.
   c. Choose **Row Height** from the context menu.
   d. Enter 24.0 as the new height.
   e. Click **OK**.

5. Insert a new row and row label above row 9.
   a. Right-click row heading **9**.
   b. Choose **Insert** from the context menu to add a new row.
   c. The new row appears directly above the originally selected row.
   d. Select cell **A9** and type Food & Beverages.
   e. Press **Enter**.

6. Hide the newly inserted row 9.
   a. Click cell **A9**.
   b. Click the **Format** button [*Home* tab, *Cells* group].
   c. Select **Hide & Unhide** in the *Visibility* category.
   d. Select **Hide Rows**.

7. Merge and center the worksheet title and date.
   a. Select **A1:H1**.
   b. Click the **Merge & Center** button [*Home* tab, *Alignment* group].
   c. Select **A2:H2** and merge and center the cells.

8. Rename *Sheet1* and color the sheet tab.
   a. Double-click the **Sheet1** tab.
   b. Type the following new name for the sheet: Location 1- Cass Lake.
   c. Press **Enter**.
   d. Click the **Format** button [*Home* tab, *Cells* group].
   e. Select **Tab Color** in the *Organize Sheets* category.
   f. Select **Green Accent 1**, **Darker 50%** (last color in the fifth *Theme Color* column).

9. Insert a new sheet.
   a. Click the bottom half of the **Insert** button [*Home* tab, *Cells* group] and select **Insert Sheet**. The sheet appears to the left of the *Location 1- Cass Lake* sheet.
   b. Click the **New Sheet** button to insert another sheet.

10. Delete the extra blank sheets.
    a. Click the **Sheet2** tab, press and hold **Shift**, and click the **Sheet3** tab. Release **Shift** (both worksheet tabs are selected).
    b. Click the **Delete** button drop-down list [*Home* tab, *Cells* group].
    c. Select **Delete Sheet** to remove the selected worksheets.

11. Create a copy of the worksheet *Location 1- Cass Lake* and rename the new worksheet tab.
    a. Right-click the **Location 1- Cass Lake** tab.
    b. Choose **Move or Copy** from the context menu.
    c. The *Move or Copy* dialog box displays.
    d. Choose **(move to end)** in the *Before Sheet* box.
    e. Check the **Create a copy** box in the bottom left corner of the window.

f. Click **OK**. The new sheet is automatically named *Location 1- Cass Lake (2)*.

g. Double-click the new worksheet tab **Location 1- Cass Lake (2)**, and type the new sheet name: Location 2- Breezy Point.

h. Press **Enter**.

i. Color the tab **Orange**, **Accent 4**, **Darker 50%** (last color in the eighth *Theme Color* column).

12. Press **Ctrl+S** to save the workbook.

13. Click the **File** tab and click **Close** to close the workbook (Figure 1-57).

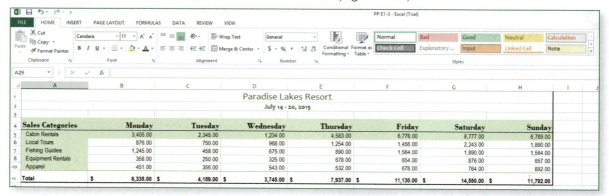

1-57 PP E1-3 completed worksheet with hidden row

SLO 1.7

Customizing the Window

In this section you explore several ways to customize the Excel window including changing workbook views, zooming options, freezing panes, splitting a worksheet into panes, and switching windows.

Workbook Views

Excel has three main views: *Normal*, *Page Layout*, and *Page Break Preview*. A fourth view, *Full Screen* view, displays a spreadsheet without screen elements so you can see more of the sheet. Each view in Excel has a specific purpose.

- *Normal* view is the default view. Use *Normal* view to create and modify spreadsheets.
- Use *Page Layout* view to apply headers and footers and to view the layout of the spreadsheet prior to distribution.
- Use *Page Break Preview* to adjust page breaks within your workbook using the drag and drop technique.
- Use *Full Screen* view to display worksheet data without the *Ribbon* and other screen elements.

The *Normal* view, *Page Layout* view, and *Page Break Preview* buttons are on the right side of the *Status bar*. You can also change views using *Normal*, *Page Layout*, and *Page Break Preview* buttons located on the *View* tab in the *Workbook Views* group (Figure 1-58).

1-58 *View* tab

1. Open a workbook. The *Normal* view displays by default.

2. Click the **View** tab.

3. Click the **Page Layout** button [*View* tab, *Workbook Views* group].
   - This view displays spreadsheet headers, footers, and page breaks (Figure 1-59).

4. Click **Page Break Preview** [*View* tab, *Workbook Views* group] to view page breaks.
   - Click and drag the dark blue page break lines to adjust page breaks (Figure 1-60).

5. Click **Normal** [*View* tab, *Workbook Views* group] to return to the default view.

6. Click **Ribbon Display Options** in the upper right corner of the Excel window and select **Auto-Hide Ribbon** to display *Full Screen* view (Figure 1-61).
   - *Full Screen* view increases the spreadsheet view by hiding the *Ribbon* and the *Status bar*.
   - The *Ribbon Display Options* menu includes three options: *Auto-Hide Ribbon*, *Show Tabs*, or *Show Tabs and Commands* (Figure 1-62). The entire *Ribbon* disappears from view when you select *Auto-Hide Ribbon*. *Show Tabs* displays *Ribbon* tabs only. Click a tab to display *Ribbon* commands. The *Show Tabs and Commands* option displays the *Ribbon* tabs and commands.

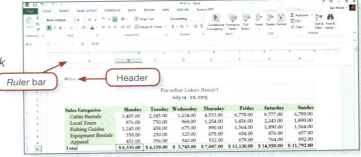

1-59 *Page Layout* view

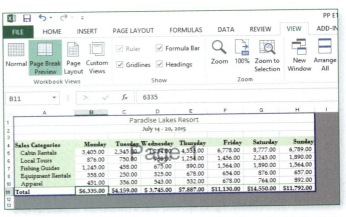

1-60 *Page Break Preview*

1-61 *Full Screen* view

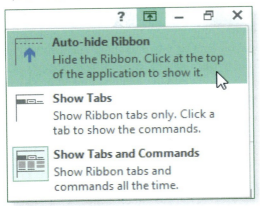

1-62 *Ribbon Display Options*

7. Click **Ribbon Display Options** and choose **Show Tabs and Commands** to display the *Ribbon* and tab commands.

▶ **ANOTHER WAY**

Use the *Status bar* buttons in the bottom right corner of the window to switch views.

Zoom Options

You can change a window's zoom level to see more of its content (zoom out) or to read the content more easily (zoom in). Zoom controls increase or decrease the magnification of the spreadsheet contents. You can increase or decrease the zoom level using *Zoom* in the *Zoom* group on the *View* tab (Figure 1-63) or the zoom controls on the *Status bar*.

1-63 *View* tab, *Zoom* options

HOW TO: Increase Zoom Using the Ribbon

1. Click the **Zoom** button [*View* tab, *Zoom* group].
   - The *Zoom* dialog box opens.
2. Click to select the radio button next to the desired *Magnification*.
   - Select **Fit selection** for a range of cells to fill the entire screen.
   - Choose **Custom** to enter an exact magnification (Figure 1-64).
3. Click **OK** to see the change in magnification in your workbook.

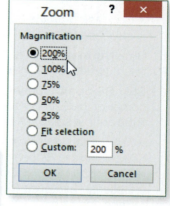

> **ANOTHER WAY**
>
> Other useful buttons are located in the *Zoom* group on the *View* tab: **100%** and **Zoom to Selection**. The *100%* option returns the magnification to the default. The *Zoom to Selection* option fills the entire screen with the range of cells selected in the worksheet.

1-64 *Zoom* dialog box

Freeze Panes

When spreadsheets are magnified or contain multiple pages, it is difficult to see all of the information on the same screen. You can use scroll bars to move to those sections that are not immediately in view, but this process is tedious if you have to scroll repeatedly. You can also *Freeze Panes* so that column and row headings display whether you are at the top, bottom, left, or right of the spreadsheet. When you apply the freeze option, the Excel window is split into one or more panes, and displays multiple areas of a spreadsheet. A darker border displays when a row or column is frozen.

HOW TO: Freeze Panes Using the Ribbon

1. Select a cell in the worksheet that is located below the rows and to the right of the columns you want to freeze.
2. Click the **Freeze Panes** button [*View* tab, *Window* group].
   - Choose **Freeze Panes** to keep rows and columns visible.
   - Select **Freeze Top Row** to keep the top row visible.
   - Choose **Freeze First Column** to keep the first column visible.
3. Select **Freeze Panes** (Figure 1-65).
   - All rows above the active cell are frozen, and all columns to the left of the active cell are frozen.

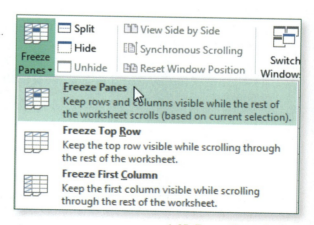

1-65 *Freeze Panes* button

4. Use the right horizontal scrolling arrow to view other columns of information.
   - Notice the row headings do not move (Figure 1-66).
5. Use the down vertical scrolling arrow to view the last row of data.
   - Notice the column headings remain constant.
6. Click the **Freeze Panes** button [*View* tab, *Window* group].
   - A new option, *Unfreeze Panes*, displays.
7. Select **Unfreeze Panes** to return the workbook to its original viewing state.

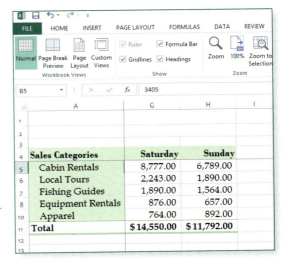

1-66 *Freeze Panes* view results

Split a Worksheet into Panes

You can use the split feature to show different parts of the same spreadsheet in separate panes. The split feature can divide a worksheet into two or four scrollable windows (panes) that you can view simultaneously. You can scroll and edit each window independently and size the panes by dragging the *Splitter bar*.

HOW TO: Split a Worksheet into Panes

1. Select the row, column, or cell where you want to split a worksheet into panes.
   - Click a cell to split a worksheet into four panes.
   - Click the first cell in the row or column to split a worksheet into two panes.
2. Click the **Split** button [*View* tab, *Window* group].
3. Adjust the size of the panes by pointing to the *Splitter bar* and dragging to reposition the splitter bar (Figure 1-67).
4. Click the **Splitter** button [*View* tab, *Window* group] to remove the splitter bar.

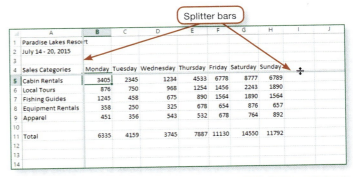

1-67 Split worksheet

Hide or Unhide Worksheets

When worksheets contain confidential information, you can hide the sheets without affecting the worksheet data or calculations in the sheet. Hidden worksheets do not appear in a printout. You can hide a worksheet using the *Ribbon* or by right-clicking a sheet tab. You cannot hide a sheet if there is only one sheet in the workbook.

HOW TO: Hide and Unhide Worksheets

1. Click the sheet tab you want to hide.
   - You can use the **Ctrl** key to select multiple sheets to hide.
2. Click the **Home** tab.
3. Click the **Format** button [*Cells* group] and choose **Hide & Unhide** in the *Visibility* group.
4. Select **Hide Sheet**. The worksheet tab does not display.
5. Click the **Format** button [*Cells* group] and choose **Hide & Unhide** in the *Visibility* group.
6. Click **Unhide Sheet** to open the *Unhide* dialog box (Figure 1-68).
7. Select the worksheet to unhide.
   - When multiple sheets are hidden, you must unhide each sheet individually.
8. Click **OK**.

1-68 *Unhide* dialog box

> ### ANOTHER WAY
> To hide the worksheet, right-click the worksheet you want to hide and choose **Hide** from the context menu. To unhide the worksheet, right click a worksheet tab and choose **Unhide**. Select the worksheet to unhide.

You can hide an open workbook window by clicking the **View** tab and clicking the **Hide** button. To unhide a workbook, click the **View** tab and click the **Unhide** button.

Switch Windows Option

The *Switch Windows* feature is useful for viewing or editing multiple open workbooks.

HOW TO: Switch Windows Using the Ribbon

1. Verify that you have more than one workbook open.
2. Click the **Switch Windows** button [*View* tab, *Window* group].
   - A list of open workbooks displays.
3. Select the workbook you want to view.
   - You can view workbooks side-by-side by selecting **View Side by Side** [*View* tab, *Window* group] (Figure 1-69).
   - The *Synchronous Scrolling* option is available when viewing two workbooks side by side. *Synchronous Scrolling* scrolls both files in the same direction at the same time. It is useful for editing different versions of similar spreadsheets or sharing information between two different workbooks.
4. Click **Maximize** to restore a workbook to full size.

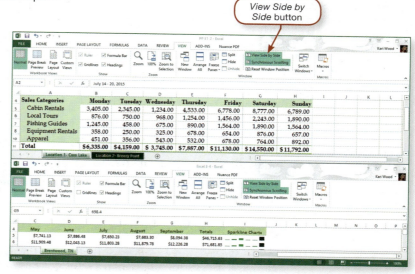

1-69 *View Side by Side*

View Multiple Worksheets at the Same Time

You can view multiple worksheets at the same time. Use the *New Window* feature to open a second window and to view different parts of the same worksheet. Use the *Arrange All* feature to position open windows. Click **Maximize** to restore a workbook to full size.

HOW TO: View Multiple Worksheets at the Same Time

1. Verify that you have more than one workbook open.
2. Click **Arrange All** [*View* tab, *Window* group] to open the *Arrange Windows* dialog box (Figure 1-70).
3. Choose an option to display more than one workbook: *Tiled, Horizontal, Vertical,* or *Cascade.*
4. Click **OK**.
5. Click **Maximize** to restore a workbook to full size.
6. Click the **View** tab, and click **New Window**.
   - A second window of the worksheet displays. Notice the change in the title bar. Each window displays a number after the name of the workbook.
7. Click **Arrange All** [*View* tab, *Window* group].
8. Choose **Vertical** in the *Arrange Windows* dialog box.
9. Select the **Windows of active workbook** check box.
10. Click **OK**.
11. Scroll the windows to display cells to edit.
12. **Close** the windows.

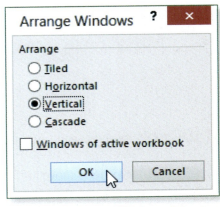

1-70 *Arrange Windows* dialog box

Finalizing a Workbook

After customizing your workbook content, structure, and format, Excel provides you with features to finalize your workbook. It's important to spell check a workbook for accuracy before printing or sending to others. You can also add document properties and a header and footer to your worksheet for document identification. If you are working with a large worksheet, you can customize page breaks and how your worksheet prints.

Check Spelling

The **Spelling** feature scans a worksheet and locates words that do not match entries in its main dictionary. You can add entries to the main dictionary such as proper names or technical terms. Duplicated words are also identified when you check spelling. You can check an entire worksheet or a selected range of cells. If you are not at the beginning of your worksheet, Excel starts spell checking at the active cell and checks to the end of the worksheet. When it reaches the end of the worksheet, a dialog box displays and asks if you want to continue checking at the beginning of the sheet. The *Spelling* dialog box displays several options when Excel finds an error. The following table describes each option.

Spelling Dialog Box Options

Option	Action
Ignore Once	Skips the word
Ignore All	Skips all occurrences of the word in the spreadsheet
Add to Dictionary	Adds the word to the default dictionary file. You can also create a custom dictionary.
Change	Changes the word to the entry you choose in the *Suggestions* box
Change All	Same as *Change*, but changes the word throughout the worksheet
Delete	Appears for duplicated words. Click to delete one occurrence of the word.
AutoCorrect	Adds the word to the list of corrections Excel makes automatically
Options	Changes the spelling options in Excel
Undo Last	Changes back to the most recent correction made
Cancel	Discontinues the checking operation

HOW TO: Spell Check a Worksheet

1. Press **Ctrl+Home** to move to the beginning of the worksheet.
2. Click the **Review** tab and click the **Spelling** button [*Proofing* group] (Figure 1-71).
3. Use the buttons on the right to change or ignore each identified error.
   - If a recommendation that is acceptable does not appear in the *Suggestions* box, edit the *Not in Dictionary* text box and click **Change**.

1-71 *Spelling* dialog box

Document Properties

Document Properties are details that you can add to any Office file. Document properties are also called ***metadata***, and you can use them to organize or to gather basic information about workbooks. Several properties are created automatically by Excel including *Creation* date, *Modified* date, *Accessed* date, and file *Size*. You can edit other document properties, such as *Title, Author, Comments, Subject,* and *Company*. You can view or edit document properties using *Backstage* view, displaying the *Document Panel,* or opening the *Property* dialog box.

HOW TO: Add Document Properties

1. Click the **File** tab to display *Backstage* view.
2. Click **Info** if it is not already selected (Figure 1-72).
   - Document property field names are listed on the left and the property fields are listed on the right.
3. Click a field property and type or edit the entry.
4. Click the **Show All/Show Fewer Properties** link at the bottom to display more or fewer document property fields.

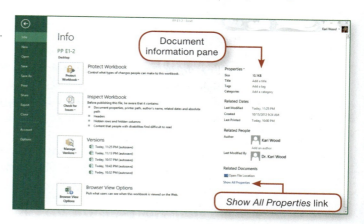

1-72 Workbook properties

Document Panel

You can view and edit document properties using the *Document* panel in *Normal, Page Layout,* or *Page Break Preview* views. The panel appears above the *Formula bar* and below the *Ribbon* (Figure 1-73). To display the *Document* panel, use the *Backstage* view. Close the *Document* panel by clicking the *Document* panel close button.

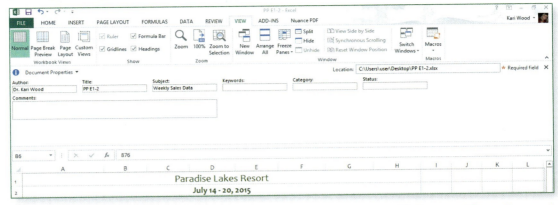

1-73 *Document Properties* panel

HOW TO: Display the Document Properties Panel

1. Click **File** to display *Backstage* view.
2. Click **Info** if it is not already selected.
3. Click the **Properties** drop-down list at the top of the *Properties* pane (Figure 1-74).
4. Select **Show Document Panel**.
   - The *Backstage* view closes and the *Document* panel displays above the *Formula bar* in the Excel window.
5. Edit or add text in the *Document Properties* fields.
6. Click **X** in the upper right corner of the *Document* panel to close the panel.

1-74 *Show Document Panel*

Advanced Properties

The ***Advanced Properties*** option displays the *Properties* dialog box. You can open the *Properties* dialog box using the *Backstage* view or the *Document* panel (Figure 1-75).

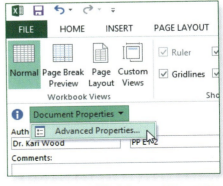

1-75 *Advanced Properties*

HOW TO: Open the Properties Dialog Box

1. Display the *Backstage* view and click **Info**.
2. Click the **Properties** button to display the drop-down list (see Figure 1-74).
3. Select **Advanced Properties**. The *Properties* dialog box opens (Figure 1-76).
   - The *General*, *Statistics*, and *Contents* tabs provide document properties that are automatically created by Excel.
   - The *Summary* and *Custom* tabs allow you to edit fields.
   - Use the *Custom* tab to add custom document property fields to your workbook.

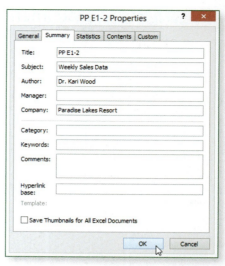

1-76 *Properties* dialog box

Page Layout

The *Page Layout* tab includes options that allow you to control the appearance of your worksheet such as margins, page orientation, and paper size (Figure 1-77). You can also use the *Page Setup* dialog box to customize worksheet settings (Figure 1-78). To view page layout changes, you can preview or print the worksheet.

Open the *Page Setup* dialog box to change multiple page setup options at one time. Click the **Page Setup**, **Scale to Fit**, or **Sheet Options** launcher on the *Page Layout* tab to open the *Page Setup* dialog box (see Figure 1-78). The following table describes each of the tabs in the *Page Setup* dialog box.

1-77 Customize page setup and print options

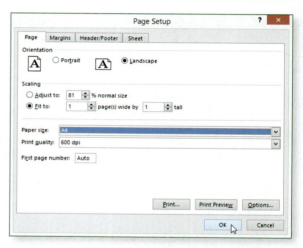

1-78 *Page* tab in the *Page Setup* dialog box

Page Setup Dialog Box Options

Tab	Tab Options
Page	Set the *Orientation* to *Portrait* or *Landscape*. *Scaling* adjusts the size of the printed worksheet as a percentage of the normal size, or you can use *Fit to* area to scale the worksheet to print on a specific number of pages. Use the *Paper size* drop-down list to select a paper size (see Figure 1-78).
Margins	Set the *Top*, *Bottom*, *Left*, and *Right* margins of the worksheet. You can also set the margins for the header and footer text in the worksheet. In the *Center on page* area, check the *Horizontally* and/or *Vertically* boxes to center the data in the worksheet on a printed page (see Figure 1-79).
Header/Footer	Add and customize headers and footers in the worksheet.
Sheet	Set the *Print area* by selecting a specified range of cells. In the *Print titles* area, you can designate certain rows or columns to repeat each time spreadsheet data spans more than one page. You can also specify printing options such as printing titles, gridlines, and row and column headings.

Margins, Page Orientation, and Paper Size

The default settings for page layout for an Excel spreadsheet include the following:

- Top and bottom margins: 0.75
- Left and right margins: 0.7
- Header and footer margins: 0.3
- Portrait orientation
- Letter size paper

You can modify each of these settings for individual worksheets or multiple worksheets. To format multiple worksheets, select the worksheet tabs. Use **Shift** to select adjacent sheets. Use **Ctrl** to select non-adjacent sheets. Right-click a sheet tab and choose **Select All Sheets** to format an entire workbook. When changing margin settings, the top and bottom margin settings must be greater than the header and footer values or the worksheet data prints over the header and footer text.

HOW TO: Customize Margins, Page Orientation, and Paper Size

1. Click the **Margins** button [*Page Layout* tab, *Page Setup* group] and select a preset option from the drop-down list.
   - Select **Custom Margins** from the *Margins* drop-down list to open the *Page Setup* dialog box to enter a precise measurement (Figure 1-79).
   - Select the **Horizontally** and/or **Vertically** check boxes in the *Center on Page* area to center your worksheet [*Page Setup* dialog box, *Margins* tab]. *Horizontally* centers data between the left and right margins. *Vertically* centers data between the top and bottom margins.

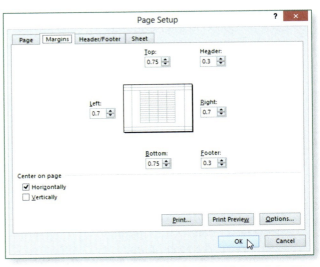

1-79 *Margins* tab in the *Page Setup* dialog box

2. Click the **Orientation** button [*Page Layout* tab, *Page Setup* group] and select **Portrait** or **Landscape** from the drop-down list.
   - When you select *Portrait*, the page is taller than it is wide; if you select *Landscape*, the page is wider than it is tall.
   - Use the *Page* tab in the *Page Setup* dialog box to change the page orientation.
   - You can also change orientation when you are ready to print. Select an option from the *Page Orientation* drop-down list in the *Print* area on the *Backstage* view.

3. Click the **Size** button [*Page Layout* tab, *Page Setup* group] and select a paper size from the drop-down list.
   - The default paper size is 8 ½"×11", which is called *Letter*.
   - Click **More Paper Sizes** to open the *Page Setup* dialog box.

Headers and Footers

Headers appear at the top of the worksheet in the *Header* area, while **footers** appear in the *Footer* area at the bottom of the worksheet. Each header and footer area has a left, middle, and right section where you can insert a page number, file name, date, or other information in text boxes.

Note that headers and footers appear on the worksheets only when you choose to add them. They do not appear on every sheet automatically. To add headers and footers to multiple worksheets at one time, select the worksheet tabs and open the *Page Setup* dialog box. Headers and footers do not display in *Normal* view. To view header and footer text, switch to *Print Layout* view or *Print Preview*.

HOW TO: Insert a Header and Footer Using the Ribbon

1. Select the worksheet.
2. Click the **Insert** tab.
3. Click the **Header & Footer** button [*Text* group].
   - The worksheet view changes to *Page Layout* view.
   - The header displays three text boxes. Information entered in the left text box is left aligned, text in the middle text box is centered, and text in the right text box is right aligned.
4. Click a text box in the header area.
   - Clicking a header or footer text box displays the *Header & Footer Tools Design* tab.
5. Click the **Design** tab to activate it (Figure 1-80).
6. Click an option in the *Header & Footer Elements* group [*Header & Footer Tools Design* tab].
   - A field is inserted with an ampersand (&) followed by the code enclosed in brackets.
   - If the header or footer contains text, you can edit or delete the contents.
   - To insert a pre-defined header or footer such as the page number or worksheet name, click the **Header** or **Footer** button [*Header & Footer Tools Design* tab, *Header & Footer* group].
7. Click **Go To Footer** [*Header & Footer Tools Design* tab, *Navigation* group].
8. Click one of the text boxes in the footer area.

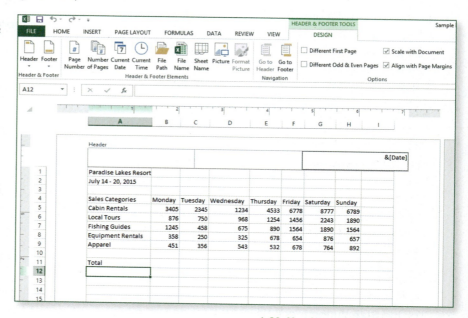

1-80 *Header area in Page Layout view*

9. Type text or click an element [*Header & Footer Elements* group].
   - If the text you type includes an ampersand (&), type two ampersands (&&) to distinguish text from the header or footer code. For example, you type "Research && Development" to display "Research & Development".
10. Scroll to the top of the worksheet and then click any cell to close the header and footer area.
    - The header and footer text displays in *Page Layout* view.
11. Switch to **Normal** view.
    - The header and footer are not visible in *Normal* view.

You can insert headers and footers using the *Page Setup* dialog box. One advantage of using the *Page Setup* dialog box to insert headers or footers is that this option allows you to add headers or footers to multiple sheets. The *Page Setup* dialog box includes preset header and footer fields located in the *Custom Header* or *Custom Footer* drop-down lists on the *Header/Footer* tab.

HOW TO: Insert Headers or Footers Using the Page Setup Dialog Box

1. Click the worksheet tab (or tabs if applying the header or footer to multiple sheets).
   - To select two or more adjacent worksheets, use **Shift**.
   - To select two or more nonadjacent sheets, use **Ctrl**.
   - To select all worksheets in the workbook, right-click a tab and click **Select All Sheets**.

2. Click the **Page Layout** tab and then click the **Page Setup** launcher [*Page Setup* group].
   - The *Page Setup* dialog box displays.

3. Select the **Header/Footer** tab.

4. Click the drop-down arrow for the *Header* or *Footer* text box to see a list of predefined headers or footers (Figure 1-81).
   - Scroll to see additional options.

5. Choose **(none)** to create a new header or footer.

6. Click the **Custom Header** or **Custom Footer** button to open the *Header* or *Footer* dialog box (Figure 1-82).

7. Type text in the *Left* section, *Center* section, or *Right* section, or click a button to insert a field code.
   - Each button has a *ScreenTip* to identify the button (Figure 1-83).

8. Click **OK** to close the *Header or Footer* dialog box.
   - The information appears in the *Header or Footer* text box.

9. Click **OK** to close the *Page Setup* dialog box.

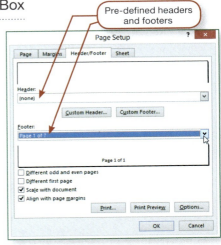

1-81 *Header/Footer* tab in the *Page Setup* dialog box

1-82 *Header* dialog box

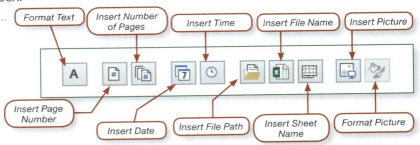

1-83 Buttons to insert header and footer content

Figure 1-83 displays the buttons available in the *Header* and *Footer* dialog boxes. When you click the *Format Text, Insert Picture,* or *Format Picture* button, another dialog box opens that provides you with additional options.

There are two ways to remove a header or footer. One method uses the *Page Setup* dialog box and the other uses the *Text* group on the *Insert* tab. Remember to use the *Page Setup* dialog box method to remove headers and footers from multiple sheets.

HOW TO: Remove Headers and Footers

1. Select the worksheet.
2. Click the **Page Layout** tab and click the **Page Setup** launcher.
3. Click the **Header/Footer** tab.
4. Click the **Header** or **Footer** drop-down list and select **(none)** (Figure 1-84).
5. Click **OK** to close the *Page Setup* dialog box.

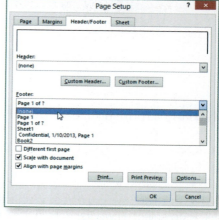

1-84 *Footer* drop-down list

> ### ANOTHER WAY
>
> To remove a header or footer, click the **Insert** tab and click **Header & Footer** [*Text* group]. Click the left, right, or center area, select the header or footer text, and press **Delete** or **Backspace**.

Page Breaks

When you complete a workbook you can preview the content before printing or distributing the workbook electronically. If the worksheet data is larger than one page, page breaks are inserted automatically. Paper size, margins, and scale options control the position of automatic page breaks. You can manually insert page breaks to change the number of rows or columns printed on the page. Use *Page Break Preview* to insert page breaks, move page breaks, or remove page breaks. Manual page breaks display as a solid line. Automatic page breaks display as a dotted or dashed line.

HOW TO: Insert a Page Break

1. Select the location to insert a page break.
   - Click the row below where you want to insert a horizontal page break.
   - Click the column to the right of where you want to insert a vertical page break.
   - Click the cell below and to the right of where you want to insert a horizontal and vertical page break.
2. Click the **Page Layout** tab.
3. Click the **Breaks** button (Figure 1-85).
4. Select **Insert Page Break**.
   - The page break displays as a solid line.

1-85 *Breaks* options

> ### ANOTHER WAY
>
> To insert a page break, right-click a row or column and choose **Insert Page Break** from the context menu.

Preview and Move a Page Break

In *Normal* view, you can use the *Breaks* command to insert, remove, and reset page breaks. You cannot drag page breaks to another location in *Normal* view. Use *Page Break Preview* to move a page break. Moving an automatic page break changes it to a manual page break.

HOW TO: Preview and Move a Page Break

1. Click the **View** tab.

2. Click the **Page Break Preview** button (Figure 1-86).

3. Drag the page break (solid line) to a new location.

   • The pointer changes to a resize pointer (two-pointed arrow) while dragging the page break.

4. Return to *Normal* view [*View* tab, *Workbook Views* group].

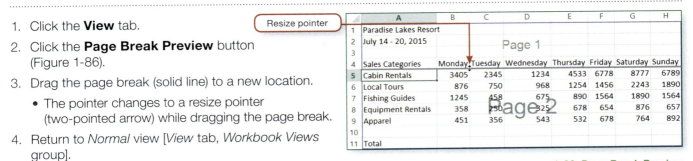

1-86 *Page Break Preview*

Remove a Manual Page Break

To remove a manual page break, use *Page Break Preview*. You cannot delete an automatic page break. You can, however, reposition an automatic page break by inserting or deleting columns and rows, changing page orientation, or adjusting column width and row height.

HOW TO: Remove a Manual Page Break

1. Switch to **Page Break Preview** [*View* tab, *Workbook Views* group].

2. Select the column or row next to the page break to be removed.

   • To delete a vertical page break, select the column to the right of the page break.
   • To delete a horizontal page break, select the row below the page break.

3. Click **Breaks** [*Page Layout* tab, *Page Setup* group] (Figure 1-87).

4. Click **Remove Page Break**.

   • To remove all manual page breaks, click **Reset All Page Breaks**.

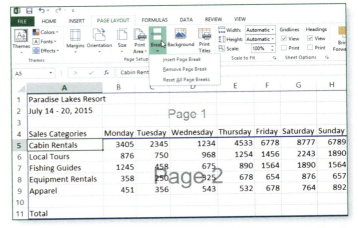

1-87 **Remove page break**

Customize Worksheet Printing

You can print an entire workbook, a single worksheet, or a section of a worksheet. You can also control the appearance of the printout by displaying gridlines, printing column letters and row numbers, or including titles that repeat on each page.

HOW TO: Print Titles, Gridlines, Column Letters, and Row Numbers

1. Click the **Page Layout** tab and locate the *Sheet Options* group (Figure 1-88).

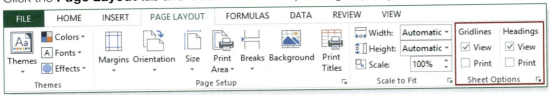

1-88 *Sheet Options*

2. Select the **Print** checkbox under *Gridlines*.

3. Select the **Print** checkbox under *Headings*.

   • Both *Gridlines* and *Row and column headings* are available in the *Print* area on the *Sheet* tab in the *Page Setup* dialog box.

4. Click the **Print Titles** button [*Page Layout* tab, *Page Setup* group] to open the *Page Setup* dialog box.

5. Click the **Rows to repeat at top** text box (Figure 1-89).

6. Drag to select the row or rows to repeat.

   • You can also type the reference of the row(s) that contains the column labels. For example, type $1:$1 to repeat the first row. Type $1:$2 to repeat the first two rows.

7. Click the **Columns to repeat at left** text box.

8. Click column **A** to select the column.

   • A second method is to type the reference of the column that contains the row labels. Type $A:$A to repeat the first column.

9. Click **OK**.

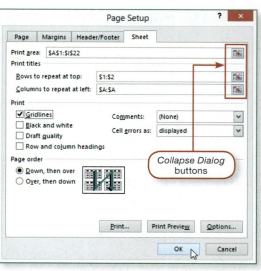

1-89 *Sheet* tab in the *Page Setup* dialog box

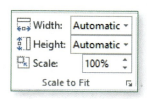

> ▶ **ANOTHER WAY**
>
> Click the **Collapse Dialog** button on the right side of *Rows to repeat at top* or *Columns to repeat at left* and select the rows or columns to repeat. Click the **Collapse Dialog** button again to expand the *Page Setup* dialog box.

Scale to Fit

The **Scale to Fit** feature expands or reduces a worksheet to fit on a specific number of pages or a specific paper size. You can adjust the worksheet as a percentage of the normal size or change the height or width values.

HOW TO: Scale to Fit

1. Click the **Page Layout** tab.

2. Select a scaling option [*Scale to Fit* group] (Figure 1-90).

   • Click the **Width** drop-down list and select the number of pages.
   • Click the **Height** drop-down list and select the number of pages.
   • Click the **Scale** up and down arrows to scale the worksheet a percentage of the normal size (100%).
   • You can also click the **Scale to Fit** launcher to display the *Page* tab in the *Page Setup* dialog box where you can make adjustments in the *Scaling* area (Figure 1-91).

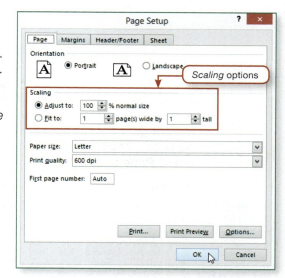

1-90 *Scale to Fit* options

1-91 *Scaling* options in the *Page Setup* dialog box

Print Area

The **print area** is the section of the worksheet that prints. A print area consists of a single cell or a range of cells. You can add cells to a print area and you can clear the print area in order to print an entire worksheet.

HOW TO: Set and Clear Print Area

1. Select the cells to print.
   - Use **Ctrl** and drag to select multiple print areas.
2. Click the **Page Layout** tab.
3. Click the **Print Area** button [*Page Setup* group] (Figure 1-92).
4. Select **Set Print Area**.
   - Change the view to *Page Break Preview* to see the print area.
   - A print area is saved when the workbook is saved.
5. To enlarge the print area, select adjacent cells, click the **Print Area** button [*Page Layout* tab, *Page Setup* group], and then select **Add to Print Area**.
   - Switch to *Page Break Preview* to view the print area.
6. To clear the print area, click the **Print Area** button [*Page Layout* tab, *Page Setup* group] and select **Clear Print Area**.

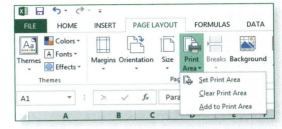

1-92 *Print Area* options

> **ANOTHER WAY**
>
> You can print part of a worksheet using the *Page Setup* dialog box. Display the **Page Setup** dialog box and select the **Sheet** tab. Type the cell range to print in the *Print area* text box. Click **OK**.

Print a Worksheet or Workbook

Once you complete a worksheet, you can preview the worksheet to verify layout and formatting changes. There are two ways to preview a worksheet. One way is to click the **File** tab and then click **Print**. The other way is to open the *Page Setup* dialog box and click **Print Preview**.

HOW TO: Preview and Print a Worksheet

1. Click the **File** tab.
2. Click **Print** (Figure 1-93). A preview of your worksheet appears on the right.
   - If the workbook is more than one page, use the **Next Page** and **Previous Page** arrows to review each page.
   - Click **Show Margins** to manually adjust the header and page margins.
   - Click **Zoom to Page** to adjust the zoom level.
3. In the *Copies* area, set the number of copies to print.
4. Select an option to print the active sheet, print the entire workbook, or print a selection.
5. Specify the pages to print.
6. Verify orientation, paper size, and margin settings.
7. Click the **Page Setup** link to display the *Page Setup* dialog box and adjust settings.
8. Click **Print**.

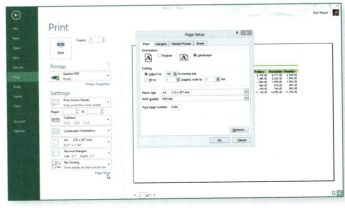

1-93 *Backstage* view: *Page Setup* dialog box

PAUSE & PRACTICE: EXCEL 1-4

For this project, you open your previous Pause & Practice file (*[your initials] PP E1-3.xlsx*) and change the display and view options, hide and unhide rows and worksheets, add document properties, and apply page setup formatting to finalize your Paradise Lakes Resorts workbook.

File Needed: *[your initials] PP E1-3.xlsx*
Completed Project File Name: *[your initials] PP E1-4.xlsx*

1. Open the *[your initials] PP E1-3* workbook.

2. Save the workbook as *[your initials] PP E1-4*.

3. Select the **Location 1 – Cass Lake worksheet**.

4. Unhide row 9 from the previous Pause & Practice (the "Food & Beverage" row).
   a. Drag to select row headings **8** and **10**.
   b. Right-click one of the selected row headings.
   c. Choose **Unhide** from the context menu. Row 9 appears between rows 8 and 10.

5. Enter the following "Food & Beverage" data in row 9 for the cell range **B9:H9**.

	B	C	D	E	F	G	H
9	254.00	209.00	198.00	402.00	519.00	677.00	399.00

6. Increase the zoom to 150%.
   a. Click the **Zoom** button [*View* tab, *Zoom* group].
   b. The *Zoom* dialog box opens.
   c. Select the **Custom** radio button and enter 150 for the magnification.
   d. Click **OK** to see the change in magnification in your workbook.

7. Use *Freeze Panes* in the worksheet.
   a. Select **B5** in the worksheet.
   b. Click the **Freeze Panes** button [*View* tab, *Window* group].
   c. Choose the **Freeze Panes** option.
   d. Use the right horizontal scrolling arrow to view the last two columns of information (Figure 1-94).

8. Hide a worksheet.
   a. Click the **View** tab and click the **100%** zoom button [*Zoom* group].
   b. Click the **Freeze Panes** button and select **Unfreeze Panes**.
   c. Right-click the **Location 2** worksheet tab.
   d. Select **Hide**.

	A	G	H
1			
2			
3			
4	**Sales Categories**	**Saturday**	**Sunday**
5	Cabin Rentals	8,777.00	6,789.00
6	Local Tours	2,243.00	1,890.00
7	Fishing Guides	1,890.00	1,564.00
8	Equipment Rentals	876.00	657.00
9	Food & Beverage	677.00	399.00
10	Apparel	764.00	892.00
11	**Total**	$ 15,227.00	$ 12,191.00

1-94 *Freeze Panes* view

9. Check the spelling of the worksheet.
   a. Click the **Spelling** button [*Review* tab, *Proofing* group].
   b. Correct any misspelled words in the worksheet.

10. Add document properties using the *Document Properties* panel.
    a. Click the **File** tab to display *Backstage* view.
    b. Click **Info** if it is not already selected.
    c. Click the **Properties** drop-down list at the top of the *Properties* pane and select **Show Document Panel**. The *Backstage* view closes and the *Document* Panel displays above the *Formula bar* in the Excel window.
    d. Add text in the following *Document Properties* fields (Figure 1-95):

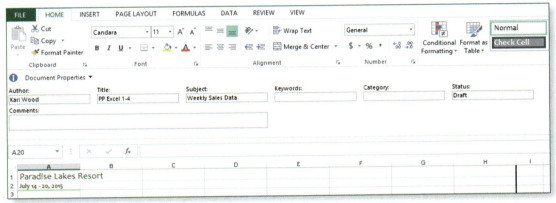

1-95 *Document* Panel

   Title: PP Excel 1-4
   Subject: Weekly Sales Data
   Status: Draft

    f. Click the **X** in the upper right corner of the *Document* Panel to close the panel.

11. Change page setup options.
    a. Click the **Page Layout** tab.
    b. Click the **Orientation** button and select **Landscape**.
    c. Click the **Page Setup** launcher to display the *Page Setup* dialog box and select the **Margins** tab.
    d. Click the **Horizontally** check box in the *Center on page* area.
    e. Click **OK** to close the *Page Setup* dialog box.

12. Add a header and footer.
    a. Click the **Page Layout** tab.
    b. Open the *Page Setup* dialog box by clicking the **Page Setup** launcher.
    c. Click the **Header/Footer** tab.
    d. Click the **Header** drop-down list and select **[your initials] PP E1-4**. The name of the file displays in the header.
    e. Click the **Footer** drop-down list and select **Page 1** to insert a page number in the footer.
    f. Click **OK** to close the *Page Setup* dialog box.

13. Select the print area and preview the worksheet.
    a. Select the cell range **A1:H11**.
    b. Select the **Page Layout** tab.
    c. Click the **Print Area** button and select **Set Print Area**.
    d. Deselect the text.
    e. Click the **File** tab and select **Print**. The workbook *Print Preview* displays.

14. Save and close the workbook (Figure 1-96).

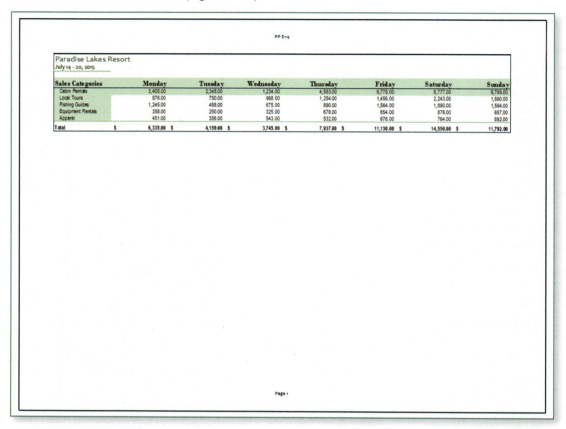

PP E1-4

Paradise Lakes Resort							
July 14 - 20, 2015							
Sales Categories	Monday	Tuesday	Wednesday	Thursday	Friday	Saturday	Sunday
Cabin Rentals	3,405.00	2,345.00	1,234.00	4,583.00	6,778.00	8,777.00	6,789.00
Local Tours	876.00	750.00	968.00	1,254.00	1,456.00	2,243.00	1,890.00
Fishing Guides	1,245.00	458.00	675.00	890.00	1,564.00	1,890.00	1,564.00
Equipment Rentals	358.00	250.00	325.00	678.00	654.00	876.00	657.00
Apparel	451.00	356.00	543.00	532.00	678.00	764.00	892.00
Total	$ 6,335.00	$ 4,159.00	$ 3,745.00	$ 7,937.00	$ 11,130.00	$ 14,550.00	$ 11,792.00

Page 1

1-96 PP E1-4 completed

Chapter Summary

1.1 Create, save, and open an Excel workbook (p. E1-3).

- When you create a blank workbook, Excel automatically assigns a file name to the file, such as *Book1*.
- You can save an Excel workbook in a variety of formats. By default, Excel workbooks are saved as *.xlsx* files.
- From the **Share** and **Export** areas of *Backstage* view, you have the option of saving in different online locations and saving a workbook as a PDF document.
- You can open workbooks from your computer, external storage device, or *SkyDrive*.

1.2 Edit a workbook by entering and deleting text, using the *Fill Handle* to complete a series, and using the cut, copy, and paste features (p. E1-6).

- When creating or editing a workbook, you can type data, import data from another file, or copy data from a web page or another source.
- Excel uses multiple pointers to indicate various selection, copying, resizing and moving options within a worksheet.
- Excel recognizes any combination of letters, numbers, spaces, and other characters as text and aligns each entry to the bottom left corner of the cell. Numeric entries align at the bottom right corner of the cell.
- Vertical alignment options include *Top Align, Middle Align,* and *Bottom Align.* Horizontal alignment options include *Align Left, Center,* and *Align Right.*
- Use the **Fill Handle** to complete lists, repeat numeric patterns, or copy cell contents to another location.
- Cut, copy, and paste data using the ***drag and drop*** method; **Cut**, **Copy**, and **Paste** buttons on the *Home* tab; the context menu; or shortcut keys on the keyboard.

1.3 Create a basic formula using *AutoSum* (p. E1-16).

- ***AutoSum*** is a button that automates the *Sum* function and other popular functions. *Sum* is used for adding values in a range.
- To adjust the cell range in a formula, use the *Formula bar* or drag the cell range border to reduce or expand the range.

1.4 Format a worksheet using different font attributes, borders, shading, cell styles, themes, and the *Format Painter* (p. E1-19).

- The default format for worksheet entries is 11 pt. Calibri.
- Customize font attributes using the *Font* group on the *Ribbon* or opening the *Format Cells* dialog box. You can change the **Font Face**, **Font Size**, **Font Style**, and **Font Type** in a single cell, a group of cells, a worksheet, or an entire workbook.
- Add borders, shading, and number formatting to a worksheet to improve readability and to add emphasis.
- The **Format Painter** option allows you to copy formatting attributes and styles from one cell to another.
- Use **Cell Styles** to format a worksheet attractively using predefined settings such as alignment, color, borders, and fill color.
- Apply ***themes*** to a workbook for consistency in color, font, and effects.

1.5 Resize, insert, delete, and hide and unhide columns and rows in a worksheet (p. E1-26).

- Control the display of data by adjusting column width or row height.
- Two methods you can use to insert or delete columns and rows are the context menu and the **Insert** or **Delete** button.
- Display multiple lines in a cell using **Wrap Text** or use **Merge & Center** to combine two or more cells.
- You can hide sensitive data in a column or incomplete information in a row using the context menu or the *Format* button.

1.6 Insert, delete, edit, format, and rearrange worksheets (p. E1-31).

- The number of worksheets contained in a workbook is limited only by the amount of your computer memory.
- The default names for the sheets within a workbook are *Sheet1, Sheet2,* and so on.
- The two methods you can use to insert or delete worksheets are the context menu and the **Insert** or **Delete** buttons.
- The context menu and the *Format* button include options to **Move** and **Copy** worksheets.

1.7 Customize the Excel window by changing views, adjusting zoom level, freezing panes, and splitting a worksheet (p. E1-36).

- Excel has three main views: **Normal**, **Page Layout**, and **Page Break Preview**.
- Display options such as **Zoom**, **Freeze Panes**, **Gridlines**, and **Headings** can help make larger spreadsheets easier to view.
- You can **Hide** and **Unhide** sheets if they include sensitive data.

1.8 Finalize a workbook by spell checking, adding document properties, applying page setup options, and printing (p. E1-41).

- Check spelling using the *Review* tab.
- Various **Document Properties** are created automatically. These include *Creation* date, *Modified* date, *Accessed* date, and file *Size*. You can add properties such as *Title*, *Author*, *Comments*, *Subject*, and *Company*.
- The *Document Information Panel* on the right side of *Backstage* view displays details that are available for update or change.
- The **Advanced Properties** option in the *Document Information* panel displays the *Properties* dialog box.
- Use *Page Setup* options to customize page layout settings and print preview to review worksheets.

Check for Understanding

In the **Online Learning Center** for this text (www.mhhe.com/office2013inpractice), there are a variety of resources that can be used to review the concepts covered in this chapter.

The following Online Learning Resources are available on the Online Learning Center:

- Multiple choice questions
- Short answer questions
- Matching exercises

Guided Project 1-1

Abdul Kohl has just been hired at Life's Animal Shelter and asked to track the organization's weekly expenses on a spreadsheet.
[Student Learning Outcomes 1.1, 1.2, 1.3, 1.4, 1.5, 1.6, 1.8]

File Needed: None
Completed Project File Name: *[your initials] Excel 1-1.xlsx*

Skills Covered in This Project

- Create and save a workbook.
- Enter text and numbers.
- Change font size and attributes.
- Create a formula using *AutoSum*.
- Use the *Fill Handle*.
- Apply *Cell Styles*.
- Apply a theme.
- Apply page layout options.

- Insert a row and adjust column width and row height.
- Rename and apply color to sheet tabs.
- Merge and center titles.
- Apply number formatting.
- Insert and delete sheets.
- Use spell check.

1. Open a new workbook.
   a. Click the **File** tab to open the *Backstage* view.
   b. Click **New** and then click **Blank workbook** to open a new blank workbook.

2. Save the workbook as *[your initials] Excel 1-1*.
   a. Press **F12** to open the *Save As* dialog box.
   b. Rename the file *[your initials] Excel 1-1* in the *File name* area.
   c. Select the folder or **Browse** to the location on your *SkyDrive*, computer, or storage device to save the workbook.
   d. Click **Save**.

3. Enter the data.
   a. Select **A1**, type Life's Animal Shelter, and then press **Enter**. Type September 1 – 7, 2015 and press **Enter**.
   b. Type the remaining data in Figure 1-97.

	A	B	C	D	E	F	G	H
1	Life's Animal Shelter							
2	September 1 - 7, 2015							
3								
4	Expense Categories	Monday						
5	Food	340.45	344.05	350.51	340.01	341.18	359.75	340.02
6	Medicine	525.33	529.31	535.25	524.59	527.99	543.39	540.01
7	Wages	675.21	580.91	575.88	579.55	680.81	750.05	565.9
8	Heat	25.75	26.01	28.05	25.03	25.99	31.04	24.99
9	Electricity	19.45	20.09	21.75	19.02	19.99	23.56	19.45
10	Total							

1-97 Excel 1-1 data

4. Use the *Fill Handle* to copy a series.
   a. Select **B4**.
   b. Place the pointer on the *Fill Handle* (small black square in the lower right corner of the cell) until the fill pointer (thin black plus sign) appears.
   c. Click and drag the fill pointer to **H4**.

5. Apply *Merge & Center* to the title and subtitle of your worksheet.
   a. Select **A1:H1** and click the **Merge & Center** button [*Home* tab, *Alignment* group].
   b. Select **A2:H2** and click the **Merge & Center** button [*Home* tab, *Alignment* group].
6. Apply *Cell Styles*.
   a. Select **A1** and click the **More** button [*Home* tab, *Styles* group].
   b. Select **Title** in the *Titles and Headings* category.
   c. Select **A2** and click the **More** button [*Home* tab, *Styles* group].
   d. Select **Heading 2** in the *Titles and Headings* category.
   e. Select **A4:A9**, hold down **Ctrl**, and select **B4:H4**.
   f. Click the **More** button [*Home* tab, *Styles* group].
   g. Select **60%, Accent 1** in the *Themed Cell Styles* category.
   h. Select **A10:H10** and click the **More** button [*Home* tab, *Styles* group].
   i. Select **Total** in the *Titles and Headings* category.
7. Apply font attributes.
   a. Select **A4:A9**, hold down **Ctrl**, and then select **B4:H4**.
   b. Click the **Bold** button [*Home* tab, *Font* group].
   c. Select **A5:A9**, hold down **Ctrl**, and then select **B4:H4**.
   d. Click the **Increase Indent** button [*Home* tab, *Alignment* group] three times.
   e. Click the **Font size** drop-down list [*Home* tab, *Font* group] and select **12 pt**.
8. Increase column width.
   a. Select **A4:H10**.
   b. Click the **Format** button [*Home* tab, *Cells* group].
   c. Select **AutoFit Column Width**. Deselect the cells.
9. Apply themes to the worksheet.
   a. Click the **Themes** button [*Page Layout* tab, *Themes* group] and choose **Integral** from the gallery (Figure 1-98).
   b. Click the **Theme Fonts** button [*Page Layout* tab, *Themes* group] and select **Franklin Gothic** from the gallery.
10. Apply font attributes to the labels in the spreadsheet.
    a. Select **A4**.
    b. Click the **Font** drop-down list [*Home* tab, *Font* group] and select **Arial**.
    c. Click the **Font Size** drop-down list and select **14**.
11. Use *AutoSum* to calculate a total and copy the formula using the *Fill Handle*.
    a. Select **B10**.
    b. Click **AutoSum** [*Home* tab, *Editing* group] and press **Enter**.
    c. Select **B10** and place the pointer on the *Fill Handle* (small black square in the lower right corner of the cell) until the fill pointer (thin black plus sign) appears.
    d. Click and drag the fill pointer to cell **H10**.
12. Apply number formatting to the numeric data.
    a. Select **B5:H10**.
    b. Click the **Accounting Number Format** button [*Home* tab, *Number* group].
13. Adjust column width.
    a. Select **A4:H10**.
    b. Click the **Format** button [*Home* tab, *Cells* group].
    c. Select **AutoFit Column Width**.

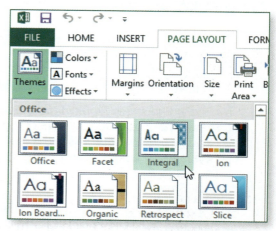

1-98 *Integral* theme button

14. Press **Ctrl+S** to save the workbook.

15. Change column width on a range of columns.
    a. Click and drag to select the column headings **B:H**.
    b. Click the **Format** button [*Home* tab, *Cells* group].
    c. Select **Column Width** from the menu.
    d. Enter 15.0 characters as the new width.
    e. Click **OK**.

16. Apply new row heights.
    a. Click row heading **4**, hold down **Ctrl**, and click row heading **10**.
    b. Right-click row heading **4**.
    c. Choose **Row Height** from the context menu.
    d. Enter 21.0 as the new height.
    e. Click **OK**.

17. Insert a new row and row heading.
    a. Right-click row heading **9**.
    b. Choose **Insert** from the context menu to add a new row. The new row appears directly above the originally selected row.
    c. Select cell **A9** and type: Cages & Equipment.

18. Increase the width of column A to **29.00**.

19. Enter the following information into the cell range **B9:H9**.

	B	C	D	E	F	G	H
9	199.03	209.25	198.90	229.05	245.09	351.98	205.55

20. Rename and color sheet tab.
    a. Double-click the **Sheet1** tab.
    b. Type the following name: Park Rapids, MN Location.
    c. Press **Enter**.
    d. Click the **Format** button [*Home* tab, *Cells* group].
    e. Select **Tab Color** in the *Organize Sheets* category to add a fill color to the background of the sheet tab.
    f. Select **Blue Accent 2**, **Darker 50%** (last color in the sixth *Theme Color* column) (Figure 1-99).

21. Insert a new sheet.
    a. Click the **Insert** button drop-down arrow [*Home* tab, *Cells* group] and select **Insert Sheet**. The new sheet named **Sheet2** appears to the left of the *Park Rapids* worksheet tab.
    b. Add another sheet to the workbook by clicking the **New Sheet** button.

22. Delete *Sheet2* and *Sheet3*.
    a. Click the **Sheet2** tab, press and hold **Shift**, click the **Sheet3** tab, and release **Shift**.
    b. Click the **Delete** button drop-down arrow [*Home* tab, *Cells* group] and select **Delete Sheet**.

23. Press **Ctrl+S** to save the workbook.

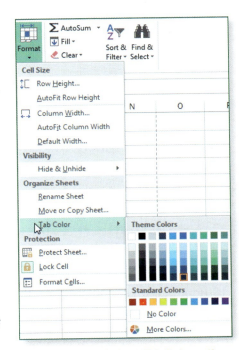

1-99 Worksheet *Tab Color* options

24. Change *Page Setup* options.
    a. Click the **Page Layout** tab and click the **Page Setup** launcher.
    b. Select the **Page** tab in the *Page Setup* dialog box.
    c. Click the **Landscape** radio button under *Orientation*.
    d. Click the **Fit to:** radio button under *Scaling* and enter 1 page wide by 1 tall.
    e. Click the **Header/Footer** tab.
    f. Click the **Header:** drop-down list and select *[your initials] Excel 1-1* from the list.
    g. Click the **Margins** tab.
    h. Click the **Horizontally** check box under *Center on page*.
    i. Click **OK**.

25. Spell check the worksheet.
    a. Press **Ctrl+Home** to go to cell **A1**.
    b. Click the **Spelling** button [*Review* tab, *Proofing* group].
    c. Correct any misspelled words.

26. Click the **File** tab and select **Print** to preview the workbook.

27. Save and close the workbook (Figure 1-100).

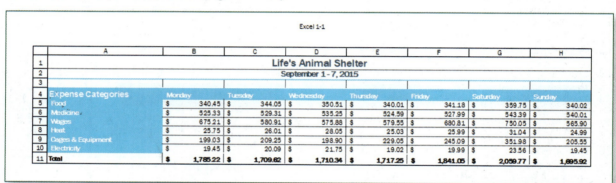

1-100 Excel 1-1 completed

Guided Project 1-2

For this project, you edit and format a spreadsheet for a sales representative for Eller Software Services. The spreadsheet contains clients' personal information and a listing of their product purchases.
[Student Learning Outcomes 1.1, 1.2, 1.3, 1.4, 1.5, 1.6, 1.7, 1.8]

File Needed: *EllerSoftwareServices-1.xlsx*
Completed Project File Name: *[your initials] Excel 1-2.xlsx*

Skills Covered in This Project

- Open and save a workbook.
- Enter and format text and numbers.
- Copy text using the *Fill Handle*.
- Create a formula using *AutoSum*.
- Apply a theme and *Cell Styles*.
- Merge and center titles and subtitles.
- Change orientation.
- Apply font attributes.

- Apply numeric formatting.
- Apply date formatting.
- Apply a border.
- Change zoom level.
- Hide and insert a row and adjust column width.
- Rename and apply color to sheet tabs.
- Use spell check.
- Apply page layout options.

1. Open a workbook.
   a. Click the **File** tab and click **Open**.
   b. Locate the folder where your files are saved.
   c. Open the workbook ***EllerSoftwareServices-1.xlsx***.

2. Rename the workbook *[your initials] Excel 1-2*.
   a. Press **F12** to open the *Save As* dialog box.
   b. Locate the folder where your files are located.
   c. Rename the file *[your initials] Excel 1-2* in the *File name* area.
   d. Click **Save**.

3. Apply a theme to the worksheet.
   a. Click the **Themes** button [*Page Layout* tab, *Themes* group].
   b. Choose **Retrospect** from the *Office* gallery.

4. Enter and format data.
   a. Select **E5**, type **MN**, and press **Enter**.
   b. Select **E5** and point to the *Fill Handle*.
   c. Click and drag the fill pointer to **E13**.
   d. Select **C5:C13**.
   e. Press **Ctrl+1** to open the *Format Cells* dialog box.
   f. Click the **Number** tab and click **Special** under *Category*.
   g. Select **Phone Number** and click **OK** to close the *Format Cells* dialog box.

5. Use *AutoSum* to calculate the total of gross sales and adjust the reference range.
   a. Type Total in **A15**.
   b. Select cell **I15**.
   c. Click **AutoSum** [*Home* tab, *Editing* group] and press **Enter**.
   d. Select **I15** and click the cell reference range in the *Formula bar*.
   e. Edit the cell range to **I13** and press **Enter**.

6. Apply *Merge & Center* to the title and subtitle of the worksheet.
   a. Select **A1:I1** and click the **Merge & Center** button [*Home* tab, *Alignment* group].
   b. Select **A2:I2** and click the **Merge & Center** button.

7. Apply *Cell Styles*.
   a. Select **A1** and click the **More** button [*Home* tab, *Styles* group].
   b. Select **Title** in the *Titles and Headings* category.
   c. Select **A2** and click the **More** button and select **Heading 2** in the *Titles and Headings* category.

d. Select **A4:A15**, hold down **Ctrl**, and then select **B4:I4**.
e. Click the **More** button and select **40%- Accent 1** in the *Themed Cell Styles* category.
f. Select **I15**, click the **More** button, and then select **Total** in the *Titles and Headings* category.

8. Apply diagonal rotation to text.
   a. Select **A4:I4**.
   b. Click the **Orientation** button [*Home* tab, *Alignment* group].
   c. Select **Angle Counterclockwise**.

9. Apply font attributes.
   a. Select the cell range **A4:A15**, hold down **Ctrl**, and click and drag to select **B4:I4**.
   b. Click the **Font size** drop-down list [*Home* tab, *Font* group] and select **12**.
   c. Click the **Font type** drop-down list [*Home* tab, *Font* group] and select **Verdana**.
   d. Click the **Bold** button [*Home* tab, *Font* group].
   e. Select the non-adjacent cell ranges **C5:C13** and **E5:F13**.
   f. Click **Center** [*Home* tab, *Alignment* group].
   g. Select **A1:A2** and click the **Increase Font Size** button [*Home* tab, *Font* group] two times.

10. Apply numeric formatting to your spreadsheet.
    a. Select **I5:I15**.
    b. Click **Comma Style** [*Home* tab, *Number* group].
    c. Select **I5**, press **Ctrl**, and select **I15**.
    d. Press **Ctrl+1** to open the *Format Cells* dialog box.
    e. Select the **Number** tab, if necessary, and select the **Accounting** category.
    f. Change the **Symbol** drop-down list to **$**.
    g. Click **OK** to close the *Format Cells* dialog box.

11. Apply date formatting to your spreadsheet.
    a. Select **H5:H13**.
    b. Click the **Short Date** format from the *Number Format* drop-down list [*Home* tab, *Number* group].

12. Increase the width of your columns.
    a. Select **A4:I15**.
    b. Click the **Format** button [*Home* tab, *Cells* group].
    c. Select **AutoFit Column Width**.

13. Press **Ctrl+S** to save the workbook.

14. Edit a cell.
    a. Double-click cell **G9** to activate edit mode.
    b. Delete the word **Software** from the cell contents and press **Enter**.

15. Change the width of a column.
    a. Click the column **G** heading to select the column.
    b. Click the **Format** button [*Home* tab, *Cells* group] and select **Column Width** from the menu.
    c. Enter 31.0 characters as the new width.
    d. Click **OK**.

16. Hide an existing row and insert a new row and row heading.
    a. Right-click row heading **10**.
    b. Choose **Hide** from the context menu.
    c. Right-click row heading **11**.
    d. Choose **Insert** from the context menu to add a new row. The new row appears directly above the originally selected row.
    e. Select cell **A11** and type Hilary Marschke.

f. Enter the following information into the cell range **B11:I11**. (Figure 1-101).

B11: 245 West
      Third Avenue
C11: 3203555443
D11: Saint Cloud
E11: MN
F11: 56301
G11: Training
H11: 11/15/2015
I11: 750.00

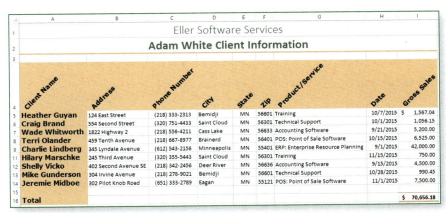

1-101 Adjusted column width

17. Rename and color a sheet tab.
    a. Double-click the **Sheet1** tab.
    b. Type the following name: MN Clients.
    c. Press **Enter**.
    d. Right-click the **MN Clients** tab.
    e. Point to **Tab Color** to add a fill color to the background of the sheet tab.
    f. Select **Orange Accent 1**, **Darker 50%** (last color in the fifth *Theme Color* column) (Figure 1-102).

18. Save the workbook.

19. Apply a bottom border.
    a. Select **A4:I4**.
    b. Press **Ctrl+1** to open the **Format Cells** dialog box.
    c. Click the **Border** tab.
    d. Select the fifth line style in the second column and select **Orange**, **Accent 1**, **Darker 50%** for the line color (last color in the fifth column).
    e. Select the bottom border button in the **Border** area (third button under the *Border* heading).
    f. Click **OK**.

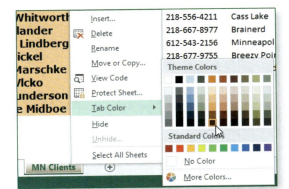

1-102 Worksheet *Tab Color* options

20. Change the zoom level.
    a. Click the **View** tab.
    b. Click **Zoom**.
    c. Select the **75% *Magnification*** level.
    d. Click **OK**.

21. Select the **Spelling** button [*Review* tab, *Proofing* group] and correct any misspellings in the worksheet.

22. Preview the worksheet.
    a. Select **Print** from the *File* tab.
    b. Review the workbook layout and format, and then return to the worksheet.
    c. Use the **Zoom** slider in the *Status bar* to return to *100%* magnification.

23. Change *Page Setup* options.
    a. Display the *Page Layout* tab and click the **Page Setup** launcher [*Page Setup* group].
    b. Select the **Page** tab and click the **Landscape** radio button under *Orientation*.
    c. Click the **Fit to:** radio button under *Scaling*, enter 1 page wide by 1 tall.

d. Select the *Margins* tab and click the **Horizontally** check box under *Center on page*.

e. Select the **Header/Footer** tab.

f. Click the **Footer:** drop-down button and select **MN Clients** to print the sheet name in the footer.

g. Click **OK**.

24. Save and close the workbook (Figure 1-103).

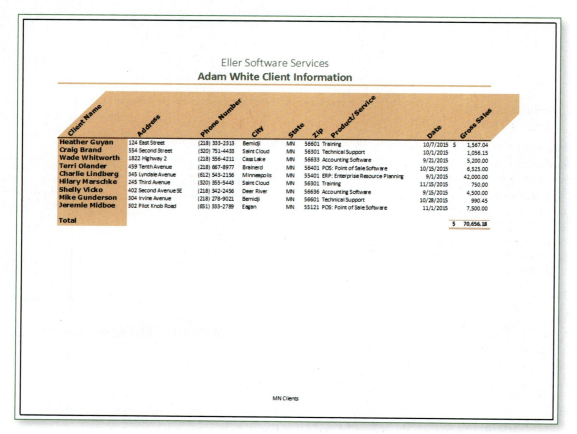

Guided Project 1-3

For this project, you create an Excel spreadsheet that consists of the product inventory information for Wear-Ever Shoes.

[**Student Learning Outcomes 1.1, 1.2, 1.3, 1.4, 1.5, 1.6, 1.7, 1.8**]

File Needed: *WearEverShoes-1.xlsx*

Completed Project File Name: *[your initials] Excel 1-3.xlsx*

Skills Covered in This Project

- Open and save a workbook.
- Enter and format text and numbers.
- Use the *Fill Handle* to copy a formula.
- Apply a theme and *Cell Styles*.
- Merge and center title and subtitle.
- Apply numeric formatting.
- Adjust column width and row height.

- Insert a column.
- Use *Page Layout* view to insert a footer.
- Move cell contents.
- Check spelling.
- Rename sheet tabs and apply color to sheet tabs.
- Apply page layout options.

1. Open and rename the workbook file.
   a. Press **Ctrl+O** to display the *Open* area.
   b. Locate the folder where your files are located.
   c. Open the workbook file ***WearEverShoes-1**.xlsx*.
   d. Press **F12** and locate the folder where your files are saved.
   e. Save the workbook as *[your initials] Excel 1-3*.

2. Click the **Themes** button [*Page Layout* tab, *Themes* group] and choose **Ion** from the gallery.

3. Increase column width.
   a. Select **A4:I12**.
   b. Click the **Format** button [*Home* tab, *Cells* group].
   c. Select **AutoFit Column Width**.

4. Apply *Cell Styles*.
   a. Select **A1**, click the **More** button [*Home* tab, *Styles* group], and select **Title** in the *Titles and Headings* category.
   b. Select **A3**, click the **More** button, and select **Heading 2** in the *Titles and Headings* category.
   c. Select **A4:A12**, press **Ctrl**, and select **B4:I4**.
   d. Click the **More** button and select **40%- Accent 1** in the *Themed Cell Styles* category.
   e. Select **B5:I12**.
   f. Click the **More** button and select **20%- Accent 2** in the *Themed Cell Styles* category.

5. Apply *Merge & Center* to the title and subtitle of your worksheet.
   a. Select **A1:I1** and click **Merge & Center** [*Home* tab, *Alignment* group].
   b. Select **A3:I3** and click **Merge & Center**.

6. Apply formatting.
   a. Select the cell range **A4:A12**, press **Ctrl**, and select **B4:I4**.
   b. Click the **Font size** drop-down list [*Home* tab, *Font* group] and select **12 pt**.
   c. Click the **Font type** drop-down list [*Home* tab, *Font* group] and select **Trebuchet MS**.
   d. Select **A4:I4** and click the **Center** button [*Home* tab, *Alignment* group].
   e. Select **I5:I12** and click the **Center** button [*Home* tab, *Alignment* group].
   f. Select **E5:E12** and click the **Increase Indent** button [*Home* tab, *Alignment* group].

7. Use the *Fill Handle* to copy a formula.
   a. Click **H5**.
   b. Point to the *Fill Handle* in the lower right corner and drag the fill pointer to **H12**.

8. Apply numeric formatting and adjust column width.
   a. Select **F5:H12**.
   b. Click **Comma Style** [*Home* tab, *Number* group].

c. Select **A4:I12**.
   d. Click the **Format** button [*Home* tab, *Cells* group] and select **AutoFit Column Width**.

9. Save your workbook (Figure 1-104).

10. Edit a cell.
    a. Double-click cell **B7** to activate edit mode.
    b. Edit the cell's contents so it appears as Pink.

1-104 Formatted worksheet

11. Change the width of a column.
    a. Click column heading **A** to select the column.
    b. Click the **Format** button [*Home* tab, *Cells* group] and select **Column Width**.
    c. Enter 24.0 as the new width and click **OK**.

12. Apply a new row height.
    a. Right-click row heading **4**.
    b. Choose **Row Height** from the context menu.
    c. Enter 21.0 as the new height and click **OK**.

13. Insert a new column and type a column heading and data in the new column.
    a. Right-click column heading **D**.
    b. Choose **Insert** from the context menu to add a new column.
    c. Select cell **D4** and type: Discontinue.
    d. Increase the width of the new column if needed to automatically fit the contents of the column.
    e. Enter the following information into the cell range **D5:D12**:

	D
5	No
6	No
7	No
8	No
9	No
10	Yes
11	No
12	Yes

14. Rename and color the sheet tab.
    a. Double-click the **Sheet1** tab.
    b. Type the following name: Northern Warehouse and press **Enter**.
    c. Click the **Format** button [*Home* tab, *Cells* group].
    d. Select **Tab Color** in the *Organize Sheets* category to add a fill color to the background of the sheet tab.
    e. Select **Dark Red, Accent 1, Darker 50%** (last color in the fifth *Theme Color* column).

15. Click the **Save** button on the *Quick Access* toolbar to save the workbook changes.

16. Move cell contents and adjust column width.
    a. Select the cell range **D4:D12**.
    b. Click the **Cut** button [*Home* tab, *Clipboard* group].

c. Click cell **K4** and click the **Paste** button [*Home* tab, *Clipboard* group].

d. Select **E4:K12**.

e. Place the pointer on the right border of the selected cell range, drag the cell range to **D4**, and release the pointer.

f. Select **B4:J12**, click the **Format** button [*Home* tab, *Cells* group], and select **AutoFit Column Width**.

17. Click the **Spelling** button [*Review* tab, *Proofing* group] and correct any misspellings in the worksheet.

18. Use *Page Layout* view to insert a footer.

a. Click the **Insert** tab and click **Header & Footer**.

b. Click the **Header & Footer Tools Design** tab.

c. Click **Go to Footer** [*Header & Footer Tools Design* tab, *Navigation* group].

d. Click in the middle section of the footer area and select **File Name** in the *Header & Footer Elements* group. Click in the worksheet to see the file name.

e. Switch to *Normal* view.

19. Change the *Page Setup* options.

a. Click the **Page Layout** tab and click the **Page Setup** launcher.

b. Select the **Page** tab from the *Page Setup* dialog box and click the **Landscape** radio button under *Orientation*.

c. Click the **Fit to:** radio button and enter 1 page wide by 1 tall.

d. Click **OK**.

20. Save and close the workbook (Figure 1-105).

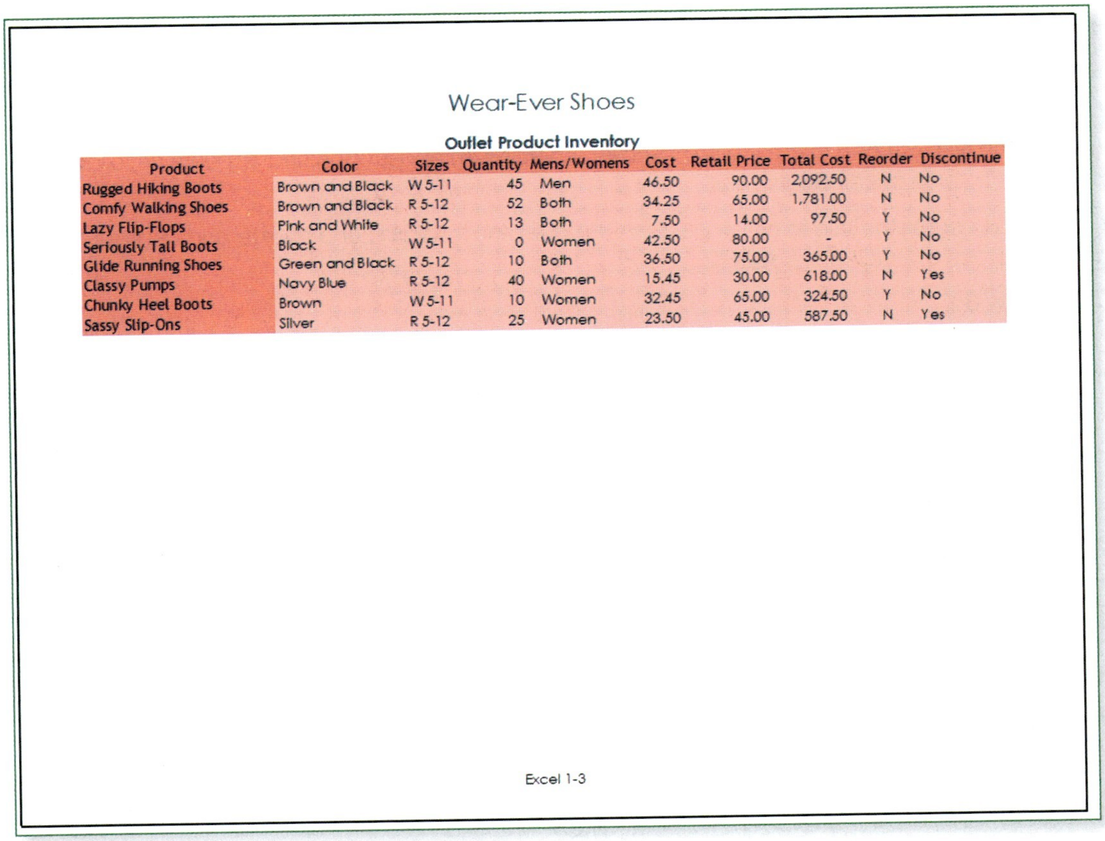

Wear-Ever Shoes

Outlet Product Inventory

Product	Color	Sizes	Quantity	Mens/Womens	Cost	Retail Price	Total Cost	Reorder	Discontinue
Rugged Hiking Boots	Brown and Black	W 5-11	45	Men	46.50	90.00	2,092.50	N	No
Comfy Walking Shoes	Brown and Black	R 5-12	52	Both	34.25	65.00	1,781.00	N	No
Lazy Flip-Flops	Pink and White	R 5-12	13	Both	7.50	14.00	97.50	Y	No
Seriously Tall Boots	Black	W 5-11	0	Women	42.50	80.00	-	Y	No
Glide Running Shoes	Green and Black	R 5-12	10	Both	36.50	75.00	365.00	Y	No
Classy Pumps	Navy Blue	R 5-12	40	Women	15.45	30.00	618.00	N	Yes
Chunky Heel Boots	Brown	W 5-11	10	Women	32.45	65.00	324.50	Y	No
Sassy Slip-Ons	Silver	R 5-12	25	Women	23.50	45.00	587.50	N	Yes

Excel 1-3

1-105 Excel 1-3 completed

Independent Project 1-4

You have just been hired as an administrative assistant at Blue Lake Sport Company. Your supervisor has asked you to convert her daily sales report into a spreadsheet that she can distribute at the department meeting.
[Student Learning Outcomes 1.1, 1.2, 1.3, 1.4, 1.5, 1.6, 1.7, 1.8]

File Needed: *BlueLakeSports-1.xlsx*
Completed Project File Name: *[your initials] Excel 1-4.xlsx*

Skills Covered in This Project

- Open and save a workbook.
- Enter and format text and numbers.
- Merge and center title and date.
- Use *AutoSum*.
- Create a formula and use the *Fill Handle*.
- Apply a theme and apply *Cell Styles*.

- Use *Page Layout* view to insert a header and footer.
- Apply page layout options.
- Adjust column width and row height.
- Rename and apply color to sheet tabs.

1. Open the workbook file *BlueLakeSport-1.xlsx*.

2. Save the presentation as *[your initials] Excel 1-4*.

3. Apply the **Slice** theme to the worksheet.

4. Edit worksheet data.
   a. Edit the title in **A1** so that the word "Sports" contains an apostrophe and appears as follows: Sport's.
   b. Edit the value in cell **B6** to 5102.

5. Merge and center the title in cell **A1** across the cell range **A1:H1**, and merge and center the date in cell **A2** across the cell range **A2:H2**.

6. Delete row **8**.

7. Use the *Fill Handle* to complete a series.
   a. Select **B4**.
   b. Use *Fill Handle* to add headings for columns **C:H**.

8. Apply *Cell Styles* to the labels in the spreadsheet.
   a. Apply the **Title Style** to **A1**.
   b. Apply the **Heading 1** style to the subtitle in **A2**.
   c. Apply the **20%- Accent 1** themed cell style to **B4:H4** and **A4:A8**.
   d. Apply the **20%- Accent 3** themed cell style to **B5:H8**.
   e. Select **A3:H3**, and apply the **Heading 1** style.

9. Format cell contents.
   a. Increase the font size of **A4:H8** to **12 pt**.
   b. Select **A5:A7** and click the **Increase Indent** button.
   c. Apply the **Comma** format to cells **B5:H8**.

10. Use *AutoSum* and the *Fill Handle* to calculate daily totals.
    a. Use *AutoSum* to create a *Sum* formula for **B8**.
    b. Use the *Fill Handle* to copy the formula in **B8** to cells **C8:H8**.

11. Apply additional formatting to the spreadsheet.
    a. Apply the **Total** cell style to cells **A8:H8**.
    b. Increase the font size to **12 pt.** in cells **B8:H8**.
    c. **Bold** all non-numeric entries in **A4:H8**.
    d. **Center** the days of the week.
    e. Select **B5:H7** and apply the *Comma Style* format.
    f. Select **B8:H8** and select **Accounting** from the *Number Format* drop-down list.

12. Adjust column width and row height.
    a. Change the width in column **A** to 22.0.
    b. Change the row height for rows **1:8** to 22.0.

13. Rename and color a sheet tab.
    a. Rename *Sheet1* Week 1 of May.
    b. Color the sheet tab **Dark Blue Accent 1**, **Darker 50%** (last color in the fifth *Theme Color* column).

14. Spell check the worksheet.

15. Apply page layout options.
    a. Change the page orientation to **Landscape**.
    b. Fit the spreadsheet to 1 page wide by 1 tall.
    c. Center the worksheet horizontally on the page.

16. Add a header and footer.
    a. Click the **Insert** tab and click **Header & Footer**.
    b. Click the left header section and add the **Sheet Name** field.
    c. Click **Go to Footer**, click the middle section, and add the **Page Number** field.
    d. Click a cell in the worksheet and switch to *Normal* view.

17. Preview the workbook.

18. Save and close the workbook (Figure 1-106).

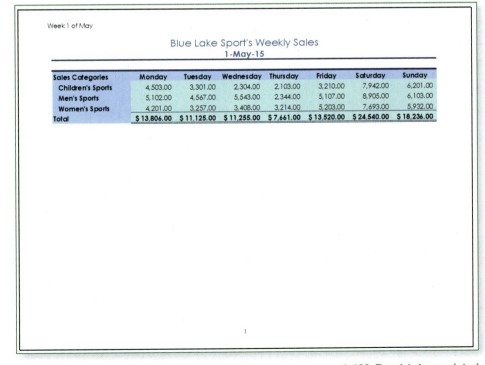

1-106 Excel 1-4 completed

Independent Project 1-5

Clemenson Imaging is a privately owned organization that employs certified staff to perform mobile medical imaging at many hospitals statewide. You have been hired as the scheduling dispatch coordinator. It is your job to schedule all the mobile technicians at various hospital locations every day. Your supervisor has requested that you convert your schedule to an Excel spreadsheet.
[Student Learning Outcomes 1.1, 1.2, 1.3, 1.4, 1.5, 1.6, 1.7]

File Needed: ***ClemsonImaging-1.xlsx***
Completed Project File Name: ***[your initials] Excel 1-5.xlsx***

Skills Covered in This Project

- Open and save a workbook.
- Enter and format text and numbers.
- Merge and center title and subtitle.
- Spell check.
- Add a border.
- Apply a theme and *Cell Styles*.

- Create a formula using *AutoSum*.
- Adjust column width and row height.
- Rename and apply color to sheet tabs.
- Apply *Freeze Panes*.
- Apply page layout options.

1. Open ***ClemsonImaging-1.xlsx*** and save it as ***[your initials] Excel 1-5***.

2. Apply the **Ion Boardroom** theme to the worksheet.

3. Edit the title in **A1** so that "LLC" appears after the word "Imaging" and appears as Clemenson Imaging LLC.

4. Merge and center the title in cell **A1** across the cell range **A1:H1** and the subtitle in cell **A2** across the cell range **A2:H2**.

5. Edit the value in cell **E7** to 3.

6. Apply *Cell Styles*.
    a. Apply the **Title** style to **A1**.
    b. Apply the **Heading 1** style to the subtitle in **A2**.
    c. Apply the **40%- Accent 2** themed cell style to **A4:H4**.

7. Apply format changes.
    a. Increase the font size of **A4:H11** to **12 pt**.
    b. Increase the indent of cells **A5:A11**.

8. Add the title Total in cell **A13** and calculate the total number of patients in **E13** using *AutoSum*. Edit the formula cell range to **E11**.

9. Apply additional formatting to the spreadsheet.
    a. Apply the **Total Cell** style to **A13:H13**.
    b. Increase the font size to **12 pt.** in cells **A13:H13**.
    c. Select **A13** and **Decrease Indent**.
    d. **Bold** and center the data in **E5:E13** and **H5:H11**.
    e. Apply **bold** format to cells **A4:H4**.

10. Adjust column widths and row heights.
    a. Change the width in column **A** to 20.0.
    b. *AutoFit* the remaining columns (**B:H**).
    c. Change the row height for rows **4** and **13** to 21.00.
    d. Delete row **12**.

11. Apply **Freeze Panes** to cell **A5**.
    a. Click the **View** tab.
    b. Select **A5**.
    c. Click **Freeze Panes** and select **Freeze Panes**.

12. Rename *Sheet1* as 12-1-2015 and color the sheet tab **Plum Accent 1, Darker 50%**.

13. Select **A4:H4** and apply a thick bottom border using the **Plum, Accent 1, Darker 50%** color.

14. Spell check the worksheet.

15. Apply page layout options.
    a. Change the orientation to **Landscape** and fit the spreadsheet to one page.
    b. Center the worksheet horizontally on the page.
    c. Add the automatic footer **12-1-2015** to the worksheet using the *Footer* drop-down list.

16. Preview the spreadsheet.

17. Save and close the workbook (Figure 1-107).

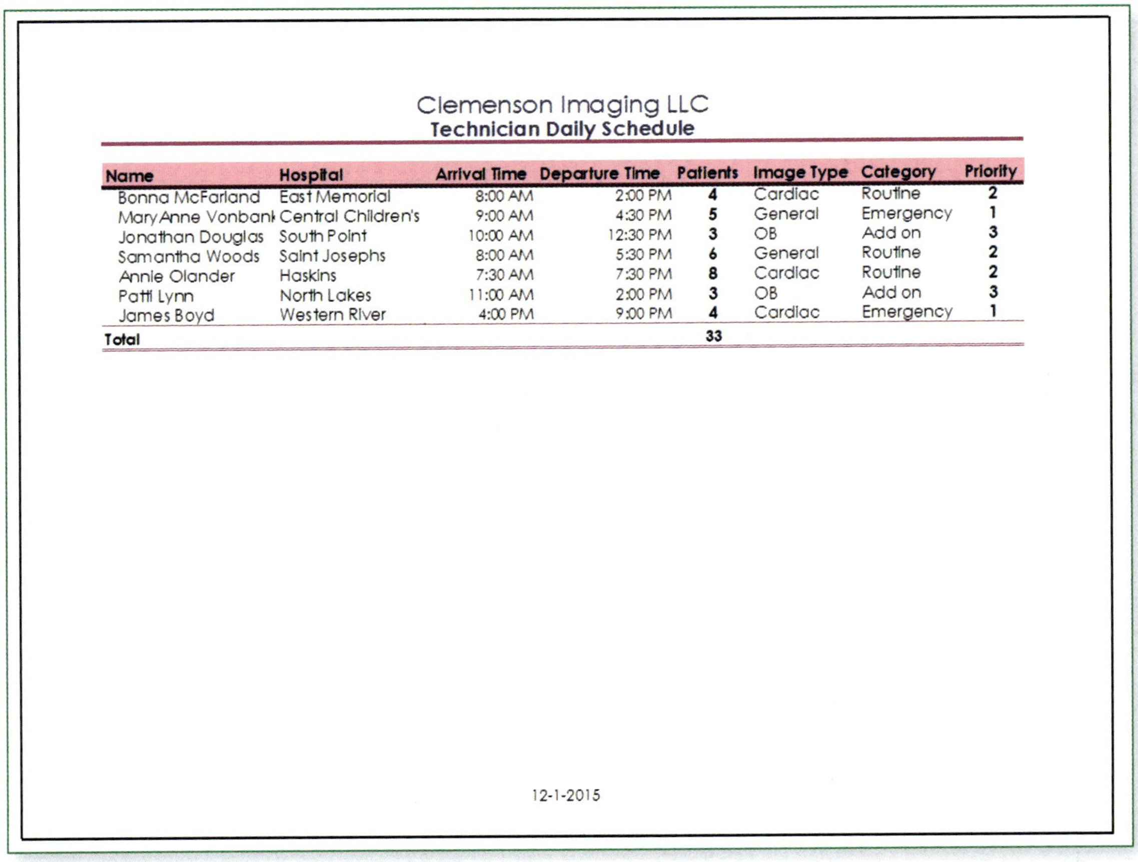

Clemenson Imaging LLC
Technician Daily Schedule

Name	Hospital	Arrival Time	Departure Time	Patients	Image Type	Category	Priority
Bonna McFarland	East Memorial	8:00 AM	2:00 PM	4	Cardiac	Routine	2
Mary Anne Vonbank	Central Children's	9:00 AM	4:30 PM	5	General	Emergency	1
Jonathan Douglas	South Point	10:00 AM	12:30 PM	3	OB	Add on	3
Samantha Woods	Saint Josephs	8:00 AM	5:30 PM	6	General	Routine	2
Annie Olander	Haskins	7:30 AM	7:30 PM	8	Cardiac	Routine	2
Patti Lynn	North Lakes	11:00 AM	2:00 PM	3	OB	Add on	3
James Boyd	Western River	4:00 PM	9:00 PM	4	Cardiac	Emergency	1
Total				33			

12-1-2015

1-107 Excel 1-5 completed

Independent Project 1-6

You have been hired as the accounts receivable clerk for a privately owned accounting company called Livingood Income Tax & Accounting. It is your job to track all the payments from clients every day. Your supervisor has requested that you convert your payment table to an Excel spreadsheet.
[Student Learning Outcomes 1.1, 1.2, 1.3, 1.4, 1.5, 1.6, 1.7, 1.8]

File Needed: None
Completed Project File Name: *[your initials] Excel 1-6.xlsx*

Skills Covered in This Project

- Create and save a workbook.
- Enter text and numbers.
- Change font size and attributes.
- Use *AutoSum*.
- Adjust column width and row height.
- Spell check.

- Apply *Freeze Panes*.
- Change zoom level.
- Apply a theme and *Cell Styles*.
- Apply page layout options.
- Hide a row.
- Rename and apply color to sheet tabs.

1. Start a new workbook and save it as *[your initials] Excel 1-6*.

2. Apply the **Organic** theme to the worksheet. Change the theme font to **Gill Sans MT**.

3. Select **A1** and type Livingood Income Tax and Accounting, press **Enter**, type Payment Schedule, and press **Enter** again.

4. Type in the remaining worksheet data from Figure 1-108.

5. Edit the title in **A1** to replace the word "and" with the symbol &.

6. Edit the value in cell **B5** to 451.25. Change "Over Due" in cell **F4** to Overdue.

7. Apply the **Title** style to **A1**.

8. Apply formatting to cell ranges.
   a. Increase the font size of **A4:G11** to **12 pt**.
   b. Select cells **B5:B11** and display the *Format Cells* dialog box. Select the **Accounting** format and change the *Symbol* to **None**.

	A	B	C	D	E	F	G
1	Livingood Income Tax and Accounting						
2	Payment Schedule						
3							
4	Invoice	Amount	Due Date	Paid	Payment Type	Over Due	Contact
5	4567	450.5	42278	Yes	Check 2005	No	No
6	3421	465.78	42248	No	Due	Yes	Letter
7	2456	250.25	42217	No	Due	Yes	Phone
8	4569	585.65	42278	Yes	Discover	No	No
9	4572	1245.89	42278	No	Due	No	No
10	1428	1245.67	42186	No	Due	Yes	Collections
11	2576	345.08	42217	Yes	Check 2345	No	No

1-108 Excel 1-6 data

9. Add the title Total in cell **A13** and calculate the total for **B13** using *AutoSum*. Adjust the cell range reference in the *Formula bar*.

10. Apply additional formatting.
    a. Apply the **Total** cell style to cells **A13:G13**.
    b. Select **A13:G13** and increase the font size to **12 pt**.
    c. **Bold** the entries in **A4:G4**.
    d. **Center** the data in **A4:G4**, **A5:A13**, **D5:D13**, and **F5:F13**.

    e. Select **A4:G4** and open the *Format Cells* dialog box. Add a thick **Green, Accent 1, Darker 50%** bottom border and a **Green, Accent 1, Lighter 80%** fill color using the second color in the fifth column.

    f. Select the cells in rows **6**, **8**, and **10** and apply the same fill color.

    g. Use the **Border** button and apply a bottom border to cells **A2:G2**.

11. Adjust column width and row height.

    a. Change the width of columns **A:G** to 14.0.

    b. Change the row height for rows **4** and **13** to 19.50.

12. Hide row **12**.

13. Rename *Sheet1* 10-27-2015 and color the sheet tab **Green, Accent 1** (first color in the fifth *Theme Color* column).

14. Spell check the worksheet.

15. Apply *Freeze Panes* to **B5**.

16. Increase the magnification of the view to **125%**.

17. Apply page layout options.

    a. Change the orientation to **Landscape** and scale the page to fit on one page.

    b. Center the worksheet horizontally on the page.

    c. Click the **Custom Header** button and add the **Insert Sheet Name** field in the *Left Header* section. Click the **Format Text** button and apply the font color **Green, Accent 1, Darker 50%** to the header field.

    d. Add the page number to the right section of the footer.

    e. Select print preview in the *Page Setup* dialog box to view your settings.

18. Save and close the workbook (Figure 1-109).

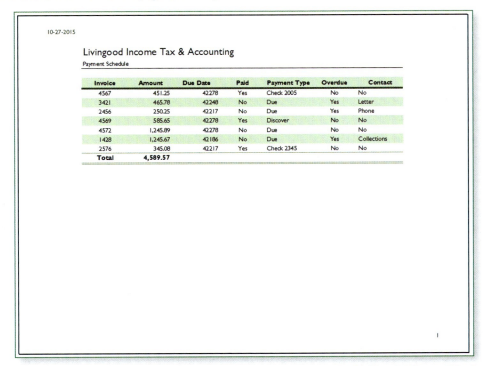

1-109 Excel 1-6 completed

E1-73

Improve It Project 1-7

For this project, you create a flight schedule for the manager of Boyd Air. You edit and format the data in a spreadsheet and add page layout formatting.
[Student Learning Outcomes 1.1, 1.2, 1.3, 1.4, 1.5, 1.6, 1.7, 1.8]

File Needed: **BoydAirFlightSchedule-1.xlsx**
Completed Project File Name: **[your initials] Excel 1-7.xlsx**

Skills Covered in This Project

- Open and save a workbook.
- Enter and format text and numbers.
- Merge and center title and subtitle.
- Format and delete rows and columns.
- Spell check.
- Use *AutoSum* to create a formula.

- Apply a theme and apply *Cell Styles*.
- Apply page layout options.
- Adjust column width and row height.
- Rename and apply color to sheet tabs.
- Freeze panes and change the zoom level.

1. Open the workbook **BoydAirFlightSchedule-01.xlsx**.

2. Rename the workbook **[your initials] Excel 1-7**.

3. Type Boyd Air in **A1** and type Flight Schedule in **A2**.

4. Merge and center the title in cell **A1** and the subtitle in cell **A2**.

5. Apply *Cell Styles* to the labels in the spreadsheet.
    a. Apply the **Title** style to **A1**.
    b. Apply the **Heading 1** style to the subtitle in **A2**.
    c. Apply the **Accent 1** cell style to **A4:F4**.
    d. Apply the **20%-Accent 1** cell style to **A5:F13**.

6. Apply formatting.
    a. Increase the font size of **A4:F4** to **14 pt**.
    b. Apply the **Total** cell style to cells **A13:F13**.
    c. **Bold** the entries in **A4:F4**.
    d. Select **A4**, **C4**, and **D4**, and click **Wrap Text** [*Home* tab, *Alignment* group].

7. Apply row and column formatting.
    a. Change the row height for row **4** to 38.00.
    b. Change the row height for row **13** to 21.00.
    c. Right align the text in **C4** and **D4**.

8. Delete row **12**.

9. Use *AutoSum* to calculate the total number of passengers.

10. Color the sheet tab **Dark Blue**, **Accent 1**, **Darker 50%** (last color in the fifth *Theme Color* column).

11. Edit the sheet tab name by deleting **Monday**.

12. *AutoFit* columns **A:F**.

13. Spell check the worksheet.

14. Apply *Freeze Panes* to **B5**.

15. Increase the magnification of the sheet to **150%**.

16. Apply page layout options.
    a. Change the orientation to **Landscape** and fit the spreadsheet to one page.
    b. Center the worksheet horizontally on the page.
    c. Add the **Insert File Name** field in the *Left Header* section and apply the font color **Dark Blue, Accent 1**.

17. Preview your settings.

18. Save and close the workbook (Figure 1-110).

Excel 1-7

Boyd Air
Flight Schedule

Flight Number	Destination	Arrival Time	Departure Time	Status	Passengers
BD 2345	Chicago, IL	8:00:00 AM	9:30:00 AM	On Time	90
BD 4567	Minneapolis, MN	9:00:00 PM	10:30:00 PM	On Time	75
BD 1234	Green Bay, WI	10:00:00 AM	12:30:00 PM	Delayed	80
BD 6578	St. Louis, MO	8:00:00 AM	9:30:00 AM	On Time	63
BD 2213	Orlando, FL	6:30:00 AM	7:00:00 AM	Delayed	90
BD 980	Fargo, ND	12:30:00 PM	2:00:00 PM	On Time	35
BD 1345	Houston, TX	4:45:00 PM	7:00:00 PM	On Time	90
Total					**523**

1-110 Excel 1-7 completed

Challenge Project 1-8

For this project, you create a spreadsheet that lists sales for a gourmet chocolate store. The sales report lists data for popular holidays within a calendar year.
[Student Learning Outcomes 1.1, 1.2, 1.3, 1.4, 1.5, 1.6, 1.7, 1.8]

File Needed: None
Completed Project File Name: *[your initials] Excel 1-8.xlsx*

Create a new workbook and save it as *[your initials] Excel 1-8*. Name the gourmet chocolate store and list five types of chocolate as row headings. For column headings, list four popular holidays for chocolate sales. Modify your workbook according to the following guidelines:

- Type sales data for each holiday.
- Include a date in the worksheet title area.
- Incorporate a theme, *Cell Styles,* and formatting.
- Use *AutoSum* to calculate totals.
- Insert header and footer text.
- Include document properties and spell check the workbook.

Challenge Project 1-9

For this project, you create a spreadsheet for a photography club. The photography club rents retail space for selling used photography equipment. The equipment available in the store includes camera bodies, lenses, tripods, and books. Each month a master list is created which includes the type of equipment for sale and current prices.
[Student Learning Outcomes 1.1, 1.2, 1.3, 1.4, 1.5, 1.6, 1.7, 1.8]

File Needed: None
Completed Project File Name: *[your initials] Excel 1-9.xlsx*

Create a new workbook and save it as *[your initials] Excel 1-9*. Modify your workbook according to the following guidelines:

- Name the photography club for the main title and create a subtitle to reflect the purpose of the spreadsheet.
- Create rows and columns of data for listing the photography equipment, price, and quantity available.
- Include other information that would be helpful to potential customers.
- Use *AutoSum* to calculate the value of the inventory.
- Incorporate a theme, *Cell Styles,* and other formatting to create a professional-looking spreadsheet.
- Include document properties and spell check the workbook.

Challenge Project 1-10

For this project, you create a spreadsheet that lists your monthly financial responsibilities. This spreadsheet is a valuable tool for money management.
[Student Learning Outcomes 1.1, 1.2, 1.3, 1.4, 1.5, 1.6, 1.7, 1.8]

File Needed: None
Completed Project File Name: *[your initials] Excel 1-10.xlsx*

Enter data for a monthly budget. Create a new workbook and save it as *[your initials] Excel 1-10*. Modify your workbook according to the following guidelines:

- Use blank rows to divide your worksheet into groups. For example, include a section for income and another section for expenses. You can create additional groups for expenses that occur monthly, quarterly, or annually.
- Insert worksheets for each month and name each sheet.
- Incorporate themes, *Cell Styles*, and formatting. (Remember that you can select multiple sheet tabs and apply Page Setup formatting to each sheet in a single step.)
- Use *AutoSum* to calculate total income and expenses.
- Include document properties and spell check the workbook.

Working with Formulas and Functions

CHAPTER OVERVIEW

Excel is a powerful tool for creating mathematical computations. You can use Excel to create a simple addition formula or a formula that includes complex calculations. When creating formulas, you can take advantage of Excel's error correcting techniques to ensure accuracy in your worksheets. This chapter introduces the basics of using formulas and functions in an Excel worksheet.

STUDENT LEARNING OUTCOMES (SLOs)

After completing this chapter, you will be able to:

SLO 2.1 Create and edit basic formulas (p. E2-79).

SLO 2.2 Use range names and relative, absolute, and mixed cell references in a formula (p. E2-83).

SLO 2.3 Apply mathematical order of operations when using parentheses, exponents, multiplication, division, addition, and subtraction (p. E2-88).

SLO 2.4 Use *AutoSum* and other common functions such as *AVERAGE, COUNT, MAX, MIN, TODAY,* and *NOW* (p. E2-93).

SLO 2.5 Apply financial, logical, and lookup functions such as *PMT, IF, VLOOKUP,* and *HLOOKUP* (p. E2-99).

SLO 2.6 Apply math and trigonometry functions such as *SUMIF, SUMPRODUCT,* and *ROUND* (p. E2-106).

CASE STUDY

In the Pause & Practice projects in this chapter, you create business workbooks related to a northern Minnesota resort business, Paradise Lakes Resort (PLR), which was introduced in Chapter 1. PLR is asking all managers to incorporate formulas into their monthly sales workbooks to determine future costs and net income projections. PLR is also considering several investment options and is using various formulas to examine and evaluate these opportunities.

Pause & Practice 2-1: Modify a workbook to include basic formulas.

Pause & Practice 2-2: Insert common functions into a workbook.

Pause & Practice 2-3: Apply financial, logical, lookup, math and trigonometry functions in a workbook.

EXCEL

Creating and Editing Basic Formulas

One reason why Excel is one of the most popular business software applications is because it gives users the ability to incorporate formulas into a workbook. A *formula* evaluates values and returns a result. Basic formula creation can involve adding weekly expenses, multiplying inventory by unit price to determine inventory value, or subtracting expenses from income. The formulas in Excel workbooks automatically update when cell values change.

Formula Syntax

The term *syntax* refers to the required parts of a formula and the rules controlling the order of the parts. As discussed in Chapter 1, the intersection of a column and row is a cell. Each cell has a *cell reference* (or cell address), which is the specific location of a cell within a worksheet. When you create formulas, you use cell references to identify cells rather than an actual number. For example, the formula to add the values in cells B5 and B6 is **=B5+B6**.

The equals sign [=] is always the first character you type when creating a formula. The equals sign alerts Excel that you are entering a formula and not text. The second component of the formula is the first cell reference (B5 in the example **=B5+B6**). The third component is the mathematical operator, which signifies the type of calculation. (In the example **=B5+B6**, the plus sign is the operator.) The final part of the sample formula is the last cell reference (B6 in the example **=B5+B6**).

Enter a Formula Using the Keyboard

There are two ways to enter cell references into a formula. You can type the formula manually using the keyboard or use the select method. Both methods require identifying the location of the formula, typing the equals sign, and then entering (by typing or selecting) the first cell reference, an arithmetic operator (+, -, *, or /), and the next cell reference. Formulas are not case sensitive, and Excel automatically changes cell references to uppercase. In both methods, you press **Enter** to complete the entry or click the **Enter** button (the check mark) on the *Formula bar*. To cancel a formula before it is complete, press **Esc**. Do not navigate using an arrow key while you are entering a formula. The cell you navigate to may accidentally be included in the formula.

HOW TO: Enter a Formula in a Cell Using the Keyboard

1. Click the cell where you want to create the formula (Figure 2-1).
2. Type = (equals sign) to begin the formula.
3. Type the first cell reference.
4. Enter the mathematical operator (+, -, *, or /).
5. Type the second cell reference.
   - Once a cell reference is entered using the keyboard, Excel color codes each cell reference.
6. Press **Enter**.
   - The result of the formula appears in the cell where the formula is located (Figure 2-2).
   - The *Formula bar* displays the formula.
   - You can use the **Enter** button (the check mark) on the *Formula bar* instead of pressing **Enter** on the keyboard (Figure 2-3). This button is only active when a cell is in **edit mode** (the insertion point is present within a cell).

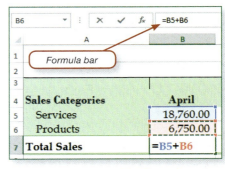

2-1 Formula syntax

2-2 Formula result

2-3 *Enter* button

Enter a Formula Using the Select Method

A popular and accurate technique of creating formulas is the ***select method***. When creating a formula, you can select a cell with your pointer instead of manually typing the cell reference, which prevents typographical errors. When you click a cell or select a cell range, Excel automatically enters the cell addresses into the formula.

HOW TO: Enter a Formula in a Cell Using Selection

1. Click the cell where you want to create the formula (Figure 2-4).
2. Type = (equals sign).
3. Using your pointer, click the first cell you want to include in the formula.
4. Enter a mathematical operator.
5. Move the pointer to the next cell reference and select the cell.
6. Click the **Enter** button on the *Formula bar* to finalize the formula.
   - If you select a cell by mistake, press **Backspace**.
   - The result of the calculation appears in the cell where the formula is located.
   - Select the cell where the formula is located to display the formula in the *Formula bar*.

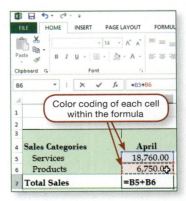

2-4 Formula syntax

Edit a Formula

There will be times when you make an error when creating a formula. You can edit a formula by double-clicking the cell where the formula is located and using edit mode to correct the formula. Another way to edit a formula is to use time-saving, color-coded editing options such as the ***Range Finder*** and ***Formula Auditing*** tools.

Range Finder

The *Range Finder* is a color-coded editing tool that applies different colors to each cell or cell range included within a formula. To activate the *Range Finder*, double-click the cell that contains the formula you want to edit or select the cell that contains the formula and click the *Formula bar*. The color-coded cells automatically appear and indicate each cell location within the formula.

HOW TO: Edit a Formula in a Cell Using the Range Finder

1. Double-click the formula you want to edit.
   - The *Range Finder* activates and the cell references appear color-coded.
   - The cell formula appears in the *Formula bar*.
2. Edit the formula.
   - Insert or delete text.
   - Drag a range finder border to move the frame to include the correct cells (Figure 2-5).
   - Drag a corner of the border to include additional cells or to reduce the number of cells.
3. Press **Enter** or click the **Enter** button on the *Formula bar* once your edit is complete.

2-5 Formula in edit mode using *Range Finder*

Formula Auditing

Formula Auditing refers to a group of editing options on the *Formulas* tab that you can use to review and correct errors in formulas. *Trace Precedents* and *Trace Dependents* are auditing tools that include a color-coded editing system. When you use these tools, different colors are applied to each cell or cell range and display arrows point to the cells and cell ranges included within a formula. *Trace Precedents* displays all cells referenced in a formula. *Trace Dependents* indicates which formulas reference a particular cell.

Evaluate Formula

Evaluate Formula is an additional auditing tool that is typically used for more complex formulas. Complex formulas may contain a syntax error. A syntax error occurs when a formula contains a typographical error, unnecessary or missing punctuation, incorrect order of arguments, or an incorrect cell reference. If your formula includes a syntax error, Excel displays an error message or returns an error code as the formula result. The *Evaluate Formula* tool reviews each part of a formula in sequence to determine where the error is.

To apply *Formula Auditing* options, display the *Formulas* tab, and choose an option in the *Formula Auditing* group (Figure 2-6). The following table describes the auditing options.

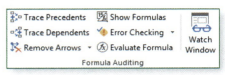

2-6 *Formula Auditing* options

Formula Auditing Tools

Button	Description
Trace Precedents	Displays arrows that point to the cells referenced in the selected formula
Trace Dependents	Displays arrows that point to the cells that contain a formula
Remove Arrows	Removes arrows for *Trace Precedents* or *Trace Dependents*
Show Formulas	Displays formulas instead of results
Error Checking	Checks for common errors
Evaluate Formula	Steps through each part of a formula
Watch Window	Adds cells to the *Watch Window*. Values are watched as the worksheet is updated.

HOW TO: Use Auditing Tools

1. Select the cell you want to edit (Figure 2-7).
2. Click the **Show Formulas** button [*Formulas* tab, *Formula Auditing* group].
   - The formula displays instead of the formula result. You may need to *AutoFit* the width of your columns to view the formula.
   - Press **Ctrl+`** to switch between formula and results views.
3. Select a cell containing a formula.

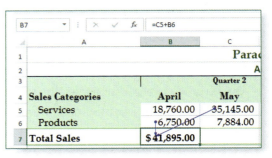

2-7 *Trace Precedents* arrows

4. Click the **Trace Precedents** button [*Formulas* tab, *Formula Auditing* group].

   - Arrows display indicating which cells in your workbook are included in the current cell's formula (see Figure 2-7).
   - Blue arrows indicate cells with no errors.
   - Red arrows indicate cells that cause errors.
   - Black arrows point from the selected cell to a worksheet icon.

5. Click **Remove Arrows** [*Formulas* tab, *Formula Auditing* group] to remove the *Trace Precedents* arrows.

6. Click a cell that is included in a formula (not the formula cell).

7. Click **Trace Dependents**.

   - An arrow displays leading from the selected cell to the formula cell.

8. Click **Remove Arrows** to remove the *Trace Dependents* arrows.

   - Click the **Remove Arrows** drop-down list to specify the type of arrow to remove.

9. Click **Show Formulas** to display formula results.

> **MORE INFO**
>
> The *Error Checking* and *Evaluate Formulas* tools are helpful if a syntax error occurs. If the error occurs because you selected the incorrect cell, it may be more useful to use *Trace Precedents*.

> **MORE INFO**
>
> To print the formula view of a spreadsheet, click the **Show Formulas** button [*Formulas* tab, *Formula Auditing* group] prior to printing the worksheet.

Message Window

There are times when a typographical error may be the cause of your syntax error. After you complete a formula containing an error, a Microsoft Excel message window may display (Figure 2-8). The window indicates an error was found, and a corrected formula appears in the box. Click **Yes** to accept the correction or **No** to edit the formula manually.

2-8 Microsoft Excel message window

Trace Error

A green triangle in the top left corner of a cell indicates that the formula in the cell may contain an error. When you select a cell with the green triangle, the *Trace Error* button displays. You can point to the button to see a ScreenTip identifying the error. Click the drop-down arrow to view a list of options to ignore or repair the error.

HOW TO: Correct a Formula in a Cell Using the Trace Error Button

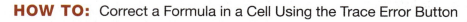

1. Click a cell with an incorrect formula (Figure 2-9).

   - The green triangle appears in the top left corner of the cell.

2. Move the pointer over the *Trace Error* button that appears to the left of the selected cell.

   - The *Trace Error* button looks like a yellow diamond with an exclamation mark (!).

2-9 Trace Error options

3. Click the **Trace Error** drop-down arrow.

4. Select an option from the *Trace Error* button list.

   • Select the **Ignore Error** option if the formula is correct.

Circular Reference

A *circular reference* occurs when a formula includes the cell address of the formula. For example, if the cell containing the formula is B7, and the syntax of the formula is =**B5+B7**, then you would have a circular reference because B7 is included in the calculation. When a circular reference occurs, a Microsoft Excel message appears (Figure 2-10). You can either click **OK** to accept the result or click **Help**.

2-10 Circular reference and Microsoft Excel message window

SLO 2.2

Working with Cell References

There are three types of cell references you can use in a formula. The type of cell references included in a formula determines the result of a formula when it is copied. The three types of cell references are *relative*, *absolute*, and *mixed*.

- *Relative cell references* identify the location of a cell. When you are creating formulas, the default cell reference is *relative*. Column and row references automatically change when you copy a formula that contains a relative cell address. The cell address **B2** is an example of a relative cell reference.

- *Absolute cell reference* is the fixed location of a cell referenced in a formula or dialog box. Absolute cell addresses include a **$** (dollar sign) around both the column and row references. Cells that contain absolute references do not change when copied. The cell address **$B$2** is an absolute cell reference. You can quickly insert dollar signs around a cell reference in the *Formula bar* by pressing **F4**.

- *Mixed cell references* contain one relative reference (either the row number or column letter) and one absolute reference (the remaining row number or column letter). The cell address **$B2** refers to an absolute column address ($B) and a relative row address (2).

- *3D cell references* indicate cells in multiple workbooks or worksheets. To create a 3D cell reference, you include the name of the workbook (if referring to a different workbook), the name of the worksheet, and the cell reference. An example of a 3D cell reference is =**'[2016 Sales.xlsx]Sheet2'!B2**. Square brackets surround the workbook name ([2016 Sales]), and an exclamation point follows the sheet name (Sheet2!). If the name of the worksheet or workbook contains non-alphabetic characters, you need to enclose the name in single quotes. Excel automatically places absolute value symbols ($) around each cell reference if you select the cell from a different workbook or worksheet rather than type the reference.

The following table lists examples of cell reference types:

Cell Reference Examples

Cell Reference	Reference Type	Description
B2	*Relative*	The cell address changes when copied.
$B$2	*Absolute*	The cell address does not change when copied.

continued

Cell Reference Examples

Cell Reference	Reference Type	Description
$B2	*Mixed*	The column portion of the cell address is absolute; the row component changes when copied.
B$2	*Mixed*	The row portion of the cell address is absolute; the column component changes when copied.
Sheet2!B2	*3D Relative*	The cell address is located on a different worksheet and changes when copied.

Copy a Formula with a Relative Cell Reference

Relative cell references within a formula adjust automatically when you copy them. For example, if you create a formula that totals the sales for the month of January, you can copy that formula to calculate the totals for February and March. The cell references change automatically.

You can use the following methods to copy formulas:

- *Fill Handle*
- *Copy* and *Paste* buttons in the *Clipboard* group on the *Home* tab
- Shortcut commands **Ctrl+C** to copy and **Ctrl+V** to paste
- *Context-sensitive menu;* right-click to display the menu
- *Control* key combined with drag and drop

HOW TO: Copy a Formula with Relative Cell References

1. Select the cell that contains the formula you want to copy (Figure 2-11).
2. Click and drag the *Fill Handle* to the destination cell or range of cells.
3. Release the *Fill Handle*.
   - The formula in the destination cell adjusts to the corresponding relative cell references.
   - Click the **Show Formulas** and **Trace Precedents** buttons [*Formulas* tab, *Formula Auditing* group] to see how the formula's cell reference changes from the source cell to the destination cell during the copy process (Figure 2-12).

2-11 Using the *Fill Handle* to copy

2-12 *Trace Precedence* arrows

After you drag the *Fill Handle* over a range, the **AutoFill Options** button displays. The drop-down list includes three options to control the fill data. Choose to *Copy Cells, Fill Formatting Only,* or *Fill Without Formatting.*

Copy a Formula with an Absolute Cell Reference

An absolute reference in a cell refers to a specific location, and it does not change when you copy or fill the formula. To change a relative cell reference to an absolute cell reference, type a **$** in front of the column letter and the row number of the cell address or select the cell address and press **F4** to insert the dollar signs quickly.

HOW TO: Copy a Formula with an Absolute Cell Reference

1. Select the cell that contains the formula you want to copy.
2. Click the *Formula bar* and click the cell reference you want to be absolute.
3. Press **F4** to change the cell address to an absolute cell reference.
4. Press **Enter** and re-select the cell to copy the formula.
5. Click and drag the *Fill Handle* to the destination cell.
6. Release the *Fill Handle.*

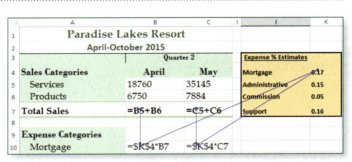

2-13 *Trace Precedence* **arrows illustrate cell references**

- The absolute cell reference remains constant when the formula is copied to the destination cell.
- Figure 2-13 displays *Trace Precedents* for the formulas with the correct formula syntax.

> **MORE INFO**
>
> **F4** is a four-way toggle key in the *Formula bar.* Press **F4** to toggle from absolute reference to mixed references to relative reference.

Range Names

You can use *range names* to navigate a worksheet or to identify a cell or group of cells (recall from Chapter 1 that a group of cells is called a *range*). Range names describe the cell or purpose of a group of cells and make it easier to interpret a formula. For example, instead of referring to cell K4 in the formula =**K4*B7**, you can name cell K4 "Mortgage", and use the range name in the formula. The example formula would change to =**Mortgage*B7**.

When you name a cell or range, the name becomes an absolute reference. The first character of a name must be a letter, an underscore (_), or a backslash (\). Range names cannot contain spaces, special characters (#, $, &), or cell references. To signify a space between words, use the underscore (_) (e.g., "Mortgage_Payment" or "MortgagePayment"). You can create a range name using the *Name* box on the *Formula bar,* the *Create from selection* button [*Formulas* tab, *Defined Names* group], or the *New Name* dialog box (Figure 2-14).

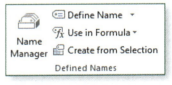

2-14 *Defined Names* **group on the** *Formulas* **tab**

To create range names using the *Name* box, select the cell or group of cells, and type the name of the range in the *Name* box.

HOW TO: Name a Cell and Use the Range Name in a Formula

1. Select the cell(s) you want to name.
2. Click the **Name** box beside the *Formula bar.*
3. Type a range name (e.g., "Tax_Rate") and press **Enter** (Figure 2-15).
4. Select the cell where you want the formula to appear and press = to begin the formula.
5. Type the beginning letters of the range name.
   - A list of names appears matching the letters typed.

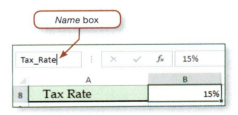

2-15 **Tax_Rate range name**

6. Double-click the range name from the list.
   - The drop-down list is known as *Formula AutoComplete*.
7. Type a mathematical operator.
8. Select the next cell reference or cell range (Figure 2-16).
9. Press **Enter**.

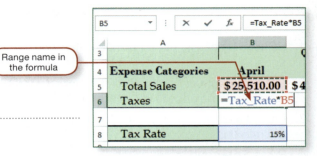

2-16 **Formula with range name**

> ## MORE INFO
>
> Manage range names by clicking the **Name Manager** button [*Formulas* tab, *Defined Names* group]. The *Name Manager* dialog box provides options for creating, editing, and deleting range names.

> ## ANOTHER WAY
>
> To insert a range name, press **F3** to display the *Paste Name* dialog box. Select a name and click **OK**.

A second method to name a range is to convert existing row and column labels to names. If a range in your worksheets contains column and or row headings, you can use these headings to name multiple cells simultaneously.

HOW TO: Name Multiple Cells Simultaneously Using the Ribbon

1. Select the range and include the row or column labels (Figure 2-17).
   - The cells and their labels must be adjacent to each other.
   - A range can consist of one cell, a range of cells, a formula, or a constant.

2. Click the **Create from Selection** button [*Formulas* tab, *Defined Names* group] to open the *Create Names from Selection* dialog box (see Figure 2-17).

3. Select the check box that best describes the label location in relation to the selected cells.

4. Click **OK**.
   - To view a list of range names, click the **Name** box arrow on the *Formula bar* (Figure 2-18).
   - The formula syntax shows the range name in place of the cell address (Figure 2-19).

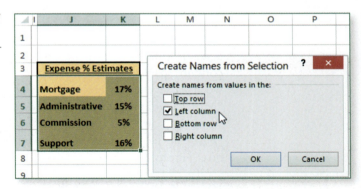

2-17 **Create Names from Selection dialog box**

2-18 **Name box**

2-19 **Formula with range name**

If you have already created formulas and are naming cells after copying formulas, select **Apply names** from the *Define Name* drop-down arrow [*Formulas* tab, *Defined Names* group] to open the *Apply Names* dialog box (Figure 2-20). Click **OK** to apply all newly created range names to existing formulas.

A third method to define range names is to use the *New Name* dialog box. The New Name dialog box includes an option to specify a range name for the entire workbook or an individual worksheet. After range names have been added to a worksheet, use the *Paste Name* dialog box to create a two-column list in a blank area of a worksheet to display defined names and their locations.

2-20 *Apply Names* dialog box

HOW TO: Use the New Name Dialog Box and the Paste Names Dialog Box

1. Select the cell range.
2. Click the **Define Name** button [*Formulas* tab, *Defined Names* group] to open the *New Name* dialog box (Figure 2-21).
3. Type the range name in the **Name** box.
4. Click the **Scope** drop-down arrow to select *Workbook* or *Worksheet.*
5. Click **OK**.
6. Click a cell in a blank area of the worksheet or a cell on a new sheet.
7. Click the **Use in Formula** button [*Formulas* tab, *Defined Names* group].
8. Select **Paste Names** to open the *Paste Name* dialog box.
9. Click **Paste List** to display the range names and their locations in the worksheet.

2-21 *New Name* dialog box

Copy a Formula with a Mixed Cell Reference

Mixed cell references are a combination of relative and absolute cell references within a single cell address. For example, you can copy a formula in a cell to another location and keep the column reference of the cell addresses constant but allow the row reference to be relative. The same rules that apply to mixed cell references apply to absolute cell references. Place a dollar sign before the part of the cell address that you want to remain absolute prior to copying.

HOW TO: Copy a Formula with a Mixed Cell Reference

1. Select the cell that contains the formula you want to copy.
2. Click the *Formula bar* and type a dollar sign next to the column letter or row number that you want to remain absolute (Figure 2-22).
3. Press **Enter**.
4. Select the cell you want to copy.
5. Click and drag the *Fill Handle* to the destination cell.
6. Release the *Fill Handle.*

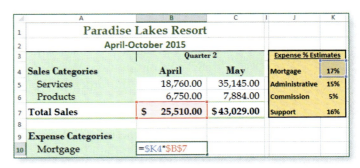

2-22 Formula with mixed cell reference

Create a Formula with a 3D Reference

Sometimes data for your formula may be located in different worksheets. For example, sales for 2015 may be saved in a different worksheet than sales for 2016. To reference cells in both sheets within a formula, you can use *3D* references. The process of using cells in other workbooks is known as ***linking workbooks***.

A formula containing a *3D* cell reference follows the same rules and requirements of non-*3D* cell references with one exception. Because a *3D* cell reference is not physically located in the same sheet as the cell containing the formula, one extra step is required when using *3D* cell references. You must click the sheet tab that contains the cell you want to use in your formula before you select the cell. To select a cell in another sheet within a different workbook, select the open workbook from the *Excel* button on the *Taskbar* and then select the worksheet tab and cell within the tab.

Sample 3D References

Active Cell	Formula	Explanation
Sheet 1 – Cell B4	=Sheet2!B2+Sheet2!B3	Adds cells B2 and B3 on sheet 2.
Sheet 1 – Cell B4	=A4+February!D5+ '[Sales.xslx]10-27-2015'!$B$10+ '[Sales.xslx]10-27-2015'!$C$12	Adds cell A4 in current sheet, D5 on the February sheet in the current workbook, and cells B10 and C12 from the 10-27-2015 worksheet in the Sales workbook.

HOW TO: Create a Formula with a 3D Relative Cell Reference

1. Click the cell where you want to create the formula.
2. Type =.
3. Select the sheet tab of the first cell in the formula.
   - If copying a cell reference from another workbook, open that workbook before creating the formula.
4. Select the cell address of the first cell of the formula.
5. Type the mathematical operator.
6. Select the sheet tab of the next cell in the formula.
7. Select the cell address of the next cell in the calculation (Figure 2-23).
8. Press **Enter** or click the **Enter** button (check mark) on the *Formula bar*.
   - You can copy a *3D* formula using the *Fill Handle*.

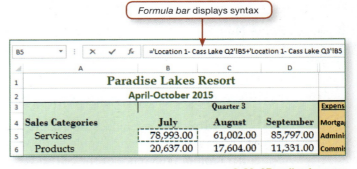

2-23 3D cell reference

SLO 2.3

Applying Mathematical Order of Operations

When you create formulas, arithmetic operators specify the type of calculation such as multiplication or addition. When more than one operator appears in a formula, it is important to understand the order in which Excel performs each operation (***mathematical order of operations***) so you create formulas that correctly calculate results.

The basic types of arithmetic operators in formulas are: addition, subtraction, multiplication, division, and exponentiation. Excel executes these operations in a specified order, but you can change the order by using parentheses.

You can use the following acronym to help remember the order: **P**lease **E**xcuse **M**y **D**ear **A**unt **S**ally. The first letter of each word in the acronym signifies an operator. The order of the words indicates which operator has precedence over another. In the event that two operators have the same level of precedence, Excel calculates the operations of the formula from left to right.

The following table describes the specific rules Excel follows in formulas with multiple operators.

Mathematical Order of Precedence in Formulas

Character	Operator Name	Order of Precedence	Acronym
()	Parentheses	First	Please
^	Exponent	Second	Excuse
*	Multiplication	Third	My
/	Division	Third	Dear
+	Addition	Fourth	Aunt
-	Subtraction	Fourth	Sally

Addition and Subtraction

Since addition and subtraction are on the same precedence level, Excel calculates from left to right if they are both included in a formula.

> For example, consider the mathematical expression: **2+5-3**.
> The addition operation (2+5) is completed first.
> The result (7) is used in the subtraction operation (7-3).
> The result is 4.

HOW TO: Use Addition and Subtraction in a Formula

1. Click the cell where you want to create the formula (Figure 2-24).
2. Type =.
3. Enter the cell address or select the first cell reference of the formula.
4. Type +.
5. Enter or select the next cell address of the calculation.
6. Type –.
7. Enter or select the last cell address of the formula.
8. Press **Enter**.
   - The result of the calculation appears in the cell containing the formula.
   - Use the *Formula bar* to view the syntax of the formula.

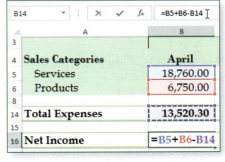

2-24 Formula with multiple operators

Multiplication and Division

Like subtraction and addition, multiplication and division are on the same precedence level. Excel calculates from left to right if multiplication and division appear in the same formula. If the syntax of the formula also includes addition or subtraction, the multiplying or dividing operators are computed before the addition or subtraction operators.

> For example, consider the mathematical expression: **2+5*3**.
> The multiplication operation (5*3) occurs first.
> The result (15) is used in the addition operation (15+2).
> The result is 17.

Conversely, consider the mathematical expression: **2*5+3**.
The multiplication operation (2*5) occurs first.
The result (10) is used in the addition operation (10+3).
The result is 13.

HOW TO: Use Multiplication and Addition in a Formula

1. Click the cell where you want to create the formula (Figure 2-25).
2. Type =.
3. Enter or select the first cell address of the formula.
4. Type +.
5. Enter or select the next cell address.
6. Type *.
7. Enter or select the last cell address of the formula.
8. Press **Enter**.

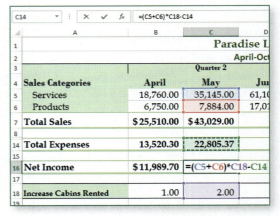

2-25 Addition and multiplication formula

Parentheses and Exponents

Excel calculates operations within parentheses before any other operation is performed. Within parentheses, Excel uses the order of operations to perform calculations.

For example, in the mathematical expression **4+(2+5)*3**.
The operation (2+5) in parentheses occurs first.
The result (7) is used in the multiplication operation (7*3).
The result (21) is used in the addition operation (21+4).
The result is 25.

HOW TO: Use Parentheses, Multiplication, Addition, and Subtraction in a Formula

1. Click the cell where you want to create the formula (Figure 2-26).
2. Type =.
3. Type ((open parenthesis).
4. Enter or select the first cell address of the formula.
5. Type +.
6. Select the next cell address and then type) (close parenthesis).
7. Type *.
8. Select the next cell address.
9. Type –.
10. Select the last cell address.
11. Press **Enter**.

2-26 Multiple operators

Exponents raise a number to a power. Use the caret symbol (^) when writing a formula that includes an exponent. The formula **3^3** raises 3 to the power of 3 and produces the result of 27.

You can use the formulas in Excel to convey calculations in a time-saving and meaningful fashion. In this project, you add formulas to a business spreadsheet that displays two quarters of sales and expenses for Paradise Lakes Resort.

File Needed: ***PLRSalesandExpenses-02.xlsx***
Completed Project File Name: ***[your initials] PP E2-1.xlsx***

1. Open the ***PLRSalesandExpenses-02.xlsx*** workbook and save the workbook as ***[your initials] PP E2-1***. (If you see a yellow bar at the top of the workbook entitled "Protected View," click **Enable Editing.**)

2. Enter an addition formula.
    a. Click cell **B7**.
    b. Type =.
    c. Select **B5**, the cell address of the first cell of the formula.
    d. Type +.
    e. Select **B6**, the next cell address of the formula.
    f. Press **Enter** or click the **Enter** button on the *Formula bar.* The syntax of the formula should read =B5+B6.

3. Copy the addition formula.
    a. Select cell **B7**.
    b. Place your pointer in the lower right corner of **B7**, click and drag the *Fill Handle* through the cell range **C7:G7**, and release the *Fill Handle* (Figure 2-27).

2-27 Using the *Fill Handle* to copy a formula

4. Create and copy the mortgage expense formula using absolute cell references.
    a. Select cell **B10**.
    b. Type the following formula to determine mortgage expenses: =K4*B7.
    c. Click to the left of the **K** column reference letter in the *Formula bar* and type $.
    d. Click to the left of the **4** row reference number and type $. You can also use **F4** to add the dollar signs in the cell reference (Figure 2-28). The formula should read: =$K$4*B7.

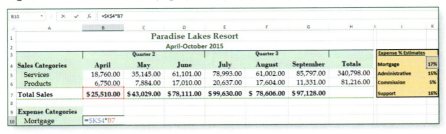

2-28 Mortgage expense formula

e. Press **Enter**.

f. Click and drag the *Fill Handle* on cell **B10** through the cell range **C10:G10**.

5. Create and copy expense formulas using multiplication and absolute cell references.

   a. Enter the formulas listed in the table at right.
   b. Select cells **B11:B14**.
   c. Use the *Fill Handle* of cell **B14** to copy the formulas to **C11:G14**.

B11	=$K$5*B7
B12	=$K$6*B7
B13	=$K$7*B7
B14	=B10+B11+B12+B13

6. Create and copy a net income formula with a *3D* reference, multiple operators, and apply the mathematical order of precedence.

   a. Click cell **B16** and type =(B5+.
   b. Select cell **B6** and type).
   c. Type -, select cell **B14**, and type -.
   d. Click the **Cass Lake Tax** sheet tab.
   e. Select **B5** on the *Cass Lake Tax* tab.
   f. Press **Enter**.
   g. Review the formula syntax. It should be =(B5+B6)-B14-'Cass Lake Tax'!B5.
   h. Select cell **B16** and place your pointer over the *Fill Handle* of cell **B16**.
   i. Use the *Fill Handle* to copy the formula to **C16:G16**.
   j. Release the pointer.

7. Use auditing tools to review the formula in cell B16.

   a. Select cell **B16**.
   b. Click **Show Formulas** and **Trace Precedents** [*Formulas* tab, *Formula Auditing* group]. The black arrow indicates a cell reference on another worksheet.
   c. Click **Remove Arrows** [*Formulas* tab, *Formula Auditing* group].
   d. Click **Show Formulas** [*Formulas* tab, *Formula Auditing* group] to return to *Normal* view.

8. Copy and paste an existing formula without the formatting.

   a. Select cell **H6** and use the *Fill Handle* to copy the formula to **H7:H16**.
   b. Click the **AutoFill Options** arrow button and select **Fill Without Formatting** to prevent overwriting existing cell formats.
   c. Delete unnecessary formulas in cells **H8, H9**, and **H15**.

9. Save and close the workbook (Figure 2-29).

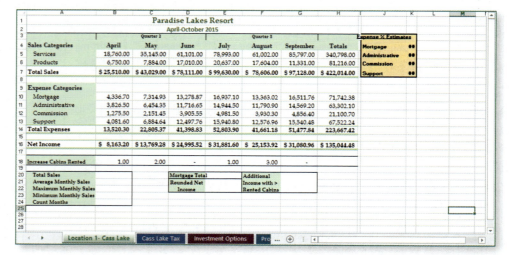

2-29 PP E2-1 completed

SLO 2.4

Working with Common Functions

Functions are pre-defined formulas and each function has a specific syntax pattern. Functions start with an equals sign (=) followed by the function name, an opening parenthesis, the arguments for the function separated by commas, and a closing parenthesis. *Arguments* are the pieces of information within parentheses that determine what value a function returns. For example, in the function =SUM(B2:B6), SUM is the function name and the cell range B2:B6 is the argument.

When you type a formula, ***Formula AutoComplete*** and ***Function Screen Tips*** appear to help you create and edit formulas. After you type an = and beginning letters of the function, *Formula AutoComplete* displays a list of functions and range names. Use the down arrow to move through the list or continue typing the function name. Press *Tab* or double-click the function name to insert it. A ScreenTip appears after you type the function name and an opening parenthesis. The ScreenTip includes the required syntax and arguments for the function. Click the ScreenTip function name to display the *Help* topic for the function.

In addition to the *AutoSum* function, which was introduced in Chapter 1 (see *SLO 1.3: Using the Sum Function*), there are other common functions that you can use to calculate values in a spreadsheet. Many times you may need to find an average or a minimum or maximum value in a range of numbers or you may want to count the numbers in a given range within a group of cells.

> ### MORE INFO
>
> Functions and formulas are similar but not exactly the same. All functions are also considered formulas, =SUM(B2:B6), but not all formulas are functions since they do not contain a function name, =B2+B3-B6.

AUTOSUM Function

As discussed in Chapter 1, the *AutoSum* button automates the insertion of the *SUM* function. Recall that when you use *AutoSum*, instead of typing a formula to add cell contents that separates each cell reference with a plus sign, you use the *SUM* function to add the cells. You can use *AutoSum* to insert the *SUM* function by clicking the *AutoSum* button in the *Function Library* group on the *Formulas* tab. In this chapter, we discuss the *AutoSum* function in more detail and explain how you can use the *AutoSum* drop-down list to insert other functions including *Average, Count Numbers, Max,* and *Min*.

HOW TO: Enter the SUM Function with AutoSum

1. Click the cell where you want to enter the function.
2. Click the **AutoSum** arrow [*Formulas* tab, *Function Library* group] (Figure 2-30).
   - When you click the upper half of **AutoSum**, the *SUM* function is inserted. Click the bottom half of **AutoSum** (the arrow) to display a list of functions.
3. Select **Sum** from the list.
   - The equals sign, function name, parentheses, and assumed cell range are entered automatically.
4. Select the cell range you wish to total if the range that Excel entered automatically is not correct.
   - The cell range appears between the parentheses in the function syntax (Figure 2-31).
5. Press **Enter**.

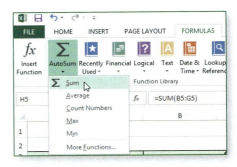

2-30 *AutoSum* function list

2-31 Selection of correct range

If you are entering multiple *AutoSum* functions in a worksheet, you can do this in one step rather than individually entering each *AutoSum* function.

HOW TO: Enter Multiple SUM Functions Simultaneously with AutoSum

1. Select the cells where you want to enter the functions (Figure 2-32).

2-32 Selected cell range for simultaneous SUM function

2. Click the **AutoSum** arrow [*Formulas* tab, *Function Library* group].
3. Select **Sum** from the list.
   - It is not necessary to press **Enter**.
   - The results appear in the cells containing the formulas.

> ### ANOTHER WAY
> *AutoSum* is also located on the *Home* tab in the *Editing* group.
> Press **Alt+=** for the *SUM* function.

> ### MORE INFO
> The *AutoSum* button is also called the **Sigma** button.

AVERAGE Function

The **AVERAGE** function calculates an average by adding cell values together and dividing the total of the values by the number of values. The *AVERAGE* function performs the calculation quickly and eliminates the need to key cell addresses and mathematical operators manually. You can apply the *AVERAGE* function by using the *AutoSum* button in the *Function Library* group on the *Formulas* tab.

HOW TO: Enter the AVERAGE Function Using the AutoSum Button

1. Click the cell where you want to enter the function.
2. Click the **AutoSum** arrow [*Formulas* tab, *Function Library* group].

3. Select **Average**.

   • The equals sign, function name, parentheses, and assumed cell range appear in the cell (Figure 2-33).

| E5 | ▼ | : | × | ✓ | fx | =AVERAGE(E5:G6) | | | | | |

AVERAGE function range

	A	B	C	D	E	F	G
3			Quarter 2			Quarter 3	
4	**Sales Categories**	**April**	**May**	**June**	**July**	**August**	**September**
5	Services	18,760.00	35,145.00	61,101.00	78,993.00	61,002.00	85,797.00
6	Products	6,750.00	7,884.00	17,010.00	20,637.00	17,604.00	11,331.00
7	**Total Sales**	$ 25,510.00	$43,029.00	$78,111.00	$99,630.00	$ 78,606.00	$97,128.00
19							
20	Quarter 3 Total Sales	$ 275,364.00		Mortgage Total		Additional	
21	Average Sales	=AVERAGE(E5:G6)		Rounded Net		Income with >	

AVERAGE function

2-33 AVERAGE function

4. Select a cell range if the range Excel automatically highlights is not correct.

   • The cell range appears between the parentheses in the function syntax.

5. Press **Enter** or click the **Enter** button on the *Formula bar*.

COUNT Functions

Although you can manually count each number in a group of cells or each cell that contains descriptive labels, *COUNT* functions provide a more error-free method to accomplish this task. To add a *COUNT* function to the worksheet, use the *AutoSum* arrow in the *Function Library* group on the *Formulas* tab (Figure 2-34).

There are several *COUNT* functions. For example, you could use a *COUNTIF* function to insert a function that calculates all cells in a range that contain the product description label "Services." The following table lists several *COUNT* functions.

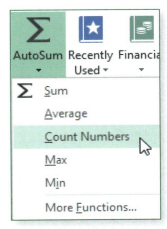

2-34 AutoSum function list

Common Count Functions

Count Functions	Description	Example Syntax
COUNT	Counts the number of cells in a range that contain numbers	=COUNT(A1:A15)
COUNTA	Counts the number of cells in a range that contain any data type, text, or numbers	=COUNTA(A1:A15)
COUNTBLANK	Counts the number of blank cells in a range	=COUNTBLANK(A1:A15)
COUNTIF	Counts the number of cells in a range based on specified criteria	=COUNTIF(A1:A15, "Services")
DCOUNT	Counts the amount of numbers in a database range that meet specified criteria	=DCOUNT(database, field, criteria)
DCOUNTA	Counts the amount of text entries in a database range that meet specified criteria	=DCOUNTA(database, field, criteria)

HOW TO: Enter the COUNT Function Using the AutoSum Button

1. Click the cell where you want to enter the function (Figure 2-35).

2. Click the **AutoSum** arrow [*Formulas* tab, *Function Library group*].

3. Select **Count Numbers** from the list to choose the *COUNT* function (see Figure 2-35).

   - The *COUNT* function counts the number of cells in a range that contain numbers.

4. Select a cell range if the range that Excel automatically highlights is not correct.

5. Press **Enter**.

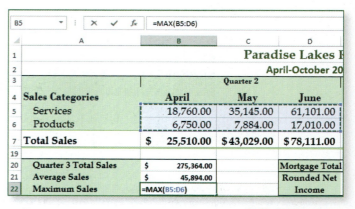

2-35 *COUNT* function

> ### MORE INFO
>
> You can use a "**?**" to take the place of one character in the *COUNT* function criteria. For example, the criteria "**Sal?**" finds results of 4-letter words beginning with *Sal* such as **Sale** or **Salt**. You can use an "*****" to represent multiple characters in criteria. For example, the criteria "**Sal***" finds results such as **Salmon** or **Salt**.

MAX and MIN Functions

The *MAX* function finds the largest value in a cell range, and the *MIN* function finds the smallest value in a cell range. To apply the *MAX and MIN* functions use the *AutoSum* arrow in the *Function Library* group on the *Formulas* tab.

HOW TO: Enter the MAX or MIN Function Using the AutoSum Button

1. Click the cell where you want to enter the function.

2. Click the **AutoSum** arrow [*Formulas* tab, *Function Library group*].

3. Select the **MAX** or **MIN** function from the list (Figure 2-36).

4. Select a cell range if the range that Excel highlights is not correct.

5. Press **Enter**.

2-36 *MAX* function

AutoCalculate

AutoCalculate allows you to view totals, averages, or other statistical information without creating a formula. The *AutoCalculate* area is located on the *Status bar*. Right-click the *Status bar* to select *AutoCalculate* options. The *Average*, *Count*, and *Sum* options are selected by default. *AutoCalculate* results do not display in the spreadsheet.

HOW TO: Use AutoCalculate for a Range of Cells

1. Select the appropriate cell range.
2. Right-click the **Status bar** to display the *Customize Status Bar* menu (Figure 2-37).
3. Select the desired functions from the shortcut menu.
   - If a function has a checkmark to the left, it is already active.
4. View the *Status bar* to see the results of selected functions (Figure 2-38).

AVERAGE: 24,441.67   COUNT: 6   SUM: 146,650.00

AutoCalculate results

2-38 *AutoCalculate* **results**

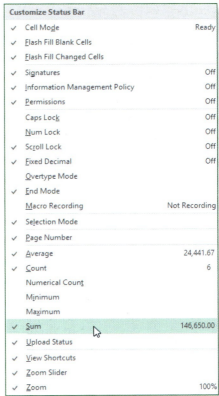

2-37 *Customize Status Bar* **menu**

TODAY and NOW Functions

Excel has 24 date and time functions. *TODAY* and *NOW* are useful functions that are often included in spreadsheets to track the current date of reports. These functions reflect your computer's date and time stamp.

The *TODAY* function uses the syntax =TODAY() to automatically insert the current date. The TODAY() function does not have any arguments. The TODAY() function updates each time the spreadsheet is opened.

The *NOW* function uses the syntax =NOW() and is similar to the *TODAY* function. However, the *NOW* function includes the current time with the date. Like the *TODAY* function, the *NOW* function is updated each time the spreadsheet opens. Several formats are available for the date and time data. For example, if you prefer to view the date as 12/21/2015, you can choose the **Short Date** format from the *Number Format* drop-down list located in the *Number* group on the *Home* tab.

The *Function Library* group on the *Formulas* tab includes a **Date & Time** button. Click the **Date & Time** arrow to view the list of date and time functions.

PAUSE & PRACTICE: EXCEL 2-2

For this project, you open your previous Pause & Practice file and insert the *SUM, AVERAGE, COUNT, MIN,* and *MAX* functions to the Paradise Lakes Resort net income spreadsheet.

File Needed: ***[your initials] PP E2-1.xlsx***
Completed Project File Name: ***[your initials] PP E2-2.xlsx***

1. Open the workbook ***[your initials] PP E2-1*** and save the workbook as ***[your initials] PP E2-2***.

2. Enter the *SUM* function using *AutoSum.*
   a. Click cell **B20**.
   b. Click the **AutoSum** arrow button [*Formulas* tab, *Function Library* group].
   c. Select **Sum**.
   d. Select the cell range **B7:G7**. Verify that the formula syntax is =SUM(B7:G7) (Figure 2-39).
   e. Press **Enter**.

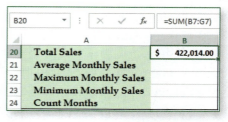

2-39 *SUM function*

3. Enter the *AVERAGE* function using *AutoSum.*
   a. Click cell **B21**.
   b. Click the **AutoSum** arrow button [*Formulas* tab, *Function Library group*].
   c. Select **Average**.
   d. Select the cell range **B7:G7**.
   e. Verify that the formula syntax is =AVERAGE(B7:G7).
   f. Press **Enter**.

4. Enter a *COUNT* function using *AutoSum.*
   a. Click cell **B24**.
   b. Click the **AutoSum** arrow button [*Formulas* tab, *Function Library* group].
   c. Select **Count Numbers**.
   d. Select the cell range **B7:G7**.
   e. Verify that the formula syntax is =COUNT(B7:G7).
   f. Press **Enter**. The formula's result should be 6.00 (Figure 2-40).

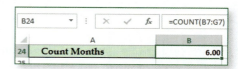

2-40 *COUNT function*

5. Enter the *MAX* function using *AutoSum.*
   a. Click cell **B22**.
   b. Click the **AutoSum** arrow [*Formulas* tab, *Function Library group*].
   c. Select **Max**.
   d. Select the cell range **B7:G7**.
   e. Verify that the formula syntax is =MAX(B7:G7).
   f. Press **Enter**.

6. Use auditing tools to review the formula in B22.
   a. Select **B22**.
   b. Click **Show Formulas** and **Trace Precedents** [*Formulas* tab, *Formula Auditing* group].
   c. Review the position of the arrows.
   d. Click **Remove Arrows** [*Formulas* tab, *Formula Auditing* group].
   e. Click **Show Formulas** [*Formulas* tab, *Formula Auditing* group] to return to *Normal* view.

7. Add absolute cell references to an existing formula.
   a. Select **B22**.
   b. Click the **Formula bar** and select the cell range **B7:G7** but not the parentheses.
   c. Press **F4** to add absolute references.
   d. Press **Enter**.
   e. Verify the formula syntax =MAX($B$7:$G$7).

8. Copy an existing formula and edit the function name.
   a. Select **B22** and use the *Fill Handle* to copy the formula to **B23**.
   b. Select cell **B23**.
   c. Click the **Formula bar** and replace the function name *MAX* with MIN.
   d. Press **Enter**.

9. Save and close the workbook (Figure 2-41).

	April	May	June	July	August	September	Totals	
Paradise Lakes Resort								
April-October 2015								
		Quarter 2			Quarter 3			**Expense % Estimates**
Sales Categories	**April**	**May**	**June**	**July**	**August**	**September**	**Totals**	Mortgage 17%
Services	18,760.00	35,145.00	61,101.00	78,993.00	61,002.00	85,797.00	340,798.00	Administrative 15%
Products	6,750.00	7,884.00	17,010.00	20,637.00	17,604.00	11,331.00	81,216.00	Commission 5%
Total Sales	$ 25,510.00	$ 43,029.00	$ 78,111.00	$ 99,630.00	$ 78,606.00	$ 97,128.00	$ 422,014.00	Support 16%
Expense Categories								
Mortgage	4,336.70	7,314.93	13,278.87	16,937.10	13,363.02	16,511.76	71,742.38	
Administrative	3,826.50	6,454.35	11,716.65	14,944.50	11,790.90	14,569.20	63,302.10	
Commission	1,275.50	2,151.45	3,905.55	4,981.50	3,930.30	4,856.40	21,100.70	
Support	4,081.60	6,884.64	12,497.76	15,940.80	12,576.96	15,540.48	67,522.24	
Total Expenses	13,520.30	22,805.37	41,398.83	52,803.90	41,661.18	51,477.84	223,667.42	
Net Income	$ 8,163.20	$ 13,769.28	$ 24,995.52	$ 31,881.60	$ 25,153.92	$ 31,080.96	$ 135,044.48	
Increase Cabins Rented	1.00	2.00	-	1.00	3.00	-		

Total Sales	$ 422,014.00		**Mortgage Total**	**Additional**
Average Monthly Sales	$ 70,335.67		**Rounded Net**	**Income with >**
Maximum Monthly Sales	$ 99,630.00		**Income**	**Rented Cabins**
Minimum Monthly Sales	$ 25,510.00			
Count Months	6.00			

Location 1- Cass Lake Cass Lake Tax Investment Options Product Cost

2-41 PP E2-2 completed

Working with Financial, Logical, and LOOKUP Functions

Excel's financial, logical, and lookup functions contain many advanced options. The *Insert Function* button automates hundreds of functions that are available in Excel. This section of the chapter focuses on using the *Insert Function* button to insert *PMT, IF, VLOOKUP,* and *HLOOKUP* functions.

The search feature within the ***Insert Function dialog box*** helps to quickly locate the function you need and tells you which arguments to include. Once the function is selected, you can complete most of the ***arguments*** (components or parts of the function) of the function by using point and click. This method can be very useful when you are not sure how to create the formula syntax or what the required arguments for a formula are. You can access the *Insert Function* button in the *Function Library* group on the *Formulas* tab (Figure 2-42) or click the **f$_x$** button located on the *Formula bar.*

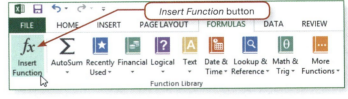

2-42 *Function Library* group

> ### ANOTHER WAY
>
> **Shift+F3** opens the *Insert Function* dialog box.

PMT Function

The *PMT* function calculates loan payment amounts. The *PMT* function assumes the borrower makes regular payments and the loan has a constant interest rate. The *PMT* function includes the principal (amount of money borrowed) and the interest rate when calculating the payment amount. It does not include other fees such as insurance costs or taxes.

The *PMT* function has five arguments, and the formula syntax for the function is:

$$=PMT(rate, nper, pv, [fv], [type])$$

- The **rate** argument is the interest rate per period for the loan; this argument is required.
- The **nper** argument is the total number of periods for repayment of the loan; this argument is required.
- The **pv** argument is the present value or the principal; this argument is required.
- The **fv** argument is the future value after you make the last payment; this argument is optional. If the fv argument is omitted, it is assumed the future value of the loan is zero.
- The **type** argument indicates when payments are due; this argument is optional. A zero or omitted argument indicates payments are due at the end of the period; this is the default setting. If the type argument is 1, payments are due at the beginning of the period.

Refer to Figure 2-43 to understand the following *PMT* function example:

The PMT function
=PMT(C8/12,F4*12,C7)

	A	B	C	D	E	F	G
1							
2		Wilson Home Entertainment Systems					
3							
4		Item Description	Equipment		Loan Term	7	
5		Purchase Price	$ 45,000.00		Payment		
6		Down Payment	$ 10,000.00		Total Interest		
7		Loan Amount	$ 35,000.00		Total Principal		
8		Annual Percentage Rate	6.5%		Total Cost of the Loan		
9							

2-43 *PMT* **function sample worksheet**

- **C8/12** is the *rate* argument and indicates an annual rate of 6.5% and that the borrower is making monthly payments (period is equal to one month), in other words 6.5% divided by 12.
- **F4*12** is the *nper* argument and indicates that the loan term is 7 years (cell F7) and there are 12 payments per year. (The total number of periods is 7 years times 12 periods per year.)
- **C7** is the *pv* argument (amount of the loan or the present value).

The result of this *PMT* function is ($519.73). The payment result is a negative number, which is indicated by the red color and the parentheses; the borrower is paying this amount and not receiving it.

HOW TO: Enter the PMT Function with the Insert Function Button

1. Click the cell where you want to enter the function.
2. Click the **Insert Function** (**f$_x$**) button to the left of the *Formula bar* to open the *Insert Function* dialog box (Figure 2-44).
3. Click the **Search for a function** box, type Payment, and click **Go**.
4. Select **PMT** from the function list and click **OK**. The *Function Arguments* dialog box opens (Figure 2-45).
5. Click the **Rate** argument text box and click the cell that contains the interest per period for the loan.

   - If the cell contains an APR (annual percentage rate), it must be converted to interest per period. Divide the interest rate by the number of payments that will be made in a year. For example, if the borrower is paying monthly, divide by 12; if the borrower is paying quarterly, divide by 4.

2-44 *Insert Function* **dialog box**

6. Click the **Nper** argument text box and click the cell that contains the term of the loan. The cell must contain the total number of periods for repayment of the loan.

   - If the loan term is in years and payments are monthly, the total number of periods is the number of years * 12.
   - If the loan term is in years and payments are quarterly, then the total number of periods is the number of years * 4.

7. Click the **Pv** argument text box and click the cell that contains the amount of the loan.

   - You can omit the last two arguments because there will be a zero balance after the last payment is made, and payments will be made at the end of each period.

8. Click **OK** to close the dialog box and insert the function.

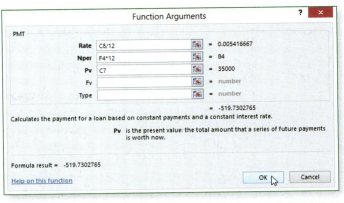

2-45 *PMT Function Arguments* **dialog box**

> ▶ **ANOTHER WAY**
>
> Use the **Financial** button [*Formulas* tab, *Function Library* group] to locate financial functions described in this section.

> ▶ **MORE INFO**
>
> To create an amortization schedule, you can use the *Loan Amortization Schedule* template in the *Templates* category from the *New* button [*File* tab]. Select the **Loan Amortization Schedule** from the *Business Schedules* subfolder located in the *Schedules* folder.

IF Function

The **IF** function evaluates a specified condition and returns one value if the condition is true and another value if the condition is false. For example, if you work for an organization that determines bonuses on the amount of sales revenue generated, you could use the *IF* function to determine if a sales goal was met and if a bonus should be paid and then calculate the amount of the bonus.

To evaluate the condition, you can use comparison operators. The table at the right lists comparison operators:

Comparison Operators

Operator	Description
=	Equal to
<>	Not equal to
>	Greater than
>=	Greater than or equal to
<	Less than
<=	Less than or equal to

The *IF* function has three arguments and the formula syntax for the function is:

=IF (logical_test, value_if_true, value_if_false)

- **The *logical_test*** argument is the value or expression to be evaluated as true or false; this argument is required. You can use any comparison operator in the logical test.

- The *value_if_true* argument is the value returned if the logical test argument is true. If the value returned is text, enclose the text in quotes.
- The *value_if_false* argument is the value returned if the logical test argument is false. If the value returned is text, enclose the text in quotes.

> **MORE INFO**
>
> Commas within a function indicate the start of a new argument, so it is a good idea to omit commas within a value argument. For example, type "5000," not "5,000," in a value argument.

Refer to Figure 2-46 to understand the following examples of using an *IF* function. The formula shown here determines if an item should be reordered:

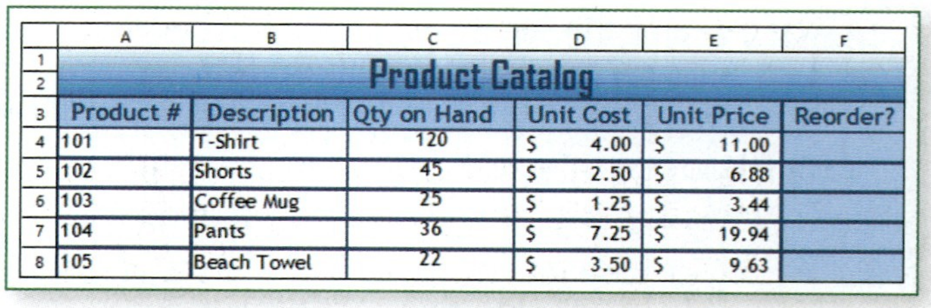

	A	B	C	D	E	F
1			**Product Catalog**			
2						
3	**Product #**	**Description**	**Qty on Hand**	**Unit Cost**	**Unit Price**	**Reorder?**
4	101	T-Shirt	120	$ 4.00	$ 11.00	
5	102	Shorts	45	$ 2.50	$ 6.88	
6	103	Coffee Mug	25	$ 1.25	$ 3.44	
7	104	Pants	36	$ 7.25	$ 19.94	
8	105	Beach Towel	22	$ 3.50	$ 9.63	

2-46 *IF* function sample worksheet

=IF(C4<=100, "Yes","No")
- C4<=100 is the *logical_test* argument and determines whether *Qty on Hand* is less than or equal to 100.
- "Yes" is the *value_if_true* argument. "Yes" is the value returned if the quantity on hand is less than or equal to 100. A "Yes" response indicates that the quantity on hand is below the minimal amount required on hand and should be reordered. The logical test argument is true if this value is returned.
- "No" is the *value_if_false* argument. "No" is the value returned if the quantity on hand is greater than 100. A "No" response indicates that it is not necessary to reorder. The logical test argument is false if this value is returned.
- The value returned for this *IF* function is "No."

The following formula is based again on information in Figure 2-46 and determines how many items to order:

=IF(C5<50,50-C5,0)
- C5<50 is the *logical_test* argument.
- 50-C5 is the *value_if_true* argument. The result of 50-C5 is the value returned if the quantity on hand is less than 50. The amount to order is calculated. The logical test argument is true if this value is returned.
- 0 is the *value_if_false* argument. 0 is the value returned if the quantity on hand is greater than or equal to 50. Reordering is not necessary. The logical test argument is false if this value is returned.
- The value returned for this *IF* function is 5.

You can insert the *IF* function by typing the formula, using the *Insert Function* button on the *Formula bar*, or using the *Insert Function* button on the *Formulas* tab.

HOW TO: Enter the IF Function

1. Click the cell where you want to enter the function.
2. Click the **Insert Function** button [*Formulas* tab, *Function Library group*] to open the *Insert Function* dialog box.

3. Type IF in the **Search for a function** box and click **Go**.

4. Select **IF** from the function list and click **OK**. The *Function Arguments* dialog box opens (Figure 2-47).

5. Click the **Logical_test** argument text box, and select the cell that will be compared.

6. Type the comparison operator or operators.

7. Click the cell that contains the comparison amount or type the value.
   - Include absolute cell references if you plan to copy the formula to another location and are referencing a cell that must remain constant.

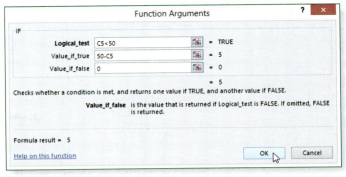

2-47 IF Function Arguments dialog box

8. Click the **Value_if_true** argument text box and click the cell that contains the true value, type the true value, or type the argument text surrounded with quotation marks.

9. Click the **Value_if_false** argument text box and click the cell that contains the false value, type the false value, or type the argument text surrounded with quotation marks.

10. Click **OK** to close the dialog box and insert the function.

> **MORE INFO**
>
> You can create nested *IF* functions that allow for more than one logical test.

LOOKUP Functions

LOOKUP functions retrieve a value from a range or table of cells located in another area of the worksheet or workbook. The two main types of *LOOKUP* functions are **VLOOKUP** (vertical lookup) and **HLOOKUP** (horizontal lookup). The *VLOOKUP* function finds a value in the first column of a range of cells and returns a value from any cell on the same row of the range. In order for the *VLOOKUP* function to work properly, the first column must be sorted in ascending order and each cell must contain a unique value.

The *VLOOKUP* function has four arguments and the formula syntax for the function is:

=VLOOKUP (lookup_value, table_array, col_index_num, [range_lookup])
- The **lookup_value** argument is required and Excel searches for this value in the first column of the cell range or table. If the cells in the first column contain text, you must enclose the text in quotes when creating the formula. When searching for the lookup value in the first column of the range, Excel finds the largest value less than or equal to the value in the first column of the range.
- The **table_array** argument is the range used for looking up data; this argument is required. You can enter a cell range or a range name. The data in the first column must be in ascending order.
- The **col_index_num** argument is the column number of the cell range or table (counting from the left); this argument is required.
- The **[range lookup]** argument is a logical value (True or False) that is used to find the nearest value (True) or an exact match (False); this argument is optional. The default value is "True."

Refer to the sample lookup table in Figure 2-48 to understand the following *VLOOKUP* function example. To find the last name of a student with a student ID of 33420, you enter the following formula:

=VLOOKUP(33420, A4:D8, 2)

- **33420** is the **lookup_value** argument (ID).
- **A4:D8** is the **table_array** argument (cell range).
- **2** is the **col_index_num** argument (the second column in the table which lists the last names of the students).
- The result of this *VLOOKUP* function is "Rosch."

To find the degree of a student with an identification number of 33420, key the following formula:

=VLOOKUP(33420,A4:D8,4)

The result of this *VLOOKUP* function is "Psychology."

Apply the *VLOOKUP* and *HLOOKUP* functions by using the *Insert Function* button on the *Formula bar* or on the *Formulas* tab or by typing the function name into a cell.

	A	B	C	D
1	**Student Data Table**			
2				
3	**ID**	**Last Name**	**First Name**	**Degree**
4	11123	Boney	John	Business
5	22234	Eisenhauer	DeAnn	Education
6	33420	Rosch	Ariel	Psychology
7	42002	Bowman	Larry	Education
8	56009	Kranz	Sandra	Accounting

2-48 Lookup table

HOW TO: Enter the VLOOKUP Function

1. Click the cell where you want to enter the function.

2. Click the **Insert Function** button [*Formulas* tab, *Function Library* group] to open the *Insert Function* dialog box (Figure 2-49).

3. Type VLOOKUP in the **Search for a function** text box and click **Go**.

4. Select **VLOOKUP** from the function list and click **OK** to open the *Function Arguments* dialog box (Figure 2-50).

5. Click the **Lookup_value** text box.

6. Click a cell in the first column of the cell range or table.

7. Click the **Table_array** argument text box and select the appropriate cell range.

   - When you drag to select, the *Function Arguments* dialog box collapses. The dialog box expands after the range is selected.
   - Apply absolute cell reference symbols to this range if you plan to copy the formula to another location.

8. Click the **Col_index_num** argument text box, and type the column number (count from the left).

   - Do not include the *Range_lookup* argument; it will default to *TRUE* and find the closest match instead of an exact match.

9. Click **OK** to close the *Functions Arguments* dialog box.

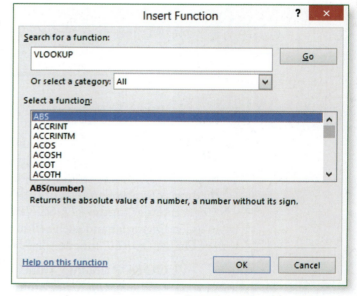

2-49 Insert Function dialog box

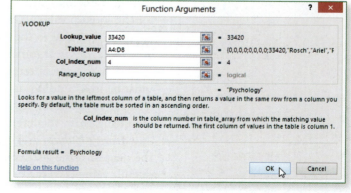

2-50 VLOOKUP Function Arguments dialog box

The **HLOOKUP** function is very similar to *VLOOKUP*. You can use *HLOOKUP* to find a value in the first row of a table or cell range and return a value from any cell in the same column of the range. Each entry in the first row must be a unique value.

The *HLOOKUP* function has four arguments, and the formula syntax for the function is:

=HLOOKUP (lookup_value, table_array, col_index_num, [range_lookup])

- The **lookup_value** argument is required and is the value Excel searches for in the first row of the cell range or table. If the cells in the first row contain text, you must enclose the text in quotes when creating the formula. When searching for the lookup value in the first row of the range, Excel finds the largest value less than or equal to the value in the first column of the range.
- The **table_array** argument is the range used for looking up data; this argument is required. You can enter a cell range or a range name. The data in the first row must be in ascending order from left to right if looking for an exact match.
- The **row_index_num** argument is the row number of the cell range or table (counting from the top); this argument is required.
- The **[range lookup]** argument is a logical value (True or False) that is used to find the nearest value (True) or an exact match (False); this argument is optional. The default value is "True."

Refer to the sample lookup table in Figure 2-51 to understand the following example:

=HLOOKUP("Last Name", A3:D8, 5)

- **Last Name** is the **lookup_value** argument found in the top row.
- **A3:D8** is the **table_array** argument (cell range).
- **5** is the **row_index_num** argument (the fifth row from the top of the cell range).
- The result of this *HLOOKUP* function is "Bowman".

	A	B	C	D
1	Student Data Table			
2				
3	ID	Last Name	First Name	Degree
4	11123	Boney	John	Business
5	22234	Esienhauer	DeAnn	Education
6	33420	Rosch	Aariel	Psychology
7	42002	Bowman	Larry	Education
8	56009	Dranz	Sandra	Accounting

2-51 Lookup table

HOW TO: Enter the HLOOKUP Function

1. Click the cell where you want to enter the function.
2. Click the **Insert Function** button [*Formulas* tab, *Function Library* group] to open the *Insert Function* dialog box.
3. Type HLOOKUP in the **Search for a function** box and click **Go**.
4. Select **HLOOKUP** and click **OK** to open the *Function Arguments* dialog box (Figure 2-52).

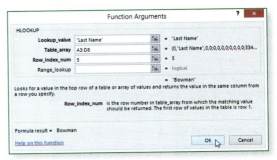

2-52 HLOOKUP Function Arguments dialog box

5. Click the **Lookup_value** argument text box and click a cell in the top row of the cell range or table.

6. Click the **Table_array** argument text box and select the cell range.
   - Be sure to apply absolute cell reference symbols to this range if you plan to copy the formula to another location.

7. Click the **Row_index_num** argument text box and type the row number (count from the top row).
   - Do not include the *Range_lookup* argument; it will default to *TRUE* and find the closest match instead of an exact match.

8. Click **OK** to close the dialog box and insert the function.

Working with Math and Trigonometry Functions

Excel includes many pre-defined math and trigonometry functions. In this section you learn to insert *SUMIF, SUMPRODUCT*, and *ROUND* functions in a spreadsheet.

SUMIF Function

The *SUMIF* function combines the *SUM* function with the logical criteria component of the *IF* function. The *SUMIF* includes cells in a calculation only if they meet a certain condition. For example, you may only want to add together cells that have values larger than 20.

The *SUMIF* function has three arguments and the formula syntax for the function is:

=SUMIF (range, criteria, [sum_range])
- The **range** argument is the range of cells to be added; this argument is required.
- The **criteria** argument defines which cells will be added (which condition must be met); this
  argument is required. Text criteria or logical or mathematical symbols must be enclosed in quotation marks (" ").
- The **[sum_range]** argument is optional. It is used to add cells that are not included in the range argument.

Refer to Figure 2-53 for an example that adds values in a range if the "*Unit Price*" value is greater than 25.

=SUMIF(E4:E6,">25",F4:F6).
- E4:E6 is the **range** argument (unit price).
- >25 is the **criteria** argument (unit price greater than 25).
- F4:F6 is the **sum_range** argument and adds the line total amounts.
- The result of this *SUMIF* function is $147.26.

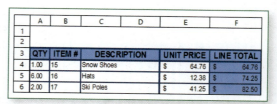

2-53 *SUMIF* **function sample worksheet**

HOW TO: Enter the SUMIF Function

1. Click the cell where you want to enter the function.
2. Click the **Math & Trig** button [*Formulas* tab, *Function Library* group] (Figure 2-54).
3. Scroll and select the **SUMIF** function. The *Function Arguments* dialog box opens (Figure 2-55).

Excel 2013 Chapter 2 Working with Formulas and Functions

4. Click the **Range** argument text box if necessary.

5. Drag to select the cell range.

6. Click the **Criteria** argument text box and type the condition.

   • Enclose the argument in quotes.

7. Click the **Sum_range** argument text box and select a range.

   • The *sum_range* identifies the actual range of cells to add. If the text box is blank, the cells in the range argument are added.

8. Click **OK**.

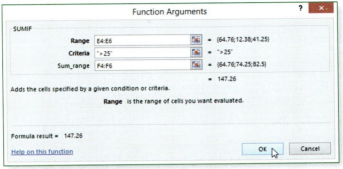

 2-55 *SUMIF Function Arguments* **dialog box**   2-54 *Math & Trig* **functions**

▶ **ANOTHER WAY**

Use *wild cards* (such as the asterisk [*]) in conjunction with criteria to sum all cells that meet corresponding criteria. For example, to sum all cells that have an associated criteria cell that begins with the letter A, type ("**A***") as the criteria.

SUMPRODUCT Function

The *SUMPRODUCT* function combines the *Sum* and *Product* mathematical operations. This function multiplies and then adds a series of arrays. An ***array*** is a range of cells in a row or column, such as A1:A4. An example of two arrays with the same dimension is A1:A5 and C1:C5. Two arrays with different dimensions are A1:A5 and C1:G1. The *SUMPRODUCT* is the sum of the products of several arrays. All arrays in a *SUMPRODUCT* function must have the same number of rows and columns.

The SUMPRODUCT function has the following arguments and the formula syntax is:

=**SUMPRODUCT (array1, array2, [array_n], ...)**

   • The ***array1*** argument is the argument that contains cells to multiply with the corresponding cells in the next array, and then those products are added together; this argument is required.
   • The ***array2*** argument must have the same number of cells and the same dimension as array1; this argument is required.

Refer to Figure 2-56 to understand the following example. The *SUMPRODUCT* function is:

=**SUMPRODUCT (A4:A6,D4:D6)**

	A	B	C	D	E
1					
2					
3	QTY	Item #	Description	Unit Price	Line Total
4	1	15	Snow Shoes	64.76	64.76
5	6	16	Hats	12.38	74.28
6	2	17	Ski Poles	41.25	82.50

2-56 *SUMPRODUCT* **function sample worksheet**

The function multiplies each specified cell in column A (quantity) times the specified cell in column D (unit price) and then adds the products.

QTY		Unit Price		Line Total
A4	*	D4	=	64.76
A5	*	D5	=	74.28
A6	*	D6	=	82.50
				221.54

The result of this *SUMPRODUCT* function is $221.54.

HOW TO: Enter the SUMPRODUCT Function

1. Click the cell where you want to enter the function.
2. Click the **Insert Function** button [*Formulas* tab, *Function Library* group] to open the *Insert Function* dialog box.
3. Type SUMPRODUCT in the **Search for a function** box and click **Go**.
4. Select **SUMPRODUCT** and click **OK** to open the *Function Arguments* dialog box (Figure 2-57).
5. Click the **Array1** argument text box and select a cell range.
6. Click the **Array2** argument text box and select a cell range.
   - Each selected array must contain the same number of cells and have the same dimensions.
7. Click **OK** to insert the function and close the dialog box.

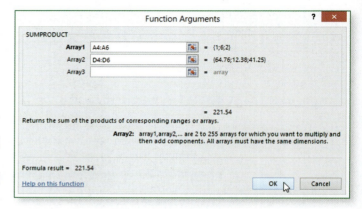

2-57 SUMPRODUCT Function Arguments dialog box

> ### MORE INFO
> Excel treats any empty cell in an array as if it has a value of 0.

ROUND Function

The *ROUND* function rounds a number to a specified number of decimal places. The *ROUND* function has two arguments and the formula syntax is:

=ROUND(number, num_digits)
- The **number** argument represents the number to round; this argument is required.
- The **num_digits** argument specifies the number of decimal places to round the number argument; this argument is required. If the *num_digits* argument is greater than zero, the number argument is rounded to the specified number of decimal places. If *num_digits* argument is zero, the number is rounded to the nearest whole number. If the *num_digits* argument is less than zero, the number is rounded to the left of the decimal point.

You can use the *ROUND* function to round the results of another formula. For example, if cell A1 contains the number 25.346, and you want to round the number to 1 decimal place, type the formula:

=ROUND(A1,1).

The result of this ROUND function is 25.3.

HOW TO: Enter the ROUND Function

1. Click the cell where you want to create the formula.
2. Click the **Insert Function** button [*Formulas* tab, *Function Library* group] to open the *Insert Function* dialog box.
3. Type ROUND in the **Search for a function** box and click **Go**.
4. Select the **ROUND** function and click **OK** to open the *Function Arguments* dialog box (Figure 2-58).
5. Click the **Number** argument text box and select a cell.
6. Click the **Num_digits** argument text box and type the number of digits you want to round the specified number.
7. Click **OK** to insert the function and close the dialog box.

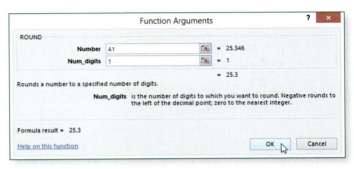

2-58 *ROUND Function Arguments* **dialog box**

> **MORE INFO**
> Excel also has a *ROUNDDOWN* function that always rounds a number down. The *ROUNDUP* function always rounds a number up.

PAUSE & PRACTICE: EXCEL 2-3

For this project, you open the previous Pause & Practice file and add the following kinds of functions: math and trigonometry, financial, logical, lookup, and date and time. These functions provide important financial information on sales and future investment opportunities to finalize the Paradise Lakes Resort workbook.

File Needed: *[your initials] PP E2-2.xlsx*
Completed Project File Name: *[your initials] PP E2-3.xlsx*

1. Open the *[your initials] PP E2-2* workbook, and save the workbook as *[your initials] PP E2-3*.

2. Enter the *SUMIF* function to determine the total mortgage.
   a. Click cell **E20**.
   b. Click the **Insert Function** button [*Formulas* tab, *Function Library* group] to open the *Insert Function* dialog box.
   c. Type SUMIF in the **Search for a function** box and click **Go**.

   d. Select **SUMIF** from the function list and click **OK** to open the *Function Arguments* dialog box.

   e. Click the **Range** argument text box and select the cell range A10:A13.

   f. Click the **Criteria** argument text box and type "Mortgage".

   g. Click the **Sum_range** argument and type H10:H13.

   h. Verify that the formula syntax is =SUMIF(A10:A13,"Mortgage",H10:H13).

   i. Click **OK**. The correct result for cell E20 is $71,742.38.

3. Enter a *SUMPRODUCT* function to determine additional income for extra rented cabins.

   a. Click cell **G20**.

   b. Click the **Insert Function** button [*Formulas* tab, *Function Library* group].

   c. Type SUMPRODUCT in the **Search for a function** box and click **Go**.

   d. Select **SUMPRODUCT** from the function list and click **OK** to open the *Function Arguments* dialog box.

   e. Click the **Array1** text box and select B16:H16.

   f. Click the **Array2** text box and select the cell range B18:H18.

   g. Verify that the formula syntax is =SUMPRODUCT(B16:H16,B18:H18).

   h. Click **OK**. The correct result for cell G20 is $143,045.12.

4. Enter a *ROUND* function to round the net income in the spreadsheet.

   a. Click cell **E21** and use the **Insert Function** button to insert the *ROUND* function.

   b. In the *Function Arguments* dialog box, type H16 in the *Number* argument text box.

   c. Type 1 in the *Num_digits* argument text box.

   d. Verify that the formula syntax is =ROUND(H16,1).

   e. Press **Enter**. The correct result for cell E21 is $135,044.50 (Figure 2-59).

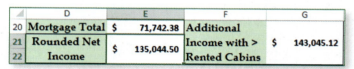

	D	E	F	G
20	Mortgage Total	$ 71,742.38	Additional	
21	Rounded Net		Income with >	$ 143,045.12
22	Income	$ 135,044.50	Rented Cabins	

2-59 *ROUND* **function results**

5. Enter a *PMT* function to determine payments if the organization were to purchase additional cabins.

   a. Click the **Investment Options** sheet tab.

   b. Click cell **B7** and use the **Insert Function** button to insert the *PMT* function.

   c. In the *Function Arguments* dialog box, click the **Rate** argument text box and click cell **B6**. Be sure to divide B6 by 12 (**B6/12**); the organization will be making monthly payments.

   d. Click the **Nper** argument text box and then click cell **B5**. Be sure to multiply B5 times 12 (**B5*12**); the organization will be making monthly payments.

   e. Click the **Pv** argument text box and then click cell **B4**.

   f. Omit the last two arguments because we want a zero balance after the last payment is made and payments will be made at the end of each period.

   g. Click **OK**.

   h. Verify that the formula syntax is =PMT(B6/12,B5*12,B4).

   i. Press **Enter**. The correct result for cell B7 is ($2,415.70) (a negative value).

6. Enter an *IF* function to determine if the organization should take out the loan for the investment. Compare the monthly payment to the lowest monthly sales total from the *Location 1- Cass Lake* sheet tab. If the monthly payment is lower, choose to make the investment.

   a. Click cell **B13** and use the **Insert Function** button to insert the *IF* function (Figure 2-60).

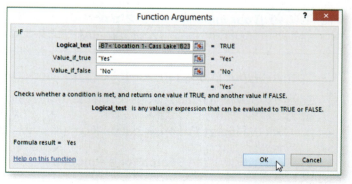

2-60 *IF Function Arguments* **dialog box**

b. In the *Function Arguments* dialog box, click the **Logical_test** argument box and then type -B7<, click the **Location 1- Cass Lake** sheet, and select **B23**.

c. Verify that the the **Logical_test** argument is -B7<'Location 1- Cass Lake'!B23.

d. Click the **Value_if_true** argument text box and type "Yes".

e. Click the **Value_if_false** argument text box and type "No".

f. Click **OK**. The result of the calculation appears in the cell containing the formula.

g. Verify that the formula syntax is =IF(-B7<'Location 1- Cass Lake'!B23,"Yes", "No").

h. Press **Enter**. The correct result for cell B13 is "Yes" (Figure 2-61).

7. Enter a *VLOOKUP* function to determine the cost of various products.

a. Select the **Product Cost** sheet tab.

b. Click cell **B4** and use the **Insert Function** button to insert the *VLOOKUP* function (Figure 2-62).

c. In the *Function Arguments* dialog box, click the **Lookup_value** argument text box and click **A4**.

d. Click the **Table_array** argument box and select the cell range **E4:G8**, and then apply absolute cell reference symbols by pressing **F4**.

e. Click the **Col_index_num** argument text box and type the column number 3.

f. Omit the **Range_lookup** argument; it will default to *TRUE* and find the closest match.

g. Click **OK**. The result of the calculation appears in B4.

h. Verify that the formula syntax is =VLOOKUP(A4,$E$4:$G$8,3).

i. Press **Enter**. The correct result in B4 is $25.50.

j. Copy the formula in **B4** to **B5:B6**. Apply **Accounting** formatting to **B4:B6**. Apply any borders needed to **A2:B6**.

8. Save and close the workbook (Figure 2-63).

	A	B
1	**New Purchase Monthly Payments**	
2		
3	Property	Cabins
4	Loan Amount	$ 450,000.00
5	Term in Years	30
6	Interest Rate	5%
7	**Payment**	($2,415.70)
8		
10		
11		
12	**Decision Table**	
13	Purchase New Property?	Yes

2-61 *PMT* **function result**

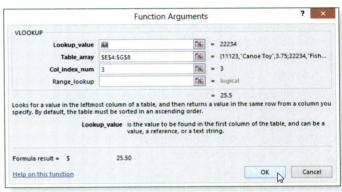

2-62 *VLOOKUP Function Arguments* **dialog box**

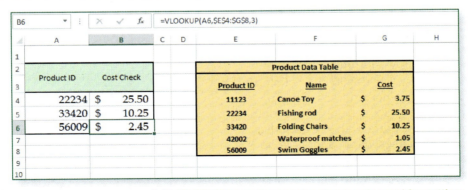

2-63 *VLOOKUP* **function results after copying and formatting**

Chapter Summary

2.1 Create and edit basic formulas (p. E2-79).

- The **syntax** of a formula refers to the required parts of the formula and the rules controlling the sequence of the parts.
- A popular and accurate technique for entering cells in formulas is the **select** method.
- Formulas calculate and update automatically when values in the worksheet change.
- Double-clicking a cell or pressing **F2** activates edit mode and allows you to modify a formula.
- The **Range Finder** is a color-coded editing tool that applies different colors to each cell or cell range within the formula syntax.
- **Formula Auditing** is a color-coded editing system that applies different colors to each cell or cell range, displays arrows pointing to cells and cell ranges included within the formula's syntax, and steps through syntax errors.
- A **syntax error** occurs when a formula contains a typographical error, unnecessary or missing punctuation, incorrect order of arguments, or an incorrect cell reference.
- The *Trace Error* button displays when a cell contains a possible error. A green triangle indicator appears in the upper left corner of the cell. You can click the down arrow to display a list of options to repair or ignore the error.
- A **circular reference** occurs when a formula includes the cell address of the formula.

2.2 Use range names and relative, absolute, and mixed cell references in a formula (p. E2-83).

- There are three basic types of cell references: **relative**, **absolute**, and **mixed**.
- Relative cell references identify the location of a cell. Relative cell addresses within a formula adjust when you copy a formula.
- Absolute cell references identify the constant location of a cell. The cell address within a formula contains a $ (dollar sign) around both the column and row parts of the cell address. Absolute cell addresses within a formula *do not* adjust when you copy a formula.
- Mixed cell references contain one relative cell address component (either the row number or column letter) and one absolute cell address component.

- **3D** cell references identify cells in worksheets other than where the formula resides. Using a *3D* cell reference in another workbook is called **linking workbooks**.
- You can apply a **range name** to a cell or groups of cells to describe the purpose of the group of cells and make it easier to interpret a formula. A range name is an absolute cell reference.
- The *Fill Handle* is a tool that allows you to copy formulas, lists, and numeric patterns.

2.3 Apply mathematical order of operations when using parentheses, exponents, multiplication, division, addition, and subtraction (p. E2-88).

- Excel follows a specified set of rules when it calculates a formula that has more than one operation.
- If the syntax of the formula includes parentheses, exponents, multiplication or division, and addition or subtraction, the operation within the parentheses is performed first, exponent operation is second, multiplying or dividing operators are computed third, and addition and subtraction are completed last.
- Use the following acronym to help remember the order of operations: **P**lease **E**xcuse **M**y **D**ear **A**unt **S**ally.

2.4 Use *AutoSum* and other common functions such as *AVERAGE, COUNT, MAX, MIN, TODAY,* and *NOW* (p. E2-93).

- Use the **AutoSum** button to insert frequently used functions.
- The **AVERAGE** function calculates an average by adding values together and dividing by the number of values.
- The **COUNT** function counts each number in a group of cells or each cell that contains specified descriptive labels.
- The **MAX** and **MIN** functions find the largest or the smallest value in a cell range.
- **AutoCalculate** allows you to view totals, averages, or other statistical information on the *Status bar* without creating any formulas.
- The **TODAY** function returns the current date each time a workbook is opened.
- The **NOW** function returns the current date and time each time a workbook is opened.

2.5 Apply financial, logical, and lookup functions such as *PMT, IF, VLOOKUP,* and *HLOOKUP* (p. E2-99).

- *Functions* are pre-defined formulas that include function names and arguments.
- The *Insert Function* dialog box automates the functions available in Excel.
- You can use the point and click method to complete most of the *arguments* (or components) of a function.
- The *PMT* function calculates payments for a loan if regular payments are made and the interest rate is constant.
- *IF* functions evaluate a specified condition and return one value if the condition is true and another value if the condition is false.
- *LOOKUP* functions retrieve a value from a range or table of cells located in another area of the worksheet.
- Two main types of *LOOKUP* functions are *VLOOKUP* (vertical lookup) and *HLOOKUP* (horizontal lookup).

2.6 Apply math and trigonometry functions such as *SUMIF, SUMPRODUCT,* and *ROUND* (p. E2-106).

- The *SUMIF* function combines the *SUM* function with the *IF* function. The *SUMIF* function includes cells in a calculation if they meet a certain condition.
- The *SUMPRODUCT* function combines the *SUM* and *PRODUCT* mathematical operations. The function multiplies and then adds together a series of *arrays*.
- The *ROUND* function rounds a value to a specified number of decimal places.

Check for Understanding

In the *Online Learning Center* for this text (www.mhhe.com/office2013inpractice), there are a variety of resources that can be used to review the concepts covered in this chapter.

The following Online Learning Resources are available in the Online Learning Center:

- Multiple choice questions
- Short answer questions
- Matching exercises

Guided Project 2-1

Courtyard Medical Plaza (CMP) is a full-service medical office complex providing customers with a variety of medical services. CMP has doctor offices, a pharmacy, x-ray and lab services, insurance and billing support, specialty physicians, optometry and dental offices, and a restaurant for clients.

  Larry Bowman is the manager for the restaurant division. He has been asked to forecast the net monthly income of the restaurant and display it on a spreadsheet. The owner has also asked to see some investment options for a new restaurant listed on the spreadsheet.
[Student Learning Outcomes 2.1, 2.2, 2.3, 2.4, 2.5, 2.6]

File Needed: **CMPRestaurantIncome-02.xlsx**
Completed Project File Name: **[your initials] Excel 2-1.xlsx**

Skills Covered in This Project

- Create and copy formulas.
- Apply mathematical order of operations.
- Use relative, absolute, and mixed cell references.
- Use *AutoSum.*

- Apply *AVERAGE, MAX,* and *MIN* functions.
- Apply the *PMT* function.
- Apply the *SUMPRODUCT* function
- Apply the *TODAY* function.
- Use formula auditing tools.

1. Open the **CMPRestaurantIncome-02.xlsx** workbook and save the workbook as **[your initials] Excel 2-1**.

2. Enter an addition formula on the *Restaurant* sheet tab to add the food and beverages sales.
   a. Click cell **B7**.
   b. Type = (equals sign).
   c. Select the first cell of the formula (**B5**), press the + (plus sign), and then select the next cell address (**B6**).
   d. Click the **Enter** button (check mark) on the *Formula bar*.
   e. Verify that the formula syntax is =B5+B6. The result of the formula is $4,251.68.

3. Copy the *Total Sales* formula from Week 1 through Week 4.
   a. Select cell **B7**.
   b. Click and drag the *Fill Handle* to cells **C7:E7**.

4. Create an addition formula to total the food monthly sales, and use the *Fill Handle* to copy the formula without formatting.
   a. Click cell **F5**.
   b. Type =.
   c. Select **B5**, press +, select **C5**, press +, select **D5**, press +, and select **E5**.
   d. Press **Enter**.
   e. Verify that the syntax of the formula is =B5+C5+D5+E5. The result of the formula is $22,333.17.
   f. Select cell **F5**.
   g. Click and drag the *Fill Handle* to cells **F6:F7**.

h. Select the **AutoFill Options** button drop-down arrow and select **Fill Without Formatting** to ensure borders are not overwritten.

i. Release the pointer. The totals for F6 and F7 are $7,546.84 and $29,880.01, respectively.

5. Create a formula to calculate the rent expense (estimated to be 17% of total sales). Apply absolute cell references and copy the rent expense formula.

   a. Select **B10** (Figure 2-64).

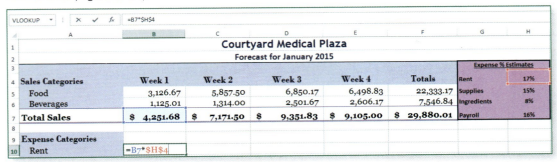

2-64 Rent expense formula with an absolute reference

   b. Type the following formula =B7*H4.
   c. Click the *Formula bar* to the left of the column letter **H** and then press **F4** to apply absolute cell references.
   d. Press **Enter**. Verify that the formula syntax is =B7*$H$4.
   e. Select **B10** and click and drag the fill pointer to cells **C10:F10**.

6. Name a cell to make it an absolute reference.

   a. Click **H7**.
   b. Click the **Name** box.
   c. Type Payroll in the *Name* box and press **Enter**.

7. Create and copy expense formulas for "Supplies", "Ingredients", and "Payroll". Use multiplication to calculate the expense and absolute cell references for the estimated percent of total sales.

   a. Enter the formulas in the table in the corresponding cells as shown in the following table.

B11	=B7*$H$5
B12	=B7*$H$6
B13	=B7*Payroll

   b. Select cells **B11:B13**.
   c. Place your pointer over the *Fill Handle* of cell range **B11:B13**.
   d. Click and drag the fill pointer through cells **C11:F13**.

8. Create an addition formula to total the expenses for week 1 and copy the formula.

   a. Click **B14**.
   b. Type = (equals sign).
   c. Select **B10** and type +.
   d. Select **B11** and type +.
   e. Select **B12** and type +.
   f. Select **B13**.
   g. Press **Enter**.
   h. Verify that the syntax of the formula is =B10+B11+B12+B13. The result of the formula is $2,380.94.
   i. Select **B14** and click and drag the *Fill Handle* to cells **C14:F14**.

E2-115

9. Create and copy a formula with multiple operators.
   a. Click **B16**.
   b. Type =(B5+B6)-B14.
   c. Press **Enter**. Verify the formula syntax is =(B5+B6)-B14.
   d. Select **B16** and click and drag the *Fill Handle* to cells **C16:F16**.

10. Use auditing tools to review a formula.
    a. Select cell **B16**.
    b. Click the **Show Formulas** button and the **Trace Precedents** button [*Formulas* tab, *Formula Auditing* group]. A blue dot appears in each cell referenced in the formula.
    c. Click the **Remove Arrows** button [*Formulas* tab, *Formula Auditing* group].
    d. Click the **Show Formulas** button [*Formulas* tab, *Formula Auditing* group] to return to results view.

11. Enter a *SUM* function to calculate monthly sales.
    a. Click cell **B20**.
    b. Click the **AutoSum** button drop-down arrow [*Formulas* tab, *Function Library* group] and select **SUM** from the drop-down list.
    c. Select the cell range **B7:E7**. Verify the formula syntax is =SUM(B7:E7).
    d. Press **Enter**. The formula result is $29,880.01.

12. Calculate average weekly sales by entering an *AVERAGE* function using the *AutoSum* button.
    a. Click cell **B21**.
    b. Click the **AutoSum** button drop-down arrow [*Formulas* tab, *Function Library* group] and select **Average** from the drop-down list.
    c. Select the cell range **B7:E7**.
    d. Press **Enter**. Verify the formula syntax =AVERAGE(B7:E7). The formula's result should be $7,470.00.

13. Calculate maximum weekly sales by entering a *MAX* function using the *AutoSum* button.
    a. Click cell **B22**.
    b. Click the **AutoSum** button drop-down arrow [*Formulas* tab, *Function Library* group] and select **Max** from the drop-down list.
    c. Select cell range **B7:E7**.
    d. Press **Enter**. Verify the formula syntax =MAX(B7:E7). The formula result is $9,351.83.

14. Use auditing tools to review a formula.
    a. Select cell **B22**.
    b. Click the **Show Formulas** button and the **Trace Precedents** button [*Formulas tab, Formula Auditing* group].
    c. Click the **Remove Arrows** button [*Formulas* tab, *Formula Auditing* group].
    d. Click the **Show Formulas** button [*Formulas* tab, *Formula Auditing* group] to return to results view.

15. Edit the maximum weekly sales formula to add absolute cell references.
    a. Select cell **B22**.
    b. Click the *Formula bar* and select the cell range **B7:E7**. Do not include the parentheses in your selection.
    c. Press **F4** key to add absolute reference symbols.
    d. Press **Enter**. The formula syntax should be =MAX($B$7:$G$7).

16. Copy an existing formula and edit the function name.
    a. Select cell **B22** and click and drag the *Fill Handle* to **B23**.
    b. Choose the **AutoFill Options** button and select **Fill Without Formatting** to ensure your borders are not overwritten.

c. Select cell **B23**.
d. Click the *Formula bar*, delete the function name **MAX**, and type **MIN**.
e. Press **Enter**. Verify the syntax of the formula is =MIN($B$7:$G$7). The formula result is $4,251.68.

17. Enter the *SUMIF* function to determine the rent total.
   a. Click cell **E20**.
   b. Click the **Insert Function** button [*Formulas* tab, *Function Library group*] to open the *Insert Function* dialog box.
   c. Type **SUMIF** in the **Search for a function** box and click **Go**.
   d. Select **SUMIF** from the function list and click **OK** to open the *Function Arguments* dialog box.
   e. Click the **Range** argument text box and select the cell range A10:A13.
   f. Click the **Criteria** argument text box and type "Rent".
   g. Click the **Sum_range** argument and type F10:F13.
   h. Verify that the formula syntax is =SUMIF(A10:A13,"Rent",F10:F13).
   i. Click **OK**. The correct result for cell E20 is $5,079.60.

18. Enter a *SUMPRODUCT* function to determine additional income for extra meal and beverage sales.
   a. Click cell **E24**.
   b. Click the **Insert Function** button [*Formulas* tab, *Function Library* group] to open the *Insert Function* dialog box.
   c. Type **SUMPRODUCT** in the **Search for a function** box and click **Go**.
   d. Select **SUMPRODUCT** and click **OK** to open the *Function Arguments* dialog box.
   e. Click the **Array1** argument text box and select the cell range **E22:F22**.
   f. Click the **Array2** argument text box and select the cell range **E23:F23**.
   g. Verify that the formula syntax is =SUMPRODUCT(E22:F22,E23:F23).
   h. Click **OK**. The correct result in E24 is $33.25. See Figure 2-65 for the complete *Restaurant* tab results.

	A	B	C	D	E	F	G	H
1				**Courtyard Medical Plaza**				
2				**Forecast for January 2015**				
3							**Expense % Estimates**	
4	**Sales Categories**	**Week 1**	**Week 2**	**Week 3**	**Week 4**	**Totals**	Rent	17%
5	Food	3,126.67	5,857.50	6,850.17	6,498.83	22,333.17	Supplies	15%
6	Beverages	1,125.01	1,314.00	2,501.67	2,606.17	7,546.84	Ingredients	8%
7	**Total Sales**	$ 4,251.68	$ 7,171.50	$ 9,351.83	$ 9,105.00	$ 29,880.01	Payroll	16%
8								
9	**Expense Categories**							
10	Rent	722.79	1,219.16	1,589.81	1,547.85	5,079.60		
11	Supplies	637.75	1,075.73	1,402.78	1,365.75	4,482.00		
12	Ingredients	340.13	573.72	748.15	728.40	2,390.40		
13	Payroll	680.27	1,147.44	1,496.29	1,456.80	4,780.80		
14	**Total Expenses**	2,380.94	4,016.04	5,237.03	5,098.80	16,732.81		
15								
16	**Net Income**	$ 1,870.74	$ 3,155.46	$ 4,114.81	$ 4,006.20	$ 13,147.21		
17								
18								
19								
20	**Total Sales**	$	29,880.01	**Rent Total**	$ 5,079.60			
21	**Average Weekly Sales**	$	7,470.00		**Meals**	**Beverages**		
22	**Maximum Weekly Sales**	$	9,351.83	**Profit per Unit**	$3.50	$1.25		
23	**Minimum Weekly Sales**	$	4,251.68	**Extra sold units**	7	7		
24				**Total Extra Profit**	$ 33.25			
25								
26								
27								
28								

Restaurant | Investment Options | ⊕

2-65 Excel 2-1 *Restaurant* tab results

19. Enter a *PMT* function on the *Investment Options* sheet tab to calculate the payment amount if the organization purchased another restaurant.
    a. Click the *Investment Options* sheet tab and select cell **B7**.
    b. Click the **Insert Function** button [*Formulas* tab, *Function Library* group].
    c. Type Payment in the **Search for a function** box and click **Go**.
    d. Select **PMT** and click **OK** to open the *Function Arguments* dialog box.
    e. Click the **Rate** argument text box, click cell **B6** (the interest rate), and type /12 (B6/12) since the organization will be making monthly payments.
    f. Click the **Nper** argument text box, click cell **B5**, and type *12 (B5*12) since the organization will be making monthly payments.
    g. Click the **Pv** argument text box and click cell **B4**, which is the amount of the loan.
    h. Omit the last two arguments because a zero balance is desired after the last payment is made and payments will be made at the end of each period.
    i. Click **OK**. The formula syntax should be =PMT(B6/12,B5*12,B4).
    j. Press **Enter**. The correct result is ($2,952.52).

20. Enter the **TODAY** function to update the worksheet date every time you open the file.
    a. Click cell **G3**.
    b. Type =TODAY() and press **Enter**. The current date appears in cell G3.

21. Save and close the workbook (Figure 2-66).

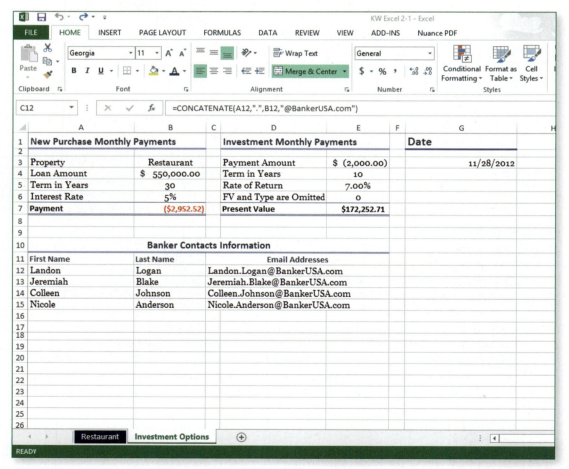

2-66 Excel 2-1 *Investment Options* tab results

Guided Project 2-2

Hamilton Civic Center (HCC) is a nonprofit community fitness center with an indoor pool, sauna, indoor track, project room, racquetball courts, meeting rooms, and a gift shop. HCC provides training and sponsors athletic and social events for adults and children. Tara Strachan is HCC's administrator for the gift shop. She has been asked to create an invoice template that links to the gift shop's product inventory spreadsheet.

[Student Learning Outcomes 2.1, 2.2, 2.3, 2.4, 2.5, 2.6]

File Needed: **HCCInvoice-02.xlsx**
Completed Project File Name: **[your initials] Excel 2-2.xlsx**

Skills Covered in This Project

- Create and copy basic formulas.
- Apply mathematical order of operations.
- Use relative, absolute, and mixed cell references.
- Apply the *VLOOKUP* function.
- Apply the *IF* function.
- Apply the *SUMIF* function.
- Apply the *TODAY* function.

1. Open the **HCCInvoice-02.xlsx** workbook from your student data files and save the workbook as **[your initials] Excel 2-2.**

2. Enter a *VLOOKUP* function with *3D* references on the *Invoice* sheet tab.
   a. Click cell **C15** on the *Invoice* sheet tab.
   b. Click the **Insert Function** button [*Formulas* tab, *Function Library* group] to open the *Insert Function* dialog box.
   c. Type VLOOKUP in the **Search for a function** box and click **Go**.
   d. Select the **VLOOKUP** function from the list and click **OK** to open the *Function Arguments* dialog box (Figure 2-67).
   e. Click the **Lookup_value** argument text box and click cell **B15** (Item #).
   f. Click the **Table_array** argument text box and click the **Gift Shop Products** sheet tab.
   g. Select the cell range **A4:F18**.
   h. Press **F4** to apply absolute cell reference symbols to the A4:F18 range.
   i. Click the **Col_index_num** argument box and type 2, the column number.
   j. Omit the **Range_lookup** argument; if you include a *Range_lookup* argument, it will default to *TRUE* and find the closest match instead of the exact match you want to find.
   k. Click **OK**. The formula syntax should be =VLOOKUP(B15,'Gift Shop Products'!$A$4:$F$18,2). The result is "Shorts" and displays in C15 on the *Invoice* tab.

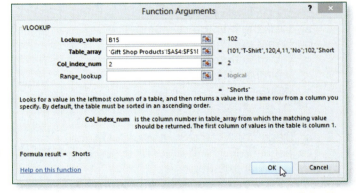

2-67 **VLOOKUP Function Arguments** dialog box

3. Copy the *VLOOKUP* formula.
   a. Select cell **C15**.
   b. Place your pointer over the *Fill Handle*.
   c. Click and drag the fill pointer through cells **C16:C17**.

4. Enter another *VLOOKUP* function with *3D* references on the *Invoice* sheet tab to insert unit price.
   a. Click cell **F15** on the *Invoice* sheet tab.
   b. Click the **Recently Used** button [*Formulas* tab, *Function Library* group].
   c. Select **VLOOKUP** to open the *Function Arguments* dialog box (Figure 2-68).
   d. Click the **Lookup_value** argument text box and click cell **B15**.
   e. Click the **Table_array** argument text box and click the *Gift Shop Products* sheet tab.
   f. Select the cell range **A4:F18** and press **F4** to apply absolute cell reference symbols to the range.
   g. Type 5 in the *Col_index_num* argument text box.
   h. Click **OK**. Verify that the formula syntax is =VLOOKUP(B15,'Gift Shop Products'!$A$4:$F$18,5). The result of the calculation is $6.88 and appears in cell F15 on the *Invoice* tab.

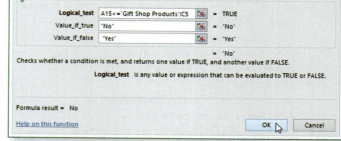

2-68 *VLOOKUP Function Arguments* dialog box

5. Copy the *VLOOKUP* formula.
   a. Select cell **F15**.
   b. Drag the *Fill Handle* through cells **F16:F17**.

6. Create an *IF* function to determine if the product is backordered.
   a. Click the **Invoice** sheet tab.
   b. Select cell **E15**.
   c. Click the **Insert Function** button [*Formulas* tab, *Function Library* group].
   d. Type IF in the **Search for a function** box and click **Go**.
   e. Select the **IF** function and click **OK** to open the *Function Arguments* dialog box (Figure 2-69).
   f. Click the **Logical_test** argument text box and click cell **A15**.
   g. Type <=.
   h. Click the **Gift Shop Products** sheet and select **C5**. The argument syntax is A15<='Gift Shop Products'!C5.
   i. Type "No" in the *Value_if_true* argument box.
   j. Type "Yes" in the *Value_if_false* argument box.
   k. Click **OK**. Verify that the formula syntax is =IF(A15<='Gift Shop Products'!C5,"No", "Yes"). The result of the calculation is "No" and displays in E15.
   l. Press **Enter**.
   m. Copy the formula in **E15** to **E16:E17**.

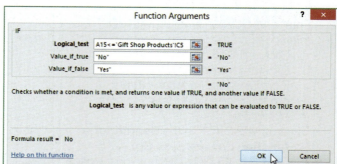

2-69 *IF Function Arguments* dialog box

7. Create a multiplication formula to calculate the sales total for shorts and use the *Fill Handle* to copy the formula.
   a. Click cell **G15**.
   b. Type =.

c. Select **A15**, type * (multiplication sign), and select **F15**.

d. Press **Enter**. Verify that the formula syntax is =A15*F15. The result should be $13.75.

e. Select cell **G15**.

f. Drag the *Fill Handle* through cells **G16:G17**. The totals for G16 and G17 should be $10.31 and $39.88.

g. Apply the **Accounting** numeric formatting to cells **F15:G17** if needed.

8. Create a *SUMIF* formula to total the line items that are not backordered.
   a. Click cell **G31** and insert the **SUMIF** function.
   b. Type E15:E17 in the *Range* argument box.
   c. Type "No" in the *Criteria* argument box.
   d. Click the **Sum_range** argument text box and select **G15:G17**.
   e. Click **OK**. Verify that the formula syntax is =SUMIF(E15:E17,"No",G15:G17). The result in G31 should be $63.94.
   f. Apply the **Accounting** formatting to **G31** if needed.

9. Create a formula with multiple operators and apply the mathematical order of precedence.
   a. Click cell **G33**.
   b. Type =G31+(G31*G32) and press **Enter**. Verify that the formula syntax is =G31+(G31*G32). The result in G33 should be $68.09.
   c. Apply the **Accounting** formatting to **G33** if needed.

10. Use auditing tools to review a formula.
    a. Select cell **G31**.
    b. Click the **Show Formulas** button and the **Trace Precedents** button [*Formulas* tab, *Formula Auditing* group].
    c. Review the formulas.
    d. Click the **Remove Arrows** button [*Formulas* tab, *Formula Auditing* group].
    e. Click the **Show Formulas** button [*Formulas* tab, *Formula Auditing* group] to return to results view.

11. Insert a date that will update every time you open the file.
    a. Click cell **E5**.
    b. Type =TODAY() and press **Enter**.
    c. Format the date to **Short Date**.

12. Save and close the workbook (Figure 2-70).

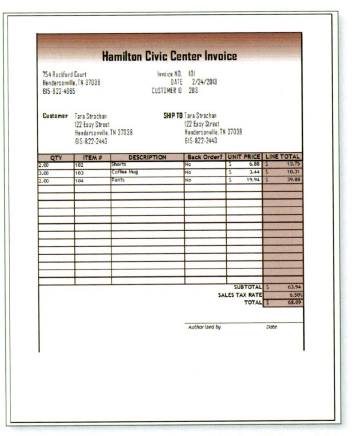

2-70 Excel 2-2 completed

Guided Project 2-3

Sierra Pacific Community College District (SPCCD) is a community college district composed of four individual community colleges. Ashlyn Varriano is the SPCCD administrator for the smallest of the four community colleges. She has been asked to explore an investment option and create an amortization schedule.

[Student Learning Outcomes 2.1, 2.2, 2.3, 2.5]

File Needed: **SPCCDInvestments-02.xlsx**
Completed Project File Name: **[your initials] Excel 2-3.xlsx**

Skills Covered in This Project

- Create and copy formulas.
- Apply mathematical order of operations.
- Use relative, absolute, and mixed cell references.
- Name cells and use the name range in a formula.
- Apply *PMT* function.

1. Open the **SPCCDInvestments-02.xlsx** workbook, and save the workbook as **[your initials] Excel 2-3**.
2. Apply range names.
   a. Select **C4:D8**.
   b. Click the **Create from Selection** button [*Formulas* tab, *Defined Names* group].
   c. Select the **Left Column** check box in the *Create Names from Selection* window. Deselect **Top row**.
   d. Click **OK**.
   e. Click the **Name** box drop-down arrow on the *Formula bar* to see a list of the new range names.
   f. Select **F4:G8**.
   g. Repeat steps 2b–d.
3. Enter the loan amount formula.
   a. Click **D7**.
   b. Type =.
   c. Select **D5** (*Purchase_Price*), press -, and select **D6** (*Down_Payment*).
   d. Press **Enter**. Verify that the formula syntax is =Purchase_Price − Down_Payment. The result of the formula should be $250,000.00.
4. Enter a *PMT* function.
   a. Click **G5**.
   b. Click the **Insert Function** button [*Formulas* tab, *Function Library* group] and insert the **PMT** function.
   c. Click the **Rate** argument box, click **D8** (named *Annual_Percentage_Rate*), and type /12 after D8 to divide it by 12 (*Annual_Percentage_Rate* /12) for monthly payments.
   d. Click the **Nper** argument box, click **G4** (*Term_of_the_Loan_in_Years*), and type *12 after G4 to multiply it by 12 (*Term_of_the_Loan_in_Years* *12) for monthly payments.
   e. Click **D7** (*Loan_Amount*) for the *Pv* argument.
   f. Click **OK**. Verify that the formula syntax is =PMT(Annual_Percentage_Rate/12,Term_of_the_Loan_in_Years*12,Loan_Amount). The correct result in G5 should be ($2,590.96).
   g. Edit the formula to create a positive number for the amortization schedule by typing a − (minus sign) in front of *Loan_Amount*. Verify that the formula syntax is =PMT(Annual_Percentage_Rate/12,Term_of_the_Loan_in_Years*12,-Loan_Amount).

5. Create a total interest formula.
   a. Click **G6** (*Total_Interest*).
   b. Type =.
   c. Select **G5** (*Payment*), type *, select **G4** (Term_of_the_Loan_in_Years), type *, type 12, type –, and select **D7** (*Loan_Amount*).
   d. Press **Enter**. Verify that the formula syntax is =Payment*Term_of_the_Loan_in_Years*12-Loan_Amount. The result of the formula should be $60,915.23.

6. Create the total principal formula.
   a. Click **G7** (*Total_Principal*).
   b. Type =.
   c. Select **G5** (*Payment*), type *, select **G4** (Term_of_the_Loan_in_Years), type *, type 12, type –, and select **G6** (*Total_Interest*).
   d. Press **Enter**. Verify that the formula syntax is =Payment*Term_of_the_Loan_in_Years*12-Total_Interest. The formula result should be $250,000.00.

7. Create an addition formula to calculate the cost of the loan.
   a. Click **G8** (*Total_Cost_of_the_Loan*).
   b. Type =.
   c. Select **G6**, type +, and select **G7**.
   d. Press **Enter**. Verify that the formula syntax is =Total_Principal+Total_Interest. The result of the formula should be $310,915.23 (Figure 2-71).

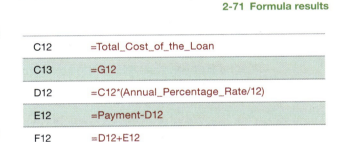

2-71 Formula results

Cell	Formula
C12	=Total_Cost_of_the_Loan
C13	=G12
D12	=C12*(Annual_Percentage_Rate/12)
E12	=Payment-D12
F12	=D12+E12
G12	=C12-F12

8. Create and copy formulas for the amortization schedule.
   a. Create the formulas listed in the table at right.
   b. Select **C13** and double-click the *Fill Handle* to copy the contents through **C14:C131**.
   c. Select the range **D12:G12**, and double-click the *Fill Handle* to copy the contents through **D13:G131**. (The values in the columns will not be correct until the formulas in all columns have been copied.)

9. Save and close the workbook (Figure 2-72).

2-72 Excel 2-3 completed

Independent Project 2-4

Central Sierra Insurance (CSI) is a multi-office insurance company that handles all lines of commercial and personal insurance policies. CEO Eliana Lingle is planning to pay a bonus to employees calculated on each employee's base monthly salary. For this project, you create a spreadsheet for Ms. Lingle to summarize the bonus payments.
[Student Learning Outcomes 2.1, 2.2, 2.3, 2.4, 2.5, 2.6]

File Needed: **CentralSierra-02.xlsx**
Completed Project File Name: **[your initials] Excel 2-4.xlsx**

Skills Covered in This Project

- Create and copy formulas.
- Apply mathematical order of operations.
- Use relative, absolute, and mixed cell references.

- Use *AutoSum.*
- Apply the *VLOOKUP* function.
- Apply the *SUMIF* function.

1. Open the **CentralSierra-02.xlsx** workbook and save the workbook as **[your initials] Excel 2-4**.

2. Create a *VLOOKUP* function to calculate the bonus amount for each employee.
   a. Click the **Employees** sheet tab, and select **I4**.
   b. Type a formula to reference the *Base Monthly Salary* amount as the *lookup_value*.
   c. Click the **Bonus** sheet tab for the *table_array* argument.
   d. Use the second column of the table for the *col_index_num*.
   e. Verify that the formula syntax is =VLOOKUP(H4,Bonus!A4:B8,2).

3. Select the formula in **I4** and apply absolute values to the cell references.

4. Copy the formula in **I4** to **I5:I13**.

5. Type a formula in **J4** to calculate the total monthly salary.
   a. Use parentheses in the formula to calculate the amount of the bonus and then add the bonus to the *Base Monthly Salary*.
   b. Copy the formula in **J4** to **J5:J13**.

6. Select **J15** and use *AutoSum* to calculate a total for the *Total Monthly Salary* column.
   a. Edit the range.
   b. Apply the **Total** cell style to **J15**.

7. Create a *SUMIF* function to calculate the total monthly salary for each office.
   a. Select **B26**.
   b. Use the information in column **D** (Branch) for the range argument.
   c. Select **D4** (Cameron Park) for the criteria argument.
   d. Use the information in column **J** (Total Monthly Salary) for the sum_range argument.

8. Edit the formula in **B26** to include absolute cell references in all cell ranges.

9. Copy and edit a formula.
   a. Select the formula in **B26** and copy the formula through **B28**.
   b. Select **B27** and change the reference from Cameron Park (**D4**) to Folsom (**D8**).
   c. Select **B28** and change the reference from Cameron Park (**D4**) to Granite Bay (**D7**).

10. Select cell **B29** and create a formula to add the salary amounts for each branch.

11. Format the data in column **I** using the **Percent Style** button.

12. Format the salary amounts in columns **H** and **J** and the "Branch Totals" section to the **Accounting** style with no symbol.

13. Select the data from **A3:J30** and change the font to **Gill Sans MT** and the font size to **11 pt**.

14. Select **E26** and type Highest Salary.

15. Type Lowest Salary in **E27** and Average Salary in **E28**.

16. Select **F26** and type =ma. When you see *MAX*, double-click to insert the function. Drag to select **J4:J13**. Press **Enter** to complete the formula.

17. Select **F27** and use the **MIN** function to calculate the lowest salary.

18. Select **F28** and use the **AVERAGE** function to calculate the average salary.

19. Select **E25** and type Salary Summary.

20. Merge and center "Salary Summary" in cells **E25** and **F25**.

21. Format the "Salary Summary" section to match the "Branch Totals" section.
    a. Apply a fill color.
    b. Apply **All Borders** from the *Borders* button drop-down list.

22. Format the two total amounts (**B29** and **J15**) to include a dollar sign.

23. Adjust column widths if necessary.

24. Save and close the workbook (Figure 2-73).

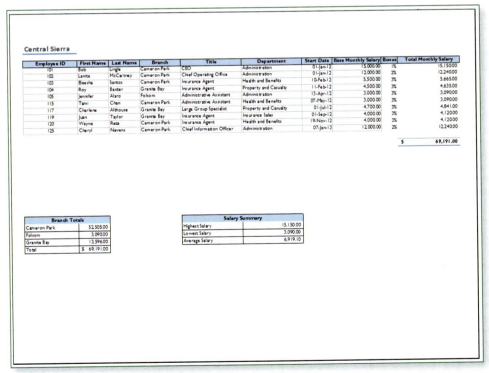

2-73 Excel 2-4 completed

E2-125

Independent Project 2-5

When San Diego Sailing received its end-of-year financial reports, its financial officers decided to evaluate the rental rates schedule for boats. You have been asked to create a spreadsheet to compare three different proposed rate changes that the group is considering implementing in the new year and to update information on the boat fleet.
[Student Learning Outcomes 2.1, 2.2, 2.3, 2.5]

File Needed: **SanDiego-02.xlsx**
Completed Project File Name: **[your initials] Excel 2-5.xlsx**

Skills Covered in This Project

- Create and copy formulas.
- Apply mathematical order of operations.
- Use relative, absolute, and mixed cell references.

- Apply the *IF* function.
- Name cells and use the name range in a formula.
- Apply the *TODAY* function.

---

1. Open the **SanDiego-02.xlsx** workbook and save the workbook as **[your initials] Excel 2-5**.

2. Select **H4** and create an *IF* function formula to determine which boats include a stove with the galley. Boats must be able to seat 8 or more people to have a stove in the galley.
   a. Use "Yes" for the *value_if_true* argument.
   b. Use "No" for the *value_if_false* argument.

3. Insert a worksheet and name the sheet Data.

4. Type the following information in the new worksheet:

	A	B
Row 3	Projected Increases	
Row 4	5% Increase	105%
Row 5	10% Increase	110%
Row 6	15% Increase	115%

5. Format the table text on the *Data* sheet.
   a. **Merge and Center** the text in **A3** over **A3:B3** and apply **bold** format.
   b. Apply **Accent 1** cell style to **A3**.
   c. Select **A3:B6** and apply the **All Borders** format.

6. Select **A4:B6** and assign range names using the **Create from Selection** button on the *Formulas* tab.

7. Select **J4** on the *Fleet* worksheet, and create a formula to calculate a 5% increase for the data in the "4 Hr. Rate" column using the range name assigned on the *Data* sheet.
   a. Type =.
   b. Select **F4** and type *.
   c. Press **F3** to open the *Paste Name* dialog box.
   d. Select **_5_Increase** and click **OK**.
   e. Press **Enter**.

8. Create formulas for **K4:O4** and copy the formulas to row 18.

9. Select the amounts in columns F, G, and J:O and apply **Currency** format with no symbol.

10. Select **A1** and type San Diego Sailing.

11. Format **A1** using the **Title** cell style and apply **bold** format. Adjust the column width.

12. Insert a row above the current row 2. Clear the formatting of the new row 2.

13. Insert the **TODAY()** function in **A2**. Format the date as **11 pt. bold** and align left.

14. Change the date format to display the month as a word followed by the day and year.

15. Apply the **All Borders** format to rows **4** through **19**.

16. Click the **Insert** tab and click the **Header & Footer** button.
    a. Switch to the *Footer* area.
    b. Click the right text box and type Page followed by a space.
    c. Click the **Page Number** button on the *Header & Footer Tools Design* tab.
    d. Click the worksheet and return to *Normal* view.

17. Paste range names in a worksheet.
    a. Click the **Data** sheet tab and select cell **A15**.
    b. Click the **Use in Formula** button [*Formulas* tab, *Defined Names* group].
    c. Click **Paste Names**.
    d. Click the **Paste List button** in the *Paste Name* dialog box.
    e. Click **OK**.

18. Save and close the workbook (Figure 2-74).

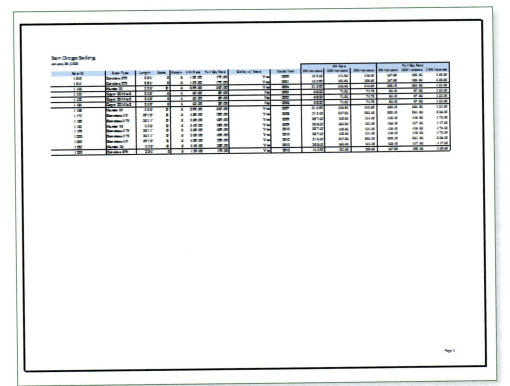

2-74 Excel 2-5 completed

Independent Project 2-6

Placer Hills Real Estate is a real estate company with regional offices throughout central California. In this project, you create a spreadsheet for the real estate company to provide summary information to its agents.
[Student Learning Outcomes 2.1, 2.2, 2.3, 2,4, 2.5]

File Needed: *PlacerHills-02.xlsx*
Completed Project File Name: *[your initials] Excel 2-6.xlsx*

Skills Covered in This Project

- Create and copy formulas.
- Apply mathematical order of operations.
- Use relative, absolute, and mixed cell references.
- Apply the AVERAGE, MAX, MIN, and COUNT functions.
- Apply the *VLOOKUP* function.

1. Open the *PlacerHills-02.xlsx* workbook and save the workbook as *[your initials] Excel 2-6*.

2. Type Placer Hills in cell **A1**, and apply the **Heading 1** style. Copy the contents of cell **A1** to the *Agent* worksheet cell **A1**.

3. Use the "SoldPrice" column data and the "ListPrice" column data on the *Listing* worksheet to calculate the percentage of list price.
   a. Select **O4**.
   b. Press = and click **N4**.
   c. Press / and click **C4**.

4. Copy the formula in **O4** to cells **O5:O12** and apply the **Percent Style** format to cells **O4:O12**.

5. Select **B20** and use the **Average** function to calculate the *Average List Price*.

6. Select **B21** and use the **Max** function to calculate the *Maximum List Price*.

7. Select **B22** and use the **Min** function to calculate the *Minimum List Price*.

8. Select **B23** and use the **Count** function to calculate the *Number of Listings*.

9. Calculate the number of brick homes by combining two functions.
   a. Select **B25**.
   b. Type =COUNTIF(
   c. Select **K4:K12**.
   d. Type ,"=Brick").
   e. Apply absolute cell references to the selected cell range.
   f. Press **Enter**.

10. Create individual formulas for **B26, B27, B29, B30, B31,** and **B32**, or copy the formula in **B25** and edit the formula.

11. Use the *VLOOKUP* function to insert the agent's last name in cells **E21:E26**.
    a. Use the agent number for the *lookup_value* argument.
    b. Use the table on the *Agent* sheet for the *table_array* argument.
    c. Use the *Last Name* column for the *col_index_num* argument.

d. Add absolute cell reference to the table_array argument.

e. Copy the formula in **B21** to **B22:B27**.

12. Select **D20:E26** and apply the **All Borders** format.

13. Format **D20:E20** with the **Accent 5** cell style and **bold** format.

14. Select **A3:O12** and apply the **All Borders** format.

15. Save and close the workbook (Figure 2-75).

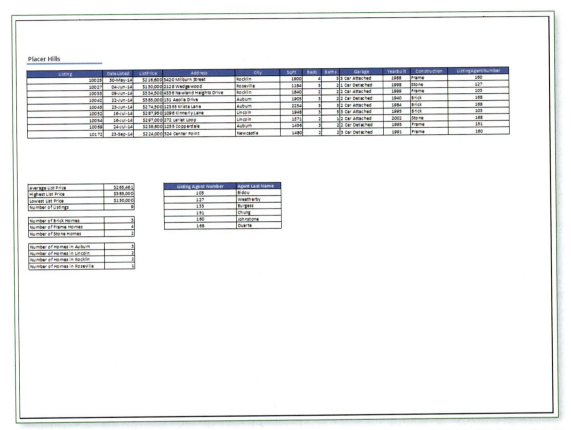

2-75 Excel 2-6 completed

Improve It Project 2-7

Mary's Rentals serves the rental equipment needs of contractors and the general public. In this exercise you create formulas and format a spreadsheet for the rental company.
[Student Learning Outcomes 2.1, 2.2, 2.3, 2.4, 2.5, 2.6]

File Needed: *MarysRentals-02.xlsx*
Completed Project File Name: *[your initials] Excel 2-7.xlsx*

Skills Covered in This Project

- Create and copy formulas.
- Apply mathematical order of operations.
- Use relative, absolute, and mixed cell references.

- Edit formulas.
- Name cells and use range names in formulas.
- Apply the *SUM* function.
- Apply the *SUMPRODUCT* function.

1. Open the **MarysRentals-02.xlsx** workbook and save the workbook as **[your initials] Excel 2-7**.

2. Select **B20** and use the *SUMPRODUCT* function to create a formula to calculate income from daily rentals.
   a. Use **C5:C12** for the *array1* argument.
   b. Use **D5:D12** for the *array2* argument.

3. Create formulas for **B21** and **B22** using *SUMPRODUCT*.

4. Select **B23** and use **Sum** to calculate total rental income for the month of March.

5. Select **C5:C12** and name the range Daily.

6. Select **E5:E12** and name the range Weekly.

7. Select **G5:G12** and name the range Monthly.

8. Select **B26** and use the *Sum* function and the *Daily* range name to calculate the number of daily rentals.
   a. Type =Su to display a list of functions beginning with "SU."
   b. Double-click **SUM**.
   c. Type da to display a list of functions and range names.
   d. Double-click **Daily**.
   e. Press **Enter**.

9. Create formulas for **B27** and **B28** using *Sum* and range names.

10. Select **B29** and create a formula to add the **Daily**, **Weekly**, and **Monthly** range names together.

11. Change the theme to **Slice**.

12. Format **A1** and **A2**.
    a. **Merge & Center** the text in **A1** over **A1:H1**, and merge and center the text in **A2** over **A2:H2**.
    b. Edit **A2** to Month of March.
    c. Apply **Accent 1** cell style to **A1**.
    d. Apply **bold** formatting to **A1** and **A2**.
    e. Change the font size of **A1** to **18 pt**.

13. Format the column headings (**A4:H4**) with cell style **20% Accent 1**.

14. AutoFit column width and row height.

15. Format the numbers in columns **D, F**, and **H** using **Accounting** style with no symbol. Apply the **Accounting** style with no symbol format to cells **B20:B22**.

16. Apply **All Borders** to A4:H12, A20:B23, and **A26:B29**.

17. Change the orientation to **landscape**.

18. Save and close the workbook (Figure 2-76).

2-76 Excel 2-7 completed

Challenge Project 2-8

In this project, you create a spreadsheet to compare three purchase options you may be considering. Plan the spreadsheet layout so that a comparison of the three options is easy to read and understand.
[Student Learning Outcomes 2.1, 2.2, 2.3, 2.5]

File Needed: None
Completed Project File Name: *[your initials] Excel 2-8.xlsx*

Create and save a workbook as *[your initials] Excel 2-8*. Enter data in a spreadsheet that will be useful in planning a major purchase such as a car or home. Modify your workbook according to the following guidelines:

- Include headings to identify the cells. Headings may include "Description," "Loan Amount," "Term of the Loan," "Interest Rate," and "Payment." Assign range names to easily identify cell references in formulas.
- Create a *PMT* formula.
- Create a payment schedule with formulas.
- Add two sheets to your workbook. Create a second spreadsheet using the original parameters except change the interest rate. Calculate the amount of payment. Create a third spreadsheet using the original parameters except change the term of the loan. Calculate the amount of the payment.
- Add another sheet to the workbook to create a side-by-side comparison of the three loan scenarios.
- Include a date formula that automatically updates when you open the spreadsheet.
- Incorporate *Themes, Cell Styles*, and formatting.
- Include document properties and spell check your workbook.

Challenge Project 2-9

In this project, you create a spreadsheet to calculate your monthly expenditures and monthly income for one year. You also calculate the percentage of total expenses each of your individual expenses represents.
[Student Learning Outcomes 2.1, 2.2, 2.3, 2.4]

File Needed: None
Completed Project File Name: *[your initials] Excel 2-9.xlsx*

Create and save a blank workbook as *[your initials] Excel 2-9*. Plan the layout of the workbook to include one sheet for expenses and one sheet for income. You may want to plan a third sheet to compare expenses with income. Modify your workbook according to the following guidelines:

- On the income sheet, list all your sources of income including full-time and part-time employment. Arrange the data so that each column heading is a month of the year.
- On the expense sheet, place the months across the sheet and the expenses in the first column.
- Create a row of cells that lists the total expenses for each month. Consider grouping expenses by month, quarter, or year. Include subtotals for each section.
- Add a formula to calculate the percentage of your total expenses each expense represents. Use an absolute cell reference in the formula.
- Use formulas to calculate your net income, average income, and maximum income.
- Add a sheet to compare projected income and projected expenses for one month to actual income and actual expenses for one month.
- Incorporate *Themes, Cell Styles*, and formatting.
- Include document properties and spell check the workbook.

Challenge Project 2-10

In this project, you create a form for a store that sells and ships merchandise. You include a lookup table to calculate shipping costs and calculate the total cost of buying an item.
[Student Learning Outcomes 2.1, 2.2, 2.3, 2.4, 2.5, 2.6]

File Needed: None
Completed Project File Name: *[your initials] Excel 2-10.xlsx*

Create and save a blank workbook as *[your initials] Excel 2-10*. Modify your workbook according to the following guidelines:

- At the top of the spreadsheet, create a section to include the name of the store, address, telephone number, web site, and store hours.
- Include bill-to and ship-to sections. Arrange and format the data.
- Include a section below the bill-to and ship-to sections to include purchasing information such as "Item Number," "Quantity," "Item Description," "Price Subtotal," "Sales Tax," "Shipping," and "Total Cost."
- Name the worksheet tab and insert a second worksheet. Name the second sheet "Shipping Charges."
- On sheet 2 ("Shipping Charges"), create a *VLOOKUP* table for shipping charges. Use a price range to calculate charges. For example, for orders up to $50, the shipping cost is $6.95; for orders of $50.01 to $100.00, the shipping cost is $8.95; etc.
- Add borders and shading as well as cell styles and a theme to format the spreadsheets attractively.
- Use 6% as the sales tax rate.
- Add range names if appropriate.
- Add formulas to calculate the cost of buying an item including tax and shipping charges.
- Test the worksheet formulas.
- Include document properties and spell check the workbook.

Creating and Editing Charts

CHAPTER OVERVIEW

In addition to building formulas and functions in a worksheet, you can use Excel to graph or chart worksheet data. After selecting the correct data in a worksheet, you can quickly create a professional-looking chart with a few clicks of the mouse. This chapter introduces you to the basics of creating, editing, and formatting Excel charts.

STUDENT LEARNING OUTCOMES (SLOs)

After completing this chapter, you will be able to:

SLO 3.1 Create, size, and position an Excel chart object and create a chart sheet (p. E3-134).

SLO 3.2 Design a chart using *Quick Layouts* and chart styles (p. E3-137).

SLO 3.3 Switch row and column data, add or remove chart elements, change chart type, and edit source data (p. E3-141).

SLO 3.4 Format chart elements with shape styles, fill, outlines, and special effects (p. E3-148).

SLO 3.5 Use images, shapes, and *WordArt* in a chart (p. E3-152).

SLO 3.6 Create a pie chart and a combination chart (p. E3-157).

SLO 3.7 Insert and format sparklines in a worksheet (p. E3-161).

CASE STUDY

In the Pause & Practice projects in this chapter, you use Excel workbooks for the northern Minnesota resort business Paradise Lakes Resort (PLR). PLR has asked its managers to develop various charts for monthly sales data to better monitor the resort's business and to help formulate goals for next year.

Pause & Practice 3-1: Create and style charts in a workbook.

Pause & Practice 3-2: Edit and format charts in a workbook.

Pause & Practice 3-3: Create a combination chart and insert sparklines in a workbook.

SLO 3.1

Creating a Chart Object and a Chart Sheet

An Excel **chart** is a visual representation of numeric data in a worksheet. A chart helps you to easily identify trends, make comparisons, and recognize patterns in the numbers. Charts are dynamic and linked to the data, so if the numbers in your worksheet change, the chart is automatically redrawn.

There are different kinds of charts, and Excel can recommend the best chart type based on your selected data range or you can choose a chart type on your own. You can display a chart in the worksheet with the data or you can place a chart on its own sheet.

Create a Chart Object

A **chart object** is a selectable object surrounded by a square border that contains many customizable chart elements like data labels or a chart title. The chart elements are displayed as selectable components within the chart object. You can size and position a chart object on a worksheet.

Source data are the cells that contain values and labels to be graphed in the chart. In Figure 3-1, the source data includes the categories names, the month names, and four values for each of three months. Each of these values is a **data point**, a cell containing a value. Each group of data points or values is a **data series**. In this example, Figure 3-1 sets up three data series for a clustered bar chart (the four items under each month). Each data series has a name (i.e., *April*, *May*, and *June*).

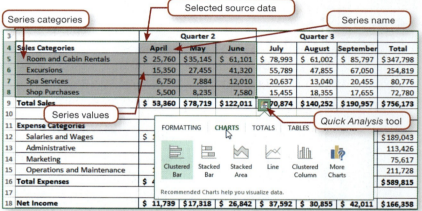

3-1 Source data and *Quick Analysis* suggestions

The text label that describes each data series is a **category label**. In Figure 3.1, the categories are the sales categories in column A (i.e., *Room and Cabin Rentals*, *Excursions*, *Spa Services*, and *Shop Purchases*).

> ### MORE INFO
>
> You can create a default chart object by selecting the appropriate data and pressing **Alt+F1**.

When you select source data that is adjacent (all the cells are next to each other), the **Quick Analysis** button appears at the lower right corner of the selection. The *Quick Analysis* tool lists tabs with the commands you are most likely to choose for your selected data, including *Charts*. After you click the *Charts* command, Excel displays recommended chart types. As you point to each chart type, you see a preview of the chart. This preview helps you to determine if you have selected the correct range. Click your preferred chart type to create a new chart object in the worksheet. The chart object is placed in the sheet next to the source data.

HOW TO: Create a Chart Object

1. Select the cell range that includes the data series and category labels you want to display in chart format.

2. Click the **Quick Analysis** button and select **Charts**.

3. Point at the preferred chart type and click to insert a chart (Figure 3-2).

> **MORE INFO**
>
> When the source data range is non-adjacent, the *Quick Analysis* tool does not display.

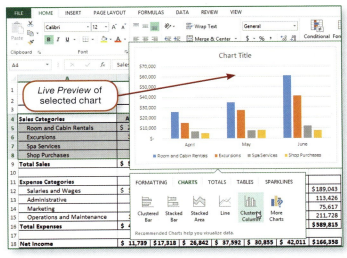

3-2 Chart object previewed

Excel Chart Types

Excel has many chart types that you can use to graph your data. Most chart types have several subtypes or variations. Excel recommends chart types based on your selected data, or you can choose the type of chart you want to use. The most common chart types are column or bar, line, and pie. Excel can also build powerful scientific and statistical charts when needed. The following table describes Excel chart types.

Excel Chart Types

Chart Type	Description	Category (Labels)	Values (Numbers)
Column	Illustrates data changes over a period of time or shows comparisons among items	Horizontal axis	Vertical axis
Bar	Displays comparisons among individual items or values at a specific period of time	Vertical axis	Horizontal axis
Pie	Uses one data series to display each value as a percentage of the whole		One data series shown by slice size
Line	Displays trends in data over time, emphasizing rate of change	Horizontal axis	Vertical axis
Area	Displays the magnitude of change over time and shows the rate of change	Horizontal axis	Vertical axis
XY (Scatter) or Bubble	Displays relationships among numeric values in two or more data series; these charts do not have a category	Horizontal axis (value 1-x)	Vertical axis (value 2-y)
Stock	Displays three series of data to show fluctuations in stock prices from high to low to close	Horizontal axis	Vertical axis
Surface	Displays optimum combinations of two sets of data on a surface	Horizontal axis (value 1-x)	Horizontal axis (value 1-x)
Radar	Displays the frequency of multiple data series relative to a center point. There is an axis for each category	NA	NA
Combo Chart	Uses two types of charts to graph values that are widely different	Either	Either

Size and Position a Chart Object

A chart object can be selected, sized, and positioned. When you select a chart object or it is active, it is surrounded by eight selection handles. A **selection handle** is a small round or rectangular shape on each corner and in the middle of each side. When you point at a selection handle, the pointer changes to a two-pointed arrow that you drag to make the chart smaller or larger. Drag a corner handle to size both height and width of the chart proportionally.

To move a chart object, point at the chart background to display a four-pointed move pointer. Then drag the chart to the desired location.

> ▶ **MORE INFO**
>
> When a chart object is selected, the *Chart Tools* tabs are visible in the *Ribbon* and three *Quick Chart Tools* are available at the top right corner of the object.

HOW TO: Move and Size a Chart Object

1. Select the chart object (Figure 3-3).

2. Place your pointer on the outside border of the chart to display a move pointer.

3. Drag the chart object to a new location and release.

4. Place your pointer on a selection handle to display a resize pointer.

5. Drag the pointer to resize the chart.

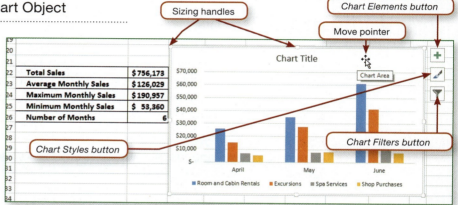

3-3 Selected chart object and move pointer

Creating a Chart Sheet

A *chart sheet* is an Excel chart that is displayed on its own sheet in the workbook. The chart sheet does not include rows, columns, and cells like a regular worksheet, but the chart is linked to its data on another worksheet.

When you create a chart from the *Quick Analysis* tool or from the *Insert* tab in the *Ribbon*, Excel creates a chart object. You can move any chart object that you have already created to its own sheet using the *Chart Tools Design* tab. When you do that, Excel moves the chart to a new sheet named *Chart1, Chart2,* and so on. You can type a new name for the chart sheet in the *Move Chart* dialog box. You can also create a new chart sheet from a new chart object.

From the *Charts* group on the *Insert* tab, you can click the **Recommended Charts** button or the specific chart type button to create the chart object.

HOW TO: Create a Chart Sheet

1. Select the cell range that includes the data series and category labels you want to display in chart format.
   - If the cell range is non-adjacent, hold down the **Ctrl** key to select each range (Figure 3-4).
2. Click the **Recommended Charts** button [*Insert* tab, *Charts* group].

3. Click the preferred chart type.

4. Click **OK**.

5. Click the **Move Chart** button [*Chart Tools Design* tab, *Location* group].

6. Click the **New sheet** radio button (Figure 3-5).

7. Type the name of the new sheet tab.

8. Click **OK**.

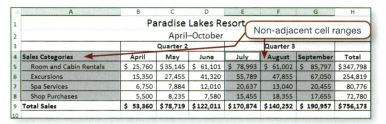

3-4 Source data ranges that are not next to each other

> ▶ **ANOTHER WAY**
> To move a chart object to its own sheet, right-click the chart object and choose **Move Chart**.

> ▶ **MORE INFO**
> You can create a default chart sheet for selected data by pressing **F11**.

3-5 *Move Chart* dialog box

SLO 3.2

Designing a Chart with Quick Layouts and Styles

Excel has many tools to help you develop consistent and appealing designs for your charts. From the *Chart Tools Design* tab, you can apply different chart layouts or choose from predefined styles. These choices affect the appearance of the entire chart.

Apply a Quick Layout

A **chart layout** is the complete set of elements that is displayed in the chart. These include parts of a chart such as the main title, axis titles, legend, and others. The *Quick Layout* command allows you to choose from 10 predefined layouts. After selecting a *Quick Layout*, you can add or remove individual chart elements, too.

To apply a *Quick Layout* use the **Quick Layout** button in the *Chart Layouts* group on the *Chart Tools Design* tab. As you point to each layout option, *Live Preview* redraws your chart so that you can decide if the layout is right for your needs.

HOW TO: Apply a Quick Layout to a Chart

1. Click the chart object or the chart sheet.

2. Click the **Quick Layout** button [*Chart Tools Design* tab, *Chart Layouts* group].

3. Point to a layout to preview its effect.

4. Click the preferred **Layout** (Figure 3-6).

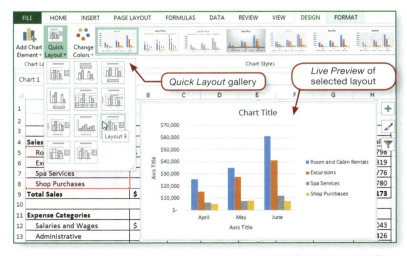

3-6 *Quick Layout* gallery

Apply a Chart Style

A **chart style** is a preset combination of colors and effects for a chart, its background, and its elements. The chart styles that are available for a chart are based on the current workbook theme. If you change the workbook theme, the chart style colors are updated, and your chart will reflect the new color palette. You can find chart styles in the *Chart Styles* group on the *Chart Tools Design* tab. Like a chart layout, you can preview the effects of a chart style as you point to each style in the gallery.

HOW TO: Apply a Chart Style

1. Select the chart object or the chart sheet.
2. Click the desired **Style** button [*Chart Tools Design* tab, *Chart Styles* group].
   - Click the **More** button [*Chart Tools Design* tab, *Chart Styles* group] to display the entire *Chart Styles* gallery (Figure 3-7).

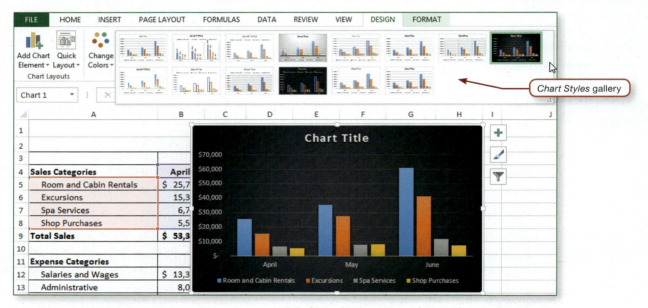

3-7 *Chart Styles* gallery and preview of selected style

> **MORE INFO**
>
> Chart styles may affect the current chart layout.

Print a Chart

You can print chart objects with the worksheet data or individually. When you want to print a worksheet with the chart object, you need to size and position the chart so that it fits on the page or scale the sheet to fit the complete worksheet contents. You can choose whether the data and chart should print in portrait or landscape orientation and you can insert headers or footers as well in a worksheet.

> **MORE INFO**
>
> Use the *Page Setup* dialog box or the *Insert* tab to insert a header or footer on a chart sheet.

You can print a chart sheet with a regular *Print* command. By default, a chart sheet prints in landscape orientation.

To print a chart object with its source data, click any cell in the worksheet. Then use the *Print* command from the *File* tab in the *Backstage* view and make your usual print choices. If you prefer to print a chart object on its own sheet, select the object first and then choose print.

HOW TO: Print a Chart with its Source Data

1. Click any cell in the worksheet.
   - To print a chart sheet, click the sheet tab.
2. Click the **File** tab to open the *Backstage* view (Figure 3-8).
3. Select **Print** at the left and set print options if necessary.
4. Click **Print**.

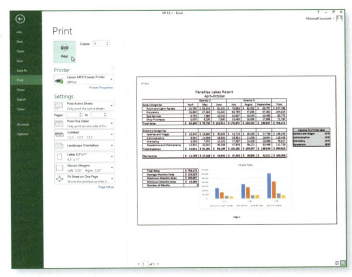

3-8 *Backstage* view, print options

PAUSE & PRACTICE: EXCEL 3-1

Charts illustrate worksheet data and make it clearer and easy to understand. For this project you insert a clustered column chart object in a worksheet that tracks sales and expenses for Paradise Lakes Resort. You also insert a clustered bar chart sheet to highlight second quarter results.

File Needed: *ParadiseLakes-03.xlsx*
Completed Project File Name: *[your initials] PP E3-1.xlsx*

1. Open the ***ParadiseLakes-03*** workbook.

2. Save this document as *[your initials] PP E3-1*.

3. Create a chart object.
   a. Select the cell range **A4:D8** for your chart.
   b. Click the **Quick Analysis** button and choose the **Charts** tab.
   c. Click **Clustered Column**.

4. Position and size the chart object.
   a. Click the chart object if it is not selected.
   b. Point at the chart area to display a move pointer.
   c. Drag the chart object so that its top left corner is at cell **C20**.

d. Point at the lower right selection handle to display a resize pointer.

e. Drag the pointer to reach cell **H35** as shown in Figure 3-9.

5. Apply a *Quick Layout.*
   a. Click the chart object if necessary.
   b. Click the **Quick Layout** button [*Chart Tools Design* tab, *Chart Layouts* group].
   c. Click **Layout 7**.

6. Create a chart sheet.
   a. Select the cell range **A4:A8**.
   b. Hold down **Ctrl** and select the cell range **E4:G8**.
   c. Click the **Recommended Charts** button [*Insert* tab, *Charts* group].
   d. Select **Clustered Bar**.
   e. Click **OK**.
   f. Click the **Move Chart** button [*Chart Tools Design* tab, *Location* group].
   g. Click the **New sheet** radio button.
   h. Type Quarter 3 as the new sheet name.
   i. Click **OK**.

7. Choose a chart style.
   a. Click the **Chart Styles** More button [*Chart Tools Design* tab, *Chart Styles* group] to display the gallery.
   b. Click **Style 10** (Figure 3-10).

8. Preview the charts.
   a. Select the **Quarter 3** sheet if necessary.
   b. Click the **File** tab to open the *Backstage* view.
   c. Click **Print** at the left to preview the chart sheet (see Figure 3-11).
   d. Click the **Back** button to return to the worksheet.
   e. Select the **Location 1 Cass Lake** sheet.
   f. Click cell **A1**.
   g. Click the **File** tab to open the *Backstage* view.
   h. Click **Print** to preview the worksheet and chart object.
   i. Click the **Back** button to return to the worksheet.

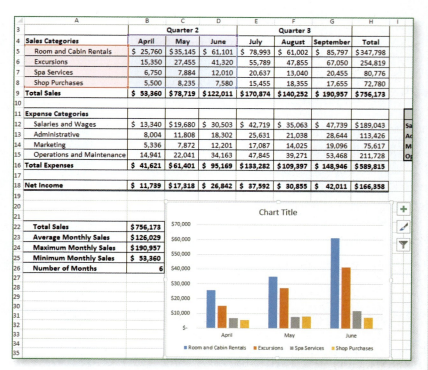

3-9 Chart object sized and positioned

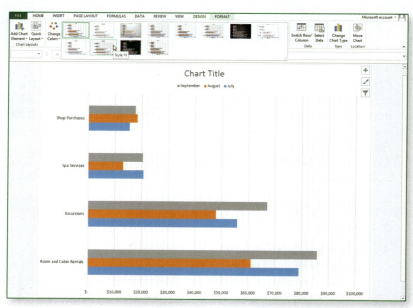

3-10 Chart sheet with new style

9. Save and close the workbook (Figure 3-11).

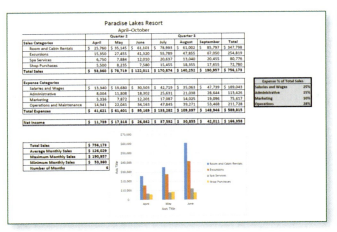

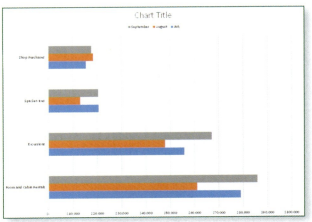

3-11 PP E3-1 completed chart object and chart sheet

SLO 3.3

Editing a Chart

You can edit a chart in many ways. For example, you will want to edit the contents of the placeholder text boxes that are inserted in your chart if you use a *Quick Layout*, or you might insert a legend to explain colors used for a data series. You can also add data labels that indicate the actual values on the chart, or you might decide to switch row and column data.

Switch Row and Column Data

When you choose a recommended chart, Excel plots the data series based on the number of rows and columns selected in the worksheet and the chart type. If you prefer, however, you can choose which data series is plotted on the X-axis and which is plotted on the Y-axis. In a column chart, by default, the X-axis is along the bottom of the chart; the y-axis is along the left.

HOW TO: Switch Row and Column Data

1. Click the chart object or chart sheet tab.

2. Click the **Switch Row/Column** button [*Chart Tools Design* tab, *Data* group] (Figure 3-12).
   - Click the **Switch Row/Column** button [*Chart Tools Design* tab, *Data* group] to toggle how the columns and rows are plotted.

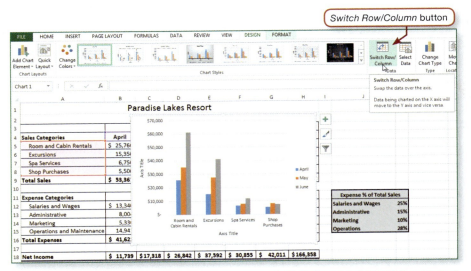

3-12 Column and row data switched

Add and Remove Chart Elements

A **chart element** is a separate, clickable, editable part of a chart. The chart layout and style that you choose affect which elements are initially displayed in a chart. You can add, remove, and format individual elements in a chart. The following table describes the chart elements.

Excel Chart Elements

Element	Description
Axis	Horizontal or vertical boundary that identifies what is plotted (the plural of axis is axes)
Axis title	Optional title for the categories or values
Chart area	Background for the chart; can be filled with a color, gradient, or pattern
Chart floor	Base or bottom for a 3-D chart
Chart title	Optional title or name for the chart
Chart wall	Vertical background or wall for a 3-D chart
Data label	Optional element that displays values with the marker for each data series
Data marker	Element that represents individual values. The marker is a bar, a column, a slice, or a point on a line
Data point	A single value or piece of data from a data series
Data series	Group of related values that are in the same column or row and translate into the columns, lines, pie slices, and other markers
Gridline	Horizontal or vertical line that extends across the plot area to help in identifying values
Horizontal (category) axis	Describes what is shown in the chart and is created from row or column headings. In a bar chart, the category axis is the vertical axis; the category axis is the horizontal axis in a column chart
Legend	Element that explains the symbols, textures, or colors used to differentiate data series
Plot area	Rectangular area bounded by the horizontal and vertical axes
Tick mark	Small line or marker on an axis to guide in reading values
Trendline	Displays averages in your data and can be used to forecast data by plotting future approximate averages
Vertical (value) axis	Shows the numbers on the chart. In a bar chart, the vertical axis is along the bottom; in a column chart, the vertical axis is along the side

You can show or remove chart elements by clicking the **Chart Elements** button to the right of the chart. When you click the button, the *Chart Elements* pane opens. In this pane, click the corresponding box to show or remove the element. To hide the pane, click the *Chart Elements* button again.

When you point at a chart element, a ScreenTip describes the element. You can click the element to select it and make it active. When a chart element is active, it is surrounded by selection handles, as shown in Figure 3-13. The name of an active element also appears in the *Chart Elements* box on the *Chart Tools Format* tab.

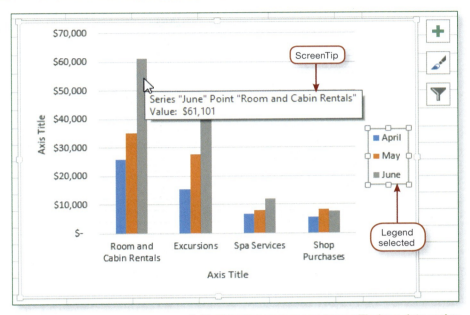

3-13 Selected legend and ScreenTip for a data series

Chart and Axes Titles

Some chart layouts include a placeholder or text box for a main chart title and axes titles. When a placeholder is shown, you need to edit the sample text to fit your data. When the layout does not include a placeholder title, you can add a placeholder or text box and then edit the text.

You can position a main chart title above the chart or within the chart area. Once you have created a text box, you can select it and move it anywhere on the chart. You can use an axis title to clarify what is represented by the categories or the values. However, keep in mind that many times an axis title is not required because the chart itself represents the data well.

HOW TO: Add a Chart Title

1. Click the chart object or chart sheet.
2. Click the **Chart Elements** button to the right of the chart.
3. Click to place a check mark next to **Chart Title** (Figure 3-14).
4. Click the menu arrow to choose a position for the title.
5. Type the title and press **Enter**.
   - To edit the chart title, triple-click the *Chart Title* placeholder, type the title, and click the chart background to deselect the element.

3-14 Chart title element added to chart object

In addition to adding and removing elements, you can edit placeholder text that is automatically placed in your chart when you select a chart layout or style. Select the element and type the new title. As you type a title, it appears in the *Formula bar*. It is placed in the chart when you press **Enter**.

If you select the placeholder element, you can triple-click the text to select all of it and display the mini toolbar. You can type new data and use the commands on the mini toolbar to reformat it. After you type the new text, click the chart background to deselect the element and complete your edit. If you press **Enter** while typing in a text box, you insert a second line for the title.

> **MORE INFO**
>
> Double-clicking a chart element opens its *Format* pane.

HOW TO: Edit Placeholder Text

1. Click the placeholder text box to display the selection handles.

2. Point at the label and triple-click to select all the text (Figure 3-15).

3. Type the new title.

4. Click the chart background to accept the edit.

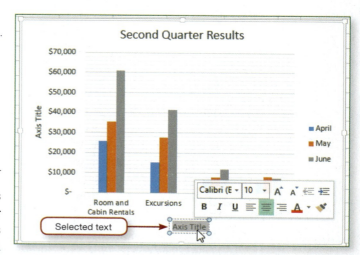

3-15 Placeholder text to be edited

You can delete chart elements when they are not necessary. For example, in a chart that illustrates dollar sales such as the one in Figure 3-15, the values on the vertical (y-axis) represent the amount of the sales. In a case like this, the vertical axis title is probably not necessary. To delete a chart element, click it to select it and press **Delete**. The chart may resize when certain elements are deleted.

Data Labels

Data labels display the value of a column, bar, pie slice, or other marker. Because the value axis uses a scale, it cannot show exact numbers, but a data label can.

HOW TO: Add Data Labels

1. Select the chart object or chart sheet.

2. Click the **Chart Elements** button to the right of the chart.

3. Click to place a check mark for **Data Labels**.

4. Click the menu arrow to choose a position for the labels (Figure 3-16).

3-16 Data labels shown outside bar markers

Data Table

A *data table* displays a table of the values of each data series based on your selected source data cells. You can add a data table to the bottom of your chart with or without legend markers (e.g., a mini legend to the left of the data table). By default, Excel does not include data tables with charts. To add a data table below your chart, use the **Data Table** button on the *Chart Tools Design* tab in the *Chart Layouts* group (Figure 3-17).

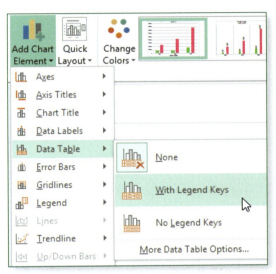

3-17 *Data Table* options

Trendlines

After adding chart elements, you may want to see any trends that occur. It is also useful to display trends in data to help predict future values. For example, a manager may need to forecast the next quarter's sales based on historical numbers. A *trendline* is a chart element that demonstrates averages in your data and that can be used to forecast data by plotting future approximate averages.

HOW TO: Add a Trendline to a Chart

1. Click the chart if it is not already selected.

2. Click the **Chart Elements** customization button in the top right corner of the chart.

3. Place your pointer over the *Trendline* check box until the arrow button appears and then click the **Trendline** arrow button.

4. Select the type of trendline you want to apply (Figure 3-18) to open the *Add Trendline* dialog box (Figure 3-19).

5. Select the data series you want to apply the *Trendline* to.

6. Click **OK** (Figure 3-20).

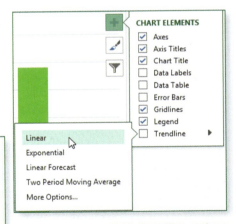

3-18 *Trendline* options

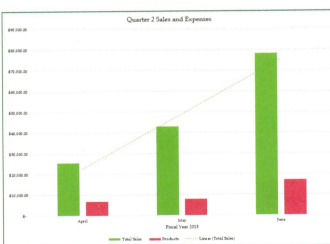

3-20 2-D clustered column chart with "Total Sales" linear trendline

3-19 *Add Trendline* dialog box

Change the Chart Type

It is possible to change the chart type. For example, you may decide to change some bar charts into column charts for consistency in a report to make it easier for your audience to quickly compare one chart to the next, or you might decide to use 3-D pie charts instead of 2-D.

> **MORE INFO**
> Excel 3-D charts add the perception of depth to a chart.

HOW TO: Change the Chart Type

1. Click the chart object or chart sheet.
2. Click the **Change Chart Type** button [*Chart Tools Design* tab, *Type* group].
3. Click the *Recommended Charts* tab.
4. Scroll the chart types in the left pane and click a tile to see a larger preview in the right pane.
5. Choose the preferred chart type and click **OK** (Figure 3-21).

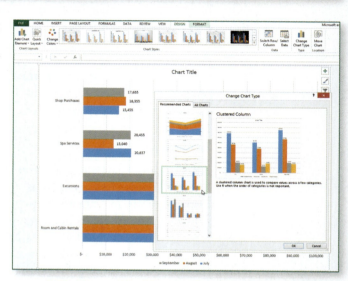

3-21 *Change Chart Type* options for selected chart sheet

Filter the Source Data

Once a chart is created, you can refine which data is displayed in the chart without changing the original source data range. This allows you to switch between several scenarios for your data without changing the underlying cell range.

You can accomplish this by applying a filter to either the values, the categories, or both. A *filter* is criteria that specifies which data is shown and which is hidden. Filters do not alter the source data range so you can return to the initial chart at any time.

HOW TO: Filter Source Data

1. Select the chart object or chart sheet.
2. Click the **Chart Filters** button in the top right corner of the chart.
   - The *Chart Filters* button is the bottom button and resembles a funnel-type filter.
3. Click to remove the check mark for the series or category you want to hide.
4. Click **Apply** (Figure 3-22).
5. Click the **Chart Filters** button to close the pane.

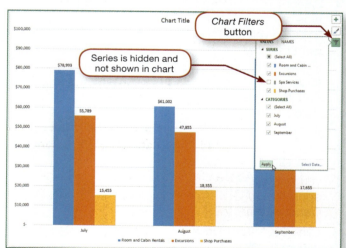

3-22 *Chart Filters* pane

Edit a Chart Data Source

In addition to filtering chart data, you can edit the existing chart data source or add a data series to a chart. In a column chart, adding a data series adds another column. To add a data series to a chart object, drag the sizing pointer in the lower right corner of the data range to expand or reduce the data range, as shown in Figure 3-23. Reducing the data range deletes the data series from the chart. To add a data series to a chart sheet, you use the *Select Data Source* dialog box.

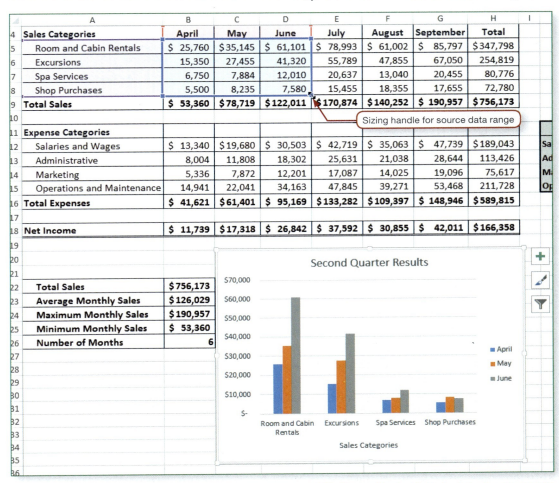

	A	B	C	D	E	F	G	H	I
4	Sales Categories	April	May	June	July	August	September	Total	
5	Room and Cabin Rentals	$ 25,760	$35,145	$ 61,101	$ 78,993	$ 61,002	$ 85,797	$347,798	
6	Excursions	15,350	27,455	41,320	55,789	47,855	67,050	254,819	
7	Spa Services	6,750	7,884	12,010	20,637	13,040	20,455	80,776	
8	Shop Purchases	5,500	8,235	7,580	15,455	18,355	17,655	72,780	
9	Total Sales	$ 53,360	$78,719	$122,011	$170,874	$140,252	$ 190,957	$756,173	
10									
11	Expense Categories								
12	Salaries and Wages	$ 13,340	$19,680	$ 30,503	$ 42,719	$ 35,063	$ 47,739	$189,043	
13	Administrative	8,004	11,808	18,302	25,631	21,038	28,644	113,426	
14	Marketing	5,336	7,872	12,201	17,087	14,025	19,096	75,617	
15	Operations and Maintenance	14,941	22,041	34,163	47,845	39,271	53,468	211,728	
16	Total Expenses	$ 41,621	$61,401	$ 95,169	$133,282	$109,397	$ 148,946	$589,815	
17									
18	Net Income	$ 11,739	$17,318	$ 26,842	$ 37,592	$ 30,855	$ 42,011	$166,358	

Sizing handle for source data range

	A	B
22	Total Sales	$756,173
23	Average Monthly Sales	$126,029
24	Maximum Monthly Sales	$190,957
25	Minimum Monthly Sales	$ 53,360
26	Number of Months	6

3-23 Chart object selected, sizing handle visible

While a chart filter does not change the source data range, editing the data source or adding a data series does change the source data range in the worksheet.

HOW TO: Add a Data Series in a Chart Sheet

1. Click the chart sheet.
2. Click the **Select Data** button [*Chart Tools Design* tab, *Data* group] to open the *Select Data Source* dialog box.
   • When the source data range is adjacent, you can click the **Collapse** button at the right of the *Chart data range* text box and drag to select a new range. Then click the **Expand** button and click **OK**.

3. Edit the cell references in the *Chart data range* text box to identify the new range (Figure 3-24).

4. Click **OK**.

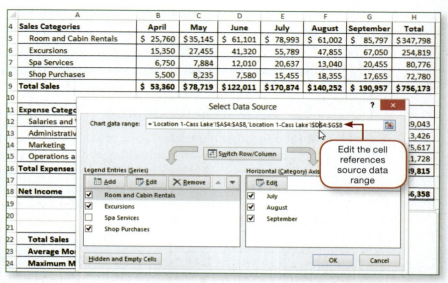

3-24 *Select Data Source* dialog box for a chart sheet

ANOTHER WAY

You can open the *Select Data Source* dialog box by clicking **Select Data** in the *Chart Filters* pane.

MORE INFO

You can apply or remove filters from the *Select Data Source* dialog box.

SLO 3.4

Formatting Chart Elements

In *SLO 3.2* and *SLO 3.3* you saw how you can quickly change the overall appearance and layout of a chart using *Quick Layouts* and *Chart Styles* and by adding or deleting chart elements. These commands are the first stages of designing a chart, but you will usually want to add your own format choices too.

Being able to personalize your charts is important. For example, your employer may have specific design requirements, or you may want to use colors and shapes from your organization or school in a chart. In either case, there are a variety of ways to enhance your charts to increase their readability.

MORE INFO

Making your own format choices enables you to distinguish your charts from those of other Excel users.

You can format each element in a chart. Some chart elements consist of a group of related elements. A data series, for example, is the group of values for a particular item. Within each data series, there are several data points. You can format the entire data series or an individual data point.

When you select an individual chart element, certain options on the *Chart Tools Design* tab apply to only that element. For example, when the chart area (background) is selected, you can change its fill or border color.

Apply a Shape Style

A **Shape Style** is a predesigned set of borders, fill colors, and effects for a chart element. **Shape fill** is the background color for the element. **Shape outline** is the border around an element. **Shape effects** include shadows, glows, bevels, or soft edges.

You choose a shape style from the gallery. As soon as you click the style, it is applied to the selected element and you see the results. There is a *Live Preview* for chart elements, and you can click the **Undo** button to remove the style if you change your mind after selecting it.

HOW TO: Apply a Shape Style

1. Click the chart element to select it.
   - Select a chart element by name by clicking the **Chart Elements** drop-down arrow [*Chart Tools Format* tab, *Current Selection* group] and choosing the element.
   - If the *Format* pane for the chart element opens, close it.
2. Click the **More** button [*Chart Tools Format* tab, *Shape Styles* group] to open the *Shape Styles* gallery (Figure 3-25).
3. Click the selected style.

3-25 *Shape Style* gallery for the chart area

Apply Shape Fill, Outline, and Effects

Once you select a chart element, you can apply fill color, set outline width and color, or special effects. These three format options are available in the *Shape Styles* group on the *Chart Tools Format* tab. If a *Shape Style* has already been applied to the object, individual choices override the style.

When you set a fill color, you choose from the workbook theme colors shown in the gallery. In addition to theme colors, the standard colors are also available, or you can build a custom color. After you choose a color, you can refine it to use a ***gradient***, a variegated blend of the color.

Live Preview is available for shape fill so you can preview the results of your choice before committing to it. To preview, just point at a color tile in the gallery. When you find the color you want, click the color tile.

The *Shape Fill*, *Shape Outline*, and *Shape Effects* buttons apply the choice you made most recently when you click the icon. To make a choice from a gallery, click the drop-down arrow for the option.

HOW TO: Apply Gradient Fill to a Chart Element

1. Click the chart element.
2. Click the **Shape Fill** button drop-down arrow [*Chart Tools Format* tab, *Shape Styles* group].
   - Click the button icon to apply the most recently used color.
3. Select the desired color.
4. Click the **Shape Fill** drop-down arrow again.
5. Choose **Gradient** (Figure 3-26) to open the gallery.
6. Click the preferred gradient.

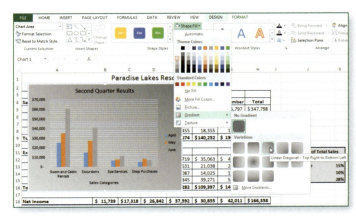

3-26 *Shape Fill* gallery and *Gradient* gallery

The outline for a shape is the border that surrounds or encircles the element. Not all chart elements are suited to an outline, but elements such as the chart or plot area often benefit from the use of an outline. When you add an outline to a chart element, you can select a weight or thickness for the line as well as a color. The thickness of an outline is measured in points, like fonts. Excel provides a gallery of weights to help you visualize the width. After you set an outline, it is easier to see the effect if you deselect the chart object.

HOW TO: Apply an Outline to a Chart Element

1. Click the chart element.
2. Click the **Shape Outline** button drop-down arrow [*Chart Tools Format* tab, *Shape Styles* group].
   - Click the button icon to apply the most recently used outline color and weight.
3. Click the desired color for the outline.
4. Click the **Shape Outline** drop-down arrow again.
5. Click **Weight**.
6. Choose a point size (Figure 3-27).

3-27 *Outline color* and *Weight* galleries

You can also apply special effects to a chart element. Popular effects include bevels and shadows, which give the element a realistic, three-dimensional look. These types of effects are best used on larger elements, such as the chart area, because they can overwhelm smaller elements.

HOW TO: Apply an Effect to a Chart Element

1. Click the chart element.
2. Click the **Shape Effects** button [*Chart Tools Format* tab, *Shape Styles* group].
3. Click the desired effect group for the object (Figure 3-28).
4. Choose the effect.

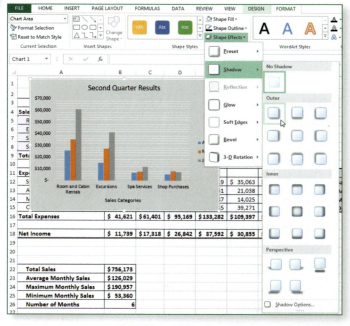

3-28 *Shape Effects* gallery for a chart object

To remove an effect, select the element and click the **Shape Effects** button drop-down arrow. Choose the type of effect and click the first option such as **No Shadow** or **No Bevel**.

The Format Task Pane

You can apply many format choices quickly from the *Chart Tools Format* tab. There are, however, several options for chart elements that are not available on the tab. Every chart element has a *Format* task pane that consolidates shape, fill, and color options and provides custom commands for the element (Figure 3-29).

To open the *Format* pane for a chart element, double-click the element or right-click it and choose *Format [Element Name]* from the menu. The *Format* pane opens to the right of the workbook window and automatically changes to reflect the selected element. For example, if you display the task pane for a data series and then select the chart title, the pane changes to the *Chart Title Format* pane.

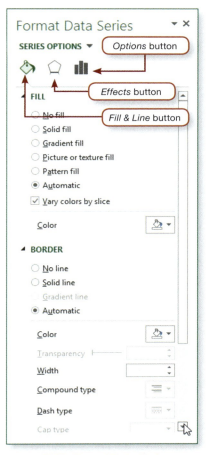

3-29 *Format Data Series* pane

> **ANOTHER WAY**
>
> Open a *Format* task pane by clicking the **Format Selection** button [*Chart Tools Format* tab, *Selection* group].

> **MORE INFO**
>
> Expand or collapse a command group in the *Format* task pane by clicking the small triangle to the left of the group name.

Most *Format* task panes have three buttons at the top: *Fill & Line*, *Effects*, and *Options*. When you click a button, the pane displays the relevant commands. *Fill & Line* and *Effects* are similar for all chart elements. The *Options* panes are specific to the element.

HOW TO: Use the Format Task Pane to Change Shape Fill

1. Double-click the chart element.
   - Verify the name of the task pane. If the wrong task pane opens, click the element again.
   - You can also select an element from the **Chart Elements** button drop-down arrow [*Chart Tools Format* tab, *Current Selection* group].
2. Click the **Fill & Line** button in the *Format* task pane.
3. Click **Fill** to expand the group.
4. Click the **Fill Color** button to open the gallery.
5. Click the desired color (Figure 3-30).

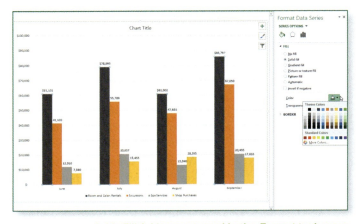

3-30 *Fill & Line* command in the *Format* task pane

There is an *Effects* command group in many *Format* task panes with the same options as the *Ribbon*. You can set shadows, bevels, glows, and more, depending on the selected element. Use these commands sparingly in most charts. Overuse of these commands can make the chart look too busy and overdesigned.

An *Options* group in a *Format* task pane is the command set that enables you to accomplish tasks that are specific to the type of element you select. For a data series in a column chart, for example, these commands determine whether numbers are shown on the right or left of the chart (secondary or primary axis), or you can choose to have the columns overlap. A pie chart, on the other hand, has series options that allow you to rotate the pie and explode the slices.

HOW TO: Use the Format Task Pane to Set Data Label Options

1. Double-click a data label element.
   - Right-click the element and choose **Format [Element Name]**.
   - If you have difficulty selecting the desired element, click the *Options* triangle next to the group name and choose the element from the drop-down list.
2. Click the **Label Options** button in the *Format* task pane.
3. Click **Label Options** or **Number** to expand the group.
4. Enter your format preferences in the task pane (Figure 3-31).

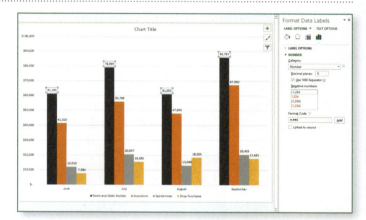

3-31 *Format Data Labels* pane

SLO 3.5

Using Images, Shapes, and WordArt in a Chart

A chart includes several selectable elements as part of its basic layout. You can add images, shapes, or *WordArt* in a chart to further personalize it. For example, a chart that illustrates the number of fish caught in a tournament could use a small image of a fish as fill for a data series rather than a fill color, or you might add a shape as a callout to a particular data point on a chart, such as a star to highlight the best sales record. You can also replace a chart title box with *WordArt* for a distinctive look.

Pictures, shapes, or *WordArt* are chart elements that you can size, position, and format.

Use a Picture as Shape Fill

In a chart, you can fill bars, columns, or pie slices with a picture that helps illustrate the data. To clarify, you might use a small stick-figure in a chart that graphs numbers of customers. You can use images that are filed on your computer or external storage device. You can search for and insert an online image, or you can copy an image from another application.

The size and design of an image are important. You cannot edit all images in Excel, so you may have to experiment with pictures to learn what works well in your charts. For example, you may not be able to change the color of a picture, or it may have a transparent background.

When you use a picture as a fill, you can use the ***Stretch*** option to stretch it across the data marker. This places a single copy of the image and stretches it to fill the shape. The ***Stack*** options resizes the picture to fit the width of the marker and repeats it to signify the values represented. There is also a ***Stack and Scale*** setting for more detailed sizing and placement of the picture.

HOW TO: Use a Picture as Fill

1. Select the data series and open its *Format* task pane.
2. Click the **Fill & Line** button in the *Format* task pane.
3. Click **Fill** to expand the group.
4. Click the **Picture or texture fill** button to open the gallery.
5. Click **Online** to search for an image or click **File** to choose a stored image.
6. Find and select the image you want to use as fill.
7. Click **Stack** to scale and repeat the image (Figure 3-32).

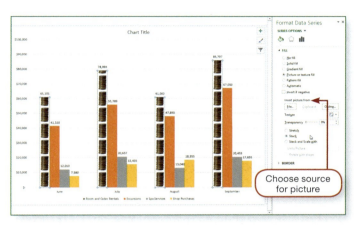

3-32 Online image used as fill for data series

Insert Shapes

Shapes such as arrows, circles, or callouts can be used to highlight important parts of a chart. For example, you can insert an arrow shape to emphasize the highest sales month or add a banner with text to congratulate the sales team.

The shapes that are available for use on a chart are the same shapes available in other Office applications. The *Shapes* gallery opens when you click the **More** button from the *Insert Shapes* group on the *Chart Tools Format* tab.

Once you place a shape in a chart, you can select it and format it from the *Picture Tools Format* tab.

HOW TO: Insert a Shape in a Chart

1. Select the chart object or chart sheet.
2. Click the **More** button [*Chart Tools Format* tab, *Insert Shapes* group].
3. Select the shape.
4. Click and drag to draw the shape on the chart (Figure 3-33).
5. Format the shape as needed.
6. Add text to the shape by right-clicking and selecting **Edit Text** from the context-sensitive menu.

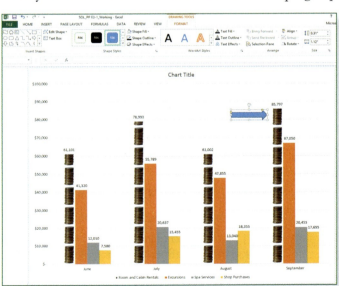

3-33 Shape inserted in chart

Use WordArt in a Chart

WordArt is a text box with preset font style, fill, and text effects. You might use *WordArt* in a chart in place of a regular chart title. You can apply a *WordArt* style to an existing chart title, or if a chart has no title, you can insert a *Text Box* shape and format it with a *WordArt* style.

HOW TO: Use WordArt in a Chart

1. Select the chart title or other chart element.
2. Click the **More** button to display *WordArt Styles* [*Chart Tools Format* tab, *WordArt Styles* group].
3. Click the preferred style (Figure 3-34).

3-34 *WordArt Style* gallery for selected chart title

PAUSE & PRACTICE: EXCEL 3-2

For this project, you open your first Pause & Practice file to edit and format the Paradise Lakes Resort charts. You switch row and column data and add and delete several chart elements. You also change the chart type so that the two charts in the workbook are consistent. Finally, you format the charts for easier reading.

File Needed: ***[your initials] PP E3-1.xlsx***
Completed Project File Name: ***[your initials] PP E3-2.xlsx***

1. Open the ***[your initials] PP E3-1*** workbook.
2. Save the workbook as ***[your initials] PP E3-2***.
3. Switch the row and column data in the chart object.
   a. Click the **Location 1-Cass Lake** worksheet tab.
   b. Click the chart object.
   c. Click the **Switch/Row Column** button [*Chart Tools Design* tab, *Data* group].

4. Add and remove chart elements.
   a. Click the **Location 1-Cass Lake** worksheet tab and select the chart object if it is not already selected.
   b. Click the **Chart Elements** button to the right of the chart.
   c. Add a title by clicking the **Chart Title** check box.
   d. Click the **Chart Title** menu arrow and choose **Above Chart**.
   e. Point at the placeholder text and triple-click.
   f. Type Second Quarter Activity.
   g. Click the chart to deselect the title.
   h. Click the horizontal axis title placeholder.
   i. Press **Delete**.
   j. Delete the vertical axis title placeholder.
   k. Double-click the legend element at the right of the chart area to open its *Format* task pane.
   l. Click the **Legend Options** button if necessary (Figure 3-35).
   m. Click the **Bottom** radio button to reposition the legend.
   n. Close the *Format Legend* task pane.

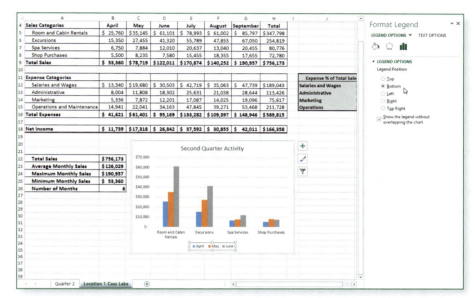

3-35 Chart in worksheet with elements added and removed

5. Change the chart type.
   a. Click the **Quarter 3** tab.
   b. Click the **Change Chart Type** button [*Chart Tools Design* tab, *Type* group] to open the *Change Chart Type* dialog box.
   c. Click the **Recommended Charts** tab.
   d. Find and select the first **Clustered Column** in the pane on the left.
   e. Click **OK**.

6. Filter the source data.
   a. Click the **Chart Filters** button in the top right corner of the chart.
   b. Click the **Excursions** check box to remove the check mark.
   c. Click **Apply**.
   d. Click the **Chart Filters** button to close the pane.

7. Apply shape styles and outlines to chart elements.
   a. Click the **Location 1-Cass Lake** tab.
   b. Click the chart object.
   c. Click the **Chart Elements** drop-down arrow [*Chart Tools Format* tab, *Current Selection* group].
   d. Choose **Plot Area** to select the plot area of the chart.
   e. Click the **More** button [*Chart Tools Format* tab, *Shape Styles* group].
   f. Click **Subtle Effect – Gold, Accent 4**.

g. Click the **Shape Outline** button drop-down arrow [*Chart Tools Format* tab, *Shape Styles* group].

h. Choose **Black, Text 1** in the top row of the *Theme Colors.*

i. Click the **Chart Elements** drop-down arrow [*Chart Tools Format* tab, *Current Selection* group].

j. Choose **Vertical (Value) Axis Major Gridlines** to select the major gridlines in the plot area.

k. Click the icon for the **Shape Outline** button [*Chart Tools Format* tab, *Shape Styles* group] to apply the last-used color (**Black, Text 1**).

l. Select the **Vertical (Value) Axis Minor Gridlines** and apply the same black outline color.

m. Click the chart area to see the change (Figure 3-36).

n. Click the **Chart Elements** drop-down arrow [*Chart Tools Format* tab, *Current Selection* group] and choose **Chart Area**.

o. Apply **Black, Text 1** for the outline.

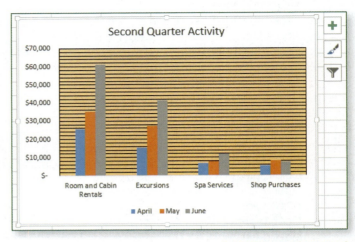

3-36 Plot area formatted

8. Use a picture as fill.

a. Click the **Quarter 3** tab.

b. Double-click one of the "Room and Cabin Rentals" columns to open the *Format Data Series* task pane.

c. Click the **Fill & Line** button.

d. Click **Fill** to expand the command group.

e. Click the **Picture or texture fill** button to open the gallery.

f. Click **Online**, type cabins in the *Office.com Clip Art* text box, and press **Enter** (Figure 3-37).

g. Choose an image and insert it.

h. Click **Stack** in the *Format Data Series* task pane.

i. Close the task pane.

3-37 Online search for a picture to use as fill

9. Use *WordArt* in a chart.

a. Triple-click the **Chart Title** placeholder to select the text.

b. Type Third Quarter Activity.

c. Click the chart area to deselect the title.

d. Triple-click the title text again.

e. From the mini toolbar, change the font size to **24 pt**.

f. Click the chart area to deselect the title.

g. Select the chart title to display the selection handles.

h. Click the **More** button [*Chart Tools Format* tab, *WordArt Style* group].

i. Choose **Fill – Black, Text 1, Shadow**.

10. Move the legend.
    a. Double-click the legend element below the chart title to open its *Format* task pane.
    b. Click the **Legend Options** button if necessary.
    c. Choose **Bottom** to reposition the legend.

11. Save and close the workbook (Figure 3-38).

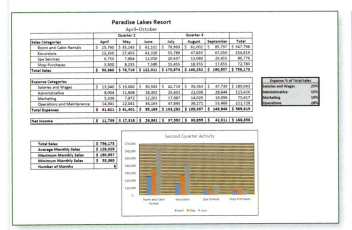

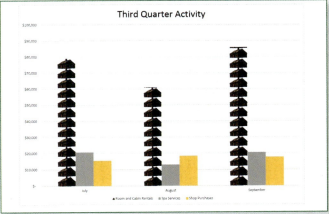

3-38 PP E3-2 completed worksheet and chart sheet

Creating and Editing a Pie Chart and a Combination Chart

When you use the *Quick Analysis* or *Recommended Charts* button, Excel chooses chart types that are suited to the data you have selected. As you develop your Excel skills and build more charts, you can choose your chart types directly from the *Charts* group on the *Insert* tab. With this method, when you click the specific chart type button, you see a small gallery with the available subtypes of the chart. As you point at each option, *Live Preview* previews the chart.

Charts created from a chart type button on the *Insert* tab are created as chart objects in the worksheet. Like any chart objects, you can move them to their own sheets.

Create a 3-D Pie Chart

A *pie chart* graphs one data series, one set of numbers. For most pie charts, you want to limit the number of categories to six or seven. A pie chart with many slices is difficult to interpret and often does not illustrate the relationship among the values. A pie chart illustrates how each number relates to the whole. In fact, you can set a value for the data series to show a percentage in the data label.

On the *Insert Pie or Doughnut Chart* button on the *Insert* tab, you can choose from a gallery of 2-D or 3-D pie types as well as a doughnut shape (see Figure 3-39). A doughnut chart is a pie chart with a hollow center. There are also two options for a pie chart with a bar or another pie chart.

HOW TO: Create a 3-D Pie Chart

1. Select the cell ranges that include the data series and the category labels.
2. Click the **Insert Pie or Doughnut Chart** button [*Insert* tab, *Charts* group] (Figure 3-39).
3. Choose **3-D Pie**.
   - Click the **Move Chart** button [*Chart Tools Design* tab, *Location* group] to move a pie chart to its own sheet.

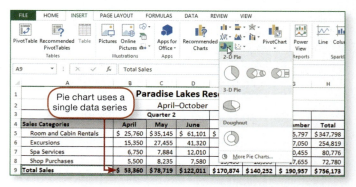

3-39 Selected data series and categories for a pie chart

Pie Chart Elements and Options

In a pie chart, the data series is represented by the whole pie. A data point is a slice of the pie. You can format the data series as a whole and you can format individual slices. It is important to note which element you have selected when you give a command. Remember the *Format* task pane. When you use it, it shows the name of the selected element. You can also view the element's name in the *Chart Elements* text box in the *Current Selection* group on the *Chart Tools Format* tab.

A pie chart can display a legend and a title. It does not, however, have axes and does not use axes titles. Data labels are often used instead of a legend for a pie chart because they show the same information. The chart area, as usual, is the background for the chart.

Pie charts do have *Quick Layouts* and *Quick Styles*. You can also set shape fill, color, and effects for the elements or objects, use a picture as fill, add an image, or insert *WordArt*.

Specialized commands for a pie chart are the angle of the first slice and the percent of explosion. The angle of the first slice allows you to rotate the pie. The first slice starts at the top of the chart at 0° (zero degrees). As you increase that value, the slice arcs to the right. *Live Preview* displays the results.

Exploding a pie slice emphasizes that slice because it moves the slice away from the rest of the pie. You set explosion as a percentage.

HOW TO: Rotate a Pie Chart and Explode a Slice

1. Double-click the pie chart to open the *Format Data Series* task pane.
   - You can also right-click the pie chart and choose **Format Data Series** to open the task pane.
2. Click the **Series Options** button to open the command group (Figure 3-40).
   - If the wrong *Format* task pane opens, click the arrow with **Series Options** and choose **Series 1**.
3. Set the angle for the first slice by dragging the slider control to the degree setting (see Figure 3-40).
   - You can also type the desired value in the text box or use the up or down spinner arrows to set a degree value.
4. Click the data point (slice) you want to explode.
   - Verify that the *Format Data Point* task pane is open.

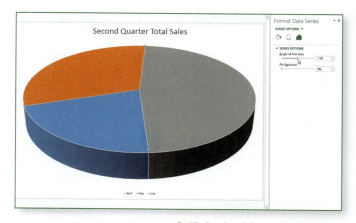

3-40 Angle of first slice adjusted

5. Set the percentage for the amount of explosion by dragging the slider control to the percent setting (Figure 3-41).
   - You can also type the new value in the text box or use the up or down spinner arrows to set a percent value.

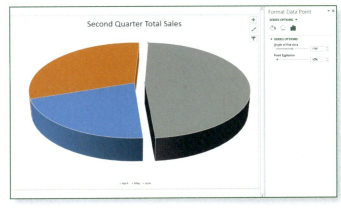

3-41 Exploded pie slice

> **MORE INFO**
>
> You can explode all the slices in a pie chart by selecting the data series, not a data point.

Create a Combination Chart

A combination chart includes two chart types such as a line chart and a column chart. Paradise Lakes Resort can use a combination chart, for example, to compare revenue from cabin and room rentals to the operations and maintenance expense. These two values reflect different types of numbers, so showing one series as a line and the other as a column focuses the revenue/expense comparison (Figure 3-42).

The most common combination of chart types is line and column, but you can also use a line and area combination. Excel offers an option to create a custom combination, but it is best to use this only after you have experience charting your data.

	A	B	C	D	E
1		**Paradise Lakes Resort**			
2		April–October			
3			Quarter 2		
4	**Sales Categories**	**April**	**May**	**June**	**July**
5	Room and Cabin Rentals	$ 25,760	$35,145	$ 61,101	$ 78,993
6	Excursions	15,350	27,455	41,320	55,789
7	Spa Services	6,750	7,884	12,010	20,637
8	Shop Purchases	5,500	8,235	7,580	15,455
9	**Total Sales**	**$ 53,360**	**$78,719**	**$122,011**	**$170,874**
10					
11	**Expense Categories**				
12	Salaries and Wages	$ 13,340	$19,680	$ 30,503	$ 42,719
13	Administrative	8,004	11,808	18,302	25,631
14	Marketing	5,336	7,872	12,201	17,087
15	Operations and Maintenance	14,941	22,041	34,163	47,845
16	**Total Expenses**	**$ 41,621**	**$61,401**	**$ 95,169**	**$133,282**

3-42 Source data for a combo chart

> **MORE INFO**
>
> Some chart types cannot be combined. If you try to do so, Excel opens a message box to inform you.

In a combination chart, you can display two sets of values with two vertical axes. The axis on the left is the primary axis; the one on the right is secondary. This option is best when the values are very different such as when comparing the number of rooms booked to dollars earned.

You can create a combination chart from the *Charts* group on the *Insert* tab as well as from the *Recommended Charts* button in the same group.

HOW TO: Create a Combination Chart

1. Select the cell ranges to be charted.
2. Click the **Insert Combo Chart** button [*Insert* tab, *Charts* group].
3. Choose the subtype (Figure 3-43).
   - You can move a combination chart to its own sheet if desired.

> ▶ **ANOTHER WAY**
>
> Create a combination chart for selected data from the **Recommended Charts** button [*Insert* tab, *Charts* group] by clicking the *All Charts* tab.

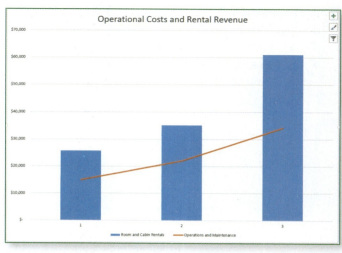

3-43 Line-Column combination chart

Combination Chart Elements and Options

A combination chart can have several data series, each shown in its own chart type. Keep this type of chart relatively simple, however, because its purpose is to compare unlike items.

A combination chart has most of the same elements as a regular column or line chart. You can apply chart styles and layouts, as well as shape fill, outline, effects, pictures, shapes, and *WordArt*, to a combination chart.

You can display or hide the secondary axis for a combination chart in the *Change Chart Type* dialog box. When you use a secondary axis, Excel builds the number scale based on the data. You can edit which data uses a line or a column from this dialog box as well (Figure 3-44).

3-44 *Change Chart Type* dialog box for a combo chart

HOW TO: Display a Secondary Axis on a Combination Chart

1. Select the chart object.
2. Click the **Change Chart Type** button [*Chart Tools Design* tab, *Type* group].
3. Choose the chart type for each series if desired.
4. Click to place or remove a check mark for a secondary axis.
5. Click **OK** (Figure 3-45).

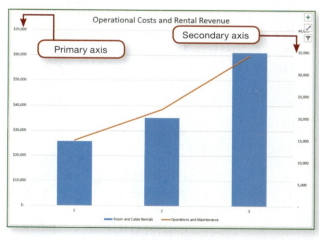

3-45 Secondary axis for a combo chart

SLO 3.7 — Inserting Sparklines in a Worksheet

Sparklines are miniature charts displayed in a cell or cell range next to your data. They can be used to illustrate trends and patterns without adding a separate chart object or sheet.

Sparklines are created from a selected data range like a chart. You can place them in a location range, usually next to the worksheet data (Figure 3-46).

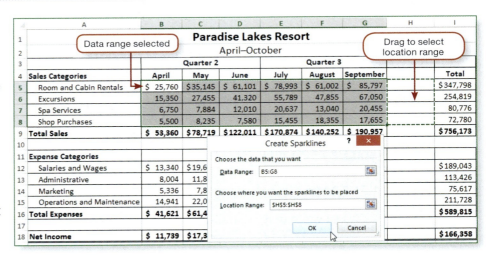

3-46 Column sparklines in a worksheet

There are three sparkline types: *Line*, *Column*, and *Win/Loss*. The *Sparklines* command is located on the *Insert* tab for the worksheet. After you insert sparklines, they act like other objects in a worksheet. The *Sparkline Tools Design* tab opens when you click the sparkline object.

To insert sparklines, you may need to insert a column at the appropriate location in your data, or, if it is empty, you may be able to use the right-most column. Depending on the type of sparkline, you may also want to increase the row height or column width to better present the sparklines.

Insert Sparklines

To insert sparklines in a worksheet, decide where you want to place them and insert a column if necessary. Select the data range that includes the values to be illustrated. This range cannot include the range where the sparklines display.

The *Sparklines* group is on the *Insert* tab and in the *Type* group on the *Sparkline Tools Design* tab.

HOW TO: Insert Column Sparklines in a Worksheet

1. Select the cell range to be used for sparklines.
   - When you select the data range first, it is displayed in the *Data Range* box within the *Create Sparklines* dialog box.
2. Click the **Column Sparkline** button [*Insert* tab, *Sparklines* group].
3. Click in the **Location Range** box.
4. Click and drag in the worksheet to select the cell range for the sparklines (Figure 3-47).
5. Click **OK**.

3-47 *Create Sparklines* dialog box

> **ANOTHER WAY**
>
> Click the **Column Sparkline** button [*Insert* tab, *Sparklines* group] and select the *Data Range* and *Location Range* from the dialog box to insert sparklines.

Sparkline Design Tools

When sparklines are selected in a worksheet, the *Sparkline Tools Design* tab opens. This context-sensitive tab includes several choices for changing the appearance of your sparklines. There is a *Shape Style* option that changes the color of the sparkline group. You can also change the color with the *Sparkline Color* command. The *Marker Color* command enables you to choose a different color for identified values in the sparklines. A **marker** for a sparkline is the data point value. You can highlight a specific value or the high, low, first, or last value as well as negative values.

Other choices on the *Sparkline Tools Design* tab are in the *Type* and *Show* groups. For example, you can change a column sparkline to a line sparkline. The *Show* commands set the color of the identified values in the data range.

HOW TO: Format Sparklines

1. Click the sparkline group in the worksheet.

2. Click the *Sparkline Line Tools Design* tab if necessary.

3. Click the **High Point** check box in the *Show* group (Figure 3-48).

   • A default color is applied to the highest value in the sparklines for each row.

4. Click the **Marker Color** button [*Sparkline Tools Design* tab, *Style* group].

5. Choose **High Point** and select a color from the gallery.

6. Click the **Sparkline Color** button [*Sparkline Tools Design* tab, *Style* group].

7. Choose a color for the sparkline group that is different from the color you chose for the *High Point*.

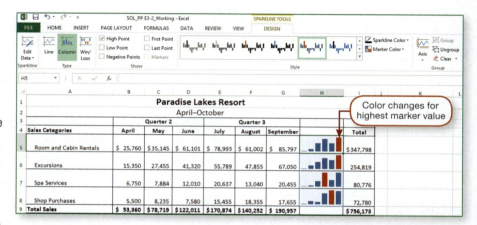

3-48 *High Point* marker selected for sparklines

Sparklines are inserted as a group in the location range. When you click any cell in the range with sparklines, the group is selected. Sparklines can be ungrouped if you need to make format choices for one sparkline cell or if you want to delete one sparkline in a range. The *Ungroup* command is in the *Group* group on the *Sparkline Tools Design* tab.

Clear Sparklines

You can remove sparklines from a worksheet with the *Clear* command in the *Group* group on the *Sparkline Tools Design* tab. After sparklines are cleared from a worksheet, you may need to delete the column where they were located or reset row heights and column widths.

HOW TO: Clear Sparklines

1. Select any cell in the sparklines range.

2. Click the **Clear Selected Sparklines** button [*Sparkline Tools Design* tab, *Group* group].

3. Choose **Clear Selected Sparklines Group**.

For this project, you continue to build Paradise Lakes' sales report by inserting a pie chart that shows the proportion of each sales category in the organization's total sales. You also insert a combination chart sheet to compare rentals and maintenance expense. Finally, you insert sparklines in the worksheet.

File Needed: *[your initials] PP E3-2.xlsx*
Completed Project File Name: *[your initials] PP E3-3.xlsx*

1. Open the *[your initials] PP E3-2* workbook.

2. Save the workbook as *[your initials] PP E3-3*.

3. Create a pie chart for total sales revenue.
   a. Select the **Location 1– Cass Lake** tab.
   b. Select cells **A5:A8** as the category.
   c. Hold down **Ctrl** and select cells **H5:H8** as the data series.
   d. Click the **Insert Pie or Doughnut Chart** button [*Insert* tab, *Charts* group].
   e. Choose **3-D Pie** (Figure 3-49).
   f. Click the **Move Chart** button [*Chart Tools Design* tab, *Location* group].
   g. Click the **New sheet** button and type Pie Chart as the sheet name.
   h. Click **OK**.

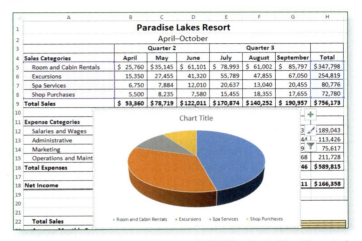

3-49 Pie chart object inserted

4. Format a pie chart.
   a. Select the **Pie Chart** tab.
   b. Click the **Chart Title** placeholder to select it and then triple-click the **Chart Title** placeholder text.
   c. Type Second and Third Quarters and press **Enter**.
   d. Type Sources of Revenue on the second line.
   e. Drag to select the first line of the title.
   f. From the mini toolbar, change the font size to **24 pt**.
   g. Drag to select the second line of the title.
   h. From the mini toolbar, change the font size to **18 pt**. (Figure 3-50).
   i. Click the chart area to deselect the title.
   j. Double-click the pie to open the *Format Data Series* task pane.

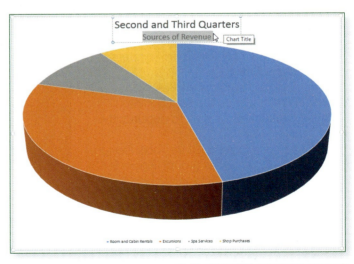

3-50 Chart titles typed and sized

   k. Click the **Series Options** button in the *Format Data Series* task pane.
   l. Click the **Room and Cabin Rentals** slice to change to the *Format Data Point* task pane.

m. Set the pie explosion percentage at **10%**.

n. Close the task pane.

o. Select the legend at the bottom of the chart to display selection handles.

p. Click the *Home* tab and change the font size to **12 pt**.

q. Point at the legend border (its edge) to display a move pointer.

r. Drag the legend object slightly closer to the chart (Figure 3-51).

s. Click the chart area to deselect the legend.

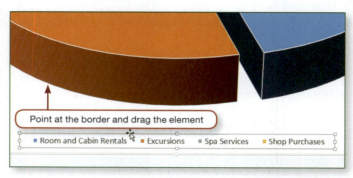

5. Create a combination chart for total sales revenue and room and cabin rentals.

   a. Select the **Location 1– Cass Lake** tab.

   b. Select cells **A4:G5** as one data series and category.

   c. Hold down **Ctrl** and select cells **A9:G9** as another data series and category.

   d. Click the **Insert Combo Chart** button [*Insert* tab, *Charts* group] (Figure 3-52).

   e. Choose **Clustered Column – Line on Secondary Axis**.

   f. Click the **Move Chart** button [*Chart Tools Design* tab, *Location* group].

   g. Click the **New sheet** button and type Combo Chart as the sheet name.

   h. Click **OK**.

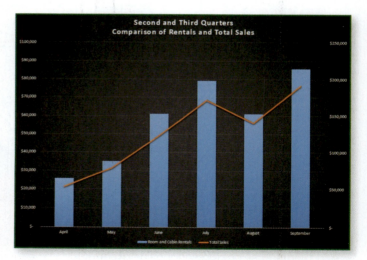

3-52 *Insert Combo Chart* button

6. Format a combination chart.

   a. Select the **Combo Chart** tab.

   b. Click to select the **Chart Title** placeholder and then triple-click the **Chart Title** placeholder text.

   c. Type Second and Third Quarters and press **Enter**.

   d. Type Comparison of Rentals and Total Sales on the second line.

   e. Click the chart area to deselect the chart title.

   f. Choose **Style 6** [*Chart Tools Design* tab, *Chart Styles* group] (Figure 3-53).

3-53 Combo chart with Style 6

7. Insert sparklines in a worksheet.

   a. Select the **Location 1– Cass Lake** tab.

   b. Right-click the column **H** heading and choose **Insert** to insert a new column.

   c. Select the cell range **B5:G8** as the data to be charted with sparklines.

   d. Click the **Column Sparkline** button [*Insert* tab, *Sparklines* group].

   e. Click in the **Location Range** box.

   f. Click and drag to select cells **H5:H8**.

   g. Click **OK**.

8. Format sparklines.
   a. Click any cell in the sparkline group.
   b. Click the **Sparkline Color** button [*Sparkline Tools Design* tab, *Style* group] and select **Green, Accent 6, Darker 25%**.
   c. While the sparkline group is selected, click the **Format** button [*Home* tab, *Cells* group] and change the **Row Height** to **30 (40 pixels)**.
   d. Set column **H** to a width of **16.00 (117 pixels)**.
   e. Click **OK**.

9. Save and close the workbook (Figure 3-54).

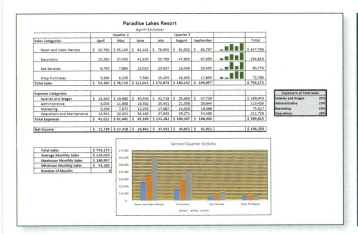

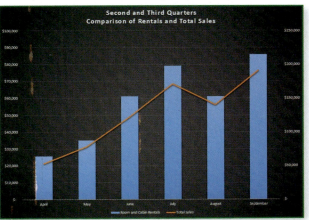

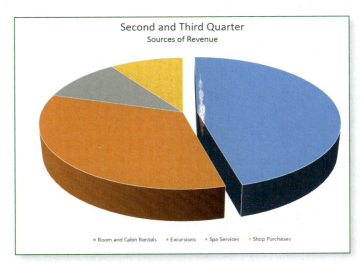

3-54 PP E3-3 completed worksheet and chart sheets

Chapter Summary

3.1 Create, size, and position an Excel chart object and create a chart sheet (p. E3-134).

- A **chart object** is a selectable object surrounded by a square border that contains many customizable chart elements like data labels or a chart title.
- Commonly used chart types are **Column**, **Line**, **Pie**, and **Bar**, but Excel can also create sophisticated statistical, financial, and scientific charts.
- The cells used to build a chart are its **source data**.
- You can size and position the chart object in a worksheet.
- A **chart sheet** is an Excel chart that is displayed on its own sheet tab in the workbook but is still linked to the source data.
- You can move a chart object to its own sheet by clicking the **Move Chart** button in the *Location* group on the *Chart Tools Design* tab.
- You can name a chart sheet tab to indicate the purpose or type of its chart.

3.2 Design a chart using *Quick Layouts* and chart styles (p. E3-137).

- A **chart layout** is a preset group of elements in a chart.
- You can apply a *Quick Layout* from the **Quick Layout** button [*Chart Tools Design* tab, *Chart Layouts* group].
- A **Chart Style** is a predefined combination of colors and effects for chart elements.
- Chart styles are based on the workbook theme.
- Apply a chart style by selecting a style from the gallery in the *Chart Styles* group on the *Chart Tools Design* tab.
- You can print a chart object with its worksheet data using the *Backstage* view.
- Print options for charts are the same as for a worksheet.
- A chart sheet prints on its own sheet in landscape orientation.

3.3 Switch row and column data, add or remove chart elements, change the chart type, and edit source data (p. E3-141).

- Excel plots source data based on the number of rows and columns selected; this determines what is shown on the horizontal or vertical axis.

- You can switch the row and column data when appropriate.
- A **chart element** is a selectable component that is part of the chart.
- Chart elements include chart and axes titles, data labels, legends, gridlines, and trendlines.
- You can change some chart types into another type. Use the **Change Chart Type** button on the *Chart Tools Design* tab.
- You can filter chart data to show or hide values or categories without changing the source data.
- Source data for a chart can be edited to add or delete a data series.

3.4 Format chart elements with shape styles, fill, outlines, and special effects (p. E3-148).

- Select a chart element with the pointer to format it or use the **Current Selection** group on the *Chart Tools Format* tab.
- A **Shape Style** is a predesigned combination of fill, borders, and effects.
- You can apply **Shape Fill**, **Shape Outline**, and **Shape Effects** separately from the *Chart Tools Format* tab.
- A chart element has its own *Format* task pane that includes fill, outline, and effects commands as well as specific options for the element.

3.5 Use images, shapes, and *WordArt* in a chart (p. E3-152).

- You can use a picture as fill for a shape.
- Select appropriately sized and designed images from your own or online sources.
- Insert shapes into a chart from the *Insert Shapes* group on the *Chart Tools Format* tab.
- You can apply **WordArt** to a chart title for special effect.
- Use the *Text Box* or *WordArt* buttons in the *Text* group on the *Insert* tab to add extra labels.

3.6 Create a pie chart and a combination chart (p. E3-157).

- A **pie chart** has one data series; it shows each data point as a part of the whole.
- Pie charts have many of the same elements as other charts, but they do not have axes.

- A **combination chart** uses two chart types to highlight differences in data or values.
- You can format a combination chart to show a secondary axis on the right side of the chart when values are widely different.

3.7 Insert and format sparklines in a worksheet (p. E3-161).

- A **sparkline** is a miniature chart in a cell or range of cells in the worksheet.
- Three sparkline types are available: **Line, Column**, and **Win/Loss**.

- Add sparklines to a worksheet from the *Sparklines* group on the *Insert* tab.
- Sparklines are grouped and can be formatted from the *Sparkline Tools Design* tab.
- Formatting options for sparklines include changing the color and identifying markers such as high and low values.
- Delete sparklines from a worksheet with the **Clear Selected Sparklines** button on the *Sparkline Tools Design* tab.

Check for Understanding

On the **Online Learning Center** for this text (www.mhhe.com/office2013inpractice), there are a variety of resources that can be used to review the concepts covered in this chapter.

The following Online Learning Resources are available on the Online Learning Center:

- Multiple choice questions
- Short answer questions
- Matching exercises

Guided Project 3-1

Life's Animal Shelter (LAS) is an animal care and adoption agency that accepts all unwanted or stray domestic animals. For this project, you create several expense charts and insert sparklines to help the agency track its expenses for the first six months of the year.
[Student Learning Outcomes 3.1, 3.2, 3.3, 3.4, 3.5, 3.6, 3.7]

File Needed: ***LASExpenses-03**.xlsx*
Completed Project File Name: ***[your initials] Excel 3-1**.xlsx*

Skills Covered in This Project

- Create a chart object.
- Create a chart sheet.
- Apply *Quick Layouts* and chart styles.
- Add and format chart elements.
- Change chart type.

- Filter the data series.
- Insert a shape in a chart.
- Create and format a combination chart.
- Insert and format sparklines in a sheet.

1. Open the ***LASExpenses-03*** workbook from your student data files folder.

2. Save the workbook as ***[your initials] Excel 3-1***.

3. Create a pie chart object.
   a. Select cells **A4:A10**. Hold down **Ctrl** and select cells **I4:I10**.
   b. Click the **Insert Pie or Doughnut Chart** button [*Insert* tab, *Charts* group].
   c. Select the **2D-Pie** chart subtype.

4. Apply a chart style.
   a. Select the chart object.
   b. Click the **More** button [*Chart Tools Design* tab, *Chart Styles* group] and select **Style 12**.

5. Edit and format chart elements.
   a. Click the chart title.
   b. Place the insertion point in front of "Totals" in the title.
   c. Type Year-to-Date Expense and press the **spacebar** once.
   d. Click the chart area to deselect the title.
   e. Select the legend element.
   f. Click the **Font Size** arrow [*Home* tab, *Font* group] and change the size to **12 pt**. (Figure 3-55).
   g. Select the chart area.

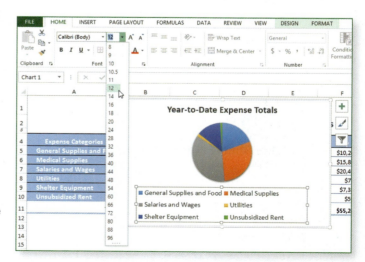

3-55 Legend selected for font size change

h. Click the **Shape Outline** button drop-down arrow [*Chart Tools Format* tab, *Shape Styles* group].
i. Choose **Black, Text 1** as the color.
j. Click the **Shape Outline** drop-down arrow again.
k. Choose **Weight** and **1 pt**.

6. Create a chart sheet.
   a. Click the pie chart object to select it.
   b. Click the **Move Chart** button [*Chart Tools Design* tab, *Location* group].
   c. Click the **New sheet** button.
   d. Type Pie Chart in the text box.
   e. Click **OK**.

7. Create a bar chart object.
   a. Click the **Half-Year Expenses** sheet tab.
   b. Select cells **A4:G10** as the source data range.
   c. Click the **Quick Analysis** button and select **Charts**.
   d. Select **Clustered Bar**.
   e. Point at the chart area to display a move pointer.
   f. Drag the chart object so its top left corner is at cell **B13**.
   g. Point at the bottom right selection handle to display a resize pointer.
   h. Drag the pointer to reach cell **G30** (Figure 3-56).

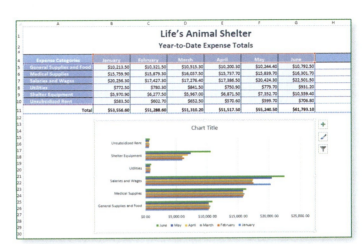

3-56 Bar chart object sized and positioned

8. Change the chart type.
   a. Click the chart object.
   b. Click the **Change Chart Type** button [*Chart Tools Design* tab, *Type* group].
   c. Click the **Recommended Charts** tab.
   d. Choose **Clustered Column** in the left pane.
   e. Click **OK**.

9. Filter the source data.
   a. Click the chart object.
   b. Click the **Chart Filters** button at the top right corner of the chart.
   c. Click to remove the check marks for **January**, **February**, and **March**.
   d. Click **Apply** in the *Chart Filters* pane (Figure 3-57).
   e. Click the **Chart Filters** button to close the pane.

10. Edit and format chart elements.
    a. Click the chart title placeholder.
    b. Point at the text and triple-click or drag to select all the text.
    c. Type Second Quarter Expenses.
    d. Click the chart area to deselect the title.

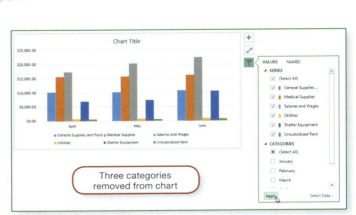

Three categories removed from chart

3-57 Chart filter applied

e. Click to select the legend element.
   f. Click the **Font Size** arrow [*Home* tab, *Font* group] and change the size to **8 pt**.
   g. Click to select the chart area.
   h. Click the **Shape Outline** button drop-down arrow [*Chart Tools Format* tab, *Shape Styles* group].
   i. Choose **Black, Text 1** as the color.
   j. Click the **Shape Outline** drop-down arrow again.
   k. Choose **Weight** and **1 pt**.

11. Create a combination chart sheet.
   a. Select cells **A8:G8**. Hold down **Ctrl** and select cells **A11:G11**.
   b. Click the **Insert Combo Chart** button [*Insert* tab, *Charts* group].
   c. Select the **Clustered Column-Line** chart subtype.
   d. Click the combo chart object to select it.
   e. Click the **Move Chart** button [*Chart Tools Design* tab, *Location* group].
   f. Click the **New sheet** button.
   g. Type Combo Chart.
   h. Click **OK**.
   i. Click the **Change Chart Type** button [*Chart Tools Design* tab, *Type* group].
   j. Click the **Secondary Axis** check box for the line chart (Figure 3-58).
   k. Click **OK**.

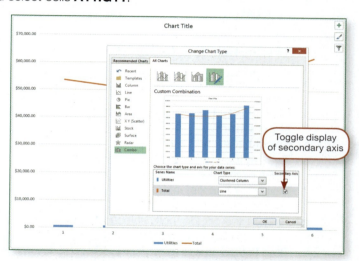

3-58 Combo chart and a secondary axis

12. Edit and format chart elements.
   a. Click the chart title placeholder.
   b. Point at the text and triple-click or drag to select all the text.
   c. Type Utilities Expense and Total Expenses.
   d. Click the chart area to deselect the title.
   e. Apply a **1 pt**. **black** outline to the chart area.

13. Insert sparklines in worksheet.
   a. Click the **Half-Year Expenses** sheet tab.
   b. Select cells **B5:G10** as the data range.
   c. Click the **Column Sparkline** button [*Insert* tab, *Sparklines* group].
   d. Click in the **Location Range** box.
   e. Click and drag to select cells **H5:H10**.
   f. Click **OK**.
   g. Click the **Format** button [*Home* tab, *Cells* group] and set the **Row Height** to **35**.
   h. Click the **Sparkline Color** button [*Sparkline Tools Design* tab, *Style* group] and select **White, Background 1, Darker 50%**.

14. Insert a shape in a chart.
   a. Click the **More** button [*Chart Tools Format* tab, *Insert Shapes* group].
   b. Select the text box shape.
   c. Draw a text box like the one shown in Figure 3-59.

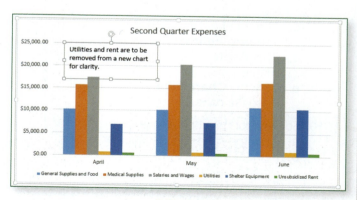

3-59 Text box shape inserted in chart

d. Type Utilities and rent are to be removed from a new chart for clarity.

e. Drag a selection handle to size the text box shape if necessary.

f. Point at an edge of the shape to display a four-pointed arrow and position it if needed.

15. Save and close the workbook (Figure 3-60).

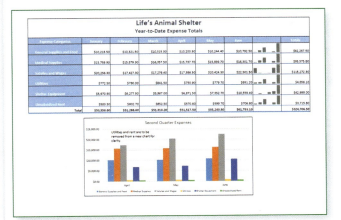

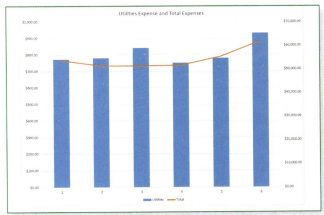

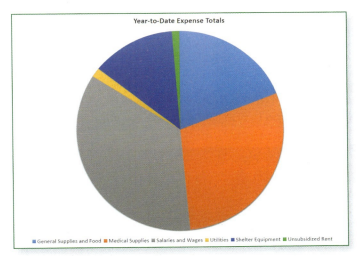

3-60 Excel 3-1 completed charts and worksheet

Guided Project 3-2

Wear-Ever Shoes is an shoe outlet with several locations. In a worksheet that tracks sales of popular items for the past six months, you create a bar chart to compare the number of pairs sold by style. You also create a combination chart to compare the number of pairs sold and the unit cost for each style.
[Student Learning Outcomes 3.1, 3.2, 3.3, 3.4, 3.5, 3.6]

File Needed: ***WearEverSales-03.xlsx***
Completed Project File Name: *[your initials] Excel 3-2.xlsx*

Skills Covered in This Project

- Create a chart sheet.
- Change the chart type.
- Apply a chart style.
- Add and format chart elements.

- Use a picture as fill.
- Create and format a combination chart.
- Use *WordArt* in a chart.

1. Open the ***WearEverSales-03*** workbook from your student data files folder.

2. Save the workbook as *[your initials] Excel 3-2*.

3. Create a column chart sheet.
   a. Select cells **A5:B16**.
   b. Click the **Quick Analysis** button and choose **Charts**.
   c. Select **Clustered Column**.
   d. Click the chart object to select it.
   e. Click the **Move Chart** button [*Chart Tools Design* tab, *Location* group].
   f. Click the **New sheet** button.
   g. Type Sales Chart.
   h. Click **OK**.

4. Change the chart type.
   a. Click the **Sales Chart** sheet tab if necessary.
   b. Click the **Change Chart Type** button [*Chart Tools Design* tab, *Type* group].
   c. Click the **Recommended Charts** tab.
   d. Choose **Clustered Bar** in the left pane.
   e. Click **OK**.

5. Apply a chart style.
   a. Select the chart sheet if necessary.
   b. Click the **Chart Styles** button in the top right corner of the chart.
   c. Select **Style 7** (Figure 3-61).
   d. Click the **Chart Styles** button to close the pane.

6. Use a picture as fill for a data point.
   a. Select the chart sheet if necessary.

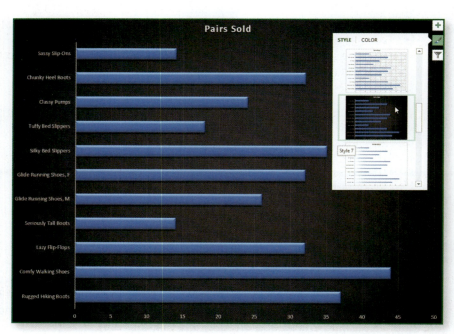

3-61 *Chart Styles* button and pane

b. Double-click any one of the bars to select the data series and open the *Format Data Series* task pane.

c. Point and click at the "Classy Pumps" bar to select it and display the *Format Data Point* task pane.

d. Click the **Fill & Line** button in the task pane.

e. Click **Fill** to expand the command group.

f. Click the **Picture or texture fill** button.

g. Click **Online** to open the *Insert Pictures* dialog box.

h. Type heels in the *Office.com Clip Art* search box and press **Enter** (Figure 3-62).

i. Select the image and click **Insert**.

j. Click **Stack** in the task pane.

k. Close the task pane and click the chart area.

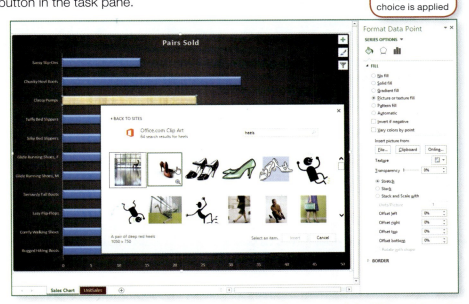

3-62 Online image search for fill in a data point

7. Create a combination chart sheet.
   a. Click the **Unit Sales** sheet tab.
   b. Select cells **A5:A16**. Hold down **Ctrl** and select cells **E5:F16**.
   c. Click the **Insert Combo Chart** button [*Insert* tab, *Charts* group].
   d. Select the **Clustered Column-Line on Secondary Axis** chart subtype.
   e. Select the combo chart object.
   f. Click the **Move Chart** button [*Chart Tools Design* tab, *Location* group].
   g. Click the **New sheet** button.
   h. Type Cost vs. Selling Price.
   i. Click **OK**.

8. Edit chart elements.
   a. Click the chart title placeholder.
   b. Select all the text in the placeholder.
   c. Type Cost and Selling Price Comparison.
   d. Select all the text in the chart title again.
   e. From the mini toolbar, change the font size to **20 pt**.
   f. Select the chart area.
   g. Apply a **1 pt**. **black** outline.

9. Use *WordArt* in a chart.
   a. Click the chart title.
   b. Click the **More** button [*Chart Tools Format* tab, *WordArt Style* group].
   c. Choose **Fill–Blue**, **Accent 1**, **Shadow**.
   d. Click the chart area to deselect the title.

10. Save and close the workbook (Figure 3-63).

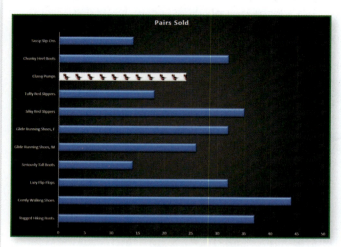

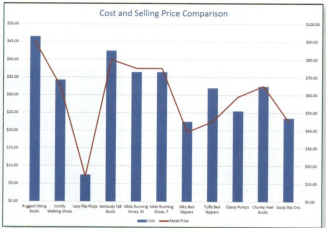

3-63 Excel 3-2 completed chart sheets

Guided Project 3-3

Blue Lake Sports has locations in several major cities and tracks sales by department in each store. For this project, you create a pie chart that shows each store's share of golf-related sales for the first quarter. You also create a line chart to illustrate week-to-week sales for specific departments in one of the stores and insert sparklines in the data.
[Student Learning Outcomes 3.1, 3.2, 3.3, 3.4, 3.6, 3.7]

File Needed: **BlueLakeSports-03**.xlsx
Completed Project File Name: **[your initials] Excel 3-3**.xlsx

Skills Covered in This Project

- Create, size, and position a pie chart object.
- Apply a chart style.
- Change chart type.
- Add and format chart elements in a pie chart.
- Create a line chart sheet.
- Apply a chart layout.
- Add and format chart elements in a line chart.
- Insert and format sparklines in a sheet.

1. Open the **BlueLakeSports-03** workbook from your student data files folder.

2. Save the workbook as **[your initials] Excel 3-3**.

3. Select the **Revenue by Department** tab.

4. Create a pie chart object.
    a. Select cells **A4:F4**, hold down **Ctrl**, and select cells **A13:F13**.
    b. Click the **Recommended Charts** button [*Insert* tab, *Charts* group].
    c. Choose **Pie** and click **OK**.

5. Apply a chart style.
    a. Select the chart object.
    b. Click the **More** button [*Chart Tools Design* tab, *Chart Styles* group].
    c. Select **Style 12**.

6. Size and position a chart object.
    a. Point at the chart area to display the move pointer.
    b. Drag the chart object so its top left corner is at cell **A21**.
    c. Point at the bottom right selection handle to display the resize pointer.
    d. Drag the pointer to cell **G36**.

7. Change the chart type.
    a. Click the pie chart object.
    b. Click the **Change Chart Type** button [*Chart Tools Design* tab, *Type* group].
    c. Click the **All Charts** tab.
    d. Choose **Pie** in the left pane.
    e. Choose **3-D Pie** and click **OK**.

8. Format pie chart elements.
    a. Double-click the pie to open the *Format Data Series* task pane.
    b. Click the **Atlanta** slice to update the pane to the *Format Data Point* task pane.
    c. Click the **Series Options** button in the *Format Data Series* task pane.
    d. Set the pie explosion percentage at **10%**.
    e. Close the task pane and click the chart area to deselect the **Atlanta** slice.

9. Add and format chart elements in a pie chart.
    a. Select the chart object if necessary.
    b. Click the **Chart Elements** button at the top right corner of the chart.
    c. Click the **Data Labels** check box (Figure 3-64).
    d. Display the submenu for **Data Labels** and choose **More Options**.
    e. In the *Format Data Point* task pane, click the **Label Options** button if necessary.

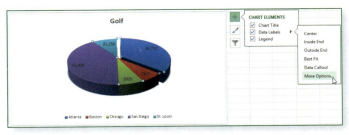

3-64 Data labels added to chart

    f. Click **Label Options** to expand the menu and click **Percentage** check box to show the percentage for each slice.
    g. Click to clear the **Value** check box and close the task pane.
    h. While the data labels are selected, press **Ctrl+B** to apply bold to the labels.
    i. While the data labels are selected, change the font size to **12 pt**. [*Home* tab, *Font* group].
    j. Click a worksheet cell to deselect the data labels and click the chart object to select it.
    k. Click the **Shape Outline** button drop-down arrow [*Chart Tools Format* tab, *Shape Styles* group] and choose **Purple, Accent 4, Darker 50%** as the color.
    l. Click the **Shape Outline** drop-down arrow again and choose **Weight** and **1 pt**.

10. Create a line chart sheet.
    a. Select the **Atlanta Revenue by Week** tab.
    b. Select cells **A4:E7**.

c. Click the **Quick Analysis** button and choose **Charts**.

d. Select **Line**.

e. Click the **Move Chart** button [*Chart Tools Design* tab, *Location* group].

f. Click the **New sheet** button.

g. Type Promo Depts.

h. Click **OK**.

11. Apply a chart layout.
    a. Select the chart sheet if necessary.
    b. Click the **Quick Layout** button [*Chart Tools Design* tab, *Chart Layouts* group].
    c. Select **Layout 5** to add a data table to the chart sheet (Figure 3-65).

12. Change the chart type.
    a. Right-click the **Promo Depts** chart and select **Change Chart Type**.
    b. On the **All Charts** tab, choose **Line with Markers** in the **Line** category.
    c. Click **OK**.

13. Edit chart elements in a line chart.
    a. Click the chart title placeholder.
    b. Type Sales for Promotion Departments and press **Enter**.
    c. Click the vertical axis title placeholder.
    d. Type Dollar Sales and press **Enter**.
    e. Click the **Chart Elements** drop-down arrow [*Chart Tools Format* tab, *Current Selection* group].
    f. Choose **Series "Apparel"** to select the line in the chart.
    g. Click the **Format Selection** button [*Chart Tools Format* tab, *Current Selection* group].
    h. Click the **Fill & Line** button in the *Format Data Series* task pane.
    i. Click **Marker** and then click **Marker Options** to expand the group (Figure 3-66).
    j. Click **Built-in** and set a size of **10 pt**.
    k. Click the **Series Options** triangle and choose **Series "Baseball"** to select that data series (Figure 3-67).
    l. Make the same marker changes for the baseball series.
    m. Select the basketball series and make the same marker changes.
    n. Close the task pane and select the chart area.

14. Insert sparklines in worksheet.
    a. Click the **Atlanta Revenue by Week** sheet tab.
    b. Right-click the **column F** heading and choose **Insert** to insert a new column.
    c. Select cells **B5:E18** as the data range.

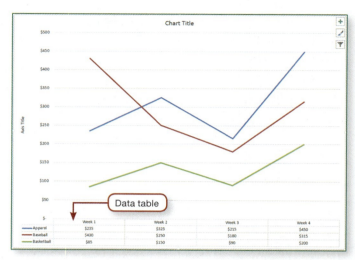

3-65 Data table added by chart layout

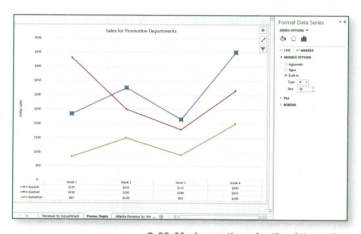

3-66 Marker options for the data series

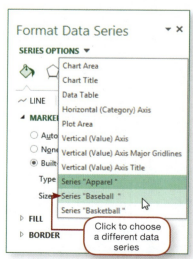

3-67 New data series selected

d. Click the **Line Sparkline** button [*Insert* tab, *Sparklines* group].

e. Click in the **Location Range** box.

f. Click and drag to select cells **F5:F18**.

g. Click **OK**.

15. Format sparklines in worksheet.

a. Click the **Format** button [*Home* tab, *Cells* group] and set the **Row Height** to **24**.

b. Click the **Format** button [*Home* tab, *Cells* group] and set the **Column Width** to **35**.

c. Click to place a check mark for **Markers** in the *Show* group in the *Sparkline Tools Design* tab.

d. Click the **Sparkline Color** button [*Sparkline Tools Design* tab, *Style* group].

e. Choose **Black, Text 1** for the line color.

16. Change the page orientation to landscape.

17. Save and close the workbook (Figure 3-68).

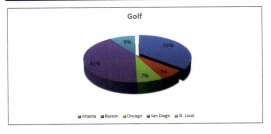

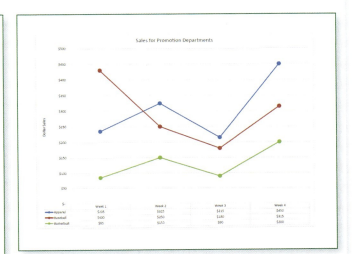

Independent Project 3-4

For this project, you create a column chart to illustrate April–September revenue for Classic Gardens and Landscapes. You also create a pie chart sheet to graph the proportion that each category contributes to total revenue.
[Student Learning Outcomes 3.1, 3.2, 3.3, 3.4, 3.5, 3.6]

File Needed: *ClassicGardensRevenue-03.xlsx*
Completed Project File Name: *[your initials] Excel 3-4.xlsx*

Skills Covered in This Project

- Create a chart object.
- Size and position a chart object.
- Edit and format chart elements.
- Edit the source data for a chart.

- Use the *SUM* function in a worksheet.
- Create a pie chart sheet.
- Use texture as fill.
- Add and format data labels in a chart.

1. Open the **ClassicGardensRevenue-03** workbook from your student data files folder.

2. Save the workbook as *[your initials] Excel 3-4*.

3. Create a *Clustered Column* chart object for cells **A4:G9**.

4. Move the chart object so that its top left corner is at cell **A12**. Size the bottom of the chart to reach cell **H30**.

5. Edit the chart title to display CGL Major Sales Revenue on one line and Second and Third Quarters on the second line.

6. Set the first line of the chart title to a font size of **20 pt**. Set the second title line to a size of **14 pt**.

7. Apply chart **Style 14** to the chart.

8. Apply a **½ point Black**, **Text 1** outline to the chart.

9. Remove the *Design Consulting* data series from the chart using the resizing pointer.

10. Enter *SUM* functions for the total column **H5:H9** and total row **B10:H10**.

11. Create a **3-D Pie** chart sheet named Revenue Breakdown for cells **A4:A9** and **H4:H9**.

12. Edit the chart title to display Revenue by Category. Set the font size to **32**.

13. Apply the **Oak** texture fill to the *Tree and Shrubbery* slice.

14. Add a data label in the center of each slice.
    a. Choose the **Accounting** format and set **0** decimal places (Figure 3-69).
    b. While the data labels are selected, set the font size to **14 pt**. and make them **bold** [*Home* tab, *Font* group].

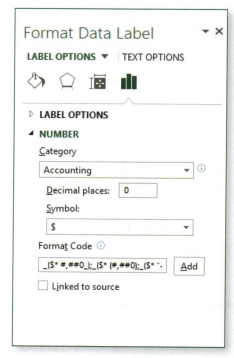

3-69 Data label options

15. Save and close the workbook (Figure 3-70).

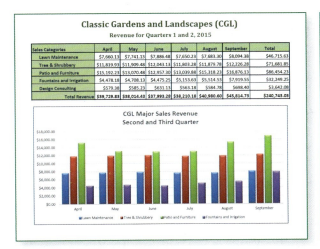
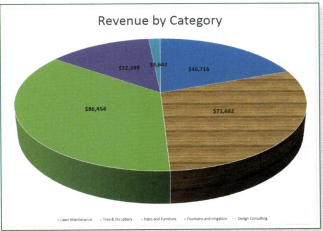

Independent Project 3-5

For this project, you create a stacked bar chart to illustrate projected tuition and fee amounts for Sierra Pacific Community College District (SPCCD). You also create a pie chart to show total projected revenue for the time period and add sparklines to the worksheet.
[Student Learning Outcomes 3.1, 3.2, 3.3, 3.4, 3.6, 3.7]

File Needed: *SierraPacificCC-03.xlsx*
Completed Project File Name: *[your initials] Excel 3-5.xlsx*

Skills Covered in This Project

- Create a chart object.
- Size and position a chart object.
- Apply a chart style.
- Switch row and column data.

- Edit chart source data.
- Create a pie chart sheet.
- Edit and format chart elements.
- Insert and format sparklines in a sheet.

1. Open the *SierraPacificCC-03* workbook from your student data files folder.

2. Save the workbook as *[your initials] Excel 3-5*.

3. Select cells **A3:E7** and create a stacked bar chart object.

4. Size and position the chart below the worksheet data in cells **A10:G28**.

5. Apply **Chart Style 6**.

6. Edit the chart title to display Tuition Revenue Projection.

7. Apply a dark blue ½ pt. outline to the chart object.

8. Switch the row and column data for the chart.

9. Edit the source data to remove the fees values from the chart.

10. Create a 3-D pie chart sheet for cells **A4:A7** and cells **G4:G7**. Move the chart to a new sheet named Total Revenue.

11. Apply **Chart Style 3** and a black ½ pt. outline.

12. Edit the chart title to Projected Revenue Sources.

13. Move the legend to the bottom and change its font size to **12 pt**.

14. Create column sparklines for cells **B4:E7** in the worksheet so that they appear in cells **F4:F7**.

15. Save and close the workbook (Figure 3-71).

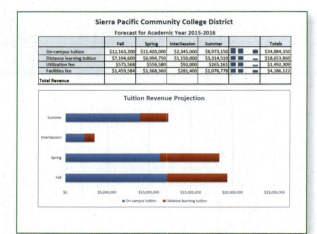
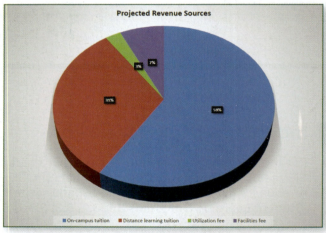

3-71 Excel 3-5 completed worksheet and chart

Independent Project 3-6

Courtyard Medical Plaza (CMP) is a full-service medical office complex providing customers with a variety of medical services in one location. For this project you create charts to illustrate data about the number of procedures performed at CMP as well as how patients come to the facility.
[Student Learning Outcomes 3.1, 3.2, 3.3, 3.4, 3.5]

File Needed: **CourtyardMedical-03.xlsx**
Completed Project File Name: **[your initials] Excel 3-6.xlsx**

Skills Covered in This Project

- *AutoFill* month names.
- Use the *SUM* function.
- Create a column chart sheet.
- Add and edit chart elements.

- Add and format a trendline in a chart.
- Insert a text box shape in a chart.
- Display gridlines in a chart.
- Use gradient fill for a chart object.

---

1. Open the **CourtyardMedical-03** workbook from your student data files folder.

2. Save the workbook as **[your initials] Excel 3-6**.

3. On the **Patient Count** worksheet, select cell **C5** and use the *Fill Handle* to complete the month names.

4. Complete the totals in **N6:N10** and **B10:M10** using the *SUM* function.
   a. Select all the values and apply **Comma Style** with no decimal places.
   b. *AutoFit* columns **B:N**.

5. Create a clustered column chart sheet named Immed Care for cells **A5:M5** and cells **A7:M7**.

6. Edit the chart title to display Immediate Care Patient Count.

7. Click the **Chart Elements** button and add a linear trendline to the chart.

8. Format the trendline.
   a. In the *Forecast* group, set the **Forward** value to **12**.
   b. Choose **Olive Green, Accent 3** for the line color.
   c. Set the **Width** of the trendline to **4 pt**.

9. Insert a text box in the chart. Draw a text box between the 300 and 400 gridlines and type The number of patients who come in for Immediate Care services will continue to grow. (Figure 3-72).

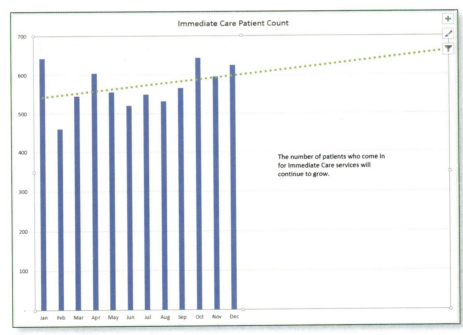

3-72 Text box shape in a chart

10. On the **Procedures Count** worksheet, select cells **A5:D16** and create a clustered column chart object. Move the chart to a new sheet named Procedures Chart.

11. Edit the chart title to display Number of Procedures on the first line and Three-Year Period on the second line.

12. Add **Primary Major Vertical** gridlines.

13. Format the plot area.
    a. Apply the fill **Tan**, **Background 2**, **Darker 10%**.
    b. Apply the **Gradient** shape fill. Choose **Linear Down**.

14. Save and close the workbook (Figure 3-73).

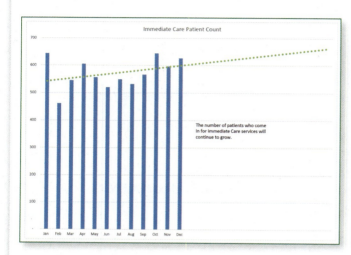
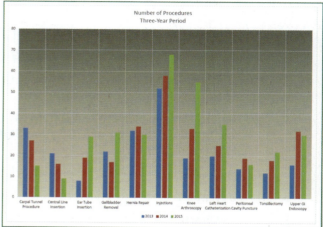

3-73 Excel 3-6 completed chart sheets

Improve It Project 3-7

Central Sierra Insurance (CSI) is a multi-office insurance company that handles commercial and personal insurance products. For this project, when you add missing data to a worksheet, the pie chart automatically updates, but the column chart incorrectly plots row and column data and does not update. To address this, you switch the row/column data and then edit the source data range.
[Student Learning Outcomes 3.2, 3.3, 3.4]

File Needed: **CentralSierraPolicies-03.xlsx**
Completed Project File Name: **[your initials] Excel 3-7.xlsx**

Skills Covered in This Project

- Insert a row within a chart source range.
- Switch row and column data.
- Apply a new color scheme to a chart and to a data series.
- Edit source data.

- Add and format elements in a 3-D chart.
- Use gradient fill for a chart object.
- Change chart type.
- Apply a chart style.
- Format chart elements.

---

1. Open the **CentralSierraPolicies-03** workbook from your student data files folder.

2. Save the workbook as **[your initials] Excel 3-7**.

3. Insert a new row at row 8.

4. In cell **A8,** type Motorcycle. In cells **B8:D8**, type these values: 15, 82, and 24.

5. Switch the row and column data for the column chart.

6. Edit the source data for the column chart to show cells **A5:D10**.

7. Change the chart color scheme to **Color 11** in the **Monochromatic** list.

8. Format chart elements.
   a. Apply the **Olive Green**, **Accent 3**, **Lighter 80%** shape fill to the **Side Wall** of the chart.
   b. Apply the **Linear Down** gradient for the shape fill.
   c. Apply the same fill and gradient to the **Walls** element.
   d. Apply the **Olive Green**, **Accent 3**, **Lighter 60%** with no gradient to the **Floor** element.

9. Change the pie chart to a **3-D Pie** and apply **Chart Style 3**.

10. Select the **Chart Area** of the pie chart and apply **Color 11** color scheme, **Olive Green**, **Accent 3**, **Lighter 80%** shape fill, and **Linear Down** gradient fill.

11. Apply a **½ pt**. **Olive Green**, **Accent 3**, **Darker 25%** outline to both chart objects.

12. Select the pie (**Series AJP**) and change the color to **Color 11** in the **Monochromatic** list.

13. Save and close the workbook (Figure 3-74).

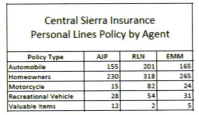

Policy Type	AJP	RLN	EMM
Automobile	155	201	165
Homeowners	230	318	265
Motorcycle	15	82	24
Recreational Vehicle	28	54	31
Valuable Items	12	2	5

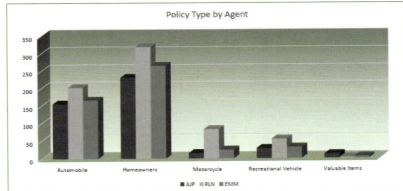

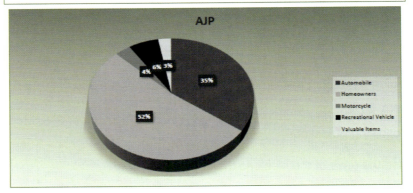

3-74 Excel 3-7 completed worksheet with charts

Challenge Project 3-8

For this project, you create a worksheet that outlines costs for trips to three of your favorite cities. From the data, you will create column or bar charts to compare the costs of the visits to each city.
[Student Learning Outcomes 3.1, 3.2, 3.3, 3.4, 3.5, 3.6]

File Needed: None
Completed Project File Name: *[your initials] Excel 3-8.xlsx*

Create a new workbook and save it as *[your initials] Excel 3-8*. Modify your workbook according to the following guidelines:

- As column headings, type the names of three cities that you would like to visit.
- As row headings, type five or six major expense categories for a trip. These might be labels such as "Air, Train, or Bus", "Hotel", "Entertainment", and similar expenses.
- Enter estimated costs for a five-day trip for each city using your own research about the city. Format your data as needed.
- Type a main and secondary title for your data.
- Create a column or bar chart sheet that compares the trips.
- Change the layout or apply a chart style.
- Use a picture as fill for one of the data series.
- Edit the chart title placeholder to display an appropriate title. Change the font size of the title to balance the chart.
- Format chart elements to create an attractive, easy-to-understand chart of your data.

Challenge Project 3-9

For this project, you create a worksheet and accompanying charts to track your daily usage of your smart phone.
[Student Learning Outcomes 3.1, 3.2, 3.3, 3.4, 3.5, 3.6]

File Needed: None
Completed Project File Name: *[your initials] Excel 3-9.xlsx*

Create a new workbook and save it as *[your initials] Excel 3-9*. Modify your workbook according to the following guidelines:

- Use the days of the week as the column headings.
- As row headings, type names of four or five tasks that you might do each day with your smart phone. You might use labels such as "Send text", "Receive phone call", "Use GPS", or similar tasks.
- Enter a value for the number of times you perform each task on each day.

- Type a main title for your data in row 1. Format your data.
- Create a column chart object that compares the number of times you did each task on Monday.
- Size and position the chart object below the worksheet data.
- Change the layout or apply a chart style.
- Edit the chart title placeholder to display an appropriate title.
- Format chart elements to create an attractive, easy-to-understand chart of your data.
- For the task with the greatest Monday value, create another column chart that displays the daily numbers for that one task.
- Size and position this chart object below the first chart.
- Format the second chart to complement the first chart.

Challenge Project 3-10

For this project, you create a worksheet and line chart that compares the temperature in your city or town at 12 noon for the past 10 days. You also insert a single sparkline in the data.
[Student Learning Outcomes 3.1, 3.2, 3.3, 3.4, 3.5, 3.6, 3.7]

File Needed: None
Completed Project File Name: *[your initials] Excel 3-10.xlsx*

Create a new workbook and save it as *[your initials] Excel 3-10*. Modify your workbook according to the following guidelines:

- In a worksheet, enter the dates for the last 10 days and enter a temperature in degrees for each date at 12 noon. Use a weather reference or your recollection of the day.
- Type a main title for your data (insert a row if necessary). Format your data.
- Create a line chart sheet that illustrates the daily temperature for 10 days.
- Change the layout or apply a chart style.
- Edit and format the chart elements as needed.
- In the worksheet, select the range of values and insert a line sparkline in the column to the right, in one cell, next to the first value.
- Format the sparkline and adjust the row height or column width to better display the sparkline.

CHAPTER 4

Importing, Creating Tables, Sorting and Filtering, and Using Conditional Formatting

CHAPTER OVERVIEW

Sharing data among software programs is essential in professional and personal work. Excel can both import data from several sources and export data in a number of formats. Because shared data is typically in the form of a list or table, Excel features a **Table** style with enhanced commands to help you manage list-type data. This chapter teaches you how to import data, create and format Excel tables, and protect your worksheets in an Excel workbook.

STUDENT LEARNING OUTCOMES (SLOs)

After completing this chapter, you will be able to:

SLO 4.1 Import data into Excel from a text file, database file, or a web site and use *Flash Fill* and data connections (p. E4-187).

SLO 4.2 Create and format an Excel table and a *PivotTable* and export data for use in other programs (p. E4-194).

SLO 4.3 Sort data by text, number, color, or icon (p. E4-205).

SLO 4.4 Apply an *AutoFilter* or an *Advanced Filter* to data (p. E4-209).

SLO 4.5 Use the *Subtotal* command and create groups and outlines (p. E4-212).

SLO 4.6 Apply and manage *Conditional Formatting* using cell rules, *Color Scales*, *Icon Sets*, and *Data Bars* (p. E4-218).

SLO 4.7 Use *Goal Seek* and protect a worksheet (p. E4-222).

CASE STUDY

For the Pause & Practice projects in this chapter, you create Excel workbooks for the northern Minnesota company, Paradise Lakes Resort (PLR), introduced in Chapters 1–3. In preparation for its annual department meetings, PLR is asking managers to import and sort data from external sources, format lists as tables and PivotTables, and subtotal data for analysis.

Pause & Practice 4-1: Import data for a workbook from text files and use *Flash Fill*.

Pause & Practice 4-2: Format an Excel list as a table, remove duplicate records, and create a *PivotTable*.

Pause & Practice 4-3: Sort and filter data in an Excel workbook and apply subtotals.

Pause & Practice 4-4: Use *Goal Seek*, apply conditional formatting, and protect a worksheet.

Importing Data

Data is available in many formats. A key Excel skill is knowing how to access and convert data for use in your Excel worksheets. *Importing* data refers to the task of obtaining data from another software program, another file format, or an Internet location. In many situations importing data saves time and increases accuracy. For example, at a retail business, you might import a supplier's catalog into a worksheet to help employees prepare routine orders. Or you might import calendar data from co-workers to build a daily schedule in a worksheet. Many companies buy customer or client lists and import the data from those lists into Excel to build prospect lists.

External data is data in a worksheet that originated in another program or format. You can import or copy external data into Excel from the *source*. The source can be a text file, a database, or a web location. If you import external data using the *Get External Data* group, you establish live connections that update the data in your worksheet if a change is made to the original data. If you simply copy data into a worksheet, you do not maintain a connection to the source. Data connections are discussed later in this section.

For most uses, it is best to import data in list format. List format features data organized in rows and columns with analogous information in the same column in each row.

Text Files

A *text file* is a document that includes basic data, no formatting, and commas or other characters to separate the data into columns and rows. Text files include *.txt* (text) documents such as those created in NotePad or WordPad. Another widely used format is *.csv* (comma separated values); you might see this type of file when you download a bank statement. Most software can save a *.prn* (printer) file, which is a simple text file that can be printed.

Text files separate data into columns, often called *fields*, in one of two ways. In one type of text file, a character, such as a comma or a tab, separates the fields. When a text file uses a special character, it is referred to as a *delimited* file (e.g., tab-delimited file). The *delimiter* in the file is the character used to separate the data.

The other text file type identifies fields or columns by a *fixed width.* Each field is a specified width, followed by a space. For example, if the first name field occupies 25 spaces and an individual's name is "Tom," it is imported as 3 characters followed by 22 empty spaces.

When you click the *From Text* button in the *Get External Data* group on the *Data* tab (Figure 4-1), the *Text Import Wizard* guides you through the data importing steps. The wizard usually is able to determine if the file you are working with is delimited or fixed width.

4-1 *Get External Data* group

> ### MORE INFO
> Many legacy or mainframe computer systems use fixed width files for data.

HOW TO: Import a Delimited Text File into a Worksheet

1. Select the cell where you want the imported data to start.
2. Click the **From Text** button [*Data* tab, *Get External Data* group].
3. Select the name of the text file in the *Import Text File* dialog box and click **Import** (Figure 4-2).
4. In the *Text Import Wizard – Step 1 of 3* window, click the **Delimited** radio button if necessary and click **Next** (Figure 4-3).

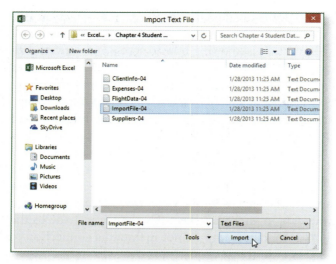

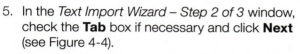

4-2 *Import Text File* dialog box

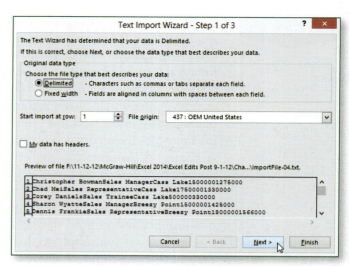

4-3 *Text Import Wizard – Step 1*

5. In the *Text Import Wizard – Step 2 of 3* window, check the **Tab** box if necessary and click **Next** (see Figure 4-4).

   - Look at the *Data preview* to determine if the correct delimiter is selected. You can try any of the listed delimiters or type a custom character.

6. Click **Finish** (Figure 4-5).

   - Select a column in the *Data preview* area and set its format in the *Column data format* group.
   - You can also format the data after it is imported.

7. Click **OK** in the *Import Data* dialog box (Figure 4-6).

   - Click **Properties** to open the *External Data Range Properties* dialog box. You can set options for imported data such as a *Refresh data* time or *Preserve cell formatting*. Click **OK** to close this dialog box.

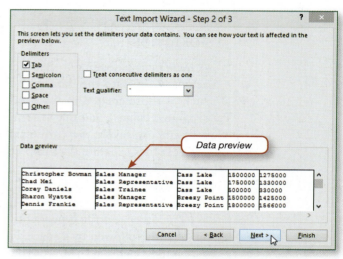

4-4 *Text Import Wizard – Step 2*

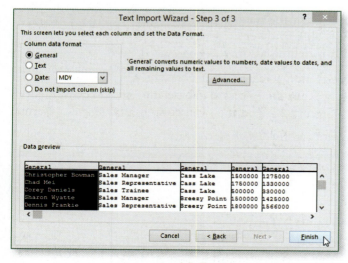

4-5 *Text Import Wizard – Step 3*

4-6 *Import Data* dialog box

E4-188

You cannot directly import text from a Word document into Excel. However, you can copy and paste data from Word into an Excel worksheet. When you paste the data in Excel, you can retain the formatting used in the Word document, or you can choose the current format in the worksheet.

HOW TO: Copy Data from a Word Document

1. Select the cell in the worksheet where you want the imported data to start.
2. Open the Word document and select the table or list you want to import to Excel.
3. Click the **Copy** button [*Home* tab, *Clipboard* group].
4. Switch to the Excel worksheet.
5. Click the **Paste** button [*Home* tab, *Clipboard* group] or press **Ctrl+V**.
   - To retain the formatting from the Word document, click the arrow with the **Paste** drop-down button to choose the option to *Match Destination Formatting*.

> **ANOTHER WAY**
> Save a Word document as a Text file (*.txt*) and import the text file into Excel.

> **MORE INFO**
> To split data in a single column into separate columns, insert as many blank columns to the right as needed for the split data. Select the column to be split and click the **Text to Columns** button [*Data* tab, *Data Tools* group]. Complete the *Convert Text to Columns Wizard* to split the column.

Access Database Files

A *database* is a collection of related tables, queries, forms, and reports. **Microsoft Access** is a relational database management system that is part of the Office suite of products. Most companies, service organizations, schools, and other enterprises keep great amounts of data in databases, so it is quite common to import data from a database for use in Excel. For example, Access cannot illustrate data in a chart. If there is chartable sales data in a database table, you can import the relevant data from Access into Excel and build the chart.

You can import a table or a query from an Access database into an Excel worksheet. To do this, you import the data as an Excel table and then you convert a table into a normal data range (this topic is covered later in this chapter).

Access database files have an *.accdb* extension. When a database includes many tables and queries, the *Select Table* dialog box opens so that you can choose the table or query you want to import.

> **MORE INFO**
> If a database has a single table or query, it is automatically imported into Excel; the *Select Table* dialog box does not open.

HOW TO: Import an Access Table into a Worksheet

1. Select the worksheet cell where you want the imported data to start.

   • Because all Access tables or queries have column or field headings, you do not need column headings in the worksheet.

2. Click the **From Access** button [*Data* tab, *Get External Data* group].

3. Select the database name in the *Select Data Source* dialog box.

4. Click **Open** (Figure 4-7).

5. Select the name of the table or query you want to import in the *Select Table* dialog box (Figure 4-8).

6. Click **OK**.

7. In the *Import Data* dialog box, select **Table** and **Existing worksheet**.

   • You can choose a new worksheet for the imported data. If you do this, the data is imported starting at cell A1.
   • Click **Properties** to change options such as refresh timing.

8. Click **OK**.

   • An Excel table displays *AutoFilter* buttons with each column heading for sorting and filtering (Figure 4-9). Filters are covered in *SLO 4.4: Filtering Data*.

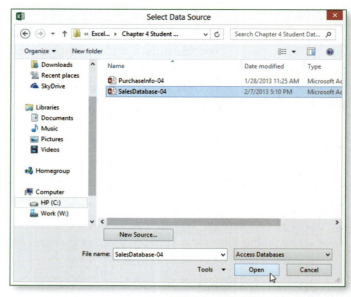

4-7 *Select Data Source* dialog box

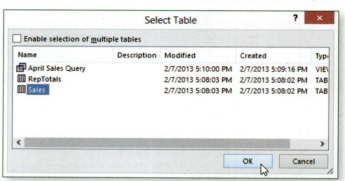

4-8 *Select Table* dialog box

> **MORE INFO**
>
> You can import tables and queries from relational databases such as SQL Server with the **From Other Sources** button [*Data* tab, *Get External Data* group].

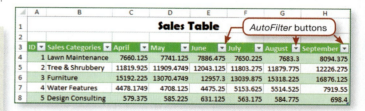

4-9 Imported Access table

Web Site Data

Many web sites include table-formatted data that you can import into a worksheet. For example, a company like Paradise Lakes Resort might import data from a web site about vacation spending so that company officers can project future rentals and purchases. Or they might import data from a weather site to build a chart about average temperatures and rainfall to plan marketing campaigns.

Web pages include a wealth of data, images, and sometimes even video. When you use the *From Web* command, data that you can import into Excel as a list or table is indicated on a web page with a small black arrow in a yellow box. This identifier enables you to easily locate which data you can import and format in columns and rows. When you click a yellow box with an arrow, the related table is selected, and the arrow changes to a green box with a check mark. The data is ready for importing.

> ▶ **MORE INFO**
> Most data that you import from another source needs to be formatted in Excel to match your other worksheet data.

Data that you import from a web page establishes a connection to the site that you can refresh whenever necessary.

HOW TO: Import Web Data into a Worksheet

1. Select the worksheet cell where you want the imported data to start.
   - Depending on how data is formatted on the web page, you may not need to insert column headings after importing.
2. Click the **From Web** button [*Data* tab, *Get External Data* group].
3. In the *New Web Query* dialog box, browse to locate the web site and data you want to import (Figure 4-10).
4. Click the **Click to select this table** arrow (yellow box with black arrow) next to the data you want to import.
   - Click the **Options** button to set options such as *Formatting* (Figure 4-11) and click **OK**.
5. Click the **Import** button in the *New Web Query* dialog box.
   - Click the **Properties** button to edit options such as *Refresh Control* or *Data Formatting and layout*. Click **OK** to save changes.
6. Click **OK** in the *Import Data* dialog box.
   - A message on screen may inform you that Excel is obtaining the data. When the import is complete, the data is displayed in the worksheet and looks similar to the example shown in Figure 4-12.

4-10 *New Web Query* window

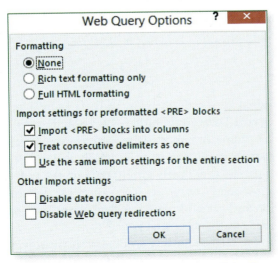

4-11 *Web Query Options* dialog box

4-12 **Data imported from a web site**

Flash Fill

Flash Fill is a new command in Excel 2013 that recognizes a pattern and duplicates it for matching cells. For example, imagine that in data that you import from a text file or a web site, individuals' first and last names are together in a single column. You want the first and last names to be in separate columns in your Excel document so in a new column in the first row, you type the first name of the first individual. When you enter the first name of the second person in the second row, *Flash Fill* completes the remaining cells in the column. The **Flash Fill Options** button appears after you press **Enter** so that you can undo the fill if necessary or accept all the suggestions.

HOW TO: Flash Fill Data in a Worksheet

1. Insert a new column to the right of the data you want to use in the *Flash Fill* column.

2. Click in the first cell in the new column for data.

3. Type the data you want to appear in the first cell in the column.

   • Figure 4-13 shows a pattern with the first and last name from the "Name" column with a period between names, followed by "@go.com."

4. Type data in the second cell following the same pattern.

   • If the *Flash Fill* suggestion list does not appear after the second item, type the third item.

5. Press **Enter** to complete the *Flash Fill*.

   • If the *Flash Fill* suggestion list does not appear, click the **Flash Fill** button [*Data* tab, *Data Tools* group] with the insertion point still in the column.

4-13 *Flash Fill* suggestion list

Data Connections

A **connection** is an identifier for data that originated outside the workbook. For any data that you import using a command in the *Get External Data* group on the *Data* tab, Excel establishes a connection that you can update, refresh, name, or remove. If you import the data from a text file or a database, you can refresh the data by importing it again. If you import the data as a web query, you can replace the data in your worksheet with current data on the web site.

A data connection to an Internet location is named *Connection*. You can access the properties for any connection and label it with a more recognizable name. A data connection to the file you import is named with the same file name as the imported file.

Depending upon your Excel options, you may see a security warning bar at the top of the worksheet when you open a workbook that has data connections. Click **Enable Editing** to work with the data.

HOW TO: Manage Data Connections

1. Click the **Connections** button [*Data* tab, *Connections* group] to open the *Workbook Connections* dialog box.

2. Select the name of the connection in the top pane (Figure 4-14).

3. Click **Refresh** to update the imported data.
   - The *Import Text File* dialog box opens if you have selected a connection for an imported text file.

4. Click the link **Click here to see where the selected connections are used** to identify where the data is located in the workbook.

5. Click **Properties** to open the *Connections Properties* dialog box.
   - You can set how the data is refreshed, change the connection name, or add a description.

6. Click **Close** to save changes.

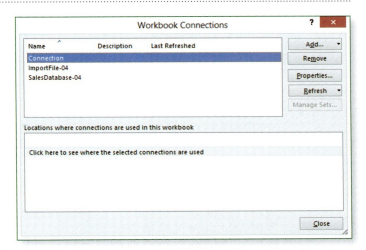

4-14 *Workbook Connections* dialog box

PAUSE & PRACTICE: EXCEL 4-1

For this project, you import data from a text file into an Excel worksheet, copy data from a Word document into the same worksheet, and use *Flash Fill* to build a worksheet for Paradise Lakes Resort.

Files Needed: ***Sales-04.xlsx***, ***ImportFile-04.txt***, and ***ImportWord-04.docx***
Completed Project File Name: ***[your initials] PP E4-1.xlsx***

1. Open the ***Sales-04*** workbook from the student data files folder. Click the **Enable Editing** button.

2. Save the workbook as ***[your initials] PP E4-1***.

3. Import data from a text file.
   a. Select cell **A3**.
   b. Click the **From Text** button [*Data* tab, *Get External Data* group].
   c. Select the ***ImportFile-04.txt*** file in the *Import Text File* dialog box.
   d. Click **Import**.
   e. Select the **Delimited** button in the *Text Import Wizard – Step 1 of 3* dialog box.
   f. Click **Next**.
   g. Place a check mark for **Tab** in the *Text Import Wizard – Step 2 of 3* dialog box.
   h. Click **Next**.
   i. Click **Finish** in the last dialog box.
   j. Click **OK** in the *Import Data* dialog box.

4. Copy data from a Word document.
   a. Select cell **A17**.
   b. Open Microsoft Word and open the ***ImportWord-04*** Word document. Click the **Enable Editing** button.
   c. Select all the data and click the **Copy** button [*Home* tab, *Clipboard* group].

d. Switch to the Excel window.
e. Click the arrow with the **Paste** button [*Home* tab, *Clipboard* group] and choose **Match Destination Formatting** (Figure 4-15).
f. Select cells **D3:E26** and apply the **Currency** number format with zero decimals.
g. Adjust the widths of columns **C:E** to 15.00.

5. Create an email address column using *Flash Fill*.
a. Insert a new column between columns **A** and **B**.
b. Type Email Address in cell **B2**.
c. Increase the width of the "Email Address" column to 37.00.
d. Type Christopher.Bowman@ somewhere.com in **B3** and press **Enter**.
e. Type Chad.Mei@somewhere.com in **B4** and press **Enter** to complete the *Flash Fill* (Figure 4-16).
f. If the *Flash Fill* suggestion list does not appear, click the **Flash Fill** button [*Data* tab, *Data Tools* group].

6. Save and close the workbook. Close the Word document.

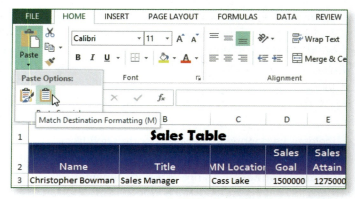

4-15 *Paste Options* for copied data

4-16 PP E4-1 completed worksheet

SLO 4.2

Creating Excel Tables

An Excel *table* is a list of related pieces of information that is formatted with a title row followed by rows of data. When your data is in table format, Excel commands allow you to organize, sort, filter, and calculate the data easily and quickly, much like a database.

The ***header row*** is the first row of the table with descriptive titles or labels. Each row of data is a ***record*** and each column is a ***field***. The label in the header row is sometimes referred to as the ***field name***. When you format your Excel data as a table, follow these guidelines to make your tables easier to use and navigate:

- Type descriptive labels in the first row and begin each label with a letter, not a number.
- Give each header a unique label; do not repeat any of the descriptive labels.
- Keep the same type of data within each column (e.g., text or values).
- Do not leave blank cells within the data.

Create an Excel Table

When data is arranged as a list and conforms to the guidelines just described, it is a straightforward format command to create an Excel table. Select the data you want to include in the table and click the **Format as Table** button in the *Styles* group on the *Home* tab. There is also a **Table** button in the *Tables* group on the *Insert* tab.

After your data is formatted as a table, each label in the header row displays an *AutoFilter* button. Recall from Chapter 3 that a *filter* specifies which data is shown and which is hidden. In other words, a filter is a criterion or a specification that data must meet to be shown. The *AutoFilter* buttons allow you to quickly hide or display rows of data. For example, you might want to display only those persons from a particular location or only those who reached a certain level of sales. In *SLO 4.4: Filtering Data*, you learn how to create and customize filters.

> **MORE INFO**
>
> The *AutoFilter* buttons do not print.

The *Table Tools Design* tab appears when any cell is selected within a table.

HOW TO: Create an Excel Table

1. Select the cells that you want to include in a table, including the header row.
2. Click the **Format as Table** button [*Home* tab, *Styles* group].
3. Choose a **Table Style** from the *Style* gallery (Figure 4-17).
4. Verify the cell range in the *Format As Table* dialog box.
   - If the cell range for the table is incorrect, drag to reselect the correct cell range in the worksheet.
5. Verify that there is a check in the **My table has headers** box in the *Format As Table* dialog box.
   - If there is no header row in the cell range you select originally, Excel inserts a row above the data and names the columns *Column1*, *Column2*, and so on. You can edit these names.
6. Click **OK** to create the table (Figure 4-18).
   - When the selected range includes imported data, you will see a message box asking to remove the connection. Click **Yes** to create the table.

4-17 Table Style gallery

Sales Table					
Name	Email Address	Title	MN Location	Sales Goal	Sales Attainment
Christopher Bowman	Christopher.Bowman@somewhere.com	Sales Manager	Cass Lake	$1,500,000	$1,275,000
Chad Mei	Chad.Mei@somewhere.com	Sales Representative	Cass Lake	$1,750,000	$1,330,000
Corey Daniels	Corey.Daniels@somewhere.com	Sales Trainee	Cass Lake	$500,000	$330,000
Sharon Wyatte	Sharon.Wyatte@somewhere.com	Sales Manager	Breezy Point	$1,500,000	$1,425,000
Dennis Frankie	Dennis.Frankie@somewhere.com	Sales Representative	Breezy Point	$1,800,000	$1,566,000
BJ Francine	BJ.Francine@somewhere.com	Sales Representative	Baudette	$1,700,000	$1,768,000
Kendal Shaedon	Kendal.Shaedon@somewhere.com	Sales Representative	Breezy Point	$1,800,000	$1,350,000
Ella Jamison	Ella.Jamison@somewhere.com	Sales Manager	Baudette	$1,500,000	$1,320,000
Alec Mikayla	Alec.Mikayla@somewhere.com	Sales Representative	Baudette	$1,700,000	$935,000
Natasha Ari	Natasha.Ari@somewhere.com	Sales Trainee	Baudette	$450,000	$409,500
Nikolai Jalowiec	Nikolai.Jalowiec@somewhere.com	Sales Manager	Walker	$1,500,000	$1,260,000
Tammy Christine	Tammy.Christine@somewhere.com	Sales Representative	Walker	$17,500,000	$9,275,000
Josie Daddiline	Josie.Daddiline@somewhere.com	Sales Representative	Walker	$17,500,000	$11,900,000
Christopher Bowman	Christopher.Bowman@somewhere.com	Sales Manager	Cass Lake	$1,500,000	$1,275,000

4-18 Formatted Excel table

> **ANOTHER WAY**
>
> Select the header and data rows and click the **Quick Analysis** tool. Choose **Tables** and click the **Table** button to format the data in a default table style.

> **MORE INFO**
>
> If you type a new label in the header row to the right of the last column, Excel makes the new label part of the table.

Table Styles

A **table style** is a predesigned set of built-in format options such as borders, fill colors, and effects for a table. A table style includes a color scheme and may display alternating fill for the rows, vertical borders, and more. You select a style when you create a table, but you can apply a different style to a table once it exists to change the look of your data. Predefined table styles are classified as *Light*, *Medium*, and *Dark*.

HOW TO: Apply a Style to an Existing Table

1. Click any cell within the table to display the *Table Tools Design* tab.
2. Click the **More** button [*Table Tools Design* tab, *Table Styles* group] to open the *Table Styles* gallery.
3. Point at a style to see a *Live Preview* of its effect on the table.
4. Click to select and apply a style.

Table Style Options

The *Table Style Options* group on the *Table Tools Design* tab includes commands for showing or hiding various parts of the table. You can hide the header row or display a total row. You can choose banded columns or rows, which alternates shading on the rows or columns. You can also hide the *AutoFilter* buttons, if you like.

If you choose to show a total row, you can choose the calculation that is displayed in the row.

HOW TO: Display a Total Row in a Table

1. Click any cell within the table.
2. Click to check the **Total Row** box [*Table Tools Design* tab, *Table Style Options* group].
   - The total row displays after the last row in the table (Figure 4-19).

4-19 Table with total row

Save a New Table Style

You may have a preference for a particular table style, or your organization may have specific requirements. You can create and name custom table styles so that you can apply preferred format choices to tables you create with one click.

In the *New Table Style* dialog box, select an individual part of a table and specify how it should be formatted. For example, you can set the first column feature a different font color or bold italic font.

When you create your own table style, it is listed in a *Custom* group at the top of the *Table Styles* gallery.

HOW TO: Save a New Table Style

1. Click any cell within a table.
2. Click the **Table Styles** More button [*Table Tools Design* tab, *Table Styles* group].
3. Click the **New Table Style** button (Figure 4-20).
4. Type a style name in the *Name* box.
5. Select a *Table Element* and click **Format** to open the *Format Cells* dialog box.
   - Make format selections on the *Font*, *Border*, or *Fill* tabs in the dialog box and click **OK**.
6. Check or uncheck the set as default box to indicate if the new style should be the default for the current document.
7. Click **OK**.

4-20 *New Table Style* dialog box

The Table Tools Group

The ***Tools*** group on the *Table Tools Design* tab has four commands: *Summarize with PivotTable*, *Remove Duplicates*, *Convert to Range*, and *Insert Slicer* (Figure 4-21). *PivotTables* are covered later in this section. First, the other three commands are introduced.

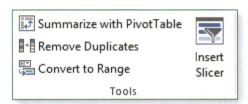

4-21 *Tools* group

A ***duplicate row*** is a row in a table that has exactly the same information in one or more columns. The *Remove Duplicates* command scans a table to locate and delete any rows with repeated data in the specified columns. In the *Remove Duplicates* dialog box, you specify which columns might have duplicate data.

HOW TO: Remove Duplicates

1. Click any cell within the table.
2. Click the **Remove Duplicates** button [*Table Tools Design* tab, *Tools* group] (Figure 4-22).
3. Place a check mark next to each column that you suspect may have duplicate data.
   - If you check all the columns, those rows containing the same data in every column are considered a duplicate and removed.
4. Click **OK**.
   - A message box indicates how many duplicate values were found and removed as well as how many unique values are still in the table (Figure 4-23).
   - This command does not preview which rows are deleted.
5. Click **OK** in the message box.

4-22 *Remove Duplicates* dialog box

4-23 *Duplicates Found* message box

In the *Tools* group, you can use the *Convert to Range* command to convert a table to a normal data in the worksheet. This removes all table formatting and the *AutoFilter* buttons.

HOW TO: Convert a Table to Range

1. Click any cell within the table.
2. Click the **Convert to Range** button [*Table Tools Design* tab, *Tools* group] (Figure 4-24).
3. Click **Yes** in the message box.

4-24 *Convert to Normal Range* dialog box

> **MORE INFO**
>
> You can show *AutoFilter* buttons in a normal data range by clicking the *Filter* button on the *Data* tab.

The *Insert Slicer* command opens a window where you can filter data to analyze smaller pieces of the whole. This command is also available for *PivotTables*, which are discussed later in this section.

Table Name and Structured References

By default, when you first create an Excel table, it is initially named *TableN* where *N* is a number. You can give an Excel table a more descriptive name using the *Table Tools Design* tab in the *Properties* group.

In an Excel table, each column is assigned a specific name based on the label in its header row. This name is known as a ***structured reference***. There is a structured reference for every column, and structured references are each preceded by the @ symbol. There are also several automatic structured references in a table. They include: #All, #Data, #Headers, #This Row, and #Totals.

You view these structured references when you build a formula by pointing to them (Figure 4-25). You can also refer to them elsewhere in the worksheet when creating a formula.

4-25 **Structured references in a table**

> **MORE INFO**
>
> To force your table formulas to use regular cell referencing in place of table headings, select **Options** from the *File* tab. Select **Formulas** on the left, navigate to the *Working with formulas* category, and remove the check next to *Use table names in formulas*.

PivotTables

A ***PivotTable*** is a summary report based on a list-type range of data in a worksheet. The list of data in a *PivotTable* is dynamic and contains movable field buttons and filter options; you can move and manipulate different components of a *PivotTable* for different analysis options.

In other words, a *PivotTable* is a separate worksheet in which you can sort, filter, and calculate large amounts of data. *PivotTables* are interactive, because you can rearrange parts of the report for analysis by clicking or dragging. Rearranging data is *pivoting* the data; pivoting allows you to look at data from a different perspective. A ***PivotChart*** can be built from a *PivotTable* and has similar features. It contains charted data that is dynamic (updates in real time) and contains the same movable field buttons and filter options that a *PivotTable* does. The *PivotChart* button is on the *PivotTable Tools Analyze* tab.

> **MORE INFO**
>
> If you create a *PivotChart* directly from list data in a worksheet, an underlying *PivotTable* is also automatically created.

PivotTables are sophisticated analysis tools. They enable you to "drill-down" into your data and assess various types of results or changes. For example, in a table or list with thousands of records, you can arrange a *PivotTable* to quickly show average sales by state, by city, or by other criteria, and, just as quickly, return to the entire list.

A *PivotTable* is based on a range of data, like a table, with a header row, although the data does not have to be formatted as an Excel table (Figure 4-26). Data for a *PivotTable* should follow the same guidelines as those recommended for an Excel table in the beginning of this section. A *PivotTable* is placed on its own sheet in the workbook.

The *Tables* group on the *Insert* tab includes the *PivotTable* button as well as the *Recommended PivotTables* button. When you are first learning about *PivotTables*, use the **Recommended PivotTables** button until you gain experience building these reports.

After you create a *PivotTable*, the *PivotTable Tools Analyze* and *Design* tabs are available for additional format choices and data commands.

	A	B	C
1			
2			
3	**Row Labels** ▾	**Sum of Sales Goal**	
4	⊟**Baudette**	5350000	
5	Alec Mikayla	1700000	
6	BJ Francine	1700000	
7	Ella Jamison	1500000	
8	Natasha Ari	450000	
9	⊟**Breezy Point**	5100000	
10	Dennis Frankie	1800000	
11	Kendal Shaedon	1800000	
12	Sharon Wyatte	1500000	
13	⊟**Cass Lake**	3750000	
14	Chad Mei	1750000	
15	Christopher Bowman	1500000	
16	Corey Daniels	500000	
17	⊟**Walker**	36500000	
18	Josie Daddiline	17500000	
19	Nikolai Jalowiec	1500000	
20	Tammy Christine	17500000	
21	**Grand Total**	50700000	
22			

4-26 An Excel *PivotTable*

> **MORE INFO**
>
> You must refresh a *PivotTable* after changes are made to the underlying worksheet data.

HOW TO: Create a PivotTable

....

1. Click anywhere within the data range.
   - The data range must have a header row.
   - You can select the entire range.

2. Click the **Recommended PivotTables** button [*Insert* tab, *Tables* group] (Figure 4-27).

- A data range in the worksheet is assumed.
- Click *Change Source Data* if the assumed range is incorrect.
- You can create a blank *PivotTable* from this dialog box.

3. Click a preview tile and review the description of the proposed *PivotTable*.

4. Select the preferred *PivotTable* and click **OK**.

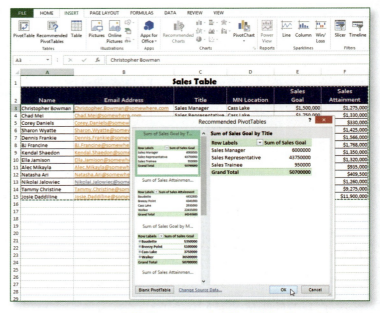

4-27 *Recommended PivotTables* for a data range

A *PivotTable* is created on a new sheet in the workbook and the *PivotTable Fields* pane opens at the right. From this pane, you can choose fields to be added to the report and hide or display other fields. You can drag field names into different areas in the pane to regroup how the data is organized.

> **MORE INFO**
>
> Delete the *PivotTable* layout by clicking the **Clear** button [*PivotTable Tools Analyze* tab, *Actions* group]. You can build a new *PivotTable* from the same data.

4-28 *PivotTable Fields* pane

In the *PivotTable* report itself, each column label includes a filter arrow so that you can hide or display selected rows. Similarly, row labels may include collapse/expand buttons to hide or show data for that part of the report. In addition, you can add a report filter by dragging a field name into the *Filter* part of the *PivotTable Fields* pane.

It takes time and practice to create a useful *PivotTable* and to understand all its features. It is a good idea to experiment as you build *PivotTables* to develop skill in placing fields, and sorting and filtering data.

HOW TO: Add a PivotTable Report Filter and Pivot Fields

1. Click anywhere in the *PivotTable*.

2. Drag the field name into the *Filter* area and release the field (Figure 4-28).

- Drag the field name from the *Choose fields to add to report* area or from another area in the *PivotTable Fields* pane.
- The field is added with a filter button in row 1 of the *PivotTable*.

3. Point and drag a field name from the *Choose fields to add to report* area into the *Values* area in the *PivotTable Fields* pane and release the field.

- A new column is added to the report (Figure 4-29).
- The calculation used for the *Values* fields is *Sum*. Change it by clicking in the column and selecting the **Field Settings** button [*PivotTable Tools Analyze* tab, *Active Field* group].

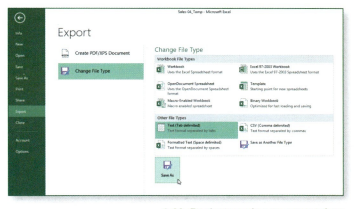

4-29 *PivotTable* results

Export Data

You have seen how you can import data from various sources for use in Excel. Similarly, you can export or save Excel data in a format that is usable in other programs and applications. For example, you can save an Excel table as a text file for use in any program that can read a text file. Since most software applications can read a text file, this is a common way to transfer or share data.

When you save worksheet data as a text file, Excel renames the sheet with the same file name that you type for the text file. You can save only one worksheet in a text file. If a workbook has multiple sheets, a message box will alert you that only the current sheet will be saved.

HOW TO: Save an Excel Table as a Text File

1. Save the workbook file you want to export.
2. Click the worksheet tab with the table or list you want to save and export.
3. Open the *Backstage* view and click **Export**.
4. Click the **Change File Type** button.
5. Select **Text (Tab delimited)** as the file type (Figure 4-30).
6. Click **Save As**.
7. Navigate to the location where you want the exported material to be saved and type the file name.
8. Click **Save**.

4-30 *Backstage* view to export data

A **SharePoint web server** is a server that runs *Microsoft SharePoint Services*, a network product that allows for collaboration and simultaneous work by groups of people via the Internet. You can export table data to a custom list on the server and make your data available for others with the *Export Table to SharePoint List Wizard*. A list on a SharePoint server stores and displays content that users can edit online. To work with the SharePoint server, you must have an Internet connection and permission from the network administrator.

HOW TO: Export an Excel Table to a SharePoint List

1. Click any cell within the table you wish to export.
2. Click the **Export** button [*Table Tools Design* tab, *External Table Data* group].
3. Select the *Export Table to SharePoint List* option.

4. Type the web address of the SharePoint site in the *Address* box (Figure 4-31).

- Check the **Create a read-only connection to the new SharePoint list** box if you do not want others to edit the data.
- Two columns are added to the table with a read-only connection. An *Item Type* column indicates whether a row represents a SharePoint list item or a folder. A *Path* column displays the folder path for a list item (mylist/foldername).

5. Type the *List* name and *Description* in the *Export Table to SharePoint List* dialog box.

- A list name is required and is displayed at the top of the list page.

6. Click **Next**.

7. Click **Finish** if the columns and data types are correct.

8. Click **OK**.

- Click the **Unlink** button [*Table Tools Design* tab, *External Table Data* group] to disconnect the Excel table from the SharePoint server.

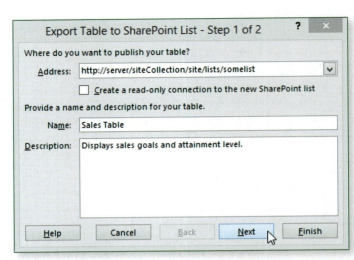

4-31 *Export Table to SharePoint List* **wizard**

> **MORE INFO**
>
> You can access and use SharePoint data in an Excel worksheet, or unlink the data to keep your own copy of the data separate.

> **ANOTHER WAY**
>
> View your SharePoint list by clicking the **Open in Browser** button [*Table Tools Design* tab, *External Table Data* group].

PAUSE & PRACTICE: EXCEL 4-2

For this project, you format data as an Excel table, add a total row, and remove duplicate records. Then you create a *PivotTable* for Paradise Lakes Resort using the Excel table as its source. Because the workbook has data connections, you will need to enable editing to work with it.

File Needed: *[your initials] PP E4-1.xlsx*
Completed Project File Name: *[your initials] PP E4-2.xlsx*

1. Open the *[your initials] PP E4-1* workbook. Click **Enable Editing**.

2. Save the workbook as *[your initials] PP E4-2*.

3. Delete column **B**.

4. Select cells **A2:E2** and clear the formats.

5. Rename the sheet tab Sales Quota Data.

6. Format the data as an Excel table.
   a. Select cells **A2:E26**.
   b. Click the **Format as Table** button [*Home* tab, *Styles* group].
   c. Select **Table Style Medium 27** from the *Style* gallery.
   d. Verify that there is a check mark for **My table has headers** in the *Format As Table* dialog box.
   e. Click **OK**.
   f. Click **Yes** in the message box about external connections (Figure 4-32).

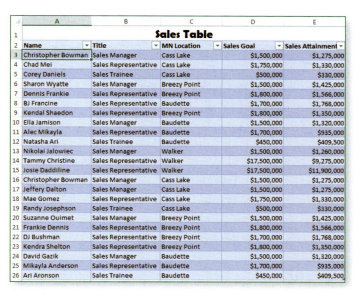

4-32 Excel data formatted as a table

7. Add a total row to a table.
   a. Click a cell within the table.
   b. Click to place a check mark for **Total Row** [*Table Tools Design* tab, *Table Style Options* group].
   c. Click cell **D27** and choose **SUM** from the drop-down list.

8. Remove duplicate rows in a table.
   a. Click a cell within the table.
   b. Click the **Remove Duplicates** button [*Table Tools Design* tab, *Tools* group].
   c. Click **Unselect All** to remove all the check marks.
   d. Click **Name** to place a check mark (Figure 4-33). If you know that duplicate data is in a specific column, you can speed up the search by choosing only that column.
   e. Click **OK** in the *Remove Duplicates* dialog box.
   f. Click **OK** in the message box.

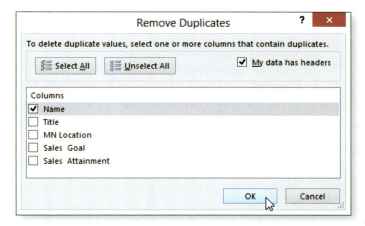

4-33 Duplicate record search in a single field

9. Create a *PivotTable*.
   a. Click cell **A3**.
   b. Click the **Recommended PivotTables** button [*Insert* tab, *Tables* group].
   c. Locate and click the **Sum of Sales Goal by MN Location (+)** preview tile.
   d. Click **OK**.
   e. Name the worksheet tab PivotTable.

10. Add a report filter in a *PivotTable*.
    a. Click a cell in the *PivotTable* to open the *PivotTable Fields* pane.
    b. Drag the **MN Location** field from the *Rows* group to the *Filters* group in the *PivotTable Fields* pane.
    c. Click the filter arrow in cell **B1** and click to place a check mark for **Select Multiple Items**.
    d. Click to remove the check marks for **Baudette** and **Breezy Point** (Figure 4-34).
    e. Click **OK**.

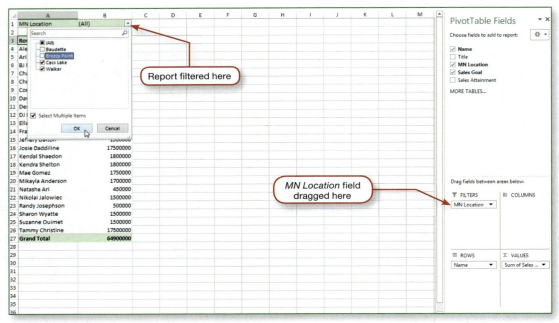

4-34 Report filter settings

11. Format data in a *PivotTable*.
    a. Right-click any cell in column B.
    b. Choose **Value Field Settings** (Figure 4-35).
    c. Click **Number Format** and set **Currency** format with no decimal places.
    d. Click **OK** to close each dialog box.

12. Save and close the workbook (Figure 4-36).

4-35 *Value Field Settings* **dialog box**

MN Location	(Multiple Items)
Row Labels	**Sum of Sales**
Chad Mei	$1,750,000
Christopher Bowman	$1,500,000
Corey Daniels	$500,000
Jeffery Dalton	$1,500,000
Josie Daddiline	$17,500,000
Mae Gomez	$1,750,000
Nikolai Jalowiec	$1,500,000
Randy Josephson	$500,000
Tammy Christine	$17,500,000
Grand Total	**$44,000,000**

4-36 PP E4-2 completed *PivotTable*

Sorting Data

Sorting is the process of arranging rows of data in an identified order. For Paradise Lakes Resort, for example, you may want to arrange the sales table by location to compare the sites. Or you may want to order the rows from best sales attainment to lowest.

You can sort data in ascending or descending order. *Ascending* order sorts data alphabetically from A to Z or numerically from smallest to largest value. In a *descending* sort, data are arranged alphabetically Z to A or numerically from largest to smallest value.

Sort Options

You can sort all Excel data that is organized in rows and columns. You can sort by one column or by multiple columns. In addition to normal text or number sorting, you can sort data by cell fill color, font color, or cell icons (from *Conditional Formatting,* covered later in this chapter in *SLO 4.6: Applying Conditional Formatting*).

The **Sort & Filter** button on the *Home* tab in the *Editing* group lists the *A to Z* sort, the *Z to A* sort, and the *Custom Sort* (multiple columns) commands. The same commands are available in the *Sort & Filter* group on the *Data* tab.

Sort Text Data

In a cell range that has a header row followed by rows of data, you can click any cell in the column you want to sort and click the appropriate button.

HOW TO: Sort Text Data by a Single Column

1. Select a cell in the column that contains the data you want to sort.
2. Click the **A to Z** button [*Data* tab, *Sort & Filter* group].
   - The records are arranged in alphabetical order based on the first character in the cell.
   - If the first character in a row is a value or special character, that record is sorted at the top.
   - Click the **Undo** button [*Home* tab, *Clipboard* group] to undo a sort.
3. Click the **Z to A** button [*Data* tab, *Sort & Filter* group].
   - The records are arranged in reverse alphabetical order based on the first character in the cell (Figure 4-37).
   - If the first character in a row is a value or special character, that record is sorted at the bottom.

	A	B	C	D	E
1			**Sales Table**		
2	**Name**	**Title**	**MN Location**	**Sales Goal**	**Sales Attainment**
3	Tammy Christine	Sales Representative	Walker	$17,500,000.00	$9,275,000.00
4	Sharon Wyatte	Sales Manager	Breezy Point	$1,500,000.00	$1,425,000.00
5	Nikolai Jalowiec	Sales Manager	Walker	$1,500,000.00	$1,260,000.00
6	Natasha Ari	Sales Trainee	Baudette	$450,000.00	$409,500.00
7	Kendal Shaedon	Sales Representative	Breezy Point	$1,800,000.00	$1,350,000.00
8	Josie Daddiline	Sales Representative	Walker	$17,500,000.00	$11,900,000.00
9	Ella Jamison	Sales Manager	Baudette	$1,500,000.00	$1,320,000.00
10	Dennis Frankie	Sales Representative	Breezy Point	$1,800,000.00	$1,566,000.00
11	Corey Daniels	Sales Trainee	Cass Lake	$500,000.00	$330,000.00
12	Christopher Bowman	Sales Manager	Cass Lake	$1,500,000.00	$1,275,000.00
13	Chad Mei	Sales Representative	Cass Lake	$1,750,000.00	$1,330,000.00
14	BJ Francine	Sales Representative	Baudette	$1,700,000.00	$1,768,000.00
15	Alec Mikayla	Sales Representative	Baudette	$1,700,000.00	$935,000.00

4-37 "Name" column sorted Z to A

> **MORE INFO**
>
> When you sort a cell range using the **A to Z** or **Z to A** buttons, complete rows of data are rearranged, not just the cells in the selected column.

To sort text data in more than one column or field, use the *Sort* dialog box. This dialog box opens when you click the **Sort** button [*Data* tab, *Sort & Filter* group] or when you choose **Custom Sort** from the **Sort & Filter** button options [*Home* tab, *Editing* group]. A common multiple column sort involves data that includes cities and states. You can first sort by state so that Alabama is before Arizona, and then within that sort, you can further sort by city. Another example of a common multiple column sort involves persons' names. When first and last names are listed in separate columns, you can sort by last name and then first name. If a list includes 15 people named "Smith," you can further sort them by first name.

The data in Figure 4-38 is sorted with a multiple sort.

	Name	Title	MN Location	Sales Goal	Sales Attainment
			Sales Table		
3	Ella Jamison	Sales Manager	Baudette	$1,500,000.00	$1,320,000.00
4	Sharon Wyatte	Sales Manager	Breezy Point	$1,500,000.00	$1,425,000.00
5	Christopher Bowman	Sales Manager	Cass Lake	$1,500,000.00	$1,275,000.00
6	Nikolai Jalowiec	Sales Manager	Walker	$1,500,000.00	$1,260,000.00
7	BJ Francine	Sales Representative	Baudette	$1,700,000.00	$1,768,000.00
8	Alec Mikayla	Sales Representative	Baudette	$1,700,000.00	$935,000.00
9	Kendal Shaedon	Sales Representative	Breezy Point	$1,800,000.00	$1,350,000.00
10	Dennis Frankie	Sales Representative	Breezy Point	$1,800,000.00	$1,566,000.00
11	Chad Mei	Sales Representative	Cass Lake	$1,750,000.00	$1,330,000.00
12	Tammy Christine	Sales Representative	Walker	$17,500,000.00	$9,275,000.00
13	Josie Daddiline	Sales Representative	Walker	$17,500,000.00	$11,900,000.00
14	Natasha Ari	Sales Trainee	Baudette	$450,000.00	$409,500.00
15	Corey Daniels	Sales Trainee	Cass Lake	$500,000.00	$330,000.00

4-38 Data sorted first by "Title" and then by "MN Location"

HOW TO: Sort Text Data by Multiple Columns

1. Select a cell in the range of cells that you want to sort.
2. Click the **Sort** button [*Data* tab, *Sort & Filter* group].
3. Check the **My data has headers** box if your data has a header row.
4. Click the **Sort by** arrow and select the column heading for the first sort (Figure 4-39).
   - The *Sort On* option specifies *Values*, *Cell Color*, *Font Color*, or *Cell Icon*. Use *Values* for sorting text or numbers.
5. Click the **Order** arrow and choose a sort option.
6. Click **Add Level** to add a second sort column.
7. Click the **Then by** arrow and select the second column heading.
8. Click the **Order** arrow and choose a sort option.
   - Click the **Options** button in the *Sort* dialog box to specify case-sensitive sorting.
9. Click **OK**.

4-39 *Sort* dialog box

Sort Data with Values

To sort data that contains values, take the same steps you took to sort text data. A value sort can be smallest to largest or largest to smallest.

Dates are treated as values. When dates are sorted smallest to largest, the earliest dates are listed first. To show the most recent date at the top of a sort, sort largest to smallest.

HOW TO: Sort Values by a Single Column

1. Select a cell in the column you want to sort.
2. Click the **A to Z** button [*Data* tab, *Sort & Filter* group].
   - If some of the beginning characters are values and some are text, rows that begin with a value are sorted first.
3. Click the **Z to A** button [*Data* tab, *Sort & Filter* group].

In a multiple column sort, you can use both a value column and a text column if necessary. The same *Sort* dialog box is used, and the *Sort On* option is *Values* for both fields. The data in Figure 4-40 is sorted first by the "MN Location" column, a text sort, and then by the "Sales Attainment" column, a value sort.

	A	B	C	D	E
1			**Sales Table**		
2	**Name**	**Title**	**MN Location**	**Sales Goal**	**Sales Attainment**
3	Natasha Ari	Sales Trainee	Baudette	$450,000.00	$409,500.00
4	Alec Mikayla	Sales Representative	Baudette	$1,700,000.00	$935,000.00
5	Ella Jamison	Sales Manager	Baudette	$1,500,000.00	$1,320,000.00
6	BJ Francine	Sales Representative	Baudette	$1,700,000.00	$1,768,000.00
7	Kendal Shaedon	Sales Representative	Breezy Point	$1,800,000.00	$1,350,000.00
8	Sharon Wyatte	Sales Manager	Breezy Point	$1,500,000.00	$1,425,000.00
9	Dennis Frankie	Sales Representative	Breezy Point	$1,800,000.00	$1,566,000.00
10	Corey Daniels	Sales Trainee	Cass Lake	$500,000.00	$330,000.00
11	Christopher Bowman	Sales Manager	Cass Lake	$1,500,000.00	$1,275,000.00
12	Chad Mei	Sales Representative	Cass Lake	$1,750,000.00	$1,330,000.00
13	Nikolai Jalowiec	Sales Manager	Walker	$1,500,000.00	$1,260,000.00
14	Tammy Christine	Sales Representative	Walker	$17,500,000.00	$9,275,000.00
15	Josie Daddiline	Sales Representative	Walker	$17,500,000.00	$11,900,000.00

4-40 Sorted data by "MN Location" and then by "Sales Attainment"

HOW TO: Sort Values and Text in Multiple Columns

1. Select a cell in the range you want to sort.
2. Click the **Sort** button [*Data* tab, *Sort & Filter* group].
3. Check the **My data has headers** box if your data has headers.
4. Click the **Sort by** arrow and select the column heading for the first sort.
5. Click the **Order** arrow and choose a sort option.
6. Click **Add Level** to add another column sort.
7. Click the **Then by** arrow and select the second column heading.
8. Click the **Order** arrow and choose a sort option.
9. Add more levels if necessary.
10. Click **OK**.

Sort by Font or Cell Color

In addition to basic sorting by the value or text content of data, you can sort data based on the font color or the cell fill color. For example, you might use color-coding in a large worksheet to identify cities, months, or individuals. You can use *Conditional Formatting* (discussed in detail later in this chapter in *SLO 4.6: Applying Conditional Formatting*) to apply fill or font color to cells. If font or fill color is used to classify data, you can group items with a sort command. In Figure 4-41 the cells with yellow fill are grouped at the top of the "Sales Attainment" column.

	A	B	C	D	E
1			Sales Table		
2	Name	Title	MN Location	Sales Goal	Sales Attainment
3	Natasha Ari	Sales Trainee	Baudette	$450,000.00	$409,500.00
4	Corey Daniels	Sales Trainee	Cass Lake	$500,000.00	$330,000.00
5	Tammy Christine	Sales Representative	Walker	$17,500,000.00	$9,275,000.00
6	Josie Daddiline	Sales Representative	Walker	$17,500,000.00	$11,900,000.00
7	Alec Mikayla	Sales Representative	Baudette	$1,700,000.00	$935,000.00
8	Ella Jamison	Sales Manager	Baudette	$1,500,000.00	$1,320,000.00
9	BJ Francine	Sales Representative	Baudette	$1,700,000.00	$1,768,000.00
10	Kendal Shaedon	Sales Representative	Breezy Point	$1,800,000.00	$1,350,000.00
11	Sharon Wyatte	Sales Manager	Breezy Point	$1,500,000.00	$1,425,000.00
12	Dennis Frankie	Sales Representative	Breezy Point	$1,800,000.00	$1,566,000.00
13	Christopher Bowman	Sales Manager	Cass Lake	$1,500,000.00	$1,275,000.00
14	Chad Mei	Sales Representative	Cass Lake	$1,750,000.00	$1,330,000.00
15	Nikolai Jalowiec	Sales Manager	Walker	$1,500,000.00	$1,260,000.00

4-41 Yellow fill sorted on top in "Sales Attainment" column

When you sort by color, there are two choices about the *Order* in the *Sort* dialog box. You set which color is to be first. Then you specify whether that color should sort to the top or the bottom. If you have three colors, you can indicate where each color should fall in the sort order.

HOW TO: Sort Data by Font or Cell Color

1. Select a cell in the column you want to sort.
2. Click the **Sort** button [*Data* tab, *Sort & Filter* group].
3. Check the **My data has headers** box if your data has headers.
4. Click the **Sort by** arrow and select the column heading for the first sort.
5. Click the **Sort On** arrow and choose **Cell Color** or **Font Color**.
6. Click the first **Order** arrow (on the left) and choose the first color (Figure 4-42).
7. Click the second **Order** arrow (on the right) and choose **On Top** or **On Bottom**.
8. Click the **Add Level** to add another column sort option as desired.
9. Click the **Then by** arrow and select the second column heading.
   - Add as many sort levels as there are colors to be sorted.
   - Choose the color and the sort position for each color.
10. Click **OK**.

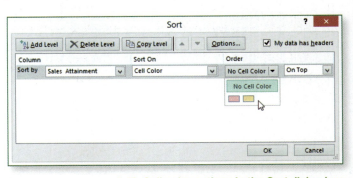

4-42 Cell color options in the *Sort* dialog box

Sort by Cell Icon

A cell icon is a small image that you can place in a cell with a *Conditional Formatting* command (see *SLO 4.6: Applying Conditional Formatting* in this chapter). You can apply icons in sets of three, four, or five, and you can sort by icon. The sorted data in Figure 4-43 has a two-set icon, sorted with the green icons on the top.

	A	B	C	D	E
1			**Sales Table**		
2	**Name**	**Title**	**MN Location**	**Sales Goal**	**Sales Attainment**
3	Tammy Christine	Sales Representative	Walker	$17,500,000.00 ⬆	$9,275,000.00
4	Josie Daddiline	Sales Representative	Walker	$17,500,000.00 ⬆	$11,900,000.00
5	Natasha Ari	Sales Trainee	Baudette	$450,000.00 ⬇	$409,500.00
6	Corey Daniels	Sales Trainee	Cass Lake	$500,000.00 ⬇	$330,000.00
7	Alec Mikayla	Sales Representative	Baudette	$1,700,000.00 ⬇	$935,000.00
8	Ella Jamison	Sales Manager	Baudette	$1,500,000.00 ⬇	$1,320,000.00
9	BJ Francine	Sales Representative	Baudette	$1,700,000.00 ⬇	$1,768,000.00
10	Kendal Shaedon	Sales Representative	Breezy Point	$1,800,000.00 ⬇	$1,350,000.00
11	Sharon Wyatte	Sales Manager	Breezy Point	$1,500,000.00 ⬇	$1,425,000.00
12	Dennis Frankie	Sales Representative	Breezy Point	$1,800,000.00 ⬇	$1,566,000.00
13	Christopher Bowman	Sales Manager	Cass Lake	$1,500,000.00 ⬇	$1,275,000.00
14	Chad Mei	Sales Representative	Cass Lake	$1,750,000.00 ⬇	$1,330,000.00
15	Nikolai Jalowiec	Sales Manager	Walker	$1,500,000.00 ⬇	$1,260,000.00

4-43 Data sorted by the cell icon in "Sales Attainment" column

HOW TO: Sort Data by Cell Icon

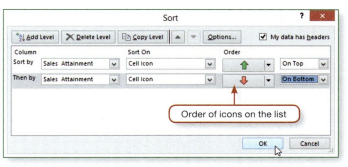

4-44 Sort dialog box

1. Select a cell with an icon in the column you want to sort.
2. Click the **Sort** button [*Data* tab, *Sort & Filter* group].
3. Check the **My data has headers** box if your data has headers.
4. Click the **Sort by** arrow and select the column heading for the first sort.
5. Click the **Sort On** arrow and choose **Cell Icon**.
6. Click the first **Order** arrow and select the first icon.
7. Click the second **Order** arrow (on the right) and choose **On Top** or **On Bottom** (Figure 4-44).
8. Click the **Add Level** button to add another sort option.
9. Click the **Then by** arrow and select the second column heading.
   - Add as many levels as there are icons.
   - Choose the sort order for each icon.
10. Click **OK**.

SLO 4.4

Filtering Data

When you work with large lists or tables, it is not practical to display thousands of rows of data on screen at once. It is easier to work with data if you filter the data to show the rows for the current month, the selected individual, or a specific product. Recall that a filter specifies which data is shown and which is hidden based on a specified criteria. When you filter data, information that doesn't meet the specified requirements is temporarily hidden.

The AutoFilter Command

Recall from earlier in the chapter that the *AutoFilter* button allows you to quickly hide or display rows of data. In list-type data or an Excel table, the **AutoFilter** command displays a filter arrow for each label in the header row. A table automatically shows *AutoFilter* arrows, but you need to activate them for a normal data range.

When you click an *AutoFilter* arrow for a header label, a pane displays sort options, filter types based on the data type, and check boxes for every piece of data. You can select check boxes to mark which records should be displayed or you can build a filter.

HOW TO: Use AutoFilters

1. Select a cell in the cell range to be filtered.
2. Click the **Filter** button [*Data* tab, *Sort & Filter* group].
3. Click the **AutoFilter** button so the column is filtered.
4. Click **(Select All)** to remove all check marks.
5. Check each record you want displayed (Figure 4-45).
6. Click **OK**.
   - Records that meet the criteria are visible with row headings in blue.
   - Records that do not meet the criteria and their row numbers are hidden.
   - A filter symbol appears with the column *AutoFilter* button (Figure 4-46).

4-45 *AutoFilter* for "MN Location"

Custom AutoFilter

From the *AutoFilter* button, you can build a custom *AutoFilter*, which is a dialog box where you build criteria. A custom *AutoFilter* gives you more options to specify how rows are displayed. You can build criteria to select ranges of data using relational operators *AND*, and *OR*. Relational operators are words like *Equals, Begins with*, or *Contains* (Figure 4-47).

The available filters depend on the type of data in the column. For example, if the column is text, *Text Filters* are available. There are also *Number Filters* and *Date Filters*.

Shows that records are filtered by this column

4-46 Filtered records

> ◢ **ANOTHER WAY**
>
> To turn off an *AutoFilter*, click the **Filter** button [*Data* tab, *Sort & Filter* group].

To remove any filter and return to the complete list, click the **Clear** button in the *Sort & Filter* group on the *Data* tab. Alternatively, you can click the *AutoFilter* button for the column and choose **Clear Filter From (ColumnName)**.

4-47 Text filters for a custom *AutoFilter*

HOW TO: Create a Custom Text AutoFilter

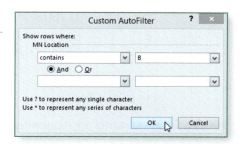

1. Select a cell in the cell range you want to filter.
2. Click the **Filter** button [*Data* tab, *Sort & Filter* group].
3. Click the **AutoFilter** button for the column you want to filter.
4. Select **Text Filters** and choose an operator.
5. Type the desired criteria in the *Custom AutoFilter* dialog box.
   - In Figure 4-48, the letter *B* is entered in the text box to filter for location names that contain the letter *B*.
6. Click **OK** in the *Custom AutoFilter* dialog box.
   - Rows that do not contain the letter *B* are hidden in Figure 4-49.

4-48 Custom AutoFilter dialog box

	A	B	C	D	E
1			**Sales Table**		
2	Name	Title	MN Location	Sales Goal	Sales Attainment
5	Natasha Ari	Sales Trainee	Baudette	$450,000.00	$409,500.00
7	Alec Mikayla	Sales Representative	Baudette	$1,700,000.00	$935,000.00
8	Ella Jamison	Sales Manager	Baudette	$1,500,000.00	$1,320,000.00
9	BJ Francine	Sales Representative	Baudette	$1,700,000.00	$1,768,000.00
10	Kendal Shaedon	Sales Representative	Breezy Point	$1,800,000.00	$1,350,000.00
11	Sharon Wyatte	Sales Manager	Breezy Point	$1,500,000.00	$1,425,000.00
12	Dennis Frankie	Sales Representative	Breezy Point	$1,800,000.00	$1,566,000.00

4-49 AutoFilter results for "MN Location" data containing the letter B

Advanced Filter

An *Advanced Filter* is similar to a query in a database. When you use an *Advanced Filter*, you build a criteria range separate from the actual data and type the criteria within that range. You can filter the data in the worksheet range or you can output data to another location on the sheet. Being able to output filter results allows you to create separate reports that include only filtered rows. An *Advanced Filter* requires more set-up work but allows you to apply more complex filters. You can even use a formula in your criteria.

To use an *Advanced Filter*, you need to create a **criteria range**. The criteria range must be at least two rows. The first row

4-50 Advanced Filter set-up and dialog box

must use column names from the worksheet data but you need not use all of them. You type the actual criteria in the second row. You can create a criteria range in empty rows anywhere on the worksheet or on another sheet. In Figure 4-50, the criteria range is A2:E3.

You can use multiple rows after the header row in the criteria range to set *AND* or *OR* conditions. If you enter criteria on the same row, they are treated as *AND* conditions. This means both criteria must be met for the record to be displayed. In Figure 4-50, "Sales Manager" in cell B3 and ">1,330,000" in cell E3 are the criteria. This is an *AND* condition because both criteria are on the same row. For an *OR* condition, use a second (or third) row in the criteria range. An *OR* filter displays the record if any one of the requirements is met.

If you want to output filtered results to another location, you also create an *extract range*. You only need to specify one row for this range, and it should include the same column headings as the data. The filter results are copied to the area below these headings and take up as many rows as necessary. In Figure 4-50, the extract range is A22:E22. Filter results appear below the extract area header.

HOW TO: Create an Advanced Filter

1. Select the header row and copy the labels to a *Criteria* area on the same worksheet or to another sheet in the same workbook.
   - If you plan to use only one or two fields in the criteria, you only need to copy those labels to the criteria range.
   - If you place the criteria range above the data, leave at least one blank row between it and the data.
2. Select the header row and copy the labels to an *Extract* area in the same worksheet.
   - The output or extract area must be on the same sheet as the data you want to filter.
   - Leave enough blank rows below the labels for the filtered results.
3. Enter the criteria in the criteria range.
4. Click the **Advanced** button [*Data* tab, *Sort & Filter* group] to open the *Advanced Filter* dialog box (see Figure 4-50).
5. Select the **Copy to another location** button to display results in the extract area.
6. In the *List range* text box, verify or select the range (including the header row).
7. In the *Criteria range* text box, select the criteria cell range in the worksheet with its header row.
   - If the criteria range is on another sheet, click the worksheet tab and then select the range.
   - You can type in cell references to identify the criteria range.
8. In the *Copy to* text box, select the extract range in the worksheet.
9. Click **OK** (Figure 4-51).

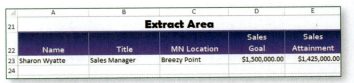

	A	B	C	D	E
21			**Extract Area**		
22	Name	Title	MN Location	Sales Goal	Sales Attainment
23	Sharon Wyatte	Sales Manager	Breezy Point	$1,500,000.00	$1,425,000.00
24					

4-51 *Advanced Filter* results for "Sales Managers" with a "Sales Attainment" greater than $1,330,000

SLO 4.5	**Using the Subtotal Command and Creating Outlines and Groups**

The **Subtotal** command automatically inserts summary rows for data that are arranged in related groups. To obtain the summary amounts, you can use functions such as *SUM, AVERAGE, MAX,* or *MIN*. Although you can insert summary rows and formulas on your own, that would be a daunting task if you had 10,000 records sorted into 200 groups. For example, you would have to insert 200 rows in the correct location for each group and then copy the formula to each of those rows. The *Subtotal* command does this automatically.

Use the Subtotal Command with SUM

The *Subtotal* command is available for a normal range of cells. The command is not available when the range is formatted as an Excel table, because a table has its own total and sorting commands. If your data is formatted as a table, you must first convert it to a normal cell range before you can display subtotals.

For the *Subtotal* command to work properly, you must sort the rows by the main field (column) to be totaled. To display sales totals by city location, for example, sort the data by the city name. The *Subtotal* command groups the rows by this field.

The *Subtotal* command formats the list data as an **outline**. An **outline** is a summary that groups records so that they can be displayed or hidden from view. The *Subtotal* button is located in the *Outline* group on the *Data* tab.

HOW TO: Display Subtotals

1. Sort the data in the first column where you want to show subtotals.
   - Convert the data to a normal range if needed.
2. Select the cell range including the header row.
3. Click the **Subtotals** button [*Data* tab, *Outline* group].
4. Click the **At each change in** arrow and choose the column heading for the subtotals.
   - This is the same column you used to sort the data.
5. Click the **Use function** arrow and choose the function.
6. In the **Add subtotal to** list, check each field that should display a subtotal.
   - You can include a subtotal for other columns (fields).
7. Choose command options such as **Replace current subtotals** and **Summary below data** (Figure 4-52) as desired.
   - You can run the *Subtotal* command numerous times with different functions to analyze data by replacing any existing subtotals.
   - You can allow a group to split across pages.
   - The "Summary" row can be placed above the data if you prefer.
   - You can remove subtotals from this dialog box.
8. Click **OK** (Figure 4-53).
   - A subtotal row appears below each group.
   - A grand total appears after the last row of data.
   - Outline buttons appear to the left of the column and row headings.
   - The outline is expanded, showing all details.

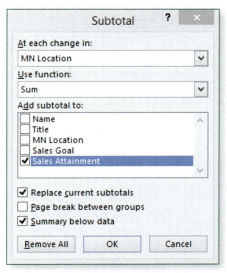

4-52 *Subtotal* dialog box

4-53 Sales Attainment subtotals for each location

> **MORE INFO**
>
> If you apply a filter to data with subtotals, you can hide the subtotal rows.

Outline Buttons

An **outline** groups and summarizes data. A worksheet can have only one outline; the outline can include all of the data on the sheet or a portion of it. Outlines have levels, indicated by the numbered buttons to the left of the column headings. Each of the *Outline Level* buttons shows increasing level of detail. The worksheet in Figure 4-53 has three levels. An outline can have up to eight levels.

Each level has an *Expand/Collapse* button. This button is a toggle and shows a minus sign (-) or a plus sign (+). When an individual group is collapsed, you do not see details for that group, only the subtotal.

HOW TO: Use Outline Buttons

1. Click a collapse button (-) to hide details for a row.
2. Click an expand button (+) to display details for a row.
3. Click the **Level 1** button (1) to reveal the grand total.
4. Click the **Level 2** button (2) to see the second outline level details (Figure 4-54).
5. Click the **Level 3** button (3) to display all details.

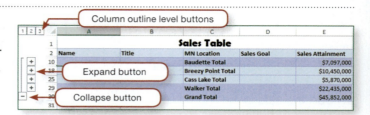

4-54 Level 2 outline results

Create an Auto Outline

If your data is consistently formatted, you can create an automatic outline. Consistently formatted data is grouped with related formulas in the same location. The formulas can be either in specific rows or columns, because an outline can use either. An **Auto Outline** inserts groups based on where the formulas are located in your data.

The data in Figure 4-55 is grouped and there is a *SUM* formula after each group. Excel can build an *Auto Outline* group from this type of data. If your data is not properly formatted, Excel displays a message that an *Auto Outline* cannot be created.

HOW TO: Apply an Auto Outline

1. Click a cell within the data range that you want to automatically outline.
2. Click the **Group** button arrow [*Data* tab, *Outline* group] and select **Auto Outline** (Figure 4-56).
   - Expand or collapse the outline to show or hide details.

	A	B	C	D
		Sales Table		
2	**Name**	**Title**	**MN Location**	**Sales**
3	Natasha Ari	Sales Trainee	Baudette	$409,500
4	Mikayla Anderson	Sales Representative	Baudette	$935,000
5	Ella Jamison	Sales Manager	Baudette	$1,320,000
6	David Gazik	Sales Manager	Baudette	$1,320,000
7	BJ Francine	Sales Representative	Baudette	$1,768,000
8	Ari Aronson	Sales Trainee	Baudette	$409,500
9	Alec Mikayla	Sales Representative	Baudette	$935,000
10	**Baudette Sales**			**$7,097,000**
11	Suzanne Ouimet	Sales Manager	Breezy Point	$1,425,000
12	Sharon Wyatte	Sales Manager	Breezy Point	$1,425,000
13	Kendra Shelton	Sales Representative	Breezy Point	$1,350,000
14	Kendal Shaedon	Sales Representative	Breezy Point	$1,350,000
15	Frankie Dennis	Sales Representative	Breezy Point	$1,566,000
16	DJ Bushman	Sales Representative	Breezy Point	$1,768,000
17	Dennis Frankie	Sales Representative	Breezy Point	$1,566,000
18	**Breezy Point Sales**			**$10,450,000**
19	Randy Josephson	Sales Trainee	Cass Lake	$330,000
20	Mae Gomez	Sales Representative	Cass Lake	$1,330,000
21	Jeffery Dalton	Sales Manager	Cass Lake	$1,275,000
22	Corey Daniels	Sales Trainee	Cass Lake	$330,000
23	Christopher Bowman	Sales Manager	Cass Lake	$1,275,000
24	Chad Mei	Sales Representative	Cass Lake	$1,330,000
25	**Cass Lake Sales**			**$5,870,000**
26	Tammy Christine	Sales Representative	Walker	$9,275,000
27	Nikolai Jalowiec	Sales Manager	Walker	$1,260,000
28	Josie Daddiline	Sales Representative	Walker	$11,900,000
29	**Walker Sales**			**$22,435,000**

4-55 Data sorted by city with formulas after each city

4-56 *AutoOutline* with two levels

Define Groups

In addition to outlining data, you can create a group, by rows or columns, for data that does not have totals or formulas. To create a group, your data must be sorted or arranged so that you can select a range of cells to indicate the group, and you can insert a summary row either above or below the group (or a summary column to the left or right of the group). You can use these blank rows to enter subtitles for the data before or after grouping.

When you work with large numbers of records in a worksheet, you can use groups to hide data that is not needed at the moment. You can concentrate only on those groups that require editing or other work.

The data in Figure 4-57 is sorted by the "Title" column, so that groups can be created for each title. Note that a blank row has been inserted after each group.

	A	B	C	D
1		**Sales Table**		
2	**Name**	**Title**	**MN Location**	**Sales**
3	Ella Jamison	Sales Manager	Baudette	$1,320,000
4	David Gazik	Sales Manager	Baudette	$1,320,000
5	Suzanne Ouimet	Sales Manager	Breezy Point	$1,425,000
6	Sharon Wyatte	Sales Manager	Breezy Point	$1,425,000
7	Jeffery Dalton	Sales Manager	Cass Lake	$1,275,000
8	Christopher Bowman	Sales Manager	Cass Lake	$1,275,000
9	Nikolai Jalowiec	Sales Manager	Walker	$1,260,000
10				
11	Mikayla Anderson	Sales Representative	Baudette	$935,000
12	BJ Francine	S		$1,768,000
13	Alec Mikayla	S		$935,000
14	Kendra Shelton	S	oint	$1,350,000
15	Kendal Shaedon	S	oint	$1,350,000
16	Frankie Dennis	S	oint	$1,566,000
17	DJ Bushman	S	oint	$1,768,000
18	Dennis Frankie	S	oint	$1,566,000
19	Mae Gomez	Sales Representative	Cass Lake	$1,330,000
20	Chad Mei	Sales Representative	Cass Lake	$1,330,000
21	Tammy Christine	Sales Representative	Walker	$9,275,000
22	Josie Daddiline	Sales Representative	Walker	$11,900,000
23				
24	Natasha Ari	Sales Trainee	Baudette	$409,500
25	Ari Aronson	Sales Trainee	Baudette	$409,500
26	Randy Josephson	Sales Trainee	Cass Lake	$330,000
27	Corey Daniels	Sales Trainee	Cass Lake	$330,000

Group dialog box:
Group ? ×
Group
● Rows
○ Columns
OK   Cancel

4-57 Data sorted by Title; blank rows inserted after each title

HOW TO: Define a Group

1. Sort the data (or arrange columns) based on the preferred grouping.

2. Insert a blank row at the end of each sort group (or at the start of each group).

   • Include a blank row above the first group if you want to display a subtitle row for each group.
   • For column data, the summary column is usually to the right of the group.

3. Select a range of cells that includes each row (or column) of your first group.

   • Do not include the blank row or column.
   • You can select the entire range in the row or column.

4. Click the **Group** button [*Data* tab, *Outline* group].

5. Choose **Rows** or **Columns** (see Figure 4-57).

   • For example, you can create column groups for data that show 12 months in the header row to group them by quarters.

6. Click **OK**.

7. Repeat steps 1-6 for each group (Figure 4-58).

Outline levels

	A	B	C	D
1		**Sales Table**		
2	**Name**	**Title**	**MN Location**	**Sales**
3	Ella Jamison	Sales Manager	Baudette	$1,320,000
4	David Gazik	Sales Manager	Baudette	$1,320,000
5	Suzanne Ouimet	Sales Manager	Breezy Point	$1,425,000
6	Sharon Wyatte	Sales Manager	Breezy Point	$1,425,000
7	Jeffery Dalton	Sales Manager	Cass Lake	$1,275,000
8	Christopher Bowman	Sales Manager	Cass Lake	$1,275,000
9	Nikolai Jalowiec	Sales Manager	Walker	$1,260,000
10				
11	Mikayla Anderson	Sales Representative	Baudette	$935,000
12	BJ Francine	Sales Representative	Baudette	$1,768,000
13	Alec Mikayla	Sales Representative	Baudette	$935,000
14	Kendra Shelton	Sales Representative	Breezy Point	$1,350,000
15	Kendal Shaedon	Sales Representative	Breezy Point	$1,350,000
16	Frankie Dennis	Sales Representative	Breezy Point	$1,566,000
17	DJ Bushman	Sales Representative	Breezy Point	$1,768,000
18	Dennis Frankie	Sales Representative	Breezy Point	$1,566,000
19	Mae Gomez	Sales Representative	Cass Lake	$1,330,000
20	Chad Mei	Sales Representative	Cass Lake	$1,330,000
21	Tammy Christine	Sales Representative	Walker	$9,275,000
22	Josie Daddiline	Sales Representative	Walker	$11,900,000
23				
24	Natasha Ari	Sales Trainee	Baudette	$409,500
25	Ari Aronson	Sales Trainee	Baudette	$409,500
26	Randy Josephson	Sales Trainee	Cass Lake	$330,000
27	Corey Daniels	Sales Trainee	Cass Lake	$330,000
28				

Collapse button

4-58 Defined groups

PAUSE & PRACTICE: EXCEL 4-3

For this project, you sort and filter data for Paradise Lakes Resort. You sort data according to location and sales values and use a *Number Filter* to display the best sales. You also build an advanced filter and include subtotals in your workbook. Because the workbook has data connections, you must enable editing.

File Needed: *[your initials] PP E4-2.xlsx*
Completed Project File Name: *[your initials] PP E4-3.xlsx*

1. Open the *[your initials] PP E4-2* workbook. Click **Enable Editing**.

2. Save the workbook as *[your initials] PP E4-3*.

3. Click the **Sales Quota Data** sheet tab.

4. Convert a table to a normal data range.
   a. Click any cell in the table.
   b. Click to remove the check mark for **Total Row** [*Table Tools Design* tab, *Table Style options* group].
   c. Click the **Convert to Range** button [*Table Tools Design* tab, *Tools* group].
   d. Click **Yes**.
   e. Select cells **A2:E25** and apply **No Fill** [*Home* tab, *Font* group].

5. Sort data in a worksheet.
   a. Click any cell in the data range.
   b. Click the **Sort** button [*Data* tab, *Sort & Filter* group].
   c. Click the **My data has headers** check box if necessary.
   d. Click the **Sort by** arrow and select **MN Location**.
   e. Choose **Values** for *Sort On* and **A to Z** for *Order*.
   f. Click the **Add Level** button.
   g. Click the **Then by** arrow and select **Sales Goal**.
   h. Choose **Values** for *Sort On* and **Largest to Smallest** for *Order* (Figure 4-59).
   i. Click **OK**. The data is sorted alphabetically first by "MN Location" and then by "Sales Goal" numbers in descending order.

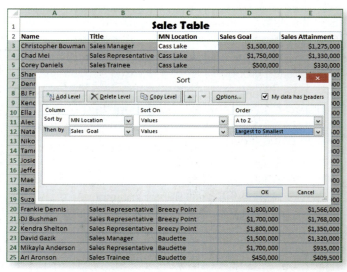

4-59 Multiple column sort with text and numeric data

6. Use a *Number AutoFilter*.
   a. Click any cell in the data range.
   b. Click the **Filter** button [*Data* tab, *Sort & Filter* group]. *AutoFilter* buttons appear with each label in the header row.
   c. Click the **AutoFilter** button for "Sales Attainment".
   d. Point at **Number Filters** and select **Greater Than Or Equal To**.
   e. In the **is greater than or equal to** text box, enter 1700000.
   f. Click **OK** (Figure 4-60).

	A	B	C	D	E
1			**Sales Table**		
2	Name ▼	Title ▼	MN Location ▼	Sales Goal ▼	Sales Attainment ⊤
3	BJ Francine	Sales Representative	Baudette	$1,700,000	$1,768,000
14	DJ Bushman	Sales Representative	Breezy Point	$1,700,000	$1,768,000
23	Tammy Christine	Sales Representative	Walker	$17,500,000	$9,275,000
24	Josie Daddiline	Sales Representative	Walker	$17,500,000	$11,900,000

4-60 *AutoFilter* results for Sales Attainment data greater than or equal to $1,700,000

7. Make a copy of the **Sales Quota Data** sheet to the right of the original.
   Hint: Right-click the worksheet tab.

8. Name the copied worksheet Advanced Filter.

9. Click the **Clear** button [*Data* tab, *Sort & Filter* group] to remove the filter.

10. Click the **Filter** button [*Data* tab, *Sort & Filter* group] to remove the *AutoFilter* buttons.

11. Create a criteria range and an extract range.
    a. Insert four rows above row 1.
    b. Select cells **A6:E6**. Copy and paste them in cells **A2:E2** and then in cells **A32:E32**.
    c. Type Criteria Area in cell **A1** and Extract Area in cell **A31**.
    d. Select **A5**, double-click the **Format Painter** button, and apply the formats to cells **A1** and **A31**. Click the **Format Painter** to turn it off.
    e. In cell **B3**, type Sales Trainee.
    f. In cell **E3**, type <400000.

12. Run an *Advanced Filter*.
    a. Click in **A7**.
    b. Click the **Advanced** button [*Data* tab, *Sort & Filter* group].
    c. Select the **Copy to another location** radio button.
    d. Verify that the correct data range is shown in the **List range** text box. If the data range is not correct, select cells **A6:E29**.
    e. Click in the **Criteria range** text box and select cells **A2:E3**.
    f. Click in the **Copy to** text box and select cells **A32:E32** (Figure 4-61).
    g. Click **OK**. Two records that meet the criteria, Corey Daniels and Randy Josephson, are displayed in rows 33:34.

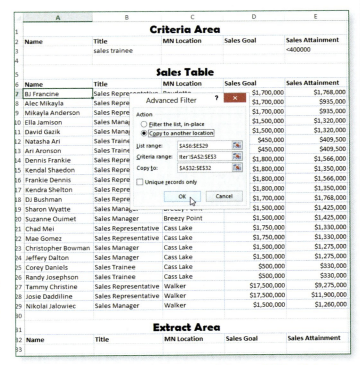

4-61 Criteria and extract ranges; *Advanced Filter* dialog box

13. Make a copy of the *Sales Quota Data* sheet to the right of the *Advanced Filter* sheet.

14. Name the copied worksheet Subtotals.

15. Click the **Clear** button [*Data* tab, *Sort & Filter* group] to remove the filter.

16. Click the **Filter** button [*Data* tab, *Sort & Filter* group] to remove the *AutoFilter* buttons.

17. Show subtotals in a list.
    a. Click a cell in the **Title** column and click the **Sort A to Z** button [*Data* tab, *Sort & Filter* group].
    b. Click the **Subtotal** button [*Data* tab, *Outline* group].
    c. Click the **At each change in** arrow and choose **Title**.
    d. Click the **Use function** arrow and choose **Average**.
    e. In the **Add subtotal to list** box, click to place check marks for **Sales Goal** and **Sales Attainment**.
    f. Click **OK** (Figure 4-62).

18. Save and close the workbook.

	A	B	C	D	E
1			**Sales Table**		
2	Name	Title	MN Location	Sales Goal	Sales Attainment
3	Ella Jamison	Sales Manager	Baudette	$1,500,000	$1,320,000
4	David Gazik	Sales Manager	Baudette	$1,500,000	$1,320,000
5	Sharon Wyatte	Sales Manager	Breezy Point	$1,500,000	$1,425,000
6	Suzanne Ouimet	Sales Manager	Breezy Point	$1,500,000	$1,425,000
7	Christopher Bowman	Sales Manager	Cass Lake	$1,500,000	$1,275,000
8	Jeffery Dalton	Sales Manager	Cass Lake	$1,500,000	$1,275,000
9	Nikolai Jalowiec	Sales Manager	Walker	$1,500,000	$1,260,000
10		**Sales Manager Average**		$1,500,000	$1,328,571
11	BJ Francine	Sales Representative	Baudette	$1,700,000	$1,768,000
12	Alec Mikayla	Sales Representative	Baudette	$1,700,000	$935,000
13	Mikayla Anderson	Sales Representative	Baudette	$1,700,000	$935,000
14	Dennis Frankie	Sales Representative	Breezy Point	$1,800,000	$1,566,000
15	Kendal Shaedon	Sales Representative	Breezy Point	$1,800,000	$1,350,000
16	Frankie Dennis	Sales Representative	Breezy Point	$1,800,000	$1,566,000
17	Kendra Shelton	Sales Representative	Breezy Point	$1,800,000	$1,350,000
18	DJ Bushman	Sales Representative	Breezy Point	$1,700,000	$1,768,000
19	Chad Mei	Sales Representative	Cass Lake	$1,750,000	$1,330,000
20	Mae Gomez	Sales Representative	Cass Lake	$1,750,000	$1,330,000
21	Tammy Christine	Sales Representative	Walker	$17,500,000	$9,275,000
22	Josie Daddiline	Sales Representative	Walker	$17,500,000	$11,900,000
23		**Sales Representative Average**		$4,375,000	$2,922,750
24	Natasha Ari	Sales Trainee	Baudette	$450,000	$409,500
25	Ari Aronson	Sales Trainee	Baudette	$450,000	$409,500
26	Corey Daniels	Sales Trainee	Cass Lake	$500,000	$330,000
27	Randy Josephson	Sales Trainee	Cass Lake	$500,000	$330,000
28		**Sales Trainee Average**		$475,000	$369,750
29		**Grand Average**		$2,821,739	$1,993,565

4-62 Completed PP E4-3 worksheet with subtotals

Applying Conditional Formatting

Conditional Formatting commands apply specified formats to cells only when the cells meet some criteria. You can use *Conditional Formatting* to highlight information in a worksheet by setting different fill colors or font styles for selected cells. For example, a sales manager might use *Conditional Formatting* to display sales amounts that are below a certain level in a bold red font.

Conditional Formatting is dynamic; the formatting adapts if the data changes. In our sales example, if sales values are updated and a particular person or department that was below the specified level has now met a goal, the bold red formatting is removed.

Basic *Conditional Formatting* commands are *Highlight Cells Rules* and *Top/Bottom Rules*. For these commands, you set the rule or criteria in a dialog box and choose the format. Another type of *Conditional Formatting* is **data visualization,** in which specified data is indicated with a fill color, a horizontal bar, or an icon within the cell. *Data visualization* commands include *Data Bars, Color Scales,* and *Icon Sets.*

Cells Rules

Highlight Cells Rules uses relational or comparison operators to determine if the value or label in a cell should be formatted. *Highlight Cells Rules* includes common operators such as *Equal to* and *Greater Than.* You can also create your own rule using other operators or a formula.

You can access all of the conditional formatting options from the *Conditional Formatting* button in the *Styles* group on the *Home* tab (Figure 4-63). You can also choose a recommended conditional formatting style from the *Quick Analysis* tool options.

4-63 *Highlight Cells Rules* menu

HOW TO: Create a "Less Than" Highlight Cells Rule

1. Select the cell range to be formatted.
2. Click the **Conditional Formatting** button [*Home* tab, *Styles* group].
3. Click **Highlight Cells Rules** and select **Less Than**.
4. In the *Format cells that are LESS THAN* box, type a value. If the number in a cell is below this value, the cell will be conditionally formatted.
   - You can click a cell in the worksheet to enter a value.
5. Click the arrow in the *with* entry box and choose a preset option (Figure 4-64).
   - Alternatively, you can choose *Custom Format* to open the *Format Cells* dialog box and build a custom format.
6. Click **OK**.

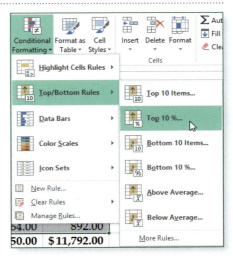

4-64 *Less Than* dialog box

Top/Bottom Rules use a ranking to format the highest (top) or lowest (bottom) items or a specified percentage of a list. You can also set a rule to format values that are above or below average (Figure 4-65). You are not limited to the percentages or numbers shown in the menu.

When you select a range of values, the *Quick Analysis* tool appears in the bottom right corner of the range. The *Totals* group typically provides likely conditional format choices. When you make your choice this way, the same dialog box opens so that you can build the format.

4-65 *Top/Bottom Rules*

HOW TO: Create a Top 10% Rule

1. Select the cell range you want to format.
2. Click the **Quick Analysis** button.
3. Click **Formatting** and choose **Top 10%** (Figure 4-66).
4. Click the arrow for the *with* box and choose **Custom Format**.
5. Click the appropriate tab to set a fill color, a font, or a border.
6. Click **OK** to close the *Format Cells* dialog box.
7. Click **OK** to close the *Top 10%* dialog box.

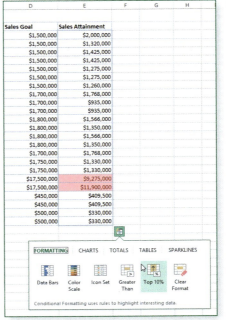

4-66 *Quick Analysis* options for conditional formatting

If you cannot find a *Highlight Cells* or *Top/Bottom* rule that fits your needs, create your own rule using operators, criteria, and formats in the *New Formatting Rule* dialog box. Options in this dialog box allow you to create a rule based on a formula as well. You can, for example, build a rule to format only cells that display a particular percentage of a specified value, such as sales that are 108% of the sales goal.

HOW TO: Create a New Conditional Formatting Rule

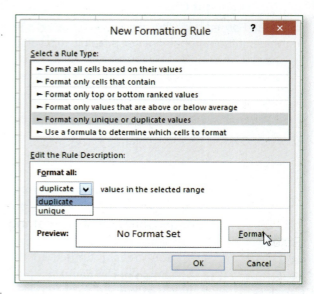

1. Select the cell range to be formatted.
2. Click the **Conditional Formatting** button [*Home* tab, *Styles* group].
3. Click **New Rule** to open the *New Formatting Rule* dialog box (Figure 4-67).
4. Select a rule type from the *Select a Rule Type* list.
5. In the *Edit the Rule Description* area, make choices to build the new rule.
   - The options that are available depend on the type of rule.
   - Click **Format** (when available) to set the format in the *Format Cells* dialog box.
   - Click **OK** to close the *Format Cells* dialog box.
6. Click **OK** to close the *New Formatting Rule* dialog box.

4-67 *New Formatting Rule* **dialog box**

Data Bars, Color Scales, and Icon Sets

Excel's data visualization *Conditional Formatting* commands format cells with icons, cell shading, or shaded bars to distinguish the values. They generally highlight the low, middle, or top values or compare the values to each other.

You can access the *Conditional Formatting* button in the *Styles* group on the *Home* tab, or the *Quick Analysis* tool. When you use the *Quick Analysis* tool, a default data bar (or other format) is applied. You can edit it by choosing a different color or style from the *Conditional Formatting* button menu.

HOW TO: Format Data with Data Bars

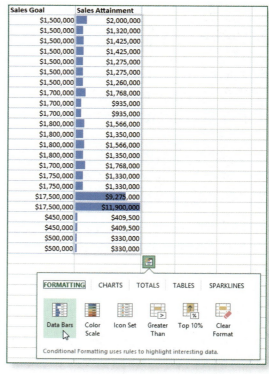

1. Select the cell range you want to format.
2. Click the **Quick Analysis** button.
3. Click **Formatting** and choose **Data Bars** (Figure 4-68).
   - A default data bar style and color are applied.
   - The length of the data bars compares the value in each cell to the other values in the selected cell range.
   - *Color Scales* use a variation of two or three colors to indicate low, middle, and high values.
   - *Icon Sets* inserts icons that represent the upper, middle, or lower values of the cell range.

4-68 *Conditional Formatting: Data Bars*

E4-220

Manage Conditional Formatting Rules

To edit, delete, or review any *Conditional Formatting* rule, use the **Manage Rules** command. You can update the range to be formatted, edit the actual format, or change the rule.

In the *Conditional Formatting Rules Manager* dialog box, you can choose to display all the rules in the worksheet or rules from other sheets in the workbook. If you choose a cell range before you give the command, the rule for the *Current Selection* is shown (Figure 4-69).

When you click **Edit Rule**, the *Edit Formatting Rule* dialog box opens. This dialog box is very similar to the *New Formatting Rule* dialog box, and you make your changes in the same way.

4-69 *Conditional Formatting Rules Manager* dialog box

HOW TO: Manage Conditional Formatting Rules

1. Click the **Conditional Formatting** button [*Home* tab, *Styles* group].
2. Choose **Manage Rules**.
3. In the *Show formatting rules for* list, make a choice.
   - If you selected a cell range, the option is *Current Selection*.
   - Choose **This Worksheet** if you did not select a range or want to see all rules in the worksheet.
4. Select the rule to edit.
5. Click **Edit Rule**.
6. In the *Select a Rule Type* list, choose another type if needed.
7. In the *Edit the Rule Description* area, make choices to change the rule.
   - The choices depend on the rule type (Figure 4-70).
   - Click **Format** when it is an option and make changes in the *Format Cells* dialog box.
8. Click **OK** to close the *Edit Formatting Rule* dialog box.
9. Click **OK** to close the *Conditional Formatting Rules Manager* dialog box and apply the change.

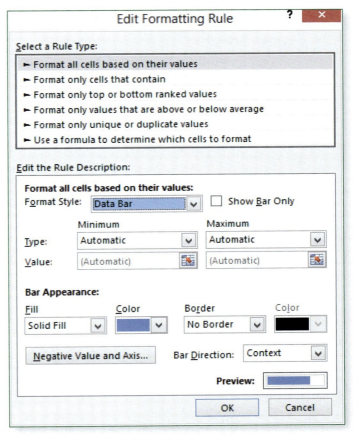

4-70 *Edit Formatting Rule* dialog box for data bars

Clear Conditional Formatting Rules

You can clear rules from a selected cell range or from an entire sheet. Access the **Clear Rules** option by clicking the *Conditional Formatting* button in the *Styles* group on the *Home* tab. For a selected range, you can click the **Quick Analysis** button and choose **Clear Format**.

HOW TO: Clear All Rules

1. Click the **Conditional Formatting** button [*Home* tab, *Styles* group].
2. Choose **Clear Rules**.
3. Click **Clear Rules from Entire Sheet** (Figure 4-71).

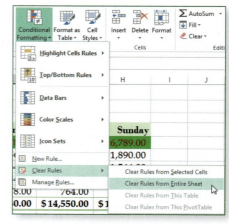

4-71 Clear Rules options

SLO 4.7

Using Goal Seek and Worksheet Protection

Goal Seek is one type of what-if analysis. It allows you to test values in a cell to "backsolve" a formula. *Backsolving* means knowing the desired results and determining the value needed to reach those results. For example, if you can afford to pay $500 per month for a new car, you can use *Goal Seek* to determine how much you can borrow and end up with a $500 per month car payment.

Worksheet protection allows you to set which cells can be edited in a worksheet. When you share work with others, worksheet protection can safeguard your work from accidental changes by others.

Use Goal Seek

Goal Seek solves a formula for one cell (one argument) in the formula. In the *Goal Seek* dialog box, you enter the cell reference for the formula in the *Set cell* text box. You type a target or goal number in the *To value* text box. For example, in Figure 4-72, an organization is solving the *PMT* function so that it results in a payment of $2,200. *Goal Seek* adjusts the interest rate (cell B6) to determine the desired payment.

You can access *Goal Seek* from the *What-if Analysis* button in the *Data Tools* group on the *Data* tab. The solution appears in the *Goal Seek Status* dialog box. You can click **OK** to accept the solution or keep the original value by clicking **Cancel**.

HOW TO: Use Goal Seek

1. Click the cell with the formula to be solved.
2. Click the **What-if Analysis** button [*Data* tab, *Data Tools* group].
3. Choose **Goal Seek**.
4. Verify the formula cell address in the *Set cell* text box.
5. Click in the *To value* text box and type in your desired formula result.
6. Click in the *By changing cell* text box and click the cell that can be adjusted (Figure 4-72).
   - In Figure 4-72, the interest rate is chosen as the value that can be adjusted.
   - *Goal Seek* can change only one cell.
   - You can key the cell reference instead of selecting the cell.
7. Click **OK**.
   - The solution is shown in the *Goal Seek Status* dialog box (Figure 4-73).
   - The solution is displayed in the cell in the worksheet.

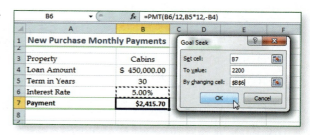

4-72 Goal Seek dialog box

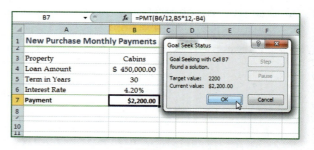

4-73 Goak Seek Status dialog box

8. Click **OK** to accept the solution.
   - You can press **Enter** to accept the solution.
   - Choose **Cancel** to ignore the solution.

Worksheet Protection

Worksheet protection is a good way to prohibit changes to your work. It employs the *Locked* cell property. This property is active for all cells in a worksheet by default. However, it has no effect until you set worksheet protection. If you set worksheet protection, no editing is possible in the sheet. When you protect a worksheet, you need to select the cells that can still be edited and disable the *Locked* property. Typically, you do this before protecting the sheet.

Unlock Worksheet Cells

When you protect a sheet, you or others may still want to edit some cells in the worksheet. In an inventory worksheet, for example, you need to update item counts, but you don't need to change the product name or code. In a protected inventory worksheet, you can unlock the item-count cells so that their values can be changed while the other values and codes cannot be edited.

The *Locked* property is on the *Protection* tab in the *Format Cells* dialog box. Open the dialog box from the *Format* button

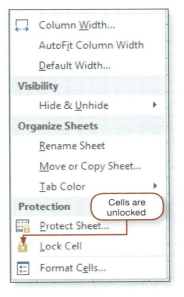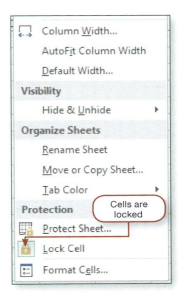

4-74 *Locked* property off and on

on the *Home* tab [*Cells* group] or by pressing **Ctrl+1**. Alternatively, you can toggle the *Locked* property on and off from the *Format* button menu. When a cell is locked, the command in the menu shows an outline; when a cell is unlocked, there is no outline (Figure 4-74).

HOW TO: Unlock Cells for Editing

1. Select the cell(s) that you still want to be able to edit.
2. Right-click a selected cell.
3. Choose **Format Cells**.
4. Click the **Protection** tab.
5. Click the **Locked** check box to remove the check mark (Figure 4-75).
6. Click **OK**.

4-75 *Format Cells* dialog box; *Protection* tab

Protect a Worksheet

The *Protect Worksheet* command includes a list of editing options that you can allow for locked cells. For example, you can allow users to select cells, but they will not be able to edit them. Or you can give users permission to format cells or to insert or delete rows or columns.

As you set worksheet protection, you can also set a password. Once this added security is enforced, all users must enter the password before they can edit anything in the worksheet. Once the password is entered, the protection is removed.

The *Protect Sheet* button is in the *Changes* group on the *Review* tab. This button is a toggle; when a worksheet is protected, it becomes the *Unprotect Sheet* button. You can also protect a worksheet from the *Format* button [*Home* tab, *Cells* group] (see Figure 4-74).

HOW TO: Protect a Worksheet

1. Unlock the cells that you want to still be able to edit.
2. Click the **Protect Sheet** button [*Review* tab, *Changes* group].
3. Check the commands that should still be available after protection is set.
4. Type a password if desired.
   - You see a placeholder as you type a password (Figure 4-76).
   - A second message box requires that you rekey the password.
   - Passwords are case sensitive.
5. Click **OK**.

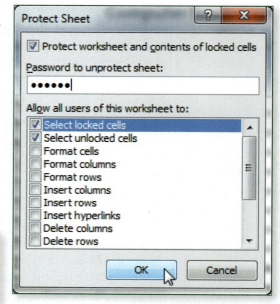

4-76 *Protect Sheet* dialog box

Unprotect a Worksheet

If you try to edit a cell in a protected sheet, a message box tells you that the sheet is protected (Figure 4-77). When a worksheet is protected, it cannot be edited until the protection is removed. If there is no password, you just need to click the **Unprotect Sheet** button.

4-77 Message window for a protected sheet

When a password has been set, you need to enter the password to remove the protection.

The *Unprotect Sheet* button is in the *Changes* group on the *Review* tab. If a password has been used, a message box for entering the password appears (Figure 4-78).

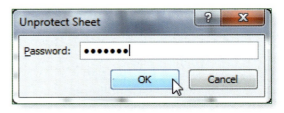

4-78 *Unprotect Sheet* dialog box

HOW TO: Unprotect a Worksheet

1. Click the **Unprotect Sheet** button [*Review* tab, *Changes* group].
2. Type the password if necessary and click **OK**.

PAUSE & PRACTICE: EXCEL 4-4

For this project, you set conditional formatting using data bars in Paradise Lakes Resort's workbook. You use *Goal Seek* to calculate a possible sales amount for one of the representatives so that average sales can reach a particular goal. Finally, you protect the worksheet but allow editing to the attainment figures.

File Needed: ***[your initials] PP E 4-3.xlsx***
Completed Project File Name: ***[your initials] PP E4-4.xlsx***

1. Open the ***[your initials] PP E4-3*** workbook. Enable editing.
2. Save the workbook as ***[your initials] PP E4-4***.
3. Click the **Sales Quota Data** sheet tab.
4. Click the **Filter** button [*Data* tab, *Sort & Filter* group] to remove the filter.
5. Apply *Conditional Formatting* using *Highlight Cells Rules*.
    a. Select cells **D3:D25**.
    b. Click the **Quick Analysis** button and choose **Formatting**.
    c. Choose **Greater Than**.
    d. Type 2000000.
    e. Select **Green Fill with Dark Green Text** from the *with* drop-down list.
    f. Click **OK**.
    g. Select cells **B3:B25**.
    h. Click the **Quick Analysis** button and choose **Formatting**.
    i. Choose **Text Contains**.
    j. Type sales trainee.
    k. Select **Light Red Fill with Dark Red Text**.
    l. Click **OK**.
6. Apply *Conditional Formatting* using *Data Bars*.
    a. Select cells **E3:E25**.
    b. Click the **Quick Analysis** button and choose **Formatting**.
    c. Choose **Data Bars**.

7. Manage *Conditional Formatting* rules.
   a. Select cells **E3:E25**.
   b. Click the **Conditional Formatting** button [*Home* tab, *Styles* group].
   c. Choose **Manage Rules**.
   d. Click **Edit Rule**.
   e. Click the **Fill** arrow and choose **Gradient Fill** (Figure 4-79).
   f. Click the **Color** arrow; choose **Gold**, **Accent 3**.
   g. Click **OK** to close the *Edit Formatting Rule* dialog box.
   h. Click **OK** to close the *Conditional Formatting Rules Manager*.

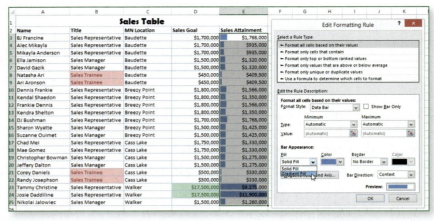

4-79 Edited rule for data bars

8. Click the **Subtotals** sheet tab.

9. Use Goal Seek.
   a. Click cell **E10**.
   b. Click the **What-if Analysis** button [*Data* tab, *Data Tools* group].
   c. Select **Goal Seek**.
   d. Type 1500000 in the *To value* box.
   e. Click in the *By changing cell* box and click cell **E5**. This finds a value for Sharon Wyatte's sales that would result in average sales of $1,500,000.
   f. Click **OK** to run *Goal Seek* (Figure 4-80). Sharon's new sales would have to reach $2,625,000.
   g. Click **OK** to accept the solution.

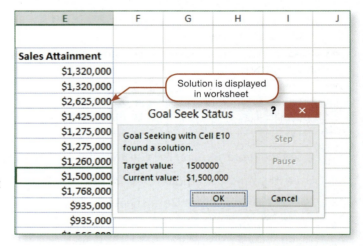

4-80 *Goal Seek* solution

10. Click the **Sales Quota Data** sheet tab.

11. Protect a worksheet with a password.
    a. Select cells **E3:E25**.
    b. Right-click a selected cell.
    c. Choose **Format Cells** from the menu.
    d. Click the **Protection** tab.
    e. Click to remove the check mark for **Locked**.
    f. Click **OK**.
    g. Click the **Protect Sheet** button [*Review* tab, *Changes* group].
    h. Show check marks for **Select locked cells** and **Select unlocked cells**.
    i. Type the password 123 and click **OK**.
    j. Retype the password and click **OK**.

12. Save and close the workbook (Figure 4-81).

	A	B	C	D	E
1			Sales Table		
2	Name	Title	MN Location	Sales Goal	Sales Attainment
3	BJ Francine	Sales Representative	Baudette	$1,700,000	$1,768,000
4	Alec Mikayla	Sales Representative	Baudette	$1,700,000	$935,000
5	Mikayla Anderson	Sales Representative	Baudette	$1,700,000	$935,000
6	Ella Jamison	Sales Manager	Baudette	$1,500,000	$1,320,000
7	David Gazik	Sales Manager	Baudette	$1,500,000	$1,320,000
8	Natasha Ari	Sales Trainee	Baudette	$450,000	$409,500
9	Ari Aronson	Sales Trainee	Baudette	$450,000	$409,500
10	Dennis Frankie	Sales Representative	Breezy Point	$1,800,000	$1,566,000
11	Kendal Shaedon	Sales Representative	Breezy Point	$1,800,000	$1,350,000
12	Frankie Dennis	Sales Representative	Breezy Point	$1,800,000	$1,566,000
13	Kendra Shelton	Sales Representative	Breezy Point	$1,800,000	$1,350,000
14	DJ Bushman	Sales Representative	Breezy Point	$1,700,000	$1,768,000
15	Sharon Wyatte	Sales Manager	Breezy Point	$1,500,000	$1,425,000
16	Suzanne Ouimet	Sales Manager	Breezy Point	$1,500,000	$1,425,000
17	Chad Mei	Sales Representative	Cass Lake	$1,750,000	$1,330,000
18	Mae Gomez	Sales Representative	Cass Lake	$1,750,000	$1,330,000
19	Christopher Bowman	Sales Manager	Cass Lake	$1,500,000	$1,275,000
20	Jeffery Dalton	Sales Manager	Cass Lake	$1,500,000	$1,275,000
21	Corey Daniels	Sales Trainee	Cass Lake	$500,000	$330,000
22	Randy Josephson	Sales Trainee	Cass Lake	$500,000	$330,000
23	Tammy Christine	Sales Representative	Walker	$17,500,000	$9,275,000
24	Josie Daddiline	Sales Representative	Walker	$17,500,000	$11,900,000
25	Nikolai Jalowiec	Sales Manager	Walker	$1,500,000	$1,260,000

4-81 Completed PP E4-4 worksheet

Chapter Summary

4.1 Import data into Excel from a text file, database file, or web site and use *Flash Fill* and data connections (p. E4-187).

- You can **import** text files in Excel including *.txt* (text) documents, *.csv* (comma separated values) files, and *.prn* (printer) files.
- The *From Text* button is in the *Get External Data* group on the *Data* tab.
- The **Text Import Wizard** guides you through the steps of importing the data.
- You can import data from a Word document and tables and queries in a Microsoft Access database into a worksheet.
- You can import table-formatted data on a web site into a worksheet using the *From Web* button on the *Data* tab.
- Imported data establishes a data connection in the workbook.
- The **Flash Fill** command copies your typing actions from nearby cells.

4.2 Create and format an Excel table and a *PivotTable*, and export data for use in other programs (p. E4-194).

- There are several methods for sorting, filtering, and calculating rows of data in Excel **tables**.
- Data that is set up like a list with a header row and the same type of data in each column can be formatted as a table.
- Create a table by clicking the **Format as Table** button in the *Styles* group on the *Home* tab or by clicking the **Quick Analysis** tool and choosing **Tables**.
- An **AutoFilter** button accompanies each label in the header row of an Excel table.
- When any cell in a table is selected, the *Table Tools Design* tab is available.
- Apply a table style by clicking the **More** button in the *Table Styles* group on the *Table Tools Design* tab.
- Save a customized table style with the *New Table Style* button in the *Table Styles* gallery in the *Table Styles* group on the *Table Tools Design* tab.
- **Table Tools** include commands to remove duplicate rows and to convert a table to a normal cell range. The *Tools* group is on the *Table Tools Design* tab.

- An Excel table is named and uses structured references (names) for each column and other predefined parts.
- A **PivotTable** is a summary report based on a cell range in the worksheet.
- For a selected cell range, use the *Recommended PivotTables* button on the *Insert* tab in the *Tables* group.
- In a *PivotTable*, fields can be repositioned to display different views of the data.
- Use the *PivotTable Fields* pane to reposition fields in a *PivotTable* report.
- Use the **Export** command in the *Backstage* view to save data in a different format.

4.3 Sort data by text, number, color, or icon (p. E4-205).

- List-type data can be sorted alphabetically or by value by one or more columns.
- Sorts can be in **ascending** order (A to Z) or **descending** (Z to A).
- Values can be sorted from smallest to largest (A to Z) or largest to smallest (Z to A).
- To sort a single column, use the *Sort A to Z* or *Sort Z to A* button in the *Sort & Filter* group on the *Data* tab.
- To sort by multiple columns, open the *Sort* dialog box by clicking the **Sort** button on the *Data* tab.
- In the *Sort* dialog box, you can choose to sort by font color, cell color, or cell icon when this type of formatting is used in the data.

4.4 Apply an *AutoFilter* or an *Advanced Filter* to data (p. E4-209).

- The **AutoFilter** command displays an *AutoFilter* button arrow in each column heading.
- Click the **AutoFilter** button to select which records are shown or hidden.
- You can build a custom *AutoFilter* using operators such as *Equals*. There are different operators for text, number, and date filters.
- An **Advanced Filter** provides sophisticated filter options such as using a formula in the filter definition.
- An *Advanced Filter* requires a criteria range in the same workbook to define the criteria.
- An *Advanced Filter* can show the filtered results separate from the actual data.
- The *Advanced* button is in the *Sort & Filter* group on the *Data* tab.

4.5 Use the *Subtotal* command and create groups and outlines (p. E4-212).

- The **Subtotal** command inserts summary rows using a function such as *SUM*, *AVERAGE*, *MAX*, or *MIN* in a normal cell range.
- The *Subtotal* command requires that the data be sorted by at least one column.
- The *Subtotal* command formats the results as an **outline**. An outline groups records so that they can be displayed or hidden.
- The *Subtotal* button is in the *Outline* group on the *Data* tab.
- The **Auto Outline** command creates groups based on formulas that are located in a consistent pattern in the data.
- The *Auto Outline* command is available from the *Group* button in the *Outline* group on the *Data* tab.
- You can manually define groups by sorting the data and using the *Group* button in the *Outline* group on the *Data* tab.

4.6 Apply and manage *Conditional Formatting* using cell rules, *Color Scales*, *Icon Sets*, and *Data Bars* (p. E4-218).

- **Conditional Formatting** formats only cells that meet specified criteria.
- Cells rules formatting uses relational or comparison operators such as *Greater Than* or *Equals*.
- In the rule dialog box, you define the rule and choose the format.
- You can create your own conditional formatting rule as well as edit existing rules with the **Manage Rules** command.

- Conditional formatting commands include *Icon Sets*, *Color Scales*, and *Data Bars*.
- An icon, color, or data bar represents a value in relation to other values in the range.
- You can **Clear Rules** from a selected cell range or from an entire sheet.

4.7 Use *Goal Seek* and protect a worksheet (p. E4-222).

- **Goal Seek** is a command that finds a solution for one of the arguments in a formula.
- In a *Goal Seek* command, you set the desired result for the formula to a value and find out how to arrive at that result by changing one cell.
- The *Goal Seek* command is part of the **What-If Analysis** button options on the *Data* tab.
- Worksheet protection is a first step in prohibiting unwanted changes to your work.
- The *Protect Sheet* button is in the *Changes* group in the *Review* tab; it is the *Unprotect Sheet* button when the worksheet is protected.
- To allow cell editing in a protected worksheet, you must disable or remove the *Locked* property for the cells you want to be able to edit.
- The *Locked* property is toggled off and on in the *Format Cells* dialog box on the *Protection* tab.
- Worksheet protection can be set with or without a password.
- Worksheet protection must be removed or turned off before the worksheet can be edited.

Check for Understanding

On the **Online Learning Center** for this text (www.mhhe.com/office2013inpractice), there are a variety of resources that can be used to review the concepts covered in this chapter.

The following Online Learning Resources are available on the Online Learning Center:

- Multiple choice questions
- Short answer questions
- Matching exercises

Guided Project 4-1

For this project you import supplier data in a text file into the inventory worksheet for Wear-Ever Shoes. You use *Flash Fill* to enter product codes and sort the data by supplier and code. You use *AutoFilter* for several tasks, use the *Subtotal* command, and work with *Goal Seek*. Finally, you protect one of the sheets in the workbook.
[Student Learning Outcomes 4.1, 4.3, 4.4, 4.5, 4.7]

Files Needed: ***WearEverInventory-04.xlsx*** and ***Suppliers-04.txt***
Completed Project File Name: ***[your initials] Excel 4-1.xlsx***

Skills Covered in This Project

- Import a text file.
- Use *Flash Fill*.
- Sort data.
- Use an *AutoFilter*.
- Create and copy a formula.

- Insert columns.
- Use the *Subtotal* command.
- Use *Goal Seek*.
- Copy and move a worksheet.
- Protect a worksheet without a password.

---

1. Open the ***WearEverInventory-04*** workbook from your student data files folder. Click the **Enable Editing** button.

2. Save the workbook as ***[your initials] Excel 4-1***.

3. Import a text file.
   a. Select cell **J4**.
   b. Click the **From Text** button [*Data* tab, *Get External Data* group].
   c. Find and select the ***Suppliers-04.txt*** file in the *Import Text File* window.
   d. Click **Import**.
   e. Select the **Delimited** button in the first *Wizard* window. Excel recognizes that this file separates the data into columns with a tab character.
   f. Click **Next**.
   g. Click to place a check mark for **Tab** if necessary.
   h. Click **Next**.
   i. Click **Finish**.
   j. Click **OK**.
   k. Use the **Format Painter** button to copy formatting from **I4** to **J4:K4**.
   l. *AutoFit* columns **J:K**.

4. Use *Flash Fill* to insert a product code.
   a. Insert a column between columns **B** and **C**.
   b. Type Code in cell **C4**.
   c. Type RHB in cell **C5**.
   d. Type r and press **Enter** in cell **C6**.

e. Type r and press **Enter** in cell **C7**. *AutoFill* completes the entries based on what is already in the column. The *Flash Fill* suggestion list does not appear because you did not type a second item to identify the pattern.

f. Click the **Fill** button [*Home* tab, *Editing* group].

g. Choose **Flash Fill**.

h. *AutoFit* column **C**.

5. Sort data in multiple columns.

a. Click any cell in cells **A5:L40**.

b. Click the **Sort** button [*Data* tab, *Sort & Filter* group].

c. Click the **My data has headers** check box if necessary.

d. Click the **Sort by** arrow and choose **Supplier**.

e. Check that **Sort On** is **Values** and **Order** is **A to Z**.

f. Click **Add Level**.

g. Click the **Then by** arrow and choose **Code**.

h. Check that **Sort On** is **Values** and **Order** is **A to Z**.

i. Click **OK** (Figure 4-82).

6. Use an *AutoFilter*.

a. Click any cell in cells **A5:L40**.

b. Click the **Filter** button [*Data* tab, *Sort & Filter* group].

c. Click the **AutoFilter** button for **Supplier** column.

d. Click **(Select All)** to remove all the check marks.

e. Click **Jennifer's Closet** to place a check mark for only that supplier.

f. Click **OK**. The data is filtered to show only records from one supplier.

7. Copy the *Northern Warehouse* worksheet.

a. Name the copied sheet Subtotals.

b. Move the *Subtotals* sheet to the right of the *Northern Warehouse* sheet.

8. Use the *Subtotal* command.

a. Click cell **K5** in the *Subtotals* sheet.

b. Click the **Filter** button [*Data* tab, *Sort & Filter* group] to remove the filter.

c. Click the **Subtotal** button [*Data* tab, *Outline* group].

d. Click the **At each change in** arrow and choose **Supplier**.

e. Click the **Use function** arrow and choose **Count**.

f. Check the **Supplier** box in the *Add subtotal to* area and remove check marks for all other fields (Figure 4-83).

g. Click **OK**. A subtotal row is inserted at the bottom of each group and shows how many products are available from each supplier.

h. Format the label in cell **J17** as **right-aligned**.

i. **Right-align** the remaining subtotal labels in column **J** (Figure 4-84).

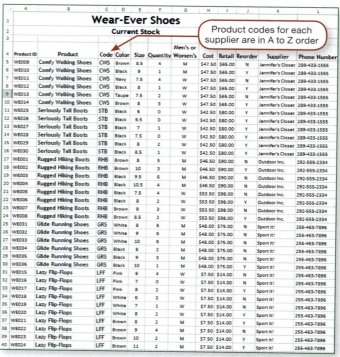

4-82 Data sorted by "Supplier" and "Code"

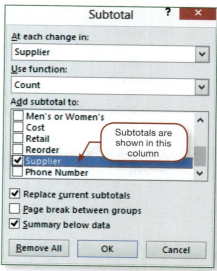

4-83 *Subtotal* dialog box to count the number of products by supplier

9. Copy the **Subtotals** sheet, name it Goal Seek, and move it to the right of the *Subtotals* sheet.

10. Prepare a *Goal Seek* worksheet.
    a. Click cell **K5** in the **Goal Seek** sheet.
    b. Click the **Subtotals** button [*Data* tab, *Outline* group].
    c. Click **Remove All** in the *Subtotal* dialog box.
    d. Insert a column between columns **I** and **J**. Type Margin in cell **J4**. Increase the width of column **J** to **7.43**.
    e. Type the profit margin formula in cell **J5** =(I5-H5)/H5 and press **Enter**. The profit margin subtracts the unit cost from the retail price and divides those results by the cost.
    f. Since the result is a percentage, format the results in cell **J5** as **Percent Style** with no decimals.
    g. Copy the formula in cell **J5** to cells **J6:J40**.
    h. Click the **Filter** button [*Data* tab, *Sort & Filter* group].
    i. Click the **AutoFilter** button for the **Margin** column.
    j. Click **(Select All)** to remove all the check marks.
    k. Click **37%** to place a check mark for that profit margin.
    l. Click **OK**. The data is filtered to show only the rows with the lowest profit margin.

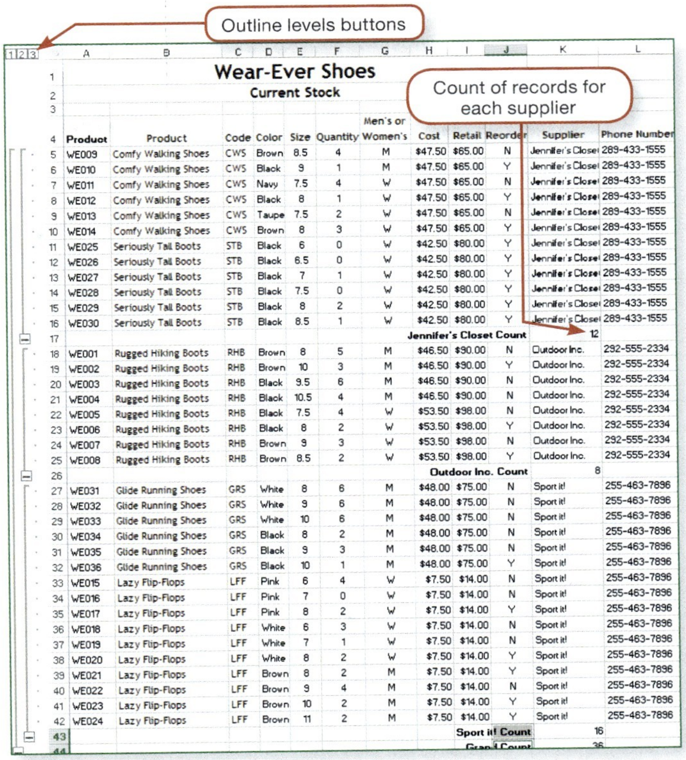

11. Use *Goal Seek*.
    a. Type New Retail Price to Reach 55% Margin in cell **N6** and make it **bold**.
    b. Click cell **J5**.
    c. Click the **What-If Analysis** button [*Data* tab, *Data Tools* group] and choose **Goal Seek**.
    d. In the *To value* box, type 55%.
    e. In the *By changing cell* box, click cell **I5** (Figure 4-85).
    f. Click **OK** to view the solution in cell **I5**.
    g. Make a note of the results and click **Cancel**.
    h. Click cell **O7** and type $73.63.

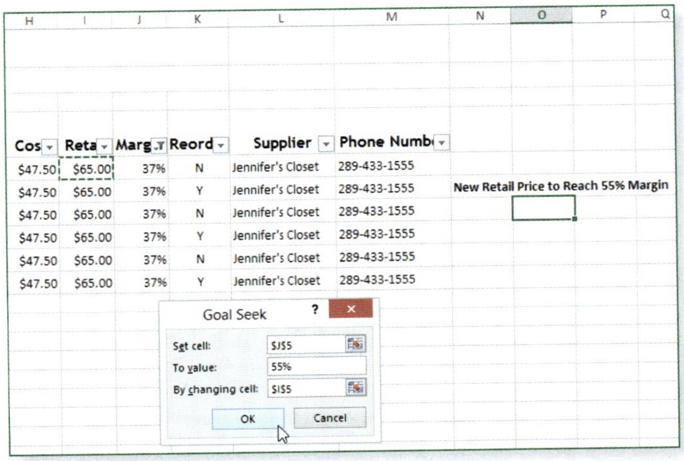

12. Protect a worksheet without a password.
    a. Click the **Subtotals** sheet tab.
    b. Click the **Protect Sheet** button [*Review* tab, *Changes* group].
    c. Verify that there are check marks for **Select locked cells** and **Select unlocked cells**.
    d. Click **OK**.

4-84 Subtotals inserted for each group

4-85 *Goal Seek* to find new retail price

13. Save and close the workbook (Figure 4-86).

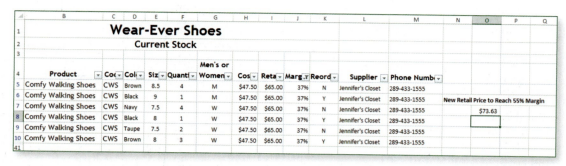

4-86 Excel 4-1 completed worksheets

Guided Project 4-2

Classic Gardens and Landscapes is building a workbook with data about sales revenue and recent promotion campaigns. You copy some data from Word and import other data from an Access database. You also use *Conditional Formatting* and create tables.
[Student Learning Outcomes 4.1, 4.2, 4.4, 4.5, 4.6]

Files Needed: ***ClassicGardensRevenue-04.xlsx***, ***SalesDatabase-04.accdb***, and ***ClassicGardensWord-04.docx***
Completed Project File Name: ***[your initials] Excel 4-2.xlsx***

Skills Covered in This Project

- Copy data from Word.
- Apply *Conditional Formatting* using an icon set.
- Import a table from a database file.
- Apply a table style.
- Insert a total row in a table.
- Use the *SUM* function.

- Insert a column.
- Copy a formula.
- Create an *Auto Outline*.
- Create a *PivotTable*.
- Set a report filter in a *PivotTable*.
- Move fields in a *PivotTable*.

---

1. Open the **ClassicGardensRevenue-04** workbook from your student data files folder. Click the **Enable Editing** button.

2. Save the workbook as **[your initials] Excel 4-2**.

3. Click the **Quarterly** sheet tab.

4. Insert six columns between columns **G** and **H**.

5. Copy data from Word.
   a. Open the Word document **ClassicGardensWord-04** from your student data files folder. Click the **Enable Editing** button.
   b. Select all the data in Word and copy it.
   c. Return to the Excel workbook.
   d. Click cell **H4**.
   e. Click the **Paste** button arrow [*Home* tab, *Clipboard* group] and choose **Match Destination Formatting**.
   f. Select cells **N5:N10** and click the *AutoSum* button [*Home* tab, *Editing* group].
   g. Select cells **B10:M10** and sum the columns.

6. Apply *Conditional Formatting*.
   a. Select cells **J5:J9**.
   b. Click the **Quick Analysis** button.
   c. Click **Formatting**.
   d. Choose **Icon Set** (Figure 4-87). The cells display an icon to represent the upper, middle, or lower values of the range.

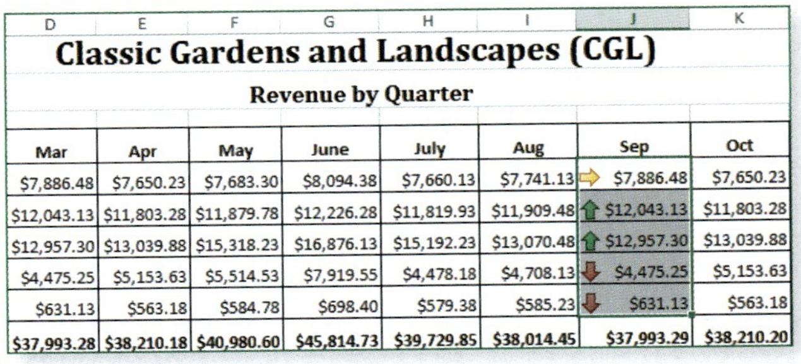

D	E	F	G	H	I	J	K
\multicolumn{8}{c}{**Classic Gardens and Landscapes (CGL)**}
\multicolumn{8}{c}{**Revenue by Quarter**}
Mar	**Apr**	**May**	**June**	**July**	**Aug**	**Sep**	**Oct**
$7,886.48	$7,650.23	$7,683.30	$8,094.38	$7,660.13	$7,741.13 ⇨	$7,886.48	$7,650.23
$12,043.13	$11,803.28	$11,879.78	$12,226.28	$11,819.93	$11,909.48 ⬆	$12,043.13	$11,803.28
$12,957.30	$13,039.88	$15,318.23	$16,876.13	$15,192.23	$13,070.48 ⬆	$12,957.30	$13,039.88
$4,475.25	$5,153.63	$5,514.53	$7,919.55	$4,478.18	$4,708.13 ⬇	$4,475.25	$5,153.63
$631.13	$563.18	$584.78	$698.40	$579.38	$585.23 ⬇	$631.13	$563.18
$37,993.28	$38,210.18	$40,980.60	$45,814.73	$39,729.85	$38,014.45	$37,993.29	$38,210.20

4-87 Icon set conditional formatting

7. *AutoFit* the columns and make sure all data is visible.

8. Click the **AutoOutline** sheet tab.

9. Enter *SUM* functions.
   a. Enter the *SUM* function in cells **E5:E18**, **I5:I18**, **M5:M18**, and **Q5:Q18**.
   b. Enter the *SUM* function in cells **R5:R18** to add the four quarter totals.
   c. Enter the *SUM* function in cells **B19:R19**.
   d. Do the same to show sums for the remaining sections on the sheet. You can hold down the **Ctrl** key, select multiple nonadjacent ranges, and click the **AutoSum** button.

10. In cell **B35**, type the formula =B19+B26+B34 and press **Enter**.

11. Copy the formula in cell **B35** to cells **C35:R35**. *Autofit* the columns.

12. Create an *Auto Outline*.
    a. Click cell **B5**.
    b. Click the **Group** button arrow [*Data tab, Outline* group] and choose **Auto Outline** (Figure 4-88). The *Auto Outline* command uses the column and row formulas to group the data.
    c. Click the **Level 2** column outline button (above the column headings). Only the quarter totals are displayed (Figure 4-89).

13. Import a table from an Access database.
    a. Click the **Table** sheet tab.
    b. Click cell **A4**.
    c. Click the **From Access** button [*Data tab, Get External Data* group].
    d. Select **SalesDatabase-04.accdb** in the *Select Data Source* window.
    e. Click **Open**.
    f. Click **tblMailings** in the *Select Table* dialog box.
    g. Click **OK**.
    h. Select **Table** and **Existing worksheet** if necessary.
    i. Click **OK**.

14. Apply a table style and show a total row.
    a. Click any cell within the table.
    b. Click the **Table Styles** More button [*Table Tools Design* tab, *Table Styles* group].
    c. Choose **Table Style Medium 15**.
    d. Click to place a check mark for **Total Row** [*Table Tools Design* tab, *Table Style Options* group].
    e. Click each cell in the range **C30:M30** and choose **SUM**.

15. Merge and center the title across **A1:N1**, and the subtitle across **A2:N2**. Set the font size of the labels to **18 pt.** (Figure 4-90).

16. Click the **PivotTable** sheet tab.

17. Create a *PivotTable*.
    a. Select cells **A3:D28**.
    b. Click the **PivotTable** button [*Insert* tab, *Tables* group]. Depending on how data is arranged, Excel cannot always recommend *PivotTable* layouts. Select the correct cell range if you did not do so before clicking the **PivotTable** button.

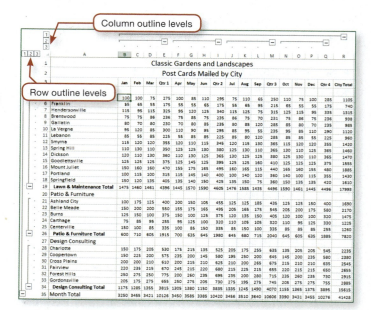

4-88 AutoOutline with three row levels and three column levels

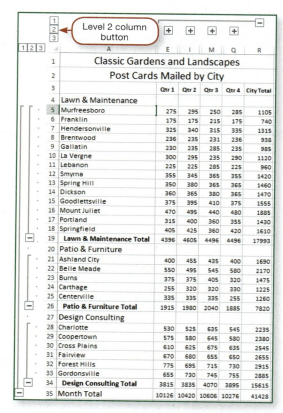

4-89 Outline collapsed at Level 2 column group

c. Select **New Worksheet** if necessary.

d. Click **OK**.

e. In the *Choose fields to add to report* area in the *PivotTable Fields* pane, click to place a check for **City, # Mailed**, and **# Responses**. These fields are shown in the report layout and in the *Row* and *Values* areas in the pane. The *Columns* area in the pane indicates that the numbers in the columns are summed or totaled in the *Grand Total* row (Figure 4-91).

f. Drag the **Department** field from the *Choose fields to add to report* area to the *Filters* area in the *PivotTable Fields* pane.

g. Click the filter arrow for the **Department** field in cell **B1**.

h. Click to place a check mark for **Select Multiple Items**.

i. Click to remove the check mark for **All**.

j. Click to place a check mark for **Landscape Design** and click **OK**.

k. Format cells **A1:B1** as bold.

l. Close the *PivotTable Fields* pane (Figure 4-92).

18. Save and close the workbook.

ID	City	Jan	Feb	Mar	Apr	May	Jun	Jul	Aug	Sep	Oct	Nov	Dec
1	Murfreesboro	100	100	75	100	85	110	75	110	65	110	75	100
2	Franklin	55	65	55	55	55	65	55	65	95	65	55	55
3	Hendersonville	115	95	115	95	120	125	115	125	75	125	115	95
4	Brentwood	75	75	86	75	85	75	86	75	70	75	86	75
5	Gallatin	80	70	80	70	80	85	80	85	120	85	80	70
6	La Vergne	95	120	85	110	90	95	85	95	55	95	85	110
7	Lebanon	85	55	85	55	85	85	85	80	120	85	85	55
8	Smyrna	115	120	120	120	110	115	120	115	130	115	120	120
9	Spring Hill	110	130	110	125	125	130	125	130	110	130	110	125
10	Dickson	120	110	130	110	130	125	130	125	125	125	130	110
11	Goodlettsville	125	125	125	125	145	125	125	125	160	125	125	125
12	Mount Juliet	150	160	160	155	175	165	160	165	115	165	160	155
13	Portland	100	115	100	115	145	140	100	140	120	140	100	115
14	Springfield	150	120	135	135	140	150	135	150	75	150	135	135
15	Ashland City	100	175	125	200	150	105	125	125	185	125	125	150
16	Belle Meade	150	200	200	155	175	165	205	165	175	205	200	175
17	Burns	125	150	100	150	100	125	120	135	150	120	100	100
18	Carthage	75	85	95	95	125	100	110	105	105	110	95	125
19	Centerville	150	100	85	100	85	150	85	150	100	85	85	85
20	Charlotte	150	175	205	175	215	135	205	175	255	135	205	205
21	Coopertown	150	225	200	235	200	145	195	250	200	145	200	235
22	Cross Plains	200	200	210	200	215	210	210	200	265	215	210	210
23	Fairview	220	235	215	245	215	220	215	225	215	220	215	215
24	Forest Hills	250	275	250	200	260	235	235	200	280	235	260	235
25	Gordonsville	205	175	275	250	275	205	275	195	275	205	275	275
Total		3250	3455	3421	3450	3585	3385	3456	3510	3640	3390	3431	3455

4-90 Imported data formatted as a table

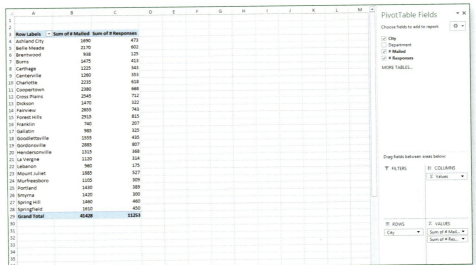

4-91 PivotTable layout

	A	B	C
1	**Department**	**Landscape Design** 🔽	← *Report Filter* button
2			
3	**Row Labels** 🔽	**Sum of # Mailed**	**Sum of # Responses**
4	Centerville	1260	353
5	Charlotte	2235	618
6	Forest Hills	2915	815
7	Gallatin	985	325
8	La Vergne	1120	314
9	Portland	1430	389
10	Springfield	1610	450
11	**Grand Total**	**11555**	**3264**

4-92 PivotTable with report filter

Guided Project 4-3

Clemenson Imaging wants to analyze expense reports from field representatives as well as its patient data and image data. To complete the necessary worksheets, you import a comma-separated text file (.csv), use the *Subtotal* command, and run *Goal Seek*. You also format data as a table and build an advanced filter. Finally, you display data in a *PivotTable*.
[Student Learning Outcomes 4.1, 4.2, 4.3, 4.4, 4.5, 4.6, 4.7]

Files Needed: *ClemensonForecasts-04.xlsx* and *ClemensonExpenseData-04.csv*
Completed Project File Name: *[your initials] Excel 4-3.xlsx*

Skills Covered in This Project

- Create an Excel table.
- Apply a table style.
- Create an *Advanced Filter*.
- Apply *Conditional Formatting*.
- Copy, move, and name a worksheet.
- Insert a row and set column widths.
- Import a comma-separated values text file.
- Sort data.

- Use the *Subtotal* command.
- Expand and collapse groups in an outline.
- Use *Goal Seek*.
- Create a *PivotTable*.
- Create a *PivotChart*.
- Unlock cells.
- Protect a worksheet with a password.

---

1. Open the **ClemensonForecasts-04** workbook from your student data files folder. Click the **Enable Editing** button.

2. Save the workbook as **[your initials] Excel 4-3**.

3. Copy the **Past&Projected** sheet and name the copied sheet Adv Filter. Move the **Adv Filter** sheet to the right of the *Past&Projected* sheet.

4. Create and format an Excel table.
   a. Select cells **A4:E60** on the *Adv Filter* sheet.
   b. Click the **Quick Analysis** tool and choose **Tables**.
   c. Click **Table**.

5. Apply a table style.
   a. Click a cell within the table.
   b. Click the **More** button [*Table Tools Design* tab, *Table Styles* group].
   c. Select **Table Style Medium 15**.

6. Create a criteria range for an *Advanced Filter*.
   a. Select cells **A4:E4** and copy and paste them to cell **G4**.
   b. Type Criteria Range in cell **G3** and set the font to **Cambria 16 pt**.
   c. Adjust column **K** width to show the complete label.
   d. Type Extract Range in cell **G8** and set the same font and size.
   e. Copy the labels from cells **G4:K4** to cell **G9**.

7. Create an *Advanced Filter*.
   a. In cell **G5**, type >12/31/16.
   b. In cell **H5**, type mri.

c. In cell **H6**, type ct scan. These criteria will find records dated 2017 or later for MRIs **and** records for CT scans from any year (Figure 4-93).

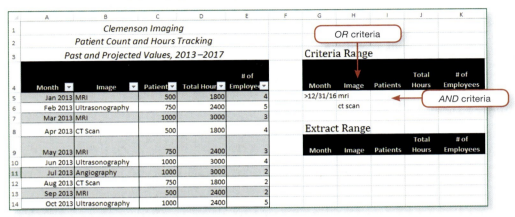

4-93 Criteria range and extract range

d. Click a cell in the table.
e. Click the **Advanced** button [*Data* tab, *Sort & Filter* group].
f. Select the **Copy to another location** radio button.
g. Verify that the **List range** is cells **A4:E60**. If the range is incorrect, click and drag to select the range. The list range includes the header row.
h. Click in the **Criteria range** box and select cells **G4:K6**.
i. Click in the **Copy to** box and select cells **G9:K9**.
j. Click **OK** (Figure 4-94). The CT scan records are from all years; the MRI records are only those from 2017 and later.

8. Apply *Conditional Formatting*.
   a. Select cells **I10:I25**.
   b. Click the **Conditional Formatting** button [*Home* tab, *Styles* group].
   c. Choose **Highlight Cells Rules** and **Greater Than**.
   d. Type 751 and choose **Green Fill with Dark Green Text**.
   e. Click **OK**.

9. Import a comma-separated values text file.
   a. Click the **Expense Info** sheet tab.
   b. Select cell **A3**.
   c. Click the **From Text** button [*Data* tab, *Get External Data* group].
   d. Find and select the **ClemensonExpenseData-04.csv** file in the *Import Text File* window.
   e. Click **Import**.
   f. Select the **Delimited** button in the first *Wizard* window. Excel recognizes that this file separates the data into columns with a comma.
   g. Click **Next**.
   h. Click to remove the check mark for **Tab** and click to place a check mark for **Comma**.
   i. Click **Finish** and click **OK**.
   j. Insert two rows at row **3**.
   k. Type Representative in cell **A4**, Date in cell **B4**, and Amount in cell **C4**.
   l. *AutoFit* column **C**.

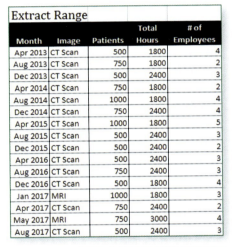

Extract Range			Total	# of
Month	Image	Patients	Hours	Employees
Apr 2013	CT Scan	500	1800	4
Aug 2013	CT Scan	750	1800	2
Dec 2013	CT Scan	500	2400	3
Apr 2014	CT Scan	750	1800	2
Aug 2014	CT Scan	1000	1800	4
Dec 2014	CT Scan	750	2400	4
Apr 2015	CT Scan	1000	1800	5
Aug 2015	CT Scan	500	2400	3
Dec 2015	CT Scan	500	2400	2
Apr 2016	CT Scan	500	2400	3
Aug 2016	CT Scan	750	2400	3
Dec 2016	CT Scan	500	1800	4
Jan 2017	MRI	1000	1800	3
Apr 2017	CT Scan	750	2400	2
May 2017	MRI	750	3000	4
Aug 2017	CT Scan	500	2400	3

4-94 *Advanced Filter* results

10. Sort data.
    a. Click cell **A5**.
    b. Click the **Sort & Filter** button [*Home* tab, *Editing* group].
    c. Choose **Sort A to Z**.

11. Use the *Subtotal* command.
    a. Click cell **A5**.
    b. Click the **Subtotal** button [*Data* tab, *Outline* group].
    c. Click the **At each change in** arrow and choose **Representative**.
    d. Click the **Use function** arrow and choose **Average**.
    e. Check the **Amount** box in the *Add subtotal to* area.
    f. Click **OK**.
    g. Format the values in column **C** as **Currency** with no decimal places.

12. Use *Goal Seek*.
    a. Type Target March Expense in cell **E4**.
    b. Click cell **C8**.
    c. Click the **What-If Analysis** button [*Data* tab, *Data Tools* group] and choose **Goal Seek**.
    d. In the *To value* box, type 600. This value sets a lower expense for Mary Jo.
    e. In the *By changing cell* box, click cell **C7**.
    f. Click **OK**.
    g. Note the target expense and click **Cancel**.
    h. Type $600 in cell **F5**.

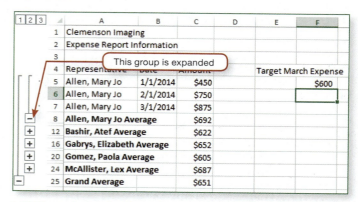

4-95 Expanded and collapsed groups after the Subtotal Command

13. Collapse outline groups.
    a. Click the collapse symbol (-) for row **12**.
    b. Click the collapse symbol (-) for each of these rows: **16**, **20**, and **24** (Figure 4-95).

14. Create a *PivotTable*.
    a. Click the **Past&Projected** sheet tab.
    b. Select cells **A4:E60**. You must select the range to display the *Quick Analysis* tool.
    c. Click the **Quick Analysis** tool and choose **Tables**.
    d. Point at several *PivotTable* options to see the *Live Preview*.
    e. Choose the option that shows a sum of each field (Figure 4-96).
    f. Rename the sheet PivotTable.

4-96 Suggested *PivotTable* choices from the *Quick Analysis* tool

15. Add a *PivotChart* to the *PivotTable* worksheet.
    a. Click a cell within the *PivotTable*.
    b. Click the **PivotChart** button [*PivotTable Tool Analyze* tab, *Tools* group].
    c. Click **Line** in the type list, and choose **Line with Markers** *PivotChart*.
    d. Click **OK**.
    e. Position the chart to the right of the *PivotTable*.
    f. In the *PivotChart Fields* pane, click to remove the check mark for **# of Employees** (Figure 4-97). The *PivotTable* and *PivotChart* are linked so that field is removed from the table and the chart. The task pane toggles between the *PivotTable* and *PivotChart* fields panes based on which element is active.

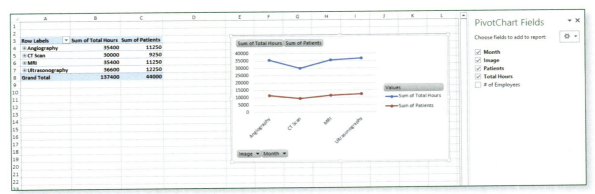

4-97 *PivotChart* and its *PivotTable*

16. Remove the *Locked* property.
    a. Click the **Past&Projected** sheet tab.
    b. Select cells **C5:E60** and right-click any cell in the range.
    c. Select **Format Cells** from the menu.
    d. Click the **Protection** tab.
    e. Clear the check mark for **Locked**.
    f. Click **OK**.

17. Protect a worksheet with a password.
    a. Click the **Protect Sheet** button [*Review* tab, *Changes* group].
    b. Click to place check marks for **Select locked cells** and **Select unlocked cells** if necessary.
    c. Type the password: 321.
    d. Click **OK**.
    e. Retype the password: 321.
    f. Click **OK**. The cells for which the *Locked* property was disabled can be edited.

18. Save and close the workbook.

Independent Project 4-4

Eller Software Services has received updated client information with sales numbers. You import the data into the worksheet, sort and filter it, and apply conditional formatting. You also format the data as an Excel table and create a *PivotTable*.
[Student Learning Outcomes 4.1, 4.2, 4.3, 4.4, 4.5, 4.6, 4.7]

Files Needed: ***EllerSales-04.xlsx*** and ***ClientInfo-04.txt***
Completed Project File Name: ***[your initials] Excel 4-4.xlsx***

Skills Covered in This Project

- Import a text file.
- Sort data.
- Use an *AutoFilter*.
- Filter data by cell color.
- Copy, name, and move a worksheet.
- Use the *Subtotal* command.

- Apply *Conditional Formatting*.
- Clear filters and conditional formatting.
- Create an Excel table.
- Create a *PivotTable*.
- Protect a worksheet with a password.

1. Open the ***EllerSales-04*** workbook from your student data files folder.

2. Save the workbook as ***[your initials] Excel 4-4***.

3. Import the ***ClientInfo-04.txt*** file in cell **A4**. The text file is tab-delimited.

4. Unhide row **10**. Fix the phone number in cell C12.

5. Set *Conditional Formatting* to show cells **I5:I13** with **Yellow Fill with Dark Yellow Text** for values that are less than **1500**.

6. Sort the data first by **Product/Service** in **A to Z** order and next by **Client Name** in **A to Z** order (Figure 4-98).

4-98 Rows sorted by "Product/Service" and then by "Client Name"

7. Display the *AutoFilter* buttons and filter the **Gross Sales** data by color to show only those cells with yellow fill.

8. Copy the **MN Clients** sheet, name the copied sheet Subtotals, and move it to the right of the *MN Clients* sheet.

9. Clear the filter and the conditional formatting on the **Subtotals** sheet.

10. Sort by **City** in **A to Z** order if necesssary.

11. Use the *Subtotal* command to show a **SUM** function in the **Gross Sales** column at each change in **City** (Figure 4-99).

4-99 Subtotal results for gross sales at each change in city

12. Copy the **Subtotals** worksheet, name the copied sheet Table Data, and move it to the right of the *Subtotals* sheet.

13. Remove all subtotals on the **Table Data** sheet.

14. Format cells **A4:I13** as an Excel table with **Table Style Medium 9**. The external connection is from the imported data; click **Yes** in the message box.

15. Display a **Total Row** in the table (Figure 4-100).

4-100 Table with total row

16. Create a *PivotTable* based on cells **A4:I13** in the **Table Data** sheet on its own sheet named PivotTable.

17. Arrange the fields in the *PivotTable* like this: **City** (*FILTERS* area), **Product/Service** (*ROWS* area), and **Gross Sales** (*VALUES* area).

18. Filter the report to display only the data for **Bemidji** and **Brainerd**.

19. Apply **Currency** style to **B4:B7**.

20. Insert a **Clustered Column PivotChart** on the *PivotTable* sheet.

21. Delete the legend from the *PivotChart* and insert the following chart title: Bemidji & Brainerd Gross Sales (Figure 4-101).

4-101 *PivotTable* with *PivotChart* results

22. Protect the **Table Data** sheet with the password **PasswordC**.

23. Save and close the workbook.

Independent Project 4-5

Boyd Air has received flight data for recent flights. After importing the data, you format it as a table and use a number filter to display the afternoon flights. Display subtotals by city of origin and use a *PivotTable* to illustrate the average capacity of the flights.
[Student Learning Outcomes 4.1, 4.2, 4.3, 4.4, 4.5]

File Needed: *FlightData-04.txt*
Completed Project File Name: *[your initials] Excel 4-5.xlsx*

Skills Covered in This Project

- Import a text file.
- Create an Excel table.
- Filter data.
- Convert a table to a normal range.
- Sort data.

- Use the *Subtotal* command.
- Copy, name, and move a worksheet.
- Create a *PivotTable*.
- Create a *PivotChart*.

1. Open a new workbook and save it as *[your initials] Excel 4-5*.

2. Import the *FlightData-04.txt* text file starting at cell **A3**. The text file is tab-delimited.

3. Click a cell within the data range and format the range as an Excel table using **Table Style Medium 21**.

4. Use the **AutoFilter** button and **Number Filters** to filter the table to display only those flights with a Departure Time after 12 PM (Figure 4-102).

5. Type Boyd Air in cell **A1**. Type Flight Statistics in cell **A2**. Set the font size to **20 pt.** for both labels.

6. Center the labels in cells **A1:A2** across the table data.

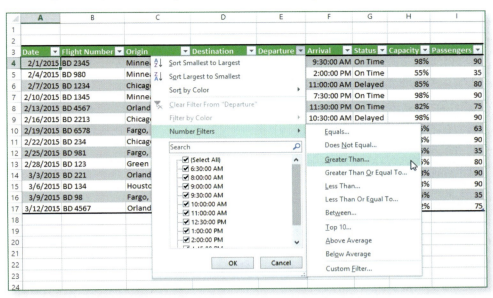

4-102 Number filter for departure time field

7. Name the worksheet Afternoon Flights.

8. Copy the **Afternoon Flights** worksheet, name the copy Subtotals, and move the **Subtotals** sheet to the right of the *Afternoon Flights* sheet.

9. On the **Subtotals** sheet, clear the filter.

10. On the **Subtotals** sheet, sort the data by **Origin** in **A to Z** order.

11. Convert the table on the **Subtotals** sheet to a normal range.

12. Select cells **A3:I17** and use the **Subtotal** command to display a sum for the **Passengers** field at each change in **Origin** (Figure 4-103). You must select the cells for the *Subtotal* command, because the main labels are not separated from the data range by a blank row.

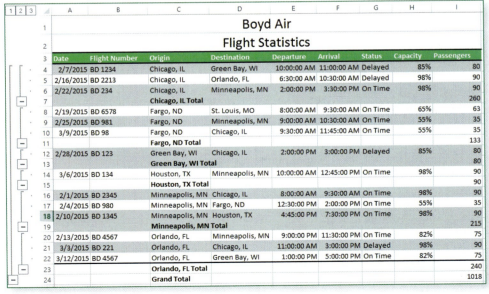

4-103 Subtotals for Passenger field at each change in Origin field

13. Copy the **Afternoon Flights** worksheet, name the copy *PivotTable Source*, and move the **PivotTable Source** sheet to the right of the *Subtotals* sheet.

14. On the **PivotTable Source** sheet, clear the filter.

15. Select cells **A3:I17** and use the **Quick Analysis** tool to create a *PivotTable* to display average of capacity by origin (Figure 4-104).

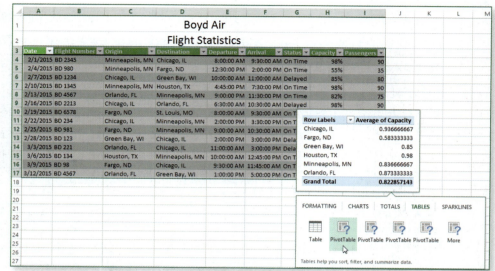

4-104 *PivotTable* suggestions from the *Quick Analysis* tool

16. Click cell **B3** in the *PivotTable*. On the *PivotTable Tools Analyze* tab, click **Field Settings** and set a **Number Format** of **Percentage** with 2 decimal places.

17. In the *PivotTable Fields* pane, place a check mark to add the **Passengers** field to the *PivotTable VALUES* area showing a sum.

18. Add a **3-D Pie PivotChart** to the sheet and position the chart to the right of the *PivotTable*.

19. Rename the worksheet *PivotTable&Chart* and close the task pane (Figure 4-105).

20. Save and close the workbook.

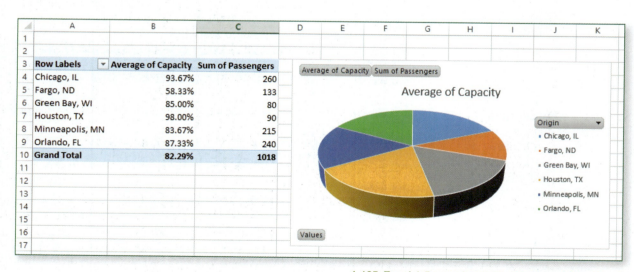

4-105 Excel 4-5 completed *PivotTable* and *PivotChart*

Independent Project 4-6

Life's Animal Shelter maintains its supplier list in a worksheet. You need to copy this data to a Word document for use by a coworker. You also need to define groups so that you can display and hide rows by supplier name.
[Student Learning Outcomes 4.1, 4.3, 4.5, 4.6, 4.7]

File Needed: **LASSuppliers-04.xlsx**
Completed Project File Name: **[your initials] Excel 4-6.xlsx**

Skills Covered in This Project

- Copy Excel data to Word.
- Sort data.
- Use *Flash Fill*.
- Insert and delete a column.

- Define a group.
- Collapse a group.
- Apply conditional formatting.
- Protect a worksheet.

1. Open the **LASSuppliers-04** workbook from your student data files folder.

2. Save the workbook as **[your initials] Excel 4-6**.

3. Select cells **A4:D18** and copy them to the *Clipboard*.

4. Open Word and create a new document. Save the document as **[your initials] Excel 4-6**. Note that because Word and Excel use different file name extensions, you can use the same file name.

5. Paste the data into Word.

6. Save and close the Word document (Figure 4-106).

7. Return to the worksheet and press **Esc** to remove the selection marquee if necessary.

8. In cell **E5**, type (651) 555-6788. In cell **E6**, start to type the number that is in cell **D6** and press **Enter** when the *Flash Fill* suggestion appears.

9. Type Phone in cell **E4**.

10. Delete column **D**.

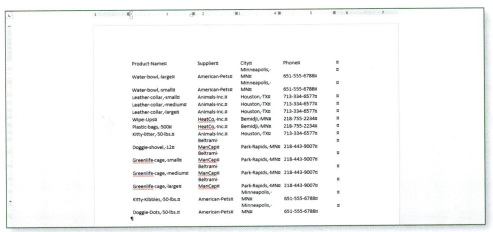

4-106 Excel data copied to Word

11. Unmerge cell **A1** and then **Merge & Center** it across cells **A1:D1**. Repeat for cell **A2** (Figure 4-107).

12. Copy the worksheet, name the copy Groups and move the copy to the right of the *LAS Suppliers* sheet.

	A	B	C	D
1	**Life's Animal Shelter**			
2	**Supplier List**			
3				
4	Product Name	Supplier	City	Phone
5	Water bowl, large	American Pets	Minneapolis, MN	(651) 555-6788
6	Water bowl, small	American Pets	Minneapolis, MN	(651) 555-6788
7	Leather collar, small	Animals Inc.	Houston, TX	(713) 334-6577
8	Leather collar, medium	Animals Inc.	Houston, TX	(713) 334-6577
9	Leather collar, large	Animals Inc.	Houston, TX	(713) 334-6577
10	Wipe-Ups	HeatCo, Inc.	Bemidji, MN	(218) 755-2234
11	Plastic bags, 500	HeatCo, Inc.	Bemidji, MN	(218) 755-2234
12	Kitty litter, 50 lbs.	Animals Inc.	Houston, TX	(713) 334-6577
13	Doggie shovel, 12	Beltrami ManCap	Park Rapids, MN	(218) 443-9007
14	Greenlife cage, small	Beltrami ManCap	Park Rapids, MN	(218) 443-9007
15	Greenlife cage, medium	Beltrami ManCap	Park Rapids, MN	(218) 443-9007
16	Greenlife cage, large	Beltrami ManCap	Park Rapids, MN	(218) 443-9007
17	Kitty Kibbles, 50 lbs.	American Pets	Minneapolis, MN	(651) 555-6788
18	Doggie Dots, 50 lbs.	American Pets	Minneapolis, MN	(651) 555-6788

4-107 **Phone numbers completed with** *Flash Fill*; **title recentered**

13. On the *Groups* sheet, select and format the labels in row **4** as **bold** and **centered**. You need to distinguish the labels in the header row from the other rows.

14. Select cells **A5:D18** and open the *Sort* dialog box. Sort by **Supplier** in **A to Z** order and then by **Product Name** in **A to Z** order.

15. Insert a blank row at row **5** and type Minneapolis in cell **A5**. Left-align the label.

16. Insert a row at row **10** and type Houston in cell **A10**. **Bold** the label.

17. Repeat step 16 for Park Rapids and Bemidji.

18. Select cells **A6:A9**. Group this data by **Rows**. Do not include the city label in the group.

	A	B	C	D
1	**Life's Animal Shelter**			
2	**Supplier List**			
3				
4	**Product Name**	**Supplier**	**City**	**Phone**
5	**Minneapolis**			
6	Doggie Dots, 50 lbs.	American Pets	Minneapolis, MN	(651) 555-6788
7	Kitty Kibbles, 50 lbs.	American Pets	Minneapolis, MN	(651) 555-6788
8	Water bowl, large	American Pets	Minneapolis, MN	(651) 555-6788
9	Water bowl, small	American Pets	Minneapolis, MN	(651) 555-6788
10	**Houston**			
11	Kitty litter, 50 lbs.	Animals Inc.	Houston, TX	(713) 334-6577
12	Leather collar, large	Animals Inc.	Houston, TX	(713) 334-6577
13	Leather collar, medium	Animals Inc.	Houston, TX	(713) 334-6577
14	Leather collar, small	Animals Inc.	Houston, TX	(713) 334-6577
15	**Park Rapids**			
20	**Bemidji**	Group can be expanded		
21	Plastic bags, 500	HeatCo, Inc.	Bemidji, MN	(218) 755-2234
22	Wipe-Ups	HeatCo, Inc.	Bemidji, MN	(218) 755-2234
23				

4-108 **Data manually defined in groups; Park Rapids group collapsed**

19. Repeat the command to group the selected data for each supplier.

20. Collapse the *Park Rapids* group (Figure 4-108).

21. Click the **LAS Suppliers** sheet tab.

22. Apply conditional formatting to show the *American Pets* supplier name with **Green Fill with Dark Green Text** (Figure 4-109).

23. Do not remove the *Locked* property for any cells, but protect the *LAS Suppliers* sheet without a password.

24. Save and close the workbook.

	A	B	C	D
1	**Life's Animal Shelter**			
2	**Supplier List**			
3				
4	Product Name	Supplier	City	Phone
5	Water bowl, large	American Pets	Minneapolis, MN	(651) 555-6788
6	Water bowl, small	American Pets	Minneapolis, MN	(651) 555-6788
7	Leather collar, small	Animals Inc.	Houston, TX	(713) 334-6577
8	Leather collar, medium	Animals Inc.	Houston, TX	(713) 334-6577
9	Leather collar, large	Animals Inc.	Houston, TX	(713) 334-6577
10	Wipe-Ups	HeatCo, Inc.	Bemidji, MN	(218) 755-2234
11	Plastic bags, 500	HeatCo, Inc.	Bemidji, MN	(218) 755-2234
12	Kitty litter, 50 lbs.	Animals Inc.	Houston, TX	(713) 334-6577
13	Doggie shovel, 12	Beltrami ManCap	Park Rapids, MN	(218) 443-9007
14	Greenlife cage, small	Beltrami ManCap	Park Rapids, MN	(218) 443-9007
15	Greenlife cage, medium	Beltrami ManCap	Park Rapids, MN	(218) 443-9007
16	Greenlife cage, large	Beltrami ManCap	Park Rapids, MN	(218) 443-9007
17	Kitty Kibbles, 50 lbs.	American Pets	Minneapolis, MN	(651) 555-6788
18	Doggie Dots, 50 lbs.	American Pets	Minneapolis, MN	(651) 555-6788

4-109 Excel 4-6 completed worksheet

Improve It Project 4-7

Eller Software Services has created a software release workbook, but the sheets contain several errors. For this project, you edit the workbook and correct sorting, filtering, and *PivotTable* problems. **[Student Learning Outcomes 4.2, 4.3, 4.4, 4.5]**

File Needed: *SoftwareRelease-04*
Completed Project File Name: *[your initials] Excel 4-7.xlsx*

Skills Covered in This Project

- Sort data.
- Remove subtotals.
- Use the *Subtotal* command.
- Edit fields in a *PivotTable*.
- Create a *PivotChart*.
- Edit chart elements.

1. Open the **SoftwareRelease-04** workbook from your student data files folder.

2. Save the workbook as *[your initials] Excel 4-7*.

3. On **Phase 1 Release Dates** sheet, click the **Name Box** arrow and select **Data** to select cells **A5:F19** by its range name. Sort the data by **Platform** in **A to Z** order and then by **Release Date** in **Oldest to Newest** order.

4. On the *Subtotals* sheet, remove the subtotals. Sort the data by **Platform** in **A to Z** order.

5. Use the **Subtotal** command to count the number of projects by platform, showing the count in the **Software Project** column.

6. On the *PivotTable* sheet, click to place check marks for **Software Project**, **Price**, and **Release Date** in the *Choose fields to add to report* area. Remove other check marks.

7. Drag the **Release Date** field into the *Filters* area in the *PivotTable Fields* task pane.

8. Use the **Report** filter to show only the projects that will be released in 2015.

9. Place the **Software Project** field in the *Values* area in the *PivotTable Fields* task pane. This field is in both the *Row* and the *Values* areas.

10. Add a **3-D Pie PivotChart** to the *PivotTable* worksheet. Place the chart to the right of the *PivotTable*.

11. Change the chart title to: Revenue by Project.

12. Click the **Field Buttons** button on the *PivotChart Tools Analyze* tab to hide the pivot buttons in the chart.

13. Close the task pane.

14. Save and close the workbook (Figure 4-110).

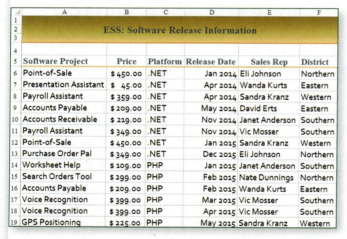

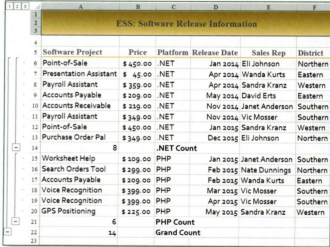

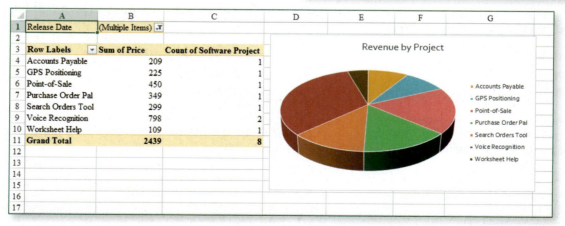

4-110 Excel 4-7 completed worksheets

Challenge Project 4-8

For this project, you import your debit or checkbook account records into an Excel workbook. You format the data as a table and sort and filter the data. Finally, you protect your data with a password.
[Student Learning Outcomes 4.1, 4.2, 4.3, 4.6, 4.7]

File Needed: None
Completed Project File Name: *[your initials] Excel 4-8.xlsx*

Create a new workbook and save it as *[your initials] Excel 4-8*. Modify your workbook according to the following guidelines:

- Import several months of your account activity from your bank's web site into the worksheet.
- If each month is a separate file on the web site, import each month separately so that the data follows one another in the sheet.
- If column headings are not included in the imported data, add headings such "Date", "Transaction", and "Balance" where appropriate.
- Format the data as an Excel table or change the style if you imported it as a table. If you have multiple tables, select all the rows and convert the tables to a normal range. Then format the entire range as a single table.
- If the records are sorted in ascending order by date, reverse the sort order.
- Review your data and apply conditional formatting to a transaction name that appears more than once or to a transaction type that you want to highlight.
- Filter the data by the color used in your conditional formatting command.
- Password protect the sheet without unlocking any cells.

Challenge Project 4-9

For this project, you build a worksheet that will allow you to analyze costs of a decorating or remodeling project in your home or apartment.
[Student Learning Outcomes 4.6, 4.7]

File Needed: None
Completed Project File Name: *[your initials] Excel 4-9.xlsx*

Create a new workbook and save it as *[your initials] Excel 4-9*. Modify your workbook according to the following guidelines:

- Type labels for at least five tasks in a decorating or remodeling project, such as "Purchase paint", "Consult with contractor", etc.
- Type an estimated cost for each task and use a *SUM* formula to show an estimated total.

- Determine a slightly lower total cost than your original estimate and use *Goal Seek* to adjust one of the tasks so that you can reach this preferred lower cost.
- Review your data and apply conditional formatting to display the two most expensive tasks in a different color.
- Add a main title to your worksheet and use different font sizes and borders to effectively display your information.

Challenge Project 4-10

For this project, you create a worksheet that lists names, birth dates, and hair color for 12 people. You format the list as a table and build a *PivotTable*.
[Student Learning Outcomes 4.2, 4.3, 4.4, 4.5]

File Needed: None
Completed Project File Name: *[your initials] Excel 4-10.xlsx*

Create a new workbook and save it as *[your initials] Excel 4-10*. Modify your workbook according to the following guidelines:

- Type your first name, your last name, your birthdate, and your hair color in four columns in a row.
- Type the same information for 11 more people, using real or fictitious data. Use birthdates that are the same year as yours as well as two other years, so that your data has only three birth years. Use only three hair colors for all your people, such as brown, blond, and red.
- Format the data as a table and apply a table style.
- Sort the date by birthdate with the youngest people listed first. Then filter the data to show only those records from the first year listed in the data.
- Make a copy of the table sheet and convert the table to normal range. Use the *Subtotal* command to count the number of persons with each hair color.
- Copy the table again for use as a *PivotTable* source. Create a *PivotTable* that displays something of interest about your list.

Microsoft® Office
IN PRACTICE

access

Creating a Database and Tables

CHAPTER OVERVIEW

Microsoft Access (Access) is the leading PC-based database management system (DBMS) software in both the personal and business market. This software makes it easy for you to ensure your data are accurate, organized, and usable. Access helps you organize and manage personal, business, and educational data in a structure known as a database. This chapter covers the basics of working with a relational database and using the Access database management system.

STUDENT LEARNING OUTCOMES (SLOs)

After completing this chapter, you will be able to:

SLO 1.1 Explain data organization concepts, use the Access *Navigation* pane, and identify objects (p. A1-3).

SLO 1.2 Create a database, set database properties, understand database object naming conventions and data types, and close a database (p. A1-11).

SLO 1.3 Create a table in *Datasheet* view, edit the default primary key, add a new field, edit field properties, save a table, and enter records into a table (p. A1-17).

SLO 1.4 Navigate table records in a datasheet and customize a datasheet by modifying field order, row height, column width, field alignment, font style and size, row colors, and gridlines (p. A1-28).

SLO 1.5 Search, sort, and filter records in a table (p. A1-36).

CASE STUDY

Throughout this book, you have the opportunity to put into practice the Access features you are learning. The case study introduces you to the **Pause & Practice** *projects in the chapter. These Pause & Practice projects are relevant and related to the case study. Each chapter contains three to five Pause & Practice projects.*

The first Pause & Practice is designed to orient you to using Access and allows you to explore the different parts of the Access interface and navigation mechanism. In this project, you open an existing database for the *College of Sciences* that tracks information

about classes it offers. The remaining Pause & Practice projects are designed to help you learn how to build a database for *Central Sierra Insurance*. Central Sierra Insurance is a multi-office insurance company that handles all lines of commercial and personal insurance policies. Central Sierra regularly hires qualified personnel, and it needs to create an effective way to organize and manage the information about its employees. Lanita McCartney has asked you to create a simple database containing information about its employees. This database is created as a blank desktop database with one table. As you progress through the Pause & Practice projects, you incorporate many of the features you are learning in this chapter to construct and enhance this database.

Pause & Practice 1-1: Open an existing database. Explore the tabs of the Access *Ribbon* and *Navigation* pane. Use *Datasheet* and *Design* view of a table.

Pause & Practice 1-2: Create a new, blank desktop database. Customize the table using *Datasheet* view to edit the primary key, add new fields, save the table, reopen the table, edit field properties, and add employee records.

Pause & Practice 1-3: Modify the table created in Pause & Practice 1-2 and refine the datasheet layout by modifying the field order, row height, field width, and field alignment; selecting a display font and size; displaying gridlines; and alternating row colors.

Pause & Practice 1-4: Use the employee table to search for data, sort the records on a single field and on multiple fields, and filter the records using single and multiple criteria.

SLO 1.1

Understanding Database Concepts

Organizations can generate a tremendous amount of data. Think about just some of the pieces of data captured by FedEx when you send a package or envelope: the sender's first and last name, sender's street address, sender's city, sender's state, sender's zip code, recipient's first and last name, recipient's street address, recipient's city, recipient's state, recipient's zip code, date sent, package weight, and type of service (e.g., next-day air, ground service). Every day, FedEx delivers millions of packages and documents. This translates into millions of sender names, addresses, recipient names, addresses, and so forth, captured each day. To stay in business, FedEx must have an efficient and effective way to capture, process, and store these data to ensure that it delivers your package on time and to the right location.

Databases are used by many organizations to manage data. A ***database*** is an organized collection of integrated and related tables. A ***database management system (DBMS)*** is software that allows you to create a database; manage the data in the database by adding, deleting, and updating records; sort and retrieve data; and create queries and reports relating to that data. In this book, you learn about Microsoft Access, the leading PC-based DBMS software application.

Using a database management system, people can build applications to allow organizations to track orders and deliveries, manage retail sales and inventory, maintain employee payroll records, update patient data, and track student progress. Throughout this chapter, you learn more about these database concepts by using the Access DBMS as you create a simple database.

Organize Data

Like the majority of the DBMSs available today, Access is a ***relational database,*** which means that the data are organized into a collection of related tables. Each table stores data about one type, or grouping, of information represented in the system. For example, a database application used by a retail store contains a table with details about its customers, a table with details about the products it sells, and a table with details about the orders its customers have made for the various products. The different tables are related, or connected, to one another through common fields.

The first step in creating a database is to determine the best way to organize the required data. To do so, you need to understand the ***hierarchy of data*** used in relational databases.

In Access, the hierarchy is organized from the smallest to the largest grouping of data. A *Field* is a collection of characters that describes one aspect of a business object or activity—a single unit of data. A *Record* is a collection of related data fields. A *Table* is a collection of related records. Visually you see the table containing rows and columns. Each row is the equivalent of a record. A row contains many different columns, or fields. A *Database* is a collection of related tables. An example of how this hierarchy works for a database that a university might use is shown in the following table.

Hierarchy of Data

Unit	Description	Examples
Field	A single unit of data	Date enrolled, student name, student ID
Record	A collection of related fields	All of the fields for one student stored together
Table	A collection of related records	A record for each of the students at the university stored together
Database	A collection of integrated and related tables	The collection of the student, faculty, and course tables for the entire university

How do you know how many tables you need or which fields belong in which tables? There are several different formal techniques you can use to help you plan the design of your database. One of the techniques is to follow a process to build an *Entity-Relationship Diagram (ERD)*. A second technique is *normalization*, in which you compare your tables with a set of rules to ensure that they are well designed. Both of these formal techniques help you create a well-designed relational database. Often the design plan is already completed for you, and you simply need to build the design. At this point, the simplest answer to the question about how many tables you need is this: Create a separate table for each major subject or grouping of information you will store in the database.

The Access Interface

The interface is what you use to interact with Access to create, modify, delete, and use different objects, or parts, of your database application. The *Ribbon* in Access contains five primary tabs: *File, Home, Create, External Data,* and *Database Tools.* Access also has several *contextual tabs* that become available to you when you are working on different tasks. The *Ribbon* provides some of the common Office functions, like copy, paste, and file management, but many of the *Ribbon* tabs are unique to Access.

> ### MORE INFO
>
> Depending on configuration changes made to the Access program installed on your computer, you may see a sixth tab titled *Add-Ins.*

Examine Access Objects

An Access database application typically contains many different components, such as tables and reports. In Access, these components are called *objects.* The major objects in Access are *tables, forms, queries,* and *reports.* At a minimum your database must contain at least one table. These objects are described in the following table.

Major Access Objects

Object	Purpose	Additional Information	Navigation Pane Icon
Table	Stores data records	Once a table is created, you can begin entering data. Create a separate table for each type or grouping of information. When you view data in a table, it appears in a tabular format, very much like a spreadsheet.	
Form	Used to create an interface to view, add, update, and delete data in a table	Although you can do these tasks directly in a table, a form usually provides an easier way to interact with the data. Forms also allow you to view only one record at a time and to view fields from multiple tables at the same time.	
Query	Used to find data in your database	Queries allow you to specify criteria to locate specific records. Queries can also be used to perform actions such as updating or deleting records.	
Report	Used to view and print the data in your database	Reports allow you to create a formatted, and more professional, way to view and print the contents of your database.	

> **MORE INFO**
>
> Forms, queries, and reports provide different ways to interact with the data in your tables. As a result, they are related to the tables on which they are based.

Access contains two additional objects: **Macros** and **Modules**. These objects allow you to add functionality to the forms and reports in your database. For example, you can add a button to a form. The button responds to various events, like **OnClick**. You can attach specific actions to these different events. For example, attach the **OpenForm** action to a button to open another form when the button is clicked.

Use the Navigation Pane

Each object in your database application is shown in the **Navigation pane.** The object is identified by its name and an icon indicating the object type.

The top bar of the *Navigation* pane contains the **Shutter Bar Open/Close** button, which opens and closes the pane.

- If the pane is closed, as shown in the left side of Figure 1-1, you will only see the phrase "Navigation pane."
- Open the *Navigation* pane by clicking the **Shutter Bar Open/Close** button.
- The objects inside your database display, as shown on the right side of Figure 1-1.

> **ANOTHER WAY**
>
> **F11** opens and closes the *Navigation* pane.

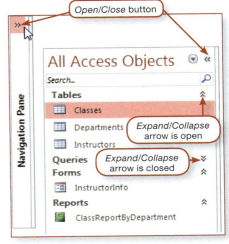

1-1 *Shutter bar* of the *Navigation* pane

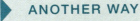

The *Navigation* pane displays your objects by **categories** and **groups.** Within the *Navigation* pane you can expand and collapse the different groups. This is useful if you have many objects in your database and wish to narrow down those that are visible. Click the **expand/collapse arrow** to the right of the group name to change the current display. When a group is collapsed, like the *Queries* group in Figure 1-1, only the name of the group displays. The objects contained within that group do not display.

You can customize what is displayed in the *Navigation* pane and the way the objects are organized by using the **Navigation menu.**

The top half of the *Navigation* menu allows you to select a category. The standard categories are:

- **Custom:** Groups objects based on custom categories that you create
- **Object Type:** Groups objects on the basis of their type
- **Tables and Related Views:** Groups different objects according to the tables on which they are based
- **Created Date:** Groups objects on the basis of the week associated with the date they were created
- **Modified Date:** Groups objects on the basis of the week associated with the date they were last modified

The bottom half of the *Navigation* menu allows you to filter by a specific group within that category. The choices in the *Filter By Group* will change based on the selected category. The filter selection is reflected in the *Title* bar of the *Navigation* pane.

The *Navigation* pane in Figure 1-1 reflects the settings selected in Figure 1-2; it shows all objects grouped by the category of *Object Type* and the filter of *All Access Objects*.

1-2 *Navigation* menu

HOW TO: Modify the Navigation Pane Category and Group Filter

1. Click the **Navigation pane arrow**, shown in Figure 1-3, to open the *Navigation* menu.
2. Select the **desired category**.
   - The *Navigation* menu closes and the *Navigation* pane updates to display the objects based on your category selection.
3. Click the **Navigation pane arrow** to open the *Navigation* menu.
4. Select the **desired filter selection**.
   - The *Navigation* menu closes and the *Navigation* pane updates to display the objects based on your filter selection.

1-3 Modify the *Navigation* pane

Use Datasheet and Design View of a Table

Because the *Table* is the primary object of a database, it is useful to dig a little bit deeper into this object as you learn about the Access interface.

Access provides two ways to view a table (Figure 1-4): *Datasheet View* and *Design View*.

- **Design View** allows you to build or modify the basic structure or functionality of an object. You see all the details, or properties, of the fields in your table in *Design* view.
- **Datasheet View** allows you to enter, modify, delete, or view the data records. You can also use *Datasheet* view to define or modify the structure of a table.

  You can open tables directly from the *Navigation* pane.

- Open a table in *Datasheet* view by double-clicking the table name in the *Navigation* pane.

1-4 View menu of a table

- Open a table in *Design* view by right-clicking the table name in the *Navigation* pane and selecting *Design View* from the context menu.
- Switch between views of an open table by clicking the *View* button arrow [*Home* tab, *Views* group] and selecting the desired view.

PAUSE & PRACTICE: ACCESS 1-1

In this project, you explore a database that tracks information about classes that are offered in the *College of Sciences.* This database contains three tables, one query, one form, and one report. You open the database, explore the Access *Ribbon,* explore the *Navigation* pane, and work with *Datasheet* and *Design* views of a table.

File Needed: ***CollegeOfSciencesClasses-01.accdb***

Completed Project File Name: None

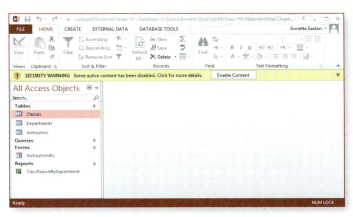

1. Open the database used by the College of Sciences.
   a. Double-click the ***CollegeOfSciences Classes-01.accdb*** file in your student data files folder. This launches Access and opens the sample database application (Figure 1-5).
   b. If prompted, click the **Enable Content** button in the *Security Warning* message bar.

1-5 CollegeOfSciencesClasses-01 database

> ### MORE INFO
>
> Because viruses and worms may be transmitted in files, Microsoft warns you when you open a database file. If you trust the source of the file, enable the content so that you can use the database.

   c. When a database is opened, Access opens the *Navigation* pane and selects the *Home* tab.

2. Explore the Access *Ribbon.*

a. Click the **File** tab to open the *Backstage* view, shown in Figure 1-6.

Select the arrow to return to the Access Ribbon

> **MORE INFO**
>
> The *Backstage* view in Access provides file management capabilities to open, close, and save a database; create a new database; and print or publish a database.

b. Click the arrow to return to the Access *Ribbon.*

c. Click the **Home** tab. The *Home* tab (Figure 1-7) offers common Office functions, the ability to change the way you view an object, and searching and sorting functions.

1-6 *Backstage* view

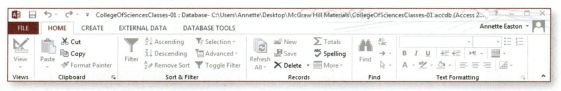

1-7 *Home* tab

d. Click the **Create** tab. The *Create* tab (Figure 1-8) creates all the objects you use in your database. The icons are grouped on the basis of the type of object you need to build.

1-8 *Create* tab

e. Click the **External Data** tab. The *External Data* tab (Figure 1-9) provides functionality to link to other applications and data files. The icons are grouped on the basis of the type of connectivity you need.

1-9 *External Data tab*

f. Click the **Database Tools** tab. The *Database Tools* tab (Figure 1-10) provides information about your database and additional functions to help you manage the database.

1-10 *Database Tools* tab

3. Explore the *Navigation* pane.
   a. Select the **Navigation pane arrow** next to *All Access Objects.* The *Navigation* menu should display as shown on the right side of Figure 1-11.
      This *Navigation* pane displays objects by the *Object Type* category, and the filter is to show *All Access Objects.*
   b. Click anywhere outside the *Navigation* menu to close the menu.
   c. In the *Navigation* pane, click the **expand/collapse arrow**, shown in Figure 1-12, at the right edge of the *Tables* group. The *Tables* group collapses, leaving no table objects visible. The arrow has changed to an expand arrow.
   d. Click the **expand/collapse arrow** in the *Tables* group to reopen the *Tables* group and display the three tables.
   e. Click the **Navigation pane arrow** next to *All Access Objects.*
   f. Select the **Tables and Related Views** category. The *Navigation* pane updates and should look similar to Figure 1-13.
      This view shows each of the tables and all of the other objects that are associated with each table. For example, the report object named *ClassReportByDepartment* is associated with each of the three tables. However, the form object *InstructorInfo* is only associated with the *Instructors* table.
   g. Click the **Navigation pane arrow**.
   h. In *Filter by Group,* select the **Departments** group.
      The *Navigation* pane now shows only the *Departments* table with the three objects that are associated with that table.
   i. Click the **Navigation pane arrow**.
   j. Click the **Object Type** category. The *Navigation* pane should have returned to show all of your objects by the *Object Type* category.

4. Explore *Datasheet* and *Design* views of a table.
   a. Double-click the **Classes** table to open the table in *Datasheet* view, as shown in Figure 1-14.

> **MORE INFO**
>
> Depending on the resolution of your monitor and the size of the Access window, you may see more or less of the table.

   b. Click the **Right arrow** key to navigate across the fields of the first record. *Datasheet* view allows you to add new fields into your table at the same time that you are looking at the data values. Look for the last column named *Click to Add.*
   c. Click the **Right arrow** key once more to navigate to the *ClassID* of the second row.

1-11 **Explore the *Navigation* pane**

1-12 ***Expand/collapse arrow***

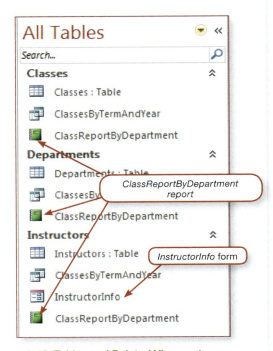

1-13 ***Tables and Related Views* category**

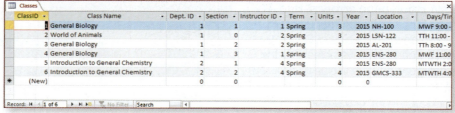

1-14 *Datasheet* view of *Classes* table

1-15 Two table views

d. Use the **Down arrow** key to navigate down to *ClassID 6,* the last of the data records. If you were to navigate into the *(New)* record, you would be able to add a new class into the table by entering the data values.

e. Click the **Home** tab. Click **View** in the *Views* group. You should be able to see the two possible table views shown in Figure 1-15.

f. Click **Design View**.

> ### ANOTHER WAY
>
> Change the view by clicking on the **Design View** button on the right side of the *Status bar.*

Your screen should be similar to that shown in Figure 1-16. *Design* view shows you the details, or properties, of the different fields in your table.

g. Use the **scroll bar** to navigate down to see all the fields in the *Classes* table. Look for the last field, *Days/Times.* You could add additional fields into the table by entering the field name into the blank row below *Days/Times.*

h. Close the *Classes* table by clicking the **X** in the upper right corner of the *Classes* table window.

i. Close the *CollegeOfSciencesClasses-01* database by clicking the **Close** button [*File* tab].

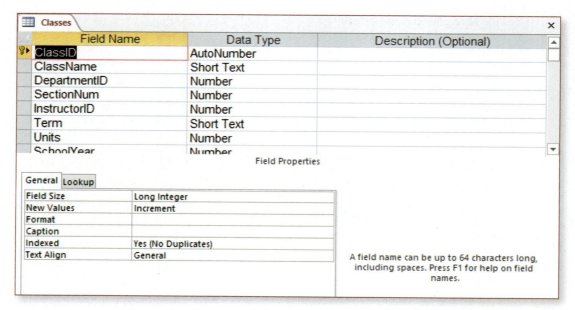

1-16 *Design* view of *Classes* table

Creating and Managing a Database

In Access, the database application file stores all of the separate objects that you create and use. The database file must be created before you can create and use any other objects. You can create a new database file by using a prebuilt template as a starting point, or you can create a blank desktop database if you wish to start from scratch.

Templates

A *template* is a pre-designed database that contains various pre-built objects. A *template* provides you with a complete, ready-to-use database application. After creating a database based on a template, you can use the new database directly or you can customize the database to better meet your needs. Templates are a great starting point if your needs are addressed in the template.

You can choose from several templates that are installed with Access. In addition, there are other templates available at Office.com.

HOW TO: Create a New Database Using a Template

1. With Access already open, if the Backstage view is not displayed, click the **File** tab to open the *Backstage* view.
2. Click the **New** button. The list of sample templates displays (Figure 1-17).
3. Select the **template** you wish to use.
4. Use the **Browse** button to browse to a location on your computer or USB drive to save the database.
5. Type the file name in the **File name** area.
6. Click the **OK** button.
7. Click the **Create** button. The new database opens.
8. If prompted, click the **Enable Content** button in the *Security Warning* message bar.

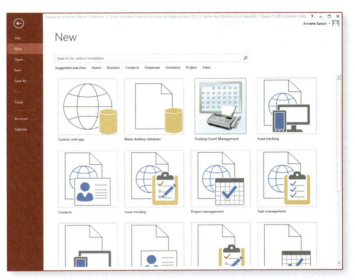

1-17 **Create a new database from a template**

> **ANOTHER WAY**
>
> **Ctrl+N** opens the *Backstage* view so you can select a new database to create.

Database Properties

Every database contains a variety of details about the database. These details, or properties, include information about the date the database was created and its author. View common file properties in the ***Database Properties*** dialog box available via the ***View and edit database properties*** link on the *Backstage* view. You can edit the properties on the *Summary* tab. However, you cannot edit properties on many of the other tabs. For example, the ***Size*** or ***Modified Properties*** on the *General tab* are automatically updated by the system.

HOW TO: View and Edit Database Properties

1. Click the **View and edit database properties** link [*File* tab, *Info* button], shown in Figure 1-18, to open the *Properties* dialog box displayed in Figure 1-19.

2. Click the **Summary** tab.

3. View the properties that have been entered.

4. Edit any desired properties. Be sure to complete any properties required by your instructor.

> **MORE INFO**
>
> Some properties may already be completed based on the settings selected when Office was installed on the computer.

5. Click the **OK** button to save and close.

1-18 Open the database properties

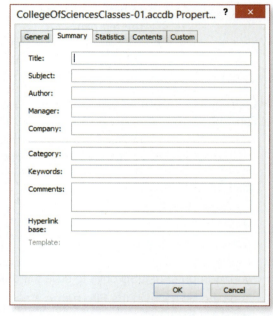

1-19 *Properties* dialog box

Create a Blank Desktop Database

Many times a template does not exist to meet your needs or it requires significant modifications to make it fit your requirements. In these cases you can create a ***Blank desktop database.*** With the *Blank desktop database* option, you create all the tables and other objects that you need. When a blank desktop database is created, Access automatically creates one new table and opens that table in *Datasheet* view.

HOW TO: Create a New Blank Desktop Database

1. With Access already open, click the **New** button [*File* tab].

> **ANOTHER WAY**
>
> **Ctrl+N** opens the *Backstage* view with *New* button selected.

2. Select the **Blank desktop database** icon (Figure 1-20).

3. Type the file name in the *File name* area.

1-20 Create a new *Blank desktop database*

4. Use the **Browse** button to browse to the location on your computer or USB drive to save the database and click the **OK** button.

5. Click the **Create** button. The database is created. A new table is automatically created and opens in *Datasheet* view.

> **MORE INFO**
>
> Access automatically assigns a generic file name to your database, such as ***Database1.accdb***. Be sure to change that name to something that is more meaningful and related to the purpose of your database.

Name Database Objects

You need to name each of the objects you create and use in Access. When you first create an object, Access assigns a generic name, such as *Table1* or *Form1*. The first time you save an object, the *Save As* dialog box prompts you to enter a different name. Database designers strongly recommend that you use a meaningful name that describes the contents of the object. For example, in the *CollegeOfSciencesClasses-01* database, the tables are named *Classes, Departments,* and *Instructors.* This makes it easy to understand the object's purpose. An object name in Access can have a maximum of 64 characters (letters, numbers, and spaces.)

In addition to selecting a name that describes the contents, the following are some additional standard naming conventions to consider:

- ***CamelCase*** notation is the practice of omitting spaces in compound words and starting each word with a capital letter. For example, *PhoneNumber* and *DepartmentName* are written using *CamelCase* notation.
- ***Leszynski*** notation is the practice of using a prefix (called a ***tag***) to indicate the type of object. For example, *tblAccounts* or *frmSales* are written using *Leszynski* notation. The most common tags are *tbl,* used for a table; *frm,* used for a form; *rpt,* used for a report; and *qry,* used for a query.

You can also combine the notations, such as in *tblStudentInformation.* In this book we use the *CamelCase* notation. Be sure to follow the naming conventions required by your instructor or employer.

Data Types

Each field in your database must be assigned a specific ***data type.*** The data type determines what properties can be manipulated and how that field can be used. Before you start to create and manipulate tables, it is important to learn about the types that are explained in the following table.

Access Data Types

Data Type	Description
Short Text	Used to store alphanumeric data (text, or combinations of text and numbers). Also used to store numbers that are not used in calculations, such as phone numbers. The maximum length is 255 characters.
Long Text	Used to store text longer than 255 characters or text containing rich text formatting. The maximum length is 65,535 characters.
Number	Used to store numbers that are used in mathematical calculations. The number can be positive or negative. There are seven field size choices for the number data type which determine the range of possible values and amount of storage space required.
Date/Time	Used to store dates and times.

(continued)

Access Data Types (continued)

Data Type	Description
Currency	Used to store numbers representing currency values. This type does not allow rounding off during calculations.
AutoNumber	Used to instruct Access to insert a unique, sequential (e.g., increments of 1) number each time a new record is added.
Yes/No	Used to store fields with two possible values, such as Yes/No, True/False, or On/Off. Displays as a check box.
OLE Object	Used to display OLE objects (e.g., spreadsheets, documents, pictures, sounds). OLE stands for object linking and embedding. This data type allows you to store objects that were created in other programs.
Hyperlink	Used to store a hyperlink to another file or web page.
Attachment	Used to attach pictures, images, and Office files. This data type is new to Access 2010 and is the recommended data type for storing images.
Calculated	Used to store the results of a calculation. Typically the equation references fields in the same table.
Lookup Wizard	Technically, this is not a data type. It is used to convert your field into a combo box that allows you to choose a value from another table or from a list of values.

Create and Save Database Objects

Databases typically contain many different objects. Each object is initially created using the *Create* tab. Once the object is created, you use one of the different views to define the object or to change the object.

HOW TO: Create a New Object

1. Click the **Create** tab on the *Ribbon.*
2. Select the **object** button of the object you wish to create.

   The button choice determines the view in which the object opens. For example, selecting the **Table** button opens a table in *Datasheet* view, whereas selecting the **Table Design** button opens a table in *Design* view.

To keep a permanent copy of an object, you need to save it. When an object is created, Access automatically assigns it a name. The first time you save an object, you are prompted to change the default name in the *Save As* dialog box.

HOW TO: Save an Object

1. Click the **Save** button [*File* tab].
2. Type the name you wish to use in the *Save As* **Object Name** box. Instead of displaying the phrase "Object Name," Access displays the type of object you are working on. For example, Figure 1-21 is a *Save As* dialog box for a form.
3. Click the **OK** button.

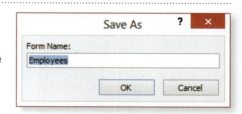

1-21 *Save As* dialog box

Sometimes you need to make a copy of an object. This may be done to have a backup of the original object or because another object has the same initial characteristics.

HOW TO: Save a Copy of an Object

1. Click the **Save As** button [*File* tab].
2. Click the **Save Object As** button in the *File Types* area and the **Save Object As** button in the *Database File Types* area as shown in Figure 1-22.
3. Click the **Save As** button to open the *Save As* dialog box (Figure 1-23).
   - Access suggests the default object name of "Copy of" and the original object name.
   - Access selects the same object type as the original object.
4. Type the name you wish to use in the *Save 'Object name' to* box.
5. Select the type of object you wish to create.
   - You can make a duplicate of the object by selecting the same object type.
   - You can create a different type of object, based on the original object's settings, by selecting another object type.
6. Click the **OK** button.

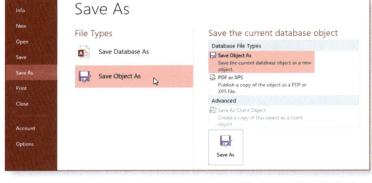

1-22 *Save Object As* button

1-23 *Save As* dialog box

Close and Open a Database

When you are finished working on a database, you should close the database file. You won't actually save the database file before closing it. Instead, you are prompted to save each of the separate database objects as you work on them. Access also automatically saves many changes to your database file, such as records you add into a table.

HOW TO: Close a Database

1. Click the **Close** button [*File* tab] to close a database.

   The current database closes. Access remains open, and you are positioned on the *Home* tab as shown in Figure 1-24. Notice that the *Navigation* pane does not display since a database is not open.

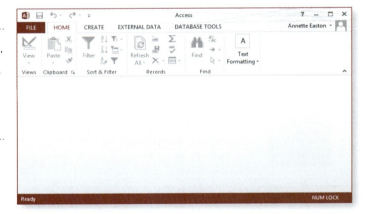

> **MORE INFO**
>
> If you are closing a database and have unsaved objects still open, Access may prompt you about saving changes to those objects.

1-24 Access *Start* page

HOW TO: Open a Database

1. Click the **Open** button [*File* tab], or press the **Ctrl+O** keys, to open an existing database.
2. Navigate to your database application file.
3. Select the **database file** and click the **Open** button.

> **ANOTHER WAY**
>
> Double-click the **file name** to open the file.

Back Up a Database

A backup copy of a database is necessary to completely restore your database. If you have several users of your database, you must be certain that all users have closed the database before you perform a backup procedure. Your organization's database administrator, in conjunction with the information systems manager, should determine a regular schedule for backups.

HOW TO: Back Up a Database

1. Click the **File** tab to open the *Backstage* view.
2. Click the **Save As** button. Your screen should be similar to that shown in Figure 1-25, with **Access Database** selected in the **Save Database As** area.
3. Select the **Back Up Database** button in the *Advanced* grouping of the *Save Database As* section.
4. Click the **Save As** button.
   - Select the desired location in which to store the backup database file.
   - Access suggests a filename, such as *PP Access 1-2_2015-03-05,* which adds today's date to the end of the file name. This is a good practice because you can quickly determine when a backup copy was created.
   - If desired, click in the **File Name** box if you wish to change the default name.
   - Click the **Save** button.

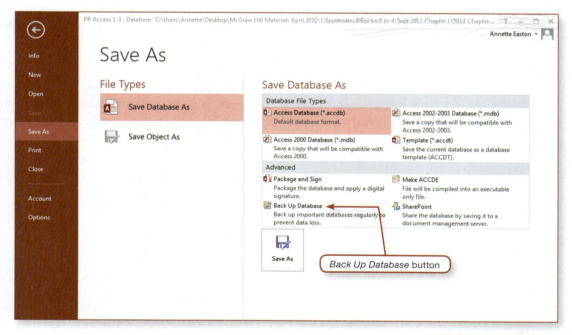

1-25 Back up a database

The *Back Up Database* option creates a copy of your database, but the current database file remains open and you continue to work in that file. If the original database file becomes damaged, copy the backup file to replace the original.

> **▶ ANOTHER WAY**
>
> Use the *Access Database* file type and select the **Save As** button to create a copy of the database. In this case, the open database switches to the new copy you created.

Creating and Using a Table in Datasheet View

Recall that when you create a new, blank desktop database, Access automatically creates one table for you. You can add tables using several different methods. In this section you learn how to use *Datasheet* view to quickly create a table and enter data records. When using a database application, *Datasheet* view is primarily used to enter, modify, delete, or view the data records.

No matter what method you use to create a table, you need to define the fields that are included within the table. You also need to describe the details, or **field properties,** of each of the fields.

> **MORE INFO**
>
> *Field properties* describe the specific details of each field. Basic field properties include the field name, type, and size.

Create a New Table in Datasheet View

Databases typically contain multiple tables. You can add a new table to your database from the *Create* tab. Tables created using the *Table* button automatically open in *Datasheet* view.

HOW TO: Create a New Table in Datasheet View

1. Click the **Create** tab on the *Ribbon*.
2. Select the **Table** button in the *Tables* group (Figure 1-26). A new table opens in *Datasheet* view.

   In Figure 1-27, notice that the *Table Tools* contextual tabs are now available, with the **Fields** tab selected.

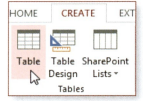

1-26 *Table* button

1-27 *Table Tools Contextual* tabs

Edit the Default Primary Key

A **primary key** is a field that contains a unique value for each record. This is the way that one record can be distinguished from another.

When a new table is created in *Datasheet* view, Access automatically includes one field, named *ID,* and designates it as the primary key. This field is assigned the *AutoNumber* data type to ensure that each record has a unique value.

> **MORE INFO**
>
> While not absolutely required, it is strongly recommended that you identify a field in each table as the primary key.

In *Datasheet* view, you can change the following field properties of the *ID primary key* field: *Name, Caption, Description,* and *Data Type.*

HOW TO: Edit the Default Primary Key

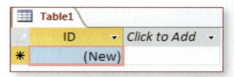

1-28 *Field Name column header*

1. Double-click the cell containing the **ID** field name (column header) in your table (Figure 1-28).

2. Type in the new name for your field and press the **down arrow** key. This action updates the change to the field name and keeps you in the same column.

3. To change the default *Data Type* of *AutoNumber,* click the **drop-down arrow** of the **Data Type** option [*Table Tools Fields* tab, *Formatting* group], as shown in Figure 1-29. Select the desired **Data Type** property.

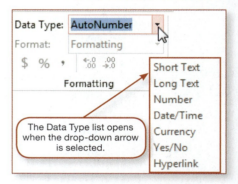

The Data Type list opens when the drop-down arrow is selected.

1-29 *Field Data Types*

Add New Fields

You create a field for each of the different pieces of information you want to keep in your table. For example, *ClassID, ClassName,* and *DepartmentID* are three of the fields in the Classes table in the *College of Sciences* database. In *Datasheet* view, you can add new fields to a table by either entering the data values directly or by entering the field names. After you have added a field, you can customize the name, caption, description, type, default value, and size properties. You can also set a few of the field validation properties. On numeric fields, you can set formatting properties.

Add New Fields by Entering Data

You can add new fields into a table by entering the data values. Add a new field by clicking in the first cell on the ***Append Row.*** The *Append Row* is always the last row in the table. It is identified with the asterisk icon in the record selector of that row. The ***Record Selector*** is the gray cell at the left side of each row in the datasheet. When you click in a field, the *Record Selector* of that row turns yellow.

A field on the *Append Row* with *(New)* displayed, as shown in Figure 1-30a, indicates an *AutoNumber* data type. The data value for this field is automatically completed by Access. You can add a new field by entering data in the cell to the right of *(New).*

If a field is blank, like the *ID* field in Figure 1-30b, first enter a value into the *ID* field and then you can add a new field by entering data in the *Click to Add* column.

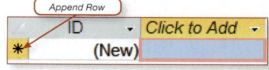

1-30a *Append Row with an AutoNumber field*

1-30b *Append Row without an AutoNumber field*

> ## MORE INFO
>
> If the *ID* field (the default primary key) does not display *(New)* in the *Append Row,* the data type has been changed from an *AutoNumber* type.

HOW TO: Add New Fields by Entering Data

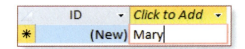

1. Click the **cell** in the first *Click to Add* column.

2. Type the data value to be entered into the cell (Figure 1-31).

1-31 **Add new field by entering data**

3. Select the **Click to Add** column header to add the field.
   - The field name changes to *Field1,* as shown in Figure 1-32.
   - *Click to Add* becomes the next column.

1-32 *Click to Add* **becomes the next column**

> ### ANOTHER WAY
> Press the **Tab** key to add the field and move to the next column.

> ### MORE INFO
> Access automatically determines a data type for the field based on the contents that you enter.

4. Repeat steps 1 through 3 to add all the additional fields to your table.

> ### MORE INFO
> You can edit the field properties as you add each field or after you add all the fields.

Add New Fields by Entering Field Names

You can add new fields into a table by entering the field name and selecting the data type.

HOW TO: Add New Fields by Entering Field Names

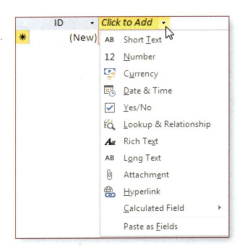

1. Click the **Click to Add** column header. The drop-down list of data types displays (Figure 1-33).

2. Select the appropriate **data type**.

3. The new field is added and assigned a default field name, such as *Field1,* as shown in Figure 1-34.

4. Type the desired **field name** in the column header.

5. Press the **Enter** key. You move to the next column with the list of data types displayed.

> ### MORE INFO
> Each field in a table must have a unique name. The name is limited to 64 characters, including letters, numbers, and spaces. Remember to follow the naming convention you are using for all database objects.

1-33 *Click to Add* **data types**

6. Repeat steps 2 through 5 to add the additional fields to your table.

1-34 **Field name column header**

7. Click the **Click to Add** column header.

8. Click the **More Fields** button [*Table Tools Fields* tab, *Add & Delete* group].

   - The *More Fields* drop-down menu, shown in Figure 1-35, provides shortcuts to some of the additional options of the basic data types.
   - Technically, these choices are not data types. Rather they assign additional formatting selections to a data type. For example, within the *Date and Time* group, there are format options for the ways to store a field with a Date/Time data type. *Short Date* formats a date to display as 12/15/2015; *Medium Date* displays as 15-Dec-15.
   - The *Quick Start* group provides a set of fields that you can add by making just one choice. For example, selecting the *Phone* quick start data type adds four fields into your table: *Business Phone, Home Phone, Mobile Phone,* and *Fax Number.*

9. Select the desired **data type**.

10. Type the desired **field name** in the column header.

11. Press the **Enter** key.

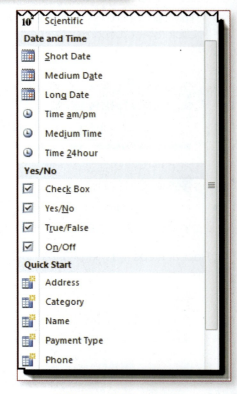

1-35 *More Fields* drop-down menu

When using the *Click to Add* option, the new field always adds to the right of the last field in your table. Occasionally you may wish to add a field between existing fields.

HOW TO: Add New Fields between Existing Fields

1. Put your pointer on the **field name** of the column to the right of where you wish to insert a new field. The selection pointer appears (Figure 1-36).

2. Click to select that column. The column is highlighted in blue.

3. Right-click to open the context menu.

4. Select the **Insert Field** button (Figure 1-37).

   The new field is inserted to the left of the selected field, as shown in Figure 1-38. It is assigned a default field name, such as *Field1*.

5. Double-click the **field name** to change the name.

1-36 Selection pointer

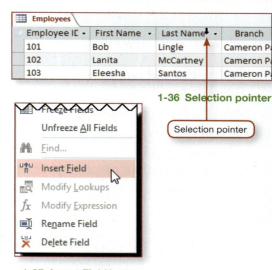

1-37 *Insert Field* button on the context menu

Employee IC ▾	First Name ▾	Field1 ▾	Last Name ▾	Bra
101	Bob		Lingle	Came
102	Lanita		McCartney	Came
103	Eleesha		Santos	Came

1-38 New field added with default field name

Delete Fields

You may need to delete a field from a table that was either created in error or is no longer needed in a table.

HOW TO: Delete a Field

1. Place your pointer above the field name of the field you wish to delete.
2. When the selection pointer appears, click to select that column.
3. Click the **Delete** button [*Table Tools Fields* tab, *Add & Delete* group] to delete the field. Access displays a message box asking you to confirm the deletion.
4. Click **Yes** to delete the field.

> **MORE INFO**
>
> The *Undo* button cannot be used to undo deletions of table fields.

Edit Properties in Datasheet View

In *Datasheet* view, you can change a limited number of the field properties. Recall that the properties of each field describe the field's details or characteristics. The majority of the field properties are changed in *Design* view. The properties that you can set in *Datasheet* view include:

- *Name:* Each field in a table must be given a unique name.
- *Caption:* The *Caption* is an alternative to the field name that displays in the datasheet. Captions often include spaces and multiple words.
- *Description:* The *Description* describes the purpose or meaning of a field if the field name by itself does not clearly convey the purpose or intended content. It displays in the lower, left-hand corner of the datasheet.
- *Data Type:* Select a data type that matches the characteristics of the stored data.
- *Field Size:* Enter the smallest, sufficient field size to ensure best performance.

HOW TO: Edit Field Properties in Datasheet View

1. Select the **cell** containing the field name (column header) you wish to change.
2. Click the **Name & Caption** button [*Table Tools Fields* tab, *Properties* group].
   - The **Enter Field Properties** dialog box opens as shown in Figure 1-39.
3. Type a new value in the *Name* property, if desired.
4. Type a value in the *Caption* property, if desired.
5. Type a value in the *Description* property, if desired.
6. Click the **OK** button to close the dialog box.
7. Click the *Data Type* option **drop-down arrow** [*Table Tools Fields* tab, *Formatting* group].
8. Select the desired **Data Type** property.
9. Type a new value in the *Field Size* property [*Table Tools Fields* tab, *Properties* group], displayed in Figure 1-40.

1-39 *Enter Field Properties* **dialog box**

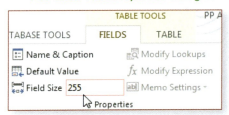

1-40 *Field Size* **property**

Save a Table

When a blank table is created, Access automatically assigns a generic name to the table, such as *Table1*. When working with a new table, you can save it by clicking the *File* tab and clicking the *Save* button. This opens the *Save As* dialog box, and you can type in a name for the table.

If you close *Table1* (the default table that comes with a new database) without saving it, Access deletes the table. This occurs even if you have entered data into the table.

HOW TO: Save a Table

1. Click the **Save** button [*File* tab].
2. Type the name you wish to use in the *Table Name* box. The first time you save changes to your table, Access prompts you to change the default table name.
3. Click the **OK** button.

> **ANOTHER WAY**
>
> **Ctrl+S** opens the *Save As* dialog box. You can also open the *Save As* dialog box by clicking the **Save** icon on the *Quick Access* toolbar or by pressing the **F12** function key.

Open a Saved Table

You can open an existing table in either *Datasheet* view or *Design* view. Once a table is open, you can easily switch views if desired.

HOW TO: Open a Saved Table in Datasheet View

1. If the *Navigation* pane is closed, click the **Shutter Bar Open/Close** button or Press **F11**.
2. Double-click the **Table** name. The table opens in *Datasheet* view.

> **ANOTHER WAY**
>
> Select the table in the *Navigation* pane and press **Enter** to open a table in *Datasheet* view.

To open a table in *Design* view, select the table in the *Navigation* pane and press **Ctrl+Enter**.

Enter, Edit, and Delete Records

Datasheet view provides an easy way to enter data values into your table, edit records already in the table, or delete records from a table.

- Enter the data by completing all the values for one record. After you finish entering the values for one record and navigate to the next record, Access automatically saves the record in the table.

> **MORE INFO**
>
> Your table must be saved at least once to initiate the automatic saving of data records.

If you realize you made an error in entering a value, there are several ways to make a correction.

- If you have navigated out of that field, click back into that field and change the value.
- If you are still typing in that field, click the *Undo* button to undo the typing in that field.

- If you have moved to the next field, undo a change to the previous field by clicking the *Undo* button.
- To undo all the changes to an unsaved record, click the *Undo* button twice.

Once you navigate out of the current record, the *Undo* command won't remove changes.

One benefit of a database is that it automatically verifies the contents of what you enter, based on the different properties you have assigned. For example, because the primary key field must have a unique value, if you enter a primary key value that is already used, Access displays an error message. Similarly, if you enter a value that violates the data type property, Access displays an error message.

HOW TO: Enter Records in a Table

1. Click the **first empty cell** in the *Append Row* (Figure 1-41).
2. Type the data value.

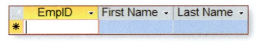

1-41 *Append row*

   - The *Append Row* asterisk changes to a pencil icon, indicating that you are editing a new record that has not yet been saved, as shown in Figure 1-42.
3. Press the **Tab** key to move to the next field.

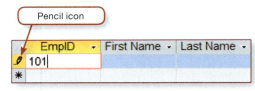

1-42 **Pencil icon indicates unsaved record**

4. Continue entering all remaining data values for the record.
5. After you enter the value in the last field, press the **Tab** key to move to the first field of the next record.

   - If you enter a duplicate value for the primary key (Figure 1-43), Access displays an error message (Figure 1-44) when you navigate out of the record.

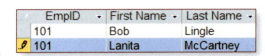

1-43 **Duplicate primary key values**

1-44 **Duplicate values error message**

- If you enter a value that does not match the data type, Access displays an error message when you navigate out of that field (Figure 1-45).

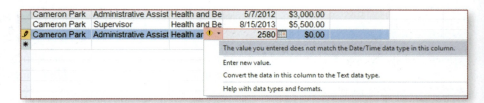

1-45 Data type error message

You can edit an existing record in a table by clicking in the cell of the field you wish to change. Make the necessary corrections in the field. When you navigate out of that field, Access automatically saves the changes.

Sometimes you need to delete a record from a table in your database.

HOW TO: Delete a Record From a Table

1. Click in the **Record Selector** cell of the record you wish to delete (Figure 1-46).
2. Click the **Delete** button in the *Records* group [*Home* tab].
   - Access displays a message box warning you about the record deletion and informing you that it is not possible to undo a delete operation.
   - Click the **Yes** button if you want to confirm the delete operation.

103	Eleesha	Santos	Camero...
104	Roy	Baxter	Granite...
115	Tami	Chan	Cameron
119	Juan	Taylor	Granite...

1-46 Select the record before deleting

PAUSE & PRACTICE: ACCESS 1-2

Businesses regularly use databases to organize and manage data in a useful and meaningful manner. For this project, you create a database to manage data about the employees of *Central Sierra Insurance*.

File Needed: None
Completed Project File Name: **[your initials] PP A1-2.accdb**

1. Create a new, blank desktop database.
   a. Open Access or click the **New** button [*File* tab] if Access is already open.
   b. Click **Blank desktop database**.
   c. Name the database [your initials] PP A1-2 in the *File Name* box.
   d. Browse to the location on your computer or storage device to save the database and click **OK**.
   e. Click **Create**. The database opens with a new table showing in *Datasheet* view (Figure 1-47).

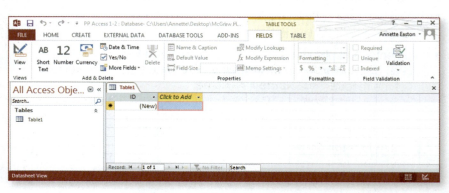

1-47 *Datasheet* view of *Table1* after a new database is created

2. Modify the default primary key.
   a. Double-click the **ID** field name (column header) in your table and type EmpID. Press the **down arrow** key to update the name and keep you in the same column.
   b. Click the **Name & Caption** button [*Table Tools Fields* tab, *Properties* group]. The *Enter Field Properties* dialog box opens (Figure 1-48).

1-48 *Enter Field Properties* **dialog box**

   c. Type Employee ID in the *Caption* property.
   d. Type Unique Employee Identification Number in the *Description* property.
   e. Click the **OK** button.
   f. Click **Short Text** in the *Data Type* selection box [*Table Tools Fields* tab, *Formatting* group] (Figure 1-49).

1-49 *Data Type* **selection box**

   g. Type 5 in the *Field Size* property [*Table Tools Fields* tab, *Properties* group].
   h. Press the **Enter** key.

3. Add new fields into the table.
   a. Click the **Click to Add** column header.
   b. Select **Short Text** in the *Data Type* selection box.
   c. Type FirstName to replace *Field1*.
   d. Press the **Enter** key to move to the next column.
   e. Continue entering the additional fields in the table using the information in the nearby table.

Data Type	Field Name
Short Text	LastName
Short Text	Branch
Short Text	Title
Short Text	Department
Date & Time	StartDate
Currency	BaseMonthlySalary

4. Save and close the table.
   a. Click the **Save** button or press **Ctrl+S** to save all of the modifications you have made to the table.
   b. Type Employees as the new table name.
   c. Click the **OK** button.
   d. Close the *Employees* table by clicking the **X** in the upper right corner of the table as shown in Figure 1-50.

1-50 Close the *Employees* table

5. Reopen the table in *Datasheet* view to edit the field properties.
   a. Double-click the **Employees** table to open it in *Datasheet* view.
   b. Click the **FirstName** field name.
   c. Click the **Name & Caption** button [*Table Tools Fields* tab, *Properties* group].
   d. Type First Name in the *Caption* property.
   e. Type Employee's First Name in the *Description* property.
   f. Click the **OK** button.

g. Type 25 in the *Field Size* property [*Table Tools Fields* tab, *Properties* group].

h. Continue changing the remaining field properties in the table using the following information. Repeat steps 5b through 5g for each field.

Field Name	Caption	Description	Size
LastName	Last Name	Employee's Last Name	25
Branch		Branch Assigned To	30
Title		Current Job Title	40
Department		Department Assigned To	40
StartDate	Start Date	Date Employment Started	N/A
BaseMonthlySalary	Base Monthly Salary	Current Base Monthly Salary	N/A

i. Click the **Save** button to save the changes to the table.

6. Enter the employee records into the *Employees* table.

a. Click **the first empty cell** in the *Append Row*. Recall that the *Append Row* is always the last row in the table. It is identified with the asterisk icon in the record selector of that row.

b. Type 101 in the *EmpID* field. Remember that if you entered a caption for a field, the caption displays as the column header in *Datasheet* view. The data entry instructions reference the actual field name.

c. Press the **Tab** key to move to the next field.

d. Type Bob in the *FirstName* field. Press the **Tab** key to move to the next field.

e. Type Lingle in the *LastName* field. Press the **Tab** key to move to the next field.

f. Type Cameron Park in the *Branch* field. Press the **Tab** key to move to the next field.

> **MORE INFO**
>
> Because you have not increased the width of any fields, you may not be able to see the entire contents of some fields. Date and Currency values that are too wide display with pound sign symbols (######).

g. Type CEO in the *Title* field. Press the **Tab** key to move to the next field.

h. Type Administration in the *Department* field. Press the **Tab** key to move to the next field.

i. Type 1/1/2012 in the *StartDate* field. Press the **Tab** key to move to the next field.

j. Type 15000 in the *BaseMonthlySalary* field. Press the **Tab** key to move to the start of the next record.

k. Continue entering the remaining records into the *Employees* table using the data values in the table below. The values that you enter are not "wrapped" in the table cells when you enter them.

Emp ID	FirstName	LastName	Branch	Title	Department	StartDate	Base Monthly Salary
102	Lanita	McCartney	Cameron Park	Chief Operating Officer	Administration	1/1/2012	12000
103	Eleesha	Santos	Cameron Park	Insurance Agent	Health and Benefits	2/10/2012	5500
104	Roy	Baxter	Granite Bay	Insurance Agent	Property and Casualty	2/11/2012	4500

Emp ID	FirstName	LastName	Branch	Title	Department	StartDate	Base Monthly Salary
115	Tami	Chan	Cameron Park	Administrative Assistant	Health and Benefits	5/7/2012	3000
119	Juan	Taylor	Granite Bay	Insurance Agent	Insurance Sales	9/1/2012	4000
120	Wayne	Reza	Cameron Park	Insurance Agent	Health and Benefits	11/19/2012	4000
125	Cheryl	Nevens	Cameron Park	Chief Information Officer	Administration	1/7/2013	12000
130	Bert	Pulido	Cameron Park	Supervisor	Health and Benefits	8/15/2013	5500
135	Elsa	Ricci	Cameron Park	Administrative Assistant	Health and Benefits	10/8/2013	2750
138	Geneva	Song	Cameron Park	Executive Assistant	Administration	10/14/2013	3750
147	George	Tipton	Folsom	Insurance Agent	Health and Benefits	1/4/2014	3900
150	Margaret	Jepson	Folsom	Insurance Agent	Property and Casualty	2/15/2014	3900
157	Eva	Skaar	Cameron Park	Large Group Specialist	Health and Benefits	4/1/2014	4500
161	Jesus	Delao	Folsom	Insurance Agent	Property and Casualty	8/25/2014	3900

7. Close the table by clicking the **X** in the upper right corner. Since the data records are automatically saved when you enter them into the table, it is not necessary to save the table before closing.

8. Reopen the *Employees* table in *Datasheet* view to verify that the records were saved.
   a. Double-click the **Employees** table to open it in *Datasheet* view. Your completed table should be similar to Figure 1-51 and display all 15 records.

9. Close the table by clicking the **X** in the upper right corner of the datasheet.

10. Close the database by clicking the **Close** button [*File* tab].

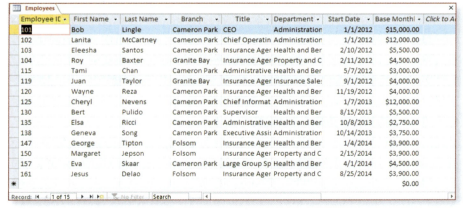

1-51 PP A1-2 completed

Exploring Datasheet View

As you have seen, you can use *Datasheet* view to add new fields into a table. However the primary use of *Datasheet* view is to enter, modify, delete, or view the data records. The *Navigation* buttons are used to move among the fields and records in *Datasheet* view. *Datasheet* view also provides many options to adjust the display of your data within a table. This section reviews how to navigate among records and how to adjust *Datasheet* view display settings.

Navigation Buttons

Access provides many different ways to navigate among the data records stored in your tables. For example, you can navigate using the keyboard arrow keys and the scroll bar. This works fine on tables that do not have too many records. However, in many cases, you may want to get to a specific record more quickly.

The **Navigation bar** provides additional methods to move among table records. It is located at the bottom left corner of a table viewed in *Datasheet* view. The *Navigation* bar, shown in Figure 1-52, contains navigation buttons, a **Filter status** message box, and a **Search** box.

1-52 *Navigation* bar

The *Navigation* buttons are located on the left side of the *Navigation* bar. The functionality of each button is explained in the following table.

Navigation Buttons in Access

Button	Description
⏮	Move to the first record of the table
◀	Move to the previous record of the table
3 of 19	The number of the current record along with the total number of records. You can type in the number of the record where you wish to move.
▶	Move to the next record in the table
⏭	Move to the last record of the table
▶⊞	Create a new record

> ▶ **ANOTHER WAY**
>
> The *Navigation* buttons can also be found under **Go To** [*Home* tab, *Find* group].

Refine the Datasheet Layout

There are several ways to adjust the default display settings in *Datasheet* view. The settings change both the view of the table on the screen and the printed contents of a table.

Sometimes you may be given specific design guidelines based on company standards. Other times you need to use your judgment to evaluate the best way to have the data display. For example, the default column width or row height of a field may not be large enough to display the entire contents. You may wish to adjust the alignment, change the display font face and font size, or adjust the row colors and display gridlines.

If you make a change to the datasheet layout that you do not like, there are several options for making a correction.

- You can repeat the steps you made to make the changes and select the previous settings.
- You can close the table without saving your changes.

Modify the Field Order

There are times when you need to modify the order in which the fields display in a datasheet. You can move a single column or you can move a group of adjacent columns.

HOW TO: Modify the Field Order

1. Place your pointer above the **field name** of the column you wish to move.
   - The selection pointer appears (Figure 1-53).
2. Click to select the **column**.
   - The cursor changes to the normal pointer (Figure 1-54).
   - The column is highlighted in blue.
3. Click, hold, and drag the pointer to move the column to the new location.
   - A black vertical line (Figure 1-55) moves with you to indicate the location where the column will be moved.
4. Release the pointer.
   - The column moves to the new location (Figure 1-56).

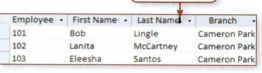

1-53 Selection pointer

1-54 Pointer

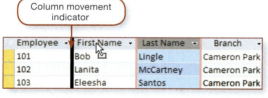

1-55 Column movement indicator   1-56 Moved column

Select a Display Font Face and Font Size

Access provides many of the standard text formatting options available in other Microsoft Office programs. These formatting options are found in the **Text Formatting** group on the *Home* tab as displayed in Figure 1-57.

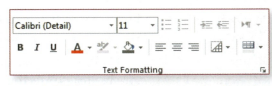

The *font face* specifies the shape of the text. The *font size* specifies the size of the text. *Font style* options include **bolding**, *italicizing*, and underlining.

Changes to a font *face,* size, or style are applied to the entire datasheet. If you want only specific content to have a different format, select the **Rich Text** option available on the **More Fields** button [*Table Tools Fields* tab, *Add & Delete* group] when adding the field in *Datasheet* view. Rich text is a special text format applied to a *Long Text* data type that allows you to store formatted text.

> **MORE INFO**
>
> The default font face and size in Microsoft Access is Calibri and 11 pt.

The type of change you wish to make determines the specific menu options you select.

- Change the font face by clicking the **Font** drop-down list in the *Text Formatting* group [*Home* tab] and selecting the desired font.
- Change the size of the font by clicking the **Font Size** drop-down list in the *Text Formatting* group [*Home* tab] and selecting the size.
- Change the style of the font by clicking the desired style button in the *Text Formatting* group [*Home* tab].

Modify the Row Height

You can adjust the row height to change the amount of space that displays between rows. When you make a change to the row height in Access, all of the rows change to the new height.

> **MORE INFO**
>
> You can also change the default font face and font size in Microsoft Access.

HOW TO: Modify the Row Height

1. Place your pointer on the **border** of a row in your table.
   - Because your changes affect all the rows, it does not matter which row you select.
   - The two-pointed arrow appears (Figure 1-58).

2. Click, hold, and drag the pointer to increase or decrease the height of the rows.
   - A black horizontal line moves with you to indicate the new height (Figure 1-59).
   - The rows change to the new height.
   - The content of columns that are narrower than needed automatically wraps within the cell as shown in Figure 1-60.

Two-pointed arrow

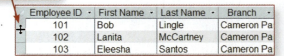

Employee ID	First Name	Last Name	Branch
101	Bob	Lingle	Cameron Pa
102	Lanita	McCartney	Cameron Pa
103	Eleesha	Santos	Cameron Pa

1-58 Two-pointed arrow

Employee ID	First Name	Last Name	Branch
101	Bob	Lingle	Cameron Pa
102	Lanita	McCartney	Cameron Pa
103	Eleesha	Santos	Cameron Pa

1-59 Row height indicator

Employee ID	First Name	Last Name	Branch
101	Bob	Lingle	Cameron Park
102	Lanita	McCartney	Cameron Park
103	Eleesha	Santos	Cameron Park

1-60 Changed row height

HOW TO: Modify the Row Height Using the Context Menu

1. Click the **Record Selector** of a row in your table.
   - Because your changes affect all the rows, it does not matter which row you select.
2. Place your pointer on the **border** of that row.
3. Right-click to open the context menu (Figure 1-61).
4. Select the **Row Height** button to open the **Row Height** dialog box.
5. Type the desired **row height**.
6. Click **OK** to close the dialog box.

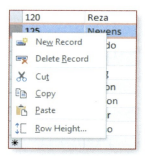

1-61 *Row* context menu

Modify the Field Width

Adjust the field width to change how much content displays. You can set each field to a desired width. You can also select a set of adjacent columns and set the same width to all of them in one operation.

HOW TO: Modify the Field Width of Selected Columns

1. Place your pointer on the right **border** of the field name of the column you wish to change.
   - The two-pointed arrow appears (Figure 1-62).
   - If you wish to change the width of adjacent columns, you must first select all of the columns. Click and hold to select the first column; drag the selection pointer to the adjacent columns (Figure 1-63).
   - Place your pointer over the **border** of the right-most field.
2. Click, hold, and drag the pointer to increase or decrease the width of the field.
   - A black vertical line moves with you to indicate the new width (Figure 1-64).
3. Release the pointer.
   - The field column(s) changes to the new width.

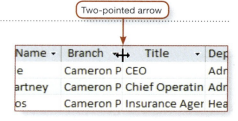

1-62 Two-pointed arrow

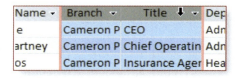

1-63 Select adjacent columns

1-64 *Field Width* indicator

> ▶ **ANOTHER WAY**
>
> To have Access *AutoFit* the column width to the widest entry, double-click instead of click and drag when the two-pointed arrow appears.

Select All button

HOW TO: Modify the Field Width of All Columns Using AutoFit

Employee ▾	First Nam ▾	Last Na
101	Bob	Lingle
102	Lanita	McCart
103	Eleesha	Santos

1-65 *Select All* button

1. Click the **Select All** button (Figure 1-65), in the upper left corner of the datasheet, to select the entire datasheet.

2. Place your pointer on the right **border** of any of the field names.

3. Double-click the **two-pointed arrow** as shown in Figure 1-66.

   - All the fields automatically adjust to their widest entry or to the width of the field caption if that is larger than the contents.

Employee ▾	First Nam ▾	Last Name ▾	Branch ▾	┿ Title ▾	Departme ▾	Sta
101	Bob	Lingle	Cameron Pa	CEO	Administrat	
102	Lanita	McCartney	Cameron Pa	Chief Opera	Administrat	
103	Eleesha	Santos	Cameron Pa	Insurance A	Health and L	3

1-66 Adjust field width of all columns

> **MORE INFO**
>
> If the width of the table window is not large enough to increase all the columns, some columns remain narrower.

> **ANOTHER WAY**
>
> You can also modify the column width by opening the context menu and selecting the *Field Width* button.

Modify the Field Alignment

The data type determines the default alignment of each field. Alignment changes are applied to the entire field, not just one cell.

- *Left-aligned data types* include *Short Text, Long Text,* and *Hyperlink.*
- *Right-aligned data types* include *Number, Date/Time, Currency,* and *Calculated.*
- *Center-aligned data types* include *Yes/No* and *Attachment.* You are not able to change the alignment of fields with the *Yes/No* and *Attachment* data types.

Change the alignment by selecting the field and then clicking the desired alignment button in the *Text Formatting* group [*Home* tab].

Display Gridlines

Gridlines help visually frame the rows and columns in a datasheet with a border. The default settings in Access display both vertical and horizontal gridlines in a gray color.

The gridline display options include:

- Both vertical and horizontal gridlines
- Only horizontal gridlines
- Only vertical gridlines
- No gridlines

To change the gridline settings, select **Gridlines** in the *Text Formatting* group [*Home* tab] (Figure 1-67), and then select the desired setting.

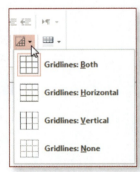

1-67 Gridlines display options

Display Alternate Row Colors

Alternate row colors help you easily scan the records and fields in your datasheet. You can change the alternating colors that are displayed or remove the colors altogether.

To change the alternate row color settings, select the *Alternate Row Color* icon in the *Text Formatting* group [*Home* tab]. Then select the desired color.

> **MORE INFO**
>
> You can also change the default gridline settings in Microsoft Access.

Use the Datasheet Formatting Dialog Box

If you are going to make several changes to the datasheet layout, you may wish to use the ***Datasheet Formatting*** dialog box.

HOW TO: Make Multiple Formatting Changes With the Datasheet Formatting Dialog Box

1. Open the *Datasheet Formatting* dialog box by clicking the **launcher** [*Home* tab, *Text Formatting* group].
2. Select the desired settings of the different options (Figure 1-68).
3. Click the **OK** button when finished.

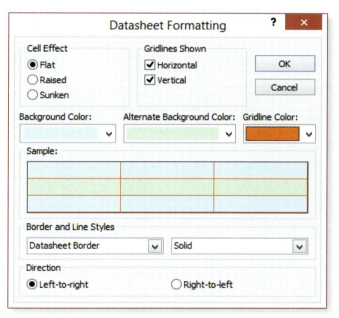

1-68 *Datasheet Formatting* dialog box

The *Datasheet Formatting* dialog box allows you to change several other formatting options that are not available through the *Home* tab. These options include the ***Cell Effect***, ***Background Color***, and ***Gridline Color***.

Save Changes

If you make changes to the design settings of the datasheet layout, you must save the table for those changes to be permanent. Select one of the previously discussed options for saving the design changes to your table.

For this project, you modify the field order, font size, row height, field width and field alignment of your *Employee* table. You also enhance the *Datasheet* view by modifying the gridline settings and alternating row colors.

File Needed: *[your initials] PP A1-2.accdb*
Completed Project File Name: *[your initials] PP A1-3.accdb*

---

1. Open the *[your initials] PP A1-2.accdb* database file that you created in Pause & Practice 1-2.

2. Save a new copy of your database.
   a. Select the **Save As** button [*File* tab]. The *Access Database* button should be selected in the *Save Database As* area.
   b. Click the **Save As** button.
   c. Select the desired location in which to store the copy of your database.
   d. Name the database [your initials] PP A1-3 in the *File name* box.
   e. Click the **Save** button.
   f. If prompted, click the **Enable Content** button in the *Security Warning* message bar.

3. Open the ***Employees*** table in *Datasheet* view. The table should appear as shown in Figure 1-69. Depending on the width of your Access window, you may see fewer columns.

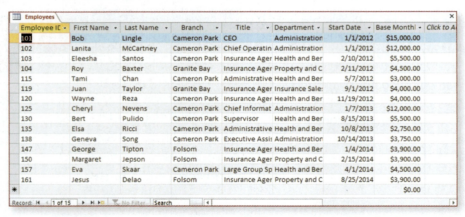

1-69 *Datasheet* **view of the** *Employees* **table**

4. Use the *Navigation* buttons to move among records.
   a. Click the **Next record** button to navigate to the second record.
   b. Click the **Next record** button three more times to navigate to the fifth record.
   c. Click the **Last record** button to navigate to the last record.
   d. Click in the **Current record** box. It changes from displaying 15 of 15 to simply displaying 15.
   e. Type 6 and press **Enter**. The sixth record should now be selected.
   f. Click the **First record** button to navigate to the first record.

5. Change the field order.
   a. Place your pointer above the **Title** field name.
   b. Click to select that column.
   c. Click, hold, and drag the pointer to the **left** of the *Branch* column.
   d. Release the pointer to move the column.
   e. Move the **Start Date** column to the right of the *Base Monthly Salary* column.

6. Change the *font face* and *size.*
   a. Click the **Font** drop-down list [*Home* tab, *Text Formatting* group].
   b. Select **Arial**.
   c. Click the **Font Size** drop-down list [*Home* tab, *Text Formatting* group].
   d. Select **12**.

7. Change the row height using the context menu.
   a. Click the **Record Selector** of a row in your table.
   b. Place your pointer on the **border** of that row.
   c. Right-click to open the context menu.
   d. Select the **Row Height** button to open the *Row Height* dialog box.
   e. Type 17 in the *Row Height* box.
   f. Click **OK**.

8. Change the column width of all columns using *AutoFit.*
   a. Click the **Select All** button in the upper left corner of the datasheet.
   b. Place your pointer on the **right border** of any of the field names.
   c. Double-click the **two-pointed arrow**. The column widths automatically adjust.
   d. Click in **any cell** to release the *Select All* setting. The table should now appear similar to that shown in Figure 1-70. If the width of the Access window was not large enough, some of the columns may display the ###### symbols. Most likely this will occur in the Base Monthly Salary or Start Date columns.

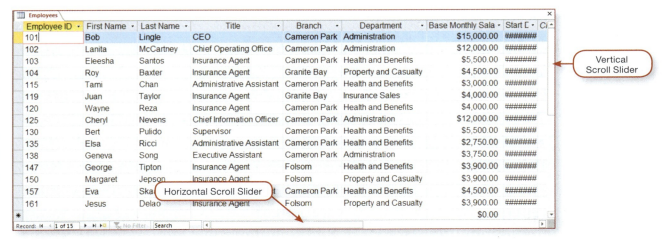

1-70 Adjusted column widths of the *Employees* table

9. If necessary, increase the width of any columns that display the ###### symbols.
   a. Move the **horizontal scroll slider** at the bottom of the datasheet to the right so that any column that contains ###### symbols moves to the middle of the window. This allows you to increase the width of this column more easily.
   b. Place your pointer on the **right border** of the field name.
   c. Click, hold, and drag the **two-pointed arrow** to the right to increase the column width. The column should now be wide enough to display the contents instead of the ###### symbols.
   d. Repeat these steps for all columns that are too narrow.

10. Change the field alignment.
    a. If necessary, move the **horizontal scroll slider** all the way to the left of the datasheet window.
    b. Select the **Employee ID** column.
    c. Click the **Center** button [*Home* tab, *Text Formatting* group].

11. Change the gridlines and alternate row colors using the *Datasheet Formatting* dialog box.
    a. Click the **launcher** [*Home* tab, *Text Formatting* group].
    b. Click the **Alternate Background Color** drop-down list in the *Datasheet Formatting* dialog box (Figure 1-71).
    c. Select **Blue-Gray**, **Text 2**, **Lighter 80%** (fourth column, second row in the *Theme Colors* category).
    d. Uncheck the **Horizontal** check box in the *Gridlines Shown* area.
    e. Click the **Gridline Color** drop-down list.
    f. Select **Blue-Gray**, **Text 2**, **Darker 25%** (fourth column, fifth row in the *Theme Colors* category).
    g. Click **OK** to close the dialog box.
    h. Click in the *Employee ID* cell for **Employee 102** as shown in Figure 1-72. Depending on your window width, you may need to scroll to see all of the columns. The slightly darker blue color shown in the second row indicates that this is the current record.

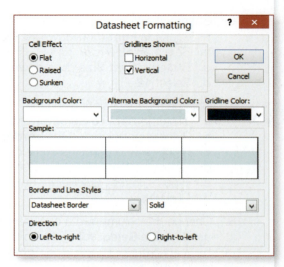

1-71 *Datasheet Formatting* dialog box

12. Press **Ctrl+S** to save the table

13. Click the **X** in the upper right corner of the datasheet to close the table.

14. Close the database by clicking the **Close** button [*File* tab].

Employee ID	First Name	Last Name	Title	Branch	Department	Base Monthly Sala	Start Date
101	Bob	Lingle	CEO	Cameron Park	Administration	$15,000.00	1/1/2012
102	Lanita	McCartney	Chief Operating Office	Cameron Park	Administration	$12,000.00	1/1/2012
103	Eleesha	Santos	Insurance Agent	Cameron Park	Health and Benefits	$5,500.00	2/10/2012
104	Roy	Baxter	Insurance Agent	Granite Bay	Property and Casualty	$4,500.00	2/11/2012
115	Tami	Chan	Administrative Assistant	Cameron Park	Health and Benefits	$3,000.00	5/7/2012
119	Juan	Taylor	Insurance Agent	Granite Bay	Insurance Sales	$4,000.00	9/1/2012
120	Wayne	Reza	Insurance Agent	Cameron Park	Health and Benefits	$4,000.00	11/19/2012
125	Cheryl	Nevens	Chief Information Officer	Cameron Park	Administration	$12,000.00	1/7/2013
130	Bert	Pulido	Supervisor	Cameron Park	Health and Benefits	$5,500.00	8/15/2013
135	Elsa	Ricci	Administrative Assistant	Cameron Park	Health and Benefits	$2,750.00	10/8/2013
138	Geneva	Song	Executive Assistant	Cameron Park	Administration	$3,750.00	10/14/2013
147	George	Tipton	Insurance Agent	Folsom	Health and Benefits	$3,900.00	1/4/2014
150	Margaret	Jepson	Insurance Agent	Folsom	Property and Casualty	$3,900.00	2/15/2014
157	Eva	Skaar	Large Group Specialist	Cameron Park	Health and Benefits	$4,500.00	4/1/2014
161	Jesus	Delao	Insurance Agent	Folsom	Property and Casualty	$3,900.00	8/25/2014
*						$0.00	

Record: 2 of 15 — Unfiltered — Search

1-72 PP A1-3 completed

Using Search, Sort, and Filter Tools to Find Records in a Table

When the number of records in a database table increases, it is important to be able to quickly and easily organize and locate specific records. Access provides a number of ways to find data, change the order of how records are displayed, and limit the records that display in the datasheet.

Search Data in a Table

The *Search* functions allow you to find data by looking for specific values. The **Search** box on the *Navigation* bar is a quick and easy way to locate the first record containing a specific value. The **Find** button in the *Find* group [*Home* tab] provides a more powerful way to search for records.

HOW TO: Find Data in a Table Using the Search Box

1. Click the **Search** box in the *Navigation* bar.
2. Enter the **Search Value** you want to locate.
   - Access evaluates the criteria as you enter each character and moves to the first field that matches those criteria as shown in Figure 1-73.

1-73 *Search* box in the *Navigation* bar

   - As you type more data into the *Search* box, Access continues to locate the first field that matches.
   - If a match is not found, the field or record that was previously selected remains highlighted.

HOW TO: Find Data in a Table Using the Find Button

1. Click the **Find** button [*Home* tab, *Find* group] (Figure 1-74).
   - If you want to search only in a specific field, select that field before you click the *Find* button.
   - The **Find and Replace** dialog box opens (Figure 1-75).

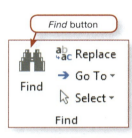

1-74 *Find* button

> **MORE INFO**
>
> The initial settings of your dialog box may be different, depending on your previous search.

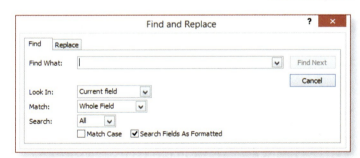

1-75 *Find and Replace* dialog box

> **ANOTHER WAY**
>
> You can also select a column and then right-click to open the context menu. Select the **Find** button to open the *Find and Replace* dialog box. You can also press **Ctrl+F** to open the *Find and Replace* dialog box.

2. Enter the **Search Value** you want to search in the *Find What* box.
3. Click the **Look In** drop-down list to select either **Current field** or **Current document**. If *Current field* is selected, the search only looks for a match in the current field.
4. Click the **Match** drop-down list to select the appropriate option.
   - **Whole Field**: The *Search Value* must match the entire contents of a field. This can be used to find an exact match.

- **Any Part of Field**: The *Search Value* must be somewhere in the field. This can be used to find a value that contains the *Search Value* anywhere in the field.
- **Start of Field**: The *Search Value* is at the beginning of the field. This can be used to find a value that starts with a certain character or number.

5. Click the **Search** drop-down list to select **All**, **Up**, or **Down**. Selecting up or down searches in that direction from the current record only.

6. Check the **Match Case** check box to limit the results to the case of the search value.

7. Click the **Find Next** button to execute the search. Access searches the table to find the first record that meets the criteria.
   - If that is the desired record, click the **Cancel** button to close the *Find and Replace* dialog box or click the **Find Next** button to continue searching.

ANOTHER WAY

You can also press **Shift+F4** to find the next record that meets the criteria.

1-76 Search item not found information message

- If the *Search Value* does not exist in the table, Access displays an information message box, shown in Figure 1-76, indicating the record was not found.

If desired, you can change data using the *Replace* tab on the *Find and Replace* dialog box. Press **Ctrl+H** to open the *Replace* tab. Enter the **Search Value** in the *Find What* box. Enter the **Replacement Value** in the *Replace With* box.

Sort Data in a Table with Datasheet View

The ***Sort*** functions allow you to organize your data. When you open a table in *Datasheet* view, by default, Access sorts the data records in ascending order by the first field. *Datasheet* view provides you with tools to perform a simple sort. You can sort the datasheet by one field, or a set of adjacent fields, in ascending or descending order.

- ***Ascending order*** is *lowest to highest* for a numeric field or *A to Z* for a text field.
- ***Descending order*** means *highest to lowest* for a numeric field or *Z to A* for a text field.

Sort Data on a Single Field

The simplest sort is to sort the datasheet on one field. You can either use the *Ascending* or *Descending* buttons in the *Sort & Filter* group [*Home* tab], or you can open the shortcut menu for the desired column.

HOW TO: Sort Data in a Table on a Single Field Using the Sort & Filter Group

1. Click the **field name** to select the column you wish to sort.
2. Click either the **Ascending** or **Descending** button in the *Sort & Filter* group on the *Home* tab (Figure 1-77).

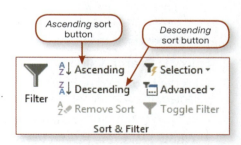

1-77 *Sort & Filter* group on the *Home* tab

- The datasheet updates to show the results of the sort. Figure 1-78 shows the employee records sorted in ascending order by the *Branch* field.
- The *Field Name* cell changes to display either an **Up** or **Down Sort indicator arrow** to the right of the drop-down arrow to visually indicate that the datasheet has been sorted on this field. If you want the table records to remain in this sorted order, you must save the table.

▶ **ANOTHER WAY**

Instead of selecting the column, you can also just click in any cell in the desired column.

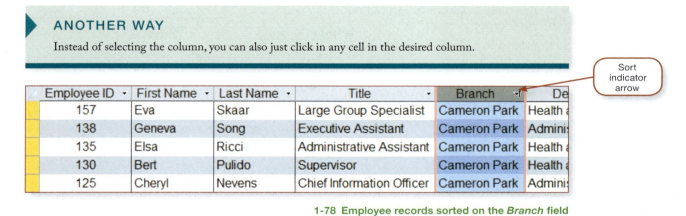

1-78 **Employee records sorted on the *Branch* field**

HOW TO: Sort Data in a Table on a Single Field Using the Shortcut Menu

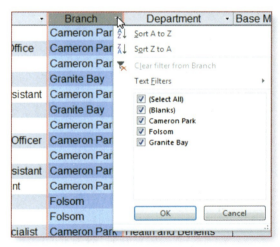

1. Click the **arrow** to the right of the **field name** you wish to sort.
   - The column turns blue, indicating it has been selected.
   - The shortcut menu opens (Figure 1-79).
2. Click either the **Sort A to Z** or **Sort Z to A** button on the shortcut menu.
   - The datasheet updates to show the results of the sort.
   - If you are sorting a numeric field, the shortcut menu options are *Sort Smallest to Largest* and *Sort Largest to Smallest*.

1-79 *Sort* shortcut menu

▶ **ANOTHER WAY**

Use **Shift+F10** to open the shortcut menu, and then type **S** for an ascending sort or type **O** for a descending sort. You can also right-click to open the context menu, then select the desired sort order.

Sort Data on Multiple Fields

Sometimes sorting your datasheet on multiple fields makes it easier to organize the data records. In *Datasheet* view, you can sort on multiple adjacent fields using the same sort order.

- The left-most selected field is sorted first.
- If there are identical items in the first field, the second field is sorted.
- This process continues for all additional selected fields.

HOW TO: Sort Data in a Table on Multiple Fields

1. Click and hold the **pointer** over the *Field Name* of the first column you want to sort. With the selection pointer still displayed, drag the pointer to the adjacent columns.

2. Release the pointer.

3. Click either the **Ascending** or **Descending** button [*Home* tab, *Sort & Filter* group].

   - The datasheet updates to show the results of the sort. Figure 1-80 shows the employee records sorted in descending order by the *Branch* [Granite Bay, Folsom, and Cameron Park] and the *Department* [Property and Casualty, Insurance, Health and Benefits, and Administration] fields.
   - In the example shown in Figure 1-80, there is a "tie" for the *Branch,* so the *Department* field determines which record appears at the top.

1-80 Employee records sorted on *Branch* and *Department* fields

> **MORE INFO**
>
> If the fields that you wish to sort together are not adjacent, you first need to move them together. Refer back to the "Modify the Field Order" section in *SLO 1.4: Exploring Datasheet View*, if neccessary.

Remove Sorting Criteria

To return the records in your datasheet to their original order, remove the *Sort* criteria.
- Click the **Remove Sort** button [*Home* tab, *Sort & Filter* group] to remove all *Sort* criteria.

> **MORE INFO**
>
> If you open a table with a previously saved sort, clicking *Remove Sort* removes the sort.

Filter Data in a Table with Datasheet View

The **Filter** functions are helpful in limiting the number of records that display in your datasheet. There are several different filter options available.

Create a Filter by Selection

Filter by Selection allows you to display only the records that match the value in the fields you have selected.

1-81 Selection button in the *Sort & Filter* group

HOW TO: Filter Data Using Filter by Selection

1. Click in the cell that contains the value you wish to filter.
   - You can select only part of the cell contents, if desired.

2. Click the **Selection** button in the *Sort & Filter* group on the *Home* tab (Figure 1-81).

- The drop-down list shows the available filter options.
- The available filter options depend on the data type of the field and what criterion is selected. If you only select part of a field, the beginning of the field, or the end of the field, the options differ.

3. Click the **desired filter option**.

- The datasheet updates to show the results of the filter.
- The *Filter status* message box changes, indicating the datasheet is filtered.
- The *Field Name* cell displays a *Filter* symbol to the right of the drop-down arrow, indicating this field has been filtered (Figure 1-82).

4. Once a filter has been applied, you can switch between viewing the complete dataset and the filtered results with the **Toggle Filter** button [*Home* tab, *Sort & Filter* group], shown in the top image in Figure 1-83. When toggled off, the *Filter status* message box, shown in the bottom image in Figure 1-83, changes to indicate that a filter exists but is toggled off.

1-82 Filtered datasheet

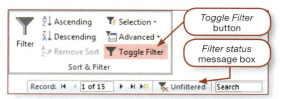

1-83 Toggle Filter button and updated *Filter status* message box

> **ANOTHER WAY**
>
> After selecting the desired cell, you can also right-click to open the context menu and then select the desired filter option.

Create a Text Filter, Number Filter, or Date Filter

A Text, Number, or *Date Filter* filters the records in your database by displaying the records that match the search criteria that you enter, instead of matching criteria you have selected from a cell. Although similar to using a *Filter by Selection*, these filters provide some additional options.

HOW TO: Filter Data Using a Text, Number, or Date Filter

1. Click the **arrow** to the right of the field name you wish to filter.
2. Click the **Text Filters** button on the shortcut menu (Figure 1-84).

- The button name is context sensitive and determined by the type of field you are filtering.
- The drop-down list displays the available filter options.
- The filter options are also context sensitive and change based on the type of field.

3. Click the desired **filter option** on the drop-down list to open the *Custom Filter* dialog box (Figure 1-85). The content of this dialog box depends on the filter option selected.

4. Type the **word or value** you wish to filter.

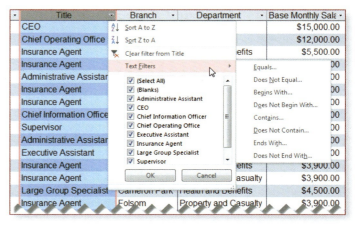

1-84 *Filter* shortcut menu

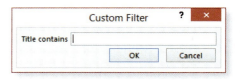

1-85 *Custom Filter* dialog box

5. Click the **OK** button.
   - The datasheet updates to show the results of the filter.
   - The *Filter status* message box changes, indicating the datasheet is filtered.
   - The *Field Name* cell displays a *Filter* symbol to the right of the drop-down arrow that indicates this field has been filtered.

Create Compound Filter Criteria

The previous examples used filters with one search value or criterion. You can create a more complex filter using compound criteria. *Compound criteria* combine more than one search value using the *AND* and *OR* logical operators.

- *AND:* The filtered records must contain all of the criteria values.
- *OR:* The filtered records must contain at least one of the criteria values.

You can specify compound criteria on one field or you can use compound criteria across several fields in your datasheet.

HOW TO: Filter Data Using "OR" Compound Criteria on One Field

1. Click the **arrow** to the right of the field name you wish to filter.
   - The shortcut menu opens.
   - Initially all the check boxes are selected.
2. Click the **(Select All)** check box to clear all the check boxes.
3. Click all of the check boxes on the shortcut menu that contain the **desired criteria** (Figure 1-86).

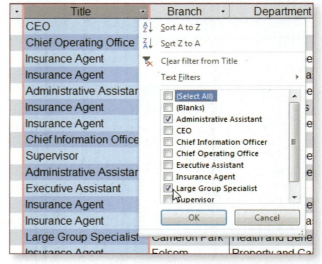

1-86 *Filter* shortcut menu showing *OR* criteria

> **MORE INFO**
>
> Selecting multiple criteria in the same field is an *OR* condition. The returned records contain the first value *or* the second value *or* the third value, and so on.

4. Click the **OK** button.
   - The datasheet updates to show the results of the filter.

HOW TO: Filter Data Using "AND" Compound Criteria on Multiple Fields

1. Click the **arrow** to the right of the first field name you wish to filter.
   - The shortcut menu opens.
   - Initially all the check boxes are selected.
2. Click the **(Select All)** check box to remove that criterion.
   - All the check boxes clear.
3. Click all of the check boxes on the shortcut menu that contain the **desired criteria**.

4. Click the **OK** button.

   - The datasheet updates to show the results of the filter.

5. Click the **arrow** to the right of the second **field name** you wish to filter.

6. Click the **(Select All)** check box to remove that criterion.

7. Click all of the check boxes on the shortcut menu that contain the desired criteria (Figure 1-87).

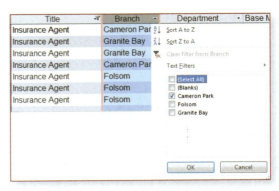

> **MORE INFO**
>
> Adding a filter to a second field is an *AND* condition. The returned records match the filter from *both* fields.

1-87 Using filters on multiple fields to create *AND* criteria

8. Click the **OK** button.

   - Only the records that meet both of the criteria display (Figure 1-88).

9. If desired, you can add a filter to additional columns by repeating the earlier steps.

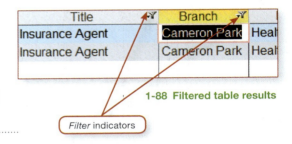

1-88 Filtered table results

Remove Filter Criteria

To return the records in your datasheet to their original unfiltered state, you must remove the *Filter* criteria. You can remove a filter from just one field or you can remove all of the filters.

HOW TO: Remove Filter Criteria from a Single Field

1. Click the **arrow** to the right of the first field name where you wish to remove a filter.

   - The shortcut menu opens.

2. Click the **Clear filter from Field Name** button to remove the filter.

   - The button will not display the phrase "Field Name", but instead will display the actual field name that has been filtered.

   - The datasheet updates to show the results of this filter being removed.

> **ANOTHER WAY**
>
> Click a cell of the desired Field. Press **Shift+F10** to open the shortcut menu, and then type **L** to select *Clear filter from Field Name*.

HOW TO: Remove Filter Criteria from All Fields

1. Click the **Advanced** button [*Home* tab, *Sort & Filter* group] to open the shortcut menu.

2. Click the **Clear All Filters** button.

For this project, you search for data in the *Employees* table using the *Search* box and the *Find* button. Next, you sort the table using single and multiple fields. You also filter the records using single and multiple criteria.

File Needed: ***[your initials] PP A1-3.accdb***
Completed Project File Name: ***[your initials] PP A1-4.accdb***

---

1. Open the ***[your initials] PP A1-3.accdb*** database file you created in Pause & Practice 1-3.

2. Save a new copy of your database.
   a. Select the **Save As** button [*File* tab]. The **Access Database** button should be selected in the *Save Database As* area.
   b. Click the **Save As** button.
   c. Select the **desired location** in which to store the copy of your database.
   d. Name the database [your initials] PP A1-4 in the *File name* box.
   e. Click the **Save** button.
   f. If prompted, click the **Enable Content** button in the *Security Warning* message bar.

3. Open the ***Employees*** table in *Datasheet* view. The changes you made to the datasheet layout in Pause & Practice 1-3 should be reflected, as shown in Figure 1-89.

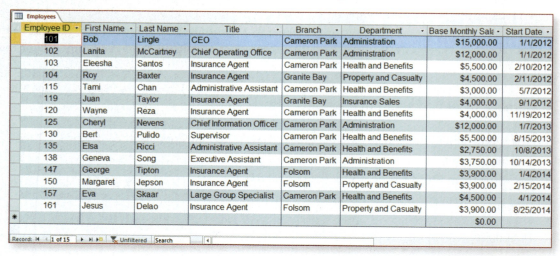

1-89 PP A1-4 Starting datasheet view

4. Use the *Search* box to find records.
   a. Type Health in the *Search* box in the *Navigation* bar. The *Department* field for **Employee 103** should be selected.
   b. Type Folsom in the *Search* box. The *Branch* field for **Employee 147** should be selected.
   c. Clear out the *Search* box.
   d. Click in the **Employee ID** cell for *Employee 101*.

5. Use the *Find* button to find records.
   a. Click the **Find** button [Home tab, *Find* group] to open the *Find and Replace* dialog box.
   b. Type Insurance in the *Find What* box.

c. If *Current document* is not displayed in the *Look In* drop-down list, click the **drop-down arrow** to select *Current document*. Then you can look for a match in all fields in the table.

d. If *Any Part of Field* is not displayed in the *Match* drop-down list, click the **drop-down arrow** to select *Any Part of Field*. Then you can find a match if the *Search Value* is somewhere in a field.

e. If *All* is not displayed in the *Search* drop-down list, click the **drop-down arrow** to select *All*. Then you can search through all the records.

f. If the **Match Case** check box is checked, uncheck that box.

g. Select the **Find Next** button to execute the search. The search starts from the currently selected field. Access searches the table to find the first record that meets the criteria. The *Title* field for **Employee 103** should be selected. If you had not clicked out of the *Branch* field in step 4d, the *Title* field for Employee 150 would have been selected.

h. Click the **Find Next** button again to find the next occurrence of *Insurance*. The *Title* field for Employee 104 should be selected.

i. Continue clicking the **Find Next** button until the *Department* field for **Employee 119** is selected.

j. Click the **Cancel** button to close the *Find and Replace* dialog box.

6. Sort the datasheet on a single field using the shortcut menu.
   a. Click the **arrow** to the right of the *Start Date* field.
   b. Click the **Sort Newest to Oldest** button on the shortcut menu. Employee 161, the most recently hired employee, should be in the first row of the datasheet.
   c. Click the **Remove Sort** button [*Home* tab , *Sort & Filter* group] to remove the sort criteria.
   d. Click in **any cell** to unselect the *Start Date* column.

7. Sort the datasheet on multiple fields using the *Sort & Filter* group.
   a. Click and hold the **pointer** over the *Branch* field name, the first column you wish to sort. With the selection pointer still displayed, drag the pointer to the *Department* field name.
   b. Release the pointer.
   c. Click the **Descending** button [*Home* tab, *Sort & Filter* group]. Employee 104, the employee from Granite Bay in the Property and Casualty department, should be in the first row of the datasheet.
   d. Click the **Remove Sort** button [*Home* tab, *Sort & Filter* group] to remove the sort criteria.
   e. Click in **any cell** to unselect the columns.

8. Filter the datasheet using *Filter by Selection*.
   a. Click after the "t" in the phrase **Insurance Agent**, in the *Title* cell for Employee 103.
   b. Click the **Selection** button [*Home* tab, *Sort & Filter* group].
   c. Select **Equals "Insurance Agent"** from the drop-down list. The datasheet should display only the seven employees who are insurance agents.
   d. Click the **arrow** to the right of the *Title* field name.
   e. Select the **Clear filter from Title** button to remove the filter. The datasheet updates to show all the records.

9. Filter the datasheet using a *Text Filter*.
   a. Click the **arrow** to the right of the *Title* field name.
   b. Select the **Text Filters** button on the shortcut menu.
   c. Click **Contains** from the drop-down list.
   d. Type Assistant in the *Title contains* box.
   e. Click the **OK** button. The datasheet should display only the three employees who have "Assistant" as part of their title.
   f. Click the **Toggle Filter** button [*Home* tab, *Sort & Filter* group] to switch back to viewing all the records.
   g. Click the **Toggle Filter** button again to switch back to the filtered records.
   h. Click the **arrow** to the right of the *Title* field name.
   i. Select the **Clear filter from Title** button to remove the filter. The datasheet updates to show all the records.

10. Filter the datasheet using compound criteria on multiple fields.
    a. Click the **arrow** to the right of the *Title* field name.
    b. Click the **(Select All)** check box to remove that criterion.
    c. Select the **Insurance Agent** check box on the shortcut menu.
    d. Click the **OK** button. The datasheet should display only the seven employees who are insurance agents.
    e. Click the **arrow** to the right of the *Branch* field name.
    f. Click the **(Select All)** check box to remove that criterion.
    g. Click the **Cameron Park** check box on the shortcut menu.
    h. Click the **OK** button. The datasheet should display only the two employees who are insurance agents at the Cameron Park branch.
    i. Click the **Advanced** button [*Home* tab, *Sort & Filter* group].
    j. Select the **Clear All Filters** button. The datasheet updates to show all the records.

11. Click the **X** in the upper right corner of the datasheet to close the table.

12. Select the **No** button when asked to save changes to the design of the *Employees* table.

13. Close the database by clicking the **Close** button [*File* tab].

Chapter Summary

1.1 Explain data organization concepts, use the Access Navigation pane, and identify objects (p. A1-3).

- The *hierarchy of data* helps organize the data into fields, records, tables, and a database.
- The *Navigation pane* displays all of the objects in your database. You can open objects directly from the *Navigation* pane.
- The major *Access objects* are *tables, forms, reports,* and *queries.*
- A database must contain at least one table.

1.2 Create a database, set database properties, understand database object naming conventions and data types, and close the database (p. A1-11).

- You can create a new database from a *template*, a ready-to-use database application that comes complete with objects already created.
- *Database properties* are details about the database including title, author, company, subject, date created, and date last modified.
- Create a *Blank desktop database* when you want to build your database application from scratch.
- *CamelCase* notation is the practice of naming objects by omitting spaces in compound words and starting each word with a capital letter.
- Each field in your database must be assigned a specific *data type* that determines what properties can be manipulated and how that field can be used.
- In *Backstage view,* you can close and open databases.

1.3 Create a table in *Datasheet* view, edit the default primary key, save a table, and enter records into a table (p. A1-17).

- Use *Datasheet view* to enter, modify, delete, or view data records.
- You can create and edit a new table using *Datasheet* view.
- Each table should have a *primary key,* a field that contains a unique value for each record.

- Add new fields in *Datasheet* view by entering data values or field names.
- The *properties* of each field describe the details or characteristics about the field. You can modify some of these properties in *Datasheet* view.
- Each table must be saved with a unique name.
- When entering records into a datasheet, Access verifies that the content of each field matches the data type. After a record is entered, it is automatically saved into the table.

1.4 Navigate table records in a datasheet and customize a datasheet by modifying field order, row height, column width, field alignment, font style and size, row colors, and gridlines (p. A1-28).

- Use the *Navigation bar* to move among records in a table.
- You can move the columns in a datasheet to change their order.
- You can change the *Font face, size,* and *style* in your datasheet. The changes are reflected in the entire datasheet.
- You can increase or decrease the *row height* in Access, but all of the rows change to the new height.
- You can adjust each column to a unique *field width.* Numeric or date fields display ##### if the column is not wide enough to display the entire contents.
- *Field alignment* dictates how content is aligned horizontally within a cell. Cells can be aligned *left, center,* or *right.*
- *Gridlines* visually frame the rows and columns in a datasheet with a border.
- *Alternating row colors* help you easily scan the records and fields in your *datasheet.*
- Use the *Datasheet Formatting dialog box* if you are going to make several changes to the datasheet layout.

1.5 Search, sort, and filter records in a table (p. A1-36).

- The *Search* box and the *Find* button allow you to find data with a specific value quickly.

- When you open a table in *Datasheet* view, the data records are sorted in ascending order by the first field.
- An **ascending order sort** is from lowest to highest; a **descending order sort** is from highest to lowest.

- In *Datasheet* view, if you sort on multiple fields, they all must be sorted in the same sort order.
- The **Filter** functions display only the set of records that meet specified criteria. The available filter options vary based on the data type of the field and what criterion is selected.

Check for Understanding

In the **Online Learning Center** for this text (www.mhhe.com/office2013inpractice), there are a variety of resources that can be used to review the concepts covered in this chapter.

The following Online Learning Resources are available in the Online Learning Center.

- Multiple choice questions
- Short answer questions
- Matching exercises

Guided Project 1-1

For this project, you create and use a new database based on the *Desktop Event Management* template. As the vice president of events for the *Green Club* at your university, you are trying to find an efficient way to keep track of the events your club has planned this semester. After creating the database, use the *Navigation* pane to explore the objects that exist in this database, edit field properties of the table, enter records, and modify the datasheet layout.
[Student Learning Outcomes 1.1, 1.2, 1.3, 1.4]

File Needed: None
Completed Project File Name: *[your initials] Access 1-1.accdb*

Skills Covered in This Project

- Create a database from a template.
- Use the *Navigation* pane.
- Edit properties in *Datasheet* view.
- Save a table.

- Enter records.
- View properties in *Design* view.
- Change the datasheet layout.
- Explore Access objects.

1. Create a new database based on a template.
   a. Open Access or click the **New** button [*File* tab] if Access is already open.
   b. Select the **Desktop Event Management** template (Figure 1-90).
   c. In the *File Name* box, enter *[your initials] Access 1-1.*
   d. If desired, click the **Browse** button to change the location in which to save your database. Click the **OK** button.
   e. Click the **Create** button. The database opens. Note: *If you experience a problem downloading the template, close the dialog box and skip to step 2.*
   f. Skip to step 3.

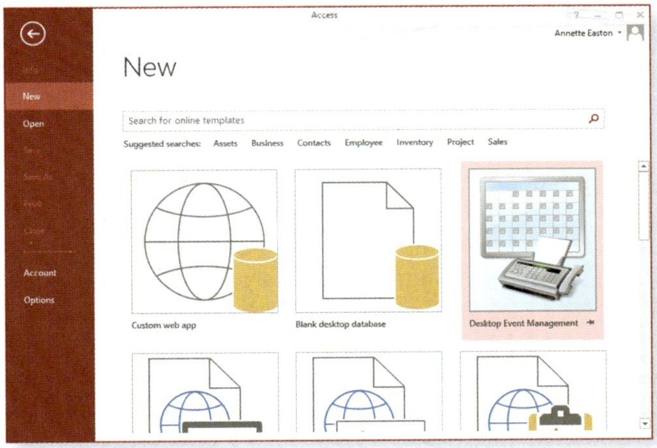

2. Open the **DesktopEventManagement-01** database from your student data files.
   a. Select the **Save As** button [*File tab*]. The *Access Database* button should be selected in the *Save Database As* area.
   b. Click the **Save As** button.
   c. Select **Yes** in the message box to have Access close the open objects.
   d. Enter *[your initials] Access 1-1* in the *File Name* box.
   e. If desired, select the location in which to save your database.
   f. Click the **Save** button. The database opens.

1-90 *Desktop Event Management* template available online

3. Click the **Enable Content** button in the *Security Warning* message bar (Figure 1-91).

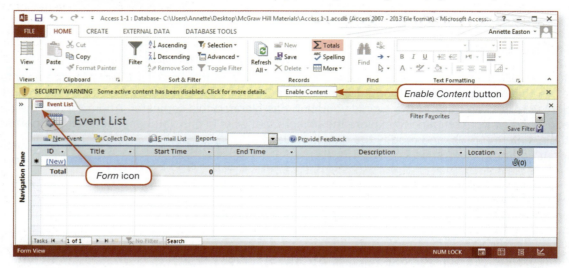

1-91 *Security Warning* message bar

The events database system is now ready to explore. This database contains many database objects that you have not yet used, like forms and reports. Often the objects in a template will contain more advanced database features. In the events database, when the database opens, an *Event List* form opens automatically. You know it is a form because the *Form* icon displays on the object tab. This form was designed to display data using a datasheet layout. You can also use this form to enter data into the database. You can now explore the database table in this template to see if it meets your needs.

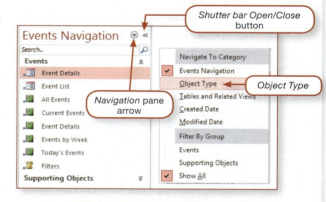

1-92 Modify the *Navigation* pane display

4. Use the *Navigation* pane to view the database objects.
    a. Click the **Shutter Bar Open/Close** button to open the *Navigation* pane. This particular template has customized the *Navigation* pane, as shown on the left side of Figure 1-92. The developers created an *Events* category to display only some the different objects.
    b. Click the **Navigation pane arrow** next to the *Events Navigation* category to open the *Navigation* menu, shown on the right side of Figure 1-92.
    c. Click the **Object Type** category.
        The *Navigation* pane should now display as shown in Figure 1-93. You can see that the Events template comes with 12 pre-built objects
        *   2 tables
        *   1 query
        *   3 forms
        *   5 reports
        *   1 macro
    d. The *Event List* form is linked to the *Events* table. If there are no records in the table, nothing displays in the form.
    e. Close the **Event List** form by clicking on the **X** in the right corner.

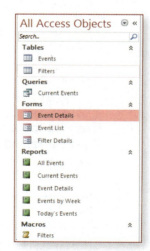

1-93 Pre-built objects in the events database

5. View the *Events* table in *Datasheet* view and edit field properties.
   a. Double-click the **Events** table to open it in *Datasheet* view. There are no records entered into the database table (Figure 1-94).

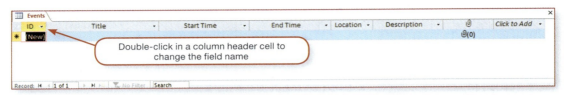

1-94 *Datasheet* view of the *Events* table

   b. Double-click the cell containing the **ID** field name (column header).
   c. Type Event ID for the field name and press the **down arrow** key.
   d. Click the **Table Tools Fields** tab. Remember that this contextual tab only displays when you are editing a table.
   e. Click the **Title** field name.
   f. Click the **Name & Caption** button [*Table Tools Fields* tab, *Properties* group].
   g. Type Event Title in the **Caption** property and click **OK**.
   h. Type 100 in the *Field Size* property [*Table Tools Fields* tab, *Properties* group].
   i. Click the **Start Time** field name. In the *Formatting* group [*Table Tools Fields* tab], notice that the *Data Type* property is set to *Date/Time,* and the *Format* property is set to *General Date*.
   j. Click the **Save** button to save the changes to the table design. With the changes to the field properties saved, the table is ready for you to begin to enter data records.

6. Enter a data record into the *Events* table to test the table structure.
   a. Click in the **Event Title** cell in the *Append Row*.
   b. Type Member Welcome and Kickoff Meeting. The pencil icon displays, indicating that this record has not yet been saved.
   c. Press the **Tab** key to move to the *Start Time* field and type 7:00 PM.
   d. Press the **Tab** key to move to the *End Time* field. The message box in Figure 1-95 opens. If a message box opens after leaving a field, it indicates that the data entered do not match what was expected for that field.
   e. Press the **OK** button to return to the *Start Time* field. It appears that this template has a discrepancy in the *Start Time* field. You need to fix this discrepancy before the Green Club can use the database. Because we need to explore this field further, delete the text you entered and leave that field blank for now.

1-95 Error message box

   f. Press the **Tab** key to move to the *End Time* field. Because you did not enter a value for the *Start Time,* leave the *End Time* field blank for now.
   g. Press the **Tab** key to move to the *Location* field and type Recreation Center Room 200.
   h. Press the **Tab** key to move to the *Description* field and type Member Meeting.
   i. Press the **Tab** key to move to the *Attachment* field.
   j. Press the **Tab** key because you do not have an attachment to enter. The pencil icon no longer displays since the record has been saved.

7. Change the layout of the *Events* table.
   a. Click to select the **Location** column.
   b. Click, hold, and drag the **pointer** to move the *Location* column to the left of the *Start Time*.
   c. Change the *Font Face* to **Times New Roman** [*Home* tab, *Text Formatting* group].
   d. Change the *Font Size* to **12** [*Home* tab, *Text Formatting* group].
   e. Click the **Select All** button, in the upper left corner of the datasheet.

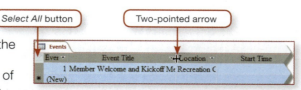

f. Place your **pointer** on the right border of any of the field names (Figure 1-96).

g. Double-click the **two-pointed arrow**. The width of all the fields should adjust to the needed width to display the cell contents. If the width of the Access window is not large enough, some of the fields will be smaller.

1-96 **Adjust field widths in the table**

h. Click the **Save** button to save the changes to the table design.

i. Close the *Events* table by clicking on the **X** in the right corner.

8. Explore the *Event List* and *Event Details* forms.
   a. Double-click the **Event List** form in the *Forms* group of the *Navigation* pane. The *Event List* form will open as shown in Figure 1-97.

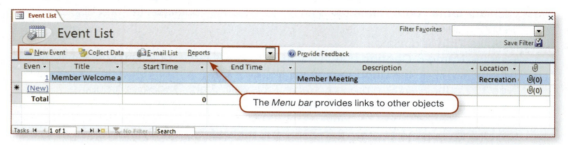

1-97 *Event List* **form**

b. The *Member Welcome* record you entered into the *Events* table displays. Recall that a form object provides a more user-friendly interface to view, add, update, and delete data in a table. It can also include additional features beyond those available in a table. For example, the *Event List* form, part of the template, has been customized to include a menu with direct links to additional forms and reports in the database.

c. Click the **New Event** button in the *Menu bar* of the *Event List* form to open the *Event Details* form (Figure 1-98). This form can be used to enter a new record into the database.

d. The properties of the time fields are not quite right at this point, so do not enter any additional data records.

e. Click the **Close** button to close the *Event Details* form.

9. Explore the other database objects.
   a. Look at the objects displayed in the *Navigation* pane. You should still see the same objects shown earlier in Figure 1-93.
   b. Look at the *Tables* group. You see the *Events* table and the *Filters* table.
   c. You also want your database to store information about the members of the Green Club. As a result, you realize that this database template is not right for you yet. You recognize that you will need to learn more about how to modify existing databases to create additional tables, or how to build your own database from scratch.

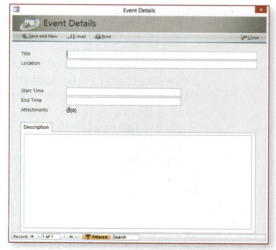

1-98 *Event Details* **form**

10. Close the *Event List* form by clicking the **X** in the right corner.

11. Close the database and Access by clicking the **X** in the right corner of the application window.

Guided Project 1-2

American River Cycling Club is a local cycling club. For this project, you create a database, containing one table, to store information about club members. After creating the database, add fields into the table, edit field properties, enter records, modify the datasheet layout, and sort and filter the data in the table.
[Student Learning Outcomes 1.2, 1.3, 1.4, 1.5]

File Needed: None
Completed Project File Name: *[your initials] Access 1-2.accdb*

Skills Covered in This Project

- Create a blank desktop database.
- Edit the default primary key.
- Add a new field into a table.
- Edit properties in *Datasheet* view.
- Save a table.

- Enter records.
- Change the datasheet layout.
- Sort data in a table.
- Filter data in a table.

1. Create a new blank desktop database.
    a. Open Access or click the **New** button [*File* tab] if Access is already open.
    b. Click **Blank desktop database**.
    c. In the *File Name* box, enter *[your initials] Access 1-2*.
    d. If desired, click the **Browse** button to change the location in which to save your database and click **OK**.
    e. Click the **Create** button. The database is created. A new table is created and opens in *Datasheet* view. If a table does not display, click the **Table** button [*Create* tab, *Tables* group] to create a new table.

2. Edit the default primary key and add new fields into the table.
    a. Double-click the cell containing the **ID** field name (column header).
    b. Type MemberID in the *Field Name* and press the **Enter** key. The *Click to Add* column to the right is selected so you can add the next field into the table.
    c. Click the **Short Text** data type to select the data type for this new field.
    d. Type FirstName in the *Field1* column header and press the **Enter** key.
    e. Click the **Short Text** data type.
    f. Type LastName in the *Field1* column header and press the **Enter** key.
    g. Add the remaining fields into the table using the information in the nearby table. Remember that you select the data type first and then enter the field name. After you enter the last field name, *CellPhoneNumber,* press the **down arrow** key to remain in that column.

Data Type	Field Name
Short Text	Address
Short Text	City
Short Text	State
Short Text	ZipCode
Hyperlink	EmailAddress
Short Text	CellPhoneNumber

    h. Press **Ctrl+S** to save all of the modifications you have made to the table.
    i. Type Members as the new table name.
    j. Select the **OK** button.

3. Edit the field properties of the *Members* table.
   a. Click the **MemberID** field name.
   b. Click the **Name & Caption** button [*Table Tools Fields* tab, *Properties* group].
   c. Type Member ID in the *Caption* property.
   d. Because the field names in this table provide a clear description of the content, it is not necessary to enter anything into the *Description* property.
   e. Click the **OK** button.
   f. Select the **FirstName** field name.
   g. Click the **Name & Caption** button [*Table Tools Fields* tab, *Properties* group].
   h. Type First Name in the *Caption* property.
   i. Click the **OK** button.
   j. Type 20 in the **Field Size** property [*Table Tools Fields* tab, *Properties* group].
   k. Change the remaining field properties in the table using the following information:

Field Name	Caption	Size
LastName	Last Name	25
Address		45
City		25
State		2
ZipCode	Zip	5
EmailAddress	Email	N/A
CellPhoneNumber	Cell Phone	12

   l. Click the **Save** button to save the changes to the table. With the changes to the field properties saved, the table is ready for you to begin to enter data records. Remember that even though you have changed the caption that displays as the column header in *Datasheet* view, the field names have not changed.

4. Enter the member records into the *Members* table.
   a. Click the **First Name** cell in the *Append Row*.
   b. Type Geneva. The pencil icon displays, indicating that this record has not yet been saved.
   c. Press the **Tab** key to move to the next field.
   d. Type Lingle in the *Last Name* field. Press the **Tab** key to move to the next field.
   e. Type 1850 Stoneridge Court in the *Address* field. Press the **Tab** key.
   f. Type Cameron Park in the *City* field. Press the **Tab** key.
   g. Type CA in the *State* field. Press the **Tab** key.
   h. Type 95682 in the *ZipCode* field. Press the **Tab** key.
   i. Type glingle@gmail.com in the *EmailAddress* field. Press the **Tab** key.
   j. Type 780-886-6625 in the *CellPhoneNumber* field. Press the **Tab** key. The pencil icon no longer displays. You move to the *MemberID* field in the *Append Row*.
   k. Tab to the **next field**. Enter the following information into the table. Remember that after you tab out of the *CellPhoneNumber* field you move to the *MemberID* field. Since that is an *AutoNumber* field, do not enter a value and simply tab to the **next field**.

FirstName	LastName	Address	City	State	Zip Code	Email	CellPhone
Cheryl	Wilson	7105 High Street	Folsom	CA	95630	cwilson@mcc.com	916-451-8325
Ryan	Thomas	2227 Alexandra Drive	Auburn	CA	95602	rthomas@gmail.com	916-753-5586

f.   Click the **Toggle Filter** button [*Home* tab, *Sort & Filter* group] to switch back to viewing all the records.

g.   Click the **Toggle Filter** button again to switch back to the filtered records.

h.   Click the **arrow** to the right of the *Email* field name.

i.   Click the **Clear filter from Email** button to remove the filter.

9.   Close the *Members* table by clicking the **X** in the right corner.

10. Celect the **No** button in the dialog box. You do not need to save any of the changes as a result of sorting or filtering the table. The completed table layout should look similar to Figure 1-102.

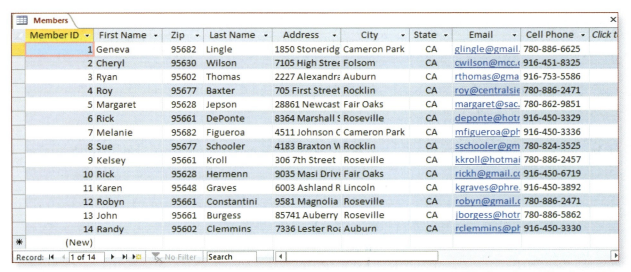

Members									
Member ID ⌄	First Name ⌄	Zip ⌄	Last Name ⌄	Address ⌄	City ⌄	State ⌄	Email ⌄	Cell Phone ⌄	Click t
1	Geneva	95682	Lingle	1850 Stoneridg	Cameron Park	CA	glingle@gmail.	780-886-6625	
2	Cheryl	95630	Wilson	7105 High Stree	Folsom	CA	cwilson@mcc.c	916-451-8325	
3	Ryan	95602	Thomas	2227 Alexandra	Auburn	CA	rthomas@gma	916-753-5586	
4	Roy	95677	Baxter	705 First Street	Rocklin	CA	roy@centralsie	780-886-2471	
5	Margaret	95628	Jepson	28861 Newcast	Fair Oaks	CA	margaret@sac.	780-862-9851	
6	Rick	95661	DePonte	8364 Marshall S	Roseville	CA	deponte@hotr	916-450-3329	
7	Melanie	95682	Figueroa	4511 Johnson C	Cameron Park	CA	mfigueroa@ph	916-450-3336	
8	Sue	95677	Schooler	4183 Braxton W	Rocklin	CA	sschooler@gm	780-824-3525	
9	Kelsey	95661	Kroll	306 7th Street	Roseville	CA	kkroll@hotmai	780-886-2457	
10	Rick	95628	Hermenn	9035 Masi Drive	Fair Oaks	CA	rickh@gmail.cc	916-450-6719	
11	Karen	95648	Graves	6003 Ashland R	Lincoln	CA	kgraves@phre	916-450-3892	
12	Robyn	95661	Constantini	9581 Magnolia	Roseville	CA	robyn@gmail.c	780-886-2471	
13	John	95661	Burgess	85741 Auberry	Roseville	CA	jborgess@hotr	780-886-5862	
14	Randy	95602	Clemmins	7336 Lester Roa	Auburn	CA	rclemmins@ph	916-450-3330	
*	(New)								

Record: ◄ ◄ 1 of 14 ► ►► ►* 🔽 No Filter   Search

1-102 **Completed *Members* table**

11. Add database properties using the *Database Properties* dialog box.

a.   Click the **File** tab to open the *Backstage* view.

b.   Click the **Info** button if it is not already selected.

c.   Click the **View and Edit Database Properties** link to open the *Database Properties* dialog box.

d.   In the *Title* area, type American River Members.

e.   In the *Author* area, type Taylor Mathos.

f.   In the *Company* area, type ARCC.

g.   Click **OK** to save the changes.

12. Close the *American River* database and Access by clicking the **X** in the right corner of the application window.

Guided Project 1-3

San Diego Sailing Club is a local sailing with a fleet of sailboats that members can rent. For this project, you create a database, containing one table, to store information about rental sailboats. After creating the database, you add fields to the table, edit field properties, enter records, modify the datasheet layout, and sort and filter the data in the table.

[**Student Learning Outcomes 1.2, 1.3, 1.4, 1.5**]

File Needed: None
Completed Project File Name: *[your initials] Access 1-3.accdb*

Skills Covered in This Project

- Create a blank desktop database.
- Edit the default primary key.
- Add a new field into a table.
- Edit properties in *Datasheet* view.
- Save a table.

- Enter records.
- Change the datasheet layout.
- Sort data in a table.
- Filter data in a table.

1. Create a new blank desktop database.
   a. Open Access or click the **New** button [*File* tab] if Access is already open.
   b. Click **Blank desktop database**.
   c. In the *File Name* box, enter *[your initials] Access 1-3*.
   d. If desired, click the **Browse** button to change the location in which to save your database and click **OK**.
   e. Click the **Create** button. The database is created. A new table is created and opens in *Datasheet* view.

2. Edit the default primary key and add new fields into the table.
   a. Double-click the cell containing the **ID** field name (column header).
   b. Type BoatID in the *Field Name.*
   c. Press the **down arrow** key to update the field name and stay in the same column.
   d. Click the **Short Text** data type [*Table Tools Fields* tab, *Formatting* group]. Because the boats already have an ID number assigned to them, do not use the *AutoNumber* data type in Access.
   e. Click the **Click to Add** column header.
   f. Click the **Short Text** data type.
   g. Type BoatType in the *Field Name* column header and press the **Enter** key.
   h. Click the **Short Text** data type.
   i. Type Length in the *Field Name* column header and press the **Enter** key.
   j. Enter the remaining fields into the table using the following information. Remember that you select the data type first and then enter the field name. After you enter the last field name, *ModelYear,* press the **down arrow** key to remain in that column.

Data Type	Field Name
Number	Seats
Number	Sleeps
Currency	FourHourRentalRate
Currency	FullDayRentalRate
Yes/No	GalleyWithStove
Short Text	ModelYear

   k. Press **Ctrl+S** to save all of the modifications you have made to the table.

   l. Type SailboatFleet as the new table name.

   m. Click the **OK** button.

3. Edit the field properties of the *SailboatFleet* table.

   a. Click the **BoatID** field name.

   b. Select the **Name & Caption** button [*Table Tools Fields* tab, *Properties* group].

   c. Type Boat ID in the *Caption* property.

   d. Because all of the field names in this table provide a clear description of their content, it is not necessary to enter any additional information in the *Description* property.

   e. Click the **OK** button.

   f. Type 4 in the *Field Size* property [*Table Tools Fields* tab, *Properties* group].

   g. Select the **BoatType** field name.

   h. Click the **Name & Caption** button [*Table Tools Fields* tab, *Properties* group].

   i. Type Boat Type in the *Caption* property.

   j. Click the **OK** button.

   k. Type 25 in the *Field Size* property [*Table Tools Fields* tab, *Properties* group].

   l. Change the remaining field properties using the following information:

Field Name	Caption	Size
Length		8
Seats		N/A
Sleeps		N/A
FourHourRentalRate	4 Hr Rate	N/A
FullDayRentalRate	Full Day Rate	N/A
GalleyWithStove	Galley w/ Stove	N/A
ModelYear	Model Year	4

   m. Click the **Save** button to save the changes to the table. With the changes to the field properties saved, the table is ready for you to begin to enter data records.

4. Enter the data records into the *SailboatFleet* table.

   a. Click the **BoatID** field cell in the *Append Row*.

   b. Type 1150. The pencil icon displays, indicating that this record has not yet been saved.

   c. Press the **Tab** key to move to the next field.

   d. Type Capri 22 Mk II in the *BoatType* field. Press the **Tab** key to move to the next field.

   e. Type 24'8" in the *Length* field. Press the **Tab** key to move to the next field.

   f. Type 6 in the *Seats* field. Press the **Tab** key to move to the next field.

   g. Type 4 in the *Sleeps* field. Press the **Tab** key to move to the next field.

   h. Type 65 in the *FourHourRate* field. Press the **Tab** key to move to the next field.

   i. Type 89 in the *FullDayRate* field. Press the **Tab** key to move to the next field.

   j. Leave the check box blank in the *GalleyWithStove* field. Press the **Tab** key to move to the next field.

   k. Type 2001 in the *ModelYear* field. Press the **Tab** key to move to the next record. The pencil icon no longer displays.

   l. Continue entering the remaining records into the table using the following information. Click the **GalleyWithStove** field check box to indicate a "Y" value.

BoatID	BoatType	Length	Seats	Sleeps	FourHour Rental Rate	FullDay Rental Rate	Galley With Stove	Model Year
1010	Catalina 270	28'4"	8	6	139	179	Y	1994
1146	Hunter 33	33'6"	10	6	299	349	Y	2000
1015	Catalina 270	28'4"	8	6	139	179	Y	1995
1185	Hunter 36	35'6"	10	6	349	389	Y	2006
1180	Beneteau 373	36'11"	10	6	369	409	Y	2006
1175	Beneteau 40	39'10"	12	6	489	529	Y	2005
1225	Hunter 36	35'6"	10	6	349	389	Y	2008
1190	Beneteau 373	36'11"	10	6	369	409	Y	2006
1200	Beneteau 373	36'11"	10	6	369	409	Y	2007
1152	Capri 22 Mk II	24'8"	6	4	65	89		2001
1205	Beneteau 40	39'10"	12	6	489	529	Y	2008
1168	Hunter 33	33'6"	10	6	299	349	Y	2004
1164	Capri 22 Mk II	24'8"	6	4	65	89		2003

5. Sort the *SailboatFleet* table.
   a. Click the **arrow** to the right of the **BoatID** field name.
   b. Click the **Sort A to Z** button on the shortcut menu. The records display in ascending order by the *BoatID* field.
   c. Click the **Save** icon on the *Quick Access* toolbar.

6. Change the layout of the *SailboatFleet* table.
   a. Change the **Font Face** to **Times New Roman** [*Home* tab, *Text Formatting* group].
   b. Change the *Font Size* to **12** [*Home* tab, *Text Formatting* group].
   c. Click and hold to select the **Length** column.
   d. Drag the selection **pointer** to select the *Seats* and *Sleeps* columns.
   e. Place your pointer on the right border of the **Sleeps** field.
   f. Double-click to adjust the *Field Width* using *AutoFit*.
   g. Select the **BoatType** field.
   h. Place your **pointer** on the right border of the *BoatType* field. The cursor changes to the two-pointed arrow.
   i. Click, hold, and drag the **pointer** to the right to increase the width of the *BoatType* field so that you can see the entire data value in the *BoatType* column.
   j. Select the **Boat ID** field.
   k. Click the **Center Alignment** button [*Home* tab, *Text Formatting* group].
   l. Select the **Length** field.
   m. Click the **Center Alignment** button.
   n. Click anywhere to deselect the column.
   o. Open the *Datasheet Formatting* dialog box (Figure 1-103) by clicking the **launcher** in the bottom right corner of the *Text Formatting* group [*Home* tab].

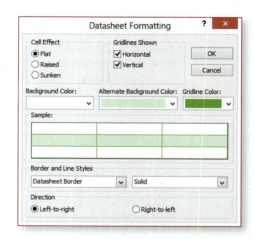

1-103 *Datasheet Formatting* dialog box

p. Click the **Alternate Background Color** drop-down list in the *Datasheet Formatting* dialog box.

q. Select **Green, Accent 6, Lighter 80%** (tenth column, second row in the *Theme Colors* category).

r. Click the **Gridline Color** drop-down list.

s. Select **Green, Accent 6, Darker 25%** (tenth column, fifth row in the *Theme Colors* category).

t. Click **OK** to close the dialog box.

u. Press **Ctrl+S** to save the changes to the layout. The updated layout should appear similar to Figure 1-104.

Boat ID	Boat Type	Length	Seats	Sleeps	4 Hr Rate	Full Day Rat	Galley w/ St	Model Year
1010	Catalina 270	28'4"	8	6	$139.00	$179.00	✔	1994
1015	Catalina 270	28'4"	8	6	$139.00	$179.00	✔	1995
1146	Hunter 33	33'6"	10	6	$299.00	$349.00	✔	2000
1150	Capri 22 Mk II	24'8"	6	4	$65.00	$89.00	☐	2001
1152	Capri 22 Mk II	24'8"	6	4	$65.00	$89.00	☐	2001
1164	Capri 22 Mk II	24'8"	6	4	$65.00	$89.00	☐	2003
1168	Hunter 33	33'6"	10	6	$299.00	$349.00	✔	2004
1175	Beneteau 40	39'10"	12	6	$489.00	$529.00	✔	2005
1180	Beneteau 373	36'11"	10	6	$369.00	$409.00	✔	2006
1185	Hunter 36	35'6"	10	6	$349.00	$389.00	✔	2006
1190	Beneteau 373	36'11"	10	6	$369.00	$409.00	✔	2006
1200	Beneteau 373	36'11"	10	6	$369.00	$409.00	✔	2007
1205	Beneteau 40	39'10"	12	6	$489.00	$529.00	✔	2008
1225	Hunter 36	35'6"	10	6	$349.00	$389.00	✔	2008
*			0	0	$0.00	$0.00	☐	

Record: 1 of 14 | No Filter | Search

1-104 Formatted datasheet layout

7. Filter the *SailboatFleet* table using compound criteria and sort the filtered results.

a. Click the **arrow** to the right of the *Seats* field name.

b. Click the **Number Filters** button on the shortcut menu.

c. Click **Greater Than** from the drop-down list (Figure 1-105).

d. Type 8 in the *Seats is greater than or equal to* box.

e. Click the **OK** button. The datasheet should display only the 11 boats that can seat at least eight people.

f. Click the **arrow** to the right of *the 4 Hr Rate* field name.

g. Click the **Number Filters** button on the shortcut menu.

h. Click **Less Than** from the drop-down list.

i. Type 350 in the *4 Hr Rate is less than or equal to* box.

j. Click the **OK** button. The datasheet should display only the six boats that can seat at least eight people and have a four-hour rate of less than or equal to $350.

k. Click to select the **Length** column.

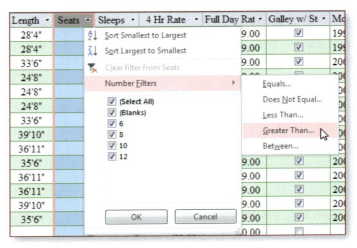

1-105 Number Filters

l. Click the **Ascending** button [*Home* tab, *Sort & Filter* group] to sort the filtered results by the *Length* field. In Figure 1-106, notice the filter symbols next to the field names of the *Seats* and *4 Hr Rate* fields and the sort symbol next to the *Length* field name.

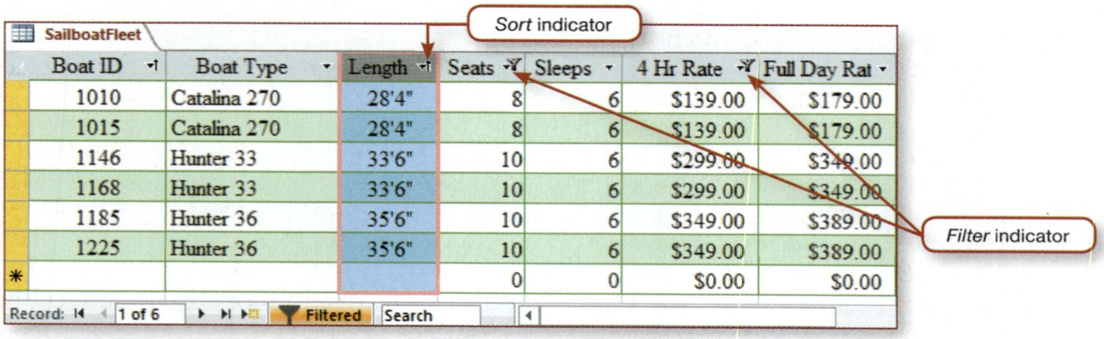

1-106 Filtered and sorted records

m. Click the **Toggle Filter** button [*Home* tab, *Sort & Filter* group] to switch back to the unfiltered records. Notice that the records remain sorted.

o. Click the **Remove Sort** button [*Home* tab, *Sort & Filter* group] to remove the sort criteria.

p. Click the **Advanced** button [*Home* tab, *Sort & Filter* group]. The shortcut menu opens.

q. Click the **Clear All Filters** button. The datasheet should update to show all the records.

8. Close the *SailboatFleet* table by clicking the **X** in the right corner.

9. Click the **No** button in the dialog box. You do not need to save any of the changes as a result of sorting or filtering the table.

10. Close the *San Diego Sailing* database by clicking the **X** in the right corner of the application window.

Independent Project 1-4

Courtyard Medical Plaza (CMP) is a full-service medical office complex. For this project, you create a database, containing one table, to store information about the physicians who work at CMP. After creating the database, you add fields into the table, edit field properties, enter records, modify the datasheet layout, and sort and filter the data in the table.
[Student Learning Outcomes 1.2, 1.3, 1.4, 1.5]

File Needed: None
Completed Project File Name: **[your initials] Access 1-4.accdb**

Skills Covered in This Project

- Create a blank desktop database.
- Edit the default primary key.
- Add a new field into a table.
- Edit properties in *Datasheet* view.
- Save a table.

- Enter records.
- Change the datasheet layout.
- Sort data in a table.
- Filter data in a table.

1. Create a new blank desktop database.
   a. Name the database **[your initials] Access 1-4**.
   b. If desired, change the location where you save the database.

2. Edit the default primary key and add new fields into the table.
   a. Change the **ID** field name to DoctorID. Keep this field as an *AutoNumber* data type.
   b. Enter the remaining fields into the table using the information in the nearby *Data Type* table. After you enter the last field name, *MoveInDate,* press the **down arrow** key to remain in that column.
   c. Save the table as Physicians.

Data Type	Field Name
Short Text	LastName
Short Text	FirstName
Short Text	OfficeNumber
Short Text	PrimarySpecialty
Date & Time	MoveInDate

3. Edit the field properties of the *Physicians* table using the information in the following *Field Name* table.

Field Name	Caption	Size
DoctorID	Doctor ID	N/A
LastName	Last Name	25
FirstName	First Name	20
OfficeNumber	Office	3
PrimarySpecialty	Specialty	30
MoveInDate	Tenant Since	N/A

4. Save the table after updating the properties.

5. Enter the data records shown in the following table into the *Physicians* table. Remember that the *DoctorID* field is automatically entered by Access.

Last Name	First Name	Office	Specialty	Tenant Since
Beyer	Robert	101	Cardiovascular Disease	2/15/2012
Scher	Elizabeth	115	Pediatrics	3/1/2014
Ostrander	Emy	101	Cardiovascular Disease	11/8/2014
Foster	Margaret	200	Pediatrics	7/1/2005
Flores	Ricardo	151	Internal Medicine	3/1/2014
Camacho	Juan	180	Dermatology	6/1/2010
Alamar	Alicia	151	Internal Medicine	2/20/2011
Hennessy	James	220	Pediatrics	7/1/2010
Plice	Rick	305	Family Medicine	3/15/2008
Dyer	Daniel	115	Pediatrics	3/1/2014
Singh	Robyn	210	Family Medicine	6/1/2013
Norman	Steven	230	Internal Medicine	12/15/2007
Ansari	Randy	180	Dermatology	4/1/2012
Pelayo	Kumara	210	Family Medicine	5/15/2007

6. Change the layout of the *Physicians* table.
   a. Change the *Font Size* to **12 pt**.
   b. Use **AutoFit** to increase the field width of the *Specialty* field.
   c. Use **AutoFit** to increase the field width of the *Tenant Since* field.
   d. **Center-align** the *Doctor ID, Office,* and *Tenant Since* fields.
   e. Change the *Alternate Row Color* to **Blue, Accent 1, Lighter 60%** (fifth column, third row in the *Theme Colors* category).
   f. Save the changes to the layout.

7. Sort the *Physicians* table in ascending order by the *Specialty* field.

8. Remove the sort criteria.

9. Filter the *Physicians* table to find the doctors who moved in on or after 1/1/2010 and who have a specialty in Pediatrics. The table should appear as shown in Figure 1-107.

10. Clear all the filters. The datasheet updates to show all the records.

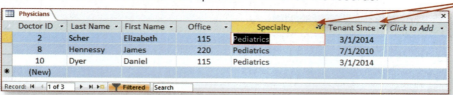

Filter indicator

1-107 Records filtered on *Specialty* and *Tenant Since*

11. Close the *Physicians* table.

12. Do not save any of the changes as a result of sorting or filtering the table.

13. Add the following database properties.
    a. *Title:* Courtyard Medical Plaza Physicians
    b. *Author:* Caroline Rios
    c. *Company:* CMP
    d. Save the changes.

14. Close the database.

Independent Project 1-5

Life's Animal Shelter (LAS) is an animal adoption agency that strives to keep its expenses down and donations up and is mainly run by volunteers. LAS does not turn any animal away, and its goal is to find homes for all animals within six months of their arrival. Julie Freed, one of the volunteers, has begun building a database for LAS. In this project, you work with her database, which currently has one table that contains information about the pets currently at LAS. Add one field into the table, edit field properties, enter data into records, modify the datasheet layout, and sort and filter the data in the table.
[Student Learning Outcomes 1.1, 1.2, 1.3, 1.4, 1.5]

File Needed: ***LifesAnimalShelter-01.accdb***
Completed Project File Name: ***[your initials] Access 1-5.accdb***

Skills Covered in This Project

- Open an existing database.
- Use the *Navigation* pane.
- Edit field properties in *Datasheet* view
- Add a new field into a table.
- Save a table.

- Enter records.
- Change the datasheet layout.
- Sort data in a table.
- Filter data in a table.

1. Open the ***LifesAnimalShelter-01*** database from your student data files.

2. Save a new copy of your database.
   a. Select the **Save As** button [*File tab*]. The *Access Database* button should be selected in the *Save Database As* area.
   b. Click the **Save As** button.
   c. Select the desired location in which to store the copy of your database.
   d. Type ***[your initials] Access 1-5*** in the *File Name* box.
   e. Click the **Save** button.

3. Enable content in the security warning.

4. Open the *Navigation* pane.

5. Open the *Pets* table in *Datasheet* view.

6. Edit the field properties of the *Pets* table using the information in the following table.

Field Name	Caption	Size
ID	Pet ID	N/A
PetName	Pet Name	15
Type		10
Breed		40
Age		8
Gender		1
Details	Why I'd make a great companion	N/A

   For several of the fields you see a *Some data may be lost* warning message display when you change the field size. The sizes provided are large enough based on the data entered, so no data will be lost. Click the **Yes** button to make the change.

7. Save the table after updating the properties.

8. Add a new field to the left of the *Details* field. Remember that the field name is still *Details* even though the caption is changed to *Why I'd make a great companion.*
   a. Select the **Details** column.
   b. Right-click to open the context menu.
   c. Select the **Insert Field** button.

9. Edit the field properties using the following information:
   a. *Field Name:* Color
   b. *Data Type:* **Short Text**
   c. *Size:* 25

10. Save the table after updating the properties of this new field.

11. Enter the data values shown in the following table into the *Color* field.

Pet ID	Pet Name	Color
1	Abby	Black
2	Alec	Tan
3	Allie	Brown
4	Barnaby	White
5	Lilith	Black/White
6	Martin	Brown Tabby/White
7	Sasha	Tan/White
8	Tate	Black/White
9	Elsa	White/Brown
10	Hubert	White/Brown
11	Bessie	Black/White
12	Connie	Tortoise Shell
13	Topaz	Brown Tabby
14	Lady	Black Brindle/White
15	Ashley	White/Brown
16	Bandit	Black/White
17	Vince	White
18	Pixie	White
19	Rocky	Tan/Black

12. Change the layout of the *Pets* table.
   a. Use **AutoFit** to decrease the field width of the *Pet ID, Type, Age,* and *Gender* fields.
   b. **Center-align** the *Pet ID* and *Gender* fields.
   c. Change the *Alternate Row Color* to **Gray-25%, Background 2, Darker 10%** (third column, second row in the *Theme Colors* category).
   d. Set the *Field Width* of the *Details* field to 60.

e. Set the *Row Height* of the table to 110.

f. Save the changes to the layout.

13. Filter the *Pets* table to find the **Dogs** and **Cats** with **Brown** as part of their coloring. The resulting table should be similar to Figure 1-108. Your records may display in a different order.

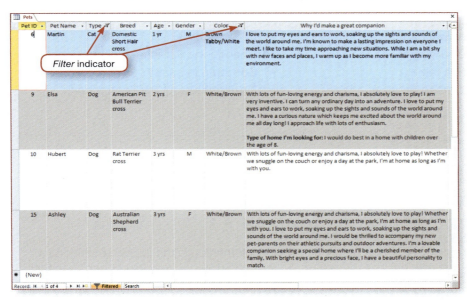

1-108 **Records filtered on** *Type* **and** *Color*

14. Sort the filtered results in ascending order by the *Gender* field.

15. Remove the sort criteria. Clear all the filters. The datasheet will update to show all the records.

16. Close the *Pets* table.

17. Do not save any of the changes as a result of sorting or filtering the table.

18. Edit the following database properties.
    a. *Company:* LAS
    b. *Author:* Student Name
    c. *Comments:* Pets table updated on [enter today's date]
    d. Save these changes.

19. Close the database.

Independent Project 1-6

Boyd Air is a national airline company. For this project you will create a database, containing one table, to store information about the airplanes in Boyd Air's fleet. After creating the database, add fields into the table, edit field properties, enter records, modify the datasheet layout, and find data using the *Search* box.
[Student Learning Outcomes 1.2, 1.3, 1.4, 1.5]

File Needed: None
Completed Project File Name: *[your initials] Access 1-6.accdb*

Skills Covered in This Project

- Create a blank desktop database.
- Edit the default primary key.
- Add new fields into a table.
- Edit properties in *Datasheet* view.
- Save a table.

- Enter records.
- Change the datasheet layout.
- Sort data in a table.
- Find data using the *Search* box.

1. Create a new blank desktop database.
   a. Name the database *[your initials] Access 1-6*.
   b. If desired, change the location to save your database.
2. Add new fields into the table.
   a. Do not make any changes to the *ID* field.
   b. Enter the remaining fields into the table using the information in the following table. After you enter the last field name, *InServiceDate,* press the **down arrow** key to remain in that column.

Data Type	Field Name
Short Text	PlaneModel
Short Text	Manufacturer
Short Text	Length
Number	FirstClassSeats
Number	CoachSeats
Date & Time	InServiceDate

   c. Save the table as Fleet.

3. Edit the field properties of the *Fleet* table using the information in the nearby table.

4. Save the table after updating the properties.

5. Enter the data records provided in the nearby table into the *Fleet* table. Remember that the *ID* field is automatically entered by Access. Remember that the *Datasheet* view of the table displays the field captions, while the following table shows the field name.

Field Name	Caption	Size
ID	Aircraft ID	N/A
PlaneModel	Model	25
Manufacturer		20
Length		7
FirstClassSeats	First Class	N/A
CoachSeats	Coach	N/A
InServiceDate	In-Service	N/A

PlaneModel	Manufacturer	Length	FirstClassSeats	CoachSeats	InServiceDate
B747-400	Boeing	231'10"	24	544	1/1/2010
Dash8	De Havilland	107'9"	0	70	3/1/2009
Dash8	De Havilland	107'9"	0	70	2/20/2010
B737-800	Boeing	129'6"	12	150	10/1/2012
A319	Airbus	111'0"	8	116	1/1/2013
B777	Boeing	242'4"	30	450	9/25/2007
A319	Airbus	111'0"	8	116	6/1/2012
A319	Airbus	111'0"	8	116	8/1/2013
B737-800	Boeing	129'6"	12	150	7/25/2012
B737-800	Boeing	129'6"	12	150	11/10/2009
B777	Boeing	242'4"	30	450	6/1/2014
B747-400	Boeing	231'10"	24	544	4/1/2010
B777	Boeing	242'4"	30	450	12/1/2011

6. Change the layout of the *Fleet* table.
   a. Change the *Font Size* to **12 pt**.
   b. Select the entire datasheet and use **AutoFit** to adjust all the fields to their correct size.
   c. **Center-align** the Aircraft ID, *First Class,* and *Coach* fields.
   d. Remove the gridlines.
   e. Save the changes to the layout.

7. Sort the *Fleet* table in descending (Newest to Oldest) order according to the *In-Service* field. The table should display similar to Figure 1-109.

8. Remove the sort criteria.

9. Use the *Search* box to find Dash8.

10. Delete the value from the *Search* box.

11. Close the *Fleet* table.

12. Do not save any of the changes as a result of sorting or filtering the table.

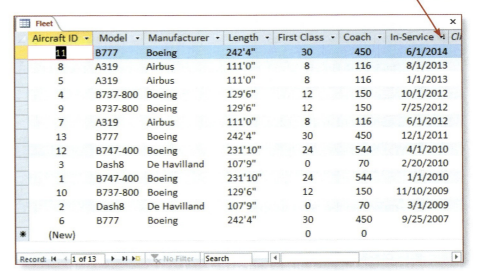

Sort indicator

1-109 Records sorted on *In-Service* field

13. Add the following database properties.
    a. *Title:* Boyd Air Fleet Data
    b. *Author:* Student Name
    c. *Company:* BoydAir
    d. Save the changes.

14. Close the database.

Improve It Project 1-7

Placer Hills Real Estate (PHRE) is a real estate company with regional offices throughout central California. Kelsey Kroll, one of the managers, had begun building a database. The database has one table that contains information about the real estate properties currently listed for sale. You add one field into the table, edit field properties, enter data into records, modify the datasheet layout, and sort and filter the data in the table.
[Student Learning Outcomes 1.1, 1.2, 1.3, 1.4, 1.5]

File Needed: **PlacerHills-01.accdb**
Completed Project File Name: **[your initials] Access 1-7.accdb**

Skills Covered in This Project

- Open a database.
- Use the *Navigation* pane.
- Edit the default primary key.
- Add a new field into a table.
- Edit properties in *Datasheet* view.
- Save a table.
- Enter records.
- Change the datasheet layout.
- Sort data in a table.
- Filter data in a table.

1. Open the **PlacerHills-01** database from your student data files.

2. Save a new copy of your database.
   a. Select the **Save As** button [*File tab*]. The *Access Database* button should be selected in the *Save Database As* area.
   b. Click the **Save As** button.
   c. Select the desired location in which to store the copy of your database.
   d. Type **[your initials] Access 1-7** in the *File Name* box.
   e. Click the **Save** button.

3. Enable content in the security warning.

4. Open the *Navigation* pane.

5. Open the *Listings* table in *Datasheet* view.

6. Edit the field properties of the *Listings* table using the information in the nearby table.
   For several of the fields, you see a *Some data may be lost* warning message when you change the field size. Because the new field sizes are sufficient for the existing data, click the **Yes** button to continue.

7. Save the table after updating the properties.

8. Add a new field to the left of the *Agent* field.

9. Edit the field properties using the following information:
   a. *Field Name:* Construction
   b. *Data Type:* Short Text
   c. *Size:* 5

10. Save the table after updating the properties.

Field Name	Caption	Size
ListingID		N/A
DateListed	Date Listed	N/A
ListPrice	List Price	N/A
Address		35
City		20
SqFt		N/A
Beds		N/A
Baths		N/A
Garage		18
YearBuilt	Built	N/A
ListingAgent	Agent	25

11. Enter the data values shown in the nearby table into the new *Construction* field.

12. Change the layout of the *Listings* table.
    a. Change the *Font Size* to **12 pt**.
    b. Select the entire datasheet and use **AutoFit** to adjust all the fields to their correct size. Remember that if the width of the Access window was not wide enough, some of the columns may still be too small. You can adjust the width of those columns individually.
    c. **Center-align** the *SqFt, Beds, Baths, Built,* and *Construction* fields.
    d. Change the gridline color to **Green 5** (seventh column, sixth row in the *Standard Colors* category).
    e. Set the row height of the table to 16.
    f. Save the changes to the layout.

13. Add the following database properties and save the changes:
    a. *Company:* PHRE
    b. *Comments:* Listings table updated [enter today's date]

14. Sort the *Listings* table in descending order by the *List Price* field. *ListingID 10024* should be at the top of the datasheet and *ListingID 10053* should be at the bottom of the datasheet.

15. Remove the sort criteria.

16. Filter the *Listings* table to find the listings of homes that are at least 2000 square feet, have 3 or 4 bathrooms, and are brick construction.

17. Sort the filtered results in ascending order by the *List Price* field. Your datasheet should be similar to the one shown in Figure 1-110.

18. Remove the sort criteria.

19. Clear all the filters. The datasheet updates to show all the records.

20. Close the *Listings* table.

21. Do not save any of the changes as a result of sorting or filtering the table.

22. Close the database.

ListingID	Construction
10022	Frame
10023	Stone
10024	Brick
10027	Stone
10030	Stone
10031	Brick
10040	Frame
10042	Brick
10043	Stone
10044	Brick
10045	Brick
10046	Brick
10048	Frame
10052	Brick
10053	Frame
10054	Stone
10060	Frame
10062	Frame
10069	Frame
10073	Brick
10074	Brick
10099	Stone
10100	Frame
10110	Stone
10116	Frame
10130	Stone
10144	Frame
10150	Brick
10165	Frame
10166	Brick
10172	Frame

Sort indicator

Filter indicator

Listing	Date Listed	List Price	Address	City	SqFt	Beds	Baths	Garage	Built	Construction	Agent
10045	4/18/2014	$274,500.00	12355 Krista Lane	Auburn	2234	3	3	2 Car Attached	1984	Brick	Kallyn Duarte
10074	5/20/2014	$329,900.00	1827 Delouch Dr	Lincoln	2575	3	3	3 Car Attached	2006	Brick	Kelly Weatherby
10031	4/2/2014	$368,505.00	2024 Brixham	Roseville	2385	3	3	2 Car Attached	1999	Brick	Kallyn Duarte
10024	3/23/2014	$675,000.00	1917 Oak Crest Dr.	Roseville	3397	4	4	3 Car Attached	2006	Brick	Jack Johnstone
*		$0.00			0	0	0		0		

Record: 1 of 4   Filtered   Search

1-110 Records sorted on *List Price*

Challenge Project 1-8

Create a database for an organization to which you belong. The database should contain one table. Create the table by adding fields and modifying properties. Enter data into the table. Ensure that the datasheet layout is easy to read.
[Student Learning Outcomes 1.2, 1.3, 1.4, 1.5]

File Needed: None
Completed Project File Name: *[your initials] Access 1-8.accdb*

Create a new database and save it as *[your initials] Access 1-8.* Modify your database according to the following guidelines:

- Enter at least five fields into the table.
- Save the table.
- Edit the field properties to match the needs of the database.
- Enter several records into the table.
- Change the layout as desired to create a professional-looking layout.
- Sort the records by one of the fields.

Challenge Project 1-9

Create a database for a small bakery. The database should contain one table to store information about the different items sold by the bakery. One of the table fields is item category. Examples of the content for the Item categories might include cupcakes, cakes, pies, cookies, and candy. Create the table by adding fields and modifying properties. Enter data into the table. Ensure that the datasheet layout is easy to read.
[Student Learning Outcomes 1.2, 1.3, 1.4, 1.5]

File Needed: None
Completed Project File Name: *[your initials] Access 1-9.accdb*

Create a new database and save it as *[your initials] Access 1-9.* Modify your database according to the following guidelines:

- Add the following fields into the table: *ItemID, ItemName, CostToMake, Mark-UpPercentage,* and *ItemCategory.*
- The *Item ID* should use an *AutoNumber* data type. Select appropriate data types for the other fields.
- Save the table.
- Edit the field properties, like the *Field Size,* to match the needs of the database.
- Enter several records into the table.
- Change the layout as desired to create a professional-looking layout.
- Find a record where the category is *Cupcakes,* using the *Search* box.
- Use the *Filter by Selection* to find all the records for which the category is *Cupcakes.*

Challenge Project 1-10

Create a database for a travel agency. The database should contain one table to store information about upcoming cruises. Create the table by adding fields and modifying properties. Enter data into the table. Ensure that the datasheet layout is easy to read.
[Student Learning Outcomes 1.2, 1.3, 1.4, 1.5]

File Needed: None
Completed Project File Name: *[your initials] Access 1-10.accdb*

Create a new database and save it as *[your initials] Access 1-10.* Modify your database according to the following guidelines:

- Add the following fields into the table: *TripID, TripName, NumberOfDays, DepartureCity, DestinationCity, DepartureDate,* and *CostPerPerson.*
- The *TripID* should use an *AutoNumber* data type. Select appropriate data types for the other fields.
- Save the table.
- Edit the field properties, like the *Field Size,* to match the needs of the database.
- Enter several records into the table for trips of various lengths. Search the web if you need help finding examples of data to enter.
- Change the layout as desired to create a professional-looking layout.
- Create a filter using compound criteria to locate all cruises that leave from a select city and have the same trip length.

Using Design View, Data Validation, and Relationships

CHAPTER OVERVIEW

In Chapter 1 you learned to use *Datasheet* view to create and view tables. Many database designers prefer to create tables in *Design* view because it is easier to change the various field and table properties. Additionally, some database properties can only be changed using *Design* view. This chapter covers the basics of creating a table in *Design* view, using data validation rules to ensure your data is valid, and creating relationships among different tables in a database.

STUDENT LEARNING OUTCOMES (SLOs)

After completing this chapter, you will be able to:

SLO 2.1 Create a table in *Design* view; add new fields; define a primary key; delete fields; save, close and open a table; and switch between *Datasheet* and *Design* views (p. A2-75).

SLO 2.2 Set field properties including *Field Size, Format, Caption, Default Value,* and *Required* (p. A2-79).

SLO 2.3 Explain data integrity and data validation concepts and options (p. A2-86).

SLO 2.4 Create field and record level validation rules, test rules, create validation text, create lookup fields, and define an input mask (p. A2-87).

SLO 2.5 Change field properties after records are added into a table (p. A2-99).

SLO 2.6 Explain relational database principles, understand the steps that must be taken to design a database, create relationships between tables, implement referential integrity, and delete and edit relationships (p. A2-104).

SLO 2.7 Import data records from Excel (p. A2-116).

SLO 2.8 Preview and print the contents of a table (p. A2-118).

SLO 2.9 Manage a database using *Compact & Repair* (p. A2-121).

CASE STUDY

Mary's Rentals is a privately owned equipment rental company. In the Pause & Practice projects in this chapter, you develop a database that contains information about the company's products. As you progress through the chapter, you incorporate many of the skills you are learning to construct and enhance this database.

Pause & Practice 2-1: Create a new blank database. Customize the table using *Design*

view to store equipment information. Add new fields, define the primary key, edit field properties, and save the table.

Pause & Practice 2-2: Refine your equipment table design by adding a field validation rule and a table validation rule, adding validation text, testing the validation rules, creating a lookup field, and defining an input mask.

Pause & Practice 2-3: Add a second table to store the service history of the equipment.

Define a relationship between the equipment and service history tables.

Pause & Practice 2-4: Import data into the service history table and print the contents of the equipment table. Use the *Compact & Repair Database* option to manage the database.

SLO 2.1

Creating a Table in Design View

Design view is used to create a table from scratch. When creating the table you define the fields that are included in the table and set their properties. You can also make changes to the fields in an existing table using *Design* view. This section teaches you to create a table in *Design* view, add new fields, define a primary key, delete fields, and save a table.

Create a New Table in Design View

You can add a new table into a database from the *Create* tab. Tables created using the **Table Design** button automatically open in *Design* view.

HOW TO: Create a New Table in Design View

1. Click the **Create** tab on the *Ribbon*.
2. Click the **Table Design** button in the *Tables* group (Figure 2-1).
   - A new table opens in *Design* view, as shown in Figure 2-2.
   - The table is assigned a generic name, such as *Table1*.
   - The *Design* tab, a **Table Tools contextual tab**, is now available and selected.
   - The new table does not contain any fields.
   - The *Design* view window is divided into two areas. The top half displays the *Field Name*, *Data Type* and *Description* for all the fields in the table. The lower half displays the detailed field properties of the selected field.

2-1 *Table Design* button on the *Create* tab

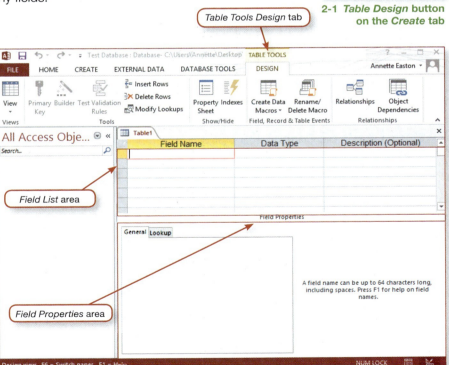

2-2 New table in *Design* view

Add New Fields

Add new fields into a table by entering a field name in the first empty row in the field list. When you add a new field you must enter values for the *Field Name* and *Data Type* properties. If you like, you can enter values for other available properties.

HOW TO: Add a New Field

1. Click the **Field Name** property box in the first empty row in the field list.
2. Type the desired name in the property box (Figure 2-3).
   - Each field must have a unique name that is limited to 64 characters.
   - The name can include letters, numbers, and spaces and most special characters.
   - The name cannot include a period (.), exclamation point (!), accent grave (`), or square brackets ([ ]).
   - Use the naming conventions required by your instructor or employer.
3. Press the **Enter** key to add the field.
   - You move to the *Data Type* property with the *Short Text Data Type* selected.
   - The *Field Properties* of this field now display in the lower half of the *Design* view window.

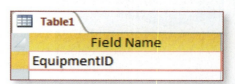

2-3 *Field Name* property box

> **ANOTHER WAY**
>
> Press the **Tab** key to add the field and move to the *Data Type* column.

4. Click the **drop-down arrow** in the **Data Type** property box (Figure 2-4).
   - The list of data types displays.
5. Select the appropriate **Data Type**.
6. Press the **Enter** key to move to the *Description* property box.
7. Type a value in the **Description** property box, if desired (Figure 2-5).
8. Press the **Enter** key to move to the *Field Name* property box of the next row.
9. Repeat steps 2 through 8 to add the additional fields into your table.

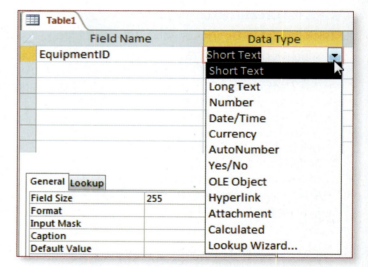

2-4 *Data Type* options in *Design* view

Description (Optional)
Unique ID assigned to each piece of equipment

2-5 Enter the field's description in the *Description* property box

Sometimes you may need to add a new field between existing fields in a table. To add this new field, you must first insert a new row. After the row has been inserted, follow the steps above to add the new field.

HOW TO: Insert a Blank Row to Add a New Field between Existing Fields

1. Click in the **Field Name, Data Type,** or **Description** property box to select the row where you want to add the new field.

> **ANOTHER WAY**
>
> Click in the **Row Selector** box to select a field. The *Row Selector* is the gray box to the left of a field name in *Design* view. The *Row Selector* of the selected row turns yellow.

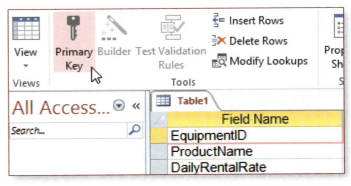

Row Selector box

2-6 *Insert Rows* Button

2. Click the **Insert Rows** button [*Table Tools Design* tab, *Tools* group] as shown in Figure 2-6.
   - A new blank row is entered above the selected field.
   - Follow the steps in the *How To: Add a New Field* to enter the details about the new field.

Define a Primary Key

Recall that a ***primary key*** is a field that contains a unique value for each record. When a table is created in *Design* view, a primary key field is not automatically assigned. You must determine which of the fields in your table uniquely identifies each record. If needed, add an additional field with an *AutoNumber Data Type* to serve as the primary key.

HOW TO: Define a Primary Key

1. Click in the **Field Name, Data Type,** or **Description** property box to select the desired field.

2. Click the **Primary Key** button [*Table Tools Design* tab, *Tools* group] (Figure 2-7).
   - The Primary Key symbol appears in the *Row Selector* box.

2-7 *Primary Key* button

Delete Fields in a Table

There may be times when you need to delete a field in a table. While this is easy to accomplish, it is important to realize that this may impact other parts of your database. If you have queries, forms, and reports that contain this field, you must also modify those objects to remove this field.

1. Click in the **Field Name, Data Type,** or **Description** property box to select the desired field.
2. Click the **Delete Rows** button [*Table Tools Design* tab, *Tools* group] (Figure 2-8).
3. If there is data in the table, Access displays an information message (Figure 2-9) asking you to confirm the deletion of the field and data in the table.

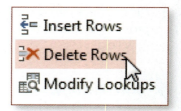

2-8 *Delete Rows* button

2-9 **Delete field confirmation message**

Save, Close, and Open a Table

The save, close, and open operations on a table work the same whether you are in *Datasheet* or *Design* view.

- Save a new table by clicking the **File** tab and clicking the **Save** button. This opens the *Save As* dialog box. Type in a new name for the table to replace the generic name assigned by Access.

> **ANOTHER WAY**
>
> Recall from Chapter 1 that you can also use **Ctrl+S**, the **Save** icon on the *Quick Access* toolbar, or the **F12** function key to open the *Save As* dialog box.

- Close a table by clicking the **X** in the upper right corner of the table.

  If you close a new table without saving it, Access deletes the table.

- Open a table in *Design* view by right-clicking the table name in the *Navigation* pane and selecting **Design View** from the context menu, as shown in Figure 2-10.

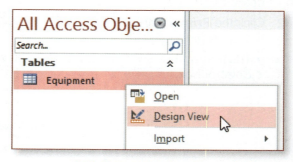

2-10 **Open a table from the context menu**

Switch between Datasheet and Design Views

Recall that **Datasheet view** is used to enter records into a table. When creating, and later using, a table, you may find that you need to switch between looking at the data records and looking at the properties of the different fields. When a table is open, Access provides two ways to easily switch between different table views.

- Select the **View** button arrow [*Home* tab, *Views* group] and then select the desired view option (Figure 2-11).
- Select the **desired view icon** from the right side of the *Status bar* (Figure 2-12), located at the bottom of the Access window.

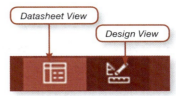

2-12 Table *View* icons in the Status bar

2-11 The *View* button

Setting Field Properties

Field properties describe the specific details of each field. When you add a field into the table, you enter values for the field name, data type, and description properties. You can set many additional field properties depending on the needs of your database. The available properties vary based on the data type of the field. Field Properties are grouped into **General** and **Lookup** properties, and are displayed on their respective tabs in the *Field Properties* area in the lower half of the *Design* view window. This section introduces the more common *General* tab field properties of **Field Size**, **Format**, **Caption**, **Default Value**, and **Required**.

In order for the changes you make on any of the properties to be permanent, you must save the table. You can save the table either after each change or after all of your changes have been made.

Be sure to select the correct field in the list of fields before setting any of the properties discussed in this section.

Set the Field Size

The *Field Size* property determines the maximum number of characters allowed in a *Short Text* field or the range of possible values in a *Number* field.

- A *Short Text* field can have a size from 0 to 255.
- A *Number* field can have seven possible field sizes that are explained in the following table.

Number Data Type Field Sizes

Field Size	Description
Byte	Stores numbers from 0 to 255. Does not use decimal places.
Integer	Stores numbers from −32,768 to 32,767. Does not use decimal places.
Long Integer	Stores numbers from −2,147,483,648 to 2,147,483,647. Does not use decimal places. This is the default field size for a number data type.
Single	Stores numbers from -3.4×10^{38} to 3.4×10^{38} with a precision of 7 significant digits.
Double	Stores numbers from -1.797×10^{38} to 1.797×10^{38} with a precision of 15 significant digits.
Replication ID	Stores a globally unique identifier (FUID) randomly generated by Access.
Decimal	Stores numbers from -10^{28} to 10^{28} with a precision of 28 significant digits.

- An *AutoNumber* field can use either the *Long Integer* or *Replication ID* field size.

The other data types do not have a *Field Size* property since their size is controlled by the database. The *Field Size* property, if available, is the first property on the *General* tab.

1. For a *Short Text* field, click in the **Field Size** property box and type the desired field size (Figure 2-13).

   • The default size of a *Short Text* field is 255.

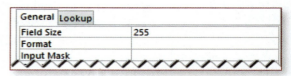

2-13 *Field Size* property

> **MORE INFO**
>
> Use the smallest field size that allows for the required processing or storage.

2. For a *Number* field, click the **drop-down arrow** in the *Field Size* property and select the desired number field size (Figure 2-14).

   • The default selection for a *Number* field is *Long Integer*.

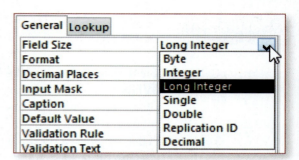

2-14 Field sizes for a *Number* data type

The Format Property

The *Format* property indicates the way a field displays in a table; it doesn't change what is actually stored. The choices available vary by the data type selected. Some data types like *Number, Currency, Date/Time,* and *Yes/No* have predefined formats from which you can select. For *Short Text* and *Long Text* data types, you can create a custom format.

To enter a value in the *Format* property box, either select the predefined format or enter the desired formatting characters.

Number and Currency Field Formats

Click the **drop-down arrow** in the *Format* property box of a *Number* or *Currency* field to display the list of predefined formats (Figure 2-15).

If you don't select a format, Access uses the *General Number* format for a number field, although it won't display in the *Format* property box. A *Currency* field defaults to the *Currency* format.

General Lookup	
Field Size	Long Integer
Format	
Decimal Places	General Number 3456.789
Input Mask	Currency $3,456.79
Caption	Euro €3,456.79
Default Value	Fixed 3456.79
Validation Rule	Standard 3,456.79
Validation Text	Percent 123.00%
Required	Scientific 3.46E+03

2-15 Predefined formats for *Number* and *Currency* data types

Date/Time Field Formats

Click the **drop-down arrow** in the *Format* property box of a *Date/Time* field to display the list of predefined formats (Figure 2-16). You can choose formats that display only the date, only the time, or both.

If you don't select a format, Access uses the *General Date* format, although it won't display in the *Format* property box.

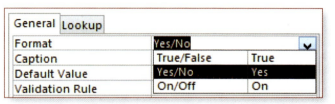

2-16 Predefined field formats for the *Date/Time* data type

Yes/No Field Formats

Click the **drop-down arrow** in the *Format* property of a *Yes/No* field to display the list of predefined formats shown in Figure 2-17.

If you don't select a format, Access uses the *Yes/No* format.

Short Text and Long Text Field Formats

Short Text and *Long Text* fields do not have any predefined formats.

2-17 Predefined field formats for the *Yes/No* data type

You can use formatting symbols to create a custom format and change the way the data display. More than one symbol may be used if multiple formatting effects are needed. Four common formatting symbols are described in the following table.

Short Text and Long Text Field Formatting Symbols

Character	Description
>	Characters display in uppercase. For example, if fl or Fl is entered into a field with a format of >, the entry displays as FL. This must be the first of the formatting symbols if multiple symbols are used.
<	Characters display in lowercase. For example, if FL or Fl is entered into a field with a format of <, the entry displays as fl. This must be the first of the formatting symbols if multiple symbols are used.
@	Enter one @ symbol for each character in the size of the field. If the field content contains fewer characters than the field size, the content displays with leading spaces. For example, if ABC is entered into a field of size 5 with a format of @@@@@, this entry displays as space, space, ABC.
[color]	Applies a color to this field only. The color must be enclosed in brackets. The possible colors are black, blue, cyan, green, magenta, red, yellow or white. This formatting symbol only works when applied in conjunction with one of the other formatting symbols. For example, a format of **>[blue]** displays that field's contents in upper case with a blue color.

Recall that *Short Text* and *Long Text* data types default to display left-justified. In Chapter 1 you learned to change the alignment of a field in *Datasheet* view. The @ character does not change the alignment, but when leading spaces are included for field contents that are less than the field size, the displayed contents does not appear to be left-justified.

The Caption Property

The *Caption* property contains the text that displays in the column header to identify a field in *Datasheet* views of tables, forms, queries, and reports. *Captions* often include spaces and multiple words as compared to the field name. Access displays the field name as the caption if you do not enter a caption value.

To enter a value for the *Caption* property, click in the **Caption** property box and type in the desired value.

Set the Default Value

You can use the *Default Value* property to automatically insert a specified value into a new record in a table. For example, Access can enter today's date into an *OrderDate* field. Or if most of a company's customers live in California, a default value of CA can be entered for the *State* field. Using a default value doesn't prevent the user from changing that value if needed (for example, when a customer is from NV instead of CA).

To enter a value in the *Default Value* property, click in the **Default Value** property box and type in the desired value.

> **MORE INFO**
>
> The default value of *Date()* enters the current date while *Now()* enters the current date and time. The *Format* property determines how the content actually displays.

Set Required Field

You can specify whether a user must enter a value into a field or whether he or she can skip the field and leave it blank. If a field must have a value you should set the *Required* property to *Yes*. The default value for the *Required* property is *No*.

To set the *Required* property, click in the **Required** property box and select **Yes**.

When building tables, you may wish to set the required property last. This allows you to more easily test different features in the table without being forced to enter a value for every field. This is especially helpful when you are adding different types of validation rules into the table. This skill is covered in the next section.

PAUSE & PRACTICE: ACCESS 2-1

For this Pause & Practice you create a new database for Ryan Thomas, operations director for Mary's Rentals. You use *Design* view to create a table to store information about the rental equipment. In addition, you modify the *Field Properties* to enhance the functionality of this table.

File Needed: None
Completed Project File Name: *[your initials] PP A2-1.accdb*

---

1. Create a new blank database.
   a. Open Access or click the **New** button [*File* tab] if Access is already open.
   b. Click **Blank desktop database**.
   c. Type *[your initials]* PP A2-1 in the *File Name* box.
   d. If desired, click the **Browse** button to change the location in which to save the database and click **OK**.
   e. Click the **Create** button. The database opens with a new table showing in *Datasheet* view.

2. Switch to *Design* view and save the table.
   a. Click the **View** button arrow [*Table Tools Fields* tab, *Views* group].
   b. Select the **Design View** option. You are prompted to save the table.
   c. Type Equipment as the new table name.
   d. Click **OK**. The table displays in *Design* view with the default primary key selected.

3. Modify the default primary key.
   a. Click in the **ID** *Field Name* property box in your table and type EquipmentID. Press the **Tab** key to move to the *Data Type* property.
   b. Click the **drop-down arrow** in the *Data Type* property box.
   c. Select the **Short Text** data type. Press the **Tab** key to move to the *Description* property.
   d. Type Unique ID assigned to each piece of equipment. in the property box. Press the **Tab** key to move to the next row (Figure 2-18).

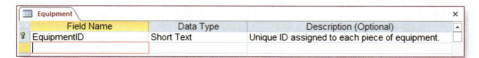

2-18 Add fields into the *Equipment* table

> ## MORE INFO
>
> The default *AutoNumber* data type was not appropriate for the *EquipmentID* field since Mary's Rentals already has assigned ID numbers to their equipment. Choose a *Short Text* data type for fields not used in arithmetic operations, even if the field contains numbers.

4. Add new fields into the table.
   a. Type ProductName in the *Field Name* property box of the second row. Press the **Tab** key to move to the *Data Type* property.
   b. Select the **Short Text** *Data Type.* Press the **Tab** key to move to the *Description* property.
   c. Do not enter a description; instead, press the **Tab** key to move to the next row.
   d. Continue adding the remaining fields into the *Equipment* table using the following information.

Field Name	Data Type	Description
Category	**Short Text**	Type of Equipment.
DailyRentalRate	**Currency**	
WeeklyRentalRate	**Currency**	Must be greater than the DailyRentalRate.
MonthlyRentalRate	**Currency**	Must be greater than the WeeklyRentalRate.
DatePurchased	**Date/Time**	Date we purchased the equipment. Not necessarily the date the equipment was made.
Comments	**Long Text**	Additional information about the equipment.

5. Save all of the modifications to the *Equipment* table.

6. Set the *Field Properties* in the *Equipment* table.
   a. Click in the **Field Name** property box of the *EquipmentID* field.
   b. Type 5 in the *Field Size* property box in the *Field Properties* area.
   c. If needed, click in the **Required** property box and select **Yes**.

d. Click in the **Field Name** property box of the *ProductName* field.

e. Continue changing the remaining field properties in the *Equipment* table using the following information.

Field Name	Field Size	Format
ProductName	45	>[Blue]
Category	30	
DatePurchased		Medium Date

The *Required* property will be set for several of the other fields in Pause & Practice 2-2 after you have added some data validation features into the table design.

7. Save the table. Your completed table design should be similar to Figure 2-19.

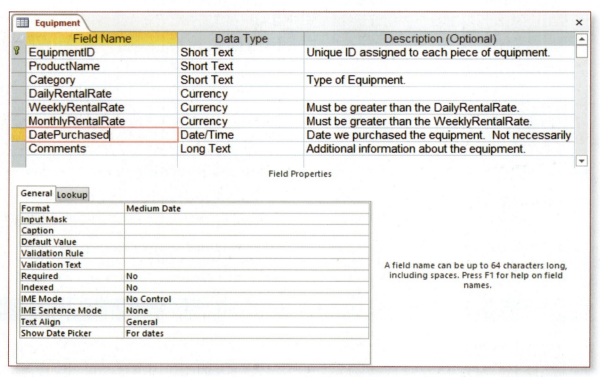

2-19 *Design* view of the completed *Equipment* table

8. Switch to *Datasheet* view.

9. Modify the field width of the *ProductName* and *Comments* columns. Recall from Chapter 1 that you can change the column width through the context menu.

a. Select the *ProductName* column.

b. Right-click to open the context menu and select the **Field Width** button.

c. Enter 23 in the *Column Width* box and press **OK**.

d. Repeat steps a through c to change the *Comments* field to a column width of 26.

10. Modify the row height of the table. Recall from Chapter 1 that you can change the row height through the context menu.
    a. Select any row in the table.
    b. Right-click to open the context menu and select the **Row Height** button.
    c. Enter 58 in the *Row Height* box and press **OK**.

11. Enter the following ten equipment records into the *Equipment* table.
    a. You are only entering values for three of the fields now since you will adjust the properties of the other fields in Pause & Practice 2-2.
    b. Access automatically displays a value of $0.00 in currency data type fields that do not have any data.
    c. If you want to force a line break in a text field, to have some text appear on a second line, press the **Ctrl+Enter** keys at the point where you want the line break to occur. For example, for EquipmentID 09863, to have "Bucket" start on a second line, press **Ctrl+Enter** after typing in "lbs".

Equipment ID	Product Name	Comments
09863	Backhoe Compact Allmand Diesel	Lift Capacity: 2100 lbs Bucket Size: 16" only
10015	Generator Portable Makita 1000W	Size: 19-1/2"L × 11-3/4"W × 17-1/2"H Weight: 55 lbs
10047	Skip Loader 4X4	Subject to Environmental Fee
10103	Generator Towable PowerPro 25KW	Overall L × W × H: 67"L × 28"W × 3"H
10129	Level Site Laser	
10235	Wheelbarrow	
10236	Snake Drain 1/2" Electric	General Brand - Easy Rooter Jr
10237	Pipeline Inspection Camera -85'	85' Cable
10283	Grinder Angle 7" w/Vacuum	Surface grinding of: Concrete, Screed, Tile Adhesives and removing thin coatings on concrete
10368	Metal Detector - Garrett ACE 250	

d. The completed table will be similar to Figure 2-20.

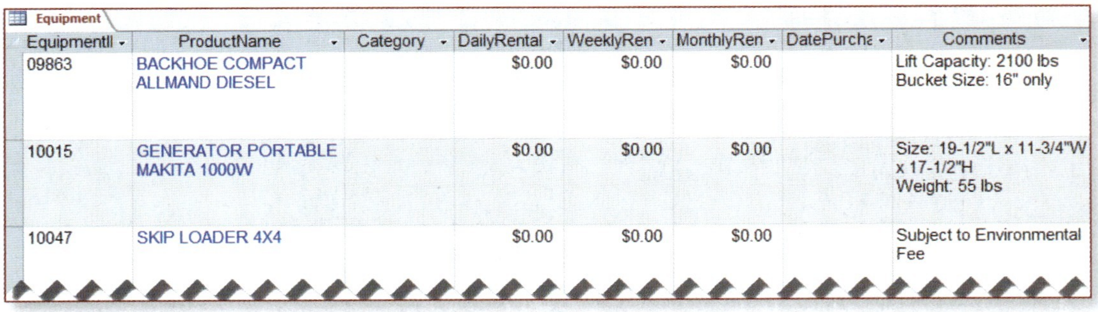

EquipmentI▾	ProductName ▾	Category ▾	DailyRental ▾	WeeklyRen ▾	MonthlyRen ▾	DatePurcha ▾	Comments ▾
09863	BACKHOE COMPACT ALLMAND DIESEL		$0.00	$0.00	$0.00		Lift Capacity: 2100 lbs Bucket Size: 16" only
10015	GENERATOR PORTABLE MAKITA 1000W		$0.00	$0.00	$0.00		Size: 19-1/2"L x 11-3/4"W x 17-1/2"H Weight: 55 lbs
10047	SKIP LOADER 4X4		$0.00	$0.00	$0.00		Subject to Environmental Fee

2-20 PP A2-1 completed

12. Save and close the table.

13. Close the database.

Understanding Data Integrity and Data Validation

The usefulness of your database depends on the quality of the data being stored. It is critical that all data entered into a table is verified to make sure that it is accurate.

The process of verifying the accuracy, or integrity, of the data is known as **data validation**. Data validation uses the data integrity rules that have been defined in the field and table properties. **Data integrity rules** ensure that the data in a database is accurate and consistent. Some of the more common data integrity rules are described in the following table.

Data Integrity Rules

Rule Focus	Description
Data Format	Ensures that a value entered into a field matches the data type established for that field; meets any size constraints; and meets any required formatting, such as beginning with a number or letter, or matching a month/day/year format.
Range	Ensures that a value entered into a field falls within the range of acceptable values that have been established.
Consistency	Ensures that a value entered into a field is consistent with a value in another field.
Completeness	Ensures that a field contains a value if it is required.

Data integrity rules are included as part of the **metadata**, the descriptions about what the different data fields represent and their formats. In Access, metadata is entered into the different field properties. An example of the metadata for the *Order Details* table in *Northwind Traders*, a sample database included with Access, is shown in Figure 2-21.

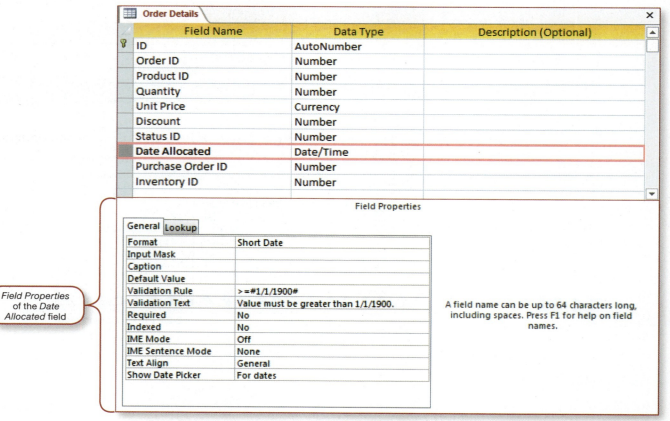

2-21 Metadata of the *Order Details* table in *Northwind Traders*

One of the key advantages to a database is that the DBMS automatically uses the metadata for the data integrity rules to perform data validation. Based on the metadata shown for the *Date Allocated* field, the database performs data validation using the following data integrity rules:

- The field must have *Date/Time* data and must follow the *Short Date* format (the *Data Type* and *Format* properties).
- The date must be greater than or equal to 1/1/1900 (the *Validation Rule* property).
- The user may leave this field blank (the *Required* property).

SLO 2.4

Integrating Data Validation in Tables

You learned how to set the *Data Type* and *Required* properties in Student Learning Outcome 2.2. The material that follows describes how to implement the *Data Format, Range,* and *Consistency* data integrity rules. In Access these can be created using field and record validation rules. This section explains how to create validation rules in *Design* view, although they can also be entered in *Datasheet* view. Additionally you learn how to use lookup fields to ensure range integrity and how to use an *Input Mask* to help users enter data in the correct format. Remember to save your table after you make changes to any of these properties.

Field Validation Rules

Field validation rules are used to create range and data format integrity rules by limiting entries to a certain range of values or making sure entries match a specified format. You enter the specific rule into the *Validation Rule* property of a field. Access checks field validation rules when a user navigates out of the field. If the data violates the rule, Access requires the user to fix the problem before he or she can leave the field.

Validation rules cannot be used on fields with data types of *Attachment, AutoNumber, OLE Object* and the *ReplicationID Field Size* choice of a *Number* field.

> **MORE INFO**
>
> If you want your rule to compare two or more fields, you must use a record validation rule.

In Access, the rules are called ***expressions***. They are written using the common operators shown in the following table.

Operators Used in Access Expressions

Arithmetic	Comparison	Logical
-	<	And
+	<=	Or
*	>	Not
/	>=	Xor
^	=	
	<>	
	Between	
	In	
	Like	

The content of your expression depends on the data type of the field, along with the specific restriction you are trying to implement. Validation rules ignore the case of the text when making an evaluation. Examples of entries for validation rules, along with an explanation of their effects, are shown in the following table.

Using and Understanding Field Validation Rules

Validation Rule Example	Explanation of Effect
<5	Value entered must be less than 5.
<> 0	Value entered must not equal 0.
>=#1/1/2015#	Value entered must be greater than or equal to 1/1/2015. *Tip: Dates must be surrounded by the # sign.*
"M" OR "F"	Value entered must be the letter M or the letter F. *Tip: Text values must be surrounded by double quotation marks.*
>=#1/1/2015# AND <#1/1/2016#	Value entered must be a date from 2015.
"A" OR > "M"	Value entered must be the letter A or a letter that comes after M in the alphabet.
IN ("CA", "NV," "AZ")	Value entered must be either CA, NV, or AZ.
Not Null	The field must be filled in. While this can be enforced by using the required property, using this validation rule allows you to include a custom validation message like "The Equipment ID field cannot be empty." *Tip: **Null** means that there is no value in the field.*

The *Yes/No* data type defaults to display data using a check box. A check indicates Yes while an unchecked box indicates No. Internally, Access stores Yes as a −1 and No as 0. Expressions written to check the contents of a *Yes/No* data type should compare the contents to either a −1 or a 0.

Use the *Like* comparison operator to find a value that is similar to (or like) something else. When using *Like*, you typically incorporate one of the **wildcard characters** available in Access. Examples of some of the wildcard characters and their effects are shown in the following table.

Using Wildcard Characters in Validation Rules

Wildcard Character	Matches	Example	Explanation of Example
?	Any single character (*numbers are also considered characters*)	Like "C????"	Values entered must be 5 characters long and begin with the letter C. *Tip: Even if the field size is larger than 5, this rule requires that exactly 5 characters are entered.*
*	Any number of characters	Like "MA*"	Values entered must begin with MA, but can be any length up to the maximum field size.
#	Any single numeric digit	Like "##"	Values entered must contain two numeric digits.

When using wildcards, the criteria of your expression must be enclosed in quotation marks. You can combine multiple wildcards to achieve the desired criteria.

HOW TO: Create a Field Validation Rule

1. Click to select the desired field.
2. Click in the **Validation Rule** property box (Figure 2-22).
3. Type in the text of the desired rule.

Default Value	
Validation Rule	...
Validation Text	

Build button

2-22 Validation Rule property box

> **ANOTHER WAY**
>
> Enter the validation rule in the *Expression Builder* dialog box. Click in the *Validation Rule* property box of the desired field. Open the *Expression Builder* dialog box by clicking the **Build** button in the *Validation Rule* property box, pressing the **Ctrl+F2** keys, or clicking the **Builder** button [*Table Tools Design* tab, *Tools* group].

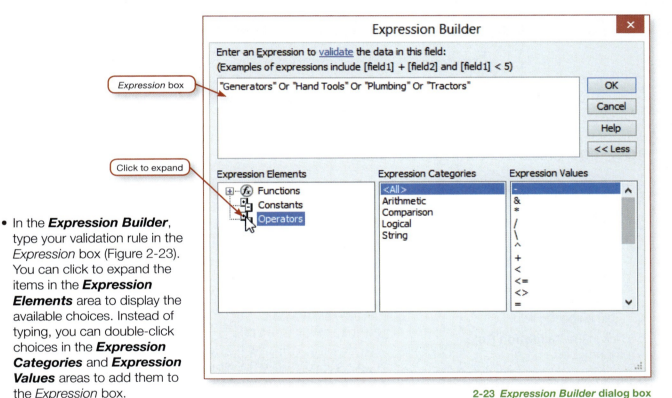

- In the **Expression Builder**, type your validation rule in the *Expression* box (Figure 2-23). You can click to expand the items in the **Expression Elements** area to display the available choices. Instead of typing, you can double-click choices in the **Expression Categories** and **Expression Values** areas to add them to the *Expression* box.

2-23 Expression Builder dialog box

Record Validation Rules

Record validation rules are used to create consistency data integrity rules by comparing fields in the same table. You can also use them to create range and data format integrity rules by limiting entries to a certain range of values or a specified format. You enter the specific rule into the *Validation Rule* property of the table. The rule is checked when a user attempts to navigate out of the record. If the data the user has entered in the record violates the rule, Access requires the user to fix the problem before he or she can leave the record.

Expressions written for a record validation rule can use the same operators and wildcard characters used in field level validation rules. However, they typically are written to compare fields. Examples of entries for record validation rules, along with an explanation of the effects, are shown in the following table.

Using and Understanding Record Validation Rules

Record Validation Rule Example	Explanation of Effect
([Field1] is Null) XOR ([Field2] is Null)	You must enter a value into either *Field1* or *Field2*, but not into both fields. *Tip: The XOR logical operator prevents both fields from having a value; both fields would be allowed to have a value if OR were used instead.*
[Field1] <> [Field2]	You may not enter the same value into both *Field1* and *Field2*.
((([Field1] > [Field2]) AND [Field2]>10))	*Field1* must be greater than *Field2* and *Field2* must have a value greater than 10. *Tip: When using the AND operator, all parts of the condition must be true.*

Substitute the actual field names in your table for the placeholders of *Field1*, *Field2*, etc. Be sure to include your field name inside of square brackets, as shown in the examples.

HOW TO: Create a Record Validation Rule

1. Click the **Property Sheet** button [*Table Tools Design* tab, *Show/Hide* group] (Figure 2-24).
   - The property sheet for the table opens, as shown in Figure 2-25.
   - This contains properties that apply to the entire table, not just a specific field.
2. Click in the **Validation Rule** property box.
3. Type the text of the desired rule directly in the property box or click the **Build** button to open the *Expression Builder* dialog box.
   - The example validation rule shown in Figure 2-26 uses the *Date()* function, which captures the current date from the computer. This example rule requires that the value in the *DatePurchased* field is greater than or equal to the current date.

2-24 *Property Sheet* button

Property Sheet   ✕

Selection type: Table Properties

General	
Read Only When Disconnected	No
Subdatasheet Expanded	No
Subdatasheet Height	0"
Orientation	Left-to-Right
Description	
Default View	Datasheet
Validation Rule	
Validation Text	
Filter	
Order By	
Subdatasheet Name	[Auto]
Link Child Fields	
Link Master Fields	
Filter On Load	No
Order By On Load	Yes

2-25 *Property Sheet* of a table

Validation Rule	[DatePurchased]>=Date()

2-26 **Example validation rule**

Test Validation Rules

When using validation rules it is important that the rules are tested. There are two different considerations for testing.

- Test to ensure the rule is written correctly.

    These tests ensure that the logic is valid and the rule works as you intended. If several fields have validation rules, it is easiest to test each rule as you write it. This helps you focus on a specific rule instead of trying to test all of them at the same time.

    To test a validation rule you must create **test data**, a set of data created to test an application. The test data should include a sample of every valid condition as well as samples of as many invalid conditions as possible. Several examples of creating test data are shown in the following table.

Test Data Examples for Validation Rules

Validation Rule	Examples of Test Data	Result of Test
"M" OR "F"	M	Valid (test of M condition); should be accepted.
	F	Valid (test of F condition); should be accepted.
	X	Invalid; error message should display.
>=#1/1/2015# AND <#1/1/2016#	12/15/2013	Invalid (below the range); error message should display.
	7/7/2015	Valid; should be accepted.
	2/13/2016	Invalid (above the range); error message should display.
([Field1] is Null) XOR ([Field2] is Null)	*Field1* null and *Field2* null	Invalid (both can't be null); error message should display.
	Field1 = 5 and *Field2* = 7	Invalid (both can't have a value); error message should display.
	Field1 null and *Field2* = 7	Valid (only *Field2* has a value); should be accepted.
	Field1 = 5 and *Field2* null	Valid (only *Field1* has a value); should be accepted.

- Test to ensure that any data already in the table is verified against the new rules.

    Test existing data by clicking the **Test Validation Rules** button [*Table Tools Design* tab, *Tools* group] (Figure 2-27).

    Access displays a message box explaining the test and alerting you to the fact that this operation could take a long time depending on the number of records of data in your table.

    If you click **Yes** to proceed, Access displays an error message (Figure 2-28) if any data is found to violate validation rules. You can select whether to continue testing other rule violations.

    If you continue testing, Access displays an error message (Figure 2-29) indicating the next rule which is violated.

2-27 *Test Validation Rules* button

2-28 **Validation rule violation warning message**

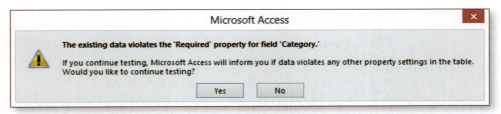

2-29 Message box for data validation errors

You must return to *Datasheet* view, locate any records that have invalid data, and then make the necessary corrections.

Create Validation Text

When data is entered that violates a validation rule, Access automatically displays a message box alerting the user to the problem, as shown in Figure 2-30. The message box text includes the condition entered into the validation rule. Unfortunately, the message is often not very clear to a typical user of your database.

2-30 Default message when entering data that violates a validation rule

You can use the ***Validation Text*** property to enter a custom message that displays instead of the default message. Be clear and concise in your message. Include the reason the entry is invalid and suggest how to correct the problem. For example, "The Date Listed must be greater than or equal to 1/1/2015" is a better error message than "Invalid entry in Date Listed field" or "Please enter a valid Date Listed."

HOW TO: Create Validation Text

1. Click to select the **desired field** or open the *Property Sheet* for the table by clicking the **Property Sheet** button [*Table Tools Design* tab, *Show/Hide* group].

2. Click in the **Validation Text** property box.

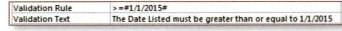

| Validation Rule | >=#1/1/2015# |
| Validation Text | The Date Listed must be greater than or equal to 1/1/2015 |

2-31 Example validation text

3. Type in the text of the desired message. An example message is shown in the *Validation Text* property box in Figure 2-31.

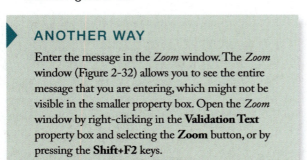

ANOTHER WAY

Enter the message in the *Zoom* window. The *Zoom* window (Figure 2-32) allows you to see the entire message that you are entering, which might not be visible in the smaller property box. Open the *Zoom* window by right-clicking in the **Validation Text** property box and selecting the **Zoom** button, or by pressing the **Shift+F2** keys.

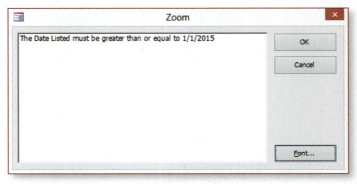

2-32 Create a custom validation text message in the *Zoom* window

Create a Lookup Field

Lookup fields display a list of data values from which the user can choose. Lookup fields are another way to implement range integrity rules and are an alternative to validation rules since they also limit what can be entered into a field. They are very helpful when the actual choices are lengthy or prone to typing mistakes. Lookup fields can be used on any field that is defined as a data type of *Number, Short Text,* or *Yes/No.* They are most commonly used on *Number* and *Short Text* fields.

The list of values in a lookup field can either be directly entered into the properties of the field or automatically filled in from values in another table or query. In this section you learn to create a lookup field by entering the list of values.

One of the choices you make when creating a lookup field is to determine the way that the list displays. This choice is made in the *Display Control* property on the *Lookup* tab. *Text* and *Number* fields have three options for the *Display Control* property. The way the control functions varies, depending on whether you are viewing the data in *Datasheet* view of a table or whether you are viewing it in a form. Since you select the type of control when creating the lookup field, it is important to understand the differences now. The three options are explained in the table below, which includes samples of how the control displays in a table or form.

Understanding Display Control Options

Display Control Choice	Explanation	Table Sample	Form Sample
Text Box	Displays the contents of a field and also allows the user to type a value into that field. This is the default choice.		
List Box	Table view: Displays as a drop-down list. The list appears when the arrow is clicked. Form view: Displays as a box showing all possible choices.		
Combo Box	Displays as a drop-down list in both table view and form view. The list appears when the arrow is clicked.		

Notice that a *List Box* and *Combo Box* display the same way in *Datasheet* view of a table but are different when displayed on a form. Because the *List Box* control takes up more space on a form, and users don't always find it intuitive to understand and don't know to make a selection, you may want to opt to use the *Combo Box* display control choice.

> **MORE INFO**
>
> Access resets the *Field Size* property of a *Short Text* field to 255 after the *Display Control* property has been changed to a *List Box* or *Combo Box.* If desired, you can change it back to a different size.

HOW TO: Create a Lookup Field by Typing in a List of Values

1. Click to select the **desired field**.

2. Select the **Lookup** tab in the *Field Properties* area in the lower half of the *Design view* window (Figure 2-33).

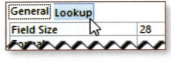

2-33 Select the *Lookup* tab

3. Click in the **Display Control** property box, click the **drop-down arrow** and select **Combo Box**.

   - Based on the selection of the *Combo Box* display control, additional properties will become available on the *Lookup* tab, as shown in Figure 2-34.

4. Click in the **Row Source** property box, click the **drop-down arrow** and select **Value List**.

   - Click the **drop-down arrow** and select **Value List**.
   - This choice indicates that you will enter the list of possible choices.

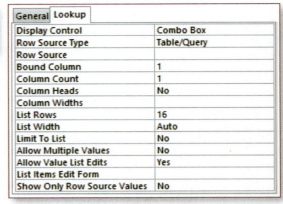

General	Lookup	
Display Control		Combo Box
Row Source Type		Table/Query
Row Source		
Bound Column		1
Column Count		1
Column Heads		No
Column Widths		
List Rows		16
List Width		Auto
Limit To List		No
Allow Multiple Values		No
Allow Value List Edits		Yes
List Items Edit Form		
Show Only Row Source Values		No

2-34 Additional properties on the *Lookup* tab

5. Type the list of choices into the **Row Source** property box.

   - Separate each choice with a **semicolon** (;).
   - If the choice contains a comma (,) as punctuation, the choice must be surrounded be quotation marks ("").

6. Edit the **List Rows** property if desired.

   - This value determines how many choices display in the list. If there are more choices than rows entered, a scroll bar automatically appears.

7. Edit the **Limit To List** property if desired.

   - This property determines whether a user can enter a value into the field that isn't located on the list.
   - Set this property to **Yes** if you want to restrict the user to picking from the list.

8. Edit the **Allow Value List Edits** property if desired.

   - This property determines whether the list of items can be edited.
   - Set this property to **Yes** if you want to allow the user to change the values in the list while entering or viewing data.
   - When the value is *Yes,* the user sees the *Edit List Items* icon appear below the list, when they are in *Datasheet* view (Figure 2-35).

   If the icon is selected, it opens the *Edit List Items* dialog box (Figure 2-36).

2-35 *Edit List Items* icon in *Datasheet* view

> ▶ **ANOTHER WAY**
>
> Open the *Edit List Items* dialog box by right-clicking in the **lookup field** and selecting the **Edit List Items** button.

   - The *Edit List Items* dialog box allows the user to add new items onto the list, change existing items, or delete items from the list.
   - Be cautious about giving this type of control to your users.

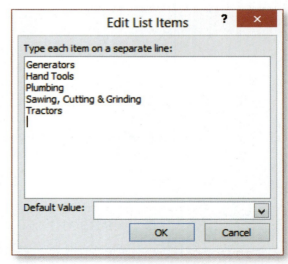

2-36 *Edit List Items* dialog box

HOW TO: Create a Lookup Field Using the Lookup Wizard

1. Click to select the **desired field**.
2. Click in the property box for the **Data Type** property and select the **arrow** to display the list of data types.
3. Select **Lookup Wizard** (Figure 2-37).
   • The *Lookup Wizard* dialog box opens.
4. Select the radio button for **I will type in the values that I want**. (Figure 2-38).
5. Click the **Next** button.
   • The next step of the *Lookup Wizard* displays.
   • Initially there are no items in the list.
6. Click the **first cell** in the *Col1* column.
7. Type the first value in the list.
8. Press the **down arrow** key to move to the next row.
9. Continue typing in all values (Figure 2-39).
10. Click the **Next** button when done entering all items on the list.
    • The final step of the *Lookup Wizard* displays (Figure 2-40).
11. The label defaults to the original field name you entered. If desired, you can change the field name here.
12. Click the **Limit To List** check box if desired.
    • This property determines whether a user can enter a value into the field that isn't located on the list.
    • Set this property to **Yes** if you want to restrict the user to picking from the list.
13. Click the **Finish** button when done.
14. If desired, you can edit the *List Rows* and *Allow Value List Edits* properties on the *Lookup* tab. These were described in the previous *How To: Create a Lookup Field by Typing in a List of Values*, steps six and eight.

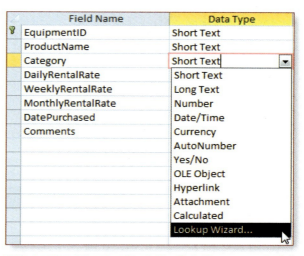

2-37 *Lookup Wizard* option in the *Data Type* property list

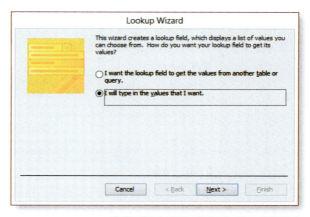

2-38 First step of the *Lookup Wizard*

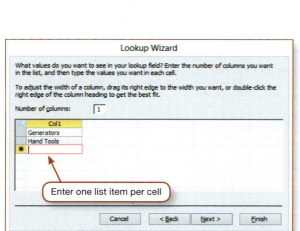

2-39 Enter choices in the second step of the *Lookup Wizard*

2-40 Last step of the *Lookup Wizard*

Define an Input Mask

An **Input mask** forces a user to enter data using a specific format. For example, you can require a user to enter a phone number with an area code in the (123) 123-4567 format. Input masks help enforce data format integrity rules.

An input mask can only be used on fields with data types of *Short Text*, *Number* (excluding *ReplicationID* field sizes), *Currency*, or *Date/Time*. You can type the mask directly into the *Input Mask* property box or you can select the *Build* button to launch the **Input Mask Wizard**. However, the *Input Mask Wizard* only works on *Short Text* or *Date* fields.

Before you learn how to create an input mask it is important to learn some fundamental rules. An input mask uses a variety of characters that control how and what kind of data is acceptable. Some common special characters are explained in the following table.

Input Mask Special Characters

Character	Explanation of Effect
0	User must enter a number (0 to 9).
9	User can enter a number (0 to 9), but it is not required.
#	User can enter a number (0 to 9), space, or plus or minus sign, but it is not required. If not filled in, Access enters a blank space.
L	User must enter a letter (A to Z, upper or lower case).
?	User can enter a letter (A to Z, upper or lower case), but it is not required.
A	User must enter a letter or a number.
a	User can enter a letter or a number, but it is not required.
!	In a text field, when fewer characters are entered than specified in the mask, the data displays right-justified with empty spaces on the left side of the mask instead of the default right side of the mask.
""	Characters entered inside of the quotation marks display as written.
\	Characters following the slash are displayed as written

An input mask contains three parts, each separated by a semicolon.

- The first part is mandatory and shows the desired formatting. Examples of the mandatory portion of an input mask are as follows.

Mask Example	Explanation of Effect
(000) 000-0000	You must enter an area code along with the phone number (0 indicates required). The phone number will be entered starting with the area code.
(999) AAA-AAAA	The phone number does not require an area code (9 indicates optional). The number portion can be numbers or digits. This mask would allow an entry of 555-STAR for the phone number.
!9999	You can enter up to four numbers (9 indicates optional). The ! symbol indicates that if fewer than four number are entered, the data displays right-justified with the empty spaces to the left, For example, if 12 is entered, it would display as " 12" instead of "12".
"WN "9999	The data must start with WN, a blank space, and be followed with up to 4 numbers. Since the ! symbol is not used, the numbers will be left-justified since the empty spaces will be to the right.

When you enter the mask characters, Access may add additional special characters to ensure the mask displays as desired. For example, if you enter (000) 000-0000 as the mask, Access converts it to \(000") "000\-0000. Access inserted the \ in front of the (symbol to indicate that this character displays as written. Access also inserted quotation marks around the) and space. Finally another \ was inserted in front of the – symbol to indicate that this character displays as written.

- The second part of the input mask is optional and indicates whether the mask characters, such as parentheses, dashes, etc., are stored with the data. Not storing the characters saves space; this can be significant in large databases. If you do store the characters make sure the field size is large enough to store the data value and the characters. The two possible symbols are 0 and 1. A 0 tells Access to store the characters; a 1 or empty tells Access not to store the characters. If this part of the mask is left blank, Access behaves as if a 1 was entered.
- The third part of the mask is also optional and specifies what symbol displays in the mask as the user enters the data. The default symbol is the _ (underscore.) You can select a different symbol if desired. If this part of the mask is left blank, Access behaves as if the _ symbol was selected.

Based on the mask characters entered, Access may add additional special characters to ensure the mask displays as desired. Three examples of input masks follow. Recall that the semicolon symbol (;) separates the different parts of the mask. The parts of each mask are identified, along with displaying a sample of how the mask would appear (Figures 2-41 through 2-43).

Example 1: \(000") "000\-0000;0;   Sample:

2-41 Example 1 *Input Mask* display

Part 1	Part 2	Part 3
\ (000") "000\-0000	0	Empty
The \ in front of the (symbol, the quotation marks around the) and space, and the \ in front of the – symbol indicate that these characters display as written.	The mask characters are stored along with the data. This format requires a field size of 14 to store the phone number digits and the mask characters, including the blank space between the area code and the number.	The default _ symbol displays as the placeholder character.

Example 2: \(999") "AAA\-AAAA;;*   Sample:

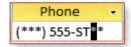

2-42 Example 2 *Input Mask* display

Part 1	Part 2	Part 3
\ (999") "AAA\-AAAA	Empty.	*
The \ in front of the (symbol, the quotation marks around the) and space, and the \ in front of the – symbol, indicates that these characters display as written.	The mask characters are not stored along with the data. This format requires a field size of ten to store the phone number.	The * symbol displays as the placeholder character.

Example 3: "WN "9999;1;_   Sample:

2-43 Example 3
Input Mask display

Part 1	Part 2	Part 3
"WN "9999	1	_
Since the database designer wanted WN and a space to appear at the beginning, she entered it inside of quotation marks.	The mask characters are not stored with the data. This format requires a field size of four to store the flight number.	The _ symbol displays as the placeholder character.

HOW TO: Create an Input Mask

1. Click to select the **desired field**.
2. Click in the **Input Mask** property box.
3. Click the **Build** button to launch the *Input Mask Wizard* dialog box (Figure 2-44).

> **ANOTHER WAY**
>
> You can type the rule directly into the property box.

4. Select the pre-formatted mask you wish to use or something close that you can modify.
5. Click the **Next** button to move to the next step of the *Input Mask Wizard* (Figure 2-45).
6. Edit the **Input Mask** as desired.
7. Edit the **Placeholder character** as desired.
8. Click the **Next** button to move to the next step of the *Input Mask Wizard* (Figure 2-46).

2-44 *Input Mask Wizard,* step one

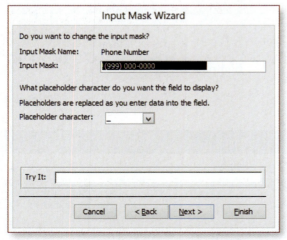

2-45 *Input Mask Wizard,* step 2

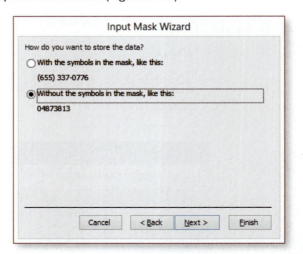

2-46 *Input Mask Wizard,* step 3

9. Select the appropriate radio button based on whether you are storing the symbols with the data. Be sure that the field width is large enough to also store the symbol since it takes space as well.

10. Click the **Finish** button.

11. Make any needed adjustments to the *Input Mask* directly in the property box.

> **MORE INFO**
>
> The input mask displays only when a user clicks into that field.

Changing Field Properties after Records Are Added into a Table

In Chapter 1 you learned to use *Datasheet* view to add records into a table. Ideally you will have decided on the final structure of all your tables before you begin to enter data, but there may be times you need to make a change to the field properties on a table that already contains data.

Making the change is straightforward. Open the table in *Design* view and follow the steps previously described for the specific property. However, making changes to the table design after records are added must be done with caution.

You just learned that the field properties are used to specify the data integrity rules. Keep in mind that changes to several of the properties may result in unintended consequences. When you save the changes, Access displays a message box warning you about the potential problems. Examples of different problem situations and the resulting warnings include the following.

- If you reduce the *Field Size,* Access warns you that data may be lost (Figure 2-47). If you click *Yes* to continue, Access truncates the contents of any data values that are larger than the new field size. Be certain that the field is large enough that you don't lose any data since you can't undo this change.

2-47 *Field Size* change warning message

- If you change the *Required* property to Yes, Access warns you that data integrity rules have changed (Figure 2-48). If you click **Yes** to test the data with the new rules, Access validates the existing data. This could take a long time depending on the number of records in the table.

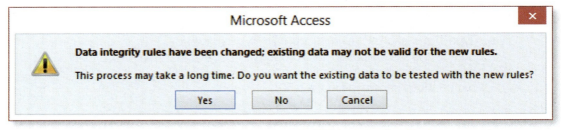

2-48 Data integrity rule change warning message

If any records violate the new rule, another message box displays, similar to Figure 2-49.

Microsoft Access

Existing data violates the new setting for the 'Required' property for field 'Category.'

Do you want to keep testing with the new setting?
* To keep the new setting and continue testing, click Yes.
* To revert to the old setting and continue testing, click No.
* To stop testing, click Cancel.

[Yes]   [No]   [Cancel]

2-49 Validation error warning message

You must decide whether to keep the new rule. This message only appears once to let you know that there is data that violates the rule, not once for each record that violates the rule. If you proceed with the change, you must open the table and individually correct each violation of this new rule.

- If you change any of the validation rules, you should test the changes as described earlier in this chapter by clicking the *Test Validation Rules* button [*Table Tools Design* tab, *Tools* group]. Again, you must individually correct each violation of a new rule.

PAUSE & PRACTICE: ACCESS 2-2

For this Pause & Practice you add features to enhance the data integrity in the *Equipment* table. You add field and record level validation rules and validation text, use the *Lookup Wizard* to create a combo box, and add an input mask. You also test the validation rules. Finally you add data into the equipment table.

File Needed: *[your initials] PP A2-1.accdb*
Completed Project File Name: *[your initials] PP A2-2.accdb*

1. Open the *[your initials] PP A2-1.accdb* database file created in Pause & Practice 2-1.

2. Save a new copy of your database as *[your initials] PP A2-2*.

3. Enable content in the security warning.

4. Open the *Equipment* table in *Design* view.

5. Add a field validation rule and validation text.
   a. Click to select the **EquipmentID** field.
   b. Click in the **Validation Rule** property box.
   c. Type Like "#####" in the *Validation Rule* property box.
   d. Click in the **Validation Text** property box.
   e. Type The Equipment ID must contain 5 numbers in the *Validation Text* property box. The completed properties should match those shown in Figure 2-50.

General	Lookup	
Field Size	5
Format	
Input Mask	
Caption	
Default Value	
Validation Rule	Like "#####"
Validation Text	The Equipment ID must contain 5 numbers
Required	Yes
Allow Zero Length	Yes
Indexed	Yes (No Duplicates)
Unicode Compression	No
IME Mode	No Control
IME Sentence Mode	None
Text Align	General

2-50 Completed properties of the *EquipmentID* field

6. Test the field validation rule.
   a. Switch to *Datasheet* view to test the rule. If prompted, save the changes to your table. You may also be prompted with a box that states that the data integrity rules have changed and asked whether you want to test the existing data. Click **No**.
   b. Click in the **EquipmentID** cell in the *Append Row*.
   c. Type A1212 in the *EquipmentID* field. This value is incorrect because it contains letters. Press the **Tab** or **Enter** key to move to the next field. A message box should display the validation text message you entered in step 5 (Figure 2-51).

2-51 Error message displays validation text from a field validation rule

   d. Press **OK** to acknowledge the error.
   e. Delete the contents and type 123 in the *EquipmentID* field. Press the **Tab** key to move to the next field. This value is incorrect because it contains only three numbers. The message box should display the validation text message.
   f. Press **OK** to acknowledge the error.
   g. Type 12345 in the *EquipmentID* field. Press **Tab** to move to the next field. This value is correct and you should be moved to the *ProductName* field.
   h. Click the **Record Selector** for *EquipmentID 12345.*
   i. Click the **Delete** button [*Home* tab, *Records* group] to delete this test record. A message box displays. Click **Yes** to confirm the deletion.
   j. Switch back to *Design* view of the table.

7. Add a record validation rule.
   a. If the *Property Sheet* for the *Equipment* table is not already open, click the **Property Sheet** button [*Table Tools Design* tab, *Show/Hide* group] to open the *Property Sheet*.
   b. Click in the **Validation Rule** property box.
   c. Click the **Build** button to open the *Expression Builder* dialog box.
   d. Enter [WeeklyRentalRate]>[DailyRentalRate] And [MonthlyRentalRate]>[WeeklyRentalRate] in the *Expression Builder.* Instead of typing the field names, you can double-click them in the *Expression Categories* area and add them to the *Expression* box. Field names added by double-clicking automatically have a blank space added before and after the name. This does not affect the expression.
   e. Press **OK** to close the *Expression Builder.*
   f. Right-click in the **Validation Text** property box and select the **Zoom** button.
   g. Type The Weekly Rate must be greater than the Daily Rate and the Monthly Rate must be greater than the Weekly Rate. in the *Zoom* window. Press **OK**.
   h. Close the *Property Sheet* window.

8. Test the record validation rule.
   a. Switch to *Datasheet* view to test the rule. If prompted, save the changes to your table. You may also be prompted that the data integrity rules have changed and asked whether you want to test the existing data. Click **No**.
   b. For *EquipmentID 09863*, type 160 in the *DailyRentalRate* field, 160 in the *WeeklyRentalRate* field, and 160 in the *MonthlyRentalRate* fields.
   c. Press the **down arrow** key to leave the current record. This causes the record level rule to execute. The message box should display the validation text message (Figure 2-52) because the *WeeklyRentalRate* is not greater than the *DailyRentalRate* and the *MonthlyRentalRate* is not greater than the *WeeklyRentalRate*. This test is checking if the *And Compound Condition* is working correctly.

2-52 Error message displays validation text from a record validation rule violation

   d. Press **OK** to acknowledge the error.
   e. Delete the contents and type 640 in the *MonthlyRentalRate* field.
   f. Press the **down arrow** key to exit the current record. The message box should display the validation text message because the *WeeklyRentalRate* is not greater than the *DailyRentalRate*, the first half of the compound condition.
   g. Press **OK** to acknowledge the error.
   h. Delete the contents and type 640 in the *WeeklyRentalRate* field.
   i. Press the **down arrow** key to exit the current record. The message box should display the validation text message because the *MonthlyRentalRate* is not greater than the *WeeklyRentalRate*, the second half of the compound condition.
   j. Press **OK** to acknowledge the error.
   k. Delete the contents and type 1920 in the *MonthlyRentalRate* field.
   l. Press the **down arrow** key to leave the current record. The record changes should be successfully saved.
   m. Switch back to *Design* view of the table.

9. Modify the *Category* field to use a *Combo Box.*
   a. Click to select the **Category** field.
   b. Click in the **Data Type** property box, click the **arrow,** and select **Lookup Wizard**. The *Lookup Wizard* dialog box opens.
   c. Select the radio button for **I will type in the values that I want**.
   d. Click the **Next** button.
   e. Leave 1 in the *Number of columns* box and click in the **first cell** in the *Col1* column.
   f. Type Generators.
   g. Press the **down arrow** key to move to the next row.
   h. Type in the values from the following table.

Category
Hand Tools
Plumbing
Sawing, Cutting & Grinding
Tractors

A2-102

i. Click the **Next** button when done entering all the items.
j. Click the **Limit To List** check box.
k. Click the **Finish** button.
l. Save your changes to the table. If an error message displays regarding converting data, click **Yes** to proceed.

10. Add an input mask to the *DatePurchased* field.
    a. Click to select the **DatePurchased** field.
    b. Click in the **Input Mask** property box.
    c. Click the **Build** button or press **Ctrl+F2**. The *Input Mask Wizard* dialog box opens.
    d. Select the **Medium Date** *Input Mask* (Figure 2-53a).
    e. Click the **Next** button. The next screen of the *Input Mask Wizard* displays the characters used in the mask along with the *Placeholder character* (Figure 2-53b).
    f. Click the **Next** button to accept the input mask without making any changes and to accept the suggested *Placeholder character*.
    g. Click the **Finish** button.

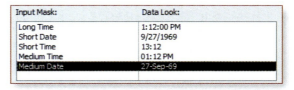

2-53a *Medium Date Input Mask* option

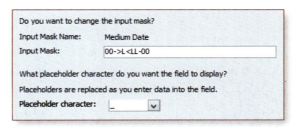

2-53b *Medium Date Input Mask* characters

11. Set the **Required** property to **Yes** for the following fields: *ProductName, Category, DailyRentalRate, WeeklyRentalRate, MonthlyRentalRate,* and *DatePurchased*.

12. Save the changes to the *Equipment* table. If prompted to test existing data against the new rules, click **No**.

13. Switch to *Datasheet* view and enter the following data values into the table. Remember that the *EquipmentID* value has already been entered. The values for the *ProductName* column, located between the *Equipment ID* and *Category* fields, have also been entered. Those data values are not repeated in the table below. Additionally, you already entered the rental rate values for the first record when you were testing the validation rules.

    Because you created an input mask for the *DatePurchased* field, those data values have been provided using the mask format to ease data entry.

Equipment ID	Category	Daily Rental Rate	Weekly Rental Rate	Monthly Rental Rate	Date Purchased
09863	Tractors	160	640	1920	09-Sep-11
10015	Generators	30	120	360	15-Dec-11
10047	Tractors	225	900	2700	08-Mar-12
10103	Generators	120	360	1080	20-Jul-12
10129	Hand Tools	60	240	720	02-Aug-12
10235	Hand Tools	10	30	60	01-Feb-13
10236	Plumbing	35	140	420	01-Feb-13
10237	Plumbing	200	800	2400	01-Feb-13
10283	Sawing, Cutting, & Grinding	120	480	1440	15-Mar-13
10368	Hand Tools	15	45	135	15-May-13

14. Save the table. The *Datasheet* view should look similar to Figure 2-54.

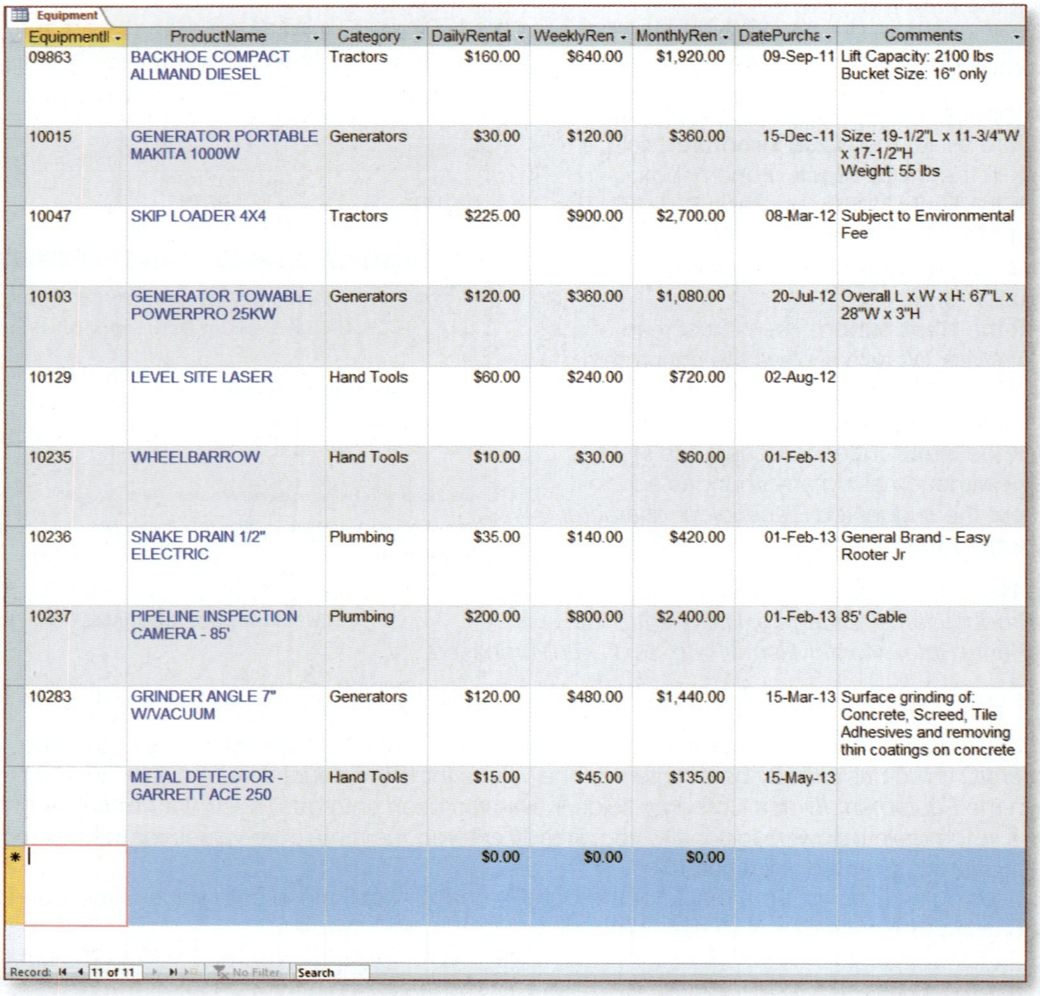

EquipmentID	ProductName	Category	DailyRental	WeeklyRen	MonthlyRen	DatePurcha	Comments
09863	BACKHOE COMPACT ALLMAND DIESEL	Tractors	$160.00	$640.00	$1,920.00	09-Sep-11	Lift Capacity: 2100 lbs Bucket Size: 16" only
10015	GENERATOR PORTABLE MAKITA 1000W	Generators	$30.00	$120.00	$360.00	15-Dec-11	Size: 19-1/2"L x 11-3/4"W x 17-1/2"H Weight: 55 lbs
10047	SKIP LOADER 4X4	Tractors	$225.00	$900.00	$2,700.00	08-Mar-12	Subject to Environmental Fee
10103	GENERATOR TOWABLE POWERPRO 25KW	Generators	$120.00	$360.00	$1,080.00	20-Jul-12	Overall L x W x H: 67"L x 28"W x 3"H
10129	LEVEL SITE LASER	Hand Tools	$60.00	$240.00	$720.00	02-Aug-12	
10235	WHEELBARROW	Hand Tools	$10.00	$30.00	$60.00	01-Feb-13	
10236	SNAKE DRAIN 1/2" ELECTRIC	Plumbing	$35.00	$140.00	$420.00	01-Feb-13	General Brand - Easy Rooter Jr
10237	PIPELINE INSPECTION CAMERA - 85'	Plumbing	$200.00	$800.00	$2,400.00	01-Feb-13	85' Cable
10283	GRINDER ANGLE 7" W/VACUUM	Generators	$120.00	$480.00	$1,440.00	15-Mar-13	Surface grinding of: Concrete, Screed, Tile Adhesives and removing thin coatings on concrete
	METAL DETECTOR - GARRETT ACE 250	Hand Tools	$15.00	$45.00	$135.00	15-May-13	
*			$0.00	$0.00	$0.00		

Record: 11 of 11   No Filter   Search

2-54 PP A2-2 completed

15. Close the table.
16. Close the database.

Understanding and Designing Relational Databases

As you learned earlier, a database is a collection of integrated and related tables. So far we have concentrated on learning the steps to build and use a table in Access. Because most databases have more than one table, the next step is to learn how to create a collection of integrated and related tables.

Relational Principles

Recall that Access is a relational database management system. The data in a *relational database* is organized into a collection of related tables. Each table stores data about one part of the system.

Consider, for example, the Mary's Rentals database. In addition to the *Equipment* table you have been working on, Mary's Rentals needs separate tables to store details about employees, customers, customer orders, information about which equipment has been rented in each order, and the service history for the equipment.

The different tables are related, or connected, to each other through common fields. You can create these relationships and view them in the ***Relationships window***. Figure 2-55 illustrates how the different tables in Mary's Rentals are connected. The lines connecting the different tables show which fields are connected to each other.

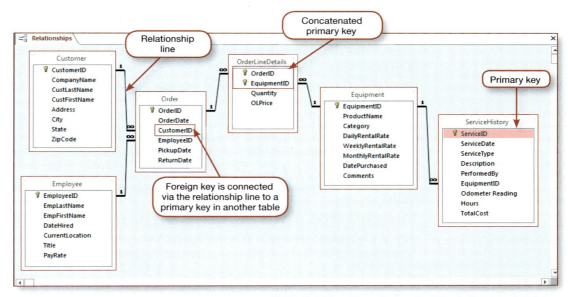

2-55 *Relationships* window for Mary's Rentals database

To be considered relational, a database must meet certain specifications. Many of the specifications are familiar to you because of the work you have already done in building tables. We use Mary's Rentals to illustrate these specifications.

- The data in the database must be stored in tables.
- The rows of the table must represent records. In the *Equipment* table, for example, each record contains the data about one particular piece of equipment.
- The columns of the table must represent fields. A field contains one specific piece of data about a record. In the *Equipment* table, *EquipmentID* and *ProductName* are the first two fields (see Figure 2-55).
- Each row must have a unique identifier or primary key. The primary key allows the DBMS to locate a specific record in the database. The primary key can either be one field in the table or a combination of several fields. If a primary key is made up of more than one field, as in the *OrderLineDetails* in Figure 2-55, it is called a ***concatenated key*** or ***composite key***.
- Each table must have a relationship with at least one other table. In order to have a relationship, the two tables must have a field in common with each other table. This common field is created by adding the primary key field from one table into the related table. In the related table, this added field is known as a ***foreign key***. After the foreign key is added into a table, you create a relationship between the two tables by linking the foreign key to the primary key. The foreign key allows you to establish the relationship with another table.

The Steps to Design a Relational Database

For a database to be of value to an organization it must be well designed. It is important to spend time early in the database development process analyzing the needs of the business so you can create a database that meets the needs of the business. The following seven steps will help you create a well-designed database:

1. **Determine the purpose of the database and the scope of the functions that will be performed**. For example, the purpose of the Mary's Rentals database is to manage inventory and customer orders. The functions that need to be performed include all tasks needed to record customers and their orders, from the initial taking of an order all the way to checking a rental return back in to the location.

   While the Mary's Rentals database does contain basic information about the employees, it does not track other human resources information like sick leave or vacation time. Those functions are outside of the scope of this database.

2. **Determine the major objects that are needed in the database to support its purpose and functions**. These objects could represent people, places, or things. Each object is built as a table. Having the data stored in separate tables helps to minimize the amount of duplicated or redundant data. This improves the overall data integrity in your database.

   In the Mary's Rentals database, examples of people objects are customers or employees. Thing objects are equipment and orders. While Mary's Rentals doesn't have any place objects, an example could be a warehouse or rental location should the company choose to store those in the system.

3. **Determine the specific details you need to capture about each object**. These details are the fields included in each table.

4. **Determine which field in each table is the primary key**. Remember that the primary key is a field that is unique across the different records. If none of the fields that you have identified in step 3 is unique, you may need to add an additional unique field that can serve as the primary key. Sometimes you might need to combine more than one field together to create a concatenated primary key.

5. **Determine the data type and size of each field**. Each field must be defined as containing only a specific type of data such as numbers, text, or dates. Additionally, you should decide how big each field can be.

   For example, you might allow 40 characters for a street address field while a zip code field should be limited to nine numbers.

6. **Determine any additional restrictions on what kinds of data can be stored in the fields**. You may wish to further limit the data that can be entered to increase data integrity.

   For example you may determine that some fields must be filled in while others are optional, or some fields may be limited to a certain list of choices.

7. **Determine how the different tables are related to each other**. This step requires that you look at your different tables and see how they are related to each other. In this way you can create a foreign key in different tables.

   One relationship in Figure 2-55 is between the *Customer* and *Order* tables. In this case the *CustomerID* was placed into the *Order* table so that the company would know which customer was associated with a particular order. You will learn how to perform this step in the next section.

Three Types of Relationships

There are three different types of relationships that may exist between tables in a database: one-to-one, one-to-many, and many-to-many. When designing your database, it is critical that you understand how your tables are related to each other and that you select the correct relationship type. One type of relationship is not better than another; a relationship is simply a reflection of the reality of how the tables are associated. The one-to-many type relationship is the most common.

Additionally, when describing table relationships, you sometimes will refer to a table based on the side of the relationship to which it belongs. For example, in a 1:M relationship, one table may be called the "1" table, while the other table may be called the "M" table. In a many-to-many relationship (M:N), the letter N is commonly used in the shorthand notation to differentiate the second side of the relationship.

One-to-One Relationship

In a ***one-to-one relationship***, one row of data in *Table A* may be associated with only one row of data in *Table B*. For example, a business may have a table containing information about employees. Since the employees frequently travel internationally, they also have another table to store information about employee passports. Each employee has only one passport and a passport belongs to only one employee.

Figure 2-56 show the visual representation of a one-to-one relationship in Access.

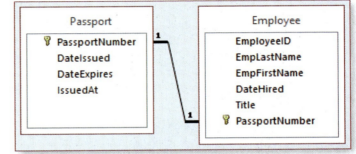

2-56 One-to-one relationship

One-to-Many Relationship

In a ***one-to-many relationship***, one row of data in *Table A* may be associated with many rows of data in *Table B*. In Mary's Rentals there is a one-to-many relationship between the *Customer* and *Order* tables. A customer can have many orders, but a particular order is associated with only one customer.

In Access, the many side of a relationship is indicated with the ***infinity symbol***. Figure 2-57 shows the visual representation of a 1:M relationship.

Many-to-Many Relationship

In a ***many-to-many relationship***, many rows of data in *Table A* may be associated with many rows of data in *Table B*. In Mary's Rentals there is a many-to-many relationship between the *Order* and *Equipment* tables. An order can be for many different pieces of equipment, and a particular piece of equipment can be on many different orders (obviously not at exactly the same time).

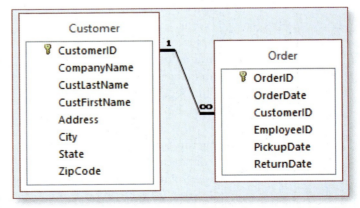

2-57 One-to-many relationship

A relational database does not directly support M:N relationships. They require the creation of a third table, *Table C*. This third table is a **junction** or **intersection table** that matches up the records across the two tables. With the creation of the junction table, the M:N relationship converts into two 1:M relationships. This results in a 1:M relationship between *Table A* and *Table C*, and another 1:M relationship between *Table B* and *Table C*.

Figure 2-58 shows the visual representation of a *M:N relationship*. The *OrderLineDetails* table is the junction table in this example. A junction table contains the *primary key* fields from each of the "1" tables. In this case, *OrderLineDetails* contains the primary key field of *OrderID* from the *Order* table and the primary key field of *EquipmentID* from the *Equipment* table. The combination of *OrderID* and *EquipmentID* creates a concatenated primary key in the junction table.

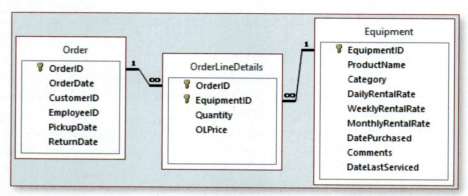

2-58 A many-to-many relationship is converted into two one-to-many relationships

Understand a Foreign Key

Recall that a foreign key is the field in common between two tables. When designing your tables it is important to know how to create a foreign key. In the seventh step of designing a database, you determine how the tables are related to each other and determine what the foreign key is. By the time you get to step 7, you already have each of the tables in your database defined.

For example, in Independent Project 1-5 in Chapter 1, you built a database containing a pet table for Life's Animal Shelter. The shelter also needs a table to store information about owners who adopt the pets. Working through step 6 of designing a database would result in the

2-59 Owner and Pet tables without a field in common

Owner and *Pets* tables shown in Figure 2-59. At this point there is not a field in common.

Step 7 requires you to identify what type of relationship exists between the *Owner* and *Pets* tables. An owner could adopt many pets but a pet belongs to only one owner. This is a 1:M relationship.

- For a 1:M relationship, you create the foreign key by taking the primary key field from the *1* table and adding it as an extra field into the *M* table. This added field is known as the foreign key.

In the Life's Animal Shelter example, you take the *OwnerID* from the *Owner* table and add it in as a foreign key into the *Pets* table (Figure 2-60). Although not required, many database designers prefer to start the foreign key field name with the letters FK.

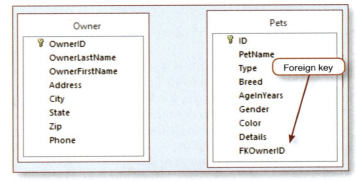

2-60 Add the foreign key into the "M" table in a relationship

- For a 1:1 relationship, you create the foreign key by taking the primary key from either table and adding it into the other table. You must set the ***Indexed*** property of the foreign key field to **Yes (No Duplicates)** for Access to recognize a 1:1 relationship.
- If you determine that you have a M:N relationship, you first need to create the junction table and convert the M:N relationship into two 1:M relationships. The junction table contains the primary key fields from each of the *1* tables, along with any other fields that describe that junction.

Remember that the foreign key field is always the primary key of another table. Sometimes it is the primary key in both. An example of this is shown and explained in Figure 2-64.

The actual addition of the foreign key into the related table is done in *Design* view of the table. When adding the foreign key field, set the field properties to be the same *Data Type* and *Field Size* as the primary key in the *1* table. The foreign key field name can be anything. Often it will be either the exact same name as the primary key or the name of the primary key preceded by FK.

Adding the foreign key into the table does not establish the relationship. This is done as a separate step, described in the next section. The addition of the foreign key just allows you to relate the tables.

Create Relationships between Tables

You can add relationships after you have added the foreign keys into the tables. Relationships should be set before any data is added into the tables that contain the foreign keys. While the process of creating the relationship is very straightforward, you need to make several decisions about how Access enforces the relationship.

Define a Relationship Using the Relationships Window

You can create a relationship directly in the *Relationships* window.

HOW TO: Define a Relationship Using the Relationships Window

1. Click the **Relationships** button [*Database Tools* tab, *Relationships* group].
   - If this is the first time you are establishing relationships for your database, the *Show Table* dialog box appears (Figure 2-61).
2. Select the **first table** to add.
3. Click the **Add** button.

2-61 *Show Table* dialog box

4. Continue adding the remaining tables.

5. Click the **Close** button when all tables have been added.

   - The tables appear in the *Relationships* window.
   - Sometimes the size of the table object is not large enough to display the entire field name of all of the table fields or to display all of the table fields. This is the case for the *Equipment* table shown in Figure 2-62.
   - If you want, you can adjust the size of the table object to see more fields.

6. Click, hold, and drag the **primary key** field from the *1* table on top of the **foreign key** field in the related table (see Figure 2-62).

   - The pointer displays a small plus sign box when it is dragged onto the related table.
   - The related table is either a *1* table or a *M* table, depending on the type of relationship.

7. Release the pointer when you are positioned on top of the **foreign key** field in the related table.

   - The *Edit Relationships* dialog box displays (Figure 2-63).

8. Verify that the field names displayed are correct. If necessary you can use the drop-down arrows to make any corrections.

9. Check the **Enforce Referential Integrity** box.

   - The check boxes for *Cascade Update Related Fields* and *Cascade Delete Related Records* become available.
   - If desired, check those boxes.

10. Click **Create**.

    - The *Relationships* window updates with the relationship line added (Figure 2-64). The *1* and infinity symbols display, indicating that referential integrity is enforced. If the two tables had a one-to-one relationship, then the *1* symbol would display on both ends.
    - As you can see in Figure 2-64, the *EquipmentID* field is the primary key of the *Equipment* table and is part of a concatenated primary key in the *OrderLineDetails* table. It also is a foreign key in the *OrderLineDetails* table since it links back to the primary key in the *Equipment* table.

11. Save the changes made to the relationships.

12. If you are finished with all changes to the relationships, click **Close** [*Relationship Tools Design* tab, *Relationships* group].

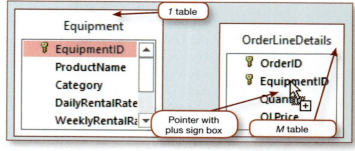

2-62 Drag the primary key to the foreign key to create a relationship

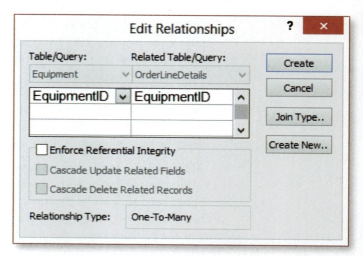

2-63 *Edit Relationships* dialog box

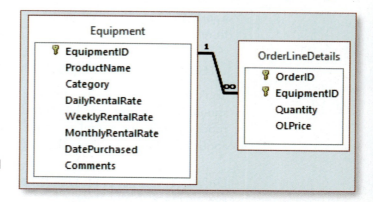

2-64 Completed relationships window

▶ ANOTHER WAY

You can create a relationship using the *Lookup Wizard* and choosing the option to lookup the field from another table.

Once a relationship has been created, when you view the *1* table in *Datasheet* view you can see the related records. A plus sign appears to the left of the first column, indicating that this table is related to another table.

- View related records by clicking the **plus sign**. The plus sign changes to a minus sign. Figure 2-65 shows the related records for *EquipmentID 10015*.
- You can enter additional records into the related table directly from this view.
- Click the **minus sign** to hide the related records.

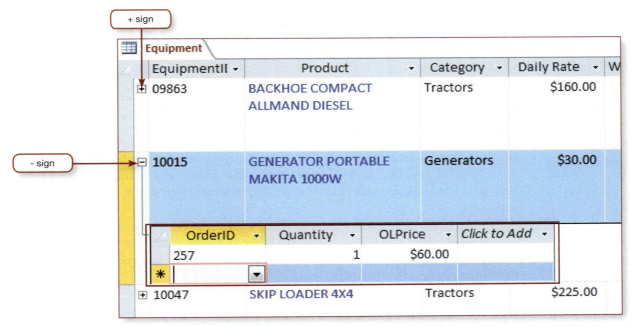

2-65 Click the plus sign to show related records in *Datasheet* view

Enforce Referential Integrity

When creating a relationship, you must decide if you want to enforce referential integrity. ***Referential integrity*** ensures that records in associated tables have consistent data. For example, if you enter a row of data in the *OrderLineDetails* table, when you enter a value in the *EquipmentID* field it should match an *EquipmentID* value that already exists in the *Equipment* table. This ensures consistency and integrity of the database.

If you create a relationship and do not enforce referential integrity, you can have records in the associated table that do not match a record in the *1* table.

For example, if a doctor's office does not require a patient to declare a primary physician, the *PhysicianID* field on a *Patient* table may be left blank. While this is possible, in the majority of cases you will want to enforce referential integrity.

Enforce referential integrity by selecting the **Enforce Referential Integrity** check box in the *Edit Relationships* dialog box.

In addition to requiring that the foreign key value of record in the associated table matches a primary key value in the *1* table, when referential integrity has been enforced Access prohibits two other actions.

- First, Access does not allow you to delete a record from the *1* table if that record has related records in an associated table. For example, at a school you may have a table with student information and another table containing information about student parking tickets. If referential integrity is enforced, Access does not allow you to delete a student record from the *Student* table if that student has any rows of data in the *ParkingTicket* table. This ensures that all parking tickets remain linked to the student who got the ticket. This restriction means that a student can't exit the school system without first paying all his parking tickets.

- Second, Access does not allow you to change the value of the primary key field in the *1* table if that record has related records in an associated table. Assuming that *StudentID* is the primary key in the *Student* table, the student is not allowed to change the value of her *StudentID* if she has any parking ticket records in the *ParkingTicket* table.

Sometimes there are valid reasons to override these constraints. If referential integrity has been enforced, the **Cascade Update Related Fields** and **Cascade Delete Related Records** options become available.

Cascade Updates

Sometimes it is desirable to allow the primary key value of the *1* table to be changed. For example, if a *StudentID* value has been stolen, the student must be assigned a new ID. In cases like this you want to be able to change the value of the primary key, and have Access find all related records and change the value in the foreign key to match the new primary key value.

To allow the primary key value to be changed and have Access cascade updates in the related table, select the **Cascade Update Related Fields** check box in the *Edit Relationships* dialog box. You can do this only if you have selected the *EnforceReferential Integrity* option in the *Edit Relationships* dialog box.

Cascade Deletes

Sometimes you want to be able to delete a record from the *1* table and have Access automatically delete all the related records in the associated table. For example, if a record is deleted from the *Order* table because an order is cancelled, all of the records in the *OrderLineDetails* table (the specific products this customer had ordered) should be deleted as well. In cases like this, you want to be able to make this deletion, and have Access delete all the related records.

To allow a record in the *1* table to be deleted and have Access delete all associated records in the related table, select the **Cascade Delete Related Records** check box in the *Edit Relationships* dialog box. You can do this only if you have selected the *Enforce Referential Integrity* option.

Save a Relationship

If you have made any changes to the relationships you need to save those changes.

Click the **Save** button on the *Quick Access* toolbar to save any changes made to the relationships.

Delete a Relationship between Tables

If a relationship has been created in error, or you need to make changes to the fields involved in the relationship, or you no longer need to have a particular relationship, you can delete it. You must close all of the tables involved in the relationship, as well as any objects that are based on those tables before you can delete a relationship.

HOW TO: Delete a Relationship between Tables

1. Click the **Relationships** button [*Database Tools* tab, *Relationships* group].
   - The *Relationships* window appears.
2. Select the **relationship line** you wish to delete (Figure 2-66).
   - The middle part of the line thickens once it has been selected.
3. Right-click the **relationship line** to open the shortcut menu.
4. Click **Delete** (Figure 2-67).
   - A confirmation message appears, asking you to confirm the deletion. Click **Yes** to confirm the deletion.
5. Click the **Save** button to save your changes.
6. If you are finished with all deletions to the relationships, click **Close** [*Relationship Tools Design* tab, *Relationships* group].

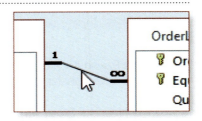

2-66 **Select the relationship line**

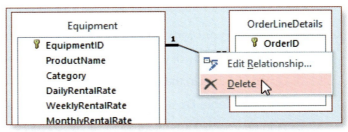

2-67 *Delete* icon in the shortcut menu

Edit a Relationship between Tables

Occasionally you need to make changes to an existing relationship between tables.

HOW TO: Edit a Relationship between Tables

1. Click the **Relationships** button [*Database Tools* tab, *Relationships* group].
   - The *Relationships* window appears.
2. Select the **relationship line** you wish to edit.
3. Click **Edit Relationships** [*Relationship Tools Design* tab, *Tools* group] (Figure 2-68).
   - The *Edit Relationships* dialog box displays (Figure 2-69).

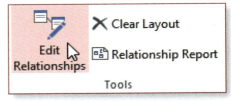

2-68 *Edit Relationships* button

> **ANOTHER WAY**
>
> Right-click the **relationship line** to open the shortcut menu and then select **Edit Relationship**.

4. Make any needed changes.
5. Click **OK**.
6. **Save** the changes made to the relationships.
7. If you are finished with all changes to the relationships, click **Close** [*Relationship Tools Design* tab, *Relationships* group].

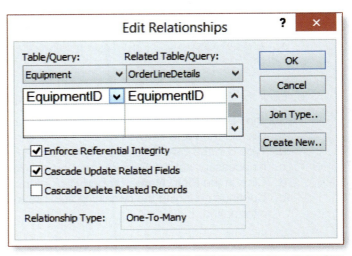

2-69 *Edit Relationships* dialog box

In this Pause & Practice, you add a second table to store the service history of the equipment. Next you define a relationship between the *Equipment* and *ServiceHistory* tables.

Files Needed: ***[your initials] PP A2-2.accdb***
Completed Project File Name: ***[your initials] PP A2-3.accdb***

1. Open the ***[your initials] PP A2-2.accdb*** database file created in Pause & Practice 2-2.

2. Save a new copy of your database as ***[your initials] PP A2-3***.

3. Enable content in the security warning.

4. Click the **Table Design** button [*Create* tab, *Tables* group] to open a new table in *Design* view.

5. Add new fields into the table.
   a. Type ServiceID in the *Field Name* property box of the first row. Press the **Tab** key to move to the *Data Type* property.
   b. Select the **Short Text** *Data Type*. Press the **Tab** key to move to the *Description* property.
   c. Type Unique ID number for the service request.
   d. Click the **Primary Key** button [*Table Tools Design* tab, *Tools* group].
   e. Press the **Tab** key to move to the next row.
   f. Continue adding the remaining fields into the table using the following information.

Field Name	Data Type	Description
ServiceDate	**Date/Time**	Date service was completed
ServiceType	**Short Text**	Indicates whether service was maintenance, repair, or inspection
Description	**Short Text**	General description of the nature of the service performed
PerformedBy	**Short Text**	Employee ID number of the repair person
FKEquipmentID	**Short Text**	Must match an EquipmentID value in the Equipment table. (This is the foreign key.)
OdometerReading	**Number**	Odometer reading at time of repair (for vehicles only)
Hours	**Number**	Total number of hours the equipment has been in use
TotalCost	**Currency**	Cost of the service (parts and labor)

6. Click the **Save** button to save the table as ServiceHistory.

7. Set the Field Properties in the *ServiceHistory* table.
   a. Click in the **Field Name** property box of the *ServiceID* field.
   b. Type 6 in the *Field Size* property box in the *Field Properties* area.
   c. If necessary, set the *Required* property to **Yes**.
   d. Click in the **Field Name** property box of the *ServiceDate* field.
   e. Continue changing the remaining field properties in the *ServiceHistory* table using the following information.

Field Name	Field Size	Format	Required
ServiceDate		General Date	Yes
ServiceType	15		Yes
Description	255		Yes
PerformedBy	3		Yes
FKEquipmentID	5		Yes
OdometerReading	Long Integer		
Hours	Long Integer		
TotalCost	Currency		Yes

8. Save the table by clicking the **Save** button.

9. Modify the *ServiceType* field to use a *Combo Box*.
   a. Click to select the **ServiceType** field.
   b. Click in the property box for the **Data Type** property, click the **arrow,** and select **Lookup Wizard**. The *Lookup Wizard* dialog box opens.
   c. Select the radio button for **I will type in the values that I want**.
   d. Click the **Next** button.
   e. Click in the **first cell** in the *Col1* column.
   f. Type Maintenance.
   g. Press the **down arrow** key to move to the next row.
   h. Type Repair. Press the **down arrow** key to move to the next row.
   i. Type Inspection.
   j. Click the **Next** button.
   k. Click the **Limit To List** check box.
   l. Click the **Finish** button. Remember that Access resets the *Field Size* to 255.
   m. Type 15 in the *Field Size* property box of the *ServiceType* field.

10. Save and close the table.

11. Create a relationship between the *Equipment* and *ServiceHistory* tables.
    a. Click the **Relationships** button [*Database Tools* tab, *Relationships* group]. If this is the first time you have established relationships for your database, the *Show Table* dialog box appears.
    b. If the *Show Table* dialog box does not display, click the **Show Table** button [*Relationship Tools Design* tab, *Relationships* group].
    c. Select the **Equipment** table and click the **Add** button.
    d. Select the **ServiceHistory** table and click the **Add** button.
    e. Click the **Close** button. The tables display in the *Relationships* window.
    f. Adjust the size of the table objects to see all of the fields.
    g. Drag the **EquipmentID** from the *Equipment* table on top of the **FKEquipmentID** in the *ServiceHistory* table. The pointer displays a small plus sign box when it is dragged onto the related table (Figure 2-70).
    h. Release the pointer when you are positioned on top of the **FKEquipmentID** field. The *Edit Relationships* dialog box displays.

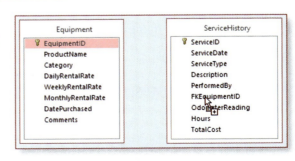

2-70 Create the relationship between the *Equipment* and *ServiceHistory* tables

i. Verify that the field names displayed are correct. If necessary use the **drop-down arrows** to make any corrections.

j. Check the **Enforce Referential Integrity** check box.

k. Check the **Cascade Update Related Fields** check box.

l. Check the **Cascade Delete Related Records** check box. The completed *Edit Relationships* dialog box should be similar to Figure 2-71.

m. Click **Create**. The *Relationships* window updates with the relationship line added (Figure 2-72). The 1 and infinity symbols display, indicating that referential integrity is enforced.

n. Save the changes made to the relationships.

o. Click **Close** (*Relationship Tools Design* tab, *Relationships* group].

12. Open the *Equipment* table in *Datasheet* view.

a. Notice the plus signs display to the left of the *EquipmentID* column.

b. Click the **plus sign** for *EquipmentID 09863* to display the related records (Figure 2-73). Since you have not yet entered any data into the *ServiceHistory* table, no related records display.

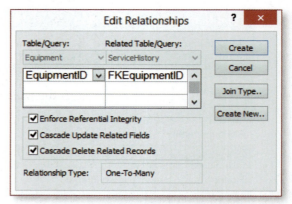

2-71 Select *Referential Integrity* options in the Edit Relationships dialog box

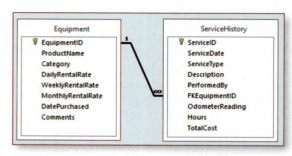

2-72 Completed relationship between the tables

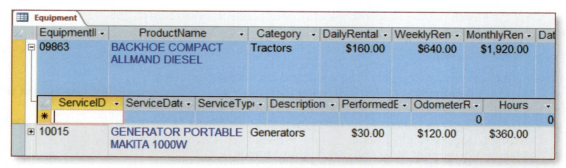

2-73 Display related records for *EquipmentID 09863*

13. Close the *Equipment* table.

14. Close the database.

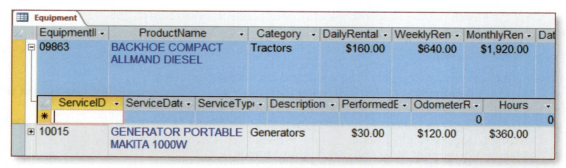

SLO 2.7

Importing Data Records from Excel

You have already learned how to enter data records into a table using *Datasheet* view. Sometimes companies may have their data stored in another file. In cases like this you can import the data records into Access instead of having to enter all the data values.

In this section you learn how to import data from an Excel file into a table that you have already created. You append (add into) the existing data records already in the table. Prior to importing the file, you need to ensure that the Excel file is formatted correctly.

- The first row of the Excel file must contain column headings that match the existing field names in the Access table.
- The data fields don't need to be in the same order.
- All of the fields in the table do not need to be in the Excel file as long as the *Required* property allows the field to be empty.
- If the fields are not of the same data type (for example the Access field data type is *Number* but the Excel file field contains *Text*), Access still imports the file but the contents of that field is left empty. In this case, the *Required* property must allow the field to be empty.

HOW TO: Import Data from Excel

1. Click the **Excel** button [*External Data* tab, *Import & Link* group].
   - The *Get External Data – Excel Spreadsheet* dialog box launches (Figure 2-74).

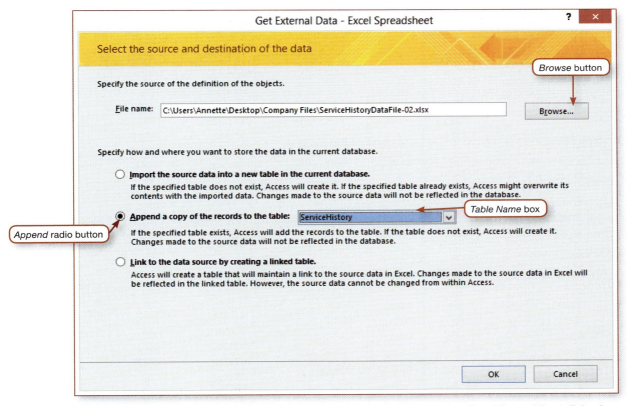

2-74 *Get External Data – Excel Spreadsheet* **dialog box**

2. Click the **Browse** button to launch the *File Open* dialog box.
3. Locate and select the Excel file that contains the records you want to import.
4. Click the **Open** button. The *File Open* dialog box closes.
5. Select the **Append a copy of the records to the table** radio button.
6. Click the **drop-down arrow** in the *table name* box and select the desired table.

7. Click **OK** to launch the *Import Spreadsheet Wizard* (Figure 2-75). The data records should display in the *Wizard* window.

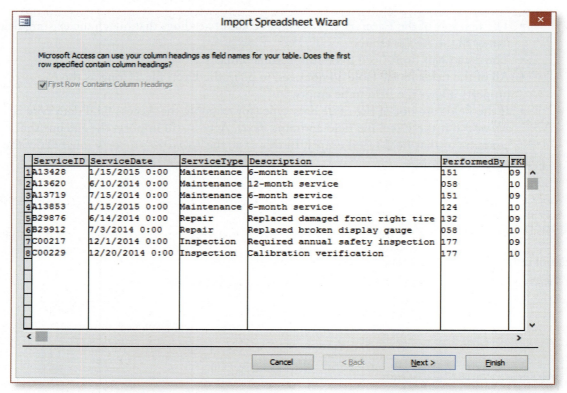

Import Spreadsheet Wizard

Microsoft Access can use your column headings as field names for your table. Does the first row specified contain column headings?

☑ First Row Contains Column Headings

	ServiceID	ServiceDate	ServiceType	Description	PerformedBy	FKI
1	A13428	1/15/2015 0:00	Maintenance	6-month service	151	09
2	A13620	6/10/2014 0:00	Maintenance	12-month service	058	10
3	A13719	7/15/2014 0:00	Maintenance	6-month service	151	09
4	A13853	1/15/2015 0:00	Maintenance	6-month service	124	10
5	B29876	6/14/2014 0:00	Repair	Replaced damaged front right tire	132	09
6	B29912	7/3/2014 0:00	Repair	Replaced broken display gauge	058	10
7	C00217	12/1/2014 0:00	Inspection	Required annual safety inspection	177	09
8	C00229	12/20/2014 0:00	Inspection	Calibration verification	177	10

Cancel   < Back   Next >   Finish

2-75 Import Spreadsheet Wizard

8. Click the **Next** button to advance to the next page of the *Wizard*.
   • Access confirms the name of the table to append the records.
9. Click **Finish**.
   • The *Wizard* displays the *Save Import Steps* screen.
   • If you are frequently going to repeat an import process, you can click the check box to save the steps to perform the action more quickly.
10. Click the **Close** button.
11. You can open the table to verify that the records were successfully added into the table.

SLO 2.8

Printing the Contents of a Table

Occasionally you may wish to print a simple list of all records in a table. You can do this with the *Print* button on the *Backstage* view. There are three options available after selecting the *Print* button.

• ***Quick Print:*** Sends the contents of the current object immediately to the printer.
• ***Print:*** Allows you to select different print options before sending the contents to the printer.
• ***Print Preview:*** Allows you to preview the way the table records will print before actually sending them to the printer.

Preview the Data Records

Previewing the way that your table records will print is a good idea. This allows you to check that the formatting is appropriate and to make changes to any settings before printing.

HOW TO: Preview the Data Records before Printing

1. Select the table you want to print from the *Navigation* pane. The table can be closed or it can be open in *Datasheet* view when you print records.
2. Click the **Print** button [*File* tab] to display the printing options.
3. Click the **Print Preview** button.
   - The *Print Preview* tab opens and shows a preview of how the table will print (Figure 2-76).
   - The default print settings include the table name and current date at the top of the report and page number at the bottom of the report. Access calls these three items *Headings.*
4. Review the *Navigation bar* to determine if there are additional pages that will print. In Figure 2-76, the darkened *Next Page* button indicates that there are additional pages.

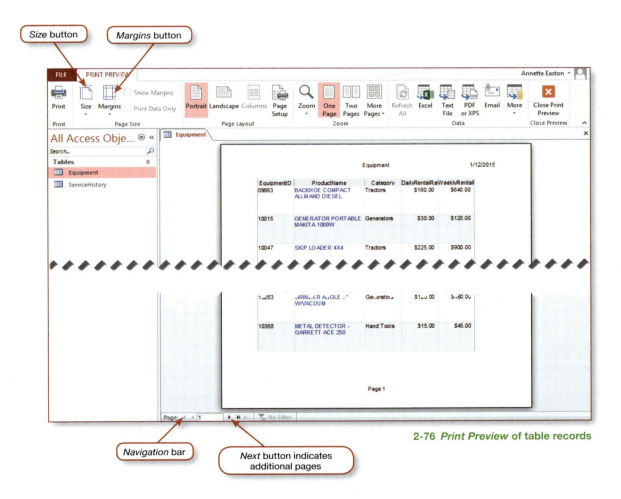

2-76 *Print Preview* of table records

5. Adjust the page orientation by selecting the **Portrait** or **Landscape** buttons [*Print Preview* tab, *Page Layout* group].
6. Adjust the paper size or margins by selecting the **Size** or **Margins** buttons [*Print Preview* tab, *Page Size* group].

7. If you want to, you can remove the *Headings* from the printout by deselecting the **Print Headings** check box on the *Print Options* tab of the *Page Setup* dialog box.

8. When ready to print, click the **Print** button [*Print Preview* tab, *Print* group] to open the *Print* dialog box.

9. You can change the number of copies, page range, and printer if desired.

10. Click **OK**.

11. Click the **Close Print Preview** button [*Print Preview* tab, *Close Preview* group].

2-77 *Page Setup* dialog box

Print the Data Records without Previewing

If you previously previewed how the table will print, you can quickly print the table records without previewing the pages.

HOW TO: Print Table Records

1. Select the **table** you want to print from the *Navigation* pane. The table can be closed or it can be open in *Datasheet* view when you print records.

2. Click the **Print** button [*File* tab] to display the printing options.

3. Click the **Print** button.
   - The *Print* dialog box displays.

4. Change the number of copies, page range, and printer if desired.

5. Click **OK**.

Managing a Database Using the Compact & Repair Database Utility

Over time, as you use your database, the database file becomes larger. Much of this is due to additional records being added into the tables. However, some of the increased size is due to certain ways that Access operates. In order to accomplish some functions, Access creates temporary objects. These objects are not always automatically deleted when the function has been performed. Additionally, when you delete database objects, that space is not always released.

As the database file grows, it takes longer to perform tasks such as adding and deleting records, querying tables, and printing reports. With really large databases this can result in a significant decrease in processing speed.

Another concern is that a database file may become corrupted. In Access this is most likely to occur if the database is shared over a network and numerous users make frequent edits to *Long Text* fields. A corrupted database doesn't typically result in lost data; rather, some of the forms or the code inside of macros may be lost or become unusable. Recall from Chapter 1 that macros are objects that add functionality to your database. For example, a macro provides the code to make a button work.

You can use the ***Compact & Repair Database*** utility to reduce the chances of corruption and to reclaim unused space from temporary and deleted objects. Before running this process be sure to create a backup copy of your database. Additionally, if this is a multi-user database, no one can be using the database at the time the *Compact & Repair* is performed.

HOW TO: Compact & Repair a Database

1. Click the **File** tab. The *Info* button should be selected.
2. Click the **Compact & Repair Database** button (Figure 2-78).
   - If Access is not able to repair everything in a corrupted database, it creates a table named *MSysCompactErrors.* This table opens automatically and contains information about the objects that could not be repaired.

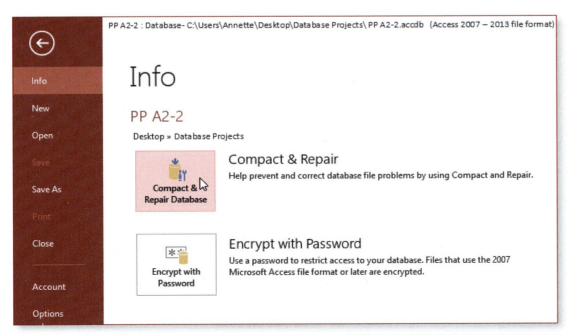

2-78 Compact & Repair Database button

In this Pause & Practice, you import data into the *ServiceHistory* table. You also print the contents of the *Equipment* table and manage the database using *Compact & Repair Database* option.

Files Needed: ***[your initials] PP A2-3.accdb***, ***ServiceHistoryDataFile-02.xlsx***
Completed Project File Name: ***[your initials] PP A2-4.accdb***

1. Open the ***[your initials] PP A2-3.accdb*** database file created in Pause & Practice 2-3.

2. Save a new copy of your database as ***[your initials] PP A2-4***. Remember to pay attention to the location where you are saving your database.

3. Enable content in the security warning.

4. Import data into the *ServiceHistory* table.
   a. Click the **Excel** button [*External Data* tab, *Import & Link* group] to launch the *Get External Data – Excel Spreadsheet* dialog box.
   b. Click the **Browse** button to launch the *File Open* dialog box.
   c. Locate and select the ***ServiceHistoryDataFile-02.xlsx*** Excel file.
   d. Click the **Open** button. The *File Open* dialog box closes.
   e. Select the **Append a copy of the records to the table** radio button.
   f. Click the **drop-down arrow** in the *table name* box and select the **ServiceHistory** table.
   g. Click **OK** to launch the *Import Spreadsheet Wizard.* The data records should display in the *Wizard* window as shown in Figure 2-79.

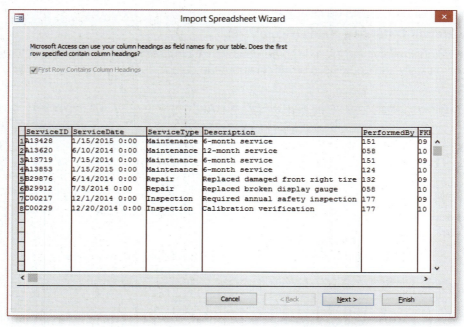

2-79 *Import Spreadsheet Wizard*

   h. Click the **Next** button to advance to the next page of the *Import Spreadsheet Wizard*.
   i. Verify that the *Import to Table* box contains the *ServiceHistory* table.
   j. Click **Finish**.
   k. Click the **Close** button. It is not necessary to save these import steps.

5. Open the *ServiceHistory* table in *Datasheet* view to verify that the eight records imported correctly.

6. Close the *ServiceHistory* table.

7. Open the *Equipment* table in *Datasheet* view.
   a. Notice the plus signs display to the left of the *EquipmentID* column.
   b. Click the **plus sign** for *EquipmentID 09863* to display the related records. You should see the four entries in the *ServiceHistory* table for this piece of equipment.
   c. Click the **minus sign** to hide the related records.

8. Prepare to print the *Equipment* table.
   a. Click the **Print** button [*File* tab] to display the printing options.
   b. Click the **Print Preview** button to open the *Print Preview* tab and view a preview of how the table will print.
   c. Click the **Landscape** button [*Print Preview* tab, *Page Layout* group] to change the page orientation.
   d. Click the **Margins** button [*Print Preview* tab, *Page Size* group].
   e. Select the **Normal** button as shown in Figure 2-80. The report preview should appear as shown in Figure 2-81. Depending on the default font or printer settings, the *Comments* field may appear on a separate page.

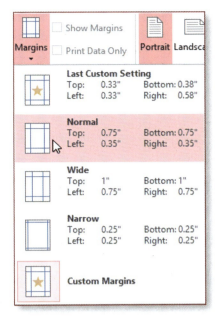

2-80 *Margins* options in *Print Preview*

EquipmentID	ProductName	Category	DailyRentalRa	WeeklyRentalf	MonthlyRental	DatePurchase	Comments
09863	BACKHOE COMPACT ALLMAND DIESEL	Tractors	$160.00	$640.00	$1,920.00	09-Sep-11	Lift Capacity: 2100 lbs Bucket Size: 16" only
10015	GENERATOR PORTABLE MAKITA 1000W	Generators	$30.00	$120.00	$360.00	15-Dec-11	Size: 19-1/2"L x 11-3/4"W x 17-1/2"H Weight: 55 lbs
10047	SKIP LOADER 4X4	Tractors	$225.00	$900.00	$2,700.00	08-Mar-12	Subject to Environmental Fee
10103	GENERATOR TOWABLE POWERPRO 25KW	Generators	$120.00	$360.00	$1,080.00	20-Jul-12	Overall L x W x H: 67"L x 28"W x 3"H
10129	LEVEL SITE LASER	Hand Tools	$60.00	$240.00	$720.00	02-Aug-12	
10235	WHEELBARROW	Hand Tools	$10.00	$30.00	$60.00	01-Feb-13	
10236	SNAKE DRAIN 1/2" ELECTRIC	Plumbing	$35.00	$140.00	$420.00	01-Feb-13	General Brand - Easy Rooter Jr
10237	PIPELINE INSPECTION CAMERA - 85'	Plumbing	$200.00	$800.00	$2,400.00	01-Feb-13	85' Cable

Equipment   1/12/2015

Page 1

2-81 *Print Preview* of *Equipment* table records

   f. If desired, click the **Print** button to open the *Print* dialog box. In the *Print* dialog box you can change the **Number of Copies**, **Print Range**, or **Printer Name**. Click the **OK** button to print the report.

9. Click the **Close Print Preview** button [*Print Preview* tab, *Close Preview* group].

10. Backup and Compact & Repair the database.
    a. Click the **Save As** button [*File* tab].
    b. Ensure that *Save Database As* is selected in *File Types.*
    c. Select **Back Up Database** in the *Save Database As* area.
    d. Click the **Save As** button.
    e. Accept the default name in the *File name* box and click the **Save** button.
    f. Click the **File** tab. The *Info* button should be selected.
    g. Click the **Compact & Repair Database** button.

11. Close the database.

Chapter Summary

2.1 Create a table in *Design* view, add new fields, define a primary key, delete fields, and save, close, and open a table (p. A2-75).

- ***Design view*** provides the most flexibility when you are creating tables and setting field properties.
- Add new fields in *Design* view by entering the field name and selecting the data type.
- Each table should have a ***primary key***, a field that contains a unique value for each record.
- You can add a new field between existing fields by inserting a row and delete a field by deleting a row.
- You must save any changes to the table design for them to be permanent.

2.2 Set field properties including *Field Size, Format, Caption, Default Values,* and *Required* (p. A2-79).

- The field properties in *Design* view are grouped into ***General*** and ***Lookup*** properties.
- The ***Field Size*** property sets the maximum number of characters allowed or the maximum value of a number.
- You can use the ***Format*** property to set the way the data displays in a table.
- You can choose from ***predefined formats*** for *Number, Currency, Date/Time,* and *Yes/No* data types.
- You can create ***custom formats*** for Short Text and *Long Text* data types.
- Customize the ***Caption*** property to change the contents that appears as a column header.
- An established ***default value*** automatically enters a value into a field.
- Require a user to enter a value for a field by setting the ***Required*** property.

2.3 Explain data integrity and data validation concepts and options (p. A2-86).

- ***Data validation*** is the process of verifying the accuracy, or integrity, of the data.
- Create ***data integrity rules*** to ensure that the data is accurate and consistent.
- ***Data format***, ***range***, ***consistency***, and ***completeness*** are the most common types of data integrity rules.

- ***Metadata*** are the descriptions about what the different data fields represent and their formats.

2.4 Create field and table level validation rules, test rules, create validation text, create lookup fields, and define an input mask (p. A2-87).

- ***Field validation rules*** create range and data format integrity rules by limiting what can be entered into a field.
- Consistency integrity rules compare fields in the same table. These ***table validation rules*** are entered into the record validation rule property for the table.
- It is a good idea to create several cases of ***test data*** and use them to test the validation rules to ensure the rule works as desired.
- You can enter custom error messages into the ***Validation Text*** property. This message displays when data is entered that violates a validation rule.
- ***Lookup fields*** display a list of pre-defined choices from which the user can select.
- Apply an ***input mask*** to a field to require the user to enter the data in a pre-defined format.

2.5 Change field properties after records are added into a table (p. A2-99).

- If you change field properties after data has been added into the tables, Access warns you that the change could result in lost data or inconsistent data.
- Pay attention to the warning messages because it may be impossible to undo some of the changes and recover any lost data.

2.6 Explain relational database principles, understand the steps that must be taken to design a database, create relationships between tables, implement referential integrity, and delete and edit relationships (p. A2-104).

- A ***relational database*** contains data that is organized into a collection of related tables. To be considered relational, a database must meet a set of specifications.
- It is important to follow the ***steps to designing a relational database*** to ensure that your set of tables and relationships are correct.

A2-125

- *Relationships* are the connections among different tables. They can be classified as **one-to-one**, *one-to-many*, and *many-to-many*.
- A *foreign key* is a field in common across tables and is the mechanism that allows tables to be related.
- Once the foreign key has been added into a table, the relationships can be established through the **Relationships window**.
- Referential integrity ensures that records in related tables are consistent.
- Depending on the needs of the business, you can decide whether to **cascade updates** and *deletes*.

2.7 Import data records from Excel (p. A2-116).

- You can import data records from an Excel file into an Access table with the *Append* option.
- The first row of the Excel file must contain the field names from the Access table. The format of the fields should match or not all the data values may be imported.

2.8 Preview and print the contents of a table (p. A2-118).

- On the *Backstage* view you can print the contents of a table.
- *Print Preview* allows you to see how the records appear before printing. In the *Print Preview* tab you can change paper size, margins, and page orientation.

2.9 Manage a database using *Compact & Repair* (p. A2-121).

- Over time the size of your database increases due to added data as well as temporary and deleted objects.
- In larger databases, functions such as adding and deleting records, querying tables, and running reports take longer.
- The **Compact & Repair Database** utility reclaims unused space and repairs databases that have become corrupted.

Check for Understanding

In the **Online Learning Center** for this text (www.mhhe.com/office2013inpractice), there are a variety of resources that can be used to review the concepts covered in this chapter.

The following Online Learning Resources are available on the Online Learning Center.

- Multiple choice questions
- Short answer questions
- Matching exercises

Guided Project 2-1

Central Sierra Insurance wants to expand the database you created in the Pause & Practice 1-4 project in Chapter 1. To ensure consistency, the starting file is provided for you. In this project, you use *Design* view to create a second table, edit field properties, and integrate data integrity rules. You also create a relationship between the two tables and enforce referential integrity constraints. Finally, you view how the table records will print using *Print Preview*. [Student Learning Outcomes 2.1, 2.2, 2.3, 2.4, 2.5, 2.6, 2.8]

File Needed: ***CentralSierra-02.accdb***
Completed Project File Name: ***[your initials] Access 2-1.accdb***

Skills Covered in This Project

- Create a table using *Design* view.
- Add fields into a table.
- Edit field properties in *Design* view.
- Use the *Lookup Wizard* to create a drop-down list.
- Save a table.
- Enter records.

- Verify the existence of a foreign key.
- Create a 1:M relationship between tables.
- Enforce referential integrity.
- View a table in *Datasheet* view and expand related records.
- Preview table results for printing.

1. Open the ***Central Sierra-02.accdb*** database file.

2. Save a new copy of your database as ***[your initials] Access 2-1***.

3. Enable content in the security warning.

4. Click the **Table Design** button [*Create* tab, *Tables* group] to open a new table in *Design* view.

5. Add new fields into the table and set field properties.
   a. Type Branch in the *Field Name* property box of the first row. Press the **Tab** key to move to the *Data Type* property.
   b. Select the **Short Text** *Data Type.* Press the **Tab** key to move to the *Description* property.
   c. Type Unique Branch Name.
   d. Click the **Primary Key** button [*Table Tools Design* tab, *Tools* group].
   e. Press the **Tab** key to move to the next row.
   f. Add the remaining fields into the table using the following information.

Field Name	Data Type	Description
Address	Short text	Street address of the branch
City	Short text	Branch city
State	Short text	Branch state

continued

Field Name	Data Type	Description
Zip	Short text	Branch Zip code
Phone	Short text	Branch main phone number
Fax	Short text	Branch main fax number

g. Click the **Save** button to save the table as Branch. It is a good idea to periodically save a table when you are creating it so you don't lose your work.

h. Click in the **Field Name** property box of the *Branch* field.

i. Type 30 in the *Field Size* property box in the *Field Properties* area.

j. If necessary, set the *Required* property to **Yes**.

k. Click in the **Field Name** property box of the *Address* field.

l. Change the remaining field properties in the *Branch* table using the following information.

Field Name	Field Size	Default Value	Required
Address	40		Yes
City	20		Yes
State	2	CA	Yes
Zip	9		Yes
Phone	10		Yes
Fax	10		No

6. Save the table by clicking the **Save** button.

7. Create an input mask for the *Zip* field.
   a. Click to select the **Zip** field.
   b. Click in the property box for the **Input Mask** property.
   c. Click the **Build** button to launch the *Input Mask Wizard*.
   d. Select the **Zip Code** *Input Mask*.
   e. Click the **Next** button.
   f. Don't make any changes to the mask or *Placeholder character*. Click the **Next** button.
   g. Select the radio button for **Without the symbols in the mask, like this**.
   h. Click the **Finish** button.
   i. Save the table.

8. Create an input mask for the *Phone* field.
   a. Click to select the **Phone** field.
   b. Click in the property box for the **Input Mask** property.
   c. Click the **Build** button to launch the *Input Mask Wizard*.
   d. Select the **Phone Number** *Input Mask*.
   e. Click the **Next** button.
   f. Don't make any changes to the mask or placeholder character. Click the **Next** button.
   g. Select the radio button for **Without the symbols in the mask, like this**.
   h. Click the **Finish** button.
   i. Save the table.

9. Create an input mask for the *Fax* field.
   a. Click to select the **Fax** field.
   b. Click in the property box for the **Input Mask** property.
   c. Click the **Build** button to launch the *Input Mask Wizard.*
   d. Select the **Phone Number** *Input Mask.*
   e. Click the **Next** button.
   f. Don't make any changes to the mask or placeholder character. Click the **Next** button.
   g. Select the radio button for **Without the symbols in the mask, like this**.
   h. Click the **Finish** button.

10. Save the table and switch to *Datasheet* view.
   a. Enter the following records into the *Branch* table.

Branch	Address	City	State	Zip	Phone	Fax
Cameron Park	3360 Coach Lane	Cameron Park	CA	95682-8454	(530) 672-3232	(530) 672-1111
Folsom	75 Natoma St, #B1	Folsom	CA	95630-2640	(916) 458-5555	(916) 458-6666
Granite Bay	6132 Del Oro Road	Granite Bay	CA	95746-9007	(916) 791-8787	(916) 791-9999

   b. Save and close the table.

11. Modify the *Department* field in the *Employees* table to use a *Combo Box.*
   a. Open the **Employees** table in *Design* view.
   b. Click to select the **Department** field.
   c. Click in the property box for the **Data Type** property, click the arrow, and select **Lookup Wizard**. The *Lookup Wizard* dialog box opens.
   d. Select the radio button for **I will type in the values that I want**.
   e. Click the **Next** button.
   f. Click in the **first cell** in the *Col1* column.
   g. Type Administration.
   h. Press the **down arrow** key to move to the next row.
   i. Type Health and Benefits. Press the **down arrow** key to move to the next row.
   j. Type Insurance Sales. Press the **down arrow** key to move to the next row.
   k. Type Property and Casualty.
   l. Click the **Next** button.
   m. Click the **Limit To List** check box.
   n. Click the **Finish** button.
   o. Save the table. If prompted to test the existing data against the new rules, click **Yes**.

12. Verify the existence of a foreign key and create a one-to-many relationship between the *Branch* and *Employees* tables.
   a. The *Branch* field is the field in common across the two tables. It is the primary key in the *Branch* table.
   b. Open both tables in *Design* view and verify that the *Branch* field has the same *Data Type* and *Field Size* in both tables.
   c. Edit the *Description* property of the *Branch* field in the *Employees* table to read Branch Assigned To – Must Match a Branch in the Branch table.
   d. Save and close any tables that you may have opened.
   e. Click the **Relationships** button [*Database Tools* tab, *Relationships* group].
   f. In the *Show Table* dialog box, select the **Branch** table and click the **Add** button.
   g. Select the **Employees** table and click the **Add** button.
   h. Click the **Close** button.

i.   Drag the **Branch** field from the *Branch* table on top of the **Branch** field in the *Employees* table. Release the pointer. The *Edit Relationships* dialog box displays.

j.   Verify that the field names displayed are correct. If necessary, use the drop-down arrows to make any corrections.

k.   Click the **Enforce Referential Integrity** check box.

l.   Click the **Cascade Update Related Fields** check box.

m.   Leave the **Cascade Delete Related Records** check box not selected. The company does not want to delete employees just because they may close a branch. This allows them to reassign employees.

n.   Click **Create**. The *Relationships* window updates with the relationship line added. The *1* and infinity symbols display, indicating that referential integrity is enforced.

o.   Save the changes made to the relationships.

p.   Click **Close** [*Relationship Tools Design* tab, *Relationships* group].

13. Enter the following record into the *Employees* table to test the new drop-down list.

Emp ID	FirstName	LastName	Branch	Title	Department	Start Date	Base Monthly Salary
200	Timothy	Hansen	Cameron Park	Insurance Agent	Health and Benefits	4/15/2015	3900

14. Save and close the table.

15. Open the *Branch* table in *Datasheet* view.
    a.   Adjust the width of the fields so that the entire field contents shows for each field.
    b.   Click the **plus sign** to the left of the *Branch* field for the *Cameron Park* branch. You should see the 11 employees assigned to Cameron Park.
    c.   Click the **minus sign** to close the related records.

16. Preview the data records in the *Branch* table before printing.
    a.   Click the **Print** button [*File* tab] to display the printing options.
    b.   Click the **Print Preview** button. The *Print Preview* tab opens and shows a preview of how the table will print.
    c.   Click the **Landscape** button [*Print Preview* tab, *Page Layout* group] to change the page orientation.
    d.   The report preview should appear as shown in Figure 2-82.
    e.   If desired, click the **Print** button to open the *Print* dialog box and click **OK** to print the report.
    f.   Click the **Close Print Preview** button.

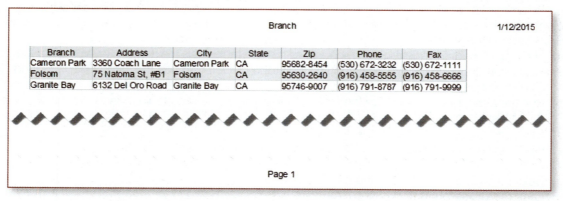

2-82 *Print Preview* of *Branch* table records

17. Save and close the *Branch* table.

18. Close the database.

Guided Project 2-2

San Diego Sailing Club wants to expand the database created in Guided Project 1-3 in Chapter 1. To ensure consistency, the starting file is provided for you. In this project, you use *Design* view to create a second table, edit field properties, and integrate data integrity rules. You also create a relationship between the two tables, enforce referential integrity constraints, and import data into the second table. Finally, you *Compact & Repair* the database.

[Student Learning Outcomes 2.1, 2.2, 2.3, 2.4, 2.5, 2.6, 2.7, 2.8, 2.9]

Files Needed: ***SanDiegoSailing-02.accdb***, ***SDRentalsDataFile-02.xlsx***
Completed Project File Name: *[your initials] Access 2-2.accdb*

Skills Covered in This Project

- Create a table using *Design* view.
- Add fields into a table.
- Edit field properties in *Design* view.
- Create a validation rule and validation text.
- Save a table.
- Create a 1:M relationship between tables.
- Enforce referential integrity.
- Import records.
- Preview a table for printing.
- *Compact & Repair* a database.

1. Open the ***SanDiegoSailing-02.accdb*** database file.
2. Save a new copy of your database as *[your initials] Access 2-2*.
3. Enable content in the security warning.
4. Click the **Table Design** button [*Create* tab, *Tables* group] to open a new table in *Design* view.
5. Add new fields into the table and set field properties.
   a. Type RentalID in the *Field Name* property box of the first row. Press the **Tab** key to move to the *Data Type* property.
   b. Select the **Short Text** *Data Type*. Press the **Tab** key to move to the *Description* property.
   c. Type Unique ID assigned to each rental.
   d. Click the **Primary Key** button [*Table Tools Design* tab, *Tools* group].
   e. Press the **Tab** key to move to the next row.
   f. Add the remaining fields into the table using the following information.

Field Name	Data Type	Description
FKBoatID	Short Text	Must match a BoatID in the SailboatFleet table
RentalDate	Date/Time	Date of rental
FourHourRental?	Yes/No	Yes is a 4-hour rental; No is a daily rental
MemberID	Short Text	ID number of Member renting the boat

A2-131

g. Click the **Save** button to save the table as SDRentals.
h. Click in the **Field Name** property box of the *RentalID* field.
i. Type 5 in the *Field Size* property box in the *Field Properties* area.
j. Type Rental ID in the *Caption* property box.
k. Change the remaining field properties in the *SDRentals* table using the following information.

Field Name	Field Size	Format	Caption
FKBoatID	4		Boat ID
RentalDate		Short Date	Rental Date
FourHourRental?		Yes/No	Four Hour Rental?
MemberID	4		Member Number

6. Save the table by clicking the **Save** button.

7. Create a field validation rule and validation text for the *RentalDate* field.
   a. Click to select the **RentalDate** field.
   b. Click in the **Validation Rule** property box.
   c. Type >=#1/1/2015#.
   d. Click in the **Validation Text** property box.
   e. Type The Rental Date must be greater than or equal to 1/1/2015.
   f. Save the table and switch to *Datasheet* view.
   g. Type 1 in the *RentalID* field. **Tab** to the *RentalDate* field and type 7/5/2013.
   h. Press the **Tab** key. The message box should display the contents of your *Validation Text* property. Click **OK**. Type 7/5/2015 in the *RentalDate* field.
   i. Press the **Tab** key. You should successfully move to the *FourHourRental?* field.
   j. Click the **Record Selector** box to select this data record and click **Delete** [*Home* tab, *Records* group] since you no longer need this sample data.
   k. Click **Yes** to confirm deletion of this record.
   l. Close the *SDRentals* table.

8. Create a one-to-many relationship between the *SailboatFleet* table and the *SDRentals* table.
   a. Click the **Relationships** button [*Database Tools* tab, *Relationships* group].
   b. In the *Show Table* dialog box, select the **SailboatFleet** table, and click the **Add** button.
   c. Select the **SDRentals** table and click the **Add** button.
   d. Click the **Close** button.
   e. Drag the **BoatID** field from the *SailboatFleet* table on top of the **FKBoatID** field in the *SDRentals* table as shown in Figure 2-83. Release the pointer. The *Edit Relationships* dialog box displays.
   f. Verify that the field names displayed are correct. If necessary, use the **drop-down arrows** to make any corrections.
   g. Click the **Enforce Referential Integrity** check box.
   h. Click the **Cascade Update Related Fields** check box.
   i. Leave the **Cascade Delete Related Records** check box not selected. The club does not want to delete rental records just because it may take a boat out of service. This allows the club to keep a record of the rental.
   j. Click **Create**. The *Relationships* window updates with the relationship line added. The *1* and infinity symbols display, indicating that referential integrity is enforced.
   k. Save the changes made to the relationships.
   l. Click **Close** [*Relationship Tools Design* tab, *Relationships* group].

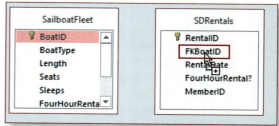

2-83 Drag the *BoatID* to the *FKBoatID* to create a relationship

9. Import data from Excel into the *SDRentals* table.
   a. Click the **Excel** button [*External Data* tab, *Import & Link* group] to launch the *Get External Data – Excel Spreadsheet* dialog box.
   b. Click the **Browse** button to launch the *File Open* dialog box.
   c. Locate and select the ***SDRentalsDataFile-02.xlsx*** Excel file.
   d. Click the **Open** button. The *File Open* dialog box closes.
   e. Select the **Append a copy of the records to the table** radio button.
   f. Click the **drop-down arrow** in the *Table Name* box and select the **SDRentals** table.
   g. Click **OK** to launch the *Import Spreadsheet Wizard.* The data records should display in the *Wizard* window.
   h. Click the **Next** button to advance to the next page of the *Import Spreadsheet Wizard.*
   i. Verify that the *Import to Table:* box contains the *SDRentals* table.
   j. Click **Finish**.
   k. Click the **Close** button.

10. Open the *SDRentals* table in *Datasheet* view. Your table should have the six records shown in Figure 2-84.

2-84 *SDRentals* table records after import

11. Edit field properties in the *SDRentals* table.
   a. Click the **Design View** icon (Figure 2-85) in the *Status bar* to switch to *Design* view.
   b. Change the *Required* property for all fields except *FourHourRental?* to **Yes**.
   c. Save the changes to your table. Access displays a message box warning you that data integrity rules have changed. Click **Yes** to test your data against the new rules.
   d. Close the *SDRentals* table.

2-85 *Design View* icon in the *Status bar*

12. View the related data in the *SailboatFleet* table.
   a. Open the *SailboatFleet* table in *Datasheet* view.
   b. Click the **plus sign** to the left of the *BoatID* field *for BoatID 1010.* You should see two rentals for this boat.
   c. Close the *SailboatFleet* table.

13. Preview the data records in the *SailboatFleet* table for printing.
   a. Select the **SailboatFleet** table in the *Navigation* pane.
   b. Click the **Print** button [*File* tab] to display the printing options.
   c. Click the **Print Preview** button. The *Print Preview* tab opens and shows a preview of how the table will print.
   d. Click the **Landscape** button [*Print Preview* tab, *Page Layout* group] to change the page orientation.
   e. Click the **Close Print Preview** button.

14. Use *Compact & Repair* to reclaim unused space.
   a. Click the **File** tab. The *Info* button should be selected.
   b. Click the **Compact & Repair Database** button.

15. Close the database.

Guided Project 2-3

American River Cycling Club wants to expand the database created in Guided Project 1-2 in Chapter 1. To ensure consistency, the starting file is provided for you. For this project, you use *Design* view to create a second table, edit field properties, and integrate data integrity rules. You also create a relationship between the two tables and enforce referential integrity constraints. Finally, you import data and view how the table records will print using *Print Preview*.
[Student Learning Outcomes 2.1, 2.2, 2.3, 2.4, 2.6, 2.7]

Files Needed: ***AmericanRiver-02.accdb***, ***RaceResultsDataFile-02.xlsx***
Completed Project File Name: ***[your initials] Access 2-3.accdb***

Skills Covered in This Project

- Create a table using *Design* view.
- Add fields into a table.
- Edit field properties in *Design* view.
- Use the *Lookup Wizard* to create a drop-down list.
- Save a table.

- Create a 1:M relationship between tables.
- Enforce referential integrity.
- Import records.
- View a table in *Datasheet* view and expand related records.

1. Open the ***AmericanRiver-02.accdb*** database file.

2. Save a new copy of your database as ***[your initials] Access 2-3***.

3. Enable content in the security warning.

4. Click the **Table Design** button [*Create* tab, *Tables* group] to open a new table in *Design* view.

5. Add new fields into the table and set field properties.
   a. Type RaceID in the *Field Name* property box of the first row. Press the **Tab** key to move to the *Data Type* property.
   b. Select the **Short Text** *Data Type.* Press the **Tab** key to move to the *Description* property.
   c. Type Unique Race ID number.
   d. Press the **Tab** key to move to the next row.
   e. Type FKMemberID in the *Field Name* property box. Press the **Tab** key to move to the *Data Type* property.
   f. Select the **Number** *Data Type.* Press the **Tab** key to move to the *Description* property.
   g. Type Must match a MemberID in the Members table.
   h. Click the **row selector** to select the *RaceID* field. Press and hold the **Shift** key. Click the **row selector** to select the *FKMemberID* field.
   i. Click the **Primary Key** button [*Table Tools Design* tab, *Tools* group]. The *Primary Key* symbol should appear on both the *RaceID* and *FKMemberID* fields, indicating a *concatenated primary key,* as shown in Figure 2-86.

Field Name	Data Type	Description (Optional)
RaceID	Short Text	Unique Race ID number
FKMemberID	Number	Must match a MemberID in the Members table

2-86 RaceID and *FKMemberID* make a concatenated primary key

   j. Click in the **Field Name** property box of the cell below *FKMemberID.*

k. Add the remaining fields into the table using the following information.

Field Name	Data Type	Description
Place	Number	Place finished in the race
Time	Date/Time	Total time
Division	Short Text	Division in which the member participated
AgeGroup	Short Text	Age group in which the member participated

l. Click the **Save** button to save the table as RaceResults.
m. Click in the **Field Name** property box of the *RaceID* field.
n. Type 3 in the *Field Size* property box in the *Field Properties* area.
o. Change the remaining field properties in the *RaceResults* table using the following information.

Field Name	Field Size	Format	Caption
FKMemberID			Member ID
Place	Integer		
Time		Short Time	
Division	1		
AgeGroup	13		

6. Save the table by clicking the **Save** button.

7. Modify the *Division* field to use a *Combo Box.*
   a. Click to select the *Division* field.
   b. Click in the property box for the *Data Type* property, click the **arrow,** and select **Lookup Wizard**.
   c. Select the radio button for **I will type in the values that I want**.
   d. Click the **Next** button.
   e. Click in the **first cell** in the *Col1* column and type M.
   f. Press the **down arrow** key to move to the next row.
   g. Type F.
   h. Click **Next**.
   i. Click the **Limit To List** check box.
   j. Click **Finish**.
   k. Change the *Field Size* property to 1. Recall that after changing a field to display with a *Combo Box*, Access resets the *Field Size* to 255.
   l. Save and close the table.

8. Create a one-to-many relationship between the *Members* table and the *RaceResults* table.
   a. Click the **Relationships** button [*Database Tools* tab, *Relationships* group].
   b. In the *Show Table* dialog box, select the **Members** table and click the **Add** button.
   c. Select the **RaceResults** table and click the **Add** button.
   d. Click the **Close** button.
   e. Drag the **MemberID** field from the *Members* table on top of the **FKMemberID** field in the *RaceResults* table as shown in Figure 2-87. Release the pointer. The *Edit Relationships* dialog box displays.

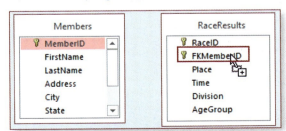

2-87 Drag the *MemberID* to the *FKMemberID* to create a relationship

A2-135

f. Verify that the field names displayed are correct. Use the **drop-down arrows** to make any corrections.

g. Click the **Enforce Referential Integrity** check box.

h. Click the **Cascade Update Related Fields** check box.

i. Leave the **Cascade Delete Related Records** check box not selected. The club does not want to delete race records just because a member may leave the club. This allows the club to keep a record of the race.

j. Click **Create**. The *Relationships* window updates with the relationship line added. The *1* and infinity symbols display, indicating that referential integrity is enforced.

k. Save the changes made to the relationships.

l. Click **Close** [*Relationship Tools Design* tab, *Relationships* group].

9. Import data from Excel into the *RaceResults* table.

a. Click the **Excel** button [*External Data* tab, *Import & Link* group] to launch the *Get External Data – Excel Spreadsheet* dialog box.

b. Click the **Browse** button to launch the *File Open* dialog box.

c. Locate and select the **RaceResultsDataFile-02.xlsx** Excel file.

d. Click the **Open** button. The *File Open* dialog box closes.

e. Select the **Append a copy of the records to the table** radio button.

f. Click the **drop-down arrow** in the *Table Name* box and select the **RaceResults** table.

g. Click **OK** to launch the *Import Spreadsheet Wizard*. The data records should display in the *Wizard* window.

h. Click the **Next** button to advance to the next page of the *Import Spreadsheet Wizard*.

i. Verify that the *Import to Table* box contains the *RaceResults* table.

j. Click **Finish**.

k. Click the **Close** button.

10. Open the *RaceResults* table in *Datasheet* view. Your table should contain the 23 records shown in Figure 2-88.

RaceID	Member ID	Place	Time	Division	AgeGroup
1	1	2	2:15	F	>=20 and <30
1	2	3	2:20	F	>=30 and <40
1	5	1	2:14	M	>=30 and <40
1	8	4	2:22	F	>=30 and <40
1	11	5	2:23	F	>=30 and <40
2	1	1	0:47	F	>=20 and <30
2	8	2	0:51	F	>=30 and <40
2	11	3	0:52	F	>=30 and <40
3	1	3	1:07	F	>=20 and <30
3	2	1	1:06	F	>=30 and <40
3	5	2	1:07	M	>=30 and <40
3	6	4	1:08	M	>=30 and <40
3	7	6	1:10	F	>=20 and <30
3	8	7	1:11	F	>=30 and <40
3	10	5	1:09	M	>=20 and <30
4	1	3	0:43	F	>=20 and <30
4	7	2	0:42	F	>=20 and <30
4	10	1	0:40	M	>=20 and <30
5	1	1	2:10	F	>=20 and <30
5	3	5	2:20	M	>=30 and <40
5	8	2	2:11	F	>=30 and <40
5	9	4	2:16	F	<20
5	12	3	2:14	F	<20
*	0	0			

Record: 1 of 23 — No Filter — Search

2-88 *RaceResults* table records after import

11. Edit field properties in the *RaceResults* table.
    a. Click the **Design View** icon in the *Status bar* to switch to *Design* view.
    b. Change the *Required* property for all fields to **Yes**.
    c. Save the changes to your table. Access displays a message box warning you that data integrity rules have changed. Click **Yes** to test your data against the new rules.
    d. Close the *RaceResults* table.

12. View the related data records in the *Members* table.
    a. Open the *Members* table in *Datasheet* view.
    b. Click the **plus sign** to the left of the *MemberID* field for *Geneva Lingle, MemberID* 1. You should see the five races in which Geneva has participated.
    c. Click the **plus sign** to the left of the *MemberID* field for the *Ryan Thomas, MemberID* 3. You should see the one race in which Ryan has participated. Your screen should look similar to Figure 2-89.
    d. Close the *Members* table.

13. Close the database.

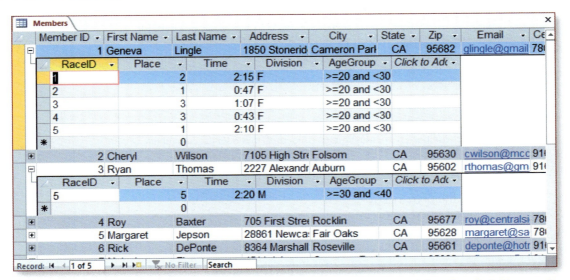

2-89 *Members* table with related *RaceResults* table records

Independent Project 2-4

Courtyard Medical Plaza wants to expand the database created in Independent Project 1-4 in Chapter 1. To ensure consistency, the starting file is provided for you. For this project, you use *Design* view to create a second table, edit field properties, integrate data integrity rules, and enter data. You also create a relationship between the two tables, enforce referential integrity constraints, and import data. Finally you preview how the records will print.
[Student Learning Outcomes 2.1, 2.2, 2.3, 2.4, 2.6, 2.7]

Files Needed: *CourtyardMedicalPlaza-02.accdb, RentInvoicesDataFile-02.xlsx*
Completed Project File Name: *[your initials] Access 2-4.accdb*

Skills Covered in This Project

- Create a table using *Design* view.
- Add fields into a table.
- Edit field properties in *Design* view.
- Create and test a record validation rule.
- Save a table.
- Enter records.

- Create a 1:M relationship between tables.
- Import records.
- Enforce referential integrity.
- View a table in *Datasheet* view and expand related records.
- Preview table results for printing.

1. Open the **CourtyardMedicalPlaza-02.accdb** database file.

2. Save a new copy of your database as *[your initials] Access 2-4*.

3. Enable content in the security warning.

4. Create a new table using *Table Design*.
   a. Add the following fields into the table and set field properties.

Field Name	Data Type	Description
InvoiceID	Number	Unique Invoice Number
InvoiceDate	Date/Time	Date Invoice created
DueDate	Date/Time	Date Bill is due
AmountDue	Currency	Total Rent amount due
FKDoctorID	Number	Must match a DoctorID in the Physicians table
Description	Short Text	Brief summary of charge(s)

   b. Set *InvoiceID* as the primary key.
   c. Save the table as RentInvoices.
   d. Change the field properties in the *RentInvoices* table using the following information.

Field Name	Field Size	Format	Caption
InvoiceID	Integer		
InvoiceDate		Medium Date	Invoice Date
DueDate		Medium Date	Due Date
AmountDue			Amount Due
FKDoctorID	Long Integer		Doctor ID
Description	40		

5. Save the table.

6. Create and test a record validation rule in the *RentInvoices* table.
   a. Open the *Property Sheet* for the *RentInvoices* table.
   b. Type [DueDate] > = ([InvoiceDate]+10) in the validation rule property for the table.
   c. Type The Due Date must be at least 10 days after the Invoice Date. as **Validation Text**.
   d. Close the *Property Sheet* window.
   e. Switch to *Datasheet* view to test the rule. If prompted, save the changes to your table.

f. Type 1 in the *InvoiceID* field. Press the **Tab** key to move to the *InvoiceDate* field.

g. Type 1/1/2015. Press the **Tab** key to move to the *DueDate* field.

h. Type 1/5/2015.

i. Press the **down arrow** key to leave the current record. The message box should display the validation text message (Figure 2-90) since the *DueDate* is not at least 10 days after the *InvoiceDate*.

j. Delete the contents and type 1/11/2015 in the *DueDate* field.

k. Verify that the record adds successfully.

l. Delete this record since you no longer need this sample data.

m. Close the *RentInvoices* table.

7. Create a one-to-many relationship between the *Physicians* table and the *RentInvoices* table.

a. Open the *Relationships* window and add the two tables.

b. Drag the **DoctorID** field from the *Physicians* table on top of the **FKDoctorID** field in the *RentInvoices* table as shown in Figure 2-91.

c. Make the correct choices to *Enforce Referential Integrity* and *Cascade Update Related Fields*.

d. Leave the **Cascade Delete Related Records** check box not selected. Courtyard Medical Plaza does not want to delete invoice records just because a doctor may move out of the office complex. This allows Courtyard Medical Plaza to keep all rental records.

e. Create the relationship.

f. Save the changes and close the *Relationships* window.

8. Import data from Excel into the *RentInvoices* table.

a. Launch the *Get External Data – Excel Spreadsheet* dialog box.

b. Locate and select the ***RentInvoicesDataFile-02.xlsx*** Excel file.

c. Append the records to the *RentInvoices* table.

d. Launch the *Import Spreadsheet Wizard*.

e. Finish the *Import Spreadsheet Wizard*. Close the *Wizard* after the records have imported.

9. Open the *RentInvoices* table in *Datasheet* view. Your table should contain 27 records.

a. Place your pointer over the right border of the *Description* field and double-click to increase the width using *AutoFit*.

b. Save the changes to your table.

10. Edit field properties in the *RentInvoices* table.

a. Use *Design* view to change the *Required* property for all fields to **Yes**.

b. Save the changes to your table. Access displays a message box warning you that data integrity rules have changed. Test your data against the new rules.

c. Close the *RentInvoices* table.

11. Open the *Physicians* table in *Datasheet* view.

a. Click the **plus sign** to the left of the *DoctorID* field for *Robert Beyer, DoctorID 1*. You should see the three invoices sent to Dr. Beyer.

2-90 Error message displays validation text from a record validation rule violation

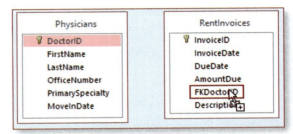

2-91 Drag the DoctorID to the FKDoctorID to create a relationship

b. Click the **plus sign** to the left of the *DoctorID* field for the *Emy Ostrander, DoctorID 3*. Notice that Dr. Ostrander does not have any invoices. Based on the way Courtyard Medical processes billing, they only send the bill to the one doctor listed on the lease. Your screen should be similar to Figure 2-92.

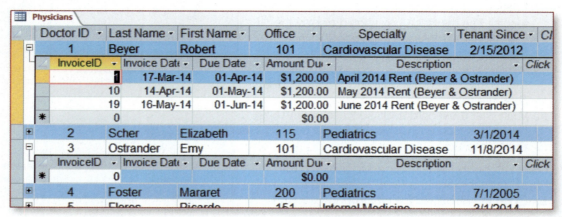

2-92 *Physicians* table with related *RentInvoices* table records

c. Close the *Physicians* table.

12. Preview the data records in the *RentInvoices* table for printing.
    a. Select the **RentInvoices** table in the *Navigation* pane.
    b. Use *Print Preview* to show a preview of how the table will print.
    c. Close the *Print Preview*.

13. Close the database.

Independent Project 2-5

Life's Animal Shelter wants to expand the database created in the Independent Project 1-5 in Chapter 1. To ensure consistency, the starting file is provided for you. In this project, you use *Design* view to create a second table, edit field properties, integrate data integrity rules, and enter data. You also create a relationship between the two tables and enforce referential integrity constraints. Finally, you add data using the relationship between tables.
[Student Learning Outcomes 2.1, 2.2, 2.3, 2.4, 2.6]

File Needed: *LifesAnimalShelter-02.accdb*
Completed Project File Name: *[your initials] Access 2-5.accdb*

Skills Covered in This Project

- Create a table using *Design* view.
- Add fields into a table.
- Edit field properties in *Design* view.
- Create an input mask.
- Create a validation rule and validation text.
- Save a table.

- Enter records.
- Create a foreign key.
- Create a 1:M relationship between tables.
- Enforce referential integrity.
- View a table in *Datasheet* view and expand related records.

1. Open the **LifesAnimalShelter-02.accdb** database file.
2. Save a new copy of your database as **[your initials] Access 2-5**.
3. Enable content in the security warning.
4. Create a new table using *Table Design*.
   a. Add the following fields into the table and set field properties.

Field Name	Data Type	Description	Field Size
OwnerID	Short Text	Unique Owner ID	4
OwnerLastName	Short Text	Last name	20
OwnerFirstName	Short Text	First name	20
Address	Short Text	Street address	40
City	Short Text		20
State	Short Text		2
Zip	Short Text	Zip Code	5
Phone	Short Text	Contact phone number	10

   b. Set *OwnerID* as the primary key.
   c. Save the table as Owner.

5. Create an input mask for the *Phone* field.
   a. Select the **Phone** field.
   b. Use the **Phone Number** *Input Mask.*
   c. Don't make any changes to the mask or placeholder character and select the radio button for **Without the symbols in the mask, like this**.
   d. Finish the *Input Mask Wizard.*

6. Save the table. Create and test a field validation rule.
   a. Select the *OwnerID* field.
   b. Type Like "####" as a validation rule.
   c. Type You must enter a 4-digit Owner ID as validation text.
   d. Save the table and switch to *Datasheet* view.
   e. Test the rule by typing 11 in the first row of the *OwnerID* column.
   f. Move to the *OwnerLastName* field. The message box should display the validation text message (Figure 2-93) since the *OwnerID* is not four digits long.
   g. Delete the contents and type 1111 into the *OwnerID* field.

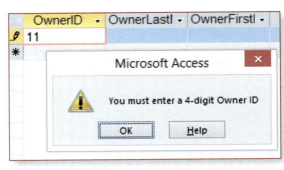

2-93 Field validation rule error message

h. Verify that you can successfully move to the *OwnerLastName* field since 1111 meets the validation rule criteria.

i. Delete this test data record.

7. Enter the following records into the *Owner* table. Life's Animal Shelter doesn't have any data about the owners stored electronically so you are unable to import any data.

Owner ID	OwnerLast Name	OwnerFirst Name	Address	City	State	Zip	Phone
0100	Smith	Albert	11 Lakewood Drive	Abilene	TX	79601	325-614-9333
0101	Weston	Mark	2601 Nonesuch Road	Abilene	TX	79606	325-555-1112
0102	Rivera	Angela	2548 Laney Road	Denton	TX	76208	940-321-8020
0103	Moyer	Silvia	6867 Anglebluff Circle	Dallas	TX	75248	972-380-6188
0104	Wills	Mason	2421 Klondike Drive	Dallas	TX	75228	214-224-5555

8. Save and close the table.

9. Determine the foreign key field.
    a. Currently there is not a field in common across the *Owner* and *Pets* tables. There is a one-to-many relationship between the two tables since an owner could adopt many pets, but each pet is adopted by only one owner.
    b. The foreign key comes by taking the primary key field from the *1* table and adding it in as an additional field in the *M* table.
    c. Open the *Pets* table in *Design* view.
    d. Add the foreign key field below the *Details* field using the following information.

Field Name	Data Type	Description	Field Size
FKOwnerID	Short Text	Must match an Owner ID in the Owner table	4

    e. Save and close the *Pets* table.

10. Create a one-to-many relationship between the *Owner* and *Pets* tables.
    a. Open the **Relationships** window and add the two tables.
    b. Enlarge the table objects, if needed, to see all of the fields.
    c. Drag the **OwnerID** field from the *Owner* table on top of the **FKOwnerID** field in the *Pets* table. Release the pointer. The *Edit Relationships* dialog box displays.
    d. Make the choices to **Enforce Referential Integrity** and **Cascade Update Related Fields**.
    e. Leave the **Cascade Delete Related Records** check box not selected. The shelter does not want to delete pet records when it deletes information about an owner.
    f. Create the relationship,
    g. Save the changes and close the *Relationships* window.

11. Enter the following data into the specified records in the *Pets* table to reflect which pets have been adopted.
    a. Open the *Pets* table in *Datasheet* view.
    b. Type 0100 in the *FKOwnerID* field for *PetID 1*.
    c. Type 0103 in the *FKOwnerID* field for *PetID 3*.
    d. Type 0100 in the *FKOwnerID* field for *PetID 12*.

e. Type 0104 in the *FKOwnerID* field for *PetID 14*.

f. Close the *Pets* table.

12. View the related data records in the *Owner* table.

a. Open the *Owner* table in *Datasheet* view.

b. Click the **plus sign** to the left of the *OwnerID* field for the *Albert Smith, OwnerID 0100.* You should see the two pets adopted by Albert.

c. Close the *Owner* table.

13. Close the database.

Independent Project 2-6

The New York Department of Motor Vehicles tracks information about drivers, including accidents in which they have been involved. The starting database file is provided for you. For this project, you use *Design* view to edit a table and integrate data integrity rules. You also create a relationship between the two tables and enforce referential integrity constraints. Finally you view how the table records will print using *Print Preview*.

[Student Learning Outcomes 2.1, 2.2, 2.3, 2.4, 2.5, 2.6, 2.8]

File Needed: ***NewYorkDMV-02.accdb***
Completed Project File Name: ***[your initials] Access 2-6.accdb***

Skills Covered in This Project

- Edit a table using *Design* view.
- Edit field properties in *Design* view.
- Create a lookup field.
- Save a table.

- Enforce referential integrity.
- View a table in *Datasheet* view and expand related records.
- Preview table results for printing.

1. Open the ***NewYorkDMV-02.accdb*** database file.

2. Save a new copy of your database as ***[your initials] Access 2-6***.

3. Enable the contents in the security warning.

4. Edit field properties of the *Ticket* table in *Design* view.

a. Select a **Short Date** *Format* for the *TicketDate* field.

b. Create a *Lookup Field* for the *PrimaryFactor* field with the following choices and limit the choices to those on the list: Alcohol, Backing Unsafely, Driver Distraction, Driver Inexperience, Failure to Keep Right, Failure to Yield R.O.W., Following too Closely, Passing/Lane Violations, Traffic Control Disregarded, Turning Improperly, Unsafe Speed.

c. Make all fields *Required.*

d. Save the changes to the table. If prompted to test existing data against the new rules, click **Yes**.

e. Close the table.

5. Edit field properties of the *Drivers* table in *Design* view.
   a. Open the *Drivers* table in *Design* view.
   b. Make all fields *Required*.
   c. Create a lookup field on the *Gender* field with the choices of M and F. Select **Yes** in the *Limit To List* property.
   d. Assign a *Default Value* of NY to the *State* field.
   e. Save the changes to the table. If prompted to test existing data against the new rules, click **Yes**.
   f. Close the table.

6. Review table relationships.
   a. Open the *Relationships* window (Figure 2-94). Notice the *Relationship line* does not have any symbols on the end points. This indicates that *Referential Integrity* has not been enforced.
   b. Close the *Relationships* window.
   c. Open the *Ticket* table in *Datasheet* view to see the impact of not *Enforcing Referential Integrity*.
   d. Enter the following test data record into the table.

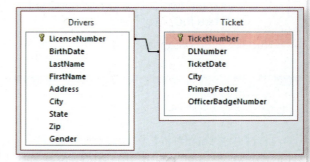

2-94 Referential Integrity is not enforced

Ticket Number	DL Number	Ticket Date	City	Primary Factor	Officer Badge Number
12345678901	999999999	1/1/2015	New York	Unsafe Speed	123456789

   e. Open up the *Drivers* table in *Datasheet* view. Keep the *Ticket* table open.
   f. Notice that there is no data record for a driver with the *LicenseNumber* of *999999999*. When *Referential Integrity* is not enforced, Access allows you to enter data records that don't need to have a corresponding record in the related table.
   g. Click to expand the **plus symbol** for *LicenseNumber 10000501 (Timothy Smith)*. You should see the two tickets Timothy received. Notice that the relationship exists even if referential integrity is not enforced.
   h. Close the *Drivers* table.
   i. Delete the test data record from the *Ticket* table.
   j. Save and close the *Ticket* table.

7. Edit referential integrity constraints.
   a. Open the *Relationships* window.
   b. Select the **Relationship line** and edit the relationship.
   c. Make the choices to **Enforce Referential Integrity** and **Cascade Update Related Fields**.
   d. Leave the **Cascade Delete Related Records** check box not selected. You do not want to delete ticket records if you delete information about a driver.
   e. Click **OK** to save the changes to the relationship.
   f. Save the changes and close the *Relationships* window.

8. Test the referential integrity constraints.
   a. Open the *Ticket* table in *Datasheet* view.
   b. Enter the following test data record into the table.

Ticket Number	DL Number	Ticket Date	City	Primary Factor	Officer Badge Number
1234567890	99999999	1/1/2015	New York	Unsafe Speed	123456789

c. Access should display a message box (Figure 2-95) indicating that you cannot add this ticket record because it requires a related record in the *Drivers* table.

2-95 Error message when referential integrity is violated

d. Change the *DLNumber* to 12344537, a valid license number, so you can get past the error message.
e. Delete the test data ticket record.
f. Close the *Ticket* table.

9. Preview the data records in the *Drivers* table for printing.
   a. Select the **Drivers** table in the *Navigation* pane.
   b. Use *Print Preview* to show a preview of how the table will print.
   c. Change the page to a **Landscape** orientation.
   d. Use the **Navigation** buttons to move to the second page.
   e. Close the *Print Preview.*

10. Close the database.

Improve It Project 2-7

Placer Hills Real Estate wants to expand the database created in the Improve It Project 1-7 in Chapter 1. To ensure consistency, the starting file is provided for you. In this project, you use *Design* view to edit properties in a table and integrate data integrity rules. You edit data records, create a relationship between the two tables, and enforce referential integrity constraints. Finally you view how the table records will print using *Print Preview*.
[Student Learning Outcomes 2.1, 2.2, 2.3, 2.4, 2.6, 2.8]

File Needed: *PlacerHills-02.accdb*
Completed Project File Name: *[your initials] Access 2-7.accdb*

Skills Covered in This Project

- Edit a table using *Design* view.
- Edit field properties in *Design* view.
- Create an input mask.
- Save a table.
- Create a foreign key.
- Create a 1:M relationship between tables.
- Enforce referential integrity.
- View a table in *Datasheet* view and expand related records.
- Preview table results for printing.

1. Open the **PlacerHills-02.accdb** database file.

2. Save a new copy of your database as **[your initials] Access 2-7**.

3. Enable the contents in the security warning.

4. Open the *Agents* table in *Datasheet* view (Figure 2-96).

Agents				
EmployeeN▾	LastName ▾	FirstName ▾	DateHired ▾	Phone ▾
103	Bidou	Simon	Sunday, August 15, 2010	5306487689
127	Weatherby	Kelly	Sunday, February 20, 2011	9169873756
133	Burgess	John	Monday, November 05, 2012	5302784699
151	Chung	Rick	Saturday, January 18, 2014	9168236940
160	Johnstone	Jack	Thursday, May 01, 2014	9165551679
160	Duarte	Kallyn	Monday, June 02, 2014	9167441614
169	Gerardo	Montoya	Friday, June 27, 2014	9165345991
*				

2-96 *Datasheet* view of the *Agents* table

   a. Look at the *DateHired* and *Phone* fields. The manager of the real estate office wants those to be formatted differently.
   b. Notice that both Jack Johnstone and Kallyn Duarte have the same value in the *EmployeeNum* field. If the employee number is supposed to be unique, something must not be set correctly with the primary key in this table.
   c. Change Kallyn Duarte's *EmployeeNum* to be 168, the correct value.

5. Change to *Design* view to make needed corrections to the *Agents* table.
   a. Notice that the table does not have a primary key. Although Access recommends that you assign a primary key in a table, Access lets you create a table without one.
   b. Set the *EmployeeNum* as the primary key.
   c. Set the *Format* property of the *DateHired* field to use *Short Date*.
   d. Create an input mask for the *Phone* field. Select the **Phone Number** *Input Mask*. Don't make any changes to the mask or placeholder character and select the radio button for **Without the symbols in the mask, like this**. Complete the *Input Mask Wizard*.
   e. Make all fields **Required**.
   f. Save the table.
   g. Switch to *Datasheet* view to ensure that the formatting shows as desired.
   h. Adjust the field width of the *DateHired* field to 13. Remember that you can select the column, right-click to open the context menu, and then select the **Field Width** button to change the width to a specific size.
   i. Adjust the field width of the *Phone* field to 16.
   j. Save and close the *Agents* table.

6. Determine the type of relationship and the foreign key field.
   a. There is a one-to-many relationship between the two tables since an agent can list many different real estate properties, but a property is listed by only one agent.
   b. The foreign key comes by taking the primary key field from the *1* table and adding it in as an additional field in the *M* table. In this case the *EmployeeNum* should also be added into the *Listings* table.
   c. Open the *Listings* table in *Datasheet* view. Notice that this table has a field that stores the agent's name. However, it doesn't have the foreign key. To minimize redundant data, you will change the *Agent* field so that it will now store the agent's employee number instead of the agent's name. This requires changing the data values as well as field properties.

7. Edit the data values in the *Agent* field in the *Listings* table.
   a. Click the **arrow** to the right of the *Agent Field Name* and select **Sort A to Z**. Because the employee name values begin with the first name, the sort isn't alphabetical by last name. However, the sort makes it easier to change the data values since all the properties by the same agent are grouped together.
   b. Change each of the six records for *Jack Johnstone* to have the value of 160 for the *Agent* field. After entering the first value, you can use copy and paste to enter the remaining values.
   c. Continue changing the remaining records using the information in the following table.

Number of Records	Agent Name	New Value for Agent Field
3	John Burgess	133
5	Kallyn Duarte	168
8	Kelly Weatherby	127
4	Rick Chung	151
3	Simon Bidou	103
2	Gerardo Montoya	169

   d. Remove the sort from the *Agent* field.
   e. Save the table.

8. Switch to *Design* view in the *Listings* table to edit the properties of the foreign key.
   a. Click in the **ListingAgent** *Field Name* property box.
   b. Change the field name to ListingAgentNumber.
   c. Change the *Description* to read Must match an EmployeeNum in the Agents table.
   d. Change the field size to 3.
   e. Save and close the table. Access warns you that the field size has been changed and that you may lose data. Your values meet this new size. Click **Yes**.

9. Create a one-to-many relationship between the *Agents* table and the *Listings* table.
   a. Open the *Relationships* window and add the two tables.
   b. Enlarge the table objects, if needed, to see all of the fields.
   c. Drag the **EmployeeNum** field from the *Agents* table on top of the **ListingAgentNumber** field in the *Listings* table as shown in Figure 2-97.
   d. Make the correct choices to **Enforce Referential Integrity** and **Cascade Update Related Fields**.
   e. Leave the **Cascade Delete Related Records** check box not selected. You do not want to delete property records just because an agent may leave the company. This allows you to keep a record of the listings.
   f. Create the relationship.
   g. Save the changes and close the *Relationships* window.

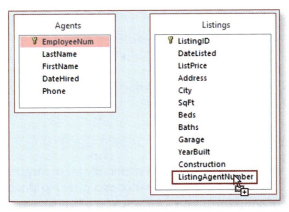

2-97 Drag the *EmployeeNum* to the *ListingAgentNumber* to create a relationship

10. Open the *Agents* table in *Datasheet* view.
    a. Click to expand the records for Kelly Weatherby. There should be eight properties listed.
    b. Close the *Agents* table.

11. Preview the data records in the *Listings* table for printing.
    a. Select the **Listings** table in the *Navigation* pane.
    b. Use *Print Preview* to show a preview of how the table will print.
    c. Change the page to **Landscape** *orientation.*
    d. Close the *Print Preview.*

12. Close the database.

Challenge Project 2-8

Modify the database you created in Challenge Project 1-8. Use *Design* view to edit field properties. Change any data that violates these properties, preview the table for printing, and *Compact & Repair* the database.
[Student Learning Outcomes 2.2, 2.3, 2.4, 2.5, 2.8, 2.9]

File Needed: *[your initials] Access 1-8.accdb*
Completed Project File Name: *[your initials] Access 2-8.accdb*

Open the database *[your initials] Access 1-8* and save a copy of it as *[your initials] Access 2-8*. Modify your database according to the following instructions:

- Edit the table in *Design* view.
- Create a validation rule and validation text for at least one of the fields in your table.
- Test the validation rule.
- Add an input mask on another field.
- As appropriate, edit *Default Value* and *Required* properties for the fields.
- Test existing records against changes to the properties.
- Correct any data values that do not meet the new data integrity rules.
- Use *Print Preview* to preview the table for printing.
- Adjust the margins and orientation to create an easy to read printout. Print the table if desired.
- Use *Compact & Repair* to reclaim any unused space.
- Save all changes to the table.

Challenge Project 2-9

Blue Lake Sports is a nationally recognized sporting goods company. It has a growing internship program at its corporate office to offer experience to college students. You have been asked to create a database to store information about the internship program. Create two tables, create a relationship between the tables, and add data into the database.
[Student Learning Outcomes 2.1, 2.2, 2.3, 2.4, 2.6]

File Needed: None
Completed Project File Name: *[your initials] Access 2-9.accdb*

Open a new database and save it as *[your initials] Access 2-9.* Modify your database according to the following instructions:

- Create a table using *Design* view to store information about the interns.
- Add a field named *InternID.* Use a *Short Text* data type and designate it as the primary key.
- Add the following fields: *LastName, FirstName, Phone, University, Major,* and *IntershipStartDate.*
- Select appropriate data types and field sizes for the fields.
- Use the *Lookup Wizard* to create a drop-down list for *University* and add at least three choices to the list.
- Save the table as *Intern.*
- Enter several records into the table.
- Create a second table using *Design* view to store information about the different departments in which an intern can work.
- Add a field named *DepartmentName.* Use a *Short Text* data type and designate it as the primary key.
- Add the following fields: *DeptMgrLastName, DeptMgrFirstName, OfficeNumber,* and *Division.*
- Select appropriate data types and field sizes for the fields.
- Use the *Lookup Wizard* to create a drop-down list for *Division* and add the choices of *Golf, Water Sports,* and *Children.*
- Save the table as *Department.*
- Enter several rows of data. Use the following values for the *DepartmentName: Sales-Golf, Accounting-Golf, HR-Golf, Sales-Water Sports, Accounting-Water Sports, HR-Water Sports, Sales-Children, Account-Children, HR-Children.*
- An intern can only be assigned to one department, but a department may have several interns. Add the correct foreign key into the *Intern* table. Don't make that field required yet.
- Create the one-to-many relationship. Enforce referential integrity and cascade updates and deletes. Save the changes to the relationship.
- Edit the data records in the *Intern* table to add values into the foreign key field. Edit the *Intern* table to make the foreign key field required.
- Save all changes to the table.
- Open the *Department* table in *Datasheet* view. Expand the plus sign for several departments to see the associated interns assigned to this department.

Challenge Project 2-10

Modify the database you created in Challenge Project 1-10 for a travel agency. Your database contains a table about upcoming cruises. Use *Design* view to create a new table to store information about the different ships on which passengers can cruise. Create a relationship between the tables, and add data into the new table.
[Student Learning Outcomes 2.1, 2.2, 2.3, 2.4, 2.6]

File Needed: *[your initials] Access 1-10.accdb*
Completed Project File Name: *[your initials] Access 2-10.accdb*

Open the database *[your initials] Access 1-10* and save a copy of it as *[your initials] Access 2-10*. Modify your database according to the following instructions:

- Create a table using *Design* view to store information about the ships.
- Add a field named *ShipID*. Use a *Short Text* data type and designate it as the primary key.
- Add the following fields: *ShipName, CruiseLineName, DateLaunched, NumberOfPassengers,* and *CountryOfRegistry.*
- Select appropriate data types and field sizes for the fields.
- Use the *Lookup Wizard* to create a drop-down list for *CruiseLineName* and add at least three choices to the list.
- Save the table as *Ships*.
- Enter several records into the table for various ships. Search the web if you need help finding examples of data to enter.
- Edit the *Trips* table you created in Challenge Project 1-10. Add the foreign key field of *ShipID*. It must have the same data type and field size you assigned in the *Ships* table.
- Create a one-to-many relationship between the two tables, since a ship can be used for many different cruises, but a specific cruise is only on one ship. Enforce referential integrity and cascade updates and deletes. Save the changes to the relationship.
- Edit the data records in the *Trips* table to add values into the *ShipID* field.
- Save all changes to the table.
- Open the *Ships* table in *Datasheet* view. Expand the plus sign for several ships to see the associated trips this ship is taking.

Creating and Using Queries

CHAPTER OVERVIEW

Queries provide a powerful way to find and analyze data in databases. In Chapter 1 you learned to use the *Search, Sort,* and *Filter* tools to find data. These are good tools but, over time as the number of records stored in your databases increases, those tools become less helpful. Learning to create and use queries helps you to quickly and easily access your data and to manage your databases. This chapter covers the basics of creating a query, adding criteria to a query, using different query options, integrating calculated fields, and creating summary queries.

STUDENT LEARNING OUTCOMES (SLOs)

After completing this chapter, you will be able to:

SLO 3.1 Use the *Simple Query Wizard* to create and run a query (p. A3-152).

SLO 3.2 Create a query in *Design* view, add fields, and save and run a query (p. A3-153).

SLO 3.3 Add a criterion to a query, use comparison operators, and create criteria with wildcards (p. A3-159).

SLO 3.4 Integrate sorting and limiting fields and records that display (p. A3-164).

SLO 3.5 Use the *AND* and *OR* operators to include multiple criteria in a query (p. A3-168).

SLO 3.6 Create a parameter query (p. A3-174).

SLO 3.7 Build a query that uses a calculated field (p. A3-178).

SLO 3.8 Create a summary query using aggregate functions (p. A3-184).

CASE STUDY

For the Pause & Practice projects in this chapter you develop queries for several different databases. As you progress through the Pause & Practice projects, you use the features you learn in this chapter to find and analyze data in a database with queries.

Pause & Practice 3-1: Create, run, and add a criterion to a query in *Design* view. Edit and save a copy of a query.

Pause & Practice 3-2: Create queries with sorting, multiple criteria, and unique values options.

Pause & Practice 3-3: Create queries using a parameter and calculated fields.

Pause & Practice 3-4: Create a summary query that uses aggregate functions.

Understanding Queries and Using the Simple Query Wizard

A *query* finds data in your database by allowing you to ask a question. For example, in a university database you can create a simple query that shows all the students. Some queries include a criterion to search for only specific records, such as "show only the students who are taking a course in the Biology department." You can also create a query that includes multiple criteria to further narrow your search. For example, a query in the Central Sierra Insurance database might use three criteria to find all of the employees who work as insurance agents in the Cameron Park branch who were hired after January 1, 2014.

You can create a query in *Design* view or with the **Query Wizard**. In this section you use the **Simple Query Wizard** option.

When you build a query you must tell Access where to find the data. The data source for a query can be a table or another query. The *Simple Query Wizard* allows you to select the specific table(s) and queries as well as the specific fields to include in the query. After you create a query, you can run it to see the results. If you need to make changes to the query once it has been created, you can edit it using *Design* view.

HOW TO: Create a Query Using the Simple Query Wizard

1. Click the **Create** tab on the *Ribbon*.
2. Click the **Query Wizard** button in the *Queries* group (Figure 3-1) to launch the *Query Wizard*.
3. Select **Simple Query Wizard** in the *New Query* dialog box (Figure 3-2).
4. Click the **OK** button.
   - The *Simple Query Wizard* launches (Figure 3-3).
   - The values displayed in the *Tables/Queries* box and the *Available Fields* window vary depending on the contents of your database.

3-1 Query Wizard button

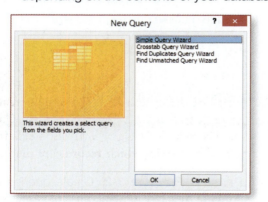

3-2 Select the query type in the New Query dialog box

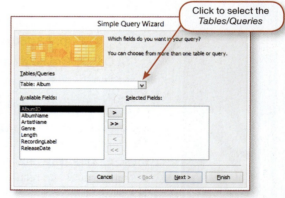

3-3 Simple Query Wizard

5. Click the **Tables/Queries** drop-down arrow and select the *Table* or *Query* name.
6. Select a **Field** to include in the query from those displayed in the *Available Fields* window.
7. Click the **Move Single Field** button.
   - The field moves into the *Selected Fields* window (Figure 3-4).
   - The *Remove Single Field* and *Remove All Fields* buttons become active.

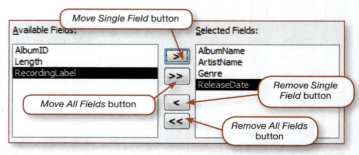

3-4 Use the Move Fields buttons to select the fields to display in a query

8. Continue moving all required fields, changing the selected *Table* or *Query* if needed.

> **ANOTHER WAY**
> Use the **Move All Fields** button (Figure 3-4) to select all of the fields in the query.

9. Click the **Next** button when you have finished adding fields. The last page of the *Simple Query Wizard* displays.
   - The *Title* box displays a default *Query Title.* The title will also be used as the *Query Name.* The default name combines the *Table Name* with the word *Query.*
   - Since you may have several queries that use the same table as the data source, be sure to create a name that describes the function of the query.
10. Change the title if desired.
11. Click **Finish** to run the query. Access automatically saves and executes the query.
    - The results show in *Datasheet* view (Figure 3-5).
    - The *Query Name* displays in the *Queries* group on the *Navigation* pane.
12. Close the query when done.

3-5 Query results display in *Datasheet* view

SLO 3.2

Creating, Running, and Editing a Query in Design View

While the *Simple Query Wizard* is useful when you want to see information quickly in your database, it doesn't allow you to take advantage of all of the options available when creating a query. As a result, the most common way to create queries is with *Query Design*. In **Query Design** you not only can specify the table(s) or queries to include, along with the fields from those objects, but you can also specify options to further restrict which records are displayed as well as how the results display.

Create a Query Based on a Single Table

You can create a new query from the *Create* tab. Queries you create using the *Query Design* button automatically open in *Design* view.

HOW TO: Create a New Query in Design View Using a Single Table

1. Click the **Create** tab on the *Ribbon.*
2. Click the **Query Design** button in the *Queries* group (Figure 3-6).
   - The *Show Table* dialog box opens with the *Tables* tab selected (Figure 3-7).

3-6 *Query Design* button

3. Select the table to use in the query. If your new query is based on an existing query instead of a table, first select the *Queries* tab in the *Show Table* dialog box and then select the query.

4. Click **Add** to add the table into the *Query Design* window (Figure 3-8).

   - The *Query Design* window is divided into two sections. The top half shows the available tables and fields. The bottom half shows the *Design grid*. The **Design grid** indicates which fields have been included in the query, along with details about criteria and how the query results display.
   - As desired, you can increase the size of the table objects in the window to display all of the fields.
   - The **Divider bar** separates the two sections. You can adjust the size of either section by moving the *Divider bar* up or down.

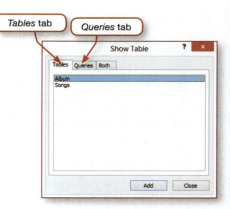

3-7 *Show Table* dialog box

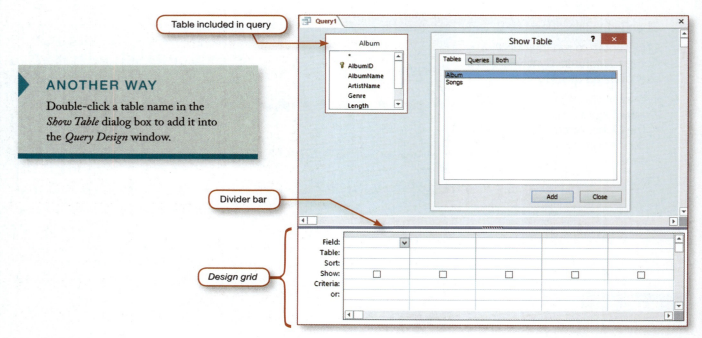

3-8 *Query Design* window

5. Click the **Close** button to close the *Show Table* dialog box.

6. The *Design* tab, a *Query Tools* contextual tab, is now available and is selected (Figure 3-9).

3-9 *Query Tools* contextual tab

Notice that the *Select* icon is chosen in the *Query Type* group [*Query Tools Design* tab] shown in Figure 3-9. This indicates that the query is a select query. You can use **select queries** to locate, or select, data in the database. They are the most common type of query. In future chapters, you will learn about some of the other query types that are action-based.

Add Fields into a Query

After you create a query, you need to add the fields into the query. Do this by putting fields into the *Design grid*. You can add as many fields as needed into the query. The query results display the fields in the order you place them into the *Design grid*.

There are three different ways to add fields into a query.

- Click, hold, and drag a field name from a *Table* displayed in the top part of the *Query Design* window to the first empty column in the *Field* row of the *Design grid*. The *Field* and *Table* row cells in the *Design grid* update to display the contents (Figure 3-10).
- Double-click a field name from a *Table* in the top part of the *Query Design* window. The field is added to the first empty column in the *Field* row of the *Design grid*.
- Click in the first empty column in the *Field* row of the *Design grid*. Click the **arrow** to display the list of field names. Select the desired field name (Figure 3-10).

To include all of the fields from a table in the query either select the * symbol from the *Table* in the top part of the *Query Design* window or select the **TableName.*** field from the drop-down list of fields displayed in the *Design grid*.

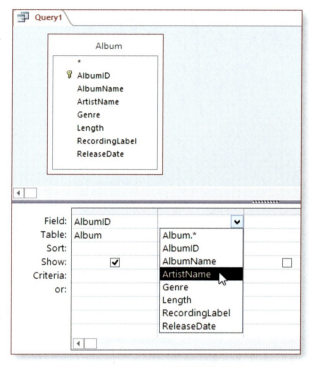

3-10 Add fields into a query

> **MORE INFO**
>
> If you want to apply criteria to individual fields, add each field separately instead of using the * symbol.

Run a Query

To see the results of a query, you need to execute, or run, the query. Running a newly written query ensures that you have created your query correctly; it is an important part of the database design and testing process.

- Click the **Run** button [*Query Tools Design* tab, *Results* group] to execute, or run, a query (Figure 3-11).

3-11 Run button

The results of the query display in *Datasheet* view (Figure 3-12). *Datasheet* view of a query operates like *Datasheet* view of a table. This means you can change, add, and delete records in this view. Making changes to the data shown in *Datasheet* view of a query changes the actual table data.

AlbumName	ArtistName	ReleaseDate
Seeds from the Underground	Kenny Garrett	10-Apr-12
Own the Night	Lady Antebellum	13-Sep-11
19	Adele	10-Jun-08
Mylo Xyloto	Coldplay	25-Oct-11
Hands All Over	Maroon 5	12-Jul-11
Waking Up	OneRepublic	17-Nov-09
Dreaming Out Loud	OneRepublic	20-Nov-07
Christina Aguilera	Christina Aguilera	15-Jul-99
Keeps Getting' Better: A Decade of Hits	Christina Aguilera	08-Sep-09
Hillbilly Bone	Blake Shelton	02-Mar-10
One of the Boys	Katy Perry	17-Jun-08
Blown Away	Carrie Underwood	01-May-12
Crazy Ex-Girlfriend	Miranda Lambert	01-May-07
Blunderbuss	Jack White	23-Apr-12

Record: 1 of 14   No Filter   Search

3-12 Query results display in *Datasheet* view

> **MORE INFO**
>
> Be careful about using the *Datasheet* view results of a query to add data. You will encounter error messages when you attempt to add data in *Datasheet* view if you have not included all the fields in a query but you have set data integrity properties to require all fields.

You can refine the datasheet layout using the skills you learned in Chapter 1. In *Datasheet* view of a query you can change the font type, font size, font color, column width, alternate row colors, and gridlines. To further customize the appearance of the query results you can use a form or report to display the query results. These objects are introduced in the next chapter.

Sometimes no records show when you run a query. This may be because no records are in the table that match your query criteria. However, if you expect results to display but none are shown when you run the query, you need to explore the potential causes. Check that the criterion value entered into the query matches the way the values are entered into the table. Additionally, verify that the query design is correct. You may have accidentally included the wrong field in the query and as a result there are no values that could match the way the criterion is entered. Finally, the data may have been entered wrong when it was added to the table.

Save a Query

When you create a query, Access automatically assigns a generic name to the query, such as *Query1*. When working with a new query, save it by clicking the **File** tab and then clicking the **Save** button. This opens the *Save As* dialog box, where you can type in a name for your query.

Since you may have several queries based on the same table, it is suggested that you create a name that describes the function of the query.

HOW TO: Save a Query

1. Click the **Save** button [*File* tab].
2. Type the name you wish to use in the *Query Name* box (Figure 3-13). The first time you save changes to your query, Access prompts you to change the default query name.
3. Click the **OK** button.

3-13 *Save As* dialog box for a query

> **ANOTHER WAY**
>
> Recall that you can also use **Ctrl+S**, the **Save** icon on the *Quick Access* toolbar, or the **F12** function key to open the *Save As* dialog box.

Once a query has been saved, it displays in the *Queries* group of the *Navigation* pane (Figure 3-14).

Open a Saved Query

Open a saved query in *Design* view by right-clicking the query name in the *Navigation* pane and selecting **Design View** from the context menu (Figure 3-15).

If you double-click a query name in the *Navigation* pane, the query executes and the results show in *Datasheet* view.

3-14 Saved queries display in the *Navigation* pane

Create a Query Based on Multiple Tables

The vast majority of databases contain multiple, related tables. As a result, some of the questions that you want to ask about the data require that you get data from more than one table. When building a query you can add more than one table into the *Query Design* window. Be sure to include only tables that are related to each other or you may end up with more records than anticipated and records may be displayed in a way that doesn't make sense.

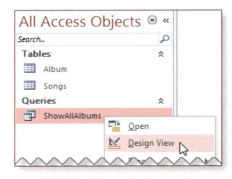

3-15 Use the context menu to open a query in *Design* view

HOW TO: Create a New Query in Design View Using Multiple Tables

1. Click the **Create** tab on the *Ribbon*.
2. Click the **Query Design** button in the *Queries* group to open the *Show Table* dialog box.
3. Select the first table you want to use in the query.

4. Click **Add** to add the table into the *Query Design* window.

5. Select the second table you want to use in the query.

6. Click **Add** to add the table into the *Query Design* window.

   - The *Query Design* window updates to show both tables (Figure 3-16).
   - A relationship line displays showing the relationship.

7. Continue adding all required tables.

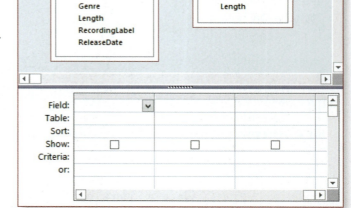

> **ANOTHER WAY**
>
> Select the first table name. Press and hold the **Shift** or **Ctrl** key. Select any additional table names. Click **Add** to add all the tables into the *Query Design* window.

3-16 *Query Design* window displays all the tables used in a query

8. Click the **Close** button to close the *Show Table* dialog box.

   - You can now add fields and run and save the query following the steps you have learned.

Edit Fields in Query Design

When building a query you may need to insert a field between two fields that already are placed in the *Design grid*. Alternatively you may need to delete a field from the *Design grid* if you determine it is no longer needed. The *Query Setup* group [*Query Tools Design* tab] contains the **Insert Columns** or **Delete Columns** buttons to add or delete a field (Figure 3-17).

3-17 *Insert Columns* and *Delete Columns* buttons

HOW TO: Insert New Fields between Existing Fields in a Query

1. Select the column in the *Design grid* to the right of where you wish to insert a new field (Figure 3-18).

2. Click the **Insert Columns** button [*Query Tools Design* tab, *Query Setup* group]. The new column is inserted and becomes the selected column (Figure 3-19).

3-18 Select a column in the *Design grid*

3. Add a field into that column by clicking in the *Field* row of the new column, clicking the arrow, and selecting the desired field name.

3-19 A new column is inserted between existing fields

HOW TO: Delete Fields From a Query

1. Select the column in the *Design grid* of the field that you wish to delete.
2. Click the **Delete Columns** button [*Query Tools Design* tab, *Query Setup* group] to delete the selected field.

SLO 3.3

Adding a Criterion to a Query

You can add a criterion into a query to search for records that meet a specific value. The type of criterion you enter, along with the way you enter the criterion, depends on the data type of the field. Use *expressions* to write the criterion. In Chapter 2 you learned to create expressions when you created a validation rule. The expressions that you write for a criterion work the same way. The criterion expression can be entered directly in the criteria cell or in the *Expression Builder.*

When you enter the specific criterion value, be sure to format the value correctly based on the data type of the field.

- Criterion for *Number, Currency* and *AutoNumber* data types includes the actual number value not surrounded by any special symbols.
- Criterion for *Short Text* and *Long Text* data types is enclosed within quotation marks. Access ignores the case of the text in the criterion when making an evaluation.
- Criterion for *Date/Time* data types is enclosed within pound (#) symbols.
- Criterion for *Yes/No* data types use either *Yes* or *No.* Use *Yes* to find records where the check box is selected and use *No* to find records where the check box is not selected.

Single Criterion

In the simplest criterion expression you only enter the criterion value. Access evaluates this criterion as an "equal to" comparison. In other words, it will find all data that is "equal to" the criterion.

HOW TO: Add a Criterion into the Query

1. Click in the cell of the **Criteria** row of the desired field.
2. Type in the text of the criterion expression you want to enter.

- The criterion shown in Figure 3-20 creates a query that finds all albums whose *Genre* is "Country".
- If your criterion value is longer than the column width, you can increase the width of the column. Position the pointer at the border of a column, above the field name. The cursor turns into the two-pointed arrow. Drag the two-pointed arrow to resize the column.

Field:	AlbumName	ArtistName	Genre
Table:	Album	Album	Album
Sort:			
Show:	☑	☑	☑
Criteria:			"Country"
or:			

3-20 Enter a criterion into a query

> **ANOTHER WAY**
>
> Open the *Expression Builder* dialog box by right-clicking and selecting the **Build** button from the context menu (Figure 3-21), clicking the **Builder** button [*Query Tools Design* tab, *Query Setup* group], or by pressing the **Ctrl+F2** keys.

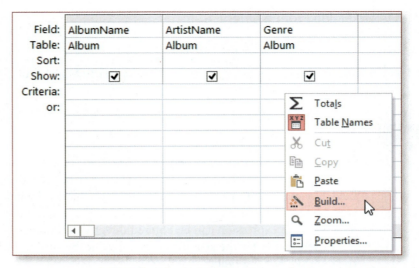

3-21 Select the *Build* button to open the *Expression Builder*

> **MORE INFO**
>
> When entering an expression, the *IntelliSense* tool may suggest a list of possible values. Figure 3-22 shows an example of the *IntelliSense* list. A description of the selected item also displays. The list automatically appears if the word you enter into an expression is a function or object name. The list updates as you keep typing. As desired, you can select an item from the list, press **ESC** to hide the list, or simply continue typing in your value.

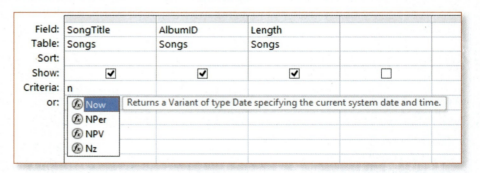

3-22 The *IntelliSense* tool suggests possible functions based on the value you have entered

After adding a criterion to a query, remember to test the query to make sure you wrote the criterion expression correctly. Test the query by running it and then comparing the results to your expected results.

If no records in the database match the query criterion, the datasheet still displays but no records appear. If this occurs and you expect that records in the table should display as a result of the query, verify that the query criterion was entered correctly or that data values were entered correctly when the record was added into the table.

Comparison Operators

When you want to search for values beyond an "equal to" comparison, you need to include a comparison operator in the expression. Usually the comparison operator appears at the beginning of the expression, although that depends on the exact structure of the expression.

The operators are summarized in the following table:

Comparison Operators

Operator	Explanation	Example
<	Less than	<5
<=	Less than or equal to	<=100
>	Greater than	>#1/1/2014#
>=	Greater than or equal to	>="B24"
=	Equal to	="CA"
<>	Not equal to	<>0
Between	Between these two values	Between 10 and 20
In	Contained in this list of values	In(1, 5, 10)
Like	Similar to this value	Like "C??"

A criterion can also have the value of **Is Null** or **Is Not Null**. Use *Is Null* to find records where the value is not entered for a specific field. Use *Is Not Null* to find records where the field contains a value.

Date/Time fields sometimes use a function as the criteria value. **Functions** are pre-built procedures that perform a specific task. A common function used with *Date/Time* fields is **Date()**, which returns the current date from your computer. For example, if you write a criterion for a *ShippingDate* as <=*Date ()*, it finds records that have a *ShippingDate* value that is on or before today's date. Additionally, a criterion for *Date/Time* fields often may include an arithmetic formula as part of the comparison. For example, in the *ShippingDate* field, the criterion of *Between Date() and Date()+7* returns the records that have a *ShippingDate* value that is one of the next 7 days.

Use Wildcards in Criteria

You can use the **Like** comparison operator in a criterion to find records containing data that is similar to, or like, the criterion value. When using *like,* you typically incorporate one of the **wildcard characters** available in Access. When you use a wildcard, the criterion of your expression must be enclosed in quotation marks, even when you use *Number, Currency,* and *AutoNumber* data types.

Examples of some of the wildcard characters and their effects in a query criterion are illustrated in the following material:

- Use the **?** wildcard character to match any single character in a specific position. Remember that numbers are also considered characters.

Field (Type and Size)	Example Criterion	Explanation of Example
PhoneNumber (Text, Size 10) *[The input mask symbols are not stored with the data.]*	Like "9??????????"	Finds records where the phone number contains 10 characters and starts with a 9.

If you use the criterion above to search the sample data shown in Figure 3-23, only the highlighted record values are returned by the query. The last record, phone number 923-1111, does start with a 9, but it is not 10 characters long.

If you wrote the criterion as *Like "9 ???????"*, which would require a value of exactly 8 characters, no records would be returned since none of the phone numbers in Figure 3-23 contains only 8 characters.

- Use the * wildcard character to match any number of characters.

3-23 Sample phone data

Field (Type and Size)	Example Criterion	Explanation of Example
SongTitle (Text, Size 70)	Like "love *"	Finds records where the song title starts with the word love. Note that there is a blank space after the letter "e" and before the asterisk.

Due to the blank space between the asterisk and the word "love", this query finds only the complete word of "love" and not songs where the title contains the letters of the word "love" within a word, such as "beloved" or "lover". This criterion would find "Love for All Seasons". However, it will not find songs with the title of "Leave Love Alone" or "Make You Feel My Love" because in these titles "love" is not the first word.

If you change the criterion to *Like "* love"*, the only songs found would be those that end with the word "love". For example, it would find "Make You Feel My Love".

If you change the criterion to *Like "* love *"*, the only songs found would be those that contain the word "love" somewhere in the middle ("love" cannot be the first or last word). This query would find "Leave Love Alone".

If you are interested in finding songs that contain the letters of the word "love", you can remove the spaces. For example, the query *Like "* love *"*, would find song titles that contain the letters of the word "love" anywhere in the title. This would find all of the songs that *Like "* love *"* found and it would also find "She Will Be Loved" and "Lovers in a Dangerous Time".

> **MORE INFO**
>
> You must pay attention to the proper placement of the * wildcard, along with any characters and spaces, to ensure that the query returns the correct results.

You can combine multiple wildcards together. For example, using the criterion of *Like "*1?"* combines the * and ? wildcards. Using this criterion on the *PhoneNumber* field in Figure 3-23 would return the phone numbers of (325) 555-1112 and ( ) 923-1111. This criterion returns records with a phone number of any length, as long as a "1" is the second to the last digit.

Field (Type and Size)	Example Criterion	Explanation of Example
SalesPrice (Currency, Size N/A)	Like "*.99"	Finds records where the sales price ends with .99.

This criterion finds records where the price is .99, 2.99, or 345.99. It will not find records where the price is 1.09 or 3.995.

- Use the **#** wildcard character to match any single numeric digit.

Field (Type and Size)	Example Criterion	Explanation of Example
SqFt (Number, Size Long Integer)	Like "2###"	Finds records where the square footage starts with a 2 and contains 4 digits.

This criterion finds houses that are in the 2,000 to 2,999 square foot range. It does not find a house with 255 square feet or with 20,000 square feet since those don't meet the 4-digit specification.

Field (Type and Size)	Example Criterion	Explanation of Example
SalesPrice (Currency, Size N/A)	Like "###.99"	Finds records where the sales price contains three digits to the left of the decimal point and ends with .99.

This criterion finds records where the price is 100.99 or 345.99. It will not find records where the price is .99, 2.99 or 1043.99.

For this Pause & Practice you use *Design* view to create queries for a music database to search for various recordings.

File Needed: ***MusicDatabase-03.accdb***
Completed Project File Name: ***[your initials] PP A3-1.accdb***

1. Open the ***MusicDatabase-03.accdb*** database file.

2. Save a new copy of your database as ***[your initials] PP A3-1***.

3. If prompted, enable content in the database.

4. Create a new query in *Design* view.
   a. Click the **Query Design** button [*Create* tab, *Queries* group] to open the *Show Table* dialog box.
   b. Select the **Album** table and click the **Add** button.
   c. Select the **Songs** table and click the **Add** button.
   d. Click the **Close** button.
   e. Double-click the **SongTitle** field from the *Songs* table in the *Query Design* window. The field is added to the first empty column in the *Design grid.*
   f. Double-click the **AlbumName** field from the *Album* table.
   g. Double-click the **ArtistName** field from the *Album* table.
   h. Double-click the **Length** field from the *Songs* table. The completed query should be similar to Figure 3-24.

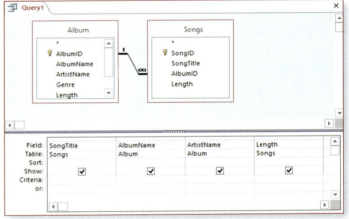

5. Click the **Run** button [*Query Tools Design* tab, *Results* group] to run the query. The query should open in *Datasheet* view and display 251 records.

6. Click the **View** button [*Home* tab, *Views* group] and select the **Design View** option to switch back to *Design* view.

3-24 Completed query design

7. Save the query.
   a. Click the **Save** button [*File* tab].
   b. Type ShowAllSongs in the *Query Name* box.
   c. Click the **OK** button. The query name displays in the *Navigation* pane in the *Queries* group.

8. Add a criterion to the query to find all of the songs by The Beatles.
   a. Type The Beatles in the **Criteria** row of the *ArtistName* field. When you enter criterion into a *Short Text* or *Long Text* field, you can either enter quotation marks around the criterion, or if you omit the quotation marks, Access automatically enters them for you.
   b. **Tab** out of that field. Notice that Access automatically puts quotation marks around the text criteria (Figure 3-25).

3-25 Query criterion

9. Click the **Run** button [*Query Tools Design* tab, *Results* group] to run the query. The query should open in *Datasheet* view and display the 40 songs by The Beatles (Figure 3-26).

10. Save a copy of this query.
    a. Click the **Save As** button [*File* tab] and select the **Save Object As** button [*File* tab].
    b. Click the **Save As** button. Access suggests the new query name of *Copy of ShowAllSongs*.
    c. Type AllSongsByTheBeatles in the *Save 'ShowAllSongs' to* box.
    d. Click the **OK** button. The two queries should now be displayed in the *Navigation* pane in the *Queries* group.
    e. Close the query.

11. Right-click the **ShowAllSongs** query name in the *Navigation* pane and select **Design View** from the context menu to open the query.

12. Add a criterion to the query to find all the songs that begin with the word "I".
    a. Type Like "I *" in the **Criteria** row of the *SongTitle* field. Be sure to enter a space after the "I" or your results include all songs where the first word begins with the letter "I" not just the ones with the word "I". This query will not find songs where the word "I" is only at the ending or in the middle of the title. This is because of the space included after the letter "I". At the end of *SLO 3.5* you will learn how to create criteria to accomplish this need.
    b. **Tab** out of that field.

13. Run the query. Your results should display 10 songs that contain the word "I".

14. Save a copy of the query using the name SongsThatStartWith"I".

15. Close the query.

16. Close the database.

SLO 3.4

More Query Options

Access provides a variety of options to help control the way query results display. For example, you may wish to have the results display in a sorted order. Or you may need to include a field in a query to apply a criterion, but you don't want that field to display in the results. At other times a query may show duplicate records and you want to show only records that contain unique values. This section describes some of the ways to control the display of query results.

Unique Values Property

A well-designed database is structured to minimize redundant data. As a result, most queries display unique records in the results. However, sometimes the structure of a particular query causes duplicated records to display.

For example, a music database may have two tables: one that stores information about each album owned and another that stores information about the songs that are on each album. The *Query* window showing those tables is displayed in Figure 3-27. As you know, it is possible for a song to appear on multiple albums. For example, "Genie in a Bottle" appears on two of Christina Aguilera's albums, *Keeps Gettin' Better: A Decade of Hits* and *Christina Aguilera*. The "Genie in a Bottle" song would appear twice in the *Songs* table, each with a unique *SongID* value.

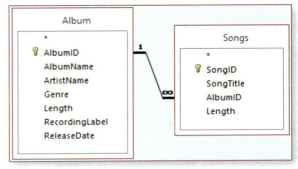

3-27 *Query* window shows the relationship between the *Album* and *Songs* tables

If you write a query to find the names of all the songs in the database, you don't necessarily need to see that song name appear once for each album that includes this song. You can use the ***Unique Values*** property to direct Access to only display records that don't include duplicated values.

> ### MORE INFO
>
> Don't confuse the *Unique Values* property with the ***Unique Records*** property. *Unique Records* checks all the fields in a table (not just those included in the query).

HOW TO: Display Unique Values in Query Results

1. Open the query in *Design* view.
2. Click the **Property Sheet** button [*Query Tools Design* tab, *Show/Hide* group] to open the *Property Sheet* for the query (Figure 3-28).
   - The *Property Sheet* opens (Figure 3-29).
   - Verify that the *Selection type* displays *Query Properties.*
   - If the *Selection Type* displays *Field Properties,* you have selected a field. Click in the top half of the *Query Design* window to switch to the *Query Properties.*
   - In the *Show/Hide* group, the *Table Names* button is highlighted when the *Design grid* displays the *Table* row below the *Field* row.
3. Click in the **Unique Values** property box and select **Yes**.
4. Close the *Property Sheet*.

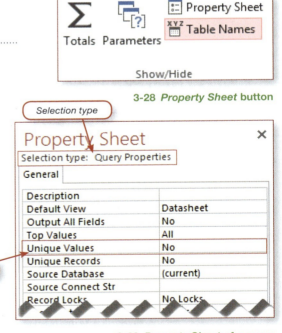

3-28 *Property Sheet* button

3-29 *Property Sheet* of a query

> ### ANOTHER WAY
>
> Press the **F4** key to open or close the *Property Sheet.*

The usefulness of the *Unique Values* property depends on the query structure. For example, if you run the query shown in Figure 3-30 you see one record for every song in the database. Setting the *Unique Values* property to *Yes* does not reduce the number of records displayed. This is because including the field of *AlbumName* creates unique records in the results (assuming the same *SongTitle* is not included on an album twice).

Field:	AlbumName	SongTitle	ArtistName
Table:	Album	Songs	Album
Sort:			
Show:	✔	✔	✔
Criteria:			

3-30 *Unique Values* property has no impact when fields create unique records

The query shown in Figure 3-31 does not include the *AlbumName* field. Setting the *Unique Values* property to *Yes* on this query results in fewer records being displayed. With this query, "Genie in a Bottle" appears only one time in the query results.

Field:	SongTitle	ArtistName
Table:	Songs	Album
Sort:		
Show:	✔	✔
Criteria:		

3-31 Not including the *AlbumName* results in unique values

Show Option for Query Fields

Most of the time, you want all of the fields placed into the *Design grid* to display in the query results. Occasionally, you don't want a field to display because it would show unnecessary or duplicated values. The query shown in Figure 3-32 displays all the songs that are on albums by "The Beatles".

Field:	SongTitle	ArtistName
Table:	Songs	Album
Sort:		
Show:	✔	✔
Criteria:		"The Beatles"
or:		

3-32 *Show* row check box for fields

This query produces a datasheet like that shown in Figure 3-33. The *ArtistName* field is needed in the query because you included a criterion on that field to limit the records displayed to songs by "The Beatles". But displaying the *ArtistName* is not really necessary here, as you know that all of these songs are by "The Beatles".

SongTitle	ArtistName
Come Together	The Beatles
Something	The Beatles
Maxwell's Silver Hammer	The Beatles
Oh! Darling	The Beatles
Octopus's Garden	The Beatles
I Want You (She's So Heavy)	The Beatles
Here Comes the Sun	The Beatles
Because	The Beatles

3-33 Query results

- To not show a query field in the query results, deselect the **Show** row check box in the *Design grid* of your query (Figure 3-34).

In order to determine if a query is working correctly, first run the query with all fields displayed so you can verify the accuracy of the query. Only after you are confident with the query design should you deselect the *Show* row check box of the appropriate fields.

Deselected *Show* check box

Field:	SongTitle	ArtistName
Table:	Songs	Album
Sort:		
Show:	✔	☐
Criteria:		"The Beatles"
or:		

3-34 Deselect *Show* row check box

Apply Sorting

Access can display the results of a query in sorted order. You can sort on one or more fields.

- To sort the results of a query, click in the **Sort** row of the desired field.
- Click the **drop-down arrow** and select **Ascending** or **Descending** (Figure 3-35).

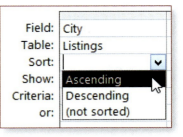

3-35 *Sort* option of a query

> ▶ **MORE INFO**
>
> To remove sorting from a field, click the **drop-down arrow** in the *Sort* row and select **(not sorted)**.

Access sorts data based on the order of the columns. If you are sorting on multiple fields, you need to decide the sorting order of the fields. For example, in a table containing a list of all properties for sale, a client may want the query results sorted by the *City, Construction,* and *SqFt* fields. There are many possible combinations of sorted results in this instance. Here we show two examples. The two sort examples shown here use an *Ascending* sort order on each field.

Figure 3-36 shows results sorted first by *City*, next by *Construction*, and last by *SqFt*. Because *City* is the first sort field and alphabetically Auburn is the first city in the database, this results in all properties in Auburn appearing first. Within the Auburn properties, homes made of brick appear first. Finally, within the "Auburn" and "Brick" properties, the property with the smallest square footage appears at the top of the list.

ListingID	Address	City	Construction	SqFt
10042	131 Aeolia Drive	Auburn	Brick	1905
10045	12355 Krista Lane	Auburn	Brick	2234
10040	3935 Cedar Mist Lane	Auburn	Frame	1056
10069	1255 Copperdale	Auburn	Frame	1456
10144	863 Holly Hill Drive	Auburn	Frame	2876
10043	1575 Oak Ridge Way	Auburn	Stone	2266
10150	423 Welterwood	Lincoln	Brick	1482
10046	1735 Andover Lane	Lincoln	Brick	1552
10052	1096 Kinnerly Lane	Lincoln	Brick	1948
10072	406 E St	Lincoln	Frame	1100
10062	2811 Cardinal Dr.	Lincoln	Frame	2061

3-36 Records sorted by the *City*, *Construction,* and *SqFt* fields

Figure 3-37 is sorted differently. In this example, the query is sorted first by *Construction*, next by *City*, and last by *SqFt*. In these results all properties with brick construction appear first. Within the "Brick" properties, those in Auburn appear first. Finally, within the "Brick" and "Auburn" properties, the smallest square footage appears at the top of the list.

ListingID	Address	Construction	City	SqFt
10042	131 Aeolia Drive	Brick	Auburn	1905
10045	12355 Krista Lane	Brick	Auburn	2234
10150	423 Welterwood	Brick	Lincoln	1482
10046	1735 Andover Lane	Brick	Lincoln	1552
10052	1096 Kinnerly Lane	Brick	Lincoln	1948
10073	736 Oakdale	Brick	Newcastle	766
10031	2024 Brixham	Brick	Roseville	2385
10024	1917 Oak Crest Dr.	Brick	Roseville	3397
10044	446 Manzanita Way	Brick	Weimer	1885
10040	3935 Cedar Mist Lane	Frame	Auburn	1056
10069	1255 Copperdale	Frame	Auburn	1456
10144	863 Holly Hill Drive	Frame	Auburn	2876
10072	406 E St	Frame	Lincoln	1100
10062	2811 Cardinal Dr.	Frame	Lincoln	2061

3-37 Records sorted by the *Construction*, *City*, and *SqFt* fields

HOW TO: Sort a Query Using Multiple Fields

1. Add the fields into in the *Design grid* from left to right based on the desired sort order.

2. If the fields are already placed in the *Design grid,* you can rearrange the column order by moving a column.

   - Select the column to be moved.
   - Position the pointer in the small row above the field name. Click and hold the pointer. A black vertical line appears to the left of the selected column (Figure 3-38).
   - Drag the field to the new location. The line moves with you to indicate the location where the column is moved.
   - Release the pointer to complete the move.

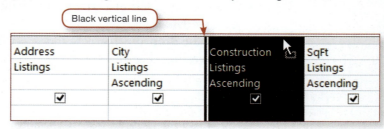

3-38 The black vertical line indicates the new location of the column

3. For each of the sort fields, click in the **Sort** row and select **Ascending** or **Descending**.

> **MORE INFO**
>
> Sometimes you may need to combine sorting and show options. For example you may wish to have the first sort field display in a different position in the query results. In this case you would include the field twice. The field would be included at the left of the query to designate the *Sort* selection and to deselect the *Show* box. The same field would be added a second time in the desired position to show the value.

SLO 3.5

Defining Multiple Criteria in a Query

The previous examples created queries that used at most one condition or criterion. Many times the questions that you want to ask about the data are more complex and require the use of compound criteria. **Compound criteria** combine more than one criterion using the *AND* or *OR* logical operators and allow you to ask questions using multiple conditions.

The AND Operator

The **AND** logical operator requires that a record meet all of the individual conditions specified in order to be included in the results. An *AND* condition can be used in one field or across multiple fields.

HOW TO: Use AND Compound Criteria in Multiple Fields

1. Click in the **Criteria** row of the first field.

2. Type in the text of the desired criterion expression.

3. Click in the **Criteria** row of the second field.

4. Type in the text of the second desired criterion expression.

5. Continue entering the criterion in the remaining fields.

   - The query shown in Figure 3-39 finds the properties in Auburn that have a list price of less than $300,000 and have more than 2,000 square feet.

3-39 Query criteria entered on the same row creates an *AND* condition

> **MORE INFO**
>
> Values entered on the same *Criteria* row of the *Design grid* create an *AND* condition.

Occasionally you need to use the *AND* operator in a single field. In these cases the *AND* operator is typically combined with another comparison operator such as *Between*, > or <. Remember that all criteria included together on a row are treated as *AND* conditions.

HOW TO: Use AND Compound Criteria in a Single Field

1. Click in the **Criteria** row of the field.
2. Type in the text of the desired condition, including the word "AND" between each part of the condition.
   - The query shown in Figure 3-40 finds sailboats that have a full day rental rate that is greater than or equal to $200 and less than or equal to $500.
   - This condition could also be written using the *Between* operator. The condition in Figure 3-41 uses *Between* and returns the same results as the condition shown in Figure 3-40 which uses the >= and <= operators.

Field:	BoatID	BoatType	Length	FullDayRentalRate
Table:	SailboatFleet	SailboatFleet	SailboatFleet	SailboatFleet
Sort:				
Show:	✔	✔	✔	✔
Criteria:				>=200 And <=500
or:				

3-40 Use the word "AND" between compound critieria in the same field

FullDayRentalRate
SailboatFleet
✔
Between 200 And 500

3-41 *Between* operator

> **MORE INFO**
>
> The case used to write "AND" has no impact on the query. "AND" or "And" or "and" all evaluate the same.

The OR Operator

The **OR** logical operator requires a record to meet at least one of the individual conditions specified in order to be included in the results. With the *OR* operator you can specify multiple criteria in one field or you can use compound criteria across several fields.

HOW TO: Use OR Compound Criteria in Multiple Fields

1. Click in the **Criteria** row of the first field.
2. Type in the text of the desired criterion expression.
3. Click in the **or** box of the second field.
4. Type in the text of the second desired criterion expression.
5. Continue entering criteria on the remaining fields, each time entering the value on the row below the last row you entered a value.
   - The query shown in Figure 3-42 finds the properties that are in Auburn or have a list price of less than $300,000 or have more than 2,000 square feet.

Field:	ListingID	Address	City	ListPrice	SqFt
Table:	Listings	Listings	Listings	Listings	Listings
Sort:					
Show:	✔	✔	✔	✔	✔
Criteria:			"Auburn"		
or:				<300000	
					>2000

Multiple criteria on different rows

3-42 Query criteria entered on different rows create an *OR* condition

Entering multiple criteria in the same field is an **OR** condition. The returned records match the first value *or* the second value *or* the third value, and so on.

HOW TO: Use OR Compound Criteria in a Single Field

1. Click in the **Criteria** row of the first field.

2. Type in the text of the desired criterion expression.

3. Click in the **or** box of the same field.

4. Type in the text of the second desired criterion expression.

5. Continue entering the additional criteria in the field, each time entering the value on the next row.

Field:	ListingID	Address	City	ListPrice	SqFt
Table:	Listings	Listings	Listings	Listings	Listings
Sort:					
Show:	☑	☑	☑	☑	☑
Criteria:			"Auburn"		
or:			"Roseville"		

3-43 Place compound critieria in separate rows of the same field to create an *OR* condition

- The query shown in Figure 3-43 finds the properties that are in Auburn or Roseville.

Combine the AND and OR Operators

You can create a query that combines both the *AND* and *OR* operators. These types of conditions can be logically complex. Keep in mind that all criteria included on a row are treated as *AND* conditions, while criteria entered on separate rows are treated as *OR* conditions.

Compare the queries in Figures 3-44 and 3-45. The query in Figure 3-44 returns all properties in Auburn that have a list price less than $300,000 and have more than 2,000 square feet, or any property in Roseville, no matter the list price or square footage. The *ListPrice* and *SqFt* criteria are only applied to the city of Auburn, because they are only included on the row with the *City* criterion for Auburn.

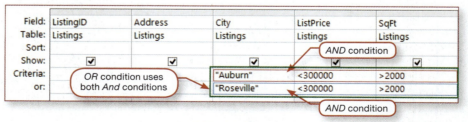

Field:	ListingID	Address	City	ListPrice	SqFt
Table:	Listings	Listings	Listings	Listings	Listings
Sort:					AND condition
Show:	☑	☑	☑	☑	☑
Criteria:	OR condition		"Auburn"	<300000	>2000
or:			"Roseville"		

3-44 The *ListPrice* and *SqFt* criteria apply only to the city of Auburn

The query in Figure 3-45 returns all properties in Auburn that have a list price less than $300,000 and have more than 2,000 square feet, or all properties in Roseville that have a list price less than $300,000 and have more than 2,000 square feet. If you want to have the *List-Price* and *SqFt* criteria apply to both cities, you need to repeat the criteria on both rows.

Field:	ListingID	Address	City	ListPrice	SqFt
Table:	Listings	Listings	Listings	Listings	Listings
Sort:					AND condition
Show:	☑	☑	☑	☑	☑
Criteria:	OR condition uses both *And* conditions		"Auburn"	<300000	>2000
or:			"Roseville"	<300000	>2000
					AND condition

3-45 The ListPrice and SqFt criteria apply to both cities

Finally consider the query in Figure 3-46. This query returns all properties in Auburn that have a list price less than $300,000, or all properties in Roseville no matter their list prices or square footages, or all properties in Lincoln with square footage between 2,000 and 3,000 square feet.

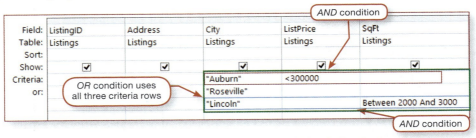

Field:	ListingID	Address	City	ListPrice	SqFt
Table:	Listings	Listings	Listings	Listings	Listings
Sort:					
Show:	☑	☑	☑	☑	☑
Criteria:			"Auburn"	<300000	
or:			"Roseville"		
			"Lincoln"		Between 2000 And 3000

AND condition

OR condition uses all three criteria rows

AND condition

3-46 The *ListPrice* criteria apply to Auburn and the *SqFt* criteria apply to Lincoln

As these examples illustrate, compound conditions can become very complex. Spend the time to understand what you need the query to do before you attempt to build the query in Access.

Now that you have learned about compound criteria, you can return to the issue in Pause & Practice 3-1 regarding not being able to find songs where the word "I" is at the end or in the middle of the title. In Pause & Practice 3-1 using the compound criteria of *Like "I *" Or Like "* I *" Or Like "* I"* would find songs that begin, contain, or end with the word "I".

PAUSE & PRACTICE: ACCESS 3-2

For this Pause & Practice you use *Design* view to create two queries for the San Diego Sailing Club database.

File Needed: *SanDiegoSailing-03.accdb*
Completed Project File Name: *[your initials] PP A3-2.accdb*

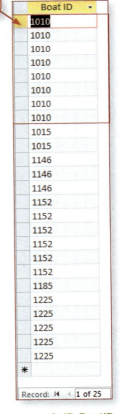

The same *Boat ID* displays many times

Boat ID ▾
1010
1010
1010
1010
1010
1010
1010
1010
1015
1015
1146
1146
1146
1152
1152
1152
1152
1152
1152
1185
1225
1225
1225
1225
1225
*

Record: ◄ ◄ 1 of 25

1. Open the **SanDiegoSailing-03.accdb** database file.

2. Save a new copy of your database as *[your initials] PP A3-2*.

3. If prompted, enable content in the database.

4. Create a new query in *Design* view. The Sailing Club wants to find out what boat types have been rented so it can decide whether to adjust pricing or marketing on some of its boat types. If a boat has been rented, a record of that rental exists in the *SDRentals* table. To help you better understand the logic involved in building queries, this query is built in stages.
   a. Click the **Query Design** button [*Create* tab, *Queries* group] to open the *Show Table* dialog box.
   b. Select the **SDRentals** table and click the **Add** button.
   c. Click the **Close** button.
   d. Click the **drop-down arrow** in the first **Field** row column in the *Design grid* and select **FKBoatID**.
   e. Click in the **Sort** row, click the **drop-down arrow**, and select **Ascending**.
   f. Click the **Run** button [*Query Tools Design* tab, *Results* group] to execute the query. The query should open in *Datasheet* view and display 25 records (Figure 3-47). Notice that in a number of instances the same *BoatID* displays multiple times, once for each time that boat was rented. Also notice that these records do not include the *BoatType;* that field needs to come from the *SailboatFleet* table.

3-47 *BoatID* query results

5. Edit the query to include the *BoatType* and display *Unique Values*.
   a. Click the **View** button [*Home* tab, *Views* group] and select the **Design View** option to switch back to *Design* view of the query.
   b. Click the **Show Table** button [*Query Tools Design* tab, *Query Setup* group].
   c. Select the **SailboatFleet** table and click the **Add** button.
   d. Click the **Close** button.
   e. Click the **drop-down arrow** in the second **Field** row column of the *Design grid* and select **SailboatFleet.BoatType**.
   f. Click the **Run** button [*Query Tools Design* tab, *Results* group] to execute the query. The query now shows the *BoatType,* but the same *BoatID* and *BoatType* still display multiple times, once for each time each boat was rented.
   g. Click the **View** button [*Home* tab, *Views* group] and select the **Design View** option to switch back to *Design* view of the query.
   h. Click the **Property Sheet** button [*Query Tools Design* tab, *Show/Hide* group] to open the *Property Sheet.*
   i. If you need to, click in the **Query Window** so that the *Selection type* in the *Property Sheet* displays *Query Properties.*
   j. Click in the **Unique Values** property box and select **Yes**. The query window should look similar to Figure 3-48.
   k. Close the *Property Sheet.*
   l. Click the **Run** button. The query should open in *Datasheet* view and display six records (Figure 3-49). Each *BoatID* now displays only once, but the *BoatTypes* are still repeated.

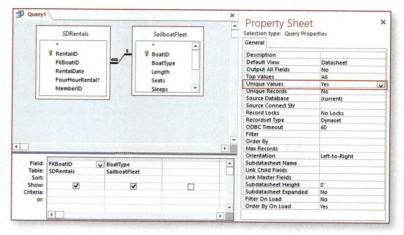

3-48 Set the *Unique Values* property in the *Property Sheet* of the query

6. Edit the query so the *Boat Type* displays only once. The *Boat Type* is displaying more than once because the *FKBoatID* field is different for each boat.
   a. Click the **View** button [*Home* tab, *Views* group] and select the **Design View** option to switch back to *Design* view of the query.
   b. Click in the **Sort** row of the **FKBoatID** field, click the **drop-down arrow**, and select **(not sorted)**.
   c. Deselect the **Show** row check box for the **FKBoatID** field.
   d. Click the **Run** button. The query should display the four boats shown in Figure 3-50.
   e. Open the **SailboatFleet** table. The query remains open as well.
   f. The club has six different types of boats. It appears that the Beneteau 373 and Beneteau 40 have not been rented since they do not appear in the query results.
   g. Close the **SailboatFleet** table.
   h. Click the **Save** button and save the query as BoatTypesRented.
   i. Close the *BoatTypesRented* query.

Boat ID	Boat Type
1010	Catalina 270
1015	Catalina 270
1146	Hunter 33
1152	Capri 22 Mk II
1185	Hunter 36
1225	Hunter 36

Record: 1 of 6

3-49 Query results with repeated *Boat Type* values

Boat Type
Capri 22 Mk II
Catalina 270
Hunter 33
Hunter 36

3-50 Unique records for *Boat Type*

7. Create a new query in *Design* view. The Sailing Club wants to find the rentals in February, 2015, that were either of a Catalina 270 boat type or were for a 4-hour rental costing more than $100 for the *FourHourRental* rate.
   a. Click the **Query Design** button [*Create* tab, *Queries* group] to open the *Show Table* dialog box.
   b. Select the **SailboatFleet** table and click the **Add** button.
   c. Select the **SDRentals** table and click the **Add** button.
   d. Click the **Close** button.
   e. Drag the **FKBoatID** field from the *SDRentals* table in the *Query Design* window to the first empty column in the *Design grid.*
   f. Drag the **RentalDate** field from the *SDRentals* table to the second column in the *Design grid.*
   g. Drag the **BoatType** field from the *SailboatFleet* table to the third column in the *Design grid.*
   h. Double-click the **FourHourRental?** field in the *SDRentals* table to move it into the *Design grid.*
   i. Double-click the **FourHourRentalRate** field in the *SailboatFleet* table to move it into the *Design grid.*
   j. Double-click the **FullDayRentalRate** field in the *SailboatFleet* table to move it into the *Design grid.*

8. Click the **Save** button and save the query as February2015Rentals.

9. Add criteria to the query.
   a. Click in the **Criteria** row of the *RentalDate* field.
   b. Type >=#2/1/2015# And <=#2/28/2015# in the *Criteria* row. If you need to, widen the *RentalDate* column to see the entire criteria.
   c. Continue entering the remaining criteria as shown in Figure 3-51. Make sure to enter values in the correct field columns and criteria rows.

Field:	FKBoatID	RentalDate	BoatType	FourHourRental?	FourHourRentalRate	FullDayRentalRate
Table:	SDRentals	SDRentals	SailboatFleet	SDRentals	SailboatFleet	SailboatFleet
Sort:				Ascending		
Show:	✔	✔	✔	✔	✔	✔
Criteria:		>=#2/1/2015# And <=#2/28/2015#	"Catalina 270"			
or:		>=#2/1/2015# And <=#2/28/2015#		Yes	>100	

3-51 Compound query criteria

10. Sort the records by the *FourHourRental?* field by clicking in the **Sort** property box and selecting **Ascending**.

11. Save the changes made to the query.

12. Click the **Run** button. The query should open in *Datasheet* view and display the eight records shown in Figure 3-52.

Boat ID ▾	Rental Date ▾	Boat Type ▾	Four Hour Re ▾	4 Hr Rate ▾	Full Day Rate ▾
1225	2/28/2015	Hunter 36	✔	$349.00	$389.00
1015	2/15/2015	Catalina 270	✔	$139.00	$179.00
1010	2/2/2015	Catalina 270	✔	$139.00	$179.00
1015	2/28/2015	Catalina 270	☐	$139.00	$179.00
1010	2/18/2015	Catalina 270	☐	$139.00	$179.00
1010	2/17/2015	Catalina 270	☐	$139.00	$179.00
1010	2/12/2015	Catalina 270	☐	$139.00	$179.00
1010	2/9/2015	Catalina 270	☐	$139.00	$179.00

Record: I◄ ◄ 1 of 8 ► ►I ►▦ ▾ No Filter Search

3-52 Completed query in *Datasheet* view

13. Close the query.

14. Close the database.

SLO 3.6

Creating and Using a Simple Parameter Query

The query examples covered so far in this chapter use criteria that have been entered into, or hardcoded into, the query. In *SLO 3.3: Adding a Criterion to a Query*, you saw a query that displayed all the country music albums—those that have a *Genre* listed as "Country". The criteria property box for that query had the value of "Country". What if you wanted to locate all the albums in a music database that are rock or jazz? You could create a separate query for each situation and enter in the specific criteria value into each query. But this would not be very efficient.

It is more efficient to create a parameter query. A **parameter query** asks you to enter the specific criteria value when you run the query. This allows you to write one query but use it for many different values of the criteria. Figure 3-53 is an example of the *Enter Parameter Value* dialog box. When you see this box, enter the specific value, such as "Country" or "Rock", click the **OK** button, and the desired results are shown.

If you enter a value that is not located in the database, the query returns an empty datasheet.

3-53 *Enter Parameter Value* dialog box

To create a parameter query, you follow the same steps you learned to create a query with criteria. However, instead of entering a specific value for the criteria, you need to format the criteria expression so that Access prompts you for a **parameter value**.

Create a Parameter

Parameters must follow a few simple rules.

- Your parameter is the specific phrase that you want to display in the dialog box, for example "Enter the Music Genre". Be sure to enter a phrase that gives clear instructions about what kind of information to enter into the dialog box, along with any formatting instructions.
- Enter your parameter into the *Criteria* row for the desired field.
- Enclose the parameter within square brackets.
- You can include a comparison operator, like < or >=, before the parameter.

HOW TO: Create a Parameter

1. In *Design* view of the query, click in the **Criteria** row of the desired field.

2. Type in the parameter. An example parameter value is shown in Figure 3-54. You can use the *Expression Builder* to enter the parameter. This may be helpful when the parameter contains a longer phrase that is harder to enter into the *Criteria* row.

Field:	AlbumName	ArtistName	Genre
Table:	Album	Album	Album
Sort:			
Show:	☑	☑	☑
Criteria:			[Enter the Music Genre]
or:			

3-54 Sample parameter

3. Click **Run** [*Query Tools Design* tab, *Results* group] to execute the query. The *Enter Parameter Value* dialog box displays. Either press **Cancel** or enter a value and press **OK**.

> **MORE INFO**
>
> The actual phrase entered inside of the square brackets has no impact on how the parameter and the query function. *[Enter the Music Genre]*, *[ ]* and *[Genre?]* all collect the same information, but the first option is more user-friendly when it appears in the dialog box.

You can include more than one parameter in the same field if you need to enter multiple values. For example, a client at the Placer Hills Real Estate Company is looking for properties between 1,800 and 2,500 square feet. You already learned how to use the *Between* operator to write a compound criteria expression. To create a more flexible query, you can incorporate multiple parameters with the *Between* operator.

HOW TO: Use Multiple Parameters in a Criterion

1. In *Design* view of the query, click in the **Criteria** row of the desired field.
2. Right-click and select **Zoom**, or press the **Shift+F2** keys, to open the *Zoom* box.
3. Type in the criteria expression including the parameters. An example expression is shown in Figure 3-55. This example includes two parameters.

> **ANOTHER WAY**
>
> The *Zoom* box is an alternative to the *Expression Builder*. It provides a larger area in which to enter an expression, but it does not show any of the *Expression Elements* displayed in the lower portion of the *Expression Builder*.

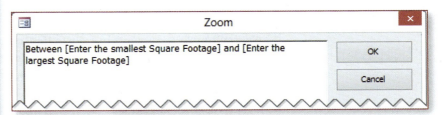

3-55 **Example expression that contains two parameters**

4. Click the **OK** button.
5. When the query is executed, the first *Enter Parameter Value* dialog box displays (Figure 3-56a). Enter the value and click **OK**. Then the second *Enter Parameter Value* dialog box displays (Figure 3-56b). After all the *Enter Parameter Value* dialog boxes have displayed, the query runs.

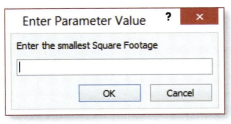

3-56a **First *Enter Parameter Value* dialog box**

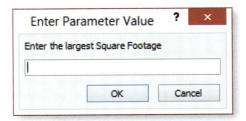

3-56b **Second *Enter Parameter Value* dialog box**

You can use parameters in more than one field in a query. For example, a realtor may want to locate the properties listed for sale in a specific city that have a list price less than a maximum dollar value. The realtor wants the query to prompt the user to specify the city and the maximum list price each time it runs. Figure 3-57 shows the *Query Design grid* for that query. When the query executes, the *Enter Parameter Value* dialog boxes display in the order that the fields are listed in the query. In this example, the *City* parameter displays before the *ListPrice* parameter. This example also includes the <= comparison operator with the *ListPrice* parameter.

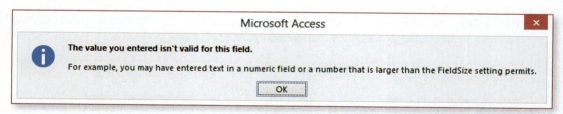

Field:	ListingID	Address	City	SqFt	ListPrice
Table:	Listings	Listings	Listings	Listings	Listings
Sort:					
Show:	✔	✔	✔	✔	✔
Criteria:			[What City?]		<=[Maximum List Price?]
or:					

3-57 *Query Design grid* with multiple parameters

The Parameter Data Type

The *Enter Parameter Value* dialog box accepts any type of input entered by the user. However, the data type of the field determines what is valid in terms of performing the actual comparison. Consider what happens when a letter is entered into the *Enter Parameter Value* dialog box of field with a number data type. When Access executes the query, if the value entered into the dialog box doesn't match the data type of the field, by default Access displays the following message: "*The expression is typed incorrectly, or it is too complex to be evaluated. For example, a numeric expression may contain too many complicated elements. Try simplifying the expression by assigning parts of the expression to variables.*"

The default error message, while absolutely correct in terms of content, may be confusing for a user. Also it is problematic that even if there are multiple *Enter Parameter Value* dialog boxes, the message only shows once when the query is executed. The user doesn't know if he or she made only one mistake or several.

To make dialog boxes easier to understand, Access allows you to specify the data type that a parameter can accept. If you have specified a data type, and the user enters a value that doesn't match the data type, a more helpful error message displays (Figure 3-58).

Microsoft Access

ℹ️ **The value you entered isn't valid for this field.**

For example, you may have entered text in a numeric field or a number that is larger than the FieldSize setting permits.

OK

3-58 Error message when the data type has been specified

If you specify the data type, Access also checks the data type when you press **OK** on the *Enter Parameter Value* dialog box. If the data type is not correct, after displaying the message box, Access returns you back to the *Enter Parameter Value* dialog box to re-enter an acceptable value.

HOW TO: Specify the Parameter Data Type

1. Click the **Parameters** button [*Query Tools Design* tab, *Show/Hide* group] (Figure 3-59).
   - The *Query Parameters* dialog box opens.
   - Recall that the *Table Names* button is highlighted when the *Design grid* displays the *Table* row.
2. Click in the first cell in the **Parameter** column.

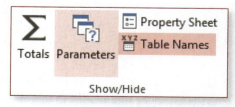

3-59 *Parameters* button

3. Type in the name of your parameter.
   - Make sure that you enter the text as it appears in the *Criteria* property box.
   - The square brackets around the text are optional.
4. Click in the **Data Type** cell.
5. Click the **drop-down arrow** and select the correct data type (Figure 3-60).
6. If needed, enter additional parameters in the dialog box.
7. Click the **OK** button when you are finished.

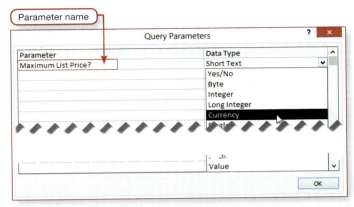

3-60 Assign a data type to a parameter

> **MORE INFO**
>
> If the parameter name entered in the *Query Parameters* dialog box does not match the parameter text in the *Criteria* row, Access still displays the *Enter Parameter Value* dialog box, but the query is not able to use the value entered since the parameters do not match.

Use Wildcards in a Parameter Query

You can use the *Like* comparison operator and wildcards in a parameter when writing the query criteria. Remember, the *Like* comparison operator can help you find records containing data that is similar to, or *like*, the criterion value. Recall that the * symbol represents any number of characters, the **?** represents any single character, and the **#** represents any single number.

There are three common ways to structure a criteria expression with a parameter that uses wildcards. You can include a wildcard symbol at the end, a wildcard symbol at the beginning, or a wildcard symbol at the beginning and the end. The following examples illustrate each of these methods. These examples also introduce the **& concatenation operator** which combines, or concatenates, two text values into one.

- *Like [Enter Prompt Text Inside the Brackets] &* " *" finds records where the data in the field begins with the value entered into the parameter. To limit the results to finding a complete word, the criteria includes a space before the asterisk. This treats the parameter value entered as a separate word, not just letters.

   Example: *Like [Enter the first word of the song] &* " *"

   Explanation: If the user enters "love" into the *Enter Parameter Value* dialog box, this query finds songs where the title starts with the word "love". For example, this query finds "Love for All Seasons" and "Love This Pain". However, it does not find the songs with the title of "Leave Love Alone", "Make You Feel My Love", or "Lovely Rita".

You can remove the space before the asterisk if you want the query to find titles that begin with the letters entered into the parameter dialog box. If "love" is entered, this criteria finds all songs where the first four letters are "love". It still finds all the songs that begin with the word "love" but it will now also find "Lovely Rita".

- *Like* "* " & *[Enter Prompt Text Inside the Brackets]* finds records where the data in the field ends with the value entered into the parameter. To limit the results to finding a complete word, the criteria includes a space after the asterisk.

Example: *Like* "* " & *[Enter the last word of the song]*

Explanation: If the user enters "love" into the *Enter Parameter Value* dialog box, this query finds songs where the title ends in the word "love". For example, the query finds "Make You Feel My Love". It does not find "Love for All Seasons", "Leave Love Alone", or "50 Ways to Leave Your Lover".

- *Like* "* " & *[Enter Prompt Text Inside the Brackets]* & "*" finds records where the data in the field contains the value entered into the parameter in the middle of the field. In this example there is a space after the first asterisk and there is a space before the second asterisk.

Example: *Like* "* " & *[Enter the song word]* & "*"

Explanation: If the user enters "love" into the *Enter Parameter Value* dialog box, this query finds songs with titles that contain the word "love" in the middle. For example, the query finds "Leave Love Alone". It would not find "Love for All Seasons", "Make You Feel My Love", or "50 Ways to Leave Your Lover". The phrase inside of the parameter was changed just to clarify the prompt. Recall that the phrase contents has no impact on the query results.

If the criterion is changed to *Like* "*" & *[Enter the letters to find in the song title]* & "*", with no spaces before or after the asterisks, and the word "love" is entered into the *Enter Parameter Value* dialog box, then all of the songs listed above would be located since this criteria searches for all titles that contain the letters "love". Additionally, a query written this way also works to display all the records if the *Enter Parameter Value* dialog box is left blank. This gives you a great deal of flexibility in returning either selected records or all records.

It is important to remember that the entry the user types in the *Enter Parameter Value* dialog box affects how the query functions. For example, with the criterion of *Like* "* " & *[Enter the song word]* & "*", if you type "love " (with a space after the "e"), Access returns a different set of records than if the user types "love" or "love " (with two spaces).

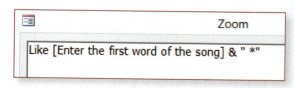

3-61 *The Zoom* box provides a large area to enter a parameter

SLO 3.7 Adding Calculated Fields to a Query

A **calculated field** is a field that gets its value from a calculation instead of a value that is entered into the field. The calculation, or formula, can reference other fields in the database. For example, if a database that stores sales transactions contains the fields of *UnitPrice* and *Quantity*, the *Total Cost* of an item purchased is calculated by multiplying the *UnitPrice* by the *Quantity*.

Unlike a regular table field, a calculated field is not stored in the database. Why not simply store the *TotalCost* field in the database instead of having the database calculate it? To help avoid redundant data and ensure integrity in your database, most database designers recommend that you don't store fields in your database if the field can be calculated using data from other fields.

When writing a formula for a calculated field, use the traditional mathematical operators shown in the following table. Remember that Access evaluates formulas using the standard order of operations. When there is more than one operator in an equation, Access evaluates the equation from left to right, performing calculations based on their precedence level.

Order of Operations Characters and Precedence Level

Character	Operator	Order of Operation
()	Parentheses	First
^	Exponent	Second
*	Multiplication	Third
/	Division	Third
-	Subtraction	Fourth
+	Addition	Fourth

▶ **MORE INFO**

Access refers to formulas as *Expressions*.

Enter a Formula in a Calculated Field

A formula for a query field has two parts that are separated by a colon (:). The first part is the name you assign to the calculated field. The second part is the formula or expression. A generic example of a formula is written as *FieldName:Expression*. The expression can reference other fields and can include other **constants**, hardcoded values entered into a formula. The expressions must obey the following rules:

- Any fields included in the expression must be enclosed within square brackets.
- Any fields that are needed in the expression must be in tables included in the query.

For example, when you apply these rules to the *Total Cost* example described earlier, the formula for a calculated field that determines the *Total Cost* of an item is written as *TotalCost:[UnitPrice]*[Quantity]*.

HOW TO: Add a Calculated Field to a Query

1. Click in the first empty column in the **Field** row of the *Design grid*.
2. Right-click and select either **Zoom** to open the *Zoom* box or **Build** to open the *Expression Builder*.

3. Enter the formula following the rules described above.

- Figure 3-62 is an example of a formula that calculates the potential commission on the sale of a home.
- Notice the different parts of the formula.

4. Click the **OK** button in the *Zoom* box or *Expression Builder* when you are finished entering the formula.

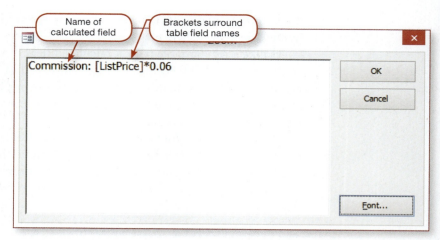

3-62 Enter the formula for a calculated field

You can adjust the *Format* properties to change how the calculated field displays.

HOW TO: Format a Calculated Field in a Query

1. Click to select the **calculated field** in the *Design grid*.
2. Press **F4** to open the *Properties Sheet* for that field.
3. Click in the **Format** property box and click the **arrow** to see the available format options (Figure 3-63).
4. Select the desired format option.
5. If needed, click in the **Decimal Places** property box and select the desired number of decimal places.
6. Press **F4** to close the *Property Sheet*.

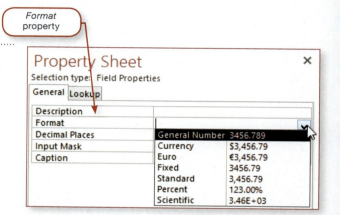

3-63 Format options

Remember to run your query to verify that your calculated field works as planned.

Troubleshoot Calculated Fields

There are three common problems you may encounter with a calculated field.

- An *Enter Parameter Value* dialog box displays when you run the query. If you are not expecting an *Enter Parameter Value* dialog box to display, pay attention to the contents of the parameter. In Figure 3-64, the dialog box is asking the user to enter a value for "List Price".

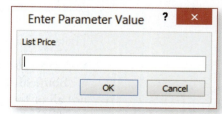

3-64 *Enter Parameter Value* dialog box for the *List Price* field

Review the formula that you have entered into the *calculated field*. Notice in Figure 3-65 that the field name enclosed in the square brackets is *List Price*. Recall that the field in the database was actually named *ListPrice* (no space between *List* and *Price*).

If this occurs, edit the expression so that it includes valid field names.

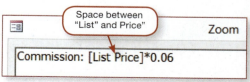

3-65 Review the field name entered into the parameter

- A field is missing a name. Each field must have a name. If you forget to include a field name when you enter the formula, Access assigns the field a generic field name such as *Expr1* by default. This default field name displays in both the *Design grid* (Figure 3-66) and the *Datasheet* view of the results (Figure 3-67). If this happens, edit the expression and change the field to an appropriate name.

3-66 A generic field name like *Expr1* is assigned by Access if you do not name the field

- The formula does not provide the correct answer. In cases like this you need to review the structure of the formula. Make sure that you have used the correct fields and have written the formula correctly according to the order of operations.

3-67 The *Expr1* field name in *Datasheet* view

Functions in a Calculated Field

Access provides a variety of *functions*, predefined formulas to perform a specific task, which you can use in a formula. Access groups the functions by the type of task they perform. The following table highlights a few of the functions available in Access.

Examples of Access Functions

Function	Category	Explanation
Max	SQL Aggregate	Finds the largest value
Round	Math	Rounds the value
UCase	Text	Converts the value to upper case
Left	Text	Finds a specific number of characters from the left of the field
IIf	Program Flow	Performs a comparison and does one of two alternatives. Referred to as the "immediate if" (IIf) function.
Year	Date/Time	Returns the year portion of a date field

A function is typically included as part of a formula. This means that when you use a function, you need to follow the general rules about how to write a formula.

Some of the functions listed in this table are described in various chapters of the book but not all of the Access functions are introduced. If you are writing a complex formula, be sure to utilize the *Access Help System* to see if there is a function that might make your task easier to complete. In this section, to help you learn how to use a function in a calculated field, the *Left* function is introduced.

The **Left** function uses the format of *Left(string, length)*. Functions typically have different parameters, or arguments, that you must include with the function. The *Left* function has two parameters: *string* and *length*. The function analyzes the content of the string parameter and extracts a certain number of characters, as indicated in the length parameter, from the left of the string parameter. For example, *Left("California",2)* returns the value of "*Ca*", while *Left("California",5)* returns the value of "*Calif*".

Both the string and length parameters are required and each can be either a field or a constant. You must enclose fields in square brackets, while text constants are enclosed in quotation marks. In the example, *Left([State],2)* the *State* field is used as the string parameter.

The example in Figure 3-68 shows a formula that finds the first character of the *First-Name* field and combines it with a period, a space, and the *LastName*. This formula displays a name as "G. Lingle" or "M. Johnson".

The formula uses the *Left* function with the & concatenation operator. Recall that **concatenation** combines different parts of an equation together. You used the & operator with the *Like* special operator to combine different parts of an expression together in *SLO 3.6: Creating and Using a Simple Parameter Query*. Often concatenation is used to combine different fields together. For example, you can use it to combine a first and last name, or to combine the city, state, and zip code into one field.

HOW TO: Use the Left Function in a Calculated Field

1. Add the fields from the database tables into the query grid.
2. Click in the first empty column in the **Field** row of the *Design grid*.
3. Right-click and select either **Zoom** to open the *Zoom* box or **Build** to open the *Expression Builder*.
4. Enter the formula, including the appropriate function.

   • The example in Figure 3-68 uses the *Left* function.

5. Click the **OK** button in the *Zoom* box or *Expression Builder* when finished entering the formula.

3-68 Example of a formula that uses the *Left* function

Remember to run your query to verify that your calculated field works. The most challenging part of working with a calculated field is not the actual process of entering the formula into a field. Rather it is the process of determining what the formula must do, structuring the formula correctly, verifying the results, and fine tuning the display formatting.

PAUSE & PRACTICE: ACCESS 3-3

For this Pause & Practice you use *Design* view to create two queries for the American River Cycling Club.

File Needed: ***AmericanRiver-03.accdb***
Completed Project File Name: ***[your initials] PP A3-3.accdb***

1. Open the ***AmericanRiver-03.accdb*** database file.
2. Save a new copy of your database as ***[your initials] PP A3-3***.
3. If prompted, enable content in the database.

4. Create a new query in *Design* view. The American River Cycling Club wants to find out which members have participated in races and what place they got in each race. They want to display the member's name, race number, and race result position. The member's name should be formatted as the first initial, a period, a space, and the last name (e.g., *G. Lingle*). To help understand the logic behind queries, you build this query in stages. Figure 3-69 illustrates the table structure of the database.

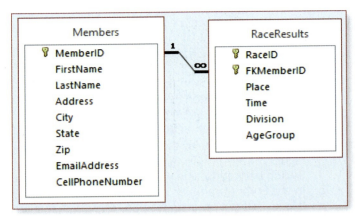

3-69 Table structure of the *American River* database

   a. Click the **Query Design** button [*Create* tab, *Queries* group] to open the *Show Table* dialog box.
   b. Select the **Members** table and click the **Add** button.
   c. Select the **RaceResults** table and click the **Add** button.
   d. Click the **Close** button.
   e. If you need to, increase the size of the table objects to display all of the fields.
   f. Click in the first column in the **Field** row of the *Design grid*.
   g. Press the **Ctrl+F2** keys to open the *Expression Builder*.
   h. Type MemberName:Left([FirstName],1) & ". " & [LastName] into the window.
   i. Click **OK**.
   j. Drag the **RaceID** field from the *RaceResults* table into the second column in the *Field* row of the *Design grid*.
   k. Drag the **Place** field from the *RaceResults* table into the third column in the *Field* row in the *Design grid*. Your completed *Design grid* should look similar to Figure 3-70.

Field:	MemberName: Left([FirstN	RaceID	Place
Table:		RaceResults	RaceResults
Sort:			
Show:	☑	☑	☑
Criteria:			
or:			

3-70 Query *Design grid*

5. Click the **Save** button and save the query as *MemberRaceResults*.

6. Click the **Run** button [*Query Tools Design* tab, *Results* group] to execute the query. The query should open in *Datasheet* view and display 34 records (Figure 3-71).

7. Save a copy of the query.
   a. Click the **Save As** button [*File* tab] and select the **Save Object As** button [*File* tab].
   b. Click the **Save As** button.
   c. Replace the suggested name by typing MemberRaceResultsPlaceParameter.
   d. Click the **OK** button. The two queries should now be displayed in the *Navigation* pane in the *Queries* group.

8. Edit the *MemberRaceResultsPlaceParameter* query to add a parameter.
   a. Click the **View** button [*Home* tab, *Views* group] and select the **Design View** option to switch back to *Design* view of the query.

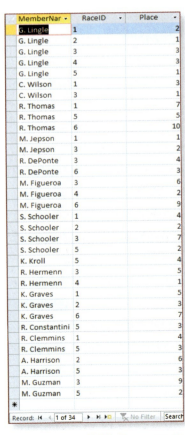

MemberNar ▾	RaceID ▾	Place ▾
G. Lingle	1	2
G. Lingle	2	1
G. Lingle	3	3
G. Lingle	4	3
G. Lingle	5	1
C. Wilson	1	3
C. Wilson	3	1
R. Thomas	1	7
R. Thomas	5	5
R. Thomas	6	10
M. Jepson	1	1
M. Jepson	3	2
R. DePonte	3	4
R. DePonte	6	3
M. Figueroa	3	6
M. Figueroa	4	2
M. Figueroa	6	9
S. Schooler	1	4
S. Schooler	2	2
S. Schooler	3	7
S. Schooler	5	2
K. Kroll	5	4
R. Hermenn	3	5
R. Hermenn	4	1
K. Graves	1	5
K. Graves	2	3
K. Graves	6	7
R. Constantini	5	3
R. Clemmins	1	4
R. Clemmins	5	3
A. Harrison	2	6
A. Harrison	5	3
M. Guzman	3	9
M. Guzman	5	2
*		

Record: I◀ ◀ 1 of 34 ▶ ▶I ▶⧉ 🗙 No Filter Search

3-71 Query results

b. Type [Show members who finished in what place? (Enter a number)] in the **Criteria** row of the *Place* field. You can use the *Zoom* box or *Expression Builder* to enter the parameter.

c. Click the **Save** button to save the query.

d. Click the **Run** button to test the query. The *Enter Parameter Value* dialog box displays (Figure 3-72).

e. Enter 1 and click the **OK** button. The query results should display the 5 records shown in Figure 3-73.

f. Switch back to *Design* view and **Run** the query again.

g. In the *Enter Parameter Value* dialog box, click the **OK** button without entering a value. The query results should display with no records showing since there are no records where the place value matches "null," or no value.

9. Close the query.

10. Close the database.

3-72 Enter Parameter Value dialog box

3-73 Query results

Creating and Using a Summary Query

As you now know, queries help locate data in a database by asking a question. Up to this point, the queries you have worked with have all been structured to find sets of records. But sometimes the question that you want answered involves getting summarized results. For example, you may want to know the total number of Pop/Rock albums that you own, or the average listing price of properties for sale, or the total number of dogs available for adoption. A *summary query* analyzes a set of records and displays summarized results.

Aggregate Functions

A summary query works by using an aggregate function. *Aggregate functions* perform calculations on a group of records. The most common aggregate functions are explained in the following table. When used in a summary query, the function calculates an answer based only on the records that match the query's criteria.

Common Aggregate Functions

Function	Explanation	Supported Data Types
Avg	Finds the average value of the field	AutoNumber, Currency, Date/Time, Number
Count	Counts the number of records that have a value in the field	All data types
Max	Finds the maximum value of the field	AutoNumber, Currency, Date/Time, Number, Short Text
Min	Finds the minimum value of the field	AutoNumber, Currency, Date/Time, Number, Short Text
Sum	Finds the total value of the field	AutoNumber, Currency, Date/Time, Number

Build a Summary Query

The basic building blocks of a summary query are the same as they are for the select queries you have already built. A summary query uses a ***Total row*** that is added into the *Design grid* of the query. Each field in the query has a value in the *Total* row of either *Group By* or the appropriate aggregate function for the field, as shown in Figure 3-74.

When you add a *Total* row to the *Design grid*, each field is initially set to *Group By*. If you don't change at least one of the fields, the query results show one record for each row of data.

Figure 3-75 shows the result of the query in Figure 3-74, with the *Total* row for all three fields set to *Group By*. The only difference between this query and one that doesn't include the *Total* row is that the results in this query are grouped by *Division* and *AgeGroup*.

If you change the query to use the *Min* function in the *Place* field, the query displays the results shown in Figure 3-76.

Compare the difference in the *Field Name* of the *Place* field between Figures 3-75 and 3-76. This revised query answers the question "What is the minimum place that our members took, grouped by division and within division by age group?" Or, in other words, "By division and age group, show the best place finish one of our members achieved in any of the races." The results show that members won a first place in every division and age group except the "less than 20 year old females" division.

To be most effective, a summary query should include only the fields that you want to group by and the fields that you want to aggregate. For example, consider the *Design grid* shown in Figure 3-77. Notice that the *First-Name* and *LastName* fields have been added and the *Min* function remains in the *Place* field.

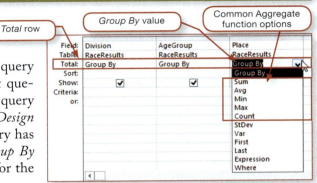

3-74 Select the aggregate function in the *Total* row

Division	AgeGroup	Place
F	<20	3
F	<20	4
F	>=20 and <30	1
F	>=20 and <30	2
F	>=20 and <30	3
F	>=20 and <30	6
F	>=20 and <30	9
F	>=30 and <40	1
F	>=30 and <40	2
F	>=30 and <40	3
F	>=30 and <40	4
F	>=30 and <40	5
F	>=30 and <40	7
M	>=20 and <30	1
M	>=20 and <30	2
M	>=20 and <30	5
M	>=20 and <30	9
M	>=30 and <40	1
M	>=30 and <40	2
M	>=30 and <40	3
M	>=30 and <40	4
M	>=30 and <40	5
M	>=30 and <40	7
M	>=30 and <40	10

3-75 All fields use *Group By* in the *Total* row

Division	AgeGroup	MinOfPlace
F	<20	3
F	>=20 and <30	1
F	>=30 and <40	1
M	>=20 and <30	1
M	>=30 and <40	1

3-76 Query results with the *Min* aggregate function

Field:	Division	AgeGroup	Place	FirstName	LastName
Table:	RaceResults	RaceResults	RaceResults	Members	Members
Total:	Group By	Group By	Min	Group By	Group By
Sort:					
Show:	✔	✔	✔	✔	✔
Criteria:					
or:					

3-77 *Design* view of query to show the highest place finish for each member

That query produces the results shown in Figure 3-78. This query returns "the highest place finish for each member." In this case the *Division* and *AgeGroup* fields only affect the order in which the records display, not which records display.

In order to get the results you desire, you need to spend some time planning out the structure of a summary query before you build it.

Division	AgeGroup	MinOfPlace	First Name	Last Name
F	<20	4	Kelsey	Kroll
F	<20	3	Robyn	Constantini
F	>=20 and <30	3	Amber	Harrison
F	>=20 and <30	1	Geneva	Lingle
F	>=20 and <30	2	Melanie	Figueroa
F	>=30 and <40	1	Cheryl	Wilson
F	>=30 and <40	3	Karen	Graves
F	>=30 and <40	2	Sue	Schooler
M	>=20 and <30	2	Marco	Guzman
M	>=20 and <30	1	Rick	Hermenn
M	>=30 and <40	1	Margaret	Jepson
M	>=30 and <40	3	Randy	Clemmins
M	>=30 and <40	3	Rick	DePonte
M	>=30 and <40	5	Ryan	Thomas

3-78 Query results show the highest place finish for each member

HOW TO: Create a Summary Query

1. Click the **Query Design** button [*Create* tab, *Queries* group].
2. Select the first table to use in the query from the *Show Table* dialog box.
3. Click the **Add** button to add the table into the *Query Design* window.
4. Continue adding all required tables.
5. Click the **Close** button to close the *Show Table* dialog box.
6. Add the desired fields into the *Design grid*.
7. Click the **Totals** button [*Query Tools Design* tab, *Show/Hide* group] (Figure 3-79).
   - The *Total* row is added into the *Design grid* below the *Table* row.
   - The *Total* row value for each field in the *Design grid* is set to *Group By*.

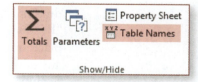

3-79 *Totals* button

> **MORE INFO**
>
> You cannot use the *Group By* choice in fields that have *Long Text, OLE Object,* and *Hyperlink* data types.

Once you have created the summary query, you need to select the appropriate aggregate functions.

HOW TO: Use an Aggregate Function in a Summary Query

1. Click in the **Total** row cell of the desired field.
2. Click the **arrow** and select the desired aggregate function (Figure 3-80).
   - The query in Figure 3-80 answers the question "How many races was each member in?"
3. Repeat steps 1 and 2 for any additional fields that will be aggregated.

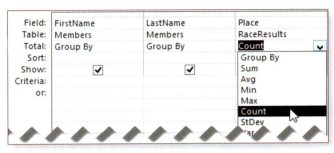

3-80 Select the aggregate function from the drop-down list

Occasionally you may want to create a summary query where you want to see multiple calculations on the same field. For example, you may want to find the best and worst place finish that each member had in a race. Or for our real estate database you might want to see the average, maximum, and minimum list price for all properties.

HOW TO: Use Multiple Aggregate Functions on a Field

1. Click in the **Total** row cell of the desired field.
2. Click the **arrow** and select the desired aggregate function.
3. Add the field into another column in the *Design grid.*
4. Click the **arrow** and select the desired aggregate function.
5. Continue adding the field and selecting the aggregate function for as many calculations as you want to include.
   - Figure 3-81 shows an example of a query that aggregates the *Average, Maximum*, and *Minimum* on the *ListPrice* field.
   - This query would produce the results shown in Figure 3-82.

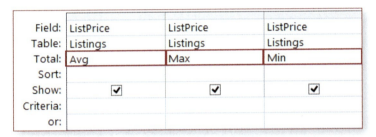

3-81 Include a field multiple times to use more than one aggregate function on the same field

3-82 Query results with multiple aggregate functions

When you use a summary query, the way that you indicate criteria changes a little. You need to select the **Where** option from the drop-down list of aggregate functions, in addition to adding the specific criteria.

HOW TO: Use Criteria in a Summary Query

1. Click in the **Total** row cell of the field that will have the criteria.
2. Click the **arrow** and select the **Where** option.
   - The *Show* row check box is deselected.
   - If desired, select the **check** box on the **Show** row to include that field in the query results.

3. Click in the **Criteria** row of the field and enter the criteria.
- Figure 3-83 shows an example of the query *Design grid* that calculates and displays the *Average ListPrice* for properties listed after *7/1/2014*.
- The query results do not include the *DateListed* since the *Show* row check box is deselected.

3-83 Select the *Where* option in the *Total* row when using criteria in a summary query

PAUSE & PRACTICE: ACCESS 3-4

For this Pause & Practice you create a summary query for the Placer Hills Real Estate Company.

File Needed: *PlacerHills-03.accdb*
Completed Project File Name: *[your initials] PP A3-4.accdb*

1. Open the *PlacerHills-03.accdb* database file.
2. Save a new copy of your database as *[your initials] PP A3-4*.
3. If prompted, enable content in the database.
4. Create a new summary query in *Design* view. The Placer Hills Real Estate Company wants to find out some summary information. By agent, the company wants to know the average list price of each agent's listings and the total number of properties each agent has listed. It wants to display the agent's first and last name, as well as the two summary fields. To help you understand the logic behind queries, you build this query in stages. Figure 3-84 shows the table structure of the database.

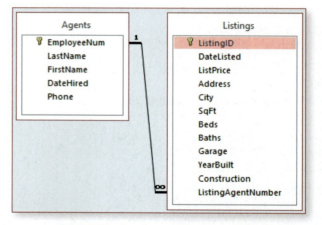

3-84 Table structure of the *Placer Hills* database

   a. Click the **Query Design** button [*Create* tab, *Queries* group] to open the *Show Table* dialog box.
   b. Select the **Agents** table and click the **Add** button.
   c. Select the **Listings** table and click the **Add** button.
   d. Click the **Close** button.
   e. Increase the size of the table objects to display all of the fields.
   f. Click the **drop-down arrow** in the first **Field** row column of the *Design grid* and select **Agents.FirstName**.
   g. Click in the second column in the **Field** row, click the **drop-down arrow**, and select **Agents.LastName**.
   h. Click in the third column in the **Field** row, click the **drop-down arrow**, and select **Listings.ListPrice**.
   i. Click in the fourth column in the **Field** row, click the **drop-down arrow**, and select **Listings.ListPrice**. (Yes, you add this field twice!)
   j. Click the **Totals** button [*Query Tools Design* tab, *Show/Hide* group] to add the *Total* row to the query.

5. Add the aggregate functions into the query.
   a. Click in the **Total** row cell of the first *ListPrice* field.
   b. Click the **arrow** and select **Avg**.
   c. Click in the **Total** row cell of the second *ListPrice* field.
   d. Click the **arrow** and select **Count**.
   e. The completed *Design grid* should look similar to Figure 3-85.

Field:	FirstName	LastName	ListPrice	ListPrice
Table:	Agents	Agents	Listings	Listings
Total:	Group By	Group By	Avg	Count
Sort:				
Show:	✔	✔	✔	✔
Criteria:				
or:				

3-85 Aggregate functions added to query

6. Click the **Save** button and save the query as *AvgListPriceAndListingCountByAgent*.

7. Click the **Run** button [*Query Tools Design* tab, *Results* group] to execute the query. The query should open in *Datasheet* view and display 7 records.

8. Adjust the column width of the *AvfOfListPrice* and *CountOfListPrice* fields to display the entire column name.
   a. Select the **AvgOfListPrice** column.
   b. Right-click to open the context menu.
   c. Select **Field Width**.
   d. Select **Best Fit**.
   e. Select the **CountOfListPrice** column.
   f. Right-click to open the context menu.
   g. Select **Field Width**.
   h. Select **Best Fit**.
   i. The *Datasheet* view should match that of Figure 3-86.

9. Click the **Save** button to save the changes.

10. Close the query.

11. Close the database.

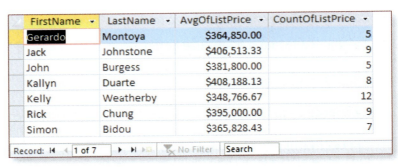

FirstName	LastName	AvgOfListPrice	CountOfListPrice
Gerardo	Montoya	$364,850.00	5
Jack	Johnstone	$406,513.33	9
John	Burgess	$381,800.00	5
Kallyn	Duarte	$408,188.13	8
Kelly	Weatherby	$348,766.67	12
Rick	Chung	$395,000.00	9
Simon	Bidou	$365,828.43	7

Record: ◄ ◄ 1 of 7 ► ►I ►⋮ 🔽 No Filter | Search

3-86 Query results for summary query

Chapter Summary

3.1 Use the *Simple Query Wizard* to create and run a query (p. A3-152).

- Use **queries** to find data in your database.
- You can build queries from tables, other queries, or both.
- The **Simple Query Wizard** lets you quickly build a query by specifying the tables or queries to use and then selecting the desired fields from those objects.
- You can edit a query created with the *Simple Query Wizard* in *Design* view.

3.2 Create a query in *Design* view, add fields, save and run a query (p. A3-153).

- The **Query Design** button opens *Design* view to build queries.
- *Design* view provides the most flexibility when creating queries.
- Add tables or queries into the *Query Design* window by selecting them from the *Show Table* dialog box.
- You must add fields into the **Design grid** if you want them to appear in the query.
- **Run** a query to execute the query and have the query locate records in the database.
- Query results display in *Datasheet* view.
- Save each query with a unique name.

3.3 Add a criterion to into a query, use comparison operators, and create criteria with wildcards (p. A3-159).

- You can add a criterion to a query to search for specific records.
- You enter a criterion **expression** into the *Criteria* row of the *Design grid*. You can type the expression directly into the *Criteria* row or enter it using the **Expression Builder**.
- Expressions can include the standard **comparison operators**.
- Combine the **Like** comparison operator with **wildcard symbols** for greater flexibility in the criterion value.

3.4 Integrate sorting and limiting fields and records that display (p. A3-164).

- Set the **Unique Values** property to have Access evaluate the fields in the query and avoid including duplicated values.

- The **Unique Records** property checks all the fields in a table, not just those included in the query.
- Deselecting the *Show* row check box prevents a field from displaying in the query results.
- Query results can be sorted in ascending or descending order in one or more fields.
- If sorting on multiple fields, the fields must be placed into the *Design grid* in order of sort priority.

3.5 Use the *AND* and *OR* operators to include multiple criteria (p. A3-168).

- **Compound criteria** combine more than one criterion using the **AND** and **OR** operators; this allows you to create a more complex query.
- Criteria written in different fields but on the same criteria row are evaluated as an *AND* comparison.
- Criteria written on different criteria rows are evaluated as an *OR* comparison.
- You can combine *AND* and *OR* operators in one query.

3.6 Create a parameter query (p. A3-174).

- A **parameter query** asks the user to enter a specific criteria value at the time the query is run.
- When a parameter query is included, the *Enter Parameter Value* dialog box displays before the query executes.
- The **parameter** is the text phrase you enter into the *Criteria* row of the field. You must enclose the parameter in square brackets.
- A query can include multiple parameters, on one or more fields.
- If you specify the data type of the parameter, Access displays a more user-friendly message if a user makes an error when entering the parameter value.
- You can combine the *Like* comparison operator with wildcard symbols for increased flexibility in a parameter.

3.7 Build a query that uses a calculated field (p. A3-178).

- **Calculated fields** get their value from a calculation instead of being stored in a table.

- Use a calculated field instead of a table field if the database can calculate the field's value using data stored in other fields.
- You can add a calculated field into the *Design grid* of a query.
- The formula expression for a calculated field is in the format *FieldName:Expression*.
- The formulas use the standard mathematical operators and order of operations.
- Access provides a variety of **functions,** which are predefined formulas that perform a specific task.
- You can include a function as part of an expression in a calculated field.

3.8 Create a summary query using aggregate functions (p. A3-184).

- A **summary query** analyzes a set of records and then displays summarized results.
- Summary queries use **aggregate functions,** functions that perform calculations on a group of records.
- Common aggregate functions include *Avg, Count, Max, Min,* and *Sum.*
- Summary queries can summarize several different fields or perform different calculations on the same field.

Check for Understanding

In the **Online Learning Center** for this text (www.mhhe.com/office2013inpractice), there are a variety of resources that can be used to review the concepts covered in this chapter.

The following Online Learning Resources are available in the Online Learning Center:

- Multiple choice questions
- Short answer questions
- Matching exercises

Guided Project 3-1

You have built a database to store information about a friend's music collection. You want to write three queries to help answer some questions about the songs in the database. To ensure consistency, the starting file is provided for you. Use *the Simple Query Wizard* to create a query, use *Design* view to edit the query, and add criteria. After saving and testing the query, save a copy of the query to add a parameter. Finally, create a third query that includes summary query capabilities. **[Student Learning Outcomes 3.1, 3.2, 3.3, 3.4, 3.5, 3.6]**

File Needed: *LargerMusicDatabase-03.accdb*
Completed Project File Name: *[your initials] Access 3-1.accdb*

Skills Covered in This Project

- Create a query using the *Simple Query Wizard.*
- Edit a query in *Design* view.
- Add compound criteria to a query.
- Execute a query.

- Save a query.
- Add a parameter to a query.
- Sort query results.
- Edit a query to add an aggregate function.

1. Open the *LargerMusicDatabase-03.accdb* database file.

2. Save a new copy of your database as *[your initials] Access 3-1*.

3. If needed, enable content in the security warning.

4. Open the *Album* table in *Datasheet* view to view the contents. You should see 27 different records.

5. Click the **plus symbol** to the left of *AlbumID 6,* to see the songs that are on Maroon 5's *Hands All Over* album.

6. Close the table.

7. Create a new query using the *Simple Query Wizard.*
   a. Click the **Query Wizard** button [*Create* tab, *Queries* group] to launch the *Query Wizard.*
   b. Select **Simple Query Wizard** in the *New Query* dialog box.
   c. Click the **OK** button to launch the *Simple Query Wizard* (Figure 3-87). Verify that the *Album* table appears in the *Tables/Queries* box.
   d. Select **AlbumName** in the *Available Fields* window.

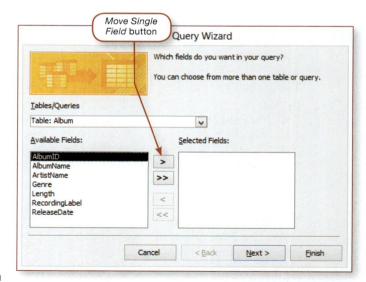

3-87 *Simple Query Wizard*

e. Click the **Move Single Field** button to move the field into the *Selected Fields* window.
f. Select **ArtistName** in the *Available Fields* window.
g. Click the **Move Single Field** button.
h. Continue moving over the **Genre** and **ReleaseDate** fields.
i. Click the **Tables/Queries** drop-down arrow and select the **Songs** table.
j. Select **SongTitle** in the *Available Fields* window.
k. Click the **Move Single Field** button. The completed *Selected Fields* window should match Figure 3-88.
l. Click the **Next** button. The second page of the *Simple Query Wizard* displays. Because of the relationship between the two tables, Access asks you whether you want a detail or summary query.
m. Leave the radio button selected for **Detail** and click the **Next** button.
n. Change the title in the *Title* box to SongsOnAlbums.
o. Click **Finish** to save and run the query. The query results should match those shown in Figure 3-89, displaying 355 total records.

3-88 Completed *Selected Fields* window

3-89 Query results of *SongsOnAlbums* query

8. Edit the query in *Design* view to add criteria to find songs on rock albums released after 1/1/2000.
   a. Click the **View** button [*Home* tab, *Views* group] and select the **Design View** option to switch back to *Design* view of the query.
   b. Type Rock in the *Criteria* row of the *Genre* field.
   c. **Tab** out of that field. Notice that Access automatically puts quotation marks around the text criteria.
   d. Click the **Run** button [*Query Tools Design* tab, *Results* group] to run the query. The query should open in *Datasheet* view and display the 93 songs that were on rock albums.
   e. Switch back to *Design* view and type >=#1/1/2000# in the *Criteria* row of the *ReleaseDate* field.
   f. Click the **Run** button [*Query Tools Design* tab, *Results* group]. The query should display 30 songs from Maroon 5's *Call and Response: The Remix Album* and John Mayer's *Born and Raised* albums.

9. Save a copy of the query.
   a. Click the **Save As** button [*File* Tab].
   b. Select the **Save Object As** button and then click the **Save As** button.
   c. Replace the suggested object name in the *Save 'SongsOnAlbums' to* box with SongsOnRockAlbumsAfterJan2000.
   d. Click **OK**.
   e. Close the query.

10. Edit the *SongsOnAlbums* query in *Design* view to add a parameter for the *ArtistName* field.
    a. In the *Queries* group of the *Navigation* pane, select the **SongsOnAlbums** query. Right-click to open the context menu and select the **Design View** option to open the query in *Design*.
    b. Type [Show songs by which Artist?] in the *Criteria* row of the *ArtistName* field.
    c. Click the **Run** button [*Query Tools Design* tab, *Results* group] to run the query. The *Enter Parameter Value* dialog box displays.
    d. Type Maroon 5 and click **OK** (Figure 3-90). The query should open in *Datasheet* view and display the 48 songs on albums released by Maroon 5.

Enter Parameter Value dialog box

3-90 Enter Parameter Value dialog box

11. Edit the query to add sorting.
    a. Click the **View** button [*Home* tab, *Views* group] and select the **Design View** option to switch back to *Design* view of the query.
    b. Click in the **Sort** row of the *ReleaseDate* field and select **Ascending**.
    c. Click the **Run** button [*Query Tools Design* tab, *Results* group] to run the query. The *Enter Parameter Value* dialog box displays.
    d. Type Maroon 5 and click **OK**.
    e. Verify that the results are displayed in ascending order on the *ReleaseDate* field.

12. Save a copy of the query.
    a. Click the **Save As** button [*File* Tab].
    b. Select the **Save Object As** button and then click the **Save As** button.
    c. Replace the suggested object name in the *Save 'SongsOnAlbums Query' to* box with SongCountArtistParameter.
    d. Click **OK**. The query opens in *Design* view.

13. Edit the query to add a *Total* row.
    a. Click the **Totals** button [*Query Tools Design* tab, *Show/Hide* group].
    b. Click in the **Total** row cell for the *SongTitle* field.
    c. Click the **drop-down arrow** and select **Count**.

14. Click the **Save** button to save the query.

15. Click the **Run** button [*Query Tools Design* tab, *Results* group] to run the query.
    a. The *Enter Parameter Value* dialog box displays.
    b. Type Maroon 5 and click **OK**.
    c. The query should open in *Datasheet* view and display the *CountOfSongs* on the 3 albums by Maroon 5 (Figure 3-91).
    d. As desired, extend the width of the *CountofSongTitle* column and save the changes to query.

AlbumName	ArtistName	Genre	ReleaseDate	CountOfSongTitle
Call and Response: The Remix Album	Maroon 5	Rock	09-Dec-08	18
Hands All Over	Maroon 5	Pop	12-Jul-11	14
Overexposed (Deluxe)	Maroon 5	Pop	17-Jul-12	16

Record: ◄ ◄ 1 of 3 ► ►► ►* No Filter   Search

3-91 Query results with Count aggregate function

16. Close the query.

17. Close the database.

Guided Project 3-2

San Diego Sailing Club wants to create two queries to summarize the total dollar value of the rentals for each boat in its fleet. To ensure consistency, the starting file is provided for you. Use *Design* view to create a summary query, edit the query, add aggregate functions, and add criteria. After saving and testing the query, create a second query that uses aggregate functions and a parameter.
[Student Learning Outcomes 3.2, 3.3, 3.4, 3.5, 3.6, 3.8]

File Needed: ***SailingDatabase-03.accdb***
Completed Project File Name: ***[your initials] Access 3-2.accdb***

Skills Covered in This Project

- Create a query using *Design* view.
- Add fields to a query.
- Add criteria to a query.
- Execute a query.

- Save and test a query.
- Save a copy of a query.
- Add a parameter.
- Use aggregate functions.

1. Open *the* **SailingDatabase-03.accdb** database file.

2. Save a new copy of your database as ***[your initials] Access 3-2***.

3. If prompted, enable content in the database.

4. Create a new summary query in *Design* view. The Sailing Club wants to find out the total dollar value of the full day rentals, by boat, from the boats that have been rented. If a boat has been rented, there is a record in the *SDRentals* table.
   a. Click the **Query Design** button [*Create* tab, *Queries* group] to open the *Show Table* dialog box.
   b. Select the **SailboatFleet** table and click the **Add** button.
   c. Select the **SDRentals** table and click the **Add** button.
   d. Click the **Close** button.
   e. Increase the size of the table objects to display all of the fields.
   f. Click the **drop-down arrow** in the first **Field** row column of the *Design grid* and select **SDRentals.FKBoatID**.
   g. Click in the second column in the **Field** row, click the **drop-down arrow**, and select **SailboatFleet.BoatType**.
   h. Click in the third column in the **Field** row, click the **drop-down arrow**, and select **SailboatFleet.FullDayRentalRate**.
   i. Click in the fourth column in the **Field** row, click the **drop-down arrow**, and select **SDRentals.FourHourRental?**.
   j. Click the **Totals** button [*Query Tools Design* tab, *Show/Hide* group].
   k. Click the **Run** button [*Query Tools Design* tab, *Results* group] to execute the query. The query should open in *Datasheet* view and display 13 records (Figure 3-92). This query only shows boats that have been rented. At most a *Boat ID* appears in two rows; one row if the *Four Hour Rental?* box is checked and another row if the *Four Hour Rental?* box is not checked.

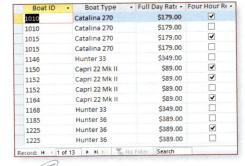

3-92 Sailboat query results

5. Edit the query to add aggregate functions. Because you are looking only for rentals that were for a full day, use the "No" value on the *FourHourRental?* field.
    a. Click the **View** button [*Home* tab, *Views* group] and select the **Design View** option to switch back to *Design* view of the query.
    b. Click in the **Total** row cell for the *FullDayRentalRate* field.
    c. Click the **drop-down arrow** and select **Sum**.
    d. Click in the **Total** row cell for the *FourHourRental?* field.
    e. Click the **drop-down arrow** and select **Where**. This causes the **Show** row check box for the *FourHourRental?* field to be deselected.
    f. Click in the **Criteria** row for the *FourHourRental?* field and enter No. The *IntelliSense* feature in Access may suggest the value of "Now" while you are typing. Press the **Esc** key to hide the list and then **tab** out of the field.
    g. The query window should look similar to Figure 3-93.

Field:	FKBoatID	BoatType	FullDayRentalRate	FourHourRental?
Table:	SDRentals	SailboatFleet	SailboatFleet	SDRentals
Total:	Group By	Group By	Sum	Where
Sort:				
Show:	✔	✔	✔	☐
Criteria:				No
or:				

3-93 *Design grid* **for the summary query with criteria**

    h. Click the **Run** button. The query should open in *Datasheet* view and display seven records (Figure 3-94). The *BoatID* now displays only once since the criteria limits the results only to the full day rentals.

6. Click the **Save** button and save the query as *SummaryOfFullDayRentalsByBoat*.

3-94 Results from completed
SummaryOfFullDayRentalsByBoat **query**

7. Verify that that query works correctly.
    a. Open the *SDRentals* table in *Datasheet* view.
    b. Click the **arrow** in the *Boat ID* field name cell.
    c. Select the **Sort A to Z** option.
    d. Click the **arrow** in the *Four Hour Rental?* field name cell.
    e. Select the **Sort Cleared to Selected** option.
    f. *Boat ID 1010* has five full day rentals. From Figure 3-92 you know that the full day rate for that boat is $179.00 and 5 × $179 = $895.00.
    g. Click the **Remove Sort** button [*Home* tab, *Sort & Filter* group].
    h. Close the *SDRentals* table. If prompted, do not save the changes to the table.

8. Save a copy of the query.
    a. Click the **Save As** button [*File* Tab].
    b. Select the **Save Object As** button and then click the **Save As** button.
    c. Replace the suggested name with SummaryOfFullDayRentalsByBoatWithParameter. This second query will allow the Sailing Club to enter the date range for the summary query and also will count the number of rentals.

9. Click the **View** button [*Home* tab, *Views* group] and select the **Design View** option to open this query in *Design* view. Add the additional fields and aggregate function.
   a. Drag the **FullDayRentalRate** field from the *SailboatFleet* table to the fifth column in the *Design grid*. (Yes, this field is in the query twice.)
   b. Click in the **Total** row cell for this field, click the **drop-down arrow**, and select **Count**.
   c. Drag the **RentalDate** field from the *SDRentals* table to the sixth column in the *Design grid*.
   d. Click in the **Total** row cell for this field, click the **drop-down arrow**, and select **Where**. This causes the **Show** row check box for the *RentalDate* field to be deselected.

10. Click the **Save** button and save the changes to the query.

11. Add two parameters to the *RentalDate* field.
    a. Click in the **Criteria** row of the *RentalDate* field.
    b. Right-click and select **Zoom**.
    c. Type Between [Enter the Start Date] And [Enter the End Date] in the *Zoom* box.
    d. Click **OK**. The query window should look similar to Figure 3-95.

Field:	FKBoatID	BoatType	FullDayRentalRate	FourHourRental?	FullDayRentalRate	RentalDate
Table:	SDRentals	SailboatFleet	SailboatFleet	SDRentals	SailboatFleet	SDRentals
Total:	Group By	Group By	Sum	Where	Count	Where
Sort:						
Show:	✔	✔	✔	☐	✔	☐
Criteria:				No		Between [Enter the
or:						

3-95 Query window with aggregate functions and a parameter

12. Click the **Run** button.
    a. Enter 2/1/2015 in the *Enter the Start Date* box of the *Enter Parameter Value* dialog box.
    b. Click **OK**.
    c. Enter 2/28/2015 in the *Enter the End Date* box of the *Enter Parameter Value* dialog box.
    d. Click **OK**.
    e. The query should open in *Datasheet* view and display the records shown in Figure 3-96.

Boat ID ▾	Boat Type ▾	SumOfFullD ▾	CountOfFullDayRe ▾
1010	Catalina 270	$716.00	4
1015	Catalina 270	$179.00	1
1152	Capri 22 Mk II	$89.00	1
1185	Hunter 36	$389.00	1

Record: I◄ ◄ 1 of 4 ► ►I ►⋈ 🔾 No Filter   Search

3-96 Query results with *Sum* and *Count* aggregate functions and parameter

13. Click the **Save** button to save the changes made to the query.

14. Close the query.

15. Reopen the query in *Design* view. Notice that Access has reordered the position of the fields. The two fields that use the *Where* option on the *Total* row have been moved to the right side of the *Design* grid. This does not affect the way the query runs.

16. Close the query.

17. Close the database.

Guided Project 3-3

Placer Hills Real Estate wants to run three queries on its database. The first query helps an agent find available properties that meet the specific criteria of her client. The second query helps the office manager determine the potential commission that agents can earn on the houses they have listed. The third query is based on the potential commission query, which you enhance to include a parameter so the manager can search only for a particular agent. To ensure consistency, the starting file is provided for you. Use *Design* view to create the queries, edit the queries, and add criteria, calculated fields, and a parameter. Save and test the queries to ensure they work correctly. **[Student Learning Outcomes 3.2, 3.3, 3.4, 3.5, 3.6, 3.7]**

File Needed: ***PlacerHills-03.accdb***
Completed Project File Name: ***[your initials] Access 3-3.accdb***

Skills Covered in This Project

- Create a query using *Design* view.
- Add fields to a query.
- Add compound criteria to a query.
- Execute a query.

- Save and test a query.
- Add calculated fields to a query.
- Add a parameter.

1. Open the ***PlacerHills-03.accdb*** database file.

2. Save a new copy of your database as ***[your initials] Access 3-3***.

3. If prompted, enable content in the database.

4. Create a new query in *Design* view to help an agent locate the potential properties that meet the requirements of her client.
   a. Click the **Query Design** button [*Create* tab, *Queries* group] to open the *Show Table* dialog box.
   b. Select the **Agents** table and click the **Add** button.
   c. Select the **Listings** table and click the **Add** button.
   d. Click the **Close** button.
   e. Increase the size of the table objects to display all of the fields.
   f. Double-click the **ListingID** field to add it into the *Design grid*.
   g. Double-click the **Address** field to add it into the *Design grid*.
   h. Double-click the **City** field to add it into the *Design grid*.
   i. Continue adding the following fields into the *Design grid*: **ListPrice, SqFt, Beds, Baths, Garage, YearBuilt, FirstName, LastName**, and **Phone**.

5. Click the **Save** button and save the query as *PropertiesForBrandonBuchanon*.

6. Add criteria to the query. A client, Brandon Buchanon, is looking for homes in Rocklin or Roseville. The properties must have at least three bedrooms and at least two bathrooms and at least 1,800 square feet. Properties must have an attached garage. In general, the list prices shouldn't exceed $550,000. However, if the house is in Rocklin, Brandon is willing to spend up to $600,000.
   a. Type Rocklin in the *Criteria* row of the *City* field.
   b. Type <=600000 in the *Criteria* row of the *ListPrice* field.

c. Continue entering the criteria displayed in Figure 3-97 into the *Design grid.* Note that the criteria for the *Garage* field is Like "*Attached".

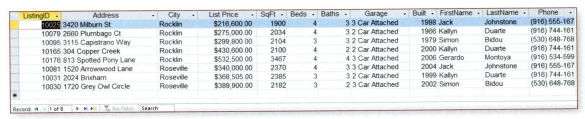

Field:	ListingID	Address	City	ListPrice	SqFt	Beds	Baths	Garage	Yea
Table:	Listings	Listings	Listings	Listings	Listings	Listings	Listings	Listings	List
Sort:									
Show:	✔	✔	✔	✔	✔	✔	✔	✔	
Criteria:			"Rocklin"	<=600000	>=1800	>=3	>=2	Like "*Attached"	
or:			"Roseville"	<=550000	>=1800	>=3	>=2	Like "*Attached"	

3-97 Enter the query criteria into the *Design grid*

7. Add sorting to the query.
   a. Select **Ascending** in the **Sort** row for the *City* field.
   b. Select **Ascending** in the **Sort** row of the *ListPrice* field.

8. Save the changes to the query and click the **Run** button [*Query Tools Design* tab, *Results* group] to execute the query. The query should open in *Datasheet* view and display the eight records shown in Figure 3-98.

ListingID	Address	City	List Price	SqFt	Beds	Baths	Garage	Built	FirstName	LastName	Phone
10025	3420 Milburn St	Rocklin	$216,600.00	1900	4	3	3 Car Attached	1988	Jack	Johnstone	(916) 555-167
10079	2660 Plumbago Ct	Rocklin	$275,000.00	2034	4	3	2 Car Attached	1966	Kallyn	Duarte	(916) 744-161
10095	3115 Capistrano Way	Rocklin	$299,800.00	2104	3	3	2 Car Attached	1979	Simon	Bidou	(530) 648-768
10165	304 Copper Creek	Rocklin	$430,600.00	2100	4	2	2 Car Attached	2000	Kallyn	Duarte	(916) 744-161
10176	813 Spotted Pony Lane	Rocklin	$532,500.00	3467	4	4	3 Car Attached	2006	Gerardo	Montoya	(916) 534-599
10081	1520 Arrowwood Lane	Roseville	$340,000.00	2370	4	3	3 Car Attached	2004	Jack	Johnstone	(916) 555-167
10031	2024 Brixham	Roseville	$368,505.00	2385	3	3	2 Car Attached	1999	Kallyn	Duarte	(916) 744-161
10030	1720 Grey Owl Circle	Roseville	$389,900.00	2182	3	2	3 Car Attached	2002	Simon	Bidou	(530) 648-768

Record: I◄ ◄ 1 of 8 ► ►I ►❏ No Filter   Search

3-98 Datasheet view of query results for *PropertiesForBrandonBuchanon*

9. Close the query.

10. Create a new query in *Design* view. The office manager wants to calculate the potential commission on the listed properties.
    a. Click the **Query Design** button [*Create* tab, *Queries* group] to open the *Show Table* dialog box.
    b. Select the **Agents** table and click the **Add** button.
    c. Select the **Listings** table and click the **Add** button.
    d. Click the **Close** button.
    e. Increase the size of the table objects to display all of the fields.
    f. Right-click in the **Field** cell of the first column and select **Zoom**.
    g. Type Agent's Name: [FirstName] & " " & [LastName].
    h. Click **OK**.
    i. Double-click the **ListingID** field to add it into the second column of the *Design grid.*
    j. Double-click the **ListPrice** field to add it into the *Design grid.*
    k. Right-click in the **Field** cell of the fourth column and select **Zoom**.
    l. Type Potential Commission: [ListPrice]*.06.
    m. Click **OK**.

11. Format the *Potential Commission* calculated field.
    a. Click to select the **Potential Commission** field. Verify that the *Show* check box is selected.
    b. Press **F4** to open the *Property Sheet.* If the *Show* check box was not selected, the *Property Sheet* displays the query properties instead of the field properties.
    c. Click in the **Format** property box.
    d. Click the **arrow** and select **Currency**.
    e. Press **F4** to close the *Property Sheet.*

12. Click the **Save** button and save the query as *PotentialCommissionByProperty*.

13. Click the **Run** button. The query should open in *Datasheet* view and display all 55 records. A sample of the results is shown in Figure 3-99.

Agent's Name	ListingID	List Price	Potential C(
Simon Bidou	10022	$337,600.00	$20,256.00
Simon Bidou	10030	$389,900.00	$23,394.00
Simon Bidou	10033	$334,500.00	$20,070.00
Simon Bidou	10040	$299,999.00	$17,999.94
Simon Bidou	10077	$625,000.00	$37,500.00
Simon Bidou	10080	$274,000.00	$16,440.00
Simon Bidou	10095	$299,800.00	$17,988.00
Kelly Weatherby	10023	$339,600.00	$20,376.00
Kelly Weatherby	10027	$130,000.00	$7,800.00
Kelly Weatherby	10048	$350,000.00	$21,000.00

14. Adjust the width of the *Agent's Name* field.
    a. Right-click in the **Agent's Name** cell to open the context menu.
    b. Select the **Field Width** button.
    c. Select **Best Fit**.

15. Click the **Save** button to save the changes to the query.

3-99 Query results showing *Potential Commission* calculated field

16. Click the **View** button [*Home* tab, *Views* group] and select the **Design View** option to switch back to *Design* view.

17. Add a parameter to find properties by agent. Because the agent's table stores the data as first and last name, you need to add those fields to the query.
    a. Double-click the **FirstName** field to add it into the *Design grid*.
    b. Double-click the **LastName** field to add it into the *Design grid*.
    c. Type [Enter the Agent's First Name] in the *Criteria* row for the *FirstName* field.
    d. Type [Enter the Agent's Last Name] in the *Criteria* row for the *LastName* field.
    e. Deselect the check box on the **Show** row for the *FirstName* field.
    f. Deselect the check box on the **Show** row for the *LastName* field.

18. Save a copy of the query.
    a. Click the **Save As** button [*File* Tab].
    b. Select the **Save Object As** button and then click the **Save As** button.
    c. Replace the suggested name with AgentParameterPotentialCommissionByProperty and click **OK**.

19. Click the **Run** button [*Query Tools Design* tab, *Results* group].
    a. Enter Gerardo in the *Enter the Agent's First Name* box of the *Enter Parameter Value* dialog box.
    b. Click **OK**.
    c. Enter Montoya in the *Enter the Agent's Last Name* box of the *Enter Parameter Value* dialog box.
    d. Click **OK**. The query should open in *Datasheet* view and display the five records shown in Figure 3-100.

20. Close the query.

21. Close the database.

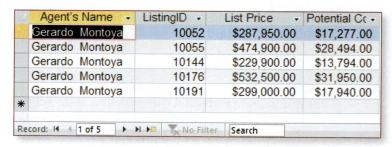

Agent's Name	ListingID	List Price	Potential C(
Gerardo Montoya	10052	$287,950.00	$17,277.00
Gerardo Montoya	10055	$474,900.00	$28,494.00
Gerardo Montoya	10144	$229,900.00	$13,794.00
Gerardo Montoya	10176	$532,500.00	$31,950.00
Gerardo Montoya	10191	$299,000.00	$17,940.00

Record: 1 of 5   No Filter   Search

3-100 Parameter query results

Independent Project 3-4

You are creating a parameter query for the music database you have worked with in previous projects. To ensure consistency, the starting file is provided for you. Use *Design* view to create the query. Edit the query to add criteria. After saving and testing the query, edit the query to add a parameter. [Student Learning Outcomes 3.2, 3.3, 3.4, 3.5, 3.6]

File Needed: *LargerMusicDatabase-03.accdb*
Completed Project File Name: *[your initials] Access 3-4.accdb*

Skills Covered in This Project

- Create a query in *Design* view.
- Edit a query in *Design* view.
- Add compound criteria to a query.
- Execute a query.
- Save a query.
- Sort query results.
- Add a parameter to a query.

1. Open the **LargerMusicDatabase-03.accdb** database file.

2. Save a new copy of your database as *[your initials] Access 3-4*.

3. If needed, enable content in the security warning.

4. Open the *Songs* table in *Datasheet* view to verify that the table contains 355 songs.

5. Close the table.

6. Create a new query in *Design* view. The query finds songs with lengths that are within a certain range.
   a. Add both tables into the *Query Design* window.
   b. Increase the size of the table objects to display all of the fields.
   c. Add the following fields into the query: **AlbumName**, **ArtistName**, **SongTitle**, and **Length**.

7. Save the query as *SongOrAlbumChoice-3To4Minutes*.

8. Edit the query to add criteria.
   a. In the *Length* field enter the following criteria: Between #0:03:00# and #0:04:00#. Due to the way Access stores times, Access changes this criteria to read: *Between #12:03:00 AM# And #12:04:00 AM#*.

9. Save the changes and **Run** the query. The datasheet should display 173 songs.

10. Change to *Design* view to edit the query and add a parameter. The parameter should allow the user to enter either the *Album Name* or the *Artist Name* to find songs.
    a. Type [Enter the Album Name] as the criterion for the *AlbumName* field.
    b. On the *Or* row, type [Enter the Artist Name] as the criterion for the *ArtistName* field.
    c. Copy the criterion in the *Length* field and paste it into the *Or* row of the *Length* field. You need the criterion to be in both the *Criteria* row and the *Or* row.

11. Sort the results to display in ascending order by song length.

12. Save the changes to the query. The completed *Design grid* should match that shown in Figure 3-101.

Field:	AlbumName	ArtistName	SongTitle	Length
Table:	Album	Album	Songs	Songs
Sort:				Ascending
Show:	☑	☑	☑	☑
Criteria:	[Enter the Album Name]			Between #12:03:00 AM# And #12:04:00 AM#
or:		[Enter the Artist Name]		Between #12:03:00 AM# And #12:04:00 AM#

3-101 *Design grid* **of query showing multiple parameters and compound criteria**

13. Run the query to verify that it works.
    a. In the **Enter the Album Name** *Enter Parameter Value* dialog box, type Keeps Gettin' Better: A Decade of Hits. Be sure to enter the parameter value exactly as written, including all punctuation and spaces, or the query will not display the correct results.
    b. In the **Enter the Artist Name** *Enter Parameter Value* dialog box, don't enter anything and click **OK**.
    c. The datasheet should show the eight (out of 16) songs from this album that meet the criteria (Figure 3-102). You can verify the song count on this album by looking in the *Songs* table for *AlbumID 14*.

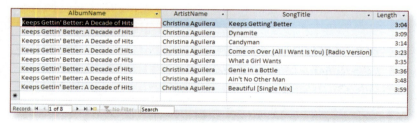

3-102 **Query results for** *Keeps Gettin' Better: A Decade of Hits*
songs between three and four minutes long

14. Switch back to *Design* view and run the query again.
    a. In the **Enter the Album Name** *Enter Parameter Value* dialog box, don't enter anything and click **OK**.
    b. In the **Enter the Artist Name** *Enter Parameter Value* dialog box, type Christina Aguilera and click **OK**.
    c. The datasheet should show the 17 (out of 28) songs from this artist that meet the criteria (Figure 3-103). You can verify the song count for this artist by looking in the *Albums* table for *Christina Aguilera* and expanding the plus symbol.

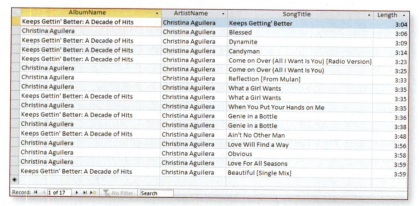

3-103 **Query results for Christina Aguilera songs between three**
and four minutes long

15. Close the query.

16. Close the database.

Independent Project 3-5

The State of New York Department of Motor Vehicles wants to create three queries. The first query provides summary data on the number of tickets by city and violation. The second query summarizes the total tickets by violation. The third query provides summary data for the total fines assessed against each driver who has had a ticket. To ensure consistency, the starting file is provided for you. Use *Design* view to create the summary queries. Edit the queries to add fields, aggregate functions, and sorting. Finally, save and run the queries.
[Student Learning Outcomes 3.2, 3.4, 3.8]

File Needed: **NewYorkDMV-03.accdb**
Completed Project File Name: **[your initials] Access 3-5.accdb**

Skills Covered in This Project

- Create a summary query in *Design* view.
- Edit a query in *Design* view.
- Add fields to a query.
- Execute a query.
- Save a query.
- Sort query results.
- Add aggregate functions.

1. Open the **NewYorkDMV-03.accdb** database file.

2. Save a new copy of your database as **[your initials] Access 3-5**.

3. If needed, enable content in the security warning.

4. Create a new summary query in *Design* view. The query counts the number of tickets issued by city and violation.
   a. Add the **Ticket** table into the *Query Design* window.
   b. Increase the size of the table object to display all of the fields.
   c. Add the following fields into the query: **City**, **PrimaryFactor**, and **TicketNumber**.
   d. Add the **Total** row to the query.
   e. **Group By** the *City* and *PrimaryFactor* fields and **Count** the *TicketNumber* field.

5. Save the query as *TicketCountByCityAndFactor*.

6. Run the query. The datasheet should display 20 records.

7. Widen the field column widths to the **Best Fit** (Figure 3-104).

8. Save the changes to the query.

9. Save a copy of the query as *TicketCountByFactor*.

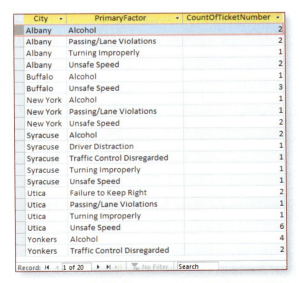

3-104 Summary query results counting tickets by city and factor

10. Edit the *TicketCountByFactor* query in *Design* view. The query should show the total tickets issued for each violation factor, sorted in descending order by count.
    a. Delete the *City* field.
    b. Sort the *TicketNumber* field in descending order.

11. Save and run the query. The datasheet should match Figure 3-105.

12. Close the query.

13. Create a new summary query in *Design* view. The query provides summary data on the total fines assessed against each driver.
    a. Add both tables into the *Query Design* window.
    b. Increase the size of the table objects to display all of the fields.
    c. Add the following fields into the query: **LicenseNumber**, **FirstName**, **LastName**, **Fine**, and **TicketNumber**.
    d. Add the **Total** row to the query.
    e. **Group By** the *LicenseNumber*, *FirstName*, and *LastName* fields, **Sum** the *Fine* field and **Count** the *TicketNumber* field.
    f. Sort the *Fine* field in descending order.

14. Save the query as *TicketsByDriver*.

15. Run the query. The datasheet should display 21 drivers who have received tickets, sorted in descending order by the total dollar amount of their fines (Figure 3-106).

16. Close the query.

17. Close the database.

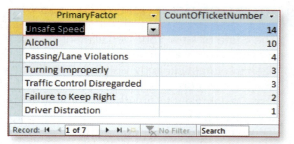

PrimaryFactor	CountOfTicketNumber
Unsafe Speed	14
Alcohol	10
Passing/Lane Violations	4
Turning Improperly	3
Traffic Control Disregarded	3
Failure to Keep Right	2
Driver Distraction	1

Record: 1 of 7   No Filter   Search

3-105 Summary query results counting tickets by factor

LicenseNum	FirstName	LastName	SumOfFine	CountOfTick
15500786	Brian	Shin	$1,010.00	4
15503625	Corey	Norman	$800.00	2
12389049	Bonnie	Hirshman	$680.00	3
39989780	Kevin	Nguyen	$535.00	3
12348279	Sharon	Altier	$510.00	3
12348692	Michael	Finch	$505.00	3
10004387	Miranda	Jones	$400.00	1
12346978	Jon	Juarez	$400.00	1
10000501	Timothy	Smith	$345.00	3
39992366	Mark	Watson	$180.00	1
12344537	Austin	Davis	$165.00	2
12346123	Claudia	Schooler	$150.00	1
18957217	Jessica	Healy	$135.00	2
15502325	Ron	Stokes	$130.00	1
12345678	Emily	Garcia	$120.00	1
10003086	Mark	Williams	$120.00	1
18955806	Nancy	Smith	$90.00	1
12388795	Caroline	Doiron	$90.00	1
12345838	Eric	Wilson	$90.00	1
10004372	Kathy	Brown	$90.00	1
10001786	Sanda	Johnson	$60.00	1

Record: 1 of 21   No Filter   Search

3-106 Summary query results of tickets by driver

Independent Project 3-6

Courtyard Medical Plaza wants to create a query to provide details about its tenants and their rental payment history. The starting database file is provided for you. Use *Design* view to create the query. Edit the query to add calculated fields. After saving and testing the query, edit the query to add a parameter.
[Student Learning Outcomes 3.2, 3.3, 3.4, 3.5, 3.6, 3.7]

File Needed: ***CourtyardMedicalPlaza-03.accdb***
Completed Project File Name: *[your initials] Access 3-6.accdb*

Skills Covered in This Project

- Create a query in *Design* view.
- Edit a query in *Design* view.
- Add compound criteria to a query.
- Execute a query.
- Save a query.
- Sort query results.
- Add a parameter to a query.

---

1. Open the **CourtyardMedicalPlaza-03.accdb** database file.

2. Save a new copy of your database as **[your initials] Access 3-6**.

3. If needed, enable content in the security warning.

4. Create a new query in *Design* view. The query should display the rental invoice history.
   a. Add both tables into the *Query Design* window.
   b. Increase the size of the table objects to display all of the fields.
   c. Add the following fields into the query: **LastName**, **InvoiceID**, **DueDate**, **DateReceived**, **AmountDue**, and **Discount**.
   d. Run the query to make sure it works. The datasheet should display 54 records.

5. Save the query as InvoiceHistory.

6. Edit the query to add calculated fields.
   a. Insert a column to the left of *InvoiceID*.
   b. In the inserted column, add a calculated field to concatenate the *FirstName* and *LastName* fields using the following formula: Doctor: [FirstName] & " " & [LastName].
   c. Don't show the *LastName* field. In the next step you will use that for query criteria.
   d. Insert a column to the left of *Discount*.
   e. In the inserted column, add a calculated field to determine the number of days early the rent was paid using the following formula: DaysPaidEarly: [DueDate] - [DateReceived].
   f. To the right of the *Discount* field enter a calculated field to determine the net amount of rent due with the following formula: NetRent: [AmountDue] - [Discount].

7. Save your changes and run the query. The datasheet should look similar to Figure 3-107 and display a total of 54 records.

Doctor ▾	InvoiceID ▾	Due Date ▾	DateReceive ▾	Amount Due ▾	DaysPaidEar ▾	Discount ▾	NetRent ▾
Robert Beyer	1	01-Apr-14	3/30/2014	$1,200.00	2	$12.00	$1,188.00
Robert Beyer	10	01-May-14	4/29/2014	$1,200.00	2	$12.00	$1,188.00
Robert Beyer	19	01-Jun-14	5/30/2014	$1,200.00	2	$12.00	$1,188.00
Robert Beyer	28	01-Jul-14	7/1/2014	$1,200.00	0		
Robert Beyer	37	01-Aug-14	8/1/2014	$1,200.00	0		
Robert Beyer	46	01-Sep-14	8/30/2014	$1,200.00	2	$12.00	$1,188.00
Elizabeth Schei	2	01-Apr-14	4/1/2014	$1,000.00	0		
Elizabeth Schei	11	01-May-14	5/1/2014	$1,000.00	0		

3-107 Query results showing concatenated and calculated fields

8. Edit the query to add parameters to search either by last name or by a date range.
   a. Type [Enter the last name or leave blank to select all doctors] as the criteria for the *LastName* field.
   b. On the *Or* row, type Between [Enter the Starting Date] And [Enter the Ending Date] as the criteria for the *DueDate* field.

9. Sort the results in ascending order by *LastName* and *DueDate*.

10. Save the query.

11. Run the query.
    a. In the **Enter the Last Name** *Enter Parameter Value* dialog box, type Flores and click **OK**.
    b. In the **Enter the Starting Date** *Enter Parameter Value* dialog box, don't enter anything and click **OK**.
    c. In the **Enter the Ending Date** *Enter Parameter Value* dialog box, don't enter anything and click **OK**.
    d. The datasheet should show the six payments received from Dr. Flores (Figure 3-108). Dr. Flores paid his rent early three months this year.

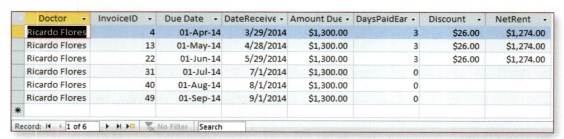

Doctor	InvoiceID	Due Date	DateReceive	Amount Due	DaysPaidEar	Discount	NetRent
Ricardo Flores	4	01-Apr-14	3/29/2014	$1,300.00	3	$26.00	$1,274.00
Ricardo Flores	13	01-May-14	4/28/2014	$1,300.00	3	$26.00	$1,274.00
Ricardo Flores	22	01-Jun-14	5/29/2014	$1,300.00	3	$26.00	$1,274.00
Ricardo Flores	31	01-Jul-14	7/1/2014	$1,300.00	0		
Ricardo Flores	40	01-Aug-14	8/1/2014	$1,300.00	0		
Ricardo Flores	49	01-Sep-14	9/1/2014	$1,300.00	0		

Record: ◄ ◄ 1 of 6 ► ►► ►▣ No Filter Search

3-108 Query results when name parameter is completed

12. Switch back to *Design* view and run the query again.
    a. In the **Enter the Last Name** *Enter Parameter Value* dialog box, don't enter anything and click **OK**.
    b. In the **Enter the Starting Date** *Enter Parameter Value* dialog box, type 6/1/2014.
    c. In the **Enter the Ending Date** *Enter Parameter Value* dialog box, type 7/1/2014.
    d. The datasheet should show the 18 invoices with a due date between 6/1/2014 and 7/1/2014 (Figure 3-109).

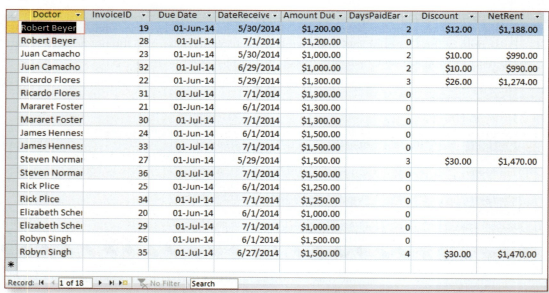

Doctor	InvoiceID	Due Date	DateReceive	Amount Due	DaysPaidEar	Discount	NetRent
Robert Beyer	19	01-Jun-14	5/30/2014	$1,200.00	2	$12.00	$1,188.00
Robert Beyer	28	01-Jul-14	7/1/2014	$1,200.00	0		
Juan Camacho	23	01-Jun-14	5/30/2014	$1,000.00	2	$10.00	$990.00
Juan Camacho	32	01-Jul-14	6/29/2014	$1,000.00	2	$10.00	$990.00
Ricardo Flores	22	01-Jun-14	5/29/2014	$1,300.00	3	$26.00	$1,274.00
Ricardo Flores	31	01-Jul-14	7/1/2014	$1,300.00	0		
Mararet Foster	21	01-Jun-14	6/1/2014	$1,300.00	0		
Mararet Foster	30	01-Jul-14	7/1/2014	$1,300.00	0		
James Henness	24	01-Jun-14	6/1/2014	$1,500.00	0		
James Henness	33	01-Jul-14	7/1/2014	$1,500.00	0		
Steven Norma	27	01-Jun-14	5/29/2014	$1,500.00	3	$30.00	$1,470.00
Steven Norma	36	01-Jul-14	7/1/2014	$1,500.00	0		
Rick Plice	25	01-Jun-14	6/1/2014	$1,250.00	0		
Rick Plice	34	01-Jul-14	7/1/2014	$1,250.00	0		
Elizabeth Sche	20	01-Jun-14	6/1/2014	$1,000.00	0		
Elizabeth Sche	29	01-Jul-14	7/1/2014	$1,000.00	0		
Robyn Singh	26	01-Jun-14	6/1/2014	$1,500.00	0		
Robyn Singh	35	01-Jul-14	6/27/2014	$1,500.00	4	$30.00	$1,470.00

Record: ◄ ◄ 1 of 18 ► ►► ►▣ No Filter Search

3-109 Query results when date parameters are completed

13. Close the query.

14. Reopen the query in *Design* view. Notice that Access has moved the *LastName* field to the right side of the *Design grid* and also entered a copy of the *DueDate* field with the *Show* row check box deselected. This is due to the way Access processes the query (Figure 3-110).

Discount	NetRent: [AmountDue	LastName	DueDate
RentInvoices		Physicians	RentInvoices
		Ascending	Ascending
☑	☑	☐	☐
		[Enter the last name]	
			Between [Enter the St

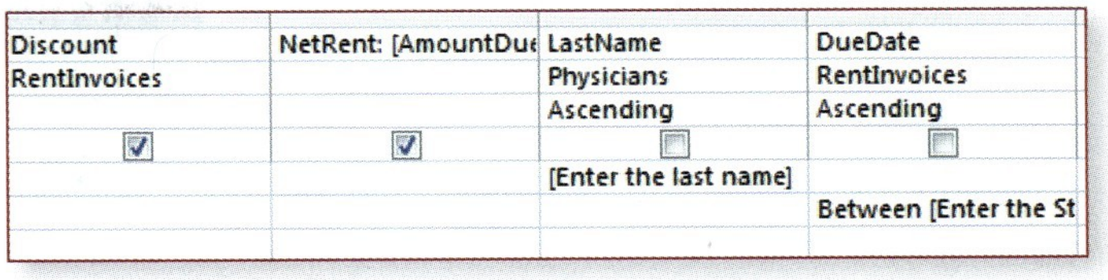

3-110 Updated *Design grid* of the query

15. Close the query.

16. Close the database.

Improve It Project 3-7

Central Sierra needs help with their database. One of the administrative assistants has created two queries to provide information about the employees. Unfortunately, the queries are not working correctly. For this project, determine why the queries don't work and make the necessary corrections. The starting file is provided for you. Use *Design* view to edit the queries. Use calculated fields, compound criteria, and parameters, and save the queries and test that they work correctly.
[Student Learning Outcomes 3.2, 3.3, 3.4, 3.5, 3.6, 3.7, 3.8]

File Needed: ***CentralSierra-03.accdb***
Completed Project File Name: ***[your initials] Access 3-7.accdb***

Skills Covered in This Project

- Edit a query in *Design* view.
- Add compound criteria to a query.
- Execute a query.
- Save a query.
- Add calculated fields to a query.
- Add a parameter to a query.

1. Open the ***CentralSierra-03.accdb*** database file.

2. Save a new copy of your database as ***[your initials] Access 3-7***.

3. Enable the contents in the security warning.

4. Run the *NewSalaryCostSummary* query. The results display in *Datasheet* view (Figure 3-111). The query is supposed to summarize results by department, and within the department by title, the total salary cost, and the total cost of potentially giving a 3% raise to all employees. You have identified several errors that need to be fixed.

First Name ▾	Last Name ▾	Title ▾	Department ▾	SumOfBas ▾	Expr1 ▾
Albert	Quiroga	Large Group Specialist	Health and Benefits	$4,500.00	4635
Bert	Pulido	Supervisor	Health and Benefits	$5,500.00	5665
Bob	Lingle	CEO	Administration	$15,000.00	15450
Charlene	Althouse	Large Group Specialist	Property and Casualty	$4,700.00	4841
Cheryl	Nevens	Chief Information Officer	Administration	$12,000.00	12360
Chris	Robles	Insurance Agent	Health and Benefits	$3,900.00	4017
Eleesha	Santos	Insurance Agent	Health and Benefits	$5,500.00	5665
Timothy	Hansen	Insurance Agent	Health and Benefits	$3,900.00	4017
Todd	DeRenzis	Administrative Assistant	Insurance Sales	$2,800.00	2884
Wayne	Reza	Insurance Agent	Health and Benefits	$4,000.00	4120

Record: I◄ ◄ 1 of 28 ► ►I ►□ 🍷 No Filter Search

3-111 *NewSalaryCostSummary* **query results**

5. Edit the query to remove the unneeded columns that cause the summary query to display too many records.
   a. Delete the *FirstName* column.
   b. Delete the *LastName* column.
   c. Save and run the query to test the results. The datasheet should now show only 14 records.

6. Edit the query to fix the calculated field name and formatting.
   a. Change the default field name of *Expr1* to SumOfPotentialNewSalary.
   b. Open the *Property Sheet* for this field and change the *Format* property to Currency.
   c. Close the *Property Sheet*.
   d. Save and run the query to test the results. The datasheet should show the improved calculated field (Figure 3-112).

Title ▾	Department ▾	SumOfBas ▾	SumOfPot ▾
Administrative Assistant	Administration	$3,000.00	$3,090.00
Administrative Assistant	Health and Benefits	$5,750.00	$5,922.50
Administrative Assistant	Insurance Sales	$5,400.00	$5,562.00
CEO	Administration	$15,000.00	$15,450.00
Chief Information Officer	Administration	$12,000.00	$12,360.00

3-112 **Query results with improvements to calculated field and removal of name fields**

7. Edit the query to fix the grouping order. The results are supposed to display the records grouped by the department, and then within each department by the job titles.
   a. Move the *Department* field to the left of the *Title* field.
   b. Save and run the query to test the results. The datasheet should show the records with the correct grouping (Figure 3-113).

Department ▾	Title ▾	SumOfBas ▾	SumOfPot ▾
Administration	Administrative Assistant	$3,000.00	$3,090.00
Administration	CEO	$15,000.00	$15,450.00
Administration	Chief Information Officer	$12,000.00	$12,360.00
Administration	Chief Operating Office	$12,000.00	$12,360.00
Administration	Executive Assistant	$3,750.00	$3,862.50
Health and Benefits	Administrative Assistant	$5,750.00	$5,922.50
Health and Benefits	Insurance Agent	$28,900.00	$29,767.00

3-113 **Query results with improved grouping**

8. Edit the query to enhance the functionality and improve the appearance. In addition to calculating the sum of both the *Base Salary* and the *Potential New Salary* fields, management would like to see the average of both of those fields, as well as the total number of employees in each area.
   a. Insert a new column to the left of the *BaseMonthlySalary* column.
   b. Click the **drop-down arrow** in the *Field* row of the inserted column and select the **EmpID** field. Set this field to use the **Count** aggregate function.

c. In the first empty column, click the **drop-down arrow** in the *Field* row and select the **BaseMonthlySalary** field. *BaseMonthlySalary* will be in the *Design grid* twice. Set this field to use the **Avg** aggregate function.

d. In the first empty column, type the following formula: AvgOfPotentialNewSalary: Avg([BaseMonthly Salary]*1.03). Set the *Total* row cell for this field to **Expression**.

e. Format this field to use **Currency**.

f. Save and run the query to test the results. The datasheet should now match that shown in Figure 3-114. Adjust the column widths as necessary to improve the appearance.

NewSalaryCostSummary

Department	Title	CountOfEn	SumOfBas	SumOfPot	AvgOfBase	AvgofPotel
Administration	Administrative Assistant	1	$3,000.00	$3,090.00	$3,000.00	$3,090.00
Administration	CEO	1	$15,000.00	$15,450.00	$15,000.00	$15,450.00
Administration	Chief Information Officer	1	$12,000.00	$12,360.00	$12,000.00	$12,360.00
Administration	Chief Operating Office	1	$12,000.00	$12,360.00	$12,000.00	$12,360.00
Administration	Executive Assistant	1	$3,750.00	$3,862.50	$3,750.00	$3,862.50
Health and Benefits	Administrative Assistant	2	$5,750.00	$5,922.50	$2,875.00	$2,961.25
Health and Benefits	Insurance Agent	7	$28,900.00	$29,767.00	$4,128.57	$4,252.43
Health and Benefits	Large Group Specialist	3	$13,500.00	$13,905.00	$4,500.00	$4,635.00
Health and Benefits	Supervisor	1	$5,500.00	$5,665.00	$5,500.00	$5,665.00
Insurance Sales	Administrative Assistant	2	$5,400.00	$5,562.00	$2,700.00	$2,781.00
Insurance Sales	Insurance Agent	1	$4,000.00	$4,120.00	$4,000.00	$4,120.00
Property and Casualty	Insurance Agent	5	$19,900.00	$20,497.00	$3,980.00	$4,099.40
Property and Casualty	Large Group Specialist	1	$4,700.00	$4,841.00	$4,700.00	$4,841.00
Property and Casualty	Supervisor	1	$5,000.00	$5,150.00	$5,000.00	$5,150.00

Record: 1 of 14 • No Filter • Search

3-114 Completed NewSalaryCostSummary query results

9. Save any changes and close the query.

10. Run the *InsuranceAgentsBranchParameter* query. Enter Folsom in the *Enter Parameter Value* dialog box. The results display in datasheet view (Figure 3-115). The query is supposed to list the insurance agents in a particular branch or show all the insurance agents if the branch prompt is left blank. You have identified several errors that need to be fixed, including that all the insurance agents displayed even though you entered a branch.

11. Edit the query to fix the parameter problem.

a. Notice that the branch parameter is actually on the *Department* field and not the *Branch* field.

b. Change that column to contain the *Branch* field.

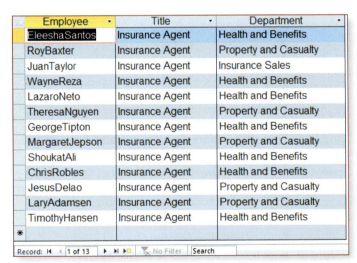

Employee	Title	Department
EleeshaSantos	Insurance Agent	Health and Benefits
RoyBaxter	Insurance Agent	Property and Casualty
JuanTaylor	Insurance Agent	Insurance Sales
WayneReza	Insurance Agent	Health and Benefits
LazaroNeto	Insurance Agent	Health and Benefits
TheresaNguyen	Insurance Agent	Property and Casualty
GeorgeTipton	Insurance Agent	Health and Benefits
MargaretJepson	Insurance Agent	Property and Casualty
ShoukatAli	Insurance Agent	Health and Benefits
ChrisRobles	Insurance Agent	Health and Benefits
JesusDelao	Insurance Agent	Property and Casualty
LaryAdamsen	Insurance Agent	Property and Casualty
TimothyHansen	Insurance Agent	Health and Benefits

Record: 1 of 13 • No Filter • Search

3-115 *InsuranceAgentsBranchParameter* query results are not correct

c. Run the query again and enter Folsom. The results now display the branch, but you still have employees from all the branches.

d. Switch to *Design* view to review the criteria. The *Branch* parameter is on the "or" row. It needs to be on the same row as "Insurance Agent".

e. Move the parameter to the criteria row to fix that problem.

f. Review the parameter. It isn't designed correctly, because it won't allow the field to be left blank and show all the insurance agents.

g. Edit the parameter as follows: Like "*" & [Enter the Branch or Leave blank to select all branches] & "*".

h. Save and run the query. Type Folsom. Only the four agents at the Folsom branch should display.

i. Run the query again and leave the dialog box empty. All 13 agents should display.

12. Edit the query to fix the *Employee* field. Notice that there isn't a space between the names.

a. Edit the formula in the *Employee* field as follows: Employee: [FirstName] & " " & [LastName].

b. Save and run the query. Enter Granite Bay. The results should match Figure 3-116 and show only the four insurance agents at the Granite Bay branch.

Employee	Title	Branch
Roy Baxter	Insurance Agent	Granite Bay
Juan Taylor	Insurance Agent	Granite Bay
Lazaro Neto	Insurance Agent	Granite Bay
Theresa Nguyen	Insurance Agent	Granite Bay
*		

Record: ◄ ◄ 1 of 4 ► ►► ►► No Filter Search

3-116 Completed *InsuranceAgentsBranchParameter* query

13. Close the query.

14. Close the database.

Challenge Project 3-8

For this project you modify the database you built in Challenge Project 2-8. Add additional data and create two queries.
[Student Learning Outcomes 3.1, 3.2, 3.3, 3.4, 3.5]

File Needed: ***[your initials] Access 2-8.accdb***
Completed Project File Name: ***[your initials] Access 3-8.accdb***

Open the database ***[your initials] Access 2-8*** and save a copy of it as ***[your initials] Access 3-8***. Modify your database according to the following instructions:

- Add at least 20 rows of additional data into the table.
- Create a query with the *Simple Query Wizard*.
- Add at least three of the fields into the query.
- Edit the query in *Design* view and enter a criterion onto one of the fields.
- Apply sorting to one of the fields.
- Save and run the query.
- Create a second query in *Design* view.

- Add all of the fields into a query.
- Add compound criteria to the query using an *OR* condition on one of the fields combined with an *AND* condition on at least one other field.
- Save and run the query.
- Adjust the width of the columns in the query so that they are sized appropriately.
- Save any changes that you made.

Challenge Project 3-9

Modify the database you created in Challenge Project 2-9 for Blue Lake Sports. Your database contains a table with information about the different departments at Blue Lake Sports and a related table with information about Interns who are working at Blue Lake. Add additional data and create one query.
[Student Learning Outcomes 3.2, 3.3, 3.4, 3.5, 3.6, 3.7]

File Needed: *[your initials] Access 2-9.accdb*
Completed Project File Name: *[your initials] Access 3-9.accdb*

Open the database *[your initials] Access 2-9* and save a copy of it as *[your initials] Access 3-9*. Modify your database according to the following instructions:

- If necessary, add additional data into the *Department* table so that you have at least 10 different departments.
- If necessary, add additional data into the *Intern* table so that there are at least 30 interns. When entering the value for the *DepartmentName* foreign key, don't assign all of the interns to the same department.
- Create a query with *Design* view.
- Add both tables into the query.
- Add the *DepartmentName* and *Division* fields (from the *Department* table).
- Add a calculated field to concatentate the intern's *FirstName* and *LastName* fields.
- Save and run the query.
- Edit the query to add a parameter. The parameter should allow the user to enter the division he or she wishes to query. Write this parameter using wildcards so that if the user leaves the *Enter Parameter Value* dialog box empty, the query returns all the records. You may want to review the *Use Wildcards in a Parameter Query* section in *SLO 3.6: Creating and Using a Simple Parameter Query* for help with this task.
- Save and run the query.
- Verify that the query works correctly when the user enters a specific division and that it returns all the records if the dialog box is left blank.
- Adjust the width of the columns in the query so that they are sized appropriately.
- Save any changes that you made.

Challenge Project 3-10

Modify the database you created in Challenge Project 2-10 for a travel agency. Your database contains a table with information about the different ships and a related table with information about upcoming cruises. Add additional data and create two queries.
[Student Learning Outcomes 3.2, 3.3, 3.4, 3.5, 3.6, 3.7, 3.8]

File Needed: *[your initials] Access 2-10.accdb*
Completed Project File Name: *[your initials] Access 3-10.accdb*

Open the database *[your initials] Access 2-10* and save a copy of it as *[your initials] Access 3-10*. Modify your database according to the following instructions:

- Add at least 10 rows of additional data into the *Trips* table. When entering the value for the *ShipID* foreign key, don't assign all of the trips to the same ship.
- Create a query with *Design* view.
- Add both tables into the query.
- Add the *ShipName, CruiseLineName,* and *NumberOfPassengers* fields (from the *Ships* table) and the *TripName* and *CostPerPerson* fields (from the *Trips* table).
- Add a field to calculate the potential revenue for each trip. The *Potential Revenue* is the *Cost PerPerson* times the *Number of Passengers.*
- Sort the results in ascending order by the potential revenue.
- Save and run the query.
- Adjust the width of the columns in the query so that they are sized appropriately.
- Save any changes that you made.
- Create a *Summary* query in *Design* view to count how many trips each Cruise Line has scheduled.
- Add both tables into the query.
- Add the *TripID* field and the *CruiseLineName* field into the query.
- Add the *Total row.*
- Count by the *TripID* field.
- Save and run the query.
- Adjust the width of the columns in the query so that they are sized appropriately.
- Save any changes that you made.

CHAPTER

4

Creating and Using Forms and Reports

CHAPTER OVERVIEW

Forms and reports enhance the usability of your Access database. Forms provide a user-friendly interface to view, add, update, and delete data in a database. Reports offer a professional way to view and print data, making it easier for your user to understand information in your database. This chapter introduces the Access tools that allow you to create and customize forms and reports.

STUDENT LEARNING OUTCOMES (SLOs)

After completing this chapter, you will be able to:

SLO 4.1 Create a simple form using quick create options; save, modify, and delete a form (p. A4-214).

SLO 4.2 Create a blank form, understand controls and control layouts, and customize a form in *Layout* view (p. A4-222).

SLO 4.3 Restrict a form to data entry, limit user edits and deletes on a form, add command buttons, and test a form (p. A4-228).

SLO 4.4 Create a simple report with the *Report Wizard*; save, modify, and delete a report (p. A4-235).

SLO 4.5 Create a blank report, understand controls and control layouts, customize a report in *Layout* view, and add a title, a date, and page numbers to a report (p. A4-242).

SLO 4.6 Enhance a report by adding grouping, sorting, and totals to a report in *Layout* view (p. A4-250).

SLO 4.7 Integrate conditional formatting into a report (p. A4-253).

SLO 4.8 Preview, modify print settings, and print a report (p. A4-256).

CASE STUDY

For the Pause & Practice projects in this chapter you develop forms and reports for several different databases. As you progress through the Pause & Practice projects in this chapter, you incorporate many of the features you learn in this chapter to build forms and reports and to display, add, edit, and delete data in a database.

Pause & Practice 4-1: Create and view forms using the *Form Wizard*, the *Form* button, and the *Split Form* button.

Pause & Practice 4-2: Create a form using the *Blank Form* button. Modify the form to restrict it to data entry, add buttons, and test the form.

Pause & Practice 4-3: Create and view a report using the *Report Wizard*. Create a report using the Blank *Report* button. Modify the report to improve its layout.

Pause & Practice 4-4: Create and preview a report with grouping and conditional formatting.

ACCESS

A4-213

Creating a Simple Form from a Table

A **form** is an object you can use to create an interface to easily view, add, update, and delete data in a database. Most forms in a database are directly connected to a table or query, the source of the data. Access calls these **bound forms** because of the link with the data source. **Unbound forms**, forms that don't have a connection to a data source, can be used to help operate the database. For example, a database may have an unbound form that contains no data but has buttons that perform different actions in the database like printing reports or opening forms. In this chapter, you learn how to create forms that are bound to a table.

Forms provide flexible access to data in a database. You can create a form with fields from one or more tables or queries. The form may also contain only a subset of the fields from the table. You also can choose to display only one record at a time or multiple records. This flexibility helps you create forms that look attractive and are more user-friendly than *Datasheet* view of a table. Ideally, a well-designed form makes it easier for your user to work with the database and prevents mistakes in adding, updating, or deleting data.

Access offers three view choices for most forms. Use **Form** view to enter and view data. **Design** view allows you to make changes to the form. **Layout** view allows you to alter the design of a form and see the effects of the changes in real time. However, not all design changes can be made in *Layout* view. Forms created with a *Datasheet* layout also have a **Datasheet** view option.

There are several different ways to create a form. These options are available in the *Forms* group [*Create* tab] (Figure 4-1). Some of the options are quick, while others take a little more effort but provide a greater deal of flexibility and allow you to create more specialized types of forms. In this section, you are introduced to three quick ways to build a form: the *Form Wizard*, the *Form*, and the *Split Form* options.

Form button — *Form Wizard* button

Form | Form Design | Blank Form | Form Wizard | Navigation | More Forms

Split Form button is available in *More Forms*

4-1 Form creation options

The Form Wizard

The **Form Wizard** steps you through the process of quickly creating a form. When you build a bound form you must tell Access where to find the data. Use the *Form Wizard* to select the specific table(s) and queries along with the specific fields to include in the form. You can also select the layout for the form. After you create the form, you can use the form to view data in your database. If you need to change the form once it has been created, edit it using *Layout* view or *Design* view.

When you use the *Form Wizard* to create a form based on one table, you can select from four different layout options.

- **Columnar:** The form displays the fields in one column (Figure 4-2). The field names are displayed to the left of the field and the name of the form is displayed in a header

Listings - Columnar Layout

ListingID	10022
Date Listed	4/24/2014
List Price	$337,600.00
Address	525 Riverdale
City	Lincoln
SqFt	2755
Beds	3
Baths	2
Garage	2 Car Detached
Built	2001
Construction	Frame
Agent	103

Record: 1 of 55 No Filter Search

4-2 Columnar form layout

section at the top of the form. A columnar layout shows only one record at a time. You use the *Navigation* buttons to move from one record to another.

- **Tabular:** The form displays the fields in a table (row and column) format (Figure 4-3). The header section at the top of the form displays the name of the form and the field names as column heads.

4-3 Tabular form layout

- **Datasheet:** The form displays in the Access *Datasheet* layout (Figure 4-4). The field names are the column heads.

4-4 Datasheet form layout

- **Justified:** The form displays the fields in a horizontal, justified layout (Figure 4-5). The field names are above each field. The form name displays in a header section. Only one record displays at a time.

4-5 Justified form layout

HOW TO: Create a Form Using the Form Wizard

1. Click the **Create** tab on the *Ribbon*.
2. Click the **Form Wizard** button [*Forms* group] to launch the *Form Wizard* (Figure 4-6).
   - The values displayed in the *Tables/Queries* box and the *Available Fields* window are based on the contents of your database.
3. Click the **Tables/Queries** drop-down arrow and select the **Table** or **Query** name.
4. Select a **Field** to include in the form from the *Available Fields* window.
   - Add fields in the order you want them to display in the form.
5. Click the **Move Single Field** button.
   - The field moves into the *Selected Fields* window (Figure 4-7).
   - The *Remove Single Field* and *Remove All Fields* buttons become active.

4-6 Form Wizard – step 1

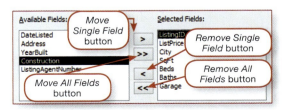

4-7 Move fields into the Selected Fields window

6. Continue moving all required fields, changing the selected *Table* or *Query* if needed.

> **ANOTHER WAY**
> Use the **Move All Fields** button (Figure 4-7) to quickly include all of the fields in the form.

7. Click the **Next** button when you are finished adding all fields. The second page of the *Form Wizard* displays (Figure 4-8).

8. Select the radio button of the form layout that you want.

9. Click the **Next** button. The last page of the *Form Wizard* displays (Figure 4-9).

10. Change the form **Title** as desired. The suggested title is the name of the table or query used to create the form. The title will also be used as the *Form Name*.

11. Click **Finish** to open the form to view the data.

   - Access automatically saves the form.
   - The form shows in *Form* view (Figure 4-10).
   - Most of the fields appear in text boxes.
   - Fields that have a lookup appear in combo boxes.
   - Fields that are a *Yes/No* data type appear as check boxes.
   - The size of a field depends on the data type and the field size.
   - The first record in the table displays.
   - The form name displays in the *Forms* group on the *Navigation* pane.

4-8 Select the form layout

4-9 Enter the form title in the last step of the *Form Wizard*

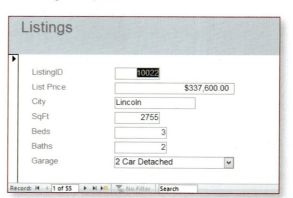

4-10 *Form* view of the completed form

12. Close the form.

The Form Button

The *Form* button is the quickest way to create a form; however, it does not give you any options during the initial creation process. After you have created the form, you can edit the form in *Layout* view or *Design* view.

HOW TO: Create a New Form Using the Form Option

1. In the *Navigation* pane, click to select the **Table** or **Query** on which to base the form.

2. Click the **Form** button [*Create* tab, *Forms* group].

3. Access creates the form and assigns the form object the same name as the table object.

4. The form opens in *Layout* view (Figure 4-11).
   - *Layout* view lets you make changes to the design of the form and, at the same time, see how the form looks with data displaying. The yellow selector border around a text box is an indicator that you are in *Layout* view.
   - The fields are placed on the form based on the order they are listed in the table.
   - Most of the fields appear in text boxes.
   - Fields that have a lookup appear in combo boxes.
   - Fields that are a *Yes/No* data type appear as check boxes.
   - All fields are assigned the same width. The height of the text boxes may be taller for fields that have a large size. The dashed border surrounding all of the fields indicates that they are grouped together to maintain uniform structure.
   - The first record in the table displays.

4-11 *Layout* **view of a form created with the** *Form* **button**

> **MORE INFO**
>
> The layout of the fields depends on the number of fields in the table and the size of the Access window when the form is created. A layout like the one shown in Figure 4-12 results if you have a smaller Access window before you click the *Form* button.

4-12 A smaller Access window results in a different field layout

The Split Form Button

A split form allows you to view data in two different ways at the same time; the top section of the form displays one record in a columnar mode while the bottom section displays a *Datasheet* view. The two sections are synchronized so when you navigate to a record in the top section, that record also displays in the lower section. This type of form allows you to see many records at once in the *Datasheet* view while giving you access to edit a single record. After you create a split form, you can use *Layout* view or *Design* view to edit it.

HOW TO: Create a Split Form Using a Single Table

1. In the *Navigation* pane, click to select the **Table** on which to base the form.

2. Click the **More Forms** button [*Create* tab, *Forms* group].

3. Select the **Split Form** option (Figure 4-13).
   - The form opens in *Layout* view (Figure 4-14).

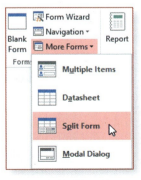

4-13 *More Forms* **button options**

4-14 Split form in *Layout* **view**

Modify a Form

After you create a form using one of the three quick methods just described, you may want to make some modifications to the form. You can modify a form using either *Design* view or *Layout* view.

Design view shows you the completed structure of the form (Figure 4-15) so you can modify any aspect of a form. *Design* view has a distinctive look, but you can also tell you are in *Design* view from the *Status bar* at the bottom of the Access window. You can modify the header, detail, and footer sections of the form. *Design* view is good for adding labels and images into a form, editing text boxes, resizing the form sections, and changing some form properties. In *Design* view, the different editing choices are organized into three **Form Design Tools** contextual tabs: **Design**, **Arrange**, and **Format**.

Layout view allows you to make changes to the design of a form while seeing how the form looks with data displaying. The *Layout* view of the form in Figure 4-15 is shown in Figure 4-16. *Layout* view looks very similar to *Form* view, but you can tell what view you are in from the *Status bar* at the bottom of the Access window. While you can use the navigation buttons to move among different records, other parts of the form are not functional in *Layout* view. For example, the *Close Form* button does not work in *Layout* view.

Since you are able to see how the data displays while modifying the design, *Layout* view is good for resizing the fields or labels, changing colors or text alignment, or applying different formats. In *Layout* view the different editing choices are organized into the same three *Form Design Tools* contextual tabs: *Design*, *Arrange*, and *Format*. However, not all editing options are available while in *Layout* view.

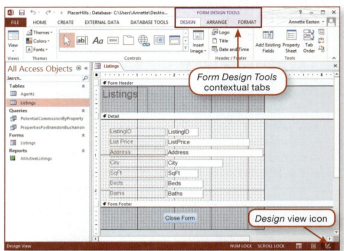

4-15 *Design* view of a form

4-16 *Layout* view of a form

HOW TO: Switch Views to Modify a Form

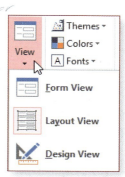

1. Click the **View** button arrow [*Home* tab].
2. Select either the **Layout** view or **Design** view option (Figure 4-17).
3. Make any desired modifications.

> ▶ **ANOTHER WAY**
>
> Select the **Layout View** or **Design View** icons from the lower right corner of the *Status bar*.

4-17 *View* options for a form

Save a Form

When you create a form using one of the three quick methods described in this section, Access automatically saves the form during the creation process. If you have made any modifications to the design of the form you need to save those changes. Save changes to a form by pressing the **Ctrl+S** keys or the **Save** icon on the *Quick Access* toolbar.

HOW TO: Save a Copy of a Form

1. Click **Save As** [*File*] tab to display the *Save As* area.
2. Click **Save Object As** in the *File Types* options. *Save Object As* should be selected in the *Database File Types* options.
3. Click the **Save As** button to open the *Save As* dialog box (Figure 4-18).
   - The name of the current object displays in the *Save "object name" to* box.
   - In Figure 4-18, "Listings" is the name of the current object.
   - The suggested name always begins with "Copy of."
4. Type the name you wish to use in the *Save "object name" to* box.
5. Click the **OK** button.

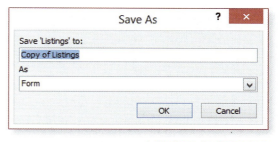

4-18 *Save As* dialog box

> ▶ **ANOTHER WAY**
>
> Press the **F12** function key to open the *Save As* dialog box.

Once a form has been saved, it displays in the *Forms* group of the *Navigation* pane (Figure 4-19). As you add more objects into your database, the number of objects displayed in the *Navigation* pane increases. This is one of the reasons why it is important to use object names that effectively and immediately convey the meaning or purpose of the object.

Forms group in *Navigation* pane

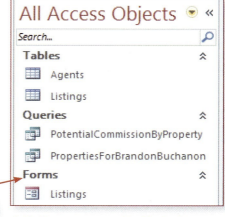

4-19 *Forms* group on the *Navigation* pane

Open a Saved Form

If you double-click a form name in the *Navigation* pane, the form opens in *Form* view. If the form was created using a *Datasheet* layout, it opens in *Datasheet* view.

Open a saved form in *Design* view or *Layout* view by right-clicking the form name in the *Navigation* pane and selecting **Design View** or **Layout View** from the context menu (Figure 4-20).

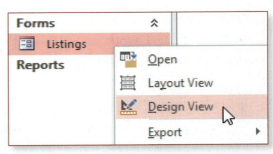

4-20 Context menu of a form

Delete a Form

Occasionally you have forms that you no longer need or want in the database. Delete a form by selecting the form name in the *Navigation* pane and clicking the **Delete** button [*Home* tab, *Records* group].

> **ANOTHER WAY**
>
> Right-click the form name in the *Navigation* pane and select **Delete** from the context menu.

PAUSE & PRACTICE: ACCESS 4-1

For this Pause & Practice you create three versions of a form using three quick creation methods. You create a form using the *Form Wizard*, the *Form* button, and the *Split Form* button.

File Needed: **PlacerHills-04.accdb**
Completed Project File Name: **[your initials] PP A4-1.accdb**

1. Open the **PlacerHills-04.accdb** database file.

2. Save the database as **[your initials] PP A4-1**.

3. If prompted, enable content in the database.

4. Create a form using the *Form Wizard*.
   a. Click the **Create** tab on the *Ribbon*.
   b. Click the **Form Wizard** button in the *Forms* group to launch the *Form Wizard*.
   c. Click the **Tables/Queries** drop-down arrow and select the **Listings** table.
   d. Click the **Move All Fields** button to move all of the fields from the *Available Fields* window to the *Selected Fields* window (Figure 4-21).
   e. Click the **Next** button to move to the second page of the *Form Wizard*.
   f. Select the **Columnar** radio button.

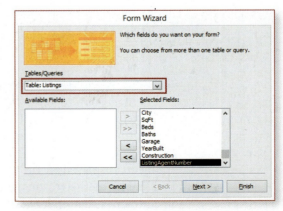

4-21 Move desired fields into the *Selected Fields* window

g. Click the **Next** button to move to the last page of the *Form Wizard*.

h. Type Listings – Form Wizard in the *Title* box.

i. Click the **Finish** button. The form opens in *Form* view (Figure 4-22).

j. Use the navigation buttons to move among records.

k. Close the form.

5. Create a form using the *Form* button.

a. In the *Navigation* pane, select the **Listings** table.

b. Click the **Form** button [*Create* tab, *Forms* group] to create the form shown in Figure 4-23. The form opens in *Layout* view. Your layout may be different depending on the size of the Access window when you created the form.

c. Click in the **Listings** label in the *Header* section. Edit the label to read Listings – Form Button.

d. Save the form. Enter Listings – Form Button as the *Form Name*.

e. Switch to *Form* view by clicking the **View** button arrow [*Form Layout Tools Design* tab, *Views* group] and selecting the **Form View** option.

f. Use the navigation buttons to move among records.

g. Close the form.

6. Create a form using the *Split Form* button.

a. In the *Navigation* pane, click to select the **Listings** table.

b. Click the **More Forms** button [*Create* tab, *Forms* group].

c. Select the *Split Form* option to create the form shown in Figure 4-24. The form opens in *Layout* view.

d. Click in the **Listings** label in the *Header* section. Edit the label to read Listings – Split Form Button.

e. Save the form. Enter Listings – Split Form Button as the *Form Name*.

f. Switch to *Form* view by clicking the **View** button arrow [*Form Layout Tools Design* tab, *Views* group] and selecting the **Form View** option.

g. Use the navigation buttons to move among records.

h. Close the form.

7. Close the database.

4-22 *Listings* form created using the *Form Wizard*

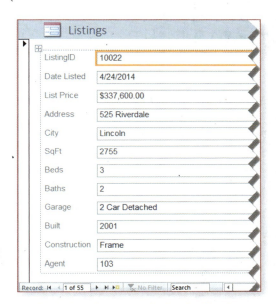

4-23 *Listings* form created using the *Form* button

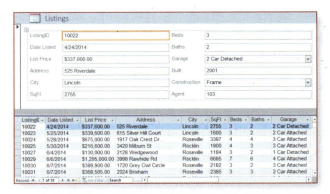

4-24 *Listings* form created using the *Split Form* option

Creating and Customizing a Form in Layout View

As you have learned, *Layout* view provides an easy way to modify a form while seeing how the form looks with data displaying. The functions of the form do not work in *Layout* view. However, you can use the navigation buttons to move among different records. In this section, you first learn how to create a blank form. After that, you explore the layout of a form and learn how to make modifications using *Layout* view.

Create a Form Using the Blank Form Button

Sometimes it is easier to start with a completely blank form and add the fields, labels, or buttons that you need directly onto the form.

HOW TO: Create a Blank Form

1. Click the **Blank Form** button [*Create* tab, *Forms* group].
2. A new blank form opens in *Layout* view (Figure 4-25a).
   - The *Field List* pane displays. The *Field List* contains the list of the tables in your database.
   - Click the **Show all tables** link to display the database tables.
   - Click the **plus sign** to expand any of the tables to see the fields in the table (Figure 4-25b).

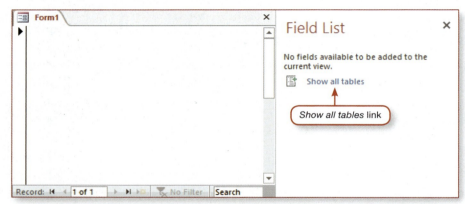

4-25a **Blank form in *Layout* view**

4-25b **Expanded *Field List***

After you create the blank form, you are ready to start adding items onto the form. Remember to save the form and any changes you make to it.

Controls

In Access, the fields, labels, buttons, and so forth are all known as *controls*. You can add controls to a form in either *Layout* view or *Design* view.

The controls are located in the *Controls* group of the *Form Layout Tools Design* tab. The controls available in *Layout* view are shown in Figure 4-26.

4-26 *Controls* group for a form

Some controls are ***bound*** to a data source, like a text box that gets its value from a field in a table. Some controls are ***unbound***, which means that they are not linked to a data source. For example, a label on a form that contains a form title is an unbound control. Finally, some controls are ***calculated***. For example, a text box that gets its value from an expression is a calculated control. The most common controls and their usage are described in the following table.

Common Form Controls

Control	Explanation
Text Box	Used to display data on a form or to accept data from a user when entering a value.
Label	Displays the content contained in its caption property. Does not accept any input from the user. You can edit the wording in a label on the form.
Button	Used to add a command button that performs an action such as *Close Form*, *Open Form*, *Delete Record*, etc.
Check Box	Used to display or accept data for a field with a *Yes/No* data type.

As you read this book you will learn more about these controls and how they are used in a database.

Control Layouts

Control layouts provide a structure that helps to align the different controls on your form. This gives your form a more uniform appearance. Forms are not required to include a control layout, although some of the form creation methods place all fields in a control layout by default. The two primary control layout options are tabular and stacked.

- A ***tabular layout*** organizes data in rows and columns. Labels identifying the different fields are above the data values. Figure 4-27 shows a tabular layout in *Layout* view. The tabular layout starts with each field having a fairly large column width. This can make it difficult to see all the fields on the screen at one time.

4-27 Tabular control layout

- A ***stacked layout*** organizes data vertically. The labels are to the left of the data control. Figure 4-28 shows a stacked layout in *Layout* view.

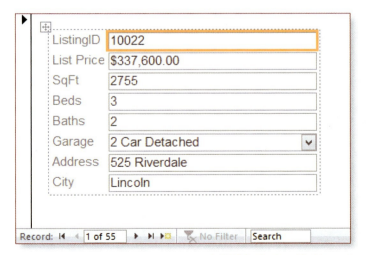

4-28 Stacked control layout

Add Fields to a Control Layout

When a new blank form is created, there are no controls initially placed on the form. You can add any desired table fields to the form in *Layout* view.

HOW TO: Add Fields into the Control Layout of a Blank Form

1. Open the form in *Layout* view.
2. If the *Field List* is not open, click the **Add Existing Fields** button [*Form Layout Tools Design* tab, *Tools* group] (Figure 4-29).

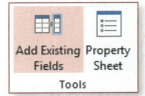

4-29 *Add Existing Fields* button

> **ANOTHER WAY**
>
> Press the **Alt+F8** keys to show or hide the *Field List*.

3. If the database tables do not show, click the **Show all tables** link to display the database tables.
4. Click the **plus sign** next to the desired table name to display the fields.
5. Double-click the desired field name.
   - The field is added into a stacked layout (Figure 4-30).
   - The most recently added field is highlighted with an orange border.
   - The next field added to the form appears below the orange-bordered field.
6. Continue adding the remaining fields.

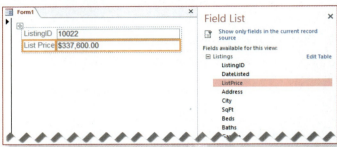

4-30 Add fields into a stacked layout of a blank form

> **ANOTHER WAY**
>
> Click and drag a field from the *Field List* into the form window to add it into the control layout.

HOW TO: Add Fields between Existing Fields in a Control Layout

1. Open the form in *Layout* view.
2. If the *Field List* is not open, click the **Add Existing Fields** button [*Form Layout Tools Design* tab, *Tools* group] or press the **Alt+F8** keys.
3. Click the **plus sign** next to the desired table name to display the fields.
4. Select the desired field name to add to the form. The field is highlighted in rose.
5. Drag the field to the desired location in the control layout. A rose-colored line indicates the position of the new field (Figure 4-31).
6. Release the pointer to add the field.

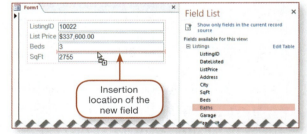

4-31 Drag a field to the desired location

Delete Fields from a Control Layout

If you use the *Form* tool, all table fields are automatically added to the control layout of the form. However, you may not want to keep all of the fields on the form. The text box and the label are two separate controls associated with a field. If you select and delete the text box, the label is automatically deleted. However, if you only select and delete the label, the text box control remains on the form. Additionally, deleting a control does not automatically delete the row or column that contains the control.

HOW TO: Delete a Field from a Control Layout

1. Open the form in *Layout* view.
2. Select the **text box control** of the field to delete.
3. If you wish to delete the text box and the row or column containing the text box, select the row or the column.
   - In a stacked layout, click the **Select Row** button [*Form Layout Tools Arrange* tab, *Rows & Columns* group].
   - In a tabular layout, click the **Select Column** button [*Form Layout Tools Arrange* tab, *Rows & Columns* group].
4. Right-click to open the context menu.
5. Select the desired **Delete** option (Figure 4-32).

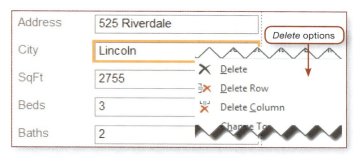

4-32 Context menu to delete a field

Customize a Form in Layout View

There are many ways to modify a form in *Layout* view. In this section, you learn how to change control layouts, adjust column widths, add and delete rows and columns in a control layout, and add a title and date to a form.

These options are available through the buttons in the *Table* and *Rows & Columns* groups on the *Form Layout Tools Arrange* tab (Figure 4-33).

4-33 Customize a form layout using options in the *Table* and *Rows & Columns* groups

Change Control Layouts

When you create a form using one of the quick create options, the form starts with either a stacked or tabular layout. As you add and delete fields on the form, you may wish to change its layout.

HOW TO: Change Control Layouts

1. Open the form in *Layout* view.
2. Click the **Arrange** tab.
3. Select one of the fields in the control layout.
   - The orange border surrounds the selected field.
4. Click the **Select Layout** button [*Form Layout Tools Arrange* tab, *Rows & Columns* group].
   - The orange border surrounds all of the controls in the layout.
5. Select either the **Stacked** or **Tabular** button [*Form Layout Tools Arrange* tab, *Table* group].
   - The form updates to show the new layout.

Adjust Column Widths

Often, the initial width of the form fields is much larger than needed. Keep in mind that in a stacked layout, all of the fields have the same width. That means that when you change the width you need to ensure that the column is wide enough to fit the largest field.

HOW TO: Change Field Column Widths

1. Open the form in *Layout* view.
2. Select the **text box control** of the desired field in the control layout.
   - The orange border surrounds the selected field.
3. Put your pointer over the right edge of the text box until it changes to a two-arrow sizing pointer.
4. Click, hold, and drag the pointer to increase or decrease the width of the text box.
   - In a stacked layout, all fields change together to maintain the same width (Figure 4-34).
   - In a tabular layout, you can set the width of each field individually (Figure 4-35).
5. The field(s) updates to show the new width.

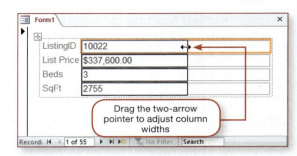

4-34 Adjust the width of all fields in a stacked layout

4-35 Adjust the width of a single field in a tabular layout

Add and Delete Rows and Columns in a Control Layout

Often you want to make minor modifications to the control layout. For example, you may want to create a second column in a stacked layout, or you may want to delete a row if you removed fields from the control layout.

HOW TO: Add a Column to a Control Layout

1. Open the form in *Layout* view.
2. Click the **Arrange** tab.
3. Select a control in the column adjacent to the place where you want to add a new column.
4. Click the **Select Column** button [*Form Layout Tools Arrange* tab, *Rows & Columns* group].
5. Click the **Insert Left** or **Insert Right** button [*Form Layout Tools Arrange* tab, *Rows & Columns* group].
   - The new column is added to the control layout (Figure 4-36).
   - A light-gray, dotted border surrounds each cell in the added column.

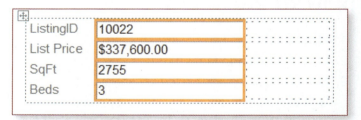

4-36 A dotted border surrounds each cell in the added column

HOW TO: Add a Row to a Control Layout

1. Open the form in *Layout* view.
2. Click the **Arrange** tab.
3. Select a control in the row adjacent to the place where you want to add a new row.

4. Click the **Select Row** button [*Form Layout Tools Arrange* tab, *Rows & Columns* group].

5. Click the **Insert Above** or **Insert Below** button [*Form Layout Tools Arrange* tab, *Rows & Columns* group].
   - The new row is added to the control layout (Figure 4-37).
   - A light-gray, dotted border surrounds each cell in the added row.

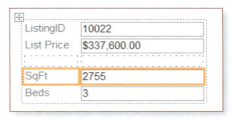

4-37 A dotted border surrounds each cell in the added row

HOW TO: Delete a Row or Column from a Control Layout

1. Open the form in *Layout* view.
2. Click the **Arrange** tab.
3. Select a control in the row or column you wish to delete.
4. Click the **Select Row** or **Select Column** button [*Form Layout Tools Arrange* tab, *Rows & Columns* group].
5. Right-click to open the context menu.
6. Select the **Delete Row** or **Delete Column** option (Figure 4-38).

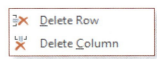

4-38 Delete options in the context menu

Move a Control within a Layout

As you make a modification to the control layout you may want to move a control from one part of the layout to another.

HOW TO: Move a Control within a Layout

1. Open the form in *Layout* view.
2. Select the control that you wish to move. The orange border surrounds that control.
3. Click in the control with the four-arrow pointer, hold, and drag the control to the new location. A rose color highlights the destination cell (Figure 4-39).

4-39 Drag a control to a new location in the form layout

> ▶ **ANOTHER WAY**
>
> Select multiple controls by pressing and holding the **Shift** key when you select controls.

Add a Title, Date, and Logo to a Form

It is good design practice to title each form. This allows the user to quickly know which form they are working with. You can also display the current date and add a logo to forms. These controls can be added to a form from the *Header/Footer* group [*Form Layout Tools Design* tab] (Figure 4-40). If the form does not already contain a *header section*, adding any of these items automatically adds a header section to the form.

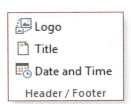

4-40 *Header/Footer* group options

Selecting either the *Logo* or the *Title* buttons adds two controls into the header section: an ***Auto_Header*** control which contains the title and an ***Auto_Logo*** control which contains the logo.

HOW TO: Add a Title, Date, or Logo to a Form in Layout View

1. Open the form in *Layout* view.
2. Click the **Design** tab.
3. Click the **Title** button [*Header/Footer* group] to add a title to the form.
   - The title is set to the form name.
4. Click the **Date and Time** button [*Header/Footer* group] to add the *Date* and/or *Time* into the header section of the form.
   - The **Date and Time** dialog box appears (Figure 4-41).
5. Select the check boxes and radio buttons corresponding to your choices.
6. Click the **OK** button.
7. Click the **Logo** button [*Header/Footer* group] to add a logo to the form.
   - The *Insert Picture* dialog box displays.
8. Select the image file to use as the logo and click **Open**.
9. Click the **Auto_Header** control and edit the contents to change the title of the form (Figure 4-42).
   - In Figure 4-42, the *Date* control is selected. Notice that the width of the control overlaps onto the *Auto_Header* control.
   - If necessary, you may adjust the width or location of these controls.

4-41 *Date and Time* dialog box

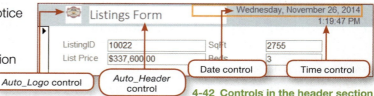

4-42 **Controls in the header section**

SLO 4.3

Facilitating Data Input with a Form

Forms allow you to view, change, or delete data already in a database or to add new data into a database. Sometimes you use a form for all these purposes, but at other times you may want to create a single purpose form. When using a form for data entry, it is important to design it to help minimize potential data entry mistakes as well as to make the data entry efficient. Use the *Property Sheet* of the form to select the desired settings to limit actions available in a form (Figure 4-43).

Restrict a Form to Data Entry

Restrict a form only to allow data entry when you don't want users to have access to all the data records that exist in the database. This allows you to limit some activities to authorized users. Additionally, this feature can prevent users from accidentally changing or deleting existing records in the table.

4-43 **Properties to limit actions available in a form**

HOW TO: Restrict a Form to Data Entry

1. Open the form in *Layout* view.
2. Click the **Design** tab.
3. Click the **Property Sheet** button [*Tools* group].

ANOTHER WAY

Press the **F4** key to open or close the *Property Sheet*.

4. In the *Selection* box of the *Property Sheet*, click the **drop-down arrow** and select **Form**.
5. If necessary, click to select the **Data** tab of the *Property Sheet*.
6. Select **Yes** in the **Data Entry** property box. The *Data Entry* property determines whether data already in the database is displayed.
7. Select **Yes** in the **Allow Additions** property box. The *Allow Additions* property determines whether a user can add data into the database.
   - Since the form does not show any existing records, the settings in the *Allow Deletions* and *Allow Edits* property boxes don't have an impact.

Limit Edits and Deletions on a Form

Sometimes you want users to be able to view existing records in a database but not to be able to edit or delete them. You can establish these limits through the *Property Sheet*.

HOW TO: Limit Edits and Deletions on a Form

1. Open the form in *Layout* view.
2. Click the **Design** tab.
3. Click the **Property Sheet** button [*Tools* group] to open the *Property Sheet*.
4. In the *Selection* box of the *Property Sheet*, click the **drop-down arrow** and select **Form**.
5. Select **No** in the *Data Entry* property box. The additional property selections you make in step 6 determine how users can access and change the data currently in the database.
6. Set the desired form properties.
   - Select **Yes** or **No** in the *Allow Additions* property box. The *Allow Additions* property determines whether a user can add data into the database. If set to *Yes*, this will override the *Data Entry* property and allow records to be added into the database.
   - Select **Yes** or **No** in the *Allow Deletions* property box. The *Allow Deletions* property determines whether a user can delete a record from the database.
   - Select **Yes** or **No** in the *Allow Edits* property box. The *Allow Edits* property determines whether a user can change values in a record in the database.

Add a Command Button

A ***command button*** is a type of control that can perform a number of different actions. For example, command buttons can be set to print the current form, close the current form, navigate to the next record, or open another form. Buttons make a form more user-friendly.

The quickest way to add a command button to a form is to use the *Command Button Wizard*. The **Command Button Wizard** creates a button and attaches all of the necessary functionality to the button. The functionality is contained in a *Macro* and is attached to the **On Click** property of the button. Recall that a **Macro** is a database object that allows you to write and attach code to different objects and controls in your database.

The *Command Button Wizard* groups the available functionality into six different categories. Those categories and the available actions are shown in the following table:

Groupings of Categories and Actions in the Command Button Wizard

Category	Actions
Record Navigation	Find Next Find Record Go To First Record Go To Last Record Go To Next Record Go To Previous Record
Record Operations	Add New Record Delete Record Duplicate Record Print Record Save Record Undo Record
Form Operations	Apply Form Filter Close Form Open Form Print a Form Print Current Form Refresh Form Data
Report Operations	Mail Report Open Report Preview Report Print Report Send Report to File
Application	Quit Application
Miscellaneous	Auto Dialer Print Table Run Macro Run Query

The *Command Button Wizard* does not launch unless you first turn on the *Control Wizards* tool. The **Control Wizards** tool directs Access to launch an available wizard when adding controls to an object.

The *Control Wizards* tool uses an on-off setting. If the icon is orange, the *Control Wizards* are on; if the icon is white, the *Control Wizards* are off.

HOW TO: Add a Command Button Using the Command Button Wizard

1. Open the form in *Layout* view.
2. Select the **Design** tab.

3. Click the **More** arrow at the far right of the *Controls* group (Figure 4-44a) to expand the *Controls* group. If the *Use Controls Wizards* button does not have a rose-colored background, select the **Use Control Wizards** button to turn on the wizard (Figure 4-44b).

4-44a *Controls* group

4-44b *Use Control Wizards* button

4. Click **Button** in the *Controls* group. Move the pointer to the desired location in the control layout and click in the cell (Figure 4-45).

5. The *Command Button Wizard* launches (Figure 4-46).

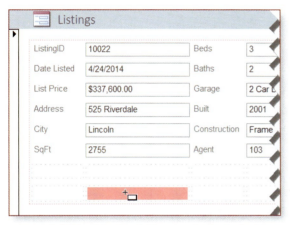

4-45 **Position the button control onto the form**

- If the *Command Button Wizard* does not launch, *Control Wizards* is not turned on.
- Delete the button that was placed on the form.
- Repeat step 3 to turn the *Control Wizards* on.
- Repeat step 4 to add a button.

6. Select a **Category** and **Action** for the button.

7. Click **Next** to move to the next page of the *Command Button Wizard*.

- Depending on the *Category* and *Action* selected, the *Command Button Wizard* may display pages asking for additional information, such as the name of a form to open.
- If prompted, select the correct answer and click **Next** to move to the next page of the wizard.

8. If prompted, choose whether you want the button to display words or an image (Figure 4-47).

9. Click **Next** to move to the last page of the wizard.

10. Enter a name for the button and click **Finish**.

- The button name is important if you are going to modify the macro code attached to the button.
- You may want the name to reference the form name and button action. For example, *ListingsFormCloseButton*.
- The button displays in the form (Figure 4-48).

4-46 *Command Button Wizard*, page 1

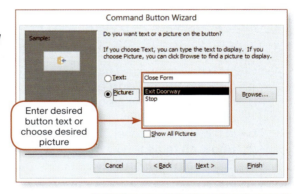

4-47 *Command Button Wizard*, page 2

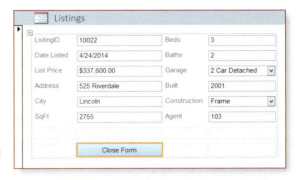

4-48 **Completed button displays on the form**

Test a Form

After you have built your form, it is important to switch to *Form* view and test the functionality of the form. You may have forgotten to add or delete a field on the form or you may want to change the text in a label to make it more user-friendly. You may also realize that you selected the wrong action to assign to a button.

Switch to *Form* view by clicking the **View** button arrow [*Form Layout Tools Design* tab] and selecting **Form View**. If you are in *Design* view, you can also press the **F5** key to switch to *Form* view.

Test the functionality of the form by performing the following tasks:

- Navigate through several records ensuring that the width of the fields is appropriate.
- Review the overall layout to ensure that the structure is easy to use and intuitive for the user.
- Test all buttons to ensure they behave as expected.
- Make any needed corrections and re-test as appropriate.

PAUSE & PRACTICE: ACCESS 4-2

For this Pause & Practice you build a form using the *Blank Form* button for the Central Sierra Insurance database. You modify the form to restrict it to data entry, add buttons, and test the form.

File Needed: **CentralSierra-04.accdb**
Completed Project File Name: **[your initials] PP A4-2.accdb**

1. Open the **CentralSierra-04.accdb** database file.

2. Save the database as **[your initials] PP A4-2**.

3. If prompted, enable content in the database.

4. Create a new form using the *Blank Form* option.
   a. Click the **Blank Form** button [*Create* tab, *Forms* group]. A new blank form opens in *Layout* view.
   b. In the *Field List* pane, click the link to **Show all tables**.
   c. Click the **plus sign** to expand the *Employees* table to see the fields in the table.
   d. Double-click the **EmpID** field to add it to the form.
   e. Double-click the **FirstName** field to add it to the form.
   f. Continue adding all the fields from the *Employees* table into the form.
   g. Close the *Field List*. The form should match Figure 4-49.

5. Modify the control layout.
   a. Click one of the fields on the form. An orange border surrounds it.

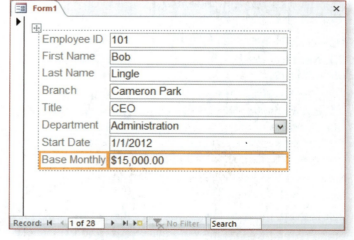

4-49 Employee form after adding all fields

b. Click the **Select Layout** button [*Form Layout Tools Arrange* tab, *Rows & Columns* group]. All the cells in the layout are bordered in orange.
c. Place your pointer over any field. Click, hold, and drag the control layout down and to the right (Figure 4-50), and then release the pointer.
d. Select the **Base Monthly Salary** label.
e. Place your pointer over the right edge of the label until it becomes a two-arrow sizing pointer.
f. Click, hold, and drag the pointer to increase the width of the label.

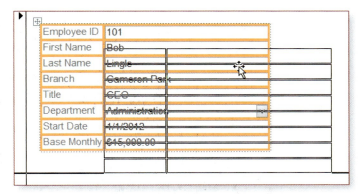

4-50 Drag the control layout to a new location

g. Navigate to record number 10. This record contains the employee with the longest title.
h. Click in the **Title** text box. Remember that the text box control displays the actual data. In this form, the text boxes are located to the right of the label.
i. Decrease the width of the text box.

6. Add a new column and new rows to the control layout.
   a. Select the **Base Monthly Salary** text box.
   b. Click the **Select Row** button [*Form Layout Tools Arrange* tab, *Rows & Columns* group].
   c. Click the **Insert Below** button [*Form Layout Tools Arrange* tab, *Rows & Columns* group] to add a blank row.
   d. Click the **Insert Below** button again to add a second blank row.
   e. Select the **Base Monthly Salary** text box.
   f. Click the **Select Column** button [*Form Layout Tools Arrange* tab, *Rows & Columns* group].
   g. Click the **Insert Right** button [*Form Layout Tools Arrange* tab, *Rows & Columns* group] to add a blank column.

7. Adjust the height and width of the new column and rows.
   a. Select a cell in the new column.
   b. Place your pointer over the right edge of the cell until it becomes a two-arrow sizing pointer.
   c. Click, hold, and drag the pointer to increase the width of the cell. Make the width approximately the same as the first column.
   d. Select a cell in the bottom blank row.
   e. Place your pointer over the bottom edge of the cell until it becomes a two-arrow sizing pointer.
   f. Click, hold, and drag the pointer to increase the height of the cell. Make the height approximately twice as high as any other row. The completed form should look similar to Figure 4-51.

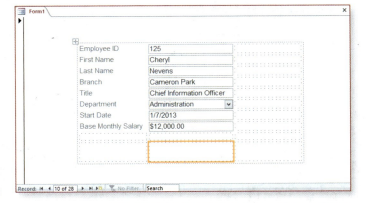

4-51 Employee form after adding and modifying rows and columns

8. Add command buttons to the form.
   a. Click the **Form Layout Tools Design** tab.
   b. Click the **More** arrow at the far right of the *Controls* group and select the **Use Control Wizards** button. The *Control Wizards* icon has a rose-colored border when it is selected.
   c. Click **Button** in the *Controls* group. Click in the left-most cell in the bottom row.

d. The *Command Button Wizard* launches. If the *Command Button Wizard* does not launch, *Control Wizards* is not turned on. Delete the button that was added to the form and go back to step 8b.

e. Select the **Record Operations** *Category* and the **Save Record** *Action* of the button.

f. Click **Next** to move to the second page of the *Command Button Wizard*.

g. Select the **Text** radio button and change the wording to read Save Employee Record.

h. Click **Next** to move to the last page of the wizard.

i. Enter AddEmpFormSaveButton as the name for the button and click **Finish**. The button displays in the form (Figure 4-52). The text in the button wraps depending on the width of the column.

4-52 Button added to form

j. Add a second button to the form. Place the button in the middle cell of the last row.

k. Select the **Record Operations** *Category* and the **Add New Record** *Action* of the button.

l. Click **Next** to move to the second page of the *Command Button Wizard*.

m. Select the **Text** radio button and change the wording to read Add New Employee.

n. Click **Next** to move to the last page of the wizard.

o. Enter AddEmpFormAddButton as the name for the button and click **Finish**.

p. Add a third button to the form. Place the button in the right-most cell of the last row.

q. Select the **Form Operations** *Category* and the **Close Form** *Action* of the button.

r. Click **Next** to move to the second page of the wizard.

s. Select the **Text** radio button and accept the existing wording of "Close Form."

t. Click **Next** to move to the last page of the wizard.

u. Enter AddEmpFormCloseButton as the name for the button and click **Finish**.

9. Add a title to the form.
   a. Click the **Form Layout Tools Design** tab.
   b. Click the **Title** button [*Header/Footer* group].
   c. Change the wording to read Add New Employee. The form should look similar to Figure 4-53.

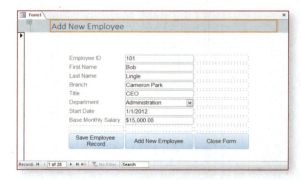

4-53 Completed form after adding a title and three buttons

10. Restrict the form to data entry.
    a. Click the **Property Sheet** button [*Form Layout Tools Design* tab, *Tools* group] to open the *Property Sheet*.
    b. In the *Selection* box of the *Property Sheet*, click the **drop-down arrow** and select **Form**.
    c. If necessary, click to select the **Data** tab.
    d. Select **Yes** in the *Data Entry* property box.
    e. Select **Yes** in the *Allow Additions* property box.
    f. Close the *Property Sheet*.

11. Save the form. Enter AddNewEmployeeForm as the *Form Name*.

12. Switch to *Form* view by clicking the **View** button arrow [*Form Layout Tools Design* tab, *Views* group] and selecting the **Form View** option. The complete form displays.

13. Test the form.
    a. Enter the data shown in Figure 4-54.
    b. Click the **Save Employee Record** button.
    c. Click the **Add New Employee** button. A blank record should display in the form.
    d. Click the **Close Form** button.

Employee ID	165
First Name	Susan
Last Name	Stone
Branch	Granite Bay
Title	Insurance Agent
Department	Health and Benefits
Start Date	9/7/2014
Base Monthly Salary	$3,800.00

4-54 Employee record values to enter in form

14. Double-click the **Employees** table to open it in *Datasheet* view.

15. Scroll down to find the new record you added into the database.

16. Close the table.

17. Close the database.

Creating a Simple Report

A *report* is an object you can use to create an organized and professional output of the data in a database. Unlike forms, reports do *not* allow you to modify the underlying data. The reports in your database are directly connected to a table or query, the source of the data.

In Chapter 2, you learned how to print the data records in a table. Reports provide a great deal more flexibility for viewing and printing the data in a database. A report can have fields from one or more tables or queries. Similar to a form, you select which fields from the tables or queries to include on the report. You also can select grouping and summarizing options when you are choosing how to display your records. This flexibility helps you create reports that look professional, in addition to being more user-friendly than *Datasheet* view of a table. Ideally, a well-designed report makes it easier for the user to understand the information contained in the database.

Creating reports is similar to creating forms. You can apply much of what you already learned about creating forms as you learn to create reports. There are several different ways to create a report. There are quick ways to create a report and some that take a little more effort but provide a great deal more flexibility when it comes to report design and specialization. In this section you are introduced to two ways to build a report, the *Report Wizard* and the *Blank Report* options. These options are available in the *Reports* group [*Create* tab] (Figure 4-55).

4-55 Report creation options

The Report Wizard

The **Report Wizard** steps you through the process of quickly creating a report. While you will probably need to fine-tune the initial report design, it provides a good starting point. The *Report Wizard* asks you which tables and queries you want to base the report on and which specific fields you want to include in the report. Additionally, you must determine if you want to group the data by any fields, sort on any fields, and choose the layout and orientation of the report. Your layout choices change based on whether you group the data or not.

The three layout choices for reports without grouping are columnar, tabular, and justified.

- A *columnar* layout displays the fields in one column (Figure 4-56). The field labels appear to the left of the data.

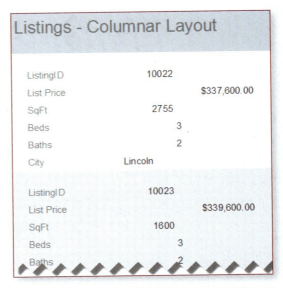

4-56 Columnar report layout

- A *tabular* layout displays the fields in a table (row and column) format. The field names display above the data (Figure 4-57).

Listings - Tabular Layout

ListingID	List Price	SqFt	Beds	Baths	Address	City
10022	$337,600.00	2755	3	2	525 Riverdale	Lincoln
10023	$339,600.00	1600	3	2	615 Silver Hill Court	Lincoln
10024	$675,000.00	3397	4	4	1917 Oak Crest Dr.	Roseville
10025	$216,600.00	1900	4	3	3420 Milburn St	Rocklin
10027	$130,000.00	1184	3	2	2128 Wedgewood	Roseville
10029	$1,295,000.00	6685	7	6	3998 Rawhide Rd	Rocklin

4-57 Tabular report layout

- A *justified* layout displays the fields in a horizontal, justified layout (Figure 4-58). The field names display above each field.

Listings - Justified Layout

ListingID	List Price		Address	City	SqFt
10022		$337,600.00	525 Riverdale	Lincoln	2755
Beds	Baths	Garage			
3	2	2 Car Detached			
ListingID	List Price		Address	City	SqFt
10023		$339,600.00	615 Silver Hill Court	Lincoln	1600
Beds	Baths	Garage			
3	2	2 Car Attached			
ListingID	List Price		Address	City	SqFt
10024		$675,000.00	1917 Oak Crest Dr.	Roseville	3397

4-58 Justified report layout

Grouping is useful when you want to organize and summarize the data in your report. For example, you could group all properties from the same city together or you could group all the songs from a particular artist together. The three layout choices for a grouped report are stepped, block, and outline.

- A *stepped* layout displays the fields in a table layout (Figure 4-59). The field names display in a row above the data. If the report is longer than one page, the field names appear at the top of each page. The grouped field displays in the left-most column. The data value appears in its own row at the start of each new grouping.

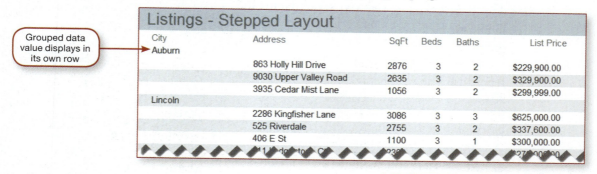

Grouped data value displays in its own row →

Listings - Stepped Layout

City	Address	SqFt	Beds	Baths	List Price
Auburn					
	863 Holly Hill Drive	2876	3	2	$229,900.00
	9030 Upper Valley Road	2635	3	2	$329,900.00
	3935 Cedar Mist Lane	1056	3	2	$299,999.00
Lincoln					
	2286 Kingfisher Lane	3086	3	3	$625,000.00
	525 Riverdale	2755	3	2	$337,600.00
	406 E St	1100	3	1	$300,000.00

4-59 Stepped layout in a grouped report

- A *block* layout is very similar to a stepped layout; it has a table layout and field names at the top. The major difference is that the grouped field appears in the same row as the first record for that grouping (Figure 4-60). If the report is longer than one page, the field names appear at the top of each page. Additionally, the data rows are grouped a little more tightly together, meaning that more data can appear on each page.

Grouped data value displays in row with other fields

4-60 Block layout in a grouped report

- An *outline* layout displays the grouped field and its label on a separate row at the start of each new grouping (Figure 4-61). The field names display above the first row of data in each grouping.

Field label and value display in a separate row

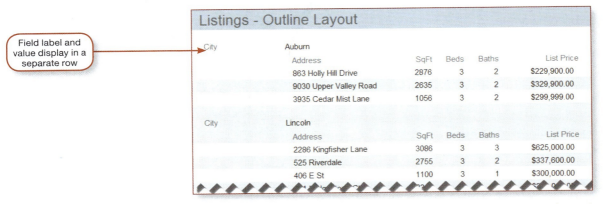

4-61 Outline layout in a grouped report

With grouped reports, you also have the option to have Access automatically calculate various summary values across the different groups. You can decide to display only the summary values (Figure 4-62) or to display both the detail records and summary values for each group (Figure 4-63).

4-62 Report with summary values only

After you have created a report using the *Report Wizard*, you can preview the report or open it in *Design* view to modify the layout. If you need to make changes to the report later, you can edit it using *Layout* view or *Design* view.

4-63 Report with detail and summary values

HOW TO: Create a Report Using the Report Wizard

1. Click the **Create** tab on the *Ribbon*.

2. Click the **Report Wizard** button in the *Reports* group to launch the *Report Wizard* (Figure 4-64).
   - The values displayed in the *Tables/Queries* box and the *Available Fields* window change based on the contents of your database.

3. Click the **Tables/Queries** drop-down arrow and select the *Table* or *Query* name.

4. Select a **Field** to include in the *Report* from those displayed in the *Available Fields* window.
   - Add fields in the order you want them to display in the report.

5. Click the **Move Single Field** button.
   - The field moves into the *Selected Fields* window.
   - The *Remove Single Field* and *Remove All Fields* buttons become active.

6. Continue moving all required fields (Figure 4-65), changing the selected *Table* or *Query* if needed.

4-64 *Report Wizard*, step 1

> **ANOTHER WAY**
>
> Use the **Move All Fields** button to quickly include all of the fields in the report.

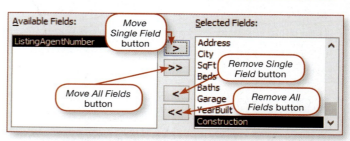

4-65 Move fields into the *Selected Fields* window

7. Click the **Next** button when you are done adding all fields. The second page of the *Report Wizard* displays (Figure 4-66).

8. Select any fields you want to use to group the data.
   - When you select fields on which to group, Access moves those fields to the left-most columns of the report.

9. Click the **Next** button. The next page of the *Report Wizard* displays (Figure 4-67).

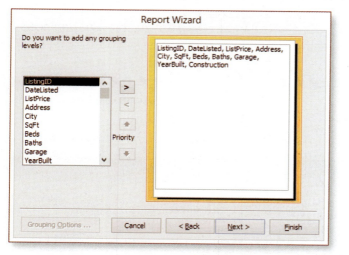

4-66 Select grouping levels

4-67 Select sorting options

10. Select any fields you want to use to sort the report and select either **Ascending** *or* **Descending** sort order.
    - If you have grouped any fields, this screen allows you to select any summary options.

11. Click the **Next** button. The next page of the *Report Wizard* displays (Figure 4-68).

12. Select the desired layout and orientation.

13. As desired, deselect the check box that fits all fields on one page. If this box is selected, some fields may not be wide enough to display their full contents.

14. Click the **Next** button. The last page of the *Report Wizard* displays (Figure 4-69).

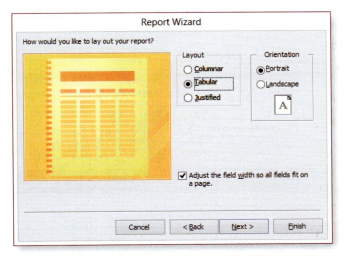

4-68 Select layout and orientation options

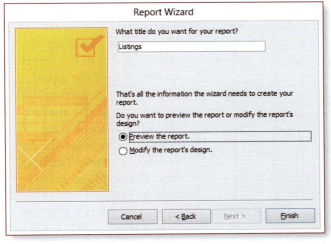

4-69 Enter the title in the last step of the *Report Wizard*

15. Change the title.

16. Select the radio button either to **Preview the report** or to **Modify the report's design**.

17. Click **Finish**.
    - Access saves the report using the name provided in the title.
    - The report shows in either *Print Preview* view or *Design* view.
    - Most of the fields appear in text boxes.
    - Fields that have a lookup appear in a combo box.
    - Fields that are a *Yes/No* data type appear as a check box.
    - The size of a field depends on the data type and the field size.
    - The *Report name displays* in the *Reports* group on the *Navigation* pane.

18. Close the report.
    - If the report was opened in *Print Preview* view, when you close *Print Preview* you are in *Design* view. You need to close that if you are done with the report.

View or Modify a Report

Access provides four different view options for a report.

- **Report** view is used to execute the report and see the results (Figure 4-70). In *Report* view you see all the data contained in the report. However, you do not see it separated into separate pages.

4-70 *Report* view of a report

- **Print Preview** view (Figure 4-71) lets you see how the report will look in print and also allows you to make modifications to the print settings, such as margins, page orientation, page size, and so forth.

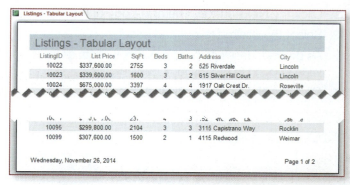

4-71 *Print Preview* view of a report

- **Design** view allows you to make changes to the report. In *Design* view the report content is organized by the section in which it appears (Figure 4-72). The three primary sections are the **Page Header**, the **Detail**, and the **Page Footer**. Some reports have additional sections based on grouping levels that have been added.

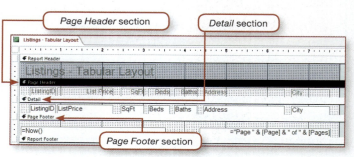

4-72 *Design* view of a report

  Design view is good for adding labels and images into a report, editing text boxes, resizing the report sections, and changing some report properties. When you are working in *Design* view, Access organizes your editing choices into four *Report Design Tools* contextual tabs: **Design**, **Arrange**, **Format**, and **Page Setup**.

- **Layout** view is a more visually oriented mode you can use to alter the design of a report and see the effects of the changes in real time. The *Layout* view of the same report shown in Figure 4-72 is shown in Figure 4-73.

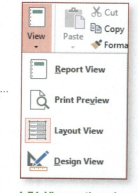

4-73 *Layout* view of a report

  Because you can see how the data displays at the same time you are able to modify the design, *Layout* view is good for resizing fields or labels, changing colors or text alignment, or applying different formats. Like *Design* view, *Layout* view organizes your editing choices into the same four *Report Design Tools* contextual tabs: *Design*, *Arrange*, *Format*, and *Page Setup*. However, not all design options are available while in *Layout* view.

HOW TO: Switch Report Views to View or Modify a Report

1. Click the **View** button arrow [*Home* tab].
2. Select the **Report View**, **Print Preview**, **Layout View**, or **Design View** option (Figure 4-74).
3. View the results or make any modifications.

> **ANOTHER WAY**
> Select a view icon from the lower right corner of the *Status bar*.

4-74 **View options for a report**

Save a Report

When a report is created using the *Report* tool or *Report Wizard* options, Access automatically saves the report during the creation process. If you have made any modifications to the design of the report, or if you created the report using any of the other options, you need to save those changes. Save changes to a report by pressing the **Ctrl+S** keys or the **Save** icon on the *Quick Access* toolbar.

HOW TO: Save a Copy of a Report

1. Click **Save As** [*File*] tab to display the *Save As* area.
2. Click **Save Object As** in the *File Types* options. *Save Object As* should be selected in the *Database File Types* options.
3. Click the **Save As** button to open the *Save As* dialog box (Figure 4-75).
   - The name of the current object displays in the *Save "object name" to* box.
   - In Figure 4-75, *Listings–Tabular Layout* is the name of the current object.
   - The suggested name always begins with "Copy of."
4. Type the name you wish to use in the *Save "object name" to* box.
5. Click the **OK** button.

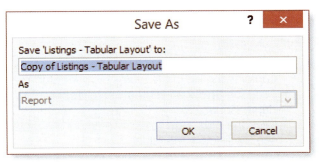

4-75 *Save As* dialog box

> **ANOTHER WAY**
>
> Press the **F12** function key to open the *Save As* dialog box.

Once a report has been saved, it displays in the *Reports* group of the *Navigation* pane.

Open a Saved Report

If you double-click a report name in the *Navigation* pane, the form opens in *Report* view.

Open a saved report in *Print Preview* view, *Design* view, or *Layout* view by right-clicking the report name in the *Navigation* pane and selecting **Print Preview, Design View,** or **Layout View** from the context menu.

Delete a Report

Occasionally you have reports that no longer are needed in the database.

Delete a report by selecting the report name in the *Navigation* pane and clicking the **Delete** button [*Home* tab, *Records* group].

> **ANOTHER WAY**
>
> Right-click the report name in the *Navigation* pane and select **Delete** from the context menu.

Creating and Customizing a Report in Layout View

In *Layout* view, you can modify a report and see how the report looks with data displaying. In this section you first learn how to create a blank report and then you explore the layout of a report and make modifications in *Layout* view.

The Blank Report Button

Sometimes it is easier to start with a completely blank report and then add the fields, labels, or other controls.

HOW TO: Create a Blank Report

1. Click the **Blank Report** button [*Create* tab, *Reports* group].
2. A new blank report opens in *Layout* view (Figure 4-76).
   - The *Field List* pane displays. The *Field List* contains the list of the tables in your database.
   - Click the **Show all tables** link to display the database tables.
   - Click the **plus sign** to expand any of the tables to see the fields in the table.

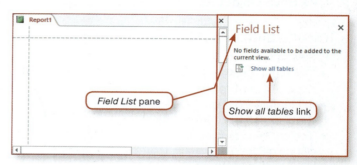

4-76 Blank report in *Layout* view

After you create the blank report, you are ready to start adding items to the report. Save the report and any changes you make to it.

Report Control Layouts

Like forms, **control layouts** provide a structure to align the controls on your report. The two primary layout options are tabular and stacked.

- *A tabular Layout* organizes data in rows and columns. Labels identifying the different fields are above the data values (Figure 4-77).

4-77 Tabular control layout in a report

- *A stacked Layout* organizes data vertically. The labels are to the left of the data control (Figure 4-78).

Add and Delete Fields in a Control Layout

A new blank report initially has no controls. You can add table fields to the report in *Layout* view.

4-78 Stacked control layout in a report

HOW TO: Add Fields into the Control Layout of a Blank Report

1. Open the report in *Layout* view.
2. If the *Field List* is not open, click the **Add Existing Fields** button [*Report Layout Tools Design* tab, *Tools* group].

> **ANOTHER WAY**
>
> Press the **Alt+F8** keys to show or hide the *Field List*.

3. Click the **plus sign** next to the table name to display the fields.
4. Double-click the field name to add the field into the report.
5. Continue adding fields.
   - The fields are added into a tabular layout (Figure 4-79).
   - The most recently added field is highlighted with an orange border.

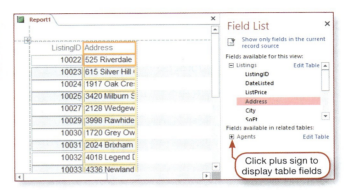

4-79 Add fields into a report

> **ANOTHER WAY**
>
> Click and drag a field into the report window to add it into the control layout.

HOW TO: Add Fields between Existing Fields in a Control Layout

1. Open the report in *Layout* view.
2. If the *Field List* is not open, click the **Add Existing Fields** button [*Report Layout Tools Design* tab, *Tools* group].
3. Click the **plus sign** next to the desired table name to display the fields.
4. Select the field name to add to the report. The selected field is highlighted in rose.
5. Drag the field to the desired location in the control layout. A rose-colored line indicates the position of the new field (Figure 4-80).

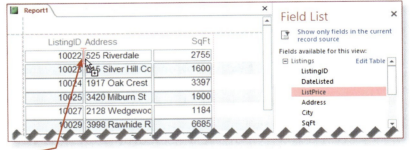

4-80 Add fields between existing fields in a control layout

> **MORE INFO**
>
> Pay attention to the rose-colored line's placement. Reports allow rows and columns to be combined. Figure 4-81 shows the new field being added into a row of a tabular layout. Figure 4-82 shows the resulting report. This could create a confusing report organization.

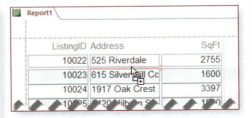

4-81 Insert a new field as a row in a tabular layout

4-82 Report after new field added

HOW TO: Delete a Field from a Control Layout

1. Open the report in *Layout* view.
2. Select the **text box control** of the field you want to delete.
3. Right-click to open the context menu.
4. Select the **Delete Row** or **Delete Column** option.

> **MORE INFO**
>
> Pay attention to the layout of the controls before you delete a field. For example, if you select a field in a tabular layout and choose the *Delete Row* option, you delete all the fields in that row, not just the selected field. Likewise, if you select a field in a stacked layout and choose the *Delete Column* option, you delete all the fields in that column, not just the selected field.

Customize a Report in Layout View

You can make a number of modifications to a report in *Layout* view. In this section, you explore the report controls, learn how to change control layouts, adjust column widths, add and delete rows and columns in a control layout, and add a title and date to a form.

Explore Report Controls

Recall that the fields, labels, buttons, and so forth are all known as *controls*. In a report, you can add controls in either *Layout* view or *Design* view. The controls are accessed in the *Controls* group of the *Report Layout Tools Design* tab. The report controls available in *Layout* view are shown in Figure 4-83.

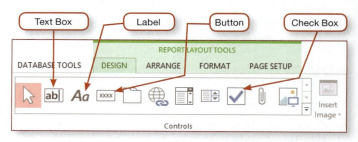

4-83 *Controls* group for a report

Like controls on forms, some controls on reports are *bound* to a data value; some are *unbound* and are not linked to a data source; and some controls are *calculated* and their value comes from an expression. As you work through the book you are introduced to a variety of report controls.

Change Control Layouts

When you create a report, the report starts with either a stacked or tabular layout. As you add and delete fields on the form, you may wish to change its layout.

HOW TO: Change Control Layouts

1. Open the report in *Layout* view.
2. Click the **Arrange** tab.
3. Select one of the fields in the control layout. The orange border surrounds that field.
4. Click the **Select Layout** button [*Report Layout Tools Arrange* tab, *Rows & Columns* group].
   - The orange border surrounds all of the controls in the layout.
5. Select either the **Stacked** or **Tabular** button [*Report Layout Tools Arrange* tab, *Table* group] (Figure 4-84).
6. The report updates with the new layout.

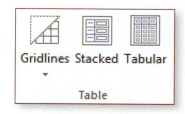

4-84 Report layout options in the *Table* group

Adjust Column Widths

Sometimes, the initial width of the report fields needs to be adjusted. Keep in mind that in a stacked layout, all of the fields have the same width. As a result, when changing the width you need to ensure that the column is wide enough to fit the largest field.

HOW TO: Change Field Column Widths

1. Open the report in *Layout* view.
2. Select the **text box control** of the field in the control layout.
   - The orange border surrounds that field.
3. Place your pointer over the right edge of the text box until it becomes a two-arrow sizing pointer.
4. Click, hold, and drag the pointer to increase or decrease the width of the text box (Figure 4-85).
   - The field(s) updates to the new width.

4-85 Adjust the width of a report field

Add and Delete Rows and Columns in a Control Layout

Often, you want to make minor modifications to the control layout. For example, you may want to create a second column in a stacked layout, or you may want to delete a row if you removed fields from the control layout. You can make these modifications using buttons in the *Rows & Columns* group of the *Report Layout Tools Arrange* tab (Figure 4-86).

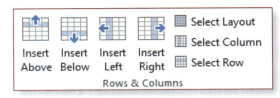

4-86 *Rows & Columns* group options

HOW TO: Add a Column to a Control Layout

1. Open the report in *Layout* view.
2. Click the **Arrange** tab.
3. Select a control in the column adjacent to where you want to add a new column.
4. Click the **Select Column** button [*Report Layout Tools Arrange* tab, *Rows & Columns* group].
5. Click the **Insert Left** or **Insert Right** button [*Report Layout Tools Arrange* tab, *Rows & Columns* group].
6. The new column is added to the control layout (Figure 4-87).

4-87 A dotted border surrounds each cell in the added column

- A light-gray, dotted border surrounds the cells in the added column.

HOW TO: Add a Row to a Control Layout

1. Open the report in *Layout* view.
2. Click the **Arrange** tab.
3. Select a control in the row adjacent to where you want to add a new row.
4. Click the **Select Row** button [*Report Layout Tools Arrange* tab, *Rows & Columns* group].
5. Click the **Insert Above** or **Insert Below** button [*Report Layout Tools Arrange* tab, *Rows & Columns* group].

   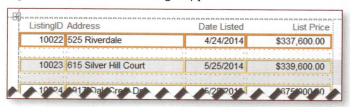

   4-88 A dotted border surrounds each cell in the added row

   - The new row is added to the control layout (Figure 4-88).
   - Notice that a new row is added below each of the existing rows in the control layout.
   - A light-gray, dotted border surrounds the cells in the new row.

HOW TO: Delete a Row or Column from a Control Layout

1. Open the report in *Layout* view.
2. Click the **Arrange** tab.
3. Select a control in the row or column you wish to delete.
4. Click the **Select Row** or **Select Column** button [*Report Layout Tools Arrange* tab, *Rows & Columns* group].
5. Right-click to open the context menu.
6. Select **Delete Row** or **Delete Column**.

Move a Control within a Layout

As you modify the control layout, you may need to move a control from one part of the layout to another.

HOW TO: Move a Control within a Layout

1. Open the report in *Layout* view.
2. Select the control that you wish to move.

   4-89 Drag a control to the new location

   - The orange border surrounds that control.
3. Click in the control with the four-arrow pointer, hold, and drag the control to the new location.
   - A rose-colored line highlights the new location (Figure 4-89).

> **ANOTHER WAY**
>
> Select multiple controls by pressing and holding the **Shift** key and selecting multiple controls. You can then move them together.

Add a Title, a Date, or Page Numbers to a Report

It is good database design to title each report. This allows the user to quickly understand the purpose of the report. You also may want to have the current date displayed in a report, and Access can also add page numbers to a report. These controls can be added to a report from the *Header/Footer* group [*Report Layout Tools Design* tab] (Figure 4-90). If the report does not already contain a header section, adding a title or the date and time automatically adds a header section to the report.

Selecting the **Title** button adds two controls into the header section, an *Auto_Header* control which contains the title and an *Auto_Logo* control which can contain a logo.

HOW TO: Add a Title, a Date, or Page Numbers to a Report in Layout View

1. Open the report in *Layout* view.
2. Click the **Design** tab.
3. Click the **Title** button [*Header/Footer* group] to add a title into the header section of the report.
   - An *Auto_Header* control is added to the header section.
   - The title is set to the report name.
4. Click the **Auto_Header** control to edit the report title.
5. Click the **Date and Time** button [*Header/Footer* group] to add the date and/or time into the header section of the report.
   - The *Date and Time* dialog box appears (Figure 4-91).
6. Select the appropriate check boxes and radio buttons to include the date and/or time with the desired formatting.
7. Click the **OK** button.
8. Click the **Page Numbers** button [*Header/Footer* group] to open the *Page Numbers* dialog box (Figure 4-92).
9. Select the radio buttons corresponding to the appropriate *Format* and *Position* of the page numbers.
   - If the *Bottom of Page* position is selected, a footer section is added to the report as needed.
10. Select the alignment of the page numbers.
11. As desired, deselect the check box to **Show Number on First Page**.
12. Click the **OK** button.
13. The title and/or date appears in the header section of the form and, based on your choice, the page numbers appear in either the header or footer section (Figure 4-93).

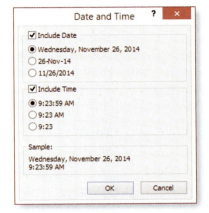

4-91 *Date and Time* dialog box

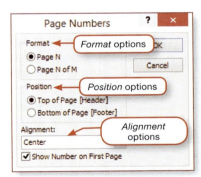

4-92 *Page Numbers* dialog box

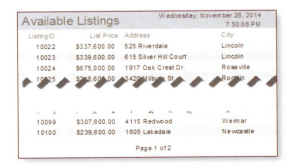

4-93 Controls in the header and footer sections

For this Pause & Practice you create two reports for the Placer Hills Real Estate database. Create one report using the *Report Wizard* and a second report using the *Blank Report* button.

File Needed: ***PlacerHills-04.accdb***
Completed Project File Name: ***[your initials] PP A4-3.accdb***

1. Open the ***PlacerHills-04.accdb*** database file.

2. Save a new copy of your database as ***[your initials] PP A4-3***.

3. If prompted, enable content in the database.

4. Create a report using the *Report Wizard*.
   a. Click the **Report Wizard** button [*Create* tab, *Reports* group] to launch the *Report Wizard*.
   b. Click the **Tables/Queries** drop-down arrow and select the **Listings** table.
   c. Click the **Move All Fields** button.
   d. Select the **ListingAgentNumber** field in the *Selected Fields* window and click the **Remove Single Field** button.
   e. Remove the *Construction*, *YearBuilt*, *Garage*, and *DateListed* fields. The *Report Wizard* should look similar to Figure 4-94.
   f. Click the **Next** button to move to the second page of the *Report Wizard*.
   g. Do not group the data. Click the **Next** button to move to the third page of the *Report Wizard*.
   h. Sort the *ListPrice* field in ascending order.
   i. Click the **Next** button to move to the fourth page of the *Report Wizard*.
   j. Select a **Tabular** layout and **Portrait** orientation.
   k. Click the **Next** button to move to the last page of the *Report Wizard*.
   l. Type Listings–Report Wizard in the *Title* box.
   m. Click the **Finish** button. The report opens in *Print Preview* view (Figure 4-95). Notice that the *ListPrice* field moved to the left-most column because you are sorting on that field.
   n. Use the navigation buttons to move among pages.
   o. Click the **Close Print Preview** button.
   p. Close the report.

4-94 Select report fields

5. Create a report using the *Blank Report* button.
   a. Click the **Blank Report** button [*Create* tab, *Reports* group] to open a new, blank report in *Layout* view.
   b. In the *Field List* pane, click the link to **Show all tables**.

4-95 Listings report created using the *Report Wizard*

c. Click the **plus sign** to expand the *Listings* table.

d. Double-click the **ListingID** field to add it to the report.

e. Double-click the **ListPrice** field to add it to the report.

f. Add the **SqFt**, **Beds**, **Baths**, **Address**, **City**, and **Garage** fields to the report. The report should look similar to Figure 4-96.

ListingID	List Price	SqFt	Beds	Baths	Address	City	Garage
10022	$337,600.00	2755	3	2	525 Riverdale	Lincoln	2 Car Detache
10023	$339,600.00	1600	3	2	615 Silver Hill	Lincoln	2 Car Attached
10024	$675,000.00	3397	4	4	1917 Oak Cre:	Roseville	3 Car Attached
10025	$216,600.00	1900	4	3	3420 Milburn S	Rocklin	3 Car Attached
10027	$130,000.00	1184	3	2	2128 Wedgew	Roseville	1 Car Detache
10029	##########	6685	7	6	3998 Rawhide	Rocklin	4 Car Attached

4-96 Add fields into a tabular layout of a blank report

g. Close the field list.

6. Save the report. Enter Listings – Blank Report Button as the *Report Name*.

7. Add a title and page numbers to the report.

   a. Click the **Design** tab.

   b. Click the **Title** button [*Header/Footer* group]. Accept the default wording of the title.

   c. Click the **Page Numbers** button [*Header/Footer* group].

   d. Select the **Page N of M** radio button in the *Format* group.

   e. Select the **Bottom of Page [Footer]** radio button in the *Position* group.

   f. Select **Left** in the *Alignment* drop-down list.

   g. Click the **OK** button.

8. Adjust the width of the report columns.

   a. Select a **text box** in the *ListingID* column.

   b. Place your pointer over the right edge of the text box until it becomes a two-arrow sizing pointer.

   c. Click, hold, and drag the pointer to decrease the width of the text box.

   d. Decrease the width of the *SqFt*, *Beds*, and *Baths* columns.

   e. As needed, increase the width of the *Address*, *List Price* and *Garage* columns.

9. Save the report.

10. Preview the report by selecting the **View** button arrow [*Report Layout Tools Design* tab, *Views* group] and selecting the **Print Preview** option. The report should look similar to Figure 4-97.

11. Click the **Close Print Preview** button.

12. Close the report.

13. Close the database.

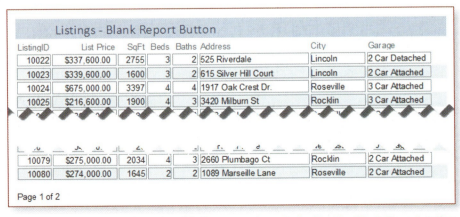

4-97 Completed listings report created using the *Blank Report* option

Grouping, Sorting, and Totals

As you learned in the *Report Wizard* section, you can choose to sort records in a report on different fields, to add grouping to a report, or to add totals to a report. Grouping is useful when you want to organize and summarize your data. For example, you could group all properties from the same city together in a real estate database or you could group all the songs from a particular artist together in a music database. When you create a grouping, Access can automatically calculate various summary values across the different groups. You can also combine sorting with the grouping. Finally, totals can also be added to a report independently of grouping or sorting being used.

You add grouping and sorting to a report using the *Group & Sort* button [*Report Layout Tools Design* tab, *Grouping & Totals* group] (Figure 4-98). Add totals using the *Totals* button [*Report Layout Tools Design* tab, *Grouping & Totals* group].

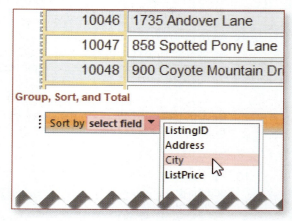

4-98 *Grouping & Totals* options

Sorting

A very useful feature in Access reports is data sorting. Sorting makes it easier to read and understand reports because it places all like data together. Access allows you to sort on multiple fields, with each field having its own sort order.

HOW TO: Add a Sort to a Report

1. Open the report in *Layout* view.
2. Click the **Design** tab.
3. Click the **Group & Sort** button [*Grouping & Totals* group] to open the *Group, Sort, and Total* pane at the bottom of the report.
4. Select the **Add a sort** option in the *Group, Sort, and Total* pane.
5. Select the field you want to sort by from the field list (Figure 4-99).
   - The report updates to display the data sorted in ascending order by the selected field.
   - The *Group, Sort, and Total* pane updates to show how the report is being sorted (Figure 4-100).
   - The default sort order is *with A on top* for text fields, *oldest to newest* for date fields, and *smallest to largest* for number fields.
6. As desired, click the arrow to the right of the default sort order to change the sort order. The default sort order in Figure 4-100 is *with A on top*.

4-99 Select a sort field

> **MORE INFO**
>
> You can add additional sorting levels to a report by clicking the **Add a sort** option.

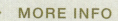

4-100 Updated *Group, Sort, and Total* pane

7. Close the *Group, Sort, and Total* pane by clicking the **X** on the *Group, Sort, and Total* header row. Be careful not to click the *Delete* symbol inside the pane or you remove the sort.

Add a Group to a Report

When you add a group in *Layout* view, a new section is added using a stepped layout. You can group on more than one field.

HOW TO: Add a Group to a Report

1. Open the report in *Layout* view.
2. Click the **Design** tab.
3. Click the **Group & Sort** button [*Grouping & Totals* group] to open the *Group, Sort, and Total* pane at the bottom of the report.
4. Select the **Add a group** option in the *Group, Sort, and Total* pane.
5. Select the field you want to group on from the field list (Figure 4-101).
   - The selected field moves to the left-most column (Figure 4-102).
   - The report changes to a stepped layout.
   - The *Group, Sort, and Total* pane updates to show how the report is being grouped (Figure 4-103).
6. As desired, click the arrow to the right of the default sort order of the grouping to change the sort order. The default sort order of the grouping in Figure 4-103 is *with A on top*.

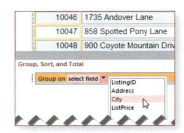

4-101 Select a group field

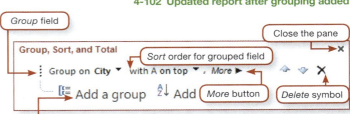

4-102 Updated report after grouping added

> **MORE INFO**
>
> You can add additional grouping levels to a report by clicking the **Add a group** option.

7. Close the *Group, Sort, and Total* pane by clicking the **X** on the *Group, Sort, and Total* header row. Be careful not to click the *Delete* symbol inside the pane or you remove the group.

4-103 Updated *Group, Sort, and Total* pane

Group and Sort Options

You can modify the report design after adding a sort or group section. You can also change the location or format of the grouping field in the control layout.

Other modifications are available. Click the **More** button in the *Group, Sort, and Total* pane to see the options shown in Figure 4-104 and explained in the following table. Click the **Less** button to close the expanded list of options.

4-104 Expanded options in *Group, Sort, and Total* pane

Options in the Group, Sort, and Total Pane

Category	Options	Explanation
Sorting	Ascending	The grouping field is sorted in ascending order.
	Descending	The grouping field is sorted in descending order.
Grouping	By entire value	The grouping is based on the entire value in the selected field.
	By partial value	The grouping is based on only part of the field. For example, in a text field, the grouping could be "by first character," which would group together all values that start with the same letter. In a date field, the grouping could be by year or month.
	Custom	The grouping is based on a specific number of characters that you provide.
Totals	Select the field and type of calculation	You choose which field in the report should be calculated, along with the calculation. Choices include *Sum*, *Avg*, *Count*, *Max*, and *Min*.
	Show grand totals	Calculates overall totals for all records.
	Show group totals as percentage of grand total	Displays the group totals as a percentage of the grand total.
	Show in header or footer section	Determines which section displays the totals.
Title		Changes the wording in the label of the grouping field.
Header section	With a header section/ without a header section	Determines whether to include a header section in the report.
Footer section	With a footer section/ without a footer section	Determines whether to include a footer section in the report.
Keep group together	Do not keep group together on one page	Allows a group to be split across multiple pages if it can't all fit in the space remaining on a page.
	Keep whole group together on one page	Starts a group on the following page if it can't all fit in the space remaining on a page.
	Keep header and first record together on one page	Prevents a header from printing on the bottom of a page unless at least one record of the group can also be printed with the header.

The wording for some of the options depends on the data type of the field. For example, an ascending sort for a text field is *"with A on top"* while an ascending sort for a date field is *"from oldest to newest."*

HOW TO: Modify Options in a Group

1. Open the report in *Layout* view.
2. Click the **Design** tab.
3. If the *Group, Sort, and Total* pane is not open, click the **Group & Sort** button [*Grouping & Totals* group].
4. Select the **More** option in the *Group, Sort, and Total* pane.
5. Select the **arrow** of the desired option and select the new option choice (Figure 4-105).

   - The report updates to reflect the new option.
   - The expanded list of options closes.

4-105 Expanded grouping options in *Group, Sort, and Total* pane

6. If you decide not to make any modifications, click the **Less** option to close the expanded list of options.
7. Close the *Group, Sort, and Total* pane by clicking the **X** on the *Group, Sort, and Total* header row.

Add Totals to a Report

You can add totals to a report to allow performance of overall calculations based on your data. Calculation options include *Sum, Average, Count Records, Count Values, Max, Min, Standard Deviation,* and *Variance*.

HOW TO: Add Totals to a Report

1. Open the report in *Layout* view.
2. Click the **Design** tab.
3. Select a **text box** in the field you want to total.
4. Select the **Totals** button in the *Grouping & Totals* group.
5. Select the desired calculation (Figure 4-106).
   - The report updates with the total added to the bottom of the report.
6. You can select another field and repeat the process to total that field as well.

4-106 *Totals* **button options**

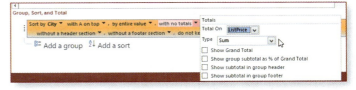

4-107 **Total options in** *Group, Sort, and Total* **pane**

SLO 4.7

Using Conditional Formatting in Reports

Conditional formatting allows you to format only values that meet a certain condition. This helps you focus the user's attention to certain records in a report.

Conditional Formatting Rules

The formatting rules are defined in the *New Formatting Rule* dialog box (Figure 4-108). When building a rule you must select the ***rule type***, conditions, and the desired formatting.

The most common rule type is *Check values in the current record or use an expression*. Use the *Compare to other records* rule type to create data bars, which allow you to compare values across data records.

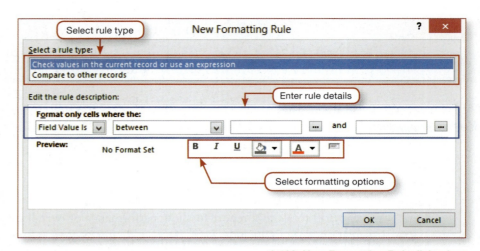

4-108 *New Formatting Rule* dialog box

Most formatting rules compare the value in a field. When you are building a rule, the dialog box options change based on the selection you make. For example, Figure 4-109a shows a rule where you enter only one data value based on the selection of the *less than* comparison. Compare this to Figure 4-109b, where you enter two data values for a *between* comparison. These figures also show examples of different formatting options.

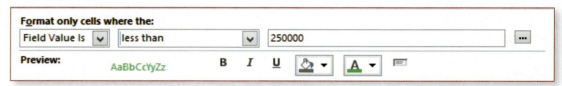

4-109a **Example rule with less than comparison and one data value**

4-109b **Example rule with between comparison and two data values**

Once you build a rule, it displays in the *Conditional Formatting Rules Manager* dialog box. You can have multiple rules in one report and even multiple rules for the same field.

When you have multiple rules, the order in which they are listed is very important, as Access stops evaluating when a match is found. For example, a report using the rules in Figure 4-110 would show a *ListPrice* that is less than 100,000 in blue instead of brown. That is because a value less than 100,000 is also less than 500,000. The evaluation stops after the condition in the first rule is met. To correct this situation, select the *Value < 500000* rule and use the down arrow key to make it the second rule instead of the first.

4-110 *Conditional Formatting Rules Manager* dialog box with multiple rules

Add Conditional Formatting to a Report

To add conditional formatting, you need to determine which fields will have formatting applied and the specific criteria you want to use to make the rule.

HOW TO: Add Conditional Formatting to a Report to Check Values in the Current Record or Use an Expression

1. Open the report in *Layout* view.
2. Click the **Format** tab.
3. Select any **text box** in the column where you wish to apply the criteria.

> **ANOTHER WAY**
>
> Select multiple fields and apply the same rule to all selected fields.

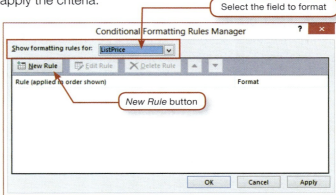

4-111 *Conditional Formatting Rules Manager* **dialog box**

4. Click the **Conditional Formatting** button [*Control Formatting* group] to open the *Conditional Formatting Rules Manager* dialog box (Figure 4-111).
   - The selected field displays in the *Show formatting rules for* box.
   - If more than one field is selected, *Multiple* displays in the box.
5. If necessary, change the field to format in the *Show formatting rules for* box.
6. Click the **New Rule** button to open the *New Formatting Rule* dialog box.
7. Select **Check values in the current record or use an expression** in the *Select a rule type* box.
8. Click the appropriate **arrows** to select the desired comparison.
9. Type the comparison values into the boxes.
10. Select formatting options as desired.
11. Click **OK**.
    - The completed rule displays in the *Conditional Formatting Rules Manager* dialog box (Figure 4-112).

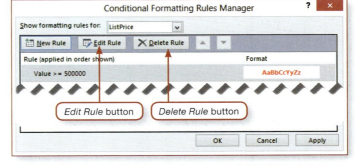

4-112 **Completed rule**

12. Add another rule to either the same field or a different field as desired.
13. Click **Apply** to have Access evaluate the data in the report and apply the formatting to the values that meet the criteria.
14. Click **OK** when you are finished building all rules.

The *Conditional Formatting Rules Manager* displays rules for only one field at a time. If you created rules for multiple fields, select the desired field first in the *Show formatting rules for* box to view the rules for that specific field.

- You can edit an existing rule by selecting the rule in the *Conditional Formatting Rules Manager* dialog box and clicking the **Edit Rule** button.
- You can delete an existing rule by selecting the rule in the *Conditional Formatting Rules Manager* dialog box and clicking the **Delete Rule** button.

Printing Reports

Reports can be viewed on screen but most reports are designed to be printed. To ensure that your report prints as desired, take the time to review it in *Print Preview* view.

Preview a Report

Recall that *Print Preview* allows you to see how your report appears on a printed page. The options on the *Print Preview* tab let you adjust the size and margins of the page, change the orientation, and change the zoom level as needed.

HOW TO: Preview a Report

1. Select the desired report in the *Navigation* pane.
2. Click the **View** button arrow [*Home* tab, *Views* group] and select the **Print Preview** option.
3. Make any desired adjustments to the report (Figure 4-113).

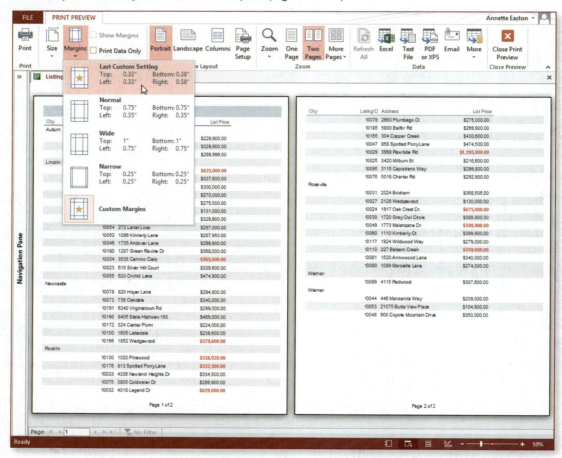

4-113 Adjust printing options while viewing a report in *Print Preview*

4. If you are ready to print, click the **Print** button [*Print Preview* tab, *Print* group] to open the *Print* dialog box. Choose desired options and click **OK** to print the report.
5. Click the **Close Print Preview** button.

Print a Report without Print Preview

If you already know that your report is designed correctly, you can print the report without previewing it first.

1. Select the desired report in the *Navigation* pane.
2. Click the **Print** button [*File* tab].
3. To print the report on the default printer without making any changes, click **Quick Print**.
4. To select a printer and printing options, click **Print** to open the *Print* dialog box. Choose desired options and click **OK** to print.

PAUSE & PRACTICE: ACCESS 4-4

For this Pause & Practice you edit a report based on a parameter query. You modify the report to add grouping and conditional formatting. Finally, you preview the report.

File Needed: ***CentralSierra-04-PP4-4.accdb***
Completed Project File Name: ***[your initials] PP A4-4.accdb***

1. Open the ***CentralSierra-04-PP4-4.accdb*** database file.
2. Save a new copy of your database as ***[your initials] PP A4-4***.
3. If prompted, enable content in the database.
4. Double-click the **EmployeesBranchParameter** query.
5. In the *Enter Parameter Value* dialog box, leave the value blank and click **OK**.
   a. The query executes and displays the results shown in Figure 4-114.
   b. The report you edit in this Pause & Practice was created using this query as the data source instead of a table.

Employee	Title	Branch	Base Monthly Salary
Bob Lingle	CEO	Cameron Park	$15,000.00
Lanita McCartney	Chief Operating Office	Cameron Park	$12,000.00
Eleesha Santos	Insurance Agent	Cameron Park	$5,500.00
Roy Baxter	Insurance Agent	Granite Bay	$4,500.00
Jennifer Alan	Administrative Assistant	Folsom	$9,000.00

4-114 *EmployeesBranchParameter* **query results**

6. Close the query.
7. Add grouping to the report.
   a. Open the *EmployeesBranchParameterReport* report in *Layout* view. The query executes.
   b. In the *Enter Parameter Value* dialog box, leave the value blank and click **OK**. The report opens in *Layout* view.
   c. Click the **Group & Sort** button [*Report Layout Tools Design* tab, *Grouping & Totals* group] to open the *Group, Sort, and Total* pane at the bottom of the report.
   d. Select the **Add a group** option in the *Group, Sort, and Total* pane.
   e. Select the **Branch** field from the *Group on select field* list (Figure 4-115).
   f. Close the *Group, Sort, and Total* pane by clicking the **X** on the *Group, Sort, and Total* header row. Be careful not to click the *Delete* symbol inside the pane or you remove the group.

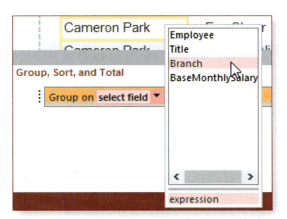

4-115 **Group on the** *Branch* **field**

8. Add conditional formatting to the report.
   a. Click any salary cell in the *Base Monthly Salary* column. All of the salary values should be highlighted.
   b. Click the **Conditional Formatting** button [*Report Layout tools Format* tab, *Control Formatting* group] to open the *Conditional Formatting Rules Manager* dialog box. *BaseMonthlySalary* displays in the *Show formatting rules for* box.
   c. Click the **New Rule** button to open the *New Formatting Rule* dialog box.
   d. Select the **Check values in the current record or use an expression** rule type in the *Select a rule type* box.
   e. Select **greater than or equal to** as the comparison.
   f. Type 10000 into the value box.
   g. Select **Bold** and a **red** font.
   h. Click **OK**. The completed rule displays in the *Conditional Formatting Rules Manager* dialog box (Figure 4-116).
   i. Click **Apply**.
   j. Click **OK**.

9. Save the report.

10. Preview the way the report will print.
    a. Right-click in the report and select **Print Preview** from the context menu.
    b. In the *Enter Parameter Value* dialog box, leave the value blank and click **OK**.
    c. Click the **Zoom** button arrow and select the **Fit to Window** option.
    d. Click the **Margins** button arrow and select the **Normal** option. If a message displays that the section width is greater than the page width, click **OK** to acknowledge the message. Your report should look similar to Figure 4-117.
    e. Close the *Print Preview* of the report.

11. Save the report.

12. Close the report.

13. Close the database.

4-116 Completed rule for *BaseMonthlySalary* field

4-117 Completed report with grouping and conditional formatting

Chapter Summary

4.1 Create a simple form using the quick create options; save, modify, and delete a form (p. A4-214).

- *Forms* allow you to view, add, update, and delete data in a database.
- You can build forms from tables, queries, or both.
- *Bound forms* are linked to the data source; **unbound forms** don't have a connection to a direct link to a data source.
- The *Form Wizard* lets you quickly build a form by specifying the tables or queries to use, selecting the desired fields and the desired layout of the form.
- You can use the *Form* button to create a form in one click.
- The *Split Form* option lets you view data in two ways on the same form by combining both a columnar display and a datasheet display.
- You can edit a form in *Design* view or *Layout* view and modify any aspect of the form's design.

4.2 Create a blank form, understand controls and control layouts, and customize a form in *Layout* view (p. A4-222).

- The *Blank Form* button lets you create a new form from scratch using *Layout* view.
- The buttons, labels, fields, and so forth that you place on a form are called **controls**.
- Controls can be **bound**, **unbound**, or **calculated**.
- *Control layouts* provide the structure that aligns the controls on a form.
- The two primary control layouts are **tabular** and **stacked**.
- You must save each form with a unique name.

4.3 Restrict a form to data entry, limit user edits and deletes on a form, add command buttons, and test a form (p. A4-228).

- When designing a form for data entry, choose design options that help minimize potential data entry errors and maximize efficiency for entering data.
- Use the *Data Entry* property of a form to restrict the form to allow data entry only when you don't want the user to be able to view data already in the database.

- Use the *Allow Edits* and *Allow Deletions* properties of a form when you want to limit the user's ability to edit or delete records in the database.
- You can add **command buttons** to a form to automate user tasks.
- Use the *Command Button Wizard* to easily add buttons to a form.
- After you build a form, test it to ensure that it functions as desired.

4.4 Create a simple report with the *Report Wizard*; save, modify, and delete a report (p. A4-235).

- Use *reports* to create an organized and professional output of the data in a database.
- You can build reports from tables, queries, or both.
- The *Report Wizard* lets you quickly build a report by specifying the tables or queries to use, selecting the desired fields, selecting any grouping or sorting options, and specifying the layout of the report.
- *Report* view executes a report and displays the results.
- *Print Preview* view shows how a report will look in print while also allowing you to make modifications to the printing settings.
- You can modify reports in *Design* view or *Layout* view.

4.5 Create a blank report, understand controls and control layouts, customize a report in *Layout* view, and add a title, a date, and page numbers to a report (p. A4-242).

- The *Blank Report* button lets you create a new report from scratch using *Layout* view.
- *Control layouts* provide the structure that aligns the controls on a report.
- The two primary control layouts are **tabular** and **stacked**.
- The buttons, labels, fields, and so forth that you place on a form are **controls**. Controls can be **bound**, **unbound**, or **calculated**.
- It is good design practice to include *titles*, *dates*, and *page numbers* on a report.
- You must save each form with a unique name.

4.6 Enhance a report by adding grouping, sorting, and totals to a report in *Layout* view (p. A4-250).

- *Sorting* the records in a report makes it easier to read and understand the data contained in the report.

- You can sort a report in *ascending* or *descending* order on one or more fields.
- Add a *group* to a report to organize and summarize the data.
- A report can contain multiple groups.
- Within a grouping level, you can choose to include *header* or *footer sections*, integrate *sorting*, and include *summary totals*.
- *Totals* allow you to perform overall calculations based on the data in the report.
- Calculation options include *Sum*, *Average*, *Count Records*, *Count Values*, *Max*, *Min*, *Standard Deviation*, and *Variance*.

4.7 Integrate conditional formatting into a report (p. A4-253).

- *Conditional formatting* allows you to format only values that meet a specified condition.

- A report can contain multiple formatting rules.
- When using multiple rules, the order of specifying the rules is important because Access stops evaluating once it finds a rule that matches the data.
- You can add, modify, and delete rules from the *Conditional Formatting Rules Manager* dialog box.

4.8 Preview, modify print settings, and print a report (p. A4-256).

- To ensure that your report prints as desired, review it in *Print Preview* view.
- You can adjust the print settings related to *page size*, *margins*, and *page orientation* using the *Print Preview* mode.
- You can print a report directly from the *Backstage* view without using *Print Preview*.

Check for Understanding

In the **Online Learning Center** for this text (www.mhhe.com/office2013inpractice), there are a variety of resources that can be used to review the concepts covered in this chapter.

The following Online Learning Resources are available in the Online Learning Center:

- Multiple Choice questions
- Short answer questions
- Matching exercises

Guided Project 4-1

In this project, you enhance the functionality of the database you built for your friend's music collection by building a form to display information about the albums and a report to show all of the songs on each album. To ensure consistency, the starting file is provided for you. Use the *Form Wizard* to create a form and *Layout* view to edit the form. Create a report using the *Report Wizard*, edit the report in *Layout* view, add totals to the report, and view the report using *Print Preview*.
[Student Learning Outcomes 4.1, 4.2, 4.4, 4.5, 4.6, 4.8]

File Needed: ***MusicDatabase-04.accdb***
Completed Project File Name: *[your initials] Access 4-1.accdb*

Skills Covered in This Project

- Create a form using the *Form Wizard*.
- Edit a form in *Layout* view.
- Add the current date to a form.
- Create a report using the *Report Wizard*.

- Edit a report in *Layout* view.
- Add totals to a report.
- View a report using *Print Preview*.

1. Open the ***MusicDatabase-04.accdb*** database file.
2. Save the database as *[your initials] Access 4-1*.
3. If prompted, enable content in the database.
4. Create a form using the *Form Wizard*.
   a. Click the **Form Wizard** button [*Create* tab, *Forms* group] to launch the *Form Wizard*.
   b. Click the **Tables/Queries** drop-down arrow and select the **Album** table.
   c. Click the **Move All Fields** button to move all of the fields from the *Available Fields* window to the *Selected Fields* window.
   d. Click the **Next** button to move to the second page of the *Form Wizard*.
   e. Select the **Columnar** radio button.
   f. Click the **Next** button to move to the last page of the *Form Wizard*.
   g. Type MusicAlbums in the *Title* box. Remember that the title also becomes the form name. Entering the title without spaces follows the CamelCase naming convention used in the book.
   h. Click **Finish**. The form opens in *Form* view.
   i. Use the navigation buttons to move to record album 25. This album has the longest album name.
5. Edit the form column widths in *Layout* view.
   a. Click the **View** button arrow [*Home* tab, *Views* group] and select **Layout View**.
   b. Close the **Field List**, if it is open.
   c. Select the **AlbumName** text box.
   d. Place your pointer at the right edge until it becomes a two-arrow sizing pointer.
   e. Click, hold, and drag the pointer to decrease the width of the text box so that it looks similar to the width in Figure 4-118.
   f. Continue changing the width of the **ArtistName**, **Genre**, **Length**, and **RecordingLabel** text boxes until your fields look similar to those in Figure 4-118.

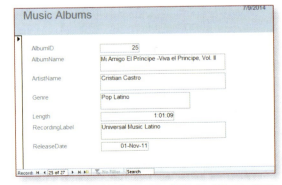

4-118 Completed *Music Albums* form

6. Edit the form header section.
   a. Click to select the **MusicAlbums** label in the header section.
   b. Click in the label to open the edit mode.
   c. Insert a space between "Music" and "Albums."
   d. Click in the header section outside of the label.
   e. Click the **Date and Time** button [*Form Layout Tools Design* Tab, *Header/Footer* group].
   f. Select the radio button to display the date using the **mm/dd/yyyy** format.
   g. Deselect the check box to **Include Time**.
   h. Click **OK**.
   i. Click the **Form View** icon in the *Status bar*. The completed form should look similar to Figure 4-118. Depending on the width of the Access window, your date field may be further to the right in your form.

7. Save the form.

8. Close the form.

9. Create a report using the *Report Wizard*.
   a. Click the **Report Wizard** button [*Create* tab, *Reports* group] to launch the *Report Wizard*.
   b. Click the **Tables/Queries** drop-down arrow in the box and select the **SongsOnAlbums** query. This report is based on a query instead of a table.
   c. Select the **AlbumName** field.
   d. Click the **Move Single Field** button.
   e. Continue adding the **ArtistName** and **SongTitle** fields. Remember that you can click the **Remove Single Field** button if you accidentally add a field that is not needed.

   f. Click the **Next** button to move to the next page of the *Report Wizard*.
   g. Choose to view the data **by Album**. The *Report Wizard* should look similar to Figure 4-119.

4-119 Select to view the data *by Album* in the *Report Wizard*

   h. Click **Next**.
   i. Do not group the data. Click the **Next** button to move to the next page of the *Report Wizard*.
   j. Do not sort the data. Click the **Next** button to move to the next page of the *Report Wizard*.
   k. Select a **Stepped** layout and **Portrait** orientation.
   l. Click the **Next** button to move to the last page of the *Report Wizard*.
   m. Type SongsOnAlbums in the *Title* box.
   n. Click the **Finish** button. The report opens in *Print Preview* view (Figure 4-120).
   o. Use the navigation buttons to move among pages.
   p. Click the **Close Print Preview** button. The report displays in *Design* view.

10. Edit the report header section.
    a. Close the **Field List** pane if it is open.
    b. Click to select the **SongsOnAlbums** label in the header section.
    c. Click in the label to open the edit mode.
    d. Insert spaces between "Songs" and "On" and "Albums."
    e. Click in the header section outside of the label.

4-120 *SongsOnAlbums* report

11. Edit the report column widths using *Layout* view.
   a. Switch the report to *Layout* view.
   b. Click the **Find** button [*Home* tab, *Find* group]. The *Find* dialog box displays.
   c. Type Moves like in the *Find What* box.
   d. Select **Any Part of Field** in the *Match* box.
   e. Click **Find Next**. The *Moves Like Jagger* song from the *Hands All Over* album by *Maroon 5* should be selected. This song has the longest song title.
   f. Close the *Find* dialog box.
   g. Place your pointer over the left edge of the text box until the pointer becomes a two-arrow sizing pointer.
   h. Click, hold, and drag the pointer towards the *ArtistName* column to increase the width of the text box. Make it large enough so you can see the entire title of the "Moves Like Jagger" song. You may need to drag the pointer a few times until you are happy with the increased size.
   i. If necessary, scroll up a little so that you can see the album name, *Hands All Over*, for this song.
   j. Click to select the **Hands All Over** text box in the *AlbumName* column.
   k. Place your pointer over the lower right corner of the text box until the pointer becomes a diagonal two-arrow sizing pointer.
   l. Click, hold, and drag the pointer down and towards the left to decrease the width of the text box while also making it taller (Figure 4-121).
   m. Click to select the **Maroon 5** text box in the *ArtistName* column.
   n. Click the left arrow key ten times to move the *ArtistName* column closer to the *AlbumName*.
   o. Click in the **AlbumName** column. Be sure that the size of this text box does not overlap with the *ArtistName* textbox. If necessary, fine-tune the width of those two text boxes.
   p. Scroll to the top of the report.
   q. Select the **ArtistName** label.
   r. Click the left arrow key 15 times to move the label to the left.

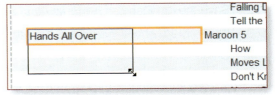

4-121 Adjust the size of the *AlbumName* column

12. Add totals to the report to count the number of songs on each album.
   a. Click the **Report Layout Tools Design** tab.
   b. Select a **text box** in the *SongTitle* column.
   c. Select the **Total** button in the *Grouping & Totals* group.
   d. Select the **Count Records** option. The report updates to display the count below the last song on each album.

13. Save the report.

14. Switch to *Print Preview* view. The complete report should look similar to Figure 4-122.

15. Close the report.

16. Close the database.

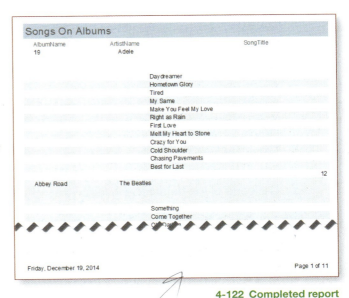

4-122 Completed report

Guided Project 4-2

San Diego Sailing Club wants to add forms and a report to its database. To ensure consistency, the starting file is provided for you. Use the *Blank Form* option to create the form and *Layout* view to modify the form, save a copy of the form, edit form properties, and add command buttons. Create a report using the *Report Wizard* and use *Layout* view to modify the report.
[Student Learning Outcomes 4.1, 4.2, 4.3, 4.4, 4.5]

File Needed: ***SanDiegoSailing-04.accdb***
Completed Project File Name: ***[your initials] Access 4-2.accdb***

Skills Covered in This Project

- Create a form using the *Blank Form* option.
- Edit a form in *Layout* view.
- Save a copy of the form.
- Add a title to a form.
- Add buttons to a form.
- Set form properties.
- Create a report using the *Report Wizard*.
- Edit a report in *Layout* view.

1. Open the ***SanDiegoSailing-04.accdb*** database file.

2. Save the database as ***[your initials] Access 4-2***.

3. If prompted, enable content in the database.

4. Create a new form using the *Blank Form* option.
   a. Click the **Blank Form** button [*Create* tab, *Forms* group]. A new blank form opens in *Layout* view.
   b. In the *Field List* pane, click the link to **Show all tables**.
   c. Click the **plus sign** to expand the *SailboatFleet* table and see the fields in the table.
   d. Double-click the **BoatID** field to add it to the form.
   e. Double-click the **BoatType** field to add it to the form.
   f. Continue adding all the fields from the *SailboatFleet* table to the form. The form should look similar to Figure 4-123.
   g. Close the *Field List*.

5. Modify the control layout.
   a. Click one of the **fields** on the form. It is surrounded by an orange border.
   b. Click the **Select Layout** button [*Form Layout Tools Arrange* tab, *Rows & Columns* group]. All the cells in the layout are bordered in orange.
   c. Move the pointer over any field. Click, hold, and drag the control layout down and to the right (Figure 4-124).
   d. Select the **Galley w/ Stove** label.

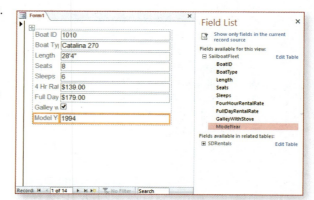

4-123 Add fields from the *SailboatFleet* table onto the form

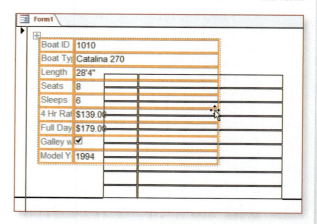

4-124 Move the control layout

e. Place your pointer over the right edge of the label until the pointer becomes a two-arrow sizing pointer.
f. Click, hold, and drag the pointer to increase the width of the label so you can read the entire label text.
g. Navigate to record number 4.
h. Click in the **BoatType** text box.
i. Decrease the width of the text box by about half.

6. Add a new column and new rows to the control layout.
   a. Select the **ModelYear** text box.
   b. Click the **Select Row** button [*Form Layout Tools Arrange* tab, *Rows & Columns* group].
   c. Click the **Insert Below** button [*Form Layout Tools Arrange* tab, *Rows & Columns* group] to add a blank row.
   d. Click the **Insert Below** button again to add a second blank row.
   e. Select the **ModelYear** text box.
   f. Click the **Select Column** button [*Form Layout Tools Arrange* tab, *Rows & Columns* group].
   g. Click the **Insert Right** button [*Form Layout Tools Arrange* tab, *Rows & Columns* group] to add a blank column.

7. Adjust the height and width of the new rows and column.
   a. Select a **cell** in the new column.
   b. Place your pointer over the right edge of the cell until the pointer becomes a two-arrow sizing pointer. Click, hold, and drag the pointer to increase the width of the cell. Make the width of the selected column approximately the same as the first column.
   c. Select a **cell** in the bottom blank row.
   d. Place your pointer over the bottom edge of the cell until the pointer becomes a two-arrow sizing pointer.
   e. Click, hold, and drag the pointer **to increase the height** of the cell. Make the height approximately twice as high as any other row. The revised form should look like Figure 4-125.

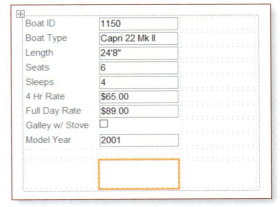

4-125 *SailboatFleetForm* **after adding a row and column**

8. Save the form. Enter SailboatFleetForm as the *Form Name*.

9. With the *SailboatFleetForm* still open, save another copy of the form by clicking **Save As** [*File* tab] and then selecting **Save Object As** and click the **Save As** button. Enter AddNewSailboatForm as the *Form Name*.

10. Add command buttons to the new form.
    a. Verify that the *AddNewSailboatForm* is open in *Layout* view. Click the **Form Layout Tools Design** tab.
    b. Click the **More** arrow at the far right of the *Controls* group and select the **Use Control Wizards** button.
    c. Click **Button** in the *Controls* group. Move the pointer to the left-most cell in the bottom row of the control layout and click. The *Command Button Wizard* launches.
    d. Select the **Record Operations** category and the **Save Record** action of the button.
    e. Click **Next** to move to the second page of the *Command Button Wizard*.
    f. Select the **Text** radio button and change the wording to read Save Sailboat Record.
    g. Click **Next** to move to the last page of the *Wizard*.
    h. Enter AddBoatFormSaveButton as the name for the button and click **Finish**. The button displays in the form.
    i. Add a second button to the form. Place the button in the middle cell of the last row.

    j. Select the **Record Operations** category and the **Add New Record** action of the button. Click **Next**.

    k. Select the **Text** radio button and change the wording to read Add New Sailboat. Click **Next**.

    l. Enter AddBoatFormAddButton as the button name and click **Finish**.

    m. Add a third button onto the form. Place the button in the right-most cell of the last row.

    n. Select the **Form Operations** category and the **Close Form** action of the button. Click **Next**.

    o. Select the **Text** radio button and use the existing "Close Form" wording. Click **Next**.

    p. Enter AddBoatFormCloseButton as the name for the button and click **Finish**.

11. Add a title control to the form.

    a. Click the **Title** button [*Form Layout Tools Design* tab, *Header/Footer* group].

    b. Change the wording to Add New Sailboat.

    c. Click in the form area to save the changes to the label. The form should look similar to Figure 4-126.

    d. Save the form.

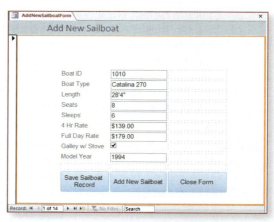

4-126 Modified *AddNewSailboatForm*

12. Restrict the form to data entry.

    a. Click the **Property Sheet** button [*Form Layout Tools Design* tab, *Tools* group] to open the *Property Sheet*.

    b. In the *Selection* box of the *Property Sheet*, click the **drop-down arrow** and select **Form**.

    c. If necessary, click to select the **Data** tab.

    d. Select **Yes** in the *Data Entry* property box.

    e. Select **Yes** in the *Allow Additions* property box.

    f. Close the *Property Sheet*.

    g. Save the form.

13. Switch to *Form* view by clicking the **View** button arrow [*Form Layout Tools Design* tab, *Views* group] and selecting the **Form View** option. The complete form displays.

14. Test the form.

    a. Enter the data shown in Figure 4-127.

    b. Click the **Save Sailboat Record** button.

    c. Click the **Add New Sailboat** button. A blank record should display in the form.

    d. Click the **Close Form** button.

Boat ID	1230
Boat Type	Catalina 270
Length	28'4"
Seats	8
Sleeps	6
4 Hr Rate	$139.00
Full Day Rate	$179.00
Galley w/ Stove	☑
Model Year	2008

4-127 Sample data

15. Modify the *SailboatFleetForm* to limit user edits and deletes.

    a. Open the **SailboatFleetForm** in *Layout* view.

    b. Click the **Form Layout Tools Design** tab.

    c. Click the **Property Sheet** button [*Tools* group] to open the *Property Sheet*.

    d. In the *Selection* box of the *Property Sheet*, click the **drop-down arrow** and select **Form**.

    e. Select **No** in the *Data Entry* property box.

    f. Select **No** in the *Allow Additions* property box.

    g. Select **No** in the *Allow Deletions* property box.

    h. Select **No** in the *Allow Edits* property box.

    i. Close the *Property Sheet*.

16. Add a title control to the form.

    a. Click the **Title** button [*Form Layout Tools Design* tab, *Header/Footer* group].

    b. Change the title wording to View Sailboat Fleet Data.

c. Click in the form area to save changes to the label.
d. Save the form.

17. Test the form.
    a. Switch to **Form** view.
    b. Navigate to record number 15 (the record you added earlier). The form should now look similar to Figure 4-128.
    c. Try to change the value in the *BoatID* text box. You should not be able to edit the value.
    d. Notice that the *New (blank) record* icon is not visible in the *Navigation* bar.
    e. Notice that the *Delete Record* button is not available in the *Records* group [*Home* tab].
    f. Close the form.

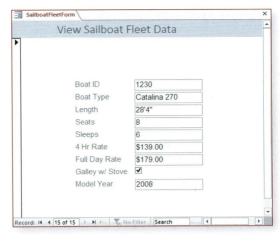

4-128 Updated *SailboatFleetForm*

18. Create a report using the *Report Wizard*.
    a. Click the **Report Wizard** button [*Create* tab, *Reports* group] to launch the *Report Wizard*.
    b. Click the **Tables/Queries** drop-down arrow and select the **SummaryOfFullDayRentalsByBoat** query.
    c. Click the **Move All Fields** button and click **Next**. The next page of the *Report Wizard* displays the grouping as shown in Figure 4-129.
    d. Click the **Next** button to move to the next page of the *Report Wizard*.
    e. Do not sort the data. Click the **Next** button to move to the next page of the *Report Wizard*.
    f. Select a **Block** layout and **Portrait** orientation. Click **Next**.
    g. Accept the suggested title.
    h. Click the **Finish** button. The report opens in *Print Preview* view (Figure 4-130).
    i. Click the **Close Print Preview** button. The report displays in *Design* view.

4-129 Suggested data grouping

4-130 *Print Preview* view of report

19. Edit the report labels using *Layout* view.
    a. Switch the report to *Layout* view.
    b. Click to select the **SummaryOfFullDay RentalsByBoat** label in the header section.
    c. Click in the label to open the edit mode.
    d. Insert a space between each of the words.
    e. Click in the header section outside of the label.
    f. Edit the labels of the column headers. Change *FKBoatID* to Boat ID and *SumOfFullDayRentalRate* to Total Income from Full Day Rentals.
    g. Save the report.
    h. Switch to *Report* view. The report should look similar to Figure 4-131.
    i. Close the report.

20. Close the database.

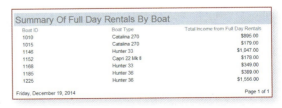

4-131 Completed report in *Report* view

Guided Project 4-3

Life's Animal Shelter wants to add a report and form to its database. To ensure consistency, the starting file is provided for you. You edit a report that was created based on a query. In *Layout* view, add a title, grouping, and totals. Next, add conditional formatting to the report, preview the results, and adjust print settings. Finally, you create a form using the *Split Form* option.
[Student Learning Outcomes 4.1, 4.5, 4.6, 4.7, 4.8]

File Needed: ***LifesAnimalShelter-04.accdb***
Completed Project File Name: ***[your initials] Access 4-3.accdb***

Skills Covered in This Project

- Modify a report in *Layout* view.
- Add grouping and sorting to a report.
- Add conditional formatting to a report.

- Add totals to a report.
- Preview a report.
- Create a form using the *Split Form* option.

---

1. Open the ***LifesAnimalShelter-04.accdb*** database file.

2. Save the database as ***[your initials] Access 4-3***.

3. If prompted, enable content in the database.

4. Open the *PetsWithoutMatchingOwner* report in *Layout* view.

5. Change the report to a landscape orientation.
   a. Click the **Report Layout Tools Page Setup** tab.
   b. Click the **Landscape** button [*Page Layout* group].

6. Adjust the width of the report columns.
   a. Click the **Report Layout Tools Arrange** tab.
   b. Select a **text box** in the *Why I'd make a great companion* column.
   c. Press and hold the **Shift** key and select the **Why I'd make a great companion** label.
   d. Press the **F4** key to open the *Property Sheet*. If necessary, click to select the **Format** tab of the *Property Sheet*.
   e. Enter 3.1 in the *Width* property. You must press **Enter** or **Tab** after entering the value so that Access recognizes a changed value.
   f. Enter 6.8 in the *Left* property.
   g. Select a **text box** in the *Breed* column.
   h. Press and hold the **Shift** key and select the **Breed** label.
   i. Enter 1.3 in the *Width* property.
   j. Select in a **text box** in the *Breed* column to select only the field and deselect the *Breed* label.
   k. Enter .5 in the *Height* property.
   l. Select a **text box** in the *Color* column.
   m. Press and hold the **Shift** key and select the **Color** label.
   n. Enter 1.5 in the *Width* property.
   o. Press **F4** to close the *Property Sheet*.
   p. Click the **right arrow** key 15 times to move the *Color* column to the right.
   q. Using Figure 4-132 as a guide, adjust the widths and placement of the *Pet Name*, *Type*, *Breed*, *Age*, and *Gender* columns. Be sure to change the size of the label of each column as well. You can either enter the property values in the *Property Sheet* or use the pointer to adjust the sizes and location.
   r. Save the report.

![Pets Without Matching Owner report showing a table with columns Pet ID, Pet Name, Type, Breed, Age, Gender, Color, Why I'd make a great companion](report)

Pet ID	Pet Name	Type	Breed	Age	Gender	Color	Why I'd make a great companion
2	Alec	Dog	Terrier cross Chihuahua	3 yrs	M	Tan	I like to take my time approaching new situations. While I am a bit shy with new faces and places, I warm up as I become more familiar with my environment. While I don't always like to be petted and held, I have a big heart and can't wait to share all of my love with a special family of my own. I'm a lovable companion seeking a special home where I'll be a cherished member of the family. With bright eyes and a precious face, I have a beautiful personality to match. **Type of home I'm looking for:** I would do best in a quiet home with no children or cats, please.
4	Barnaby	Rabbit	American cross	2 yrs	M	White	With my adorable long ears and fun-loving personality, I can't wait to find a special family and home. I like to take my time...

Friday, December 19, 2014

4-132 *PetsWithoutMatchingOwner* report

7. Edit the header and footer sections.
   a. Click the **Report Layout Tools Design** tab.
   b. Click the **text box** containing the *Date*.
   c. Click the **right arrow** key to move the field to the right. Repeat this action until the field is on the right edge of the header.
   d. Click in the title label.
   e. Change the label to Pets Available for Adoption.
   f. Click outside of the label to save the changes.
   g. Scroll down to the bottom of the report and select the **page number** text box.
   h. Click the **right arrow** key to move the field to the right. Repeat this action until the field is moved to the right side of the report.

8. Add grouping and sorting to the report.
   a. Click the **Group & Sort** button [*Report Layout Tools Design* tab, *Grouping & Totals* group] to open the *Group*, *Sort*, and *Total* pane at the bottom of the report.
   b. Select the **Add a group** option in the *Group*, *Sort*, and *Total* pane.
   c. Select the **Type** field from the *Group on select field* list.
   d. Select the **Add a sort** option in the *Group*, *Sort*, and *Total* pane.
   e. Select the **ID** field from the *Sort by select field* list.
   f. Select the **More** option in the *Group*, *Sort*, and *Total* pane.
   g. Select the **do not keep group together on one page** arrow and select the **keep header and first record together on one page** option (Figure 4-133).

   4-133 *Keep header and first record together on one page* option

   h. Close the *Group*, *Sort*, and *Total* pane by clicking the **X** on the *Group*, *Sort*, and *Total* header row. Be careful not to click the *Delete* symbol inside the pane or you remove the group.
   i. Scroll to the top of the report. The first record should be for "Martin", *Pet ID* number 6. Because the grouping uses a stepped layout, the word "Cat" appears in the *Type* column on the line above Martin.

9. Add conditional formatting to the report.
   a. Click any **cell** in the *Gender* column.
   b. Click the **Conditional Formatting** button [*Report Layout tools Format* tab, *Control Formatting* group] to open the *Conditional Formatting Rules Manager* dialog box. *Gender* displays in the *Show formatting rules for* box.

c. Click the **New Rule** button to open the *New Formatting Rule* dialog box.

d. Select the **Check values in the current record or use an expression** rule type in the *Select a rule type* box.

e. Select **equal to** as the comparison.

f. Type **M** into the value box.

g. Select **bold** and a **dark blue** font.

h. Click **OK**. The completed rule displays in the *Conditional Formatting Rules Manager* dialog box (Figure 4-134).

i. Click **Apply**.

j. Click **OK**.

k. Save the report.

4-134 Conditional formatting rule

10. Add totals to the report to count how many of each type of pet are available.

a. Select a text box in the **Pet ID** column.

b. Select the **Totals** button in the *Grouping & Totals* group.

c. Select the **Count Records** option. The report updates to show the total at the end of each group.

d. If needed, increase the height of the text box that displays the total value for the record count for the group as well as for the overall total.

e. Save the report.

11. Preview the report.

a. Select the **View** button arrow [*Report Layout Tools Design* tab, *Views* group] and select the **Print Preview** option. The report should look similar to Figure 4-135.

b. Click the **One Page** button [*Print Preview* tab, *Zoom* group].

c. Use the navigation arrows to move among pages.

d. Click the **Close Print Preview** button.

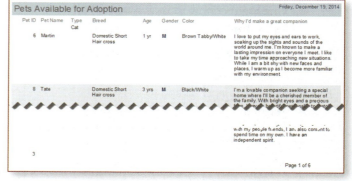

4-135 *Print Preview* of completed report

12. Close the report.

13. Create a form using the *Split Form* button.

a. In the *Navigation* pane, click to select the **Owner** table.

b. Click the **More Forms** button [*Create* tab, *Forms* group].

c. Select the *Split Form* option to create the form shown in Figure 4-136. Depending on the width of the Access window, your form may display the fields in one column in the top half of the form.

d. Save the form. Accept the suggested form name. Click **OK**.

e. Switch to *Form* view by clicking the **View** button arrow [*Form Layout Tools Design* tab, *Views* group] and selecting the **Form View** option.

f. Use the navigation buttons to move among records.

g. Close the form.

14. Close the database.

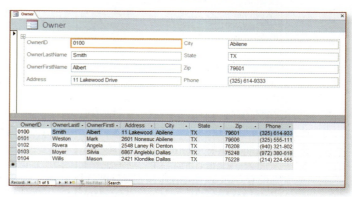

4-136 Completed split form

Independent Project 4-4

American River Cycling wants to add a report and form to its database. To ensure consistency, the starting file is provided for you. Create a form with the *Form* tool. Edit the form in *Layout* view and add buttons. Create a report using the *Blank Report* option. In *Layout* view, modify the layout and add a title and grouping. Preview the results.
[Student Learning Outcomes 4.1, 4.2, 4.3, 4.5, 4.6, 4.8]

File Needed: ***AmericanRiver-04.accd***
Completed Project File Name: ***[your initials] Access 4-4.accdb***

Skills Covered in This Project

- Create a form using the *Form* tool.
- Edit the form in *Layout* view.
- Add the current date to a form.
- Add buttons to a form.
- Set form properties.

- Create a blank report.
- Edit the report in *Layout* view.
- Add grouping to a report.
- Preview a report.

1. Open the ***AmericanRiver-04.accdb*** database file.

2. Save the database as ***[your initials] Access 4-4***.

3. If prompted, enable content in the database.

4. Create a form using the *Form* button.
   a. Select the **RaceResults** table and create a new form using the **Form** button. Your form should look similar to Figure 4-137, although the layout may be different depending on the size of the Access window when you created the form.

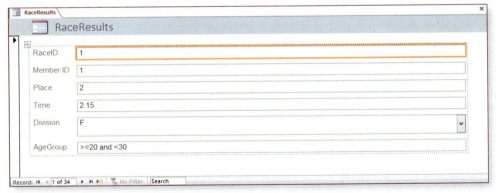

4-137 *RaceResults* form created with *Form* button

   b. Save the form as ViewRaceResults.

5. Edit the form in *Layout* view.
   a. Edit the *RaceResults* label to read Member Race Results.
   b. Decrease the column width of the fields to be about 1" wide.
   c. Add two rows below the *AgeGroup* field.

d. Move the control layout down and to the right as shown in Figure 4-138.

e. Add the date to the form. Choose the *DD-Mon-YY* format. If necessary, deselect the **Include Time** check box so that only the date is added.

f. Decrease the width of the date.

6. Add a button to the form.

a. Add a command button into a cell in the second added row that will close the form (*Form Operations* category).

b. Choose text to display in the button and accept the suggested wording.

c. Save the button as *ViewRace ResultsFormCloseButton*.

d. If necessary, increase the height of the button.

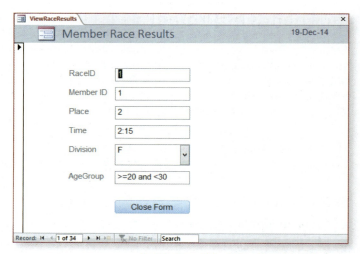

4-138 Completed *ViewRaceResults* form

7. Edit the form properties to limit user edits and deletes.

a. In the property sheet of the form, set the *Data Entry*, *Allow Additions*, *Allow Deletions*, and *Allow Edits* properties to **No**.

b. Close the property sheet.

c. Save the form.

8. Switch to *Form* view. The complete form should look similar to Figure 4-138.

a. Use the navigation buttons to move among records.

b. Close the form.

9. Create a report using the *Blank Report* button.

a. Add all the fields from the *Members* table. The report should look similar to Figure 4-139.

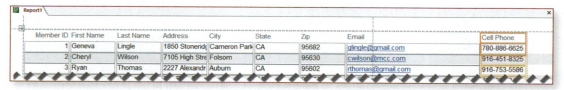

4-139 Add fields into a blank report

10. Add grouping into the report.

a. Group the report on the *City* field.

b. Save the report as ClubMembers.

11. Modify the layout of the report.

a. Select the **Report Layout Tools Page Setup** tab.

b. Click **Margins** [*Page Size* group] and select **Normal**.

c. Change the page layout to **Landscape**.

d. Adjust the width of the report columns to look similar to the columns in Figure 4-140.

e. Enter List of Club Members as the title of the report.

f. Add page numbers to the bottom of the report. Use the *Page N of M* format and center the alignment.

12. Save the changes made to the report.

13. View the report in *Print Preview*.
  a. Adjust the zoom to **One Page**. The report should look similar to Figure 4-140.

City	Member ID	First Name	Last Name	Address	State	Zip	Email	Cell Phone
List of Club Members								
Auburn								
	3	Ryan	Thomas	2227 Alexandra Drive	CA	95602	rthomas@gmail.com	916-753-5586
	14	Randy	Clemmins	7336 Lester Road	CA	95602	rclemmins@phre.com	916-450-3330
	18	Dean	Teague	2112 Stonebrook Court	CA	95602	teague.dean@sac.rr.com	916-599-2222
Cameron Park								
	7	Melanie	Figueroa	4511 Johnson Court	CA	95682	mfigueroa@phre.com	916-450-3336
	1	Geneva	Lingle	1850 Stoneridge Court	CA	95682	glingle@gmail.com	780-886-6625
Fair Oaks								
	10	Rick	Hermenn	9035 Masi Drive	CA	95628	rickh@gmail.com	916-450-6719
	5	Margaret	Jepson	28861 Newcastle Road	CA	95628	margaret@sac.rr.com	780-862-9851
Folsom								
	2	Cheryl	Wilson	7105 High Street	CA	95630	cwilson@mcc.com	916-451-8325
Lincoln								
	11	Karen	Graves	6003 Ashland Road	CA	95648	kgraves@phre.com	916-450-3892
Rocklin								
	4	Roy	Baxter	705 First Street	CA	95677	roy@centralsierra.com	780-886-2471
	8	Sue	Schooler	4183 Braxton Way	CA	95677	sschooler@gmail.com	780-824-3525
Roseville								
	12	Robyn	Constantini	9581 Magnolia Way	CA	95661	robyn@gmail.com	780-886-2471
	6	Rick	DePonte	8364 Marshall Street	CA	95661	deponte@hotmail.com	916-450-3329
	13	John	Burgess	85741 Auberry Road	CA	95661	jborgess@hotmail.com	780-886-5862
	15	Amber	Harrison	488 Yale Drive	CA	95661	aharrison24@gmail.com	780-824-1111
	16	Mark	Pohlman	7377 Acorn Glen Loop	CA	95661	mpohlman@hotmail.com	916-541-5339

Page 1 of 2

4-140 *Print Preview* of completed report

  b. Close *Print Preview*.
14. Close the report.
15. Close the database.

Independent Project 4-5

The State of New York Department of Motor Vehicles wants to add a form and a report to its database so users can more easily view the information about drivers. To ensure consistency, the starting file is provided for you. Create a split form and edit the form in *Layout* view. Next, create a report using the *Blank Report* option. In *Layout* view, modify the layout, add a title, grouping, sorting, and totals. Preview the results.
[Student Learning Outcomes 4.1, 4.2, 4.3, 4.5, 4.6, 4.8]

File Needed: ***NewYorkDMV-04.accdb***
Completed Project File Name: ***[your initials] Access 4-5.accdb***

Skills Covered in This Project

- Create a form using the *Form* tool.
- Edit a form in *Layout* view.
- Add the current date to a form.
- Move fields within the control layout.
- Test the functionality of a form.

- Create a blank report.
- Edit a report in *Layout* view.
- Add grouping and sorting to a report.
- Add totals to a report.
- Preview a report.

---

1. Open the **NewYorkDMV-04.accdb** database file.

2. Save the database as **[your initials] Access 4-5**.

3. If prompted, enable content in the database.

4. Create a form using the *Split Form* button. Recall that when using the *Split Form* button, the width of the Access window affects whether the fields are placed in one or two columns. Adjust the size of the Access window to ensure that the initial layout of the form includes two columns.

   a. If necessary, click the **Restore Down** button so that the Access window is not maximized.

   b. Click the **Create** tab. If needed reduce the width of the Access window so that there is minimal extra space to the right of the icons displayed in the ribbon.

   c. Create a split form based on the *Drivers* table. Your form should look similar to Figure 4-141. If your form does not have 2 columns, close the form without saving. Adjust the height and width of the Access window to make it a bit smaller and then create the form again.

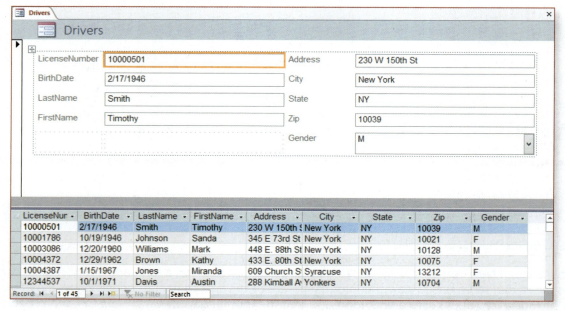

4-141 Split form based on *Drivers* table

   d. Save the form as DriverInformation.

5. Edit the form in *Layout* view.

   a. In the datasheet portion of the form, decrease the column width of the *State*, *Zip*, and *Gender* fields and increase the width of the *Address* field.

b. In the single record portion of the form, change the label for *LicenseNumber* to *License#* and insert spaces between the words in the labels for *BirthDate*, *LastName* and *FirstName*.

c. Add the date and time to the form. Accept the suggested date and time format.

6. Move controls within the layout to customize the layout.
   a. Add two rows below the *Gender* field so you have some room to move the different fields.
   b. Add one row above the *License#* field.
   c. Move the *License#* label to the cell in the top row.
   d. Move the *License#* text box to the cell below the label.
   e. Continue moving the labels and text boxes so that your fields are placed similar to those in Figure 4-142. You may have to move some labels and text boxes to a temporary location in the layout during this process.

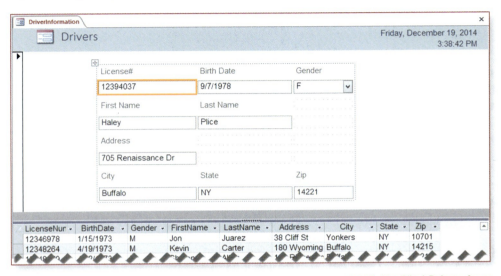

4-142 Modified *Drivers* form

f. Delete any unused rows and columns in the layout.
g. Adjust the height and width of the different rows and columns to match Figure 4-142.
h. Move the control layout from the far left so that its location is similar to the location in Figure 4-142.
i. Save the form.

7. Switch to *Form* view and practice using a form to add and delete records.
   a. Use the navigation buttons to move among records.
   b. Use the **New** (blank) record button to add a new record. Enter the following data values: *LicenseNum#:* 39995000, *BirthDate:* 3/16/1997, *Gender:* M, *FirstName:* Max, *LastName:* Sutton, *Address:* 12846 Sandy Point Drive, *City:* Utica, *State:* NY, *Zip:* 13502.
   c. Navigate to the first record.
   d. Navigate back to the last record. This should be the record you added.
   e. Navigate to the sixth record. This should be *Steve Miller's* record.
   f. Delete the record by selecting the **Delete Record** button [*Home* tab, *Records* group].
   g. Close the form when done.

8. Create a report using the *Blank Report* button.
   a. Add all the fields from the *Tickets* table.

9. Modify the layout of the report.
   a. Modify the column labels to match those shown in Figure 4-143.

Ticket Number	DL Number	Ticket Date	City	Primary Factor	Officer #	Fine
4235879527	12348279	7/5/2014	Buffalo	Unsafe Speed	A00032567	$360.00
4235879530	12346123	7/7/2014	New York	Passing/Lane Violations	A00061444	$150.00

4-143 Adjusted column width of report fields

   b. Adjust the width of the report fields, including the labels, so they are similar to the widths of the columns in Figure 4-143.
   c. Enter Ticket Report by City for the title of the report.
   d. Add page numbers to the bottom of the report. Use the *Page N of M* format and center the alignment.
   e. Save the report as TicketsByCity.

10. Add grouping and sorting to the report.
    a. Group the report on the *City* field.
    b. Sort the report on the *Ticket Date* field in from *oldest to newest* order.
    c. Save the report.

11. Add totals to the report.
    a. Calculate the average dollar value of the *Fine* field.
    b. If necessary, increase the height of the average cell.
    c. On the *Report Layout Tools Format* tab, apply the **bold** format to the *Average* text box.
    d. Save the report.

12. View the report in *Print Preview*.
    a. Adjust the zoom to **One Page**.
    b. Navigate to the second page of the report.
    c. Notice that the Utica group of tickets is spread across two pages.
    d. Close *Print Preview*.

13. In the *Group, Sort,* and *Total* pane, choose **keep whole group together on one page**.

14. Save the report.

15. Preview the report again.
    a. Adjust the zoom to **One Page**. The report should look similar to Figure 4-144.
    b. Navigate to the second page.
    c. Notice that the Utica tickets are all on the second page.
    d. Close *Print Preview*.

16. Close the report.

17. Close the database.

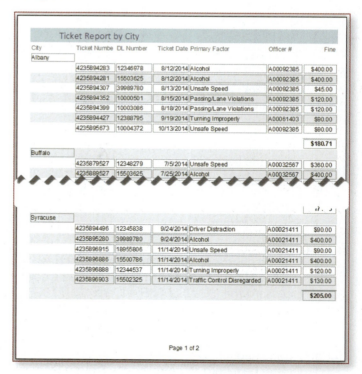

4-144 Completed *TicketsByCity* report

Independent Project 4-6

Courtyard Medical Plaza wants to add a form and a report to its database. To ensure consistency, the starting file is provided for you. Create a blank form and modify the form in *Layout* view. Edit properties to restrict the form to data entry and add buttons. Next, create a report using the *Report Wizard*. In *Layout* view, modify the layout, add sorting, and add conditional formatting. Finally, preview the results.
[Student Learning Outcomes 4.2, 4.3, 4.4, 4.5, 4.6, 4.7, 4.8]

File Needed: ***CourtyardMedicalPlaza-04.accdb***
Completed Project File Name: ***[your initials] Access 4-6.accdb***

Skills Covered in This Project

- Create a form using the *Form* tool.
- Edit a form in *Layout* view.
- Add the current date to a form.
- Move fields within the control layout.
- Restrict a form to data entry.
- Test the functionality of a form.

- Create a report using the *Report Wizard*.
- Edit a report in *Layout* view.
- Add grouping and sorting to a report.
- Add totals to a report.
- Add conditional formatting to a report.
- Preview a report.

1. Open the ***CourtyardMedicalPlaza-04.accdb*** database file.
2. Save the database as ***[your initials] Access 4-6***.
3. If prompted, enable content in the database.
4. Create a form using the *Blank Form* button.
   a. Add all the fields from the *Physicians* table to the form.
   b. Close the field list.
   c. Save the form as AddNewPhysician.
5. Edit the form in *Layout* view, add a new column and new rows to the control layout, and modify their size.
   a. Move the *Specialty* label and text box to appear above the *Office* label and text box.
   b. Add two rows below the *Tenant Since* row.
   c. Add one column to the right side of the layout.
   d. Adjust the width of the columns so that all three are of similar size.
   e. Adjust the height of the last row. Make the height approximately twice as high as any other row.
6. Add command buttons, a title, and the date to the form.
   a. Add a button into the bottom row of the left-most column to save a record [*Record Operations Category*].
   b. Change the wording to Save Physician Record.
   c. Name the button AddPhysicianFormSaveButton.
   d. Add a second button into the bottom row of the middle column to add a new record [*Record Operations Category*].
   e. Change the wording to Add New Physician.
   f. Name the button AddPhysicianFormAddButton.
   g. Add a third button into the bottom row of the right-most column to close the form [*Form Operations Category*].
   h. Use the existing wording for the button.
   i. Name the button AddPhysicianFormCloseButton.

j. Add a title to the form. Enter
   Add New Physician for the title.
k. Add the date to the form. Use the
   DD-Mon-YY format. If necessary,
   deselect the **Include Time** check
   box so that only the date is added.
l. Adjust the size and placement of
   the title and date to look similar to
   Figure 4-145.
m. Save the changes to the form. The
   revised form should look similar to
   Figure 4-145.

7. Restrict the form to data entry.
   a. In the form properties, select **Yes** in
      the *Data Entry* property box.
   b. Select **Yes** in the *Allow Additions* property box. Recall that when both the *Data Entry* and *Allow Additions* properties are set to *yes*, the values in the *Allow Deletions* and *Allow Edits* properties do not have an impact.
   c. Save the form.
   d. Switch to *Form* view. Verify that icons available in the *Navigation* bar allow you only to add records and not edit or delete existing records.
   e. Close the form.

8. Create a report using the *Report Wizard*.
   a. Launch the *Report Wizard*.
   b. Add all the fields from the *RentInvoices* table in the following order: *InvoiceID*, *FKDoctorID*, *InvoiceDate*, *Description*, *DueDate*, *DateReceived*, *AmountDue*, and *Discount*.
   c. On the second page of the *Report Wizard*, accept the suggested grouping by *FKDoctorID*.
   d. On the sort order and summary page of the *Report Wizard*, add summary options to display the *Sum* of the *AmountDue* field. Select the **Detail and Summary** radio button for the *Show* option.
   e. Choose a **stepped** layout and **Landscape** orientation.
   f. Accept the suggested title.
   g. Click the **Finish** button. The preview of the report should look similar to Figure 4-146. Don't worry if some of your fields display the ### signs indicating that the column width is too narrow. You resize the columns in step 9. The wording for the summary line was automatically added using the totals created by the *Wizard*.

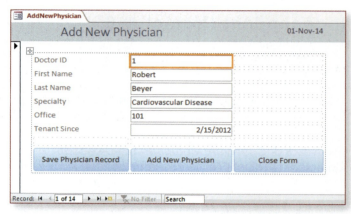

4-145 *AddNewPhysician* form

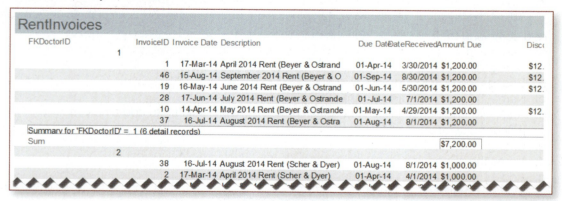

4-146 *RentInvoices* report created using the *Report Wizard*

h. Close *Print Preview*.

9. Edit the report using *Layout* view.
   a. Decrease the width of the *FKDoctorID* column.
   b. Move the *InvoiceID* label and text box to the left by selecting both of them and using the left arrow key.
   c. Move the remaining fields and adjust the column widths as needed so that your report matches the report in Figure 4-147.

4-147 *RentInvoices* report after editing the layout

   d. Adjust the width of the text boxes that display the totals so that they are large enough to display the values.
   e. Save the report.
   f. Switch to *Report* view. The report should look similar to Figure 4-147.
   g. Switch back to *Layout* view.

10. In the *Group*, *Sort*, *and Total* pane, add an *oldest to newest* sort on the *Invoice Date* field.

11. Add conditional formatting to the report so that any *Discount* values that *are greater than or equal to* $20 display in a **bold**, **green** font.

12. Save your changes.

13. View the report in *Print Preview*.
   a. Adjust the zoom to **One Page**. The report should look similar to Figure 4-148.

RentInvoices

FKDoctorID	InvoiceID	Invoice Date	Description	Due Date	DateReceived	Amount Due	Discount
1							
	1	17-Mar-14	April 2014 Rent (Beyer & Ostrander)	01-Apr-14	3/30/2014	$1,200.00	$12.00
	46	15-Aug-14	September 2014 Rent (Beyer & Ostrander)	01-Sep-14	8/30/2014	$1,200.00	$12.00
	19	16-May-14	June 2014 Rent (Beyer & Ostrander)	01-Jun-14	5/30/2014	$1,200.00	$12.00
	28	17-Jun-14	July 2014 Rent (Beyer & Ostrander)	01-Jul-14	7/1/2014	$1,200.00	
	10	14-Apr-14	May 2014 Rent (Beyer & Ostrander)	01-May-14	4/29/2014	$1,200.00	$12.00
	37	16-Jul-14	August 2014 Rent (Beyer & Ostrander)	01-Aug-14	8/1/2014	$1,200.00	
Summary for 'FKDoctorID' = 1 (6 detail records)							
Sum						$7,200.00	
2							
	38	16-Jul-14	August 2014 Rent (Scher & Dyer)	01-Aug-14	8/1/2014	$1,000.00	

Sum						$7,800.00	
5							
	4	17-Mar-14	April 2014 Rent (Flores & Alamar)	01-Apr-14	3/29/2014	$1,300.00	$26.00
	40	16-Jul-14	August 2014 Rent (Flores & Alamar)	01-Aug-14	8/1/2014	$1,300.00	
	49	15-Aug-14	September 2014 Rent (Flores & Alamar)	01-Sep-14	9/1/2014	$1,300.00	

Saturday, November 01, 2014   Page 1 of 3

4-148 Completed *RentInvoices* report

   b. Close *Print Preview*.

14. Close the report.

15. Close the database.

Improve It Project 4-7

Mary's Rentals wants to improve its database. To ensure consistency, the starting file is provided for you. You improve the functionality of a form by modifying the layout, adding a button, and limiting edits and deletes. Improve the usability of a report by modifying the layout and adding grouping and sorting. Finally, preview how the report will print.
[Student Learning Outcomes 4.2, 4.3, 4.5, 4.6, 4.8]

File Needed: **MarysRentals-04.accdb**
Completed Project File Name: **[your initials] Access 4-7.accdb**

Skills Covered in This Project

- Edit a form in *Layout* view.
- Add a title and date to a form.
- Move fields within the control layout.
- Add a button to a form.
- Set properties to limit user edits and deletes.
- Test the functionality of a form.
- Edit a report in *Layout* view.
- Add grouping and sorting to a report.
- Preview a report.

---

1. Open the **MarysRentals-04.accdb** database file.

2. Save the database as **[your initials] Access 4-7**.

3. If prompted, enable content in the database.

4. Edit the *ViewEquipment* form in *Layout* view.
   a. Increase the column width of the labels so that the entire caption displays.
   b. Edit the label contents to insert blank spaces between the words. For example, change *EquipmentID* to *Equipment ID*.
   c. Increase the column width of the text boxes so that the entire contents displays.
   d. Add a title and date to the form so that your form header looks like Figure 4-149.
   e. Adjust the size and placement of the title and date to look like Figure 4-149.
   f. Move the control layout down and to the right as it is in Figure 4-149.
   g. Add a blank row to the bottom of the layout.
   h. Adjust the height of the added row. Make the height approximately one and a half times as high as the starting height.
   i. Select both cells in the bottom row and press the **Merge** button [*Form Layout Tools Arrange* tab, *Merge/Split* group].

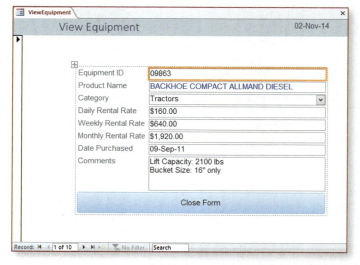

4-149 Completed *ViewEquipment* form

5. Add a command button to the form.
   a. Add a button to close the form [*Form Operations Category*] into the last row of the control layout.
   b. Use the existing wording for the button.
   c. Name the button ViewEquipmentFormCloseButton.
   d. Save the changes to the form. The revised form should look similar to Figure 4-149.

6. Edit the form properties to restrict user additions, edits, and deletes.

7. Test the form.
   a. Save the form.
   b. Switch to *Form* view and navigate through the records.
   c. Try to change the value of one of the fields. That action should be restricted.
   d. Close the form.

8. Edit the *ServiceHistory* report in *Layout* view.
   a. Remove the *FK* from the *FKEquipmentID* label.
   b. Edit the captions in the labels to insert spaces between the words. If necessary, increase the width of the labels to show the entire contents.
   c. On the *Report Layout Tools Format* tab, **center** the alignment of the *Service Date* label and text box and the *Hours* label and text box.
   d. Change the *Total Cost* label to be **right aligned**.
   e. Notice in Figure 4-150 that the size of the *Performed By* and *Odometer Reading* labels is wider than the corresponding text box. This was caused by inserting the space into the caption.

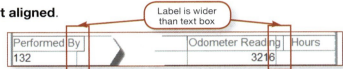

4-150 **Label sizes wider than corresponding text box**

   f. You can adjust the width of the text boxes to improve the alignment as desired.

9. Add grouping and sorting into the report.
   a. Group the report on the *FKEquipmentID* field.
   b. Change to the option to **keep header and first record together on one page**.
   c. Sort the report on the *Service Date* field in *oldest to newest* order.
   d. Save the report.

10. View the report in *Print Preview*.
   a. Adjust the zoom to **One Page**. The report should look similar to Figure 4-151.
   b. Close *Print Preview*.

11. Close the report.

12. Close the database.

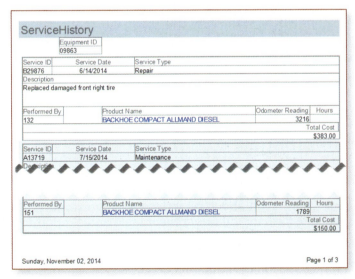

4-151 **Completed *ServiceHistory* report**

Challenge Project 4-8

For this project you modify the database you built in Challenge Project 3-8 by creating one form and two reports.
[Student Learning Outcomes 4.1, 4.2, 4.3, 4.4, 4.5, 4.6, 4.8]

File Needed: *[your initials] Access 3-8.accdb*
Completed Project File Name: *[your initials] Access 4-8.accdb*

Open the database *[your initials] Access 3-8* and save a copy of it as *[your initials] Access 4-8*.

Modify your database according to the following instructions:

- Create a form for your table using the *Form Wizard*.
- Add all the fields to the form.
- Adjust the column widths as necessary so they are sized appropriately.
- Change the form properties to restrict the form to limit user edits and deletes.
- Add one button to the form to close the form.
- Save the form and view it in *Form* view to ensure it works as desired.
- Create a report using the *Wizard* to show all the fields from one of your queries.
- Adjust the column widths as necessary so they are sized appropriately.
- Save the report and view it in *Print Preview* to ensure that it will print as desired.
- Create a second report using the *Blank Report* option.
- Add all the fields from the table into the report.
- Edit the layout as needed to adjust the column widths and page orientation.
- Add a title and page numbers to the report.
- Group the report on one of the fields.
- Save the report.
- View the report in *Print Preview* to ensure that it will print as desired.
- Save any changes that you made.

Challenge Project 4-9

Modify the database you created in Challenge Project 3-9 for Blue Lake Sports. Your database contains a table with information about the different departments at Blue Lake Sports and a related table with information about the interns who are working at Blue Lake, along with the query you created. Create a form for the *Department* table and a report for the *Intern* table.
[Student Learning Outcomes 4.2, 4.3, 4.5, 4.6, 4.7, 4.8]

File Needed: *[your initials] Access 3-9.accdb*
Completed Project File Name: *[your initials] Access 4-9.accdb*

Open the database *[your initials] Access 3-9* and save a copy of it as *[your initials] Access 4-9*.

Modify your database according to the following instructions:

- Create a form for the *Department* table using the *Blank Form* tool.
- Add all the fields to the form.
- Adjust the column widths as necessary so they are sized appropriately.
- Add a title to the form.
- Add a button to the form to close the form.
- Save the form and view it in *Form* view to ensure it works as desired.
- Create a report using the *Blank Report* tool to show all the fields in the *Intern* table.
- Adjust the column widths as necessary so they are sized appropriately.
- Group the report on the *DepartmentName* field.
- Sort the records by intern last name.
- Add totals to count the total number of interns in each department.
- Add conditional formatting to the university field. Make the font a different color for each of the university values contained in the database. You need to add several rules for the university field (one for each value).
- Edit the title of the report to indicate the contents.
- Save the report.
- View the report in *Print Preview* and adjust the orientation and margins as necessary.
- Save any changes that you made.

Challenge Project 4-10

Modify the database you created in Challenge Project 3-10 for a travel agency. Your database contains a table with information about the different ships and a related table with information about upcoming cruises, along with the queries you added. Add a form to allow new ships to be added into the database. Add a report to display trip information, grouped by number of days. Modify both the form and report to improve the overall functionality.
[Student Learning Outcomes 4.2, 4.3, 4.4, 4.5, 4.6, 4.8]

File Needed: *[your initials] Access 3-10.accdb*
Completed Project File Name: *[your initials] Access 4-10.accdb*

Open the database *[your initials] Access 3-10* and save a copy of it *as [your initials] Access 4-10*.

Modify your database according to the following instructions:

- Create a form for the *Ships* table using the *Blank Form* tool.
- Add all the fields to the form.

- Adjust the column widths as necessary so they are sized appropriately.
- Add a title to the form.
- Change the form properties to restrict the form to data entry.
- Add three buttons to the form: *Save Ship Record*, *Add New Ship*, and *Close the Form*.
- Save the form and view it in *Form* view to ensure it works as desired.
- Create a report using the *Report Wizard* to show all the fields in the *Trips* table.
- Adjust the column widths as necessary so they are sized appropriately.
- Group the report on the *Number of Days* field.
- Sort the records by cost per person.
- Add totals to calculate the average cost per person.
- Edit the title of the report to indicate the contents.
- Save the report.
- View the report in *Print Preview* and adjust the orientation and margins as necessary.
- Save any changes that you made.

Microsoft® Office
IN PRACTICE

powerpoint

CHAPTER

1

Creating and Editing Presentations

CHAPTER OVERVIEW

Microsoft PowerPoint is the leading presentation software. Whether you need to create a quick display or a very polished presentation with dazzling graphics, creative animation effects, and video, PowerPoint has all the tools you need. You can use PowerPoint for slide shows with computer projection equipment in meeting rooms, for self-running presentations viewed by individuals, or for presentations shown on the web. This chapter covers the basics of starting and editing a PowerPoint presentation.

STUDENT LEARNING OUTCOMES (SLOs)

After completing this chapter, you will be able to:

SLO 1.1   Create, open, and save a presentation (p. P1-3).

SLO 1.2   Develop presentation content by adding slides, choosing layouts, moving and resizing placeholders, editing text, and reusing slides from another presentation (p. P1-14).

SLO 1.3   Rearrange presentation content by moving, copying and pasting, duplicating, and deleting slides (p. P1-22).

SLO 1.4   Use the *Slide Master* to change theme colors and fonts (p. P1-26).

SLO 1.5   Use headers and footers to add identifying information (p. P1-29).

SLO 1.6   Insert, resize, and align a picture from a file (p. P1-33).

SLO 1.7   Apply and modify transition effects to add visual interest (p. P1-35).

SLO 1.8   Preview a presentation and print slides, handouts, and outlines (p. P1-37).

SLO 1.9   Change presentation properties (p. P1-39).

CASE STUDY

Hamilton Civic Center (HCC) is a nonprofit community fitness center with an indoor pool, sauna, indoor track, exercise room, racquetball courts, and meeting rooms. HCC partners with the local hospital to bring doctors and nurses in to provide classes on a variety of health and wellness issues for adults. It also works with local schools to support their *academic programs and sponsors events for children, including a summer day care program.*

For the Pause & Practice projects in this chapter, you create and modify a presentation about training for an upcoming marathon that is being promoted to members by the Civic Center.

Pause & Practice 1-1: Create a presentation and develop text content.

Pause & Practice 1-2: Impose consistency to a presentation's design.

Pause & Practice 1-3: Add interest with pictures and apply transitions. Print supplements.

SLO 1.1

Creating, Opening, and Saving Presentations

In this section, you explore how to start and view a PowerPoint presentation and to save a presentation in different formats. It is important to save a presentation before closing it so you can access it again if necessary. If you close the presentation before saving it, your content is lost.

Create a Presentation

When PowerPoint first opens, you are presented with several ways to start a new presentation or open an existing presentation. Clickable images called *thumbnails* have a name below each one. If you prefer to work on text content only, click the **Blank Presentation** thumbnail to go directly to your first slide so you can begin developing content.

Other thumbnails represent built-in *Themes* that provide a unified look for all the slides in a presentation. One theme has a plain, dark background while most of them have a background design. When you click a theme, a dialog box opens where you can choose from different color combinations called *Variants*. Then you start developing content.

The following examples demonstrate ways to start a presentation.

HOW TO: Create a Presentation When First Opening PowerPoint

1. Open PowerPoint and you will automatically see the *Backstage* view (Figure 1-1).
2. Click the **Blank Presentation** theme to go directly to your first slide.

Or

3. Click a **Theme** to open a dialog box (Figure 1-2).
4. Click the arrow buttons below the slide to see h ow colors are applied to different layouts.

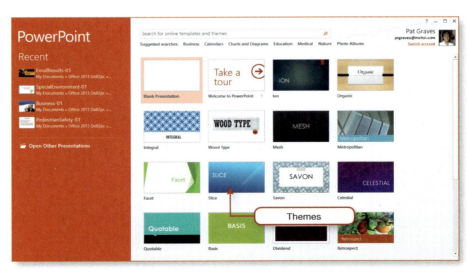

1-1 PowerPoint *Backstage* view

5. Select one of four *Variants* that provide different color combinations.

6. Click **Create**.

1-2 Theme *Variants*

When you create a new presentation, the PowerPoint title bar displays the generic name *Presentation1*. When you create additional new presentations, PowerPoint names them *Presentation2*, *Presentation3*, and so on, until you save the presentations and the new names appear in the title bar.

> **MORE INFO**
>
> When your content is complete, save your presentation (discussed on pages P1-10–P1-13) and then close it. Click the **File** tab, and then click **Close**. To close PowerPoint, click the **Close** button in the upper right corner of the title bar.

HOW TO: Create a New Presentation when PowerPoint is Open

1. Click the **File** tab to open the *Backstage* view.
2. Click the **New** button.
3. Select a *Theme* and *Variant*.
4. Click **Create**.

Or

5. Press **Ctrl+N** to open a new blank presentation.

Themes simplify the process of creating professional-looking presentations. They provide consistent background graphics, colors, and font settings. For more on selecting different theme colors and fonts, see *SLO 1.4: Working with Themes*.

A ***template*** contains the characteristics of a theme and usually provides sample content you can edit for your own slides or delete if you want only the background a template provides. Many themes and templates are available at Office.com and the online collection is ever-growing. You can save downloaded themes and templates so they are available for future use.

> **MORE INFO**
>
> Your computer must be connected to the Internet to download themes and templates.

HOW TO: Create a New Presentation from Online Templates and Themes

1. Click the **File** tab to open the *Backstage* view.
2. Click the **New** button. In the search box, type a keyword and click the **Start searching** button (Figure 1-3). Available templates and themes appear.
   - Filter your results by typing the word or before another search word and searching again.

Or

3. Click one of the *Suggested searches* for general topics, and available templates and themes will appear.
   - Filter your results by clicking one of the terms in the *Category* list on the right (Figure 1-4).
   - Filter your results by typing the word or before another search word and searching again.
4. Click a template thumbnail to open a dialog box to review other slides in addition to the title slide. Some templates include a description.
5. Click **Create**.
6. The presentation opens; it may contain sample content that you need to delete before adding your content.

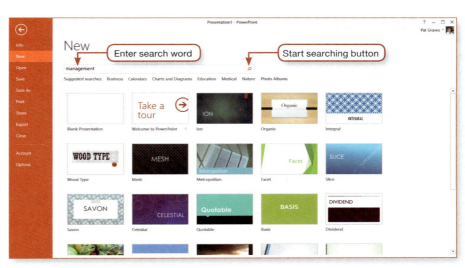

1-3 Search for online themes and templates

1-4 Search results for online themes and templates

You can use an existing presentation to start a new presentation. To do this, open a presentation file from a source such as your computer, USB drive, local network, cloud space such as SkyDrive, or an email attachment.

HOW TO: Open a Recent Presentation

1. With PowerPoint open, click the **File** tab to open the *Backstage* view.
2. Click the **Open** button.

3. Select **Recent Presentations** below the *Open* title.

4. Click a presentation on the right (Figure 1-5) to open it.

Or

5. Select your **SkyDrive**, then click **Browse** to locate the file (Figure 1-6).

1-5 **Open a recent presentation**

1-6 **Open a presentation saved on your *SkyDrive***

> **MORE INFO**
>
> For instructions to set up a SkyDrive account, refer to *SLO 1.1 Using Windows 8 and Office 2013 in Office Chapter 1, Windows 8 and Office 2013 Overview.*

Or

6. Select **Computer** and then click **Browse** to locate the file on your computer or other place such as a USB drive or local network (Figure 1-7).

7. Select the file and click **Open**.

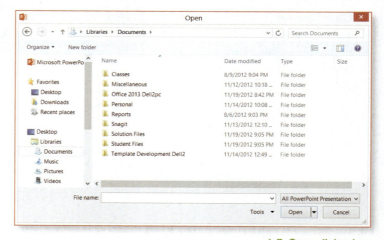

1-7 ***Open* dialog box**

> **ANOTHER WAY**
>
> **Ctrl+O** opens the *Backstage* view where you can open a presentation.

Views

PowerPoint provides different views to help you create slides, organize them, and display them in a slide show. When you start a new presentation, it opens in *Normal* view. The *Ribbon* is displayed across the top of the window and has nine tabs with commands organized in groups (Figure 1-8). Additional tabs, such as the *Drawing Tools Format* tab, open depending on what you are doing. Some tabs contain commands similar to those in Word, whereas other tabs display features that are unique to PowerPoint.

1-8 PowerPoint *Ribbon* with *Home* tab displayed

The area below the *Ribbon* is divided into two panes that display slide thumbnails on the left and a large area for working on individual slides. You can change views using commands on the *View* tab [*View* tab, *Presentation Views* group] (Figure 1-9) or the *View* buttons on the *Status bar* at the bottom of the window.

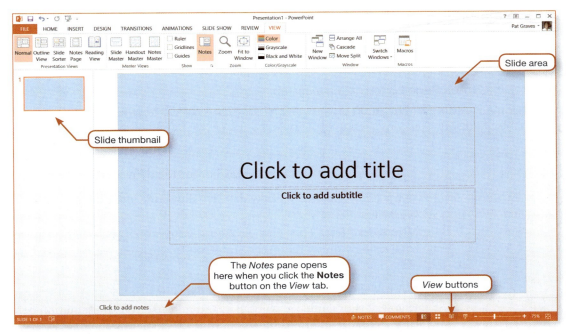

1-9 *Normal* view with *View* tab and *Notes* pane displayed

The five *Presentation Views* with commands on the *View* tab include the following:

- **Normal:** This is the default view where you enter the content of the slides and move between slides as you develop them. Click the *Normal* button or the *Notes* button to open a *Notes* pane below the slide to add speaker notes for individual slides.
- **Outline View:** This view expands the pane at the left of your slide area to show slide titles and bulleted text. Slide thumbnails are not displayed.

- **Slide Sorter:** This view displays slides as thumbnails so it is easy to reorganize slides and apply transition effects to control how the slides advance.
- **Notes Page:** This view displays each slide on a page with space below the slide where you can type speaker notes. You can also use the *Notes* pane below each slide to type speaker notes.
- **Reading View:** This view displays the slide show at full-screen or another window size controlled by the viewer. Navigation controls are in the *Status bar* at the bottom of the window.
- **Slide Master, Handout Master, and Notes Master:** These views are used to make changes that affect the whole presentation.

View Buttons are located on the *Status bar* to provide easy access regardless of which tab is currently open (Figure 1-10).

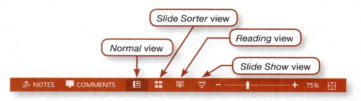

1-10 *View* buttons

HOW TO: Change Views

1. Click the **View** tab. Note that *Normal* is selected in the *Presentation Views* group.
2. Click the **Outline** button on the *View* tab.
3. Click the **Slide Sorter** button on the *View* tab or *Status bar*.
4. Click the **Notes Page** button on the *View* tab.
5. Click the **Reading View** button on the *View* tab or *Status bar*. To return to *Normal* view, click the **Normal** button on the *Status bar*.

Two more views are very important for the delivery of your presentation.

- **Slide Show view:** This view displays slides one at a time at full-screen size for audience viewing.
- **Presenter View:** This view displays speaker notes and other features that are helpful for delivering a presentation. For more on this feature, see *Presenter View* in *SLO 3.5: Controlling Display Options*.

While developing your presentation, test it in *Slide Show* view so you can see the content in the way your audience will see it, and rehearse your presentation before using it.

Start a presentation slide show from the beginning by pressing **F5**; start with the current slide by clicking the **Slide Show** button on the *Status bar*. You may also use buttons on the *Slide Show* tab (Figure 1-11).

1-11 *Slide Show* tab

HOW TO: Start a Presentation from the Slide Show Tab

1. Click the **Slide Show** tab.
2. Click the **From Beginning** button [*Start Slide Show* group] to display slides from the beginning, regardless of which slide is the current slide.
3. Click the **From Current Slide** button to display slides starting with the current slide.
4. To move through the slides, click the screen or press one of several keys on the keyboard: **spacebar**, **arrow keys**, **Enter**, **Page Down**, or **N**.

Adjust Pane Sizes in Normal View

You can adjust the pane size to help you better focus on one aspect of your presentation. For example, you can make slide thumbnails larger or increase the area for notes. In each case, the slide becomes a little smaller.

HOW TO: Adjust Pane Sizes

1. Point to the border line separating the slide thumbnails and the slide area until your pointer turns into a sizing pointer with two arrows (Figure 1-12).
2. Click and drag the pane border to the right to make the thumbnails larger and to the left to make the thumbnails smaller.
3. If the *Notes* pane is not open, click the **Notes** button [*View* tab, *Show* group].
4. With the sizing pointer, click and drag the pane border line between the *Slide* area and the *Notes* pane up to make the *Notes* pane larger or down to make it smaller.
5. With the sizing pointer, click and drag the *Notes* pane border line down to the bottom of the window or click the **Notes** button to remove this area.

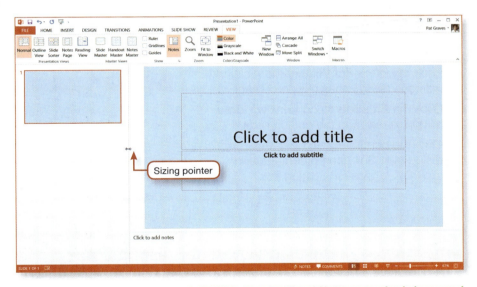

1-12 Slide thumbnail and *Notes* pane size is increased

Use Zoom

Use *Zoom* to increase the size of the slide on which you are working when you need to see detail. You can set a specific magnification level by using the *Zoom* dialog box or adjust the magnification by using the *Zoom* slider. You can use *Zoom* on the *Slide Sorter* view also.

HOW TO: Use the Zoom Dialog Box

1. Click the **Zoom** button [*View* tab, *Zoom* group].
2. Select a preset zoom percentage or enter a percentage number such as 200% (Figure 1-13).
3. Click **OK**. The slide size is increased and you can see only a portion of the slide
4. Click the **Fit slide to window** button [*View* tab, *Zoom* group] to return to the default setting so the entire slide is displayed.

1-13 *Zoom* dialog box

The *Zoom* controls are located on the right side of the *Status bar* and the current slide size percentage is shown. At 100%, the slider is in the center. Drag the slider or click the **Zoom** buttons to adjust the slide size.

HOW TO: Use the Zoom Controls

1. Click the **Zoom Out** button several times to decrease the view to 50% (Figure 1-14).
2. Drag the *Zoom* slider to the center.
3. Click the **Zoom In** button several times to increase the view to 150%.
4. Click the left or right of the *Zoom* slider to increase or decrease the percentage.
5. Click the **Fit slide to current window** button to return to the default setting.
6. Click the percentage to open the *Zoom* dialog box. Select a percentage and click **OK** to close the dialog box.

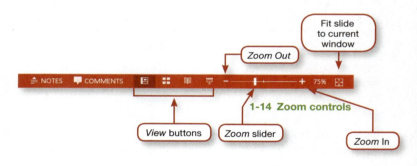

1-14 Zoom controls

Save and Close a Presentation

PowerPoint gives each new presentation a generic name, so you should name each presentation the first time you save it.

HOW TO: Save a Presentation

1. Click the **File** tab to open the *Backstage* view.
2. Click **Save** or **Save As** to display the *Save As* area (Figure 1-15).
3. Select the place where you want to save your presentation. You can save to your SkyDrive, computer, or other place such as a different web location.
4. Select a folder in the *Current Folder* or *Recent Folders* area or click the **Browse** button to open the *Save As* dialog box (Figure 1-16).

5. Browse to the folder on your computer or other place to save the file.

6. Type the file name in the *File name* area.

7. Click the **Save** button.

1-15 *Save As* area on the *Backstage* view

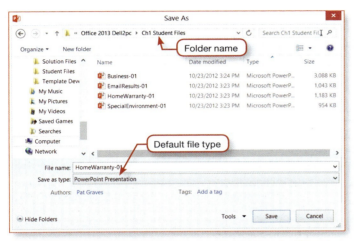

1-16 *Save As* dialog box

When saving for the first time, you can also click the **Save** button on the *Quick Access* toolbar, or press **Ctrl+S**, to open the *Save As* area on the *Backstage* view. As you make revisions to your presentation, simply clicking the **Save** button on the *Quick Access* toolbar will resave it with the same name in the same location.

If you want to create a second version of that file, then click the **File** tab and the **Save As** button to resave it with a different name in the same or different location. The original presentation is not affected by any changes you make to the second presentation.

ANOTHER WAY

Press **F12** to open the *Save As* dialog box.

You can save PowerPoint presentations in a variety of formats. By default, PowerPoint 2013 presentations are saved with the *.pptx* file extension. To change the type of presentation format, select the format of your choice from the *Save as type* area in the *Save As* dialog box (Figure 1-17).

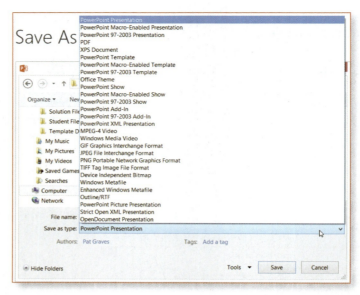

1-17 *Save As* file types

The following table lists some of the available formats that are most commonly used for PowerPoint.

Save Formats

Type of Presentation	File Extension	Uses of this Format
PowerPoint Presentation	.pptx	PowerPoint presentation compatible with 2007–2013 software versions that use an XML-enabled file format. This is the default file format.
PowerPoint 97-2003 Presentation	.ppt	PowerPoint presentation compatible with 1997–2003 software versions. Current software features are not supported.
PDF (Portable Document Format)	.pdf	Similar to pictures of slides, with each slide shown as a separate page. The file size may be smaller than the original presentation, so this format often works well for presentations distributed electronically.
PowerPoint Template	.potx	PowerPoint template that can be used to format future presentations.
Windows Media Video or MPEG-4 Video	.wmv or .mp4	PowerPoint presentation saved as a video that will play on many media players. Three resolution sizes are available, and all create large file sizes.
Outline/RTF	.rtf	A presentation text-only outline with a small file size for easy sharing.
PowerPoint Picture Presentation	.pptx	PowerPoint presentation that converts each slide into an image. It helps to reduce file size or create images for inclusion in other documents.
Open Document Presentation	.odp	PowerPoint presentation that can be opened in applications that use the *Open Document Presentation* format, such as Google.Docs or Open Office.org.

> **MORE INFO**
>
> Other file formats are used to save individual slides or images on slides. These graphic file formats include .jpg, .png, .tif, .bmp, .wmf, or .emf. These formats are explained on page P1-34.

When you are finished with a presentation, save your final version and then close the presentation. Click the **File** tab, and then click **Close**. To close PowerPoint, click the **Close** button in the upper right corner of the title bar.

Share and Export Options

From the *Backstage* view you have options for ***sharing*** (Figure 1-18) or ***exporting*** (Figure 1-19) your presentation using different file formats. Although these options take advantage of the distribution capabilities of Microsoft Office, not all classroom computer lab configurations permit access to shared online sites or network locations.

1-18 *Share* options

Share

- ***Invite People:*** Saves your presentation to a *SkyDrive* location so you can share it with people.
- ***Email:*** Sends your presentation as an attachment in the file type you choose.
- ***Present Online:*** Requires a Microsoft account so people can link to your slide show through a web browser.
- ***Publish Slides:*** Sends presentation files to a shared library or SharePoint site.

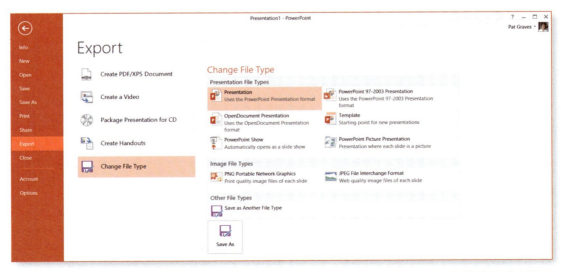

1-19 *Export* options

Export

- *Create PDF/XPS Document:* Preserves formatting and reduces file size for easier distribution.
- *Create a Video:* Saves your presentation as a video.
- *Package Presentation for CD:* Saves your presentation and all linked or embedded files.
- *Create Handouts:* Transfers slides and notes to a Word document that you can re-format.
- *Change File Type:* Saves your presentation or individual slides in different file formats.

SLO 1.2 # Adding and Editing Presentation Text

As you begin developing presentation content, you will enter most text and objects such as pictures, tables, and charts using *placeholders* on slides in *Normal* view. By default, these place-holders have no fill color or border, but you may choose to emphasize them by adding color. You can resize placeholders as needed to fit text content. Usually, slide titles and subtitles contain a single line of text; body placeholders contain bulleted text.

When PowerPoint first opens or when you start a blank presentation, the first slide has a *Title Slide* layout with two placeholders: a presentation title and a subtitle. You can add text directly into these placeholders or you can type slide titles and bulleted text in *Outline* view. The font, font size, and alignment are preset, but you can change them as you develop your presentation.

As you write text, keep in mind that it should be brief, straight to the point, and easy to read.

Add Slides and Choose Layouts

After a title slide, PowerPoint automatically inserts a *Title and Content* layout when you click the **New Slide** button. This layout is the one used for developing most slides; it has a placeholder for the slide title and a placeholder for inserting bulleted text or graphic elements. From that point forward, each time you click the top of the **New Slide** button, you add a new slide with the same layout as the previous one unless you use the **Title Slide** layout again. If you click the **New Slide** list arrow (bottom half), you see a gallery of layouts such as the ones shown in Figure 1-20 for a blank presentation.

Layouts control the position of placeholders on a slide and provide a starting point for your slide designs. You can change layouts or

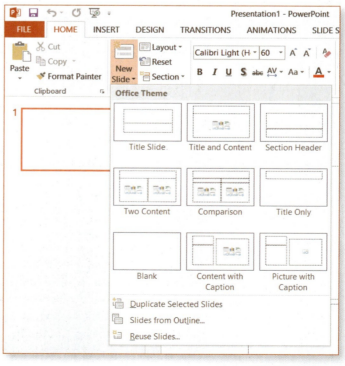

1-20 Slide layouts

customize each slide for the content you are developing. The available layouts vary based on the current theme. The most common layouts are described in the following table.

Slide Layouts

Layout Name	Layout Description
Title Slide	This layout is used for a presentation's opening slide. It contains a title and subtitle placeholder.
Title and Content	This slide layout makes up the body of a presentation. It contains a placeholder for the slide title and a larger placeholder for many different kinds of content.
Section Header	Similar to a title slide layout, it has a title and subtitle placeholder. Depending on the theme being used, it usually has a different appearance from the title slide. Slides with this layout can divide a lengthy presentation or introduce different topics or speakers.
Two Content	This layout has a slide title placeholder and two smaller content placeholders to display either two brief lists or a list and a graphic object, such as a picture or chart.
Comparison	This layout is similar to the *Two Content* layout, but it works better for comparing two lists because it provides a heading area above each content placeholder.
Title Only	Only one placeholder is provided for the title (usually at the top) of the slide.
Blank	This layout has no placeholders.
Content with Caption	This layout is similar to the *Two Content* layout, but one area is designated for the content, such as a table or chart, while the other area is meant for descriptive text.
Picture with Caption	This layout has a large area for a picture and another area for descriptive text.

HOW TO: Choose and Change Slide Layouts

1. Click the **New Slides** button [*Home* tab, *Slides* group] to insert a slide with the default layout after the current slide.
2. Click the **New Slides** list arrow [*Home* tab, *Slides* group], and select the layout you want from the *Office Theme Layout* gallery.
3. To change the layout of a selected slide, click **Layout** [*Home* tab, *Slides* group].
4. From the *Office Theme Layout* gallery, select the layout you want. Repeat this process to try another layout.
5. Click the **Undo** button to remove the layout change.

Enter Text in Placeholders

When you first see placeholders on slides, they appear as boxes with a thin border. When you click inside the placeholder, it becomes active with a blinking insertion point where you can type or edit text (Figure 1-21). Click the border to select the placeholder (Figure 1-22). In both cases, sizing handles that are small white squares appear on the corners and sides. A rotation handle that is a circular arrow appears at the top.

Dotted line border shows text can be entered or edited

Click to add title

Click to add subtitle

1-21 Edit text in a selected placeholder

Keep the wording of titles concise so the text does not become too small. Depending on the font that is used, title text for individual slides is usually 36–44 points. When using the *Title Slide* layout, the title text is usually 54–72 points.

In body placeholders, a bullet automatically appears when you type text and press **Enter**. Bullets help mark the beginning point, so people recognize items as separate. You can also add subpoints that are indented below a bulleted item. Be sure your list is very concise, usually no more than six items, and the text size is 20–28 points. Larger font sizes are very important if you are presenting in a large room so your audience can read slide text from a distance. However, if you are preparing a presentation to be viewed on a computer or online, you can use smaller font sizes.

Bulleted lists are appropriate when items require no particular order. If you need to show items in order, use a numbered list instead.

1-22 Selected placeholder to move or resize

HOW TO: Work with Lists

1. In the body placeholder, click after the first bullet and type the text.

2. Press **Enter** to type another bulleted item in the same position (the list level).

3. To indent a bulleted item to the right (Figure 1-23), press **Tab** or click the **Increase List Level** button [*Home* tab, *Paragraph* group] (Figure 1-24).

4. If you need to enter several text slides, click the **Outline View** button [*View* tab, *Presentation Views* group] to display all slide titles and bulleted text on the left of the window.

5. Use *Outline View* to move a bulleted item to the left to create a slide title.

   a. Position your insertion point before the text to move left (Figure 1-25).
   b. Press **Shift+Tab** or click the **Decrease List Level** button [*Home* tab, *Paragraph* group].
   c. Change text capitalization as needed for a title (Figure 1-26).

6. To switch to a numbered list, click the **Numbering** button [*Home* tab, *Paragraph* group].

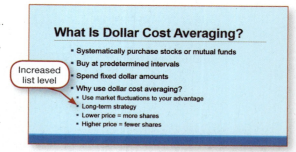

1-23 Bulleted list slide

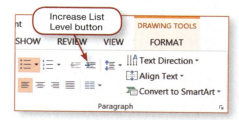

1-24 Paragraph group on the *Home* tab

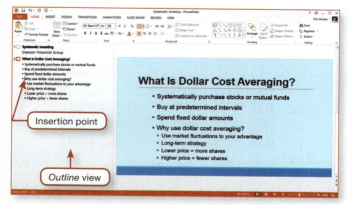

1-25 Slide with bulleted text before list level changes

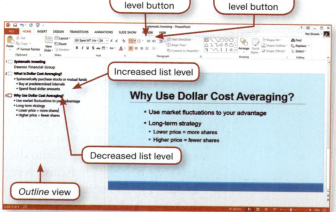

1-26 New slide created by decreasing the list level

Move, Align, and Resize Placeholders

To move a placeholder, point to the border so your pointer changes to a move arrow (with four points) and then drag the placeholder to its new position.

Align text within placeholders using the buttons on the *Home* tab in the *Paragraph* group.

- *Horizontal alignment:* **Left, Center, Right,** or **Justified** (rarely used on slides) buttons
- *Vertical alignment:* **Top, Middle,** or **Bottom** buttons

Align placeholders with one another or with the slide by clicking the **Align** button in the *Arrange* group on the *Drawing Tools Format* tab (Figure 1-27). Select from the following alignment options from the drop-down list:

- *Horizontal alignment:* **Left, Center, Right**
- *Vertical alignment:* **Top, Middle, Bottom**

1-27 Alignment options

To increase or decrease placeholder size, point to one of the corner or side *sizing* handles (Figure 1-28) until your pointer changes to a two-pointed arrow (Figure 1-29). Drag to resize. The corner sizing handles move diagonally to change both the horizontal and vertical dimensions at the same time.

1-28 Sizing handles on a placeholder

You can control the way placeholders and other objects are resized by pressing one of three keys as you drag:

- *Ctrl:* The placeholder size changes from a fixed center point.
- *Shift:* The height and width proportions are maintained as the size changes.
- *Ctrl+Shift:* The placeholder resizes from the center and remains in proportion.

1-29 Sizing pointers

Another way to precisely resize a placeholder is to enter the exact dimensions on the *Drawing Tools Format* tab.

All of these techniques for moving, aligning, and resizing also apply to pictures and other objects. If you make a change to a slide layout that you do not like, click the **Reset** button in the *Slides* group on the *Home* tab.

Edit Text

As you are writing text, you can cut, copy, or paste text. All of your font commands, such as bold, italic, underline, font, and font size are available in the *Font* group on the *Home* tab. Also, these text formatting options are available on the mini toolbar (Figure 1-30), which appears when text is selected. You can undo or redo actions using commands on the *Quick Access* toolbar.

1-30 **Mini toolbar**

Notice that your pointer changes when you are working with text. When you see a blinking insertion point, PowerPoint is waiting for you to type text. When you point to text, your pointer changes to a text selection tool so you can click and drag to select text.

ANOTHER WAY

Ctrl+X	Cut
Ctrl+C	Copy
Ctrl+V	Paste
Ctrl+Z	Undo
Ctrl+Y	Redo

HOW TO: Delete Text

1. Press **Delete** to remove text to the right of the insertion point.
2. Press **Backspace** to remove text to the left of the insertion point.
3. Select text and press **Delete** to remove several words at one time.

Click outside a text placeholder to deselect it. Handles no longer appear.

Change Text Case

Text case refers to how text is capitalized. Sometimes text appears in a placeholder in uppercase (all capital) letters. Be careful when using uppercase letters, because text may not be as easy to read as text with initial caps (the first letter only is capitalized). People are more experienced at reading lowercase text and, therefore, can generally read that text faster. Also, uppercase words in email are thought to represent shouting, and this negative connotation might carry over to your presentation if you overuse capital letters. Use uppercase letters when you really want to emphasize selected words or brief phrases.

HOW TO: Change Case

1. Select the text to be changed.
2. Click the **Change Case** button [*Home* tab, *Font* group].
3. Choose from the options **Sentence case**, **lowercase**, **UPPERCASE**, **Capitalize Each Word**, or **tOGGLE cASE** (Figure 1-31).

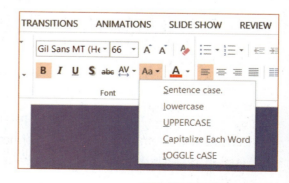

1-31 *Change Case* options

Change List Bullet Symbols

If a bullet that automatically appears seems inappropriate or if its color blends too much with the slide background, you can change the bullet symbol.

HOW TO: Change Bullet Symbols

1. Select the text where you want to change the bullet.
2. Click the **Bullets** button list arrow [*Home* tab, *Paragraph* group] and then select **Bullets and Numbering** to open the *Bullets and Numbering* dialog box.
3. Select one of the pre-defined bullets (Figure 1-32).
4. In the *Size* box, enter a different number to increase or decrease the bullet size.
5. Click the **Color** button to select a different bullet color.
6. Click the **Customize** button to open the *Symbol* dialog box (Figure 1-33), where you can select from many symbols displayed in several fonts.
7. After you select a symbol, click **OK** to add that symbol to the *Bullets and Numbering* dialog box.
8. Select the bullet and click **OK** to change the bullets on selected text.

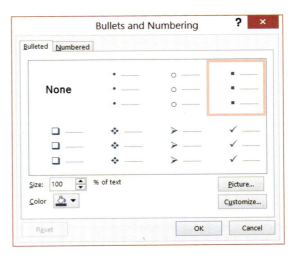

1-32 *Bullets and Numbering* dialog box

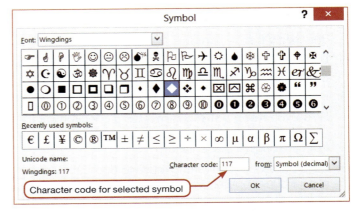

1-33 *Symbol* dialog box

The three **Wingdings** fonts have most of the available character bullets from the *Symbols* dialog box. You can also select picture bullets that are more decorative from the *Bullets and Numbering* dialog box.

The Format Painter

To copy formatting changes from text, shapes, or pictures and apply these changes to another selection, use the **Format Painter**. You can apply the changes on the same slide or on different slides.

HOW TO: Use the Format Painter

1. Select the text or other object with the format that you want to copy.
2. Click **Format Painter** [*Home* tab, *Clipboard* group] (Figure 1-34).

1-34 *Format Painter* button on the *Home* tab

3. Your pointer changes to a paintbrush.

4. Select the text or other object and click to apply the formatting.

5. If you want to apply the change to multiple selections, double-click the **Format Painter** button. Press **Esc** to stop formatting.

Reuse Slides from Another Presentation

You can add slides from another presentation without opening it as long as you can access the location where it is stored.

HOW TO: Reuse Slides

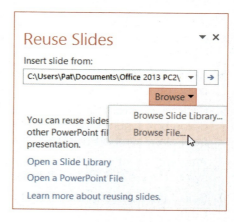

1-35 *Reuse Slides* task pane

1. In the thumbnail area, click between two slides where you want the new slide inserted.

2. Click the **New Slide** button arrow [*Home* tab, *Slides* group] and select **Reuse Slides** from the bottom of the *Office Theme Layout* gallery.

3. In the *Reuse Slides* pane that automatically opens, click **Browse** and then click **Browse File** (Figure 1-35).

4. Find the location where your existing presentation file is saved and select the file name.

5. Click **Open**. The slides in this second presentation appear in the *Reuse Slides* pane (Figure 1-36).

6. Point to each of the slide thumbnails so you can read the slide titles.

7. Select the **Keep source formatting** checkbox at the bottom of the *Reuse Slides* pane if you want the inserted slides to retain their design from the original presentation.

8. Click the slides you want to reuse to duplicate them in your current presentation. By default, the reused slides will appear with the formatting of your current presentation.

9. Click the **Close** button at the top of the *Reuse Slides* pane.

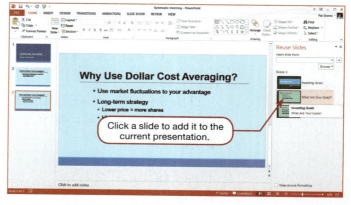

1-36 Reuse slides

> ### MORE INFO
>
> When task panes open, they are docked on the right side of the PowerPoint window. If you have a wide computer screen and you are using PowerPoint in a window size that does not fill the screen, you can drag a task pane away from the window so your slide size becomes larger. Double-click the task pane to dock it on the right of the window again.

Check Spelling and Word Usage

PowerPoint's *AutoCorrect* feature fixes many simple errors as you are typing. You can customize *AutoCorrect* options. Even when using *AutoCorrect,* you still need to check for errors when your presentation is complete. If your audience sees mistakes when viewing your slide show, your credibility is undermined. After using PowerPoint's spelling feature, carefully read the content to find any words that may have been missed, such as names or words that might not be in the spelling dictionary.

HOW TO: Check Spelling

1. From any slide in your presentation, click the **Spelling** button [*Review* tab, *Proofing* group] (Figure 1-37).

2. From the *Spelling* pane that opens on the right (Figure 1-38), consider each word that is identified and whether or not the suggested spelling is correct.

3. Click the **Audio** button on the *Spelling* pane to hear the word pronounced.

4. Click the **Change** button to insert a suggested spelling; click the **Ignore** button if you want to skip the suggestion.

5. When the spell check is complete, click **OK**.

6. Click the **Close** button at the top of the *Spelling* pane.

1-37 *Spelling* button on the *Review* tab

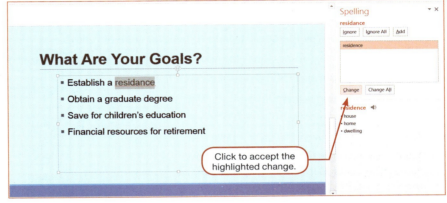

1-38 *Spelling* pane

If you want to replace an awkward word or one that is used too frequently, use PowerPoint's ***Thesaurus*** to find a more appropriate word.

HOW TO: Use the Thesaurus

1. Click in the word you want to change.

2. Click the **Thesaurus** button [*Review* tab, *Proofing* group]. Your word is selected and the *Thesaurus* pane opens (Figure 1-39).

3. Your selected word appears in the search box, and words with similar meanings appear below it.

4. Click a word from this list to see more options; click the **Back** arrow to return to the original list.

5. On a highlighted word in the list, click the **Down** arrow and choose **Insert** to replace the selected word.

6. Click the **Close** button at the top of the *Thesaurus* pane.

1-39 *Thesaurus* word choices

SLO 1.3

Rearranging Slides

When developing a presentation, you might need to move between slides as ideas occur to you or when you have new information to add. You can rearrange slides at any time. However, always carefully examine your sequence when all slides are complete. The final order must be logical to you and to your audience.

Move between Slides

In *Normal* view, you can move between slides by clicking the **Next** and **Previous** buttons, clicking scroll arrows, or dragging the scroll box on the right of the window. You can also click thumbnails or use keyboard shortcuts.

HOW TO: Move between Slides

1. Click the **Next** button or the **scroll down arrow** to go to the next slide (Figure 1-40).
2. Click the **Previous** button or **scroll up arrow** to go to the previous slide.
3. Click above or below the scroll box to move one slide at a time.
4. Drag the *Scroll* box up or down to move to a specific slide, using the slide indicator.
5. Click a slide thumbnail to make that slide active.
6. Press the following shortcut keys:

   - First slide **Home**
   - Last slide **End**
   - Next slide **Page Down** or **down arrow**
   - Previous slide **Page Up** or **up arrow**

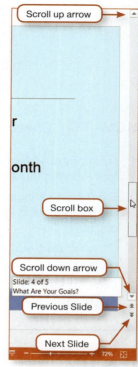

1-40 Move between slides

Copy, Paste, and Duplicate Slides

To reuse a slide's content or format, copy the thumbnail. The original slide remains in its position. Paste the copied slide where you need it and edit the text.

HOW TO: Copy and Paste Slides

1. Select the thumbnail of the slide to be copied (Figure 1-41).
2. Press **Ctrl+C** or click the **Copy** button [*Home* tab, *Clipboard* group] to copy the slide.
3. Move the insertion point to the place between slides where you want the copied slide to appear.
4. Press **Ctrl+V** or click the **Paste** button [*Home* tab, *Clipboard* group] to paste the slide.
5. You can also right-click a slide thumbnail and then select **Copy** or **Paste** from the shortcut menu.
6. On the new slide, edit the text with new content.

1-41 Copy and paste a selected slide

Duplicating slides is similar to *Copy* and *Paste,* except it requires only one step to make the second slide.

HOW TO: Duplicate Slides

1. Select the thumbnail of the slide to be duplicated.
2. Press **Ctrl+D** to duplicate the slide. The second slide is placed immediately after the original slide.
3. You can also right-click a slide thumbnail and select **Duplicate Slide** from the shortcut menu.

Select Multiple Slides

If you need to make the same changes to more than one slide, you can select more than one slide thumbnail.

HOW TO: Select Multiple Slides

1. To select multiple slides in order, select the first slide and then press **Shift** while you click the last slide (Figure 1-42).
2. To select multiple nonadjacent slides (not in order), select the first slide and then press **Ctrl** while you click each of the slides you need to select (Figure 1-43).

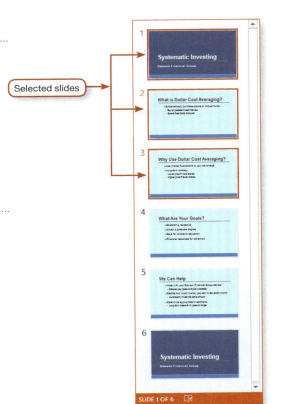

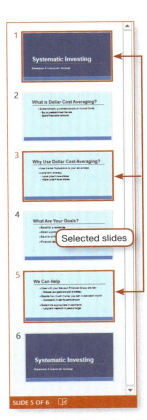

1-42 Adjacent slides selected

1-43 Nonadjacent slides selected

Rearrange Slide Order

You can rearrange slides at any time while developing a presentation. You can drag slide thumbnails up or down. On the *Outline* view, you can drag the slide icons. You can also cut slides and paste them into a different position. However, when your presentation has more slides than can be seen in the thumbnail pane, it is best to rearrange slides using *Slide Sorter* view (Figure 1-44).

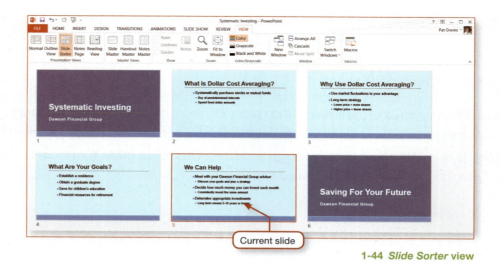

The *Slide Sorter* view enables you to see your presentation as a whole. The thumbnails are arranged from left to right in rows. By default, they are shown at a 100% size. Click the **Zoom In** button to increase the slide thumbnail size if you need to see the slide content better; click the **Zoom Out** button to decrease the slide thumbnail size and see more slides at one time.

HOW TO: Rearrange Slides in Slide Sorter View

1. Click the **Slide Sorter** button on the *Status bar*.
2. Click the **Zoom In** or **Zoom Out** buttons to adjust the size of the thumbnails.
3. Click and drag the slide thumbnails into their new positions (Figure 1-45).

Delete Slides

Remove slides by deleting slide thumbnails in *Normal* view and *Slide Sorter* view or by deleting the slide icon in *Outline* view. You can also use the **Cut** button on the *Home* tab in the *Clipboard* group. This method is helpful because if you change your mind about the deletion later, you can paste the deleted slides back into the presentation from the *Clipboard*.

HOW TO: Delete Slides

1. Right-click the slide thumbnail (or the *Slide* icon in *Outline* view) and click **Delete Slide** from the shortcut menu.
2. Select the slide thumbnail (or the *Slide* icon in *Outline* view) and press **Delete**.
3. Select the slide thumbnail (or the *Slide* icon in *Outline* view) and click **Cut** [*Home* tab, *Clipboard* group].

In this project, you develop the text for a presentation about upcoming marathon events. At the Hamilton Civic Center, this presentation promotes event preparation for participants. You start with a blank presentation, add slides, reuse slides from another presentation, and make format changes.

File Needed: ***MarathonInfo-01.pptx***
Completed Project File Name: **[your initials] PP P1-1.pptx**

1. Start a new presentation. Press **Ctrl+N**, or click the **File** tab, click **New**, and then click **Blank Presentation**.

2. Name and save the presentation.
   a. Press **F12** to open the *Save As* dialog box.
   b. Browse to the location where you want to save your files.
   c. Type [your initials PP P1-1] in the *File name* area (Figure 1-46).
   d. Be sure that the *Save as type* says "PowerPoint Presentation."
   e. Click **Save**. The *Save As* dialog box closes.

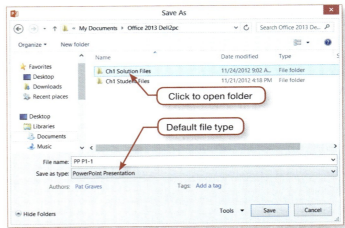

1-46 *Save As* dialog box

3. On slide 1, type the following text in the placeholders:

Title	Take the Right Steps
Subtitle	Train for a Marathon

4. Click the **New Slide** button [*Home* tab, *Slides* group] twice to add two new slides that automatically have the *Title and Content* layout. Type the following text in slides 2 and 3:

Slide 2 Title	What Is Your Goal?
Bulleted items	Run the second half faster
	Beat a time you've run before
	Or
	Finish the marathon
Slide 3 Title	Start Early to Be Ready
Bulleted items	Begin 5–16 weeks in advance
	Get a physical check up
	Prepare gear for running
	Join a training group
	Enjoy camaraderie
	Be accountable
	Run 3-4 times a week

5. Change slide 3 to a *Two Context* layout and adjust the text.
   a. Select slide 3 and click the **Layout** button [*Home* tab, *Slides* group]. Next, select the **Two Content** layout.
   b. Select the last four bulleted items on the left placeholder and press **Ctrl+X** to cut them.

c. Click in the right placeholder and press **Ctrl+V** to paste them.

d. If an extra bullet appears after the last text, delete it by pressing the Backspace key.

e. Select the middle two bulleted items on the right place-holder and press **Tab** or click the **Increase List Level** button [*Home* tab, *Paragraph* group] to format them as sub-points under the first-level item (Figure 1-47).

1-47 *Two Content* layout

6. Insert three slides from another presentation after slide 3.

   a. Click the **New Slide** list arrow and select **Reuse Slides**.

   b. On the *Reuse Slides* pane, click **Browse**; then select **Browse file** and locate your student files.

   c. Select the presentation ***MarathonInfo-01*** and click **Open**. (This presentation has spelling errors that you will fix later.)

   d. Click three slides (Figure 1-48) to insert them: "Practice Runs," "Eat Energy Foods," and "Get Running Apparel."

   e. Close the *Reuse Slides* pane.

1-48 *Reuse slides*

7. Rearrange six slides. Click the thumbnails and drag them up or down so the six slides are in this order: "Take the Right Steps," "What is Your Goal?," "Start Early to Be Ready," "Get Running Apparel," "Eat Energy Foods," and "Practice Runs."

8. Insert a new slide.

   a. With slide 6 selected, click the **New Slide** list arrow and select the **Title Only** layout.

   b. In the title placeholder, type Look It UP! (Figure 1-49).

   c. Select the title text and change the font size to **72 pts**.

   d. Select this slide thumbnail and press **Ctrl+D** to duplicate it to create slide 8.

> Look It UP!

1-49 **Placeholder text resized**

9. Edit and duplicate slide 8.

   a. On slide 8, edit the title text and type Mark It DOWN!

   b. Select this slide thumbnail and press **Ctrl+D** to duplicate it to create slide 9.

10. On slide 9, edit the title text and type See You THERE!

11. Click the **Spelling** button [*Review* tab, *Proofing* group] and correct each of the spelling errors.

12. Save the presentation. You will continue to work on this presentation for *Pause & Practice PowerPoint 1-2* and *PowerPoint 1-3*.

SLO 1.4

Working with Themes

You can use the same themes for presentations, documents, and worksheets created in all Microsoft Office applications to create a cohesive look. In PowerPoint, the **Slide Master** stores information about slide backgrounds, layouts, and fonts for each theme. Changing the *Slide Master* can help you work more efficiently because the entire presentation is affected. In this section, you change theme colors and fonts. In Chapter 3 you create unique backgrounds.

When you start a new presentation and search online, you may find themes or templates that contain artwork or pictures that fit your topic perfectly. The file names you see below each thumbnail do not distinguish between themes and templates. Many of the presentations that appear in a search will have the PowerPoint default file extension (.pptx). Those saved as template files will have a different file extension (.potx). Depending on how your software is set up, you may not see these file extensions when you open files.

You can search through general categories or enter a specific search word to get more targeted results. Themes and templates are provided by Microsoft and other companies.

Your searches will provide results that include the following:

- *Theme:* A slide show with only background graphics and text treatments but no content. Different layouts control where slide objects are positioned. You can control design elements with the *Slide Master* to create custom designs.
- *Template:* A slide show with the characteristics of a theme but also with sample content on several slides. You can edit the content or remove individual slides you do not need to create your presentation. You can control design elements with the *Slide Master* to create custom designs.
- *Template, title slide only:* While the thumbnail may show a title slide, that slide might be the only content in the presentation. Other slides may be blank or have no related graphic background. The *Slide Master* has not been used.
- *Template, individual slide only:* Some thumbnails show only a single diagram or chart that can be revised for a new presentation. Usually, the *Slide Master* has not been used.
- *Different slide sizes:* Two slide sizes will appear. The thumbnails that have an almost square appearance are shown in a 4:3 aspect ratio, the ratio of width to height, which has been the standard for many years. The thumbnails in a wide-screen size are shown in a 16:9 aspect ratio, which is the newer size that reflects the shape of current computer screens.

People who see a lot of presentations become very familiar with the designs that appear in common software. So seeing a presentation with a contemporary looking design that truly fits the topic is refreshing. Caring enough to match your theme to your topic speaks volumes to people about your preparedness and competence. Consider carefully what you select so the design is suitable for your topic and for how your presentation will be used.

HOW TO: Apply a Theme to an Existing Presentation

1. Click the **Design** tab.
2. Click the **More** list arrow in the *Themes* gallery to see additional themes.
3. Point to a thumbnail to see a live preview of that theme on the current slide (Figure 1-50).
4. Click the thumbnail to apply the theme.

1-50 *Themes* gallery

Use the Slide Master to Change Theme Colors

When you choose theme colors for your slide show, consider colors that are appropriate for your topic. Also consider where you will present. Because of room lighting, colors for a slide show projected on a large-screen are not as clear or vibrant as what you see on the computer screen directly in front of you. These differences can influence your color choices. Be sure your text is easy to read with a high contrast between the text and background colors (dark on light or light on dark).

Every presentation, even a blank one, begins with a set of colors that have been chosen to work well together. With each built-in theme, PowerPoint provides *Variants* on the *Design* tab that show different theme colors. Many more theme colors are available from the *Design* tab and from the *Slide Master* tab. Generally, the *Design* tab is best to use when you want to change only theme colors or theme fonts. You will use this technique in Chapter 3 when you customize theme colors and theme fonts.

It is best to use the *Slide Master* tab to change theme colors or theme fonts when you want to make additional changes to customize slide layouts or background graphics such as to add a company logo to all slides in a presentation.

HOW TO: Change Theme Colors

1. Click the **View** tab.
2. Click the **Slide Master** button [*Master Views* group] (Figure 1-51).
3. Click the **Colors** button [*Slide Master* tab, *Background* group] (Figure 1-52).
4. A list of theme colors appears and you see a live preview of those colors as you point to each one. The blank, Office theme will show a live preview only if the background colors have been changed.
5. Click a theme color name to apply it.
6. Select one or more Slide Master layouts on the left and click the **Background Styles** button [*Slide Master* tab, *Background* group] to change the background to light or dark variations.
7. Click the **Close Master View** button [*Slide Master* tab, *Close* group].

1-51 *Slide Master* button on the *View* tab

1-52 *Slide Master* tab and *Theme Colors*

The first two colors shown represent the background and text colors; the remaining six show accent colors. For more on customizing theme colors, see *SLO 3.1: Creating Custom Theme and Background Colors.*

Not all of the themes you find online permit color changes in the same way. It depends on how the background design was created originally.

Use the Slide Master to Change Theme Fonts

Select your fonts carefully. Some seem very traditional and serious; others appear more playful and flamboyant. Use fonts that are appropriate for your presentation topic.

Consider how legible the font is with the background color you are using. In some fonts, the letters appear very thin and are not easy to read unless you make the text bold. Also consider the issues related to where you present. The lighting and room size affect how readable the text is on a large screen and you must use large font sizes. If you design a presentation to be displayed for a single person on your notebook or tablet computer, you can use smaller font sizes.

Every presentation, even a blank one, begins with a pair of *Theme Fonts*. The heading font is used for slide titles and the body font is used for all other text. Sometimes the same font is used for both. You can view or change *Theme Fonts* from the *Design* tab or from the *Slide Master* tab.

HOW TO: Change Theme Fonts

1. Click the **View** tab.
2. Click the **Slide Master** button [*Master Views* group].
3. Click the **Fonts** button [*Slide Master* tab, *Background* group] (Figure 1-53).
4. A list of Theme Fonts appears and you see a live preview of Theme Fonts applied to placeholder text as you point to each pair.
5. Click a Theme Font pair to apply it.
6. Click the **Close Master View** button [*Slide Master* tab, *Close* group].

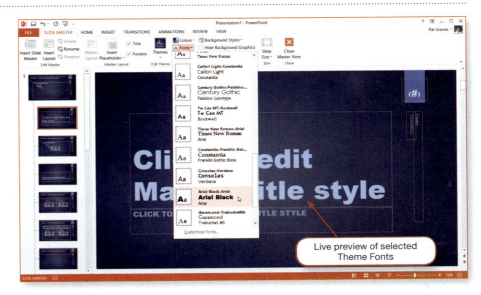

1-53 *Slide Master* tab and *Theme Fonts*

Inserting Headers and Footers

If you want to include identifying information on all slides of a presentation, use the ***Header & Footer*** command on the *Insert* tab (Figure 1-54). Footers are displayed on every slide with placeholders for the date and time, slide number, and footer text. These placeholders often appear across the bottom of the slide, but depending on the theme, they may appear in different places. You can choose to show footers on all slides or only on selected slides.

Create a Slide Footer

When you enter information using the *Header and Footer* dialog box, placeholders appear on the slides. You can move these placeholders if you wish.

HOW TO: Create a Slide Footer

1. Click the **Insert** tab.
2. Click the **Header & Footer** button [*Text* group].
3. In the *Header and Footer* dialog box, click the **Slide** tab (Figure 1-55).
4. Click the check boxes to select the following:
   a. **Date and time:** Choose between **Update automatically** to show the current date or **Fixed** to enter a specific date.
   b. **Slide number:** Each slide is numbered.
   c. **Footer:** Type text you want to appear on each slide.
5. Check the box for **Don't show on title slide** if you do not want footer information to appear on any slide created with the *Title Slide* layout.
6. Click the **Apply** button to apply the settings only to the current slide.
7. Click the **Apply to All** button to apply the settings to all slides.

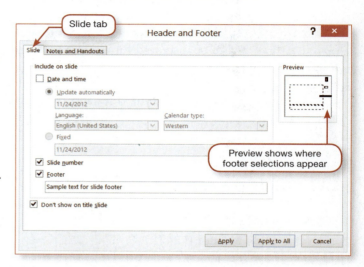

1-55 *Slide* tab on the *Header* and *Footer* dialog box

Create a Notes and Handouts Header

Because notes and handouts are usually printed documents, they can include header information that appears at the top of each page. Control all settings for notes and handouts in the same way you control slide footers.

HOW TO: Create a Notes and Handouts Header

1. Click the **Insert** tab.
2. Click the **Header & Footer** button [*Text* group].
3. In the *Header and Footer* dialog box, click the **Notes and Handouts** tab (Figure 1-56).
4. Click the check boxes to select the following:
   a. **Date and time:** Choose between **Update automatically** to show the current date or **Fixed** to enter a specific date.
   b. **Page number:** Each page is numbered.

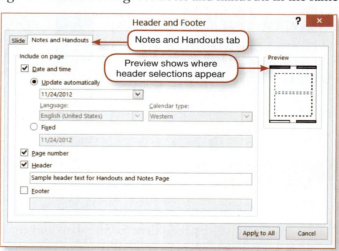

1-56 *Notes and Handouts* tab in the *Header and Footer* dialog box

c. **Header:** Type text you want to appear on each page.

d. **Footer:** Type text you want to appear on each page.

5. Click the **Apply to All** button to apply your settings to all pages.

If you leave items blank in the *Header and Footer* dialog box, empty placeholders show on your slide, but no information appears in *Slide Show* view.

PAUSE & PRACTICE: POWERPOINT 1-2

For this project, you continue working on the presentation you created in *Pause & Practice: PowerPoint 1-1*. You apply a theme then change theme colors and fonts to revise two individual slides. Finally, you add a footer to your slides and add page numbering to the notes and handout pages.

File Needed: ***[your initials] PP P1-1.pptx***
Completed Project File Name: ***[your initials] PP P1-2.pptx***

1. Open and rename the presentation file.
    a. Click the **File** tab; then click the **Open** button.
    b. Locate the folder where your files are saved.
    c. Open the presentation file **[your initials] PP P1-1**.
    d. Click the **File** tab; then click **Save As** or press **F12**.
    e. Locate the folder where your files are saved.
    f. Save the presentation as **[your initials] PP P1-2**.

2. Apply a theme.
    a. Click the **Design** tab.
    b. Click the **More** button [*Themes* group] to open the *Themes* gallery (Figure 1-57).
    c. Click the **Facet** theme so it is applied to all slides.

3. Change the background style.
    a. Click the **View** tab.
    b. Click the **Slide Master** button.
    c. Scroll to the top of the slide master layouts and select the first layout (Facet Slide Master) so your color change is applied to all slides.
    d. Click the **Colors** button [*Slide Master* tab, *Background* group].
    e. Scroll down the list and select the **Aspect** theme.
    f. Click the **Background Styles** button [*Slide Master* tab, *Background* group].
    g. Select **Style 4**, which applies a solid black background (Figure 1-58).

1-57 *Themes* **gallery**

1-58 *Background Styles*

4. Change the fonts.
   a. Click the **Fonts** button [*Slide Master* tab, *Background* group].
   b. Scroll down the list and click the **TrebuchetMS** font pair (Figure 1-59).
   c. Click the **Close Master View** button [*Slide Master* tab].

5. On slide 1, modify the title and subtitle text.
   a. Select all of the title text and make these changes:
      • Apply **bold**, change to **left alignment**, and increase the font size to **60 pts**. [*Home* tab, *Font* group].
      • Click the **Arrange** button [*Home* tab, *Drawing* group], **Align**, and select **Align Top**.
      • Select the word **Right**. Click the **Change Case** button [*Home* tab, *Font* group] and select **UPPERCASE**.
      • Resize the placeholder on the right by dragging the horizontal sizing handle so the text fits on one line.
   b. Select the subtitle and make these changes:
      • Apply **bold**, change to **left alignment**, and increase the font size to **36 pts**. [*Home* tab, *Font* group].
      • Position the subtitle below the title.

6. On slide 2, change the bullet.
   a. Select the bulleted text and click the **Bullets** list arrow [*Home* tab, *Font* group].
   b. Select **Bullets and Numbering**.
   c. Change the *Size* to **100%** of text.
   d. Click the **Color** button and select **Red**, **Accent 2** (Figure 1-60).
   e. Click the **Customize** button to open the *Symbol* dialog box. Change the font (if necessary) to **Wingdings** (Figure 1-61)
   f. Scroll down and select the **solid square** (Character code 110) and click **OK**.
   g. Click **OK** again to close the *Bullets and Numbering* dialog box.
   h. Click to put your insertion point before the word "Or" on the third bulleted item.
   i. Press **Backspace** to remove the bullet from this item only. Make this text bold.

7. Add a slide footer.
   a. On slide 2, click the **Header & Footer** button [*Insert* tab, *Text* group] (Figure 1-62).
   b. On the *Slide* tab, select **Slide number** and **Footer**.
   c. In the *Footer* text box, type Take the Right Steps, Train for a Marathon.
   d. Select **Don't show on title slide**.

1-59 *Theme* font change

1-60 Change bullet size and color

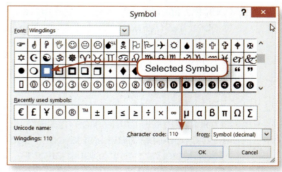

1-61 *Symbol* dialog box

e. Click the **Apply** button. The dialog box closes and the footer appears only on this slide.

f. Select the footer text and the page number. Increase the font size to **18 pts**.

8. Add page numbers for a handout.
   a. On slide 2, click the **Header & Footer** button [*Insert* tab, *Text* group].
   b. Click the **Notes and Handouts** tab.
   c. Select **Page number**.
   d. Click the **Apply to All** button and the dialog box closes.

9. Save the presentation.

1-62 *Header and Footer* dialog box with changes

SLO 1.6

Working with a Picture from a File

There is an old adage, "A picture is worth a thousand words." That saying is still true today, because pictures bring a sense of realism to a presentation. Select pictures appropriate for your topic. Include pictures obtained from web sites only if you have the permission of the image owner to avoid copyright infringement. For academic purposes, you may include images if you reference their sources as you would any other research citation.

Insert a Picture

PowerPoint supports different graphic file types, so you can insert almost any digital image from a camera, or one created by scanning a document, into a slide show. To insert a picture, click the **Picture** button in the *Images* group on the *Insert* tab. Be aware that pictures can increase the file size of your presentation dramatically.

HOW TO: Insert a Picture

1. Click the **Insert** tab.
2. Click the **Pictures** button.
3. Select the drive and folder where your picture is saved.
4. Select the file you want to insert (Figure 1-63).
5. Click **Insert**.

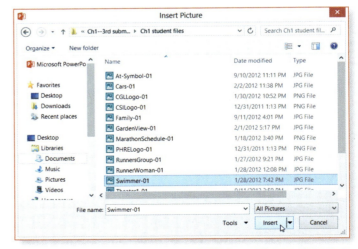

1-63 *Insert Picture* dialog box

Graphic File Formats

Picture File Type	Extension	Uses of This Format
JPEG (Joint Photographic Experts Group)	.jpg	Designed for photographic images. Handles gradual color blending and complex graphics well. Produces a smaller file size than most other formats because of compression.
PNG (Portable Network Graphics)	.png	Handles photographic images and complex graphics well. Originally designed for web applications, this format works well for presentations also. Supports transparency so areas removed from the image appear blank on the slide.
GIF (Graphics Interchange Format)	.gif	Suited for line art and simple drawings, but not optimal for photographs because it only supports 256 colors. Used for simple animated graphics. Does not handle gradual color blending well. Supports transparency.
Windows Metafile and Enhanced Windows Metafile	.wmf and .emf	Used for many Windows illustrations available through searches using the Clip Art task pane.
Device Independent Bitmap	.bmp	Images usually display well in their original size, but if you increase size, the image will be distorted.
TIFF (Tagged Image File Format)	.tiff	Designed for print publications. Produces high-quality images with large file sizes. Supports transparency.

Resize a Picture

You can make a picture smaller and still retain its clarity, but some pictures cannot be made larger without becoming blurred or distorted.

To resize a picture, point to one of the corner or side sizing handles and drag it. The corner sizing handles move diagonally to change both horizontal and vertical dimensions at the same time.

You can precisely resize a picture by entering the exact dimensions on the *Picture Tools Format* tab that appears when a picture is selected. When changing the size of pictures, maintain the correct ratio between height and width to avoid distorting the image. The selected picture of the swimmer in Figure 1-64 is shown in the original size on the left. The pictures on the right were resized horizontally to be too wide and too narrow.

If you change the size incorrectly, restore the picture's original dimensions by clicking the **Reset Picture** button in the *Adjust* group on the *Picture Tools Format* tab (Figure 1-65).

1-64 Resizing examples

1-65 *Picture Tools Format* **tab**

Align a Picture

As you place pictures and other graphic objects on slides, consider how they are aligned on the slide and how they align with other objects on the slide. Everything on the slide should align in some way. You can align pictures and other objects with each other or on the slide by clicking the *Align* button in the *Arrange* group on the *Picture Tools Format* tab and selecting the alignment from the drop-down list (Figure 1-66).

- **Horizontal alignment:** *Left, Center,* or *Right*
- **Vertical alignment:** *Top, Middle,* or *Bottom*

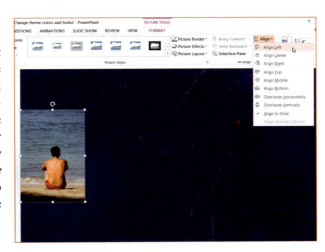

1-66 Left align on the slide

SLO 1.7 **Applying Transitions**

A **transition** is the visual effect of movement that occurs when one slide changes into another slide. Each transition effect in PowerPoint provides a different type of movement. You can find these in the *Transition to This Slide* gallery on the *Transitions* tab (Figure 1-67).

1-67 *Transitions* tab

Each slide can have only one transition. You can set transitions for one slide at a time in *Normal* view or apply the same transition to all slides. If you want to use different transitions, select thumbnails in *Normal* view or *Slide Sorter* view. Once a transition has been applied, an icon symbolizing movement appears with the slide thumbnails.

Although it is possible to apply different transitions on every slide in a presentation, it is neither practical nor advisable. People are very accustomed to PowerPoint use today and know that slides are going to change in some way. Random movements using many different transitions do not entertain an audience and may be distracting or even annoying. Control movement skillfully to reinforce your message. Some people prefer to use a "quiet" transition for most of a presentation (sort of like turning pages in a book or an e-reader). They apply a more "energetic" transition to key slides to grab attention or signal the beginning of a new topic. Use the *Slide Sorter* view to see more slides at once and decide which slides might benefit from a different movement.

In the *Timing* group, the **Advance Slide** options control whether slides advance **On Mouse Click** (the default) or after a specific number of seconds that you choose. Sound can also be associated with a transition.

HOW TO: Apply Transitions

1. Select the slide thumbnail where you want a transition to appear.
2. Click the **Transitions** tab.

3. Click the **More** button [*Transition to This Slide* group] to see additional transitions (Figure 1-68) organized by the following categories:

   a. *Subtle*
   b. *Exciting*
   c. *Dynamic Content*

4. Apply one transition to all slides in the presentation.

   a. Select a transition effect for the current slide.
   b. Be sure **On Mouse Click** is checked.
   c. Click the **Apply to All** button [*Timing* group]

5. Apply more than one transition.

   a. Click the **Slide Sorter** button on the *Status bar*.
   b. Press **Ctrl** as you click to select two or more slides that should have a different transition.
   c. Click a different transition effect and a live preview shows on the selected slides.
   d. Be sure **On Mouse Click** is checked (Figure 1-69).

6. Click the **Normal View** button on the *Status bar*.

   a. Select the first slide and click **Preview** [*Transitions* tab, *Preview* group] to test the movement.
   b. Click the **Next Slide** button and click **Preview** again for each slide.

7. Click the **Slide Show** tab.

   a. Click the **From Beginning** button to view the slide show from the first slide.
   b. Click to advance from slide to slide.

1-68 *Transitions* gallery

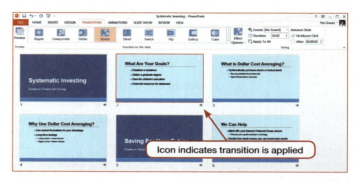

1-69 Change transitions on selected slides in *Slide Sorter* view

Duration, shown in seconds, controls how fast the slides change. Duration seconds vary based on the selected transition effect. Movement might be barely visible if the duration is fast; a slower duration of five or more seconds can make the movement much more noticeable. Enter a different number to change the duration and experiment to see what works best for your content.

Select Effect Options

Effect Options control the direction of transition movement and options vary based on the transition. Each transition can have only one effect option.

HOW TO: Select Effect Options

1. In *Slide Sorter* view, select the slide (or slides) with the same transition.
2. Click the **Transitions** tab.
3. Click the **Effect Options** button to see a drop-down list showing directional movements (Figure 1-70).
4. Select an option to apply it.
5. Repeat this process if you have more than one transition.

6. Click **Preview** to test the movement in *Normal View*.

7. Click the **Slide Show** tab.

8. Click the **From Beginning** button to view the slide show from the first slide.

9. Click to advance from slide to slide.

1-70 *Transition Effect* options

Exploring Print Options

You may want to proofread your presentation content on paper or review the slides with a colleague. Or you may want to prepare audience handouts or your own printed materials to use while you are giving the presentation. PowerPoint 2013 provides convenient ways to preview and print presentation slides, handouts, notes pages, or outlines.

Preview a Presentation

Before printing, check your slides to ensure everything looks as you intended. The *Backstage* view [*File* tab, *Print* button] displays each slide or handout page in your presentation as it will look when printed. Use the navigation controls at the bottom of the window to go through the slides or pages one at a time. You can also press **Page Up** or **Page Down**, or you can use the scroll bar on the right. Adjust slide sizes using the *Zoom* controls on the lower right.

The look of your slides in *Backstage* view is influenced by the selected printer. If you are using a color printer, the preview image is shown in color; if it prints in black and white, the preview image will be shown in *grayscale* (shades of black). In a work setting, you may have a small desktop printer for printing rough draft copies with black print and a network printer for printing more expensive, high-quality color pages. If you design slides in color and plan to print slides or handouts in grayscale, preview your slides to make sure that all text is readable. You may need to adjust some colors to get good results.

In *Backstage* view, select a printer from the available list of local and network printers. Print **Settings** are shown as buttons with the current setting displayed. Click the list arrow for a list of the following options:

- **Which Slides to Print:** Choose among *Print All Slides, Print Selection, Print Current Slide,* or *Custom Range* using slide numbers entered in the *Slides* box (e.g., slides 1-3 or slides 1-3, 5, 8).
- **What to Print:** Choose *Full Page Slides, Notes Pages, Outline,* or *Handouts.* You can print handouts with three to nine slides on a page using a horizontal or vertical arrangement on the page. You can also specify *Frame Slides, Scale to Fit Paper* (makes slides larger), or *High Quality.*
- **Print Side:** Choose between *Print One Side* or *Print Both Sides.* However, not all printers can print on both sides.
- **Print Order:** Choose between *Collated* and *Uncollated.* Usually slides print in order, but you may want to print multiple copies page by page.
- **Orientation:** Choose between *Landscape* and *Portrait.* By default, slides print in landscape orientation; notes and handouts print in portrait orientation. This option is not available if you are printing full-size slides.
- **Color Range:** Choose among *Color, Grayscale,* or *Pure Black and White.*

Below the print *Settings* in *Backstage* view, you can click the **Edit Header & Footer** link to open the *Header and Footer* dialog box and then enter or revise information.

Print a Slide

The default print settings print each slide on letter-size paper. Adjust settings as needed to print the current or selected slides.

HOW TO: Print a Slide in Grayscale

1. Click the **File** tab.
2. Click the **Print** button on the left.
3. For *Settings*, choose the options you need, such as the following:
   a. Which Slides to Print: **Print Current Slide**.
   b. What to Print: **Full Page Slides**.
   c. Print Order: **Collated**.
   d. Color Range: **Grayscale** (Figure 1-71).
4. Enter the number of copies, if you need more than one.
5. Click the **Print** button at the top.

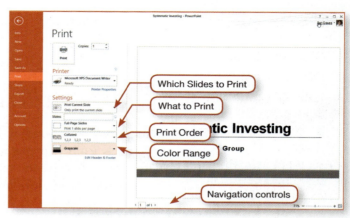

1-71 Print settings for a full-size slide

Print a Handout

Handouts print one to nine slides on a page. You can use these pages as audience handouts or for your own reference during a presentation. Selecting *Scale to Fit Paper* makes the slides larger. *Framing* shows the shape of slides, which is helpful when printing slides with a white background on white paper. Depending on the number of slides, changing the page orientation to landscape can make slides larger.

When preparing handouts for an audience, consider which slides will be important for the audience to have. If not all slides are necessary, you can specify which slides to include and perhaps reduce the number of pages required for printing.

HOW TO: Print a Handout for Selected Slides in Color

1. Click the **File** tab.
2. Click the **Print** button on the left.
3. Select a color printer.
4. For *Settings*, choose the options you need, such as the following:
   a. Which Slides to Print: Enter the specific slides needed (such as **1**, **3–4**, **6**) in the *Slides* box to print a *Custom Range*.
   b. What to Print: **6 Slides Horizontal**, **Collated**, and **Portrait Orientation**.
   c. Color Range: **Color** (Figure 1-72).
5. Enter the number of copies, if you need more than one.
6. Click the **Print** button at the top.

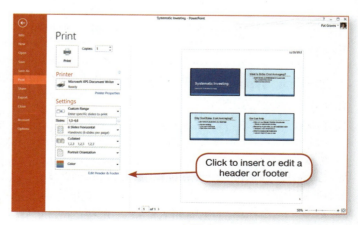

1-72 Print settings for a handout

Print an Outline

If a presentation consists of mostly slides with bulleted lists, printing an outline is a very concise way to display the content. Only the text is shown.

HOW TO: Print an Outline in Pure Black and White

1. Click the **File** tab.
2. Click the **Print** button on the left.
3. For *Settings*, choose the options you need, such as the following:
   a. Which Slides to Print: **Print All Slides**.
   b. What to Print: **Outline**.
   c. What Side: **Print One Sided**.
   d. Print Order: **Collated**.
   e. Orientation: **Portrait Orientation**.
   f. Color Range: **Pure Black and White** (Figure 1-73).
4. Enter the number of copies, if you need more than one.
5. Click the **Print** button at the top.

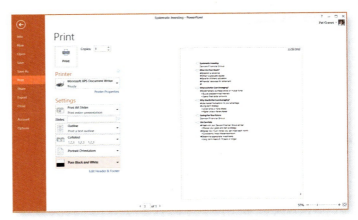

1-73 Print settings for an outline

Applying Properties

PowerPoint automatically records information in your presentation file, such as the file size, creation date, and number of slides. These *document properties,* also called *metadata,* can help you manage and track files. Click the **File** tab and click the **Info** button to see these properties on the right side of the *Backstage* view. You can edit some of these properties, such as title and author, in this view.

HOW TO: Change Properties Using Backstage View

1. Click the **File** tab.
2. Click the **Info** button.
3. Document properties are listed on the right. Point to the fields to see which ones you can edit (Figure 1-74).
4. Click **Show All Properties** to access additional information.
5. Click in a **field** and type information to edit the document property.

1-74 Document properties on *Backstage* view

SLO 1.9 Applying Properties   P1-39

Change Document Panel Information

You can change additional properties, such as subject, keywords, or category, using the *Document Properties* panel that appears in the PowerPoint window between the *Ribbon* and the slide area.

HOW TO: Change Properties Using the Document Panel

1. Click the **File** tab.
2. Click the **Info** button.
3. Click the **Properties** list arrow at the top of the *Properties* area.
4. Select **Show Document Panel** (Figure 1-75). The *Backstage* closes, and the *Document Properties Panel* displays (Figure 1-76).
5. Click in the fields and type appropriate information.
6. Click the *Document Properties* **Close** button at the top right of the panel to close the panel.

1-75 *Properties* options

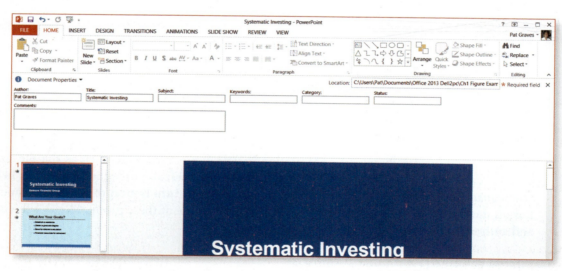

1-76 *Document Properties* Panel

Review Advanced Properties

The *Properties* dialog box displays properties organized in the following five tabs: *General, Summary, Statistics, Contents,* and *Custom.*

HOW TO: Change Properties Using the Properties Dialog Box

1. Click the **File** tab.
2. Click the **Info** button.
3. Click the **Properties** list arrow at the top of the *Properties* area.

4. Select **Advanced Properties**. The *Properties* dialog box is displayed (Figure 1-77).

5. Tabs display properties automatically generated by PowerPoint.

6. Click the **Summary** and **Custom** tabs to add or edit information.

7. Click **OK** to close the *Properties* dialog box.

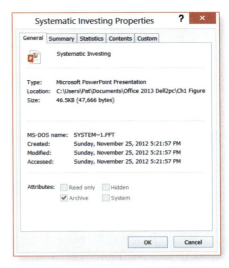

1-77 *Properties* dialog box

> **ANOTHER WAY**
>
> Open the *Advanced Properties* dialog box from the *Document* Panel by clicking **Document Properties** and selecting **Advanced Properties**.

PAUSE & PRACTICE: POWERPOINT 1-3

For this final Pause & Practice project, you finish the presentation about training for a marathon. You insert, resize, and align several pictures, apply transitions, change the presentation properties, and print a handout.

Files Needed: *[your initials] PP P1-2.pptx MarathonInfo-01.pptx*, *RunnersGroup-01.jpg*, *RunnerWoman-01.jpg*, and *MarathonSchedule-01.png*
Completed Project File Name: *[your initials] PP P1-3.pptx*

1. Open and rename the *[your initials] PP P1-2* presentation.
   a. Click the **File** tab and click the **Open** button.
   b. Locate your saved files.
   c. Open the *[your initials] PP P1-2* presentation.
   d. Click the **File** tab; then click **Save As**.
   e. Browse to the location on your computer or storage device to save the presentation.
   f. Save this presentation as *[your initials] PP P1-3*.

2. On slide 1, insert, resize, and align a picture on the slide.
   a. Click the **Insert** tab; then click the **Pictures** button.
   b. Locate the folder where your student files are saved.
   c. Select *RunnersGroup-01.jpg* and click **Insert** (or double click the file name) to insert the picture (Figure 1-78). (The .jpg file name extension may not show in your file list.)
   d. Resize the picture using the horizontal sizing arrows so it is **8.5"** wide. Because the picture is already blurred to reflect the speed of running, it looks fine when you stretch the picture.
   e. With the picture selected, click the **Align** button [*Picture Tools Format* tab, *Arrange* group].
      • Select **Align Bottom** (Figure 1-79).
      • Repeat to select **Align Right**.

1-78 Picture of runners inserted

1-79 Picture resized and aligned

3. On slide 6, repeat the process to insert a picture and align it.
   a. Click the **Insert** tab and click the **Pictures** button.
   b. Locate the folder where your files are saved.
   c. Select *RunnerWoman-01.jpg* and click **Insert** (or double click the file name) to insert the picture.
   d. No resizing is required for this picture.
   e. With the picture selected, click the **Align** button [*Picture Tools Format* tab, *Arrange* group] and select **Align Right** (Figure 1-80).

1-80 Picture aligned

4. With slide 6 selected, add a new slide and insert a picture of a table.
   a. Click the **New Slide** list arrow [*Home* tab, *Slides* group].
   b. Select the **Title Only** layout.
   c. Type the title Upcoming Marathons.
   d. Click the **Insert** tab; then click the **Pictures** button.
   e. Locate the folder where your files are saved.
   f. Select *MarathonSchedule-01.jpg* and click **Insert** (or double click the file name) to insert the picture.
   g. Move the table so it is approximately centered in the black area (Figure 1-81).

1-81 Picture of table inserted and positioned

5. On slides 8, 9, and 10, only the large title text appears. Resize the placeholders horizontally on the right side so the text fits in the placeholder without extra horizontal space or word wrapping.

6. On slide 10, change the font color for the word "THERE!" to **Tan, Text 2**.

7. On slides 8, 9, and 10, adjust where the text aligns. Repeat this process for each slide.
   a. Select the title text placeholder and click the **Align** button [*Drawing Tools Format* tab, *Arrange* group].
   b. Click **Align** and select the following alignment:

   Slide 8: **Align Left**, **Align Top** (Figure 1-82)
   Slide 9: **Align Center**, **Align Bottom**
   Slide 10: **Align Right**, **Align Middle**

1-82 Title placeholder aligned top and left

8. Apply one transition to all slides and a different transition to selected slides.
   a. Click the **Slide Sorter** button [*Status bar*].
   b. Press **Ctrl+A** to select all slides.
   c. Click the **Transitions** tab.
   d. Click the **Wipe** transition from the gallery.
   e. Click **Effect Options** [*Transition* tab, *Transition to This Slide* group].
   f. Select **From Left** (Figure 1-83).
   g. Click off a slide to remove the selections.

1-83 *Transition Effect* options

h. Select each of the following slides and apply transitions and effect options from the *Transition* tab to emphasize the content with different movements:

Slide 1: **Zoom**, **In**
Slide 7: **Doors**, **Vertical**
Slide 8: **Pan**, **From Bottom**
Slide 9: **Pan**, **From Top**
Slide 10: **Pan**, **From Left**

i. Press **Ctrl+A** to select all slides.
j. Click **Preview** [*Transitions* tab] to see the movements in *Slide Sorter* view.
k. Click the **Slide Show** button [*Status bar*] and click to advance each slide so you can see the movements in *Slide Show* view.

9. Now change some of the presentation properties.
   a. Click the **File** tab, then the **Info** button.
   b. Under *Properties*, change the *Title* to Train for a Marathon.
   c. Click the **Properties** button, then click **Show Document** Panel (Figure 1-84). Type the following information in the respective fields:

Author:	Your Name *(unless it already appears)*
Title:	Train for a Marathon *(already entered)*
Subject:	Athletic Event Promotion
Comments:	This presentation will be shown at the Civic Center to explain how to get ready for upcoming marathon events.

   d. Click the **Close** button to close the *Document Properties* panel.

1-84 *Document Properties* Panel

10. Print slides as a handout.
    a. Click the **File** tab, then the **Print** button on the left.
    b. Select the appropriate printer.
    c. Change the following *Settings* by clicking the **list arrow** for each option (repeat as necessary to make more than one change) (Figure 1-85):

    Which Slides to Print: **Print All Slides**
    What to Print: **Handouts, 6 Slides Horizontal, Frame Slides, Scale to Fit Paper**
    Print Order: **Collated**
    Orientation: **Portrait**
    Color Range: **Grayscale** (or **color** if you prefer)

1-85 *Print* settings

    d. Preview the handout by clicking the navigation buttons so you can see both pages.
    e. Click the **Print** button at the top of the *Backstage* view.

11. Press **Ctrl+S** to save the presentation (or click the **Save** button on the *File* tab or the *Quick Access* toolbar).

Chapter Summary

1.1 Create, open, and save a presentation (p. P1-3).

- You can start creating a presentation with a blank presentation, a *theme*, an existing presentation, or a *template*.
- Different *views* in PowerPoint enable you to look at your content in different ways.
- The *Zoom* feature allows you to adjust the size of the slide on which you are working.
- The standard file format for presentation files has an extension of *.pptx*.
- In *Backstage* view, PowerPoint provides a variety of save and send options. For example, you can save a presentation as a *PDF* file or email a presentation file as an attachment.
- Additional themes and templates are available at Office.com.

1.2 Develop presentation content by adding slides, choosing layouts, moving and resizing placeholders, editing text, and reusing slides from another presentation (p. P1-14).

- Use *placeholders* for presentation text and objects such as pictures, tables, and charts. You can resize, reposition, and align text placeholders on slides.
- The *New Slide* button displays a gallery of slide layouts with placeholders arranged for different content.
- You can make font changes using commands on the *Home* tab or the mini toolbar.
- *Change Case* changes the way words are capitalized.
- In bulleted lists, you can change the bullet symbol, size, and color.
- Use the *Format Painter* to copy formatting from one object and apply it to another object.
- The *Reuse Slides* feature enables you to insert slides from another presentation.
- Although potential spelling errors are automatically marked, you also can use the *Spelling* dialog box to check for errors.
- Use the *Thesaurus* to find synonyms for words in your presentation.

1.3 Rearrange presentation content by moving, copying and pasting, duplicating, and deleting slides (p. P1-22).

- You can move selected slides using a variety of methods to rearrange their sequence.
- *Copy*, *paste*, *duplicate*, and *delete* slides using the *Slides* tab or *Slide Sorter* view.

1.4 Modify a theme to change slide size and use the Slide Master to change theme colors and fonts (p. P1-26).

- Presentation *themes* provide a cohesive look through the consistent use of backgrounds, designs, colors, and font treatments.
- Consider the topic and tone of your presentation when choosing theme colors and fonts.

1.5 Use headers and footers to add identifying information (p. P1-29)

- *Footers* usually appear at the bottom of slides but can appear in other locations. They are applied to all slides or to individual slides.
- Both *headers* and *footers* are used for notes pages and handouts. They are applied to all pages.

1.6 Insert, resize, and align a picture from a file (p. P1-33).

- PowerPoint supports different *graphic file types*; you can insert almost any digital image into slide shows.
- Use *sizing handles* or enter exact dimensions to increase or decrease a picture's size.
- Avoid distortion when resizing pictures by maintaining accurate height and width ratios.
- You can *align* pictures with one another or with the slide.

1.7 Apply and modify transition effects to add visual interest (p. P1-35).

- A *transition* is the visual effect that appears when one slide changes into another slide.
- The *Effect Options* command enables you to control the direction of transition movement.
- You can apply transitions to one slide or to all slides in a presentation.

1.8 Preview a presentation and print slides, hand-outs, and outlines (p. P1-37).

- *Backstage* view allows you to examine each slide in your presentation before printing.
- The printer you select influences how slides appear in *Backstage* view.
- **Grayscale** shows shades of black.
- **Print settings** control which slides to print, what to print, and the print order, orientation, and color range.

1.9 Change properties (p. P1-39).

- Document properties are automatically recorded in your presentation file.
- You can add properties such as subject, keywords, or category to help manage and track files.
- Edit document properties in *Backstage* view under *Info* or by opening either the *Document Properties* panel or the *Advanced Properties* dialog box.

Check for Understanding

In the **Online Learning Center** for this book (www.mhhe.com/office2013inpractice), there are a variety of resources that can be used to review the concepts covered in this chapter.

The following Online Learning Resources are available in the Online Learning Center:

- Multiple choice questions
- Short answer questions
- Matching exercises

Guided Project 1-1

Jason Andrews is a sales associate for Classic Gardens and Landscaping (CGL) and frequently talks to customers when they visit the CGL showroom. For this project, you prepare a presentation he can use when introducing customers to CGL services.
[Student Learning Outcomes 1.1, 1.2, 1.3, 1.4, 1.5, 1.6]

Files Needed: *GardenView-01.jpg* and *CGLLogo-01.png*
Completed Project File Name: *[your initials] PowerPoint 1-1.pptx*

Skills Covered in This Project

- Create a new presentation using a theme.
- Change theme colors.
- Change theme fonts.
- Add slides.
- Change font size.
- Rearrange slides.

- Use the Format Painter.
- Insert a footer.
- Check spelling.
- Adjust placeholder position.
- Insert a picture.
- Save a presentation.

1. Create a new presentation using a theme.
   a. Click the **File** tab, then click **New**.
   b. Double-click the **Ion** theme (Figure 1-86).

2. Save the presentation as *[your initials] PowerPoint 1-1*.

3. Change the theme colors.
   a. Click the **Slide Master** button [*View* tab, *Master Views* group].
   b. Select the first layout on the left, **Ion Slide Master**, so your color changes are applied to all slides.
   c. Click the **Colors** button [*Slide Master* tab, *Background* group].
   d. Scroll down the list and click the **Paper** theme.
   e. Click the **Background Styles** button [*Slide Master* tab, *Background* group] and select **Style 3** (Figure 1-87).

4. Change the theme fonts.
   a. Click the **Theme Fonts** button [*Slide Master* tab, *Background* group].
   b. Scroll down the list and click the **Candara** font group.
   c. Click the **Close Master View** button [*Slide Master* tab].

1-86 Ion theme selected

1-87 Background Style 3

5. Type the following text in the placeholders on slide 1:

Title	Creating Beautiful Outdoor Spaces
Subtitle	Jason Andrews, Sales Associate

6. Apply **bold** and a **shadow** [*Home* tab, *Font* group] to both the title and subtitle. Change the title font size to **66 pts**. and the subtitle font size to **28 pts**. [*Home* tab, *Font* group].

7. Add slides.
   a. Click the **New Slide** button [*Home* tab, *Slides* group] to add a new slide that automatically has the **Title and Content** layout. Type the following text for slide 2:

Slide 2 Title	Our Services
Bulleted items	Garden center
	Tree nursery
	Gift shop
	Delivery and installation
	Patios and irrigation systems

   b. Repeat this process to create three new slides with the following text:

Slide 3 Title	Available Products
Bulleted items	Shrubs, perennials, annuals
	Soils and mulches
	Garden décor including fountains
	Shade trees and evergreen screening trees
	Flowering or ornamental trees
	Trees and plants for Christmas

Slide 4 Title	Why Sustainable Design?
Bulleted items	Energy efficiency increased
	Water efficiency increased
	Dependency on chemicals decreased
	Vigor assured through native and hardy plants

Slide 5 Title	We Make It Easy
Bulleted items	We can do the entire project or we can assist
(indent as shown)	You can do as much, or as little, as you like
	We will provide:
	Landscape design planning or just advice
	Soil testing
	Low-cost delivery
	Fountain set up

   c. Click the **New Slide** list arrow [*Home* tab, *Slides* group] and click the **Title Slide** layout. Type this text in the placeholders:

Title	Call for a Consultation
Subtitle	615-792-8833

8. Move the slide 5 thumbnail before slide 4.

9. Apply bold and use the *Format Painter*.
   a. On slide 2, select the title text and apply **bold**.
   b. Double-click the **Format Painter** button [*Home* tab, *Clipboard* group] so you can apply this change more than one time.

c. Press **Page Down** and click the title text on slide 3 to apply the same change.

d. Repeat for slides 4 and 5.

e. Click the **Format Painter** button or press **Esc** to stop applying formatting.

10. Increase the font size on other slides.

a. On slide 2, select the bulleted text placeholder and click the **Increase Font Size** button [*Home* tab, *Font* group] to increase the font size to **24 pts**.

b. Repeat for slides 3-5. On slide 4, the font size for level 2 bulleted text changes to **20 pts**.

c. On slide 6, increase the font size for the phone number to **32 pts**.

11. Create a footer with the company name in the footer text.

a. Click the **Header & Footer** button [*Insert* tab, *Text* group].

b. On the *Slide* tab, select **Date and time** with **Update automatically**, **Slide number**, and **Footer** (Figure 1-88).

c. In the *Footer* text box, type Classic Gardens and Landscapes.

d. Select **Don't show on title slide**.

e. Click the **Apply to All** button.

12. Click the **Spelling** button [*Review* tab, *Proofing* group] and correct any spelling errors you find.

13. Make the title slide look more distinctive by adjusting the placeholders and inserting the company logo and a picture.

a. On slide 1, select the subtitle and click the **Change Case** button; then select **Capitalize Each Word**.

b. Click the **Insert** tab; then click the **Pictures** button.

c. Locate the folder where your files are saved.

d. Select *GardenView-01.jpg* and click **Insert** to insert the picture.

e. Align the picture, title, and subtitle as shown in Figure 1-89.

f. Follow the same procedure to insert the logo, which is a picture file named *CGLLogo-01.png*.

14. Resize the logo width to **5.5"** [*Picture Tools Format* tab, *Size* group] and the height will automatically adjust. Position the logo as shown in Figure 1-89.

15. Save and close the presentation (Figure 1-90).

1-88 *Header and Footer* dialog box

1-89 **Completed title slide**

1-90 **PowerPoint 1-1 completed**

Guided Project 1-2

Solution Seekers, Inc., a management consulting firm, is preparing a series of brief presentations to be used in a training program for new hires. For this project, you develop a presentation about how to get better results when writing email messages.
[Student Learning Outcomes 1.1, 1.2, 1.3, 1.6, 1.7, 1.8, 1.9]

Files Needed: ***EmailResults-01.pptx***, ***EmailContent-01.pptx***, and ***AtSymbol-01.jpg***
Completed Project File Name: ***[your initials] PowerPoint 1-2.pptx***

Skills Covered in This Project

- Open a presentation.
- Change bullets.
- Reuse slides from another presentation.
- Rearrange slides.
- Check spelling.
- Adjust placeholder position.
- Insert a picture.
- Apply transitions.
- Preview a presentation.
- Change presentation properties.
- Print a handout.
- Save a presentation.

1. Open and rename a presentation.
   a. Open the ***EmailResults-01*** presentation from your student files.
   b. Press **F12** to open the *Save As* dialog box and save this presentation as ***[your initials] PowerPoint 1-2***.

2. On slide 2, change the bullets to emphasize them more.
   a. Select the bulleted text.
   b. Click the **Bullets** list arrow [*Home* tab, *Paragraph* group].
   c. Select **Bullets and Numbering**.
   d. Click the **Color** button and select **Brown**, **Text 2** (Figure 1-91).
   e. Change the size to **80%** of text.
   f. Click the **Customize** button and change the font (if necessary) to **Wingdings 2** (Figure 1-92).
   g. Select the bold **X** (Character code 211) and click **OK** to close the *Symbol* dialog box.
   h. Click **OK** again to close the *Bullets and Numbering* dialog box.

3. Reuse slides from another presentation.
   a. Click the **New Slide** list arrow and select **Reuse Slides**.
   b. On the *Reuse Slides* pane, click **Browse**; then select **Browse file** and locate your student files.
   c. Select the presentation **EmailContent-01** and click **Open**. (This presentation has spelling errors that you will fix later.)

1-91 Change bullet color

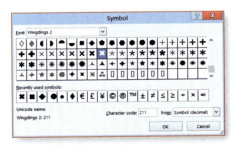

1-92 Change bullet symbol

d. On the *Reuse* Slides pane (Figure 1-93), click all four slides to insert them.
e. Close the *Reuse Slides* pane.

4. On the *Slides* tab, rearrange the six slides in this order: "Getting Results with Email," "Ask These Questions, Why?," "Write a Meaningful Subject Line," Organize It!," and "Keep It Short."

5. Click the **Spelling** button [*Review* tab, *Proofing* group] and correct each of the spelling errors.

6. Use the *Format Painter* to change bullets.
   a. On slide 2, select the body placeholder with the bulleted text.
   b. Double-click the **Format Painter** button [*Home* tab, *Clipboard* group] so you can apply what you have copied more than one time.
   c. Press **Page Down** and click the list on slide 3 to apply the change for the first-level bullets.
   d. Repeat for slides 4 and 5.
   e. Press **Esc** to end formatting.

1-93 *Reuse Slides* pane

7. On slide 3, move the picture down so it does not overlap the listed text.

8. On slide 6, use a different picture and adjust text position.
   a. Delete the picture on the right.
   b. Click the **Insert** tab; then click the **Pictures** button.
   c. Locate the folder where your student files are saved.
   d. Select *AtSymbol-01.jpg* and click **Insert** to insert the picture.
   e. Adjust the size of the title and subtitle placeholders to fit the text; then position them both on the gold shape.
   f. Align the picture, title, and subtitle as shown in Figure 1-94.

1-94 **Completed ending slide**

9. Apply one transition to all slides.
   a. Click the **Slide Sorter** button [*Status bar*].
   b. Press **Ctrl+A** to select all slides.
   c. Click the **Transitions** tab.
   d. Click the **Switch** transition from the gallery.

10. Change the movement direction.
    a. With all slides selected, click **Effect Options** [*Transition* tab, *Transition to This Slide* group] (Figure 1-95).
    b. Select **Left**.

1-95 *Effect Options*

11. Preview the presentation.
    a. Click **Preview** [*Transitions* tab] to examine the movements in *Slide Sorter* view.
    b. Click off a slide to remove the selections.
    c. Click the **Slide Show** button [*Status bar*] and advance through the slides to see the movements in *Slide Show* view.

12. Change some of the presentation properties.
    a. Click the **File** tab, then the **Info** button.
    b. Click the **Properties** button; then click **Show Document Panel**. Type this information in the respective fields.

    Author: Your Name *(unless it already appears)*
    Title: Getting Results with Email *(already entered)*
    Subject: Writing
    Comments: This presentation is for the new hire seminar.

    c. Click the **Close** button to close the *Document Properties* panel.

13. Print slides as a handout.
    a. Click the **File** tab, then the **Print** button on the left.
    b. Select the appropriate printer.
    c. Change the following *Settings* by clicking the button list arrow for each option:

    Which Slides to Print: **Print All Slides**
    What to Print: **Handouts, 6 Slides Horizontal, Frame Slides, Scale to Fit Paper**
    Print Order: **Collated**
    Orientation: **Portrait**
    Color Range: **Grayscale** (or **Color** if you prefer)

    d. Click the **Print** button at the top of the *Backstage* view.

14. Save and close the presentation (Figure 1-96).

1-96 PowerPoint 1-2 completed

Guided Project 1-3

At Placer Hills Real Estate, realtors are always thinking of ways to help sellers make their homes more marketable and help buyers find the right home. For this project, you prepare a presentation for real-tors to use when they speak with individual clients to explain how sellers can provide an added-value benefit by offering a home warranty.
[Student Learning Outcomes 1.1, 1.2, 1.5, 1.6, 1.7, 1.9]

Files Needed: *PHRELogo-01.png* and *HomeWarranty-01.pptx*
Completed Project File Name: *[your initials] PowerPoint 1-3.pptx*

Skills Covered in This Project

- Create a new presentation using an online template.
- Change font size.
- Adjust picture position.
- Insert a picture.
- Reuse slides from another presentation.
- Check spelling.
- Insert a footer.
- Apply transitions.
- Change presentation properties.
- Save a presentation.

---

1. Create a new presentation using an online template.
   a. Click the **File** tab; then click **New**.
   b. In the search box, type the search term real estate and click the **Start Searching** button or press **Enter**.
   c. Select the **For sale design template** (Figure 1-97) and click **Create** to download it. Although it is called a template, it contains only background graphics and no content that you need to remove. This template uses the 4:3 aspect ratio. (If you are unable to download the file, it is available as the presentation **ForSale-01.pptx** in your student files.)

1-97 Online real estate themes and templates

2. Save the presentation as **[your initials] PowerPoint 1-3**.

3. Type the following text in the placeholders on slide 1:

   Title Gremlin-Proof Sales
   Subtitle Angie O'Connor
      Sales Associate

4. Increase the font size of the title to **60 pts**. and move the placeholder down slightly.

5. Insert the PHRE company logo.
   a. Click the **Picture** button [*Insert* tab, *Images* group] and locate your student files.
   b. Select **PHRELogo-01.png** and click **Insert** (or double-click the file name) to insert the picture.
   c. Position this logo in the upper left as shown in Figure 1-98.

1-98 Completed title slide

6. Reuse slides from another presentation.
   a. Click the **New Slide** list arrow and select **Reuse Slides**.
   b. On the *Reuse Slides* pane, click **Browse**. Select **Browse file** and locate your student files.
   c. Select the presentation **HomeWarranty-01** and click **Open**.
   d. On the *Reuse Slides* pane (Figure 1-99), click slides 2–6 to insert them.
   e. Close the *Reuse Slides* pane.

7. Click the **Spelling** button [*Review* tab, *Proofing* group] and correct any spelling errors.

8. On slide 6, resize the picture on the top to stretch it to the top of the slide.

9. Add a footer to all slides except the title slide.
   a. Click the **Header & Footer** button [*Insert* tab, *Text* group].
   b. On the *Slide* tab, select *Slide number* and *Footer*.
   c. In the *Footer* text box, type Placer Hills Real Estate.
   d. Select *Don't show on title slide*.
   e. Click the **Apply to All** button.

10. Apply one transition to all slides.
    a. Click the **Slide Sorter** button [*Status bar*].
    b. Press **Ctrl+A** to select all slides.
    c. Click the **Transitions** tab.
    d. Click the **More** button to open the gallery; then click the **Box** effect.
    e. Click **Effect Options** [*Transitions* tab, *Transition to This Slide* group].
    f. Select **From Bottom** (Figure 1-100).
    g. Click **Preview** [*Transitions* tab] to see the movements in *Slide Sorter* view.
    h. Click the **Slide Show** button [*Status bar*] and advance through the slides to see the movements in *Slide Show* view.
    i. Double-click slide 1 to return to *Normal* view.

1-99 *Reuse Slides* pane

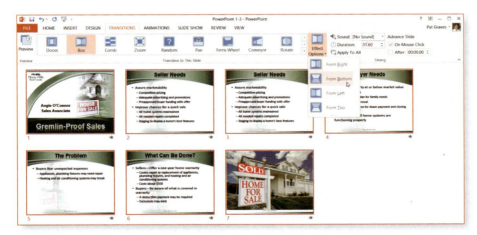

1-100 Transition Effect Options

11. Change some of the presentation properties.
    a. Click the **File** tab; then click the **Info** button.
    b. Click the **Properties** button; then click **Show Document Panel**. Type the following information in the respective fields:

Author	Angie O'Connor
Title	Gremlin-Proof Sales
Subject	Sales Strategies
Comments	Seller can offer a home warranty to encourage buyer purchase.

    c. Click the **Close** button to close the *Document Properties Panel*.

12. Save and close the presentation (Figure 1-101).

1-101 PowerPoint 1-3 completed

Independent Project 1-4

Wilson Home Entertainment Systems (WHES) assists customers with everything from a single television purchase to a home network installation to the design and construction of an elaborate home theater. In this project, you work on a presentation that sales representatives can use to demonstrate the capabilities of WHES to potential customers.
[Student Learning Outcomes 1.1, 1.2, 1.4, 1.6, 1.7, 1.9]

Files Needed: *SpecialEnvironment-01.pptx*, *WHESLogo-01.png*, *Family-01.jpg*, and *Theater1-01.jpg*
Completed Project File Name: *[your initials] PowerPoint 1-4.pptx*

Skills Covered in This Project

- Open a presentation.
- Add slides.
- Apply a theme.
- Change theme colors.
- Insert a picture.

- Adjust placeholders.
- Check spelling.
- Apply transitions.
- Change presentation properties.
- Save a presentation.

1. Open the presentation **SpecialEnvironment-01**.

2. Save the presentation as **[your initials] PowerPoint 1-4**.

3. After slide 1, insert two new slides. Type the following text for slides 2 and 3:

Slide 2 Title	Our Residential Services
Bulleted items	Design
	Sales
	Installation
	Maintenance

Slide 3 Title	Sales
Bulleted items	Authorized dealer for the highest-quality home theater technology in the industry
	Televisions
	Video Projectors
	Blu-Ray Players
	Audio Systems

4. Apply a theme and change theme colors.
    a. Select the **Integral** theme and the third **Variant** (Figure 1-102).
    b. Click the **View** tab then the **Slide Master** button.
    c. Scroll to the top of the layouts and select the first layout, *Integral Slide Master Layout* on the left so your color changes are applied to all slides.
    d. Click the **Colors** button.
    e. Scroll down the list and click the **Orange Red** theme colors.
    f. Click the **Close Master View** button.

1-102 **Change Variant**

5. On slide 1, insert different pictures.
    a. Delete the popcorn picture.
    b. Delete the subtitle placeholder.
    c. From your student files, insert **Family-01.jpg** and **WHESLogo-01.png**.
    d. Increase the family picture size (height **5"** and width **7.52"**) and align it on the top right (Figure 1-103).
    e. Align the logo on the bottom right.
    f. Move the title placeholder up and resize it so it fits in the red area on the left and word wraps as shown. Make the text **bold**, change the font color to **White**, increase the font size to **66 pts**., and apply a **shadow**.

1-103 **Completed title slide**

6. Click the **Spelling** button and correct any spelling errors you find.

7. On slide 2, increase the text size and insert a picture.
    a. Select the bulleted text placeholder and change the font size to **40 pts**.
    b. From your student files, insert **Theater1-01.jpg** and increase the picture size (height **5"** and width **7.52"**) and align it on the bottom right.

8. On slide 6, increase the picture size (height **2.18"** and width **9"**) and center it horizontally in the space below the text.

9. Apply one transition to all slides.
    a. In *Slide Sorter* view, select all the slides and apply the **Cube** transition.
    b. Apply the **From Right** effect option.
    c. Double-click slide 1 to return to *Normal* view.

10. Insert the following presentation properties using the **Document Properties Panel:**

Author	Liam Martin
Title	Create Your Special Environment
Subject	Residential Services

11. Save and close the presentation (Figure 1-104).

1-104 PowerPoint 1-4 completed

Independent Project 1-5

The Advising Offices in the Sierra Pacific Community College (SPCC) District work to assist students throughout the completion of their academic programs. Because SPCC has a large population of students who are retraining themselves for different types of employment, job-related information is especially important. For this project, you prepare a presentation about writing resumes.
[Student Learning Outcomes 1.1, 1.2, 1.3, 1.4, 1.7, 1.8]

File Needed: ***ResumeUpdates-01.pptx***
Completed Project File Name: ***[your initials] PowerPoint 1-5.pptx***

Skills Covered in This Project

- Open a presentation using an online template.
- Add slides.
- Reuse slides from another presentation.
- Rearrange slides.
- Change theme colors.
- Change bullets.
- Adjust placeholders.
- Check spelling.
- Apply transitions.
- Print a handout.
- Save a presentation.

1. Create a new presentation from an online template.
   a. Click the **File** tab; then click **New**.
   b. In the search box, type business woman design template and press **Enter**.
   c. Select the **Business woman design template** (Figure 1-105) and click **Create** to download it. This template uses the 4:3 aspect ratio. (If you are unable to download the file, it is available as the presentation *Business-01.pptx* in your student files.)

2. Save the presentation as *[your initials] PowerPoint 1-5*.

3. On slide 1, type the following text:

   1-105 Online business woman themes and templates

   Title   Resume Updates
   Subtitle   Your First Impression

4. After slide 1, insert two new slides. Type the following text for slides 2 and 3:

   Slide 2 Title   Accomplishments, Not Duties
   Bulleted items Include only the most impressive details about your career
                   Quantify your day-to-day tasks
                      How many times?
                      What was the result?
                      How much money was saved?

   Slide 3 Title: Proofread
   Bulleted items Employers take spelling and grammar errors as signs of carelessness
                   Ask a trusted friend or colleague to look at your resume

5. Reuse slides from another presentation.
   a. Click the **New Slide** list arrow and select **Reuse Slides**.
   b. On the *Reuse Slides* pane, click **Browse** and select **Browse file**. Locate the student file *ResumeUpdates-01* and click **Open**.
   c. On the *Reuse Slides* pane, click all three slides to insert them.
   d. Close the *Reuse Slides* pane.

6. Move the slide 3 (*Proofread*) thumbnail to the end of the presentation.

7. Change theme colors.
   a. Click the **View** tab; then the **Slide Master** button.
   b. Select the first *Master Layout* on the left so your color changes are applied to all slides.
   c. Click the **Colors** button and select the **Blue II** theme colors (Figure 1-106).
   d. Click the **Close Master View** button.

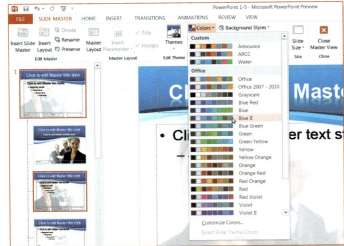

1-106 Change theme colors

8. On slide 2, change the bullets to emphasize them more.
   a. Select the level 1 bulleted text.
   b. Click the **Bullets** list arrow and select **Bullets and Numbering**.
   c. Click the **Color** button and select **Dark Teal**, **Text 2**.
   d. Change the size to **80%** of text if necessary.
   e. Click the **Customize** button and change the font to **Wingdings 2** (Figure 1-107).
   f. Select the large diamond (Character code 191) and click **OK** to close the *Symbol* dialog box.
   g. Click **OK** again to close the *Bullets and Numbering* dialog box.

9. On slide 2, resize the top of the bulleted text placeholder by dragging it down so the text does not overlap the decorative blue title area. Repeat for all other slides.

10. Use **Format Painter** to change the level 1 bullets on all other slides.

11. On slide 1, change the title and subtitle placeholders to **Left alignment**; then align both placeholders on the left (but not to the slide) (Figure 1-108).

12. Click the **Spelling** button and correct any spelling errors you find.

13. Apply one transition to all slides.
   a. Click the **Transitions** tab and apply the **Reveal** transition.
   b. Apply the **Through Black from Right** effect option.
   c. Click **Apply To All**.

14. Print slides as an outline (Figure 1-109).
   a. Click the **File** tab; then click the **Print** button on the left.
   b. Select the appropriate printer.
   c. Change the following *Settings* by clicking the list arrow for each option as necessary:

   Which Slides to Print: **Print All Slides**
   What to Print: **Outline**
   Print Side: **Print One Sided**
   Print Order: **Collated**
   Orientation: **Portrait**
   Color Range: **Grayscale**

   d. Click the **Print** button at the top of the *Backstage* view.

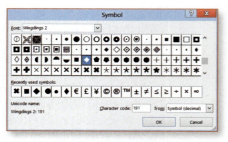

1-107 Change bullet symbol

1-108 Completed title slide

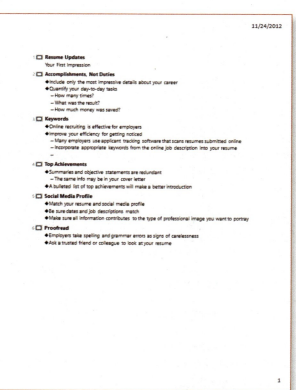

1-109 Outline

15. Save and close the presentation (Figure 1-110).

1-110 PowerPoint 1-5 completed

Independent Project 1-6

At the Hendersonville Civic Center, workshops are given for the community to address fitness, health, and wellness issues. For this project, you develop a presentation for an upcoming series about helping families become more active.
[Student Learning Outcomes 1.1, 1.2, 1.3, 1.4, 1.5, 1.6, 1.7, 1.9]

Files Needed: **PedestrianSafety-01.pptx**, **Walk1-01.jpg**, and **Walk2-01.jpg**
Completed Project File Name: **[your initials] PowerPoint 1-6.pptx**

Skills Covered in This Project

- Create a new presentation using a theme.
- Change case.
- Reuse slides from another presentation.
- Check spelling.
- Change theme colors.
- Change theme fonts.
- Rearrange slides.
- Insert a picture.
- Adjust placeholders.
- Insert a footer.
- Apply transitions.
- Change presentation properties.
- Save a presentation.

1. Create a new presentation and select the **Retrospect** theme and **Green** variant.

2. Save the presentation as *[your initials] PowerPoint 1-6*.

3. On slide 1, type the following text:

   Title   Pedestrian Safety Matters
   Subtitle   Keeping That New Year's Resolution To Be More Active

4. Select the subtitle text and change the case to **Capitalize Each Word**.

5. Click the **New Slide** list arrow and select **Reuse Slides**.
   a. On the *Reuse Slides* pane, click **Browse**. Select **Browse file** and locate your student file *PedestrianSafety-01*. Click **Open**.
   b. On the *Reuse Slides* pane, click all slides to insert them.
   c. Close the *Reuse Slides* pane.

6. Click the **Spelling** button [*Review* tab, *Proofing* group] and correct any spelling errors.

7. Click **View**, then **Slide Master**, and change theme colors and fonts.
   a. Change the colors to **Yellow Orange** and the background style to **Style 6**.
   b. Change the font to **Arial Black-Arial** (the font pairs are not listed in alphabetical order).
   c. Click **Close Master View**.

8. Adjust slide order to match the sequence shown in Figure 1-111.

1-111 Slide order

9. On slide 1, insert a picture and resize the placeholders.
   a. From your student files, insert the picture *Walk1-01.jpg*.
   b. Change the picture height to **7.5"** and align it to the slide on the top right.
   c. Adjust the size of the title and sub-title placeholders so the text wraps as shown in Figure 1-112.

10. On slide 2, put your insertion point in front of the word "Guard" and press **Enter**.

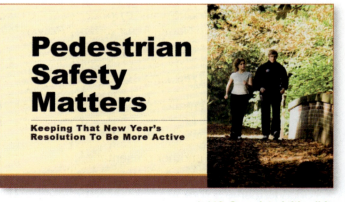

1-112 Completed title slide

11. Add a footer to all slides except the title slide.
    a. Click the **Header and Footer** button.
    b. On the *Slide* tab, select *Slide number* and *Footer*.
    c. In the *Footer* text box, type Pedestrian Safety Matters.
    d. Select **Don't show on title slide**.
    e. Click the **Apply to All** button.

12. On slide 6, insert a picture and resize the placeholder.
    a. From your student files, insert the picture **Walk2-01.jpg**.
    b. Change the picture height to **7.5"** and align it to the slide on the top right.

13. Apply one transition to all slides.
    a. In *Slide Sorter* view, select all the slides.
    b. Select the **Push** transition and apply the **From Right** effect option.

14. Preview the transitions in *Slide Show* view.

15. Change these presentation properties using the *Document Properties* panel.

    Author   Anna Lorenzo
    Title   Pedestrian Safety Matters
    Subject   Active Lifestyle

16. Click the **Close** button to close the *Document Properties* panel.

17. Save and close the presentation (Figure 1-113).

1-113 PowerPoint 1-6 completed

Improve It Project 1-7

For this project, you revise a presentation for Margaret Jepson, insurance agent at Central Sierra Insurance. You apply a design theme, adjust its appearance, and add other information to the slide show, including a picture.
[Student Learning Outcomes 1.1, 1.2, 1.3, 1.4, 1.5, 1.6, 1.7, 1.8, 1.9]

Files Needed: *TotaledCar-01.pptx*, *Cars-01.jpg*, and *CSILogo-01.png*
Completed Project File Name: *[your initials] PowerPoint 1-7.pptx*

Skills Covered in This Project

- Open a presentation.
- Change theme colors.
- Check spelling.
- Insert a picture.
- Adjust placeholders.
- Insert a footer.
- Apply transitions.
- Change presentation properties.
- Print a handout.
- Save a presentation.

1. Open the presentation *TotaledCar-01*.

2. Save the presentation as *[your initials] PowerPoint 1-7*.

3. Use the *Slide Master* to change the theme colors and fonts.
   a. Theme colors: **Yellow**
   b. Theme background style: **Style 6**
   c. Theme font: **Gil Sans MT**

4. Check spelling and correct any spelling errors.

5. On slide 1, make text changes and insert a picture and logo (Figure 1-114).
   a. Change the title font size to **66 pts.**, make the text fit on two lines, and position the placeholder on the right of the slide beside the picture.
   b. Delete the subtitle placeholder.
   c. Insert **Cars-01** and align it on the left of the slide.
   d. Insert **CSILogo-01**, change the width to **5"**, and position it below the title text on the lower right of the slide.

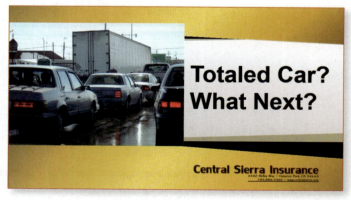

1-114 Completed title slide

6. On slide 5, make the following changes:
   a. Change the slide layout to **Title Only**.
   b. Change the font size to **54 pts**. and apply right alignment.
   c. Align the placeholder on the middle right of the slide.

7. Add header and footer text and slide numbering to all slides except the title slide.

   Slide footer text: The Totaled Car
   Handout header text: Central Sierra Insurance

8. Apply the **Reveal** transition to all slides with the **Through Black from Right** effect option.

9. Change the effect option on slide 5 to **Through Black from Left**.

10. Preview the transitions.

11. Change these presentation properties using the **Document Properties Panel**.

   Author: Margaret Jepson
   Title: Totaled Car? What Next?
   Subject: Accident Insurance

12. Print a handout with 6 slides on a page, horizontal, framed, and sized to fit paper.

13. Save and close the presentation (Figure 1-115).

1-115 PowerPoint 1-7 completed

Challenge Project 1-8

For this project, tell the story of your favorite vacation. Create six slides that introduce the topic and describe your main points with bulleted lists. Insert photographs to illustrate locations and resize them to fit with related text.
[Student Learning Outcomes 1.1, 1.2, 1.4, 1.5, 1.6, 1.7, 1.8, 1.9]

File Needed: None
Completed Project File Name: *[your initials] PowerPoint 1-8.pptx*

Create a new presentation and save it as *[your initials] PowerPoint 1-8*. Modify your presentation according to the following guidelines:

- Select an appropriate theme from Office.com for your topic.
- Use different slide layouts for variety.
- Insert three or more pictures.
- Add a footer.
- Apply transitions.
- Check spelling and include document properties.
- Print a handout.

Challenge Project 1-9

Think about different jobs for which you are qualified. On the Internet, research four different jobs and identify several characteristics and requirements for each job. Many online resources provide job-related information, such as www.careerbuilder.com.
[Student Learning Outcomes 1.1, 1.2, 1.3, 1.4, 1.5, 1.6, 1.7, 1.8, 1.9]

File Needed: None
Completed Project File Name: *[your initials] PowerPoint 1-9.pptx*

Create a new presentation and save it as *[your initials] PowerPoint 1-9*. Modify your presentation according to the following guidelines:

- Select an appropriate theme and use the Slide Master to make color and font changes as needed for your topic.
- Create a distinctive title slide.
- Write bulleted lists describing the characteristics and requirements of each different job with no more than seven lines of text on each slide.
- Apply transitions.
- Check spelling and include document properties.
- Print handouts with six slides on a page.

Challenge Project 1-10

For this project, develop a presentation about how a presenter can manage nervous tendencies when presenting in front of an audience. Include information from your own experiences and refer to online resources, such as www.presentationmagazine.com.
[Student Learning Outcomes 1.1, 1.2, 1.3, 1.4, 1.5, 1.6, 1.7, 1.8, 1.9]

File Needed: None
Completed Project File Name: *[your initials] PowerPoint 1-10.pptx*

Create a new presentation and save it as *[your initials] PowerPoint 1-10*. Modify your presentation according to the following guidelines:

- Select an appropriate theme and use the Slide Master to make color and font changes as needed for your topic.
- Create a distinctive title slide.
- Write bulleted lists describing typical causes of nervousness and suggest ways to control nervousness when presenting.
- Insert pictures to illustrate concepts.
- Apply transitions.
- Check spelling and include document properties.
- Print an outline of the presentation.

Illustrating with Pictures and Information Graphics

CHAPTER OVERVIEW

In our world today, we are surrounded by information graphics. We see them in television programming, web sites, and published material of all kinds. We interpret signage that helps us get from place to place and readily recognize many iconic images that help us with everyday tasks. These graphics communicate visually and can be more effective than long passages of text.

PowerPoint gives you the ability to create information graphics—to visually display information in ways that help an audience quickly grasp the concepts you are presenting. You can choose from many options, such as adding shapes or color for emphasis, pictures to illustrate, diagrams to show processes, and charts to show data relationships.

STUDENT LEARNING OUTCOMES (SLOs)

After completing this chapter, you will be able to:

SLO 2.1 Work with shapes, select theme colors and standard colors, and apply styles (p. P2-67).

SLO 2.2 Create interesting and eye-catching text with *WordArt* styles and text effects (p. P2-75).

SLO 2.3 Search for pictures and illustrations, modify picture appearance, and compress picture file size (p. P2-78).

SLO 2.4 Organize information in a grid format using tables and customize the arrangement of columns and rows (p. P2-85).

SLO 2.5 Emphasize portions of a table by applying styles, colors, and effects (p. P2-90).

SLO 2.6 Show processes and relationships with *SmartArt* graphics (p. P2-94).

SLO 2.7 Improve the appearance of *SmartArt* graphics by applying styles, colors, and effects (p. P2-97).

SLO 2.8 Create charts that show relationships between data values and emphasize data in different ways (p. P2-101).

SLO 2.9 Enhance a chart by applying preset styles or manually customizing individual chart elements (p. P2-105).

CASE STUDY

Classic Gardens and Landscapes (CGL) is a landscape design company that creates beautiful and low-maintenance landscapes for outdoor living spaces. Frank and Sandra Hunter recently bought a home with minimal landscaping from a builder. They contacted Gerod Sunderland, a landscape designer for CGL, to discuss improvements.

POWERPOINT

Gerod visited the property and designed plans with several options for trees, shrubs, and plants. You have been asked to prepare a presentation illustrating his key points for his meeting with the Hunters.

Pause & Practice 2-1: Add visual interest with picture enhancements and creative text designs.

Pause & Practice 2-2: Prepare a table.

Pause & Practice 2-3: Create an organization chart and convert text to a *SmartArt* graphic.

Pause & Practice 2-4: Create column and pie charts with an enhanced appearance.

Working with Shapes, Colors, and Styles

Shapes can emphasize key points. For example, an arrow can point to an object, or a line can connect two related objects. You can draw a variety of shapes using PowerPoint's *Shapes* gallery; each shape has both an outline and fill color. The *Quick Style*, *Color*, and *Effects* galleries make it easy to customize shapes and the other objects you use to illustrate your slides.

Shapes and Text Boxes

To insert a shape, select the shape you want from the *Shapes* gallery [*Insert* tab, *Illustrations* group] and use the following features to draw and adjust your shape:

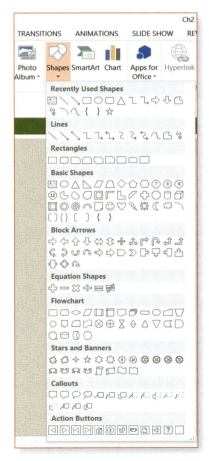

- **Crosshair:** A large plus sign used to draw the shape
- **Sizing handles:** Squares on the corners and sides of the shapes used to change shape size
- **Rotation handle:** Circular arrow on the top used to make shapes angle
- **Adjustment handle:** Squares used to change curves or points

You can add text to shapes and format the text as you do text in a placeholder or in a text box. However, the text in shapes or in text boxes does not appear in *Outline* view.

The *Shapes* gallery (Figure 2-1) is on the *Home* tab, the *Insert* tab, and the *Drawing Tools Format* tab. Shapes are grouped in the following categories:

- *Recently Used Shapes*
- *Lines*
- *Rectangles*
- *Basic Shapes*
- *Block Arrows*
- *Equation Shapes*
- *Flowchart*
- *Stars and Banners*
- *Callouts*
- *Action Buttons*

2-1 Shapes gallery

HOW TO: Insert a Shape

1. Click the **Insert** tab.
2. Click the **Shapes** button [*Illustrations* group] to display the *Shapes* gallery.
3. Select the shape you want and your pointer becomes a crosshair (Figure 2-2).
4. Click and drag to draw the shape in the approximate size you need (Figure 2-3). The shape appears with sizing handles and a rotation handle. It may have adjustment handles.
5. Press the **Shift** key while you drag to make oval shapes round, make rectangles square, and make lines straight.
6. Add text if needed.
7. Resize the shape if necessary and move it to the appropriate position on the slide.

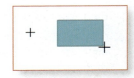

2-2 Crosshair and crosshair drawing a shape

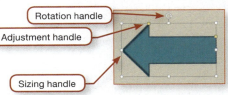

2-3 Shape with handles

When you need more than one of the same shape, you can efficiently draw them using *Lock Drawing Mode*.

HOW TO: Insert Multiple Shapes

1. Click the **Insert** tab.
2. Click the **Shapes** button [*Illustrations* group] to display the *Shapes* gallery.
3. Right-click the shape you want, and click **Lock Drawing Mode** (Figure 2-4).
4. Draw the first shape. Repeat to draw more of the same shape.
5. When you are finished, press **Esc** to turn off **Lock Drawing Mode**.

2-4 *Lock Drawing Mode*

When you select an existing shape, the *Drawing Tools Format* tab opens and the *Shapes* gallery is displayed on the left. If the existing shape does not fit your purpose, you can easily change the shape.

HOW TO: Change a Shape to Another Shape

1. Select the shape to be changed.
2. Click the **Edit Shape** arrow [*Drawing Tools Format* tab, *Insert Shapes* group] (Figure 2-5).
3. Select **Change Shape** and click a different shape from the *Shapes* gallery.
4. Click **Undo** to return to your original shape.
5. Click a blank area of the slide to deselect the shape.

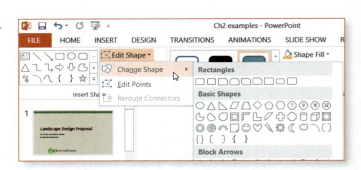

2-5 *Change Shape*

Using *text boxes*, you can add text anywhere on a slide without using placeholders. For example, you can add notations to identify slide objects or insert brief phrases you want to emphasize. Text boxes can be sized and moved around like any other shape.

HOW TO: Insert a Text Box

1. Click the **Insert** tab.

2. Click the **Text Box** button and your pointer changes to an insertion point. Create a text box using one of the following methods:

   - Begin typing at the insertion point and the text box grows to fit the text you type in it. The *Home* tab opens.
   - Click to change the pointer to a crosshair and draw a text box (Figure 2-6) in the approximate width you need. The *Home* tab opens. The text box height adjusts as you type text.

3. Resize if necessary by dragging sizing handles or entering height and width sizes [*Drawing Tools Format* tab, *Size* group] (Figure 2-7).

4. Click and drag the text box to move it to an appropriate position on the slide.

2-6 Draw a text box

2-7 Size measurements

Style Galleries

Different *Style* galleries provide collections of preset effects for shapes, pictures, or other objects. You can customize all effects using the related button such as **Shape Effects**, **Picture Effects**, or **Text Effects** to access drop-down galleries. You can choose from *Shadow, Reflection, Glow, Soft Edges, Bevel,* or *3D Rotation*. These options are described in the following table. The *Transform* effect is only available for **Text Effects**. You can also apply one or more effects without first using styles from a gallery.

Style Effect Options

Effect	Options
Shadow	**Shadow** effects appear in three groupings. An **Outer** shadow shows behind an object from different directions. An **Inner** shadow makes part of the object looked raised. A **Perspective** shadow makes an object "float" with the shadow below.
Reflection	A **Reflection** shows a mirror image below an object, like a reflection on a shiny surface or on water. You can control how close the reflection is to the object.
Glow	**Glow** provides a colored area around an object that fades into the background color on your slide. It is not available for text. Glow colors by default are based on the current theme colors but you can use other colors. The size of the *Glow* is measured in points.
Soft Edges	Some objects, such as pictures or text boxes, have a straight edge on all sides. **Soft Edges** creates a feathered edge that gradually blends into the background color. The size of the blending area is measured in points from the edge of the object inward. The larger the point size, the less you see of the object.
Bevel	**Bevel** effects add light and dark areas to create a dimensional appearance. Objects or text can look raised or inset.
3D Rotation	**3D Rotation** effects include **Parallel**, **Perspective**, and **Oblique** options that create an illusion of depth by rotating an object from front to back.
Transform	**Transform** is a *Text Effect* used to change the shape of words. It is not available for shapes.

The width of your PowerPoint window affects how galleries are displayed on the various tabs where they appear. If you have a narrow PowerPoint window, you need to click a quick style button to open a gallery. If your window is wide, part of a gallery is displayed and you click the **More** button to open the complete gallery.

2-8 *Shape Outline Weight*

Adjust Outline Weight and Style

You can emphasize an outline by making it wider with a contrasting color; you can deemphasize an outline by making it thinner. You can choose to show no outline or match its color to the shape to make the outline disappear. Select a shape and click the **Shape Outline** button [*Drawing Tools Format* tab, *Shape Styles* group]. Choose one of the following options to see drop-down lists of options (Figure 2-8):

- **Weight:** Displays line thickness measured in points
- **Dashes:** Displays lines made with various combinations of dots and dashes (Figure 2-9)
- **Arrows:** Displays arrowheads or other shapes for both ends of a line.

At the bottom of each drop-down list, select **More Lines** to open the *Format Shape* pane (Figure 2-10) where you can customize the following *Line* options:

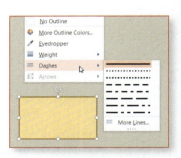

2-9 *Shape Outline Dashes*

- **Color:** Provides color choices
- **Transparency:** Adjusts transparency percentages
- **Width:** Controls the thickness of lines measured in points
- **Compound type:** Provides outlines with two or more lines in different thicknesses
- **Dash type:** Displays lines made with various combinations of dots and dashes
- **Cap type:** Controls the look (*Square, Round,* or *Flat*) of the ends of lines; it is usually applied to single lines or arrows
- **Join type:** Controls the look (*Round, Bevel, Miter*) for the connection point where two lines meet (for example, at the corner of a rectangle or square)
- **Begin and End Arrow type:** Controls the shape for both ends of an arrow
- **Begin and End Arrow size:** Controls the size of the shape at both ends of an arrow

The *Format Shape* pane is a convenient place to change many options. Figure 2-10 shows the *Fill & Line* tab with *Line* options displayed because a line was selected when the pane opened. Different options appear if you have a shape selected or if you choose a *Gradient* line. Above *Line* you can select *Fill* to change shape colors. You can click the arrow in front of these options to expand or collapse each list.

2-10 *Format Shape* pane

Additional tabs include *Effects, Size & Properties,* and *Picture* with related options on each tab. Click the buttons at the top of the pane to select different tabs.

▶ **ANOTHER WAY**
Right-click a shape and then select **Format Shape** from the shortcut menu to open the *Format Shape* pane.

Themes and Standard Colors

As you learned in Chapter 1, each PowerPoint *Theme* starts with a set of *Theme Colors* that provide background and accent colors. When you apply *Theme Colors* for shapes and text, these colors automatically change when you select a different set of *Theme Colors.*

Consider all of the colors used throughout your presentation when you make color choices because some colors seem more appropriate than others. This section explains how colors are arranged in PowerPoint and describes different ways to "mix" custom colors. The same techniques for choosing colors apply to color fills or outline colors.

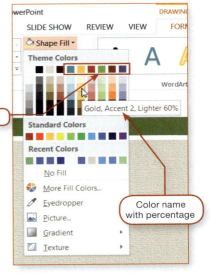

2-11 *Theme Colors* gallery

Change Solid and Gradient Fill Colors

To change the color of a selected shape, click the **Shape Fill** button [*Drawing Tools Format* tab, *Shape Styles* group] to open the ***Theme Colors*** gallery (Figure 2-11). Notice the colors arranged in the first row. The first four colors represent background and text colors; however, you can use these colors for other slide objects as well. The remaining six colors represent accent colors. These colors appear when viewing gallery styles and some effects. Beneath each color on the first row is a column of lighter and darker shades (shown as percentages) of that color. When you point to any color, a ScreenTip shows its name.

Below the *Theme Colors* is a single row of ***Standard Colors*** arranged in the order of a rainbow. When standard colors are used, they remain in effect even if *Theme Colors* change.

Gradient colors blend two or more colors together. Using the *Format Shape* pane, you can select from preset colors or customize your own gradient color by changing the colors and how they blend.

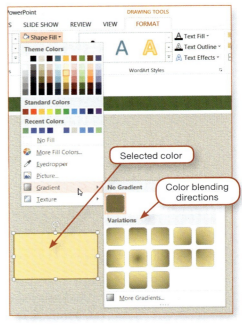

2-12 Gradient color variations for the selected color

HOW TO: Change Gradient Colors Using the Format Shape Pane

1. Select a slide object and click the **Shape Fill** button [*Drawing Tools Format* tab, *Shape Styles* group].
2. Select **Gradient** to select from a gallery of light and dark variations of the current fill color that blend the colors in different directions (Figure 2-12).

3. Click **More Gradients** at the bottom of the gallery to open the *Format Shape* pane to customize the colors.

4. Under *Fill* options, select **Gradient fill** and make selections from the following:
   - *Preset gradients:* Theme color variations (Figure 2-13)
   - *Type: Linear, Radial, Rectangular,* or *Path*
   - *Direction:* Options change based on the selected *Type.*
   - *Angle:* The percentage changes with each *Type* and *Direction.*
   - *Gradient stops:* Shapes on the gradient bar slider that you can move to control where colors change (Figure 2-14)

5. Each *Gradient stop* can be changed in the following ways to control color blending:
   - *Delete a stop:* Click the **Remove Gradient Stop** button or drag the stop off the slider.
   - *Add a stop:* Click the **Add Gradient Stop** button and click on the slider where you want it to appear.
   - *Color:* Select the stop; then change the color.
   - *Position:* Enter a different percentage or drag the stop on the slider to change its position.
   - *Transparency:* Click the arrows to change the percentage. When *Transparency* is 0%, the color is opaque (solid); as the percentage increases, the color becomes increasingly transparent and more of the background color shows through.
   - *Brightness:* Click the arrows to change the percentage. As the percentage decreases from 100%, the color softens.

6. Check **Rotate with shape** to maintain the color settings when a shape or text is rotated so it angles on the slide.

7. Under *Line* options, *select* **No line** or **Solid line** to control whether or not an outline shows around a shape or text.

8. Click **Close** and the new color is applied.

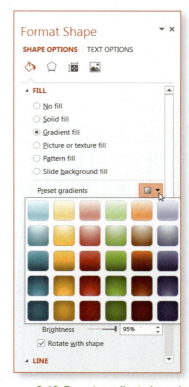

2-13 Preset gradients based on theme colors

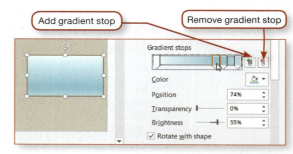

2-14 Gradient stops

> **MORE INFO**
>
> To apply gradient colors to *WordArt*, click the **Text Fill** button [*Drawing Tools Format* tab, *WordArt Styles* group] and select **Gradient** or select **Text Options**, then **Gradient fill** on the *Format Shape* pane.

Select Custom Colors

The *Colors* dialog box provides many solid color options on two tabs so you can either pick from displayed colors or mix a custom color. The new color appears on the lower right so you can compare it to the original color. Custom colors are not affected by any changes made to theme colors.

HOW TO: Use the Standard Tab to Select a Color

1. Select a shape and click the **Shape Fill** button [*Home* tab or *Drawing Tools Format* tab, *Shape Styles* group].
2. Click **More Fill Colors** to open the *Colors* dialog box.
3. On the *Standard* tab (Figure 2-15), colors are arranged in a honeycomb shape with colors blending from white to black below.
4. Click a color to apply it and notice the *New* color that appears on the right above the *Current* color.
5. Adjust the *Transparency* as needed.
6. Click **OK** to apply the new color.

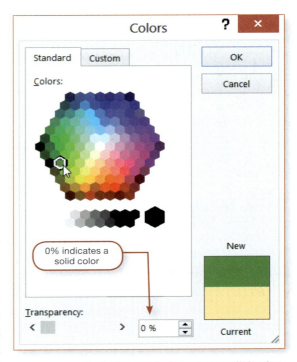

2-15 *Standard* tab on *Colors* dialog box

When you need more precision in selecting a color, use the *Custom* tab on the *Colors* dialog box. Colors are arranged like a rainbow and you drag a crosshair to select a different color. You drag the crosshair up or down to change the color intensity and then move a slider to adjust how light or dark the color appears. **Color model** information is shown on the *Custom* tab also. The **RGB** model is typically used for computer displays and colors are formed by blending values of the three numbers for *Red, Green,* and *Blue.* Highly saturated colors at the top have higher number values (255 maximum). You can use these numbers to match colors in different shapes and in different presentations.

HOW TO: Use the Custom Tab to Mix a Color

1. Select a shape and click the **Shape Fill** button [*Home* tab or *Drawing Tools Format* tab, *Shape Styles* group].
2. Click **More Fill Colors** to open the *Colors* dialog box.
3. On the *Custom* tab (Figure 2-16), a crosshair is positioned for the *Current* color.
   - Drag the crosshair to select a different color.
   - When the crosshair is at the top, colors are highly **saturated** (intense and vibrant).
   - As you move the crosshair down, colors become less saturated (duller and less intense).
4. Use the slider on the right to adjust the amount of white and black in the color to raise and lower the **luminosity** (lightness).
5. The current color and the new color appear in the lower right.
6. Adjust the *Transparency* as needed.
7. Click **OK** to apply the new color.

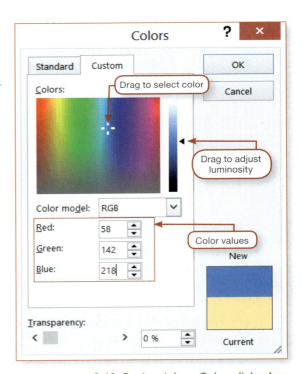

2-16 *Custom* tab on *Colors* dialog box

Use the Eyedropper for Color Matching

You can match the exact color of an object in PowerPoint with the ***Eyedropper*** and apply it to a shape.

HOW TO: Use the Eyedropper

1. Have an object, such as a picture, and the shape to be changed on the same slide. Select the shape.
2. Click the **Shape Fill** button and select **Eyedropper**.
3. As you move your pointer (now an eyedropper) around the picture, a live preview of each color appears. Pause to see a ScreenTip showing the *RGB* (Red Green Blue) values (Figure 2-17).
4. Click to select the color.

Or

5. Press **Esc** to cancel the eyedropper without selecting a color.

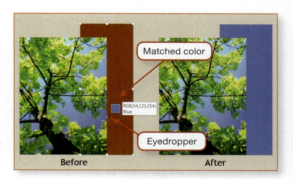

2-17 *Eyedropper* live preview and *RGB* colors

To match a color anywhere on your computer screen, left-click and hold as you drag the eyedropper pointer to other areas of the screen outside of PowerPoint.

Apply Picture, Texture, or Pattern Fills

You can fill *WordArt* and other shapes with more than colors. The following options are available from the *Shape Fill* drop-down list or from the *Format Shape* pane.

- *Texture:* Applies an image such as woven fabric or wood
- *Pattern:* Applies a mixture of two colors in various dotted or crosshatch designs
- *Picture:* Fills the *WordArt* or shape with a picture from a file or from the *Office.com Clip Art* collection

2-18 *Texture* fills

HOW TO: Apply Texture and Pattern Fills

1. Select a shape and click the **Shape Fill** button [*Drawing Tools Format* tab, *Shape Styles* group].
   - Select **Texture** to open the gallery (Figure 2-18).
   - Click a texture to apply it.

2. Select a shape and right-click. Click **Format Shape** from the callout menu to open the *Format Shape* pane.

- Select **Pattern fill** (Figure 2-19).
- Click a pattern to apply it.
- Change *Foreground* and *Background* colors as needed.

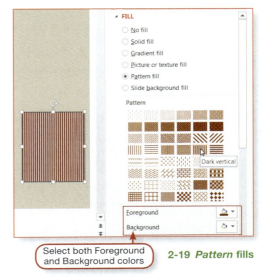

You can also use the *Format Background* pane to insert textures and adjust how they are positioned. Inserting pictures from the *Office.com Clip Art* collection is covered in *SLO 2.3 Working with Pictures*.

Select both Foreground and Background colors

2-19 *Pattern* fills

SLO 2.2

Adding Text Effects and WordArt

You can apply interesting **text effects** for many purposes. For example, you can make slide titles more attractive and easier to read, or you can provide a bold focal point on a slide. One way is to start by inserting **WordArt**.

HOW TO: Apply Text Effects with WordArt

1. Click the **WordArt** button [*Insert* tab, *Text* group] to choose a style from the *WordArt Quick Styles* gallery (Figure 2-20).

2. The gallery has preset text effects showing a variety of solid, gradient, and pattern fill colors.

3. Click to select a *WordArt* style.

4. A text box is inserted on your slide with sample text that you edit to create a *WordArt* object (Figure 2-21).

5. Use the *Font* group [*Home* tab] to make the following changes:

- Select a different font or attribute such as bold or italic.
- Change the font size by entering a point size or using the **Increase Font Size** and **Decrease Font Size** buttons.
- Click the **Character Spacing** button to make letters fit more closely or to spread letters apart.

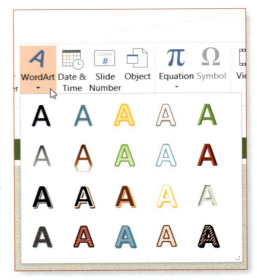

2-20 *WordArt Quick Styles* gallery

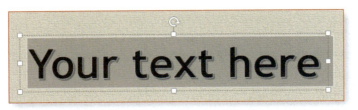

2-21 *WordArt* as it first appears

You can also start with text in a placeholder or text box and then apply text effects. With either method, you use commands on the *WordArt Styles* group [*Drawing Tools Format* tab] (Figure 2-22) to customize your text. These commands—*Text Fill, Text Outline, and Text Effects*—are similar to the *Shape* commands.

2-22 *WordArt Styles* group

HOW TO: Apply Text Effects to Existing Text

1. Select a *WordArt* object or text in a placeholder or text box.
2. Click the **More** button [*Drawing Tools Format* tab, *WordArt Styles* group] to open the *Quick Styles* gallery (Figure 2-23).
3. Point to a style to see a live preview applied to your text.
4. Click a style to apply it.
5. Use the *WordArt Styles* group [*Drawing Tools Format* tab] to make the following changes:
   - Click the **Text Fill** button to select **Theme** or other color options.
   - Click the **Text Outline** button to select **Theme** or other color options as well as line weight and style.
   - Apply different *Text Effects* (*Shadow, Reflection, Glow, Bevel, 3D Rotation,* or *Transform*).
6. With the WordArt object selected, right-click and then click **Format Shape** to open the *Format Shape* pane. Select **Shape Options** or **Text Options** and make adjustments as needed.

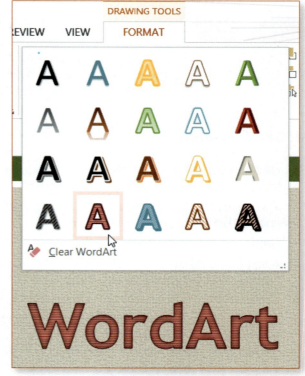

2-23 *WordArt* with style changed

Changing the text outline color and increasing line weight emphasizes the outline just as it does on shapes. Different line styles can create interesting effects. Using pictures or patterns as fill colors can add a creative touch when text is shown in a large size. A variety of different color and effects are shown in Figure 2-24.

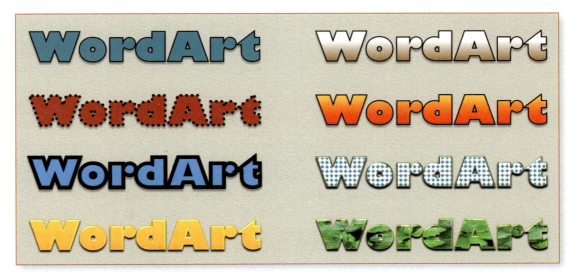

2-24 Sample fill and line effects

> **ANOTHER WAY**
>
> Select the text in a *WordArt* object and right-click. Click **Format Text Effects** from the shortcut menu to open the *Format Shape* pane with *Text Options* listed.

Transform effects are unique to text and make a word or phrase warp to fit different shapes or follow a path. For example, text can angle, flow in a circle, and arc up or down. As you point to different *Transform* effects, a live preview shows how your text will look in that shape. Once a *Transform* effect has been applied, text size is not limited to the font size because you can drag the *WordArt* sizing handles. Some *Transform* effects also provide one or more pink adjustment handles that control the slant of letters or the curve of text.

HOW TO: Apply a Transform Effect

1. Select a *WordArt* object.
2. Click the **Text Effects** button [*Format* tab, *WordArt Styles* group].
3. From the drop-down list, select **Transform** (Figure 2-25).
4. On the *Transform* gallery, point to an effect to see a live preview applied to your text.
5. Click an effect to apply it.
6. Adjust as needed using sizing and adjustment handles.

2-25 *Transform Fade Up* effect

Working with Pictures

In Chapter 1, you learned how to insert pictures from files, change their size, and align them on the slide. In this section, you use PowerPoint's search capabilities to find images to help illustrate presentation concepts.

Online Pictures and Illustrations

Use PowerPoint's **Insert Pictures** dialog box to search for pictures (digital photographs or illustrations) in the *Office.com Clip Art* collection. You can search the web using *Bing Image Search* but pictures you find may have licensing restrictions or require fees. You can also browse for images you have saved in your *SkyDrive* location.

When the search results appear, each picture has a ScreenTip identifying its name and a magnifying button you can click to temporarily increase the thumbnail size.

On the lower left of the dialog box, the picture name appears with its dimension in pixels and the name of the company providing the picture. A **pixel** is an abbreviated term for *picture element,* a single unit of information about color.

HOW TO: Search for and Insert a Picture or Illustration

1. On a slide, click the **Online Pictures** button [*Insert* tab, *Images* group] (Figure 2-26) to open the *Insert Pictures* dialog box.
2. In the *Search* box, type the search word (Figure 2-27).
3. Click the **Search** button (or press **Enter**) to activate the search.
4. Thumbnails of all the pictures that match your search word appear (Figure 2-28).
5. Click to select the picture you want.
6. Press **Ctrl** while you click to select more than one picture.
7. Click the **Insert** button. The picture will download and the *Insert Pictures* dialog box will close.

2-26 *Online Pictures* button

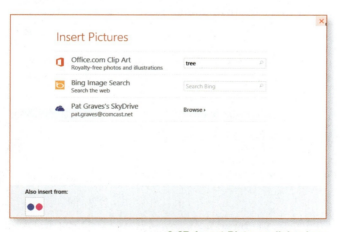

2-27 *Insert Pictures* dialog box

Selected picture name and size

2-28 *Pictures from search*

> ▶ **MORE INFO**
>
> You can open the *Insert Pictures* dialog box when creating a new slide by clicking the **Online Pictures** button on the content placeholder.

Apply Picture Quick Styles

When you have selected a picture, the *Picture Tools Format* tab becomes available. Different quick styles allow you to frame pictures, give them a 3D appearance, add a reflection, or apply other treatments. You can customize each of these options using the *Picture Effects* drop-down galleries.

When you use multiple pictures in a presentation, try to maintain consistency and use the same or a similar style for each of them. If you use different styles, be sure you have a reason for making them look different so the effects do not appear random.

HOW TO: Apply a Picture Style

1. Select a picture and click the **Picture Tools Format** tab.
2. Click the **More** button on the gallery [*Picture Styles* group] to see the pre-defined effects (Figure 2-29).
3. Drag your pointer over the styles to see a live preview applied to your picture. A ScreenTip showing the style name appears.
4. Click a style to apply it to your picture.
5. To change to a different style, simply select a different one.

2-29 **Picture style applied**

Picture Effects are similar to *Shape Effects*. Each different effect has many options you can adjust.

HOW TO: Apply or Modify Picture Effects

1. Select a picture and click the **Picture Effects** button [*Picture Tools Format* tab, *Picture Styles* group].
2. As you point to each effect, a drop-down gallery (Figure 2-30) provides many variations. Select **Options** at the bottom of each *Effects* drop-down gallery and make the needed changes to fine-tune a specific effect.
3. You can also right-click the picture and select **Format Picture** from the short-cut menu to open the *Format Picture* pane where you can make changes.
4. To remove a picture style, select the picture and click the **Reset Picture** button [*Picture Tools Format* tab, *Adjust* group].

2-30 *Picture Effects*

Crop a Picture

You can *crop* (trim) unwanted areas of a selected picture by dragging black *cropping handles* on the corners and sides of the picture that appear when **Crop** is selected. When you point to these handles, your pointer changes to a shape that resembles the handle. Be careful when dragging to be sure you are moving a cropping handle and not a sizing handle.

HOW TO: Crop a Picture

1. Select a picture and click the **Crop** button [*Picture Tools Format* tab, *Size* group].

2. Drag one or more cropping handles toward the center of the picture; the area to be removed from the edges is grayed out (Figure 2-31).

3. When you are satisfied, click the **Crop** button again to accept this change.

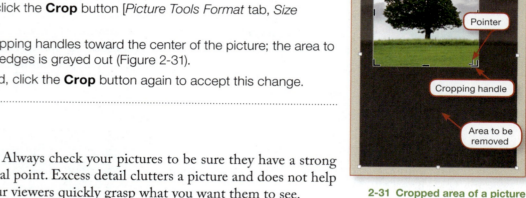

Always check your pictures to be sure they have a strong focal point. Excess detail clutters a picture and does not help your viewers quickly grasp what you want them to see.

2-31 Cropped area of a picture

Change Picture Colors

Pictures are digital photographs usually made up of many colors to achieve the realism that they portray. If an image is faded or if you want a muted image for a background area so text is easy to read, PowerPoint's *Color* feature allows you to apply different color options.

HOW TO: Change Picture Colors

1. Select a picture you want to change.

2. Click the **Color** button [*Picture Tools Format* tab, *Adjust* group].

3. A gallery appears showing different color options (Figure 2-32). The current option within each group is highlighted.

4. Click an option to apply it.

5. Click **Picture Color Options** to open the *Format Picture* pane with the **Picture Color** options listed where you can make your selections.

6. Options include the following:

   • **Color Saturation:** Colors are more muted as you move from the center to the left as saturation becomes lower; colors are more intense as you move from the center to the right as saturation increases.

2-32 *Color* gallery

- **Color Tone:** Colors on the left have cool tones and lower temperature values; colors on the right have warm tones and higher values.
- **Recolor:** Options on the first row include *Grayscale, Sepia, Washout,* and percentages of *Black and White.* The second and third rows display dark and light monotone variations of accent colors.

Set a Transparent Color

An image with a white background works well on a slide with a white background (or on a typical Word document) because you see just the image. However, a white background can detract from an image if you place it on a slide background with a contrasting color.

Use the ***Set Transparent Color*** feature to remove a single-color background. Because this feature removes only one color, it does not work well for pictures that have a lot of detail and many colors.

HOW TO: Set a Transparent Color

1. Select a picture.
2. Click the **Color** button [*Picture Tools Format* tab, *Adjust* group].
3. Click **Set Transparent Color** and your pointer changes to a pen tool.
4. Point to the area of the picture you want to remove, and click.
5. All of the pixels with that color value disappear, revealing what is behind the picture (Figure 2-33).

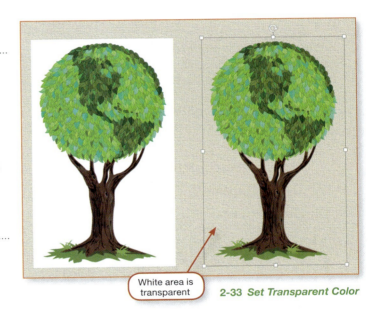

White area is transparent

2-33 Set Transparent Color

Compress Pictures

Pictures can greatly increase your presentation file size. You can ***compress*** single pictures or all pictures at one time to reduce the picture resolution depending on the quality you need. For print you generally need a higher resolution, and for on-screen viewing a lower resolution is usually fine. Resolution options are expressed in *pixels per inch (ppi)—Print (220 ppi), Screen (150 ppi),* and *E-mail (96 ppi).* The ppi measurement for viewing on screen is very different from the *dots per inch (dpi)* print measurement for printing on paper. An inexpensive printer can produce 1,200 or more *dpi,* which produces crisp, clear letterforms that are easy to read on paper.

Deleting cropped areas of pictures removes unused information and, therefore, reduces file size. Compression only affects how the pictures display in the presentation file and not the original picture files.

HOW TO: Compress Picture File Size

1. Select a picture.

2. Click the **Compress Picture** button [*Picture Tools Format* tab, *Adjust* group].

3. On the *Compress Pictures* dialog box (Figure 2-34), deselect **Apply only to this picture** if you want the compression to apply to all pictures in the presentation.

4. If you have cropped pictures, select **Delete cropped areas of pictures**.

5. Select the appropriate *Target output*.

6. Click **OK** to close the dialog box.

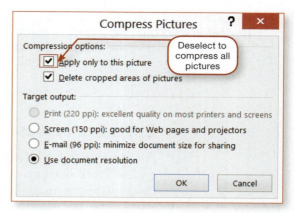

2-34 *Compress Pictures* dialog box

PAUSE & PRACTICE: POWERPOINT 2-1

When Gerod Sunderland shares his landscaping proposal with homeowners, he provides detailed printed information and uses a presentation to illustrate concepts. In this project, you add pictures and other objects to his presentation and apply a variety of styles and colors to enhance the content.

File Needed: *LandscapingProposal-02.pptx*
Completed Project File Name: *[your initials] PP P2-1.pptx*

1. Open the presentation *LandscapingProposal-02*.

2. Save the presentation as *[your initials] PP P2-1*.

3. Add a rectangle.
   a. On slide 1, click the **Shapes** button [*Insert* tab, *Illustrations* group].
   b. Select the rectangle shape.
   c. Click and drag to draw a rectangle across the slide.
   d. Change the rectangle height to **.4"** and width to **13.33"** [*Drawing Tools Format* tab, *Size* group].
   e. Click the **Shape Fill** button [*Drawing Tools Format* tab, *Shape Styles* group] and select **Brown, Accent 5, Darker 25%**.
   f. Click the **Shape Outline** button and select **No Outline**.
   g. Position the rectangle below the white line as shown in Figure 2-35.

2-35 Change *Shape Fill* color

4. Add text effects.
   a. On slide 1, select the title and click the **Text Effects** button [*Drawing Tools Format* tab, *Word Art Styles* group].
   b. Select **Bevel** and then **Circle**.
   c. Repeat to select **Shadow** and then **Offset Diagonal Bottom Right** (Figure 2-36).

5. Add a frame shape.
   a. On slide 3, click the **Shape** button [*Insert* tab, *Illustrations* group] and select the **Frame** shape under the *Basic Shapes* heading.
   b. Click and drag to draw a frame.
   c. In the frame shape type Allow three days.
   d. Change the font size to **24 pts**.
   e. Adjust the frame size with a height of **1"** and width of **3.3"** [*Drawing Tools Format* tab, *Size* group].

6. Change to a different shape and color.
   a. Click the **Edit Shape** button arrow [*Drawing Tools Format* tab, *Insert Shapes* group] and select **Change Shape**.
   b. Click the **Bevel** shape under the *Basic Shapes* heading.
   c. Change the *Shape Fill* to **Tan**, **Background 2**, **Darker 25%**.
   d. Position this shape below the bulleted text (Figure 2-37).

7. On slide 8, add *WordArt* text.
   a. Click the **WordArt** button [*Insert* tab, *Text* group].
   b. Select the style **Gradient fill - Green, Accent 4, Outline - Accent 4.**
   c. In the *WordArt* text box type Thank you for your business!
   d. Move the *WordArt* object so it is at the top of the picture (Figure 2-38).
   e. Change the *Character Spacing* [*Home* tab, *Font* group] to **Tight**.

8. Change the *WordArt* gradient fill and outline colors.
   a. Click the **Text Fill** button [*Drawing Tools Format* tab, *WordArt Styles* group] and select **Gradient**.
   b. Click **More Gradients** to open the *Format Shape* pane.
   c. Select the second gradient stop (at Position **4%**) and click the **Remove gradient stop** button.
   d. Select the left gradient stop (at Position **0%**) and change the color to **Green**, **Accent 4**, **Lighter 40%**.
   e. Select the right gradient stop and change the color to **Green**, **Accent 4**, **Darker 50%** (Figure 2-39).
   f. Close the *Format Shape* pane.
   g. Click the **Text Outline** button and change the outline color to **Black**, **Text 1**.

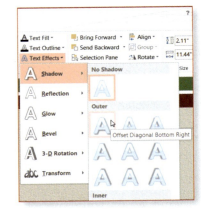

2-36 Apply *Text Effects*

2-37 Text box positioned below list

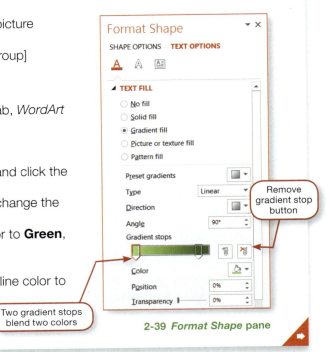

2-38 *WordArt* with gradient

2-39 *Format Shape* pane

9. Apply a *Transform* effect to the *WordArt.*
   a. Click the **Text Effects** button [*Format* tab, *WordArt Styles* group]. From the drop-down list, select **Transform**.
   b. On the *Transform* gallery, click the **Deflate Bottom** effect (Figure 2-40).
   c. Resize the *WordArt* to fit across the top of the picture (Figure 2-41).

10. Apply effects and use the *Format Painter.*
    a. On slide 2, select the left list heading placeholder.
    b. Change the text to **bold**.
    c. Click the **Shape Fill** button [*Drawing Tools Format* tab, *Shape Styles* group] and select **Texture**.
    d. Click the **Parchment** option.
    e. Click the **Format Painter** button [*Home* tab, *Clipboard* group]. Click the list heading placeholder on the right to apply the same changes.

11. On slide 3, search for and insert a picture.
    a. Click the **Online Pictures** button [*Insert* tab, *Images* group] to open the *Insert Pictures* dialog box.
    b. In the *Office.com* search box, type the word soil.
    c. Click **Search** (or press **Enter**) to activate the search.
    d. Locate the picture shown in Figure 2-42.
    e. Click **Insert**.

12. On slide 3, resize and crop the picture.
    a. Resize the picture to a height of **6"** and the width automatically adjusts to **4.01"** [*Picture Tools Format* tab, *Size* group].
    b. Click the **Crop** button [*Picture Tools Format* tab, *Size* group] and crop a little space from all four edges to focus more on the plant.
    c. Click the **Crop** button again to accept the crop.
    d. Click the **More** button [*Picture Tools Format* tab, *Picture Styles* group] and select the **Rotated**, **White** picture style.
    e. Position the picture on the right (Figure 2-43).

13. On slide 1, insert a picture.
    a. Click the **Online Pictures** button [*Insert* tab, *Images* group] to open the *Insert Pictures* dialog box.
    b. In the *Office.com* search box, type the word leaf.
    c. Locate the picture of a red maple leaf on a white background (Figure 2-44).

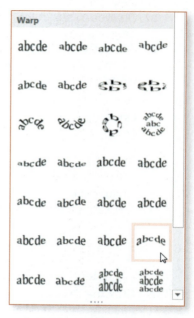

2-40 *WordArt Transform* **gallery**

2-41 *Deflate Bottom Transform* **effect applied and adjusted**

2-42 *Online Pictures* **search results**

d. Select the thumbnail and click **Insert**.

e. On the *Picture Tools Format* tab, change the leaf height to **5"** and the width automatically adjusts.

f. With the leaf selected, click **Color** [*Picture Tools Format* tab, *Adjust* group].

g. Select **Set Transparent Color** and your pointer changes to a pen tool.

h. Click the white area around the leaf so it becomes transparent.

i. Position the leaf on the right (Figure 2-44).

14. Compress a picture file size.

a. Select the leaf and click **Compress Pictures** [*Picture Tools Format* tab, *Adjust* group].

b. Deselect **Apply only to this picture**.

c. For the *Target output,* select **Use document resolution**.

d. Click **OK**.

15. Save and close your presentation.

2-43 Completed slide 3

2-44 Completed slide 1

Creating a Table

Tables show data in an organized and easy-to-read way because information is arranged in *columns* (vertical) and *rows* (horizontal). The intersection of a column and row is a *cell*. *Border* lines and *shading* show the table structure. Working with PowerPoint tables is much like working with tables in Word.

Once you create a table, you can change its size as well as column width and row height. Use table formatting to emphasize the contents in different ways and help your audience interpret the data. If you plan to project your slides on a large screen, be sure your table information is concise so you can use a minimum font size of 20 points. If a table requires a lot of detailed information, then prepare the table as a full-page handout with body text at an 11–12 point size. You can prepare a PowerPoint slide to reference the handout as you explain the table, or perhaps show on a slide only a portion of the table.

Insert and Draw Methods

You can create a table using the **Table** button [*Insert* tab, *Tables* group]. As you drag over the columns and rows to select them, the table dimensions (such as *3×4 Table*) are shown at the top of the drop-down list. The first number represents columns and the second number represents rows. By default, columns and rows appear on the slide with even sizing, but you can adjust column width and row height as you add information.

HOW TO: Insert a Table and Select Columns and Rows

1. Display the slide where you want the table.
2. Click the **Insert** tab.
3. Click the **Table** button [*Tables* group] to open the drop-down list (Figure 2-45).
4. Drag across and down to select the number of columns and rows you need.
5. Click to insert the table.

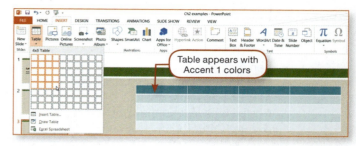

2-45 Table cells selected

By using the **Insert Table** command [*Insert* tab, *Tables* group], you can create a table by entering a specific the number of columns and rows.

HOW TO: Insert a Table and Enter the Number of Columns and Rows

1. Display the slide where you want to insert the table.
2. Click the **Insert** tab.
3. Click the **Table** button [*Tables* group] to open the drop-down list.
4. Click **Insert Table** and the *Insert Table* dialog box opens (Figure 2-46).
5. Specify the number of columns and rows you need.
6. Click **OK** to close the *Insert Table* dialog box and insert the table.

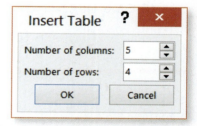

2-46 *Insert Table* dialog box

> ### ANOTHER WAY
> When you add a new slide, click the **Table** icon in the empty content placeholder and enter the number of columns and rows to create a table. The table width will be slightly wider than when you click the **Insert** button to create a table.

The final way to create a table is by drawing the table area and dividing it into columns and rows.

HOW TO: Draw a Table

1. Display the slide where you want the table.
2. Click the **Insert** tab.
3. Click the **Table** button [*Tables* group] to open the drop-down list.

4. Click **Draw Table** and your pointer changes to a pen tool.

5. Drag to create the table size you want.

6. Click the **Draw Table** button [*Table Tools Design* tab, *Draw Borders* group] to activate the pen tool again, and drag the pen within the table to insert horizontal and vertical lines that divide the table into rows and columns (Figure 2-47).

7. Press **Esc** to turn off the pen tool.

2-47 Draw Table

Regardless of the method you use to create a table, the *Table Tools Design* tab (Figure 2-48) and *Table Tools Layout* tab (Figure 2-49) are available when the table is active.

2-48 Table Tools Design tab

2-49 Table Tools Layout tab

Move and Select

Your insertion point indicates where you are within a table to add text. To move from cell to cell, use one of the following methods:

- Press **Tab** to move to the next cell on the right (or the first cell in the next row).
- Press **Shift+Tab** to move to the next cell on the left.
- Click a cell to move the insertion point to that cell.
- Use arrow keys to move in different directions from the current cell.

Where you point within a table influences whether you select individual cells, columns, rows, or the entire table. Your pointer changes to a selection pointer (a black arrow that points in different directions based on what you are selecting).

HOW TO: Select Cells, Columns, Rows, and the Table

1. To select a cell, point inside the left border and click when your pointer turns into a black arrow.

2. To select a column, use one of the following methods:
   - Point above its top border and click when your pointer turns into a downward-pointing black arrow (Figure 2-50).
   - Move your insertion point to any cell in the column. Click the **Select** button [*Table Tools Layout* tab, *Table* group] and click **Select Column**.

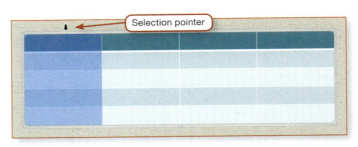

2-50 Select table column

3. To select a row, use one of the following methods:
   - Point outside the table to the left of a row and click when your pointer turns into a right-pointing black arrow (Figure 2-51).
   - Move your insertion point to **any cell** in the row. Click the **Select** button [*Table Tools Layout* tab, *Table* group] and click **Select Row**.

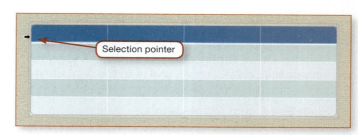

2-51 **Select table row**

4. To select multiple cells, columns, or rows, use one of the following methods:
   - Drag across adjacent cells.
   - Press **Shift** as you click additional adjacent cells.

5. To select an entire table, use one of the following methods:
   - Drag across all cells in the table.
   - Move your insertion point to any cell in the table. Click the **Select** button [*Table Tools Layout* tab, *Table* group] and click **Select Table**.

Insert and Delete Rows and Columns

After you begin entering table content, you may need to add rows or columns. You can change a table's structure in several ways:

- Insert rows above or below the current row.
- Insert columns to the left or right of the current column.
- Delete rows and columns.

HOW TO: Insert and Delete Rows and Columns

1. Click inside the table.
2. Click the **Table Tools Layout** tab.
3. Insert a row or column.
   - Click in a table cell next to where you want to add a column or row.
   - Click the **Insert Above** or **Insert Below** buttons [*Rows & Columns* group] to add rows.
   - Click the **Insert Left** or **Insert Right** buttons [*Rows & Columns* group] to add columns.
4. Delete a row or column.
   - Click in a table cell where you want to delete a column or row.
   - Click the **Delete** button and select **Delete Columns** or **Delete Rows** [*Rows & Columns* group] (Figure 2-52).

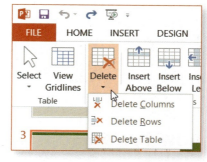

2-52 *Delete* button

> ▶ **ANOTHER WAY**
>
> Right-click a row or column and insert or delete rows and columns by selecting the appropriate option from the mini toolbar.

Merge and Split Cells

You can **merge** (combine) two or more cells in a row or column. For example, you can combine all the cells in the top row of a table so a title spans all columns (see Figure 2-53). You can **split** (divide) any single cell into two or more cells.

HOW TO: Merge and Split Cells

1. Select the cells to be merged.
   - Click the *Table Tools Layout* tab.
   - Click the **Merge Cells** button [*Merge* group] to combine those cells into one cell.
2. Select the cell (or cells) to be split.
   - Click the *Table Tools Layout* tab.
   - Click the **Split Cells** button [*Merge* group] to open the *Split Cells* dialog box and enter the number of columns and rows that you need.
   - Click **OK** to close the dialog box.

> ▶ **ANOTHER WAY**
> Click the **Eraser** button [*Table Tools Design* tab, *Draw Borders* group] and your pointer turns into an eraser. Click a border within the table to remove it and merge cells.

Adjust Sizing

You often need to resize tables to fit information appropriately. Column widths will vary based on content, but row height should usually be consistent.

HOW TO: Resize a Table, Cells, Columns, and Rows

1. Resize a table.
   - Enter sizes in the *Height* and *Width* boxes [*Table Tools Layout* tab, *Table Size* group].
   - Click and drag table sizing handles as you would to resize a shape.
2. Resize a cell, column, or row.
   - Point to a cell, column, or row inside a border. When your pointer changes to a splitter (Figure 2-53), click and drag to make the cell, column, or row larger or smaller.
   - Select the cell, column, or row you want to change; then enter the size you want in the *Height* and *Width* boxes [*Table Tools Layout* tab, *Cell Size* group].
3. To resize a column to fit the text within it, point to a border and double-click when your pointer changes to a splitter.
4. To evenly distribute column width or row height,
   - Select the columns or rows to be changed.
   - Click the **Distribute Rows** or **Distribute Columns** buttons [*Table Tools Layout* tab, *Cell Size* group].

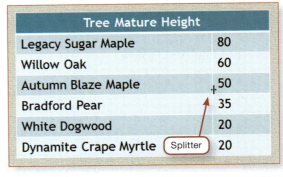

Tree Mature Height	
Legacy Sugar Maple	80
Willow Oak	60
Autumn Blaze Maple	50
Bradford Pear	35
White Dogwood	20
Dynamite Crape Myrtle (Splitter)	20

2-53 Change column width

> **MORE INFO**
>
> To maintain column width proportions, press **Shift** as you drag table sizing handles or select **Lock Aspect Ratio** before entering *Height* or *Width* sizes.

SLO 2.5

Enhancing a Table

You can format text in a table as you can any other text such as changing alignment and applying *WordArt Quick Styles*. You can also change cell margins and text direction. The following are table formatting options:

- Apply a *Table Style*.
- Customize the style by changing effect options.
- Add shading, borders, and other effects to cells, columns, or rows.

Table Style Options and Effects

On the *Table Tools Design* tab, **Table Styles** provide a gallery of built-in options for a table's design. The first style on each row of options is shown in black and white while the other six styles are in theme accent colors. Table styles are arranged in the following categories:

- *Best Match for Document*
- *Light*
- *Medium*
- *Dark*

Each table style is influenced by the features checked for **Table Style Options** [*Table Tools Design* tab]. Fill colors that emphasize table cells vary depending on which of the following options you select:

- **Header Row** or **Total Row:** The first or last row has a darker color and has bold text in a contrasting color.
- **First Column** or **Last Column:** The first or last column has a darker color and has bold text in a contrasting color.
- **Banded Rows** or **Banded Columns:** The rows or columns have alternating colors. *Banded Rows* makes reading across the table easier. *Banded Columns* emphasizes the separate columns.

HOW TO: Apply a Table Style with Header Row and Banded Rows

1. Click anywhere in the table you want to change.
2. Click the **Table Tools Design** tab.
3. Check **Header Row** and **Banded Rows** [*Table Style Options* group].
4. Click the **More** list arrow in the *Table Styles* group to see the complete gallery. The current style is highlighted.
5. Point to a style to see a live preview (Figure 2-54). ScreenTips identify each style name.
6. Click a style to apply it.

2-54 *Table Styles*

If you want to clear table formatting, click the **More** button [*Table Tools Design* tab, *Table Styles* group] and click **Clear Table**. To emphasize the table or cells within the table, such as a heading row, you can apply effects.

HOW TO: Apply Table Effects

1. Select the table, or the cells, to be changed.
2. Click the **Effects** button [*Table Tools Design* tab, *Table Styles* group (Figure 2-55).
3. Click one of the following effects and select a specific option:
   - **Cell Bevel**
   - **Shadow**
   - **Reflection**

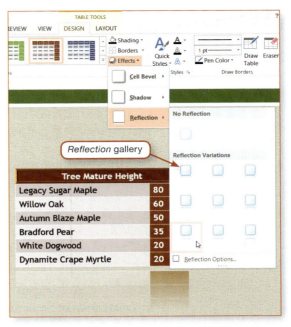

2-55 *Reflection Effects*

Shading and Border Colors

After you apply a built-in table style, you can change colors to emphasize your content or better match other aspects of your presentation. Select the cells you want to change and use the **Shading** button [*Table Tools Design* tab, *Table Styles* group] to select a different color (Figure 2-56). The icon for this button is the same as a **Shape Fill** button.

2-56 *Row shading emphasizes text*

Border lines separate cells and outline the edge of the table. Some table styles do not show border lines. To add lines, use the **Borders** button [*Table Tools Design* tab, *Table Styles* group] and each available option shows where the border line will be applied when that option is selected (Figure 2-57). Make sure to select the appropriate area before you apply the border change. If you want to make the border lines thicker, increase the **Pen Weight** [*Table Tools Design* tab, *Draw Borders* group] before you apply the border change. You can remove borders from selected cells by clicking the **Borders** button and selecting **No Border**.

Also, you can apply, change, and remove borders using the *Pen* tools [*Table Tools Design* tab, *Draw Borders* group].

- *Pen Color:* Change line color.
- *Pen Style:* Choose a different line style.
- *Pen Weight:* Change line thickness.
- *Draw Table:* Draw table area as well as column and row border lines.
- *Eraser:* Remove border lines.

2-57 *Border color and weight changed*

It may take a little practice to use the pen to change table lines and not start a new table. The *Eraser* removes each line you click.

Cell Alignment

Within cells, text is aligned on the left by default, which is appropriate for words and phrases. However, numbers should usually be right-aligned to make it easy for your audience to interpret values.

If cells have a single line of text, center the text vertically in the cells. If some cells contain more text than other cells, top alignment generally works best because it imposes consistency. Bottom alignment works well for column headings when they have more than one line of text.

Click the **Align** buttons [*Table Tools Layout* tab, *Alignment* group] and choose from the following horizontal and vertical alignment options:

- *Horizontal alignment:* Align Text Left, Center, Align Text Right
- *Vertical alignment:* Align Top, Center Vertically, Align Bottom

Cell Margins and Text Direction

Some space is needed between the border lines that define a cell and the text that goes in the cell. The default *Internal Margin* spacing is *Normal.* You can change the spacing by clicking the **Cell Margins** button [*Table Tools Layout* tab, *Alignment* group] and choose from one of the following options (Figure 2-58):

2-58 *Cell Margins* increased

- *Normal:* .05" top/bottom, .1" left/right
- *None:* 0" all sides
- *Narrow:* 0.05" all sides
- *Wide:* 0.15" all sides

Click **Custom Margins** to open the *Cell Text Layout* dialog box to enter other measurements.

If text becomes too long to fit in a cell, you can change from the default horizontal direction. Be careful when using this option because your text may not be as easy to read. Click **Text Direction** and choose one of the following four options (Figure 2-59):

- **Horizontal**
- **Rotate all text 90°**
- **Rotate all text 270°**
- **Stacked**

2-59 *Text Direction* options

For this project you create a table of costs, insert a row of data, and format the table to blend with other colors used in the landscaping presentation. You also add a text box to show an alternative cost.

File Needed: ***[your initials] PP P2-1.pptx***
Completed Project File Name: ***[your initials] PP P2-2.pptx***

1. Open the presentation ***[your initials] PP P2-1*** and save it as ***[your initials] PP P2-2***.

2. Create a table.
    a. On slide 4, click the **Table** button on the content placeholder.
    b. On the *Insert Table* dialog box, enter 4 columns and 5 rows. Click **OK** to close the dialog box.
    c. Type the following table text. It will first appear as shown in Figure 2-60.

Item	Quantity	Cost Each	Totals
Trees—shade	3	500	1,500
Trees—ornamental	3	150	450
Perennials	30	12	360
Hydroseeding sq. ft.	8,000	.10	800

Item	Quantity	Cost Each	Totals
Trees—shade	3	500	1,500
Trees—ornamental	3	150	450
Perennials	30	12	360
Hydroseeding sq. ft.	8,000	.10	800

2-60 Table as it first appears

    d. Select all table **cells** and change the font size to **20 pts**.

3. Adjust table sizing and alignment.
    a. Make each column the appropriate size for its content by pointing to each line separating the columns, including the right side of the table, and double-clicking when your pointer changes to a splitter.
    b. Select the "Quantity," "Cost Each," and "Totals" columns and click the **Align Right** button [*Table Tools Layout* tab, *Alignment* group].

4. Insert rows and add text.
    a. Click in the "Perennials" cell and click the **Insert Above** button [*Table Tools Layout* tab, *Rows & Columns* group].
    b. Add the following row text:
        Shrubs   10   40   400
    c. Click in the "Hydroseeding" cell and click the **Insert Below** button [*Table Tools Layout* tab, *Rows & Columns* group].
    d. On this new row, select the last three cells and click the **Merge Cells** button [*Table Tools Layout* tab, *Merge* group].
    e. Add the following row text:
        Total   3,510

5. Select styles, options, and shading.
    a. Click the **More** button [*Tables Tools Design* tab, *Table Styles* group] and select the **Medium Style 3, Accent 4** style.
    b. Select **Header Row**, **Total Row**, and **Banded Rows** [*Tables Tools Design* tab, *Table Style Options* group].

c. Select each of the rows with gray shading and click the **Shading** button [*Table Tools Design* tab, *Table Styles* group]; then select **Green**, **Accent 4**, **Lighter 80%**.

d. Select the last row and click the **Shading** button and select **Green**, **Accent 4**, **Lighter 60%**.

e. Select the first row and click the **Effects** button [*Table Tools Design* tab, *Table Styles* group], click **Cell Bevel**, and select **Circle** (Figure 2-61).

Item	Quantity	Cost Each	Totals
Trees—shade	3	500	1,500
Trees—ornamental	3	150	450
Shrubs	10	40	400
Perennials	30	12	360
Hydroseeding sq. ft.	8,000	.10	800
Total			3,510

2-61 Style, row shading, and *Bevel* effect applied

6. Add borders and a shadow effect.
   a. Select the first column.
   b. Click the **Pen Color** button [*Table Tools Design* tab, *Draw Borders* group] and select **Black**.
   c. Click the **Pen Weight** button [*Table Tools Design* tab, *Draw Borders* group] and select **1 pt**.
   d. Click the **Border** button [*Table Tools Design* tab, *Table Styles* group] and select **Left Border**.
   e. Select the last column.
   f. Click the **Border** button and select **Right Border**.
   g. Select the table and click the **Effects** button [*Table Tools Design* tab, *Table Styles* group]. Click **Shadow** and select **Offset Diagonal Bottom Right**.

7. Move the table so it is centered on the slide.

8. Insert a text box.
   a. Click the **Text Box** button [*Insert* tab, *Text* group] and click the slide to start a text box. Type the following text:
      Sod cost for 8,000 sq. ft. @ .60 = $4,800
   b. Change the font size to **20 pts** [*Home* tab, *Font* group].
   c. Click the **Shape Fill** button [*Home* tab, *Drawing* group] and select **Green**, **Accent 4**, **Lighter 60%**.
   d. Resize the text box as necessary so the text fits on one line. Move it to the lower right of the slide (Figure 2-62).

9. Save and close your presentation.

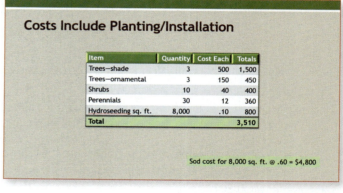

2-62 Completed table

SLO 2.6

Creating a SmartArt Graphic

To clearly illustrate concepts such as processes, cycles, or relationships, you can create a diagram using *SmartArt graphics* to help your audience see connections or sequences. This is a very important communication strategy; the shapes of the diagram are concisely labeled for each concept and the shapes you use can help people recognize relationships. For example, you can show subtopics radiating from a central topic or sequential steps in a work flow.

The *SmartArt Tools Design* tab (Figure 2-63) provides options for the overall design and styles of the *SmartArt* graphics. You can add shapes and rearrange the order of shapes.

The *SmartArt Tools Format* tab (Figure 2-73) provides options to customize shape and text styles, fill colors, outline colors, and effects.

2-64 *SmartArt Tools Format* tab

SmartArt Layouts

SmartArt layouts (diagrams) are organized by type in the *Choose a SmartArt Graphic* dialog box; each type is described in the following table. When you select a layout, PowerPoint provides more information about using that specific layout.

SmartArt Graphic Types and Purposes

Type	Purpose
List	Illustrates non-sequential or grouped information
Process	Illustrates sequential steps in a process or workflow
Cycle	Illustrates a continuing sequence or concepts related to a central idea
Hierarchy	Illustrates a decision tree or top-to-bottom relationship such as an organizational chart
Relationship	Illustrates concepts that are connected such as contrasting, opposing, or converging
Matrix	Illustrates the relationship of four parts to the whole
Pyramid	Illustrates proportional or interconnected relationships
Picture	Shows pictures as integral parts of many different diagrams
Office.com	Shows diagrams from layouts on Office.com

HOW TO: Create a SmartArt Graphic

1. Display the slide where you want to insert the *SmartArt* graphic.
2. Click the **Insert** tab.
3. Click the **SmartArt** button [*Illustrations* group] to open the *Choose a SmartArt Graphic* dialog box.
4. Select a type from the list on the left (Figure 2-65).
5. Click a layout in the gallery to select it.
6. Click **OK** to close the dialog box. The *SmartArt* graphic appears on the slide with sample text.

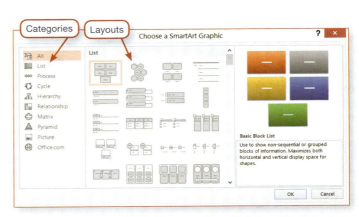

2-65 *Choose a SmartArt Graphic* dialog box

When you insert a *SmartArt* graphic using the **SmartArt** button on the *Insert* tab, the initial size of the *SmartArt* frame may be different than if you inserted the *SmartArt* graphic using the content placeholder on a new slide with a Title and Content layout. You may need to resize the frame for your content and to fit appropriately on your slide.

If the layout you choose has picture placeholders on the shapes, such as the *Continuous Picture List* layout shown in Figure 2-66, click each picture icon to open the *Insert Pictures* dialog box. Locate the picture you want to insert and click **Insert**. The picture is sized automatically and shaped to fit the current picture placeholder.

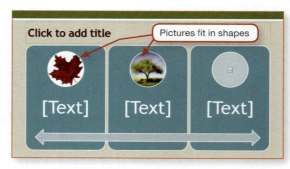

2-66 *SmartArt Continuous Picture List* layout

Add Text

Keep text very concise because space is limited for each shape within the *SmartArt* frame. *List* layouts often work well if you have both Level 1 and Level 2 information (shown as indented text in a bulleted list).

Use the Text Pane

You can enter text using the *Text Pane* [*SmartArt Tools Design* tab, *Create Graphic* group] just as you would a bulleted list. As you enter text in the *Text Pane*, it also appears in the *SmartArt* shapes. Text becomes smaller in the shapes as you enter more text. You can resize or move the *Text Pane*.

Typically, only a few words appear in each shape. After the first bulleted text is entered (Level 1 text), press **Enter** to add a second bullet. If the layout you are using has enough space, press **Tab** to indent for Level 2 text. Notice in Figure 2-67 that Level 1 text is in a shape and Level 2 text is in a bulleted list below the shape.

HOW TO: Type SmartArt Text Using the Text Pane

1. Open the *Text Pane,* if necessary, by using one of the following methods:
   • Click the **Text Pane** button [*SmartArt Tools Design* tab, *Create Graphic* group].
   • Click the **Text Pane** control on the left side of the *SmartArt* frame.
2. Type text after the first bullet to add Level 1 text.
3. Press **Enter** to add a new item. Another shape appears in your diagram, and shape sizes automatically adjust.
4. Press **Tab** to indent for Level 2 text (Figure 2-67).
5. Use arrow keys to move through the listed items.
6. To remove a shape, delete the related bulleted text in the *Text Pane.*

2-67 *SmartArt Text Pane*

Enter Text in SmartArt Shapes

You can type text directly into each *SmartArt* shape.

HOW TO: Type Text in SmartArt Shapes

1. Close the *Text Pane* by clicking the **Close** button in the top-right corner of the pane.
2. Click each *SmartArt* shape to select it and type your text. A dashed border appears as you type or edit your text.
   - Pressing **Tab** does not move your insertion point between shapes.
   - You cannot drag text into a *SmartArt* shape, but you can paste copied text.
3. Press **Delete** to remove a selected shape.
4. Click outside the *SmartArt* frame, or press **Esc**, when you are finished (Figure 2-68).

2-68 Completed picture *SmartArt* graphic

Convert Text to a SmartArt Graphic

You can change bulleted text to a *SmartArt* graphic.

HOW TO: Convert Text to a SmartArt Graphic

1. Select the bulleted text placeholder or the text within the placeholder that you want to convert to a *SmartArt* graphic.
2. Click the **Home** tab.
3. Click the **Convert to SmartArt Graphic** button [*Paragraph* group] (Figure 2-69). The gallery displays layouts that are designed to show listed information.
4. Select the layout you want and click **OK** to close the dialog box and insert the *SmartArt* graphic.

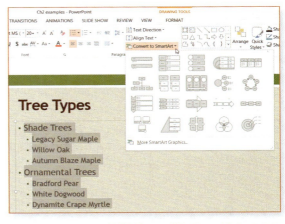

2-69 Convert to *SmartArt* graphic

SLO 2.7

Enhancing a SmartArt Graphic

When you create a *SmartArt* graphic, by default it appears using the first accent color in the current color theme. You can customize many style options and colors using the *SmartArt Tools Design* tab as well as rearrange shape order, add shapes, or change layouts.

SmartArt Styles

The **SmartArt Styles** gallery provides different effects for emphasizing the diagram shapes. In the **3-D** category, the layouts have a dimensional effect. When choosing these layouts, be sure that your diagram is not distorted or difficult to interpret.

HOW TO: Apply SmartArt Styles

1. Select the *SmartArt* graphic.
2. Click the **SmartArt Tools Design** tab.
3. Click the **More** button [*SmartArt Styles* group] to open the *SmartArt Styles* gallery (Figure 2-70).
4. Point to a style to see a live preview.
5. Click a style to apply it.

2-70 *SmartArt* graphic styles

Change Colors

How color is applied can help to differentiate between the various parts of a *SmartArt* graphic. The **Change Colors** gallery provides a quick way to change all the colors at the same time. Color options are arranged in categories; some show variations of the same color while others have different colors.

Individual shape colors within a *SmartArt* graphic can be changed as you would any other shape.

HOW TO: Change SmartArt Colors

1. Select the *SmartArt* graphic.
2. To change colors for the entire diagram, click the **Change Colors** button [*SmartArt Tools Design* tab, *SmartArt Styles* group] and select a gallery option (Figure 2-71) to apply it.
3. To change the color of a selected shape within a diagram, click the **Shape Fill** button or the **Shape Outline** button [*SmartArt Tools Format* tab, *Shape Styles* group] and choose an appropriate color.

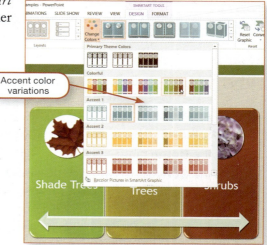

2-71 *SmartArt* graphic *Change Colors* options

Change Layouts

You may find that the *SmartArt* layout you have chosen does not fit your particular process or the relationship you are trying to show. Or you might need a layout that would better fit two levels of information.

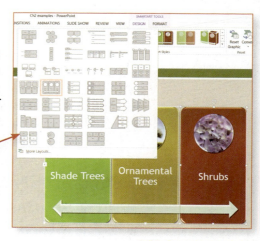

HOW TO: Change Layouts

1. Select the *SmartArt* graphic.
2. On the *SmartArt Tools Design* tab, click the **More** button [*Layouts* group] to open the *Layouts* gallery (Figure 2-72).

2-72 *SmartArt* layouts

3. Point to a layout to see a live preview of the current layout.
4. Click **More Layouts** to open the *Choose a SmartArt Graphic* dialog box.
5. Select an appropriate type from the list on the left.
6. Double-click a **layout** to apply it, or select the layout and then click **OK**.

Add Shapes

The ***Add Shape*** button on the *SmartArt Tools Design* tab inserts shapes in relation to the selected shape. The available options include the following:

- *Add Shape After*
- *Add Shape Before*
- *Add Shape Above*
- *Add Shape Below*
- *Add Assistant*

Being able to control where a new shape appears is important. For example, you can add shapes to an organization chart as new employees are hired. Adding a shape before or after a selected shape could show a new managerial position at the same level. Adding a shape above a selected shape could show a director position above a managerial position. Adding a shape below a selected shape could show a subordinate position reporting to a manager. An Assistant shape is only available for organization charts.

HOW TO: Add Shapes

1. Select the shape closest to where you want to add a shape.
2. Click the **SmartArt Design Tools** tab.
3. Click the **Add Shape** button list arrow [*Create Graphic* group] (Figure 2-73) and select the position where you want to add the new shape.

2-73 *Add Shape* options

To change the flow of a diagram, click the **Right to Left** button [*SmartArt Tools Design* tab, *Create Graphic* group].

PAUSE & PRACTICE: POWERPOINT 2-3

For this project you create an organization chart showing the CGL employees who will be managing various aspects of the landscaping for Frank and Sandra Hunter. You also convert one of the existing lists to a *SmartArt* graphic and rearrange slide objects for an interesting appearance. The *SmartArt* styles applied blend with other colors in the presentation.

File Needed: *[your initials] PP P2-2.pptx*
Completed Project File Name: *[your initials] PP P2-3.pptx*

1. Open the presentation *[your initials] PP P2-2* and save it as *[your initials] PP P2-3*.

2. Create a new slide.
   a. On slide 1, click the **New Slide** button list arrow and select the **Title and Content** layout.
   b. Type the slide title Your CGL Team.
   c. Click the **Insert a SmartArt Graphic** button on the content placeholder to open the *Choose a SmartArt Graphic* dialog box.
   d. Select the *Hierarchy* type from the list on the left.
   e. Click the **Organization Chart** layout and click **OK** to close the dialog box and insert the *SmartArt* graphic.

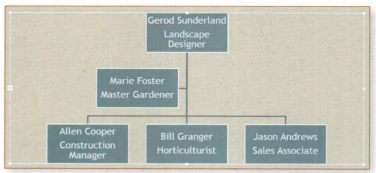

2-74 **Organization chart**

3. Add the text displayed in Figure 2-74 to the shapes. Press **Enter** after each name and let the job titles word wrap as needed.

4. Make changes to the organization chart using the *SmartArt Tools Design* tab.
   a. Change the flow by clicking the **Right to Left** button [*Create Graphic* group].
   b. Click the **More** button [*SmartArt Styles* group] and select the **Inset** effect (Figure 2-75).
   c. Click the **Change Colors** button [*SmartArt Styles* group] and select **Gradient Loop, Accent 4** (Figure 2-76).

2-75 *SmartArt* **graphic styles**

5. Change bulleted text to *SmartArt*.
   a. On slide 4, select the bulleted text and click the **Convert to SmartArt** button [*Home* tab, *Paragraph* group].
   b. Click the **Vertical Bullet List**. The *SmartArt* list fills the slide and is too large since other objects are already on the slide (Figure 2-77).

6. Make changes to the *SmartArt* graphic so it fits on the slide with the other objects.
   a. Select all shapes and change the font to **24 pts**.
   b. Select the *SmartArt* frame and resize it to better fit the text as shown (Figure 2-78).
   c. Change the style to **Inset** [*SmartArt Tools Design* tab, *SmartArt Styles* group].

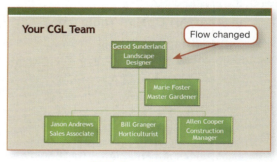

2-76 **Completed organization chart**

2-77 *SmartArt* **graphic shapes as they originally appear**

2-78 Resize the *SmartArt* graphic

2-79 Completed slide

   d. Click the **Change Colors** button [*SmartArt Tools Design* tab, *SmartArt Styles* group] and select **Colored Fill - Accent 4**.

   e. Rearrange slide objects as displayed in Figure 2-79. Be careful to point to the *SmartArt* frame when moving it so the whole diagram moves and not just an individual shape within the frame.

7. Save and close your presentation.

SLO 2.8 Creating a Chart

Charts help viewers interpret data and make comparisons. If you have lots of data, then create your chart in Excel and copy it to a PowerPoint slide. However, for most situations, Power-Point's *Chart* feature will provide all the options you need.

    To insert a chart in PowerPoint 2013, click the **Insert Chart** button on a new slide content placeholder or click the **Insert** tab and then click the **Chart** button [*Illustrations* group] to add a chart to an existing slide. You can choose a chart type to control how data is represented such as with columns, bars, lines, or pie slices. The following table lists chart types and describes their purposes.

Chart Types and Purposes

Type	Purpose
Column	Shows a comparison of values or data changes over time. Categories are shown on the horizontal axis and values are shown on the vertical axis. Columns may be clustered to show a range of values or groupings. Columns in a category may be stacked to emphasize the total category value rather than the subsections that make up the category.
Line	Shows data changes over time; works well to show trends with data plotted at even intervals. Categories are shown on the horizontal axis and values are shown on the vertical axis.
Pie	Shows the values in a data series in proportional sizes that make up a whole pie. Values cannot be negative or zero values. Percentages or actual values can be displayed near or on pie slices. This category also includes *Doughnut* charts that also show parts of a whole but can contain more than one data series as rings.
Bar	Similar to column charts except bars are horizontal; works well for comparison of values.
Area	Shows data changes over time; emphasizes the total value of a trend.
X Y (Scatter)	Shows the relationships between several data series using values on both the X and Y axes; works well to emphasize where data sets have similar values. This category also includes *Bubble* charts.
Stock	Shows fluctuation of stock prices with high, low, and close values displayed over time.

(continued)

Type	Purpose
Surface	Shows the differences between two sets of data. Instead of values, the color bands represent the same range of values as in a topographic map showing land elevations.
Radar	Shows the combined values of several data series with values relative to a center point.
Combo	Combines two charts such as a column chart with a line chart displayed over it.

> **MORE INFO**
>
> Use *Help* to search for "chart types" to see examples and get tips on how to arrange data in a worksheet.

The *Chart Tools Design* tab (Figure 2-80) and the *Chart Tools Format* tab (Figure 2-81) are available when a chart is active.

2-80 *Chart Tools Design* tab

2-81 *Chart Tools Format* tab

When you insert a chart in PowerPoint, a **spreadsheet** opens with sample data in rows and columns. A group of data values from each column is a **data series**; a group of data values from each row is a **category**. You can edit the sample data by entering your own information or you could copy and paste data from Excel, Word, or Access. If you need to revise the data in Excel, click the **Excel** button in the spreadsheet title bar.

Because the spreadsheet and PowerPoint chart are linked, the changes you make to the spreadsheet are automatically reflected in the chart.

HOW TO: Insert a Chart

1. Click the **Insert** tab; then click the **Chart** button [*Illustrations* group]. You can also click the **Insert Chart** button on a new slide content placeholder.

2. In the *Insert Chart* dialog box (Figure 2-82), chart categories are listed in the left pane and a variety of chart layouts for each category appear in the right pane. A ScreenTip identifies chart names.

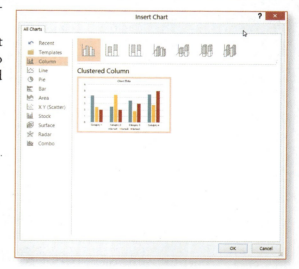

2-82 *Insert Chart* dialog box

3. Click a layout to select a chart.

4. Click **OK** to close the dialog box.

5. A spreadsheet automatically opens showing sample data that you edit (Figure 2-83).

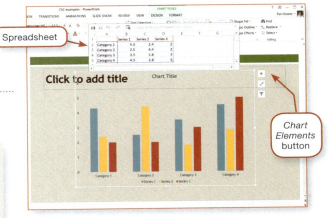

2-83 Spreadsheet linked to a chart

> **MORE INFO**
>
> The chart frame that appears on your slide when it is inserted using the *Insert* tab may be sized differently than when you insert a chart on a new slide from the *Title and Content* placeholder. Resize the chart frames as needed.

The chart frame displays ***chart elements***, the objects that make up the chart. Chart elements vary based on the type of chart used. You can see which chart elements are shown by clicking the **Chart Elements** button, the top button on the right of the chart frame. You can add or remove elements by changing selections from the list. Other chart elements appear in the list box in the *Current Selection* group on the *Chart Tools Format* tab and in the *Format* pane when you are working on the chart. The following table defines chart elements.

Chart Elements and Definitions

Element	Definition
Y-Axis (Vertical)	Also called the *Value Axis;* displayed vertically with numbers usually arranged on the left of a chart
X-Axis (Horizontal)	Also called the *Category Axis;* displayed horizontally with word or number labels across the bottom of the chart
Axis Titles	Both the Y-Axis and the X-Axis can include titles
Chart Area	The background area where the entire chart is displayed in a frame
Chart Title	A chart may include a title
Data Labels	Used to identify series and category names; may include values
Data Markers	The graphical representation of values shown as columns, bars, slices, or data points
Data Table	The data that creates the chart shown in table format below the chart
Error Bars	Used to show margins of error or standard deviation amounts
Gridlines	Lines that appear behind a chart to help the viewer judge values
Legend	The key that identifies the data series by color
Plot Area	The rectangle between the vertical and horizontal axes that is behind the data markers
Tick Marks	Used to identify the categories, values, or series on each axis
Trendline	Shows averages on 2-D charts that are not stacked and can extend beyond actual data to predict future values

Enter Data and Edit

After you replace the spreadsheet sample data with your data, you can close the spreadsheet. If you need to revise the data as you work on the chart in PowerPoint, you can open the spreadsheet again.

HOW TO: Edit Data in the Spreadsheet

1. Select the chart you want to modify.
2. Click the top of the **Edit Data** button [*Chart Tools Design* tab, *Data* group] (Figure 2-84) to open the spreadsheet. (If you need to modify the data in Excel, click the **Edit Data** button list arrow and choose **Edit Data in Excel 2013**.)
3. Resize the spreadsheet window, if necessary, to display all of your data.
4. Replace cell contents (Figure 2-85) by clicking in the **cell** and typing your data.
5. To move around in the spreadsheet,
   - Press **Enter** to move the insertion point down one row.
   - Press **Tab** to move the insertion point to the next cell on the right.
   - Press **Shift+Tab** to move to the next cell on the left.
   - Press arrow keys to move in any direction.
6. Click the spreadsheet **Close** button to return to PowerPoint.

2-84 *Edit Data* button

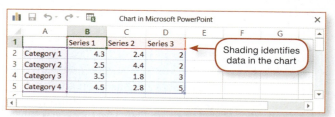

2-85 **Default spreadsheet data**

> ### MORE INFO
>
> Remove the sample data on the spreadsheet by clicking the **Select All** button (above the row 1 heading and to the left of the column A heading) and pressing your keyboard **Delete**.

Rows and columns on the spreadsheet may need adjustments.

- If a cell displays number signs (#) rather than the data you entered, the cell is not wide enough to display cell contents. You need to make the column wider.
- Be sure the shading correctly identifies the category, series, and data cells. If necessary, drag the sizing handles to adjust.
- If you need to add new columns or rows, edit the spreadsheet in Excel.

HOW TO: Modify the Spreadsheet

1. Select the chart you want to modify.
2. Click the top of the **Edit Data** button [*Chart Tools Design* tab, *Data* group].
3. Adjust column width. Position your pointer on the vertical line to the right of the column heading (Figure 2-86); then use one of these methods:
   - Drag to the correct width.
   - Double-click and the column automatically expands to fit the widest data entered in that column.

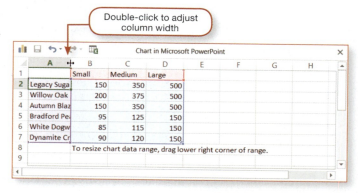

2-86 **Adjust column width**

- Right-click and select **Column Width**, then width number on the *Column Width* dialog box. Click **OK** to close the dialog box.

4. To add columns and rows, click the **Edit Data** button list arrow [*Chart Tools Design* tab, *Data* group] and choose **Edit Data in Excel 2013**.

- Click in the column to the right of where you want to add a column.
- Click in the row below where you want to add a row.
- Click the **Insert Cells** button [*Home* tab, *Cells* group] and select the option you need to insert cells, columns, or rows.

5. If necessary, resize the shaded areas on the spreadsheet so the data is accurately represented on your chart.

In PowerPoint, switch the data series by clicking the **Switch Row/Column** button [*Chart Tools Design* tab, *Data* group].

Change Chart Type

Click the **Change Chart Type** button [*Chart Tools Design* tab, *Type* group] to open the *Change Chart Type* gallery where you can choose from the many different layouts. For example, Figure 2-87 shows data in a line chart and Figure 2-88 shows the same data in a clustered column chart.

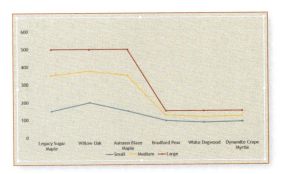

2-87 Line Chart

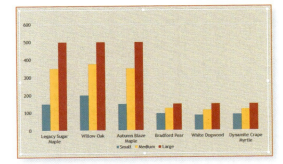

2-88 Clustered column chart

> **MORE INFO**
>
> If your PowerPoint window is narrow, you may need to click the **Quick Styles** button [*Chart Tools Design* tab] to open the *Chart Styles* gallery.

SLO 2.9

Enhancing a Chart

You can change the look of a chart by applying preset styles or manually customizing individual chart elements.

Chart Styles

The **Chart Styles** gallery [*Chart Tools Design* tab] provides preset effects for chart elements including the chart background. Click the **More** button to see styles arranged by number. Click a style to apply it (Figure 2-89).

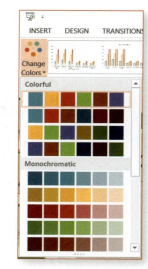

2-89 *Chart Styles* gallery

2-90 *Chart Colors* gallery

Click the **Change Colors** button [*Chart Tools Design* tab] to select *Colorful* or *Monochromatic* (shades of one color) combinations based on theme colors (Figure 2-90). The colors you choose then show in all the available chart styles. Be careful when selecting colors so the chart shapes (columns, bars, lines, or pie slices) are easy to distinguish for value comparisons. The colors also need to coordinate with your overall presentation (Figure 2-91).

If possible, avoid arranging red and green colors together. People who have difficulty recognizing different colors are most likely to have problems with red and green because they can look beige or gray.

> **ANOTHER WAY**
> You can also access *Chart Styles* and *Chart Colors* using the **Chart Styles** button on the right of each chart.

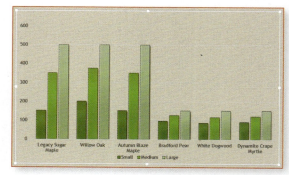

2-91 **Chart style applied**

Format Chart Elements

You can select chart elements (objects) and apply formatting in several ways.

HOW TO: Format a Chart Element

1. Use one of these methods to select a chart element and open the appropriate *Format* pane:
   - Select an element directly on the slide then double-click or right-click to open the appropriate *Format* pane for that element.
   - Click the **Chart Elements** button on the right of the chart, select a particular element, then click **More Options** to open the appropriate *Format* pane.
   - Use the *Chart Elements* list box [*Chart Tools Format* tab, *Current Selection* group] to select the element you need to change and then click **Format Selection** to open the *Format* pane for that element.

2. Use one or more of these commands on the *Chart Tools Format* tab:

- Click the **More** button [*Shape Styles* group] and select a style.
- Click the **Shape Fill**, **Shape Outline**, or **Shape Effects** buttons [*Shape Styles* group] and choose appropriate colors and effects (Figure 2-92).
- When text is selected, click the **WordArt Quick Styles** button and select from the gallery of effects. You can also click the **Text Fill**, **Text Outline**, or **Text Effects** buttons [*WordArt Styles* group] and choose appropriate colors and effects.

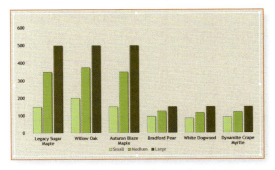

2-92 Colors changed on data series

To change the chart area size, point to any handle (the white squares on the chart frame) and resize by dragging. You can resize chart elements, but be careful not to distort size relationships.

HOW TO: Change the Chart Background

1. Select the chart.
2. Click the **Chart Tools Format** tab.
3. Click an element in the *Chart Elements* list box [*Current Selection* group].
4. Click the **Format Selection** button and the appropriate pane opens with options specific to each different element. Some options are available for 3-D charts only.
5. Chart background elements will vary based on the chart type. They may include:

- *Chart Area*
- *Plot Area*
- *Back Wall*
- *Side Wall*
- *Walls*
- *Floor*

You can fill elements of a chart with pictures. While a chart area picture might provide an interesting background, be careful when using pictures to avoid making the chart cluttered or the text difficult to read. The goal is always to create a chart that is easy to interpret.

In Figure 2-93, the plot area has a gradient fill with the darkest color at the bottom which helps to emphasize the height of the columns. In Figure 2-94, the chart type is a *3-D Column Chart*. The column heights (especially for the shorter columns) are not as easy to compare in this chart as they are in Figure 2-93.

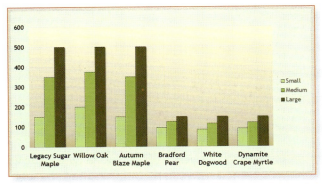

2-93 Chart plot area with gradient fill

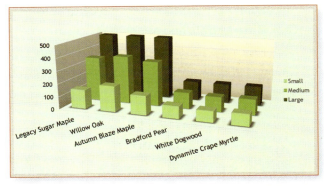

2-94 Chart with *3-D Rotation*

Legends and Labels

The *legend* identifies each data series by color. It is usually displayed on the right, but you can move it to other positions, display it horizontally above or below the plot area, or remove it.

HOW TO: Change Legend Position and Colors

1. To change the selected legend's position, use one of the following methods:
   - Click the **Chart Tools Format** tab, select **Legend** in the *Current Selection* list box, and click **Format Selection** to open the *Format Legend* pane.
   - Right-click the legend and choose **Format Legend** to open the *Format Legend* pane and select a different position. Deselect **Show the legend without overlapping the chart** if you want the legend to appear over the plot area that can be resized if necessary (Figure 2-95).
   - Click the **Chart Elements** button beside the chart, select the **Legend** list arrow, and then select the appropriate position.
   - Select the legend and drag it to another position within the chart area.

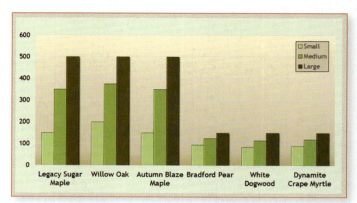

2-95 Legend moved

2. To change the selected legend's fill and outline colors, use one of the following methods:
   - Click the **Chart Tools Format** tab, click the **Shape Fill** or **Shape Outline** buttons, and select different colors.
   - Right-click the legend and choose **Format Legend** to open the *Format Legend* pane. Click the **Fill & Line** tab and then select appropriate fill and border colors. Click **Close**.

3. To remove a selected legend, use one of the following methods:
   - Click the **Chart Elements** button beside the chart and deselect the **Legend**.
   - Press **Delete**.

Labels appear in different places based on the chart style. Use the *Format Data Labels* pane to customize labels.

HOW TO: Change Chart Labels

1. Select the chart and then click the **Chart Element** button beside the chart.
2. Click **Data Labels** and select the position.
3. Click **More Options** to open the *Format Data Labels* pane.
4. Change *Label Options* to control what is displayed as well as the position.
5. Change *Text Options* to control fill and outline colors.

Using data labels above or inside columns enables the viewer to see the exact data value as well as the size relationships that the columns represent. However, the columns must be wide enough to display the numbers without overlapping. If they are too narrow (Figure 2-96), using a data table for this purpose will be more effective (Figure 2-97).

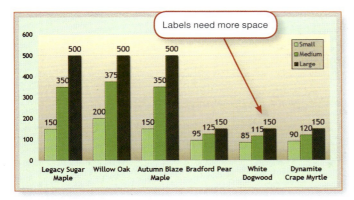

2-96 Data labels

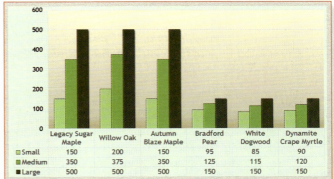

2-97 Data table

Separate a Pie Slice

You can separate pie chart slices (called *exploding*) by dragging the pie slices away from the center. However, when all slices are separated, no single slice is emphasized. To emphasize just one slice, it is best to first design a pie chart as you want it to look and then pull that slice away from the pie. Consider, also, how your colors are applied so the most noticeable or brightest color is used for the slice that you want to emphasize (Figure 2-98).

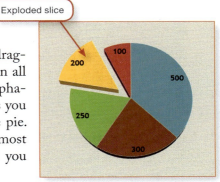

2-98 3-D pie chart with exploded slice

HOW TO: Explode a Pie Slice

1. Click a pie to select the pie object.
2. Click again to select just one pie slice. Check the handles to be sure you have selected the correct slice and not a label on the slice.
3. Drag slightly away from the center of the pie so the slice is emphasized.

As you drag a pie slice away from the center, the remainder of the pie becomes smaller. You may need to make the whole pie larger by resizing the plot area. Removing the legend creates more space for the pie, too. Pie charts are easier to interpret when short labels are shown directly on or beside slices instead of in a legend.

PAUSE & PRACTICE: POWERPOINT 2-4

For this project you create a pie and two clustered column charts showing the cost distribution for CGL landscaping, cost comparisons for tree sizes, and the height of mature trees being considered for the new landscape.

File Needed: **[your initials] PP P2-3.pptx**
Completed Project File Name: **[your initials] PP 2-4.pptx**

1. Open the presentation file **[your initials] PP P2-3** and save it as **[your initials] PP P2-4**.

2. Create a 3-D pie chart.
   a. On slide 6, "Cost Distribution," click the **Insert Chart** button on the content placeholder.
   b. Select the **Pie** chart type then select the **3-D Pie** layout. Click **OK**.
   c. Replace the spreadsheet sample data with the data in the following list and resize the columns as needed:

	Cost
Trees—Shade	1,500
Trees—Ornamental	450
Shrubs	400
Perennials	360
Hydroseeding sq. ft.	800

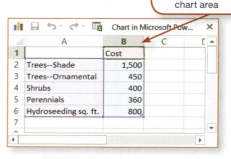

2-99 Spreadsheet linked to a chart

3. Be sure all chart data is selected. Resize the spreadsheet so you can proof all entries (Figure 2-99).

4. Close the spreadsheet.

5. Make changes to the chart.
   a. In the chart area, delete the *Cost* chart title because it duplicates the slide title.
   b. Click **Style 3** [*Chart Tools Design* tab, *Chart Styles* group].
   c. Select **Chart Area** [*Chart Tools Format* tab, *Current Selection* group] and click the **Shape Fill** button [*Chart Tools Format* tab, *Shape Styles* group]; then select **No fill**.
   d. Select the **Series "Cost" Data Labels** [*Chart Tools Format* tab, *Current Selection* group] and increase the font size to **20 pts**. [*Home* tab].
   e. Select the **Legend** and increase the font size to **20 pts**. [*Home* tab].
   f. Move the legend to the upper right of the **Chart Area.**
   g. Select the **Plot Area** and increase the size of the plot area to make the pie larger (Figure 2-100).
   h. Select the single slice for "Trees—Ornamental" and explode that slice by dragging it down slightly.

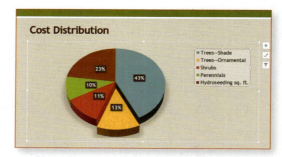

2-100 Slice exploded and legend repositioned

6. Create a clustered column chart.
   a. On slide 7, "Tree Size Cost Comparisons," click the **Insert Chart** button on the content placeholder.
   b. Click the **Clustered Column** layout and click **OK**.
   c. Replace the spreadsheet data with the following data:

	Small	Medium	Large
Legacy Sugar Maple	150	350	500
Willow Oak	200	375	500
Autumn Blaze Maple	150	350	500
Bradford Pear	95	125	150
White Dogwood	85	115	150
Dynamite Crape Myrtle	90	120	150

d. Close the spreadsheet. If you need to check the data, click the **Edit Data** button [*Chart Tools Design* tab, *Data* group].

e. Change the chart style to **Style 8** [*Chart Tools Design* tab, *Chart Styles* group] which has a dark fill for the chart area.

7. Click the **Chart Elements** button on the right side of the chart (Figure 2-101). Select the following: **Axes, Axis Titles, Data Table, Gridlines,** and **Legend**. The **Data Table** automatically appears below the columns.

a. Make adjustments to the following chart elements:

Axis Titles: Edit the *Primary Vertical (Y-axis)* rotated text by typing Tree Cost. Delete the *Primary Horizontal (X-axis) title* text below the data table.

Legend: Select the **Legend** and click **Format Selection** [*Chart Tools Format* tab, *Current Selection* group] to open the *Format Legend* pane. Deselect *Show the legend without overlapping the chart* and select the **Right Legend Position**. Move the legend to the right of the plot area.

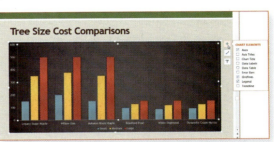

2-101 Clustered column chart with data table, axis title, and legend

b. Select each of the following chart elements and click **Shape Fill** [*Chart Tools Format* tab, *Shape Styles* group] to change the colors:

Chart Area: **Tan, Background 2, Darker 10%**
Plot Area: **Tan, Background 2**
Legend: **Tan, Background 2, Darker 10%**
Large Series: **Green, Accent 4, Darker 50%**
Medium Series: **Green, Accent 4**
Small Series: **Green, Accent 4, Lighter 40%**

c. Make all text **black**. Increase the font size on the axis title and legend to **20 pts**. Increase the table text and axis number to **18 pts**. The completed slide is shown in Figure 2-102.

2-102 Column fill colors changed

8. Create another clustered column chart.

a. On slide 8, "Growth Potential" click **Chart** [*Insert* tab, *Illustrations* group] because this slide does not have a content placeholder.

b. Click the **Clustered Column** layout and click **OK** to close the dialog box.

c. Replace the spreadsheet data with the following data:

	Height
Legacy Sugar Maple	80
Willow Oak	60
Autumn Blaze Maple	50
Bradford Pear	95
White Dogwood	20
Dynamite Crape Myrtle	20

d. This data is in one data series, so delete the extra columns in the spreadsheet. Be sure you delete the entire spreadsheet columns so the PowerPoint chart columns can expand in the available space (Figure 2-102). An empty column in the spreadsheet creates too much blank space between columns in the PowerPoint chart.

e. Select spreadsheet **Column C** and **Column D** headings and the entire columns are selected.

f. Right-click, then click **Delete**, and the columns appear blank.

g. Check to be sure the data is correctly selected and adjust borders if necessary.

h. Close the spreadsheet.

i. The chart area is smaller than in the previous chart because you inserted the chart directly on the slide rather than inserting it through a content placeholder that is in a larger size.

9. Make changes to the chart.

a. Increase the chart area to a width of **10"** and height of **5.5"** [*Chart Tools Format* tab, *Size* group] and position it evenly on the slide (Figure 2-103).

b. Delete the chart title and the legend.

c. Click the **More** button [*Chart Tools Design* tab, *Chart Styles* group] and change the chart style to **Style 14**.

d. Select the columns and change the color to **Green**, **Accent 4**.

e. Make the text **black** and increase the font size.

- *Vertical (Value) Axis:* **bold** and **20 pts**.
- *Horizontal (Category) Axis:* **bold** and **18 pts**.

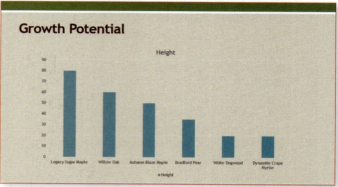

2-103 Column chart as it first appears

10. Select the *Chart Area* and apply a picture fill.

a. Click the **Shape Fill** button [*Chart Tools Format* tab, *Shape Styles* group] and select **Picture** to open the *Insert Pictures* dialog box.

b. In the *Office.com* search box, enter the search word tree and click **Search**.

c. On the *Insert Pictures* dialog box, scroll down the gallery to locate the picture of "Trees with the leaves changing color for autumn" (Figure 2-104) and click **Insert**.

d. If the *Format Chart Area* pane is not open, double-click the picture. Change the *Transparency* percentage to **60%**.

e. Close the *Format Chart Area* pane.

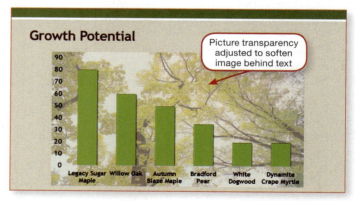

2-104 Chart resized, colors changed, and picture fill

11. Click the **Transitions** tab, apply the **Wipe** transition to all slides, and change the *Effect Options* to **From Left**.

12. Save and close your presentation.

Chapter Summary

2.1 Work with shapes, select theme colors and standard colors, and apply styles (p. P2-67).

- Change shape size by entering exact height and width sizes or by dragging sizing handles.
- Use **Lock Drawing Mode** to draw the same shape multiple times.
- Use **text boxes** to position text anywhere on a slide.
- PowerPoint's various **Styles** galleries provide collections of preset effects for shapes, pictures, or other objects.
- When you apply **Theme Colors** to shapes, the colors change when a different theme is applied.
- **Standard** colors do not change when a different theme is applied.
- Highly **saturated** colors are intense and vibrant; colors that are not saturated are muddy and dull.
- **Luminosity** is a measure of lightness that is adjusted by the amount of white or black in the color.
- Computer screens use the **RGB** color model that displays colors by blending values for *red, green,* and *blue.*
- The **Eyedropper** is used to match any color on your computer screen.

2.2 Create interesting and eye-catching text effects with *WordArt* (p. P2-75).

- The **WordArt Styles** gallery shows a collection of preset **Text Effects**.
- The **Transform** effect makes text warp into different shapes or follow a path.
- You can fill *WordArt* with solid or gradient colors, textures, patterns, or pictures.
- **Line Weight** is the line thickness measured in points.
- **Dashes** show lines with a combination of dots and dashes.
- Use the **Line Style** option on the **Format Shape** dialog box to customize line styles.

2.3 Search for pictures and illustrations, modify picture appearance, and compress picture file size (p. P2-78).

- Use the **Insert Pictures** dialog box to search for online pictures and illustrations.
- The **Picture Styles** gallery shows a collection of preset **Picture Effects**.

- To remove a picture style, click the **Reset Picture** button.
- **Cropping** trims unwanted areas of a selected picture.
- Increase **Color Saturation** to make picture colors more vibrant; decrease color saturation to make picture colors more muted.
- **Color Tone** changes a picture's cool or warm tones.
- Select **Color** and then **Recolor** to change a picture's color to a monotone color.
- The **Set Transparent Color** feature can make one color in a picture transparent. This feature works well to remove white backgrounds.
- **Compressing** pictures reduces the file size of your presentation.

2.4 Organize information in a grid format using tables and customize the arrangement of columns and rows (p. P2-85).

- You can insert and delete table **columns** and **rows**.
- Table **cells** can be **merged** or **split** to create multiple cells.
- **Column width** usually varies based on content; **row height** is usually a consistent size.

2.5 Emphasize portions of a table by applying styles, colors, and effects (p. P2-90).

- You can apply **WordArt Styles** to table text.
- **Table Styles** provide options for a table's design using theme accent colors.
- **Table Style Options** control how columns and rows are emphasized to feature areas of the table.
- **Border lines** or **shading** can separate cells.
- Horizontal cell alignment options include **Align Text Left**, **Center**, or **Align Text Right**; vertical cell alignment options include **Align Top**, **Center Vertically**, or **Align Bottom**.

2.6 Show processes and relationships with *SmartArt* graphics (p. P2-94).

- Use **SmartArt graphics** to create diagrams that illustrate concepts such as processes, cycles, or relationships.
- **SmartArt layouts** are organized by categories.
- Each layout includes information about how you can use it or the meaning it conveys.

- Type text directly in each *SmartArt* shape or type in the *Text Pane.*
- Change bulleted text to a *SmartArt* graphic by clicking the **Convert to SmartArt Graphic** button.

2.7 Improve the appearance of *SmartArt* graphics by applying styles, colors, and effects (p. P2-97).

- *SmartArt Styles* provide a gallery of effect options.
- The **Change Colors** button provides a gallery of color options arranged in categories.
- The *Add Shapes* button inserts shapes in relation to the selected shape.
- You can format or individually resize shapes within a *SmartArt* graphic.

2.8 Create charts that show relationships between data values and emphasize data in different ways (p. P2-101).

- Charts in PowerPoint are linked to spreadsheets in Excel; therefore, changes made to data in the worksheet automatically appear in the chart that represents the data.

- A group of data values is a *data series.*
- *Chart Layouts* are arranged in categories including **Column**, **Line**, **Pie**, **Bar**, and **Area**.
- The *Chart Area* displays the entire chart including all **Chart Elements**.
- The *Plot Area* provides a background for *Data Markers*, the columns, bars, or slices that represent data.

2.9 Enhance a chart by applying preset styles or manually customizing individual chart elements (p. P2-105).

- *Chart Styles* provide a gallery of preset effects for chart elements.
- The *legend* is a key that identifies each data series by color.
- The *Change Colors* button provides a gallery of colorful or monochromatic colors for chart elements.
- You can customize chart elements individually to enhance their appearance.
- To emphasize a pie slice, you can **explode** it by separating the slice from the rest of the pie chart.

Check for Understanding

In the *Online Learning Center* for this text (www.mhhe.com/office2013inpractice), there are a variety of resources that can be used to review the concepts covered in this chapter.

The following Online Learning Resources are available in the Online Learning Center:

- Multiple choice questions
- Short answer questions
- Matching exercises

Guided Project 2-1

Guest satisfaction has always been important to the success of Paradise Lakes Resort (PLR) in Minnesota. The general manager plans to use feedback from social media to identify problems and to guide improvements at the resort. In this project you illustrate a presentation the general manager will use to explain these concepts to employees at BLR.
[Student Learning Outcomes 2.1, 2.2, 2.3, 2.6, 2.7]

File Needed: *SocialMedia-02.pptx*
Completed Project File Name: *[your initials] PowerPoint 2-1.pptx*

Skills Covered in This Project

- Insert an online picture.
- Apply a picture style.
- Adjust size dimensions.
- Apply text effects.

- Insert a text box.
- Create a *SmartArt* graphic.
- Apply a *SmartArt* style and effects.

1. Open the presentation *SocialMedia-02*. This design theme shows slide titles at the bottom of all slides except the title slide.

2. Save the presentation as *[your initials] PowerPoint 2-1*.

3. On slide 1, search online for a picture.
   a. Click the **Insert** tab.
   b. Click the **Online Pictures** button to open the *Insert Pictures* dialog box.
   c. In the *Office.com* search box, type the word lake and click **Search**.
   d. Locate the picture showing two chairs on a deck facing the lake (Figure 2-105) and click **Insert**.
   e. Apply the **Metal Oval** picture style [*Picture Tools Format* tab, *Picture Styles* group].
   f. Resize the picture width to **6"** and the height automatically adjusts.
   g. Position the picture on the lower left.

2-105 Title slide

4. On slide 1, adjust the title text to complement the wood decking shown in the picture.
   a. Increase the font size to **60 pts**.
   b. Adjust the placeholder so it fits the text and move it up slightly.
   c. Click the **Text Fill** button [*Drawing Tools Format* tab, *WordArt Styles* group], select **Texture**, and select **Medium Wood**.

d. Click the **Text Effects** button, select **Shadow**, and select **Shadow Options**. The *Format Shape* pane opens.

e. Change the following settings:
Transparency: **20%**
Blur: **5 pt**.
Angle: **50°**
Distance: **3 pt**.

f. Close the *Format Shape* pane.

5. On slide 1, make the subtitle **bold** and increase the font size to **32 pts**. Adjust the placeholder size so it fits the text and move it down.

6. After slide 2, insert a new slide with a *Title and Content* layout.

7. On slide 3, add text and a shape.
   a. Type the slide title Why Social Media?
   b. Type the following bulleted text:

   Revenue
   Market Share
   Guest Satisfaction
   Guest Loyalty

2-106 Slide 3 with a shape

   c. Resize the bulleted list placeholder so it fits the text and move the text to the right (Figure 2-106).
   d. To show that each item in the list is increasing, click the **Shape** button [*Insert* tab, *Illustrations* group] and select the *Up Arrow* shape.
   e. Draw an arrow (height **3.5"** and width **2.5"**); then position the arrow to the left of the text.
   f. With the arrow selected, click the **More** button [*Drawing Tools Format* tab, *Shape Styles* group] and apply the **Intense Effect, Orange, Accent 1**.

8. After slide 4, insert a new slide with a *Blank* layout.

9. On slide 5, create a *SmartArt* graphic using a cycle layout and insert an additional shape.
   a. Click the **Insert** tab.
   b. Click the **SmartArt** button and select the **Cycle** type.
   c. Select the **Continuous Cycle** layout and click **OK**.
   d. Add the following text to each shape starting with the top shape and continuing in a clockwise direction around the circle:

   More Rentals
   Rentals
   Social Media Comments
   Improvements
   Better Social Media Comments

   e. With the Better Social Media Comments shape selected, click the **Add Shape** list arrow [*SmartArt Tools Design* tab, *Create Graphic* group] and select **Add Shape After**.
   f. In the new shape, type Higher Ratings.
   g. Click the **Intense Effect** style [*SmartArt Tools Design* tab, *SmartArt Styles* group].

h. Select all the shapes, change the font size to **20 pts.**, and apply **bold**.

i. With all the shapes selected, resize the shapes horizontally so the word "Improvements" fits on one line (Figure 2-107).

10. Insert a text box.

   a. Click the **Text Box** button [*Insert* tab, *Text* group] and click inside the cycle diagram.

   b. Type the following text on two lines:

   With the help of NewMediaMarketing.com

   c. Change the font size to **20 pts**. and center the text.

   d. Adjust the text box size, if necessary.

2-107 Slide 4 with *SmartArt graphic and effects added*

11. Click the **Reveal** button [*Transitions* tab, *Transition to This Slide* group] and then click **Apply To All**.

12. Save and close the presentation (Figure 2-108).

2-108 PowerPoint 2-1 completed

Guided Project 2-2

In this project, you prepare a presentation with key points essential to maintain a healthy lifestyle and show examples of weight loss calorie requirements for men and women at different ages. The doctors at Courtyard Medical Plaza will use this presentation to encourage clients to be more active.
[Student Learning Outcomes 2.1, 2.2, 2.3, 2.4, 2.5, 2.6, 2.7]

File Needed: *StayingActive-02.pptx*
Completed Project File Name: *[your initials] PowerPoint 2-2.pptx*

Skills Covered in This Project

- Apply text effects.
- Create a *SmartArt* graphic.
- Apply a *SmartArt* style and effects.
- Insert an online picture.
- Crop a picture.

- Apply a picture style.
- Adjust size dimensions.
- Insert a text box.
- Insert and format a table.

1. Open the presentation **StayingActive-02**.

2. Save the presentation as **[your initials] PowerPoint 2-2**.

3. On slide 1, select the title text and make these changes using the *Drawing Tools Format* tab, *WordArt Styles* group.
    a. Click the **Text Effects** button, click **Transform**, and select **Square**. Text fills the title placeholder.
    b. Click the **Text Fill** button, select **Texture**, and click **More Textures** to open the *Format Shape* pane.
    c. Select **Pattern fill** and change the *Background Color* to **Teal**, **Accent 6**.
    d. Select the **Large checker board** pattern.
    e. Click the **Text Outline** button and change the color to **Black, Background 1**.
    f. Click the **Text Effects** button and select **Glow**. Select **Glow Options** to open the *Format Shape* pane.
    g. For *Glow,* change the *Color* to **Green, Accent 1, Lighter 60%**; the *Size* to **10 pt**.; and the *Transparency* to **20%** (Figure 2-109).
    h. Close the *Format Shape* pane.

2-109 *Text Effects* for presentation title

4. On slide 2, insert a *SmartArt* graphic and modify the style using the *SmartArt Tools Design* tab.
    a. Click the **SmartArt** button on the content placeholder.
    b. Select the **Hierarchy** type and the **Horizontal Hierarchy** layout. Click **OK** to close the dialog box.
    c. Delete the three shapes on the right.
    d. Click the **Text Pane** button on the left of the SmartArt frame.
    e. After the first bullet, type Keep Moving; then type the following items after the indented bullets:

    Moderate Intensity Activity
    Count Steps (Press **Enter** to add another bullet.)
    Combine Aerobic and Strengthening

    f. Close the *Text Pane*.

g. Apply the *Subtle Effect* style [*SmartArt Styles* group].
h. Click the **Change Colors** button and select **Colorful Range**, **Accent Colors 5 to 6** (Figure 2-110).

2-110 *SmartArt graphic* **with effects added**

5. On slide 3, search for a picture and apply a picture style.
   a. Click the **Online Pictures** button [*Insert* tab, *Images* group] to open *the Insert Pictures* dialog box.
   b. Search for a picture using *Office.com* and the search word **gardening**.
   c. Select the picture "Women smiling while gardening" and click **Insert**.
   d. Resize the picture (height **4.5"** and width will automatically change to the same size since this picture is square).
   e. Move the picture to the right of the slide.
   f. Apply the *Rotated White* picture style [*Picture Tools Format* tab, *Picture Styles* group].

6. On slide 5, repeat the process in step 5 to search for a picture using the search word walk.
   a. Select the picture "Family of four walking on the beach" and click **Insert**.
   b. Click the **Crop** button [*Picture Tools Format* tab, *Size* group] and crop the picture on the top and left to focus only on the family. Click **Crop** again to accept your change.
   c. Apply the same style to match the previous picture.
   d. Resize the picture (height **5"** and width will automatically change).
   e. Move the picture to the right of the slide.

7. After slide 6, insert a new slide with a *Title and Content* layout.

8. On slide 7, add text.
   a. Type the title text **Calorie Examples**.
   b. Insert a text box with the text **Gaining 5 pounds a year** and position it below the slide title. Apply **bold** and change the font size to **20 pts**.

9. On slide 7, insert a table, add text, and modify formatting.
   a. Click the **Table** button on the content placeholder and enter **6** columns and **5** rows on the *Insert Table* dialog box. Click **OK** to close the dialog box.
   b. Type the text shown in Figure 2-111 using a font size of **20 pts**.
   c. Resize the last column so the heading text fits on one line.

Shading reflects the same person at two ages

Age	Height	Weight	Maintain	Fat Loss	Extreme Fat Loss
20	5 ft 10 in	200	2,647	2,118	1,600
25	5 ft 10 in	225	2,769	2,215	1,800
30	6 ft 2 in	240	2,916	2,333	1,920
35	6 ft 2 in	265	3,038	2,430	2,120

2-111 **Table with formatting changes**

   d. Make the column width fit each column by double-clicking the border line between columns.
   e. Select all cells and change to **Center** alignment [*Table Tools Layout* tab, *Alignment* group].
   f. Change the *Pen Color* to **Black** and the *Pen Weight* to **1 pt**. [*Table Tools Design* tab, *Draw Borders* group].
   g. Click the **Borders** button, and select **All Borders** [*Table Tools Design* tab, *Table Styles* group].
   h. Select the top table row and change the *Text Fill* to **Black** [*Table Tools Design* tab, *WordArt Styles* group].
   i. Select the second and third rows and change the *Shading* to **Green**, **Accent 1**, **Lighter 80%** [*Table Tools Design* tab, *Table Styles* group].
   j. Select the fourth and fifth rows and change the *Shading* to **Green**, **Accent 1**, **Lighter 60%**.
   k. Move the table up slightly and center it on the slide.

10. On slide 7, duplicate the table and edit the text in the second table.
    a. Select the table and press **Ctrl+D** to duplicate it. Position the second table centered near the bottom of the slide.
    b. Edit the table content (Figure 2-112).

Age	Height	Weight	Maintain	Fat Loss	Extreme Fat Loss
20	5 ft 7 in	150	2,041	1,633	1,225
25	5 ft 7 in	175	2,163	1,730	1,400
30	5 ft 9 in	180	2,204	1,763	1,440
35	5 ft 9 in	205	2,325	1,860	1,640

2-112 Table with formatting changes

11. On slide 7, insert and format a shape to label table contents.
    a. Click the **Shapes** button [*Insert* tab, *Illustrations* group] and select the **Oval**. Draw an oval shape and adjust its size (height **0.9"** and width **2"**) [*Drawing Tools Format* tab, *Size* group].
    b. Type the word Female with **black** text and **bold**.
    c. Click the **Shape Outline** button [*Drawing Tools Format* tab, *Shape Styles* group] and change the outline color to **Teal, Accent 6**.
    d. Click the **Edit Shape** button [*Drawing Tools Format* tab, *Insert Shapes* group] and select **Change Shape**. Select **Explosion 1**.
    e. Position this shape at the left corner of the bottom table (Figure 2-113).

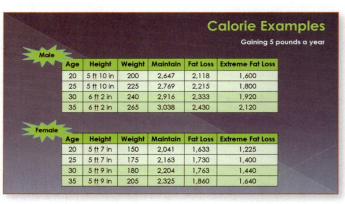

2-113 Slide 7 completed tables

12. Select the shape and press **Ctrl+D** to duplicate it.
    a. Position the second shape at the left corner of the top table.
    b. Change the text to Male.

13. After slide 7, insert a new slide with a *Title and Content* layout.

14. On slide 8, insert a table and add text.
    a. Type the title Make It Fun.
    b. Click the **Table** button on the content placeholder. Enter 2 columns and 8 rows and click **OK**.
    c. Type the following text:

Exercise Benefits	Motivation
Control weight	Enjoy the activities
Improve health	Keep it a priority
Boost immune system	Vary activities
Control appetite	Share with a friend
Feel more energetic	Enjoy companionship
Be more relaxed	Set realistic goals
Raise self-confidence	Reward yourself

15. On slide 8, make the following changes to the table:
    a. Select the table. If necessary, change the *Pen Color* to **Black** and the *Pen Weight* to **1 pt**. Click **All Borders**.
    b. Change the font size for all text to **20 pts**.
    c. Change the heading row text to **black**.

d. Select all cells and click the **Center Vertically** button [*Table Tools Layout* tab, *Alignment* group].

e. Change the table size (height **4.5"** and width **9"**) and center it horizontally on the slide.

16. Apply the **Cube** transition to all slides.

17. Save and close the presentation (Figure 2-114).

2-114 PowerPoint 2-2 completed

Guided Project 2-3

Solution Seekers, Inc., has been asked to develop a presentation for a meeting of personnel managers about salary trends for information technology workers. In the current economy, some jobs are paying less than they were a few years ago. For this project, you prepare tables and charts showing average salaries and salary changes for selected jobs.
[Student Learning Outcomes 2.1, 2.2, 2.3, 2.5, 2.6, 2.7, 2.8]

File Needed: *InfoTechSalaries-02.pptx*
Completed Project File Name: *[your initials] PowerPoint 2-3.pptx*

Skills Covered in This Project

- Convert text to a *SmartArt* graphic.
- Apply a *SmartArt* style and effects.
- Create a pie chart.
- Format a table.
- Create a column chart.

- Apply chart styles.
- Format chart elements.
- Insert *WordArt* and apply effects.
- Apply a picture style.
- Insert and align text boxes.

1. Open the presentation ***InfoTechSalaries-02***

2. Save the presentation as ***[your initials] PowerPoint 2-3***.

3. On slide 2, convert the bulleted text to a *SmartArt* graphic and modify the style and colors.
   a. Select the bulleted text and click the **Convert to SmartArt** button [*Home* tab, *Paragraph* group].
   b. Select **More SmartArt Graphics** to open the *Choose a SmartArt Graphic* dialog box.
   c. Select the **Relationship** type and the **Counterbalance Arrows** layout. Click **OK** to close the dialog box.
   d. Apply the **Cartoon** style [*SmartArt Tools Design* tab, *SmartArt Styles* group].
   e. Select the down arrow shape pointing to "Fewer Layoffs" and click the **Shape Fill** button list arrow [*SmartArt Tools Format* tab, *Shape Styles* group].
   f. Select **Gradient** and under *Dark Variations,* click **Linear Down** to emphasize the downward movement.
   g. Select the up arrow and repeat step f to apply a **Linear Up** gradient (Figure 2-115).

2-115 Slide 2 *SmartArt graphic* with color changes

4. After slide 2, insert a new slide with a *Title and Content* layout.

5. On slide 3, create a pie chart and modify it.
   a. Type the slide title **Employee Salary Satisfaction**.
   b. Click the **Chart** button in the content placeholder.
   c. Click the **Pie** chart type; then select the **3-D Pie**. Click **OK** to close the dialog box.
   d. Replace the spreadsheet data with the data shown in Figure 2-116. Close the spreadsheet.
   e. Drag the chart title to the top left of the chart area. Increase the font size to **24 pts**. [*Home* tab, *Font* group].
   f. Click the **Chart Elements** button on the right side of the slide and select **Legend**. Click **Right**.
   g. Increase the font size to **20 pts**. and drag the legend to the bottom right of the chart area.

	A	B
1		Satisfaction %
2	Very Satisfied	13
3	Somewhat Satisfied	36
4	Undecided	16
5	Somewhat Dissatisfied	24
6	Very Dissatisfied	11
7		

2-116 Spreadsheet linked to a chart

h. Click the **Chart Elements** button again and select **Data Labels**. Click **Inside End**.

i. Click the **Chart Elements** list box arrow and select **Series "Satisfaction%" Data Labels** [*Chart Tools Format* tab, *Current Selection* group]. Increase the font size to **24 pts.** and apply **bold** (Figure 2-117).

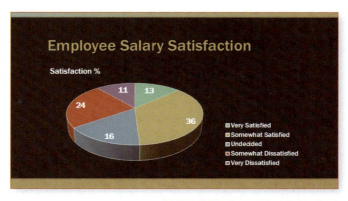

2-117 Slide 3 completed pie chart

6. On slide 4, modify table formatting.
a. Select the table. Increase the font size to **20 pts**.
b. Select **Header Row** and **Banded Rows** [*Table Tools Design* tab, *Table Style Options* group].
c. Apply the **Themed Style 1, Accent 2** style [*Table Tools Design* tab, *Table Styles* group].
d. Increase the table height to **4"** and click the **Center Vertically** button [*Table Tools Layout* tab].
e. Select columns 2–4 and change to **Right** alignment.

7. After slide 4, insert a new slide with a *Title and Content* layout.

8. On slide 5, create a column chart and modify it.
a. Type the title **Salary Change, Selected Jobs**.
b. Click the **Chart** button on the content placeholder.
c. Select the **3-D Clustered Column** and click **OK**.
d. Replace the spreadsheet data with the data shown in Figure 2-118. Select **Column D**, right-click, and select **Delete**. By removing the blank column, the chart displays correctly with no blank space. Close the spreadsheet.
e. Delete the chart title.
f. Click the **Chart Elements** button on the right side of the chart, select **Legend**, and then click **More Options** to open the *Format Legend* pane. Select **Top Right** and deselect **Show the legend without overlapping the chart**.
g. Click the **Shape Fill** button [*Table Tools Format* tab, *Shape Styles* group] and change the legend color to **Brown, Accent 2, Darker 50%**.
h. Click the chart frame to select the **Chart Area** and change the **Shape Fill** color to **Teal, Accent 1, Darker 50%**.
i. Select the **Legend** and increase the font size to **18 pts**. Repeat to increase the **Vertical (Value) Axis** font size to **18 pts**.
j. Select the **Horizontal (Category) Axis** and increase the font size to **20 pts**. (Figure 2-119).
k. On slide 6, apply the *Moderate Frame, Black* picture style [*Picture Tools Format* tab, *Picture Styles* group].

	A	B	C
1		2013	2014
2	Project Manager	101,256	104,897
3	Applications Developer	86,783	90,250
4	Security Analyst	79,498	82,663
5	Network Manager	61,245	62,871
6	Technical Support	53,387	52,296
7	Help Desk	41,854	41,532
8			

2-118 Spreadsheet linked to a chart

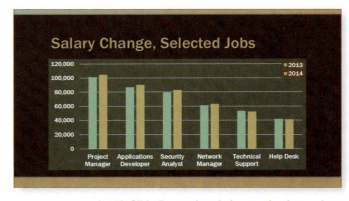

2-119 Slide 5 completed clustered column chart

9. On slide 6, insert *WordArt* text.

    a. Click the **WordArt** button [*Insert* tab, *Text* group] and select the **Fill - White, Text 1, Outline - Background 1, Hard Shadow - Background 1** style (Figure 2-120).

    b. Type the text **Employees Are Valuable** and move this text above the picture.

    c. Click the **Text Effects** button [*Drawing Tools Format* tab, *WordArt Styles* group], select **Shadow**, and click **Offset Diagonal Bottom Right**.

    d. Click the **Text Outline** button [*Drawing Tools Format* tab, *WordArt Styles* group] and select **Black, Background 2**.

    e. Deselect the *WordArt* text.

2-120 **Slide 6 picture style, text effects, and text boxes**

10. On slide 6, insert text boxes.

    a. Click the **Text Box** button [*Insert* tab, *Text* group] and type the first salary of **$74,270**. Change the font color to **black**, increase the font size to **20 pts**., and apply **bold**.

    b. Position this salary below the first person on the left of the picture.

    c. With the salary text box selected, press **Ctrl+D** and position the duplicated text box below the second person. Repeat for the remaining figures.

    d. Edit the text boxes to change the salaries to **$62,844**, **$54,340**, and **$48,982**.

    e. Select all of the salary text boxes and click the **Arrange** button [*Drawing Tools Format* tab, *Drawing* group]. Select **Align** and **Align Bottom** (Figure 2-120).

11. Apply the **Blinds** transition to all slides; then apply the **Zoom** transition to slide 6.

12. Save and close the presentation (Figure 2-121).

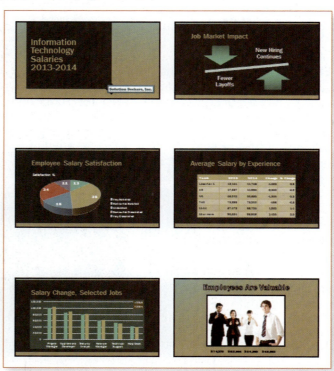

2-121 **PowerPoint 2-3 completed**

Independent Project 2-4

At Pool & Spa Oasis, sales associates must educate new spa owners about keeping spa water safe with proper maintenance. For this project, you prepare a presentation that emphasizes the routine to follow, explains pH level numbers, and lists available products that are typically used to balance water. [Student Learning Outcomes 2.1, 2.2, 2.3, 2.4, 2.5, 2.6, 2.7]

Files Needed: ***Balancing-02.pptx***
Completed Project File Name: ***[your initials] PowerPoint 2-4.pptx***

Skills Covered in This Project

- Insert *WordArt* and apply effects.
- Adjust size dimensions.
- Insert an online picture.
- Apply a picture style.
- Create a *SmartArt* graphic.

- Apply a *SmartArt* style and effects.
- Insert and format a table.
- Insert a text box.
- Change solid and gradient colors.

1. Open the presentation ***Balancing-02.***

2. Save the presentation as ***[your initials] PowerPoint 2-4.***

3. On slide 1, change the title text arrangement.
   a. Delete the title text "Balancing Act," but leave the word "The" as shown.
   b. Insert *WordArt* with the style **Fill – White, Outline – Accent 1**, **Glow – Accent 1**.
   c. Type Balancing Act.
   d. Click **Text Effects**, select **Shadow**, and **Offset Right**. Click **Shadow Options** to open the *Format Shape* pane and change the *Transparency* setting to **30%**.
   e. Change the *Character Spacing* to **Tight**.
   f. Apply the *Transform* text effect of **Cascade Up**.
   g. Increase the *WordArt* size to height **3"** and width **9"** and position as shown in Figure 2-122.
   h. Close the *Format Shape* pane.

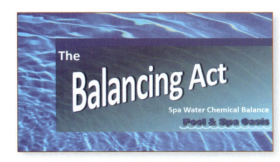

2-122 Slide 1 with *WordArt*

4. On slide 2, the bulleted list placeholder has a fill color so it cannot be resized without distorting the slide. Adjust text spacing and insert a picture.
   a. On the last bulleted item, place your insertion point in front of the word "such" and press **Shift+Enter**.
   b. Search on *Office.com* using the search word swim and insert the picture "Young woman in swimming pool."
   c. Resize the picture (height **5.5"** and the width will automatically change to **3.71"**).
   d. Apply the **Bevel Rectangle** picture style.
   e. Position the picture as shown in Figure 2-123.

2-123 Slide 2 with inserted picture and picture style

5. On slide 4, insert a *SmartArt* graphic, add text, and change formatting.
   a. Insert a *SmartArt* graphic from the *Process* category with the **Continuous Block Process layout**.
   b. In the three shapes, type Test Water, Add Necessary Products, and Enjoy!
   c. Resize the *SmartArt* graphic (height **5"** and width **9.5"**).
   d. Apply the **Polished** SmartArt style.
   e. Select the arrow and apply **Gradient** colors. Select **More Gradient** to open the *Format Shape* pane. Select a **Linear** type and **Linear Right** direction and three gradient stops.

   First stop: Position **0%**, **Light Turquoise, Background 2, Darker 50%**
   Second stop: Position **40%**, **Light Turquoise, Background 2, Darker 10%**
   Third stop: Position **100%**, **Light Turquoise, Background 2**

   f. Close the *Format Shape* pane.
   g. Apply **bold** to all *SmartArt* text (Figure 2-124).

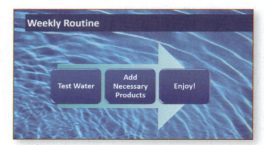

2-124 Slide 4 *SmartArt graphic* with style and color changes

6. On slide 5, insert a table, add text, and change formatting.
   a. Insert a table with 3 columns and 4 rows.
   b. Select **Header Row** and **Banded Rows**.
   c. Type the following text:

Level	Numbers	Results
High	8.0	Scale, Alkaline
Good	7.2 – 7.6	Ideal pH Range
Low	6.0	Corrosion, Acidic

   d. Change the font size to **20 pts**. for all table text.
   e. Apply the **Themed Style 1, Accent 1** table style.
   f. Select each column and adjust the cell width as follows: left column is **1.5"**, middle column is **2.75"**, and right column is **2.75"**.
   g. Change the alignment on the middle column to **Center**.
   h. Center the table on the slide.

7. On slide 5, insert a text box below the table.
   a. Type Drain and replace spa water every 60-90 days.
   b. Change the font size to **20 pts**.
   c. Change the shape fill to **Turquoise, Accent 3, Lighter 40%**.
   d. Resize the text box, if necessary, to fit the text and position it below the table aligned with the right of the table.

8. Copy the table on slide 5.

9. On slide 6, paste the table and make revisions.
   a. Delete the middle column and make the table **9"** wide.
   b. Delete the table text and add three rows.
   c. Type the following text:

Products	Purpose
Sanitizer	Type needed depends on sanitizer system
Test Strips	Measures chemical levels
Shock Treatment	Breaks down organic or unfiltered material
Total Alkalinity	Increases or decreases to balance pH levels
Calcium Increaser	Balances dissolved calcium
Stain and Scale Prevention	Removes metallic impurities

d. Adjust the column width as needed to avoid word wrapping.

e. Center the table on the slide.

10. Apply the **Ripple** transition with the **From Top-Left** effect option to all slides.

11. Save and close the presentation (Figure 2-125).

2-125 PowerPoint 2-4 completed

Independent Project 2-5

Prospective home buyers need to understand mortgage requirements and how to prepare to apply for a mortgage. Angie O'Connor at Placer Hills Real Estate frequently discusses these issues with clients, so she wants to use a presentation on her notebook computer to help guide her discussions with clients. For this project, you develop the presentation.

[Student Learning Outcomes 2.1, 2.3, 2.4, 2.5, 2.6, 2.7, 2.8]

File Needed: ***PreparetoBuy-02.pptx***
Completed Project File Name: *[your initials] **PowerPoint 2-5.pptx***

Skills Covered in This Project

- Insert an online picture.
- Crop a picture.
- Apply a picture style.
- Adjust size dimensions.
- Insert a chart and edit data.
- Apply chart styles.

- Format chart elements.
- Insert text boxes.
- Insert and format a table.
- Convert text to a *SmartArt* graphic.
- Apply a *SmartArt* style and effects.

1. Open the presentation ***PreparetoBuy-02*** that has a Standard size (4:3 aspect ratio). The slide size is 10" x 7.5" compared to the slide size of 13.333" x 7.5" for the Widescreen (16:9 aspect ratio).

2. Save the presentation as *[your initials]* ***PowerPoint 2-5***.

3. On slide 1, search at *Office.com* for the picture shown in Figure 2-126 using the search word home.
   a. Insert the picture and crop it slightly on the left to remove part of the sky.
   b. Resize the picture so it is **3"** wide and the height remains in proportion.
   c. Apply the **Moderate Frame, Black** picture style.
   d. Align the picture on the right side of the slide. The black frame portion extends beyond the slide on the right.

2-126 Slide 1 with inserted picture and picture style

4. On slide 4, insert a chart showing how fixed mortgage rates have changed over time.
   a. Click the **Line** chart type; then select the **Line with Markers** chart layout. Click **OK**.
   b. Replace the spreadsheet data with the data shown in Figure 2-127.
      - Increase the selection area to include *row 10* to avoid error messages.
      - Delete *Column D* so the corresponding chart area is correct with no blank space.
      - Close the spreadsheet.

5. The chart now shows accurate information, but it is difficult to distinguish the data series lines from the gridlines in the background. The data markers that reflect the value of each number can barely be seen (Figure 2-128). The following changes will make the chart easier to interpret.

	A	B	C	
1		Rate	Points	Co
2	1974	9.19	1.2	
3	1979	11.2	1.6	
4	1984	13.88	2.5	
5	1989	10.32	2.1	
6	1994	8.38	1.8	
7	1999	7.44	1	
8	2004	5.84	0.7	
9	2009	5.04	0.7	
10	2014	3.95	0.8	
11				

2-127 Spreadsheet linked to a chart

6. Delete the chart title.

7. Change the chart area *Shape Fill* to **Blue-Gray**, **Accent 5**, **Darker 25%**.

8. Select the "Rate" series line, right-click, and select **Format Data Series** to open the *Format Data Series* pane (Figure 2-129).

   a. Click the **Fill & Line** tab at the top of the pane. Select *Line* options and make one change:
      - *Width:* **3 pt**.

   b. Select *Marker* options and make changes so the marker on the selected series line is more noticeable. Click the option name to access the choices for each option.
      - *Marker Options:* **Built-in**, *Type* **Square**, *Size* **15** (Figure 2-130)
      - *Fill:* **Solid fill**, **Color Dark Red**, **Accent 1**, **Lighter 40%**

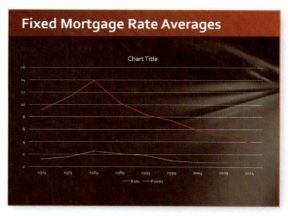

2-128 Line chart as it first appears

9. Select the "Points" series line and make the following similar changes:

   a. For *Line* options, make two changes:
      - *Line Color:* **Solid line**, **Brown**, **Accent 3**
      - *Line Style:* **Width**, **3 pt**

   b. Click the **Marker** button and make two changes:
      - *Marker Options:* **Built-in** *Type* **Diamond**, *Size* **20**
      - *Marker Fill:* **Solid fill**. **Brown**, **Accent 3**, **Lighter 40%**

2-129 *Format Data Series* pane

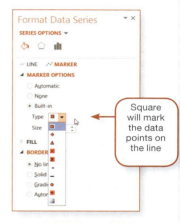

2-130 *Format Data Series* pane with *Marker* options

10. Close the *Format Data Series* pane.

11. Increase the font size to **16 pts**. and make the text **bold** for the *Horizontal (Category) axis* and the *Vertical (Value) axis*.

12. Move the chart area up slightly to make room for a source notation at the bottom of the slide.

   a. Insert a text box and type the following:

      Information based on Freddie Mac survey data
      http://www.freddiemac.com/pmms

   b. Position the text box as displayed in Figure 2-131.

13. On slide 5, insert a table with 5 columns and 3 rows. Make the following changes:

   a. Type the text shown in Figure 2-132.
   b. Select columns 2–4 and change to **Center** alignment.
   c. In the first row, change to **Bottom** alignment and change the row *Shading* to **Dark Red, Accent 1**.
   d. Align the table in the horizontal and vertical center on the slide.

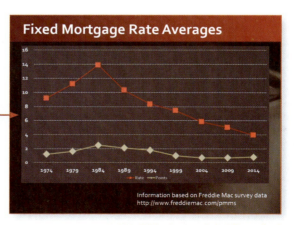

2-131 Slide 4 completed line chart

14. Insert a text box above the table.
    a. Type $250,000.
    b. Change the font to **40 pts**. and **bold**.

15. Insert a text box below the table.
    a. Type the following text on three lines:

    Lender rates are influenced by credit scores.
    Plan for a 20% down payment to avoid cost of points.
    Add taxes and insurance premiums.

    b. Position the text boxes as shown in Figure 2-132.

2-132 Slide 5 table with text
boxes added

16. On slide 6, convert the list to a *SmartArt* graphic.
    a. Select the bulleted text and convert it to the **Vertical Curved List** *SmartArt* layout.
    b. Resize the *SmartArt* frame on the right so it fits the longest line of text.

17. Make the following changes to the *SmartArt* graphic:
    a. Change the colors to **Colorful Range, Accent 4 to 5**.
    b. Apply the **Moderate Effect SmartArt** style.
    c. Select all of the white circles and change the *Shape Fill* to **Dark Red, Accent 1** and apply the *Bevel* effect of **Cool Slant**.
    d. Center the *SmartArt* graphic on the slide (Figure 2-133).

2-133 Slide 6 SmartArt graphic
with style and effects changed

18. Apply the **Shape** transition with the **Out** effect option to all slides.

19. Save and close the presentation (Figure 2-134).

2-134 PowerPoint 2-5 completed

Independent Project 2-6

Kathy Sung, Director of Services at Life's Animal Shelter (LAS), will talk to a luncheon group of businesspeople to explain the important work of LAS and to solicit financial support. For this project you develop the presentation she will use to explain the needs of LAS and describe ways people can contribute through donations or by volunteering their time.

[Student Learning Outcomes 2.1, 2.2, 2.3, 2.4, 2.5, 2.6, 2.7]

Files Needed: *YouCanHelp-02.pptx, CountryStroll-02.jpg, DayCare-02.jpg, Food-02.jpg, Groom-02.jpg,* **and** *RoyalTreatment-02.jpg*
Completed Project File Name: *[your initials] PowerPoint 2-6.pptx*

Skills Covered in This Project

- Insert an online picture.
- Apply text effects.
- Apply a picture style.
- Set transparent color.
- Recolor a picture.
- Adjust size dimensions.

- Insert a text box.
- Insert and format a table.
- Convert text to a *SmartArt* graphic.
- Create a *SmartArt* graphic with pictures.
- Apply a *SmartArt* style and effects.

1. Open the presentation *YouCanHelp-02*.

2. Save the presentation as *[your initials] PowerPoint 2-6*.

3. On slide 1, change the title text fill to **Dark Red**, **Accent 1**, **Darker 25%**. Apply the *Bevel* text effect of **Angle**.

4. Change the font size to **80 pts**. and resize the placeholder on the right so one word is on each line.

5. Use the *Insert Pictures* dialog box to search for three pictures from Office.com and insert them on slides. Type the search word dog.
   a. On slide 1, add the picture of a German Shepherd dog with a white background.
   b. On slide 2, add the picture of three boys with a dog on grass.
   c. On slide 3, add the picture of a Golden Retriever dog with a white background.

6. On slide 1, adjust the picture.
   a. Increase the picture size (height **5.9"** and width **4.7"**).
   b. Use *Set Transparent Color* to remove the white area in the picture.
   c. Position the dog picture as shown in Figure 2-135.

7. On slide 2, adjust the picture.
   a. Decrease the picture size (height **5.84"** and width **8"**).
   b. Apply the *Moderate Frame, Black* picture style.
   c. Center the picture horizontally and position it near the top of the slide.

2-135 Slide 1 with picture added, white background removed

8. Insert a text box below the picture and type the following text on two lines:

Our operating funds come through donations and pet adoption fees.

   a. Change the text to **White** and font size to **20 pts**.
   b. Change the *Shape Outline* to **White** and the *Weight* to **3 pts**.
   c. Change the *Shape Fill* to **Black**.
   d. Center the text box horizontally below the picture (Figure 2-136).

9. On slide 3, adjust the picture.
   a. Use *Set Transparent Color* to remove the white area in the picture.
   b. Increase the picture size (height **5.23"** and width **6"**).
   c. Position the picture as shown in Figure 2-137.

10. Select the slide 2 thumbnail and press **Ctrl+C** to copy it.
   a. Put your insertion point after slide 3 and press **Ctrl+V** to paste the copied slide.

11. Make changes to the new slide 4.
   a. In the text box, replace the text with the words **We Need Your Help!**
   b. Resize the text box to fit the text and center it horizontally under the picture.
   c. Select the picture and click the **Color** button.
   d. In the *Recolor* group click the **Orange, Accent color 2, Dark** option (Figure 2-138).

12. On slide 5, convert the list to a *Vertical Bullet List SmartArt* graphic.
   a. Increase the *SmartArt* frame height to **4.7"** so the text size increases.
   b. Reduce the width to **9"**).
   c. Center the *SmartArt* horizontally.
   d. Apply the **Cartoon** *SmartArt* style as displayed in Figure 2-139.

13. On slide 6, convert the list to a **Picture Lineup** *SmartArt* graphic. Click the **Picture** icon on each shape to open the *Insert Pictures* dialog box. Browse to locate your student files and insert the following pictures going from left to right (Figure 2-140):

1	*DayCare-02*
2	*CountryStroll-02*
3	*RoyalTreatment-02*
4	*Food-02*
5	*Groom-02*

Each picture is automatically resized to fit the SmartArt shape where it is inserted.

2-136 Slide 2 with picture and text box

2-137 Slide 3 with picture added, white background removed

2-138 Slide 4 with picture recolored

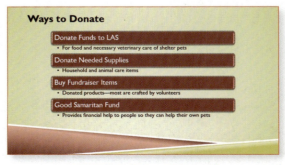

2-139 Slide 5 *SmartArt* graphic converted from bulleted text

14. After slide 6, insert a new slide with a *Title and Content* layout.
    a. Type the title Items We Need
    b. Insert a table with 3 columns and 5 rows.
    c. Type the table text shown in Figure 2-141.
    d. Increase the font size to **20 pts**.
    e. Adjust column width so each column fits the longest line of text.
    f. Center the table on the slide.

15. Apply the *Gallery* transition to all slides.

16. Save and close the presentation (Figure 2-142).

2-140 Slide 6 *SmartArt* graphic picture layout

Cleaning	Paper Products and Bedding	Dog and Cat Play
Bleach	Paper Towels	Dog and Cat Treats
Pine Sol	Paper Plates	Chewies
Mop Heads	Plastic Containers with Lids	Collars
Towels	Blankets	Leashes

2-141 Table text

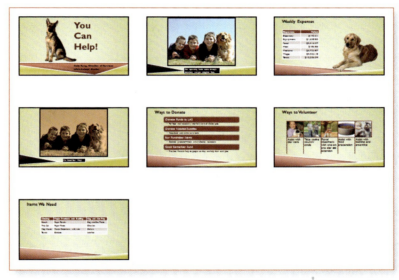

2-142 PowerPoint 2-6 completed

Improve It Project 2-7

The Hamilton Civic Center needs a presentation to explain benefits of yoga and encourage members to join yoga classes. In this project you revise a presentation to give it a cohesive look and illustrate it with pictures, a *SmartArt* graphic, and a table. You apply various styles and effects for a contemporary appearance.
[Student Learning Outcomes 2.2, 2.3, 2.4, 2.5, 2.6, 2.7]

File Needed: ***Yoga-02.pptx***
Completed Project File Name: ***[your initials] PowerPoint 2-7.pptx***

Skills Covered in This Project

- Apply text effects.
- Insert an online picture.
- Apply a picture style.
- Reposition slide objects.

- Convert text to a *SmartArt* graphic.
- Apply a *SmartArt* style and effects.
- Format a table.
- Compress pictures.

---

1. Open the presentation **Yoga-02** that has a Standard size (4:3 aspect ratio). The slide size is 10" x 7.5" compared to the slide size of 13.333" x 7.5" for the Widescreen (16:9 aspect ratio).

2. Save the presentation as *[your initials]* **PowerPoint 2-7**.

3. Make the title slide more dynamic.
   a. Search online at Office.com and insert a yoga picture.
   b. Apply a **Bevel Rectangle** picture style.
   c. Select the title placeholder; then click **Text Effects** from the *WordArt Styles* group. Select **Transform** and then select **Wave 1**.

2-143 **Title slide**

4. Recolor the logo.
   a. Select the logo and then click **Color**. Select the *Recolor* option **Blue**, **Accent color 5 Light** to replace the black with a color that will better match theme colors.
   b. Use *Set Transparent Color* to remove the white so your background color shows.
   c. Make the logo width **2.5"** and the height will automatically adjust.

5. Size and position title slide objects as shown in Figure 2-143.

6. On slide 3, change the listed text to a *SmartArt* graphic.
   a. Click the **Convert to SmartArt** button and select the **Vertical Block List**.
   b. Apply the **White Outline** *SmartArt* style.
   c. Click **Change Colors** and apply the **Colorful Range – Accent Colors 4 to 5** (Figure 2-144).

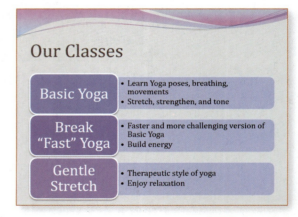

2-144 **SmartArt**

7. On slides 4 and 5, search online at *Office.com* for appropriate yoga pictures and insert them.
   a. Resize and position the pictures appropriately.
   b. With a picture selected, click **Compress Pictures**. Use document resolution, delete cropped areas of pictures, and apply compression to all pictures.

8. On slide 6, modify the table.
   a. Increase the font size to **20 pts**.
   b. Apply the **Medium Style 2 – Accent 4** table style.
   c. Select the title row, click **Cell Bevel,** and apply the **Riblet** effect.
   d. Add a **1 pt** border to all cells using the **Blue, Accent 4, Darker 50%** pen color (Figure 2-145).

9. Apply the **Dissolve** transition to all slides.

10. Save and close your presentation (Figure 2-146).

Classes	Days	Hours
Basic Yoga	Mon/Wed	4:15 – 5:15 p.m.
Break "Fast" Yoga	Tues/Thurs	7:00 – 8:10 a.m.
Gentle Stretch	Fri	10:00 – 11:30 a.m.

2-145 Slide 6 table

2-146 PowerPoint 2-7 completed

Challenge Project 2-8

For this project, do some online comparison shopping for items you would be likely to buy such as clothing, household products, or automotive supplies. Prepare slides describing the products and apply text effects to the slide titles. Prepare a chart that shows costs either for the same product at several stores or similar products at the same store.

[Student Learning Outcomes 2.1, 2.2, 2.3, 2.4, 2.5, 2.6, 2.7, 2.8]

File Needed: None
Completed Project File Name: **[your initials] PowerPoint 2-8.pptx**

Create a new presentation and save it as **[your initials] PowerPoint 2-8**. Modify your presentation according to the following guidelines:

- Select an appropriate theme and make color and font changes as needed for your topic.
- Prepare a title slide and product description slides.
- Search online for a related image and insert it on the title slide.
- Create a table summarizing some of your findings.
- Create two charts to compare specific items.

Challenge Project 2-9

Using data from the United States Department of Labor published online by the Bureau of Labor Statistics (http://www.bls.gov) prepare a presentation explaining some current trends in the labor force. For example, you could show unemployment rate comparisons from different regions or wage estimates for various occupations in different states.
Student Learning Outcomes 2.1, 2.2, 2.3, 2.4, 2.5, 2.6, 2.7, 2.8]

File Needed: None
Completed Project File Name: **[your initials] PowerPoint 2-9.pptx**

Create a new presentation and save it as **[your initials] PowerPoint 2-9**. Modify your presentation according to the following guidelines:

- Select an appropriate theme and make color and font changes as needed for your topic.
- Create a title slide using a *Transform* text effect.
- Include several bulleted slides describing current trends.
- Search for appropriate pictures, resize as needed, and apply a picture style to each one.
- Prepare a table showing salaries for several jobs in different locations or for data changing over time.
- Prepare a chart comparing employment statistics from your state or region.

Challenge Project 2-10

Using information from one of your favorite coffee or soft drink manufacturers, such as the information you can find at www.thecoca-colacompany.com or www.pepsico.com, prepare a presentation comparing different products. You could show the diversity of the product line or list promotional products with pricing. From financial information provided on the sites, you could feature total revenue, total profits, or other interesting performance data in your presentation.
[Student Learning Outcomes 2.1, 2.2, 2.3, 2.4, 2.5, 2.6, 2.7, 2.8]

File Needed: None
Completed Project File Name: *[your initials] PowerPoint 2-10.pptx*

Create a new presentation and save it as *[your initials] PowerPoint 2-10*. Modify your presentation according to the following guidelines:

- Select an appropriate theme and make color and font changes as needed for your topic.
- Create a distinctive title slide using *WordArt*.
- Search online for appropriate pictures and insert three or more.
- Adjust picture sizes and apply picture styles.
- Prepare slides listing key factors contributing to the company's growth.
- Prepare a *SmartArt* graphic illustrating a specific process or relationship from historical or operational information.
- Create a chart showing comparisons for data such as net revenue or operating profit.

Preparing for Delivery and Using a Slide Presentation

CHAPTER OVERVIEW

In this chapter you learn more methods to help you work with PowerPoint more efficiently and effectively. This chapter teaches you how to create new theme colors customized for your topic, apply animation so selected slide objects appear just at the right time in your presentation, and link to a video from a web site. You also explore PowerPoint's rehearsal features to help you perfect your delivery timing and techniques, project your presentation more effectively, and prepare a presentation to be self-running. Finally, you learn how to save a presentation so it can be distributed on a CD.

STUDENT LEARNING OUTCOMES (SLOs)

After completing this chapter, you will be able to:

SLO 3.1 Create custom theme and background colors (p. P3-139).

SLO 3.2 Apply animation to add interest and reinforce content (p. P3-147).

SLO 3.3 Link to an online video (p. P3-149).

SLO 3.4 Use rehearsal techniques to prepare for presentation delivery (p. P3-156).

SLO 3.5 Control display options for different screen sizes (p. P3-159).

SLO 3.6 Present effectively and professionally using projection equipment (p. P3-164).

SLO 3.7 Use annotation pens to highlight information and save presentation markings (p. P3-167).

SLO 3.8 Prepare a self-running presentation that loops (p. P3-170).

SLO 3.9 Use the *Package Presentation for CD* feature to prepare a slide show for display on other computers (p. P3-171).

CASE STUDY

Specialists at Solution Seekers, Inc., frequently present to both large and small groups as they work with clients to improve business performance. Davon Washington is creating a series of seminars for new hires to help them be more productive and professional. For this project, you work with Davon to finish the presentation he has developed about presentation planning.

Pause & Practice 3-1: Create custom theme and background colors. Add interest with animation and video.

Pause & Practice 3-2: Rehearse a presentation and prepare for a widescreen display.

Pause & Practice 3-3: Practice slide show delivery features.

Pause & Practice 3-4: Prepare a self-running presentation and package a presentation to a folder.

POWERPOINT

Creating Custom Theme and Backgrounds Colors

Themes create a unified appearance for your presentation. When you use themes effectively, the information you present on a topic is seen by your viewers as one "package" and not a collection of random slides. You may need to match specific colors in a company logo or a school's colors, so in this section you will prepare custom theme colors that create a unique palette and help you work more efficiently. Then you will explore different ways to apply pattern, gradient, and picture fills and consider some issues to keep in mind when applying these fills to slide backgrounds.

Custom Theme Colors

As you worked with shapes, colors, and styles in previous chapters, you saw how theme colors are arranged across the top of the *Theme Colors* gallery. Recall that various percentages of each color appear below the top row colors (Figure 3-1). This section takes a closer look at where PowerPoint automatically applies theme colors to various graphics you create.

Four sample slides are shown in Figure 3-2. These samples feature the *Facet* theme and the *Blue* color theme. The background for these slides is white (Background 1) with decorative shapes in Background 2, Text 2, and Accent 1 colors.

3-1 *Theme Colors* gallery

- **Slide 1:** The photograph has a border color of Text 2.
- **Slide 2:** The first row of circles shows background and text colors. The second row of circles shows Accent colors 1–6.
- **Slide 3:** The bullets and the *SmartArt* shapes are shown in the Accent 1 color.
- **Slide 4:** Accent 2 color variations are applied to the table; the chart shows Accent colors 1–6 based on the order data is entered on the spreadsheet.

Accent colors (Figure 3-3) appear from left to right in both the *Shape Styles* gallery and the *Table Styles* gallery (Figures 3-4 and 3-5). Other galleries show options in a similar way.

You can boost productivity by creating custom theme colors because the colors you choose are available to you in the galleries as you develop your slide show. When you save custom theme colors, the colors are also available to use again in another presentation. Keep the following guidelines in mind when you create custom theme colors:

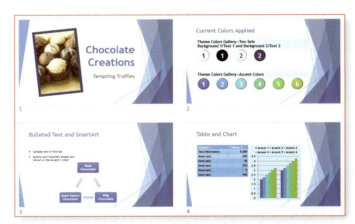

3-2 **Sample slides showing graphics with the *Facet* theme**

3-3 *Blue* **theme accent colors**

- Select your background color first and then select other colors that work well on the background.

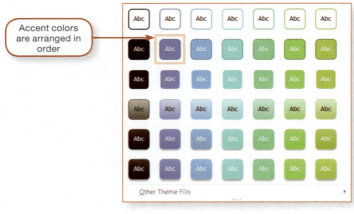

Accent colors are arranged in order

3-4 *Shapes Styles* gallery

All ▾

Best Match for Document

Light

Medium

Clear Table

3-5 *Table Styles* gallery

- Pick a text color that has a high contrast with your background color so words are easy to read.
- The Accent 1 theme color appears first when you draw shapes and is the first choice in galleries for table and *SmartArt* effects.

The following example illustrates how to change theme colors from the *Design* tab to a new set of colors that is more appropriate for a presentation about chocolate.

HOW TO: Create New Theme Colors

1. Start a new presentation using a design theme or open an existing presentation.

2. Click the **More** button [*Design* tab, *Variants* group].

3. Select **Colors** to open the list of built-in theme colors. The current theme colors are selected (Figure 3-6).

4. Select **Customize Colors** to open the *Create New Theme Colors* dialog box (Figure 3-7). For this example, the *Text/Background – Dark 1* (black) color does not change.

5. Change each color as needed to create your custom theme. This example has a brown and

Office | Current Office Theme Colors
Office
Office 2007 - 2010
Grayscale
Blue Warm
Blue
Blue II
Blue Green
Green
Green Yellow
Yellow
Yellow Orange
Orange
Orange Red
Red Orange
Red
Red Violet
Violet
Violet II
Median
Paper
Marquee
Slipstream
Aspect

Customize Colors...
Reset Slide Theme Colors

3-6 *Theme Colors* gallery

Create New Theme Colors

Theme colors

Text/Background - Dark 1
Text/Background - Light 1
Text/Background - Dark 2
Text/Background - Light 2
Accent 1
Accent 2
Accent 3
Accent 4
Accent 5
Accent 6
Hyperlink
Followed Hyperlink

Sample

Text   Text

Hyperlink   Hyperlink
Hyperlink   Hyperlink

Name: Custom 1

Reset   Save   Cancel

3-7 *Create New Theme Colors* dialog box showing *Blue* theme colors

yellow color palette that works for a presentation about chocolate (Figure 3-8).

- Click the **list arrow** on a color button to open the *Theme Colors* gallery.
- Click **More Colors** to open the *Colors* dialog box.
- Click the *Standard* or *Custom* tab, choose a color, and click **OK**.
- Repeat for each of the colors you want to change.

6. Name the new custom theme.

7. Click the **Save** button. The new custom theme is automatically applied and the name will appear in the *Custom* section of your list of available theme colors so you can use it again.

▶ ANOTHER WAY

Use the *Design* tab when you need to customize colors and fonts. When you also need to change background graphics or insert pictures such as a company logo, use the *Slide Master* tab to make all changes.

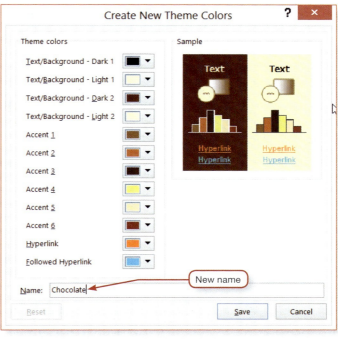

3-8 *Create New Theme Colors* dialog box showing custom colors

Figure 3.9 shows sample slides with the new colors. Controlling color this way is much more efficient than using an existing theme and having to select a custom color each time you create various illustrations. If any slide text, such as a slide title, retains the original colors, click the **Reset** button [*Home* tab, *Slides* group] to update the colors.

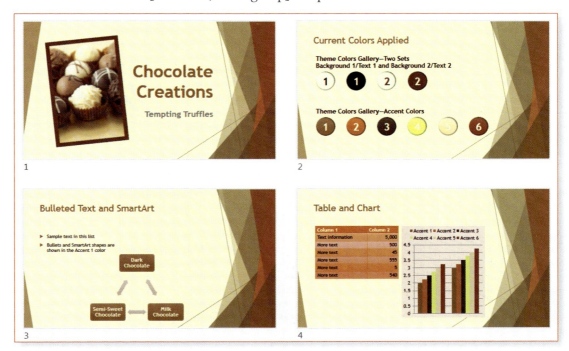

3-9 Chocolate theme colors applied to sample slides

Color combinations influence the tone of your presentation. Your options are endless, but you may want to consider a few of the following tonal effects:

- Varied and vibrant, or similar with subtle differences
- Soothing and tranquil, or lively and energetic
- Youthful or mature
- Historic or high tech

When you think about colors for your topic, consider your audience and be respectful of cultural differences. People tend to assign meaning to colors based on their cultural background and life experiences. A few examples of colors that have symbolic meaning include the following:

- *White:* Purity and cleanliness in the American culture, death in some other cultures
- *Red:* Health (red blood) in the medical field, loss (negative values) in the financial field
- *Green:* Sickness (infection) in the medical field, wealth (money) in the financial field

> **MORE INFO**
>
> To examine this concept further, look online for information about color meaning, symbolism, or the psychology of color.

Custom Background Colors

The *Format Background* pane has options similar to those you have used on the *Format Shape* pane (*See SLO 2.1: Working with Shapes, Colors, and Styles*). When you change background colors, text colors do not change. Also, the position of placeholders or the graphic shapes that are included on some design themes do not change.

When you choose colors and creative effects for backgrounds, remember that your color choices will fill the entire slide area behind everything else you design on a slide. These changes are visible throughout the presentation if you apply them to all slides, so you should examine your changes at full screen size to be sure you are satisfied with the results.

You need to consider how your background affects text, too. If a theme or template has graphic shapes included in a background, then a solid color background fill is a good choice. Select a color that has a strong contrast from the color used for text (light on dark or dark on light).

Format a Background with Pattern and Gradient Fills

Two colors (the *Foreground* and the *Background*) create pattern fills. Two similar colors make a subtle pattern; two contrasting colors make the pattern more obvious. Notice the differences in two title slides prepared using the *Whisp* theme (Figure 3-10).

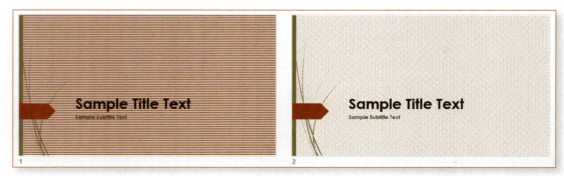

3-10 *Whisp* theme title slide with two background patterns

- *Slide 1 (Left):* Contrasting colors in a bold pattern make the title text difficult to read.
- *Slide 2 (Right):* The same colors with a subtle pattern improve the appearance.

HOW TO: Add a Background Pattern Fill

1. Point to the slide background and right-click to open the shortcut menu.
2. Click **Format Background** to open the *Format Background* pane.
3. Select the **Pattern fill** option.
4. Choose an appropriate *Foreground Color* and *Background Color*.
5. Choose one of the patterns.
6. By default, this change is applied to the current slide only. Click **Apply to All** to apply this change to the entire presentation.
7. If you want to restore the background's original design, click **Reset Background**.
8. Close the *Format Background* pane.

> ### ANOTHER WAY
> To open the *Format Background* pane, click the **Format Background** button on the *Design* tab or click the **Background Styles** list arrow [*Slide Master* tab, *Background* group] and then click **Format Background**.

You can use preset gradient colors based on theme colors or select custom colors. You first choose the type of gradient such as *Linear, Radial, Rectangular, Path,* or *Shade from title.* Then you choose the direction of color change. Based on these choices, gradient stops appear on the color bar. Move, delete, or add gradient stops to control how the colors blend. The color change is more gradual with more distance between the stops. Compare the title slides of the *Whisp* design theme shown in Figures 3-11 and 3-12. These two slides started with the same preset gradient fill of *Bottom Spotlight – Accent 4* with a type of *Linear.* The settings were changed differently.

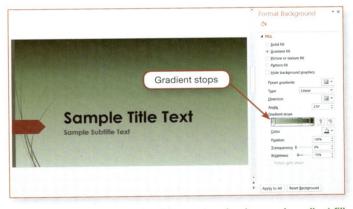

3-11 *Whisp* theme title slide with a custom background gradient fill

Figure 3-11

- *Linear Up* direction
- Three gradient stops are used

Figure 3-12

- *Linear Diagonal – Top Left to Bottom Right* direction
- The three gradient stops on the left of the color bar are close together for a defined color change; the three right stops are spread apart for a more gradual color change.

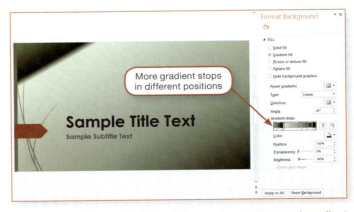

3-12 *Whisp* theme title slide with a custom background gradient fill showing different gradient stops

HOW TO: Add a Background Gradient Fill

1. Point to the slide background and right-click to open the shortcut menu.
2. Click **Format Background** to open the *Format Background* pane.
3. Select the **Gradient fill** option.
4. Click the **Preset gradients** list arrow and select a color style.
5. Click the **Type** list arrow and choose one of the options: *Linear*, *Radial*, *Rectangular*, *Path*, or *Shade from title*.
6. Click the **Direction** list arrow and choose a direction for color blending if one is available.
7. The **Angle** degree is available only for the *Linear* type and it automatically adjusts based on the direction you choose. You can type a different number or click the spin box to change the number in 10 degree increments.
8. Add or remove gradient stops.
    - To add gradient stops, click the **Add gradient stop** button.
    - To remove gradient stops, click the **Remove gradient stop** button or drag the gradient stop off the color bar.
9. Change colors by selecting a gradient stop and clicking the **Color** button. Choose a different color.
10. To change color blending, select the gradient stop and drag it to a different position on the color bar. If you want to change the order, drag the stops to rearrange them. For precise adjustments, change percentages for each stop position.
11. Adjust *Brightness* and *Transparency* as needed.
12. By default, this change is applied to the current slide only. Click **Apply to All** to apply this background to every slide in your presentation.
13. Close the *Format Background* pane.

> **ANOTHER WAY**
>
> You can access various *Background Styles* [*Design* tab, *Variants* group or *Slide Master* tab, *Background* group] that show light and dark color combinations based on theme colors.

Format a Background with Picture and Texture Fills

Pictures help you tell your story, communicate without words, and convey emotions that are difficult to express in words. Pictures can provide a dramatic background for your presentation. However, they provide some special challenges when text is displayed over pictures because of the many colors that are used in pictures. Textures have similar issues if they use many colors or show a lot of detail. Pictures in a small size can be used as textures to fill a slide with many small pictures. The examples in this section will show you several ways to combine background pictures and text.

HOW TO: Add a Background Picture Fill

1. Point to the slide background and right-click to open the shortcut menu.
2. Click **Format Background** to open the *Format Background* pane.
3. Select the **Picture or texture fill** option.
4. Click the **File** button to insert a picture from your collection.
5. Click the **Online** button to search for a picture using the *Insert Picture* dialog box.
    - Type your search word and click the **Search** button or press **Enter**.
    - Select the picture you want to use and click **Insert**.

6. To soften the picture colors so text and other objects on the slide are easy to see, use one of the following methods:
   - On the *Format Background* pane, increase the *Transparency* percentage. This setting mutes the colors but the original colors are still evident.
   - Click **Picture** at the top of the *Format Background* pane; then click **Picture Color**. Click **Presets** to choose from different saturation levels or click **Recolor** to choose from dark and light accent colors for a monotone effect. If you decide not to change colors, click the **Reset** button to restore the picture to its original state.
7. By default, this change is applied to the current slide only. Click **Apply to All** to apply this background to every slide in your presentation.
8. To restore the background to its original state, click the **Reset Background** button.
9. Close the *Format Background* pane.

▶ **MORE INFO**
You can change a slide background at any time while you are working on a presentation.

The following figures show some options you can explore using the *Format Background* pane to soften background pictures or use placeholder fill colors to make text over pictures or textures easy to read. In these examples, a single flower that is almost a square image (Figure 3–13) is used in different ways. In Figures 3-13–3-17, the first slide illustrates a problem while the other two slides show possible solutions.

Notice the following characteristics for the slides shown in Figure 3-14:

522 x 529 pixels @ 72 ppi

3-13 A flower used in backgrounds

- *Slide 1 (Left):* Because this picture is almost square (522 × 529 pixels) when it is stretched to fit the width of a widescreen display (height 7.5" and width 13.333"), part of the flower is cut off at the top and bottom. This is not necessarily a problem, just something that happens if you use a square picture. The title text, however, is not easy to read over the dark colors of the flower. This is a problem as your slide text should be legible no matter what designs you use.
- *Slide 2 (Center):* The title placeholder is the same width as the slide. A dark red fill is applied and the white text has a shadow so now the text is easy to read.
- *Slide 3 (Right):* The title placeholder treatment is the same as slide 2. The picture was recolored using the preset *Black and White: 25%* color. This creates a more abstract image.

3-14 A large square picture used as a background fill with color changes

Notice the following characteristics for the three slides shown in Figure 3-15:

- **Slide 4 (Left):** The actual size of this large flower does not fill the slide, so now the complete flower is displayed. The *Tile picture as texture* option was selected with *Alignment* changed to *Center. **Tiling** causes the picture to be repeated to fill the slide area so parts of the flower are shown around the center flower. Like slide 1 in Figure 3-14, the text is difficult to read.
- **Slide 5 (Center):** The title placeholder resembles slide 2 in Figure 3-14, but this time the fill color transparency is 30%. More of the flower shows through, yet the text is still easy to read.
- **Slide 6 (Right):** The picture was recolored with preset *Gray – 25%, Background color 2 Light.* Black text is used with no shadow. (This was done because black text with a black shadow makes the text look blurred.)

3-15 A large square picture used as a tiled background fill with color changes

If you tile a picture or texture that is small, many images fill the screen for an effect like wallpaper. If these images still seem too large, you can adjust the *Tiling Options* and reduce the *Scale* percentage to display each image in a smaller size. *Offset* points control how much the tiled images are indented from the left (*Offset X*) and top (*Offset Y*).

Notice the following characteristics for the three slides shown in Figure 3-16:

- **Slide 7 (Left):** The *Tile picture as texture* option was selected so many of these small flower images (200×203 pixels) fill the screen. For an appropriate fit on the slide, *Alignment* was changed to *Top left;* then *Offset* and *Scale* were adjusted. Like slide 4 in Figure 3-15, the text is difficult to read.
- **Slide 8 (Center):** The flower picture was recolored with preset *Grayscale.* The title placeholder colors were changed to a black fill with red text. The placeholder size was increased, too, for greater emphasis.
- **Slide 9 (Right):** The repeating picture for this slide is a small rectangle (40 by 77 pixels) with a bevel effect to make it look like a real tile. The title text is left aligned and the placeholder is filled with a gold color. A rectangle was added on the right so the date would be easy to read and to help create an asymmetrical focal point with the single large flower. This flower has a transparent background rather than white as in the previous examples.

3-16 Small pictures tiled for a background fill with color changes

Textures available on the *Format Background* pane are small images, so it is generally best to tile them because the effect is more pleasing. When stretched to fill a slide, the textures will appear blurred. Notice the following characteristics for the slides shown in Figure 3-17:

- **Slide 10 (Left):** The *Paper bag* texture was applied and it is blurred.
- **Slide 11 (Center):** The same texture was tiled so multiple small images repeat and no other change was made.
- **Slide 12 (Right):** The same texture was tiled and the *Mirror type* changed to *Both* so this creates an interesting pattern with horizontal and vertical mirror images.

3-17 The same texture used as a background fill with different settings

SLO 3.2

Applying Animation

Animation is the movement of objects on a slide. Animation can make your presentation more dynamic and keep your audience focused on concepts.

You can observe creative animation techniques by noticing how objects and text move in movies or in television commercials. As you decide what effects to use, try to select movements that enhance your content and support your message. Animation can be overdone when it is not used skillfully. Be sure you are applying animation for the right reasons and not just for entertainment value. Use animation sparingly because too much can be distracting.

When planning movement, also consider the transitions (the movement between slides). When a presentation is supporting a speaker, you want to keep the transitions calmer and apply animation effects to draw attention to information on selected slides only.

Add Entrance, Exit, and Emphasis Effects

Animation effects are arranged in three categories that are shown in different colors on the gallery (Figure 3-18):

3-18 *Animations* gallery

- *Entrance:* A movement that occurs when an object appears on the slide (green)
- *Emphasis:* A movement that calls attention to an object that remains on the slide (yellow)
- *Exit:* A movement that occurs when an object leaves the slide (red)

Note that some effects are for text only. When animating objects, those effects are gray in the gallery and are not available.

HOW TO: Apply an Animation Effect

1. Select the text or object to be animated.
2. Click the **Animations** tab.
3. Click the **More** button on the *Animations* gallery to see all available effects.
   Or
   If the *Animations* gallery is not open because your PowerPoint window is narrow, click the **Add Animation** button [*Advanced Animation* group] to open the gallery.
4. Click an effect to apply it. A number appears on the slide, showing that the object is animated.
5. Click the **Preview** button to test the animation.
6. Repeat to animate additional objects as desired. Each animated object is numbered in sequence to show animation order.
7. To remove an animation, click the animation number and press **Delete**.

> ### MORE INFO
> Animation numbers are displayed only when the *Animations* tab is open.

Effect Options, Timing, and Duration

Each different animation effect has options that control the direction of movement.

HOW TO: Change Effect Options

1. Select the animated object.
2. Click the **Effect Options** button [*Animations* tab, *Animation* group].
3. Select an appropriate **Direction** and **Sequence** if it is available.

For the *Float In* effect shown in Figure 3-19, two directions are available. Other effects have many different options. You select only one direction for each animation.

The sequence shown in this figure is *By Paragraph.* Animation numbers display before each bulleted text item so they appear individually. If you choose *As One Object,* only one animation number displays and the complete list appears at the same time. If you choose *All at Once,* the same animation number displays for each text item and the complete list appears at the same time.

3-19 Animation and effect options applied

Some people are critical of animating text because viewers cannot read text until it stops moving. If you are going to spend significant time discussing each item in a list, adding each item as you start talking about it makes sense. However, animating a list has no value if you are only making brief statements or discussing the complete list in general terms.

You can adjust animation *timing* using the following commands on the *Animations* tab in the *Timing* group:

- **Start:** This controls when animation begins. With *On Click* the speaker controls the timing; *With Previous* or *After Previous* makes animation occur automatically.
- **Duration:** By default, the time to complete each animation ranges from .50 to 2.00 seconds depending on the movement. Increasing the duration seconds extends the time an object is moving so the movement appears slower.
- **Delay:** The default is no delay, but you can enter seconds in the spin box to make the animation begin after a specified time.
- **Reorder Animation:** When multiple objects are animated, click *Move Earlier* or *Move Later* to adjust the sequence of animation.

HOW TO: Adjust Animation Timing and Duration

1. Select the animated object.
2. Click the **Start** list box arrow [*Animations* tab, *Timing* group] and select from *On Click*, *With Previous*, or *After Previous* (Figure 3-20).
3. Increase or decrease **Duration** by editing the time or clicking the spin box arrows.
4. Enter seconds or click the **Delay** spin box to specify the time (in seconds) before the animation starts.
5. Click the **Preview** button to test the animation.
6. Reorder animation if necessary using the *Move Earlier* and *Move Later* buttons.

3-20 *Animations* tab, *Timing* group

When you animate several objects, check the animation numbers to be sure the objects will appear in the order you want (Figure 3-21).

If your presentation is designed to support you as a speaker, coordinate the animation timing with your speaking. This technique usually works best in small segments only because precise timing is almost impossible to predict when you are presenting in real time to an audience. If you are designing a self-running presentation for a trade show exhibit, for example, your animation can be much more dramatic and extensive because the slide show is not dependent on a speaker's pace.

3-21 Numbers indicate animation order

SLO 3.3

Linking to an Online Video

Many videos are available online, but not all of them can be played within PowerPoint. When you search for a video using the *Insert Video* dialog box, the videos found from YouTube are most likely to play within PowerPoint as long as you have Internet access. You click **Insert** to put the video on your slide, but the actual video is not saved in your presentation.

An image of the video will appear and the necessary information to link to it is saved in your presentation.

When you search for videos, you may find a compelling interview or demonstration that will enliven your presentation, but be sure the video fits your topic and adds value.

HOW TO: Link a Presentation to an Online Video

1. Be sure your computer has Internet access. Select the PowerPoint slide where you want to show the video.
2. Click the **Insert** tab.
3. Click the **Video** button list arrow [*Media* group] and select **Online Video** (Figure 3-22) to open the *Insert Video* dialog box (Figure 3-23). The search options that appear depend on how your software is installed.
4. Type a search word in one of the search boxes, *Bing Video Search* or *YouTube* if it is available, and click the **Search** button.
5. Available video clips (brief video segments) appear with ScreenTips that identify names.
   - The video name, source, and number of minutes appear in the lower left corner of the dialog box (Figure 3-24). You may want to use this information in a source notation.
6. Click **Insert** and the video will appear on your slide. Below the video, add the appropriate source information as needed.

3-22 *Video* button on the *Insert* tab

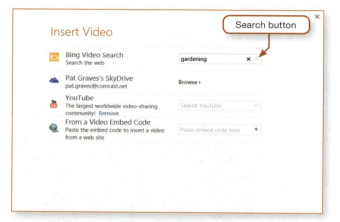

3-23 *Insert Video* dialog box showing search options

3-24 *Insert Video* dialog box showing search results

> ### MORE INFO
> A linked video will not play in a presentation that you send by email.

Play the Online Video

To play an online video in PowerPoint, the computer used to display your presentation must have Internet access.

The clarity you see in playback depends on the resolution of the original video and how it was compressed for online distribution. Resolution is expressed in pixel width and height. With more pixels, image clarity and detail improve.

As with all computer technology, video capabilities continue to improve and many videos can be played at full-screen size from their online source. However, video sharing sites often provide video in the standard definition size (640×480 pixels) or even smaller. Be careful when increasing the video size on your slide to avoid degrading image quality. Test how the video plays before you use it in your presentation.

HOW TO: Play an Online Video

1. In *Normal* view, select the video object.

2. If you wish, increase the size of the video by using one of these methods:
   - Drag handles.
   - Enter specific **Height** and **Width** measurements [*Video Tools Format* tab, *Size* group].
   - Click the *Size* launcher to open the *Format Video* pane (Figure 3-25). Click the *Size & Properties* option at the top of the pane. Adjust size by changing **Height** and **Width** measurements or changing the **Scale Height** and **Scale Width** measurements.

3. On the *Format Video* pane, check **Lock aspect ratio** and **Relative to original picture size** to maintain dimensions as your resize.

4. Check **Best scale for slide show** to select a different resolution.

5. Reposition the video as needed.

6. Notice the clarity of the video as you test it in the next steps. If the image is degraded, click the **Reset** button on the *Format Video* pane. You can also click the **Reset Design list arrow** [*Video Tools Format* tab, *Adjust* group] and click **Reset Design & Size** to restore the video to its original dimensions.

3-25 *Format Video* pane

7. To play the video in *Normal* view:
   - Click the **Play** button [*Video Tools Playback* tab, *Preview* group] to activate the video.
   - If the video can play within PowerPoint, a timeline will appear below the video with playback controls you can use to pause, mute, and access other options (Figure 3-26).
   - Click the **Play** button on the video to play it.

8. To play the video in *Slide Show* view:
   - Click the **Slide Show** button [*Status* bar] to start your slide show on the current slide.
   - Click the **Play** button on the video.
   - The same timeline described in step 7 appears at the bottom of the video as it plays.
   - Press **Esc** to stop the slide show and return to *Normal* view.

3-26 *Video playing in Normal view*

9. To make the video start automatically in *Slide Show* view:
   - Click the **Start** list box arrow [*Video Tools Playback* tab, *Video Options* group] and select **Automatically**.
   - If the video can be played at full screen size, select **Play Full Screen** [*Video Tools Playback* tab, *Video Options* group].
   - Click the **Slide Show** tab and the **From Beginning** button [*Start Slide Show* group]. Advance to the slide with the video to test that it begins playing automatically.

10. Move your pointer so it does not appear on the video while it is playing.

11. When the video is complete, advance to the next slide.

> **MORE INFO**
>
> If you find an online video that you want to use in PowerPoint, you may be able to link to it without searching for it in PowerPoint. You can copy the video's embed codes (the host web address, name of the video, and playback size information) that are included with a video in a sharing section on the host page. Then open the *Insert Video* dialog box and paste the embed codes. Information to link to the video is saved in your presentation, so Internet access is required to play the video.

Obtain Permission

Linking to a video for classroom purposes falls under the guidelines of *fair use* for education, and crediting the source may be sufficient. However, business use is different. Just like television programming or movies in a theater, videos are copyrighted by the creator. You need permission before you link to, display, or distribute video that is copyrighted. Obtaining permission is time consuming and can be expensive. If the creator does not give you permission, you must find another video and start the process again.

HOW TO: Obtain Permission to Use an Online Video

1. From the web site where the video is posted, identify the user name of the creator.
2. Click a link to go to more profile information or, in some cases, another web site.
3. Look for terms of use and find contact information.
4. Send an email message explaining the following:
   - How you want to use the video
   - What portion of the video you will use
   - When you will use the video
   - How you will show credits on the slide where the video is displayed such as in Figure 3-26
   - Your contact information for the creator's response

With the dynamic nature of the web, a video you find may be available for only a limited time. You may need to request a high resolution copy of the video, and the creator may charge you for this service.

> **MORE INFO**
>
> The *Copyright Act of 1976* is the primary basis of copyright law in the United States. It specifies fair use that permits limited use for such purposes as research, teaching, and scholarship. The *Digital Millennium Copyright Act of 1998* addresses issues of online copyright infringement.

PAUSE & PRACTICE: POWERPOINT 3-1

Davon Washington has almost finished the slide show for his seminar on presentation planning. In this project you create custom theme colors that better match the Solution Seekers, Inc., logo, modify a background style, animate several slide objects, and link to a video on a web site. You will later change the slide size from standard to widescreen.

File Needed: **PresentationPlanning-03.pptx**
Completed Project File Name: **[your initials] PP P3-1.pptx**

1. Open the presentation **PresentationPlanning-03**.

2. Save the presentation as **[your initials] PP P3-1**.

3. Create new theme colors.
   a. Click the **More** button [*Design* tab, *Variants* group].
   b. Select **Colors** and click **Customize Colors** to open the *Create New Theme Colors* dialog box (Figure 3-27).
   c. Change four colors. For each change, click the **color list arrow** and select **More Colors**. Click the **Custom** tab and enter the numbers for *Red*, *Green*, and *Blue* from the following table.

3-27 Original theme colors

	Text/Back-ground – Light 2	Accent 1	Accent 2	Accent 3
Red	234	3	102	181
Green	214	110	0	139
Blue	184	131	51	128

   d. Name the new custom theme Planning (Figure 3-28).
   e. Click the **Save** button. The new custom theme is saved in the *Custom* section of your list of available theme colors.

4. On slide 1, apply a gradient fill.
   a. Point to the slide background and right-click.
   b. Select **Format Background** to open the *Format Background* pane.
   c. Select the **Gradient fill** option.
   d. Click the **Type** list arrow and choose **Linear**.
   e. Click the **Direction** list arrow and **Linear Diagonal – Top Right to Bottom Left**.
   f. The *Angle* percentage automatically adjusts to 135°.
   g. If necessary, click the **Add gradient stop** button so you have four gradient stops.

3-28 *Planning* theme colors

h. Click each gradient stop from left to right (Figure 3-29) and adjust the *Color*, *Position*, *Brightness*, and *Transparency* to the values shown in the following table:

Gradient Stops	Stop 1	Stop 2	Stop 3	Stop 4
Color	Dark Teal, Accent 1	Dark Teal, Accent 1, Lighter 60%	Tan, Text 2	Tan, Text 2, Darker 50%
Position	0%	30%	70%	100%
Transparency	0%	50%	0%	0%
Brightness	0%	0%	0%	−50%

i. The title slide gradient fill is shown in Figure 3-30.

3-30 Title slide with new design

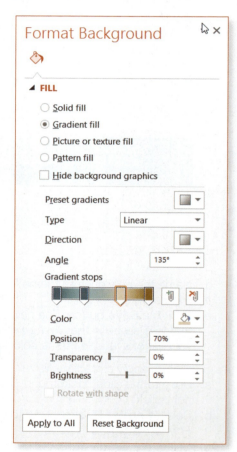

3-29 Gradient stops adjusted

5. On slide 14, create a *Picture fill* background.
   a. On the *Format Background* pane, select **Picture or texture fill** and click the **Online** button to open the *Insert Pictures* dialog box.
   b. In the *Office.com Clip Art* search box, type audience and click **Search**.
   c. Select the picture "Instructor speaking to a group of students" (Figure 3-31) and click **Insert**.

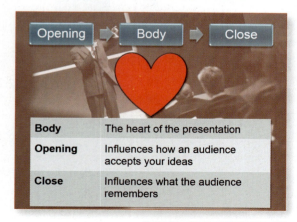

3-31 Background picture fill

d. Click the **Picture** button at the top of the *Format Background* pane and then select **Picture Color**.
e. Click the **Recolor** list arrow, and choose **Brown, Accent color 3 Light**.
f. Close the *Format Background* pane.

6. On slide 4, select the text box "Possible body sequence" and change the *Shape Fill* color to **Tan, Background 2, Darker 50%** and the *Shape Outline* color to **Dark Teal, Accent 1** (Figure 3-32).

7. On slide 13, change the *Text fill* color for the text at the top of the slide to **Brown, Text 2, Lighter 50%**.

8. Apply a transition.
   a. Click the **Transitions** tab and apply the **Wipe** transition.
   b. Click the **Effect Options** button and select **From Left**.
   c. Click **Apply to All** [*Timing* group].

9. Apply animation.
   a. Click the **Animations** tab and repeat steps b–g for each object in the following table.
   b. Select the **text or object** to be animated.
   c. Click the **More** button on the *Animation* gallery or click the **Add Animation** button [*Advanced Animation* group] if the gallery is not open.
   d. Click an **effect** to apply it.
   e. Click the **Effect Options** button and select the listed **Direction** and **Sequence** or **Amount**.
   f. Adjust settings for *Start*, *Duration*, and *Delay*.
   g. Click the **Preview** button or **Slide Show** button to test the animation.

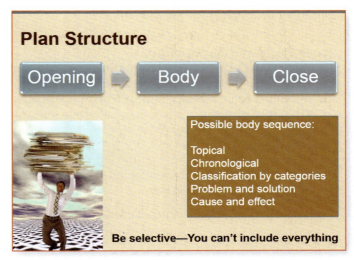

3-32 *SmartArt* resized and text box colors changed

Slide	Object	Animation Effect	Effect Options	Start	Duration	Delay
4	Possible body sequence text box	Fade (Entrance)	As One Object	On Click	02.00	None
5	First impression text	Wave (Emphasis)	By Paragraph	After Previous	00.50	None
7	Quoted text	Bounce (Entrance)	As One Object	After Previous	02.00	01:00
8	Road picture	Grow & Turn (Entrance)	None	With Previous	02.00	01:00
13	Prepare text	Float In (Entrance)	Float Up	After Previous	01.00	None
13	Slide show text	Float In (Entrance)	Float Up, By Paragraph	After Previous	01.00	01:00
14	Heart	Spin (Emphasis)	Clockwise, Two Spins	With Previous	02.00	None

10. Insert a new blank slide after slide 14.

11. On slide 15, click the **Video** button list arrow [*Insert* tab, *Media* group] and select **Online Video** to open the *Insert Video* dialog box.
    a. In the *Bing Video Search* box (or the *YouTube Search* box if it is available), type the search words presentation skills and click **Search**.
    b. From the search results, select an appropriate video from *YouTube* and click **Insert**.
    c. The video appears in a small size. Increase the size so the width is approximately **5"** wide.
    d. Center the video on the slide.
    e. Click the **Play** button [*Video Tools Playback* tab, *Preview* group] to activate the video.
    f. Click the **Play** button on the video to test it.
    g. If necessary, reduce the size of the video for a clear image.
    h. Add source information below the video.

12. Test all of your transitions and animations in your presentation.

13. Save and close the presentation.

SLO 3.4

Using Rehearsal Techniques

Everyone, no matter how experienced, can benefit from rehearsing a presentation. Practicing your delivery ensures that each slide's information supports what you are saying. Practice builds confidence, too.

Speaker Notes

Speaker notes help you remember what you need to say in your presentation, but they should never include text that would tempt you to read to your audience. Notes should be your personal reminders, such as items to emphasize or terminology to define. Notes should not be a script for everything you are going to say. For example, you could include statistics you want to mention, a quote you want to say but not show on a slide, a list of upcoming events, or additional resources for your audience. Even if you don't use the speaker notes you prepare, having them available while you present can be comforting and help to reduce nervousness.

As you think about what to include in your notes, plan for smooth and logical transitions between the various topics of your presentation. You can compose your notes using the *Notes* pane in *Normal* view or you can change to *Notes Page* view.

HOW TO: Use the Notes Pane in Normal View

1. In *Normal* view, the *Notes* pane is below the slide.

2. If the *Notes* pane is not showing, click the **Notes** button [*View* tab, *Show* group].

3. You can expand the *Notes* pane by dragging the border up (Figure 3-33).

4. If you drag the border too low and the *Notes* pane disappears, click the **Notes** button or the **Normal** button to restore it.

3-33 Increased *Notes* pane size

The *Notes Page* view provides much more space to type text than you have when using the *Notes* pane in *Normal* view.

HOW TO: Use Notes Page View

1. Click the **Notes Page** button [*View* tab, *Presentation Views* group] to show a slide as it will print.
2. Type your text in the text box below the slide to add notes (Figure 3-34).

You may want to increase the font size before you print the pages because large text is easier for you to see on a lectern or podium while you are speaking. You will need your notes to be visible even if overhead lighting is dimmed so slide colors display better on the projection screen.

> **ANOTHER WAY**
> Some people find that printed handouts with a few handwritten reminders work well for speaker notes.

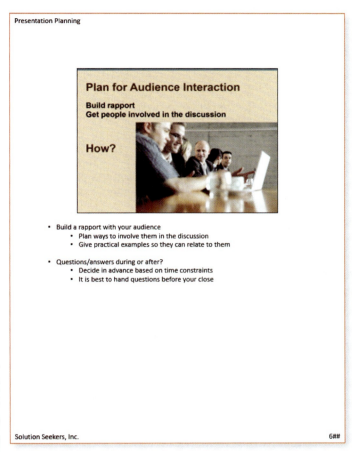

3-34 *Notes Page* view with slide and text

HOW TO: Print Notes Pages

1. Click the **File** tab and click **Print**.
2. For *Print Layout*, choose **Notes Pages** and check **Scale to Fit Paper** to make the slide images larger (Figure 3-35).
3. Omit the **Frame Slide** option for *Notes Pages*. A single-line border around the entire page is unnecessary.
4. Click the **Print** button.

Rehearse Timings

PowerPoint's ***Rehearse Timings*** feature makes it easy to judge the pace of your presentation. When you use this feature to rehearse, the time you spend on each slide is recorded as you move through the presentation. The timings that you save from

3-35 Print settings for *Notes Pages*

rehearsing appear below each slide in *Slide Sorter* view. This view enables you to see the "big picture" aspect of your presentation. You can compare the time spent on each slide and make decisions to spend less time on some slides and more time on other slides where the content takes longer to explain. You can save the timings to automate the presentation and make it self-running. If you are presenting to an audience, remove the timings so you can control when the slides advance.

HOW TO: Rehearse Timings

1. Click the **Rehearse Timings** button [*Slide Show* tab, *Set Up* group] and your slide show will start.

   3-36 Current slide time and total elapsed time

   - A *Recording* dialog box appears in the upper left corner (Figure 3-36). It shows the time each slide is displayed and the total elapsed time.
   - Click the **Next Slide** button (or press the **spacebar**) to advance.
   - Click the **Pause** or **Repeat** buttons as needed.

2. When you reach the end of your presentation, a message will ask if you want to save your timings.

3. Click **Yes** and the timings, in seconds, will display below each slide in *Slide Sorter* view (Figure 3-37). (The seconds shown in this example are brief because they were recorded when testing the presentation. The times would be much longer in an actual presentation.)

3-37 Slide timings appear below each slide thumbnail

In rehearsal, go through your presentation and practice what you will say while each slide is displayed. Use printed notes pages while you are practicing. If possible, stand to replicate more closely the experience you will have when speaking to your audience. Sometimes knowing how and where to stand in relation to the keyboard and monitor you are using takes a little practice. Your body posture is important. Good posture makes you appear confident and it positively affects how your voice projects. If possible, rehearse with the equipment you will use to deliver the presentation.

Set Timings Manually

You can enter all timings manually, but it is quicker to rehearse your presentation, save the timings, and adjust the time as needed for individual slides.

HOW TO: Modify Timings

1. Click the **Transitions** tab and be sure the **After** option is selected [*Transitions* tab, *Timing* group] and second numbers are showing (Figure 3-38).

2. For each slide, change the number of seconds as needed to increase or decrease the amount of time the slide is displayed.

3. If you want the slides to advance automatically, deselect the **On Mouse Click** option.

4. To remove the timings, click the **Record Slide Show** button list arrow [*Slide Show* tab, *Set Up* group], select **Clear**, and then select **Clear Timing on Current Slide** or **Clear Timings on All Slides** (Figure 3-39).

3-38 *Timings* group on the *Transitions* tab

3-39 *Clear Timings* options

Prepare for Mishaps

Be sure you have backup copies of your presentation in case you experience equipment failure and you need to switch to a different computer. In a worst-case situation, where both your computer and projector have malfunctioned, you can present using your handouts to support what you say. All experienced presenters encounter such problems at some time during their careers.

SLO 3.5

Controlling Display Options

As you learned in Chapter 1, themes and templates that you obtain online are available in different sizes called **Standard** and **Widescreen**. The default sizing for PowerPoint 2013 is *Widescreen* but for previous versions of PowerPoint it was *Standard*. Therefore, you may encounter files that require updating to fit your current screen size, or you may need to adjust the size of your presentation to fit an older projection screen in a room where you will give your presentation.

Adjust Slide Size

Today widescreen computers (like television screens) use a 16:9 or 16:10 aspect ratio (the ratio of width to height). A slide show designed in the 16:9 aspect ratio takes advantage of this wide horizontal space because it fills the screen. A slide show designed in the 4:3 aspect ratio (more square) and displayed on a widescreen will be positioned in the center of the screen with black areas on both sides. Both of these slide sizes are available on the *Design* tab in the *Customize* group and you can change from one to the other by clicking the **Slide Size** button and choosing **Standard (4:3)** or **Widescreen (16:9)**. Two other sizes are available on the *Slide Size* dialog box and you can create a custom size if necessary. These sizes are listed in the following table and illustrated as blue and green thumbnails in Figure 3-40:

Slide Sizes

Aspect Ratios	Width in Inches	Height in Inches
Standard 4:3	10	7.5
16:9	10	5.625
16:10	10	6.25
Widescreen 16:9	13.333	7.5

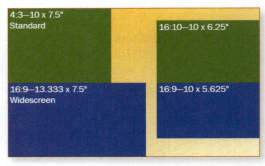

3-40 Screen sizes

The two wide sizes available in the *Slide Size* dialog box look smaller in Figure 3-40 because their width is 10", the same as the Standard 4:3 width. On your computer screen they will look almost the same as the *Widescreen* size, but ruler measurements and object sizes will be different because of the difference in width and height.

Changing between slide show sizes is a simple process, but necessary adjustments after the change can be time consuming. You need to consider how the change affects the text and graphics on your slide. Both *Standard* and *Widescreen* sizes have the same vertical measurement, so the width is what changes and adjustments are usually needed to make slide objects fit appropriately.

If you change from 4:3 to one of the other sizes (16:9 or 16:10), the vertical size is reduced, which compresses the slide vertically. Pictures or text in placeholders may not fit appropriately.

Be aware of these height and width differences when changing slide sizes. If you think you may need to change back to your original size, save the original presentation as a separate file before you begin making changes for the new size. By doing this, you can avoid all the resizing changes that would be necessary to return to the original size.

HOW TO: Change the Aspect Ratio

1. Click the **Design** tab.
2. Click the **Slide Size** button [*Customize* group]; then click either **Standard (4:3)** or **Widescreen (16:9)**.
3. Click **Custom Slide Size** to open the *Slide Size* dialog box. Sizes for printing and four sizes for on-screen viewing are available. You can choose from the following:
   - *On-screen Show (4:3):* 10×7.5" (Standard)
   - *On-screen Show (16:9):* 10×5.625"
   - *On-screen Show (16:10):* 10×6.25"
   - *Widescreen (16:9):* 13.333×7.5"
4. Click **OK** (Figure 3-41).

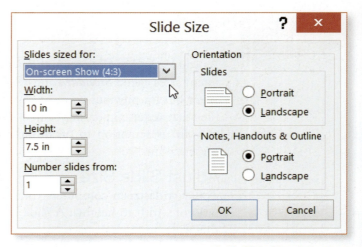

3-41 *Slide Size* dialog box

Presenter View

Presenter View allows you to display your presentation on the screens of two monitors or a monitor and a projector. PowerPoint can automatically detect when two monitors are connected and will recognize one monitor as your main monitor for *Presenter View* and extend the display to the second monitor for your full-screen slide show. Using *Presenter View* is helpful because while you are speaking you can:

- View the current slide and see the next slide in your presentation.
- Click thumbnails to display slides out of sequence.
- Have speaker notes available on the monitor for easy reading instead of needing printed notes.
- Make the screen that's visible to your audience black yet still have speaker notes available to you.
- Magnify sections of a slide.
- Use convenient navigation and pen tools.

Your monitor shows your view of the presentation and includes the displayed slide, the navigation tools, the next slide, and an area for notes. When you are using a second monitor (or projector), only the slide is displayed on that monitor for your audience. You can click the **Display Settings** button to swap between the monitors used for *Presenter View* and your full-size slide show.

If you do not have two monitors connected to your computer, you can still use *Presenter View* by pressing **Alt+F5**.

HOW TO: Use Presenter View

1. Click the **Slide Show** tab.
2. Select **Use Presenter View** [*Monitors* group] (Figure 3-42).
   - If you are using two monitors, confirm that the monitor you want your audience to see the slide show on appears in the *Show Presentation On* list box. Click the **From Beginning** button to start your slide show.
   - If you are using one monitor, press **Alt+F5**.

3-42 *Use Presenter View* option on the *Slide Show* tab

3. Review your slide show using *Presenter View* (Figure 3-43).
   - Click the **Advance to the next slide** button in the navigation area to move through your slides.
   - Click the **See all slides** button to see slide thumbnails. Click a thumbnail to display a different slide out of sequence.
   - Click the **Zoom into the slide** button, then drag the selection area over an object or text you want to magnify, and then click. That portion of the screen is displayed for your audience. Click the same button again (now **Zoom out**) to return to normal screen size.
   - Notice the slide show time displayed above the slide.
   - Press **Esc** to exit the slide show.

3-43 *Presenter View*

For this project, you add speaker notes, print notes pages, and rehearse a presentation. You will save the presentation in its original standard size and then resave it in the widescreen size. For the widescreen version, you will adjust object positioning as needed and then use *Presenter View* to display your slide show.

File Needed: ***[your initials] PP P3-1.pptx***
Completed Project File Name: ***[your initials] PP P3-2a.pptx*** and ***[your initials] PP P3-2b pptx***.

1. Open the presentation ***[your initials] PP P3-1***.

2. Save the presentation as ***[your initials] PP P3-2a***.

3. Create a visual transition between topics. Insert a new slide with the *Section Header* layout after slides 3, 9, and 15. On each of these new slides, delete the subtitle placeholder and type the title text as follows:
   a. Slide 4 title: Presentation Structure (Figure 3-44).
   b. Slide 10 title: Presentation Practice.
   c. Slide 16 title: Summary.

4. Prepare speaker notes for two slides that do not have notes.
   a. On slide 11, click the **Notes Page** button [*View* tab, *Presentation Views* group].
   b. Add the following text with blank space for easy reading (Figure 3-45):
      - Print slide with discussion points below
        - Make notes brief (like cue cards)
        - Keep text large so it is easy to read
      - Can be a "safety net" (builds confidence)
      - Use to rehearse a presentation
      - Do not read during a presentation
   c. On slide 12, add the following text:
      - Experience is the best teacher
      - Identify strengths and develop them
      - Identify weaknesses and work to overcome them
      - Reduce tendency to be nervous
   d. Click the **Normal** button [*View* tab, *Presentation Views* group].

5. Print notes pages for slides 11 and 12.
   a. Click the **File** tab and click **Print**.
   b. Select the appropriate printer and make sure that you are printing just one copy.
   c. For *Slides,* type 11–12 to print a Custom Range.
   d. For *Print Layout,* choose **Notes Pages** and select **Scale to Fit Paper** (Figure 3-46).
   e. Click the **Print** button.

Presentation Structure

3-44 *Section Header* slide layout

3-45 *Notes Page* view with text

3-46 Print settings for *Notes Pages*

6. Rehearse your presentation and save timings.
   a. Click the **Slide Show** tab.
   b. Click the **Rehearse Timings** button [*Set Up* group].
   c. Using the *Recording* dialog box, click the **Next Slide** button to advance each slide after approximately 3–5 seconds (for the purpose of practicing this feature).
   d. At the end of your presentation, click **Yes** to save your timings.
   e. Click the **Slide Sorter** button [*Status bar*] to see the timings displayed below each slide.

7. Beginning with slide 1, change how slides advance and modify presentation timings.
   a. Click the **Transitions** tab.
   b. Deselect **On Mouse Click** [*Transitions* tab, *Timing* group].
   c. Change the *After* timing to **3** seconds (shown as 00:03:00).
   d. Click the **Apply To All** button.
   e. Change the *After* timing on the *Section Header* slides (slides 4, 10, and 16) to **1** second (shown as 00:01) (Figure 3-47).

3-47 **Rehearsal timings modified**

8. Save the presentation to preserve the standard size (4:3 aspect ratio, 10×7.5") on the *[your initials] PP P3-2a* file.

9. Save the presentation again as *[your initials] PP P3-2b* to create a separate file for a widescreen size (16:9 aspect ratio, 13.333×7.5").

10. Click the **Slide Size** button [*Design* tab, *Customize* group] and select **Widescreen (16:9)**.

11. Slide objects are not aligned as they were in the standard size (Figure 3-48). Slide title text remains in the same position, but space has been added to both sides of the slide to stretch slides from 10" wide to 13.333" wide.

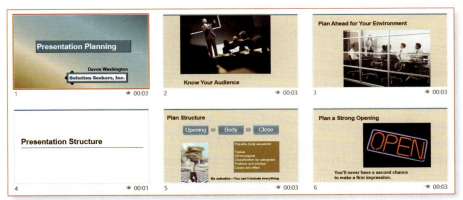

3-48 **Slide object alignment changed with widescreen size**

12. On some slides, the new object position is acceptable. Double-click Slide 1 to return to *Normal* view. Change the following slides as described (Figure 3-49):
    a. **Slide 1:** Increase the size of the title placeholder by dragging the right sizing handle to the edge of the slide (*Width* **11.2"**). Move the logo and name to the right.
    b. **Slide 2:** Left align the picture. Move the text to the left about **.5"** from the edge of the slide.
    c. **Slide 3:** Right-align the picture.
    d. **Slide 9:** Right-align the picture and the text below it. Move the slide title down.
    e. **Slide 12:** Right-align the picture. Resize the title placeholder so it fits the text and move the title down so it is closer to the picture.

3-49 Alignment adjusted on selected slides

13. Review your presentation using *Presenter View*.
    a. Click the **Slide Show** tab.
    b. Click **Use Presenter View** [*Monitors* group].
    c. Review your slides.
       • If you have two monitors, click the **From Beginning** button [*Start Slide Show* group].
       • If you have one monitor, press **Alt+F5**.

14. Save and close the presentation.

Presenting Using Projection Equipment

When facing the front of a presentation room, the ideal location for a speaker is to the left of the projection screen. People are conditioned to read from left to right, so it is natural for the audience to first look at you and then at the projection screen. Many situations are less than ideal, however, so be flexible when you cannot control the speaker area. Keep the following guidelines in mind:

• Become familiar with your equipment so you won't feel awkward using it.
• If possible, load your slide show before the audience enters the room so you are not seen scrambling around with preliminary preparations. Arrive early and test your presentation to be sure all content works correctly.
• Allow time to relax before your presentation starts. Almost everyone feels nervous before a presentation begins. This reaction is normal and just shows you are respectful of the situation. Harness your nervous energy in a positive way.
• Have your title slide displayed as people enter the room.
• If possible, greet people to make them feel welcome. Let people know that you are glad to have the opportunity to share with them.

Position Equipment

Using a computer while you speak creates some challenges. You may have a tablet computer to control your slide show, but it must work with your projector. If you are using a desktop or notebook computer, you must see the computer screen when facing the audience and be able to access the computer to advance slides. In some presentation rooms, you may need to place your computer on a table. A podium (or lectern) may be available to hold your computer and/or printed notes pages. Be careful, however, that the podium does not create a barrier between you and the audience. Move away from it when you can.

3-50 Poor electrical connections

Even if your computer has a wireless Internet connection and is running on battery power, you may need to manage power cords for other equipment. Connections may not be convenient. (Figure 3-50). Be sure to keep cables and cords away from the area where you and audience members will be walking or tape cords to the floor.

Navigate in a Slide Show

You have advanced through a slide show by pressing the spacebar or clicking on a slide. You can use other methods to advance, to go to specific slides, or to end a slide show.

During a slide show, navigation buttons are on the lower left of each slide. They are barely noticeable unless you point to that area. Use buttons (Figure 3-51) to move between slides or to bring up a shortcut menu of presentation options.

3-51 Slide show navigation buttons

Control Slide Display

The audience needs to focus on you, the speaker. Slides support your message, but you may not want a slide displayed all the time. Also, going from a blank screen to your next slide can seem more dramatic.

Blank Slides

If you know in advance that you need to discuss something unrelated to your slides, then plan ahead and place one or more slides with a black background in specific places in your slide show.

During a presentation, you can blank the screen by pressing **B** to display an empty black screen or **W** to display an empty white screen. Be careful about using the white option, however, because an all-white screen can create glare that will be unpleasant for your audience.

Hide and Reveal Slides

Hiding a slide is helpful when you have information that is not essential to your presentation but you want to have that slide available if you need it depending on time and audience interest. For example, you could hide slides containing information such as:

- References
- Additional pictures
- Additional details about a topic
- Optional charts, diagrams, or tables

To hide the current slide, click the **Hide Slide** button [*Slide Show* tab, *Set Up* group] (Figure 3-52). You can hide multiple slides by selecting thumbnails on the *Slides* pane or in *Slide Sorter* view. In *Normal* and *Slide Show* views, the slide thumbnail for a hidden slide appears grayed out with a diagonal line through the slide number.

During a slide show, you can display a hidden slide by typing the slide number and pressing **Enter**.

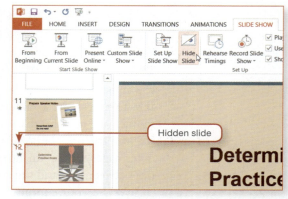

3-52 *Hide Slide* button and hidden slide 12

> ▶ **MORE INFO**
> You can print hidden slides. Click the **File** tab and then select **Print.** Click the **Print All Slides** option and select **Print Hidden Slides**.

Use Keyboard Shortcuts

Keyboard shortcuts are convenient if you have easy access to your keyboard while speaking.

Slide Show Navigation Shortcuts

Press	Action
N, spacebar, right arrow, down arrow, **Enter**, or **Page Down**	Advance to the next slide.
P, Backspace, left arrow, up arrow, or **Page Up**	Go to the previous slide.
Slide number, then **Enter**	Go to a particular slide.
Ctrl+S	Open *All slides* dialog box, select slide, and click **Go To**.
B or period	Blanks the screen to black.
W or comma	Blanks the screen to white.
S	Stop or restart an automatic show.
plus sign	Zoom in.
minus sign	Zoom out.
H or slide number, **Enter**	Go to a hidden slide.

The presentation shortcut menu is available during a slide show by right-clicking when you point anywhere on a slide.

Remote Control and Laser Pointer

A **remote control** enables you to move away from your computer as you are presenting. If you do this, you can interact with your audience more naturally because you don't need to stay close to your computer to control how slides advance. Remote control devices come in many styles from small clickers to clickers that resemble pens with USB storage. When presenting, be sure you have extra batteries available for the remote control.

Some remote controls have a built-in *laser pointer,* or you can purchase a separate pointing device. A laser pointer shows a small dot (usually red) on the slide where you point. PowerPoint's laser pointer feature resembles this dot. To use this feature, press **Ctrl** while you are pointing on the screen and your pointer changes to a dot that can be red, green, or blue.

HOW TO: Change Laser Pointer Color

1. Click the **Set Up Slide Show** button [*Slide Show* tab, *Set Up* group] to open the *Set Up Show* dialog box (Figure 3-53).

3-53 Changing laser pointer color

2. Click the **Laser pointer color** list box arrow and select **green or blue**.
3. Click **OK**.

A dot on the screen directs audience attention to a particular location. Be sure you show the dot long enough for your audience to find it and keep the dot steady. Do not bounce it around on the screen with random movements because this distracts viewers. A very small pointer movement on your computer screen makes a large movement on a projection screen.

SLO 3.7

Using Annotation Pens

During a presentation, you can call attention to information by writing or drawing on slides. These markings are called *ink annotations.* While controlling the pointer to write with a hand-held mouse is a little awkward, you can record audience feedback and make simple drawings on slides. When you reach the end of your presentation, you can save ink annotations. All markings, even if you draw a rectangle, are saved as lines and not as shapes.

Select Pen Style and Ink Color

To write or draw on a slide, use the *Pen.* To add a color overlay on text, use the *Highlighter* just as you would mark text to highlight information on paper. When you change *Ink Color,* be sure the color you select contrasts with the slide background so it is easy to see.

HOW TO: Use the Pen and Highlighter

1. Start a slide show and go to the slide you want to annotate.
2. Select the *Pen* or *Highlighter* using one of the following methods:
   - Click the **Pen** button in the navigation area (Figure 3-54) to open the shortcut menu. Select an option as desired.

Or

   - Right-click anywhere on the slide to open the shortcut menu and select **Pointer Options**. Select an option as desired (Figure 3-55).
3. Begin writing or drawing on one or more slides.
4. To remove markings, select the **Eraser** options from the shortcut menu. Click markings to delete each continuous pen stroke (Figure 3-56).
5. To change annotation color, select the **Ink Color** option from the shortcut menu and then select a different color.
6. At the end of a presentation, click **Keep** to save ink annotations. The markings are saved as lines that you can edit.

3-54 Navigation area

3-55 Shortcut menu

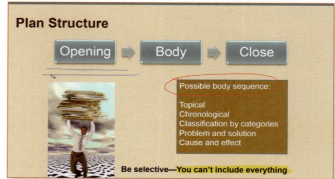

3-56 Ink annotations and the *Eraser* tool

Pen tools are available in *Presenter View,* also. You can control many of these options during a slide show using keyboard shortcuts summarized in the following table:

Ink Markup Shortcuts

Press	Action
Ctrl+P	Changes the pointer to a pen.
Ctrl+A	Changes the pointer to an arrow.
Ctrl+E	Changes the pointer to an eraser.
Ctrl+M	Shows or hides ink markup.
E	Erases markings on the screen.

For this project, you use PowerPoint features to present more effectively. You hide and reveal slides, blank slides, practice with the laser pointer, change pen colors, use the pen and highlighter, and save annotations.

File Needed: *[your initials] PP P3-2b.pptx*
Completed Project File Name: *[your initials] PP P3-3.pptx*

1. Open the presentation *[your initials] PP P3-2b*.

2. Save the presentation as *[your initials] PP P3-3*.

3. Click the **Transitions** tab and change the slide transitions.
   a. Select **On Mouse Click** and deselect **After** [*Timing* group].
   b. Click **Apply To All** [*Timing* group].

4. Select slide 4 and click the **Hide Slide** button [*Slide Show* tab, *Set Up* group].
   a. Start a slide show from slide 3 to confirm that you automatically advance directly from slide 3 to slide 5.
   b. On slide 6, type 4 and press **Enter** to show the hidden slide.

5. In *Slide Show* view, practice blanking slides.
   a. Press **B** to blank a slide to black. Press **B** to return to the slide.
   b. Press **W** to blank a slide to white. Press **W** to return to the slide.
   c. Press **Esc** to exit *Slide Show* view.

6. Change the laser pointer color.
   a. Click the **Set Up Slide Show** button [*Slide Show* tab, *Set Up Slide Show* group] to open the *Set Up Show* dialog box.
   b. Click the **Laser Pointer** list box arrow and select **blue**.
   c. Click **OK**.
   d. In *Slide Show* view, press **Ctrl** while you move your pointer to practice using the laser pointer.

7. Use the pen and highlighter.
   a. In *Slide Show* view, go to slide 7.
   b. Right-click to open the shortcut menu, select **Pointer Options**, and then select **Ink Color**. Select the standard color **Blue**.
   c. Use the **Pen** to draw a rectangle around the word "How" (Figure 3-57).
   d. Right-click to open the shortcut menu, select **Pointer Options**, and then select **Ink Color**. Select **Yellow**.
   e. Right-click to open the shortcut menu, select **Highlighter**, and then highlight the word "involved."

3-57 Pen color changed

   f. Type 13 and press **Enter** to go to slide 13. Use the **Highlighter** to highlight the words "Get help" and "feedback."
   g. Type 17 and press **Enter** to go to slide 17. Use the **Highlighter** to highlight the words "heart," "how an audience," "accepts," "what the audience," and "remembers."
   h. Right-click to open the shortcut menu, select **Pointer Options**, and then select **Eraser**. Click to remove the highlights from the words "how an audience" and "what the audience."
   i. Advance to the end of the presentation and click **Keep** to save your annotations.

8. Save and close your presentation.

Preparing a Self-Running Presentation

A self-running slide show, also referred to as a *kiosk presentation*, can be set up to run continuously without someone being present to advance the slides of the presentation. This type of presentation works well for trade shows or open house events where people walk up to a computer screen and watch the slide show. For example, self-running presentations can be used for marketing products to customers or to educate patients in medical office waiting rooms. You can record narration to accompany the slides. You can also set up the slide show to *loop* so it will automatically repeat and cycle continuously from beginning to end.

Record a Slide Show with Narration

To record voice narration for your presentation, your computer must have a microphone and sound card. Like rehearsal, you can use this feature to practice what you will say during a presentation and evaluate your vocal qualities. You can also make a narrated slide show available as a complete presentation to distribute on CDs or DVDs or to post online for viewers.

Prepare carefully to decide what you will say as each slide is displayed. Use notes pages or other resources as references.

HOW TO: Record Narration

1. Click the **Slide Show** tab.
2. Click the **Record Slide Show** button list arrow [*Set Up* group] and then select **Start Recording from Beginning** or **Start Recording from Current Slide** to open the *Record Slide Show* dialog box.
3. Select **Slide and animation timings**.
4. Select **Narrations and laser pointer**. (This option is available only if your computer has a microphone.)
5. Click **Start Recording** (Figure 3-58).
6. A *Recording* box appears in the top left corner of the screen. You can advance, pause, or resume recording in the same way you do when you rehearse a presentation (see *Section 3.4: Using Rehearsal Techniques*).
7. Speak clearly into your microphone as each slide is displayed.
8. At the end of the presentation, the narration and slide timings will automatically be saved.
9. Separate audio files are recorded on each slide and an audio icon appears in the lower right. Review your slide show and listen to your narration.
10. Save your presentation.

3-58 *Record Slide Show* dialog box

Press **Esc** if you need to end the slide show before reaching the last slide. You can clear timing or narration on the current slide or all slides. When you play back a narration, the recording is synchronized with the presentation.

HOW TO: Clear Timings or Narration

1. Click the **Slide Show** tab.
2. Click the **Record Slide Show** button list arrow [*Set Up* group] and then select **Clear**.
3. Select from these options:

   Clear Timing on Current Slide   *Clear Timings on All Slides*

   Clear Narration on Current Slide   *Clear Narrations on All Slides*

If you need to display the slide show without narration, click the **Set Up Show** button [*Slide Show* tab, *Set Up* group]. Select **Show without narration** and click **OK**.

Set Up a Kiosk Presentation with Looping

Depending on how you plan to use it, a kiosk presentation may need different design guidelines than a slide show that is shown by a presenter. While other presentations provide minimal text because the slides support the speaker's message, a kiosk presentation may contain more information because it is a stand-alone product. If your kiosk presentation is displayed in a public place with a lot of distractions, then splashy graphics can be used to grab attention. On the other hand, if your kiosk presentation is for educational purposes in a quiet setting such as a doctor's office, the slides might be designed more like pages in a book with smaller text and more detailed information.

HOW TO: Set Up a Kiosk Presentation

1. Click the **Slide Show** tab.
2. Click the **Set Up Slide Show** button [*Set Up* group] to open the *Set Up Show* dialog box (Figure 3-59).
3. Choose the following settings:
   - For *Show type,* select **Browsed at a kiosk (full screen)**.
   - For *Show options*, **Loop continuously until 'Esc'** is automatically selected and grayed out because you chose a kiosk.
   - For *Show slides*, select **All** or enter the first and last slide numbers you want to display.
   - For *Advance slides*, **Use timings**, **if present** is automatically selected for a kiosk.
   - If you are using more than one monitor, select the appropriate monitor for the slide show.
   - For *Resolution*, select **Use Current Resolution** or the highest resolution possible for your equipment.
   - For a kiosk presentation, **Use Presenter View** is not available.
4. Click **OK**.
5. Save the presentation with these changes.

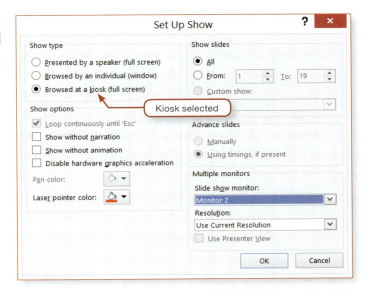

3-59 *Set Up Show* dialog box

SLO 3.9

Packaging a Presentation to a CD or Folder

The *Package Presentation for CD* feature allows you to easily transport one or more presentations for use on another computer. You can copy your presentation file and any linked files to a blank CD (CD-R, recordable or CD-RW, rewritable) or to a folder on your computer, network location, or removable drive.

HOW TO: Save a Presentation to a CD or Folder

1. Insert a CD in your CD/DVD drive if you are saving to that location.
2. Click the **File** tab and select **Export**.

3. Select **Package Presentation for CD**. Click the **Package for CD** button to open the *Package for CD* dialog box.

4. Type a name for the CD (Figure 3-60).

5. Click the **Options** button to open the *Options* dialog box (Figure 3-61) and choose from the following options:

- *Linked Files:* Preserves links and copies any external files such as audio or video files.
- *Embedded TrueType fonts:* Assures that the fonts used in your presentation are available on the playback computer.
- *Password:* Enhances security for opening or modifying a presentation.
- *Inspect:* Checks for inappropriate or private information.

6. Click **OK**.

7. To save the presentation use one of the following methods:

- Click the **Copy to CD** button and click **Yes** to verify that you want to include linked files.
- Click the **Copy to Folder** to open the *Copy to Folder* dialog box (Figure 3-62). Type a name for the folder and browse for the location to save the presentation. Select the option to **Open folder when complete** if you want to see all the files that are copied. Click **OK**.

8. When the packaging process is complete, click **No** to indicate that you don't need to make another copy. Click **Close**.

9. Test the presentation by loading it from the folder or from the CD.

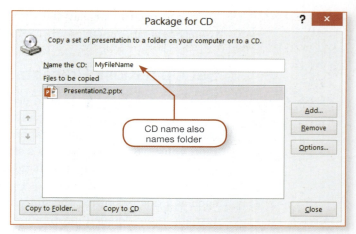

3-60 *Package for CD* dialog box

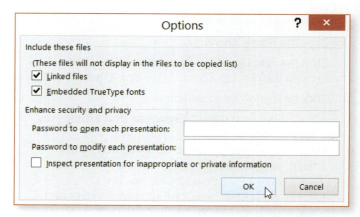

3-61 *Options* dialog box

3-62 *Copy to Folder* dialog box

> **MORE INFO**
>
> If file size requirements exceed the storage capacity of a CD, you can convert your slide show to a video and then use DVD burning software to save the files to a DVD. PowerPoint does not support direct burning to DVDs.

This project consists of two parts. You record a presentation with audio in Part A if you have a microphone connected to your computer. In Part B, you prepare a kiosk presentation, set it up to loop so it is self-running, and then use the *Package Presentation for CD* feature to save it to a folder.

File Needed: ***[your initials] PP P3-2b.pptx***
Completed Project File Name: ***[your initials] PP P3-4b.pptx***

Part A (Microphone Required)

1. Open the presentation ***[your initials] PP P3-2b***.

2. Save the presentation as ***[your initials] PP P3-4a*** and change to *Slide Sorter* view.

3. For the purpose of this project, you need only slides 1–5. Delete all other slides in the presentation.

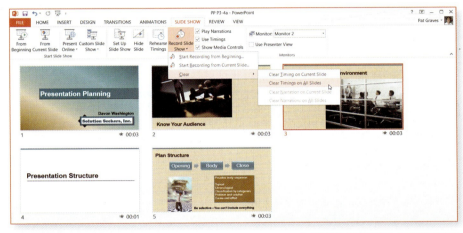

3-63 Clear timings on all slides

4. Remove the timings.
   a. Click the **Record Slide Show** button list arrow [*Slide Show* tab, *Set Up* group] and select **Clear**.
   b. Select **Clear Timings on All Slides** (Figure 3-63).

5. Click the **Notes Page** button and add notes to two slides.
   a. For slide 2, add four items after the first line of text:
      - What is their background?
      - What is their educational level?
      - How familiar are they with your topic?
      - Are they likely to be accepting of your ideas or resistant?
   b. For slide 3, add two items to the bulleted text:
      - Overall cleanliness and organization of the room
      - Temperature level for comfort
   c. Print the notes pages.

6. Using the notes pages as a reference, click the **Record Slide Show** button list arrow [*Slide Show* tab, *Set Up* group] and select **Start Recording from Beginning**.
   a. Select **Slide and animation timings** and **Narrations and laser pointer** (Figure 3-64).
   b. Click **Start Recording**.
   c. Speak clearly into your microphone as you go through the slide show.
   d. At the end of the presentation, click **Yes** to save your timings and narration.

3-64 *Record Slide Show* dialog box

7. Review the presentation and listen to the narration.

8. Save and close the presentation.

Part B

1. Open the presentation **[your initials] PP P3-2b**.

2. Save the presentation as **[your initials] PP P3-4b**.

3. For the purpose of this project, apply timing so slides change rapidly.

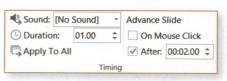

3-65 *Timing* group on the *Transitions* tab

   a. Confirm that **On Mouse Click** [*Transitions* tab, *Timing* group] is not selected.
   b. Change the *After* seconds to **00:02:00**.
   c. Click **Apply to All** (Figure 3-65).

4. Click the **Set Up Slide Show** button [*Slide Show* tab, *Set Up* group] to open the *Set Up Show* dialog box.

   a. Select the following settings (Figure 3-66):
      • For *Show type*, select **Browsed at a kiosk (full screen)**.
      • For *Show options*, **Loop continuously until 'Esc'** is automatically checked for a kiosk.
      • For *Show slides*, select **All**.
      • For *Advance slides*, **Use timings, if present** is automatically checked for a kiosk.
   b. Select the appropriate monitor. **Use Presenter View** is not available because you selected a kiosk.
   c. Click **OK**.

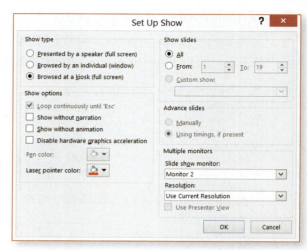

3-66 *Set Up Show* dialog box

5. Use the *Package Presentation for CD* feature to save a presentation to a folder.
   a. Click the **File** tab and select **Export**.
   b. Click **Package Presentation for CD** and click the **Package for CD** button to open the *Package for CD* dialog box.
   c. Type Planning for the name of the CD.

6. Click the **Options** button to open the *Options* dialog box and select the following:
   • Choose **Linked Files** to preserve links and copy any external files such as audio or video files.
   • Choose **Embedded TrueType fonts** to assure that the fonts you use in your presentation are available on the playback computer.

7. Click **OK** and the dialog box closes.

8. Click the **Copy to Folder** button to open the *Copy to Folder* dialog box. The name you typed for the CD automatically appears.
   a. Click **Browse** to open the *Choose Location* dialog box and find the place where you want to save the presentation. Click **Select** and the dialog box closes.
   b. Select the option to **Open folder when complete**.
   c. Click **OK** and the dialog box closes.
   d. If you receive a message about including linked files, click **Yes**.

9. A *File Explorer* window opens showing the files in the open *Planning* folder.

10. Close the *Package for CD* dialog box.

11. Close your original **[your initials] PP P3-4b** presentation.

12. Test the saved presentation by loading it from the *Planning* folder. Double-click the **[your initials] PP P3-4b** file name.

13. Close the presentation and folder.

Chapter Summary

3.1 Create custom theme colors and background styles (p. P3-139).

- Design themes create a unified appearance for your presentation.
- The Accent 1 theme color is the color that appears, by default, each time you draw a shape.
- Create custom theme colors by selecting different colors for background, text, and accent colors. Select the background color first and then select other colors that work well on that background.
- Modify backgrounds using the *Format Background* dialog box to apply a custom pattern, gradient, or picture fill.
- Carefully control how text is placed over background pictures and other fills so text is easy to read.

3.2 Apply animation to add interest and reinforce content (p. P3-147).

- Animation adds movement to slide objects and text.
- Animation is applied through **Entrance**, **Exit**, and **Emphasis** effects.
- If more than one animation is used, each animation is numbered in sequence.
- **Effect Options** control the direction and sequence of movement.
- Animation can start **On Click**, **With Previous**, or **After Previous**.
- **Duration** is the time that it takes to complete an animation.

3.3 Link to an online video (p. P3-149).

- Search for an online video using the *Insert Video* dialog box.
- You need Internet access and a video must currently be available online if you want to link to it during a PowerPoint presentation.
- Some video can be played at full screen size.
- Playback controls appear at the bottom of the video.

3.4 Use rehearsal techniques to prepare for presentation delivery (p. P3-156).

- Type speaker notes using the *Notes* pane or *Notes Page* view.

- Print speaker notes for reference during a presentation.
- Use **Rehearse Timings** to practice and judge the pace of your presentation.
- You can manually adjust timings to increase or decrease the time a slide is displayed.
- Prepare backup copies of your presentation and your notes.

3.5 Control display options for different screen sizes (p. P3-159).

- The shape of your slides varies based on the aspect ratio (the ratio of width to height) you use.
- PowerPoint's default aspect ratio is *Widescreen 16:9;* the *Standard 4:3* is available.
- *Presenter View* displays the current slide, next slide, notes, and navigation controls on one monitor, while the slide show displays on a second monitor or projection screen.
- *Presenter View* can be used with one monitor.

3.6 Present effectively and professionally using projection equipment (p. P3-164).

- Use the slide show toolbar, shortcut menu, or keyboard shortcuts to navigate to different slides in a presentation.
- To blank a slide to black, press **B**; to blank a slide to white, press **W**.
- When you **Hide** a slide, it is still in the presentation but will not display during a slide show unless you go to that specific slide.
- Use **remote controls** to advance slides so you can move away from your computer.
- Use PowerPoint's **laser pointer** to place a dot on the slide during a slide show.

3.7 Use annotation pens to highlight information and save presentation markings (p. P3-167).

- Use the **Pen** or **Highlighter** to mark or draw on a slide during a slide show.
- Use the **Eraser** to remove markings during a slide show.
- These markings, called **ink annotations**, can be saved at the end of the presentation.

3.8 Prepare a self-running presentation that loops (p. P3-170).

- If your computer has a microphone, you can include narration in a presentation.
- A self-running presentation, a *kiosk presentation*, is set to automatically loop so it runs continuously.
- Use the *Set Up Show* dialog box to set up a kiosk presentation.

3.9 Use the *Package Presentation for CD* feature to prepare a slide show for display on other computers (p. P3-171).

- The *Package Presentation for CD* feature saves linked files to a CD or other location.
- To assure that the fonts you used to create your presentation are available on the computer you will use to display your presentation, select *Embedding TrueType Fonts*.

Check for Understanding

In the *Online Learning Center* for this text (www.mhhe.com/office2013inpractice), there are a variety of resources that can be used to review the concepts covered in this chapter.

The following Online Learning Resources are available in the Online Learning Center:

- Multiple choice questions
- Short answer questions
- Matching exercises

Guided Project 3-1

One of the community colleges in the Sierra Pacific Community College District has finished construction of a new building for its business program. A dedication ceremony and open house is planned. In this project, you finalize the presentation for this special program and prepare a kiosk presentation to be displayed on monitors throughout the building while people tour after the opening ceremony. You save the standard slide size version in Part A and then change to a widescreen version in Part B.
[Student Learning Outcomes 3.1, 3.2, 3.4, 3.5, 3.6, 3.8]

File Needed: **Dedication-03.pptx**
Completed Project File Names: **[your initials] PowerPoint 3-1a.pptx** and **[your initials] PowerPoint 3-1b.pptx**

Skills Covered in This Project

- Apply a background picture fill.
- Apply animation and effect options.
- Create and print notes pages.
- Rehearse a presentation and save timings.
- Change to a widescreen slide size.

- Use *Presenter View.*
- Use slide show navigation tools, use keyboard shortcuts, and insert blank slides.
- Prepare a kiosk presentation.

Part A

1. Open the presentation **Dedication-03** that has a standard size (4:3 aspect ratio, 10 x 7.5").

2. Save the presentation as **[your initials] PowerPoint 3-1a**.

3. Apply a background picture fill with a softened effect to all slides.
   a. Right-click to open the shortcut menu. Click **Format Background** to open the *Format Background* pane.
   b. Select the **Picture or texture fill** option.
   c. Click the **Online** button to open the *Insert Pictures* dialog box.
   d. In the *Office.com Clip Art* search box, type the word building and click the **Search** button (or press **Enter**).
   e. Select the picture, "Office building with reflection" shown in Figure 3-67 and click **Insert**.
   f. Click the **Picture** button at the top of the pane and then click **Picture Color**. Click the **Recolor** list arrow and select **Blue, Accent color 2, Dark**.
   g. Click **Apply to All** so this slide is used as the background for all slides.

3-67 *Insert Picture* dialog box with search results

4. On slides 1 and 2, restore the background picture to its original color. On the *Format Background* pane under *Picture Color*, click the **Reset** button for each slide.

3-68 **Slide title moved down**

5. On slide 2, delete the subtitle placeholder and move the title down slightly (Figure 3-68).

6. On slide 6, change the background color to black.
   a. On the *Format Background* pane, click **Fill** at the top of the pane if it is not selected. Select the **Solid fill** option.
   b. Click the **Color** list arrow and select **Black**, **Background 1**.
   c. Close the *Format Background* pane.

7. Select slide 2 and press **Ctrl+D** to duplicate. Move the new slide to the end of the presentation so it becomes slide 9. Change the slide 9 title text to Take a Tour.

8. Apply a transition to all slides.
   a. Click the **Transitions** tab and apply the **Shape** transition.
   b. Click the **Effect Options** button and select **Diamond**.
   c. Click **Apply to All** [*Timing* group] (Figure 3-69).

3-69 *Transition Effect Options*

9. Apply animation on four slides and change effect options as shown in the following table.
   a. Select the text or object to be animated.
   b. Click the **More** button on the *Animation* gallery. If the *Animation* gallery is not displayed, click the **Add Animation** button [*Animations* tab, *Advanced Animation* group].
   c. Click an effect to apply it.
   d. Click the **Effects Options** button [*Animations* group] to apply *Direction*, *Sequence*, or *Amount* settings.
   e. Adjust settings for *Start* and *Duration*.
   f. Click the **Preview** button or **Slide Show** button to test the animation.

Slide	Object	Animation Effect	Effect Options	Start	Duration
1	Text box for agenda	*Wipe* (Entrance)	*From Bottom, By Paragraph*	*On Click*	00.50
3	Picture	*Shape* (Entrance)	*Out, Diamond*	*After Previous*	02:00
7	Text box for space design	*Zoom* (Entrance)	*Object center, As One Object*	*On Click*	00:50
7	Text box for wireless access	*Zoom* (Entrance)	*Object center, As One Object*	*On Click*	00:50
8	Text box for donors	*Wipe* (Entrance)	*From Bottom, All At Once*	*After Previous*	00:50

10. Prepare speaker notes on two slides.
   a. Click the **Notes Page** button [*View* tab, *Presentation Views* group].
   b. Click the **Zoom** button and increase the *Percent* to **150%** so you can more easily see the text. Click **OK**.
   c. Add the following text with a blank line between each item on two notes pages (Figure 3-70):

   Slide 1: Welcome the audience.
   Review today's agenda—go through animation.

   Slide 9: The tours will now begin and last until 4 p.m.
   Student leaders are available outside this auditorium to guide small groups.
   Or tour on your own.

3-70 *Notes Page* view showing speaker notes

   d. Click the **Normal** button to return to *Normal* view.

11. Print notes pages for slides 4 and 5.
   a. Click the **File** tab and click **Print**.
   b. Select the appropriate printer and make sure that you are printing just one copy.
   c. For *Slides*, type 4–5 to print a *Custom Range*.
   d. For *Print Layout*, choose **Notes Pages** and check **Scale to Fit Paper** (Figure 3-71).
   e. Click the **Print** button.

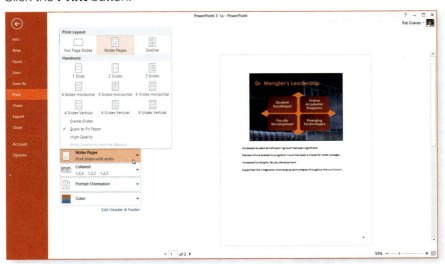

3-71 Print view of notes page

12. Rehearse and save timings.
    a. Click the **Rehearse Timings** button [*Slide Show* tab, *Set Up* group].
    b. Using the *Recording* dialog box, click the **Next Slide** button to advance each slide after approximately 3–5 seconds.
    c. At the end of your presentation, click **Yes** to save your timings. The timings are displayed below each slide in *Slide Show* view.

13. Save the presentation to preserve the current standard (4:3) slide size.

Part B

14. Resave the presentation as ***[your initials] PowerPoint 3-1b***.

15. Deselect the **After** timings [*Transitions* tab, *Timing* group] and click **Apply To All**.

16. Click the **Slide Size** button [*Design* tab, *Customize* group] and click **Widescreen (16:9)** (Figure 3-72). The slide size has changed from 10" to 13.333" wide.

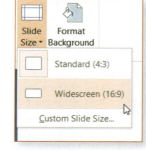

3-72 Slide Size

17. Reposition objects on the following slides to fit the widescreen size:
    a. ***Slide 1:*** Right-align the text box.
    b. ***Slide 2:*** Move the slide title to the left to match other slide titles.
    c. ***Slide 7:*** Right-align both text boxes (Figure 3-73).
    d. ***Slide 8:*** Move the text at the top of the slide to the left. Right-align the text box.
    e. ***Slide 9:*** Move the slide title to the left to match other slide titles.

18. Use *Presenter View* to review your presentation.
    a. Click the **Slide Show** tab.
    b. Click **Use Presenter View** [*Monitors* group].
    c. Start your presentation.
       • If you have two monitors, click the **From Beginning** button [*Start Slide Show* group].
       • If you have one monitor, press **Alt+F5**.
    d. Click the **Presenter View** right arrow button to advance slides as you review them.
    e. Click the **Zoom into the slide** button to magnify a section of the slide. Click **Zoom Out** to return to the normal slide size (Figure 3-74).
    f. Click the **See all slides** button to view thumbnails of all slides. Click to display different slides.
    g. Press **Esc** to exit *Presenter View*.

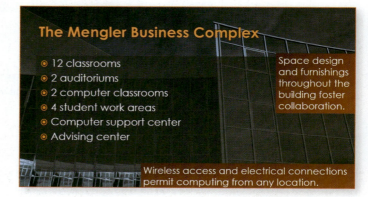

3-73 Text boxes right-aligned

3-74 Presenter View

19. In *Slide Show* view, practice use of navigation tools, keyboard shortcuts, and blanking slides.
    a. Click the **right arrow** button in the slide navigation area to advance slides.
    b. Click the **Menu** button in the slide navigation area to open the shortcut menu and go to a specific slide.
    c. Right-click to open the shortcut menu and go to a specific slide.
    d. Press **N** to advance to the next slide; press **P** to go to the previous slide.
    e. Type 6 and press **Enter** to go to slide 6.
    f. Press **B** to blank a slide; press **B** to view the screen again.

20. Prepare a kiosk presentation with looping.
    a. Select the **After** timing [*Transitions* tab, *Timing* group] and click **Apply To All** so timings will be available for the kiosk presentation.
    b. On slides 1 and 7, select each animated object and change **Start** [*Animations* tab, *Timing* group] to **After Previous**.
    c. Click the **Set Up Slide Show** button [*Slide Show* tab, *Set Up* group] to open the *Set Up Show* dialog box.
    d. Select the following settings:
        • *For Show type*, select **Browsed at a kiosk (full screen)**.
        • *For Show options*, **Loop continuously until 'Esc'** is automatically selected for a kiosk.
        • *For Show slides*, select **All**.
        • *For Advance slides*, **Use timings**, **if present** is automatically selected for a kiosk.
    e. Select the appropriate monitor.
    f. Click **OK**.

21. Test the presentation to make sure slide transitions and animations work correctly.

22. Save and close the presentation (Figure 3-75).

3-75 PowerPoint 3-1 completed

Guided Project 3-2

For the second training session for new hires on presenting effectively, Davon Washington, Management Consultant at Solution Seekers, Inc., is preparing guidelines for designing slides and developing content in a visual way. For this project, you finish the presentation that Davon has prepared and save it on a CD so participants can refer to it after the session.
[Student Learning Outcomes 3.1, 3.2, 3.3, 3.4, 3.7, 3.9]

Files Needed: *SlideShowDevelopment-03.pptx*, *Background-03.jpg*, and *Applause-03.jpg*
Completed Project File Names: *[your initials] PowerPoint 3-2.pptx* and folder *Develop Slides*

Skills Covered in This Project

- Apply a background picture fill.
- Create custom theme colors.
- Apply animation and effect options.
- Link to an online video.
- Create and print notes pages.
- Add ink annotations.
- Use the *Package Presentation for CD* feature.

---

1. Open the presentation **SlideShowDevelopment-03**.

2. Save the presentation as *[your initials] PowerPoint 3-2*.

3. Apply a background picture fill to all slides.
   a. Right-click and select **Format Background** to open the *Format Background* pane.
   b. Select the **Picture or texture fill** option.
   c. Click the **File** button to open the *Insert Pictures* dialog box.
   d. Locate the student file **Background-03** and click **Insert** (Figure 3-76).
   e. Click **Apply to All** so this picture is the background for all slides.

3-76 Title slide with new background picture fill

4. On slide 12, repeat step 3 to apply a different background picture, **Applause-03**, for this slide only.
   a. Change the *Offset left* to **−9%** and the *Offset top* to **−5%** for better picture positioning. (*Offset right* is 0% and *Offset bottom* is −9%.)
   b. Close the *Format Background* pane.

5. Prepare a new custom color theme to blend with the background picture.
   a. Click the **More** button [*Design* tab, *Variants* group].
   b. Select **Colors** and click **Customize Colors** to open the *Create New Theme Colors* dialog box.
   c. Change five accent colors.
      - For each change, click the color list arrow and select **More Colors** to open the *Colors* dialog box.
      - Click the **Custom** tab and enter the numbers for *Red*, *Green*, and *Blue* shown in the following table.

	Accent 1	Accent 2	Accent 3	Accent 4	Accent 5
Red	255	157	255	38	95
Green	247	175	217	203	30
Blue	220	210	82	236	60

    d. Name the new custom theme Development (Figure 3-77).

    e. Click the **Save** button.

6. Adjust text and object colors on the following selected slides:

    a. **Slide 3:** Change the black text on the *SmartArt* shapes to white.

    b. **Slide 4 and 5:** Click **Reset** [*Home* tab, *Slides* group] so the list bullet updates for the new *Accent 1* color.

    c. **Slide 7 and 11:** Change the *SmartArt* graphic color. Click the **Change Colors** button [*SmartArt Tools Design* tab, *SmartArt Styles* group] and select the **Colored Fill – Plum, Accent 5** style (Figure 3-78).

    d. **Slide 12:** Change the text box *Shape Fill* to **Plum, Accent 5**.

3-77 New theme colors

7. Apply a transition to all slides.

    a. Click the **Transitions** tab and apply the **Reveal** transition.

    b. Click the **Effect Options** button and the select **Smoothly from Right**.

    c. Change the *Duration* to **02:00** [*Timing* group].

    d. Click **Apply to All**.

8. Apply animation on four slides and change effect options as shown in the following table.

    a. Select the text or object to be animated.

    b. Click the **Animations** tab and click the **More** button on the *Animation* gallery. (Click the **Add Animation** button [*Advanced Animation* group] if the gallery is not open.)

    c. Click an effect to apply it.

    d. Click the **Effects Options** button to apply *Direction*, *Sequence*, or *Amount* settings.

    e. Adjust settings for *Start and Duration* as needed to match the table.

    f. Click the **Preview** button or **Slide Show** button to test the animation.

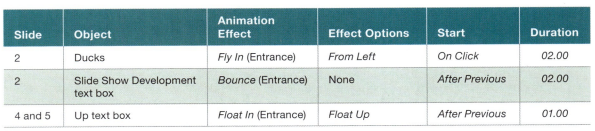

3-78 SmartArt recolored

Slide	Object	Animation Effect	Effect Options	Start	Duration
2	Ducks	*Fly In* (Entrance)	*From Left*	*On Click*	02.00
2	Slide Show Development text box	*Bounce* (Entrance)	None	*After Previous*	02.00
4 and 5	Up text box	*Float In* (Entrance)	*Float Up*	*After Previous*	01.00

(Continued)

Slide	Object	Animation Effect	Effect Options	Start	Duration
4 and 5	Down text box	*Float In* (Entrance)	*Float Down*	*After Previous*	*01.00*
6	Color wheel	*Spin* (Emphasis)	*Clockwise, Two Spins*	*After Previous*	*03.00*
12	Text box	*Wheel* (Entrance)	*2 Spokes, As One Object*	*After Previous*	*02.00*

9. After slide 11, insert a new blank slide.

10. On the new slide 12, find and insert an online video.
    a. Click the **Insert** tab.
    b. Click the **Video** button list arrow [*Media* group] and select **Online Video** to open the *Insert Video* dialog box.
    c. Use the search words presentation slide design and select an appropriate video. Click **Insert**.
    d. Increase the size of the video (*Width* **6.5"**) if the quality remains acceptable.
    e. Below the video, add the appropriate source information.
    f. Play the video in *Slide Show* view, by clicking the **Start** button on the video.
    g. Press **Esc** to exit *Slide Show* view.

11. Beginning on slide 1, click the **Notes Page** button [*View* tab, *Presentation Views* group] and advance through all slides and read the speaker notes to review tips for slide design.

12. Print notes pages for slides 7 and 11.
    a. Click the **File** tab and click **Print**.
    b. Select the appropriate printer and make sure that you are printing just one copy.
    c. For *Slides,* type 7, 11 to choose a *Custom Range*.
    d. For *Print Layout*, choose **Notes Pages** and check **Scale to Fit Paper** (Figure 3-79).
    e. Click the **Print** button.

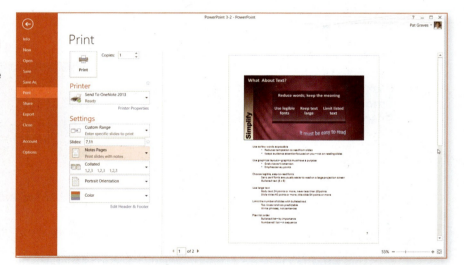

3-79 Print *Notes Pages*

13. Add ink annotations on slides 4, 5, and 7.
    a. In *Slide Show* view, go to slide 4.
    b. Right-click to open the shortcut menu and select **Pointer Options** and **Highlighter**. Highlight the word "organization."
    c. On slide 5, repeat step 14b and highlight the words "creative thinking."
    d. On slide 7, right-click to open the shortcut menu. Select **Pointer Options** and **Pen**. Circle the words "Reduce words" and "keep the meaning."
    e. Advance to the end of the presentation and click **Keep** to save your ink annotations.

14. Save the presentation (Figure 3-80).

15. Use the *Package Presentation for CD* feature to save the presentation to a folder.
    a. Click the **File** tab and select **Export**.
    b. Click **Package Presentation for CD** and click the **Package for CD** button to open the *Package for CD* dialog box.
    c. Type Develop Slides to name the CD.
    d. Click the **Options** button to open the *Options* dialog box and select **Linked Files** and **Embedded TrueType fonts**.
    e. Click **OK**.
    f. Click the **Copy to Folder** button to open the *Copy to Folder* dialog box. The folder name appears and is the same name you typed for the CD. Deselect the **Open folder when complete** option (Figure 3-81).
    g. Browse for the location to save the presentation and click the **Select** button.
    h. Click **OK** to close the *Copy to Folder* dialog box.
    i. A message appears asking if you want to include linked files. Click **Yes**.
    j. Another message appears telling you that ink annotations will not be included. Click **Continue**.
    k. Close the *Package for CD* dialog box.
    l. Close the presentation.

16. Test the presentation.
    a. Open the folder where you "packaged" the presentation. Notice that additional files have been saved in this folder.
    b. Double-click the file name in the folder to open the presentation. If you receive a security warning, click the **Enable** button. Test the presentation and then close it.
    c. To show the presentation from a different computer, the online video link will be broken. You will need to delete the existing video and insert the video again from the presentation computer.

3-80 PowerPoint 3-2 completed

3-81 *Package for CD* and *Copy to Folder* dialog boxes

Guided Project 3-3

At an upcoming meeting of the American River Cycling Club, Eric Salinas is giving a presentation about the importance of knowing your target heart rate and exercising with your heart rate at an appropriate target level. For this project, you finalize the presentation.
[Student Learning Outcomes 3.1, 3.3, 3.4, 3.5, 3.8]

Files Needed: **HeartRateARCC-03.pptx** and **RiderAir.jpg**
Completed Project File Name: **[your initials] PowerPoint 3-3.pptx**

Skills Covered in This Project

- Create custom theme colors.
- Apply a background picture fill.
- Link to a video on a web site.
- Use *Presenter View*.
- Create and print notes pages.
- Record a presentation with narration.
- Prepare a kiosk presentation.

1. Open the presentation **HeartRateARCC-03**.
2. Save the presentation as **[your initials] PowerPoint 3-3**.
3. Prepare a new custom color theme to blend with the heart picture on slide 3.
   a. Click the **More** button [*Design* tab, *Variants* group].
   b. Select **Colors** and click **Customize Colors** to open the *Create New Theme Colors* dialog box.
   c. For each change, click the **Color** list arrow and select **More Colors** to open the *Colors* dialog box. Click the **Custom** tab and enter the numbers for *Red*, *Green*, and *Blue* shown in the following table for four colors.

	Text/Background – Dark 2	Accent 1	Accent 2	Accent 3
Red	24	36	204	227
Green	66	99	0	108
Blue	77	116	0	9

3-82 New ARCC color theme

   d. Name the new custom theme ARCC (Figure 3-82).
   e. Click the **Save** button and the new colors will automatically be applied to all slides.

4. Format the title slide by adding a background picture fill.
   a. Right-click and select **Format Background** to open the *Format Background* pane.
   b. Select the **Picture or texture fill** option.
   c. Click the **File** button to open the *Insert Pictures* dialog box.
   d. Locate the student file **RiderAir-03** and click **Insert**.

e. Click **Picture** at the top of the pane and select **Picture Color**. Click the **Recolor** list arrow and select **Black and White**, **25%** (Figure 3-83).

f. Close the *Format Background* pane.

3-83 **Completed title slide**

5. On the title slide, increase the subtitle font size to **36 pt.** and resize the placeholder so one word fits on each line.

6. On slide 5, find and insert an online video.
   a. Click the **Insert** tab.
   b. Click the **Video** button list arrow [*Media* group] and select **Online Video** to open the *Insert Video* dialog box.
   c. Use the search words Col de la Madone and select an appropriate video. Click **Insert**.
   d. Position the video to the left of the picture and increase the video size (*Width* **5.5"**) if the quality remains acceptable.
   e. Below the video, add the appropriate source information.
   f. Play the video in *Slide Show* view by clicking the **Start** button in the middle of the video.

7. Apply a transition. Choose the **Cube** [*Transitions* tab, *Transition to This Slide* group] with the **From Right** effect options. Click **Apply To All**.

8. Use *Presenter View* to review your presentation.
   a. Click the **Slide Show** tab.
   b. Click **Use Presenter View** [*Monitors* group].
   c. Start your presentation.
      - If you have two monitors, click the **From Beginning** button [*Start Slide Show* group].
      - If you have one monitor, press **Alt+F5**.
   d. Click the **Presenter View** right arrow button to advance slides as you review them.
   e. If the notes text seems too small, click the **Make the text larger** button to adjust the text size in the *Notes* pane and then scroll to read the text (Figure 3-84).
   f. Press **Esc** to end the slide show.

3-84 *Presenter View*

9. Print notes pages for slides 3 and 4.
   a. Click the **File** tab. Click **Print**.
   b. Select the appropriate printer and make sure that you are printing just one copy.
   c. For *Slides,* type 3–4 to choose a *Custom Range*.
   d. For *Print Layout,* choose **Notes Pages** and select **Scale to Fit Paper**.
   e. Click the **Print** button.

10. Record a slide show with narration.
    a. Click the **Record Slide Show** button [*Slide Show* tab, *Set Up* group] and select **Start Recording from Beginning** to open the *Record Slide Show* dialog box.

b. Select both options and click **Start Recording** (Figure 3-85). The *Recording* dialog box appears.

c. Speak clearly into your microphone as each slide is displayed.

d. Click the **Next Slide** navigation button to advance each slide.

3-85 *Record Slide Show* **dialog box**

11. Prepare a kiosk presentation with looping.
    a. Click the **Set Up Slide Show** button [*Slide Show* tab] to open the *Set Up Show* dialog box.
    b. Select the *Show type* **Browsed at a kiosk (full screen)**.
    c. For *Show slides* select **All**.
    d. Select the appropriate monitor.
    e. Click **OK**.

12. Save and close your presentation (Figure 3-86).

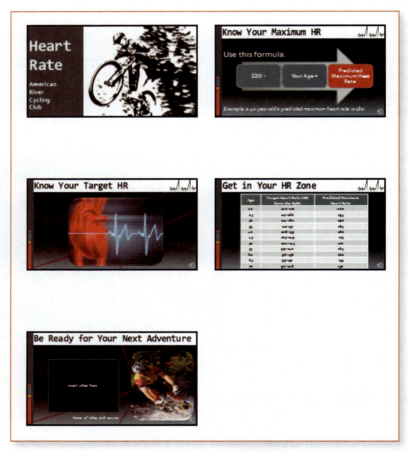

3-86 **PowerPoint 3-3 completed**

Independent Project 3-4

The sales representatives at Wilson Home Entertainment Systems review acceptable viewing distances when talking with clients who are in the early stages of planning a home theater or media room. They discuss options for televisions or projection systems for the spaces being planned. For this project, you complete a presentation to prepare clients for an in-home consultation.
[Student Learning Outcomes 3.1, 3.2, 3.4, 3.6, 3.7, 3.8]

File Needed: *ScreenSizes-03.pptx*, *TVCabinet-03.jpg*, and *Projector-03.jpg*
Completed Project File Name: *[your initials] PowerPoint 3-4.pptx*

Skills Covered in This Project

- Apply a background picture fill.
- Apply animation and effect options.
- Create and print notes pages.
- Rehearse a presentation and save timings.
- Use slide show navigation tools, keyboard shortcuts, and blank slides.
- Hide and reveal slides.
- Use the laser pointer feature.
- Use annotation pens.
- Prepare a kiosk presentation.

1. Open the presentation **ScreenSizes-03**.

2. Save the presentation in its current standard slide size as **[your initials] PowerPoint 3-4**.

3. Using the *Format Background* pane, change the background fill on three slides to a picture fill.
   a. **Slide 5:** Insert **TVCabinet-03** from your student files.
   b. **Slide 6:** Search *Online* using the *Insert Pictures* dialog box and the search word television. Locate a picture of a wall-mounted flat screen television (Figure 3-87).
   c. **Slide 7:** Insert **Projector-03** from your student files.
   d. Close the *Format Background* pane.

3-87 Background picture fill

4. Apply the **Vortex** transition with the **From Bottom** effect option. Change the *Duration* to **3.00**. Apply these settings to all slides (Figure 3-88).

5. Apply animation on four slides and change effect options as shown in the following table:

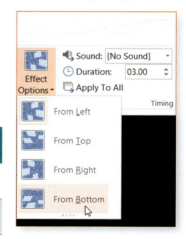

3-88 *Vortex* transition

Slide	Object	Animation Effect	Effect Options	Start	Duration
2	Question mark	*Spin* (Emphasis)	*Clockwise, Two Spins*	*After Previous*	02.00
5, 6, 7	Text box	*Fly In* (Entrance)	*From Top-Left, As One Object*	*After Previous*	00.50

6. Prepare speaker notes on the following three slides. Insert blank space between each item.
   a. **_Slide 5:_** Provides storage for related equipment and media.
      Select appropriate height for viewing.
      Some cabinets have a lift to hide TV when not in use.
   b. **_Slide 6:_** Creates an uncluttered, contemporary look.
      Where will you keep related equipment?
   c. **_Slide 7:_** Most equipment is concealed in some way.
      Projector
      Receiver
         Sound system
         DVD player
      Remote controls operate equipment.
      Wires and cables are in the walls.

7. Print notes pages for slides 5, 6, and 7 (Figure 3-89).

8. Rehearse the presentation and save timings.

9. Modify the timings to advance each slide after approximately 3–5 seconds.

10. Hide slide 4.

11. In *Slide Show* view, practice the following slide show features:
    a. Use the navigation area buttons.
    b. Right-click and use the shortcut menu.
    c. Use keyboard shortcuts.
    d. Blank slides.
    e. Go to the hidden slide 4.
    f. Point to slide objects with the laser pointer.

3-89 Notes page

12. Use the *Set Up Show* dialog box to change *Advance Slides* to **Manually**. Click **OK**.

13. Add annotations on slides 3 and 4 using the **Pen** with **Red** ink and keep annotations. Use *Presenter View* and practice making annotations on the presenter slide.
    a. **_Slide 3:_** Circle the "55-60" and "100" screen sizes.
    b. **_Slide 4:_** Go to this hidden slide and circle the following phrases in the bulleted items: "level with the middle," "reduce color clarity," and "visibility at all seats."
    c. Keep ink annotations.

14. Use the *Set Up Show* dialog box to prepare a kiosk presentation with looping.
    a. For *Advance Slides*, select **Use timings, if present**.
    b. Select **Browsed at a kiosk (full screen)** and show **All** slides.
    c. Select the appropriate monitor.
    d. Click **OK**.

15. Save and close the presentation (Figure 3-90).

3-90 PowerPoint 3-4 completed

Independent Project 3-5

For the third training session for new hires on presenting effectively, Davon Washington, Management Consultant at Solution Seekers, Inc., is preparing guidelines for delivering a presentation with projection equipment. For this project, you finish the presentation that Davon has prepared.
[Student Learning Outcomes 3.1, 3.2, 3.4, 3.5, 3.7, 3.8]

File Needed: **PresentationDelivery-03.pptx**
Completed Project File Name: **[your initials] PowerPoint 3-5.pptx**

Skills Covered in This Project

- Apply a background picture fill.
- Apply animation and effect options.
- Create and print notes pages.
- Hide and reveal slides.
- Rehearse a presentation and save timings.
- Use *Presenter View.*
- Use ink annotation pens.
- Record a presentation with narration.

1. Open the presentation **PresentationDelivery-03**.

2. Save the presentation as **[your initials] PowerPoint 3-5**.

3. On slide 3, make the following changes:
   a. From the *Block Arrows* category in the *Shapes* gallery, select the **right arrow** and draw an arrow (*Height* **1.7"** and *Width* **4"**). The **Shape Fill** color is **Dark Red**, **Accent 1**.
   b. Apply the *Shape Effect* of **Shadow**, **Offset Bottom**.
   c. Adjust the arrow position as shown in Figure 3-91.
   d. Delete the "Answer" text box.

4. Apply the **Fade** transition with the **Smoothly** effect option. Change the *Duration* to **01.00**. Apply these settings to all slides.

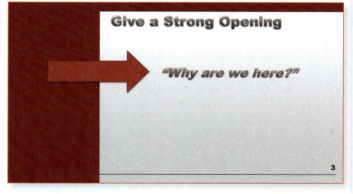

3-91 Shape added

5. Apply animation on five slides and change effect options as shown in the following table.

Slide	Object	Animation Effect	Effect Options	Start	Duration
2	Text, You get only one . . .	*Bounce* (Entrance)	*As One Object*	*After Previous*	*02.00*
5	Butterfly image	*Grow & Turn* (Entrance)	*None*	*After Previous*	*02.00*
7	Graphic	*Wipe* (Entrance)	*From Left*	*After Previous*	*02.50*
11	Text, Make it memorable	*Bounce* (Entrance)	*As One Object*	*After Previous*	*02.00*
12	Success shape	*Grow/Shrink* (Emphasis)	*Both, Larger*	*After Previous*	*02.50*

6. Prepare speaker notes on two slides. Apply bullets and indent the bulleted text (Figure 3-92).

   a. *Slide 2:* Never underestimate the importance of a first impression
        If possible, welcome people as they arrive for your presentation

   b. *Slide 9:* Be careful with how you use humor
       • Use humor only if it is appropriate
       • Avoid jokes—you could unintentionally offend someone
     Humor works best when it fits the presentation and seems natural
       • Break the ice
       • Be yourself; be real
       • Make your audience feel comfortable
     Choose stories or examples from your own experience

7. Print notes pages for slides 5, 6, and 7.

8. Hide slide 8.

9. Review the presentation to check transitions and animations.
   a. On the *Transitions* tab, deselect **On Mouse Click**.
   b. Change *After* to **00:03:00** seconds.
   c. Click **Apply To All**.
   d. Start your slide show from the beginning and review all slide movements.

3-92 Notes with bullets and indents

10. Use *Presenter View* to review your presentation and make ink annotations.
   a. Deselect **Use Timings** [*Slide Show* tab, *Set Up* group] so you can advance through the slides at your own pace.
   b. Select **Use Presenter View**.
   c. Press **Alt+F5** to begin the presentation.
   d. Navigate through slides using the *Presenter View* arrow buttons.
   e. Click the **See all slides** button and click thumbnails to move to different slides.
   f. Add annotations on the following slides using the **Pen** with **Blue** ink. If you are not satisfied with your markings, then use the **Eraser** and try again.
       • *Slide 2:* Circle the words "Be professional."
       • *Slide 4:* Draw a rectangle around the words "Eye Contact" and "Smile" (Figure 3-93).
       • *Slide 7:* Circle the words "Avoid monotone."
       • *Slide 10:* Circle "End on time."
   g. At the end of the presentation, click **Keep** to save annotations.

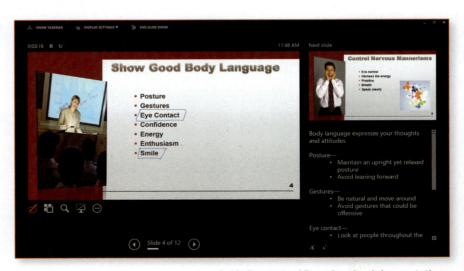

3-93 *Presenter View* showing ink annotations

11. If you have a microphone on your computer, record a slide show with narration.
    a. Print notes pages for additional slides where you need reminders of what to discuss.
    b. On the *Slide Show* tab, click **Record Slide Show** and select both **Slide and animation timings** and **Narrations and laser pointer**.
    c. Begin on the first slide and speak clearly into your microphone as each slide is displayed.
    d. Save and close your presentation (Figure 3-94).

3-94 PowerPoint 3-5 completed

Independent Project 3-6

At the Hamilton Civic Center (HCC), classes are offered for a variety of fitness activities. For this project, you complete a presentation to promote the water aerobics classes at several community events. It will also be used as a self-running presentation at the HCC front desk.
[Student Learning Outcomes 3.1, 3.2, 3.3, 3.4, 3.5, 3.6, 3.8]

File Needed: *WaterAerobics-03.pptx*
Completed Project File Names: *[your initials] PowerPoint 3-6a.pptx* and *[your initials] PowerPoint 3-6b.pptx*

Skills Covered in This Project

- Create custom theme colors.
- Modify background fill colors.
- Change object colors on selected slides.
- Apply animation and effect options.
- Change to a widescreen slide size.
- Hide and reveal a slide.
- Use slide show navigation tools, keyboard shortcuts, and blank slides.
- Link to an online video.
- Prepare a kiosk presentation.

---

1. Open the presentation **WaterAerobics-03**.

2. Save the presentation as **[your initials] PowerPoint 3-6a**.

3. Use the *Create New Theme Colors* dialog box to create a custom theme. Change four colors according to the *Red*, *Green*, and *Blue* numbers shown in the following table. Name the custom theme Water and save it (Figure 3-95).

3-95 *Water* theme colors

	Text/ Background - Dark 2	Accent 1	Accent 3	Accent 5
Red	7	53	16	255
Green	55	151	89	51
Blue	99	241	100	153

4. Change the background colors.
   a. Click the **More** button [*Design* tab, *Variants* group] and select **Background Styles**. Click **Style 2** so a light blue is applied to all slides in the presentation.
   b. On slides 1 and 8, use the *Format Background* pane to change the **Solid Fill** to **Dark Blue**, **Text 2**.
   c. On slides 1 and 8, change the color for the text at the bottom of these slides to **White, Background 1** (Figure 3-96).

5. Change the color for the following two objects to **Pink, Accent 5**:
   a. *Slide 3:* Text Fill for "Fun"
   b. *Slide 4:* Shape Fill for the table heading row

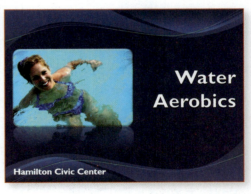

3-96 Title slide in standard slide size

6. Type the following speaker notes on slide 4 (Figure 3-97):

   Swimming classes, scuba classes, and the local swim team practice sessions are scheduled at other times.
   Check with the front desk for unscheduled time when the pool is open.
   Each class is 6 weeks long.

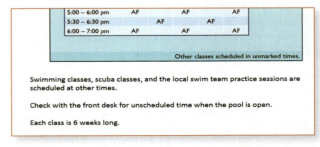

3-97 Notes page

7. Apply the **Ripple** transition with the **From Top-Left** effect option. Apply this transition to all slides.

8. Apply animation on four slides and change effect options as shown in the following table:

Slide	Object	Animation Effect	Effect Options	Start	Duration
2	Bulleted list	*Fly In* (Entrance)	*From Bottom-Right, By Paragraph*	*After Previous*	*01.00*
3	Bulleted list	*Fly In* (Entrance)	*From Bottom, As One Object*	*After Previous*	*01.00*
3	*WordArt* "Fun"	*Bounce* (Entrance)	*As One Object*	*After Previous*	*02.50*
5	Text box	*Wipe* (Entrance)	*From Left, As One Object*	*After Previous*	*02.00*

9. Save the presentation to preserve the file in the **Standard 4:3** slide size.

10. Resave the presentation as *[your initials] PowerPoint 3-6b*.

11. Click the **Design** tab and change *Slide Size* to **Widescreen 16:9**.
    a. Make the following adjustments so objects better fit the wider screen size:
       - *Slide 1:* Increase the picture size (*Height* **4"** and *Width* **6"**). Move the picture and text as shown in Figure 3-98.
       - **Slide 4:** Resize the text box on the right so the text fits on four lines (Figure 3-99). Align it to the slide on the right.
       - **Slide 4:** Right-align the text box at the bottom of the slide and then extend the left end of the box to fit across the bottom of the slide.
       - **Slide 5:** Repeat the same alignment and size increase process for the text box at the bottom of the slide.

12. Hide slide 5.

13. Use *Slide Show* view to practice the following features:
    a. Use the navigation buttons.
    b. Right-click and use the shortcut menu.
    c. Use keyboard shortcuts.
    d. Blank slides.
    e. Go to the hidden slide 5.
    f. Point to slide objects with the laser pointer.

14. After slide 4, insert a new slide with the *Title Only* layout. Type the title Learn Online.

3-98 Title slide in widescreen slide size

3-99 Text boxes adjusted

15. On slide 5, use the *Insert Video* dialog box to find and insert an online video.
    a. Use the search words water aerobics exercises and select an appropriate video. For referencing purposes, write down the name of the video and online source from the lower left of the dialog box. Click **Insert**.
    b. Increase the video size if the quality remains acceptable.
    c. Below the video, add the name of the video and online source.
    d. Test the video in *Slide Show* view to be sure it plays correctly.

16. Rehearse the presentation and save timings.
    a. Modify the timings to advance each slide after approximately 3–5 seconds.

17. Set up a kiosk presentation so it automatically loops.
    a. Show all slides and use timings.

18. Test the presentation and make any needed timing adjustments.

19. Save and close the presentation (Figure 3-100).

3-100 PowerPoint 3-6 completed

Improve It Project 3-7

Delivering news that employees may perceive as bad news is a difficult task. Improve this text-only presentation about presenting news to employees. Use existing slide text to create notes pages. Create custom theme colors. To communicate the message in a more visual way, add *SmartArt* graphics, brief text, and appropriate pictures. The figures in this section provide slide examples; your slides may differ slightly from these examples.
[Student Learning Outcomes 3.1, 3.2, 3.4, 3.8]

File Needed: ***Announcement-03.pptx***
Completed Project File Names: ***[your initials] PowerPoint 3-7.pptx***

Skills Covered in This Project

- Create custom theme colors.
- Modify slide content using pictures. *SmartArt,* and text boxes.
- Create and print notes pages.

- Apply appropriate transitions.
- Rehearse a presentation and save timings.
- Prepare a kiosk presentation.

1. Open the presentation ***Announcement-03***.

2. Save the presentation as ***[your initials] PowerPoint 3-7***.

3. Create custom theme colors. Change five colors and save the custom theme with the name Announce.

	Text/Background - Dark 2	Text/Background - Light 2	Accent 1	Accent 2	Accent 3
Red	38	255	255	124	204
Green	19	230	153	26	236
Blue	0	193	0	26	255

4. On slide 1, make the text more distinctive.
   a. Apply bold to the slide placeholders.
   b. Increase the title text **66 pts.** and "Big" to **96 pts**. Change the font color to **Orange**, **Accent 1**, **Lighter 40%**.
   c. Increase the subtitle text to **32 pts**. and "You" to **48 pts**. (Figure 3-101).

3-101 **Revised title slide**

5. On slide 2, use the existing bulleted text to create a notes page.
   a. Click the **Notes** button so you can see the *Notes* pane in *Normal* view. Increase the size of the *Notes* pane so you can see it while you are working on each slide.
   b. Copy the existing bulleted text and paste it in the *Notes* pane. Arrange this text neatly (Figure 3-102).

6. On slide 2, show that "change" can be perceived as both good and bad (Figure 3-103).
   a. Replace the bulleted text with three short items: Fear, Dread, Be resistant. Resize the body placeholder and move it to the lower right.

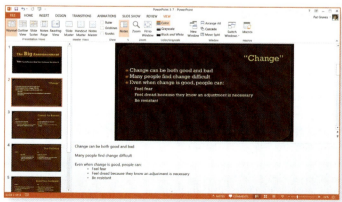

3-102 *Notes* pane expanded

b. Use the search word anxiety to find a similar picture and insert it. Apply the **Rounded Corner Diagonal**, **White** picture style and change the **Picture Border** to **Black**, **Background 2**.

c. Insert a *SmartArt* **Opposing Arrows** layout from the *Relationship* category. Type the text Good and Bad. Apply the **Inset** *SmartArt Style.*

d. Resize chart objects and position them as shown in Figure 3-103.

3-103 Slide 2 revised

7. Prepare the remaining notes pages on slides 3-6:
   a. Cut the existing bulleted text and paste this text on notes pages for each slide. Also include the words "Do" and "Don't."
   b. On each slide, delete the title and heading placeholders.

8. On slide 3, using a picture, emphasize what you should and should not do to control rumors (Figure 3-104).
   a. Insert a text box and type Don't create false expectations. Change the font size to **24 pts**. and emphasize the word "Don't" by increasing the font size to **32 pts**. and changing the color to **Orange**, **Accent 1**. Change the shape fill color to **Black**, **Background 2** (this is a very dark brown).

3-104 Slide 3 revised

   b. Duplicate this text box and change the text to Do explain things in a positive way.
   c. Use the search word excitement to find a similar picture and insert it. To match the picture on slide 1, apply the **Rounded Corner Diagonal**, **White** picture style and change the **Picture Border** to **Black**, **Background 2**.

9. On slide 4, using a picture, emphasize what you should and should not do in your delivery of bad news (Figure 3-105).
   a. Copy the "Don't" and "Do" text boxes from slide 3 and paste them on slide 4. Change the slide 4 text boxes to: Don't be insincere or "slick" and Do be confident and caring.
   b. Use the search word relax to find a similar picture and insert it. Apply the same picture style.
   c. Resize the picture and position objects as shown.

3-105 Slide 4 revised

10. On slide 5, using a picture, emphasize what you should and should not do to reflect your understanding of your audience (Figure 3-106).
    a. Copy the "Don't" and "Do" text boxes from slide 4 and paste them on slide 5. Change the slide 5 text boxes to: Don't be condescending and Do show your understanding.
    b. Use the search word meeting to find a similar picture and insert it. Apply the same picture style.
    c. Resize the picture and position objects as shown.

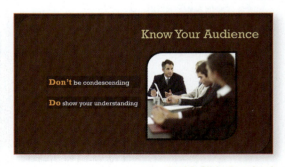

3-106 Slide 5 revised

11. On slide 6, using a picture, provide a strong summary statement (Figure 3-107).
    a. Insert a text box and type this text: Treat people as you would like to be treated.
    b. Make the text bold, increase the font size to **32 pts**., and change the shape fill to **Black, Background 2**.
    c. Use the search word meeting to find a similar picture and insert it. Apply the same picture style.
    d. Resize the picture and position objects as shown.

12. Apply the **Gallery** transition to all slides.

13. Print notes pages for slides 2-5.

14. Rehearse the presentation and save timings.

15. Modify the timings and change the *After* seconds to **00:03:00**.

16. Set up the slide show for a kiosk presentation.

17. Save and close the presentation (Figure 3-108).

3-107 Slide 6 revised

3-108 PowerPoint 3-7 completed

Challenge Project 3-8

For this project, explain the benefits of tablet computing and factors to consider when purchasing a tablet. Using sources such as www.pcmag.com, list some of the top-rated products and their prices. Describe common features, applications, and accessories.
[Student Learning Outcomes 3.1, 3.2, 3.3, 3.4, 3.5, 3.9]

File Needed: None
Completed Project File Name: *[your initials] PowerPoint 3-8.pptx*

Create a new presentation and save it as *[your initials] PowerPoint 3-8*. Modify your presentation according to the following guidelines:

- Select an appropriate theme and create custom theme colors for a high-tech appearance.
- Change to a widescreen format.
- Include pictures from www.pcmag.com or other sources and credit the source below each picture.
- Animate approximately three objects for emphasis and apply appropriate effects.
- Rehearse the presentation and save timings.
- Link to an online video.
- Prepare a slide listing your references and include it as the last slide in your presentation.
- Use *Package Presentation for CD* to save the presentation to a folder.

Challenge Project 3-9

Prepare a presentation to promote a student or civic organization. Use pictures and very brief text to convey the aim and purpose of the organization. Consider using an organization chart to illustrate the officer or committee structure. Apply styles and text treatments consistently.
[Student Learning Outcomes 3.1, 3.2, 3.3, 3.4, 3.6, 3.9]

File Needed: None
Completed Project File Name: *[your initials] PowerPoint 3-9.pptx*

Create a new presentation and save it as *[your initials] PowerPoint 3-9*. Modify your presentation according to the following guidelines:

- Select an appropriate theme and then create custom theme colors for your topic.
- Modify backgrounds by applying a gradient fill to all slides and a picture fill to one slide.
- Design slides with a variety of illustration techniques and minimal text.
- Add transitions and animations with appropriate effects.
- Create and print notes pages.
- Include an online video if one is available and credit your source.
- Prepare a slide listing your references and include it as the last slide in your presentation.
- Rehearse the presentation and use a variety of navigation techniques.
- Use *Package Presentation for CD* to save your presentation to a folder.

Challenge Project 3-10

Create a presentation about living green. Focus on ways to conserve water and other resources. Use web sites such as www.mygreenside.org and others. Prepare a slide listing your references and include it as the last slide in your presentation.
[Student Learning Outcomes 3.1, 3.2, 3.3, 3.4, 3.6, 3.8]

File Needed: None
Completed Project File Name: *[your initials] PowerPoint 3-10.pptx*

Create a new presentation and save it as *[your initials] PowerPoint 3-10*. Modify your presentation according to the following guidelines:

- Create custom theme colors that fit the "green" topic.
- Modify backgrounds and use at least one picture fill.
- Design slides with a variety of illustration techniques and minimal text.
- Add transitions and animations with appropriate effects.
- Create and print notes pages.
- Include an online video about "green" living and credit your source.
- Hide slides and blank slides.
- Rehearse the presentation, save timings during the rehearsal and then modify timings.
- Prepare a kiosk presentation.

appendices

Common Office 2013 Keyboard Shortcuts

Action	Keyboard Shortcut
Save	Ctrl+S
Copy	Ctrl+C
Cut	Ctrl+X
Paste	Ctrl+V
Select All	Ctrl+A
Bold	Ctrl+B
Italic	Ctrl+I
Underline	Ctrl+U
Close *Start* page or *Backstage* view	Esc
Open *Help* dialog box	F1
Switch windows	Alt+Tab

Word 2013 Keyboard Shortcuts

Action	Keyboard Shortcut
File Management	
Open a new blank Word document	Ctrl+N
Save	Ctrl+S
Open *Save As* dialog box	F12
Open an existing document from the *Backstage* view	Ctrl+O
Open an existing document from the *Open* dialog box	Ctrl+F12
Close a document	Ctrl+W
Editing	
Toggle on/off *Show/Hide*	Ctrl+Shift+8
Copy	Ctrl+C
Cut	Ctrl+X
Paste	Ctrl+V
Bold	Ctrl+B
Italic	Ctrl+I
Underline	Ctrl+U
Left align text	Ctrl+L
Center text	Ctrl+E
Right align text	Ctrl+R
Justify text	Ctrl+J

Action	Keyboard Shortcut
Single line spacing	Ctrl+1
Double line spacing	Ctrl+2
1.5 line spacing	Ctrl+5
Undo	Ctrl+Z
Repeat/Redo	Ctrl+Y
Insert line break	Shift+Enter
Insert page break	Ctrl+Enter
Insert column break	Ctrl+Shift+Enter
Insert non-breaking space	Ctrl+Shift+spacebar
Copy formatting	Ctrl+Shift+C
Paste formatting	Ctrl+Shift+V
Increase font size	Ctrl+Shift+. (Ctrl+>)
Decrease font size	Ctrl+Shift+, (Ctrl+<)
Insert an endnote	Alt+Ctrl+D
Insert a footnote	Alt+Ctrl+F
Update field	F9
Open Panes and Dialog Boxes	
Print area on the *Backstage* view	Ctrl+P
Open *Font* dialog box	Ctrl+D
Open *Spelling and Grammar* pane	F7
Open *Thesaurus* pane	Shift+F7
Open *Navigation* pane	Ctrl+F
Open *Find and Replace* dialog box with the *Replace* tab selected	Ctrl+H
Open *Find and Replace* dialog box with the *Go To* tab selected	Ctrl+G or F5
Open *Insert Hyperlink* dialog box	Ctrl+K
Open Word Help dialog box	F1
Selection and Navigation	
Select all	Ctrl+A
Turn selection on (continue to press F8 to select word, sentence, paragraph, or document)	F8
Move the insertion point to the beginning of the document	Ctrl+Home
Move the insertion point to the end of the document	Ctrl+End
Move the insertion point to the beginning of a line	Ctrl+left arrow
Move the insertion point to the end of a line	Ctrl+right arrow
Switch window	Alt+Tab

Excel 2013 Keyboard Shortcuts

Action	Keyboard Shortcut
File Management	
Open a new blank workbook	Ctrl+N
Open an existing workbook from the *Backstage* view	Ctrl+O
Open an existing workbook from the *Open* dialog box	Ctrl+F12
Close	Ctrl+W
Save	Ctrl+S
Move to cell A1	Ctrl+Home
Next worksheet	Ctrl+Page Down
Previous worksheet	Ctrl+Page Up
Editing	
Cut	Ctrl+X
Copy	Ctrl+C
Paste	Ctrl+V
Undo	Ctrl+Z
Repeat/Redo	Ctrl+Y
Underline	Ctrl+U
Bold	Ctrl+B
Italic	Ctrl+I
Open *Format Cells* dialog box	Ctrl+1
Edit mode (insertion point appears within the cell)	F2
Manual line break in a cell	Ctrl+Enter
Toggle between formula view and results view	Ctrl+~
Customizing Sheets	
Hide row	Ctrl+9
Hide column	Ctrl+0
Unhide row	Ctrl+Shift+(
Insert dialog box (cell, row, or column)	Ctrl+plus sign (+)
Insert worksheet	Shift+F11
Insert chart object	Alt+F1
Formula Creation	
Open *Insert Function* dialog box	Shift+F3
Insert a plus sign	Shift+=
Insert a multiplication sign	Shift+8
Insert an exponent sign	Shift+6
Insert an open parenthesis	Shift+9

Action	Keyboard Shortcut
Insert a closed parenthesis	Shift+0
Insert the *SUM* function	Alt+=
Absolute symbol toggle	F4
Open *Paste Name* dialog box (insert range name)	F3

Access 2013 Keyboard Shortcuts

Action	Keyboard Shortcut
Database File Management	
Open a new blank database	Ctrl+N
Open an existing database	Ctrl+O
Editing	
Cut	Ctrl+X
Copy	Ctrl+C
Paste	Ctrl+V
Working with Objects	
Open or close *Navigation* pane	F11
Open selected object in the default view	Enter
Open selected object in *Design* view	Ctrl+Enter
Save a database object; if first time saving the object, opens the *Save As* dialog box	Ctrl+S
Open the *Save As* dialog box	F12
Open shortcut menu for the selected object	Shift+F10
Working with Text and Data	
Move to next field in a table, query, or form	Tab
Move to preceding cell in a table, query, or form	Shift+Tab
Insert line break when entering data in a *Short Text* or *Long Text* field	Ctrl+Enter
Undo changes to current field. Undoes all changes if more than one field on current record has been changed.	ESC
Switch between *Edit* mode (insertion point displayed) and *Navigation* mode	F2
Select current column (works in *Navigation* mode only)	Ctrl+spacebar
Increase selection to add adjacent column to the right	Shift+right arrow
Increase selection to add adjacent column to the left	Shift+left arrow
Open *Find and Replace* dialog box	Ctrl+F
Open *Find and Replace* dialog box with the *Replace* tab selected	Ctrl+H
Find next	Shift+F4

Action	Keyboard Shortcut
Working in Design View	
Open *Expression Builder* dialog box	Ctrl+F2
Open *Zoom* window	Shift+F2
Open or close the *Properties* window for the selected control	F4
Show or hide *Field* list	Alt+F8
Switch to *Form* view from *Design* view	F5
Print Preview Shortcuts	
Open *Page Setup* dialog box from *Print Preview* view	S
Open *Print* dialog box from *Print Preview* view	P or Ctrl+P

PowerPoint 2013 Keyboard Shortcuts

Action	Keyboard Shortcut
File Management	
Open a new blank presentation	Ctrl+N
Open an existing presentation from the *Backstage* view	Ctrl+O
Open an existing presentation from the *Open* dialog box	Ctrl+F12
Open *Save As* dialog box	F12
Save	Ctrl+S
Editing	
Cut	Ctrl+X
Copy	Ctrl+C
Paste	Ctrl+V
Duplicate slides	Ctrl+D
Undo	Ctrl+Z
Redo	Ctrl+Y
Soft return, causes text to wrap to the next line	Shift+Enter
Slide Movement in Normal View	
Move to first slide	Home
Move to last slide	End
Move to next slide	Page Down or down arrow
Move to previous slide	Page Up or up arrow
Move from the slide title to the body placeholder	Ctrl+Enter
Slide Movement in Slide Show View	
Start a presentation slide show from the beginning	F5
Open *Presenter View* and start a slide show	Alt+F5

Action	Keyboard Shortcut
Advance to the next slide	N, spacebar, right arrow, down arrow, Enter, or Page Down
Go to the previous slide	P, Backspace, left arrow, up arrow or Page Up
Go to a particular slide	Slide number, Enter
Go to a particular slide by opening *All Slides* dialog box and selecting a slide title	Ctrl+S
Go to a hidden slide	H or slide number, Enter
Blanks the screen to black	B or period
Blanks the screen to white	W or comma
Stop or restart an automatic show	S or +
Ink Markup in Slide Show View	
Change pointer to pen	Ctrl+P
Change pointer to arrow	Ctrl+A
Change pointer to eraser	Ctrl+E
Show or hide ink markup	Ctrl+M
Erase markings on the screen	E

glossary

3D cell reference Cell address that is not physically located in the same sheet as the cell containing the reference.

3D Rotation Style effect option that includes parallel, perspective, and oblique options to create an illusion of depth.

A

absolute cell reference Cell address that contains dollar signs ($) which prevent the specified cell address from being altered during a copy process.

Access table Database object that stores a collection of related records.

active cell Selected cell in a worksheet; a border around the selected cell and the displayed cell address in the name box indicates which cell is considered active in a worksheet.

adjustment handle Square that shapes curves or points.

Advanced Filter Filter option that hides rows of data that are unnecessary and exports rows that fit a criteria; allows for more advanced filtering options such as multi-level criteria.

aggregate function Function that performs calculations on a group of records such as *AVERAGE*, *COUNT*, and *SUM*.

alignment Arrangement of cell contents in relation to the left and right sides of a cell (horizontal) and the top and bottom of a cell (vertical).

Allow Additions property Form property that controls whether the form allows users to enter data into the database.

Allow Deletions property Form property that controls whether the form allows users to delete a record from the database.

Allow Edits property Form property that controls whether the form allows users to change data in the database.

alternative text (alt text) Information tag that appears when a reader places the pointer on a table or graphic object; also used with screen readers to accommodate those with visual impairments.

AND logical operator Operator that requires that a record meet all of the individual conditions to be included in the results.

animation Movement of objects on a slide.

app Short for application; software program or Windows 8 application or accessory.

append row Last row in a table, indicated by an asterisk; enter data values into the fields in the append row to add a new record into the table.

area chart Chart type that shows data changes over time; emphasizes the total value of a trend.

argument Information within parentheses in a function that determines what value a function returns.

array Range of cells such as A1:A4 or series of numbers such as 1, 2, 3, 4, 5.

arrow Line style that provides arrowheads or other shapes for both ends of a line.

arrow settings Line option that controls the size of the shape at both ends of an arrow.

ascending order Sort order that arranges data from lowest to highest for a numeric field or from A to Z for a text field.

AutoCalculate Tool in the status bar that displays sums, averages, counts, minimum, and maximum values for cells.

AutoComplete Feature that fills in the complete day, month, or date as you type.

AutoCorrect Feature that corrects commonly misspelled words.

AutoCorrect Options smart tag Tag that appears by a word that has been automatically corrected.

AutoFilter A filter option in which drop-down arrows appear on column headings and filter data that is not relevant based on specified criteria.

AutoFit Formatting option that automatically adjusts column width or row height to reveal all the contents within a column or row; also referred to as *AutoFit Column Width*.

AutoFormat Feature that controls the formatting of items such as numbered and bulleted lists, fractions, ordinal numbers, hyphens and dashes, quotes, indents, and hyperlinks.

AutoNumber data type Data type used to store a unique number, automatically assigned by Access.

AutoOutline An option that creates groupings based on pre-existing formulas in your data and displays buttons that you can use to collapse or expand groups of data.

axis title Chart element that names the horizontal and vertical axes using placeholders or textboxes.

B

Backstage view Area of an Office application where you perform common actions (such as *Save*, *Open*, *Print*, and *Share*) and change application options; document properties are displayed here.

Banded Columns *Table Style* option featuring columns that have alternating colors.

Banded Rows *Table Style* option featuring rows that have alternating colors.

bar chart Chart type that is similar to a column chart with bars shown horizontally.

bar tab stop Tab that inserts a vertical line at the tab stop.

Bevel Style effect option that applies light and dark areas to create a dimensional appearance so objects and text look raised or inset.

bibliography List of the sources used in a report.

bibliography style Style that determines the formatting of sources and citations in a report.

blank workbook Pre-built and ready-to-use template with default fonts, font sizes, themes, and margins; all new blank workbooks are based on the blank workbook template.

block layout Report layout option available when grouping records that displays the fields in a row and column format with the field names displayed as column heads; the grouped field displays in the left-most column but on the same row as the first record for the grouping.

bookmark Location in a document that is electronically marked and can be linked to a hyperlink or cross-reference.

border Line around text, paragraph, page, cell, table, or graphic object.

bound control Control that gets its value from a field in a table.

bound form Form that is directly connected to a table or query as the data source.

bulleted list Unordered list of items; a bullet symbol precedes each item, and a left and hanging indent controls left alignment.

C

calculated control Control that gets its value from an expression.

calculated field Field that gets its value from a calculation instead of a value that is entered into the field.

CamelCase notation Naming convention for object and field names in which spaces are omitted between compound words and each word starts with a capital letter.

cap type Line option that controls the look of the ends of lines; usually applied to single lines or arrows.

caption Descriptive text that appears above or below a graphic.

caption property Field property used to create a caption that displays in the column header in datasheet view of a table and in the labels on forms and reports; captions often include spaces and multiple words and are more readable than a field name.

Cascade Delete Related Records Referential integrity option that allows you to delete a record from a table even if there are matching records in related tables; also deletes all matching records from related tables.

Cascade Update Related Fields Referential integrity option that allows a primary key value to be changed in a record in one table and automatically updates the foreign key values in matching records in related tables.

category Group of data values from each row in a spreadsheet.

category axis (X-axis) Horizontal border in the plot area that measures charted data.

category label Text label in a row or column that describes a data series in a chart.

cell Intersection of a column and a row.

cell address Letter of the column and number of the row that represent the location of a cell; also referred to as a cell reference.

cell margins Space around the top, bottom, left, and right of the text inside a table cell.

cell reference Column letter and row number that represent the location of the cell; also referred to as a cell address.

cell selector Pointer that selects a cell of a table.

cell style Set of built-in formats, which include a variety of borders, shading, alignment, and other options.

center tab stop Tab that centers text at the tab stop.

Change Case Button used to change text from the case shown to a different case such as uppercase to lowercase.

Change Colors Gallery that lists different color combinations for SmartArt layouts that are based on theme colors.

character spacing Space between letters and words.

chart Object that displays numeric data in the form of a graph to compare data values or display data trends.

chart area One of several chart background elements; background area where the entire chart is displayed in a frame.

chart element One of the components that make up a chart, such as chart floor, chart area, data series, chart wall, etc.

chart label A title, legend, or data table used to organize chart data.

chart object An object that represents a chart in a workbook.

Chart Style Tool that allows you to quickly apply a set of built-in formats to alter the look of a chart.

Chart Styles Gallery that lists preset effects for chart elements.

chart title Chart element that names the chart using placeholders or text boxes.

chart type Category of charts that represent data using various shapes and subtypes.

check box Box that allows you to choose one or more from a group of options.

check box control Control on a form or report used to display data for a field with a Yes/No data type; when used on a form, it can also accept data when a user enters a value.

circular reference Error that occurs when a formula includes the cell address of cell where the formula is located.

citation Abbreviated source information in the body of the report that credits the source of information referred to in a document.

Clear Formatting Command that removes formatting from selected text and formats the text in *Normal* style.

clip art Electronic graphical image.

Clipboard Location where multiple copied items from an Office file or other source such as a web page are stored.

Clipboard pane Pane that displays the contents of the *Clipboard*.

Color Saturation Color option that controls the intensity of a color; colors that are vibrant are highly saturated and colors that are muted have a low saturation level.

Color Tone Color option that controls temperature values to make a picture's colors more cool or warm.

column Vertical grouping of cells in a table or a vertical area of text in a document.

columnar layout Form or report layout that displays the fields in one column with the field names displayed to the left of the field.

column break Formatting option that ends a column and pushes subsequent text to the next column.

column chart Chart type that shows a comparison of values or data changes over time.

column selector Pointer that selects a column of a table.

combo chart Chart type that is a combination of two chart types such as a column chart with a line chart.

***Command Button* control** Control on a form or report used to perform an action such as *Close Report* or *Open Form*.

Command Button Wizard Tool that guides you through the steps of creating a command button control and assigning an action to the button.

Compact and Repair Database utility that removes unused space from a database to help improve performance; can be used to repair a database in which some objects have become corrupted.

comparison operator A symbol, such as = or >, used to compare two values in an expression.

completeness rule Data integrity rule that ensures a value is entered if required.

compound criteria Criteria used in filters or expressions that combine more than one value using the *AND* and *OR* logical operators.

compound type Line option that provides outlines with two or more lines that vary in thickness.

Compress Pictures Command that reduces presentation file size by reducing picture resolution.

concatenate Combine multiple parts of an equation together into one piece; often used in an expression to combine several fields together.

concatenated key Primary key made up of more than one field; also known as a composite key.

conditional formatting Formatting that is automatically applied only to data values that meet a specific condition.

consistency rule Data integrity rule that ensures a value in one field is consistent with a value in another field.

constant Hardcoded value that does not change, which is entered into a formula.

content control field Word field in which you type custom information such as the date or year.

context menu Menu of commands that appears when you right-click text or an object.

context-sensitive Describes menu options that change depending on what you have selected.

continuous section break Formatting option that divides a document into different sections on the same page so sections can be formatted independently of each other; can also be used at the end of columns to balance column length.

control Item on a form or report such as a text box, label, or command button; used to enter, edit, or display data, or perform tasks in the database.

control layout Structure that helps to align the different controls on a form or report.

Control Wizards Tool that directs Access to launch an available wizard when adding controls to an object in the database; for example, the *Control Wizards* tool must be turned on for the *Command Button Wizard* to activate.

copy Duplicate text or other information.

criteria area Range of cells in a spreadsheet designated for customized criteria for *Advanced Filter* options.

criterion (pl. criteria) Expression entered into a query to limit and focus results.

crop Trim unwanted areas of a selected picture.

crosshair Large plus sign tool used to draw a shape.

cross-reference Note in a document that directs readers to another location in a document.

custom dictionary Location in Office where words that you add are stored.

cut Remove text or other information.

Cycle *SmartArt* graphic type used to illustrate a continuing sequence or concepts related to a central idea.

D

dash type Line option that displays lines made with various combinations of dots and dashes.

dashes Line styles that combine dots and dashes to make different patterns.

database An organized collection of integrated and related tables.

database management system (DBMS) Software that allows a user to create a database; manage the data in the database by adding, deleting, and updating records; sort and retrieve data; and create queries and reports relating to that data.

***Data Entry* property** Form property that determines whether existing data in the database is displayed on the form.

data format rule Data integrity rule that ensures a value entered into a field matches the data type of the field.

data integrity rules A set of rules that ensures data in a database is accurate and consistent.

data label Label that lists the value, category name, or series name of a component of a chart.

data marker Symbol that represents a single point or value in a charted range of cell information; graphical representation of values shown as columns, bars, slices, or data points.

data point One cell in a data series that is included in a chart.

data series Group of data values.

datasheet layout Form layout that displays the fields in *Datasheet* view.

***Datasheet* view** View option that allows you to enter, modify, view, or delete data; available in a table, query, or form.

data table Chart element that shows the data that creates a chart in table format below a chart; table of the values of each data series based on selected source data cells.

data type Field property that determines the type of data that can be entered in a field, what properties can be manipulated, and how that field can be used.

data validation Process of verifying the accuracy of data entered into a table.

***Date* function** Function that obtains the current date from your computer.

decimal tab stop Tab that aligns text at the decimal point at the tab stop.

default Setting that is automatically applied by an application unless you make specific changes.

default value property Field property that sets a value to automatically be entered into a field.

Delay Animation timing command used to make an animation begin at a specified time.

delimited Data file type option that ensures that columns are created based on characters in your file instead of a specified amount of space between data.

descending order Sort order that arranges data from highest to lowest for a numeric field or from Z to A for a text field.

Design view View option that allows you to build or modify the basic structure or functionality of a database object.

destination cell Cell you paste content to after cutting or copying.

dialog box Window that opens and displays additional features.

Different First Page Formatting option that imposes first-page header or footer content that differs from the other headers and footers in a document.

Different Odd & Even Pages Formatting option that imposes headers and/or footers that differ on odd and even pages.

Distribute Columns Table option that evenly distributes column width.

Distribute Rows Table option that evenly distributes row height.

document property Information about a file such as title, author name, subject, etc.

document property field Word field that displays the document property contents in the body, header, or footer of a document.

drop-down list List of options that displays when you click a button.

duplicate Create a copy of an object or a slide.

duration Length of time; controls the speed of transitions and animations in a slide show.

dynamic Describes results that adjust in real time to data changes.

E

effect Formatting feature such as shadow, glow, or soft edges added to an element.

Effect Option Command that controls the direction of slide transitions and animation movement.

Emphasis Animation effect that calls attention to an object that remains on the slide.

endnote Reference, citation, or other text that appears at the end of a document.

Entity-Relationship Diagram (ERD) Diagram used to plan database design.

Entrance Animation effect that occurs when an object appears on the slide.

Excel Start page Opening area of Excel where you can create a new blank workbook, open a previously saved workbook, or create a new workbook from an Excel template.

Excel Table Group of data with an applied *Table* format that allows data to be manipulated within the table independently of the data outside the table.

Exit Animation effect that occurs when an object leaves the slide.

explode Separate pie chart slices.

expression Type of formula used to write validation rules, perform calculations, create query criteria, control macros, and group and sort data in a report.

Expression Builder dialog box Window that provides easy access to tools used to create expressions.

external data Data from an outside source exported into Excel that can be updated whenever a change is made to the original data in its original location.

extract Create a regular folder from a zipped folder.

extract area Range of cells in the spreadsheet designated for customized results from *Advanced Filter* application.

Eyedropper Tool used to match the exact color of an object.

F

field Collection of characters that describes one aspect of a business object or activity (a single unit of data).

field handle Area to select a document property of content control field.

field properties Description of the specific details of each field in a table; basic field properties include the field name, data type, and field size.

File Explorer Window where you browse for, open, and manage files and folders (formerly called Windows Explorer).

file name extension A series of letters automatically added to a file name that identifies the type of file.

fill handle Small black square that appears in the bottom right corner of a cell and changes to a thin black plus sign pointer that can be dragged to copy or fill a series.

filter Feature that limits the data records that display in a datasheet.

Filter by Selection Filter option that displays only the records that match the value in specific fields you have selected.

Find Feature that searches a file to locate specific text and/or formatting.

first line indent Horizontal space between the first line of a paragraph and the left margin.

fixed width Data file type option that ensures that columns are determined by a specified amount of space (e.g., every inch).

Flash Fill *AutoFill* option that recognizes and implements patterns to quickly complete column or row data.

footer Displays content at the bottom of a document page or object.

footnote Reference, citation, or other text that appears at the bottom of a page.

foreign key Field in one table that is also the primary key in another table; used to create relationships between tables.

form Database object used to enter, modify, view, or delete data from a table.

Form button Tool that allows you to quickly create a form; no options are provided during the initial creation process.

Form view View option used to enter and view data.

Form Wizard Tool that guides you through the steps to create a form.

Format Painter Tool that duplicates formatting choices such as font, font size, line spacing, indents, bullets, numbering, styles, etc. from one selection to another selection.

Format property Property that indicates the way a field displays in a table.

formula Mathematical syntax in a cell that calculates and updates results.

Formula Auditing Color-coded editing tool that applies colors to cell ranges and displays lines that point to the cell ranges in a formula's syntax.

Formula bar Area directly below the *Ribbon* that displays cell contents such as formula syntax, numbers, and letters; cell contents can be edited in the *Formula bar*.

Freeze Panes View option that allows you to scroll vertically or horizontally while keeping column and row headings visible.

function Predefined formula that performs a specific task.

G

gallery Group of options on a tab.

Glow Style effect option that provides a colored area around an object that fades into the background color on the slide.

Goal Seek Tool that determines and adjusts the value of a cell until a condition is met in a different cell.

Gradient Option that blends two or more colors or light and dark variations of the current fill color in different directions.

graphics Visual objects such as pictures, clip art, shapes, *SmartArt*, charts, and *WordArt*.

grayscale A range of shades of black in a display or printout.

gridlines Lines that visually frame rows and columns; in PowerPoint, horizontal or vertical lines (depending on the chart type) that appear behind chart elements such as columns or bars or that can be displayed on a slide as an aid to alignment.

group Area on a tab that contains related commands and options; option used to organize data in a report so that similar records appear together.

H

Handout Option that displays or prints 1–9 slides on a page.

hanging indent Additional horizontal space between second and carryover lines of a paragraph and the left margin.

header Displays content at the top of a document or object.

header row First row of a table.

Hierarchy *SmartArt* graphic type used to illustrate a decision tree or top-to-bottom relationship such as an organization chart.

horizontal alignment Content positioning option that aligns material in relation to the left, center, right, or middle (justified) of the page or slide; can also refer to the position of objects in relation to each other.

hyperlink Text or an object that a reader can click to be taken to another location in the document, to a web page, or to a different file.

I

import Transfer data from an application or browser into Excel.

indent Increase the distance between the cell contents and the left boundary of the cell.

ink annotations Markings that call attention to information you mark by writing or drawing on slides.

Input Mask property Property used to specify the format for data entered into a field.

Input Mask Wizard Tool that guides you through the steps to define an input mask; only available on *Short Text* or *Date* fields.

insert control Button that allows you to quickly insert a row or column into a table.

IntelliSense Tool that suggests a list of possible values when you enter an expression.

J

join type Line option that controls the look of the connection point where two lines meet, such as the corner of a rectangle.

junction table Table created to link the two tables in a many-to-many relationship; also known as an intersection table.

justified alignment Content positioning option that aligns material with both the left and right margins.

justified layout Form or report layout option that displays the fields in a horizontal, justified layout with field names displayed above each field.

K

kerning Space between letters in a proportional font.

keyboard shortcut Key or combination of keys that you press to apply a command.

kiosk presentation Self-running slide presentation that automatically loops.

L

label Cell entry that begins with a letter; text in a worksheet that identifies a title and subtitle, row and column headings, and other descriptive information.

label control Control on a form or report that displays the content of the caption property of a field.

landscape orientation Page layout option in which the page is oriented so it is wider than it is tall.

Layout Controls the position of placeholders on a slide.

Layout view Form or report view option used to make design changes to the object and see the effects of the changes in real time.

leader Series of dots or characters that fills the blank space between text and a tab stop.

left indent Horizontal space between a paragraph and the left margin.

left tab stop Tab that aligns text at the left of the tab stop.

legend Descriptive text or key that describes a data series.

Leszynski notation Naming convention for object and field names in which a prefix (called a "tag") is added to a name to indicate object type.

line break Formatting option that controls where lines begin and end, which can be used to keep lines together in a bulleted or numbered list.

line chart Shows data changes over time.

line spacing Amount of space between lines of text within a paragraph.

linking workbooks Process of referring to cells from another workbook in the current workbook.

List *SmartArt* graphic type used to illustrate non-sequential or grouped information.

live preview Display option that allows you to temporarily apply and view a style or formatting feature.

Lock Aspect Ratio Command used to maintain proportion when entering object height or width sizes.

Lock Drawing Mode Tool used to draw more than one of the same shape.

Long Text **data type** Data type used to store alphanumeric data longer than 255 characters or text containing rich text formatting.

lookup field Field used to display a list of data values that users can select to store in the field.

Lookup Wizard Tool that guides you through the steps to create a lookup field.

loop Cycle continuously in a slide show from beginning to end and automatically repeat.

M

many-to-many relationship Relationship between tables in a database where many rows of data in one table can be associated with many rows of data in a related table.

margin Blank space at the top, bottom, left, or right of a document; in a text box, the space between the outside of the box and the text within the box; in a table, the space between a cell border and the cell text.

mathematical order of operations Set of rules that establishes the sequence that operations are performed in multiple-operation expressions and formulas.

Matrix *SmartArt* graphic type used to illustrate the relationship of four parts to the whole.

maximize Increase the size of the window of an open Office file so it fills the entire computer monitor.

Merge Cells Command that combines two or more cells in a row or column.

metadata All properties that describe what data fields in a table represent.

Microsoft account Free account that gives you access to an email account, *SkyDrive* online storage area, and Office Web Apps.

mini toolbar Toolbar listing formatting options that appears when you select text or right-click.

minimize Place an open Office file on the taskbar so it is not displayed on the desktop.

mixed cell reference Cell address that contains one relative cell address component (either the row number or column letter) and one absolute cell address component (the remaining row number or column letter).

Monochromatic Color combinations containing only shades of one color.

multilevel list Customized list that includes a combination of numbers, letters, or bullets.

N

Name **box** Area of the *Formula bar* that displays the cell address of the currently active cell; used to navigate in a worksheet and to name cells.

Navigation **bar** Area at the bottom left corner of a table that contains buttons used to move among table records in *Datasheet* view.

non-breaking space Formatting option that keep words together so they are not separated by word wrap at the end of a line.

normalization Database design process to create well-structured database tables.

normal range Range of cells that does not contain a *Table* format, *AutoFilter* buttons, or an outline and allows you to apply *Subtotals*.

Normal **template** Predesigned and ready-to-use document that includes default fonts, font sizes, line and paragraph spacing, styles, and margins; new blank document.

Normal **view** Default view option where you enter the content of slides and move between slides as you develop them.

Notes Page **view** Option that displays each slide on a page with space below the slide where you can type speaker notes.

null Value in a field that indicates that nothing was ever entered in that field.

number data type Data type used to store numbers in fields that are used in mathematical calculations.

numbered list List that arranges items in order; a number or letter precedes each item, and a left and hanging indent controls left alignment.

NumPages **field** Word field that lists the number of pages in a document.

O

object Major component in an Access database.

Office Web Apps Free online application software you can use to create, save, and edit Office files.

one-to-many relationship Relationship between tables in a database where a row of data in one table can be associated with many rows of data in a related table.

one-to-one relationship Relationship between tables in a database where a row of data in one table can be associated with only one row of data in a related table.

operating system Software that makes a computer function and controls the working environment.

OR **logical operator** Operator that requires that a record meet at least one individual condition to be included in the results.

outdent Negative indent that lines up information outside the left or right margins.

outline Border around selected element.

outline layout A report layout available when grouping records. Displays the grouped field and its label on a separate row at the start of each grouping. The field names are displayed as column heads above the first row of data in each grouping.

Outline view Expands the pane at the left of the slide area to show slide titles and bulleted text.

P

Package Presentation for CD Feature that saves a presentation and related files to a CD or a folder.

page break Formatting option that controls where text on a page ends.

page number field Word field that lists the page number.

paragraph alignment Formatting option that determines how a paragraph is positioned horizontally on the page.

paragraph break Formatting option that you insert when you press **Enter** at the end of a word, line, or paragraph.

paragraph spacing Amount of spacing before and after a paragraph.

paragraph symbol Icon that indicates a paragraph break.

parameter Specific phrase (entered in the *criteria* box of a query field) that displays in the *Enter Parameter Value* dialog box when a parameter query is run.

Parameter Query Query that asks a user to enter a specific criterion value.

paste Place text or other objects that have been stored on the *Clipboard* in a new location.

Pattern Background color Color used with a foreground color to create a pattern.

Pattern Fill Option that applies a mixture of two colors to shapes in various dotted or crosshatch designs.

Pattern Foreground color Color used with a background color to create a pattern.

PDF (portable document format) File format used to convert a file into a static image.

Pen Tool used to write or draw on a slide during a slide show.

Picture Fill *Shape Fill* option that fills the *WordArt* or shape with a picture from a file or from the Office.com clip art collection.

picture layout *SmartArt* graphic type used to show pictures as integral parts of many different diagrams.

pie chart Chart type that shows the values in a data series in proportional sizes that make up a whole pie.

PivotChart Charted data that is dynamic (updates in real time) and contains the same movable field buttons and filter options that a *PivotTable* does.

PivotTable List of data that is dynamic and contains movable field buttons and filter options; a user can physically move different components of a *PivotTable* for different analysis options.

pixel Abbreviated term for picture element, a single unit of information about color.

placeholder In PowerPoint, the area of a slide where you can add text, tables, charts, and pictures. In Word, text that temporarily marks a spot in a document where a citation is missing and needs to be completed.

Plot Area One of several chart background elements; the rectangle between the vertical and horizontal axes that is behind the data markers.

pointer Small icon, such as a block plus sign, thin black plus sign, or white arrow, that appears and moves when you move your mouse or touch your touchpad.

portrait orientation Page layout option in which the page is oriented so it is taller than it is wide.

position A character-spacing option that raises or lowers text by a designated number of points.

Presenter View Option that displays slides, speaker notes, a timer, and features helpful for a speaker; can be displayed on just one monitor or can be displayed on one monitor while the presentation is displayed at full-screen size on a second monitor or projector.

primary key Field that contains a unique value for each record in a table; allows one record to be distinguished from another.

print area Range of cells to be printed.

Print Preview Print option that allows you to see how a document, spreadsheet, or database object will look when printed and to make changes to the printing options before printing.

Process *SmartArt* graphic type used to illustrate sequential steps in a process or workflow.

program options Area in each Office application where you can make changes to the program settings.

protection Layer of security you can apply to a worksheet that allows various cells to be accessible while others are not.

Pyramid *SmartArt* graphic type used to illustrate proportional or interconnected relationships.

query Database object used to find data in a database.

Q

Quick Access toolbar Area located above the *Ribbon* with buttons you use to perform commonly used commands.

Quick Analysis Tool that analyzes cell data and provides charts, colors, and formula suggestions.

Quick Layout Tool that allows you to quickly change both the design and labeling elements of a chart instead of changing individual attributes manually.

Quick Style Tool that allows you to quickly apply a combination of color schemes and formats to alter the look of a chart.

R

radar chart Chart type that shows the combined values of several data series with values relative to a center point.

radio button Round button you click to choose one option from a list.

range Group of cells.

Range Finder Color-coded editing tool that applies colors to each cell or range included in a formula's syntax.

range name A customized name for a cell or range of cells; describes the cell or purpose of a group of cells and makes it easier to interpret a formula..

range rule Data integrity rule that ensures a value in a field falls within an established range of acceptable values.

Reading view Option that displays a slide show at full-screen or alternate window size determined by the viewer.

Recolor Changes picture colors to monotone color variations.

record Collection of related data fields.

record validation rule Validation rule that compares fields in the same table; entered into the *Validation Rule* property of a table.

Recycle Bin Location where deleted files and folders are stored.

redo Repeat an action.

reference marker Number, letter, or symbol that marks a footnote or endnote in the body of a document.

referential integrity The quality of consistency in data entered into related tables; enforcing referential integrity prevents a record in one table from referencing a record that does not exist in a related table.

Reflection Style effect option that shows a mirror image below an object.

Rehearse Timings Feature that helps you to judge the pace of the presentation.

relational database Database in which data is organized into a collection of related tables.

Relationship *SmartArt* graphic type used to illustrate concepts that are connected such as contrasting, opposing, or converging.

relative cell reference Default cell address in Excel; a cell address that changes in the destination cell when copied.

remote control Device that enables a speaker to control a slide show when he or she steps away from the computer during a presentation.

Reorder Animation Animation timing command used to adjust animation sequence.

Replace Feature that searches a file to locate specific text and/or formatting and replace it with specified replacement text and/or formatting.

report Database object used to view and print data in a database.

Report view Report view option that shows all of the data contained in the report; displays in a continuous layout, which does not separate the data into separate pages.

Report Wizard Tool that guides you through the steps to create a report.

Required property Field property that indicates whether a value must be entered into a field or if it can be skipped and left blank.

Reset Picture Command used to restore a picture's original characteristics and dimensions.

resizing pointer Pointer that resizes a graphic object or a table column or row.

restore down Decrease the size of the window of an open Office file so it does not fill the entire computer monitor.

RGB model Typically used for computer displays; colors are formed by blending values of the three numbers for red, green, and blue.

Ribbon Bar that appears at the top of an Office file window and displays available commands.

right indent Horizontal space between a paragraph and the right margin.

right tab stop Tab that aligns text at the right of the tab stop.

rotation handle Tool that appears on an object that you can use to rotate a graphic object.

row Horizontal grouping of cells.

row selector Pointer that selects a row of a table.

ruler Vertical or horizontal guide that displays measurements within the margins of a document.

S

sans serif font One of several font typefaces with letters that do not include structural details (flair).

scale Character-spacing option that changes spacing by a designated percentage.

ScreenTip Descriptive information about a button, drop-down list, launcher, or gallery selection that appears when you place your pointer on the item.

section break Formatting option used to break a document into different sections so sections can be formatted independently of each other.

select method Technique of selecting cell addresses to create a formula.

Select Query Query that locates, or selects, data in a database.

selection/move pointer Four-pointed arrow that selects and moves objects.

serif font One of several font typefaces with letters that feature structural details (flair).

Set Transparent Color Feature that removes one color from a picture; used to remove solid backgrounds.

shading Fill color applied to text, paragraph, page, cell, table, or graphic object.

Shadow Style effect option that provides dimension by inserting a shadow behind or below an object.

shape Graphic object that can be drawn, such as a line, arrow, circle, or rectangle.

shape adjustment handle Yellow diamond that changes the contour of a shape.

shape effect Format feature, such as *Shadow*, *Reflection*, or *Glow*, applied to a graphic object.

shape fill Color that fills a shape or graphic object.

shape outline Border around a graphic object.

Shape Style Set of built-in formats for shapes that include borders, fill colors, and effect components.

SharePoint web server Web server that runs Microsoft's *SharePoint Services* and allows groups of people to share information.

Short Text data type Data type used to store alphanumeric data; the maximum length is 255 characters.

Show check box Box in *Design* view of a query that indicates whether a field used in a query displays in the query results.

Show/Hide Button that displays or hides paragraph breaks, line breaks, spaces, tabs, and other formatting symbols in a document.

Simple Query Wizard Tool that guides you through the steps to create a query.

sizing handles Squares on the corners and sides of an object that resize the object.

SkyDrive Online storage area that is a part of your Microsoft account where you can store and access documents from any computer with an Internet connection.

Slicer Pop-up filtering-menu based on the headings in a table.

slide layout Slide development feature with built-in placeholders for text and other content such as tables, charts, or SmartArt.

Slide Master Feature that stores information about slide backgrounds, layouts, and fonts for each theme.

Slide Show view Option that displays slides in sequence at full-screen size for audience viewing.

Slide Sorter view Option that displays slides as thumbnails.

SmartArt Object that presents information in graphical format.

SmartArt graphics Graphics used to illustrate concepts such as processes, cycles, or relationships.

SmartArt Styles Gallery that lists different effects for emphasizing shapes within a layout.

Soft Edges Style effect option that creates a feathered edge, which gradually blends into the background color.

soft page break Formatting option that allows text to flow to the next page when it reaches the bottom margin of a page.

sort Feature that arranges text, table rows, or records in alphabetical or numerical order.

source Complete bibliographic reference for a book, journal article, or web page.

source cell Cell you cut or copy from when cutting or copying.

source data Data and label cells that are included in chart creation.

Sparklines Miniature chart-like graphics you can add to data in a specified cell.

speaker notes Reminders to help the speaker present that are entered into the Notes pane and are visible in Notes Pane view.

Split Cells Command that divides a single cell into two or more cells.

Split Form Option that allows you to view data two different ways at the same time; the top section of the form displays a columnar layout and the bottom section of the form displays a datasheet layout.

spreadsheet Data displayed in columns and rows.

stacked layout Control layout that organizes the data vertically.

standard slide sizing Display option size that uses a 4:3 aspect ratio.

Start Animation timing command that controls when animation begins.

stepped layout Report layout option available when grouping records; displays the fields in a row and column format with the field names displayed as column heads; the grouped field displays in the left-most column.

stock chart Chart type that shows fluctuation of stock prices with high, low, and close values displayed over time.

Style gallery Collection of preset effects for text, shapes, pictures, or other objects.

style Set of built-in formats, which include a variety of borders, shading, alignment, and other options.

subtotals Tool that allows you to group data and quickly apply functions, such as SUM, AVERAGE, MAX, or MIN, to data in a selected cell range.

summary query Query that analyzes a set of records and displays summarized results.

surface chart Chart type that shows the differences between two sets of data.

syntax Rules that dictate how the various parts of a formula must be written.

T

tab Area on the Ribbon that lists groups of related commands and options.

table Database object that stores a collection of related records.

table of contents List of topics in a document; lists headings in the document and related page numbers.

table selector handle Handle that appears at the upper left of a table when the pointer is on a table.

table style Built-in formats for tables, which include a variety of borders, shading, alignment, and other options.

tab selector Button at the top of the vertical ruler where you select the type of tab stop you want to set on the ruler.

tab stop Marker that controls where the insertion point stops when Tab is pressed.

tabular layout Form or report layout option that displays the fields in a row and column format with the field names displayed as column heads.

target frame Window where a reader is directed when a hyperlink document or web site opens.

Taskbar Horizontal area at the bottom of the Windows desktop where you can launch programs or open folders.

task pane Area at the left or right of an Office application window where you can perform tasks.

template Predesigned and ready-to-use document, workbook, database, or slide presentation that includes formulas, formatting, and viewing options.

test data A set of data created to test a database application to ensure that the system performs as desired.

text box Area where you can type text.

text box control Control on a form or report used to display data; when used on a form, it can also accept data when a user enters a value.

text files Files such as.txt (text) documents, .csv (comma separated values) files, and .prn (printer) files.

text pane Area where you enter text for SmartArt shapes.

text wrapping Formatting option that controls how text wraps around a graphic.

Texture Fill Shape Fill option that applies an image such as woven fabric or wood.

theme Collection of fonts, colors, and effects that you can apply to an entire document, workbook, or presentation.

theme colors Set of background and accent colors.

theme fonts Pair of fonts used for a presentation's headings and body text.

Thesaurus Resource tool that lists synonyms for a selected word.

thumbnail Small picture of an image or layout.

tick marks Symbols that identify the categories, values, or series on an axis.

total row Row added into *Design* view of query that specifies the aggregate function to perform.

Trace Dependents Color-coded auditing tool that displays formulas referenced within a selected formula.

Trace Precedents Color-coded auditing tool that displays the cells within a selected formula.

Transform Style effect option used to change the shape of words.

transition Visual effect that occurs when one slide changes into another slide.

Transparency Color setting that is adjusted by percentage to allow the background to show through objects.

Trendline Tool that calculates and plots averages and forecasts averages based on previously plotted data and numbers.

U

unbound control Control that is not linked to a data source.

unbound form Form that does not have a connection to a data source.

undo Reverse an action.

Unique Records **property** Query property that directs Access to display only records that do not include duplicated values; checks all fields in the table, whether or not they have been included in the query.

Unique Values **property** Query property that directs Access to display only records that do not include duplicated values in the fields included in the query.

unlock Format applied to cells prior to applying protection to a worksheet to allow access to specified cells.

V

Validation Rule **property** Property used to set limits on acceptable values that can be entered into a field.

Validation Text **property** Property used to enter a custom message that displays when a validation rule is violated.

value Number that you type in a cell for numbers, currency, dates, and percentages.

value axis (Y-axis) Vertical border in the plot area that measures charted data.

vertical alignment Content positioning option that aligns material in relation to the top, bottom, or middle of the page or slide; can also refer to the position of objects in relation to each other.

W

weight Thickness of an outline measured in points.

white space Blank space around text and objects in a document; improves the readability of a document and prevents the document from appearing cluttered.

widescreen slide sizing Display option size that uses a 16:9 aspect ratio; a 16:10 aspect ratio is also available.

wildcard character Symbol used in an expression in a query to find records that match, or in a validation rule to require data being entered to match a specific character, number, or pattern.

Windows desktop Working area in Windows.

Windows Start page Opening area of Windows where you select and open programs or apps.

WordArt Graphic object that visually enhances text.

word wrap Formatting option that ensures that text automatically continues to the next line when a line ends at the right margin.

workbook Complete Excel file including all of its worksheets.

worksheet Individual sheet within a workbook; also referred to as a sheet; comparable to a page in a book.

worksheet tab Area near the bottom left of the Excel window that displays the name of the worksheet.

Wrap Text Formatting tool that enables you to display the contents of a cell on multiple lines.

X

X-axis Axis displayed horizontally, usually on the bottom of a chart; also called the category axis.

XY chart Chart type that shows the relationships between several data series using two value axes.

Y

Y-axis Axis displayed vertically, usually on the left of a chart; also called the value axis.

Z

zipped (compressed) folder Folder that has a reduced file size and can be attached to an email.

zoom Change file display size.

index

Symbols

wildcard character, A2-88, A3-162, A3-177
(pound signs), in any cell, E1-21
symbols, columns displaying, A1-34
$ (dollar sign), in absolute cell addresses, E2-83
() parentheses operator, A3-179
* (asterisk), as a wildcard for a string of characters, W2-95
* (multiplication) operator, A3-179
* wildcard character, A2-88, A3-162, A3-177
? concatenation operator, A3-178
? wildcard character, A2-88, A3-161, A3-177, W2-95
^ (caret symbol), for an exponent, E2-90
^ (exponent) operator, A3-179
< (less than) operator, A3-161
<= (less than or equal to) operator, A3-161
<> (not equal to) operator, A3-161
> (greater than) operator, A3-161
>= (greater than or equal to) operator, A3-161
= (equal to) operator, A3-161
− (minus sign), clicking, A2-111, A2-123, A2-130
− (subtraction) operator, A3-179
/ (division) operator, A3-179
+ (addition) operator, A3-179
+ (plus sign). See plus sign (+)

Numbers

1:1 (one-to-one) relationship, A2-107
1:M (one-to- many) relationship, A2-107
2D pie type, gallery of, E3-157
2D-Pie chart subtype, E3-168
3D category, P2-97
3D cell references, E2-83, E2-88, E2-92
3D charts, E3-146
3D Clustered Column, P2-123
3D Column Chart, P2-107
3D pie chart
    creating, E3-158, P2-110
    with exploding slice, P2-109
3D Pie PivotChart, E4-244, E4-248
3D Pie type, E3-157, P2-122
3D Rotation effect, P2-69
72 pt. (point), W1-37

A

A to Z button, E4-205, E4-206
absolute cell references, E2-83, E2-84–E2-85, E2-91–E2-92, E2-98
Abstract content control field and type, W3-171
.accdb extension, E4-189, O1-15
.accdt extension, O1-15
accent colors, P2-71
Access 2013
    database files, E4-189–E4-190
    described, A1-2, E4-189, O1-6
    Help System, A3-181
    launching, O1-8
    Start page, A1-15
    views available in, O1-32
Access database. See database
Access database (2000-2003 format) file type, O1-15
Access Database button, A1-43
Access database file type, O1-15
Access expressions. See expressions
Access Help dialog box, O1-10
Access interface, A1-4–A1-7
Access objects. See objects
Access template file type, O1-15
Accounting Number Format button, E1-25
Accounting numeric formatting, applying, E2-121
active cell, E1-6
Add a group option, in the Group, Sort, and Total pane, A4-251, A4-257, A4-269
Add a sort option, in the Group, Sort, and Total pane, A4-250, A4-269
Add Chart Element, displaying data labels, E3-145
Add Chart Elements button, E3-142
Add Existing Fields button, A4-224, A4-243
Add Gradient Stop button, P2-72, P3-144, P3-153
Add New Placeholder option, W3-137
Add Shape button, P2-99
Add Shape tab, P2-116
Add subtotal to list box, E4-218
Add to Dictionary option, W1-32
Add to Print Area, E1-51
Add Trendline dialog box, E3-145
Add-Ins tab, A1-4
addition, in a formula, E2-90
addition (+) operator, E2-89
addition formula, E2-89, E2-91, E2-116
adjacent cells, selecting, E1-10
adjacent columns, selecting, A1-31
adjustment handle, P2-67
Adobe Acrobat, O1-21
Adobe Reader, O1-20–O1-21
Advance Slide options, in the Timing group, P1-35
Advance to next slide button, P3-161
Advanced button, E4-212, E4-217, E4-237
Advanced Filter, E4-211
    creating, E4-212, E4-236–E4-237
    criteria range for, E4-236
    running, E4-217
Advanced Filter dialog box, E4-212
Advanced Properties dialog box, P1-41
Advanced Properties option, E1-43
After spacing, W1-37
After timing, P3-181
aggregate functions, A3-184–A3-185, A3-187, A3-189, A3-196, A3-197
Align buttons, P1-17, P1-35, P1-42, P2-92, W4-221, W4-230, W4-235
Align Center button, W4-238
Align Center Left button, W4-207
Align options, W4-222
Align Text button, P3-154
alignment, of information in a cell, E1-8
alignment buttons, W4-222
Alignment group, E1-8, W4-203
Alignment launcher, E1-9
alignment options, within the cell of a table, W4-203
All Apps, displaying, O1-3
All Charts tab, E3-175, E3-176
All slides dialog box, P3-166
Allow Additions property box, A4-229, A4-266
Allow Deletions property box, A4-229, A4-266
Allow Edits property box, A4-229, A4-266
Allow Value List Edits property, A2-94
Alt key, adjusting a tab stop, W2-69
Alt Text tab, in the Table Properties dialog box, W4-204
Alt+=, opening the SUM function, E2-94
Alt+Ctrl+D, inserting an endnote, W3-130
Alt+Ctrl+F, inserting a footnote, W3-130
Alt+Enter, entering a manual line break, E1-28
Alt+F1, creating a default chart object, E3-134
Alt+F5
    with one monitor, P3-180, P3-187
    using Presenter View, P3-161
Alt+F8, showing or hiding the Field List, A4-224, A4-243
Alternate Background Color drop-down list, A1-35
Alternate Row Color icon, A1-32
alternate row colors, displaying, A1-32
alternative text (Alt text), W4-204
amortization schedule, creating, E2-101
AND compound criteria, in a single field, A3-169
AND conditions, setting, E4-211
AND logical operator, A1-41, A3-168–A3-169
AND operators, combining with OR, A3-170–A3-171